THE CONTEXT OF SCRIPTURE

VOLUME I

Canonical Compositions from the Biblical World

THE CONTEXT OF SCRIPTURE

Canonical Compositions, Monumental Inscriptions, and Archival Documents from the Biblical World

General Editor	William W. Hallo
Associate Editor	K. Lawson Younger, Jr.
Project Editor	David E. Orton

TUTA SUB AEGIDE PALLAS · 1683 ·

The Context of Scripture

VOLUME I

Canonical Compositions from the Biblical World

Editor

WILLIAM W. HALLO

Associate Editor

K. LAWSON YOUNGER, JR.

Consultants

HARRY A. HOFFNER, JR.
ROBERT K. RITNER

BRILL
LEIDEN · NEW YORK · KÖLN
1997

This book is printed on acid-free paper.

Cover: "Man and his God" (Text 1.179) lines 97-112, on a tablet from the collections of the University Museum, University of Pennsylvania (CBS 15205), published by Samuel Noah Kramer in M. Noth & D. Winton Thomas (eds.), *Wisdom in Israel and in the Ancient Near East* (FS H.H. Rowley; VTS 3; Leiden: E.J. Brill, 1960), Pl. iv (opp. p. 175).

Library of Congress Cataloging-in-Publication Data

The context of Scripture / editor, William W. Hallo ; associate editor, K. Lawson Younger.
p. cm.
Includes bibliographical references and index.
Contents: v. 1. Canonical compositions from the biblical world.
ISBN 9004106189 (alk. paper)
1. Bible. O.T.—Extra-canonical parallels. 2. Middle Eastern literature—Relation to the Old Testament. 3. Bible. O.T.—History of contemporary events—Sources. 4. Middle Eastern literature—Translations into English. I. Hallo, William W. II. Younger, K. Lawson.
BS1180.C66 1996
220.9'5—dc21 96-48987
CIP

Die Deutsche Bibliothek – CIP-Einheitsaufnahme

The context of scripture : canonical compositions, monumental inscriptions, and archival documents from the biblical world / ed. William W. Hallo. – Leiden ; New York ; Köln : Brill
NE: Hallo, William W. [Hrsg.]
Vol. 1 Canonical compositions from the biblical world. – 1997
ISBN 90-04-10618-9

ISBN 90 04 10618 9 (*Vol. 1*)
ISBN 90 04 09629 9 (*Set*)

PRINTED IN THE NETHERLANDS

CONTENTS

HITTITE CANONICAL COMPOSITIONS

PREFACE

The genesis of this project may be said to lie in the four Summer Seminars for College Teachers which the undersigned conducted under the auspices of the National Endowment for the Humanities at Yale in 1978, 1980, 1987 and 1990. In these, I sought to salvage what was worthwhile of the older comparative approach to biblical history and literature by replacing it with the more nuanced "contextual approach." Nearly fifty papers by the participating scholars resulted from these seminars, and most of them were published, together with my introductory essays, in the four volumes that go under the general title of *Scripture in Context*.[1] The fourth of these volumes was edited by K. Lawson Younger, Jr., who had written and published his doctoral dissertation at Sheffield.[2] He was in contact with David Orton at the very time that Dr. Orton was moving from Sheffield to Leiden to take up the post of Senior Editor (Religion) for E. J. Brill. At the same time (Spring 1991), I was spending a sabbatical in Leiden, so Orton sought me out at Younger's suggestion to assess my interest in a major new project to bring ancient Near Eastern texts to bear on the study of biblical literature and history. I was interested in what promised to serve as a test of some of my long-held and long-taught methodologies: not only the contextual approach, but also my taxonomy of ancient documentation, and my theories of translation. I submitted a detailed proposal in which my conception of such a project was outlined. This became the basis of further discussions with Dr. Orton in Leiden, at the International Conference of the Society of Biblical Literature in Rome (1991), and the World Congress of Jewish Studies in Jerusalem (1993). At the last venue, in particular, I had the opportunity to test some of the proposals on a well informed and critical audience by presenting portions of what is now the introduction to the present volume.[3] Trenchant advice was offered, i.a., by the late Jonas C. Greenfield.

After lengthy negotiations, a contract was signed and I then proceeded to secure the collaboration of Prof. Younger as Associate Editor. He has been a tower of strength to the project, lending his expertise in all matters relating to West Semitic and often enough to the other four sections as well. In addition, he prepared camera-ready copy of all the contributions. In matters Egyptian, I consulted my then Yale colleague Robert Ritner (now of the University of Chicago), and in matters Hittite, I benefitted from the wise counsel of Harry A. Hoffner, Jr. (University of Chicago).

My own task consisted in the first place of preparing the initial outline of texts to be translated. In their selection I was guided by a number of principles. Other things being equal (though they rarely are), preference was given to newly recovered or newly (re-)edited texts, though place was also made for some of the well-known older stand-bys; to texts able to be presented in their entirety; to well-preserved rather than fragmentary texts; and to texts whose relevance for biblical studies, by way either of comparison or of contrast, had been demonstrated or argued in the secondary literature. All four of these criteria were rarely met by any one text, and when they were, it was not always possible to find a translator for them.

On the whole, however, we consider ourselves fortunate in attracting so many of the leading talents in the field for this ambitious enterprise. All of them deserve unstinted thanks, with special credit to those recruited late in the day who thus had to meet tight deadlines (see the List of Contributors to Volume 1, below).

The aim was to provide the best and latest possible translations in every case. In a few instances this combination could be achieved only by reprinting previously published versions, and making special arrangements to this end. A list of the publishers who graciously cooperated in this regard follows this Preface.

To deal with so many contributors and publishers required the capable help of an administrative assistant furnished by the publisher in the person, initially, of Anne Folkertsma and, subsequently, of Mattie Kuiper. Thanks to the marvels of modern communication, it was possible to maintain almost instantaneous three-way contact among them and the three editors. But even the best mechanical devices are only as proficient as those who handle them, and Mesdames Folkertsma and Kuiper both performed to perfection. Without their steady ministrations, the project could not have reached its present milestone. A special tribute is due to David Orton, who not only conceived the project, but who lent it his unflagging support and provided experienced counsel at editorial meetings in Leiden (1992-96), and at SBL meetings in Chicago (1994) and Philadelphia (1995).

---

[1] See below, Abbreviations and Symbols, s.v. *SIC* 1-4.

[2] K. Lawson Younger, Jr., *Ancient Conquest Accounts: A Study in Ancient Near Eastern and Biblical History Writing* (JSOTSup 98; Sheffield, JSOT Press, 1990).

[3] See below, Introduction with n. 1.

Some of the aids to the reader, notably the index, glossary, and gazetteer, are of necessity postponed to the third and concluding volume in the series. But it is hoped that even without them, the present initial volume will take its place as a *vade mecum* in the libraries of all those interested in the ancient Near East, its ongoing rediscovery, and its bearing on "The Context of Scripture."

William W. Hallo
October 3, 1996

ACKNOWLEDGEMENTS

The following publishers permitted the reprinting of portions of books:

Texts 1.24; 1.26; 1.27; 1.28; 1.30; 1.31; 1.35; 1.36; 1.38; 1.39; 1.40; 1.41; 1.46; 1.47; 1.48; 1.53; 1.54 (pp. 36-37, 41-46, 48-50, 61-68, 77-93, 110-125, 130-136): Miriam Lichtheim, *Ancient Egyptian Literature*. 3 Volumes. The University of California Press,© 1973-1980. Regents of The University of California.

Text 1.56 (pp. 150-151): Reprinted by permission of the editors of the *Journal of Ancient Near Eastern Society* 14 (1982).

Text 1.80 (p. 215) : Reprinted from *Journal of Near Eastern Studies*. The University of Chicago Press.© 1986 by the University of Chicago. All rights reserved.

Text 1.99; 1.100 (pp. 309-327, 327-328): Reprinted from *Journal of Near Eastern Studies* 43 (1984) and 51 (1992) by permission of The University of Chicago Press.© 1984 and 1992 by The University of Chicago. All rights reserved.

Texts 1.108; 1.109; 1.110; 1.113; 1.131 (pp. 381-391, 404-416, 453-457): © Stephanie Dalley 1989. Reprinted from *Myths from Mesopotamia* translated by Stephanie Dalley (1989) by permission of Oxford University Press.

Texts 1.111; 1.114; 1.115; 1.116; 1.117; 1.129; 1.130; 1.132; 1.133; 1.151; 1.152; 1.153; 1.154 (pp. 390-402, 416-419, 449-453, 461, 485-495): Translation is reprinted, with permission, from *Before the Muses: An Anthology of Akkadian Literature* by Benjamin R. Foster (CDL Press, 1993).

N.B. the explanatory material (introductions, biblical analogies and notes) is the work of the editors.

Texts 1.158; 1.170; 1.173 (pp. 511-513, 545-548, 552-557): Reprinted from Thorkild Jacobsen, *The Harps that once ... Sumerian Poetry in Translation* (1987) by permission of Yale University Press.

Text 1.171 (pp. 548-550) : Reprinted from D. Katz, *Gilgamesh and Agga*, Library of Oriental Texts 1 (1993) by permission of Styx Publications.

ABBREVIATIONS AND SYMBOLS

AA	*Archäologischer Anzeiger.*
ÄA	Ägyptologische Abhandlungen.
AAA	*Annals of Archaeology and Anthropology* (University of Liverpool).
AAT	Ägypten und Altes Testament.
AB	Anchor Bible.
ABC	A. K. Grayson. *Assyrian and Babylonian Chronicles.* Locust Valley, NY: J. J. Augustin, 1975.
ABD	D. N. Freedman, Editor. *The Anchor Bible Dictionary.* 5 Vols. New York: Doubleday, 1992.
ABL	R. F. Harper. *Assyrian and Babylonian Letters.* London/Chicago, 1892-1914.
ACF	*Annuaire du Collège de France.*
ACh	C. Virolleaud. *Astrologie Chaldéenne.*
ActOr	*Acta Orientalia.*
ActSum	*Acta Sumerologica.*
ADAIK	Abhandlungen des Deutschen Archäologischen Instituts Kairo.
AEL	M. Lichtheim. *Ancient Egyptian Literature: A Book of Readings.* 3 vols. Berkeley, Los Angeles, and London: University of California, 1973-1980.
AEO	*Ancient Egyptian Onomastica. Text.* 2 vols. Oxford: Oxford University Press, 1947.
AfO	*Archiv für Orientforschung.*
AGI	*Archivio Glottologico Italiano.*
AHAW	Abhandlungen der Heidelberger Akademie der Wissenschaften.
AHw	W. von Soden. *Akkadisches Handwörterbuch.* Wiesbaden, 1959-1975.
AION	*Annali dell' Istituto Universitario Orientale di Napoli*
AIONSup	Annali dell' Istituto Universitario Orientale di Napoli, Supplemento
AJA	*American Journal of Archaeology*
AJBI	*Annual of the Japanese Biblical Institute*
AJSL	*American Journal of Semitic Languages*
ALASP	Abhandlungen zur Literatur Alt-Syrien-Palästinas. Münster: Ugarit-Verlag.
ALASP 1	M. Dietrich and O. Loretz. *Die Keilalphabete. Die Phönizisch-kanaanäischen und altarabischen Alphabete in Ugarit.* 1988.
ALASP 2	J. Tropper. *Der ugaritische Kausativstamm und die Kausativbildungen des semitischen. Eine morphologisch-semantische Untersuchung zum Š-Stamm und zu den umstrittenen nichtsibilantischen Kausativstämmen des Ugaritischen.* 1990.
ALASP 3	M. Dietrich and O. Loretz. *Mantik in Ugarit Keilalphabetische Texte der Opferschau — Omensammlungen — Nekromantie.* Mit Beiträgen von H. W. Duerbeck, J.-W. Meyer, and W. C. Seitter. 1990.
ALASP 7	M. Dietrich and O. Loretz, Editors. *Ugarit — ein ostmediterranes Kulturzentrum im Alten Orient.* 1994.
AnBib	Analecta Biblica.
ANET	J. B. Pritchard, Editor. *Ancient Near Eastern Texts Relating to the Old Testament.* 3d ed. with supplement. Princeton, NJ: Princeton University Press, 1969.
AnOr	Analecta Orientalia.
AnSt	*Anatolian Studies.*
AO	*Aula Orientalis.* Revista de estudios del próximo oriente antiguo.
AOAT(S)	Alter Orient und Altes Testament (Sonderreihe).
AoF	*Altorientalische Forschungen.*
AOS	American Oriental Series.
AOSup	Aula Orientalis Supplementa.
APAW	Abhandlungen der Preussischen Akademie der Wissenschaften.
ARAB	D. D. Luckenbill. *Ancient Records of Assyria and Babylonia.* 2 Vols. Chicago, 1926-27.
Arch.	*Archaeologia.*
ARI	A. K. Grayson. *Assyrian Royal Inscriptions.* 2 Vols. Wiesbaden: Otto Harrassowitz, 1972-76.
ARM(T)	*Archives royales de Mari* (texts in transliteration and translation).
ArOr	*Archiv Orientální.*
AS	Assyriological Studies.
ASAE	*Annales du Service des Antiquités de l'Égypte.*
Asarh.	R. Borger. *Die Inschriften Asarhaddons Königs von Assyrien. AfO* Beiheft 9. Graz: Ernst Weidner, 1956.
ASOR	American Schools of Oriental Research.
ASORDS	American Schools of Oriental Research Dissertation Series.
ASSF	Acta Societatis Scientiarum Fennicae.
Assur	*Assur.* Monographic Journals of the Near East. Malibu: Undena, California.
Aspects	A. Spalinger. *Aspects of the Military Documents of the Ancient Egyptians.* YNER 9. New Haven and London: Yale University Press, 1983.
ASTI	*Annual of the Swedish Theological Institute.*
ATANT	Abhandlungen zur Theologie des Alten und Neuen Testaments.
BA	*Biblical Archaeologist.*
BAH	Bibliothèque archéologique et historique.
BAL[2]	R. Borger. *Babylonische-assyrische Lesestücke.* 2nd ed. AnOr 54. Rome: Pontificium Institutum Biblicum, 1979.
BAM	F. Köcher. *Die babylonisch-assyrische Medizin in Texten und Untersuchungen.* Berlin, 1963.
BaM	*Baghdader Mitteilungen.*
BAR	*Biblical Archaeology Review.*
BASOR	*Bulletin of the American Schools of Oriental Research.*
BASORSup	Bulletin of the American Schools of Oriental Research Supplementary Studies.
BBVO	Berliner Beiträge zum Vorderen Orient. Berlin.
BdÉ	Bibliothèque d'étude.
BE	Babylonian Expedition of the University of Pennsylvania, Series A: Cuneiform Texts.
BeO	*Bibbia e oriente.*
BES	Brown Egyptological Studies.
BDB	F. Brown, S. R. Driver and C. A. Briggs. *A Hebrew and English Lexicon of the Old Testament with an Appendix containing the Biblical Aramaic.* Oxford: Clarendon Press, 1907.
BFOP	Babylonian Fund Occasional Publications.
BHLT	A. K. Grayson. *Babylonian Historical-Literary Texts.* Toronto and Buffalo, 1975.
BHS	K. Elliger, W. Rudolph, et al., Editors. *Biblica hebraica stuttgartensia.* Stuttgart, 1977.
BIFAO	*Bulletin de l'Institut Français d'Archéologie Orientale.*
BiMes	Bibliotheca Mesopotamica.
BiOr	*Bibliotheca Orientalis.*
BJRL	*Bulletin of the John Rylands Library.*
BJS	Brown Judaic Studies.
BKAT	Biblischer Kommentar: Altes Testament.
BM	British Museum.
BM	B. R. Foster. *Before the Muses.* 2nd edition. 2 vols. Bethesda, MD: CDL Press, 1996.
BMOP	British Museum Occasional Paper. London: British Musuem.
Bo	Inventory numbers of Boghazköy tablets excavated 1906-12.
BP	William W. Hallo. *The Book of the People.* BJS 225. Atlanta: Scholars Press, 1991.
BR	*Biblical Research.* Chicago.

BSOAS	*Bulletin of the School of Oriental and African Studies.*
BSAg	*Bulletin of Sumerian Agriculture.*
BTAVO	Beihefte zum Tübinger Atlas des Vorderen Orients. Wiesbaden.
BTB	*Biblical Theology Bulletin.*
BWANT	Beiträge zur Wissenschaft vom Alten und Neuen Testament.
BWL	W. G. Lambert. *Babylonian Wisdom Literature.* Oxford: Clarendon Press, 1960.
BZ	*Biblische Zeitschrift.*
BZAW	Beihefte zur Zeitschrift für die alttestamentliche Wissenschaft.
CAD	A. L. Oppenheim, et al., Editors. *The Assyrian Dictionary of the Oriental Institute of the University of Chicago.* Chicago: The Oriental Institute, 1956-.
CAH^3	*The Cambridge Ancient History.* 3d ed. Cambridge: Cambridge University Press, 1973-75.
CANE	J. M. Sasson, Editor. *Civilizations of the Ancient Near East.* 4 Vols. New York: Scribner, 1995.
CBC	Cambridge Bible Commentary.
CBQ	*Catholic Biblical Quarterly.*
CBQMS	Catholic Biblical Quarterly Monograph Series.
CCT	Cuneiform Texts from Cappadocian Tablets.
CdÉ	*Chronique d'Égypte.*
CH	R. F. Harper. *The Code of Hammurabi.*
CHD	H. G. Güterbock and H. A. Hoffner, Jr., Editors. *The Hittite Dictionary of the Oriental Institute of the University of Chicago.* Chicago: The Oriental Institute, 1989-
CIS	*Corpus Inscriptionum Semiticarum.* Paris, 1881.
COS	W. W. Hallo, Editor. *The Context of Scripture.* 3 Volumes. Leiden: E. J. Brill, 1997-.
CRAIBL	*Comptes rendus de l'Académie des inscriptions et belles lettres.*
CT	Cuneiform Texts from Babylonian Tablets in the British Museum.
CTA	A. Herdner. *Corpus des tablettes en cunéiformes alphabétiques découvertes à Ras Shamra-Ugarit de 1929 à 1939.* Mission de Ras Shamra 10. BAH 79. Paris: Imprimerie Nationale; Geuthner, 1963.
CTH	Laroche, E. *Catalogue des textes hittites.* Paris: Klincksieck, 1971.
DCPP	E. Lipiński, et al., Editors. *Dictionnaire de la Civilisation Phénicienne et Punique.* Paris: Brepols.
DDD	*The Dictionary of Deities and Demons.* Leiden: Brill.
DM	*Deir el-Medineh* (Ostraca).
DNWSI	J. Hoftijzer and K. Jongeling. *Dictionary of the North-West Semitic Inscriptions.* Handbuch der Orientalistik 1/21. Leiden: E. J. Brill, 1995.
DOTT	D. Winton Thomas, Editor. *Documents from Old Testament Times.* London, 1958.
Dreams	A. L. Oppenheim. *The Interpretation of Dreams in the Ancient Near East, With a Translation of an Assyrian Dream-Book.* Transactions of the American Philosophical Society, n.s. 46/3. Philadelphia: The American Philosophical Society, 1956.
EA	J. A. Knudtzon, et al., Editors. *Die El-Amarna-Tafeln.* Vorderasiatische Bibliothek 2. Leipzig, 1915.
EAK	*Einleitung in die assyrischen Königsinschriften.* R. Borger, Vol. 1. W. Schramm, Vol. 2.
EI	*Eretz-Israel.*
ELS	P. Attinger. *Elements de linguistique sumerienne.* OBO, Sonderband. 1993.
Emar	D. Arnaud. *Recherches au pays d'Aštata, Emar VI.e: textes sumériens et accadiens, texte.* Paris: Éditions Recherche sur les Civilisations, 1986.
EPRO	Études préliminaires aux religions orientales dans l'empire Romain. Leiden.
Erl.	K. Sethe. *Erläuterung zu den aegyptischen Lesestücken.* Leipzig, 1929.
Erra	L. Cagni. *L'Epopea de Erra.* Studi semitici 34. Rome, 1969. Idem. *The Poem of Erra.* SANE 1/3. Malibu, 1977.
ERTR	Egyptian Religious Texts and Representations.
EVO	*Egitto e Vicino Oriente.*
FAOS	Freiburger Altorientalische Studien.
FAT	Forschungen zum Alten Testament.
FDD	B. R. Foster. *From Distant Days: Myths, Tales, and Poetry of Ancient Mesopotamia.* Bethesda, MD: CDL Press, 1995.
FIFAO	Fouilles de l'Institut Français d'Archéologie Orientale.
FOTL	R. Knierim and G. M. Tucker, Editors. *The Forms of Old Testament Literature.* Grand Rapids: Eerdmans.
FRLANT	Forschungen zur Religion und Literatur des Alten und Neuen Testament.
FTH	A. R. Millard, et al., Editors. *Faith, Tradition and History.* Winona Lake, IN: Eisenbrauns, 1994.
GAG	W. von Soden. *Grundriss der Akkadischen Grammatik.* AnOr 33. Rome, 1952.
GM	*Göttinger Miszellen.*
HAK	H. Hunger. *Babylonische und assyrische Kolophone.* AOAT 2. Keukirchen-Vluyn: Neukirchener Verlag, 1968.
HAE	J. Renz and W. Röllig. *Handbuch der Althebräischen Epigraphik.* 3 Volumes. Darmstadt: Wissenschaftliche Buchgesellschaft, 1995.
HED	J. Puhvel. *Hittite Etymological Dictionary.* 2 Vols. in 1. Berlin, 1984.
HHI	H. Tadmor and M. Weinfeld. *History, Historiography and Interpretation. Studies in Biblical and Cuneiform Literatures.* Edited by H. Tadmor and M. Weinfeld. Jerusalem: The Magnes Press, 1983.
Hiero. Texts	British Museum. *Hieroglyphic Texts from Egyptian Stelae, etc.* 2nd ed. London, 1961-.
HKL	R. Borger. *Handbuch der Keilschriftliteratur.* 3 Vols. Berlin, 1967-1973.
HO	J. Černý and A. H. Gardiner. *Hieratic Ostraca I.* Oxford: Griffith Institute, 1957.
HPBM 2	E. A. W. Budge, Editor. *Hieratic Papyri in the British Museum.* 2nd series. London: British Museum, 1923.
HPBM 3	A. H. Gardiner. *Hieratic Papyri in the British Museum.* 3rd series. 2 Vols. London: British Museum, 1935.
HPKMB	Hieratische Papyrus aus dem königlichen Museen zu Berlin.
HS	*Hebrew Studies.*
HSM	Harvard Semitic Monographs.
HSS	Harvard Semitic Studies.
HT	Hittite Texts in the Cuneiform Character in the British Museum. London, 1920.
HTR	*Harvard Theological Review.*
HSAO	D. O. Edzard, Editor. *Heidelberger Studien zum alten Orient.* Wiesbaden, 1967.
HUCA	*Hebrew Union College Annual.*
HUCASup	Hebrew Union College Annual, Supplements.
HW 1., 2., 3., Erg.	J. Friedrich. *Hethitisches Wörterbuch.* Heidelberg, 1952(-54).
HW^2	J. Friedrich and A. Kammenhuber. *Hethitisches Wörterbuch.* 2nd ed. Heidelberg, 1975-.
IBoT	Istanbul Arkeoloji Müzelerinde Bulunan Boğazköy Tabeltleri(nden Seçme Metinler). Istanbul, 1944, 1947, 1954; Ankara, 1988.
IBS	Innsbrucker Beiträge zur Kulturwissenschaft (Sonderheft). Innsbruck.
ICC	International Critical Commentary.
IDB	G. A. Buttrick, Editor. *The Interpreter's Dictionary of the Bible.* 4 Vols. New York and Nashville: Abingdon, 1962.
IEJ	*Israel Exploration Journal.*
IF	*Indogermanische Forschungen.*

IM — *Istanbuler Mitteilungen.*
IntB — G. A. Buttrick, Editor. *The Interpreter's Bible.* 12 Vols. New York and Nashville: Abingdon, 1951-57.
IRSA — E. Sollberger and J.-R. Kupper. *Inscriptions royales sumériennes et akkadiennes.* Paris: Cerf, 1971.
JANES — *Journal of the Ancient Near Eastern Society.*
JAOS — *Journal of the American Oriental Society.*
JARCE — *Journal of the American Research Center in Egypt.*
JBL — *Journal of Biblical Literature.*
JCS — *Journal of Cuneiform Studies.*
JEA — *Journal of Egyptian Archaeology.*
JEOL — *Jaarbericht van het Vooraziatisch-Egyptisch Genootschap: Ex Oriente Lux.*
JESHO — *Journal of the Economic and Social History of the Orient.*
JETS — *Journal of the Evangelical Theological Society.*
JIES — *Journal of Indo-European Studies.*
JJS — *Journal of Jewish Studies.*
JNES — *Journal of Near Eastern Studies.*
JNSL — *Journal of Northwest Semitic Languages.*
JPOS — *Journal of the Palestine Oriental Society.*
JQR — *Jewish Quarterly Review.*
JRAS — *Journal of the Royal Asiatic Society.*
JSOR — *Journal of the Society of Oriental Research.*
JSOT — *Journal for the Study of the Old Testament.*
JSOTSup — Journal for the Study of the Old Testament, Supplement Series.
JSS — *Journal of Semitic Studies.*
JSSEA — *Journal of the Society for the Study of Egyptian Antiquity.*
JSSSup — Journal of Semitic Studies, Supplement Series.
KAI — H. Donner and W. Röllig. *Kanaanäische und aramäische Inschriften.* 3 Vols. Wiesbaden, 1962-64.
KAR — E. Ebeling. *Keilschrifttexte aus Assur religiösen Inhalts.*
KAT — Kommentar zum Alten Testament.
KB[1] — L. Koehler and W. Baumgartner. *Lexicon in Veteris Testamenti Libros.* Leiden: Brill, 1958.
KB[3] — L. Koehler, W. Baumgartner, and J. Stamm, et al., Editors. *Hebräisches und aramäisches Lexikon zum Alten Testament.* Leiden: Brill, 1967.
KBo — *Keilschrifttexte aus Boghazköi.* (vols. 1-22 are a subseries of WVDOG). Leipzig & Berlin.
KlF — *Kleinasiatische Forschungen.*
KKU — W. Sallaberger, *Der Kultische Kalender der Ur III Zeit.* Untersuchungen zur Assyriologie und Vorderasiatischen Archäologie 7/1. Berlin & New York: de Gruyter, 1993.
KRI — K. A. Kitchen. *Ramesside Inscriptions, Historical and Biographical.* Oxford, 1969-.
KTU — M. Dietrich, O. Loretz, and J. Sanmartín. *Keilalphabetische Texte aus Ugarit einschliesslich der keilalphabetischen Texte außerhalb Ugarits.* Teil 1 *Transkription.* AOAT 24/1. Kevelaer: Butzon & Bercker; Neukirchen-Vluyn: Neukirchener Verlag, 1976.
KTU[2] — M. Dietrich, O. Loretz, and J. Sanmartín. *The Cuneiform Alphabetic Texts from Ugarit, Ras Ibn Hani, and Other Places* (*KTU*: Second, enlarged edition). Münster: Ugarit-Verlag, 1995.
KUB — *Keilschrifturkunden aus Boghazköi.* Staatliche Museen zu Berlin, Vorderasiatische Abteilung. Berlin: Akademie Verlag, 1921-.
KZ — *Historische Sprachforschung = Zeitschrift für Vergleichende Sprachforschung* ("*Kuhns Zeitschrift*")
LAPO — Littératures anciennes du Proche-Orient.
LAS — S. Parpola. *Letters from Assyrian Scholars to the Kings Esarhaddon and Assurbanipal.* 2 Vols. AOAT 5. Neukirchen-Vluyn, 1970, 1983.
LCL — Loeb Classical Library.
LdÄ — Lexikon der Ägyptologie.
LIH — L. W. King. *The Letters and Inscriptions of Hammurabi.*
LMAOS — Liverpool Monographs in Archaeology and Oriental Studies.
LKA — E. Ebeling. *Literarische Keilschriftexte aus Assur.*
LSS — Leipziger semitistische Studien.
LV — Late Version.
MAOG — Mitteilungen der altorientalischen Gesellschaft.
MARI — *Mari, Annales de recherches interdisciplinaires.*
MÄS — Münchner ägyptologische Studien.
MAV — Middle Assyrian Version.
MDAIK — Mitteilungen des deutschen archäologischen Instituts, Abteilung Kairo.
MDOG — Mitteilungen der deutschen Orient-Gesellschaft.
MIO — *Mitteilungen des Instituts für Orientforschung.*
MLE — *Materiali lessicali ed epigrafici.*
MMEW — A. Livingstone. *Mystical and Mythological Explanatory Works of Assyrian and Babylonian Scholars.* Oxford: Oxford University Press, 1986 (reprint 1987).
MRS — Mission de Ras Shamra. Paris.
MSL — *Materialien zum sumerischen Lexikon; Materials for the Sumerian Lexicon.*
MVAG — Mitteilungen der vorderasiatisch-ägyptischen Gesellschaft.
NABU — *Nouvelles assyriologiques brèves et utilitaires.*
NAWG — Nachrichten der Akademie der Wissenschaften in Göttingen.
Nbn. — J. N. Strassmaier. *Inschriften von Nabonidus.*
OA — *Oriens Antiquus.* Rivista del Centro per le Antichità e la Storia dell'Arte del Vicino Oriente.
OBO — Orbis Biblicus et Orientalis.
OBV — Old Babylonian Version.
OCPR — E. Matsushima, Editor. *Official Cult and Popular Religion in the Ancient Near East: Papers of the First Colloquium on the Ancient Near East - The City and Its Life, held at the Middle Eastern Culture Center in Japan (Mitaka, Tokyo), March 20-22, 1992.* Heidelberg: Winter, 1993.
OECT — Oxford Editions of Cuneiform Texts.
OIP — The University of Chicago, Oriental Institute Publications.
OLA — Orientalia lovaniensia analecta.
OLP — *Orientalia lovaniensia periodica.*
OLZ — *Orientalistische Literaturzeitung.*
Or — *Orientalia.* n.s.
OrSuec — *Orientalia Suecana.*
OTL — The Old Testament Library, Westminster Press.
OTS — Oudtestamentische Studiën.
PAAJR — *Proceedings of the American Academy of Jewish Research.*
PAPS — *Proceedings of the American Philosophical Society.*
PBS — Publications of the Babylonian Section, University Museum, University of Pennsylvania.
PEQ — *Palestine Exploration Quarterly.*
PIBA — *Proceedings of the Irish Biblical Association.*
PIHANS — Publications de l'Institute historique et archéologique néerlandais de Stamboul.
PJ — *Palästina-Jahrbuch.*
PKB — J. A. Brinkman. *A Political History of Post-Kassite Babylonia 1158-722 B.C.* Rome, 1968.
POTT — D. J. Wiseman, Editor. *Peoples of Old Testament Times.* Oxford: Clarendon.
PRU — J. Nougayrol/Ch. Virolleaud. *Le Palais royal d'Ugarit.* II-VI. MRS. Paris: Imprimerie Nationale, 1955-1970.
PSBA — *Proceedings of the Society of Biblical Archaeology.*
PSD — Å. Sjöberg, Editor. *The Sumerian Dictionary of the University Museum of the University of Pennsylvannia.* Philadelphia, 1948-.
PPYEE — Publications of the Pennsylvania-Yale Expedition to Egypt.

R	H. C. Rawlinson, *The Cuneiform Inscriptions of Western Asia.*
RA	*Revue d'assyriologie et d'archéologie orientale.*
RAI	*Recontre Assyriologique Internationale.*
RAI 26	B. Alster, Editor. *Death in Mesopotamia.* Mesopotamia 8. Copenhagen: Akademisk Forlag.
RAI 38	*La circulation des biens, des personnes et des idées dans le Proche-Orient ancien: Actes de le XXXVIIIe R.A.I.* Paris: Editions Recherche sur les Civilisations, 1992.
RAKM	H. D. Galter, Editor. *Die Rolle der Astronomie in den Kulturen Mesopotamiens.* Beiträge zum 3. Grazer Morgenländischen Symposion (23.-27. September 1991). Graz: GrazKult.
RÄRG	H. Bonnet. *Reallexikon der ägyptischen Religionsgeschichte.* Berlin, 1952.
ResQ	*Restoration Quarterly.*
RB	*Revue biblique.*
RdÉ	*Revue d'Égyptologie.*
RES	*Répertoire d'epigraphie sémitique.*
RGBK	B. Janowski, et al., Editors. *Religionsgeschichtliche Beziehungen zwischen Kleinasien, Nordsyrien und dem Alten Testament. Internationales Symposion Hamburg 17.-21. März 1990.* OBO 129. Freiburg/Schweiz: Universitätsverlag.
RGTC	Réportoire géographique des textes cunéiformes, B TAVO, Reihe B 7,1ff. Wiesbaden, 1974-.
RHA	*Revue hittite et asianique.*
RHR	*Revue de l'histoire des religions.*
RIDA	*Revue internationale des droits de l'antiquité.* 3rd series. Brussels.
RIH	Field numbers of tablets excavated at Ras Ibn-Hani.
RIMA 1	*The Royal Inscriptions of Mesopotamia. Assyrian Periods.* Volume 1. A. K. Grayson. *Assyrian Rulers of the Third and Second Millennia BC (To 1115 BC).* Toronto: University of Toronto, 1987.
RIMA 2	*The Royal Inscriptions of Mesopotamia. Assyrian Periods.* Volume 2. A. K. Grayson. *Assyrian Rulers of the Early First Millennium BC* (1114-859 BC). Toronto: University of Toronto, 1991.
RISA	G. A. Barton. *The Royal Inscriptions of Sumer and Akkad.* Library of Ancient Semitic Inscriptions 1; New Haven: Yale, 1929.
RlA	E. Ebeling and B. Meissner, et al., Editors. *Reallexikon der Assyriologie.*
RS	Field numbers of tablets excavated at Ras Shamra.
RSF	*Rivista di Studi Fenici.*
RSO	*Rivista degli Studi Orientali.*
RSOu	Ras Shamra - Ougarit. Publications de la Mission Française Archéologique de Ras Shamra - Ougarit. Paris: Éditions Recherche sur les Civilisations, 1983-.
RSOu 3	M. Yon, Editor. *Le centre de la ville. 38e-44e campagnes (1978-1984).* RSOu 3. Paris: Éditions Recherche sur les Civilisations, 1987.
RSOu 4	D. Pardee. *Les textes para-mythologiques de la 24e campagne (1961).* RSOu 4. Paris: Éditions Recherche sur les Civilisations, 1988.
RSOu 6	M. Yon, et al., Editors. *Arts et industries de la pierre.* RSOu 6. Paris: Éditions Recherche sur les Civilisations, 1991.
RSOu 7	P. Bordreuil, Editor. *Une bibliothèque au sud de la ville.* RSOu 7. Paris: Éditions Recherche sur les Civilisations, 1991.
RSOu 11	M. Yon, M. Sznycer, P. Bordreuil, Editors. *Le Pays d'Ougarit autour de 1200 av.J.C. Historie et archéologie. Actes du Colloque International, Paris, 28 juin — 1er juillet 1993.* RSOu 11. Paris: Éditions Recherche sur les Civilisations, 1995.
RT	*Recueil de travaux relatifs à la philologie et à l'archéologie égyptiennes et assyriennes.*
SAA	State Archives of Assyria.
SAAB	*State Archives of Assyria Bulletin.*
SAAS	State Archives of Assyria Studies.
SAHG	A. Falkenstein and W. von Soden. *Sumerische und akkadische Hymnen und Gebete.* Zürich and Stuttgart, 1953.
SÄK	*Studien zur altägyptischen Kultur.*
SANE	Sources from the Ancient Near East.
SAOC	Studies in Ancient Oriental Civilizations. Chicago: The Oriental Institute.
SARI	Jerrold S. Cooper. *Sumerian and Akkadian Royal Inscriptions.* Vol. 1: *The Pre-Sargonic Texts.* The AOS Translation Series 1. New Haven, CN: AOS, 1986.
SBAW	Sitzungsberichte der bayerischen Akademie der Wissenschaften.
SBH	G. A. Reisner. *Sumerisch-babylonische Hymnen nach Thontafeln griechischer Zeit.*
SBL	Society of Biblical Literature.
SBLDS	Society of Biblical Literature Dissertation Series.
SBLRBS	SBL Resources for Biblical Study.
SBLWAW	SBL Writings of the Ancient World.
SBT	Studies in Biblical Theology.
SBV	Standard Babylonian Version.
SCO	*Studi Classici e Orientali.*
ScrHier	Scripta Hierosolymitana.
SDB	*Supplément au Dictionnaire de la Bible.* Paris.
SEL	*Studi Epigrafici e Linguistici sul Vicino Oriente antico.*
SGL	A. Falkenstein and J. van Dijk. *Sumerische Götterlieder.* Heidelberg, 1959.
Shnaton	*Shnaton. An Annual for Biblical and Ancient Near Eastern Studies.* (Hebrew).
SJOT	*Scandinavian Journal of the Old Testament.*
SIC 1	C. D. Evans, W. W. Hallo, and J. B. White, Editors. *Scripture in Context: Essays on the Comparative Method.* Pittsburgh, 1980.
SIC 2	W. W. Hallo, J. C. Moyer, and L. G. Perdue, Editors. *Scripture in Context II: More Essays on the Comparative Method.* Winona Lake, Indiana, 1983.
SIC 3	W. W. Hallo, B. W. Jones, and G. L. Mattingly, Editors. *The Bible in the Light of Cuneiform Literature. Scripture in Context III.* Ancient Near Eastern Texts and Studies 8. Lewiston: Mellen, 1990.
SIC 4	K. L. Younger, Jr., W. W. Hallo, and B. F. Batto. Editors. *The Canon in Comparative Perspective. Scripture in Context IV.* Ancient Near Eastern Texts and Studies, 11. Lewiston, NY: The Edwin Mellen Press, 1991.
SMEA	*Studi micenei ed egeo-anatolici.*
SO	*Sources orientales.*
SÖAW	Sitzungsberichte der österreichischen Akademie der Wissenschaft, Phil.-hist. Kl., Vienna.
SPAW	Sitzungsberichte der Preussischen Akademie der Wissenschaft, Phil.-hist. Kl., Berlin.
SPHC	*Select Papyri in the Hieratic Character from the Collections of the British Museum.* Part 2. London, 1860.
SRT	E. Chiera. *Sumerian Religious Texts.* Upland, PA, 1924.
SSEAJ	*Society for the Study of Egyptian Antiquities Journal.*
SSI	J. C. L. Gibson. *Textbook of Syrian Semitic Inscriptions.* 3 Vols. Oxford, 1973-79.
SSU	Studia Semitica Upsaliensia.
StBoT	Studien zu den Boğazköy Texten.
STT	O. R. Gurney, J. J. Finkelstein and P. Hulin. *The Sultantepe Tablets.*
Studia Aramacia	M. J. Geller, J. C. Greenfield, and M. P. Weitzman, Editors. *Studia Aramaica: New Sources and New Approaches.* JSS Supplement 4. Oxford: Oxford University Press, 1995.
Studies Alp	H. Otten, H. Ertem, E. Akurgal and A. Süel, Editors. *Hittite and Other Anatolian and Near Eastern Studies*

in Honour of Sedat Alp. Ankara: Türk Tarih Kurumu Basımevi, 1992.

Studies Ahlström W. B. Barrack and J. R. Spencer, Editors. *In the Shelter of Elyon: Essays on Ancient Palestinian Life in Honor of G. W. Ahlström*. JSOTSup 31. Sheffield: JSOT, 1984.

Studies Bounni P. Matthiae, et al., Editors. *Resurrecting the Past. A Joint Tribute to Adnan Bounni*. Uitgaven van het Nederlands Historisch-Archaeologisch Instituut te Istanbul 67. Istanbul: Nederlands Historisch-Archaeologisch Instituut te Istanbul, 1990.

Studies Brunner M. Görg, Editor. *Fontes atque Pontes. Eines Festgabe für Hellmut Brunner*. AAT 5. Wiesbaden: Otto Harrassowitz, 1983.

Studies Brunner-Traut I. Gramer-Wallert and W. Helck, Editors. *Festschrift für Emma Brunner-Traut*. Tübingen: Attempto Verlag, 1992.

Studies Cazelles A. Caquot and M. Delcor, Editors. *Mélanges bibliques et orientaux en l'honneur de M. Henri Cazelles*. AOAT 212. Kevelaer: Butzon & Bercker; Neukirchen-Vluyn: Neukirchener Verlag, 1981.

Studies Dussaud *Mélanges syriens offerts à Monsieur René Dussaud: secretaire perpetuel de l'Academie des inscriptions et belles-lettres*. 2 Vols. BAH 30. Paris: Geuthner, 1939.

Studies Ehrman Y. L. Arbeitman, Editor. *Fucus. A Semitic/Afrasian Gathering in Remembrance of Albert Ehrman*. Current Issues in Linguistic Theory 58. Philadelphia: Benjamins, 1988.

Studies Fecht J. Osing and G. Dreyer, Editors. *Form and Mass, Festschrift für G. Fecht*. AAT 12. Wiesbaden: Otto Harrassowitz, 1987.

Studies Fensham W. T. Claassen, Editor. *Text and Context. Old Testament and Semitic Studies for F. C. Fensham*. JSOTSup 48. Sheffield: JSOT Press, 1988.

Studies Finkelstein M. deJong Ellis, Editor. *Essays on the Ancient Near East in Memory of Jacob Joel Finkelstein*. Memoirs of the Connecticut Academy of Arts and Sciences, December, 19. Hamden, CT: Connecticut Academy of Arts and Sciences, Transactions, 1977.

Studies Fitzmyer M. P. Horgan and P. J. Kobelski, Editors. *To Touch the Text. Biblical and Related Studies in Honor of Joseph A. Fitzmyer, S.J.* New York: Crossroad, 1989.

Studies Freedman C. Meyers and M. O'Connor. *Essays in Honor of David Noel Freedman in Celebration of his Sixtieth Birthday*. Winona Lake, IN: Eisenbrauns, 1983.

Studies Galling A. Kuschke and E. Kutsch, Editors. *Archäologie und Altes Testament. Festschrift für Kurt Galling zum 8. Jan. 1970*. Tübingen: Mohr (Siebeck), 1970.

Studies Gibson N. Wyatt, W. G. E. Watson and J. B. Lloyd, Editors. *Ugarit, Religion and Culture. Proceedings of the International Colloquium on Ugarit, Religion and Culture Edinburgh, July 1994. Essays Presented in Honour of Professor John C. L. Gibson*. UBL 12. Münster: Ugarit-Verlag, 1996.

Studies Glueck James A. Sanders, Editor. *Near Eastern Archaeology in the Twentieth Century. Essays in Honor of Nelson Glueck*. Garden City, NY: Doubleday, 1970.

Studies Gordon H. A. Hoffner, Jr., Editor. *Orient and Occident. Essays Presented to Cyrus H. Gordon on the Occasion of his Sixty-fifth Birthday*. AOAT 22. Kevelaer: Butzon & Bercker; Neukirchen-Vluyn: Neukirchener Verlag, 1973.

Studies Gordon² G. Rendsburg, et al., Editors. *The Bible World. Essays in Honor of Cyrus H. Gordon*. New York: KTAV/New York University, 1980.

Studies Griffith S. R. K. Glanville, Editor. *Studies Presented to F. Ll. Griffith*. London: Oxford University Press, 1932.

Studies Güterbock K. Bittel, et al., Editors. *Anatolian Studies Presented to Hans Gustav Güterbock on the Occasion of his 65th Birthday*. PIHANS 33. Istanbul: Nederlands Historisch-Archaeologisch Instituut in het Nabije Oosten, 1974.

Studies Güterbock² H. A. Hoffner, Jr., and G. Beckman, Editors. *Kaniš-šuwar. A Tribute to Hans G. Güterbock on his Seventh-Fifth Birthday*. AS 23. Chicago: The Oriental Institute of the University of Chicago.

Studies Hallo M. E. Cohen, D. C. Snell and D. B. Weisberg, Editors. *The Tablet and the Scroll: Near Eastern Studies in Honor of William W. Hallo*. Bethesda, MD: CDL, 1993.

Studies Hospers H. L. J. Vanstiphout, et al., Editors. *Scripta Signa Vocis: Studies about Scripts, Scriptures, Scribes, and Languages in the Near East, Presented to J. H. Hospers by his Pupils, Colleagues, and Friends*. Groningen: Egbert Forsten, 1986.

Studies Hughes *Studies in Honor of George R. Hughes*. SAOC 39. Chicago: Oriental Institute of the University of Chicago.

Studies Jacobsen S. J. Lieberman, Editor. *Sumerological Studies in Honor of Thorkild Jacobsen*. AS 20. Chicago: University of Chicago Press, 1976.

Studies Kramer B. L. Eichler, et al., Editors. *Kramer Anniversary Volume*. AOAT 25. Neukirchen-Vluyn: Neukirchener Verlag.

Studies Kramer² Jack M. Sasson, Editor. *Studies in Literature from the Ancient Near East ... Dedicated to Samuel Noah Kramer*. AOS 65. New Haven: American Oriental Society, 1984.

Studies Kraus G. van Driel, et al., Editors. *Zikir Šumim. Assyriological Studies Presented to F. R. Kraus on the Occasion of his Seventieth Birthday*. Nederlands Instituut voor het Nabije Oosten Studia Francisci Scholten Memoriae Dicata 5. Leiden: Brill, 1982.

Studies Kutscher A. F. Rainey, Editor. *kinattūtu ša dārâti: Raphael Kutscher Memorial Volume*. Tel Aviv Occasional Publications 1. Tel Aviv: Institute of Archaeology of Tel Aviv University, 1993.

Studies Laroche E. Masson, Editor. *Florilegium Anatolicum. Mélanges offerts à Emmanuel Laroche*. Paris: Éditions E. de Boccard, 1979.

Studies Leslau A. S. Kaye, Editor. *Semitic Studies in Honor of Wolf Leslau on the Occasion of his Eighty-fifth Birthday November 14th, 1991*. 2 Volumes. Wiesbaden: Harrassowitz, 1991.

Studies Loewenstamm Y. Avishur and J. Blau, Editors. *Studies in Bible and the Ancient Near East Presented to Samuel E. Loewenstamm on His Seventieth Birthday*. Jerusalem: Rubenstein, 1978.

Studies Meek W. W. McCullough, Editor. *The Seed of Wisdom: Essays in Honour of T. J. Meek*. Toronto: University of Toronto Press, 1964.

Studies Moran T. Abusch, J. Huehnergard and P. Steinkeller, Editors. *Lingering Over Words: Studies in Ancient Near Eastern Literature in Honor of William L. Moran*. HSS 37. Atlanta: Scholars Press, 1990.

Studies Naster R. Doncel and R. Lebrun, Editors. *Archéologie et religions de l'Anatolie ancienne: mélanges en l'honneur du professor Paul Naster*. Homo Religiosus 10. 2 Volumes. Louvain-la-Neuve: Centre d'histoire des religions, 1983.

Studies Oppenheim R. D. Biggs and J. A. Brinkman, Editors. *From the Workship of the Assyrian Dictionary. Studies Presented to A. Leo Oppenheim*. Chicago: University of Chicago Press, 1964.

Studies Otto J. Assmann, E. Feucht and R. Grieshammer, Editors. *Fragen an die Altägyptischen Literature. Studien zum Gedenken an E. Otto*. Wiesbaden: Harrassowitz, 1977.

Studies Pope J. H. Marks and R. M. Good, Editors. *Love and Death in the Ancient Near East: Essays in Honor of Marvin H. Pope*. Guilford: Four Quarters Publishing Company, 1987.

Studies Reiner — F. Rochberg-Halton, Editor. *Language, Literature, and History: Philological and Historical Studies presented to Erica Reiner*. AOS 67. New Haven: American Oriental Society, 1987.

Studies Rowley — M. Noth, Editor. *Wisdom in israel and in the Ancient Near East Presented to Professor Harold Henry Rowley*. VTSup 3. Leiden: E. J. Brill, 1955.

Studies Sachs — E. Leichty, et al., Editors. *A Scientific Humanist: Studies in Memory of Abraham Sachs*. Occasional Publications of the Samuel Noah Kramer Fund 9. Philadelphia: University Museum, 1988.

Studies Schott — W. Helck, Editor. *Festschrift für Siegfried Schott zu seinem 70. Geburtstag am 20. August 1967*. Wiesbaden: Harrassowitz, 1968.

Studies Seeligmann — Y. Zakovits and A. Rofé, Editors. *Sepher Yiṣḥaq Arieh Seeligmann*. Jerusalem: Rubenstein, 1983.

Studies Segert — E. M. Cook, Editor. *Sopher Mahir: Northwest Semitic Studies Presented to Stanislav Segert*. Santa Monica, 1990 = *Maarav* 5-6.

Studies Sjöberg — H. Behrens, et al., Editors. *Dumu-e$_2$-dub-ba-a. Studies in Honor of Åke W. Sjöberg*. Occasional Publications of the Samuel Noah Kramer Fund 11. Philadelphia: University Museum, 1989.

Studies Speiser — William W. Hallo, Editor. *Essays in Memory of E. A. Speiser*. AOS 53. New Haven: American Oriental Society, 1968.

Studies Stinespring — J. M. Efird, Editor. *The Use of the Old Testament in the New and Other Essays. Studies in Honor of William Franklin Stinespring*. Durham: Duke University Press, 1972.

Studies Tadmor — M. Cogan and I. Eph᾿al, Editors. *Ah, Assyria, ... Studies in Assyrian History and Ancient Near Eastern Historiography Presented to Hayim Tadmor*. ScrHier 33. Jerusalem: The Magnes Press, 1991.

Studies Talmon — M. Fishbane and E. Tov, Editors. *'Sha'arei Talmon': Studies Presented to Shemaryahu Talmon*. Winona Lake, IN: Eisenbrauns, 1992.

Studies Wilson — G. Kadish, Editor. *Studies in Honor of John A. Wilson*. SAOC 35. Chicago: University of Chicago Press, 1969.

Studies Wright — F. M. Cross, W. E. Lemke, and P. D. Miller, Editors. *Magnalia Dei, The Mighty Acts of God: Essays on the Bible and Archaeology in Memory of G. Ernest Wright*. Garden City, NY: Doubleday, 1976.

SWBAS — The Social World of Biblical Antiquity Series.

TB — *Tyndale Bulletin*.

TCL — Musée du Louvre, Département des Antiquités orientales, *Textes cunéiformes*.

TCS — Texts from Cuneiform Sources.

TDOT — G. Johannes Botterweck and H. Ringgren, Editors. *Theological Dictionary of the Old Testament*. Rev. ed. Trans. by J. T. Willis. Grand Rapids: 1974-.

THeth — Texte der Hethiter. Heidelberg: Carl Winter Verlag.

ThS — Theologische Studien.

TLB — Tabulae cuneiformes a F. M. Th. de Liagre Böhl collectae.

TLZ — *Theologische Literaturzeitung*.

TMH — Texte und Materialien der Frau Professor Hilprecht Collection of Babylonian Antiquities im Eigentum der Universität Jena. Leipzig, 1932-37.

TUAT — O. Kaiser, Editor. *Texte aus der Umwelt des Alten Testaments*. Gütersloh, 1984-.

TZ — *Theologische Zeitschrift*.

UBL — Ugaritisch-Biblische Literatur.

UET — Ur Excavations, Texts.

UF — *Ugarit-Forschungen*.

Ugaritica 5 — C. F. A. Schaeffer, Editor. *Ugaritica* 5. MRS 16; BAH 80. Paris: Imprimerie Nationale; Geuthner.

Ugaritica 6 — J.-C. Courtois, Editor. *Ugaritica* 6. MRS 17; BAH 81. Paris: Mission Archéologique de Ras Shamra; Geuthner.

Ugaritica 7 — C. F. A. Schaeffer, Editor. *Ugaritica* 7. MRS 18; BAH 99. Paris: Mission Archéologique de Ras Shamra; Geuthner.

UMBS — University of Pennsylvania. The University Museum, Publications of the Babylonian Section.

Unity and Diversity — H. Goedicke and J. J. M. Roberts, Editors. *Unity and Diversity: Essays in the History, Literature, and Religion of the Ancient Near East*. Baltimore and London: The Johns Hopkins University Press, 1975.

Urk. IV — K. Sethe and W. Helck, Editors. *Urkunden des ägyptischen Altertums, Abteilung IV: Urkunden der 18. Dynastie*. Fascicles 1-22. Leipzig and Berlin, 1906-1958.

UT — C. H. Gordon. *Ugaritic Textbook*. AnOr 38. Rome: Pontifical Biblical Institute, 1965.

VAB — Vorderasiatische Bibliothek.

VAT — Tablets in the collections of the Staatliche Museen, Berlin.

VO — *Vicino Oriente*.

VT — *Vetus Testamentum*.

VTSup — Supplements to Vetus Testamentum.

Wb — A. Erman and H. Grapow, Editors. *Wörterbuch der ägyptischen Sprache*. 7 Vols. Leipzig, 1926-1963.

WBC — Word Biblical Commentary.

WCJS — *World Congress of Jewish Studies*.

WHJP — World History of the Jewish People.

WMANT — Wissenschaftliche Monographien zum Alten und Neuen Testament.

WO — *Die Welt des Orients*.

WVDOG — Wissenschaftliche Veröffentlichungen der Deutschen Orient-Gesellschaft.

YBC — Yale Babylonian Collection.

YES — Yale Egyptological Studies.

YNES — Yale Near Eastern Researches.

YOS — Yale Oriental Series. Babylonian Texts.

YOR — Yale Oriental Series. Researches.

ZA — *Zeitschrift für Assyriologie und vorderasiatische Archäologie*.

ZÄS — *Zeitschrift für ägyptische Sprache und Altertumskunde*.

ZAW — *Zeitschrift für die alttestamentliche Wissenschaft*.

ZDMG — *Zeitschrift der deutschen morgenländischen Gesellschaft*.

ZDPV — *Zeitschrift des deutschen Palästina-Vereins*.

ZThK — *Zeitschrift für Theologie und Kirche*.

GENERAL ABBREVIATIONS

Abbr.	abbreviation
Akk.	Akkadian
ANE	ancient Near East
Aram.	Aramaic
BH	Biblical Hebrew
ca.	circa
col(s).	column(s)
ED	Early Dynastic Period
ed.	edition
Eg.	Egyptian
esp.	especially
GN	geographical name
Heb.	Hebrew
imperf.	imperfect
JPS	Jewish Publication Society
K	Kuyunjik Collection, British Museum
KJV	King James Version
LH	Late Hebrew
LXX	Septuagint
MH	Middle Hittite
MS	Middle Hittite Script
ms(s)	manuscript(s)
MT	Masoretic Text
n(n).	note(s)
NJPS	*New Jewish Publication Society translation*
NRSV	New Revised Standard Version
NS	New Hittite Script
n.s.	New Series
OB	Old Babylonian
obv.	obverse
OH	Old Hittite
P.	Papyrus
perf.	perfect
Phil.-hist. Kl.	Philosophisch-historische Klasse
Phoen.	Phoenician
pl.	plural
pl(s).	plate(s)
prep.	preposition
r.	reverse
rev.	revised
SBV	Standard Babylonian Version
Sel.	Selection
Sum.	Sumerian
WS	West Semitic
Sam.	Samaritan Pentateuch
Ug.	Ugaritic

ABBREVIATIONS OF BIBLICAL BOOKS (INCLUDING THE APOCRYPHA)

Gen	Genesis
Exod	Exodus
Lev	Leviticus
Num	Numbers
Deut	Deuteronomy
Josh	Joshua
Judg	Judges
1-2 Sam	1-2 Samuel
1-2 Kgs	1-2 Kings
Isa	Isaiah
Jer	Jeremiah
Ezek	Ezekiel
Hos	Hosea
Joel	Joel
Obad	Obadiah
Amos	Amos
Jonah	Jonah
Mic	Micah
Nah	Nahum
Hab	Habakkuk
Zeph	Zephaniah
Hag	Haggai
Zech	Zechariah
Mal	Malachi
Ps (*pl.*: Pss)	Psalm(s)
Job	Job
Prov	Proverbs
Ruth	Ruth
Cant	Canticles (= Song of Songs)
Eccl (= Qoh)	Ecclesiastes (= Qoheleth)
Lam	Lamentations
Esth	Esther
Dan	Daniel
Ezra	Ezra
Neh	Nehemiah
1-2 Chr	1-2 Chronicles
Add Esth	Additions to Esther
Bar	Baruch
Bel	Bel and the Dragon
1-2 Esdr	1-2 Esdras
4 Ezra	4 Ezra
Jdt	Judith
Ep Jer	Epistle of Jeremiah
1-2-3-4 Macc	1-2-3-4 Maccabees
Sir	Sirach (Ecclesiasticus)
Sus	Susanna
Tob	Tobit
Wis	Wisdom

TALMUDIC SOURCES

b. Šabb.	*Babylonian Talmud, Šabbat*
b. ᶜAbod. Zar.	*Babylonian Talmud, ᶜAboda Zara*
y. Sanh. 18a	*Jerusalem Talmud, Sanhedrin*

LIST OF CONTRIBUTORS

JAMES P. ALLEN
Metropolitan Musuem of Art

BENDT ALSTER
University of Copenhagen

RICHARD H. BEAL
University of Chicago

GARY BECKMAN
University of Michigan

CHAIM COHEN
Ben Gurion University of the Negev

BILLIE JEAN COLLINS
Emory University

STEPHANIE DALLEY
Oxford University

AARON DEMSKY
Bar-Ilan University

D. O. EDZARD
University of Munich

GERTRUD FARBER
University of Chicago

DANIEL FLEMING
New York University

BENJAMIN R. FOSTER
Yale University

MICHAEL V. FOX
University of Wisconsin, Madison

GENE B. GRAGG
University of Chicago

ANN K. GUINAN
University of Pennsylvannia

WILLIAM W. HALLO
Yale University

WOLFGANG HEIMPEL
University of California, Berkeley

JAMES K. HOFFMEIER
Wheaton College

HARRY A. HOFFNER, JR.
University of Chicago

TH. P. J. VAN DEN HOUT
University of Amsterdam

VICTOR HUROWITZ
Ben Gurion University of the Negev

THORKILD JACOBSEN ‡
Harvard University

DINA KATZ
Leiden

JACOB KLEIN
Bar-Ilan University

BARUCH A. LEVINE
New York University

MIRIAM LICHTHEIM
University of California, *retired*

ALASDAIR LIVINGSTONE
University of Birmingham

TREMPER LONGMAN III
Westminster Theological Seminary

GREGORY MCMAHON
University of New Hampshire

ALAN MILLARD
University of Liverpool

DENNIS PARDEE
University of Chicago

ROBERT K. RITNER
University of Chicago

YITSCHAK SEFATI
Bar-Ilan University

NILI SHUPAK
University of Haifa

RICHARD C. STEINER
Yeshiva University

H. L. J. VANSTIPHOUT
University of Groningen

K. LAWSON YOUNGER, JR.
LeTourneau University

‡ Deceased

INTRODUCTION

ANCIENT NEAR EASTERN TEXTS AND THEIR RELEVANCE FOR BIBLICAL EXEGESIS[1]

William W. Hallo

Classical and Near Eastern parallels have been used to illuminate the biblical text for as long as there have been biblical studies. Already according to Philo Judaeus, writing in Greek and living in the shadow of the great Greek library of Alexandria[2] in the first half century of the Common Era,[3] Abraham "becomes a speculative philosopher,"[4] a role-model for the sect of Jewish ascetics that he described as Therapeutae.[5] Nine centuries later, Saadiah Gaon,[6] likewise born in Egypt[7] but living in the equally stimulating atmosphere of Abbasid Baghdad,[8] freely employed his knowledge of Arabic to solve cruces of Biblical Hebrew.[9] But it again took almost another millennium before biblical names, words, and themes, were to be juxtaposed, not just to those of the contemporary world, but to those long lost to sight and mind in the buried cities of the past.

The nineteenth century of our era opened Egypt and the Asiatic Near East to large-scale excavations, and witnessed the decipherments of the hieroglyphic and cuneiform scripts. The results revolutionized what can best be described as "the first half of history" — that 2500-year stretch between the invention of these earliest forms of writing and their replacement by the simpler "alphabetic" scripts of the Hebrew and Greek traditions, and their derivations.[10] The period 3000-500 BCE (more or less), ostensibly the context of the biblical record, was thrown into wholly new relief. The inevitable transformation of biblical studies was not long in ensuing.

It is sufficient to recall in this connection those great syntheses that characterized German biblical scholarship of the comparative variety[11] beginning in 1872 with Eberhard Schrader and his *The Cuneiform Inscriptions and the Old Testament*.[12] A second, revised edition appeared as early as 1883, and twenty years later, in 1903, the compendium, by now classic, was completely revised and updated by two leading Assyriologists of the time, Heinrich Zimmern and Hugo Winckler.[13] Winckler had himself entered the lists with a compendium of his own by now in its second edition.[14]

The following year, 1904, the scope of coverage was extended to the hieroglyphic sources from Egypt in *The Old Testament in the Light of the Ancient East*, by Alfred Jeremias.[15] The popularity of this work can be judged by the fact that it went through three further editions, each one thoroughly revised.[16]

Meantime Hugo Gressmann widened the scope of such works still further by introducing the pictorial element in "Ancient Near Eastern Texts and Pictures to the Old Testament," in two volumes and as many editions.[17]

---

[1] In their original form, these remarks were presented to the Eleventh World Congress of Jewish Studies, Jerusalem, June 25, 1993. Their concluding portion appeared in *Proceedings of the Eleventh World Congress of Jewish Studies. Division A: The Bible and Its World* (Jerusalem: World Union of Jewish Studies, 1994) 9-15.

[2] Edward A. Parsons, *The Alexandrian Library* (Amsterdam: Elsevier, 1952).

[3] Ca. 20 BCE - 50 CE.

[4] Samuel Sandmel, "Philo's place in Judaism: a Study of Conceptions of Abraham in Jewish Literature," *HUCA* 25 (1954) 209-238; 26 (1955) 151-332, esp. p. 288. Reprinted as *Philo's Place in Judaism* (Cincinnati: Hebrew Union College Press, 1956).

[5] In his *De Vita Contemplativa*; see Sandmel, ibid., 315-317.

[6] 882-942 CE.

[7] Specifically in Pithom, in the Fayyum District, some 150 miles south of Alexandria.

[8] Jacob Lassner, *The Topography of Baghdad in the Early Middle Ages: Texts and Studies* (Detroit: Wayne State University, 1970); Guy LeStrange, *Baghdad During the 'Abbasid Caliphate* (London: Oxford University Press, 1900).

[9] Solomon L. Skoss, *Saadia Gaon. the Earliest Hebrew Grammarian* (Philadelphia: Dropsie College Press, 1955).

[10] W. W. Hallo, "The first half of history," *Yale Alumni Magazine* 37/8 (May, 1974) 13-17.

[11] Cf. the brief survey by W. W. Hallo, "German and Jewish Culture: Land of Two Rivers?" *Shofar* 7/4 (Summer 1989) 1-10.

[12] *Die Keilinschriften und das Alte Testament* (Giessen, 1872; 2nd ed., 1883).

[13] *Die Keilinschriften und das Alte Testament* (Berlin: Reuther & Richard, 1903).

[14] *Keilinschriftliches Textbuch zum Alten Testament* (Leipzig, 1892, 1903). A third ed. appeared in 1909.

[15] *Das Alte Testament im Lichte des Alten Orients* (Leipzig: J. C. Hinrichs, 1904).

[16] 1906, 1916, 1930.

[17] *Altorientalische Texte und Bilder zum Alten Testament* (Tübingen: J. B. Mohr, 1909; 2nd ed., Berlin/Leipzig: W. de Gruyter, 1926-27).

The appeal of these works of synthesis was by no means limited to a German-speaking readership. On the contrary, many of them appeared in English translations and have been cited by their English titles here. Thus Schrader appeared in translation as early as 1885-8,[18] and Jeremias in 1911.[19] At the same time, German scholarship, both biblical and ancient Near Eastern, was having a profound impact in the English-speaking world through more personal, direct means: British and particularly American students coming to Germany for graduate and post-graduate study on the one hand, and on the other, German scholars coming to American universities to teach. Among many other examples of the former category, we may cite Julian Morgenstern, who received a doctorate in Assyriology from Heidelberg in 1904 with a dissertation on "The Doctrine of Sin in the Babylonian Religion."[20] A good example of the latter category would be Paul Haupt (1858-1926), brought from Göttingen in 1885 to head the new Oriental Seminary at the Johns Hopkins University in Baltimore.

Haupt's most famous student, and the leading figure in the comparative approach to biblical studies in America through most of the twentieth century, was unquestionably William F. Albright (1891-1971).[21] Last of the polymaths who were equally at home in cuneiform, hieroglyphics, and Northwest Semitics, he had to forego a career in Assyriology or Egyptology on account of defective eyesight, but continued to integrate every new archaeological and epigraphic discovery into his ever expanding panorama of the total experience of biblical Israel. Beginning with a dissertation on "The Assyrian Deluge Epic" written under Haupt in 1916 but never published, he spent the years between the two world wars in publishing an unending stream of articles; then, beginning in 1940, he devoted himself to longer monographic works, elegant and wide-ranging syntheses of his views on biblical history, archaeology, literature, religion and theology. The volumes entitled *From the Stone Age to Christianity: Monotheism and the Historical Process* (1940), *The Archaeology of Palestine* (1949), *The Biblical Period from Abraham to Ezra: an Historical Survey* (1963), *History, Archaeology and Christian Humanism* (1964), and *Yahweh and the Gods of Canaan* (1968) attest to his scope.

Although the German model of compendia of comparative texts was thus avoided by Albright, it was followed by other American scholars, notably R. W. Rogers[22] and G. A. Barton,[23] whose *Archaeology and the Bible* appeared in its seventh and last edition in 1937. But with the approach of the Second World War and the shift of Ancient Near Eastern scholars and scholarship to America, the creation of a new compendium on an American model became a top priority. In James B. Pritchard an editor was found who was able to carry the task forward. He recruited Albright and a dozen other leading (North) American specialists,[24] among them four outstanding emigre scholars.[25] He used Gressmann as his proximate and most recent model, both in the initial selection of texts[26] and in the creation of a companion volume of pictures[27] which was his own work based on his archaeological training and interests.

Pritchard's volume, or *ANET* as it is frequently called, quickly established itself as the pre-eminent compendium of its kind in the post-war period. Comparable efforts by British, French and even German teams made no attempt to replace it, but rather to offer complementary works answering to different requirements. Thus for example the British "Society for Old Testament Study" published *Documents from Old Testament Times* (1958) on the occasion of its fortieth anniversary. But D. Winton Thomas, its editor, had no intention of matching or even approaching the scope of *ANET* (which was freely cited in the volume). The French series *Littératures anciennes du Proche-Orient*, published under the patronage of École Biblique et Archéologique Française of Jerusalem, covers much of the same ground as *ANET* and does so, if anything, more extensively. But its separate volumes are appearing at lengthy intervals as each is completed by the relevant contributor(s); hence the series cannot replace *ANET* as a handy reference work covering all or at least most of the "ancient Near Eastern texts relating to the Old Testament." Even the Germans have re-entered the lists with *Texte aus der Umwelt des Alten Testaments*, edited by Otto Kaiser. In three volumes, it is an ambitious attempt to revive the older tradition of German compendia and to combine that with some of the best features of the newer ones — including the depth of the French series and the breadth of *ANET*. But in spite of its title, it makes little or no reference to biblical parallels or contrasts.

[18] Translated by O. C. Whitehouse from the 2nd German edition (London and Edinburgh: Williams and Norgate, 2 vols. = Theological Translation Fund Library, 33, 38).

[19] Translated from the 2nd German ed. 2 vols. (London: Williams and Norgate = Theological Translation Library 28-29). The American edition (New York: Putnam's) was edited by the Assyriologist C. H. W. Johns.

[20] Morris Lieberman, "Julian Morgenstern - Scholar. Teacher, Leader," *HUCA* 32 (1961) 1-9.

[21] See most recently *BA* 56/1 (March, 1993) for articles by J. M. Sasson, N. A. Silberman, W. W. Hallo, W. G. Dever and B. O. Long "celebrating and examining W. F. Albright."

[22] *Cuneiform Parallels to the Old Testament* (New York: Eaton & Mains, 1912; 2nd ed. 1926).

[23] *Archaeology and the Bible* (Philadelphia: American Sunday-School Union, 1916; 7th ed., 1937).

[24] T.J. Meek (Toronto) was a Canadian.

[25] A. Goetze and A. L. Oppenheim for the 1st ed. (1950); A. Jamme and F. Rosenthal were added in the 2nd ed. (1955).

[26] See his preface to *Ancient Near Eastern Texts Relating to the Old Testament* (Princeton: Princeton University Press, 1950) xv.

[27] J. B. Pritchard, *The Ancient Near East in Pictures Relating to the Old Testament* (Princeton: Princeton University Press, 1954).

As for *ANET* itself, it has spawned a veritable cottage-industry of by-products. Mention has already been made of the companion volume of *The Ancient Near East in Pictures* (1954) familiarly known as *ANEP*. There have also been two combined abridgements of *ANET* and *ANEP*, published respectively in 1958[28] and 1975,[29] both widely used as textbooks. There is a 1969 volume combining the new material of the third edition of *ANET* with a second edition of *ANEP*.[30] Finally there is the third edition of *ANET* itself, which appeared at the same time. But unlike the previous two editions, the new edition did not so much break new ground as give wider circulation to new translations of Ancient Near Eastern texts that had appeared elsewhere in the interim. To quote my own review at the time,

> The great appeal of (*ANET*) rested on sound foundations: for the first time it assembled some of the most significant Ancient Near Eastern texts in authoritative, generously annotated English translations based on the accumulated insight of several generations of scholarship scattered, till then, in a bewildering variety of publications not readily accessible to the average biblical scholar. The new edition (1969) fulfills some of the same desiderata .... But by its very nature it is essentially different from the original edition, for in great measure it concentrates on texts newly discovered or recovered, and by and large available in current publications, for the most part in English, which are complete with readable translations and scholarly apparatus.[31]

The trend noted in my review was not about to stop. On the contrary, the trickle observed there has meantime become a mighty stream. As ever more new texts are made available, the relationship between biblical and ancient Near Eastern studies has assumed an ever growing importance if only as measured by the sheer output of books and articles inspired by their comparison. Moshe Yitzhaki of Bar-Ilan University has even devised a whole new "bibliometric approach" to provide such a yardstick.[32] Defining "citation analysis" as "the analysis of the reference in scholarly publications of a certain subject field in order to describe patterns of citation,"[33] he applies this new technique to the fields of biblical and ancient Near Eastern studies and concludes that, at least in the small and somewhat random sample tested, "the figures indicate a relatively low use of the research literature of one field by the other."[34]

If his sample is representative, we face an anomalous situation: an ever increasing stream of ancient Near Eastern texts — recovered, reconstructed, edited and translated — which is relevant for biblical studies, but a statistical reluctance to employ them. Under the circumstances, a new compendium is called for all the more urgently. We do not, it is true, need a new *ANET* to provide us with a first authoritative English rendering of the texts, and as far as I know none is contemplated. But we do need a new compendium to assemble the existing renderings, update them where necessary, and indicate their relevance for biblical scholarship. That is what *The Context of Scripture* proposes to do. The project was conceived by David E. Orton, Senior Editor of E. J. Brill Publishers, and developed along lines set forth in a detailed proposal submitted to him by the undersigned in 1991. The collaboration of K. Lawson Younger, Jr. of LeTourneau University (Longview, Texas) as Associate Editor was secured shortly thereafter.

How does the new compendium differ from its predecessors? This question will here be considered from two perspectives — what may be called the horizontal and the vertical dimensions respectively — and the resulting theoretical formulations will then be illustrated with a concrete example or two.

The "context" of a given text may be regarded as its horizontal dimension — the geographical, historical, religious, political and literary setting in which it was created and disseminated. The contextual approach tries to reconstruct and evaluate this setting, whether for a biblical text or one from the rest of the ancient Near East.[35] Given the frequently very different settings of biblical and ancient Near Eastern texts, however, it is useful to recognize such contrasts as well as comparisons or, if one prefers, to operate with negative as well as positive comparison.[36] According to Pritchard, already Gressmann had maintained that "translations should serve ... not only for comparison and illustration, but for contrast."[37]

---

[28] J. B. Pritchard, ed., *The Ancient Near East: An Anthology of Texts and Pictures* (Princeton: Princeton University Press, 1958).

[29] J. B. Pritchard, ed., *The Ancient Near East, Vol. II: A New Anthology of Texts and Pictures* (Princeton: Princeton University Press, 1975).

[30] J. B. Pritchard, ed., *The Ancient Near East: Supplementary Texts and Pictures Relating to the Old Testament* (Princeton: Princeton University Press, 1969).

[31] W. W. Hallo, "Review of *ANET* (3rd ed.)," *JAOS* 90 (1970) 525.

[32] Moshe Yitzhaki, "The Relationship Between Biblical Studies and Ancient Near East Studies: a Bibliometric Approach," *ZAW* 99 (1987) 232-248.

[33] Ibid., 235.

[34] Ibid., 248.

[35] W. W. Hallo, "Compare and Contrast: the Contextual Approach to Biblical Literature," in *SIC* 3 1-30; idem, *The Book of the People* (Brown Judaic Studies 225; Atlanta: Scholars Press, 1991) chapter 2: "The Contextual Approach."

[36] Hallo, "New Moons and Sabbaths: a Case Study in the Contrastive Approach," *HUCA* 48 (1977) 1-18.

[37] *ANET* (1st ed., 1950) p. xiv.

But even where (positive) comparison is asserted, it is useful to raise questions of category and genre so that, as nearly as possible, like is compared with like. In the present project, the broader literary context, or category, will actually serve as the basic unit of organization. That is, recognizing that the relevant corpus has outgrown the bounds of a single volume, even a folio-sized volume, its three volumes are devoted respectively, to "canonical," "monumental" and "archival" texts from the ancient Near East. Since the biblical text (in its "canonical" form) is entirely canonical in the sense in which I choose to employ that term,[38] the reader will be immediately alerted to the categorical contrasts involved even when a comparison is suggested.

On a lower level of literary context, due attention is paid to genre (Gattung) and to the associated concept of life setting ("Sitz im Leben"). Thus, for example, within the volume devoted to "canonical" texts, the basic division is by "focus": divine, royal, or individual, with the divine focus embracing such genres as myths, hymns, prayers, divination, incantations and rituals. Finally, the questions of where, when and in what direction an alleged borrowing may have occurred is occasionally raised in the commentary, even if the question frequently cannot be answered.

But a text is not only the product of its contemporary context, its horizontal locus, as it were, in time and space. It also has its place on a vertical axis between the earlier texts that helped inspire it and the later texts that reacted to it. We can describe this feature of its interconnectedness as its vertical or, in line with current usage, its intertextual dimension. The field of biblical studies has been rather slow to employ the term itself and the field of ancient Near Eastern studies even slower.[39] But of course the concept as such has long been part of the stock-in-trade of both fields. Thus it is wholly appropriate to call attention to perceived instances of intertextuality both within each linguistic tradition and among separate traditions — and to do so, not in more or less random footnotes or enigmatic indices, but overtly and systematically in the margins of the translations.

The translations themselves, however, need to meet new standards if they are to serve as springboards for the recognition and designation of contextual and intertextual comparisons and contrasts. There is no need, it is true, to translate every significant text *de novo*, to reinvent the wheel, so to speak. But one can aspire to match the native terms and idioms with their English counterparts in such a way as to approach the ideal of a 1:1 relation in which each word (and only that word) is rendered by a given English equivalent, each derivative of that word with a derivative of that equivalent. This ideal cannot, of course, be carried out perfectly in practice, not even when the target language is German, though it was attempted with great determination by Martin Buber and Franz Rosenzweig in their translation of the Bible,[40] nor in French, where the same principle was applied by Andre Chouraqui, and certainly not in English, where a similar effort by Everett Fox has now given us a valuable new translation of the Pentateuch.[41] Nor has the method ever been applied to ancient Near Eastern texts *apart* from the Bible. But with the help of a data base, it should theoretically be possible — though difficult in practice — to make the attempt, and to see how many improvements emerge in the understanding, both of the text itself and of its relation to other texts.

To illustrate all the theoretical principles outlined above would take at least a half dozen examples, preferably chosen from a wide variety of ancient literary corpora. But the salient points can be illustrated adequately by one example that, for all its brevity, has a fairly wide set of evidentiary implications. The "Sumerian Sargon Legend" has been known in part since 1916 from an Uruk tablet subsequently acquired by the Louvre Museum,[42] and was duly noted in studies of Mesopotamian historiography, notably by H. G. Güterbock in 1934.[43] But a larger and nearly complete tablet belonging to the composition was excavated at Nippur in the season of 1951-52, assigned to the Baghdad Museum, and finally published by Jerrold Cooper and Wolfgang Heimpel in 1983. Thus nearly seventy years elapsed before the full import of the text emerged.[44]

Apart from sharing a common protagonist, the text as reconstituted has little or nothing to do with the better known Akkadian Sargon Legend, sometimes cited as a possible source of the Moses birth legend, though with little justifica-

---

[38] W. W. Hallo, "The Concept of Canonicity in Cuneiform and Biblical Literature: a Comparative Appraisal," in *SIC* 4, 1-19.

[39] Hallo, "Proverbs Quoted in Epic," in *Studies Moran*, 203-217, esp. 203-205. It should be noted that Moran himself used the term "intertextuality" already in *Studies Reiner*, 253 (end).

[40] Hallo, "Notes on Translation," *EI* 16 (H. M. Orlinsky Volume, 1982) 99*-102*; *idem*, "Franz Rosenzweig übersetzt," in Wolfdietrich Schmied-Kowarzik, ed., *Der Philosoph Franz Rosenzweig* (1886-1929) (Freiburg/München: Karl Alber, 1988) 1:287-300.

[41] *The Five Books of Moses ... a New Translation with Introduction, Commentary and Notes by Everett Fox* (Schocken Bible 1) (New York: Schocken, 1995).

[42] Vincent Scheil, "Nouveaux renseignments sur Šarrukin d'après un texte sumérien," *RA* 13 (1916) 175-179; republished by Henri de Genouillac, *Textes réligieux sumériens du Louvre 2* (TCL 16. Paris: Geuthner, 1930) No. 73.

[43] H. G. Güterbock, "Die historische Tradition und ihre literarische Gestaltung bei Babyloniern und Hethitern," *ZA* 42 (1934) 1-91, 44 (1938) 45-149, esp. 42:37f.

[44] J. S. Cooper and Wolfgang Heimpel, "The Sumerian Sargon Legend," *JAOS* 103 (1983) 67-82; republ. in J. M. Sasson, ed., *Studies ... dedicated to Samuel Noah Kramer* (AOS 65; 1984) 67-82.

tion.[45] It is in Sumerian, a product most likely of the neo-Sumerian period (ca. 2100-1800 BCE in linguistic terms), while the later text is in Akkadian, quite possibly commissioned by Sargon II of Assyria (722-705 BCE) or at least intended to celebrate his earlier namesake. The Sumerian text is, of course, not included in *ANET*, but as now known it includes at least one passage that bears comparison with a biblical pericope.

Lines 53-56 as translated by Cooper read:

> In those days, writing on tablets certainly existed,
> but enveloping tablets did not exist;
> King Urzababa, for Sargon, creature of the gods,
> Wrote a tablet, which would cause his own death, and
> He dispatched it to Lugalzagesi in Uruk.

As both editors noted, "Line 53 parodies the famous passage in *Enmerkar and the Lord of Aratta* 503ff."[46] — a passage, it may be added, not without its own echoes in the biography of Moses.[47] What was quickly pointed out by others, however, was that the motif of a king dispatching a potential rival to a third party carrying instructions to that party to put the rival to death so that the messenger becomes the means to his own demise, corresponds to a familiar folklore motif,[48] with echoes not only in the Bible but also in classical literature and even in Hamlet.

In the Iliad, Bellerophon was sent to the king of Lycia with a similarly deadly message. In 2 Samuel 11, King David rid himself of Uriah with a message that Uriah carried to David's general Joab. These parallels have been recognized in varying degrees by Herman Vanstiphout,[49] Veronika Afanas'eva,[50] and especially Bendt Alster.[51] They show that the Uriah pericope is made up, at least in part, of traditional literary topoi or folkloristic motifs, and justify the inclusion of the newly recovered Sumerian legend in the discussion of the biblical treatment of the theme.

The most recent treatment of the Uriah pericope well illustrates the use and usefulness of ancient Near Eastern parallels for the understanding of biblical texts — if only by showing the danger of ignoring them. In "Nations and nationalism: adultery in the House of David," Regina M. Schwartz uses the pericope to condemn not only David, his people, and all his progeny, but those who have repossessed the City of David and the land of Israel in his name to this day.[52] The study fails, not because of its political overtones, but because it presumes the historical validity of the episode, utterly ignoring its literary character. Where but in the Bible could one find national literature preserving the materials for so scathing a self-examination? And within the Bible, where more so than in the "court history of David" in 2 Samuel? And what if the author has not written history, but woven a traditional story of the "deadly letter" into an imaginative recasting of the succession narrative? Familiarity with the motif and its antiquity would at least suggest this alternative possibility.

The Sumerian Sargon Legend well illustrates the vertical component we have spoken of, depending as it does quite clearly on the earlier Sumerian Epic of Enmerkar and the Lord of Aratta, and echoed as we have seen by the later stories of Uriah in 2 Samuel and Bellerophon in the Iliad. But it also illuminates the "horizontal" context of any given text. Its focus on royalty in general, and on the spectacular rise to power of Sargon of Akkad in particular, is of a piece with the literary and ideological interests of the Ur III and Isin I dynasties of the neo-Sumerian cultural era (ca. 2100-1800 BCE).

It allows us to raise the same question as one which has repeatedly been raised with regard to comparable biblical material, namely: can we, in fact should we, separate literary and ideological considerations in assessing ancient sources? Can we and should we divide our sources strictly into literary and historical ones?

I have long pleaded for using literary and historical sources to illuminate each other — treating literary sources as precious aids in reconstructing history, and reconstructing history as the essential context for literature.[53] Recently,

[45] Brian Lewis, *The Sargon Legend: a Study of the Akkadian Text and the Tale of the Hero Who Was Exposed at Birth* (ASORDS 4; 1980); cf. *ANET* 119; Hallo, *The Book of the People*, 47f., 130f.

[46] *JAOS* 103 (AOS 65) 82. For this passage see below, p. 546 and G. Komoróczy, "Zur Atiologie der Schrifterfintlung im Enmerkar-Epos," *AoF* 3 (1975) 19-24; but more recently H. L. J. Vanstiphout, "Enmerkar's Invention of Writing Revisited," in *Studies Sjöberg*, 515-524.

[47] Hallo, *BP*, 48f., 183f., with earlier literature.

[48] K 789 in Stith Thomson's Index.

[49] H. L. J. Vanstiphout, "Some Remarks on Cuneiform ecritures," in *Studies Hospers*, 217-234, esp. pp. 224, 233, n. 65.

[50] V. K. Afanas'eva, "Das sumerische Sargon-Epos. Versuch einer Interpretation," *AoF* 14 (1987) 237-246. According to Alster *ZA* 77:171, Afanas'eva already made her views known at the *RAI* in Leningrad in 1984.

[51] B. Alster, "A Note on the Uriah letter in the Sumerian Sargon Legend," *ZA* 77 (1987) 169-173; *idem*, "Lugalbanda and the Early Epic Tradition in Mesopotamia," in *Studies Moran*, 59-72, esp. pp. 70f.

[52] *Critical Inquiry* 19 (1992) 131-150. My thanks to Jacob Lassner for calling the article to my attention.

[53] Cf. most recently Hallo, "The Limits of Skepticism," *JAOS* 110 (1990) 187-199, esp. pp. 189f. with nn. 20-41.

Marc Brettler has come to a similar conclusion from other premises. Using the story of Ehud as his point of departure, he faults both those who, like Robert Alter, see it as "only" literature, and those who, like Baruch Halpern, see it as genuine history.

The tale of Ehud has, in fact, more in common with the Uriah pericope than at first meets the eye — including the echo of a traditional motif first associated with the great kings of the Sargonic dynasty in Mesopotamia. I refer to the assassination of a ruling monarch by an ostensibly unarmed courtier. In the Mesopotamian historiographic tradition as enshrined in its most characteristic form, the omen literature, the dastardly deed was committed by resort to the cylinder seal, or more particularly (in my opinion) to the wooden pin on which it was mounted and by which it was attached to a necklace worn by its owner; if sharpened to a point, this pin could serve as a deadly weapon when whipped off the neck and plunged into the body of the unsuspecting victim, as was apparently the fate of no less than three of the Sargonic kings: Rimush, probably his (twin?) brother Man-ishtushu, and Shar-kali-sharri. The case of Ehud, who rid Israel of its Moabite oppressor with a well-timed thrust from the dagger concealed on his right side under his cloak, is not so very different, considering the relatively greater rarity of cylinder-seals in Israel.[54]

Thus I do not necessarily agree with Brettler in regarding the chief historical value of the Ehud story as lying in the attitude toward Moab on the part of Israel in the time of the author of the pericope (whenever that was!) that it reveals, but I agree with him in seeing the value of a concept of "literature as politics."[55] Such a concept had previously been recognized in Assyrian literature by Peter Machinist,[56] as Brettler later acknowledged,[57] and before that in Hittite literature by Harry Hoffner,[58] and in Egyptian literature by R. J. Williams.[59] What it implies is the rejection of any hard-and-fast dichotomy between "history" and "literature" in favor of a recognition that, often enough, history *is* literature, and vice versa. The old conceit held that biblical literature can be validated as history only when reflected in extra-biblical historical sources such as the Stele of Merneptah or the Mesha Stele, but is falsified as history and reduced to "mere literature" when anticipated or echoed in extra-biblical *literary* sources such as the Akkadian Sargon Legend or now the Sumerian Sargon Legend. This alone would justify a separation of the comparative material into historical monuments, canonical compositions, and archival documents. But the new attitude goes further. It recognizes that the assessment of a biblical text, so far from ending with the identification of an extra-biblical parallel, begins there.

In conclusion, the combination of an intertextual and a contextual approach to biblical literature holds out the promise that this millennial corpus will continue to yield new meanings on all levels: the meaning that it holds for ourselves in our own contemporary context, the meanings it has held for readers, worshippers, artists and others in the two millennia and more since the close of the canon; the meaning that it held for its own authors and the audiences of their times; and finally the meanings that it held when it was part of an earlier literary corpus. It is to the clarification of that oldest level of meaning that *The Context of Scripture* is dedicated.[60] It may also serve as a memorial to Pritchard, whose death occurred on January 1, 1997, as this volume was going to press.

---

[54] Hallo, "'As the Seal upon Thine Arm': Glyptic Metaphors in the Biblical World," in Leonard Gorelick and Elizabeth Williams Forte, eds., *Ancient Seals and the Bible* (Occasional Papers on the Near East 2/1; 1983) 7-17 and pl. xii, esp. pp. 13f.; *idem*, "'As the Seal upon Thy Heart': Glyptic Roles in the Bibiical World," *Bible Review* 1/1 (February 1985) 20-27, esp. p. 26.

[55] Marc Brettler, "The Book of Judges: Literature as Politics," *JBL* 108 (1989) 395-418.

[56] P. Machinist, "Literature as Politics: the Tukulti-Ninurta Epic and the Bible," *CBQ* 38 (1976) 455-482.

[57] *HUCA* 62:285, n. 1.

[58] H. A. Hoffner, Jr., "Propaganda and Political Justification in Hittite Historiography," in *Unity and Diversity*, 49-62.

[59] R. J. Williams, "Literature as a Medium of Political Propaganda in Ancient Egypt," in *Studies Meek*, 14-30.

[60] Scripture is here citied from and defined as the Hebrew (and Aramaic) Bible. This is not to deny the relevance of ancient Near Eastern parallels for New Testament studies, but that is a subject for another book and another editor.

EGYPTIAN CANONICAL COMPOSITIONS

A. DIVINE FOCUS

1. COSMOLOGIES

FROM THE "BOOK OF NUT" (1.1)

James P. Allen

This text consists of a series of captions accompanying the image of the goddess Nut stretched out as a representation of the sky, held off the earth by the atmosphere (Shu). Originally perhaps of Middle Kingdom composition, it appears on ceilings of the cenotaph of Seti I (Dynasty 19, ca. 1291–1279 BCE) at Abydos and the tomb of Ramesses IV (Dynasty 20, ca. 1163-1156 BCE) at Thebes; the texts were also copied, with exegesis, in two Demotic papyri of the second century CE. Together, the representation and its texts describe the ancient Egyptian concept of the universe.

Outside the Cosmos (Texts Dd-Ee, on Nut's right)
The uniform darkness,[1] ocean[2] of the gods, the place from which birds come: this is from her northwestern side up to her northeastern side, open to the Duat that is on her northern side,[a] with her rear in the east and her head in the west. These birds exist with their faces as people and their nature as birds, one of them speaking to the other with the speech of crying.[3] After they come to eat plants and to get nourished in the Black Land, alighting under the brightness of the sky, then they change into their nature of birds.

(Text L, above Nut) The upper side of this sky exists in uniform darkness,[b] the southern, northern, western and eastern limits of which are unknown,[c] these having been fixed in the Waters,[d] in inertness.[4] There is no light of the Ram there:[5] he does not appear there — (a place) whose south, north, west and east land is unknown[c] by the gods or akh's,[6] there being no brightness there. And as for every place void of sky and void of land,[7] that is the entire Duat.

a Job 26:7

b Job 18:18

c Job 38:19

d Gen 1:7

Description of Nut (Texts Ll, Gg, Q, and P)
Her right arm is on the northwestern side, [the left] on the [north]eastern side. Her head is the western Akhet, her mouth is the west.[8] (*The goddess's mouth is labeled*) Western Akhet, (*her crotch*) Eastern Akhet.

Cycle of the Sun (Texta Aa-Bb, to the winged sun-disk at Nut's mouth)
The Incarnation[9] of this god enters at her first hour of evening,[10] becoming effective again in the embrace[11] of his father Osiris, and becoming purified therein. The Incarnation of this god rests from life in the Duat at her second hour of pregnancy.[12] Then the Incarnation of this god is governing the westerners, and giving directions in the Duat. Then the Incarnation of this god comes forth on earth again, having come into the world, young, his physical strength growing great again, like the first occasion of his original state. Then he is evolved into the great god, the winged disk. When this god sails to the limits of the basin of the sky, she causes him to enter again into night,

[1] Lit., "joined darkness" (*kkw zmꜣw*). See Parker 1960:52. In the Book of Gates this term refers to hours 2-11 of night — i.e., those whose darkness is unbroken by light.

[2] Lit., "cool waters" (*qbḥw*), a term for the sky, specifically as a medium for travelling by boat (e.g., Pyr. 374c, 465a, 873c-d, 917a-b, 1049a, 1990b).

[3] Possibly for *mdw rmṯ* "human speech," though the determinatives indicate otherwise. Cf. Hornung 1963-1967:1 138, 3-4: "There is heard the sound of something in this cavern like the sound of men wailing."

[4] Verbal noun of *njnj* "be slack, inert" (*Wb* 2:203, 7; 275, 2-16). In creation accounts the term usually connotes the potentiality for movement and life.

[5] The Demotic text (pCarlsberg I 2, 27) glosses this line "There is no rising of the Sun there." The ram is a frequent image of the sun: Hornung 1973:85-87, pl. 5.

[6] That is, by the forces and elements of nature ("gods") and the deceased human beings who have made a successful transition to life after death with the gods ("akh's"): Allen 1988b:45.

[7] Perhaps "every void place of sky or earth," but the repetition of *šw* "void" suggests the reading adopted here (*šw n* for *šw m*). The text evidently defines the Duat as part of the world space surrounded by the universal Waters, but neither sky nor earth.

[8] Or "Her head is in the western Akhet, her mouth is in the west," but the label "Western Akhet" on Nut's cheek suggests an identification.

[9] The physical manifestation of a divinity (god, king, or deceased): von Beckerath 1984:39.

[10] The first hour of night, beginning at sunset: Parker 1960:35, 62.

[11] Lit., "inside the arms" (*ḫnw ˁwj*). The term refers to the usual means by which the *ka*, or life force, was passed: Pyr. 1653a.

[12] "Pregnancy" (*bkꜣt*) is the term used of hours 2-4 of night: Parker 1960:35. Here it refers to the beginning of the second hour past sunset, when the sun's light disappears from the sky as it enters the Duat.

into the middle of the night,[13] and as he sails inside the dusk these stars are behind him. When the Incarnation of this god enters her mouth, inside the Duat, it stays open after he sails inside her, so that these sailing stars[14] may enter after him and come forth after him. Where they course, is to their locales.

(Texts G, F, and E, to the sun-disk before Nut's foot)
The redness[15] after birth, as he becomes pure in the embrace of his father Osiris. Then his father lives, as he becomes effective [again] through him, as he opens in his splitting[16] and swims in his redness.

(Texts M-O, to the sun-disk on Nut's foot)
The Incarnation of this god comes forth from her rear. Then he is on course toward the world, apparent and born. Then he produces himself above. Then he parts the thighs of his mother Nut. Then he goes away to the sky.

(Texts J-K and H, to the winged scarab at Nut's thigh)
When the Incarnation of this god comes forth from the Duat, these stars come forth after him at the birthplace.[17] Then he is reared in the birthplace. Then he becomes effective again through his father Osiris, in the Abydene nome, on the first occasion of his original state. Then he is evolved and goes away to the sky, in the hour of "She Has Gone to Rest."[18] Then he is dominant, having come into the world. Then his heart and his physical strength evolve. Then Geb sees the Chick,[19] when the Sun has shown himself as he comes forth. Then he is entered into this (winged scarab).[20] Then he is evolved, like his original evolving in the world on the first occasion.

[13] Hours 5-8 of night: Parker 1960:35.

[14] A *hapax* (*sqdw*) evidently referring to the stars' motion through the sky. The Demotic text has *sbꜣw* "stars" (pCarlsberg I 3, 34).

[15] Written ideographically with the red crown, but the interpretation of the Demotic text is clear: "The redness comes after birth. It is the color that comes in the sundisk at dawn ... his rays being upon earth in the color named ... The red crown is that which is read 'redness'" (pCarlsberg I 2, 1-3; Parker 1960:49).

[16] Following the text of Seti I. The Demotic text glosses: "It opens to the sky" (pCarlsberg I 1, 39; Parker 1960:48).

[17] The Demotic text has *msqtt* "Milky Way" (pCarlsberg I 2, 4/6), but the earlier texts both have *nmstt* — possibly an *m*-formation of *msj* "give birth," with dissimilation **mmstt* > *nmstt*.

[18] The ninth hour of night: Parker 1960:51.

[19] Referring to the newborn sun. The word (*w*) is evidently the otherwise unattested origin of the phonetic value *w* of the quail-chick, its meaning suggested by the determinative of the seated child. The Demotic text has *ẖ* "newborn" (pCarlsberg I 2, 18).

[20] The demonstrative either modifies the picture of the winged scarab (suggested by a space left blank in the text), or is used as a noun. The Demotic text explains: "that is to say, the form of the Scarab that is in [the picture]" (pCarlsberg I 1, 28-29; Parker 1960:46).

REFERENCES

Frankfort 1933 I:72-86, II pl. 81; Parker 1960 I:36-94, pl. 30-51; Hornung 1972:485-86; Allen 1988a:1-9.

FROM COFFIN TEXTS SPELL 714 (1.2)

James P. Allen

This text is part of a series inscribed on coffins of the First Intermediate Period and Middle Kingdom, designed to aid the deceased's spirit in its daily journey from the Netherworld of the tomb to the world of the living. This particular spell, in which the deceased is identified with the primordial source of all matter as it first existed within the primeval waters, has so far been found only on one coffin.

The background of creation (CT VI 343j)
I am the Waters, unique, without second.

The evolution of creation (CT VI 343k-344d)
That is where I evolved,
on the great occasion of my floating that happened to me.[1]
I am the one who once evolved —
Circlet,[2] who is in his egg.

I am the one who began therein, (in) the Waters.
See, the Flood is subtracted from me:[a]
see, I am the remainder.[3]
I made my body evolve through my own effec-

a Gen 1:6-7

[1] The text opens with the universal waters as speaker, but from here to the end of the spell the speaker is Atum: cf. CT II 34g-h "Then said Atum to the Waters: I am floating, very weary." See n. 3 below.

[2] The term is a *hapax* (*ḏbnn*), evidently a diminutive of *ḏbn* "circle." Both this and the following phrase refer to Atum's primordial, unevolved state.

[3] These two lines use mathematical terminology — *prj* "be subtracted" (*Wb* I 525, 1) and *wḏꜣ* "remainder" (*Wb* I 400, 19) — to describe the distinction that existed between the primordial singularity of matter (Atum) and its environment (the universal waters).

tiveness.[4]
I am the one who made me.
I built myself as I wished, according to my heart.[5]

[4] An abstract (ʾḫw) denoting the quality of productive action, akin to magic: Friedman 1984-85; Borghouts 1987.
[5] The seat of thought and emotion. These three lines indicate that Atum's evolution into the created world reflected his own concept of the world as it should be.

REFERENCES

CT VI 343j-344d; Faulkner 1977:270; Allen 1988a:13-14.

FROM PYRAMID TEXTS SPELL 527 (1.3)

James P. Allen

The Pyramid Texts were inscribed on the walls of the substructures of royal pyramids at the end of the Old Kingdom, with the same purpose as their descendants, the Coffin Texts. This spell begins by describing the material derivation of the first two elements of the world — the atmospheres above and below the earth (Shu and Tefnut) — from the single source of all matter (Atum), as a "mythological precedent" for the daily rebirth of the deceased king.

The birth of Shu and Tefnut from Atum (Pyr. 1248)
Atum evolved[1] growing ithyphallic,[2] in Heliopolis. He put his penis in his grasp that he might make orgasm with it,[3] and the two siblings were born — Shu and Tefnut.

[1] Following the text of Merenre (M). Pepi I (P) has "Atum is the one who evolved." The text of Pepi II (N) is a reinterpretation, with initial "Atum Scarab" as vocative and the following lines as imperatives.
[2] Lit., "as one who comes extended," (*m jw sʾw jr.f*), where the self-referential *jr.f* indicates either the reflexive nature of the action or its relationship with the action of Atum's "evolution."
[3] Atum's masturbation is one of the metaphors employed in Eg. cosmogonies to explain the physical origin of the world from a single material source: Allen 1988a:14.

REFERENCES

Pyr. 1248a-d; Faulkner 1969:198; Allen 1988a:13-14.

FROM PYRAMID TEXTS SPELL 600 (1.4)

James P. Allen

The beginning of this spell, another "mythological precedent," combines three images of the first moments of creation. The first lines invokes the divine source of all matter (Atum) in his evolution as the sun ("Scarab") and the world-space within the primeval waters. This is followed by references to the "etymological" origin of Shu and Tefnut and to the source of their life force.

Atum as the First Things (Pyr. 1652-1653a)
Atum Scarab![1]
When you became high, as the high ground,
when you rose, as the benben[2] in the Phoenix[3]
Enclosure in Heliopolis,
you sneezed Shu, you spat Tefnut,[4]

[1] Referring to Atum in his ultimate evolution, the rising sun. The sun was often represented as a scarab beetle (*ḫprr*) through "etymological" association with the verb *ḫpr* "evolve."
[2] A pyramidion or squat obelisk representing the primeval hill, first Place to emerge at the creation. The root of the word, *bn* "swell up," also appears in *wbn* "rise, swell forth" (used of the sun at sunrise), and *bnw* "heron, phoenix" (see next note).
[3] Eg. *bnw* "heron," a metaphor for the rising sun through etymological association (*wbn* "rise"). The Greek concept of the phoenix rising from its own ashes derives from this image, but is not found as such in Eg. sources.
[4] "Etymological" explanations of Atum's first two evolutions: *jšš* "sneeze" and *tf* "spit." For the meaning of *jšš*, cf. *jšš ṯʾw* "sneeze air": Parker et al. 1979:71 and pl. 27, 17.

and you put your arms about them, as the arms of *ka*,
that your ka might be in them.[5]

[5] The image of the *ka* passed by means of an embrace reflects the hieroglyphic spelling of the word (*kꜣ*) as a pair of upraised arms. In Eg. thought, the *ka* is a spiritual aspect of men and gods, a kind of animating force, passed from the creator to the king, from the king to his subjects, and from a father to his children. The word is also the root of a derived abstract *kꜣw* "sustenance." Though usually represented only by its hieroglyph, the ka was occasionally depicted as a "twin" of the king's image — hence the older translation "double." See Allen 1988b:43-44.

REFERENCES

Pyr. 1652a-1653a; Faulkner 1969:246-247; Allen 1988a:13-14.

FROM COFFIN TEXTS SPELL 75 (1.5)

James P. Allen

Spells 75–81 of the Coffin Texts, which identify the deceased as a manifestation (*ba*) of the first element of the world (*Shu*), are a major source for the evolutionary view of creation promulgated in Heliopolis. In at least two MSS (S1C and S2C), these seven spells were treated as a single text, with the title "Spell of the *ba* of Shu and evolution into Shu" (CT I 314a). Spell 75, one of the most frequently copied of all Coffin Texts, describes the birth of Shu. In the cosmogony of Heliopolis, this is the first stage in the evolution of Atum that produced the created world.

Shu's relationship to Atum (CT I 314/315b-326/327a)
I am the *ba*[1] of Shu, the self-evolving[2] god:
it is in the body of the self-evolving god that I have evolved.

I am the *ba* of Shu, the god mysterious(?)[3] of form:
it is in the body of the self-evolving god that I have become tied together.

I am the utmost extent[4] of the self-evolving god:
it is in him that I have evolved.

I am the one who stills the sky for him,
I am the one who silences the earth for him.[5] [a]

I am the one who foretells him when he emerges from the Akhet,[6]
putting fear of him into those who seek his identity.

I am one who is millions, who hears the affairs of millions.
I am the one who transmits the word of the self-evolving god to his multitude.

I am the one who officiates over his boat-crew,
being stronger and more raging[7] than every Ennead.

The origin of Shu (CT I 326/327b-338/339b)
The speech of the original gods, who evolved after me, has been repeated to me,[8] when they asked of the Waters my evolution, seeing my strength in the great boat that the self-evolving god sails, and how I have acted[9] [b] among them, causing my reputation according to my evolution. I shall speak. Become still, Ennead! Become silent, gods, and I will tell you my evolution myself. Don't ask my evolution of the Waters.

a Hab 2:20
b Lam 3:63; Ps 139:2

[1] The term *ba* (*bꜣ*) denotes an aspect by which a god, person, or thing can be recognized. The *ba* is a nonphysical concept, perhaps best defined as the sum of an entity less its material form — in the case of human beings, somewhat akin to the notion of "soul" or personality. The *ba* of a deceased person traveled between the mummy, where it spent the night, and the world of daylight, where it was reunited with its life force (ka) to live as an "effective being" (akh). This mobile quality, combined with the hieroglyphic writing of the word (with the jabiru bird), gave rise to the common representation of the *ba* as a human-headed bird. See Zabkar 1968; Allen 1988b:43.

[2] "Self-evolving" (*ḫpr ḏs.f*) is a common epithet of the creator god, denoting his independence from external causality: Allen (1988b) 17. The term is used most often, and par excellence, of Atum, who evolved into the created world.

[3] The meaning of the term *sfg* is uncertain. The phrase "*sfg* of form" is used elsewhere of the sun (Pyr. *1061f = CT III 74e) and in the context of judgement (CT II 58a, 62d, 63f). The translation "mysterious" is based on Pyr. 665a, where *sfg* occurs in parallel with *štꜣ* "secret" (see n. 15 below). The term also occurs in the description of a god "*sfg* of body, (but) with many vessels": Vernus (1978) 183.

[4] Lit., "the one who is in the limit" (*jmj ḏr*).

[5] A reference to the quelling of chaos attendant on the creation, with its establishment of order.

[6] The creation of the atmosphere produced a void in the universal waters, into which the sun could rise for the first time. Shu thus "foretells" the sunrise.

[7] The term (*ḏnd*, later *dndn*) describes a quality directed against an enemy (*Wb* V 579, 4 = 471, 4/22 — here, against the enemies of the sun); it is also used of fire (*Wb* V 471, 23; cf. *Wb* V 530, 1, and the spelling in CT IV 328g). The M-Ann. MS substitutes "aggressive" (*ꜥḥꜣ.kw*).

[8] Variant "I have heard" in some MSS (M-Ann., G1C, A1T).

[9] Lit., "how I stood up and sat down" (*ꜥḥꜥ.n.j ḥms.n.j*): see Williams 1969:94.

When the Waters saw me, I was already evolved. He does not know where I evolved. He did not see with his face how I evolved.[10]

It is in the body of the great self-evolving god
that I have evolved,
for he created me in his heart,
made me in his effectiveness,
and exhaled me from his nose.[11]

Shu's nature (CT I 338/339c-344/345c and 354/355b-358/359a)
I am exhale-like of form,
created by that august self-evolving god
who strews the sky with his perfection,
the total of the gods' forms,[12]
whose identity the gods who sail him do not know,
whom the "sunfolk"[13] follow.

It is in his feet that I have grown,
in his arms that I have evolved,
in his limbs that I have made a void.

He created me himself in his heart,
he made me in his effectiveness.
I was not born by birth.

...

I am one exhale-like of form.
He did not give me birth with his mouth,
he did not conceive me with his fist.[14]

He exhaled me from his nose,
he made me in the midst of his perfection,
which excites those who are in the inaccessible places[15]
when he strews the sky with his perfection.

Shu's relationship to the rest of creation (CT I 372/373b-376/377c, 384b-385c, and 405b-c)
I do not have to listen to magic:[16]
I evolved before it.

My clothes are the wind of life:[17] [c]
it came forth about me, from the mouth of Atum.

I evolved in the god who evolved on his own,
alone, older than the gods.

I am the one who touches[18] for him the height of the sky.[d]
I am the one who brings to him his effectiveness,
who unites for him his million of ka placed in protection of his associates.[19]

...

For it is through creation in its entirety that I evolved,[20]
at the utterance of that august self-evolving god
who does not turn back on what he has said.[21] [e]
For I am the one who made to the limit, according to his command.

...

I am the god mysterious(?)[22] of form,
but I am in the utmost extent of sunlight.

c Gen 2:7; 6:17; 7:15; 7:22
d Job 22:12
e Jer 4:28

[10] Compare the description of the Waters in the "Book of Nut" (above, text 1.1) as existing "above" the sky. Shu, as the void, is distinct from the universal waters, and thus cannot be "known" by them.

[11] A two-stage description of Shu's birth, from the creator's original concept "in his heart" to the "effective" action that produced Shu. The third line refers to the "etymological" etiology of Shu, by "sneezing" (*jšš*).

[12] A reference to Atum's name (*j.tmw*), which is formed from the root *tm* "finish, end, complete," also found in the noun *tmw* "totality." As the singularity from which all matter derived, Atum is the sum of all the forces and elements of the created world (the gods).

[13] A general term for humanity, as the people on whom the sun shines: Gardiner 1947 I:111*-112*.

[14] These lines evidently contrast Shu's "immaterial" nature, as air, with the standard metaphors for his etiology via Atum's "sneezing" and masturbation.

[15] The term "inaccessible places" (*štꜣw*) is a designation of the Duat: Hornung (1975-76) I 4; II 49, 99 nn. 15-16. The sun's passage through this region at night "excites" (makes active) the beings who dwell in this region in a state of "inertness."

[16] Magic (*ḥkꜣ*, *ḥkꜣw*) broadly denotes the power to produce an effect by indirect means, somewhat akin to the western notion of sympathetic magic. In creation accounts, magic is the link between the creator's concept of the world and its physical evolution. It was considered a natural force, and thus a god (Heka, Hike). See Ritner 1993:4-28.

[17] Shu's "clothing" is a metaphor for the physical effect of the air, otherwise invisible. The same concept is elaborated in greater detail in CT Spell 80 (CT II 29f-31a). See p. 12 below.

[18] Variants have "who unites" (*dmḏ*: B1C) and "who ties together" (*ṯꜣz*: CT I 377d).

[19] The term "associates" (*wnḏwt*) derives from a designation of domesticated animals (*Wb* I:326, 2-4). As used here it evidently refers to the totality of humankind: compare the description of people as "noble animals" (*ʿwt špst*) in pWestcar 8, 17, and "the animals of the god" (*ʿwt nt nṯr*) in the Instruction for Merikare (pPetersburg 1116A 12, 1). See texts 1.11 and 1.35 below.

[20] Lit., "it is through making completely that I evolved" (*ḫpr.n.j js m ʿ jrt mj qd*). Variants have "through the one who made completely" (*m ʿ jr mj qd*: B1C, B2L, B1P), "through making similarly to me" (*m ʿ jrt my r.j*: M3C, M5C, M28C), and "it is through my agency that doing similarly has evolved entirely" (*ḫpr.n js m ʿ.j jrt my r ḏr*: S1-2C, T3C, M23C, G1T). The reference is evidently to Shu's causal priority over the rest of creation.

[21] A reference to the concept of creation by means of the spoken word, and to its irreversible nature.

[22] See n. 3 above.

REFERENCES

CT I 314/315b-405c; de Buck 1947; Faulkner 1964; Zandee 1971-72; Faulkner 1973:72-77; Allen 1988a:14-18.

FROM COFFIN TEXTS SPELL 76 (1.6)

James P. Allen

This text continues the tale of Shu's birth by describing how the structure of the world-space and its contents derive from the initial creation of the atmosphere. It also contains one of the first references to the four negative qualities of the primordial waters, later developed by the theologians of Hermopolis into a cosmogony of four divine couples, the Ogdoad.

Initial invocation: the deceased as Shu (II 1a-2a)
O you eight Infinite Ones,[1] who are at the parts of the sky,[a]
whom Shu made from the efflux[2] of his limbs,
who tie together the ladder[3] for Atum!

Come to meet your father in me!
Give me your arms,
tie together a ladder for me.

I am the one who created you,
I am the one who made you,
as I was made by my father Atum.

Shu's nature (CT II 2b-3c)
I am weary at the Uplifting of Shu,[4]
since I lifted my daughter Nut atop me
that I might give her to my father Atum in his utmost extent.

I have put Geb under my feet:
this god is tying together the land for my father Atum,
and drawing together the Great Flood for him.

I have put myself between them
without the Ennead seeing me.[5]

Shu's birth (CT II 3d-4d)
It is I who am Shu,
whom Atum created on the day that he evolved.[6]
I was not built in the womb,[b]
I was not tied together in the egg,
I was not conceived by conception.

My father Atum sneezed me in a sneeze of his mouth,[7]
together with my sister Tefnut.
She emerged after me,
while I was still hooded with the air of the Phoenix's[8] throat,
on the day that Atum evolved[9] —
out of the Flood, out of the Waters,
out of darkness, out of lostness.[10] [c]

Shu's relationship to the gods (CT II 5a-6b)
It is I who am Shu, father of the gods,
in search of whom, together with my sister Tefnut,
Atum once sent his Sole Eye.[11]
I am the one who made brightening the darkness possible for it.[12]
It found me as a man of infinite number:[13]
I am the begetter of repeated millions —
out of the Flood, out of the Waters,
out of darkness, out of lostness.[c]

It is I who am Shu, begetter of the gods.

a Deut 30:4
b Isa 44:2, 24; 49:5; Job 31:5
c Gen 1:2; 2 Sam 22:12; Ps 18:12; 88:6; Job 10:22; 22:11; 38:19

[1] Four or eight gods (*ḥḥw*) thought to assist Shu in holding the waters of the universe off the earth.
[2] A term (*rdw*) broadly denoting a material link between two things: for example, clouds are the "efflux" of the atmosphere, Shu.
[3] A metaphor for ascent to the realm of the sky.
[4] Term (*wṯzw šw*) referring to Shu's activity in holding the universal waters off the earth, often represented pictorially by the image of a male god (Shu) standing on the prone body of Geb, the earth, with arms upraised beneath the extended body of the sky (Nut).
[5] The "Ennead" here refers to the subsequent generations of gods, whose evolution followed that of Shu.
[6] The term "day" (here written with divine determinative, like the name Re) is a metaphor for the simultaneity of creation: Atum's evolution into the created world is equivalent to the birth of Shu, which created the world space within the universal waters.
[7] See p. 7, n. 4.
[8] See n. 3 to Pyramid Texts Spell 600 (p. 7). The term here is used in reference to Atum's solar aspect.
[9] See n. 6 above.
[10] These four terms refer to qualities of the primordial waters, defined in contrast to those of the created world: watery (*nwj*), vs. the "dryness" (*šw*) of the world; infinite in expanse (*ḥḥw*), vs. the world's "limits" (*ḏrw*); darkness (*kkw*), vs. light; and *tnmw*, an abstract from the verb *tnm* "become lost, go astray," probably referring to the chaotic or unknowable nature of the waters, in contrast to the order and tangibility of creation (Allen 1988a:20). The same qualities appear in the description of the universal waters in the "Book of Nut" (above text 1.1). As early as the Middle Kingdom, they were recognized as gods by the theologians of Hermopolis, and codified with four female counterparts into the Ogdoad. In the Coffin Texts, however, only the names of the Flood (*ḥḥw*) and the Waters (*nwj*) are written with divine determinatives; "darkness" and *tnmw* are treated as abstracts. In the Hermopolitan system, the last term is replaced by the god Amun (*jmnw* "hidden") and his counterpart, Amaunet.
[11] The term "eye" (*jrt*) is often used as a metaphor for the physical sun as an aspect of the creator or sun-god. The present passage refers to the sun as the final cause of creation, on whose behalf the world space was created.
[12] A similar line occurs in Spell 80 (CT II 30b) (see p. 12). The translation adopted here follows the text of B1Bo and G1T, with addition of the participle *jr* "who made possible" that appears in the other copies and in the parallel from Spell 80.
[13] Compare the phrase *z n nḥḥ* "a man of eternity" (i.e., someone who will live forever), in the tale of the Eloquent Peasant (Peas. B1, 126; see text 1.43 below).

REFERENCES

CT II 1a-6b; Faulkner 1973:77-80; Zandee 1973a; Allen 1988a:18-21.

FROM COFFIN TEXTS SPELL 78 (1.7)

James P. Allen

This text follows Coffin Texts Spell 76 after a few lines (Spell 77) that describe the birth of Shu through the combined metaphors of masturbation and spitting. The major theme in Spell 78 is the identification of this event with the evolution of Time in its two aspects: the permanent pattern of existence, identified with Tefnut; and the eternal repetition of life, identified with Shu.

Shu as the atmosphere (CT II 19a-b)
I am the *ba*[1] of Shu,
to whom was given Nut atop him and Geb under his feet.
I am between them.

Shu as the cycle of time (CT II 22a-b)
I am Eternal Recurrence, father of an infinite number.[2]
My sister is Tefnut, daughter of Atum, who bore the Ennead.

Tefnut as the pattern of time (CT II 23a-c)
I am the one who bore repeated millions for Atum:
Eternal Sameness is (my sister) Tefnut.[3]

[1] See n. 1 to Coffin Texts Spell 75 (p. 8).
[2] The word *nḥḥ* "Eternal Recurrence" derives from the root *ḥḥ* "million, infinite number" and denotes eternity conceived as the eternal repetition of the daily cycle of life. A dynamic concept, associated with the verbs *ḫpr* "evolve" and *ᶜnḫ* "live," it is exemplified on the cosmic scale in the daily setting and rising of the sun, and on the human scale in the cycle of generations. See Assmann 1975a. Its etiology here is equated with the birth of Shu, perhaps because both *nḥḥ* and *šw* are grammatically masculine.
[3] Following A1C, with the addition of *snt.j (pw)* from the other MSS. The word *ḏt* "Eternal Sameness" denotes eternity as the unchanging pattern of existence, established at the creation. It is a stable concept, associated with the verb *wnn* "exist" and exemplified in the concept of *mᵓᶜt* (Maat) "(natural) order." See Assman (1975). Spell 78 equates its genesis, and that of *mᵓᶜt*, with the birth of Tefnut, Shu's coeval "twin," probably because all three are grammatically feminine.

REFERENCES

CT II 19a-23c; Faulkner 1973:81-82; Zandee 1973b; Allen 1988a:21-27.

FROM COFFIN TEXTS SPELL 80 (1.8)

James P. Allen

Following a short reprise of Spell 76 (Spell 79), this text continues the temporal theme first sounded in Spell 78 and expands it through the additional concepts of Life, identified with Shu, and the natural Order of the universe, associated with Tefnut. As part of its exposition, the spell concentrates on the notion of the One (Atum) evolving into the multiplicity of life. This includes the phenomenon of generational death and rebirth (codified in Osiris and Isis), the creation of people, and the interrelationship of all living things. The spell's physical description of Shu as the atmosphere is one of the clearest statements of the Egyptian concept of divinity immanent in the elements of nature. Together with a short summation (Spell 81), this text completes the theological exposition of the meaning of Shu's birth that began in Spell 75.

Introduction (CT II 23d-28d)
O you eight Infinite Ones — an infinite number of Infinite Ones,[1]
who encircle the sky with your arms,
who draw together the sky and horizon[2] of Geb!
Shu has given you birth
out of the Flood, out of the Waters,
out of lostness, out of darkness,[3] [a]
that he might allot you to Geb and Nut,
Shu being Eternal Recurrence,

a Gen 1:2; 2 Sam 22:12; Ps 18:12; 88:6; Job 10:22; 22:11; 38:19;

[1] See n. 1 to Coffin Texts Spell 76, p. 10.
[2] Eg. *ᵓkr*, a term for the visible interface of sky and earth, often represented as a two-headed lion (east and west).
[3] See n. 10 to Coffin Texts Spell 76, p. 10.

and Tefnut, Eternal Sameness.[4]

The nature of Shu (CT II 28e-32a)
I am the *ba*[5] of Shu, who is at the Great Flood,
who goes up to the sky as he wishes,
who goes down to the earth as his heart decides.

Come in excitement[6] to greet the god in me!
I am Shu, child of Atum.

My clothing is the air of life,[b]
which emerged for it around me, from the mouth of Atum
and opens for it the winds on my path.
I am the one who made possible the sky's brilliance after the Darkness.

My skin is the pressure[7] of the wind,
which emerged behind me from the mouth of Atum.
My efflux[8] is the storm-cloud[9] of the sky,
my fumes[10] are the storm[9] of half-light.

The length of the sky is for my strides,
and the breadth of the earth is for my foundations.[c]

I am the one whom Atum created,
and I am bound for my place of Eternal Sameness.
It is I who am Eternal Recurrence,
who bore repeated millions;
whom Atum sneezed,
who emerged from his mouth,
as he used his hand that he desired, in order to let fall for the earth.[11]

The origin of Shu and Tefnut (CT II 32b-35h)
Then said Atum:

b Gen 2:7; 6:17; 7:15, 22; Job 38:9

c Gen 13:17

d Is 44:24

My living daughter is Tefnut.
She will exist with her brother Shu.
Life is his identity,
Order[12] is her identity.

I shall live with my twins, my fledglings,
with me in their midst —
one of them at my back,
one of them in my belly.

Life will lie with my daughter Order —
one of them inside me,
one of them about me.

It is on them that I have come to rely,[13]
with their arms about me.

It is my son who shall live,
he whom I begot in my identity,
for he has learned how to enliven the one in the egg, in the respective womb,
as people, that emerged from my eye[14] —

(the eye) that I sent forth when I was alone [d] with the Waters, in inertness,
not finding a place in which I could stand or sit,
before Heliopolis had been founded, in which I could exist;
before the Lotus[15] had been tied together, on which I could sit;
before I had made Nut so she could be over my head and Geb could marry her;
before the first Corps[16] was born,
before the original Ennead had evolved and started existing with me.

Then said Atum to the Waters:
I am floating, very weary,[17] the natives inert.[18]

---

[4] See nn. 2-3 to Coffin Texts Spell 78, p. 11.

[5] See n. 1 to Coffin Texts Spell 75, p. 8.

[6] The Eg. root *ḥᶜj* or intensive *ḥᶜjᶜj* seems to denote arousal, sexual or otherwise, at the sight of someone or something, often from a state of prior inactivity. In the creation accounts it usually has a milder connotation of simple activity.

[7] An abstract (*mḏdw*) from the verb *mḏd* "press (*Wb med* I:416), strike (*Wb* II:191, 14-192, 2), adhere to (*Wb* II:192,3-5)," which seems to have the root meaning of forceful touching or pressure. The sentence is evidently an attempt to explain the physical reality of air, which is otherwise unseen.

[8] See n. 2 to Coffin Texts Spell 76, p. 10.

[9] For these terms (*qrr* and *nšnj*, respectively), see Roccati 1984:346.

[10] A term (*jdt*) used of a god's scent (Pyr. 456a; Urk IV 339,15). It is a byproduct of burning incense (Simpson 1974 pl. 31 ANOC 69.1 vert. 4-5) and gives off smoke (Pyr. 365b).

[11] These lines are a conflation of the two metaphors used to describe the etiology of Shu, etymological (*jšš* "sneeze") and physical (masturbation). The image of Atum "desiring" his hand reflects its deification — thus transforming the metaphor of masturbation into the more usual one of birth.

[12] The term "order" (*mᵓᶜt*) is a fundamental component of the Eg. world-view, a concept combining the western notions of natural law and social and moral norms. Order was established as part of the creation itself, as a force of nature and thus divine (Maat). Like the other forces and elements of the world, it is unchanging, a quality expressed here by its equation with the temporal concept of Eternal Sameness. The opposite of order is disorder or chaos (*jzft*), which equally has both social and moral as well as natural aspects. The most recent comprehensive study is Assmann 1990.

[13] Lit., "I have stood up" (*ᶜḥᶜ.n.j*): cf. *Wb* I :219, 18. The same usage appears in Hornung 1975-76 II:38, 13.

[14] A reference to the "etymological" etiology of human beings (*rmṯ*) from the "tears" (*rmyt*) of the sun (the creator's "eye").

[15] The Lotus (*qᵓd*: cf. Pyr. 284c, 541d; CT I 94b) is part of an early Eg. metaphor for the first act of life following the creation — the initial sunrise from the opening petals of a lotus flower growing on the first Place, the primeval Hill.

[16] A term (*ẖt*, lit., "body") for the group of gods usually known as the Ennead.

[17] In creation accounts, weariness (*wrḏ*), like inertness (see n. 4 to the "Book of Nut," p. 5), connotes the potentiality for activity — here, Atum's potentiality for the evolution that will produce the created world.

[18] See note 17. "Natives" (*pᶜwt*) is a term normally used of the Egyptians as original inhabitants of Egypt: Gardiner 1947 I:108*-110*.

It is my son Life, who lifts up my heart, that will enliven my heart[19]
when he has drawn together these very weary limbs of mine.

The Waters said to Atum:
Kiss[20] your daughter Order.
Put her to your nose and your heart will live.
They will not be far from you —
that is, your daughter Order and your son Shu, whose identity is Life.
It is of your daughter Order that you shall eat,
it is your son Shu that shall elevate you.

Shu as Life (CT II 35i-36e and 39b-40b)
I, in fact, am Life, son of Atum —
from his nose he bore me,
from his nostrils I emerged.
I shall put myself at his collar,
that he may kiss me and my sister Order,
when he rises every day and emerges from his egg,
when the god is born in the emergence of sunlight[21]
and homage is said to him by those whom he begot.
...

I am Life, lord of years,
Life of Eternal Recurrence, lord of Eternal Sameness —
the eldest that Atum made with his effectiveness,[22]
when he gave birth to Shu and Tefnut in Heliopolis,
when he was one and evolved into three,
when he parted Geb from Nut,
before the first Corps was born,
before the two original Enneads evolved and were existing with me.

In his nose he conceived me,
from his nostrils I emerged.

e Gen 1:6

f Gen 2:7; 7:22; Job 27:3

He has placed me at his collar
and he does not let me get far from him.

The process of Life (CT II 40c-43h)
My identity is Life, son of the original god:
I live in the ...(?)[23] of my father Atum.
I am Life at his collar, the one who freshens the throat —
whom Atum made as Grain when he sent me down to this land,
and to the Isle of Fires, when my identity became Osiris, son of Geb.[24]
I am Life, for whom the length of the sky and the breadth of Geb were made:
it is from me that presented offerings emerge for the god.[25]

My father Atum will kiss me as he emerges from the eastern Akhet;
his heart will rest at seeing me as he proceeds in rest to the western Akhet.

He will find me on his way,
and I will tie on his head and enliven his uraeus.[26]

I will fix the head of Isis on her neck,
and assemble Osiris's bones.
I will make firm his flesh every day
and make fresh his parts every day —
falcons living off birds, jackals off prowling,
pigs off the highlands, hippopotami off the cultivation,
men off grain, crocodiles off fish,
fish off the waters in the Inundation[27] [e] —
as Atum has ordered.

I will lead them and enliven them,
through my mouth, which is Life in their nostrils.[f]
I will lead my breath into their throats,
after I have tied on their heads by the Annunciation[28] that is in my mouth,

[19] The text employs two different terms for "heart" here. The first, *jb*, is the more common term, usually connoting the heart as the seat of thought and emotion (compare the English "lift the spirits"). The second, *ḥ*ˀ*tj*, often has a more physical connotation, as here.

[20] Or perhaps "inhale." The verb (*sn*) denotes an action of the nose rather than the lips.

[21] Following B7C, the only MS with *m* "in." The other copies apparently read "when the god is born and sunlight is sent forth" (*ms.t nṯr pr.t j*ˀ*ḫw*).

[22] See n. 4 to Coffin Texts Spell 714, p. 7.

[23] A word (*bznw*) of unknown meaning, perhaps a mineral: Harris 1961:190-191.

[24] These two lines define the realm of life. In the world of the living, it is embodied in grain, the fundamental staple of the Eg. diet. In the Duat, it is concentrated within the mummy of Osiris, the source of all potential life.

[25] The presentation of offerings was the major component of Eg. rituals, in both divine and mortuary cults. It was perhaps the chief responsibility of the Egyptians to their gods. See Assmann 1970:63-65. In mortuary cults, food and drink were offered so that the deceased might benefit from the life-sustaining force within them.

[26] The term "uraeus," a Greek vocalization of Eg. *j*ᶜ*rt*, refers to the protective serpent usually depicted on the forehead of gods and the king.

[27] Following B1C, the only copy with initial ᶜ*nḫ* "live off." In the other MSS, these clauses specify what is meant by "make fresh his parts," with the first noun in each clause in apposition to "his parts" and the prepositional phrase indicating the means. The position of human beings in this list is noteworthy — as part rather than the apex of the natural order. Contrast Gen 1:26.

[28] "Annunciation" (*ḥw*) denotes the power of bringing about a result by enunciating it with the tongue. It is often divinized (Hu) and usually paired with Perception (*sj*ˀ, Sia), the power of conceptualization associated with the heart. Annunciation was considered an aspect of magic (see n. 16 to Coffin Texts Spell 75, p. 9), exercised by the creator and the king.

which my father Atum, who emerged from the eastern Akhet, has given me.
I will enliven the little fish[29] and the crawling things on Geb's back.
I, in fact, am Life that is under Nut.

[29] A *hapax* (*ḥḏḏw*) probably identical with the Ptolemaic *ḥḏw* "fish, fowl" (*Wb* III:355, 19-20). The determinative here indicates a kind of fish.

REFERENCES

CT II 27d-43h; Faulkner 1973:83-87; Zandee 1974; Allen 1988a:21-27.

FROM PAPYRUS BREMNER-RHIND (1.9)

James P. Allen

The papyrus from which this text is taken (pBM 10188) is a collection of theological treatises and magic spells against the dangers of the Netherworld (represented in sum by the demon Apophis), compiled from various sources at the beginning of the Ptolemaic Period. This selection, originally composed perhaps as early as the Ramesside Period, describes the evolution of multiplicity from the unity of Atum, who is both the "Lord to the Limit" (of the created world) and the sun at the dawn of creation ("Evolver").[1] It is unusual for its use of abstract terminology, based on the verb *ḫpr* "evolve,"[2] in addition to the physical metaphors that Egyptian theologians regularly used to describe the process of creation.

Title (26,21) SCROLL OF KNOWING THE EVOLUTION of the Sun AND OF OVERTHROWING APOPHIS. RECITATION.

Evolution of the many from the one (26,21-24)
The Lord to the Limit, speaking after he evolved:
I am the one who evolved as Evolver.
When I evolved, evolution evolved.
All evolution evolved after I evolved,
evolutions becoming many in emerging from my mouth,
without the sky having evolved,
without the earth having evolved,
without the ground or snakes[3] having been created in that place.
I became tied together in them[4] out of the Waters, out of inertness,
without having found a place in which I could stand.[a]

I became effective in my heart,
I surveyed with my face.
I made every form alone,
without having sneezed Shu,
without having spat Tefnut,[5]
without another having evolved and acted[6] with me.

I surveyed in my heart by myself
and the evolutions of evolutions became many,
in the evolutions of children
and in the evolutions of their children.

The first generation (26,24-27,2)
I am the one who acted as husband with my fist:
I copulated with my hand,
I let fall into my own mouth,
I sneezed Shu and spat Tefnut.[7]
It is my father, the Waters, that tended them,
with my Eye[8] after them since the time they became apart from me.
After I evolved as one god,
that was three gods with respect to me.

The sun (27,2-4)
When I evolved into this world,

[a] Job 26:7

[1] The papyrus contains two versions of this text. The second, with the same title, is slightly longer (28, 20-29, 6).

[2] The text uses three writings of this root: (1) that of the verb and its conjugated forms (*sḏm.f*, *sḏm.n.f*, and participle), with bookroll determinative; (2) the same spelling with plural strokes, apparently with the meaning of the infinitive "(process of) evolution" (only in 26, 22); (3) a form with written (curl) *w* (*ḫprw*), plural strokes, and the determinatives of the upright mummy and falcon on a standard. The last is evidently a concrete noun, and is treated grammatically as plural ("evolutions").

[3] The word (*ḏdft*) is a collective, and includes worms and crawling insects such as centipedes, as well as snakes. These forms of life were viewed by the Egyptians as chthonic beings, primordial to the creation.

[4] The pronoun probably refers to the elements of the created world mentioned in the preceding lines. "Tie together" (*ṯˀz*) is an Eg. idiom for physical realization.

[5] A reference to the "etymological" etiology of these two gods, via "sneezing" (*jšš* : *šw*) and "spitting" (*tf* : *tfnt*).

[6] Or "who acted for himself" (*jr n.f*).

[7] These lines represent an attempt to syncretize the "etymological" and physical explanations of the birth of Shu and Tefnut. Atum's semen is envisioned as falling into his mouth, from which it is "sneezed" and "spat" to produce the two gods.

[8] A metaphor for the sun as a manifestation of the creator.

Shu and Tefnut grew excited in the inert waters[9]
in which they were,
and brought me my Eye after them.[10]

And after I joined together my parts,
I wept over them:
that is the evolution of people,
from the tears that came from my Eye.[11]

She raged against me after she returned
and found I had made another in her place
to replace her as (my) effective one.
So I promoted her place on my face,
and afterward she began to rule this entire land.[12]

b Job 31:2; Is 5:24

c Gen 1:24

When their rage fell to their roots [b]
I replaced what she had taken from her.[13]

The creation of multiplicity (27,4-6)
When I emerged from the roots
I created all the snakes and everything that
evolved from them.[14] [c]
Then Shu and Tefnut gave birth to Geb and Nut.
Then Geb and Nut gave birth to Osiris, Horus
Fore-Eyed,[15] Seth, Isis and Nephthys,
from one womb,[16] (one) after the other,
and they gave birth to their multitude in this
world.

[9] The writing combines that of *nwj* "the Waters" and *nnw* "inertness," and may reflect the variant form of the former name (Nun), which is derived from the same root as *nnw*.

[10] See n. 6 to Coffin Texts Spell 80, p. 12. In this case, the "excitement" of Shu and Tefnut refers to their evolution as a void in the universal waters, which produces a space for the sun ("my Eye") to appear in.

[11] See n. 14 to Coffin Texts Spell 80, p. 12.

[12] These lines are a logical outgrowth of the metaphor of the sun as the creator's eye. Its departure into the world at the dawn of creation leaves a void in Atum's "face," which he fills by making a new eye to serve as his "effective" instrument in governing the world. The conflict between the two is resolved by Atum's promotion of the eye to his uraeus.

[13] The parallel text (29,4-5) has "Her anger fell to her roots because of the roots I replaced in her, (but) she became soothed when her place in my face was promoted, and she began to rule the entire land." On that basis, the present sentence seems to mean "When the rage of my eye and its replacement abated(?), I replaced what my new eye had taken from the previous one." The referents of the third-person pronouns, however, are unclear, and the interpretation of the phrase "fall to the roots" (*ḫr r wꜣbw*) as an idiom for "abate" is speculative; for the latter, cf. the idiom *sḫr r tꜣ* "throw to the ground," used of removing defects (*Wb* IV:258, 1).

[14] "Emerging from the roots" (*prj m wꜣbw*) is otherwise unattested, but evidently refers to Atum's transition from his primordial state of existence to his ultimate realization as the created world. The "snakes and all that evolved from them" are the chthonic elements of Atum's first evolution (see n. 3 above).

[15] "Fore-eyed" (*ḫntj-n-jrtj*, lit., "forward of eyes") is an epithet of Horus in his solar aspect.

[16] I.e., all from the womb (*ẖt* "body") of Nut. The text omits the second "one," probably from haplography (*m ẖt wꜥt* <*wꜥ*> *m sꜣ wꜥ*).

REFERENCES

Faulkner 1933:59, 15-61, 12; Faulkner 1937:172-73; Faulkner 1938:41-42; *ANET* 6-7; Piankoff 1955:24; Sauneron 1959):48-51; Allen 1988a:28-30.

FROM COFFIN TEXTS SPELL 335 = BOOK OF THE DEAD SPELL 17 (1.10)

James P. Allen

This spell, the most frequently copied of all major Egyptian funerary texts, equates the deceased's passage from the tomb to daylight with the sun's journey from night to day, a theme summarized in its title. It originated in the Coffin Texts and was subsequently incorporated in their New Kingdom descendant, the so-called Book of the Dead, which was known by the same title. Almost from its inception, the spell accumulated extensive glosses on the original text. The excerpt below contains its opening lines along with the most important of their glosses from both the Coffin Texts and Book of the Dead.[1] The text deals with the concept of the sunrise as both the culminating act of Atum's evolution and the determining factor in the newly-created world.

Title (CT IV 184/185a)
SPELL FOR EMERGING BY DAY IN THE NECROPOLIS.[2]

Introduction (CT IV 184/185b-186/187a)
The word evolved, totality was mine[3] when I existed alone.

[1] The translation is based on the earlier, Coffin Texts version, which is generally better than the later copies in the Book of the Dead. The glosses from the Book of the Dead are based on the archetype text established by Rößler-Köhler 1979.

[2] The Eg. *prt m hrww* "emerging by day" is ambiguous: "emerging into daylight" is also possible. In Urk IV 148, 12, the phrase is contrasted with *nwyt m grḥ r jz* "returning by night to the tomb," suggesting the translation adopted here.

[3] Most copies have *mdt*, a concrete noun meaning "word, content (of a letter or decree), matter, affair"; the abstract *mdw* "speech, speaking" appears in M4C, T2Be, and M1NY. The latter, plus the determinative of the "man with hand to mouth" in T1C, M7-8C, and T3Be, indicates that the reference here is to the creator's *fiat* ("word") rather than to the act of creation itself ("matter, affair"). Book of the Dead copies have generally reinterpreted the line as *ḫpr mdt n nb tmw* "The word of the Lord of Totality evolved."

The first sunrise (CT IV 186/187b)
I am the Sun[4] in his first appearances.

Glosses (CT IV 187d-f, BD 17)

CT That is him rising in the east of the sky. Variant: it is the beginning of the Sun appearing over the world.

BD Who then is he? It is the Sun when he began the reign he has exercised. It is the Sun's beginning to appear in the kingship he has exercised, when Shu's uplifting had not yet evolved and he was on the high ground[5] in Hermopolis, when the children of exhaustion[6] had been given to him as the Hermopolitans.[7]

The sun as Atum (CT IV 188/189a-190/191b)
I am the great self-evolving god,

Glosses (CT IV 188/189b-c, BD 17)

CT Who is he, the great self-evolving one? It is water: it is the Waters, father of the gods.

BD Variant: it is the Sun.

who created his identities,[8] lord of the Enneads,

Glosses (BD 17)[9]

BD Who then is he? It is the Sun when he created the identities of his parts. It is those gods who are after him evolving.

the unopposable one of of the gods.

Glosses (CT IV 191c-d, BD 17)

CT Who is it? It is Atum in his disk.

BD Variant: it is the Sun rising in the eastern Akhet of the sky.

The sun determines time (CT IV 192/193a)
Yesterday is mine;[a] I know tomorrow.

a Ps 90:4

Glosses (CT IV 192/193b-c and 193d-f, BD 17)

CT As for yesterday, it is Osiris; as for tomorrow, it is the Sun. Who is it? The day of We Are Enduring. It is the burial of Osiris and causing his son Horus to rule.[10]

BD Who then is he? As for yesterday, it is Osiris; as for tomorrow, it is the Sun, on the day when the enemies of the Lord to the Limit were destroyed and his son Horus was caused to rule. Variant: It is the day of We Are Enduring. It is the burial of Osiris being directed by his father the Sun.

The sun establishes order (CT IV 194/195a-196/197a)
The gods' battleship/battleplace[11] was made in accordance with my say.

Glosses (CT IV 194/195b-d, BD 17)

CT As for the god's battleplace, it is the West. It was made in order to battle the gods' enemies.[12]

BD What then is it? It is the West. It was made for the gods' *ba*'s in accordance with the command of Osiris, lord of the western cemetery. Variant: It is the West. This is what the Sun caused every god to descend to. Then he fought it[13] for them.

I know the identity of that great god who is in it.

Glosses (CT IV 196/197c, BD 17)

CT The Acclaimed,[14] the Sun, is his identity.

BD Who then is he? It is Osiris. Variant: the Acclaimed, the Sun, is his identity. It is the *ba* of the Sun, by means of which he himself copulates.

---

[4] Eg. *rʿw* (Re, Ra). Book of the Dead copies substitute "Atum."

[5] A reference to the primeval hill, the first Place to emerge at the creation.

[6] The root *bdš* is used both of physical and moral exhaustion. Here, however, it appears to be a synonym for the "inert" (see n. 4 to the "Book of Nut," p. 5) and chaotic qualities of the primeval waters, since the "children of exhaustion" (*msw bdšt*) — a term that normally describes the sun's enemies in the Duat — are clearly equated here with the Ogdoad (see next note).

[7] I.e., the four pairs of gods representing the negative qualities of the universal waters, focus of the Hermopolitan cosmogony (see n. 10 to Coffin Texts Spell 76, p. 10).

[8] A few MSS have reinterpreted the relative clause as "for whom the lord of the Ennead created" (*qmꜣ.n n.f nd psḏt*) or "who created the Enneads for himself" (*qmꜣ n.f psḏwt*); the standard text is preserved in Book of the Dead copies. Establishment of the name (*rn*) of a thing creates its "identity": thus, the evolution of Atum into the substance of the world is equivalent to the "naming" of his parts, as explained in the gloss to this line.

[9] This line has no glosses in the Coffin Texts.

[10] These glosses are among the most informative sources for the Eg. concept of linear time. The past (*sf* "yesterday") is equated with the preceding generation (Osiris) and death ("the burial of Osiris"), the future with the present generation (Horus) and the sunrise. Together, the two form a permanent pattern of existence ("the day of We Are Enduring").

[11] "Battleship" is undoubtedly the original text, as indicated by the next line. A number of copies have reinterpreted the word as "battleplace," and this in turn seems to have served as the basis of the gloss. Of the Coffin Texts MSS that have glosses, only two (B1Y and B9C[a]) show the ship determinative; one of these (B9C[a]) has the unique gloss *nšm[t] pw* "It is the *nšmt* boat (of Osiris)" (the gloss of B1Y is lost).

[12] This sentence appears only in M1C and M54C. Both copies read *jr.n.t.s r sʿḥꜣ ḫftjw nṯrw*; the context, and later versions, suggest the meaning "battle" for the rare infinitive *sʿḥꜣ* (*Wb* IV 53,1) rather than the normal causative "cause to battle." The Book of the Dead's "for the god's *ba*'s" (*n bꜣw nṯrw*) first appears in the Coffin Texts MS BH1Br.

[13] Evidently referring to the West; but cf. Rößler-Köhler 1979:172-73 (26*).

[14] The epithet "Acclaimed" (*ḥknw*) reappears in the New Kingdom "Litany of the Sun," where the solar deity is called *ḥkn n jrt.f* "acclaimed because of his eye": Hornung 1975-76 I:35.

The sun as the determinant of all things (CT IV 198/199a-200/201a)
I am the great Phoenix[15] that is in Heliopolis,
the accountant[16] of that which exists.

Glosses (CT IV 200b-203b)[17]
CT Who then is he? It is Osiris. As for that which exists, it is Eternal Recurrence and Eternal Sameness. As for Eternal Recurrence, it is day; as for Eternal Sameness, it is night.[18]

[15] See n. 3 to Pyramid Texts Spell 600, p. 7.

[16] Lit., "the one who pertains to allotting" (*jrj sjpt*): cf. Englund 1978:81.

[17] The Book of the Dead glosses are essentially the same as those of the Coffin Texts.

[18] The identification of the sun as Osiris evidently refers to the moment when the two join in the depths of the Duat, thus regenerating Osiris and giving the sun the power of rebirth. At this point the two gods are one, as shown by a relief in the tomb of Nefertari that depicts a mummified body (Osiris) with ram's head and solar disk (the sun), identified by the labels "It is the Sun resting in Osiris, Osiris resting in the Sun": Hornung 1973: pl. 5. This is the defining moment of all existence ("that which exists"), when its permanent pattern ("Eternal Sameness") is reaffirmed for yet another daily cycle ("Eternal Recurrence") (see nn. 2-3 to Coffin Texts Spell 78, p. 11). In keeping with the concept of time elaborated in a preceding gloss (see n. 10, above), the text also identifies the former with the past ("night") and the latter with the future ("day").

REFERENCES

CT IV 184/185a-201f; Faulkner 1973:262-269; Rößler-Köhler 1979:157-158, 212-215; Allen 1988a:30-35.

COFFIN TEXTS SPELL 261 (1.11)

James P. Allen

While the Heliopolitan accounts of creation concentrate primarily on the material origins of the world, they also acknowledge the role played by magic, the divine force that translated the creator's will into reality.[1] In Egyptian thought, magic has two components: conceptualization ("Perception"), which takes place in the heart; and Annunciation, the creative expression of a thought through the medium of the spoken word. Spell 261 of the Coffin Texts identifies the deceased with this force; as such, it presents a good exposition of the role that magic played in the creation.[2]

Title (CT III 382a)
EVOLVING INTO MAGIC.

Invocation (CT III 382b-d)
O noble ones who are before the Lord of Totality![3]
Behold, I am come to you.
Be afraid of me, in accordance with what you have learned.

The role of Magic (CT III 382e-387b)
I am the one whom the Sole Lord made[4]
before two things had evolved in this world,[5]
when[6] he sent his sole eye,[7]
when[8] he was one,
when something came from his mouth,
when his million of ka was in protection of his associates,[9]
when he spoke with the one who evolved with him, than whom he is mightier,[10]
when he took Annunciation in his mouth.[11]
I, in fact, am that son of Bore-All,[12]

[1] For a discussion of the Eg. concept of magic, see Ritner 1993:4-28.

[2] The spell exists in two versions, one from Asyut, preserved in four copies, and the other from el-Bersheh, for which only one MS survives. The translation here is based on the Asyut copies, with the more important variants from the Bersheh version noted in the notes.

[3] The "Lord of Totality" (*nb tmw*) is an epithet of Atum (*j.tmw*), reflecting his role as material source of the created world. The "noble ones who are before" him are the gods.

[4] Variant "I am the identity that the Sole Lord made" (S1C^b). The Bersheh version replaces this line with the clause "about the identity of the Sole Lord" continuing the preceding sentence.

[5] I.e., when Atum was still one and had not yet evolved into the multiplicity of the world.

[6] Bersheh version "after."

[7] See n. 11 to Coffin Texts Spell 76, p. 10.

[8] Bersheh version "because."

[9] The same phrase occurs in Coffin Texts Spell 75; see p. 9, n. 19. The Bersheh version adds "who shine in his eye."

[10] The Bersheh version has "when he spoke to Scarab" (see n. 1 to Pyramid Texts Spell 600, p. 7), suggesting that the reference here is to the sun.

[11] See n. 28 to Coffin Texts Spell 80, p. 13. The idiom *jtj ḥw* "take Annunication" may have the sense of "starting to announce": cf. Lacau and Chevrier 1977 I:123 n. e, and compare English "take flight."

[12] There is no obvious referent for the demonstrative *pw* "that," unless it is meant to relate the term "son" to the preceding description. The Bersheh version adds "born without a mother." "Bore-All" (*ms tmw*) is another epithet of Atum.

and I am the protection[13] of that which the Sole Lord commanded.
I am the one who gave life to the Ennead.[14]
I am Acts-As-He-Likes, father of the gods, high of stand,[15]
who made the god functional in accordance with that which Bore-All commanded,
a noble god, who speaks and eats with his mouth.[16]

The status of Magic (CT III 387c-389e)
Become still for me!
Bow down to me!
I have come to tread on the bulls of the sky and sit on the bulls of the sky[17]
in my great rank of Lord of Ka's,[18] the heir of Atum.
I have come to take my seat and receive my rank.

All was mine before you evolved, gods.[19] [a]
Go down, you who came at the end![20]
I am Magic.

[a] Prov 8:22-31

[13] S1C[a] adds a human determinative, perhaps indicating "I am the magician."
[14] The Bersheh version adds "the met one of the gods, that which they met without that noble one, lord of the noble ones, having made them" — evidently referring to the priority of magic.
[15] Referring to the standard on which the gods' images were carried.
[16] "Eating with the mouth" reflects a common concern of the Coffin Texts for the deceased's ability to use his bodily functions properly after death. Here the deceased, as magic, "speaks" as well as "eats" with this faculty.
[17] A reference to the four winds (CT II 399a), here exemplifying the deceased's control (as magic) over the forces and elements of nature.
[18] See n. 5 to Pyramid Texts Spell 600, p. 8.
[19] Note the same phrase used of the creator himself in the opening lines of Coffin Texts Spell 335 (p. 15 above).
[20] I.e., who evolved after magic itself.

REFERENCES

CT III 382a-389e; te Velde 1970:180; Faulkner 1973:199-201; Allen 1988a:37-38; Ritner 1993:17.

FROM COFFIN TEXTS SPELL 647 (1.12)

James P. Allen

The conceptual link between the creator's *fiat* and its material realization in the forces and elements of the world was conceptualized by the theologians of Memphis in the creative role of their god Ptah. The earliest exposition of this theology appears in Spell 647 of the Coffin Texts. Attested in only one copy, it is a long spell identifying the deceased with all aspects of the Memphite god. The excerpts below concern Ptah's role in the creation.

Title (CT VI 267a)
PROTECTION THROUGH PTAH.

Ptah's etiology (CT VI 267f-s)
Thus said Atum:
"Let my vertebra be fixed,
let my egg be firm on the vertebrae of the Great Flood.[1]
Oh, oh, my son!
How good is your disposition,
how creative is he whom I have begotten!"
That is the evolution of my identity of Ptah,
good of disposition, great of strength.[2]
"He to whom report is made in the palace of the lord of life,
to whom his places report,
for whom his ranks are promoted beyond those greater than him,"
said Perception[3] about me.
That is the evolution of my identity of helper,
lord of order, Scribe at the fore of the Great House.[4]
Order is excited at my command [for] life and dominion.[5]
Thoth is on my "great flood" against that from

[1] This sentence establishes the evolutionary background to Ptah's origin: Atum's desire to evolve precedes Ptah's role in that process.
[2] Ptah was frequently called "good of disposition" (*nfr ḥr*) because of his reputation for answering prayers. The adjective "creative" (*ptḥ*, from a rare verb meaning "sculpt, fashion") supplies the etymological origin of the god's name (*ptḥ*): see Osing 1976:652-53. The concept of "(physical) strength" (*pḥtj*), paronomastic with the name, refers to the effectiveness of Ptah's role in creation.
[3] Perception (*sjꜣ*) denotes the power of conceptualization based on observation. As here, it is frequently deified (Sia), and coupled with Annunciation, which it logically precedes (see n. 28 to Coffin Texts Spell 80, p. 13).
[4] The epithet "helper" (*smy*) evidently reflects Ptah's reputation for answering prayers (see n. 2 above). The phrase "lord of order" (*nb mꜣꜥt*) probably refers to his role in the creation (see next note); it is also used of the sun/Atum (CT I 352/353d; VII 268a, 279b-c). The role of scribe reflects Ptah's function as intermediary to the creator; the "Great House" (*pr wr*) is the archetypical royal shrine of Upper Egypt.
[5] This line explains what is meant by the epithet "lord of order": Ptah's commands activate ("excite": see n. 6 to Coffin Texts Spell 80, p. 12) the natural and moral order of the world.

which my pen is barred,
there being nothing the gods can do.[6]

Ptah establishes order (CT VI 267t-268b)
I am one noble in his place,
who is in the heart of the Lord of the Shrine.[7]
I emerge from and enter into the shrine of the Lord to the Limit,
elevating Order on the offering-slab of Shu and him in the sarcophagus,[8]
causing the Sound Eye[9] to enter,
punishing disorder in the council,[10]
and driving off the Sun's abomination from his boat,
while every god is exalting me,
every akh is in awe of me,
and the subjects are worshipping my goodness.[11]

Ptah governs all life (CT VI 268c-o, 269j-k, and 269r-u)
I am the one who makes plants grow,
who makes green the shores of the Nile Valley;
lord of desert lands, who makes green the wadis,
chief of the Nubians, Asiatics, and Libyans.
The Nine Bows have been netted for me,
and totality has been given me by the Sun, Lord to the Limit.

I am South of His Wall,[12] sovereign of the gods.
I am king of the sky,
distributor of ka's,[13] who officiates over the Two Lands;
distributor of ka's, who gives *ba*'s,[14] manifestations,[15] ka's, and beginnings.
I am distributor of ka's, and they live according to my action:
when I wish, I make it possible for them to live,
there being none of them who can speak to me
except for [the one who made] that unique identity of mine,
because I am Annunciation in his mouth and Perception in his body.
...
I emerge from and enter into [the shrine of the Lord] to the Limit,
telling him the conduct of the Two Lands
in accordance with how I make it possible for them to live there,
...
giving life and conducting gifts to the gods who have offerings.[16]

It is I who am lord of life, who officiates in Nut,[17]
while Seth is my escort because he knows the conduct of what I do.
I am the lord of life.

[6] Ptah's role as "scribe" involves the participation of Thoth, god of writing. The meaning of "on my great flood" (*ḥr mḥt.j wrt*) is uncertain: it may be a "cosmogonic" variant of the idiom "on the water" (*ḥr mw*), meaning "loyal." Thoth's assistance insures that Ptah's "written" commands cannot be opposed.

[7] The phrase "in the heart" (*jmj jb*) is normally used by officials to indicate their access to the king. While it probably carries this connotation here as well, it also has a deeper meaning, since the spell later describes Ptah's relationship to the creator as "Annunciation in his mouth and Perception in his body." The "Lord of the Shrine" is Atum, as the next line indicates; the "shrine" here is a metaphor for the created world.

[8] Ptah's actions establish the order of creation, both in the world of the living ("Shu") and in the Duat, the domain of Osiris ("him in the sarcophagus").

[9] The Sound Eye (*wḏ*ꜣ*t*) is a metaphor for the sun as an aspect of Horus, the god of kingship: Ptah's role makes the sunrise possible.

[10] "Disorder" (*jzft*) is the opposite of natural and moral law (*m*ꜣꜥ*t* "order"). As "lord of order," Ptah evaluates the actions of each individual at the final judgement in the "council" (*ḏ*ꜣ*ḏ*ꜣ*t*) of gods.

[11] The beings mentioned in the last three clauses are three of the four classes of sentient beings recognized by the Egyptians: the gods are the original forces and elements of the created world; the akh's (ꜣ*ḫjw*) are human beings who have died and joined the gods in an "effective" (ꜣ*ḫ*) form of new life; the word "subjects" (*rḫwt*) denotes the living (as subjects of the pharaoh). The fourth class of sentient beings is that of the dead, human beings who have not made a successful transition to new life after death and now float lifeless in the waters of the Duat. All four classes are mentioned later in this spell (CT VI 269p), as "people, gods, akh's, and the dead."

[12] A frequent epithet of Ptah, referring to the location of his major temple in Memphis, outside the "White Walls" that delimited the town for much of its early history.

[13] This phrase (*nḥb-k*ꜣ*w*) denotes a deity (Neheb-kau) specifically associated with the transmission of life force (ka), for unknown reasons depicted (as here, via the determinative) as a serpent. The transmission of ka's is a prime function of kingship (see n. 5 to Pyramid Texts Spell 600, p. 8).

[14] See n. 1 to Coffin Texts Spell 75, p. 8.

[15] The word is an abstract from the verb *ḫ*ꜥ*j* "appear," here denoting "appearance" as a verbal noun (the act of appearing) rather than a concrete term (the outward appearance of something).

[16] See n. 25 to Coffin Texts Spell 80, p. 13.

[17] I.e., in the boat of the sun, which sails across the waters of the sky (Nut) during the day.

REFERENCES

CT VI 267a, 267f-268o, 269j-k/r-u; Faulkner 1977:221-23; Allen 1988a:38-42.

FROM A RAMESSIDE STELA (1.13)

James P. Allen

In the Middle Kingdom Coffin Texts, the creative role of Ptah is clearly secondary to that of Atum, the material source of creation. In the New Kingdom, however, it evolved into a full cosmogony in its own right, combining the intellectual principle of Ptah with the material role of Ta-tenen ("Rising Land"), the deified Primeval Hill representing the first instance of created matter. One of the most concise expositions of this Memphite system appears on a private stela of the Ramesside Period, now in Copenhagen (GNC 897/AEIN 54).

Introduction (col. 1)
Yours truly[1] is worshipping your perfection,
great Ptah, South of His Wall,[2]
Ta-tenen in the midst of the Walls.[3]

Ptah as creator (cols. 1-4)
Noble god of the first occasion,
who built people and gave birth to the gods,[4]
original one who made it possible for all to live;
in whose heart it was spoken, who saw them evolve,
who foretold what was not and thought of what is.
There is nothing that has evolved without him,
he whose evolution is their evolution[5] in the course of each day,
anterior to what he has determined.

Ptah as king (cols. 4-5)
You have set the world to its laws as you made it,
and the Black Land is fixed under your command, like the first occasion.

[1] This expression (*b*ʾ*k jm*, lit., "the servant there") derives from the epistolary style of the Middle Kingdom, where it is regularly used as a circumlocution for the first person when addressing someone of higher rank.
[2] See n. 12 to Coffin Texts Spell 647, p. 19.
[3] A short form of the original name of Memphis, "White Walls."
[4] Cf. Urk IV 1850,2-3 "Ta-tenen, who caused people and the gods to evolve."
[5] In the Eg., a relative clause impossible to render in grammatical English: lit., "he who they evolved when he evolved" (*ḫpr.w ḫpr.f*).

REFERENCES

Koefoed-Petersen 1936:57; Koefoed-Petersen 1948:37 and pl. 37A; Assmann 1975b:466; Allen 1988a:38-42.

FROM THE BERLIN "HYMN TO PTAH" (1.14)

James P. Allen

Although much of what we know about Egyptian cosmogony derives from funerary compositions such as the Pyramid Texts, Coffin Texts, and Book of the Dead, informative reflections of these creation accounts are also preserved in hymns designed for use in daily temple rituals. One such hymn to Ptah, preserved on a papyrus from the reign of Ramesses IX now in Berlin (pBerl. 3048), is an important source for the Memphite cosmogony centered on the creative role of Ptah Ta-tenen.

Introduction (2,1-2 and 3,1-2)
Worshipping Ptah, father of the [god]s,
Ta-tenen, eldest of the originals, [at] daybreak.[1]
[Recitation]:
Greetings, Ptah, father of the gods,
Ta-tenen, eldest of the originals,
...
who begot himself by himself, without any evolving[2] having evolved;
who [craf]ted[3] the world in the design of his heart;
evolution of his evolutions,[2]
model who gave birth to all that is,
begetter who created what exists.[4]

[1] The hymn was designed to be used in the ritual of opening the god's shrine at daybreak.
[2] This text uses virtually the same orthography as that of Papyrus Bremner-Rhind (see p. 14, n. 2) to distinguish the various forms of the root *ḫpr* — verb ("evolve"), infinitive ("[process of] evolution"), and concrete noun ("evolution," here both singular and plural).
[3] A reference to Ptah's association with the work of artisans. The high priest of Ptah in Memphis was called "greatest of the directors of artistry" (*wr ḫrp ḥmwt*).
[4] These two lines display a subtle use of wordplay and grammatical gender, contrasting "model" (fem. *twt*) and "begetter" (masc. *wtt*), and associating the notion of "birth" with the former and "creation" with the latter.

Ptah as creator (4,3-5,1)
PHARAOH[5] has come before you, Ptah:
he has come before you, god distinguished of form.
Greetings before your originals,
whom you made after you evolved in the god's body,
(you) who built his body by himself,
without the earth having evolved, without the sky having evolved,
without the waters having been introduced.[6]

You tied together the world, you totalled your flesh,
you took account of your parts and found yourself alone,
place-maker, god who smelted[7] [a] the Two Lands.

There is no father of yours who begot you in your evolving,
no mother of yours who gave you birth:
your own Uniter,[8] [b]
active one who came forth active.

When you stood up on the land in its inertness,
it drew together thereafter,
you being in your form of Ta-tenen,
in your evolution of the one who totals the Two Lands.[9]

The one whom your mouth begot and your arms have created[10] —
you took him from the Waters,
your action modelling your perfection:
your son, distinguished in his evolving,
who dispels for you the uniform darkness[11] with the radiance of his two eyes.[12]

Ptah's character (11,4-8)
O be fearful of him, O be afraid of him —
this god who made your needs.
Give adulation to his might
and become content in the presence of his two sound eyes.[12]

Since his words are the balance of the Two Lands,[13]
there is no bypassing the utterance he has made.[14]

The great identity that lays storms,
which [every] face fears when his *ba*[15] [e]volves;
magic that has control of the gods,
whose respect is great in the Ennead:
the reckoning [of him] is in what he has begun,
his control is among that which he has made.

a Is 44:24
b Gen 2:7; Isa 29:16; Jer 18:6

[5] A generic designation, which would have been replaced by the name of the ruling pharaoh in the actual ritual.
[6] Written here as the term for the physical substance rather than the name of the universal waters. The former was thought to derive from the latter, entering the world from under the earth or, as the Nile, through caverns in the south of Egypt.
[7] A further reference to Ptah's association with craftsmanship: in this case, metalworking.
[8] Lit., "your own Khnum." Khnum (*ẖnmw*), whose name means "uniter," was the deity who formed the physical substance of each individual like a vessel of clay on a potter's wheel. Cp. Gen 2:7; Isa 29:16; Jer 18:6. See Gordon 1982:203-214.
[9] The Two Lands (Upper and Lower Egypt) were united (*dmḏ* "combine, total") both physically and symbolically at the site of Memphis.
[10] Referring to the sun, as the last clause of this sentence makes clear. In another section of this hymn (10,3-5), the sun, speaking as Ptah's "eldest son," says of him: "I came forth from him, the lord of all people, who created me in the Waters, raised up the sky for me and supported the earth for me, and sails me in the body of Nut."
[11] The darkness before creation (dispelled by the first sunrise) and still existing unbroken in the universal waters outside the world: see n. 1 to the "Book of Nut," p. 5.
[12] The sun and moon, which were identified respectively as the right and left eyes of the solar aspect of Horus.
[13] The phrase "balance of the Two Lands" (*mḫꜣt tꜣwj*) carries a dual connotation here: as the measure of the natural and moral order (*mꜣꜥt*) established by the creator's "words" with the creation of the world, and as a reference to Memphis, which was often described by the same phrase (see n. 9 above).
[14] A reference to the immutability and permanence of the natural order. Compare the description of the creator in Coffin Texts Spell 75 as the god "who does not turn back on what he has said" (p. 9).
[15] Referring to the sun as a manifestation (*ba*) of Ptah: here written like the homonymous word "Ram," often used of the sun.

REFERENCES

Möller 1905:36-46; Wolf 1929; Sauneron 1953; Assmann 1975b:322-33; Allen 1988a:38-42.

FROM THE "MEMPHITE THEOLOGY" (1.15)

James P. Allen

Perhaps the most famous of all Egyptian creation accounts is preserved on a worn slab of black granite, created for erection in the temple of Ptah at Memphis during the reign of the Nubian pharaoh Shabaqo and now in the British Museum (BM 498). As its dedicatory text records, the stone was purportedly inscribed in order to preserve a much older document, probably on papyrus or leather; lacunae deliberately incorporated in the copy support this claim. For a long time the original was thought to derive from the Old Kingdom or even earlier, but advances in our understanding of Egyptian grammar and theology have now made a date in the Nineteenth

Dynasty more likely.[1] The text is remarkable not only for its history but more importantly for the content of its closing section, translated here.

Dedication (line 2)

His Incarnation[2] copied this writing anew in the house of his father Ptah South of His Wall,[3] when His Incarnation found it as something that the predecessors had made, worm-eaten and unknown from beginning to end. Then [His Incarnation] copied [it] anew — and it is better than its former state — for the sake of his name enduring and making his monuments last in the house of his father Ptah South of His Wall, for the length of eternity, as something that the Son of Re [SHABAQO] [4] did for his father Ptah Tatenen that he might achieve given life eternally.

Creation by thought and expression (cols. 53-56)

There was evolution into Atum's image through both the heart and the tongue.[5] And great[6] and important is Ptah, who gave life to all the [gods] and their ka's as well through this heart and this tongue, as which Horus and Thoth have both evolved by means of Ptah.[7]

It has evolved that heart and tongue have control of [all] limb[s], show[ing] that he is preeminent in every body and in every mouth — of all the gods, all people, all animals, and all crawling things that live — planning and governing everything he wishes.[8]

His Ennead is before him, in teeth and lips[9] — that seed and those hands of Atum: (for) Atum's Ennead evolv[ed] through his seed and his fingers, but the Ennead is teeth and lips in this mouth that pronounced the identity of everything, and from which Shu and Tefnut emerged and gave birth to the Ennead.

The eyes' seeing, the ears' hearing, the nose's breathing of air send up (information) to the heart, and the latter is what causes every conclusion[10] to emerge; [a] it is the tongue that repeats what the heart plans.

The result of creation (cols. 56-58)

So were all the gods born, Atum and his Ennead as well, for it is through what the heart plans and the tongue commands that every divine speech[11] has evolved.

So were the male life-principles made and the female life-principles set in place[12] [b] — they who make all food and every offering[13] — through that word that makes what is loved and what is hated.[14]

So has life been given to him who has calm and

a Deut 29:3
b Gen 1:27

[1] For the dating see Schlögl 1980:110-117. Junge (1973) has argued that the text is an original composition of the 25th Dyn.

[2] The standard form of reference to the ruling pharaoh as the current "incarnation" of kingship: see n. 9 to the "Book of Nut," p. 5.

[3] For this epithet, see n. 12 to Coffin Texts Spell 647, p. 19.

[4] The name inside the cartouche was erased, but can be restored on the basis of the prenomen elsewhere on the stone.

[5] These words begin a new section, the final one on the stone. What precedes is the script of a ritual commemorating the unification of the Two Lands and the founding of Memphis, and a list of the various forms of Ptah. The sentence reads lit., "(Something) evolved through the heart, (something) evolved through the tongue, into the image of Atum," with the subject of the verbs unexpressed. The word *tjt* "image" is used of depictions and hieroglyphic signs; the sense here is evidently that the world, which evolved from Atum, is an "image" of its material source. This text uses the words *jb* and *ḥꜣtj* interchangeably for "heart," although the sense is that normally associated with the former, as the seat of thought and emotion, rather than the latter, which often denotes the physical organ.

[6] The word *wr* "great" connotes both status and age: as the link between the creator's expressed thought and its realization in the "image of Atum," Ptah is prior to all other forces and elements of the created world. This creative function is consonant with the principle of "in-formation" that Ptah represents, exemplified in his role as patron of sculptors: the link between the concept of a statue in the sculptor's mind and its ultimate material realization.

[7] Thoth, the power of rationalization, and Horus, the force of kingship, reflect the operation of "heart" (thought) and "tongue" (command) in the created world. These principles, like all the other forces and elements of nature, came into being through Ptah's mediation.

[8] This sentence continues the theme stated in the final clause of the preceding sentence. The principle of expressed thought, which produced the created world, continues to affect it, thus showing that Ptah's mediation is still operative.

[9] This clause echoes a line from the much older Pyramid Texts: "My lips are the two Enneads: I am the great expression" (Pyr. 1100a-b): see Schott 1938. The initial pronoun "his" evidently refers to Ptah: although he is not otherwise associated with the Ennead, its gods derive from his action, as the following clauses make clear.

[10] Like its English calque, the Eg. *ʿrqyt* derives from a root meaning "conclude," which is used both in the sense of "complete, finish" and "understand" (*Wb* I:212, 3-6, 10-15). The entire sentence explains how the material principle embodied in the Ennead can be derived from the intellectual principle of thought and expression: like a "conclusion" expressed in speech, the created world is the expression of the creator's concept of it.

[11] The phrase "divine speech" is the Eg. term for the hieroglyphic writing system, concrete symbols (*tjt* "image": see n. 5, above) of mental concepts. The entire created world ("Atum and his Ennead as well") is thus a hieroglyphic text of the creator's original concept.

[12] The text here employs both the generic term for life force, *kꜣ* (ka: see n. 5 to Pyramid Texts Spell 600, p. 8), which is grammatically masculine, and its much rarer feminine counterpart *ḥmwst*.

[13] The two terms used here relate grammatically to their subjects: masculine *ḏfꜣw* "food" and feminine *ḥtpt* "offerings." The link between life force (*kꜣ*) and food (including food offerings) is reflected in the abstract *kꜣw* "sustenance," a concept that underlies the present passage.

[14] The significance of this final clause is unclear. Doing "what is loved and what is hated" are concepts normally associated with moral order, which is the subject of the next line. On that basis it has been suggested that the sentence should end with "through that word" and that the next sentence began with a conjoined clause that has been omitted: "<So has order been given> to the one who does what is loved

death given to him who has wrongdoing.[15] [c]

So was made all construction and all craft, the hands' doing, the feet's going, and every limb's movement, according as he governs that which the heart plans, which emerges through the tongue, and which facilitates[16] everything.

The role of Ptah (cols. 58-61)

It has evolved that Ptah is called "He who made totality and caused the gods to evolve," since he is Ta-tenen,[17] who gave birth to the gods, from whom everything has emerged — offerings and food, gods' offerings, and every good thing. So is it found understood[18] that his physical strength is greater than the gods'.

c Deut 30:15; Eccl 7:12

d Gen 2:2

So has Ptah come to rest after his making everything [d] and every divine speech[19] as well, having given birth to the gods, having made their towns, having founded their nomes, having set the gods in their cult-places, having made sure their bread-offerings, having founded their shrines, having modelled their bodies to what contents them. So have the gods entered their bodies — of every kind of wood, every kind of mineral, every kind of fruit, everything that grows all over him,[20] in which they have evolved.

So were gathered to him all the gods and their ka's as well, content and united in the lord of the Two Lands.[21]

<and disorder given> to the one who does what is hated": Sethe 1928:64-65. The use of the demonstrative ("that word"), however, suggests a following relative clause.

[15] The establishment of moral order is used here to exemplify the creation of order (*mꜣꜥt*) as part of the natural world.

[16] Lit., "which makes the help (of)" (*jrrt smw*): see Grdseloff 1952. This sentence concludes and summarizes the text's exposition of creation through expressed thought.

[17] Ptah is here equated with the Memphite god representing the first matter to emerge at creation (the primeval hill). This in turn is the source of all subsequent matter in the world, which is the subject of this and the following paragraph.

[18] Or "found recognized" (*gm s(j)ꜣ* rather than *gm sꜣ*): Allen 1988a:93. The verb *sjꜣ*, which denotes the faculty of Perception (see n. 28 to Coffin Texts Spell 80, p. 13) is perhaps more appropriate to the text; its operation via the senses was described at the end of the preceding section.

[19] See n. 11 above.

[20] As Ta-tenen, the physical earth: see n. 17 above.

[21] This line, which identifies Ptah as king, ends the cosmogonic exposition of the text. It also reflects the ritual that precedes the cosmogony (see n. 5 above), and introduces the final few columns on the stone (61-64), which summarize the themes of the ritual.

REFERENCES

Breasted 1902; Erman 1911; Sethe 1928:1-80; Junker 1939; *ANET* 4-6; Sauneron 1959:62-64; Lichtheim 1973:51-57; Allen 1988a:42-47.

FROM PAPYRUS LEIDEN I 350 (1.16)

James P. Allen

While the cosmogonies of Heliopolis and Memphis were concerned with the material source and the means of creation, respectively, that of Thebes was devoted to its ultimate cause, the creator himself, conceptualized in the god Amun. Among the many texts of New Kingdom and later date describing the role of Amun in the creation, the most extensive is that preserved on a papyrus from the end of Ramesses II's reign, now in Leiden (I 350). It is divided into a series of eulogies, artificially numbered as "chapters," each dealing with a different aspect of the god.[1] The five "chapters" excerpted below deal most directly with Amun's nature and his role as creator.

Amun as self-generating (2,25-28)

40TH CHAPTER.

The one who crafted himself, whose appearance[2] is unknown.
Perfect aspect, who evolved into a sacred emanation.[3]
Who built his processional images and created himself by himself.
Perfect icon,[4] whom his heart made perfect.
Who tied his fluid together with his body

[1] The papyrus originally contained 26 "chapters," of which 22 are preserved. The numbering is artificial, by units (1-9, the first four lost), tens (10-90), and hundreds (100-800). Most "chapters" begin and end with a word similar in sound to the number. The text also employs "verse points," superlinear dots that mark the end of each line.

[2] The term (*qj*) refers to the external appearance of something, its way of acting, or its situation (*Wb* V:15, 6-16, 8) — in essence, the means by which something is perceived by others.

[3] This term, whose root (*bsj*) means "introduce," refers to the sun (*Wb* I:475, 2), here as the means by which Amun is "introduced" into the world.

[4] The word literally means "controller" (*sḫm*): see Hornung 1971:52-53.

to bring about his egg in his secret interior.
Evolution of evolution,[5] model of birth.
Who finished himself in proper order,[6]
[...] who crafted 40.[7]

Amun as the source of all evolution (3,22-28)
80TH CHAPTER.
The Hermopolitans[8] were your first evolution
until you completed these,[9] while you were alone.
Your body was secreted among the elders,[10]
you hiding yourself as Amun,[11] at the head of the gods.
You made your evolution into Ta-tenen,
in order to cause the original ones to be born from your first original state.
Your perfection was raised aloft as Bull of His Mother,[12]
and you distanced yourself as the one in the sky, fixed in the sun.
You are come in fathers, maker of their sons,
in order to make functional heirs for your children.
You began evolution with nothing,[13]
without the world being empty of you on the first occasion.
All gods are evolved after you,
[...].[14]

Amun as the source of creation (3,28-4,8)
[90TH CHAPTER].
The Ennead is combined in your body:
your image[15] is every god, joined in your person.
You emerged first, you began from the start.
Amun, whose identity is hidden[16] [a] from the gods;
oldest elder, more distinguished than these.
Ta-tenen,[17] who smelted [himself] by himself, in Ptah:
the toes of his body are the Hermopolitans.
Who appeared in the Sun, from the Waters, that he might rejuvenate.
Who sneezed, [as Atum, from] his [mouth,
and gave birth to] Shu and Tefnut combined in manifestation.
Who appears on his throne as his heart prompts,
who rules for himself all that is, in his [disk].
Who ties together for himself the kingship of Eternal Recurrence,
down to Eternal Sameness, permanent as Sole Lord.
Light was his evolution on the first occasion,[b]
with all that exists in stillness for awe of him.
He honked by voice, as the Great Honker,[18]
at the District,[19] creating for himself while he was alone.
He began speaking[20] in the midst of stillness,
opening every eye and causing them to look.
He began crying out while the world was in stillness,[c]
his yell in circulation while he had no second,
that he might give birth to what is and cause them to live,
and cause every person to know the way to walk.[c]
Their hearts live when they see him.
His are the effective forms of the Ennead.[21]

Amun as pre-existing (4,9-11)
100TH CHAPTER.
Who began evolution[22] on the first occasion.
Amun, who evolved in the beginning, with his

a Judg 13:18
b Gen 1:3-5
c Ps 143:8

[5] This text uses the same orthographic conventions as those found in a similar phrase predicated of Ptah in the "Berlin Hymn": see n. 2 to that text (p. 20).

[6] Lit., "orderliness" (*bw m*ᵓᶜ) an abstract formed from the root of the word *m*ᵓᶜ*t* "order." The verse point here has been placed erroneously after *bw* and before *m*ᵓᶜ.

[7] The meaning of this phrase is unknown: one or more key words have been lost at the beginning of the line.

[8] I.e., the Ogdoad. The word here is a nisbe (*ḫmnjw*) from the name of Hermopolis (*ḫmnw*), itself a reference to the Ogdoad (*ḫmnt* "group of eight"), and used as a play on the "chapter" number (*ḫmnw* "80").

[9] The notion of "completing" (*km*) has a dual reference here. Amun "completes" the Ogdoad through the creation; he also "completes" them as the fourth of four pairs, together with his female counterpart Amaunet.

[10] I.e., the gods of the Ogdoad, who, as qualities of the primeval waters, existed before all the other gods.

[11] A reference to the etymology of Amun's name (*jmnw* "hidden").

[12] This term is normally used of Amun's solar aspect. Amun created the sky and is immanent in the sun, son of the sky (Nut): he is thus the male sexual partner ("bull") of his own mother.

[13] Or "you began to evolve." The line reads *š*ᵓᶜ*.n.k ḫpr nn wnt*, lit., "You began evolving without what exists."

[14] Some two lines (6 verses) are lost.

[15] For this term (*tjt*) see the "Memphite Theology," p. 22, n. 5.

[16] This phrase (*jmn rn.f*) is occasionally used as a fuller form of Amun's name, and is perhaps its origin.

[17] Ta-tenen, the primeval hill, occurs first in the list of Amun's creations as the first element of the created world to emerge from the universal waters. The name (*t*ᵓ*-ṯnnj* "land that becomes distinct") also reflects the adjectival phrase used of Amun in the preceding line (*ṯnj r nn* "more distinguished than these").

[18] The goose was sacred to Amun, probably because its morning honking suggested the god's voiced that "spoke" the first dawn into existence — as indicated by this and the following lines.

[19] Probably a reference to the primeval hill, the first Place ("District").

[20] Lit., "He parted words" (*wp.f mdwt*). The phrase recalls the idiom "part the mouth" (*wpj r*) for "speak" (*Wb* II :300, 1-2) and is used here as a conscious parallel to "opening the eye" (*wn jrt*) in the following line.

[21] The reading of the final word is uncertain. "Ennead" (*psḏt*) is possible, and seems required by the homonomy with the "chapter" number (here, *psḏww* "90") that usually ends each "chapter."

[22] Or "began to evolve": cf. n. 13 above.

emanation unknown,
no god evolving prior to him,
no other god with him to tell of his appearance,[23]
there being no mother of his for whom his name was made,
and no father of his who ejaculated him so as to say "It is I."[24]
Who smelted his egg by himself.
Icon[25] secret of birth, creator of his (own) perfection.
Divine god, who evolved by himself
and every god evolved since he began himself.

Amun as transcendent (4,12-21)
200TH CHAPTER.
Secret of evolution (but) glittering of forms,
wonderful god of many evolutions.
All gods boast in him,
in order to magnify themselves in his perfection, like his divinity.
The Sun himself is joined with his person.
It is he who is the Great One in Heliopolis,[26]
who is also called Ta-tenen.
Amun, who emerged from the Waters that he might lead everyone.
Another of his evolutions is the Hermopolitans.
Original one who begot the original ones and caused the Sun to be born,
completing himself in Atum,[27] one body with him.
It is he who is the Lord to the Limit, who began existence.
His *ba*, they say, is the one who is in the sky.[28]
It is he who is the one who is in the Duat,[29] foremost of the east.
His *ba* is in the sky, his body in the west,
and his cult-image in Southern Heliopolis,[30] elevating his appearances.
Amun is one, hiding himself from them.[31]
He is concealed from the gods, and his aspect is unknown.
He is farther than the sky, he is deeper than the Duat.[32] [d]
No god knows his true appearance,[33]
no processional image of his is unfolded through inscriptions,[34]
no one testifies to him accurately.
He is too secret to uncover his awesomeness,
he is too great to investigate, too powerful to know.
Instantaneously falling face to face into death
is for the one who expresses his secret identity,[e] unknowingly or knowingly.[35]
There is no god who knows how to invoke him with it.
Manifest one whose identity is hidden,[e] inasmuch as it is inaccessible.[36]

Amun as One (4,21-26)
300TH CHAPTER.
All the gods are three:
Amun, the Sun, and Ptah, without their seconds.
His identity is hidden in Amun,
his is the Sun as face, his body is Ptah.[37]
Their towns are on earth, fixed for Eternal Recurrence:
Thebes, Heliopolis, and Memphis, unto Eternal Sameness.

d Prov 25:2-3
e Judg 13:18

[23] See n. 2 above.
[24] These two lines may reflect Eg. customs in naming a newborn: Zandee 1947:74; Posener 1970:204-205.
[25] See n. 4 above.
[26] I.e., Atum. The first sixteen lines of this "chapter," dealing with Amun's perceptibility through nature, explain his relationship to the other major cosmogonic systems (Heliopolis, Memphis, and Hermopolis), and to the two major forces in the created world (the sun, in the world of the living, and Osiris, in the Duat).
[27] This line (*tm.f sw m tmw*) is similar to the one that established the etymology of Amun's name in the "80th Chapter" (see n. 11 above).
[28] I.e., the sun, which is the primary manifestation (*ba*) of Amun in the created world.
[29] I.e., Osiris.
[30] This phrase was often used as a designation of Thebes, reflecting its theological prominence, similar to that established earlier for Heliopolis.
[31] Having dealt with the many immanent means through which Amun can be perceived, the text now turns to a discussion of his true nature, which, by contrast, is imperceptible, unknowable, and one. "Them" refers to all the gods mentioned in the preceding lines.
[32] These two phrases describe the limits of the created world. As the creator, Amun must necessarily be separate from the world he has created.
[33] See n. 2 above.
[34] This line refers to the frequent scenes of the god's bark carried in procession, sculpted on temple walls throughout Egypt.
[35] Rather than a prescription for punishment, these lines reflect the philosophical contradiction inherent in a knowledge of Amun's true nature. In Eg. epistemology, knowledge entails the internalization of external reality: "perception" (*sjꜣ*), which takes place in the heart. Since Amun transcends all created beings, his subordination in this manner is physically impossible, thus producing instant annihilation for the perceiver.
[36] A summation of the entire "chapter": although the nature of Amun can be perceived to some extent through what he has created (*bꜣy* "manifest one," lit., "*ba*-like"), Amun himself transcends creation ("whose identity is hidden") and is therefore physically unknowable ("inaccessible" to knowledge).
[37] The Eg. construction (3 *pw nṯrw nbw*) is ambivalent as to subject and predicate; in this case, however, the list of three gods in the next line identifies "three" as the predicate. Although the "chapter" begins with a triad, the pronoun "his" in its second sentence reveals that its true subject is the oneness of God: hidden in his true nature (*jmn rn.f*: see n. 16 above), but manifest in the sun (his "face") and in the physical substance ("his body") of which all created matter partakes (Ptah here in his role as Ta-tenen: see n. 17 to the "Memphite Theology," p. 23). The "chapter" also unites the three cosmogonies associated with these aspects of God, which is the subject of the lines that follow.

When a message is sent from the sky, it is heard in Heliopolis,
and repeated in Memphis to (Ptah) of good disposition,[38]
put in a report, in Thoth's writing,
for the town of Amun, bearing their concerns,
and the matter is answered in Thebes
by an Oracle emerging,[39] intended for the Ennead.[40]
Everything that comes from his — Amun's — mouth,[41]
the gods are bound by it, according to what has been decreed.
When a message is sent, whether for killing or for giving life,[f]
life or death are in it for everyone
except him — Amun together with the Sun [and Ptah:] total, 3.[42]

f 1 Sam 2:6

[38] See n. 2 to Coffin Texts Spell 647, p. 18.

[39] The word translated as "Oracle" here is the phrase *ḫr.tw* "one says" with divine determinative.

[40] All divine decisions reflect the original process of creation: the creator's spoken word activates Atum's evolution ("heard in Heliopolis"), via the mediation of Ptah ("repeated in Memphis"), and results in physical reality ("intended for the Ennead").

[41] The expression used here (*prt m r* "what emerges from the mouth") is also an idiom for "utterance."

[42] All creation is affected by the creator's word except for the creator himself; this includes the sun and Ptah, who are merely aspects of Amun.

REFERENCES

Gardiner 1905; Erman 1923; Zandee 1947; Fecht 1964:46-52; Assmann 1975b:312-21; Allen 1988a:48-55.

FROM COFFIN TEXTS SPELL 1130 (1.17)

James P. Allen

Egyptian cosmogonies were concerned primarily with explaining the origin of the world and its elements. The creation of human beings was considered part of this process, and as such was not given special attention in and of itself: if noted at all, it is usually explained by a simple "etymological" metaphor, which derives people (*rmṯ*) from the "tears" (*rmyt*) of the creator's eye. By the same token, the establishment of social and moral norms is generally absent from the creation accounts, since these were considered part of the natural order governing the operation of the world as a whole. Spell 1130 of the Coffin Texts is perhaps the major exception to this tradition. Like all Egyptian cosmogonies, it equates the creation with the establishment of order and the attendant quelling of chaos; but unlike most, it describes this process in largely human terms — the relationship of people to nature and to one another. The spell is also unusual in its reference to the end of the world, which is conceived essentially as a return to chaos, a reversal of the process of creation itself.

Introduction (CT VII 461c-462c)

RECITATION BY INACCESSIBLE-OF-IDENTITIES, the Lord to the Limit, speaking before those who still the storm during the sailing of the entourage:[1] Please proceed in calm, and I will repeat to you the four deeds[2] that my own heart did for me inside the Coil[3] [a] for the sake of stilling disorder.[4]

The establishment of order (CT VII 462d-464f)

I have done four good deeds inside the portal of the Akhet.[5]
I have made the four winds,[b]
so that every person might breathe in his area.[6]
That is one of the deeds.
I have made the great inundation,
so that the poor might have control like the rich.[7] [c]
That is one of the deeds.
I have made every person like his fellow.[d]

a Prov 8:27
b Jer 39:46; Eze 37:9; Zec 2:6; Dan 7:2; 8:8; 11:4
c 1 Sam 2:7; Prov 22:2
d Jer 4:22

[1] The "entourage" are the gods that accompany the sun in his voyage by boat across the waters of the Duat, by night, and remove the dangers of the Duat from his path ("who still the storm"). This introduction sets the scene of the spell at night, which is equivalent to the situation before creation.

[2] The translation "deeds" is somewhat misleading. The term (*ẓp*) is closer to the English concepts "occasion, event, happening."

[3] The "Coil" (*mḥn*) is a metaphor for the primeval singularity from which the world evolved, envisioned as a coiled serpent.

[4] The act of creation involved both the establishment of order and the consequent stilling of disorder.

[5] I.e., within the space between the Duat and the visible horizon: thus, before the first sunrise at the dawn of creation.

[6] Air is one of the two prime requisites of life: as all living things have life in common, so too do they benefit from the universal presence of air.

[7] Food, the second necessity of life, derives in Egypt from the Nile, either directly or, through its irrigation of the land, indirectly. Like air, the river's inundation exists without regard to social distinctions — here, between poor (*ḥwrw*) and rich (*wsr*, lit., "powerful").

I did not decree that they do disorder:
it is their hearts that break what I said.[8]
That is one of the deeds.
I have made their hearts not forget the West,
for the sake of making offerings to the nome gods.[9]
That is one of the deeds.

The operation of order in the world (CT VII 464g-467d)
I made the gods evolve from my sweat,
while people are from the tears of my Eye.[10]

I shine anew every day in this my rank of Lord to the Limit.
I made night for Weary-hearted,[11]
while I am bound for sailing aright in my boat.
I am lord of the Flood[12] in crossing the sky.
I do not have to show respect for any of my parts:[13]
Annunciation and Magic are felling for me that evil-charactered one[14]
that I might see the Akhet and come to sit at its head,
that I might separate the needy from the rich,[15] [e]
and do likewise to the disorderly.
Life is for me, I am its lord:
the scepter will not be taken from my hand.

The end of creation (CT VII 467e-468b)
And when I have spent millions of years between
myself and that Weary-hearted one, the son of Geb,[16]
I will come to sit with him in one place,
and mounds will become towns, and towns mounds:
one enclosure will destroy the other.[17]

e Jer 22:16; Ps 35:10; 72:4

[8] Since creation involved the establishment of order, subsequent disorder in the world derives not from the creator but from human failings. The phrase "what I said" here refers not to a code of divine law, but to the order of creation itself, which arose with the creation from the creator's *fiat* (cf. n. 21 to Coffin Texts Spell 75, p. 9). Social inequality is a prime source of disorder in the world; thus, the natural order must necessarily involve no such distinctions: "I have made every person like his fellow."

[9] All people are conscious of their mortality and the fact that they will have to find acceptance in the company of the gods after death. Thus, offerings are presented to the gods in this life in that anticipation: see n. 25 to Coffin Texts Spell 80, p. 13.

[10] Although both people and the gods derive from the creator, the latter evolved directly from the creator's substance ("sweat": cf. n. 2 to Coffin Texts Spell 76, p. 10), whereas people are a secondary creation, here explained "etymologically" (see n. 14 to Coffin Texts Spell 80, p. 12).

[11] An epithet of Osiris, denoting both his inert state and his potentiality for life: cf. n. 17 to Coffin Texts Spell 80, p. 12.

[12] Variant "lord of Eternal Recurrence" (*nḥḥ*). Either suits the context: the sky is the surface of the "Flood" (*ḥḥw*), and the sun's daily cycle defines the eternal repetition of life.

[13] All of creation is the creator's "parts," derived from him: he is therefore prior to and greater than any of them.

[14] "Evil-charactered" (*ḏw qd*) is an epithet of Apophis, the serpent that opposes the sun's journey through the Duat. "Annunciation" and "Magic" are two of the gods in the sun's "entourage" (see n. 1 above): for these gods, see n. 28 to Coffin Texts Spell 80, p. 13, and n. 16 to Coffin Texts Spell 75, p. 9, respectively.

[15] Like the dawn of creation, sunrise from the Akhet each morning reestablishes the order of the created world — here exemplified in its social component. "Separation" (*wḏ*ᶜ) is a term deriving from Eg. jurisprudence: *wḏ*ᶜ *mdw* "judgement" is lit., "separating the matter." Note the repeated theme of social inequality, here involving the needy (*m*ᵓ*r*) vs. the rich (*wsr*: see n. 7 above).

[16] See n. 11 above. The line refers to the daily cycle of the sun, which travels from daylight ("myself") to the Duat, where it joins with the body of Osiris and receives the power of rebirth. This cycle is the determinant of "Eternal Recurrence": see n. 18 to Coffin Texts Spell 335, p. 17.

[17] I.e., all things will return to their original state of oneness. Atums's unification with Osiris reflects the state farthest removed from that of life, but also contains, through Osiris, the hope of rebirth once again (see the preceding note).

REFERENCES

CT VII 461c-468b; *ANET* 7-8; Lichtheim 1973:131-33; Faulkner 1978:167-169; Hermsen 1991:227-234.

BOOK OF THE DEAD 175 (1.18)
"Rebellion, Death and Apocalypse"

Robert K. Ritner

Through a series of dialogues between divine speakers, this famous theological treatise details the corruption of the original creation with the introduction of death and concomitant anxiety regarding an afterlife, as well as apocalyptic pronouncements of the world's ultimate dissolution and recreation. A final section relates an ontological myth describing the origin of ritual, deities and names. Thought to have been composed as early as the First Intermediate Period (Kees 1956:207), the six surviving manuscripts range in date from the 18th Dynasty to the Roman Period.[1] In addition to the basic manuscript in Naville (1886, vol. 1, pls. cxcviii-cxcix), primary bibliography may be found in Hornung (1979:517-518), adding the published translations in Allen (1974:183-185), Barguet (1967:260-263), Faulkner (1985:175), Hornung (1979:365-371), and Wilson (*ANET* 9-10). No previous translation has included detailed critical analysis of the differing versions.

SPELL FOR NOT DYING AGAIN.[2] WORDS SAID BY the Osiris NN:
"O, Thoth, what is it that has happened through the children of Nut? They have made war. They have raised disturbance. When they committed evil, then they created rebellion. When they committed slaughter, then they created imprisonment. Indeed, they have converted what was great into what is small in all that I have done.

Hail(?),[3] O great one Thoth" - so says Atum.

"You shall not see evil. You shall not suffer. Curtail their years, hasten their months, since they have betrayed secrets[4] in all that you have done."

"Mine is your palette, O Thoth. To you I have brought your ink pot. I am not among those who betray their secrets. No injury shall be done through me."

WORDS SAID BY the Osiris NN:
"O, Atum,[5] what does it mean that I go to the desert, the Land of Silence, which has no water, has no air, and which is greatly deep, dark, and lacking?"[6]
"Live in it in contentment."[7]
"But there is no sexual pleasure in it."
"It is in exchange for water and air and sexual pleasure that I have given spiritual blessedness, contentment in exchange for bread and beer" — so says Atum.
"It is too much for me, my lord, not to see your face."[8]
"Indeed, I shall not suffer that you lack."[9]
"But every god has taken his throne[10] in the bark Millions (of Years)."
"Your throne belongs to your son Horus" - so says Atum.[11] "He now will dispatch the elders.[12] He now will rule the two banks.[13] He will inherit the throne[14] which is in the Island of Flames."
"Then command that the god see his equal,[15] for my face will see the face of my lord Atum."[16]
"What is the span[17] of my life" — so says Osiris.
"You shall be for millions of millions (of years),[19] a lifetime of millions.[20] Then I shall destroy all that I have made. This land will return into the Abyss, into the flood as in its former state. It is I who shall remain together with Osiris, having made my transformations into other snakes[21] which mankind will not know, nor gods see. How beautiful is that which I have done for Osiris, exalted more than all the gods! I have given to him rulership[22] in the desert, the Land of Silence, while his son Horus is the heir upon his throne[23] which is in the Island of Flames. I have made his seat[24] in the bark of Millions (of Years). I have caused that he dispatch the elders.[25] I have caused that his monuments be founded, while love of him is on earth, while the falcon is distant,[26] secure in

[1] Sources labeled following Szczudloska 1963 and Kees 1930, adding Lute 1977 as Ke.
[2] Lb adds "in the Necropolis;" Kd substitutes: "Spell for Revivifying in the Necropolis, giving love to the blessed spirit before the great god who is in the underworld." The term *nn* is the deceased individual, equated with Osiris, whose name is inserted here.
[3] Cf. (?) Coptic *miok* "hail."
[4] Lit., "inflicted damage to secrets."
[5] Later variants Lb and Sp add "(my) lord" before Atum. The early text Jl reads instead "That which Osiris said to Atum."
[6] Or "unfathomable/boundless." Lit., "of seeking."
[7] Possibly conclusion of preceding sentence (as Allen): "while one lives in it in contentment." Negated in late editions Sp and Kd: "(Indeed), one does not live in it in contentment." Jl and Eb add signs suggesting "contentment of the Land of Silence."
[8] So Jl; reduced in Eb and Ke to "See your face;" Sp: "It is too painful for me, lord Atum, not to see your face;" similarly Kd, but moving "lord Atum" to the end of the sentence.
[9] Sp adds: "You are for millions of millions (of years)!"
[10] So Jl, Eb and Ke; all others: "seated himself."
[11] Jl drops "so says Atum;" Kd consistently misunderstands "so says" as "to be good." Sp reads "... your son Horus as the sun disk on earth."
[12] Sp and Kd: "those elder than him."
[13] Eb reads "your throne," while Ke has "his throne."
[14] Jl: "He will be my heir of my throne;" Sp and Kd: "he being (your) heir of (your) throne."
[15] So Jl and Sp; Lb inserts "me" after "command;" Eb and Ke read "Then command that I see his equal." Kd is garbled: "while there is no god, his second or his third."
[16] Late versions Lb, Sp, and Kd read "your sacred face."
[17] Dropped in Ke.
[18] Late versions add "there" (i.e., in the underworld).
[19] Lb inserts "— so says Atum."
[20] Lb and Ke read "a great lifetime of millions." Eb and Ke insert "I have caused that he dispatch the elders," wrongly displaced from below. Sp contains a long and broken interpolation.
[21] Eb and Ke read "worms."
[22] Eb and Ke read "I have given to him the desert," and Eb confuses "Land of Silence" with "while then."
[23] Jl reads "my heir of my throne."
[24] Eb and Ke insert "provision for" his seat.
[25] Displaced above by Eb and Ke. Kd reads "those elder than him."
[26] Eb and Ke simplify "Horus is secure in his palace ..." All other variants favor the translation "be distant" and not the homophonous "Horus (the falcon)."

his palace through the desire of founding his monuments.[27] I have sent[28] the soul of Seth[29] distinct from all[30] the gods. I have caused that his soul be under guard in the bark[31] through the desire that he not frighten the god's limbs."

"O, my father Osiris, may you do for me what your father Re did for you. May I endure upon earth,[32] may I found my throne, may my heir be healthy, may my tomb stand firm. They are my servants upon earth.[33] May my enemies be as split sycamore figs,[34] with Selqet over their bonds.

I am your son, O my father Re. May you make for me this life, prosperity, and health,[35] while the falcon is distant,[36] secure in his palace. May one go forth to this lifetime of one who seeks for reverence among these revered ones."[37]

The sound of praise is in Heracleopolis, joy in Naref, since Osiris has appeared as Re, having inherited his throne, ruling the two banks completely.[38] The Ennead is satisfied concerning it; Seth is as a great split sycamore fig.

"O[39] my lord Atum," so says Osiris.[40] "May Seth be afraid of me when he sees that my form is as your form. May all people come to me — all patricians, all commoners, all sunfolk, gods, blessed spirits and the dead — in bowing when they see me, since you have placed fear of me and created respect for me."

Then Re [acted] in accordance with all that he said.[41] Then Seth came with his head downcast, touching the earth, since he had seen what Re had had done for Osiris. Blood then descended from his nose. Then Re[42] hacked the blood that came forth from his nose. That is how there came to be the ritual hacking of the earth in Heracleopolis.[43]

Then Osiris became ill in his head, through the heat of the *Atef*-crown that was on his head — on the first day when he put it on his head — [44] through the desire that the gods might fear him. Then Re returned in peace to Heracleopolis[45] to see his son[46] Osiris, and he found him sitting in his house, his head fallen into swelling[47] through the heat of the *Atef*-crown that was on his head.[48] Then Re emptied out these swellings, extracting the blood, pus and corruption, so that they ended up in a swamp. Then Re said to Osiris: "From the blood and pus descended from your head you have made a swamp." Thus came to be the great[49] swamp that is in Heracleopolis.

Then Osiris said to Re: "How healthy and how relieved is my face! How uplifted I am regarding what you commanded for my face regarding the ornament."[50]

Then Re [said] to Osiris: "Let your face be secure, your front be uplifted! How great is fear of you, how vast your respect! Behold the beautiful name come forth to you from my mouth! Behold your name remains for millions of many millions (of years)"! That is how there came to be the name of Harsaphes, foremost of his place[51] in Heracleopolis, while the great[52] *Atef*-crown is on his head, with millions and hundreds of thousands[53] of bread, beer, bulls for slaughter,

[27] Kd substitutes "this land."
[28] So Jl, garbled elsewhere.
[29] Lb, Sp and Kd all add "to the West."
[30] Dropped only by Jl.
[31] Eb alone omits "in the bark."
[32] Late versions all in third person.
[33] Sp reads "that which Pharaoh desires." Kd substitutes "since he loves Osiris on earth."
[34] Sp specifies "great" split figs.
[35] Sp adds "on earth."
[36] Eb and Ke again simplify "Horus is secure in his palace." Kd terminates the spell with "The falcon is established."
[37] Eb and Ke substitute "May you cause that this my lifetime attain to that of one who seeks ..." Jl and Sp conclude the section with variants of "How happy is (your) heart."
[38] Texts for this final section in Kees 1930.
[39] Garbled in Sp.
[40] Sp adds "to Re."
[41] So Jl. Sp: "Good is that which Re did for Osiris when he acted in accordance with all that he said"
[42] So Jl. Lb and Sp substitute "Osiris."
[43] Jl omits "in Heracleopolis."
[44] Only in Sp.
[45] Jl ends clause here.
[46] Only in Sp.
[47] So Jl. Lb has "swollen;" Sp reads "weighted down."
[48] Final phrase in Sp.
[49] Jl reads "this noble swamp."
[50] So Jl. Lb seemingly corrupt: "My front is uplifted. Command the chief of craftsmen since ..."
[51] Lb reads "name."
[52] So Lb and Sp.
[53] Lb adds "tens of thousands and thousands."

birds for wringing, everything good and pure,[54] greater than the fluid of his spirit, while his spirit is before him, the spirit of sexual pleasure elevating to him all offerings.[55]

Then Re said to him: "How beautiful is this that has been done[56] for you. Never has the like been done."[57]

Then Osiris said: "It is by the authoritative power of my speech that I did it. How good is the king with authoritative utterance in his mouth!"

Then Re said to Osiris: "Behold, goodness has come forth to you from my mouth. By means of it your primal state has come into being. Then your name is fixed through it for millions of millions (of years)."[58] That is how the name of Heracleopolis came to be.[59]

"How great is fear of you, how vast your respect! So long as there exists Horus, son of Osiris, born of Isis the goddess, may I exist as he exists, may I endure as he endures, my years like his years, his years like my years on earth for millions of many millions (of years)."[60]

Words to be said over an image of NN made of lapis lazuli, given to a man at his neck. It is a great protection on earth and enhances a man in the necropolis. It gives love of him to people, gods, blessed spirits and the dead. It protects him from the assault of a god and protects a man from everything evil.[61] Truly effective, (proved) millions of times.

[54] So Lb and Sp.

[55] So Jl. Lb and Sp have instead: "greater than the flood waters on the river to count, the recurrence of his offerings by the millions fixed before him, while drunkenness by the thousands elevates to him his offerings of all good things."

[56] Jl reads "that I have done."

[57] Jl adds "for me."

[58] So Sp. Lb is corrupt, and Jl reads "Its name thereby is for millions of millions (of years)."

[59] So Jl. Lb reads "That is how it became very great in Heracleopolis."

[60] Further fragmentary passages in Sp only.

[61] So Jl. Lb reads "It is effective for the one who recites it in the necropolis. May you not be silent." Sp reads "It is effective for the one who recites the book on earth, and effective for him in the necropolis. May you not be silent about it."

REFERENCES

Naville 1886 1:cxcviii-cxcix; Allen 1974:183-185; Barguet 1967:260-263; Faulkner 1985:175; Hornung 1979:365-371, 517-518; Kees 1930; 1956; *ANET* 9-10.

COFFIN TEXT 157 (1.19)
"Cultic Abomination of the Pig"[a]

Robert K. Ritner

This spell for "Knowing the Souls of Pe" (with its descendant Book of the Dead 112) provides a theological explanation for the Egyptian pork taboo, a prohibition never uniformly accepted (Darby et al. 1977:171-209; Miller 1990). The conclusion to the companion Coffin Text spell 158 is instructive: "Not to be said while eating pork." No less interesting is the medical aspect of spell 157, since it details the first recorded opthalmological exam, perhaps including reference to a type of eye chart with "strokes." The form of the myth is aetiological, explaining the origin of animals and customs.

BEING ORDAINED FOR FOODSTUFFS IN THE NECROPOLIS, PRAISE AND LOVE ON EARTH, AND EXISTENCE AMONG THE FOLLOWING OF HORUS AND HIS ATTENDANTS. A MYSTERY KNOWN IN THE ESTATE (IN PE). KNOWING THE SOULS OF PE.

a Lev 11:7-8; Isa 65:2-5; 66:3, 17

O female souls of night, female marsh dwellers, Mendesian women, women of the Mendesian nome, dwellers in the Mansion of Iapu, shadowy ones ignorant of praise, brewers of Nubian beer, do you know the reason for which Pe was given to Horus? You do not know it, but I know it. It was Re who gave it in recompense for the mutilation in his eye. I know it. It was the case that Re said to Horus: "Let me see your eye since this has happened to it." He then saw it and he said: "Look, pray, at that stroke while your hand covers the healthy eye which is there." Then Horus looked at that stroke. Horus then said: "Behold, I see it completely white." THAT IS HOW THE ORYX ("See-white") CAME TO BE.

Re then said: "Look at that black pig." Then Horus looked at that black pig. Then Horus cried out over the condition of his throbbing ("raging") eye, saying: "Behold, my eye feels as at that first wound which Seth inflicted against my eye."

Then Horus lost consciousness ("swallowed his heart") before him. Re then said: "Place him on his bed until he is well." It was the case that Seth made transformations against him as that black pig. Then he cast a wound into his eye. Re then said: "Abominate the pig for Horus." "Would that he be well," SO SAID THE GODS. THAT IS HOW THE ABOMINATION OF THE PIG CAME TO BE FOR HORUS BY THE GODS AND THEIR FOLLOWERS.

NOW when Horus was in his childhood, his sacrificial animal came to be a pig though his eye had not yet suffered. As for Imsety, Hapy, Duamutef, and Qebehsenuef, their father is Horus the elder and their mother is Isis. It was the case that Horus said to Re: "Give to me two in Pe and two in Hierakonpolis from this corpus of brethren to be with me in eternal assignment so that the earth might flourish and disturbance be extinguished in this my name of Horus upon his papyrus column."[1]

I KNOW THE SOULS OF PE: ONE IS HORUS; ONE IS IMSETY; ONE IS HAPY.

[1] An image commonly found on healing stelae known as "Horus cippi," used to avert and cure the wounds of scorpions and snakes.

REFERENCES

Textual edition: de Buck 1938:326-348. Further discussion and translations: *ANET* 9-10; Faulkner 1973:135-136.

BOOK OF THE DEAD 112 (1.20)
(Variant of CT 157)

Robert K. Ritner

The primary manuscript (18th Dynasty) appears in Naville (1886: pl. cxxiv), with translations in Barguet (1967:148-150), Allen (1974:91) and Faulkner[1] (1985:108-109). A vignette depicts the seated gods Horus, Imsety and Hapy.

Spell for Knowing the Souls of Pe.
It is NN who shall say: "O marsh dwellers, those among the marsh dwellers, Mendesian women, those of the Mendesian nome, lady trappers[2] who are in Pe, shadowy ones who know no return, brewers of beer who knead bread, do you know the reason for which Pe was given to Horus? I know it, but you do not know it. It was Re who gave it in recompense for the mutilation in his eye by this which Re said to Horus: 'Let me see this which happened in your eye.' When Re investigated, then he saw. Re then said to Horus: 'Look, pray, at that black boar.' Then he looked. And then his throbbing ("raging") eye suffered greatly. Horus then said to Re: 'Behold, my eye feels as at that wound which Seth inflicted against my eye.' The he lost consciousness ("swallowed his heart"). Re then said to the gods: 'Place him on his bed. Let him recover.' It was the case that Seth had made his transformations into a black boar. Then that one cast a wound into his eye. Re then said to the gods: 'Let the pig be abominated for Horus. Let him recover.' That is how the pig came to be the abomination of Horus by the Ennead that is in his following.[a]

a Lev 11:7-8; Deut 14:3, 8; Isa 65:2-5; 66:3, 17

When Horus was in his youth, his sacrificial animal came to be as his cattle and his pigs, though his followers abominate (them). Imsety, Hapy, Duamutef, and Qebehsenuef, (he is) their father, and Isis is their mother. Horus then said to Re: 'May you give to me two brothers in Pe, and the remaining two in Hierakonpolis from this corpus together with me, to be in eternal assignment so that the earth might flourish, and disturbance be extinguished. That is how his name came to be as 'Horus upon his Papyrus Column.' I know the souls of Pe. One is Horus. One is Imsety. One is Hapy.

Lift up your heads, O gods who are in the underworld. It is so that you might see him having become as a great god that I have come before you."

[1] Translation conflated with Coffin Text 157 version.
[2] Or "weavers."

REFERENCES

Naville 1886: pl. cxxiv; Barguet 1967:148-150; Allen 1974:91; Faulkner 1985:108-109.

2. OTHER MYTHS

THE REPULSING OF THE DRAGON (1.21)
(Coffin Text 160)

Robert K. Ritner

During the course of each day's journey, the sun god confronted a serpent adversary[a] whom he vanquished with the assistance of the militant god Seth and the force of divine magic. Within the following Coffin Text spell, this battle with the "dragon" is located at Bakhu, the mountainous western support of heaven where the sun sets. Elsewhere the serpent is styled Apep (Apopis), who threatens to devour the solar boat in the seventh and twelfth hours of night and thereby destroy the created order, returning the world to a state of chaos. Various temple, and even private, rituals were devised to ensure the victory of Re and the consequent maintenance of world stability (Ritner 1993:210-212). By the recitation of a victorious "mythic precedent" on the divine plane, this Coffin Text spell was designed to accomplish a variety of positive goals for the living and the dead, including protection against deadly serpents.[a]

(Spell for) ENDURING ON EARTH, NOT EATING EXCREMENT IN THE NECROPOLIS,[1] NOT PERISHING IN THE NECROPOLIS BY A LIVING OR DEAD *BA*-SPIRIT, NOT DYING BY MEANS OF A SERPENT,[2] ENTERING AND EXITING THROUGH THE EASTERN PORTALS OF HEAVEN, BEING HEALTHY ON EARTH BY A LIVING OR DEAD *BA*-SPIRIT, HAVING POWER OVER OFFERINGS THAT AN HEIR MAKES FOR HIS FATHERS IN THE NECROPOLIS,[3] KNOWING THE SPIRITS OF THE WEST.

a Isa 51:9

I know that mountain of Bakhu upon which the sky leans. Of crystal(?) it is, 300 rods in its length, 120 rods in its width. On the east of this mountain is Sobek, Lord of Bakhu. Of carnelian is his temple. On the east of that mountain is a serpent, 30 cubits in his length, with three cubits of his forefront being of flint. I know the name of that serpent who is on the mountain. His name is "He overthrows."[4] Now at the time of evening he turns his eye over against Re, and there occurs a halting among the (solar) crew, a great astonishment(?) within the voyage, so that Seth bends himself against him.[5] What he says as magic: Let me stand against you so that the voyage be set right. O you whom I have seen from afar, close your eye since I have bound you![6] I am the male! Cover your head so that you may be well and I may be well![7] I am "Great of Magic."[8] I have used (it) against you. What is it? It is effectiveness.[9]

O you who goes on his belly, your strength belongs to your mountain. But watch me as I go off with your strength in my hand! I am one who lifts up[10] strength. I have come just so that I might plunder the (serpent-formed) earth gods.

As for Re, may he who is in his evening (i.e. Re) be satisfied with me when we have circled the sky, while you (the serpent) are in your fetters. It is what has been commanded against you in the divine presence. Thus does Re set[11] in life.

I KNOW THE SOULS OF THE WEST. ONE IS RE.[12] ONE IS SOBEK, LORD OF BAKHU. ONE IS HATHOR, LADY OF THE EVENING.[13]

[1] An unfortunate fate of the damned, whose world and bodily functions are reversed.
[2] A variant adds: "being healthy on earth," displaced from below.
[3] Displaced in two variants to the end of the text.
[4] Variant "He who is in his burning."
[5] Perhaps a reference to Seth's standard posture in lancing the serpent adversary at the prow of the solar bark.
[6] Variants substitute: "Close your eye, be veiled for me!"
[7] Variants conclude: "since I am hostile."
[8] See Ritner 1993:19, n. 78.
[9] Variants have: "This effective power, what is it?"
[10] Or "displays/wears."
[11] The term forms a pun with "be satisfied" at the beginning of the paragraph.
[12] Variant "Atum," the form of the sun god at sunset.
[13] Variant. "Seth. Lord of life."

REFERENCES

Primary textual edition: de Buck 1938:373-388. Further discussion and translations: *ANET* 11-12; Faulkner 1973:138-139.

THE LEGEND OF ISIS AND THE NAME OF RE (1.22)
(P. Turin 1993)

Robert K. Ritner

Few texts illustrate so clearly the ritual significance of the personal name. Felt to be an intrinsic element and source of power, the name did not simply identify but defined an individual.[1] [a] For hostile purposes, the destruction of a name could effect the death or misfortune of its owner, and this belief underlies both the prominent role of naming in execration texts (see text 1.32 below) and the well attested expunging of royal names in dynastic feuds. Divinities were often said to have secret names guarded from devotees and other deities alike. The inherent power of such divine names is stated directly in the late Papyrus BM 10188, in which Re-Atum declares: "Magic is my name."[2] In similar fashion, bodily "relics" are repositories of personal energy and equally subject to manipulation. In this spell, it is the spittle of the creator that serves to animate lifeless clay, in conformity with traditional Egyptian accounts of the creation.

SPELL of the divine god, who came into being by himself, who made heaven, earth, water, the breath of life, fire, gods, men, flocks, herds, reptiles, birds, and fish, the kingship of gods and men altogether,[3] with limits beyond numerous years, [...] and with numerous names. One did not know that (name); one did not know this (name).

Now, Isis was a wise woman. Her heart was more devious than millions among men; she was more selective than millions among the gods; she was more exacting than millions among the blessed dead. There was nothing that she did not know in heaven or earth, like Re, who made the substance of the earth. The goddess planned in her heart to learn the name of the noble god.

Now, Re entered every day in front of the crew (of the solar bark), being established on the throne of the two horizons. A divine old age had weakened his mouth so that he cast his spittle to the earth. He spat out, it lying fallen upon the ground. Isis kneaded it for herself with her hand, together with the earth that was on it. She formed it into a noble serpent; she made (it) in the form of a sharp point. It could not move, though it lived before her. She left it at the crossroads by which the great god passed in accordance with his heart's desire through his Two Lands.[4] The noble god appeared outside, with the gods from the palace in his following, so that he might stroll just like every day. The noble serpent bit him, with a living fire coming forth from his own self.[5] It raged(?) among the pines. The divine god worked his mouth; the voice of his majesty reached up to heaven. His Ennead said: "What is it? What is it?" His gods said: "What? What?" He could not find his speech to answer concerning it. His lips were quivering, and all his limbs were trembling. The poison seized upon his flesh as the inundation seizes what is behind it. The great god regained his composure[6] and cried out to his followers: "Come to me, you who have come to be from my body, gods who came forth from me, so that I might let you know its development. Something painful has stabbed me. My heart does not know it. My eyes did not see it. My hand did not make it. I cannot recognize it among any of the things that I have made. I have not tasted a suffering like it. There is nothing more painful than it."

"I am a noble, son of a noble, the fluid of a god come forth from a god. I am a great one, son of a great one. My father thought out my name. I am one who has numerous names and numerous forms. My form exists as every god. I am called Atum and Horus of Praise. My father and mother told me my name. I have hidden it in my body from my children[7] so as to prevent the power of a male or female magician from coming into existence against me. I went outside to see what I had made, to stroll in the Two Lands that I created, and something stung me. I do not know it. It is not really fire; it is not really water, though my heart is on fire and my body is trembling, all my members giving birth to a chill."

"Let the children of the gods be brought to me, whose words are magically effective, who know their spells, whose wisdom reaches up to heaven!"

The children of the god then came, each man of them bearing his boasting.[8] Isis came bearing her

a Gen 3:19-20

[1] Cf. Gen 3:19-20, where the naming of creatures by Adam signifies man's control over them.
[2] See Ritner 1993:26.
[3] Lit., "as a single thing."
[4] Egypt.
[5] The serpent's fiery venom derives ultimately from the god's own fluids.
[6] Lit., "established his heart."
[7] Or "at my birth."
[8] Following P. Chester Beatty XI, 2/8 (*ib*ᶜ < ᶜ*b*ᶜ); Turin 1993 has *ikb* "mourning."

effective magic, her speech being the breath of life, her utterance dispelling suffering, her words revivifying one whose throat is constricted. She said: "What is it, what is it, my divine father? What, a serpent has inflicted weakness upon you? One of your children has raised his head against you? Then I shall overthrow it by efficacious magic, causing him to retreat at the sight of your rays."

The holy god opened his mouth: "It was the case that I was going on the road, strolling in the Two Lands and the deserts. My heart desired to see what I had created. I was bitten by a serpent without seeing it. It is not really fire; it is not really water, though I am colder than water and hotter than fire, my entire body with sweat. I am trembling, my eye unstable; I cannot see. Heaven beats down rain upon my face in the time of summer!"[9]

THEN SAID Isis to Re: "Say to me your name, my divine father, for a man lives when one recites in his name." [b]

(Re said:) "I am[10] [c] the one who made heaven and earth, who knit together the mountains, who created that which exists upon it. I am the one who made the water, so that the Great Swimming One[11] came into being. I made the bull for the cow,[12] so that sexual pleasure came into being. I am the one who made heaven and the mysteries[13] of the horizons; I placed the *ba*-spirits of the gods inside it. I am the one who opens his two eyes so that brightness comes into being, who closes his two eyes so that darkness comes into being, according to whose command the inundation surges, whose name the gods do not know. I am the one who made the hours so that the days came into being. I am the one who divided the year, who created the river.[14] I am the one who made living fire, in order to create the craft of the palace. I am Khepri in the morning, Re at noon, and Atum who is in the evening."

b Gen 32:27, 29; Exod 20:7

c Exod 3:13-14

The poison was not repelled in its course; the great god was not comforted.

Then Isis said to Re: "Your name is not really among those that you have said to me. Say it to me so that the poison might go out, for a man lives when one pronounces his name."

The poison burned with a burning; it was more powerful than flame or fire.

Then the majesty of Re said: "May you give to me your two ears, my daughter Isis, so that my name might go forth from my body to your body. The most divine one among the gods had hidden it, so that my status might be broadened within the Bark of Millions.[15] If there occurs a similar occasion when a heart goes out to you, say it to your son Horus after you have bound him by a divine oath, placing god in his eyes."[16] The great god announced his name to Isis, the Great One of Magic.

"Flow out, scorpions! Come forth from Re, Eye of Horus! Come forth from the god, flame of the mouth.[17] I am the one who made you; I am the one who sent you. Come out upon the ground, powerful poison! Behold, the great god has announced his name. Re lives; the poison is dead. NN, born of NN, lives; the poison is dead, through the speech of Isis the Great, the Mistress of the Gods, who knows Re by his own name."

Words to be recited over an image of Atum and of Horus-of-Praise, a figure of Isis, and an image of Horus,[18] DRAWN (ON) THE HAND OF THE SUFFERER AND LICKED OFF BY THE MAN; DO LIKEWISE ON A STRIP OF FINE LINEN, PLACED ON THE SUFFERER AT HIS THROAT. THE PLANT IS SCORPION PLANT. GROUND UP WITH BEER OR WINE, IT IS DRUNK BY THE MAN WHO HAS A SCORPION STING. IT IS WHAT KILLS THE POISON — TRULY EFFECTIVE, (PROVED) MILLIONS OF TIMES.[19]

[9] A reference to his fevered sweat, contrasted with the typically cooling water of the Nile.
[10] Cf. Exod 3:13-14.
[11] A name of the heavens, symbolized by a celestial cow bearing the bark of the sun.
[12] Common Eg. euphemisms for penis and vagina, see Ritner 1987 col. 645.
[13] Not a verb, contra Borghouts "(I made) the horizon inaccessible."
[14] The connection is logical in Egypt, where the fluctuation of the Nile determined the seasons.
[15] The solar bark.
[16] A reference to the injured eye of Horus, cured by Isis after an attack by Seth. Cf. text 1.20 above.
[17] Venom.
[18] Shown in a vignette on the Turin papyrus.
[19] For discussion, see Ritner 1993:95.

REFERENCES

Primary manuscript: P. Turin 1993 (19th Dyn.): Pleyte and Rossi 1869-76 pls. cxxxi:12 - cxxxiii:14; and lxxvii + xxi:1-5; excerpted in Möller 1927:29-32. Other contemporary exemplars: HO 2 and HO 3, 2; O. Deir el-Medineh 1263; and Papyrus Chester Beatty 11. Bibliography and translations: *ANET* 12-14; Borghouts 1978:51-55; Ritner 1993:76, n. 337. For methodological commentary, see Ritner (ibid., 76, 83, 95-96, and 164).

THE LEGEND OF ASTARTE AND THE TRIBUTE OF THE SEA (1.23)
P. Amherst (Pierpont Morgan) XIX-XXI

Robert K. Ritner

The tattered remains of a once magnificent manuscript, the "Astarte Papyrus" nevertheless provides tantalizing evidence of Egyptian traditions regarding the Asiatic goddess who had been adopted into cult and mythology by the beginning of the New Kingdom. While this legend has been shown to have an indigenous Egyptian setting, it is yet parallel to, and likely inspired by, the Ugaritic story of the Fight between Baal and the sea god Yam (text 1.86), whose Semitic name is also used for the threatening deity in the Egyptian tale. Helck, in contrast, has suggested that the tale is an adaptation derived from the Hurrian "Song of Ullikummi." In the Egyptian legend, the Sea seems to threaten to overwhelm heaven, earth and mountains unless provided with tribute. When Astarte is sent to deliver the tribute, the Sea demands further that she be given to him in marriage, perhaps with a dowry including the seal of the earth god and the beads of the sky goddess. From other sources, it appears that the Sea is ultimately vanquished in combat by Seth (the Egyptian counterpart of Baal), mentioned in the fragmentary concluding lines.

(Col. 1) [...] ... his two bulls. "Let me praise [...] ... Let me praise the [earth(?) ...] ... Let me praise the sky [in its(?)] place [...] the earth." [...] Ptah. Now after [...] the earth. The earth rested[1] [...] "[...] I strip off her [....."] Then they bent like .... [...] Then [each(?)] man embraced [his fellow(?). Now] after [seven(?)] days, the sky did [...] descending upon [...] the Sea. The [... the] earth gave birth[a] to [..] the four banks of the [Sea(?)][2] [...] in its midst like the suspension [...] his throne of Ruler. He [...] carry for him the tribute. [...] in the council. Then Renenutet carried [...] as Ruler [...] sky. Now, behold, one brought to him the tribute [...] or his [...] he will seize us as plunder [...] our own to [...] Renenutet his tribute in silver and gold, lapis lazuli [and turquoise(?)...] the boxes. Then they said to the Ennead: "[...] the tribute of the Sea, so that he might hear for us [all] the matters [of the earth(?)], protected from his hand. Will he [...]"

a Isa 51:10; Jer 5:22; Ps 104:6-9; Job 38:8-11

(Col. 2) [...] Now they were fearful of [...] the [tribute] of the Sea. Give [...] the tribute of the Sea. [...] evil. Renenutet took a [...] Astarte. Then the[3] [...] said: "[...] birds hear what I might say. May you[4] not depart [...] another." Hurry, go to Astarte [...] her house. And you should cry out below [the window of the room in which(?)] she sleeps. And should say to her: "If you are [awake, ...] If you are asleep, may I wake you. [... the] Sea as Ruler over the [earth and the mountains and(?)] the sky. Please, may you come before them at this [moment."(?) ...] Asiatics. Then Astarte [...][5] the daughter of Ptah. Now [...] of the Sea, the [...] "[...] you go yourself bearing the tribute of [the Sea" ...] Then Astarte wept [...] its[6] Ruler was silent. [...] "Lift up your[7] face. [...] Lift up your face. And you should [...] away." Then he lifted up [his face ...] the [...] singing and laughing at him. [... Then the Sea] saw Astarte while she was sitting on the edge of the Sea. Then he said to her: "Where have you come from, O daughter of Ptah, O angry and raging goddess? Have you worn out your sandals that are on your feet; have you frayed your clothes that are on you, by the going and coming that you have done from the sky and the earth?" Then [Astarte] said to him [...]

(Col. 3) *The Sea instructs Astarte to carry a message to the Ennead, probably demanding the goddess in marriage as security against his further depredations.*

[... say to Ptah before(?)] the Ennead. "If they give to me Your[8] [daughter(?) ...] them. What would I do against them for my part?" Astarte heard what the Sea said to her. She lifted herself up to go to the Ennead to the place where they were gathered. The greater ones saw her; they stood up before her. The lesser ones saw her; they lay down on their bellies. She was given her throne and she sat down. She was presented with the (Col. 4) [tribute of the Sea(?) ...] [the] earth [...] the beads. [...] Then the beads [...] the messenger of Ptah going to say these words to Ptah and to Renenutet. Then Renenutet took off

[1] Or "became satisfied."
[2] Or, as restored by Gardiner, "the four regions of the [earth]."
[3] Masculine.
[4] Masculine.
[5] Long lacuna, followed by a determinative suggesting "compel/strike."
[6] Or "his."
[7] Masculine.
[8] Masculine.

the beads that were on her neck. Behold, she placed [them] on the balance [...]

(Col. 5) [...] Astarte. "O my [...] It means an [argument(?)] with the Ennead. Therefore he will send and he will demand [...] the seal of Geb [...] the balance in it." Then (Col. 6) [...] (Col. 7) [...] my basket of [...] (Cols. 8-9) [...] (Col.10) [... tribute(?)] of the Sea [... pass(?)] by the gates [...] the gates, go out (Col. 11) [...] If they come again [...] (Cols. 12-13) [...] (Col. 14) [... the] Sea. And he shall [...] to cover the earth and the mountains and (Col. 15) [the sky.(?)] [...] to fight with him to the effect that [...] he sat down calmly. He will not come to fight with us. Then Seth sat down. [...]

(Verso) [...] "Behold, I[9] am with your[10] [...]" The Sea left [...] the seven [...] together with the sky and [...]

[9] Masculine.
[10] Masculine.

REFERENCES

Text: Gardiner 1932a:74-85; 1932b:76-81. Studies: *ANET* 17-18; Stadelmann 1975; Helck 1983; van Dijk 1986:31-32; Ritner 1989:112-113.

THE DESTRUCTION OF MANKIND (1.24)

Miriam Lichtheim

This mythological tale forms the first part of a longer text known as "The Book of the Cow of Heaven," which is inscribed in five royal tombs of the New Kingdom (the tombs of Tutankhamun, Seti I, Ramses II, Ramses III, and Ramses VI). The first part relates how the sun-god Re set out to destroy the human race because mankind was plotting rebellion against him. But after an initial slaughter, carried out by the "Eye of Re," the sun-god relented and devised a ruse to stop the goddess from further killing. The interest of the tale lies, of course, in the theme of human wickedness arousing the divine wrath and resulting in a partial destruction of mankind, a theme that received its classic treatment in the Mesopotamian and biblical stories of the Flood.

The second part of the text (not translated here) tells how the sun-god, weary of government, withdrew into the sky and charged the other great gods with the rule of heaven and earth.

Though recorded in the New Kingdom, the text is written in Middle Egyptian, and it probably originated in the Middle Kingdom. The tale thus stands apart from stories which are written in Late Egyptian, the vernacular of the New Kingdom.

(1) It happened [in the time of the majesty of] Re, the self-created, after he had become king of men and gods together: Mankind plotted against him, [a] while his majesty had grown old, his bones being silver, his flesh gold, his hair true lapis lazuli. When his majesty perceived the plotting of mankind against him, his majesty said to his followers: "Summon to me my Eye,[1] and Shu, Tefnut, Geb, Nut, and the fathers and mothers who were with me when I was in Nun,[2] and also the god Nun; and he shall bring his courtiers (5) with him. But bring them stealthily, lest mankind see, lest they lose heart.[3] Come with them (the gods) to the Palace, that they may give their counsel. In the end I may return to Nun, to the place where I came into being."

a Gen 6:5-7, 11-13; 11:4

The gods were brought, the gods were lined up on his two sides, bowing to the ground before his majesty, that he might make his speech before the eldest father, the maker of mankind, the king of people.[4] They said to his majesty: "Speak to us, that we may hear it." Then Re said to Nun: "O eldest god in whom I came into being, and ancestor gods, look, mankind, which issued from my Eye,[5] is plotting against me. Tell me what you would do about it, for I am searching. I would not slay them until I have heard what you might (10) say about it."

Then spoke the majesty of Nun: "My son Re, god greater than his maker, more august than his creators, stay on your throne! Great is fear of

[1] The eye of the sun-god is viewed as a being distinct from him.
[2] The primordial water in which creation began.
[3] Lit., "lest their heart flee."
[4] The god Nun.
[5] An allusion to the idea that mankind (*rmṯ*) issued from a tear (*rmyt*) of the sun-god. See above Coffin Texts Spell 80 (above text 1.8, p. 12, n. 14).

you when your Eye is on those who scheme against you." Said the majesty of Re: "Look, they are fleeing to the desert, their hearts fearful that I might speak to them." They said to his majesty: "Let your Eye go and smite them for you, those schemers of evil! No Eye is more able to smite them for you. May it go down as Hathor!"

The goddess returned after slaying mankind in the desert, and the majesty of this god said: "Welcome in peace, Hathor, Eye who did what I came for!" Said the goddess: "As you live for me, I have overpowered mankind, and it was balm to my heart." Said the majesty of Re: "I shall have power over them as king (15) by diminishing them." Thus the Powerful One (Sakhmet) came into being.[6]

The beer-mash of the night for her who would wade in their blood as far as Hnes.[7] Re said: "Summon to me swift, nimble messengers that they may run like a body's shadow!" The messengers were brought immediately, and the majesty of this god said: "Go to Yebu and bring me red ochre[8] in great quantity!" The red ochre was brought to him, and the majesty of this god ordered the Side-Lock Wearer in On[9] to grind the ochre, while maidservants crushed barley for beer. Then the red ochre was put into the beer-mash, and it became like human blood; and seven thousand jars of beer were made. Then the majesty of the King of Upper and Lower Egypt, Re came together with the gods to see the beer.

Now when the day dawned (20) on which the goddess would slay mankind in their time of traveling south,[10] the majesty of Re said: "It is good;[11] I shall save mankind by it!" And Re said: "Carry it to the place where she plans to slay mankind!" The majesty of King Re rose early before dawn, to have this sleeping draught poured out. Then the fields were flooded three palms high with the liquid [b] by the might of the majesty of this god. When the goddess came in the morning she found them flooded, and her gaze was pleased by it.[12] She drank and it pleased her heart. She returned drunk without having perceived mankind. The majesty of Re said to the goddess: "Welcome in peace, O gracious one!" Thus beautiful women came into being in the town of Imu.[13]

b Gen 7:19-20

[6] A word play on *sḫm*, "power," and *sḫmt*, the lion-goddess Sakhmet.
[7] This sentence serves as introduction to what follows.
[8] Or hematite.
[9] The high priest of Re in Heliopolis.
[10] Emend to "her time of traveling south"?
[11] I.e., "the beer is good."
[12] Or, "her face was beautiful in it"?
[13] A word play on *im*ꜣ, "gracious."

REFERENCES

Maystre 1941; Erman 1927:47-49; *ANET* 10-11; Piankoff 1955:27-29; Brunner-Traut 1965:69-72; Lichtheim *AEL* 2:197-199.

3. HYMNS

THE GREAT CAIRO HYMN OF PRAISE TO AMUN-RE (1.25)
P. Cairo 58038 (P. Bulaq 17)

Robert K. Ritner

While the initial sections of this universalist hymn are carved on a statue of the Second Intermediate Period (12th-17th Dynasties; see Hassan 1928:157-193), the best preserved manuscript is a Theban papyrus of the early 18th Dynasty (Amenhotep II). The papyrus text is published in Mariette (1872: pls. xi-xiii) and excerpted in Möller (1927:33-34). Commentary, bibliography, and translations are found in Grébaut 1874; Wilson *ANET*; Assmann 1975b:199-207, 549-553; and Römer 1987. Later New Kingdom excerpts are well-attested on ostraca from Deir el-Medineh (see Römer 1987:406).

I. ADORATION OF Amon-Re,
The bull resident in Heliopolis, Chief of all the gods,
The good god, the beloved,
Who gives life to every warm being
And to every good herd.[1]

[1] The Eg. creator is commonly described as a "Good Shepherd." Many similar references follow.

Hail to you, Amon-Re, Lord of the Thrones of the Two Lands,
Foremost of Karnak,
Bull of his Mother,[2] foremost of his fields,
Wide of stride, foremost of Upper Egypt,
Lord of the Medjay[3] Nubians, Ruler of Punt,
Oldest One of heaven, Eldest of earth,
Lord of what exists, enduring in all things.[4]

UNIQUE ONE, LIKE WHOM[5] AMONG the gods?
Goodly bull of the Ennead,
Chief of all the gods,
Lord of Truth, Father of the gods,
Who made mankind, who created the flocks,
Lord of what exists, who created the tree of life, [a]
Who made the herbage, who vivifies the herd,
Goodly Power, whom Ptah engendered,
Youth, beautiful of (2/1) love,
To whom the gods speak praise,
Who made what is below and what is above, illuminating the Two Lands,
Ferried across the sky in peace,
King of Upper and Lower Egypt, Re, triumphant, Chief of the Two Lands,
Great of strength, Lord of respect,
Chief who made the land in its entirety.

WHOSE PLANS ARE MORE EXALTED THAN those of any god,
At whose beauty the gods rejoice,
For whom jubilation is spoken in the great shrine of El-Kab,
With festal processions in the fire shrine at Pe,
Whose fragrance the gods love,
When He returns from Punt,[6]
Great of perfume, when He descends {from} the Medjay,[7]
Beautiful of face, returned from God's land.

DOGGING whose feet are the gods,
As they recognize His Majesty as their Lord,
Lord of fear, rich in terror,
Great in wrathful manifestations, powerful in appearances,[8]
Whose offerings flourish, who made food-stuffs,
Jubilation to you, who made the gods,
Who suspended heaven, who laid down the ground!
(3/1) CAESURA

II. Awake soundly, Min-Amon,
Lord of eternity, who made endlessness,
Lord of praise, foremost of the [Ennead],[9]
Whose horns are firm, whose face is beautiful,
Lord of the uraeus, lofty of plumage,
With beautiful fillet, lofty of White Crown,
Before whom coil the two uraeus cobras,
Fragrant One who is in the palace,
(with) Double Crown, Headdress, Blue Crown,
Beautiful of face when He receives the *Atef*-Crown,
Whom Upper and Lower Egypt love,
Lord of the Double Crown when He receives the *Ames*-sceptre,
Lord of the *Mekes*-sceptre, bearer of the Flail.

GOODLY Ruler HAVING APPEARED WITH THE WHITE CROWN,
Lord of solar rays, who made brightness,
To whom the gods speak jubilation,
Who extends His arms to the one He loves,
While His enemies fall to the flame.
It is His Eye that overthrows the rebels,
Placing its spear into the one who sucks up the Abyss,[10]
Forcing (4/1) the villain to disgorge what it has swallowed.

HAIL TO YOU, Re, Lord of the Two Truths,
Whose shrine is hidden, Lord of the gods,
Khepri in the midst of His bark,
Who issued command that the gods might be,
Atum, who made the common man,
Who distinguished their forms, who made their lives,
Who separated the races,[11] one from another,
Who hears the prayer of the one who is in distress,
Graciously disposed when He is entreated.

WHO RESCUES THE FEARFUL FROM THE HAND OF THE BRAZEN,
Who judges the wretch and the ruined,

a Gen 2:9; 3:22, 24; Prov 3:18

[2] An epithet designating the creator as self-begotten, who impregnated his own mother.
[3] The Beja nomads, living between the Nile and the Red Sea.
[4] For this pantheistic notion, cf. the daily ritual, text 1.34 below.
[5] Lit., "like whom (of) the gods" *mi m (n) nṯr.w*. Translators have assumed wrongly that the writing here and in col. 9/3 must be an error for *imy nṯr.w* "among" the gods, though elsewhere *imy* is written standardly (e.g., col. 3/3, 5/4, 9/6, etc.). Wilson (*ANET* 365) suggests "like the fluid(?) of the gods."
[6] Source of incense and exotic African produce, thought to be inland Somalia.
[7] Erroneously written "when He sends the Medjay."
[8] The final word has been added in red as a correction.
[9] Restored from statue BM 40959, right side, line 4 (Hassan 1928).
[10] Apep (Apopis).
[11] Lit., "colors."

Lord of perception, with effective utterance
on his mouth,
For love of whom the Inundation has come,
Lord of sweetness, rich in love,
Coming so that the common man might live,
Who gives movement to every eye,
Formed in the Abyss,
Whose grace created brightness,
At whose beauty the gods rejoice,
(5/1) Their hearts living when they see him.
CAESURA

III. Re, REVERED IN KARNAK,
Grand of appearances in the Mansion of the
Benben,[12]
Heliopolitan, Lord of the new moon festival,
For whom are performed the six-day and
quarter month festivals,
Sovereign — life, prosperity, health! — Lord
of all the gods,
Falcon(?)[13] in the midst of the horizon,
Chief of patricians of the Land of Silence,[14]
Whose name is hidden from His children
In this His name of "Amon."[15]

HAIL TO YOU WHO ARE IN PEACE,
Lord of joy, powerful in appearances,
Lord of the uraeus, lofty of plumage,
With beautiful fillet, lofty of White Crown,
You, whom the gods love to see,
The Double Crown fixed on Your brow,
Love of You pervading the Two Lands,
Your rays shining in the eyes.
The patricians are happy when You rise;
The flocks languish when You shine.
Love of You is in the southern heaven,
(6/1) Your sweetness in the northern heaven.
Your beauty captivates hearts,
Love of You wearying the limbs,[16]
Your beautiful form relaxing the hands.
Thoughts go astray at the sight of you.

YOU ARE the Sole One,[17] WHO MADE [ALL]
THAT EXISTS,
One, alone, who made that which is,
From whose two eyes mankind came forth,
On whose mouth the gods came into being,
Who made the herbage [for] the herds,[18]
The tree of life[b] for the sunfolk,
Who made that on which the fish live [in]
the river,
And the birds flying through heaven,
Who gave breath to the one in the egg,
Who vivifies the son of the slug,

b Gen 2:9; 3:22, 24; Prov 3:18

Who made that on which the gnat lives,
The worm and the flea likewise,
Who made the sustenance of the mice in
[their] holes,
Who vivifies the winged creatures in every
tree.

HAIL TO YOU, WHO DID THIS ENTIRELY,
One, alone, with numerous arms,
Who spends the night (7/1) watchful, while
everyone sleeps,
Who seeks what is useful for his flock,
Amon, enduring in all things,
Atum, Horachty,
Praise to you, as they all say.
Jubilation to you, because you have wearied
yourself with us.
Let the earth be kissed for you, because you
have created us.

HAIL TO YOU — by all flocks,
Jubilation to you — by all foreign lands,
To the heights of heaven, to the breadth of
the earth,
To the depths of the ocean,
The gods bowing to Your Majesty,
Exalting the might of Him who created
them,
Rejoicing at the approach of Him who begot
them,
Saying to you: "Come in peace,
Father of the fathers of all the gods,
Who suspended heaven, who laid down the
ground.

WHO MADE WHAT EXISTS, WHO CREATED
THAT WHICH IS,
Sovereign, — life, prosperity, health! —
Chief of the gods.
Let us adore your might (8/1) in as much as
you have made us,
Let {us} act for you because you have borne
us.
Let us give you jubilation because you have
wearied yourself with us."

HAIL TO YOU, WHO MADE ALL THAT EXISTS,
Lord of Truth, Father of the gods,
Who made mankind, who created the flocks,
Lord of Grain,
Who made the life of the desert flocks,
Amon, the bull, beautiful of face,
Beloved in Karnak,
Grand of appearances [in] the Mansion of
the Benben,

[12] The primordial mound first risen from the Abyss.
[13] Assuming an unorthographic spelling; otherwise: "when he is viewed."
[14] The underworld.
[15] See "The Legend of Isis and the Name of Re," text 1.22 above. The name Amon means "hidden."
[16] So great is the love that it overwhelms the bearer.
[17] Or, "Sole Image, who made ..."
[18] Provided with five determinatives for specificity: ox, ibex, goat, pig and ram.

Repeating investitures[19] in Heliopolis,
Who judges the two contestants[20] in the great broad hall,
Chief of the Great Ennead.

SINGLY UNIQUE ONE, WITHOUT HIS SECOND,
Foremost of Karnak,
Heliopolitan, foremost of His Ennead,
Living on Truth every day,
Horizon-dweller, Horus of the East,
For whom the desert creates silver and gold,
Genuine lapis lazuli for love of him,
Balsam and various incenses among the Medjay,
(9/1) Fresh myrrh for your nostrils,
O Beautiful of face, returned {from} the Medjay,
Amon-Re, Lord of the Thrones of the Two Lands,
Foremost of Karnak,
Heliopolitan, foremost of His harem.
CAESURA

IV. Unique king, like whom among the gods?
With numerous names, the number unknown,
Who rises in the eastern horizon,
Who sets in the western horizon,
Who overthrows His enemies
In the course of every day,[21]
Whose two eyes[22] Thoth elevates,
Pacifying Him with his efficacious spells,
At whose beauty the gods rejoice,
He whom His solar apes exalt.[23]
Lord of the Night bark and the Day bark,
They traversing for you the Abyss in peace,

YOUR CREW IN JOY,
When they see the rebel overthrown,
His body licked by the knife,
(10/1) The flame having eaten him,
His *ba*-spirit more destroyed than his corpse.
That VILLAIN,[24] his movement is removed,
While the gods rejoice,
The crew of Re at peace,
Heliopolis rejoicing,
For the enemies of Atum are overthrown,
Karnak at peace, Heliopolis rejoicing.
The Lady of Life, her heart is glad,
For the enemy of her lord is overthrown,
The gods of Babylon[25] in jubilation,
Those in their shrines kissing the ground,

WHEN THEY SEE THE ONE MIGHTY IN HIS STRENGTH,
Power of the gods,
True One, Lord of Karnak,
In this Your name of Maker of Truth,
Lord of sustenance, bull of offerings,
In this Your name of Amon, Bull of His Mother,
Maker of all peoples,
Creator and Maker of all that exists,
In this Your name (11/1) of Atum-Khepri,[26]
Great falcon, with festive breast,
Beautiful of face, with festive chest,
Pleasing of form, lofty of feather,
Before whom the uraeus cobras sway,
To whom the hearts of patricians draw near,
For whom the sunfolk turn about,
Who makes festive the Two Lands in His epiphanies.
Hail to You, Amon-Re, Lord of the Thrones of the Two Lands,
Whose city desires that he rise!

IT IS COMPLETED, satisfactorily, as found.

[19] Lit., "diadems."
[20] Horus and Seth.
[21] Another uncertain verse is added as a correction in red above the line: "On the morning of his birth every day." See Römer 1987:422-423.
[22] The sun and the moon.
[23] The apes whose antics announce the rising sun.
[24] The Apep serpent.
[25] Eg. Babylon, a suburb of modern Cairo.
[26] "All peoples" (*tʾ-tm.w*) provides a pun with Atum (*Tmw*), and "Creator" (*sḫpr*) a pun with Khepri (*Ḫpri*).

REFERENCES

Assmann 1975b:199-207, 549-553; Grébaut 1874; Hassan 1928:157-193; Mariette 1872: pls. xi-xiii; Möller 1927:33-34; Römer 1987:406; *ANET* 365.

THE GREAT HYMN TO OSIRIS (1.26)
(On the Stela of Amenmose — Louvre C 286)

Miriam Lichtheim

A round-topped limestone stela, 1.03 x 0.62 m, of fine workmanship dating from the 18th Dynasty. In the lunette there are two offering scenes showing, on the left, the official Amenmose and his wife Nefertari seated before an offering table and, on the right, a lady named Baket, whose relationship to Amenmose is not stated. Before Amenmose stands a son with his arms raised in the gesture of offering. Another son stands behind the couple, and more sons and daughters are seated below. A priest also performs offering rites before the lady Baket. Below the scenes is the hymn to Osiris in twenty-eight horizontal lines.

This hymn contains the fullest account of the Osiris myth extant in Egyptian, as distinct from Greek, sources. Allusions to the Osiris myth are very frequent in Egyptian texts, but they are very brief. It seems that the slaying of Osiris at the hands of Seth was too awesome an event to be committed to writing. Other parts of the story could be told more fully, especially the vindication of Osiris and of his son Horus, to whom the gods awarded the kingship of Egypt that had belonged to Osiris. The latter, though resurrected, no longer ruled the living but was king of the dead in the netherworld. The final part of the hymn praises the beneficent rule of Horus and, since each living Pharaoh represented Horus, the praise is directed to the reigning king as well.

(1) Adoration of Osiris by the overseer of the cattle of [Amun], [Amen]mose, and the lady Nefertari. He says:

Hail to you, Osiris,
Lord of eternity, king of gods,
Of many names, of holy forms,
Of secret rites in temples!
Noble of *ka* he presides in Djedu,[1]
He is rich in sustenance in Sekhem,[2]
Lord of acclaim in Andjty,[3]
Foremost in offerings in On.[4] [a]
Lord of remembrance in the Hall of Justice,[5]
Secret *ba* of the lord of the cavern,
Holy in White-Wall,[6]
Ba of Re, his very body.
Who reposes in Hnes,[7]
Who is worshiped in the *naret*-tree,
That grew up to bear his *ba*.[8]
Lord of the palace in Khmun,[9]
Much revered in Shashotep,[10]
Eternal lord who presides in Abydos,[11]
Who dwells distant in the graveyard
Whose name endures in people's mouth.

Oldest in the joined Two Lands,
Nourisher[12] before the Nine Gods,
Potent spirit among spirits.
Nun has given him his waters,
Northwind journeys south to him,
Sky makes wind before his nose,
That his heart be satisfied.
Plants sprout by his wish,
Earth grows its food for him,
Sky and its stars obey him,
The great portals open for him.
Lord of acclaim in the southern sky,
Sanctified in the northern sky,
The imperishable stars are under his rule,
The unwearying stars are his abode.
One offers to him by Geb's command,
The Nine Gods adore him,
Those in the *Duat* kiss the ground,
Those on high[13] bow down.
The ancestors rejoice to see him,
Those yonder are in awe of him.

The joined Two Lands adore him,
When His Majesty approaches,
Mightiest noble among nobles,
Firm of rank, of lasting rule.
Good leader of the Nine Gods,
Gracious, lovely to behold,

a Gen 41:45, 50; 46:20; Ezek 30:17

[1] Busiris.
[2] Letopolis.
[3] The Ninth Nome of Lower Egypt.
[4] Heliopolis.
[5] Lit., "the Two Justices" (or, "the Two Truths"), the name of the hall in the netherworld in which the judgment of the dead takes place.
[6] Memphis and its nome.
[7] Heracleopolis Magna.
[8] According to the tradition of Herakleopolis the tomb of Osiris was located in that town, and the sacred *naret*-tree grew over the tomb and sheltered the *ba* of Osiris.
[9] Hermopolis.
[10] Hypselis.
[11] The hymn enumerates the chief cult centers of Osiris from north to south, beginning with Busiris, his foremost northern center of worship, and ending with Abydos, his main cult center in Upper Egypt.
[12] *Ḏfꜣ* is abundance of food personified as a divinity. Cf. below, notes 15 and 17.
[13] I.e., those buried in the high ground of the desert tombs.

Awe inspiring to all lands,
That his name be foremost.
All make offering to him,
The lord of remembrance in heaven and earth,
Rich in acclaim at the *wag*-feast,
Hailed in unison by the Two Lands.
The foremost of his brothers,
The eldest of the Nine Gods,
Who set Maat throughout the Two Shores,
Placed the son on his father's seat.
Lauded by his father Geb,
Beloved of his mother Nut,
Mighty when he fells the rebel,
Strong-armed when he slays his foe.
Who casts fear of him on his enemy,
Who vanquishes the evil-plotters,
Whose heart is firm when he crushes the rebels.

Geb's heir (in) the kingship of the Two Lands,
Seeing his worth he gave (it) to him,
To lead the lands to good fortune.
He placed this land into his hand,
Its water, its wind,
Its plants, all its cattle.
All that flies, all that alights,
Its reptiles and its desert game,
Were given to the son of Nut,
And the Two Lands are content with it.
Appearing on his father's throne,
Like Re when he rises in lightland,
He places light above the darkness,
He lights the shade with his plumes.[14]
He floods the Two Lands like Aten[15] at dawn,
His crown pierces the sky, mingles with the stars.
He is the leader of all the gods,
Effective in the word of command,
The great Ennead praises him,
The small Ennead loves him.

His sister was his guard,
She who drives off the foes,
Who stops the deeds of the disturber
By the power of her utterance.
The clever-tongued whose speech fails not,
Effective in the word of command,
Mighty Isis who protected her brother,
Who sought him without wearying.
Who roamed the land lamenting,
Not resting till she found him,
Who made a shade with her plumage,
Created breath with her wings.
Who jubilated, joined her brother,
Raised the weary one's inertness,

b Gen 3:22

Received the seed, bore the heir,
Raised the child in solitude,
His abode unknown.
Who brought him when his arm was strong
Into the broad hall of Geb.

The Ennead was jubilant:
"Welcome, Son of Osiris,
Horus, firm-hearted, justified,
Son of Isis, heir of Osiris!"
The Council of Maat assembled for him
The Ennead, the All-Lord himself,
The Lords of Maat, united in her,
Who eschew wrongdoing,
They were seated in the hall of Geb,
To give the office to its lord,
The kingship to its rightful owner.
Horus was found justified,
His father's rank was given him,
He came out crowned by Geb's command,
Received the rule of the two shores.

The crown placed firmly on his head,
He counts the land as his possession,
Sky, earth are under his command,
Mankind is entrusted to him,
Commoners, nobles, sunfolk.[16]
Egypt and the far-off lands,
What Aten encircles is under his care,
Northwind, river, flood,
Tree of life,[b] all plants.
Nepri gives all his herbs,
Field's Bounty[17] brings satiety,
And gives it to all lands.
Everybody jubilates,
Hearts are glad, breasts rejoice,
Everyone exults,
All extol his goodness:
How pleasant is his love for us,
His kindness overwhelms the hearts,
Love of him is great in all.

They gave to Isis' son his foe,
His attack collapsed,
The disturber suffered hurt,
His fate overtook the offender.
The son of Isis who championed his father,
Holy and splendid is his name,
Majesty has taken its seat,
Abundance is established by his laws.
Roads are open, ways are free,
How the two shores prosper!
Evil is fled, crime is gone,
The land has peace under its lord.
Maat is established for her lord,

[14] *Šw* is written, but *šwt* must have been intended. Note the word play on *šw(t)*, "shade," and *šwty*, "plumes."

[15] Though written without the divine determinative, the word *itn* has probably already assumed the connotation of a divinity. The divine determinative is also lacking in the two occurrences of *dfꜣ*, "Abundance," where the personification is clear.

[16] The population of Egypt and mankind as a whole.

[17] See note 12.

One turns the back on falsehood.
May you be content, Wennofer![18]
Isis' son has received the crown,
His father's rank was assigned him
In the hall of Geb.
Re spoke, Thoth wrote,
The council assented,
Your father Geb decreed for you,
One did according to his word.

An offering which the king gives (to) Osiris Khentamentiu, lord of Abydos, that he may grant an offering of bread and beer, oxen and fowl, ointment and clothing and plants of all kinds, and the making of transformations: to be powerful as Hapy, to come forth as living *ba*, to see Aten at dawn, to come and go in Rostau,[19] without one's *ba* being barred from the necropolis.

May he be supplied among the favored ones before Wennofer, receiving the offerings that go up on the altar of the great god, breathing the sweet northwind, drinking from the river's pools: for the *ka* of the overseer of the cattle of [Amun], [Amen]mose, justified, born of the lady Henut, justified, and of his beloved wife, [the lady Nefertari, justified].

[18] A name of Osiris.
[19] A name for the necropolis and specifically that of Giza.

REFERENCES

Moret 1931; Erman 1927:140-145; Lichtheim *AEL* 2:81-86.

TWO HYMNS TO THE SUN-GOD (1.27)
From a Stela of the Brothers Suti and Hor — BM 826

Miriam Lichtheim

In the course of the 18th Dynasty, the rise to prominence of Amun of Thebes resulted in his assimilation to the supreme god, the sun-god Re. Furthermore, the conceptual dominance of sun worship had turned the sun-god into the all-embracing creator-god who manifested himself in many forms and under many names. Thus he absorbed Amun and Horus, and he was Atum, Harakhti, and Khepri. And his visible form, the sun-disk (Aten) became yet another manifestation of the god himself. The hymns to the sun-god of the twin brothers Suti and Hor, who lived in the reign of Amenhotep III, address the god in these various forms, and they accord a prominent place to the Aten, the most recently evolved personification of the god. In the first hymn the sun-god is addressed as Amun, Harakhti, Re, and Khepri; in the second hymn he is Aten, Khepri, and Horus.

The hymns are inscribed on a rectangular stela in door form, of gray granite and measuring 1.44 x 0.88 m. The central portion of the surface is carved to resemble a round-topped stela. In the lunette are the standing figures of Anubis and Osiris who are adored by the brothers Suti and Hor and their wives. The figures of the worshiping couples have been erased. Below the figures are twenty-one horizontal lines of text. The first hymn ends in the middle of line 8. The second runs from the middle of line 8 to near the end of line 14. The remaining lines consist of personal statements and prayers of the two brothers.

First Hymn

(1) Adoration of Amun when he rises as Harakhti by the overseer of the works of Amun, Suti, (and) the overseer of the works of Amun, Hor. They say:

Hail to you, Re, perfect each day,
Who rises at dawn without failing,
Khepri who wearies himself with toil!
Your rays are on the face, yet unknown,
Fine gold does not match your splendor;
Self-made you fashioned your body,
Creator uncreated.
Sole one, unique one, who traverses eternity,
[Remote one],[1] with millions under his care;
Your splendor is like heaven's splendor,
Your color brighter than its hues.
When you cross the sky all faces see you,
When you set you are hidden from their (5)
sight;
Daily you give yourself at dawn,
Safe is your sailing under your majesty.
In a brief day you race a course,
Hundred thousands, millions of miles;
A moment is each day to you,
It has passed when you go down.
You also complete the hours of night,
You order it without pause in your labor.

[1] What is written is *ḥry wꜣwt*, "who is above the ways," but perhaps *ḥryw*, "remote," was intended.

Through you do all eyes see,
They lack aim when your majesty sets.
When you stir to rise at dawn,
Your brightness opens the eyes of the herds;
When you set in the western mountain,
They sleep as in the state of death.

Second Hymn
Hail to you, Aten of daytime,
Creator of all, who makes them live!
Great falcon, brightly plumed,
Beetle who raised himself.
Self-creator, uncreated,
Eldest Horus within Nut,
Acclaimed (10) in his rising and setting.
Maker of the earth's yield,
Khnum and Amun of mankind,
Who seized the Two Lands from great to small.
Beneficent mother of gods and men,
Craftsman with a patient heart,
Toiling long to make them countless.
Valiant shepherd who drives his flock,
Their refuge, made to sustain them.
Runner, racer, courser,
Khepri of distinguished birth,
Who raises his beauty in the body of Nut,
Who lights the Two Lands with his disk.
The Two Lands' Oldest who made himself,
Who sees all that he made, he alone.
Who reaches the ends of the lands every day,
In the sight of those who tread on them.
Rising in heaven formed as Re,
He makes the seasons with the months,
Heat as he wishes, cold as he wishes.
He makes bodies slack, he gathers them up,
Every land rejoices at his rising,
Every day gives praise to him.

Prayers
The overseer of works, Suti; the overseer of works, (15) Hor. He says:

I was controller in your sanctuary,
Overseer of works in your very shrine,
Made for you by your beloved son,
The Lord of the Two Lands, *Nebmare*,[3] given life.
My lord made me controller of your monuments,
Because he knew my vigilance.
I was a vigorous controller of your monuments,
One who did right (*maat*) as you wished.
For I knew you are content with right,
You advance him who does it on earth.
I did it and you advanced me,
You made me favored on earth in Ipet-sut,[4]
One who was in your following when you appeared.[5]
I was a true one who abhors falsehood,
Who does not trust the words of a liar.
But my brother, my likeness, his ways I trust,
He came from the womb with me the same day.

The overseer(s) of Amun's works in Southern Ipet,[6] Suti, Hor.

When I was in charge on the westside,
He was in charge on the eastside.
We controlled great monuments in Ipet-sut,
At the front of Thebes, the city of Amun.
May you give me old age in your city,
My eye <beholding> your beauty;
A burial in the west, the place of heart's content,
As I join the favored ones who went in peace.
May you give me sweet breeze when I land,
And [garlands][7] on the day of the *wag*-feast.

[2] Or, "when he embraces them?" But a contrast with slackness is more plausible.
[3] Amenhotep III. The two brothers were architects in the service of this king.
[4] Karnak.
[5] When the statue of Amun appeared in a festival procession.
[6] Luxor.
[7] The *sšdw* received on a feast day must be decorative ribbons, scarves, or garlands rather than wrappings.

REFERENCES

Text: *Hiero. Texts*, Part 8:22-25 and pls. xxi; Varille 1942; *Urk. IV* 1943-1947; Stewart 1957:3-5. Translations: Sainte Fare Garnot 1948; 1949; Helck 1961; Fecht 1967; *ANET* 367-368; Lichtheim *AEL* 2:86-89.

THE GREAT HYMN TO THE ATEN (1.28)
In the Tomb of Ay — West Wall, 13 Columns

Miriam Lichtheim

The texts in the tomb of the courtier Ay have yielded the most extensive statements of Aten worship. Here we have not only several short hymns and prayers but, above all, the long text which has come to be known as "The Great Hymn to the Aten." The east wall of the tomb is inscribed with three hymns and prayers to the Aten and to the king, and the west wall contains the great hymn. The long text columns begin at the top of the wall. Below the text are the kneeling relief figures of Ay and his wife.

"The Great Hymn to the Aten" [a] is an eloquent and beautiful statement of the doctrine of the one god. He alone has created the world and all it contains. He alone gives life to man and beast. He alone watches over his creations. He alone inhabits the sky. Heretofore the sun-god had appeared in three major forms: as Harakhti in the morning, as Khepri in midday, and as Atum in the evening. His daily journey across the sky had been done in the company of many gods. It had involved the ever-recurring combat against the primordial serpent Apopis. In traversing the night sky the god had been acclaimed by the multitudes of the dead who rest there; and each hour of the night had marked a specific stage in his journey. Thus the daily circuit of the sky was a drama with a large supporting cast. In the new doctrine of the Aten as sole god all these facets were eliminated. The Aten rises and sets in lonely majesty in an empty sky. Only the earth is peopled by his creatures, and only they adore his rising and setting.

(1) Adoration of *Re-Harakhti-who-rejoices-in-lightland In-his-name-Shu-who-is-Aten*, living forever; the great living Aten who is in jubilee, the lord of all that the Disk encircles, lord of sky, lord of earth, lord of Lower Egypt, who lives by Maat, the lord of the Two lands, *Nefer-kheprure, Sole-one-of-Re*; the Son of Re who lives by Maat, the Lord of Crowns, *Akhenaten*, great in his lifetime; (and) his beloved great Queen, the Lady of the Two Lands, *Nefer-nefru-Aten Nefertiti*, who lives in health and youth forever. The Vizier, the Fanbearer on the right of the King, ----- [Ay]; he says:[1]

Splendid you rise in heaven's lightland,
O living Aten, creator of life!
When you have dawned in eastern lightland,
You fill every land with your beauty.
You are beauteous, great, radiant,
High over every land;
Your rays embrace the lands,
To the limit of all that you made,
Being Re, you reach their limits,[2]
You bend them <for> the son whom you love;
Though you are far, your rays are on earth,
Though one sees you, your strides are unseen.

When you set in western lightland,
Earth is in darkness as if in death;[b]
One sleeps in chambers, heads covered,
One eye does not see another.
Were they robbed of their goods,
That are under their heads,
People would not remark it.
Every lion comes from its den,
All the serpents bite;[3]
Darkness hovers, earth is silent,
As their maker rests in lightland.

Earth brightens when you dawn in lightland,
When you shine as Aten of daytime;
As you dispel the dark,
As you cast your rays,
The Two Lands are in festivity.
Awake they stand on their feet,
You have roused them;
Bodies cleansed, (5) clothed,
Their arms adore your appearance.
The entire land sets out to work,[c]
All beasts browse on their herbs;
Trees, herbs are sprouting,
Birds fly from their nests,
Their wings greeting your *ka*.[d]
All flocks frisk on their feet,
All that fly up and alight,
They live when you dawn for them.
Ships fare north, fare south as well,
Roads lie open when you rise;
The fish in the river dart before you,
Your rays are the midst the sea.[e]

Who makes seed grow in women,
Who creates people from sperm;
Who feeds the son in his mother's womb,
Who soothes him to still his tears.
Nurse in the womb,
Giver of breath,
To nourish all that he made.
When he comes from the womb to breathe,
On the day of this birth,
You open wide his mouth,

a Cf. Ps 104
b Ps 104:20
c Ps 104:23
d Ps 104:12
e Ps 104:25-26

[1] Though the hymn was undoubtedly composed for recitation by the king, inscribed in the tomb of Ay, it was adapted to recitation by the courtier.

[2] The sentence consists of a wordplay on r^{c}, "Sun," and r^{c}, "end," "limit."

[3] This is one of several passages that recall similar formulations in Ps 104 and have led to speculations about possible interconnections between the Hymn to the Aten and the psalm. The resemblances are, however, more likely to be the result of the generic similarity between Eg. hymns and biblical psalms. A specific literary interdependence is not probable. For many of the generic similarities, see Auffret 1981:133-316.

You supply his needs.
When the chick in the egg speaks in the shell,
You give him breath within to sustain him;
When you have made him complete,
To break out from the egg,
He comes out from the egg,
To announce his completion,
Walking on his legs he comes from it.

How many are your deeds.[f]
Though hidden from sight,
O sole God beside whom there is none! [g]
You made the earth as you wished, you alone,
[h] All peoples, herds, and flocks;
All upon the earth that walk on legs,
All on high that fly on wings,[h]
The lands of Khor and Kush,
The land of Egypt.
You set every man in his place,
You supply their needs;
Everyone has his food,
His lifetime is counted.
Their tongues differ in speech,
Their characters likewise;
Their skins are distinct,
For you distinguished the peoples.[4]

You made Hapy in the *Duat*,[5]
You bring him when you will,
To nourish the people,
For you made them for yourself.
Lord of all who toils for them,
Lord of all lands who shines for them,
Aten of daytime, great in glory!
All distant lands, you make them live,
You made a heavenly Hapy descend from them;
(10) He makes waves on the mountains like the sea,
To drench their fields and their towns.
How excellent are your ways, O Lord of eternity!
A Hapy from heaven for foreign peoples,
And all lands' creatures that walk on legs,
For Egypt the Hapy who comes from the *Duat*.[6]

f Ps 104:24
g Isa 43:10
h-h Ps 8:7-8

Your rays nurse all fields,
When you shine they live, they grow for you;
You made the seasons to foster all that you made,
Winter to cool them, heat that they taste you.
You made the far sky to shine therein,
To behold all that you made;
You alone, shining in your form of living Aten,
Risen, radiant, distant, near.
You made millions of forms from yourself alone,
Towns, villages, fields, the river's course;
All eyes observe you upon them,
For you are the Aten of daytime on high.
... --- ...[7]

You are in my heart,
There is no other who knows you,
Only your son, *Neferkheprure, Sole-one-of-Re*,
Whom you have taught your ways and your might.
<Those on> earth come from your hand as you made them,
When you have dawned they live,
When you set they die;
You yourself are lifetime, one lives by you.
All eyes are on <your> beauty until you set,
All labor ceases when you rest in the west;
When you rise you stir [everyone] for the King,
Every leg is on the move since you founded the earth.
You rouse them for your son who came from your body,
The King who lives by Maat, the Lord of the Two Lands,
Neferkheprure, Sole-one-of-Re,
The Son of Re who lives by Maat, the Lord of crowns,
Akhenaten, great in his lifetime;
(and) the great Queen whom he loves, the Lady of the Two Lands,
Nefer-nefru-Aten Nefertiti, living forever.

[4] The Hymn to the Aten expresses the cosmopolitan and humanist outlook of the New Kingdom at its purest and most sympathetic. All peoples are seen as the creatures of the sun-god, who has made them diverse in skin color, speech, and character. Their diversity is described objectively, without a claim of Eg. superiority. On the theme of the differentiation of languages see Sauneron 1960:31-41.

[5] The netherworld.

[6] Hapy, the inundating Nile, emerges from the netherworld to nourish Egypt, while foreign peoples are sustained by a "Nile from heaven" who descends as rain.

[7] Several obscure sentences containing corruptions and a lacuna.

REFERENCES

Text: Davies 1903-08 6:29-31 and pls. xxvii and xli; Sandman 1938:93-96. Translation: *ANET* 369-371; Gardiner 1961:225-227; Simpson 1973:289-295; Lichtheim *AEL* 2:96-100; Studies: Auffret 1981:133-316.

4. PRAYERS

PRAYER TO RE-HARAKHTI (1.29)

Michael V. Fox

This is an individual supplication in a fairly stereotypic form, probably designed for use by different people in various situations. The worshipper asks for acceptance of his prayers without praying for anything in particular and confesses his sins and folly without reference to specific transgressions.

The worshipper seems to be a pilgrim to the temple at Heliopolis. The prayer is an expression of "personal piety," a form of religion prominent in the Ramesside period (see, e.g., Fecht 1965). It emphasizes the individual's humility and frailty and his dependence on god.

Some biblical psalms speak out of a similar context: a pilgrim expressing his confidence and joy when visiting the temple, where he imagines himself dwelling always in God's presence. Compare Pss 23:6; 26:8; 27:4; 84, esp. vv 3, 5, 11; 42:3; 43:3-4; 122:1. Other psalms resemble this prayer in confessing frailty and sinfulness, e.g. Pss 25:7; 51; 40:13.

Prayer to Pre^{c}-Harakhty[1]

Come to me, Pre^{c}-Harakhty,
that you may perform (your) will.
You are the one who takes action,
there being none who takes action apart from you,
but (one can act) only if you are acting with him.[2]

Come to me, Atum, every day!
You are the noble god.
My heart has gone forth,
travelling southward to Heliopolis.
[...]
My heart rejoices,
my bosom exults.

Hear my prayers —
my supplications by day,
my hymns by night.
For my petitions are constant in my mouth,
They are heard throughout the day.[4]

O sole one, unique![5]
O Pre^{c}-Herakhty,
the likes of whom does not exist here.
Protector of millions,
who deliverers hundreds of thousands,
the helper of the one who cries to him,
the lord of Heliopolis.[6]

Visit not my many offenses upon me,
I am one ignorant of himself.
I am a mindless man,
who all day follows his mouth,
like an ox after grass.[7]

If my evenings (?) [...]
I am one who to whom repose comes.
I spend the day walking about
in the (temple) court, [a]
I spend the night [...][8]

a Ps 84:3, 5, 11; 42:3; 43:3-4

[1] Text: Pap. Anastasi II, 10, 1-11, 2; late New Kingdom (Gardiner 1937:18-19). Translations and bibliography: Caminos 1954:60ff.; *ANET* 379; Assmann no. 176; Barucq and Daumas 1980:145-46. The text appears in an anthology of model texts for scribal students. Pre^{c}-Harakhty is a Late Eg. name of the sun god in his daytime form; Re-Harakhti is the more common earlier name.

[2] Stanza I (invocation) plays on the word *iri*, "do," "take action," "perform," "create," etc. The theme is that God alone can act effectively of his own accord. Similar phraseology is elsewhere used in praising a god as *creator*, but the theme here seems to be God's effectiveness in general.

[3] Stanza II (invocation) declares the worshipper's delight in God's presence.

[4] In Stanza III (appeal), the worshipper calls upon god to hear his prayers.

[5] "Sole One" or "unique" (*w*^{c}) is a common sobriquet of gods. It praises a particular god's uniqueness without denying the existence of other gods. See Hornung 1982:185-86, 230-37.

[6] Stanza IV (praise) is a series of epithets praising the god as protector and deliverer.

[7] In Stanza V (confession), the penitent declares his weakness and ignorance. He says that he follows his mouth—his ungoverned desires—as thoughtlessly as a grazing ox does his.

[8] Stanza VI (confidence) is uncertain and incomplete. The penitent finds serenity in the "temple court" (uncertain, but the divine determinative shows that it is a location associated with the temple). There he spends his days and (possibly) his nights.

REFERENCES

Assmann 1975b; Barucq and Daumas 1980; Caminos 1954; Fecht 1965; Gardiner 1937; Hornung 1982.

5. HARPERS' SONGS

THE SONG FROM THE TOMB OF KING INTEF (1.30)

Miriam Lichtheim

The song is preserved in two New Kingdom copies. First, on pages vi, 2-vii, 3, of the Ramesside Papyrus Harris 500 (= P. British Museum 10060); and, second, carved on a wall of the tomb of Paatenemheb from Saqqara, now in Leiden, which dates from the reign of Amenhotep IV (Akhenaten). The latter copy, which is incomplete, is written above the heads of a group of four musicians led by a blind harpist. The song's introductory line states that it reproduces a song inscribed in the tomb of a King Intef — a name that was borne by a number of kings of the 11th and of the 17th Dynasties. Since the two New Kingdom copies reproduce a genuinely Middle Egyptian text, we need not doubt that an original text, carved in a royal tomb of the Middle Kingdom, existed.

The phrase "make holiday" (*ir hrw nfr*), which the singer of the *Intef Song* addresses to the audience, was a term employed in situations of daily life as well as in reference to death and the afterlife. Furthermore, it is known that funerary banquets were held in the cemeteries on feast days. It is thus quite possible that Harpers' Songs were sung at such funerary banquets, and that they employed the "make holiday" theme in its multiple meanings. In the context of the funerary banquet the various meanings would blend into one.

The theme of sorrow over death properly belonged to the Laments on Death which were an integral part of the burial ceremony. What is noteworthy is that these laments juxtapose sorrow and joy in a manner similar to the *Intef Song* and subsequent Harpers' Songs, and move rapidly back and forth between grief and joy:

> I have wept, I have mourned!
> O all people, remember getting drunk on wine,
> With wreaths and perfume on your heads![1]

The dead too had joy: "How good is this which happens to him!"[2]

Given the multiple meanings of the "make holiday" theme, it follows that it was not the use of this theme which made the *Intef Song* so startling, but rather its skepticism concerning the reality of the afterlife and the effectiveness of tomb-building. It was this skepticism which injected a strident note of discord into a class of songs that had been designed to praise and reassure. The incongruity is of the same order as that which one observes in the *Dispute between a Man and His Ba*. For there the *ba*, though itself the guarantor of immortality, is given the role of denigrating death and immortality, denying the worth of tombs, and counseling enjoyment of life. The incongruity was not lost on the Egyptians, as the subsequent development of Harpers' Songs reveals. The Harpers' Songs of the New Kingdom show two responses to the *Intef Song*: an outright rejection of its "impious" thoughts, and a toning down of its skepticism so as to remove the sting. Both solutions are found side by side in two Harpers' Songs carved on the walls of the New Kingdom tomb of a priest Neferhotep.[3]

The objection to the skeptic-hedonistic message is phrased thus:

> I have heard those songs that are in the tombs of old,
> And what they relate in extolling life on earth,
> And in belittling the land of the dead.
> Why is this done to the land of eternity,
> The just and fair that holds no terror?

There follows the praise of eternal life.

The toning down of the skeptical approach took various forms, and resulted in Harpers' Songs that were eclectic and lacked unity. But though toned down, the note of skepticism could be heard, sometimes faintly, sometimes clearly, in Harpers' Songs and in other compositions, as a haunting suspicion that the struggle to win immortality was at best beset by uncertainties and at worst, futile.

(vi 2) Song which is in the tomb of King Intef, the justified, in front of the singer with the harp.

He is happy, this good prince!
⌜Death is a kindly fate⌝.[4]

[1] See Lüddeckens 1943:149-150; the passage is from a Saqqara tomb in Leiden (Holwerda-Boeser 1905-1932 4:pl. 15).

[2] Lüddeckens 1943:100: *wꜣḏ wy nn ḫpr n.f*, from Theban tomb number 49.

[3] Theban tomb number 50; see Lichtheim 1945:178ff, and below, pp. 49-50.

[4] *Šꜣw nfr ḥḏy* has been variously interpreted. In Lichtheim 1945:192, I emended *ḥḏy* to *ḫpr* in accordance with the parallel introductory phrase in the first Harper's Song of the Tomb of Neferhotep. Ferdern (1946:259) proposed a different division of the sentences: *wꜣḏ pw sr pn/ nfr šꜣw/ nfr ḥḏy*, and rendered, "A happy one is this prince; good is the destiny; good is the injury." Wilson (*ANET* 467) retained the

A generation passes,[a]
Another stays,
Since the time of the ancestors.
The gods who were before rest in their tombs,
Blessed (vi 5) nobles too are buried in their
tombs.
(Yet) those who built tombs,
Their places are gone,
What has become of them?
I have heard the words of Imhotep and Harde
def,[5]
Whose sayings are recited whole.
What of their places?
Their walls have crumbled,
Their places are gone,
As though they had never been! [b]
None comes from there,
To tell of their state,
To tell of their needs,
To calm our hearts,
Until we go where they have gone!

a Eccl 1:4
b Eccl 1:11
c Eccl 11:9-10
d Eccl 3:22

Hence rejoice in your heart! [c]
Forgetfulness profits you,[6]
Follow your heart as long as you live!
(vi 10) Put myrrh on your head,
Dress in fine linen,
Anoint yourself with oils fit for a god.[7]
Heap up your joys,
Let your heart not sink!
Follow your heart and your happiness,[d]
Do your things on earth as your heart commands!
When there comes to you that day of mourning,
The Weary-hearted[8] hears not their mourning,
Wailing saves no man from the pit!

Refrain (vii 2): Make holiday,
Do not weary of it!
Lo, none is allowed to take his goods with him,
Lo, none who departs comes back again!

earlier division and translated: "Prosperous is he, this good prince/ Even though good fortune may suffer harm." In addition, some have wanted to read *wḏ* rather than *wʾḏ*. But *wʾḏ* is strongly supported by the parallel phrases in the *Totenklagen*. The sentence *wʾḏ wy nn ḫpr n.f* from Theban tomb number 49 recurs in Theban tomb number 106 in the form of a quotation (See Lüddeckens 1943:100-101), thereby showing that it was the proper thing to say at a funeral.

I now attempt yet another rendering, in which *ḥḏy* is taken to be a noun denoting destruction, i.e., death, and *šʾw nfr*, though undoubtedly a euphemism for death, is retained in its literal meaning, the whole being a nominal sentence without *pw*.

The new interpretation of the whole song which Lorton (1968:45ff) tried is entirely mistaken.

5 The two famous sages of the Old Kingdom, who were worshiped as gods. An Instruction ascribed to Imhotep, the vizier of King Djoser, has not come to light.

6 Contrary to my earlier rendering I now divide *wḏʾ.k ib.k rs/ mhʾ ib ḥr sʾḫ n.k*; for I have become convinced that any overlong and unbalanced sentence in a poetic text is the result of wrong division and mistranslation.

7 Lit., "with the genuine marvels that belong to a god."

8 The god Osiris.

REFERENCES

Text: Budge 1910:23-24, pls. xlv-xlvi; Müller 1899:29-30, pls. xii-xvi; Holwerda-Boeser 1905-1932 4:pl. 6 (the tomb copy). Translation: Erman 1927:133-134; Breasted 1933:163-164; Lichtheim 1945:192-193; *AEL* 1:194-197; *ANET* 467-468; Daumas 1965:404.

THE SONG FROM THE TOMB OF NEFERHOTEP (1.31)
(Theban Tomb No. 50)

Miriam Lichtheim

When they first appeared in the Middle Kingdom, the texts known as Harper's Songs were designed to praise death and the life after death. But in the famous *Harper's Song from the Tomb of King Intef*, preserved in a papyrus copy, the praises of the afterlife were replaced by anxious doubts about its reality, and by the advice to make merry while alive and to shun the thought of death. Such a skeptic-hedonistic message may have originated in songs sung at secular feasts; but when transmitted as a funerary text inscribed in a tomb and addressed to the tomb-owner, the message became incongruous and discordant. The incongruity did not pass unnoticed. In the tomb of the priest Neferhotep there are three Harper's Songs, each expressing a particular response. One song continued the skeptic-hedonistic theme but blended it with elements of traditional piety in an attempt to tone down and harmonize the contrary viewpoints. The second song is an outright rejection of skepticism and hedonism, coupled with a praise of the land of the dead. The third is a description of life after death in traditional ritualistic terms. Thus, the three songs in one and the same tomb reflect the Egyptian preoccupation with the nature of death and the varying and conflicting answers and attitudes which continued side by side.

The second and third songs, and the figures of the harpers who recite them, form part of a banquet scene on the left rear wall of the hall. The first song occurs in the context of an offering-table scene, in the passage leading from the hall to the inner shrine. The second song, the one that deliberately rejects the skeptic message, is translated below.

Says the singer-with-harp of the divine father of Amun, Neferhotep,[1] justified:

All ye excellent nobles and gods of the graveyard,
Hearken to the praise-giving for the divine father,
The worship of the honored noble's excellent *ba*,
Now that he is a god everliving, exalted in the West;
May they[2] become a remembrance for posterity,
For everyone who comes to pass by.

I have heard those songs that are in the tombs of old,
What they tell in extolling life on earth,
In belittling the land of the dead.[3]
Why is this done to the land of eternity,
The right and just that has no terrors?
Strife is abhorrent to it,
No one girds himself against his fellow;
This land that has no opponent,
All our kinsmen rest in it
Since the time of the first beginning.
Those to be born to millions of millions,
All of them will come to it;
No one may linger in the land of Egypt,
There is none who does not arrive in it.[4]
As to the time of deeds on earth,[a]
It is the occurrence of a dream;[5]
One says: "Welcome safe and sound,"
To him who reaches the West.

a Job 4:12-21; 7:7-9; 10:20-21 Ps 62:9

[1] The name and priestly title of the tomb-owner. The harpist remains unnamed.
[2] The praises.
[3] In these lines the singer explicitly refers to harper's songs that express skepticism (see the previous song).
[4] The thought expressed in this quatrain occurs in almost identical terms in hymns to Osiris, where it is the god, rather than the land of the dead, to whom all must come; see Louvre Stela C 218 (Pierret 1874-1878 2:134-138) and BM Stela 164 (*Hiero. Texts*, 9:25-26 and pls. xxi-xxia).
[5] Note the appearance of the thought that life is a dream.

REFERENCES

Text: Pierret 1874-1878 2:134-138; Gardiner 1913:165-170; Erman 1927:253-254; *Hiero. Texts*, 9:25-26, pls. xxi-xxiA. Translation: Lichtheim 1945:178-212 and pls. i-vii; *AEL* 2:115-116; *ANET* 33-34.

6. DIVINATION, INCANTATION, RITUAL

EXECRATION TEXTS (1.32)

Robert K. Ritner

From the Old Kingdom through the Roman era, priests performed official ritual cursings of the potential enemies of Egypt. The ceremonies included the breaking of red pots[1] [a] and figurines inscribed with formal "Execration Texts" listing Nubians, Asiatics, Libyans, living and deceased Egyptians, as well as generally threatening forces. The texts themselves contain no explicit curses, but instead serve to identify the fate of the enemies with that of the destroyed pot or image. The texts were seemingly compiled by the state chancellory, since they were updated to reflect changes in rulers and territories. This translation follows the Middle Kingdom Berlin bowls (mid-12th Dynasty), supplemented by slightly earlier parallel texts from an intact deposit at the Nubian fortress of Mirgissa.

A. Nubia

The ruler of Kush, Auau, born of [...], and all the stricken ones[2] who are with him.
The ruler of Saï, Seteqtenkekh, and all the stricken ones who are with him.
The ruler of Webasepet, Bakuayt, called

a Jer 19:1-11; Amos 1:2-4; Num 22-24

[1] Cp. the biblical "Oracles against the Nations" where the places named become the target of magic or divine action (e.g., Isa 13-27; Jer 45-51; Ezek 25-29; Amos 1-2; Zeph 2; Zech 9 and scripture note *a* above). See Ritner 1993:140, n. 623.
[2] For the corrected reading and prospective nuance of "captive," see Ritner 1993:141, n. 628.

Tchay, born of Ihaas, born to Wenkat, and all the stricken ones who are with him.

The ruler of Webasepet, Iauny, born of Gemhu[(?) ...], born to Ti[...], and all the stricken ones who are with him.

The Medjay, Wah-ib, born of [...]tpuhia, born to Wenkat, and all the stricken ones who are with him.

The ruler of Ausheq, and all the stricken ones who are with him.

Every Nubian of Kush, of Muger, of Saï, of Irs[...], of Nasem, of Rida, of Irsukhet, of Iamnas, of Ia[...], [of ...]amu, of Tuksa, of Bahass, of Ma[...]ia, of Ibis, of Gas(?), of Ausheq, of Webasepet, of Iaat-..., of Iaat, of Tcheksis, of Megseruia, of Ruhpubawit(?),

Their strong men, their messengers, their confederates, their allies, who will rebel, who will plot, who will fight, who will say[3] that they will fight, who will say that they will rebel, in this entire land.

B. Asia

The ruler of Iy-anq,[4] [b] *Erum*,[5] and all the stricken ones who are with him.

The ruler of Iy-anq, *Abi-yamimu*,[6] and all the stricken ones who are with him.

The ruler of Iy-anq, Akirum,[7] and all the stricken ones who are with him.

The ruler of Shutu,[8] [c] Ayyabum,[9] and all the stricken ones who are with him.

The ruler of Shutu, Kushar,[10] and all the stricken ones who are with him.

The ruler of Shutu, Zabulanu,[11] and all the stricken ones who are with him.

The ruler of *ʾIymwʿrrw*, *Ḫâlu-barîḫ*,[12] and all the stricken ones who are with him.

[b] Num 13:22-33; Deut 2:10; Josh 11:21-22; 14:6-15; 15:13-19
[c] Num 24:17
[d] Josh 13:3; Judg 1:18
[e] Josh 15:8

The ruler of *Qhrmw*, ʿAmmu-(y)atar,[13] and all the stricken ones who are with him.

The ruler of *Qhrmw*, *Hmṯnw*, and all the stricken ones who are with him.

The ruler of *Qhrmw*, ʿAmmu-yakûn,[14] and all the stricken ones who are with him.

The ruler of Arḥâbu,[15] *ʿprwhq*, and all the stricken ones who are with him.

The ruler of Arḥâbu, *Iymʿnʿwmw*, and all the stricken ones who are with him.

The ruler of *ʾIsinw*, *Iykwḏdʾ*'s son *ʿmmwtʾi*, and all the stricken ones who are with him.

The ruler of *ʾIsinw*, *ʿwḏwšnw*, and all the stricken ones who are with him.

The ruler of *ʾIsinw*, *Mʾʾmwt*, and all the stricken ones who are with him.

The ruler of *ʾInhiʾ*, Malkî-ilum,[16] and all the stricken ones who are with him.

The ruler of *ʾInhiʾ*, *ʾqḥm*, and all the stricken ones who are with him.

The ruler of *ʾInhiʾ*, Kamarum,[17] and all the stricken ones who are with him.

The ruler of *ʾInhiʾ*, Yapʿânu,[18] and all the stricken ones who are with him.

The ruler of *ʾqhi*, *Iyqʾḏmw*, and all the stricken ones who are with him.

The ruler of *ʾqhi*, *Šmšwʾirʾim*, and all the stricken ones who are with him.

The ruler of ʿIrqatum,[19] *Iʾwmqhti*, and all the stricken ones who are with him.

The ruler of Ashkelon,[20] [d] *Ḫʾykm*,[21] and all the stricken ones who are with him.

The ruler of Ashkelon, *Ḫkṯnw* (?), and all the stricken ones who are with him.

[The ruler of ..., and all the stricken ones who are] with him.

The ruler of Mutî-ilu,[22] *Mnṯm*, and all the stricken ones who are with him.

The ruler of Jerusalem,[23] [e] Yaqar-ʿAmmu,[24]

---

[3] Or "think."
[4] Wilson (*ANET* 329) notes the suggested relation of *ʾIyʿnq* to ʿAnaqim "giants" in Canaan; see also Lipiński 1974:41-48.
[5] So suggested by Wilson (*ANET* 328) for *ʿʾm*.
[6] So suggested by Wilson (*ANET* 328) for *ʾIbiymʿmʿw*.
[7] So suggested by Wilson (*ANET* 328) for *ʿkʾm*.
[8] Wilson (*ANET* 329) suggests the identification of *Šwtw* with Moab on the basis of Num 24:17, "sons of Sheth."
[9] Wilson (*ANET* 329) identifies *ʾIybm* with cuneiform Ayyab, "Job."
[10] Suggested by Wilson (*ANET* 329) for *Kwšr*.
[11] Wilson (*ANET* 329) identifies *Ṯbʾnw* with cuneiform for "Zebulon."
[12] Lit., *Ḫʾwbʾḥ*, see: Albright 1934:7.
[13] Lit., *ʿmmwitʾ*, see: Albright 1934:7.
[14] Lit., *ʿmmwikn*, see: Albright 1934:7.
[15] Lit., *ʾIʾḥbw*, see: Albright 1934:7.
[16] Lit., *Mʾ(?)kʾm*, see: Albright 1934:7.
[17] Lit., *Kmʾm*, see: Albright 1934:7.
[18] Lit., *Iypʿnw*, see: Albright 1934:7.
[19] Lit., *ʿʾqtm*, see: Albright 1934:7.
[20] Wilson (*ANET* 329) identifies *ʾIsqʾnw* with cuneiform "Ashqaluna."
[21] Wilson (*ANET* 329) suggests a vocalization Khalu-kim.
[22] So Albright 1934:7, for *Mwitʾ*.
[23] Hieroglyphic *ʾwšʾmm*.
[24] Hieroglyphic *ʾIyqʾʿmw*.

and all the stricken ones who are with him.
The ruler of Jerusalem, Seti-ᶜAnu,[25] and all the stricken ones who are with him.
The ruler of *ᶜḫmt*, [...]*ks*ᵓ*m*, and all the stricken ones who are with him.
The ruler of Alhânu,[26] *Iym*ᶜ*i*ᵓ*w*, and all the stricken ones who are with him.
All rulers of ᵓ*Iysipi*, and all the stricken ones who are with them.
All the Asiatics of Byblos,[f] of Ullaza, of Iy-anq, of Shutu, of ᵓ*Iymw*ᶜ*rrw*, of *Qhrmw*, of *Arḥâbu*, of Yarmût,[27] of ᵓ*Inhi*ᵓ, of ᵓ*qhi*, of ᶜIrqatum, of Yarmût (sic.), of *Isinw*, of Ashkelon, of *Dmit*ᵓ*iw*, of Mutî-ilu, of Jerusalem, of Alhânu, of ᵓ*Iysipi*,
Their strong men, their messengers, their confederates, their allies, the tribesmen in Asia, who will rebel, who will plot, who will fight, who will say that they will fight, who will say that they will rebel, in this entire land.

C. Libya
The chiefs in Libya, all Libyans and their rulers.
Their strong men, their messengers, their confederates, their allies, who will rebel, who will plot, who will fight, who will say that they will fight, who will say that they will rebel, in this entire land.

D. Egyptians
All people (i.e., "Egyptians"), all patricians, all commoners, all men, all eunuchs, all women, all nobles, who will rebel, who will plot, who will fight, who will say that they will fight, who will say that they will rebel, every rebel who will say that he will rebel, in this entire land.
The deceased[28] Ameni, tutor of Sit-Bastet, who raised Sit-Hathor, daughter of Neferu.
The deceased Senwosret-seneb, the younger, called "Little One," tutor of Sit-Ipi, daughter of Sit-Hathor, who raised Kamu, daughter of Sit-Hathor.
The deceased Sehetep-ib, tutor of Sit-Hathor, who raised Iwt-rehu-ankh.
The deceased Sobekhotep, born of Renes-ankh.
The deceased Seni-ankh, born of Iwrw, born to Hetepi.
The deceased Senwosret, called Witu, born to Ameny.
The deceased Amenemhat, born of Hepiu, born to Mutchau.
The deceased Ameny, born of Hetep, born to Senwosret.

E. Evil Things
Every evil word, every evil speech, every evil slander,[29] every evil intent, every evil plot, every evil fight, every evil disturbance, every evil plan, every evil thing, every evil dream in every evil sleep.

f Josh 13:5

[25] Hieroglyphic *Sṯ*ᶜ*nw*.
[26] So Albright 1934:7 for ᵓ*I*ᵓ*hnw*.
[27] So Albright 1934:7 for ᵓ*Iy*ᵓ*mwt*.
[28] For the corrected reading, see Ritner 1993:141, n. 627.
[29] Or "incantation."

REFERENCES

Texts: Sethe 1926; Koenig 1990. Translations and studies: *ANET* 328-329; Ritner 1993:136-190.

DREAM ORACLES (1.33)
(P. Chester Beatty III, P. BM 10683)

Robert K. Ritner

The Chester Beatty "Dream Book" is currently the oldest surviving manual of dream interpretation. Perhaps deriving from a 12th Dyn. original, the present manuscript dates from the 19th Dynasty and was the property of senior scribes at the royal workmen's village of Deir el-Medineh.[1] The book comprises eleven columns in tabular form, each preceded by the vertically-written heading: "If a man see himself in a dream." The horizontal lines of the columns briefly detail the dream image, whether or not it is favorable, and the prognostication for the dreamer. The text is arranged in discrete units, with good dreams listed before bad ones (highlighted by red ink), and a concluding incantation to avert any evil results. The entire pattern was repeated twice, once for "followers" of Horus and again for those associated with Seth.[2] The interpretations are often based on religious symbolism or paronomasia ("puns"), with many sexual situations and ironic reversals.[3]

For the Egyptians, as for many cultures, dreams provided a point of contact between the divine and human worlds, so that dreams might be sought for inspiration or healing (incubation), or for communication with the dead; see Vernus 1986. Conversely, enemies might send evil dreams, and the execration texts (above, pp. 50-52) specifically combat "every evil dream in every evil sleep." For other protections against night terrors, see Ritner 1990.

If a man see himself in a dream: [a]

[a] Gen 37:5-10; 40:5-41, 36; 1 Sam 28:6; Dan 2:1-45; Jer 29:8-9

(2/7) Shooting at a target. [Good.] It means something good will happen to him.
(2/9) [Mentioning] his wife to a husband. Good. It means the retreat of evils attached to him.
(2/11) His penis having become large. Good. It means an increase of his property.
(2/12) [Taking(?)] a bow in his hand. Good. The giving to him of his (most) important office.
(2/13) Dying adversely. Good. It means living after the death of his father.
(2/14) Seeing the god who is above.[4] Good. It means much food.
(2/20) His mouth filled with dirt. Good. Living off[5] of his townsmen.
(2/21) Eating the flesh of a donkey. Good. It means his promotion.[6]
(2/22) Eating the flesh of a crocodile. Good. [It means] living off[7] the property of an official.
(2/24) Looking through a window. Good. The hearing of his cry by his god.
(2/25) Being given papyrus reeds. Good. It means hearing his cry.
(2/26) Seeing himself atop a house. Good. [It means] finding something.
(3/2) [Seeing] himself in mourning. Good. An increase of his property.
(3/3) His hair having become long.[8] Good. It means something at which his face will light up (i.e., "be be joyful").
(3/4) Being given white bread. Good. It means something [at which his face] will light up.[9]
(3/5) Drinking wine. Good. It means living in Truth.
(3/7) Copulating with his mother ... Good. [It means] cleaving to him by his relatives.
(3/8) Copulating with his sister. Good. It means the transferral to him of property.
(3/17) Being given a head. Good. The opening of his mouth to speak.
(4/1) Killing a snake. Good. Killing a quarrel.[10]
(4/2) Seeing his face as a panther. Good. Acting as chief.
(4/3) Seeing a large cat. Good. It means a large harvest will occur for him.[11]
(4/4) Drinking wine. Good. The opening of his mouth to speak.[12]
(4/5) Binding malefic people at night. Good. Taking away the speech of his enemies.
(4/6) Crossing in a ferry-boat. Good. It means coming forth from all quarrels.[13]
(4/7) Seated on a sycamore. Good. Driving off all his ills.
(4/12) Destroying his clothes. Good. Releasing him from all ills.
(4/13) Seeing himself dead. Good. A long life before him.
(4/14) Binding his own two legs. Good. It means dwelling among his townsmen.
(4/15) Falling from a wall. Good. It means coming forth from all quarrels.[14]
(5/5) [Drinking] his own urine. Good. It means eating[15] the property of his son.
(5/19) Submerging in the Nile. Good. It means purification from all evil.[16]
(6/1) Burying an old man. Good. It means prosperity.
(6/24) Seeing Asiatics. Good. The love of his father when he dies comes into his presence.
(7/4) Drinking warm beer. BAD. It means suppurating illness infects him.
(7/6) Chewing cucumber. BAD. It means quarrel-

[1] For the date, see Gardiner 1935:8-9. For the owners of the papyrus, see Pestman 1982.
[2] Corresponding to the two personality types recognized in Eg. wisdom literature: the ideal, restrained man (of Horus) and the intemperate man (of Seth).
[3] Since words were felt sacred, and not the chance products of linguistic history, puns were believed to express inherent links between individual words and concepts. For ironic reversals, note the many favorable dreams entailing death or mourning — suggesting an inheritance for the dreamer.
[4] Perhaps a reference to the moon god, see van Dijk 1986:37.
[5] Lit., "eating."
[6] A pun on *ꜥꜣ* "donkey" and *sꜥꜣ* "make great/promote."
[7] Cf. 2/20. The rapacious crocodile is here a symbol of the bureaucratic official.
[8] Probably a symbol of mourning.
[9] A pun on *ḥḏ* "white" and *ḥḏꜣi* "light up/be bright."
[10] Lit., "words."
[11] A pun on *mꜣiw ꜥꜣ* "large cat" and *šmw ꜥꜣ* "large harvest."
[12] Cf. 3/5 and 3/15.
[13] Lit., "words."
[14] Lit., "words."
[15] Or figuratively "living off."
[16] Probably a reference to divinization by drowning in the Nile.

ing[17] with him occurs when he is met.
(7/8) Eating a filleted catfish. BAD. His seizure by a crocodile.
(7/11) Seeing his face in a mirror. BAD. It means another wife.
(7/12) God dispelling his tears. BAD. It means fighting.
(7/13) Seeing himself enchanting[18] his side. BAD. Exacting property from him.
(7/17) Copulating with a woman. BAD. It means mourning.
(7/18) Bitten by a dog. BAD. His being touched by magic.[19]
(7/19) Bitten by a snake. BAD. It means the occurrence of a quarrel against him.[20]
(7/20) Measuring barley. BAD. It means the occurrence of a quarrel against him.
(7/21) Writing upon a papyrus roll. BAD. The reckoning of his transgressions by his god.
(7/22) Moving his house. BAD. [It means] his illness.
(7/23) Enchanted by another with his spell.[21] BAD. It means mourning.
(7/24) Acting as helmsman in a boat. BAD. Regarding any judgment of him, he will not be victorious.
(7/25) His bed catching fire. BAD. It means the driving off of his wife.
(7/27) Being pricked by a thorn. BAD. It means telling lies.
(7/28) Seeing the trapping of birds. BAD. It means the seizure of his property.[22]
(8/1) Seeing his penis hard. BAD. Victory to his enemies.[23]
(8/5) Looking into a deep well. BAD. Putting him in prison.
(8/6) He catching on fire. BAD. His being slaughtered.
(8/12) His teeth falling out.[24] BAD. It means the death of a man among his dependants.
(8/13) Seeing a dwarf. BAD. Taking away half of his life.
(8/25) Carrying off temple goods. BAD. Seizure of his property before him.
(9/3) An Asiatic cloak upon him. BAD. His removal from his office.
(9/9) Seeing a woman's vulva. BAD. The ultimate in misery against him.
(9/10) Uncovering his own rear. BAD. He will be orphaned in the end.[25]
(9/14) Placing his face to the ground. BAD. The seeking of something from him by the dead.
(9/15) Seeing a blazing fire. BAD. It means the seizure of his son or his brother.
(9/16) Copulating with a sow. BAD. Being deprived of his property.[26]
(9/22) Copulating with his wife in the daylight. BAD. The seeing of his transgressions by his god.
(9/27) Guarding monkeys. BAD. A reversal is before him.
(9/28) Bringing mice from the field. BAD. A bad heart.
(10/9) Breaking a pot with his feet. BAD. It means fighting.[27]
(10/10-10/19) WORDS SAID BY A MAN WHEN HE AWAKENS IN HIS PLACE.

"Come to me, come to me, my mother Isis! Behold, I am seeing what is far from me in my city."

"Behold me, my son Horus, as one come forth bearing away what you have seen, so that your deafness be ended as your dream recedes, and fire go forth against him who frightens you. Behold, I have come so that I might see you, that I might drive off your ills, and that I might eradicate all terror."[28]

"Hail, good dream seen (by) night and by day. Drive off every evil terror that Seth, son of Nut, has made. As Re is victorious against his enemies, so I am victorious against my enemies."

THIS SPELL IS SAID by a man when he awakes in his place. *Pesen*-loaves are placed in (his) presence with some fresh herbs moistened with beer and myrrh. The man's face is to be wiped with them and all evil dreams that he has seen are driven off.

[17] Lit., "words."
[18] Gardner 1935:16, followed by Wilson (*ANET* 495), assume a garbled writing and translate "with a pain in his side."
[19] For the fear of hostile magic, see Ritner 1993:20-22.
[20] Cf. 4/1.
[21] For the defensive need to preserve the secrecy of spells, see Ritner 1993:202-204.
[22] A pun on *ḥm* "trapping" and *nḥm* "seizure."
[23] A pun on *nḫt* "firm/strong" and *nḫtw* "victory."
[24] Lit., "down from him."
[25] A pun on *pḥ.wy* "rear" and *pḥw* "end." Likely a reference to the orphaned Horus; cf. "The Tale of Horus and Seth."
[26] For the unlucky nature of the pig, see text 1.19 above.
[27] Cf. the execration ritual of breaking pots, noted above, p. 50.
[28] Lit., "redness," see Ritner 1993:170, n. 787.

REFERENCES

Text: Gardiner 1935:9-23. Translations: *ANET* 495; Borghouts 1978:3-4.

DAILY RITUAL OF THE TEMPLE OF AMUN-RE AT KARNAK (1.34)
P. Berlin 3055 - A Selection

Robert K. Ritner

Dating from the 22nd Dynasty, this Theban ritual papyrus is one of the best sources for the standardized morning liturgy used for divine and royal cults throughout Egypt from the New Kingdom until Roman times. The Seti temple at Abydos depicts thirty-six chapters or "spells," with nineteen represented at the Ptolemaic temple of Edfu and six at the contemporary temple of Dendera. In contrast, this Berlin papyrus adapted for Amon (together with P. Berlin 3014 + 3053 designed for his consort Mut), contains sixty-six recitations. No single source provides the complete ritual, but the constituent elements are easily reconstructed. The royal representative enters the chapel, censes and opens the *naos* to reveal the cult image. Thereafter follow spells of prostration, praise and offerings, after which the cult statue is removed, salved, clothed, adorned, and provided with unguent and eye-paint. In the concluding rites, fresh sand is strewn on the chapel floor, and the god is purified by water and natron and replaced in the *naos*. On exiting, the priest sweeps away his footprints, banishing impurities and demonic forces.

BEGINNING OF THE SPELLS[1] of the divine ritual enacted in the temple of Amon-Re, king of the gods, in the course of every day by the chief *wab*-priest[2] who is in his daily service.

SPELL FOR striking the fire.
WORDS TO BE SAID: "Come, come in peace, Eye of Horus, luminous, sound, rejuvenated in peace! May it shrine like Re in the two horizons, since the power of Seth has hidden himself before the Eye of Horus, who took it and brought it to put in its place for Horus. Concerning his Eye, Horus is triumphant, while the Eye of Horus repels the enemies of Amun-Re, Lord of the Thrones of the Two Lands, in all their places. May the King give an offering! I am pure."

SPELL FOR taking the censer.
WORDS TO BE SAID: "Hail to you, [censer of the gods] who are in the following of Thoth; my arms are upon you as (those of) Horus, my hands upon you like (those of) Thoth, my fingers on you like (those of) Anubis, foremost of the divine booth.[3] I am the living servant of Re. I am a *wab*-priest, since I am pure (*wab*). The purity of the gods is my purity. May the King give an offering! I am pure."

[SPELL FOR] PLACING the incense-bowl on the censer arm.

WORDS TO BE SAID: "Hail to you, incense-bowl of [...] the field in Mendes, the clay in Abydos. I am purified by the Eye of Horus so that I might perform the rites with you, they being pure for Amon-Re, Lord of the Thrones of the Two Lands, and his Ennead. May the King give an offering! I am pure."

SPELL FOR putting incense on the flame.
WORDS TO BE SAID: "To the *ba*-soul of the East, to Horus of the East, to Kamutef[4] within the solar disk, to the Terrible One who shines with his two Sound Eyes, to Re-harakhti,[5] the great god, the winged power, foremost of the two southern conclaves of heaven."

SPELL FOR advancing [to] the sacred place.[6]
WORDS TO BE SAID: "O *ba*-souls of Heliopolis, as you are sound, so I am sound, and vice-versa. Your *ka*-spirits are sound precisely because my *ka*-spirit is sound before all the *ka*-spirits of the living. As all live, so I live. The two jugs of Atum are the protection of my body. For me Sakhmet the great, beloved of Ptah, placed life, stability and dominion around all my flesh by an oath of Thoth. I am Horus the chief, beautiful of respect, lord of terror, great of respect, high of plumage, great in Abydos. May the King give an offering! I am pure."

ANOTHER SPELL.
"Awake happily in peace, Karnak, mistress of the temples of the gods and goddesses who are in her! O gods and goddesses who are in Karnak, gods and goddesses who are in Thebes, gods and goddesses who are in Heliopolis, gods and goddesses who are in Memphis, gods and goddesses who are in heaven, gods and goddesses who are in the earth, gods and goddesses who are in the South, North, West and East, the kings of Upper and Lower Egypt, children of kings, who took the White Crown, who made monuments for

[1] The translation "spell" has been adopted to conform with the rendering of the same Eg. term in so-called "magical" texts. One could as easily adopt "recitation" or "utterance" for all contexts. There is no distinction in Eg. terminology — or theology — between official cultic "recitations" and private magical "spells"; see Ritner 1993:41-42.

[2] Lit., "pure priest."

[3] The embalming booth.

[4] "Bull of His Mother," an epithet of Min-Amun.

[5] A fusion of Re and "Horus of the Two Horizons."

[6] The holy of holies or *naos* in which the divine image resides.

Amun in Karnak, may you awaken, may you be in peace. May you awaken happily in peace."

SPELL FOR breaking the cord.[7]
WORDS TO BE SAID: "The cord is broken, the seal is loosened. Bringing to you the Eye of Horus, I have come. You have your Eye, O Horus."

SPELL FOR breaking the clay seal.
WORDS TO BE SAID: "The clay seal is broken, the waters are breached, the vessels[8] of Osiris are drained. I have come not to drive the god away from his throne. It is to put the god upon his throne that I have come. May you be established upon your great throne, O Amun-Re, Lord of the Thrones of the Two Lands. I am the one whom the gods initiated.[9] May the King give an offering! I am pure."

SPELL FOR unfastening the *naos*.[10]
WORDS TO BE SAID: "The finger of Seth is withdrawn from the Eye of Horus so that it be well. The finger of Seth is released from the Eye of Horus so that it be well. The hide is loosened from the back of the god.[11] O Amun-Re, Lord of the Thrones of the Two Lands, receive for yourself your two plumes and your White Crown as the Eye of Horus, the right (plume) being the right Eye, the left (plume) being the left Eye. You have your beauty, O Amun-Re, Lord of the Thrones of the Two Lands. Naked one, be clothed. Dressed one, be dressed, though I am but a prophet. It is the king who sent me to see the god."[12]

SPELL FOR revealing the god.
WORDS TO BE SAID: "The doors of heaven are opened. The doors of the earth are opened. Hail to Geb, as the gods have said, established on their thrones. The doors of heaven are opened so that the Ennead might shine. As Amun-Re, Lord of the Thrones of the Two Lands, is exalted, so the great Ennead is exalted upon their thrones. You have your beauty, O Amun-Re, Lord of the Thrones of the Two Lands. Naked one, be clothed. Dressed one, be dressed."

SPELL FOR seeing the god.
WORDS TO BE SAID: "My face is protected from[13] the god and vice-versa. O gods, make way for me so that I might pass. It is the king who has sent me to see the god."

SPELL FOR kissing the ground.
WORDS TO BE SAID: "I have kissed the ground; I have embraced Geb. For Amun-Re, Lord of the Thrones of the Two Lands, have I performed the chants {by which}[14] I am purified for him. You have your sweat, O gods. You have your perfumes, O goddesses. You have the perfumes of your bodies.[15] My kiss is life for Pharaoh, praise for the Lord of the Two Lands."[16]

SPELL FOR prostrating.[17]
WORDS TO BE SAID: "Hail to you, Amun-Re, Lord of the Thrones of the Two Lands, enduring upon your great throne. I have prostrated (myself) through fear of you, fearful of your dignity. I have embraced Geb and Hathor so that she might cause that I be great. I shall not fall to the slaughter of this day."

SPELL FOR prostrating and for rising.
WORDS TO BE SAID: "Hail to you, Amun-Re, Lord of the Thrones of the Two Lands. I have not acted with your secretions;[18] I have not removed your dignity.[19] I have not conflated your appearance with that of another god.[20] I have prostrated myself through fear of you, so that I might perceive what you desire. You shall not fall to your enemies on this day. Your enemies whom you hate, may you overthrow them as your enemies of this day.[21] There is no wretchedness for the one who adores his lord."

SPELL FOR kissing the ground with the face bowed.

WORDS TO BE SAID: "I have kissed the ground with my face bowed; I have caused Truth to ascend to you. There is no god who has done

[7] The knotted and sealed cord securing the door of the *naos*.
[8] As noted by Wilson, the breaking of the seal is symbolized by the opening of a clay dam. The term "vessels" designates the arteries and veins of the god, from which flow the waters of the Nile.
[9] Moret translates: "who enters (to) the gods."
[10] The parallel ritual for the goddess Mut reads "drawing back the bolt."
[11] Perhaps a reference to a shroud placed over the statue at night.
[12] In theory, only the king should be able to confront the statue of the god. Of necessity, this privilege was delegated to local high priests as royal representatives.
[13] Moret translates "protection for the god."
[14] Restored from the Abydos variant.
[15] The "sweat" and "secretions" of the gods are perfume.
[16] Moret translates: "I have smelled (these things) so that Pharaoh live and the Lord of the Two Lands be adored."
[17] Lit., "placing (oneself) upon the belly."
[18] All fluids are restored to the gods to avoid potential misuse as in "The Legend of Isis and the Name of Re" (text 1.22 above).
[19] See above, n. 14.
[20] Lit., "I have not caused your color to resemble another god."
[21] Probably the enemies included in the daily execration rite; see text 1.32 above.

what I have done. I have not lifted up my face. I have not inflicted impurities. I have not conflated your appearance with that of another god."
... (col. 5, 3)

SPELL FOR adoring Amun.
WORDS TO BE SAID: "Into your presence Pharaoh has come, O male one of the gods, primordial one of the Two Lands, He of the Sacred Arm,[22] Amun-Re, Lord of the two plumes, great one with the crown of greatness on your head, king of the gods resident in Karnak, image of Amun,[23] enduring in all things in your name of 'Amun, more powerful than all the gods.' They will not turn their backs on you in their name of 'Ennead.'"[24]

[22] The epithets describe the standard posture of the male, ithyphallic creator with upraised arm.
[23] *Contra* Assmann, who translates: "You are Amun."
[24] A pun on *psḏ* "back" and *psḏ.t* "ennead."

REFERENCES

Text: Königlichen Museen zu Berlin (1901: pls. I-XXXVII). Translations: Moret 1902; Roeder 1960:72-141; *ANET* 325-326; Assmann 1975:260-273; and Barta 1980: cols. 841-45.

B. ROYAL FOCUS

1. INSTRUCTIONS

MERIKARE (1.35)

Miriam Lichtheim

The text is preserved in three fragmentary papyri which only partly complement one another. They are Papyrus Leningrad 1116A, dating from the second half of the 18th Dynasty; P. Moscow 4658, from the very end of the 18th Dynasty; and P. Carlsberg 6, from the end of the 18th Dynasty or later. Unfortunately, the most complete manuscript, P. Leningrad, is also the most corrupt. The numerous lacunae and the many scribal errors make this text one of the most difficult.

The work is cast in the form of an Instruction spoken by an old king to his son and successor. The fragmentary beginning has preserved the name of the son: Merikare. But that of the father is lost except for the still visible outline of the cartouche and traces of two vertical hieroglyphs forming the end of the king's name. This name is assumed to be that of one of the several kings of the 9th/10th Dynasties who bore the nomen Khety (Akhtoi). However, since the order of the kings of this dynasty has not yet been fully clarified, it has not been determined which of the several Khetys preceded Merikare. J. von Beckerath (1966:13-20) has proposed as the most suitable candidate the Khety whose prenomen was Nebkaure.

As an Instruction, it continues the genre Instruction which originated in the Old Kingdom. But a new element has been added: it is a royal instruction, and specifically, a royal testament. It is the legacy of a departing king which embodies a treatise on kingship.

The treatise on kingship in the form of a royal testament is a literary genre that was to flourish many centuries later in the Hellenistic world and subsequently in the Islamic East as well as in medieval Europe: the *speculum regum*. It is, of course, not possible to draw a connecting line from the ancient Egyptian type to its Hellenistic and medieval counterparts — far too little is preserved from all ancient literatures to make it possible to reconstruct their interconnections — but it is interesting to see the emergence of the genre. Not that the Instruction to Merikare was the first work of this type (an Instruction of an earlier king Khety is referred to in the text), but it is the earliest preserved, and probably also an early work of the genre, for it shows compositional weaknesses that suggest experimentation.

I believe the work to be pseudepigraphic in the sense of not having been composed by King Khety himself, but genuine in the sense of being a work composed in the reign of King Merikare, designed to announce the direction of his policy and containing valid, rather than fictitious, historical information.

Set beside such literary antecedents as the Maxims of Ptahhotep, the work shows intellectual and literary progress. Its morality has grown in depth and subtlety; and there is a parallel growth in the ability to formulate concepts, and to develop themes and topics at greater length. A fully sustained compositional coherence as found in comparable works of the 12th Dynasty has not been achieved. There are several instances in which the same topic reappears in different places, and in which a buildup to a climax is deflected. Yet an overall plan and progression can be recognized.

The first major portion, of which almost nothing is preserved, deals with rebellion and how to overcome it. The second major section gives advice on dealing wisely and justly with nobles and commoners and is climaxed by a view of the judgment in the hereafter. Next comes advice on raising troops and on performing the religious duties. Then follows the "historical section" in which the old king describes his accomplishments and advises on how to continue them. At this point there is the beginning of a paean on the glory of kingship which is interrupted by a reference to the tragic destruction of monuments in the holy region of Abydos, a matter that had previously been alluded to. This leads to a reflection on divine retribution and rises to the recognition that the deity prefers right doing to rich offerings. Then comes the true climax: a hymn to the creator god, the benefactor of mankind. The concluding section exhorts acceptance of the royal teachings.

The scribes of the New Kingdom divided the work into sections by means of rubrication. At an average such sections consist of twelve sentences and clauses. Where these rubrics were logical I have maintained them; but not all of the rubrics of the principal manuscript, P. Leningrad, are judicious, for the scribes often introduced rubrics mechanically without regard to content. The major topics encompass more than one rubricated section. The building blocks within each section are the small units of two, three, and four sentences, which are joined together by parallelism in its several forms, such as similarities, elaborations, and contrasts. And since all sentences and clauses are of approximately the same length, there results a clearly marked, regular, sentence rhythm.

All Instructions are composed in this rhythmic style marked by symmetrical sentences which I call the orational style. On occasion, when specific events are told, it turns into prose. At other moments it rises into poetry, as in the hymn to the creator-god which crowns the Instruction addressed to Merikare.

------
(25) The hothead[1] is an inciter of citizens,
He creates factions among the young;
If you find that citizens adhere to him,

Denounce him before the councillors,
Suppress [him], he is a rebel,
The talker is a troublemaker for the city.
Curb the multitude, suppress its heat,
------
(30) ------
May you be justified before the god,
That a man may say [even in] your [absence]
That you punish in accordance [with the crime].
Good nature is a man's heaven,
The cursing of the [furious] is painful.

If you are skilled in speech, you will win,
The tongue is [a king's] sword;
Speaking is stronger than all fighting,
The skillful is not overcome.
------ on the mat,
The wise is a [⌜school⌝][2] to the nobles.
Those who know that he knows will not attack him,
No [crime] occurs when he is near;
Justice comes to him distilled,
Shaped in the sayings of the ancestors.
(35) Copy your fathers, your ancestors,

See, their words endure in books,
Open, read them, copy their knowledge,
He who is taught becomes skilled.
Don't be evil, kindness is good,
Make your memorial last through love of you.
Increase the [people], befriend the town,
God will be praised for (your) donations,
One will ------
Praise your goodness,
Pray for your health ---.

Respect the nobles, sustain your people,
Strengthen your borders, your frontier patrols;
It is good to work for the future,
One respects the life of the foresighted,
While he who trusts fails.
Make people come [to you] (40) through your good nature,
A wretch is who desires the land [of his neighbor],
A fool is who covets what others possess.
Life on earth passes, it is not long,
Happy is he who is remembered,
A million men do not avail the Lord of the Two Lands.
Is there [a man] who lives forever?
He who comes with Osiris passes,
Just as he leaves who indulged himself.

Advance your officials, so that they act by your laws,
He who has wealth at home will not be partial,
He is a rich man who lacks nothing.
The poor man does not speak justly,
Not righteous is one who says, "I wish I had,"
He inclines to him who will pay him.
Great is the great man whose great men are great,
Strong is (45) the king who has councillors,
Wealthy is he who is rich in his nobles.
Speak truth in your house,
That the officials of the land may respect you;
Uprightness befits the lord,
The front of the house puts fear in the back.[3]

Do justice, then you endure on earth;
Calm the weeper, don't oppress the widow,
Don't expel a man from his father's property,
Don't reduce the nobles in their possessions.
Beware of punishing wrongfully,
Do not kill, it does not serve you.
Punish with beatings, with detention,
Thus will the land be well-ordered;
Except for the rebel whose plans are found out,
For god knows the treason plotters,
(50) God smites the rebels in blood.
He who is merciful --- lifetime;
Do not kill a man whose virtues you know,

[1] The *ẖnn-ib*, the person whose heart is inflamed.
[2] In place of Gardiner's restoration, "schoolhouse," Williams 1964:16, has proposed "storehouse."
[3] The "back of the house" is the rear where women, children, and servants had their quarters.

With whom you once chanted the writings,
Who was brought up ... --- before god,
Who strode freely in the secret place.
The *ba* comes to the place it knows,
It does not miss its former path,
No kind of magic holds it back,
It comes to those who give it water.

The Court that judges the wretch,[4]
You know they are not lenient,
On the day of judging the miserable,
In the hour of doing their task.
It is painful when the accuser has knowledge,
Do not trust in length of years,
They view a lifetime in an hour!
When a man remains over after death,
His deeds are set beside him as treasure,
And being yonder lasts forever.
A fool is who does what they reprove!
He who reaches them without having done wrong
Will exist there like a god,
Free-striding like the lords forever!

Raise your youths and the residence will love you,
Increase your subjects with ⌜recruits⌝,[5]
See, your city is full of new growth.
Twenty years the youths indulge their wishes,
Then ⌜recruits⌝ go forth ...
Veterans[6] return to their children ...
......[7]
I raised troops from them on my accession.
Advance your officials, promote your [soldiers],
Enrich the young men who follow you,
Provide with goods, endow with fields,
Reward them with herds.

Do not prefer the well born to the commoner,
Choose a man on account of his skills,
Then all crafts are done --- ...
Guard your borders, secure your forts,
Troops are useful to their lord.
Make your monuments [worthy] of the god,
This keeps alive their maker's name,
A man should do what profits his *ba*.
In the monthly service, wear the white sandals,
Visit the temple, rob ⌜observe⌝[8] the mysteries,
Enter the shrine, eat bread in god's house;
Proffer libations, multiply the loaves,
Make ample the daily offerings,
It profits him who does it.
Endow your monuments according to your wealth,
Even one day gives to eternity,
An hour contributes to the future,
God recognizes him who works for him.
......[9]
Troops will fight troops
As the ancestors foretold;
Egypt fought in the graveyard,
Destroying tombs in vengeful destruction.
As I did it, so it happened,
As is done to one who strays from god's path.
Do not deal evilly with the Southland,
You know what the residence foretold about it;
As this happened so that may happen.
⌜Before they had trespassed⌝ ... ---
I attacked This ⌜straight to⌝ its southern border ⌜at Taut⌝,
I engulfed it like a flood;
King Meriyebre, justified, had not done it;
Be merciful on account of it,
------ renew the treaties.
No river lets itself be hidden,
It is good to work for the future.

You stand well with the Southland,
They come to you with tribute, with gifts;
I have acted like the forefathers:
If one has no grain to give,
Be kind, since they are humble before you.
Be sated with your bread, your beer,
Granite comes to you unhindered.
Do not despoil the monument of another,
But quarry stone in Tura.
Do not build your tomb out of ruins,
(Using) what had been made for what is to be made.
Behold, the king is lord of joy,
You may rest, sleep in your strength,
Follow your heart, through what I have done,
There is no foe within your borders.

I arose as lord of the city,
Whose heart was sad because of the Northland;
From Hetshenu to ⌜Sembaqa⌝, and south to Two-Fish Channel[10]

---

[4] Baer would render *sꜣry* as the "oppressed" and *wḏꜥ* as "providing justice" to the aggrieved, whence the judgment would be the vindication of those who were wronged on earth, rather than a general judgment of the dead. My feeling is that an overall judgment is envisaged in the passage as a whole; but the first part may well be the vindication of the innocent.

[5] *Šwt* in Ptahhotep, line 489 means "neighbors, friends, helpers," or the like. Here it has been thought to mean "feathers" in the sense of "Nachwuchs" (Volten 1945:20), "recruits" (Wilson 1964:16-19), or "milice active" (Posener 1964:305).

[6] *Sꜥḳyw*, "veterans" (Volten, Posener), but it is uncertain.

[7] One obscure sentence.

[8] *Kfꜣ ḥr sštꜣ* has been translated "reveal the mysteries," except by Gardiner who rendered "be discreet concerning the mysteries." On *kfꜣ* in the compound *kfꜣ ib* see Litcheim *AEL* 1:78 n. 27.

[9] Four sentences which, though free of lacunae, are very obscure. The word written *tww.k* has been rendered as "your statues," but I cannot believe that the king is speaking of dispatching royal statues to foreign countries.

[10] Lit., "its southern border at Two-Fish Channel." The "Two Fish Channel," known from P. Westcar IX, 16 and elsewhere, appears to be the name for the Nile branch in the nome of Letopolis, i.e., the southernmost part of the Canopic branch. In this passage it designates the

I pacified the entire West as far as the coast of the sea.
It pays taxes, it gives cedar wood,[11]
One sees juniper wood which they give us.
The East abounds in bowmen,
⸢Their labor⸣ ------
The inner islands are turned back,
And every man within,
The temples say, "you are greater (85) than I."[12]

The land they had ravaged has been made into nomes,
All kinds of large towns [rare in its];
What was ruled by one is in the hands of ten,
Officials are appointed, tax-[lists drawn up].
When free men are given land,
They work for you like a single team;
No rebel will arise among them,
And Hapy will not fail to come.
The dues of the Northland are in your hand,
For the mooring-post is staked in the district I made in the East
From Hebenu to Horusway;[13]
It is settled with towns, filled with people,
Of the best in the whole land,
To repel (90) attacks against them.
May I see a brave man who will copy it,
Who will add to what I have done,
A wretched heir would ⸢disgrace⸣ me.

But this should be said to the Bowman:[14]
Lo, the miserable Asiatic,
He is wretched because of the place he's in:
Short of water, bare of wood,
Its paths are many and painful because of mountains.
He does not dwell in one place,
Food propels his legs,
He fights since the time of Horus,
Not conquering nor being conquered,
He does not announce the day of combat,
Like a thief who darts about a group.[15]

But as I live (95) and shall be what I am,
When the Bowmen were a sealed wall,
I breached [their strongholds],
I made Lower Egypt attack them,
I captured their inhabitants,
I seized their cattle,
Until the Asiatics abhorred Egypt.
Do not concern yourself with him,
The Asiatic is a crocodile on its shore,
It snatches from a lonely road,
It cannot seize from a populous town.

Medenyt has been restored to its nome,
Its one side is irrigated as far as Kem-Wer,
It is the ⸢defense⸣ against the Bowmen.[17]
(100) Its walls are warlike, its soldiers many,
Its serfs know how to bear arms,
Apart from the free men within.
The region of Memphis totals ten thousand men,

southern boundary of the western Delta.

[11] *Mrw*-wood is rendered "Zedernholz" by Helck 1961-70 esp. 5:906. The Merikare passage conveys the fact that imports of foreign timber again reach the Heracleopolitan realm.

[12] I.e., the temples (or: "administrative districts?") of the central Delta, called "the inner islands," acknowledge the king and pay homage to him.

[13] Kees (1962:6) insisted that Hebenu is not an unknown locality in the eastern Delta, as Scharff and Volten had thought, but is the well-known metropolis of the sixteenth nome of Upper Egypt, hence that the king is speaking of an extensive system of border strongholds which stretched from the eastern side of the sixteenth nome all the way to the northeastern Delta, to the border fortress of Sile, where the "Horus-way," the road to Palestine, began. "Horusway" and "Horusways" are synonymous with Sile.

[14] This celebrated passage has been reexamined by Seibert 1967:90-98. The principal difficulty lies in *štʾw m ḫt ʿšʾw*, which had been rendered "difficult from many trees," despite the fact that an arid landscape cannot have many trees. Drioton (1960:90-91) proposed the meaning "debarred from having many trees." Seibert takes *m ḫt* to be the compound preposition "after," to which he assigns the meaning "despite," and proposes to read: *šrʾw m ḫt ʿšʾ <ny> wʾwt iry/ḳsn m-ʿ ḏww*, which he renders, "verborgen trotz der Menge der Wege dahin/ (und) schlimm durch Berge." However, the meaning "despite" assigned to the alleged *m-ḫt* is impossible in this context. Only when *m-ḫt* serves as conjunction in a temporal clause can it acquire the overtone of "despite," as in the two references from Urk. 1:49 and 1:283, cited in *Wb.*, 3 345.21, and in Edel 1955-64:§797: *m-ḫt nn ḏd.n.(i)*, and *m-ḫt nn wḏ.n ḥm.(i)*, where the literal meaning "after" has the overtone "despite," as is possible in any language. Said in a tone of rebuke, the sentence "after I told you to stay at home, you went out," means "despite my telling you to stay at home." But the spatial preposition "after" is not capable of such manipulation: "after many paths" does not yield "despite many paths."

I divide the sentences into: *ʾhw m mw/ štʾw m ḫt/ ʿšʾw wʾwt iry/ ḳsn m-ʿ ḏww*; and following Drioton I take *štʾw m ḫt* to mean "debarred from trees." For *ʾhw*, the meaning "short of," "lacking," is inescapable (Volten: "kümmerlich;" Seibert: "dürftig"), and it agrees with the *sʾhhw* of Ptahhotep line 485, which I have rendered "deprived." As to the initial *ḳsn pw n bw ntf im*, Seibert rightly pointed out that the *n* cannot be ignored, hence "he (the Asiatic) is wretched." It may be recalled that the personal use of *ḳsn pw* occurs twice in Ptahhotep, lines 81 and 446.

[15] *Šnʿ*, "dart about," as in *Peasant*, B i 61. The Moscow var. has *šn-ʿ*, an unknown compound for which Seibert proposed the meaning "to ban."

[16] I.e., the east bank of the twenty-second nome was recovered by the Heracleopolitans and brought under cultivation up to the point where it joined the Fayum which they had held all along. This rendering was suggested to me by K. Baer. On *km-wr* of the Fayum see Yoyotte 1962:116f.

[17] While P. Leningrad has *ḥpʾ*, "navel-cord," P. Carlsberg has *ḥpw* with fighting-man determinative. Scharff and Volten chose *ḥpw* and assigned it the meaning "Abwehr." Wilson and others preferred "navel cord." In any case "it" refers to Medenyt; hence the town and its nome are either "the defense against" the Asiatics or the "point of entry" that attracts the Asiatics.

Free citizens[18] who are not taxed;
Officials are in it since the time it was residence,
The borders are firm, the garrisons valiant.
Many northerners irrigate it as far as the Northland,
Taxed with grain in the manner of free men;[19]
Lo, it is the gateway of the Northland,
They form a dyke as far as Hnes.[20]
Abundant citizens are the heart's support,
Beware of being surrounded by the serfs of the foe,
Caution prolongs life.

If your southern border is attacked,
The Bowmen will put on the girdle,
Build buildings in the Northland!
As a man's name is not made small by his actions,
So a settled town is not harmed.
Build ------
The foe loves destruction and misery.
King Khety, the justified, laid down in teaching:
He who is silent toward violence diminishes the offerings.
God will attack the rebel for the sake of the temple,
He will be overcome for what he has done,
He will be sated with what he planned to gain,
He will find no favor on the day of woe.
Supply the offerings, revere the god,
Don't say, "it is trouble," don't slacken your hands.
He who opposes you attacks the sky,
A monument is sound for a hundred years;[22]
If the foe understood, he would not attack them,[23]
There is no one who has no enemy.

The Lord of the Two Shores is one who knows,
A king who has courtiers is not ignorant;
As one wise did he come from the womb,
From a million men god singled him out.
A goodly office is kingship,
It has no son, no brother to maintain its memorial,
But one man provides for the other;
A man acts for him who was before him,
So that what he has done is preserved by his successor.
Lo, a shameful deed occurred in my time:
The nome of This was ravaged;
Though it happened through my doing,
I learned it after it was done.[24]
There was retribution for what I had done,
For it is evil to destroy,
Useless to restore what one has damaged,
To rebuild what one has demolished.
Beware of it! A blow is repaid by its like,
To every action there is a response.

While generation succeeds generation,
God who knows characters is hidden;
One can not oppose the lord of the hand,[25]
He reaches all that the eyes can see.
One should revere the god on his path,
Made of costly stone, fashioned of bronze.[26]
As watercourse is replaced by watercourse,
So no river allows itself to be concealed,
It breaks the channel in which it was hidden.
So also the *ba* goes to the place it knows,
And strays not from its former path.
Make worthy your house of the west,
Make firm your station in the graveyard,[27]
By being upright, by doing justice,
Upon which men's hearts rely.
The loaf[28] of the upright is preferred
To the ox of the evildoer.
Work for god, he will work for you also,
With offerings that make the altar flourish,
With carvings that proclaim your name,
God thinks of him who works for him.

Well tended is mankind — god's cattle,
He made sky and earth for their sake,
He subdued the water monster,[29] [a]
He made breath for their noses to live.
They are his images, [b] who came from his body,
He shines in the sky for their sake;
He made for them plants and cattle,
Fowl and fish to feed them.
He slew his foes, reduced his children,

a Isa 27:1; Pss 74:14; 104:26; Job 3:8; 26:13; 41:1

b Gen 1:26-27

[18] Here, above in line 86 and below in line 103 I have, following Volten, rendered *wʿbw* as "free men" rather than "priests." But it is uncertain; see Volten's discussion 1945:54.

[19] If *bʾkw* is the passive, as I think it is, then the next sentence, *swʾt pw ḥr.i n ir st*, "it means surpassing me for him who does it," is out of place here.

[20] "Dyke" here is surely metaphorical for "protection." A real dyke all the way from the Delta to Heracleopolis is hardly possible.

[21] *N in.tw ḥr mw.f*, "one will not bring him on one's water." "To be on someone's water" is usually taken to mean "to be loyal to someone." This passage suggests a broader meaning, a mutual relationship of friendship and favor.

[22] Posener 1965:345 read the numeral "hundred" after *rnpt*.

[23] The sentence *m mrwt smnḫ ir.t.n.f* etc. which follows here is out of place; it recurs in its proper context in line 118.

[24] The destruction of tombs in the Thinite nome during warfare against the Thebans had already been mentioned in line 70. Here the king takes the blame for the action of his troops.

[25] The sun-god in his aspect as creator.

[26] Apparently a reference to the cult statues of the gods carried in procession during festivals.

[27] See Lichtheim *AEL* 1:59, n. 3. Here in Merikare the advice on tomb-building is spiritualized: the funerary monument is to be built on right doing.

[28] *Bit*, "loaf," rather than "character," as suggested by R. Williams 1964:19.

[29] A reference to the concept of a primordial water monster, defeated at the time of creation.

When they thought of making rebellion.[30]
He makes daylight for their sake,
He sails by to see them.
He has built (135) his shrine around them,
When they weep he hears.
He made for them rulers in the egg,
Leaders to raise the back of the weak.
He made for them magic as weapons
To ward off the blow of events,
Guarding[31] them by day and by night.
He has slain the traitors among them,
As a man beats his son for his brother's sake,
For god knows every name.

Do not neglect my speech,
Which lays down all the laws of kingship,
Which instructs you, that you may rule the land,
And may you reach me with none to accuse you!
Do not kill (140) one who is close to you,
Whom you have favored, god knows him;
He is one of the fortunate ones on earth,
Divine are they who follow the king!
Make yourself loved by everyone,
A good character is remembered
[When his time] has passed.
May you be called "he who ended the time of trouble,"
By those who come after in the House of Khety,
In thinking[32] of what has come today.
Lo, I have told you the best of my thoughts,
Act by what is set before you!

[30] An allusion to the myth of the "destruction of mankind," a text that forms part of the composition known as "the book of the cow of heaven," which is inscribed on the walls of three royal tombs of the 19th Dynasty; see above, text 1.24.

[31] *Rsi*, "to watch," not *rswt*, "dream," as suggested by Federn 1960:256-257.

[32] Reading *iw ḏd tw.k*, and taking *ntyw m pḥwy m pr Ḫty* in the temporal sense, in accordance with Posener 1966:345. On *m sšꜣw* see Lichtheim *AEL* 1:79 n. 50; the rendering of *m sšꜣw* as "in contrast" negates the whole thrust of the king's speech — the description of his achievements which his son is asked to emulate and surpass.

REFERENCES

Text: Golenischeff 1916 pls. ix-xiv; Volten 1945:3-82 and pls. 1-4. Translation: Gardiner 1914:20-36; Erman 1927:75-84; *ANET* 414-418; Scharff 1936 (lines 69-110 and most of lines 111-144); Lichtheim *AEL* 1:97-109. Discussion: Posener 1950; 1962; 1963; 1964; 1965; 1966; Drioton 1960:90-91; Williams, 1964:16-19; Seibert, 1967:90-98; Müller 1967:117-123; Kees 1962:86.

AMENEMHET (1.36)

Miriam Lichtheim

When first studied, the text was regarded as the genuine work of King Amenemhet I, composed by him after he had escaped an attempt on his life. The currently prevailing view is that the king was in fact assassinated in the thirtieth year of his reign, and that the text was composed by a royal scribe at the behest of the new king, Sesostris I.

The attack on the king's life is told in a deliberately veiled manner; yet there are sufficient hints in the account and elsewhere in the text to convey to the Middle Kingdom audience that the speaker is the deceased king who speaks to his son in a revelation, and to later audiences, including the sophisticated one of the New Kingdom, that the work was composed by a court writer.

It is a powerful and imaginative composition, distinguished by its personal tone and by the bitterness born of experience with which the old king castigates the treachery of his subjects, and warns his son not to place trust in any man. The theme, then, is regicide. In contrast with the theme "national distress," regicide was not a topic that could be treated fully and openly, for it conflicted too strongly with the dogma of the divine king. Hence the work is the only one of its kind.

The orational style is used throughout, except in the description of the assassination which is rendered in prose.

The text was preserved in Papyrus Millingen of the 18th Dynasty, a copy of which was made by A. Peyron in 1843. Subsequently the original papyrus was lost. Portions of the work are preserved on three wooden tablets of the 18th Dynasty, some papyrus fragments, and numerous ostraca of the New Kingdom.

The line numbers are those of Papyrus Millingen, which is a good manuscript but fragmentary in the final portion.

(I.1) Beginning of the Instruction made by the majesty of King Sehetepibre, son of Re, Amenemhet, the justified,[1] as he spoke in a revelation of truth, to his son the All-Lord. He said:

[1] In Papyrus Chester Beatty IV, a New Kingdom scribe drew up a list of famous authors of the past and assigned the composition of the In-

Risen as god,[2] hear what I tell you,
That you may rule the land, govern the shores,
Increase well-being!
Beware of subjects who are nobodies,
Of whose plotting one is not aware.[3]
Trust not a brother, know not a friend,
Make no (I.5) intimates, it is worthless.
When you lie down, guard your heart yourself,
For no man has adherents on the day of woe.
I gave to the beggar, I raised the orphan,[a]
I gave success to the poor as to the wealthy;
But he who ate my food raised opposition,[b]
He whom I gave my trust used it to plot.[4]
Wearers of my fine linen looked at me as if they were needy,[5]
Those perfumed with my myrrh ⌜poured water while wearing it⌝.[6]
You my living peers, my partners among men,
Make for me mourning such as has not (I.10) been heard,
For so great a combat had not yet been seen!
If one fights in the arena forgetful of the past,
Success will elude him who ignores what he should know.

It was after supper, night had come. I was taking an hour of rest, lying on my bed, for I was weary. As my heart (II.1) began to follow sleep, weapons for my protection were turned against me,[7] while I was like a snake of the desert. I awoke at the fighting, ⌜alert⌝,[8] and found it was a combat of the guard. Had I quickly seized weapons in my hand, I would have made the cowards retreat ⌜in haste⌝. But no one is strong at night; no one can fight alone; no success is achieved without a helper.

(II.5) Thus bloodshed occurred while I was without you; before the courtiers had heard I would hand over to you; before I had sat with you so as to advise you.[9] For I had not prepared for it, had not expected it, had not foreseen the failing of the servants.

Had women ever marshaled troops? [c]
Are rebels nurtured in the palace?
Does one release water that destroys the soil
And deprives people of their crops?[10]
No harm had come to me since my birth,
No one equaled me as a doer of deeds.

(II.10) I journeyed to Yebu, I returned to the Delta,
Having stood on the land's borders I observed its interior.
I reached the borders of ⌜the strongholds⌝[11]
By my strength and my feats.
I was grain-maker, beloved of Nepri,
Hapy honored me on every field.
None hungered in my years,
None (III.1) thirsted in them,
One sat because I acted and spoke of me,
I had assigned everything to its place.
I subdued lions, I captured crocodiles,
I repressed those of Wawat,
I captured the Mediai,
I made the Asiatics do the dog walk.

I built myself a house decked with gold,
Its ceiling of lapis lazuli,
Walls of silver, floors of [acacia wood],
(III.5) Doors of copper, bolts of bronze,
Made for eternity, prepared for all time,
I know because I am its lord.
Behold, much hatred is in the streets,
The wise says "yes," the fool says "no,"
For no one knows it ⌜without your presence⌝,[12]
Sesostris my son!
As my feet depart, you are in my heart,

a Job 29:12
b Job 29-30
c Judg 4-5

struction of Amenemhet to a scribe by the name of Khety. Whether or not his attribution was correct, it reveals that the New Kingdom scribe understood the pseudepigraphic nature of the work (see Posener 1956:67). But as regards the audience of the Middle Kingdom, it seems to me probable that it took the work to be the genuine testament of King Amenemhet; for pseudepigrapha would lose much of their effectiveness if they were not, at least initially, believed to be the works of the men whose name they bore.

[2] The much debated introductory passage was reexamined by Goedicke 1968:15-21 who made a case for taking *ḏd.f ḫʿ m nṯr* as a single sentence, in accordance with the verse-points, and having it refer to the dead king who is "risen as god," rather than to the accession of Sesostris I. If so taken, however, the address to Sesostris becomes very abrupt, consisting only of "listen to me," and the sentence lacks balance. Helck summarized the previous renderings and preferred to take *ḫʿ* as imperative, "rise," rather than the participle, "risen."

[3] As Helck and Goedicke observed, the two *tmmt* refer back to *smdt*. I take the passage to mean that subjects who are unknown are dangerous because they can plot in secrecy. *Ḫrw* in the sense of "plot" is well attested (see Volten 1945:108).

[4] Lit., "he whom I gave my hands."

[5] Following Gardiner 1939:483, I read *sšwyw*, rather than *šw*, "grass."

[6] *Sti mw* has generally been interpreted as an act of disrespect or defiance, e.g., Helck: "spuckten vor mir aus." The inner logic of the composition requires, however, that the king, looking back on the treacherous behavior of the plotters, should describe it in terms of covert acts, since any open defiance would have drawn immediate punishment. The "pouring water" in *Admonitions*, 7, 5, suggests a menial task.

[7] I take *spẖr* in the literal sense of "turn around."

[8] The meaning of *iw.i n ḥʿw.i*, "I being to my body" is uncertain. Gardiner's "by myself" was disputed by Anthes and Helck; the latter suggested "kam zu mir," i.e., "became alert."

[9] I.e., the old king was prevented from "sitting together" with his son in a formal ceremony of abdication.

[10] The context here, and in *Neferti*, line 46, suggests tnat *iryt* means "produce" and "crops."

[11] For *ḫpšwt* Gardiner (1939:493) proposes "frontier-strongholds," while Helck assumes a corrupted writing of *ḫpš*, the constellation "great bear."

[12] The three sentences recur in *Admonitions*, 6, 13. Helck has pointed out that *msyt* is a corruption of *msḏ*, "hatred." The third sentence is obscure.

My eyes behold you, child of a happy hour
⸢Before the people as they hail you⸣.
I have made the past and arranged the future,
I gave you the contents of my heart.
You (III.10) wear the white crown of a god's son,
The seal is in its place, assigned you by me,
Jubilation is in the bark of Re,
Kingship is again what it was in the past!
......[13]
Raise your monuments, establish your strongholds,
Fight ....[14]

[13] A garbled sentence, not preserved in P. Millingen.
[14] The two concluding sentences are corrupt.

REFERENCES

Text: Griffith 1896:35-51; Maspero 1914; Volten 1945:104-128; Lopez 1963:29-33; Helck 1969. Translation: *BAR* 1:474-483; Erman 1927:72-74; *ANET* 418-419; Lichtheim AEL 1:135-139. Discussion: Posener 1956; Gardiner 1939:479-496; Malinine 1934:63-74; de Buck 1939:847-852; 1946:183-200; Faulkner 1932:69-73; Anthes 1957:176-190; 1958:208-209; Goedicke 1968:15-21.

2. HISTORIOGRAPHY

KING LISTS (1.37)

James K. Hoffmeier

King-lists of various types abound in ancient Egyptian sources. Technically, a collection of three or more names is a "group" and a true king-list arranges names in proper historical order and provides the length of reign. Following this definition, the only Egyptian source that meets these requirements is the Turin Canon, and it is not fully preserved. Nevertheless, the term king-list has been applied to a wider variety of lists, including the funerary offering lists, such as those at Karnak, Abydos and Sakkara. Such "cultic assemblages of deceased kings," as Donald Redford calls them, are abundant, and vary considerably in length. Of this type, dozens are known, but they are rarely consulted in historical reconstructions because of their brevity and, in some cases, confused order.

While no direct ties exist between the Old Testament and the king-lists presented here, they do shed light on genealogical lists such as those found in Genesis, 1 Chronicles and elsewhere. The Turin Canon contains what is believed to have been an exhaustive list of kings who ruled beginning with Meni (Menes) down into the empire period, complete with the duration of reigns. Prior to the beginning of 1st Dynasty in column II of the papyrus, the initial column contains a list of deities who are called "king of Upper and Lower Egypt." Following this title, the deity's name is written in a cartouche, the cylindrical enclosure reserved for royal names. The length of the reigns are also added after the name, and the figures are extremely long, e.g. Thoth 7726 years and another deity whose name is lost, 7718 years. Once the dynastic kings are introduced, the figures are realistic. A parallel might be drawn between this practice and that found in the Sumerian King-list and the Genesis 5 and 11 genealogies. In both of these cases, very long reigns are listed prior to the flood, but the numbers are reduced significantly thereafter. Unfortunately, the fragmentary state of column I prevents us from knowing how the Egyptian scribes understood the difference between the pre-dynastic divine rulers and Meni and his successors. The inclusion of pre-dynastic (legendary?) divine rulers along with historical kings from the 1st Dynasty on, indicates that the Egyptians made no distinction between "historical" and "mythic" or "legendary" individuals as modern historians do.

Unlike the original Turin Canon, the famous king-lists at Abydos and Sakkara are not complete lists of the kings from Dynasties 1-19. Rather they are selective. For instance, the kings of the 1st and 2nd Intermediate periods, as well as Queen Hatshepsut and Akhenaten, Smenkhkare, Tutankhamun, and Ay, the so called Amarna kings are omitted in the Abydos list. Similar selectivity is found in the Sakkara list. The practice of omitting entire epochs, such as the Amarna and Hyksos periods, were ways that later kings could expunge embarrassing forebears and not make offerings to them. On the other hand, there is no evidence that superfluous names were added to the Egyptian lists. Selectivity, apparently, violated no literary or political expectations in ancient Egypt. By extension, it holds that the omission of individuals or groups of ancestors from Israelite genealogies in the Bible was practiced for ideological or structural purposes, while not violating any Near Eastern canons of historiography.

1. KARNAK LIST (1.37A)

A small chapel once stood in Thutmose III's Akh-menu temple complex at Karnak. Over 150 years ago it was removed to the Louvre in Paris. While its list is offertory in nature, it is made up of seated figures of the kings with various regal titles before the cartouche. The names are grouped in eight parts, but the particular alignments are not always clear. The importance of these name-lists is that they include names omitted from AL and SL, such as earlier Theban 11th Dynasty kings, and some from 2nd Intermediate Period, are included. There has been considerable scholarly discussion about the criteria used for the compilation of the lists. Suggestions include that these were monarchs who actually ruled from Thebes or those who engaged in building activities there; that the figures represent actual statues of royal forebears at Karnak or that lists were comprised of ancient offering lists. Regardless of how this list originated, its use for historical reconstruction is of limited value.

(*Group I*)
1. [lost]
2. Sneferu
3. Sahure
4. Inen/Iny
5. Isesi
6. [lost]
7. [lost]
8. Sekhemre-semntawyre

(*Group II*)
1. [lost]
2. Intef
3. In[tef]
4. Mon[tuhotep]
5. Mayor Int[ef]
6. [Sa Re T]eti
7. [P]epy
8. Merenre

(*Group III*)
1. Sehetepibre (Amenemhet I)
2. Nebkaure (Amenemhet II)
3. [lost]
4. [lost]
5. Maakherure (Amenemhet IV)
6. Sobekneferu
7. Intef

(*Group IV*)
1. Kheperkare (Senusert I)
2. Sekennenre
3. Senakhtenre
4. Niuserre
5. Nebkheperre (Senusert II)
6. Nebhepetre (Montuhotep II)
7. Sneferkare
8. //////re

(*Group V*)
1. [lost]
2. Khaneferre
3. Khasekhemre
4. Sekhemre-snefertawy
5. Sekhemre-khuitawy
6. Seankhibre
7. Sewadjenre
8. ////kau-[re]

(*Group VI*)
1. [lost]
2. Merisekhemre
3. Merikaure
4. ///s re-wesertawy
5. ////////re
6. Snefer///re
7. Khahe[tep]re
8. Khaankhre

(*Group VII*)
1. [Sekhem]re-wahkhau
2. Sewahenre
3. Merihetepre
4. Khuitawyre
5. [lost]
6. [lost]
7. Sekhemre-wadjkhau

(*Group VIII*)
1. ///////re
2. Snefer///re
3. Sewadjenre
4. Sekhemre-[///]tawy
5. [lost]
6. [lost]
7. [lost]

2. ABYDOS LIST (AL) (1.37B)

In the cenotaph of Seti I at Abydos, which was completed by Ramesses II, is found a sequential list of kings from Dynasty 1 through reigning monarch Seti of Dynasty 19. To the left of the list, stand Seti and crown-prince Ramesses who holds a papyrus containing the list that is recorded to the right. The accompanying inscription indicates that the list was made up of the beneficiaries of the offerings being made. Because this list was made up of the royal ancestors whom the reigning monarch wished to honor, it was selective. Thus while historians may wish to consult this list, and ones like it (e.g. the Sakkara list), it is not relied upon for historical reconstruction without the aid of more complete lists, like the Turin Canon or an annalistic report such as the Palermo Stone.

(*Dynasty 1*)
1. Meni
2. Teti
3. Iti
4. Ita
5. Semti
6. Merpabia
7. (Not translatable)
8. Qebeh

(*Dynasty 2*)
9. Bedjau
10. Kakau
11. Baninetjer
12. Wadjnes
13. Sendi
14. Djadjay

(*Dynasty 3*)
15. Nebka
16. //djeser-sa
17. (Djeser)-teti
18. Sedjes
19. Neferkare

(*Dynasty 4*)
20. Sneferu
21. Khufu
22. Djedefre
23. Khaefre
24. Menkaure
25. Shepseskaf

(*Dynasty 5*)
26. Userkaf
27. Sahure
28. Kakai
29. Reneferef
30. Niuserre
31. Menkauhor
32. Djedkare
33. Unas

(*Dynasty 6*)
34. Teti
35. Userkare
36. Meryre (Pepy I)
37. Merenre
38. Neferkare (Pepy II)
39. Merenre-Antyemsaef

(*1st Intermediate Period*)
40. Netjerkare
41. Menkare
42. Neferkare
43. Neferkare-Neby
44. Djdekare-Shema
45. Neferkare-Khenedu
46. Merenhor
47. Sneferka
48. Nikare
49. Neferkare-Teruru
50. Neferkahor
51. Neferkare-Pepysenb
52. Sneferka-Anu
53. Ka[//]kaure
54. Neferkaure
55. Neferkauhor
56. Neferirkare

(*Dynasty 11*)
57. Nebhepetre (Montuhotep II)
58. Sankhkare (Montuhotep III)

(*Dynasty 12*)
59. Sehetepibre (Amenemhet I)
60. Kheperkare (Senusert I)
61. Nebkaure (Amenemhet II)
62. Khakheperre (Senusert II)
63. Khakaure (Senusert III)
64. Nimaare (Amenemhet III)
65. Maakherure (Amenemhet IV)

(*Dynasty 18*)
66. Nebpehtyre (Ahmose)
67. Djeserkare (Amenhotep I)
68. Aakheperkare (Thutmose I)
69. Aakheperenre (Thutmose II)
70. Menkheperre (Thutmose III)
71. Aakheperrure (Amenhotep II)
72. Menkheperrure (Thutmose IV)
73. Nebmaatre (Amenhotep III)
74. Djeserkheperure-setepenre (Horemheb)

(*Dynasty 19*)
75. Menphtyre (Ramesses I)
76. Menmaatre (Seti I)

3. SAKKARA KING LIST (SL) (1.37C)

Carved on the Sakkara tomb of the "Overseer of Works" from the reign of Ramesses II is the so called "Sakkara King List." Like its counterpart at Abydos, this is an offering list which originally recorded the names of 58 monarchs. Above each cartouche is the word *nsw*, "king" with determinative of a seated king, a white or red crown; they alternate throughout. Below each cartouche is the epithet *m*ꜣꜥ *ḫrw*, "justified," indicating that these kings were deceased. While this list is laid out much like Seti I list from Abydos, it includes kings not mentioned at Abydos. For instance, while AL records the names of eight 1st Dynasty kings, SL has but two. Among those excised is Meni, the legendary Menes of Herodotus. Owing to the selectivity, and sequential problems with this list, it is not relied upon in serious historical reconstruction.

(Dynasty 1)
1. Merbiapen
2. Qebehu

(Dynasty 2)
3. Baunetjer
4. Kakau
5. Banetjeru
6. Wadjnes
7. Senedj
8. Neferkare
9. Neferkasokar
10. Hudjefa
11. Beby

(Dynasty 3)
12. Djeser
13. Djeser-Teti
14. Nebkare
15. Huny

(Dynasty 4)
16. Sneferu
17. Khufu
18. Djedefre
19. ////uf
20. [lost]
21. [lost]
22. [lost]
23. [lost]
24. [lost]

(Dynasty 5)
25. Userka[ef]
26. [S]ahure
27. Neferirkare
28. Shepseskare
29. Khaneferre
30. Menkahor
31. Maakare
32. Unas

(Dynasty 6)
33. Teti
34. Pepy (I)
35. Merenre
36. Neferkare (Pepy II)

(Dynasty 11)
37. Nebhepetre (Montuhotep II)
38. Sankhkare (Montuhotep III)

(Dynasty 12)
39. Sehetepibre (Amenemhet I)
40. Kheperkare (Senusert I)
41. Nebkare (Amenemhet II)
42. Khakhepere (Senusert II)
43. Khakare (Senusert III)
44. [Nimaa]re (Amenemhet III)
45. Maakherure (Amenemhet IV)
46. Sobekkare

(Dynasty 18)
47. Nebpehtyre (Ahmose)
48. Djeserkare (Amenhotep I)
49. [lost] (Thutmose I)
50. [lost] (Thutmose II)
51. [lost] (Thutmose III)
52. [lost] (Amenhotep II)
53. [lost] (Thutmose IV)
54. [lost] (Amenhotep I)
55. [Djeserkhepere S]etepen[re] (Horemeheb)

(Dynasty 19)
56. Men [pehtyre] (Ramesses I)
57. Men [maatre] (Seti I)
58. [Usermaatre] Setepenre (Ramesses II)

4. TURIN CANON (1.37D)

Located in the Museo Egizio in Turin, Italy, this papyrus is the most important source for the historical and chronological reconstruction of ancient Egypt. It is more than a list. Rather it originally contained a sequence of kings from Dynasty 1, with regnal years assigned to each king. Beginning with Menes (Meni), it continues down to the 19th Dynasty, the period to which this papyrus dates. According to Sir Alan Gardiner who published a hieroglyphic transcription of the hieratic original (1959), it is a "genuine chronicle remarkably like the Manetho of Africanus and Eusebius" (1962:47). This papyrus was apparently in near perfect condition when discovered by Drovetti in 1822 in western Thebes. However, by the time Champollion studied it a few years later, it was regrettably in a poor, fragmented state, with large sections having been lost or destroyed in the intervening years. This sad fact has long been lamented by historians because knowledge of certain kings and durations of certain reigns remain lost. Nevertheless, the Turin canon continues to be the most important document from pharaonic times for historical reconstruction. The list begins with a series of deities, such as Seth, Horus and Thoth who are called "King of Upper and Lower Egypt" and whose names are written in a cartouche. Following this in column II is the sequence of kings beginning with Meni, the legendary Menes. In the following translation, the three columns represent: the column and line number of the manuscript, the royal name, and the year/month/day.

(Dynasty 1)

II.11	Meni	lost
II.12	It//	lost
II.13	lost	lost
II.15	//[H]ori	lost

II.16	Semti	lost
II.17	Merbiapen	lost
II.18	Semsem	lost
II.19	[Ke]beh	lost
II.20	Bau[netjer]	lost
II.21	[Ka]kau	lost

(*Dynasty 2*)

II.22	[Bau]netjeren	lost
II.23	lost	lost
II.24	Senedj	lost
II.25	Aaka	lost
III.1	Neferkasokar	8 / 3 /[//]
III.2	Hudjefa	[11]/ 8 / 4
III.3	Bebty	27 / 2 / 1

(*Dynasty 3*)

III.4	Nebka	19/0/0
III.5	Djeserit	19
III.6	Djeserti	6
III.7	[Hudje]fa	6
III.8	Hu[ni]	24 / [lost]

(*Dynasty 4*)

III.9	Sneferu	24 / [lost]
III.10	[Khufu]	23 /[lost]
III.11	[Djedefre]	8 /[lost]
III.12	Kha[efre]	lost
III.13	lost	lost
III.14	[Menkaure]	18 /[lost]
III.15	lost	4
III.16	lost	2

(*Dynasty 5*)

III.17	[User]ka[f]	7
III.18	[Sahure]	12
III.19	lost	lost
III.20	lost	7
III.21	lost	// + 1
III.22	lost	11
III.23	Menkauhor	8
III.24	Djedy (Djedkare)	28
III.25	Unas	30

(*Dynasty 6*)

IV.1	lost	lost
IV.2	lost	lost / 6 / 21
IV.3	lost	20
IV.4	lost	44
IV.5	[Pepi II]	90 + X
IV.6	[Merenre]	1 / 1 /
IV.7	lost	lost
IV.8	Nitikerty	lost
IV.9	Neferka, child	lost
IV.10	Nefer	2 / 1 / 1
IV.11	Ibi	4 / 2
IV.12	lost	2 / 1 / 1
IV.13	lost	1 / 0 /1/2 day
IV.14-19	[Poorly prserved or lost]	

(*Dynasties 9-10*)

IV.20	Neferkare	lost
IV.21	Khety	lost
IV.22	Senenh///	lost
IV.23	////////	lost
IV.24	Mer/////	lost
IV.25	Shed////	lost
IV.26	H//////	lost

(*Dynasty 11*)

V.1-11	lost	lost
V.12	Wah///	lost
V.13	lost	lost
V.14	lost	49
V.15	lost	8
V.16	Nebhepetre	51
V.17	Sankhka[re]	12
V.18	Total 143 years	

(*Dynasty 12*)

V.19	[Kings of]the Capital Itjtawy	
V.20	[Sehet]epib[re]	lost
V.21	[Kheper] ka[re]	45/ lost
V.22	lost	10 +
V.23	lost	19 / lost
V.24	lost	30+ /lost
V.25	lost	40+ /lost
VI.1	Maakherure	9 / 3 / 27
VI.2	[Sobek]nefer[u]re	3 / 10 / 14
VI.3	Kings of the [Capital Itjtawy] 8, total 213 / 1 / 16	

(*Dynasty 13*)

VI.5	[Khitawy]re	2 / 3 /24
VI.6	[Sekhemka]re	lost
VI.7	//amenemhet	3 /lost
VI.8	Sehetepibre	1
VI.9	Iufni	lost
VI.10	Sankhibre	lost
VI.11	Smenkare	lost/lost/4
VI.12	Sehetepibre	lost/lost/3
VI.13	Sewadjkare	lost/lost/6
VI.14	Nedjemibre	/ /lost
VI.15	Re-Sobek[hote]p	2
VI.16	Ren[se]neb, he function for 4 months	
VI.17	Autibre	/ 7 /
VI.18	Sedjefakare	lost
VI.19	Sekhemre-khuitawy-Sobekhetep	lost
VI.20	User[ka]re - //re//ndjer	lost
VI.21	[Smenekh]kare the General	lost
VI.22	/////ka[re] - Intef	lost
VI.23	/////ib-Seth	blank
VI.24	Sekhemkare-Sobekhetep	3 / 2/lost
VI.25	Khasekhemre-Neferhotep	11/ 1 /lost
VI.26	Sihathor	lost/ 3 /lost
VI.27	Khaneferre-Sobekhetep	lost
VII.1	Khahetepre	4 / 8 / 29
VII.2	Wahibre-Iaib	10 / 8 / 28
VII.3	Merneferre	23 / 8 / 18
VII.4	Merhotepre	2 / 2 / 9
VII.5	Seankhenswadjtu	3 / 2 / lost
VII.6	Mersekhemre-Ined	3 / 1 / 1

VII.7	Sewadjkare-Hori	5 / 8 /
VII.8	Merika[//]-Sobek[hetep]	2/ // / 4
VII.9	lost	lost/lost/11
VII.10	lost	lost/lost/3
VII.11	lost	lost
VII.12	lost	lost
VII.13	////mose	lost
VII.14	////maatre- [I]bi	lost
VII.15	////webenre-Hor[i]	lost
VII.16	////kare	lost
VII.17	////enre	lost
VII.18	//////re	lost
VII.19	lost	lost
VII.20	lost	lost
VII.21	///rre	lost
VII.22	Merkheperre	lost
VII.23	Merika[re]	lost
VIII.1	Nehesy	lost/ 3 /
VIII.2	Khatyre	lost/3 /
VIII.3	Nebefautre	1 / 5 / 15
VIII.4	Sehebre	3 / lost / 1
VIII.5	Merdjefare	3 /lost
VIII.6	Sewadjkare	1 / lost
VIII.7	Nebdjefare	1 / lost
VIII.8	Webenre	1
VIII.9	lost	1 / 1 / lost
VIII.10	/// djefa[re]	4 /
VIII.11	///[w]eben[re]	3 /
VIII.12	Autibre	lost
VIII.13	Heribre	lost/lost/ 29
VIII.14	Nebsenre	lost / 5 / 20
VIII.15	//////re	lost / lost / 21
VIII.16	Sekheperenre	2 / /1
VIII.17	Djedkherure	2 / /5
VIII.18	Sankhibre	lost / lost / 19
VIII.19	Nefertumre	lost / lost / 18
VIII.20	Sekhem//re	lost
VIII.21	Kakemutre	lost / lost
VIII.22	Neferibre	lost / lost
VIII.23	Ia////re	lost / lost
VIII.24	Kha///re	lost
VIII.25	Aaka///re	lost
VIII.26	Smen///re	lost
VIII.27	Djedi///re	lost
IX.1-6	lost	lost
IX.7	Senefer[ka/]re	lost
IX.8	Men////re	lost
IX.9	Djedi//[re]	lost
IX.10-13	lost	lost
IX.14	Inek///	lost
IX.15	Ineb///	lost
IX.16	Ip////	lost
IX.17-27	lost	lost
IX.28	////ren-Hapu	lost
IX.29	///ka[re?]-Nebennati	lost
IX.30	///ka[re?]-Bebnem	lost
IX.31	lost	lost
X	lost	lost
X.20	Khamudy	
X.21	[Total of] Foreign [Chieftains] 8, they functioned 100+ years.	
X.21-30	(very fragmentary)	
(Dynasty 17)		
XI.1	Sekhemre-////	3 /
XI.2	Sekhemre-////	16 /
XI.3	Sekhemre-s[menttawy]	1 /
XI.4	Sewadje[n]re	///1 /
XI.5	Nebiryautre	29 /
XI.6	Nebitautre	lost
XI.7	Semen[wadj?]re	lost
XI.8	Seweser///re	12 /
XI.9	Sekehre-Shedwaset	lost
XI.10-15	lost	lost
XI.16	Weser///re	lost
XI.17	Weser/////	lost
XI.18-end	(lost or too fragmentary for translation)	

REFERENCES

Caulfeild and Saint Thomas 1902:pl.43; Gardiner 1959; 1962:430-445; Kitchen 1992:328-329; Redford 1986; Swelim 1983; *Urk IV*.

C. INDIVIDUAL FOCUS

1. NARRATIVES

SINUHE (1.38)

Miriam Lichtheim

The numerous, if fragmentary, copies of this work testify to its great popularity, and it is justly considered the most accomplished piece of Middle Kingdom prose literature.

The two principal manuscripts are: (1) P. Berlin 3022 (abbr., B) which dates from the 12th Dynasty. In its present state, it lacks the beginning of the story and contains a total of 311 lines; (2) P. Berlin 10499 (abbr., R) which contains 203 lines and includes the beginning. It dates to the end of the Middle Kingdom.

A third major copy is on a large ostracon in the Ashmolean Museum, Oxford, which gives 130, partly incomplete, lines. It is, however, an inferior copy, dating to the 19th Dynasty. Its principal value lies in the detailed commentary of its editor, J. Barns. In addition, small portions of the text are preserved on papyrus fragments and on numerous ostraca.

The present translation uses as principal manuscripts the text of R for the beginning and of B for the bulk, and incorporates an occasional variant from other manuscripts.

(R 1) The Prince, Count, Governor of the domains of the sovereign in the lands of the Asiatics, true and beloved Friend of the King, the Attendant Sinuhe, says:

I was an attendant who attended his lord, a servant of the royal harem, waiting on the Princess, the highly praised Royal Wife of King Sesostris in Khenemsut, the daughter of King Amenemhet in Kanefru, Nefru, the revered.[1]

Year 30, third month of the inundation, day 7: the god ascended to his horizon. The King of Upper and Lower Egypt, *Sehetepibre*, flew to heaven and united with the sun-disk, the divine body merging with its maker. Then the residence was hushed; hearts grieved; the great portals were shut; (10) the courtiers were head-on-knee; the people moaned.

His majesty, however, had despatched an army to the land of the Tjemeh, with his eldest son as its commander, the good god Sesostris. He had been sent to smite the foreign lands and to punish those of Tjehenu.[2] (15) Now he was returning, bringing captives of the Tjehenu and cattle of all kinds beyond number. The officials of the palace sent to the western border to let the king's son know the event that had occurred at the court. The messengers met him on the road, (20) reaching him at night. Not a moment did he delay. The falcon flew with his attendants, without letting his army know it.

But the royal sons who had been with him on this expedition had also been sent for. (B 1) One of them was summoned while I was standing (there). I heard his voice, as he spoke, while I was in the near distance. My heart fluttered, my arms spread out, a trembling befell all my limbs. I removed myself in leaps, to seek a hiding place. I put (5) myself between two bushes, so as to leave the road to its traveler.

I set out southward. I did not plan to go to the residence. I believed there would be turmoil and did not expect to survive it. I crossed Maaty near Sycamore; I reached Isle-of-Snefru.[3] I spent the day there at the edge (10) of the cultivation. Departing at dawn I encountered a man who stood on the road. He saluted me while I was afraid of him. At dinner time I reached "Cattle-Quay." I crossed in a barge without a rudder, by the force of the westwind. I passed to the east of the quarry, (15) at the height of "Mistress of the Red Mountain." Then I made my way northward. I reached the "Walls of the Ruler," which were made to repel the Asiatics and to crush the Sand-

[1] Sinuhe was specifically in the service of Princess Nefru, the wife of Sesostris I, the latter being co-regent at the time of his father's death. Khenemsut and Kanefru are the names of the pyramids of Sesostris I and Amenemhet I.

[2] Tjemeh and Tjehenu designated two distinct Libyan peoples who merged in the course of time. In this story the terms are used interchangeably.

[3] Goedicke (1957:77-85) has made it plausible that *M*$^{\supset c}$*ty* was not a lake but a name for the Giza region (see also Gauthier 1925-31 4:218 on a town *M*$^{\supset c}$*ty*), and that Isle-of-Snefru and Isle-of-Kem-Wer were not islands. Sinuhe is traveling south along the edge of the western desert, until he crosses the Nile at a spot the name of which Goedicke explained as "Cattle-Quay." He landed in the vicinity of the "Red Mountain" (today's Gebel al-Ahmar), and only then did he decide to flee the country and hence turned northward.

farers. I crouched in a bush for fear of being seen by the guard on duty upon the wall.

I set out (20) at night. At dawn I reached Peten. I halted at "Isle-of-Kem-Wer." An attack of thirst overtook me; I was parched, my throat burned. I said, "This is the taste of death." I raised my heart and collected myself when I heard the lowing sound of cattle (25) and saw Asiatics. One of their leaders, who had been in Egypt, recognized me. He gave me water and boiled milk for me.[a] I went with him to his tribe. What they did for me was good.

a Judg 4:19; 5:25

Land gave me to land. I traveled to Byblos; I returned to Qedem. I spent (30) a year and a half there. Then Ammunenshi,[4] the ruler of Upper Retenu, took me to him, saying to me: "You will be happy with me; you will hear the language of Egypt." He said this because he knew my character and had heard of my skill, Egyptians who were with him having borne witness for me. He said to me: "Why (35) have you come here? Has something happened at the residence?" I said to him: "King Sehetepibre departed to the horizon, and one did not know the circumstances." But I spoke in half-truths:[5] "When I returned from the expedition to the land of the Tjemeh, it was reported to me and my heart grew faint. It carried (40) me away on the path of flight, though I had not been talked about; no one had spat in my face; I had not heard a reproach; my name had not been heard in the mouth of the herald. I do not know what brought me to this country; it is as if planned by god. As if a Delta-man saw himself in Yebu, a marsh-man in Nubia."

Then he said to me: "How then is that land without that excellent god, fear of whom was throughout (45) the lands like Sakhmet in a year of plague?" I said to him in reply: "Of course his son has entered into the palace, having taken his father's heritage."

He is a god without peer,
No other comes before him;
He is lord of knowledge, wise planner, skilled leader,
One goes and comes by (50) his will.

He was the smiter of foreign lands,
While his father stayed in the palace,
He reported to him on commands carried out.

He is a champion who acts with his arm,
A fighter who has no equal,
When seen engaged in archery,
When joining the melee.

Horn-curber who makes hands turn weak,
His foes (55) can not close ranks;
Keen-sighted he smashes foreheads,
None can withstand his presence.

Wide-striding he smites the fleeing,
No retreat for him who turns him his back;
Steadfast in time of attack,
He makes turn back and turns not his back.

Stouthearted when he sees the mass,
He lets not slackness fill his heart;
(60) Eager at the sight of combat,
Joyful when he works his bow.

Clasping his shield he treads under foot,
No second blow needed to kill;
None can escape his arrow,
None turn aside his bow.

The Bowmen flee before him,
As before the might of the goddess;
As he fights he plans the goal,
(65) Unconcerned about all else.

Lord of grace, rich in kindness,
He has conquered through affection;
His city loves him more than itself,
Acclaims him more than its own god.

Men outdo women in hailing him,
Now that he is king;
Victor while yet in the egg,
Set to be ruler since his birth.

Augmenter of those born with him,
(70) He is unique, god-given;
Happy the land that he rules!

Enlarger of frontiers,
He will conquer southern lands,
While ignoring northern lands,
Though made to smite Asiatics and tread on Sand-farers!

"Send to him! Let him know your name as one who inquires while being far from his majesty. He will not fail to do (75) good to a land that will be loyal to him."

He said to me: "Well then, Egypt is happy knowing that he is strong. But you are here. You shall stay with me. What I shall do for you is good."

[4] K. Baer would read the name as Amorite ^{c}Ammulanasi, "God is verily (my) prince." On the name pattern see Huffmon (1965:223, 240). I retain the reading "Ammunenshi" largely because I adhere to the method of transliterating the Eg. consonantal script with a minimum of vocalization and without regard for actual pronunciation.

[5] Some scholars have adopted the rendering, "It was told to me incorrectly" (see Barns 1952:5 n. 23). I do not find this convincing. Sinuhe's "half-truths" consist in pretending that the death of the old king was reported to him when in fact he had only overheard a conspiratorial message, and in disclaiming any knowledge of the circumstances.

He set me at the head of his children. He married me to his eldest daughter.[b] He let me choose for myself of his land, (80) of the best that was his, on his border with another land. It was a good land called Yaa. Figs were in it and grapes. It had more wine than water. Abundant was its honey,[c] plentiful its oil. All kinds of fruit were on its trees. Barley was there and emmer, and no end of cattle of all kinds. (85) Much also came to me because of the love of me; for he had made me chief of a tribe in the best part of his land. Loaves were made for me daily,[6] and wine as daily fare, cooked meat, roast fowl, as well as desert game. (90) For they snared for me and laid it before me, in addition to the catch of my hounds. Many sweets were made for me, and milk [c] dishes of all kinds.

b Gen 30:16-30; Exod 2:21

c Exod 3:8; Num 13:27

d-d 1 Sam 17

I passed many years, my children becoming strong men, each a master of his tribe. The envoy who came north or went south to the residence (95) stayed with me. I let everyone stay with me. I gave water to the thirsty; I showed the way to him who had strayed; I rescued him who had been robbed. When Asiatics conspired to attack the Rulers of Hill-Countries,[7] I opposed their movements. For this ruler of (100) Retenu made me carry out numerous missions as commander of his troops. Every hill tribe against which I marched I vanquished, so that it was driven from the pasture of its wells. I plundered its cattle, carried off its families, seized their food, and killed people (105) by my strong arm, by my bow, by my movements and my skillful plans. I won his heart and he loved me, for he recognized my valor. He set me at the head of his children, for he saw the strength of my arms.

There came a hero of Retenu,[8] [d]
To challenge me (110) in my tent.
A champion was he without peer,
He had subdued it all.
He said he would fight with me,
He planned to plunder me,
He meant to seize my cattle
At the behest of his tribe.

The ruler conferred with me and I said: "I do not know him; I am not his ally, (115) that I could walk about in his camp. Have I ever opened his back rooms or climbed over his fence? It is envy, because he sees me doing your commissions. I am indeed like a stray bull in a strange herd, whom the bull of the herd charges, (120) whom the longhorn attacks. Is an inferior beloved when he becomes a superior? No Asiatic makes friends with a Delta-man. And what would make papyrus cleave to the mountain? If a bull loves combat, should a champion bull retreat for fear of being equaled? (125) If he wishes to fight, let him declare his wish. Is there a god who does not know what he has ordained, and a man who knows how it will be?"

At night I strung my bow, sorted my arrows, practiced with my dagger, polished my weapons. When it dawned Retenu came. (130) It had assembled its tribes; it had gathered its neighboring peoples; it was intent on this combat.

He came toward me while I waited, having placed myself near him. Every heart burned for me; the women jabbered. All hearts ached for me thinking: "Is there another champion who could fight him?" He <raised> his battle-axe and shield,[9] (135) while his armful of missiles fell toward me. When I had made his weapons attack me, I let his arrows pass me by without effect, one following the other. Then, when he charged me, I shot him, my arrow sticking in his neck. He screamed; he fell on his nose; (140) I slew him with his axe. I raised my war cry over his back, while every Asiatic shouted. I gave praise to Mont, while his people mourned him. The ruler Ammunenshi took me in his arms.

Then I carried off his goods; I plundered his cattle. What he had meant to do (145) to me I did to him. I took what was in his tent; I stripped his camp. Thus I became great, wealthy in goods, rich in herds. It was the god who acted, so as to show mercy to one with whom he had been angry, whom he had made stray abroad. For today his heart is appeased.[d]

A fugitive fled (150) his surroundings — [10]
    I am famed at home.
A laggard lagged from hunger —
    I give bread to my neighbor.
A man left his land in nakedness —
    I have bright clothes, fine linen.
A man ran for lack of one to send —
    I am (155) rich in servants.
My house is fine, my dwelling spacious —

[6] Or: "supplies of mint-drink;" see Barns 1952:9 n. 38.

[7] Sinuhe is on the side of the *ḥḳꜣw ḫꜣswt*, the "rulers of mountainlands," the term from which the name "Hyksos" was derived.

[8] In this passage Sinuhe's prose assumes the symmetrical rhythm of poetry.

[9] The insertion of a verb still seems to me the best solution for this much debated passage. Weapons, including a shield, do not simply "fall" from a fighter. Only missiles, whether arrows or javelins, "fall." An alternative might be to take *ꜥḥꜥ.n* not as the auxiliary but as the verb "to stand" referring to shield and axe. The champion held his shield and axe in readiness while shooting his missiles.

[10] Westendorf (1968:128) gave a new analysis and translation of this beautiful poem which climaxes the account of Sinuhe's career abroad. While it is true that the preposition *n* in all four occurrences here has the meaning "because of," to translate it thus would destroy the attempt to render the poem as a poem. The change of mood, from Sinuhe's exultation over his success to his intense longing for the lost homeland,

My thoughts are at the palace!

Whichever god decreed this flight, have mercy, bring me home! Surely you will let me see the place in which my heart dwells! What is more important than that my corpse be buried in the land (160) in which I was born![e] Come to my aid! What if the happy event should occur![11] May god pity me! May he act so as to make happy the end of one whom he punished! May his heart ache for one whom he forced to live abroad! If he is truly appeased today, may he hearken to the prayer of one far away! May he return one whom he made roam the earth to the place from which he carried him off!

e Gen 49:29-32

(165) May Egypt's king have mercy on me, that I may live by his mercy! May I greet the mistress of the land who is in the palace! May I hear the commands of her children! Would that my body were young again! For old age has come; feebleness has overtaken me. My eyes are heavy, my arms weak; (170) my legs fail to follow. The heart is weary; death is near. May I be conducted to the city of eternity! May I serve the Mistress of All! May she speak well of me to her children; may she spend eternity above me![12]

Now when the majesty of King Kheperkare was told of the condition in which I was, his majesty sent word (175) to me with royal gifts, in order to gladden the heart of this servant like that of a foreign ruler. And the royal children who were in his palace sent me their messages. Copy of the decree brought to this servant concerning his return to Egypt:

> Horus: Living in Births; the Two Ladies: Living in Births; the King of Upper and Lower Egypt: *Kheperkare*; the Son of Re: (180) *Sesostris*, who lives forever. Royal decree to the Attendant Sinuhe:
>
> This decree of the King is brought to you to let you know: That you circled the foreign countries, going from Qedem to Retenu, land giving you to land, was the counsel of your own heart. What had you done that one should act against you? You had not cursed, so that your speech would be reproved. You had not spoken against the counsel of the nobles, that your words should have been rejected. (185) This matter — it carried away your heart. It was not in my heart against you. This your heaven in the palace lives and prospers to this day.[13] Her head is adorned with the kingship of the land; her children are in the palace. You will store riches which they give you; you will live on their bounty. Come back to Egypt! See the residence in which you lived! Kiss the ground at the great portals, mingle with the courtiers! For today (190) you have begun to age. You have lost a man's strength. Think of the day of burial, the passing into reveredness.
>
> A night is made for you with ointments and wrappings from the hand of Tait. A funeral procession is made for you on the day of burial; the mummy case is of gold, its head of lapis lazuli. The sky is above you as you lie in the hearse, oxen drawing you, musicians going before you. The dance of (195) the *mww*-dancers is done at the door of your tomb; the offering-list is read to you; sacrifice is made before your offering-stone. Your tomb-pillars, made of white stone, are among (those of) the royal children. You shall not die abroad! Not shall Asiatics inter you. You shall not be wrapped in the skin of a ram to serve as your coffin.[14] Too long a roaming of the earth! Think of your corpse, come back!

This decree reached me while I was standing (200) in the midst of my tribe. When it had been read to me, I threw myself on my belly. Having touched the soil, I spread it on my chest.[15] I strode around my camp shouting: "What compares with this which is done to a servant whom his heart led astray to alien lands? Truly good is the kindness that saves me from death! Your *ka* will grant me to reach my end, my body being at home!"

Copy of the reply to this decree:

> The servant of the Palace, Sinuhe, (205) says:[16] In very good peace! Regarding the matter of this flight which this servant did in his ignorance. It is your *ka*, O good

occurs in the last distich (as Westendorf suggested), and provides the transition to the prayers for return.

[11] I.e., "what if death should occur while I am still abroad?" So with Westendorf 1968:129-130.

[12] In this context the "Mistress of All" could be either the queen or the goddess Nut. The latter interpretation was preferred by Sander-Hansen 1955-1957:147.

[13] The queen is meant.

[14] The Ashmolean Ostracon (Barns 1952:2, 48) reads: *n ᵓir.tw ḏri.k*, and Barns suggests to read *nn ᵓir.tw ḏri.k* (1952:21 n. 18). But since elsewhere *ḏrit* means "container," "coffin," I assume the same word here and, following the text of B, take it to mean that the ram's skin will not be Sinuhe's coffin.

[15] As a gesture of humility.

[16] This translation of Sinuhe's reply to the king's letter follows in essentials that of Barns 1967:6-14.

god, lord of the Two Lands, which Re loves and which Mont lord of Thebes favors and Amun lord of Thrones-of-the-Two-Lands, and Sobk-Re lord of Sumenu, and Horus, Hathor, Atum with his Ennead, and Sopdu-Neferbau-Semseru the Eastern Horus, and the Lady of Yemet — may she enfold your head — and the conclave upon the flood, and Min-Horus of the hill-countries, and Wereret lady of (210) Punt, Nut, Haroeris-Re, and all the gods of Egypt and the isles of the sea — may they give life and joy to your nostrils, may they endow you with their bounty, may they give you eternity without limit, infinity without bounds! May the fear of you resound in lowlands and highlands, for you have subdued all that the sun encircles! This is the prayer of this servant for his lord who saves from the West.

The lord of knowledge who knows people knew (215) in the majesty of the palace that this servant was afraid to say it. It is like a thing too great to repeat. The great god, the peer of Re, knows the heart of one who has served him willingly. This servant is in the hand of one who thinks about him. He is placed under his care. Your Majesty is the conquering Horus; your arms vanquish all lands. May then your Majesty command to have brought to you the prince of Meki from Qedem, (220) the mountain chiefs from Keshu, and the prince of Menus from the lands of the Fenkhu. They are rulers of renown who have grown up in the love of you. I do not mention Retenu — it belongs to you like your hounds.

Lo, this flight which the servant made — I did not plan it. It was not in my heart; I did not devise it. I do not know what removed me from my place. It was like (225) a dream. As if a Delta-man saw himself in Yebu, a marsh-man in Nubia. I was not afraid; no one ran after me. I had not heard a reproach; my name was not heard in the mouth of the herald. Yet my flesh crept, my feet hurried, my heart drove me; the god who had willed this flight (230) dragged me away. Nor am I a haughty man. He who knows his land respects men. Re has set the fear of you throughout the land, the dread of you in every foreign country. Whether I am at the residence, whether I am in this place, it is you who covers this horizon.[17] The sun rises at your pleasure. The water in the river is drunk when you wish. The air of heaven is breathed at your bidding. This servant will hand over his possessions (235) to the brood[18] which this servant begot in this place. This servant has been sent for! Your Majesty will do as he wishes! One lives by the breath which you give. As Re, Horus, and Hathor love your august nose, may Mont lord of Thebes wish it to live forever!

I was allowed to spend one more day in Yaa, handing over my possessions to my children, my eldest son taking charge of my tribe; (240) all my possessions became his — my serfs, my herds, my fruit, my fruit trees.[f] This servant departed southward. I halted at Horus-ways. The commander in charge of the garrison sent a message to the residence to let it be known. Then his majesty sent a trusted overseer of the royal domains with whom were loaded ships, (245) bearing royal gifts for the Asiatics who had come with me to escort me to Horus-ways. I called each one by his name, while every butler was at his task. When I had started and set sail, there was kneading and straining beside me, until I reached the city of Itj-tawy.

f Gen 25:5; Deut 21:15-17

When it dawned, very early, they came to summon me. Ten men came and ten men went to usher me into the palace. My forehead touched the ground between the sphinxes, (250) and the royal children stood in the gateway to meet me. The courtiers who usher through the forecourt set me on the way to the audience-hall. I found his majesty on the great throne in a kiosk of gold.[19] Stretched out on my belly, I did not know myself before him, while this god greeted me pleasantly. I was like a man seized by darkness. (255) My *ba* was gone, my limbs trembled; my heart was not in my body, I did not know life from death.

His majesty said to one of the courtiers: "Lift him up, let him speak to me." Then his majesty said: "Now you have come, after having roamed foreign lands. Flight has taken its toll of you. You have aged, have reached old age. It is no small matter that your corpse will be interred without being escorted by Bowmen. But don't act thus, don't act thus, speechless (260) though your

[17] Or: yours is all that the horizon covers.

[18] Taking *ṯꜣt* to mean "progeny, brood," as proposed by Barns 1952:26 n. 36.

[19] There is no need to transpose the word before *nt ḏꜥm* if it is read as *wmt.t* (not *wmt*), this being the word for "enclosure" (see *Wb.* 1:307). I take it to refer to the light, kiosk type of structure which was built over the dais on which the throne stood, and surrounded the throne on three sides.

name was called!" Fearful of punishment[20] I answered with the answer of a frightened man: "What has my lord said to me, that I might answer it? It is not disrespect to the god![21] It is the terror which is in my body, like that which caused the fateful flight! Here I am before you. Life is yours. May your Majesty do as he wishes!"

Then the royal daughters were brought in, and his majesty said to the queen: "Here is Sinuhe, (265) come as an Asiatic, a product of nomads!" She uttered a very great cry, and the royal daughters shrieked all together. They said to his majesty: "Is it really he, O king, our lord?" Said his majesty: "It is really he!" Now having brought with them their necklaces, rattles, and sistra, they held them out to his majesty:[22]

> Your hands (270) upon the radiance, eternal king,
> Jewels of heaven's mistress!
> The Gold[23] gives life to your nostrils,
> The Lady of Stars enfolds you!
>
> Southcrown fared north, north crown south,
> Joined, united by your majesty's word.
> While the Cobra decks your brow,
> You deliver the poor from harm.
> Peace to you from Re, Lord of Lands!
> Hail to you and the Mistress of All!
>
> Slacken your bow, lay down your arrow,
> (275) Give breath to him who gasps for breath!
> Give us our good gift on this good day,[24]
> Grant us the son of north wind, Bowman born in Egypt!
>
> He made the flight in fear of you,
> He left the land in dread of you!
> A face that sees you shall not pale,
> Eyes that see you shall not fear!

His majesty said: "He shall not fear, he shall not (280) dread!" "He shall be a Companion among the nobles. He shall be among the courtiers. Proceed to the robing-room to wait on him!"

I left the audience-hall, the royal daughters giving me their hands. (285) We went through the great portals, and I was put in the house of a prince. In it were luxuries: a bathroom and mirrors.[25] In it were riches from the treasury; clothes of royal linen, myrrh, and the choice perfume of the king and of his favorite courtiers were in every (290) room. Every servant was at his task. Years were removed from my body. I was shaved; my hair was combed. Thus was my squalor returned to the foreign land, my dress to the Sand-farers. I was clothed in fine linen; I was anointed with fine oil. I slept on a bed. I had returned the sand to those who dwell in it, (295) the tree-oil to those who grease themselves with it.

I was given a house and garden that had belonged to a courtier. Many craftsmen rebuilt it, and all its woodwork was made anew. Meals were brought to me from the palace three times, four times a day, apart from what the royal children gave without a moment's pause.

(300) A stone pyramid was built for me in the midst of the pyramids. The masons who build tombs constructed it. A master draughtsman designed in it. A master sculptor carved in it. The overseers of construction in the necropolis busied themselves with it. All the equipment that is placed in (305) a tomb-shaft was supplied. Mortuary priests were given me. A funerary domain was made for me. It had fields and a garden in the right place, as is done for a Companion of the first rank. My statue was overlaid with gold, its skirt with electrum. It was his majesty who ordered it made. There is no commoner for whom the like has been done. I was in (310) the favor of the king, until the day of landing[26] came.

(Colophon) It is done from beginning to end as it was found in writing.

---

[20] The Ashmolean Ostracon (Barns 1952:2, 49) reads: "fear your punishment," seems to me inferior.

[21] Read: *n ḥr-ᶜ n nṯr is pw*, and see Barns's note on *ḥr-ᶜ*, "shortcoming," (1952:30-32 n. 50).

[22] The princesses hold out the emblems sacred to Hathor and perform a ceremonial dance and a song in which they beg a full pardon for Sinuhe. The song was studied by Brunner 1955:5-11.

[23] Epithet of Hathor.

[24] Reading *imi n.n ḫnt.n nfr m hrw pn nfr*, according to Barns (1952:2, 58 and p. 33 n. 58).

[25] Following Sander-Hansen (1955-1957:149) in taking *ᶜmw nw ᵓḫt* to mean "mirrors."

[26] The day of death. Through its beginning and its ending, the story is given the form of the tomb-autobiography in which the narrator looks back on his completed life.

REFERENCES

Publication: Gardiner 1909; Blackman 1932:1-41; Barns 1952; Sethe 1924:3-17; 1927:5-21. Translation and commentary: Gardiner 1916; Grapow 1952. Translation: Erman 1927:14-29; Lefèbvre 1949:1-25; *ANET* 18-22; Edel 1968:1-12; Lichtheim *AEL* 1:222-235. Analysis and evaluation: Posener 1956:87-115. Comments (selection): Alt 1923:48-50; 1941:19ff; Blackman 1930:63-65; 1936:35-40; de Buck 1932:57-60; Clère 1939a:16-29; 1939b 2:829ff.; Brunner 1955:5-11; 1964:139-140; Goedicke 1957:77-85; 1965:29-47; Huffmon 1965; Yoyotte 1964:69-73; Lanczkowski 1958:214-218; Barns 1967:6-14; Westendorf 1968:125-131.

THE SHIPWRECKED SAILOR (1.39)

Miriam Lichtheim

The tale is set in a narrative frame. A high official is returning from an expedition that apparently failed in its objective, for he is despondent and fearful of the reception awaiting him at court. One of his attendants exhorts him to take courage, and as an example of how a disaster may turn into a success, tells him a marvelous adventure that happened to him years ago. At the end of his tale, however, the official is still despondent.

The only preserved papyrus copy of the tale was discovered by Golenischev in the Imperial Museum of St. Petersburg. Nothing is known about its original provenience. The papyrus, called P. Leningrad 1115, is now in Moscow. The work, and the papyrus copy, date from the Middle Kingdom.

(1) The worthy attendant said: Take heart, my lord! We have reached home. The mallet has been seized, the mooring-post staked, the prow-rope placed (5) on land. Praise is given, god is thanked, everyone embraces his fellow. Our crew has returned safely; our troops have had no loss. We have left Wawat behind, we have passed (10) Senmut; we have returned in safety, we have reached our land. Now listen to me, my lord! I am not exaggerating. Wash yourself, pour water over your fingers. You must answer (15) when questioned. You must speak to the king with presence of mind. You must answer without stammering! A man's mouth can save him. His speech makes one forgive him. (20) But do as you like! It is tiresome to talk to you.

But I shall tell you something like it that happened to me. I had set out to the king's mines, and had gone (25) to sea in a ship of a hundred and twenty cubits in length and forty cubits in width. One hundred and twenty sailors were in it of the pick of Egypt. Looked they at sky, looked they at land, their hearts were stouter (30) than lions. They could foretell a storm before it came, a tempest before it broke.

A storm came up while we were at sea, before we could reach land. As we sailed (35) it made a ⌜swell⌝, and in it a wave eight cubits tall. The mast — it (the wave) struck (it).[1] Then the ship died. Of those in it not one remained. I was cast (40) on an island by a wave of the sea. I spent three days alone, with my heart as companion. Lying in the shelter of trees I hugged (45) the shade.

Then I stretched my legs to discover what I might put in my mouth. I found figs and grapes there, all sorts of fine vegetables, sycamore figs, unnotched and notched,[2] (50) and cucumbers that were as if tended. Fish were there and fowl; there is nothing that was not there. I stuffed myself and put some down, because I had too much in my arms. Then I cut a fire drill, (55) made a fire and gave a burnt offering to the gods.

Then I heard a thundering noise and thought, "It is a wave of the sea." Trees splintered, (60) the ground trembled. Uncovering my face, I found it was a snake that was coming. He was of thirty cubits; his beard was over two cubits long. His body was overlaid (65) with gold; his eyebrows were of real lapis lazuli. He was bent up in front.

Then he opened his mouth to me, while I was on my belly before him. He said to me: "Who brought you, who brought you, fellow, (70) who brought you? If you delay telling me who brought you to this island, I shall make you find youself reduced to ashes, becoming like a thing unseen." <I said>: "Though you speak to me, I do not hear (75) it; I am before you without knowing myself." Then he took me in his mouth, carried me to the place where he lived, and set me down unhurt, (80) I being whole with nothing taken from me.

Then he opened his mouth to me, while I was on my belly before him. He said to me: "Who brought you, who brought you, fellow, who brought you to this island (85) of the sea, whose two sides are in water?" Then I answered him, my arms bent before him. I said to him: "I had set out (go) to the mines on a mission of the king in a ship of a hundred and twenty cubits in length and forty cubits in width. One hundred and twenty sailors were in it of the pick of Egypt. (95) Looked they at sky, looked they at land, their hearts were stouter than lions. They could foretell a storm before it came, a tempest before it struck. Each of them — his heart was stouter, (100) his arm stronger than his mate's. There was no fool among them. A storm came up while we

[1] The sentence has been read as: *in ḫt ḥw n.i s(t)*, and rendered as "the mast (or, a piece of wood) struck the wave for me," thereby flattening it and thus helping the sailor, while the ship nevertheless sank. But the sense is poor, for the context leads one to expect that the wave hit the ship and sank it. I believe that the element *n.i* is not the preposition with suflix but rather the common graphic peculiarity of the spelling of *ḥwi*, "to strike," and also of *ḥwi*, "to flood," with an intrusive *n.i* (see *Wb*. 3:49). I also take the *s* to be the suffix referring to the wave; and the dependent pronoun *sw* needs to be added as the object. This admittedly imperfect solution is presented largely in order to emphasize that the passage remains problematic.

[2] I.e., unripe and ripe figs; the ripe ones were notched, as was explained by Keimer 1928:288ff. and 1928:50ff.

were at sea, before we could reach land. As we sailed it made a ⌜swell⌝, and in it a wave (105) eight cubits tall. The mast — it struck (it). Then the ship died. Of those in it not one remained, except myself who is here with you. I was brought to this island (110) by a wave of the sea."

Then he said to me: "Don't be afraid, don't be afraid, fellow; don't be pale-faced, now that you have come to me. It is god who has let you live and brought you to this island of the *ka*.[3] (115) There is nothing that is not in it; it is full of all good things. You shall pass month upon month until you have completed four months in this island. Then (120) a ship will come from home with sailors in it whom you know. You shall go home with them, you shall die in your town.

"How happy is he who tells what he has tasted,[4] when the calamity has passed. (125) I shall tell you something similar that happened on this island. I was here with my brothers and there were children with them. In all we were seventy-five serpents, children and brothers, without mentioning a little daughter whom I had obtained through prayer. Then a star (130) fell, and they went up in flames through it. It so happened that I was not with them in the fire, I was not among them. I could have died for their sake when I found them as one heap of corpses."

"If you are brave and control your heart, you shall embrace your children, you shall kiss your wife, you shall see your home. It is better than everything else. (135) You shall reach home, you shall be there among your brothers."

Stretched out on my belly I touched the ground before him; then I said to him: "I shall speak of your power to the king, I shall let him know (140) of your greatness. I shall send you *ibi* and *ḥknw* oils, laudanum, *ḥsyt*-spice, and the incense of the temples which pleases all the gods. I shall tell what happened to me, what I saw of your power. One will praise god for you in the city before the councillors of the whole land. I shall slaughter (145) oxen for you as burnt offering; I shall sacrifice geese to you. I shall send you ships loaded with all the treasures of Egypt, as is done for a god who befriends people in a distant land not known to the people."

Then he laughed at me for the things I had said, which seemed foolish to him. (150) He said to me: "You are not rich in myrrh and all kinds of incense. But I am the lord of Punt, and myrrh is my very own. That *ḥknw*-oil you spoke of sending, it abounds on this island. Moreover, when you have left this place, you will not see this island again; it will have become water."

Then the ship (155) came, as he had foretold. I went and placed myself on a tall tree, I recognized those that were in it. When I went to report it, I found that he knew it. He said to me: "In health, in health, fellow, to your home, that you may see your children! Make me a good name in your town; that is what I ask (160) of you." I put myself on my belly, my arms bent before him. Then he gave me a load of myrrh, *ḥknw*-oil, laudanum, *ḥsyt*-spice, *tišpss*-spice, perfume, eyepaint, giraffe's tails, great lumps of incense, (165) elephant's tusks, greyhounds, long-tailed monkeys, baboons, and all kinds of precious things.

I loaded them on the ship. Then I put myself on my belly to thank him and he said to me: "You will reach home in two months. You will embrace your children. You will flourish at home, you will be buried."[5]

I went down to the shore (170) near the ship; I hailed the crew which was in the ship. I gave praise on the shore to the lord of the island, those in the ship did the same. We sailed north to the king's residence. We reached the residence in two months, all as he had said. I went in to the king; (175) I presented to him the gifts I had brought from the island. He praised god for me in the presence of the councillors of the whole land. I was made an attendant and endowed with serfs of his.

See me after (180) I had reached land, after I saw what I had tasted! Listen to me! It is good for people to listen.

He said to me: "Don't make an effort, my friend. Who would give water at dawn (185) to a goose that will be slaughtered in the morning?"[6]

(Colophon) It is done from beginning to end as it was found in writing, by the scribe with skilled fingers, Imenaa, son of Imeny — life, prosperity, health!

[3] The expression "island of the *ka*" is curious. Gardiner rendered it as "phantom island" (1908:65).

[4] Eg. says "to taste" for "to experience."

[5] This has been the usual rendering of *rnpy.k m ẖnw ḳrst.k*, in which *ẖnw* was taken to mean "home," as it does elsewhere in the tale, and *ḳrst.k* to stand for *ḳrs.tw.k*. Brunner-Traut (1963:9) now renders: "und wirst dich in deinem Grabe verjüngen." This is grammatically perfect, but I find the older rendering more plausible, since the emphasis of the tale is on the "return home."

[6] For this timeless proverb see Spalinger 1984.

REFERENCES

Publication: Golenischev 1912; 1916:pls. 1-8; Erman 1906:1-26; Blackman 1932:41-48. Translation: Erman 1927:29-35; Lefebvre 1949:29-40; Keimer 1928a:288 ff.; 1928b:50 ff.; Gardiner 1908:65; Brunner-Traut 1963:5-10; Lichtheim *AEL* 1:211-215.

THE TWO BROTHERS (1.40)
(P. D'Orbiney = P. BM 10183)

Miriam Lichtheim

This is a complex and vivid tale, rich in motifs that have parallels in later literatures. The two protagonists have some connection with a myth of the two gods, Anubis and Bata, that was told as a tradition of the Seventeenth Nome of Upper Egypt. The myth is preserved in a late form in the Papyrus Jumilhac (see Vandier 1962). More important than the mythological connection is the depiction of *human* characters, relationships, and feelings in a narration of sustained force. The episode of Bata and his brother's wife has a remarkable similarity with the tale of Joseph and Potiphar's wife, a similarity that has often been commented on. References to the recurrence in other literatures of the tale's folkloristic motifs will be found in the works cited, especially in Lefebvre's and Brunner-Traut's comments to their translations.

Papyrus D'Orbiney is written in a beautiful hand by the scribe Ennana who lived at the end of the 19th Dynasty.

(1.1) It is said, there were two brothers, of the same mother and the same father. Anubis was the name of the elder, and Bata the name of the younger. As for Anubis, he had a house and a wife; and his young brother was with him as if he were a son. He was the one who made clothes for him, and he went behind his cattle to the fields. He was the one who did the plowing, and he harvested for him. He was the one who did for him all kinds of labor in the fields. Indeed, his young brother was an excellent man. There was none like him in the whole land,[a] for a god's strength was in him.

Now when many days had passed, his young brother [was tending] his cattle according to his daily custom. And he [returned] to his house in the evening, laden with all kinds of field plants, and with milk, with wood, and with every [good thing] of the field. He placed them before his [elder brother], as he was sitting with his wife. Then he drank and ate and [went to sleep in] his stable among his cattle.

Now when it had dawned and another day had come, [he took foods] that were cooked and placed them before his elder brother. Then he took bread for himself for the fields, and he drove his cattle to let them eat in the fields. He walked behind his cattle, and they would say to him: "The grass is good in such-and-such a place." And he heard all they said and took them to the place of (2.1) good grass that they desired. Thus the cattle he tended became exceedingly fine, and they increased their offspring very much.

Now at plowing time his [elder] brother said to him: "Have a team [of oxen] made ready for us for plowing, for the soil has emerged and is right for plowing. Also, come to the field with seed, for we shall start plowing tomorrow." So he said to him. Then the young brother made all the preparations that his elder brother had told him [to make].

Now when it had dawned and another day had come, they went to the field with their [seed] and began to plow. And [their hearts] were very pleased with this work they had undertaken. And many days later, when they were in the field, they had need of seed. Then he sent his young brother, saying: "Hurry, fetch us seed from the village." His young brother found the wife of his elder brother seated braiding her hair. He said to her: "Get up, give me seed, (3.1) so that I may hurry to the field, for my elder brother is waiting for me. Don't delay." She said to him: "Go, open the storeroom and fetch what you want. Don't make me leave my hairdo unfinished."

Then the youth entered his stable and fetched a large vessel, for he wished to take a great quantity of seed. He loaded himself with barley and emmer and came out with it. Thereupon she said to him: "How much is what you have on your shoulder?" He said to her: "Three sacks of emmer and two sacks of barley, five in all, are on my shoulder." So he said to her. Then she [spoke to] him saying: "There is [great] strength in you. I see your vigor daily." And she desired to know him as a man. She got up, took hold of him, and said to him: "Come, let us spend an hour lying together.[b] It will be good for you. And I will make fine clothes for you."

Then the youth became like a leopard in [his] anger over the wicked speech she had made to

a Job 1:8; 2:3

b Gen 39:7

him; and she became very frightened. He rebuked her, saying: "Look, you are like a mother to me; and your husband is like a father to me. He who is older than I has raised me. What (4.1) is this great wrong you said to me? Do not say it to me again! But I will not tell it to anyone. I will not let it come from my mouth to any man." He picked up his load; he went off to the field. He reached his elder brother, and they began to work at their task. When evening had come, his elder brother returned to his house. And his young brother tended his cattle, loaded himself with all things of the field, and drove his cattle before him to let them sleep in their stable in the village.

Now the wife of his elder brother was afraid on account of the speech she had made. So she took fat and grease and made herself appear as if she had been beaten, in order to tell her husband, "It was your young brother who beat me." Her husband returned in the evening according to his daily custom. He reached his house and found his wife lying down and seeming ill. She did not pour water over his hands in the usual manner; nor had she lit a fire for him. His house was in darkness, and she lay vomiting.

Her husband said to her: "Who has had words with you?" She said to him: "No one has had words with me except your (5.1) young brother. When he came to take seed to you, he found me sitting alone. He said to me: 'Come, let us spend an hour lying together; loosen[1] your braids.' So he said to me. But I would not listen to him. 'Am I not your mother? Is your elder brother not like a father to you?' So I said to him. He became frightened and he beat <me>, so as to prevent me from telling you. Now if you let him live, I shall die! Look, when he returns, do [not let him live]![2] For I am ill from this evil design which he was about to carry out in the morning."[3]

Then his elder brother became like a leopard. He sharpened his spear and took it in his hand. Then his elder <brother> stood behind the door <of> his stable, in order to kill his young brother when he came in the evening to let his cattle enter the stable. Now when the sun had set he loaded himself with all the plants of the field according to his daily custom. He returned, and as the lead cow was about to enter the stable she said to her herdsman: "Here is your elder brother waiting for you with his spear in order to kill you. Run away from him." He heard what his lead cow said, and (6.1) when another went in she said the same. He looked under the door of his stable and saw the feet of his elder brother as he stood behind the door with his spear in his hand. He set his load on the ground and took off at a run so as to flee. And his elder brother went after him with his spear.

Then his young brother prayed to Pre-Harakhti, saying: "My good lord! It is you who judge between the wicked and the just!" And Pre heard all his plea; and Pre made a great body of water appear between him and his elder brother, and it was full of crocodiles. Thus one came to be on the one side, and the other on the other side. And his elder brother struck his own hand twice, because he had failed to kill him. Then his young brother called to him on this side, saying: "Wait here until dawn! When the Aten has risen, I (7.1) shall contend with you before him; and he will hand over the wicked to the just! For I shall not be with you any more. I shall not be in the place in which you are. I shall go to the Valley of the Pine."

Now when it dawned and another day had come, and Pre-Harakhti had risen, one gazed at the other. Then the youth rebuked his elder brother, saying: "What is your coming after me to kill me wrongfully, without having listened to my words? For I am yet your young brother, and you are like a father to me, and your wife is like a mother to me. Is it not so that when I was sent to fetch seed for us your wife said to me: 'Come, let us spend an hour lying together?' But look, it has been turned about for you into another thing." Then he let him know all that had happened between him and his wife. And he swore by Pre-Harakhti, saying: "As to your coming to kill me wrongfully, you carried your spear on the testimony of a filthy whore!" Then he took a reed knife, cut off his phallus, and threw it into the water; and the catfish swallowed it. And he (8.1) grew weak and became feeble. And his elder brother became very sick at heart and stood weeping for him loudly. He could not cross over to where his young brother was on account of the crocodiles.

Then his young brother called to him, saying: "If you recall something evil, will you not also recall something good, or something that I have done

[1] *Wnḫ* here does not mean "to put on"; on the contrary, it means "to loosen" one's braids, as a woman does when she lies down. This meaning of *wnḫ* is known from the medical texts; see von Deines and Westendorf 1961-1962 2:194, where the authors write: "Der Terminus *wnḫ* bezeichnet eine Lösung zweier Teile von einander, ohne dass eine vollständige Trennung erfolgt."

[2] Or restore: "You shall kill him."

[3] Lit., "yesterday." The day ended at sunset.

for you? Go back to your home and tend your cattle, for I shall not stay in the place where you are. I shall go to the Valley of the Pine. But what you shall do for me is to come and look after me, when you learn that something has happened to me. I shall take out my heart and place it on top of the blossom of the pine. If the pine is cut down and falls to the ground, you shall come to search for it. If you spend seven years searching for it, let your heart not be disgusted. And when you find it and place it in a bowl of cool water, I shall live to take revenge on him who wronged me. You will know that something has happened to me when one puts a jug of beer in your hand and it ferments. Do not delay at all when this happens to you."

Then he went away to the Valley of the Pine; and his elder brother went to his home, his hand on his head and smeared with dirt.[4] When he reached his house, he killed his wife, cast her to the dogs,[c] and sat mourning for his young brother.

[c] 2 Kgs 9:30-37

Now many days after this, his young brother was in the Valley of the Pine. There was no one with him, and he spent the days hunting desert game. In the evening he returned to sleep under the pine on top of whose blossom his heart was. And after (9.1) many days he built a mansion for himself with his own hand <in> the Valley of the Pine, filled with all good things, for he wanted to set up a household.

Coming out of his mansion, he encountered the Ennead as they walked about administering the entire land. Then the Ennead addressed him in unison, saying: "O Bata, Bull of the Ennead, are you alone here, having left your town on account of the wife of Anubis, your elder brother? He has killed his wife and you are avenged of all the wrong done to you." And as they felt very sorry for him, Pre-Harakhti said to Khnum: "Fashion a wife for Bata, that he not live alone!" Then Khnum made a companion for him who was more beautiful in body than any woman in the whole land, for <the fluid of> every god was in her. Then the seven Hathors came <to> see her, and they said with one voice: "She will die by the knife."

He desired her very much. She sat in his house while he spent the day (10.1) hunting desert game, bringing it and putting it before her. He said to her: "Do not go outdoors, lest the sea snatch you. I cannot rescue you from it, because I am a woman like you. And my heart lies on top of the blossom of the pine. But if another finds it, I shall fight with him." Then he revealed to her all his thoughts.

Now many days after this, when Bata had gone hunting according to his daily custom, the young girl went out to stroll under the pine which was next to her house. Then she saw the sea surging behind her, and she started to run before it and entered her house. Thereupon the sea called to the pine, saying: "Catch her for me!" And the pine took away a lock of her hair. Then the sea brought it to Egypt and laid it in the place of the washermen of Pharaoh. Thereafter the scent of the lock of hair got into the clothes of Pharaoh. And the king quarreled with the royal washermen, saying: "A scent of ointment is in the clothes of Pharaoh!" He quarreled with them every day, and (11.1) they did not know what to do.

The chief of the royal washermen went to the shore, his heart very sore on account of the daily quarrel with him. Then he realized[5] that he was standing on the shore opposite the lock of hair which was in the water. He had someone go down, and it was brought to him. Its scent was found to be very sweet, and he took it to Pharaoh.

Then the learned scribes of Pharaoh were summoned, and they said to Pharaoh: "As for this lock of hair, it belongs to a daughter of Pre-Harakhti in whom there is the fluid of every god. It is a greeting to you from another country. Let envoys go to every foreign land to search for her. As for the envoy who goes to the Valley of the Pine, let many men go with him to fetch her." His majesty said: "What you have said is very good." And they were sent.

Now many days after this, the men who had gone abroad returned to report to his majesty. But those who had gone to the Valley of the Pine did not return, for Bata had killed them, leaving only one of them to report to his majesty. Then his majesty sent many soldiers and charioteers to bring her back, and (12.1) with them was a woman into whose hand one had given all kinds of beautiful ladies' jewelry. The woman returned to Egypt with her, and there was jubilation for her in the entire land. His majesty loved her very very much, and he gave her the rank of Great Lady. He spoke with her in order to make her tell about her husband, and she said to his majesty: "Have the pine felled and cut up." The king sent soldiers with their tools to fell the pine.

[4] Gestures of mourning.

[5] *Smn*, "to establish," evolved to include the meanings "to record" and "to determine." Hence the chief washerman did not "stand still" but rather he "determined" or "realized" that he was standing opposite the lock of hair.

They reached the pine, they felled the blossom on which was Bata's heart, and he fell dead at that moment.

When it had dawned and the next day had come, and the pine had been felled, Anubis, the elder brother of Bata, entered his house. He sat down to wash his hands. He was given a jug of beer, and it fermented. He was given another of wine, and it turned bad. Then he took his (13.1) staff and his sandals, as well as his clothes and his weapons, and he started to journey to the Valley of the Pine. He entered the mansion of his young brother and found his young brother lying dead on his bed. He wept when he saw his young brother lying dead. He went to search for the heart of his young brother beneath the pine under which his young brother had slept in the evening.[6] He spent three years searching for it without finding it.

When he began the fourth year, his heart longed to return to Egypt, and he said: "I shall depart tomorrow." So he said in his heart. When it had dawned and another day had come, he went to walk under the pine and spent the day searching for it. When he turned back in the evening, he looked once again in search of it and he found a fruit. He came back with it, and it was the heart of his young brother! He fetched a bowl of cool water, placed it in it, and sat down according to his daily <custom>.

When night had come, (14.1) his heart swallowed the water, and Bata twitched in all his body. He began to look at his elder brother while his heart was in the bowl. Then Anubis, his elder brother, took the bowl of cool water in which was the heart of his young brother and <let> him drink it. Then his heart stood in its place, and he became as he had been. Thereupon they embraced each other, and they talked to one another.

Then Bata said to his elder brother: "Look, I shall change myself into a great bull of beautiful color, of a kind unknown to man, and you shall sit on my back. By the time the sun has risen, we shall be where my wife is, that I may avenge myself. You shall take me to where the king is, for he will do for you everything good. You shall be rewarded with silver and gold for taking me to Pharaoh. For I shall be a great marvel, and they will jubilate over me in the whole land. Then you shall depart to your village."

When it had dawned (15.1) and the next day had come, Bata assumed the form which he had told his elder brother. Then Anubis, his elder brother, sat on his back. At dawn he reached the place where the king was. His majesty was informed about him; he saw him and rejoiced over him very much. He made a great offering for him, saying: "It is a great marvel." And there was jubilation over him in the entire land. Then the king rewarded his elder brother with silver and gold, and he dwelled in his village. The king gave him many people and many things, for Pharaoh loved him very much, more than anyone else in the whole land.

Now when many days had passed, he[7] entered the kitchen, stood where the Lady was, and began to speak to her, saying: "Look, I am yet alive!" She said to him: "Who are you?" He said to her: "I am Bata. I know that when you had the pine felled for Pharaoh, it was on account of me, so that I should not live. Look, (16.1) I am yet alive! I am a bull." The Lady became very frightened because of the speech her husband had made to her. Then he left the kitchen.

His majesty sat down to a day of feasting with her. She poured drink for his majesty, and he was very happy with her. Then she said to his majesty: "Swear to me by God, saying: 'Whatever she will say, I will listen to it!'" He listened to all that she said: "Let me eat of the liver of this bull; for he is good for nothing." So she said to him. He became very vexed over what she had said, and the heart of Pharaoh was very sore.

When it had dawned and another day had come, the king proclaimed a great offering, namely, the sacrifice of the bull. He sent one of the chief royal slaughterers to sacrifice the bull. And when he had been sacrificed and was carried on the shoulders of the men, he shook his neck and let fall two drops of blood beside the two doorposts of his majesty, one on the one side of the great portal of Pharaoh, and the other on the other side. They grew into two (17.1) big Persea trees, each of them outstanding. Then one went to tell his majesty: "Two big Persea trees have grown this night — a great marvel for his majesty — beside the great portal of his majesty." There was jubilation over them in the whole land, and the king made an offenng to them.

Many days after this, his majesty appeared at the audience window of lapis lazuli with a wreath of all kinds of flowers on his neck. Then he <mounted> a golden chariot and came out of the palace to view the Persea trees. Then the Lady came out on a team behind Pharaoh. His majesty sat down under one Persea tree <and the Lady under the other. Then Bata> spoke to his wife: "Ha, you false one! I am Bata! I am alive

6 The phrasing fails to take into account that the pine has been felled.

7 The bull.

⌜in spite of you⌝. I know that when you had <the pine> felled for Pharaoh, it was on account of me. And when I became a bull, you had me killed."

Many days after this, the Lady stood pouring drink for his majesty, and he was happy with her. Then she said to his majesty: "Swear to me by God, saying: 'Whatever she will say, I will listen to it!' So you shall say." He listened (18.1) to all that she said. She said: "Have the two Persea trees felled and made into fine furniture." The king listened to all that she said. After a short while his majesty sent skilled craftsmen. They felled the Persea trees of Pharaoh, and the Queen, the Lady, stood watching it. Then a splinter flew and entered the mouth of the Lady. She swallowed it, and in a moment she became pregnant. The king <ordered> made of them[8] whatever she desired.

Many days after this, she gave birth to a son. One went to tell his majesty: "A son has been born to you." He was fetched, and a nurse and maids were assigned to him. And there was jubilation over him in the whole land. The king sat down to a feast day and held him on his lap. From that hour his majesty loved him very much, and he designated him as (19.1) Viceroy of Kush. And many days after this, his majesty made him crown prince of the whole land.

Now many days after this, when he had spent [many years] as crown prince of the whole land, his majesty flew up to heaven.[9] Then the king[10] said: "Let my great royal officials be brought to me, that I may let them know all that has happened to me." Then his wife was brought to him. He judged her in their presence, and they gave their assent. His elder brother was brought to him, and he made him crown prince of the whole land. He <spent> thirty years as king of Egypt. He departed from life; and his elder brother stood in his place on the day of death.

(Colophon) It has come to a good end under the scribe of the treasury, Kagab, and the scribes of the treasury, Hori and Meremope. Written by the scribe Ennana, the owner of this book. Whoever maligns this book, Thoth will contend with him.

[8] The Persea trees.
[9] I.e., the king died.
[10] Bata.

REFERENCES

Publication: *SPHC* pls. 9-19; Möller 1927 1:1-20; Gardiner 1932b:9-29; Translation: Lefèbvre 1949:137-158; Schott 1950:193-204; Brunner-Traut 1963:28-40; Wente 1973:92-107. Comments: Yoyotte 1952:157-159; Vandier 1962:45-46, 105-106, 114-115; Jesi 1962:276-296; Blumenthal 1973:1-17; von Deines and Westendorf 1961-62 2:194; Lichtheim *AEL* 2:203-211.

THE REPORT OF WENAMUN (1.41)
(P. Moscow 120)

Miriam Lichtheim

In its present state the papyrus consists of two pages with a total of 142 lines. The first page has numerous lacunae, and the end of the story is missing. The papyrus was written at the end of the 20th Dynasty, that is to say, directly after the events which the report relates. Whether or not the report reflects an actual mission, it depicts a true historical situation and a precise moment. It is the third decade of the reign of Ramses XI (1090-1080 BCE), during which the king yielded power to the two men who shared the effective rule of Egypt: Herihor in the south and Smendes in the north. The empire had been lost, and thus so simple an enterprise as the purchase of Lebanese timber could be depicted as a perilous adventure.

What makes the story so remarkable is the skill with which it is told. The Late-Egyptian vernacular is handled with great subtlety. The verbal duels between Wenamum and the prince of Byblos, with their changes of mood and shades of meaning that include irony, represent Egyptian thought and style at their most advanced. What *Sinuhe* is for the Middle Kingdom, *Wenamun* is for the New Kingdom: a literary culmination. The differences between them are not only that the one reflects political power and the other political decline, but more importantly that almost a millennium of human history has gone by, a time during which the peoples of the ancient world lost much of their archaic simplicity. Wenamun stands on the threshold of the first millennium BCE, a millennium in which the modern world began, a world shaped by men and women who were the likes of ourselves.

(1.1) Year 5,[1] fourth month of summer, day 16, the day of departure of Wenamun, the Elder of the Portal of the Temple of Amun, Lord of Thrones-of-the-Two-Lands, to fetch timber for the great noble bark of Amun-Re, King of Gods, which is upon the river and [is called] Amun-user-he.[2]

On the day of my arrival at Tanis, the place where Smendes and Tentamun are,[3] I gave them the dispatches of Amun-Re, King of Gods. They had them read out before them and they said: "I will do, I will do as Amun-Re, King of Gods, our lord has said."

I stayed until the fourth month of summer in Tanis. Then Smendes and Tentamun sent me off with the ship's captain Mengebet,[4] and I went down upon the great sea of Syria in the first month of summer,[5] day 1. I arrived at Dor,[6] a Tjeker town; and Beder, its prince, had fifty loaves, one jug of wine, (1.10) and one ox-haunch brought to me. Then a man of my ship fled after stealing one vessel of gold worth 5 *deben*, four jars of silver worth 20 *deben*, and a bag with 11 *deben* of silver; [total of what he stole]: gold 5 *deben*, silver 31 *deben*.

That morning, when I had risen, I went to where the prince was and said to him: "I have been robbed in your harbor. Now you are the prince of this land, you are the one who controls it. Search for my money! Indeed the money belongs to Amun-Re, King of Gods, the lord of the lands. It belongs to Smendes; it belongs to Herihor, my lord, and (to) the other magnates of Egypt. It belongs to you; it belongs to Weret; it belongs to Mekmer; it belongs to Tiekerbaal, the prince of Byblos!"[7] He said to me: "Are you serious? ⌜Are you joking?⌝ Indeed I do not understand the demand you make to me. If it had been a thief belonging to my land who had gone down to your ship and stolen your money, I would replace it for you from my storehouse, until (1.20) your thief, whatever his name, had been found. But the thief who robbed you, he is yours, he belongs to your ship. Spend a few days here with me; I will search for him."

I stayed nine days moored in his harbor. Then I went to him and said to him: "Look, you have not found my money. [Let me depart] with the ship captains, with those who go to sea."

[The next eight lines are broken. Apparently the prince advises Wenamun to wait some more, but Wenamun departs. He passes Tyre and approaches Byblos. Then he seizes thirty *deben* of silver from a ship he has encountered which belongs to the Tjeker. He tells the owners that he will keep the money until his money has been found. Through this action he incurs the enmity of the Tjeker].

They departed and I celebrated [in] a tent on the shore of the sea in the harbor of Byblos. And [I made a hiding place for] Amun-of-the-Road[8] and placed his possessions in it. Then the prince of Byblos sent to me saying: "[Leave my] harbor!" I sent to him, saying: "Where shall [I go]? ------. If [you have a ship to carry me], let me be taken back to Egypt." I spent twenty-nine days in his harbor, and he spent time sending to me daily to say: "Leave my harbor!"

Now while he was offering to his gods, the god took hold of a young man [of] his young men and put him in a trance. He said to him:[9] "Bring [the] god up! Bring the envoy who is carrying him! (1.40) It is Amun who sent him. It is he who made him come!" Now it was while the entranced one was entranced that night that I had found a ship headed for Egypt. I had loaded all my belongings into it and was watching for the darkness, saying: "When it descends I will load the god so that no other eye shall see him."

Then the harbor master came to me, saying: "Wait until morning, says the prince!" I said to him: "Was it not you who daily took time to come to me, saying: 'Leave my harbor'? Do you now say: 'Wait this night,' in order to let the ship that I found depart, and then you will come to say: 'Go away'?" He went and told it to the prince. Then the prince sent to the captain of the ship, saying: "Wait until morning, says the prince."

When morning came, he sent and brought me up, while the god rested in the tent where he was on the shore of the sea. I found him seated in his

[1] The year date is reckoned by the "Renaissance Era" introduced by Herihor in the 19th regnal year of Ramses XI. The month dates given for the beginning of Wenamun's journey are garbled and require emendation. This first date might be emended to "second month of summer."

[2] The name of the great processional bark of Amun of Thebes.

[3] Smendes, the ruler of Tanis, subsequently became the first king of the 21st Dyn. The fact that, in the tale, his wife Tentamun is always mentioned together with him suggests that she was an important person, perhaps a Ramesside princess, who shared the rule with her husband.

[4] The captain is a Syrian, and so apparently is the crew; but the ship is in the service of Egypt.

[5] Emend to: "first month of the inundation."

[6] A port town on the coast of northern Palestine, controlled by the Tjeker, a people belonging to the "sea peoples" who, having failed to invade Egypt, had settled on the Palestinian coast. Concerning Dor, see now Stern 1994.

[7] I.e., the stolen money was intended for the persons with whom Wenamun expected to do business.

[8] The statuette which represented Amun in his aspect of protector of travelers.

[9] I.e., the man in a trance says to the prince.

upper chamber with his back against a window, and the waves of the great sea of Syria broke behind (1.50) his head. I said to him: "Blessings of Amun!" He said to me: "How long is it to this day since you came from the place where Amun is?" I said to him: "Five whole months till now." He said to me: "If you are right, where is the dispatch of Amun that was in your hand? Where is the letter of the High Priest of Amun that was in your hand?" I said to him: "I gave them to Smendes and Tentamun." Then he became very angry and said to me: "Now then, dispatches, letters you have none. Where is the ship of pinewood[10] that Smendes gave you? Where is its Syrian crew? Did he not entrust you to this foreign ship's captain in order to have him kill you and have them throw you into the sea? From whom would one then seek the god? And you, from whom would one seek you?" So he said to me.

I said to him: "Is it not an Egyptian ship? Those who sail under Smendes are Egyptian crews. He has no Syrian crews."[11] He said to me: "Are there not twenty ships here in my harbor that do business with Smendes? As for Sidon, (2.1) that other (place) you passed, are there not another fifty ships there that do business with Werekter and haul to his house?"

I was silent in this great moment. Then he spoke to me, saying: "On what business have you come?" I said to him: "I have come in quest of timber for the great noble bark of Amun-Re, King of Gods. What your father did, what the father of your father did, you too will do it." So I said to him. He said to me: "True, they did it. If you pay me for doing it, I will do it. My relations carried out this business after Pharaoh had sent six ships laden with the goods of Egypt, and they had been unloaded into their storehouses. You, what have you brought for me?"

He had the daybook of his forefathers brought and had it read before me. They found entered in his book a thousand *deben* of silver and all sorts of things. (2.10) He said to me: "If the ruler of Egypt were the lord of what is mine and I were his servant, he would not have sent silver and gold to say: 'Carry out the business of Amun.' It was not a royal gift that they gave to my father! I too, I am not your servant, nor am I the servant of him who sent you! If I shout aloud to the Lebanon, the sky opens and the logs lie here on the shore of the sea! Give me the sails you brought to move your ships, loaded with logs for <Egypt>! Give me the ropes you brought [to lash the pines] that I am to fell in order to make them for you ---. ------ that I am to make for you for the sails of your ships; or the yards may be too heavy and may break, and you may die <in> the midst of the sea. For Amun makes thunder in the sky ever since he placed Seth beside him![12] Indeed, Amun has (2.20) founded all the lands. He founded them after having first founded the land of Egypt from which you have come. Thus craftsmanship came from it in order to reach the place where I am! Thus learning came from it in order to reach the place where I am![13] What are these foolish travels they made you do?"

I said to him: "Wrong! These are not foolish travels that I am doing. There is no ship on the river that does not belong to Amun. His is the sea and his the Lebanon of which you say, 'It is mine.' It is a growing ground for Amun-user-he, the lord of every ship. Truly, it was Amun-Re, King of Gods, who said to Herihor, my master: 'Send me!' And he made me come with this great god. But look, you have let this great god spend these twenty-nine days moored in your harbor. Did you not know that he was here? Is he not he who he was? You are prepared to haggle over the Lebanon with Amun, its lord? As to your saying, the former kings sent silver and gold: If they had owned life and health, they would not have sent these things. (2.30) It was in place of life and health that they sent these things to your fathers! But Amun-Re, King of Gods, he is the lord of life and health, and he was the lord of your fathers! They passed their lifetimes offering to Amun. You too, you are the servant of Amun!

If you will say 'I will do' to Amun, and will carry out business, you will live, you will prosper, you will be healthy; you will be beneficent to your whole land and your people. Do not desire what belongs to Amun-Re, King of Gods! Indeed, a lion loves his possessions! Have your scribe brought to me that I may send him to Smendes and Tentamun, the pillars Amun has set up for the north of his land; and they will send all that is needed. I will send him to them, saying: 'Have it brought until I return to the south; then I shall refund you all your expenses.'"[14] So I said to him.

[10] Or, "for (the transport of) the pine wood."

[11] Wenamun claims that Syrian crews who sail for Egypt are Egyptian crews.

[12] Seth was equated with the Syrian Baal and both were storm gods.

[13] The gist of the prince's speech is that, though Egypt was created by Amun before all other lands and is thus the motherland of all the arts, the civilization of Syria is now fully grown and no longer dependent on Egypt.

[14] I.e., after Wenamun has returned to Thebes, his master Herihor will reimburse Smendes and Tentamun.

He placed my letter in the hand of his messenger; and he loaded the keel, the prow-piece, and the stern-piece, together with four other hewn logs, seven in all, and sent them to Egypt. His messenger who had gone to Egypt returned to me in Syria in the first month of winter, Smendes and Tentamun having sent: (2.40) four jars and one *kakmen*-vessel of gold; five jars of silver; ten garments of royal linen; ten *ḫrd*-garments[15] of fine linen; five hundred smooth linen mats; five hundred ox-hides; five hundred ropes; twenty sacks of lentils; and thirty baskets of fish. And she had sent to me:[16] five garments of fine linen; five *ḫrd*-garments of fine linen; one sack of lentils; and five baskets of fish.

The prince rejoiced. He assigned three hundred men and three hundred oxen, and he set supervisors over them to have them fell the timbers. They were felled and they lay there during the winter. In the third month of summer they dragged them to the shore of the sea. The prince came out and stood by them, and he sent to me, saying: "Come!" Now when I had been brought into his presence, the shadow of his sunshade fell on me. Then Penamun, a butler of his,[17] intervened, saying: "The shadow of Pharaoh, your lord, has fallen upon you." And he was angry with him and said: "Leave him alone."

As I stood before him, he addressed me, saying: "Look, the business my fathers did in the past, I have done it, although you did not do for me what your fathers did for mine. Look, the last of your timber has arrived and is ready. Do as I wish, and come to load it. For has it not been given to you? (2.50) Do not come to look at the terror of the sea. For if you look at the terror of the sea, you will see my own! Indeed, I have not done to you what was done to the envoys of Khaemwese,[18] after they had spent seventeen years in this land. They died on the spot." And he said to his butler: "Take him to see the tomb where they lie."

I said to him: "Do not make me see it. As for Khaemwese, the envoys he sent you were men and he himself was a man. You have not here one of his envoys, though you say: 'Go and see your companions.' Should you not rejoice and have a stela [made] for yourself, and say on it: 'Amun-Re, King of Gods, sent me Amun-of-the-Road, his envoy, together with Wenamun, his human envoy, in quest of timber for the great noble bark of Amun-Re, King of Gods. I felled it; I loaded it; I supplied my ships and my crews. I let them reach Egypt so as to beg for me from Amun fifty years of life over and above my allotted fate.' And if it comes to pass that in another day an envoy comes from the land of Egypt who knows writing and he reads out your name on the stela, you will receive water of the west like the gods who are (2.60) there."

He said to me: "A great speech of admonition is what you have said to me."[19] I said to him: "As to the many <things> you have said to me: if I reach the place where the High Priest of Amun is and he sees your accomplishment, it is your accomplishment that will draw profit to you."

I went off to the shore of the sea, to where the logs were lying. And I saw eleven ships that had come in from the sea and belonged to the Tjeker (who were) saying: "Arrest him! Let no ship of his leave for the land of Egypt!" Then I sat down and wept. And the secretary of the prince came out to me and said to me: "What is it?" I said to him: "Do you not see the migrant birds going down to Egypt a second time? Look at them traveling to the cool water![20] Until when shall I be left here? For do you not see those who have come to arrest me?"

He went and told it to the prince. And the prince began to weep on account of the words said to him, for they were painful. He sent his secretary out to me, bringing me two jugs of wine and a sheep. And he sent me Tentne, an Egyptian songstress who was with him, saying: "Sing for him! Do not let his heart be anxious." And he sent to me, (2.70) saying: "Eat, drink; do not let your heart be anxious. You shall hear what I will say tomorrow."

When morning came, he had his assembly summoned. He stood in their midst and said to the Tjeker: "What have you come for?" They said to him: "We have come after the blasted[21] ships that you are sending to Egypt with our enemy." He said to them: "I cannot arrest the envoy of Amun in my country. Let me send him off, and you go

[15] The nature of *ḫrd* is not known. Černý (1958:208-209) suggested the meanings "awning," and "veil." To my knowledge Eg. art never depicts the wearing of veils.

[16] Tentamun had sent a personal gift to Wenamun.

[17] An Eg. in the service of the prince of Byblos.

[18] We do not know to whom the prince is referring. A vizier Khaemwese served under Ramses IX.

[19] This reply of the prince seems to be ironic.

[20] I.e., Wenamun has now been abroad for more than a year and is thus witnessing for the second time the annual flight to Egypt of migratory birds.

[21] It looks as if the verb *ḳnḳn*, "to beat," is here used idiomatically as a curse word. Cf. the name *ḳnḳn-tꜣ* given to a lonely foreign place in P. Anastasi IV.12,6 (Gardiner 1937:48).

after him to arrest him."

He had me board and sent me off from the harbor of the sea. And the wind drove me to the land of Alašiya.[22] Then the town's people came out against me to kill me. But I forced my way through them to where Hatiba, the princess of the town was. I met her coming from one of her houses to enter another. I saluted her and said to the people who stood around her: "Is there not one among you who understands Egyptian?" And one among them said: "I understand it." I said to him: "Tell my lady that I have heard it said as far away as Thebes, the place where Amun is: 'If wrong is done in every town, in the land of Alašiya right is done.' Now is wrong done here too every day?"

She said: "What is it (2.80) you have said?" I said to her: "If the sea rages and the wind drives me to the land where you are, will you let me be received so as to kill me, though I am the envoy of Amun? Look, as for me, they would search for me till the end of time. As for this crew of the prince of Byblos, whom they seek to kill, will not their lord find ten crews of yours and kill them also?" She had the people summoned and they were reprimanded. She said to me: "Spend the night ______[23]

[22] Alašiya is thought to be Cyprus, but the identification is not certain.

[23] The remainder of the report is lost.

REFERENCES

Publication: Golenishchev 1899:74-102; Gardiner 1932b:61-76; Korostovtsev 1960. Translation: Erman 1900:1-14; 1927:174-185; Lefebvre 1949:204-220; *ANET* 25-29; Gardiner 1961:306-313; Edel 1968:41-48; Wente 1973:142-155; Lichtheim *AEL* 2:224-230. Comments: Nims 1968:161-164.

2. "PROPHECY"

THE ADMONITIONS OF AN EGYPTIAN SAGE: THE ADMONITIONS OF IPUWER (1.42)

Nili Shupak

The "Admonitions" was composed during the First Intermediate period (c.a. 2000 BCE) or the late Middle Kingdom.[1] The text is preserved on Papyrus Leiden 344, dating to the 18th or 19th Dynasty (1580-1200 BCE).

The original composition contained a narrative frame which has been lost, and which established the setting of the utterances of the sage as a council at the royal court, in a manner similar to that of the "Prophecies of Neferti" (text 1.45 below).

The speeches of the sage are arranged in six poems, each of which opens with an identical formula,[2] although the poems are not continuous with regard to content.

A considerable portion of this work is concerned with an account of ordeals and calamities of the times. The second part of the composition consists of exhortations to the people to repent by destroying the enemy and fulfilling their religious obligations. The climax of the work is in the third part, which portrays an ideal monarch who will rehabilitate the country,[3] and concludes by pinning the blame for the decline into evil days on an unnamed regnant king[4] and presenting the fortunate conditions in store for Egypt once the nation is redeemed. The composition closes with an obscure passage which speaks of an aged monarch, and may allude to actual historical circumstances.

The work, which is clearly a document of social criticism and contains some sections referring to events in the future,[5] has common features with the biblical prophecy.[6] Note: l.p.h. = "life, prosperity, health!" — the traditional blessing over the king.

[1] For a review of the various scholarly opinions concerning the date of "The Admonitions" see: Barta 1974:21. Some scholars, however, believe that this text is a pure literary fiction and does not relate to any historical situation; see: Lichtheim *AEL* 1:149-150; Hornung 1990:190.

[2] The same device is used in "The Eloquent Peasant" and "The Dispute between a Man and His *Ba*"; see: Shupak 1989-1990, Table II, 38-39, and text 1.43 below.

[3] For an alternative explanation see n. 34, below.

[4] It has been proposed that "The Admonitions" of Ipuwer are addressed to Pepi II, one of the kings of the Sixth Dynasty.

[5] Scholarly opinion is divided as to whether these sections which describe the redemption of the land contain a prediction of things to come or merely express a yearning for better days.

[6] On the question of the existence of prophecy in the biblical sense in Ancient Egypt see: Shupak 1989-1990.

Calamities of the Times (1.1-10.6)

Introduction (1.1-1.9)

(1.1) The doorkeepers say: "Let us go and plunder" ...,
The washerman refuses to carry his load [...],
The bird [-catchers] have drawn up in line of battle,
[The inhabitants] of the Delta marshes carry shields ...,
A man looks upon his son as his enemy ...,
(1.8) The virtuous man goes in mourning because of what has happened in the land ...
(1.9) Foreigners[7] have become Egyptians[8] everywhere.

First Poem (Introduction Formula — iw ms) (1.9-6.14)

(1.9) Indeed, the face is pale,
(1.10) What the ancestors foretold has happened [...].[9]
Indeed [...] the land is full of gangs,
A man goes to plough with his shield ...
Indeed, the Nile overflows, none plough for it;
Everyone says: "We do not know what has happened throughout the land."
(2.4) Indeed, women are barren, and none conceive,
Khnum[10] does not create because of the condition of the land,
(2.4-2.5) Indeed, poor men have become owners of wealth,
He who could not make for himself sandals owns riches.[11]
(2.6-7) Indeed, many dead are buried in the river,
The stream is a grave, and the tomb has become a stream.
(2.7-2.8) Indeed, the noblemen are in mourning and the poor man is full of joy,
Every town says: "Let us expel the powerful among us."
Indeed, men are like ibises; dirt is throughout the land,
There is none indeed whose clothes are white at this time.

a Exod 7:14-25; Pss 78:44; 105:29

Indeed, the land turns around like a potter's wheel,
The robber is a possessor of riches and [the rich man has become (?)] a plunderer ...
(2.10) Indeed, the river is blood, yet one drinks from it,[a]
Men shrink from people and thirst after water.
Indeed, gates, columns and walls are burning,
While the hall of the palace l.p.h. stands firm and endures ...
(2.12-2.13) Indeed, crocodiles are glutted on their catch,
People go to them of their own will ...
(2.14) Indeed, the well born man ... passes without being recognized,
The child of his lady has become the son of his maid.
(3.1) Indeed, the desert is throughout the land,
The nomes are laid waste,
Foreign tribes[12] come into Egypt ...
(3.6) Indeed, the builders [of pyramids have become] farmers of fields,
Those who were in the sacred bark are yoked [to it].[13]
None, indeed, sail northward to (3.7) Byblos[14] today,
What shall we do for cedar trees for our mummies?
The priests are buried with their produce,
The [chiefs] are embalmed with their oil,
As far as (3.9) Crete,[14] they come no more,
Gold is lacking ...
(3.10-3.13) Indeed, Elephantine and Thines (?) [the dominion of] Upper Egypt are not taxed because of civil war.
Lacking are grain, charcoal ...
To what purpose is a treasure-house without its revenues?
Glad indeed is the heart of the king, when gifts come to him.
Look, every foreign country [says?]: "This is our water![15] This is our fortune!"
What shall we do about it? All is ruin!

[7] Eg. *ḫ*ꜣ*styw*, a nisbe adjective derived from *ḫ*ꜣ*st* "foreign country," used here as term for Asiatics; cf. line 4.5 and n. 19, below.

[8] Lit., "have become people."

[9] The contemporary disasters are represented as a fulfilment of what was foretold (*sr*) by the ancestors. *Sr*, foretelling, also appears in connection with the ancestors in "The Instructions Addressed to Merikare" 69-71. On the relationship between prediction and the genre of speculative wisdom literature see: Shupak 1989-1990:25-28 and cf. also "The Prophecies of Neferti" notes 5, 16; see above, p. 63.

[10] Cf. 5.7.

[11] The stylistic device appearing here, i.e., series of contrasts to highlight the absurdity of the current state of affairs — a reversed social order, is a dominant feature in "The Admonitions;" cf. 2.4-2.8; 2.14; 3.6; 7.8-8.5. This device is common in the Eg. as well as the biblical wisdom literature; cf. "The Eloquent Peasant" n. 32 and "The Prophecies of Neferti" n. 29.

[12] Lit., "bowmen" Eg. *pḏtyw*. The word is often used in "The Admonitions" to denote the Asiatics cf. 14.13 and also 2.2; 15.1 (untranslated); see also n. 19, below.

[13] The passage probably refers to the change in occupation of the funerary professionals who, owing to lack of needed materials, turned to agriculture; see Goedicke 1967:93.

[14] This section (3.6-3.9) relates to a break in trade between Egypt and her significant commercial partners, Byblos and Crete. Byblos supplied Egypt with timber from early dynastic times; strong cultural contacts between Egypt and Crete existed during the Hyksos times and the 18th Dynasty, when goods such as textiles and carpets were imported to Egypt from the Aegean.

[15] Obscure phrase which may have here a figurative sense, i.e., "This is our fate"; see: Faulkner 1964:26; Lichtheim *AEL* 1:161 n. 7.

Indeed, merriment has perished, is [no longer] made,
There is groaning throughout the land mingled with laments ...
(4.2-4.3) Indeed, great and small [say] "I wish I were dead,"
Little children say "He should not have caused [me] to live."[16] [b]
Indeed, the children of princes are dashed against walls,
And the infants[17] are laid on the high ground.
Indeed, those who were in the place of embalming are laid on high ground,
And the secrets of the embalmers are thrown away ...
(4.5) Indeed, the whole Delta will no longer be hidden,[18]
Lower Egypt will trust trodden roads.
What shall one do? ...
Behold, it is in the hands of those who do not know it, like those who know it,
The foreigners are skilled in the crafts of the Delta ...[19]
Indeed, all maid servants are rude in their tongue,
When their mistress speaks it is irksome to the servants ...

(5.2-5.3) Indeed, princes are hungry and perish,
Servants are served ...
Indeed, the hot-tempered man says: "If I knew where god is, then I would serve him."
Indeed, [justice][20] is throughout (5.4) the land in its name,
but what they (men) do in appealing to it, is wrong ...
Indeed, all animals, their hearts weep,
Cattle moan because of the state of the land.
Indeed, the children of princes are dashed against walls,
The infants are laid on the high ground,
(5.7) Khnum groans in weariness ...
(5.9-5.11) Indeed, a slave (?) [has the power?] throughout the land,

b Job 3:3ff., 20-22; 10:18-19; 13:15; 14:13; 17:13-14

The strong man sends to all people.[21]
A man strikes his maternal brother —
What has been done?
Indeed, the ways are (blocked), the roads are watched,
Men sit in the bushes, until the night traveller comes, in order to plunder his load.
What is upon him is taken away;
He is thrashed with blows of a stick and criminally slain.

Indeed, perished is what yesterday was seen ...
If only this were the end of men,
No conceiving, no birth,
Then the land would be quiet of noise, and tumult be no more.
Indeed [men eat] herbs and wash (them) down with water,
No seeds nor herbs are found for the birds ...
(6.5-6.6) Indeed, the writings of the private council-chamber[22] are taken away,
Laid bare are the secrets which were in it ...
(6.7-6.8) Indeed, (public) offices are opened and their records are taken,
The serf becomes lord of serfs. (?)
Indeed, [scribes?] are killed and their writings stolen,
Woe is me because of the misery of this time!
Indeed, the scribes of the land-register — their writings are destroyed,
The grain of Egypt is common[23] property.
Indeed, the laws of the council-chamber are thrown out,
Men walk on them in public places,
Beggars break them up in the streets.
Indeed, the beggar has attained the state of the Nine Gods,[24]
The instructions of the House of the Thirty[25] are divulged.
(6.12) Indeed, the great council chamber is a public resort,
Beggars come and go in the Great Houses.[26]
Indeed, the children of princes are cast out in the streets,

[16] The attitude of despair and weariness with life which is echoed in the utterances of Ipuwer (cf. 2.12-2.13 above) is also expressed in "The Dispute between a Man and His *Ba*" (see *COS* 3) where the hero longs for death (cf. 20.21); and Job persistently wishes for death throughout his bewailings, cf. Scripture References *b*.

[17] Lit., "Children of neck," i.e., infants who when carried by their parents clasp them round the neck.

[18] Alternative reading: "will not be seen". Eg. *dgi* has double meaning, "to hide" and "to see." Here both senses are appropriate.

[19] The picture drawn in this passage of the Delta overflowing with Asiatics is similar to that appearing in other texts relating to the second millennium BCE (cf. "The Prophecies of Neferti" n. 8). It seems that the Asiatics have adapted the Eg. culture and replaced the Egyptians in key positions; see Van Seters 1964:21.

[20] On "justice" (*m*ꜣ*ꜥt*) and its antonym "wrong" (*isft*), see "The Eloquent Peasant" n. 27 (p. 100, below).

[21] This sentence appears with a slight difference in "The Dispute between a Man and His *Ba*" 107 (see *COS* 3).

[22] Lines 6.5-6.12 may refer to the activity of the *ḫnrt*, the Great Prison at Thebes, which was the center for the administration of justice; see: Van Seters 1964:18.

[23] Lit., "I go get it."

[24] Eg. *Psḏt*.

[25] The law court in Upper Egypt consisted of thirty judges who also functioned as district chiefs.

[26] The six "Great Houses," already known from the Old Kingdom, were the law courts to which all the Eg. judges belonged.

The wise man says: "Yes", the fool says: "No"
And it is pleasing to him who knows nothing about it.[27]

Second Poem (Introduction Formula — mṯn, mṯn is) (7.1-9.7)

(7.1) Behold, the fire has risen high,
Its burning goes forth against the enemies of the land.
Behold, things have been done that have not happened for a long time,
The King has been disposed of by beggars.
Behold, he who was buried like a falcon ... has no bier,
What the pyramid concealed has become empty.
Behold, it has befallen that the land is deprived of kingship by a few people who ignore the custom,
Behold, men have fallen into rebellion against the Uraeus.[28]

The [...] of Re, who pacifies the Two Lands,
(7.4) Behold, the secrets of the land, whose limits are unknown, are divulged,
The Residence is thrown down in a minute ...
(7.5) Behold, the Ḳrḥt serpent[29] is taken from his hole,
The secrets of Egypt's kings are bared ...
(7.8) Behold, the possessors of tombs are cast on high ground,
He who could not make a grave is [possessor] of a treasury.
Behold, the change among the people:
He who could not build a room for himself is (now) a possessor of walls ...
Behold, noble ladies are on rafts,
Magnates are in the workhouse;
He who could not even sleep on a wall is (now) possessor of a bed ...
(7.11-7.12) Behold, the possessors of robes are (now) in rags,
He who never wove for himself is (now) the possessor of fine linen.
Behold, he who never built for himself a boat is (now) the possessor of ships,
He who possessed the same looks at them, (but) they are not his ...
(8.1) Behold, he who had no property is (now) a possessor of wealth,
The magnate sings his praise.
Behold, the poor of the land have become rich,
The possessor of property has become one who has nothing ...
Behold, he whose hair had fallen out and lacked oil,
Has become a possessor of jars of sweet myrrh.
(8.5) Behold, she who had no box is a possessor of a coffer,
She who looked at her face in the water is possessor of a mirror.
Behold, a man is happy when he eats his food,
Consume your goods in gladness,
Without being hindered by anybody;
It is good for a man to eat his food,
God commands it for him whom he favours ...
(9.2) Behold, all the offices, they are not in their (right) place,
Like a herd running at random without its herdsman,[30]
Behold, cattle stray and there is none to collect them ...
(9.3) Behold, a man is slain beside his brother ...
(9.5) Behold, he who had no dependents (?) is (now) a lord of serfs,
He who was a [magnate] does commission himself ...

Third Poem (Introduction Formula — ḥḏ) (9.8-10.6)

(9.8) Destroyed is [...] in that time ...
Destroyed is [...]
Their food [is taken?] from them ...
(10.3) Lower Egypt weeps,
The storehouse of the king is the common property of everyone;
The entire palace l.p.h. is without its revenues:
To it belong wheat and barley, fowl and fish
To it belong white cloth and fine linen, copper and oil ...

Exhortations (10.6-11.11)

Fourth Poem (Introduction Formula: ḥḏ) (10.6-10.12)

Destroy the enemies of the noble Residence,
Splendid of magistrates ...
(10.7) Destroy the enemies of the noble Residence ...
(10.8) [Destroy the enemies] of the formerly noble Residence,
Manifold of laws ...

Fifth Poem (Introduction Formula: sḫ͗) (10.12-11.10)

Remember to immerse [...][31]
Him who is in pain when (?) he is sick in his body ...

[27] This sentence also appears in "The Instruction of Amenemhet" (text 1.36 above) XIV b-c.
[28] Eg. *iʿrt*, symbol of Eg. kingship.
[29] The Ḳrḥt serpent was a guardian spirit.
[30] See note 37, below.
[31] According to a different view the following section (10.12ff.) does not deal with a call for pious conduct but rather recalls the golden past, when the right order prevailed see: *ANET* 443 n. 33 and Lichtheim *AEL* 1:162 n. 23.

Remember to ... to fumigate with incense,
To offer water in a jar in the early morning.
(11.1-11.2) Remember [to bring] the fatted *r* geese, *trp* geese and *st* geese,
To offer offerings to the gods.
Remember to chew natron and to prepare white bread,
A man (should do it) on the day of wetting the head.[32]
(11.3-11.4) Remember to erect flagstaffs and to carve stelae,
The priest cleansing the shrines,
The temple being plastered (white) like milk.
Remember to make pleasant the perfume of the sanctuary,[33]
To set up the bread-offerings.
Remember to observe regulations, to adjust dates,
To remove him who enters the priestly office with impure body, for to do so is wrong ...
(11.6) Remember to slaughter oxen ...
Remember to come forth pure ...

Redemption (11.11-13.9)

Criticism of the Sun-God and the Description of the Ideal Monarch (11.11-12.11)[34]

(11.11) Lack of people ... Re who commands [...] worshipping him ...
Behold, why does he see (11.13) to fashion (men)?
The timid man is not distinguished from the violent one.[35]
He has brought coolness upon the heat,[36]
(12.1) Men say: "He is the herdsman of all, and there is no evil in his heart."
His herds are few (but) he spends a day collecting them,[37] [c]
(12.2) (Because) fire is in their heart.
Would that he had perceived their nature in the first generation,
Then he would have smitten the evil,
He would have stretched out his arm against it,
He would have destroyed (12.3) their seed and their heirs,
While the people still desired to give birth.
Sadness overwhelms, misery is everywhere ...
(12.4) Combat has gone forth,
(12.5) The redresser of evil is one who commits it.
There is no pilot in their hour,
Where is he today?
Is he asleep?[d] Behold (12.6), his power is not seen ...

Criticism of the King (12.11-13.9)

Authority, Knowledge and Truth[38] are with you,
Yet confusion is what you set throughout the land,
And the noise of tumult.
Behold, one fights against another,
For men obey[39] what you have commanded.
If three men travel (12.14) on the road,
They are found to be only two,
For the many kill the few.
Does a herdsman desire death?
Then may you command it done ...
It is your doing that brought those things to pass,
You have told lies.
The land is weed which destroys men,
None is named among the living.
All these years are strife,
A man is murdered on his roof top ...
(13.5) O that you could taste something of the misery of it,
Then you would say ...

The Happy Days (Contrasted with the Contemporary Adversities) (13.9-16.1)

Sixth Poem (Introduction Formula: iw ir.f ḥmw nfr)

[It is indeed good] when ships sail upstream ...

c Jer 3:15; 23:1-4; Ezek 34; 37:24; Mic 5:3-5; Zech 9:16

d 1 Kgs 18;27; Ps 44:24; 121:4

[32] Moistening the head, like cleansing the mouth with natron, were probably some kind of purifactory rites.

[33] Lit., "the horizon."

[34] The following section is very problematic and has been discussed at length in research. Scholarly opinion is divided as to whether we are dealing here with criticism directed to god Re, (see Gardiner 1909b:13-14, 79-80; Barta 1974:22-29; Lichtheim *AEL* 1:162 n. 24) or with a description of an ideal redeemer (see *ANET* 443 n. 36).

The translation given here assumes that the main part of the section is indeed addressed to Re and goes back to primeval times, since some of the details presented here (see 11.11-11.13; 12.2-3) accord with the famous myth about the "Destruction of Mankind" (text 1.25 above). But some lines (11.13: "He has ... heat"; 12.1; 12.5: "There is no pilot ..."; 12.6) undoubtedly refer to the image of the redeemer king, a motif characteristic of this literary genre appearing also in "The Prophecies of Neferti" (58-62); see: Shupak 1989-1990:31-34 and text 1.45.

[35] Re is rebuked for his passive behaviour: He did not discern the bad character of the human beings so he is responsible for its existence. The idea that evil in man's nature is not the work of the creator accords with *CT* 1130 where the god declares: "I made every man equal to his fellow and I forbade them to do wrong but their hearts disobeyed."

[36] Coolness of temperament is a quality that is mentioned repeatedly in the wisdom texts as well as the autobiographical and king's court writings. The ideal king is he who cools the heat (cf. "Seḥetep-ib-Ra" St 3.5). Heat as a metaphor for anger and hot temper reappears in 12.2.

[37] The image of the ruler as herdsman of his people is common in the literature of the Ancient Near East. In relation to the god Re it comes also in "The Instructions Addressed to Merikare" (text 1.35, above) 130. For further examples see Van Seters 1964:19; for biblical parallels see: Scripture References *c*.

[38] Ḥu, Sia and Maat are the three divine attributes in the possession of the king. In the following section Ipuwer rebukes the king and blames him for being the cause of the calamities and miseries that have fallen on the land. Since the three attributes mentioned above and the title "herdsman" may also refer to the god Re, some scholars believe that he is the one addressed here. See: Fecht 1972:87-88; Otto 1951:6.

[39] Lit., "imitate." *Sni* has double meaning "to imitate," "copy" and "to disobey," "go beyond"; cf. Shupak 1993:80-81. Since in the fol-

(13.10) It is indeed good when [...]
[It is indeed] good when the net is drawn,
And birds are tied up [...] ...
It is indeed good when the hands of men build pyramids,
(13.13) Ponds are dug and orchards made for the gods.
It is indeed good when people are drunk,
When they drink *myt* and their hearts are glad ...
It is indeed good when shouting is in (men's) mouths ...
(14.1) It is indeed good, when beds are made ready,
The head-rests of magistrates are safely secured ...
The door is shut upon him who slept in the bushes,
(14.10) [...] [in their midst] like Asiatics ...[40]
None are found who would stand up to protect them ...
Every man fights for his sister and to save his own skin.
(14.11) Is it the Nubians? Then we will protect ourselves!
Warriors are made many in order to repel foreigners;[41]
Is it the Libyans? Then we will turn them back!
The Medjai are pleased with Egypt.
How does it come that every man kills his brother?
The troops (15.1) we raised for ourselves have become foreigners and taken to ravaging,
What has come to pass has caused the Asiatics to know the state of the land ...

(15.13) What Ipuwer said when he answered the majesty of the All-Lord:[42]
[...] all herds ...
You have done what pleases their heart,
You have nourished the people among them,
Yet, they cover (16.1) their faces in fear of tomorrow.

Obscure Proverb (16.1-17.2)
(16.1) There was an old man who was about to die,
While his son was a child without knowledge;
He has not yet opened his mouth to speak to you,
When you seize and kill him (?)

lowing lines the stress is laid on the king's guilt and he is blamed as well for telling lies, the first sense of *sni* seems to be more appropriate.

[40] Different poeple are listed here among Egypt's enemies: The Asiatics (Eg. *Styw*) in the north (cf. "The Prophecies of Neferti" 18.32-33, 63.66ff. and ibid. n. 8.), the Nubians (Eg. *Nḥsyw*) in the south, and the Libyans (Eg. *Ṯmḥyw)* in the west. The Medjai (Eg. *Mḏ*ᵓ*yw)* whose home was the Nubian western steppe are distinct here from the other Nubian people since, being regimented as professional soldiers and desert police, they were in friendly contact with Egypt. Cf. Van Seters 1964:14-15. For the historical and political setting of this section see ibid., 14-16, 22.

[41] See note 12, above.

[42] Here for the first time appears the name of the speaker, a sage called Ipuwer. The words of Ipuwer are represented as a reply to the king whose speech may have preceded in the original text, but is not to be found in the present manuscript. For a different opinion, assuming that relics of the king's words are to be found in 14.10ff., see: Lichtheim *AEL* 1:162 n. 29.

REFERENCES

Barta 1974:19-33; Faulkner 1964:24-36; Fecht 1972; Gardiner 1909; Goedicke 1967:93-95; Hornung 1990:83-100, 190-191; Lichtheim *AEL* 1:149-163; Otto 1951; Shupak 1989-90:1-40; 1993; Van Seters 1964:13-23; Westendorf 1973:41-44; *ANET* 441-444.

THE ELOQUENT PEASANT (1.43)

Nili Shupak

This work was composed during the Middle Kingdom (in the 12th or 13th Dynasty)[1] and has been preserved on four papyri of that time. Three of these, known as B1 and B2 and R, are now in Berlin, and the fourth, Pap. Butler, is in London.

The composition, which pertains to the class of speculative wisdom literature, contains a narrative frame and text set out in verse form. This structure is common to works composed during that period, such as "The Admonitions of an Egyptian Sage," "The Prophecies of Neferti," "The Dispute between a Man and his *Ba*." The frame narrates the circumstances that gave rise to the peasant's complaint, i.e., his having been robbed of his property. The body of work consists of nine complaints that the peasant addresses to the high steward Rensi, son of Meru. These are spoken in an eloquent rhetorical style in which images and proverbs are employed, as well as word plays and assonances.

The grievances that the peasant puts to the judge contain no more than allusions to his private misery and are primarily concerned with the broad issue of doing justice. This is, therefore, essentially a moral document which

[1] This date of composition was recently demonstrated by Berlev 1987; see also Parkinson 1991a.

is at once an earnest appeal for the preservation of social order and justice (*mꜣꜥt*) and a condemnation of the corruption of the times.

Frame-Story: Introduction (R1-41)
There was a man Khu-n-Anup was his name. A peasant of Salt-Field[2] was he. He had a wife. [M]ryt was her name.

This peasant said to his wife: "Behold, I am going down to Egypt to bring provisions from there for my children. Go and measure for me the barley (4) which is in the storehouse, the (barley) remaining from [yesterday]."[3] Then he measured [twenty]-six gallons of barley. Then this peasant said to his wife: "Behold, (I give) you twenty gallons of grain for provisions for you and your children and you will make for me six gallons into bread and beer for every day (on which) [I will live]."[4]

(7) This peasant went down to Egypt after he had loaded his donkeys with vines, rushes, natron, salt, wood ... panther skins, wolf hides ... (35) full (measure) of all the good products of Salt-Field.

This peasant went south toward Herakleopolis[5] and he reached the region of Per-fefi north of Medenit.[6]

He met a man there standing on the river bank, Nemty-nakht was his name. He was son of a man whose name was Isri and he was a subordinate of the high steward, Rensi, son of Meru.

Frame-Story (cont.): The Robbery (R 42-60; B1 1-30)
Then this Nemty-nakht said, when he saw this peasant's donkeys which were tempting to his heart, "Would that I had some effective idol[7] that I might steal the goods of this peasant with it!" Now the house of Nemty-nakht was at the beginning of a path[8] which was narrow, not so wide as to exceed the width of a loin-cloth. One side of it was under water; the other side of it was under barley. And then this Nemty-nakht said to his servant "Go and bring me a cloth[9] from my house." It was brought to him immediately. Then he spread it out on the beginning of the path so that its fringe was on the water and its hem on the barley.

This peasant came along the public road.[10] Then this Nemty-nakht said, "Be careful peasant. (2) Will you tread on my clothes?" And then this peasant said "I shall do as you wish, my way is good."[11]

So he went upwards. And then this Nemty-nakht said, "Will my barley be your path?" Then this peasant said "My way is good. The bank is high. The (only) way is under barley, for you are blocking our path with your clothes. Will you then not let us pass by on the road?"

(R 59) He had just reached saying (this) word (B1 9) when one of these donkeys filled his mouth with a wisp of barley. Then this Nemty-nakht said: "Behold, I will take away your donkey, peasant, for eating my barley. Behold, it will tread out (grain) because of its offense (13)."[12]

And then this peasant said "My course is good. (Only) one (wisp) has been damaged. Could I buy back my donkey for its (the wisp's) value if you seize it for filling its mouth with a wisp of barley? (15-16). But I know the lord of this district, it belongs to the high steward Rensi, son of Meru. He indeed is one who punishes every robber in this land. Shall I be robbed in his district?"

(19) This Nemty-nakht said: "Is this the proverb which men say: 'The name of a poor man is pronounced for his master's sake?' I am the one who is speaking to you, yet the high steward it is whom you have invoked!" Then he took a stick of green tamarisk and thrashed all his limbs with

[2] Eg. *Sḫt-ḥmꜣt*; usually identified with Wadi Natrun northwest of Herakleopolis.
[3] Thus Parkinson 1991b; for other reconstructions see: Lichtheim *AEL* 1:170: "[last year];" Perry 1986:98: "[the harvest]."
[4] Alternative reconstruction: "(in which) [I shall travel]." See: Lichtheim *AEL* 1:170.
[5] Eg. *Nn-nsw*. Herakleopolis was the capital of the 9th and 10th Dynasties.
[6] The locations of Per-fefi and Medenit are unknown. For most recent suggestion see Kuhlmann 1992:205-207.
[7] This is the common interpretation of the Egyptian word *šsp*. For another translation *šsp*-cloth, see Perry 1986:125-127.
[8] The meaning of *smꜣ tꜣ n rꜣ wꜣt* is obscure and various interpretations have been suggested: a crossing, riverside path, a point at which the narrow path merged with the public road, landing place. The best solution would be to suppose that *smꜣ tꜣ* marks the merging of Nemty-nakht's private home path with the public road, which narrowed at that point so that it could be covered by a garment. Cf. Lichtheim *AEL* 1:183 n. 5.
[9] Eg. *ifd* is a four-cornered fringed piece of cloth and it signifies here the usual man's garment (Cf. B1 2 where it is replaced by *ḥbsw*-clothes). Nemty-nakht placed his own garment on the road. According to the ancients a man's garment contains his identity and has magical properties, therefore damaging a man's garment was considered a disgrace to him. See: Shupak 1992:7 n. 22.
[10] Lit., "On the way of all people."
[11] Eg. *nfr mṯn*. Meaning: my conduct is proper, my intentions are pure.
[12] Nemty-nakht confiscated the donkey. See: Perry 1986:141. For the custom of confiscating the property of a debtor as a pledge in the ancient world see: Shupak 1992:8 n. 28.

it, and his donkeys (24) were seized and driven into the district.

Then this peasant wept very greatly because of the pain of what had been done to him. And then this Nemty-nakht said "Do not raise your voice peasant! Behold you are in the city of the Lord of Silence."[13]

Then this peasant said: "You beat me, you steal my goods and now you take away the complaint[14] of my mouth! O Lord of Silence may you give me back my property! Then I shall stop screaming which you fear."

Frame-Story (cont.): The Peasant Appealed to Rensi Son of Meru (B1 31-51)

Then this peasant spent a period of ten days appealing to[15] Nemty-nakht who did not pay attention to it (32). So this peasant went[16] to Herakleopolis to appeal to the high steward, Rensi, son of Meru. He met him going out of the door of his house to his court[17] boat. And then this peasant said, "Would that I might be permitted to inform you concerning this complaint. It is a case[18] of letting your favourite servant come to me so that I might send him back to you about it."

And then the high steward Rensi, son of Meru, allowed his favorite servant to go in front of him and this peasant sent him concerning his case in its entirety.

Then the high steward Rensi, son of Meru accused[19] this Nemty-nakht before the magistrates[20] who were at his side. And then they said to him "Probably it is a peasant of his who has gone to someone else beside him. Behold, that is what they do to a peasant of theirs who goes to (46) others beside them. Is it a case of one punishing this Nemty-nakht for a little natron and a little salt? Let him be ordered to give compensation[21] for it, and he will give compensation."

Then the high steward Rensi, son of Meru, was silent; he did not reply to these magistrates; he did not reply to the peasant.

First Petition (B1 52-71)

Then this peasant came to appeal to the high steward Rensi, son of Meru; he said:

"High steward, my lord,
Greatest of the great, leader of all that is and all that is not!
If you embark on a lake of justice[22]
May you sail on it with fair breeze,
Let not the fastener[23] of your sail unravel!
Your boat shall not lag,
No misfortune shall take your mast,
Your yards will not break (59) ...
You will not taste the river's evils,
You will not see the face of fear.[24]
(62) [a] For you are father to the orphan,
Husband to the widow,
Brother to the rejected woman,
Apron[25] to the motherless. [a]

Let me make your name in this land according to every good law:[26]

Leader free from covetousness,
A great man free from baseness,
(67) Destroyer of falsehood,

a-a Exod 22:22-23; Deut 10:18; 14:28-29; 24:17-22; 27:19; Prov 23:10; Job 24:3

[13] The epithet "Lord of silence" designates Osiris, the god of the dead; cf. *Urk.* IV 1031.

[14] Eg. *nḫwt* means complaint and at times bears the sense of lamentation; see: "Admonitions of an Egyptian Sage" (text 1.42) 2.7; 3.14.

[15] Eg. *spr*, to appeal, which appears at the beginning of each new complaint of the peasant, is a legal terminus technicus of a kind prevalent in our text; cf. Shupak 1992:10-11.

[16] Another variant: "sailing south" (R 82).

[17] *ᶜrryt* denotes an administrative body or institution or location involved in legal procedures. Here it appears in connection with a boat's structure *ḳ͗ḳ͗w n ᶜrryt* — court boat, and relates to the custom of the Egyptian judges to circulate throughout the kingdom to make themselves available to anyone wishing to approach them in legal matters. See Shupak 1992:16-18.

[18] The Egyptian word *sp* is used in this text in its technical sense — a case; cf. B1 46-47, 203. See Shupak 1992:12.

[19] For the legal aspect of *srḫ* — to accuse see Shupak 1992:11.

[20] The magistrates — *srw* were involved in the legal system and served as judges. See: Shupak 1992:6.

[21] *Ḏbꜣ* — compensation is a terminus technicus related to the execution of a sentence. See: Shupak 1992:13.

[22] The comparison of the judge to a sailor and the metaphor of navigation for the administration of land affairs are common in our text: cf. B1 89-91, 156-158, 221, 278-279; B2 98-103 and "Rekhmire" *Urk.* IV 1077, 3. Rensi is described as a sailor sailing on a lake of truth (*mꜣᶜt* — see n. 27) relating to his lawful administration which is based on justice. Cf. "The Instruction of Ptahhotep" 93.

[23] *Ndbyt* — meaning uncertain. See Perry 1986:180-185.

[24] "The face of fear" — meaning the crocodile, "the lord of fear" *Urk.* IV 616,9; cf. "The Dispute between a Man and His Ba" 79 (see *COS* 3), where the drowned children see the "face of the crocodile."

[25] The high official's garment, called an apron, is mentioned here in connection with its owner's functions of protecting the lower class. In Egypt and throughout the Ancient Near East the rulers were considered protectors of the poor and the oppressed, patron to widows and orphans; cf. "Rekhmire": *Urk* IV 1078, 6-10; "The Instruction Addressed to Merikare" 47; "The Instruction of Amenemhet" I 6-7. For more parallels from Egypt as well as from Mesopotamia see: Perry 1986:196-204; Fensham 1962.

[26] "Name" relates to the high steward's title consisting of five great names enumerated in the following lines. The title which emphasizes the duties of the high official, is analogous to the fivefold royal titulary.

[27] "Justice" — Eg. "maat" (*mꜣᶜt*). The good judge is one who "does maat" and destroys its antonyms i.e., *isft* — wrong (B1 67) and *grg* — falsehood (cf. B1 159 - 160, 182, 197). In a period of anarchy falsehood replaces *mꜣᶜt* (B1 198 cf. B1 182) and also: "The Prophecies of Neferti" 68-69; "The Complaints of Khakheperre-sonb" Recto 11, and "The Admmonitions of an Egyptian Sage," 5.3-5.4; "The Dispute between a Man and his *Ba*," 122-123 (see *COS* 3).

Creator of justice,[27]
Who comes at (68) the voice of the caller,[28] [b]
When I speak may you hear!
Do justice you praised one,
Whom the praised ones praise!
Remove my grief, I am burdened with sorrow,
I am weak on account of it,
Examine me, I am lacking!"

Frame-Story (cont.) (B1 71-87, R 117-138)

Now this peasant made this speech in the time of the majesty of King of Upper and Lower Egypt Nebkaure, the justified. Then the high steward Rensi, son of Meru, went before his majesty. He said: "My lord, I have found one of those peasants who is really eloquent of speech.[29] His goods have been stolen, and, behold, he has come to appeal to me about it." And then his majesty said: "If you wish to see me in health, you shall retain him here without replying to anything he says. In order to keep him (80) talking, be silent. Then have it brought to us in writing, that we may hear it. But provide for his wife and his children. For one of those peasants comes here (only) just before his house is empty. And provide for this peasant himself. You shall cause food to be given to him without letting him know that it is you who are providing it."

Then he was given ten loaves and two jugs of beer every day. The high steward Rensi, son of Meru, gave it. He gave it to a friend of his and he gave it to him (the peasant). Then the high steward Rensi, son of Meru, wrote to the mayor of Salt-Field about providing food for this peasant's wife, a total of three measures of grain every day.

Second Petition (B1 88-138)

Then this peasant came to appeal to him a second time; he said:

"High steward, my lord
Greatest of the great, richest of the rich,
Great for his great ones, rich for his rich ones!
Steering oar of heaven, beam of earth,
Plumb-line which carries the weight![30]
(91) Steering oar, do not diverge
Beam, do not tilt
Plumb-line, do not swing awry!

The great lord takes possession of the ownerless, stealing from the lonely man. Your portion is in your house: a jug of beer and three loaves. But what are you doing to satisfy the hunger of your dependents? A mortal man, along with his underlings, must die. Will you be a man of eternity?[31]

Is it not wrong: a balance that tilts,
A plummet that strays,
(97) The straight becoming crooked?
Behold, justice flees from you,
Banished from its (98) seat! [c]
When the magistrates do wrong,[32] [d]
[e]When he who is in charge of examining the plea shows partiality,[33]
When judges snatch what has been stolen.[e]
He who trims a matter's rightness makes it swing awry,
The breath-giver languishes on the ground (?)" ...
(104) This peasant said:
[f] "The measurer of grain-piles trims for him self.
He who fills for another diminishes the other's share;[f]
He who should rule by law, commands theft,
Who then will punish wrongdoing?
The straightener of another's crookedness supports another's crime ...

(115) You are strong and mighty. Your arm is active, your heart greedy, mercy has passed you by ... (121) He who has bread should be merciful. Violence is for the criminal; robbing suits him who has nothing. The stealing done by the robber is the misdeed of one who is poor. One cannot reproach him; he (merely) seeks for himself.[g] But you are sated with your bread, drunken with your beer, rich in all" ...

Third Petition (B1 139-193)

Then this peasant came to appeal to him a third time; he said:

b Exod 22:22, 26; 2 Kgs 4:1; 8:3, 5; Job 19:7;
c Eccl 3:16
d Eccl 5:7
e-e Lev 19:15; Deut 1:17; Prov 18:5; 24:23; 28:21
f-f Deut 25:13-15; Prov 20:10, 23; 11:1
g Prov 6:30

[28] The judge's basic duty is "to come at the voice of the caller," i.e., to listen to the complaint. This obligation is clearly explained in "The Installation of the Vizier Rekhmire" (13-14) and in "The Instruction of Ptahhotep" (264-276); cf. also *Urk.*IV 1082, 15-16 and "The Stele of Mentuḥotep" 11-12, 14.

[29] Eg. *nfr mdt*, lit. good, fine speech; a saying that is perfect in form as well as in content. See: Shupak 1993:325-326, 332.

[30] The image of balance as a symbol of justice and honesty occurs often in the tale (cf. B1 96-97, 148-149, 160-162, 311-313; B2 92-93). The judge whose duty is to oversee justice is likened to it, as well as some parts of his body (cf. B1 92-93, 165-167). See: Gardiner 1923:10 n. 4; Herrmann 1963; Perry 1986:253-261, 332-333.

[31] Cf. "The Instruction Addressed to Merikare" (text 1.35 above) 41-42, 53-57.

[32] Here follows a section consisting of oppositions that are intended to point out the ironies in the current state of affairs. This literary pattern is characteristic of the genre of speculative wisdom literature; cf: B1 247 ff; "The Admonitions of an Egyptian Sage" n. 11; "The Complaints of Khakheperre-sonb." n. 16; "The Prophecies of Neferti" n. 29 and "The Dispute between a Man and his *Ba*," 113ff (see *COS* 3). It appears also in biblical wisdom; cf. Eccl 10:6-7, 3:16, 7:15, 8:10; Prov 30:22-24.

[33] "Shows partiality" Eg. *rdi ḥr gs* lit., "incline sideways." This is a legal terminus technicus probably derived from the image of scales. Cf. B1 149, 312-313 and see: Shupak 1992:15-16.

"High steward, my lord,
You are Re, the lord of heaven, with your courtiers.
Men's sustenance is from you as from the flood,
You are Hapy who makes green the fields
And re-establishes destroyed mounds.[34]
Punish the robber and protect the miserable.
(144) Be not flood against the pleader! ...
(148) Does the hand-balance deviate?
(148-149) Does the stand-balance tilt?[35]
[h] Does Thoth[36] show favour
So that you may do wrong? ...[h]
(156) By the sail-wind you should steer,
Control the waves to sail aright,
Guard from landing by the helm-rope ...
(160) Speak not falsely — you are the standard,
You are the one with the hand-balance,
If it tilts you may tilt ...
(165) Your tongue is the plummet,
Your heart is the weight,
Your two lips are its arms (167) ...

(180) Hearer, you hear not! Why do not you hear! ... (182) When the secret of truth is found, falsehood is thrown on its back on the ground. Trust not the morrow before it has come;[i] one knows the trouble in it."[37]

h-h Prov 21:2; 24:12; 16:2; Job 31:6

i Prov 16:9; 19:21; 27:1

Now this peasant had made this claim[38] to the high steward Rensi, son of Meru, at the entrance of the judgement hall.[39] Then he had two guards stand up against him bearing whips and they thrashed all his limbs. The peasant said:

"The son of Meru goes on erring. His face is blind to what he sees, deaf to what he hears, forgetful about what he should have remembered.

Behold, you are a town (190) without a mayor,
Like a group without its ruler,
Like a ship without a captain,
Like a band without a leader.
Behold, you are an officer who steals,
A mayor who accepts (bribes),
A district overseer who should punish crime
Who is the model for him who does (it)."

Fourth Petition (B1 194-225)

And then this peasant came to appeal to him a fourth time ... he said:

(197) "Goodness is destroyed, none adhere to it
(198) Throwing falsehood's back to the ground (has also perished)[40] ...

(201) Who can sleep until daybreak? Gone is working by night, travel by day[41] and letting a man defend his own right case.[42]

Behold, it is of no use telling you this; mercy has passed you by. How miserable is the wretch whom you have destroyed! ...

(215) He who eats tastes; he who is asked answers; he who sleeps sees (217) the dream; and a judge who deserves punishment is a model for him who does evil. Fool, you are attacked! Ignorant man you are questioned! ...

(221) Steersman, let not drift your boat
Life-sustainer, let not one die
Provider, let not one perish.
Shadow, be not sunlight
Shelter, let not the crocodile snatch!
The fourth time I apply to you! Shall I go on all day!"

Fifth Petition (B1 225-239)

And then this peasant came to appeal to him a fifth time; he said:

"High steward, my lord ... (231) Rob not a poor man of his property, a weak man whom you know. Breath to the poor is his property; he who takes it away stops up his nose. You are appointed to investigate complaints and pass judgement between two (litigants),[43] to punish the robber. But behold, supporting the thief is what you do! One puts his trust in you, but you have become a

[34] The reference here is to the fertilizing process performed by the Nile, whereby the river first destroys the land and then rebuilds it. Cf. B1 144. See: Gilula 1978:129-130.

[35] Eg. *rdi ḥr gs;* see n. 33, above.

[36] Thoth, the god of wisdom and writing is in charge of writing down the results of the judgement of the dead, alluded to here. Thoth is the ideal judge "who never inclined sideways" (B1 268-269). Cf. also B1 305, where the writing instruments with which Thoth recorded justice are enumerated.

[37] The idea that the knowledge of the future is hidden from human beings is common to the Egyptian and biblical wisdom literature. Cf. "The Instruction of Kagemni" II 2; "The Instruction of Ptahhotep" 343; "The Instruction of Anii" 8, 9-10; "The Instruction of Amenemope" 19, 10-13; Prov 17:9, 19:21, 27:1. For more parallels from the New Kingdom see Lichtheim 1983:7 and Griffiths 1960:219-222.

[38] The Egyptian word *mdt* usually meaning "words", "matter", designates "complaint", "claim", in legal context. Cf. B1 234, B2 118 and see Shupak 1992:12 n. 46.

[39] Eg. *ʿryt* see n. 17, above.

[40] See n. 27, above.

[41] For a similar description of dangers and bloodshed on the highways, see "The Admonitions of an Egyptian Sage" (text 1.42 above) 12.13.

[42] Lit., "letting a man stand up to his case," i.e., to defend his case in the court. Cf. "The Installation of a Vizier" (5) where the vizier is warned to enable man to present his arguments in court.

[43] Lit., "you are appointed to hear (*sḏm*) complaints and to cut (*wḏʿ*) between two." The double task of the judge is marked by two verbs: *sḏm* appearing in legal context often means "to investigate" and *wḏʿ* has the sense of "to adjudicate between two litigants," "to pass judgement." Cf. B1 217, 269, B2 133.

transgressor. You were placed as a dam for the poor, as a safeguard against drowning. But, behold, you are his lake, a water pourer!"

Sixth Petition (B1 239-265)

And then this peasant came to appeal to him a sixth time; he said:

"High steward, my lord! ...
(247) Look with your own eyes:
The arbitrator is a robber,
The peace-maker is one who makes grief,
He who should soothe causes suffering ...
(260)You are learned, skilled, accomplished,
But not in order to plunder!
You should be the model for all men,
But your affairs are crooked!
(263) The standard for all men cheats the whole land! ..."

Seventh Petition (B1 266-289)

And then this peasant came to appeal to him a seventh time; he said:

"High steward, my lord!
You are the steering oar of the whole land,
This land sails around by your command.
(268) You are brother to Thoth,
The judge who is not partial ...[44]

(275) Indeed my belly is full, my heart is heavy. Therefore it has come out from my belly.[45] When there is a breach in a dam its waters rush out. (278) So my mouth opened to speak.

I have fought my sounding pole.[46] I have boiled (279) out my water. I have emptied what was in my belly;[47] I have washed my soiled linen. My speech is over; my grief is all before you.

Eighth Petition (B1 289-322)

Then this peasant came to appeal to him an eighth time; he said:

"High steward, my lord ...
(303) Do justice for the Lord of Justice[48]
Whose justice is always true;
(305) Pen, papyrus, palette of Thoth,[49]
May you be afar from wrongdoing!
When good is good, it is really good.
For justice is for eternity;
It enters the Necropolis with its doer,[50]
When he is buried and interred.
His name does not pass from the earth,
He is remembered because of (his) goodness,
This is the rule of god's command.

The hand-balance — it tilts not; the [51] stand-balance — it leans not to one side. (313) Whether I come or whether another comes, you will have to address (us). Do not answer (us) with the answer of silence.[52] Do not attack one who cannot attack you. You have no pity, you are not troubled, you are not disturbed! You do not repay my good speech[53] which comes from the mouth of Re himself ..."

Ninth Petition (B2 91-115)

And then this peasant came to appeal to him a ninth time; he said:

"High steward, my lord! (92-93) The tongue is men's stand-balance. It is the hand-balance that detects deficiency. Punish him who should be punished ... (98) If falsehood walks it goes astray. It cannot cross in the ferry; it cannot advance. He who is enriched by it has no children, has no heirs on earth. He who sails (102) with it cannot reach land; (103) his boat cannot moor at its landing place ... (113) Behold, I have been appealing to you (but) you do not listen to it. I shall go and appeal to Anubis about you."[54]

Frame-Story: Conclusion (B2 115-142)

And then the high steward, Rensi, son of Meru caused two guards to go to bring him back. Then this peasant was fearful, thinking it was done so as (118) to punish him for the claim he made ... (123) And then the high steward, Rensi, son of Meru said: "Just stay here so you can hear your petitions."

Then he caused them to be read from a new papyrus-roll, each petition in its turn.

[44] Alternative interpretation: "who investigates without being partial." On "being partial" see n. 33, above.

[45] In the Egyptian perception the heart is the seat of wisdom and intellect and it dwells within the belly. When a man expresses his thoughts it is as if his heart was going out of his belly. Cf. "The Instruction of Amenemope" 22, 11-16; "The Instruction of Kheti" XXV B-C.

[46] See: Gardiner 1923:17 n. 10.

[47] The comparison of the act of giving voice to one's troubles to a purgation, an "emptying of the belly," is widespread in the Egyptian wisdom literature. It derives from the belief that the belly is the seat of human thought and intelligence; cf. "The Complaints of Khakheperre-sonb" Recto 3 and n. 7; "The Instruction of Ptahhotep" 266-267; "The Stele of Mentuḥotep" 11-12.

[48] "Lord of Justice" may apply to Re, the sun god who is the creator of Maat-justice. But it may equally denote Thoth, "the ideal judge" (see n. 36 above) or another god, since various gods carried this epithet. See: *ANET* 410, n. 25.

[49] See note 36, above.

[50] The high official is warned that after his death — when his heart will be weighed up against the emblem of justice — he will have to pay for his misdeeds. Cf. "The Instruction Addressed to Merikare" (text 1.35 above) 127-128; "The Instruction of Phaḥḥotep" 84-99.

[51] See n. 30, above.

[52] Alternative interpretation: "Answer not as one who addresses a silent man"; "silent man" denoting the petitioner.

[53] See n. 29, above.

[54] Being disenchanted with the corrupt legal system of mere mortals the peasant asked in his final appeal for the help of Anubis, i.e., he expressed his desire to consult the oracle, one of the means of passing a verdict in Egypt. See: Shupak 1992:11 n. 39. Similarly, the biblical Job disappointed by his friends' counsels appealed to God as the last means of restoring justice to earth.

The high steward, Rensi, son of Meru, presented them to his majesty, the King of Upper and Lower Egypt, Nebkaure, the justified. And then it pleased the heart of his majesty more than anything in this whole land. And then his majesty said: (133) "May you yourself judge, son of Meru!" And then the high steward, Rensi son of Meru, caused two guards to go to [bring Nemty-nakht] (135). He was brought and a report was made of [all his property] ... his wheat, his barley, his donkeys ... of this Nemty-nakht [which was given] to this peasant ...

REFERENCES

ANET 407-410; *Urk.* IV ; Berlev 1987:78-83; Fensham 1962:129-139; Gardiner 1923:5-23; Gilula 1978:129-130; Griffiths 1960:219-221; Herrmann 1963:106-115; Kuhlmann 1992:191-207; Lichtheim *AEL* 1:169-184; 1983; Parkinson 1991a:171-181; 1991b; Perry 1986; Shupak 1992:1-18; 1993.

THE COMPLAINTS OF KHAKHEPERRĒ-SONB (1.44)

Nili Shupak

The work was composed during the Middle Kingdom and has been preserved on a writing tablet from the 18th Dynasty. This tablet, no. 5645 in the BM, is the single surviving copy. The author is a priest of Heliopolis and his name contains the pronomen of Sesostris II who ruled during the 12th Dynasty.

Unlike other compositions pertaining to the genre of speculative wisdom literature — "The Eloquent Peasant," "The Prophecies of Neferti," "The Admonitions of an Egyptian Sage," and "The Dispute between a Man and His *Ba*" — this one does not contain a narrative frame in prose that serves as a setting for a rhetoric section in verse. But it has a title which is usually characteristic of the wisdom instructions (*Lebenslehre*) and which informs us of the nature of the subject and gives us the name of the author.[1]

The items enumerated in the title as making up the contents of the work are called — "words," "maxims," and "phrases."[2] These words are used again in the prologue of Khakheperre-sonb's instruction where he announces his literary ambition to say things that have never been said before.[3] Nevertheless, when he comes to speak of the grievous state of society, his observations differ in no way from the utterances of either his predecessors or those who would come after him. Like them Khakheperre-sonb gives an account of adversities and calamities falling on the land and describes the ruin of the country. It also contains social admonition concerning inversion of normal social hierarchies and religious censure.

It is not clear whether the text is complete or not; it may have continued on another tablet. The author Khakheperre-sonb was famous in the Ramesside period, as one may conclude from the appearance of his name among the eight great Egyptian scribes in Papyrus Chester Beatty IV. On the manuscript, the verses of the composition are marked off by red dots.

Title (Recto 1)
The collection of words,[4]
The gathering of maxims,
The quest of phrases [a] with a searching heart,[5] [b]
Made by the priest of Heliopolis, the ...
Khakheperre-sonb called Ankhu.

a Eccl 12:9
b Eccl 1:13, 17; 8:16; 9:1

Prologue: the Aim of the Composition or the Author's Literary Ambitions (Recto 2-7)
He says:
Would I had unknown phrases,
Maxims that are strange,
Novel untried words,

[1] For a discussion of parallels to Khakheperre-sonb's title and prologue in the Egyptian wisdom instructions ("The Instruction of Ptaḥḥotep" [1; 47-50], "The Instruction of Amenemope" [1, 1-12; 1, 13-3, 7 etc.), and in the biblical wisdom literature (Prov 1:1, 2-6; 30:1; 31:1; Eccl 1:1, 12) see: Shupak 1990:84-85.

[2] See n. 4, below.

[3] For a different explanation of the aim and message of Khakheperre-sonb see Ockinga 1983:89-90.

[4] The three terms appearing here — "words" (*mdwt*), "maxims" (*ṯsw*) and "phrases" (*ḫnw*) are repeated in the next section, which stands in chiastic parallelism with it. These terms belong to the terminology of the wisdom literature and are regularly applied to wisdom utterances. In the speculative compositions they are used to designate the complaints and exhortations of the authors. Thus the sayings of "The Eloquent Peasant" are "phrases" (B1 280); Neferti is able to address "some good words" and "chosen maxims" to the king (l. 7-8, 13 and see "The Prophecies of Neferti" n.1). For discussion of the etymology and the semantics of *mdwt*, *ṯsw*, *ḫnw* and their parallels in biblical Hebrew, see Shupak 1993:313-321, 324-325.

[5] In Recto 1-4 Khakheperre-sonb expresses his desire to say new things. These concerns of the Egyptian priest are very similar to those of the architect Amenḥetep of the 18th Dynasty and his Hebrew counterpart Ecclesiastes. Amenḥetep sings his own praise as one who "has a hearing heart seeking (*ḏʿr.f*) counsel regarding strange things, like one whose heart understands them" (*Urk.* IV 1817,8-9); cf. Khakheperre-sonb's "the quest (*ḏʿr*) of phrases with searching heart." This spirit of inquiry is also characteristic of Ecclesiastes who uses his heart as an

Void of repetitions;
Not maxims of past speech,[6]
(3) Spoken by the ancestors.

I empty my belly of that which is in it,[7]
In loosing all that I have said (before);
For what has been said is repetition,
When what was said is said.
There is no boasting in the speech of the ancestors,
When those of later times find them.

(5) One who has spoken should not speak,[8]
But one should speak who has something to speak,
May another find what he will speak,
Not a teller of tales afterwards,[9]
This is vain endeavour, it is lies,
And no one will mention his name to others.[c]

I said this in accord with what I have seen:[10]
From the first generation,
Down (7) to those who come after,
They imitate[11] that which is past.[d]

The Author's Complaint about His Inability to Speak to His Heart about It (Recto 7-9)
Would that I knew what others do not know,[12]
Things that have never been repeated,
Then I would say them and my heart would answer me![13] [e]
(8) Then I would explain to it my distress,
Then I would shift to it the burden which is on my back,
The matters that oppress me,
I would express to it what I suffer through it[14]
(9) And I would say "ah" with relief.

The Calamities of the Times: The Description of the Ruined Land (Recto 10-12)
I meditate on what has happened,[15]
The events that have passed throughout the land.
Changes have taken place, it is not like last year,
One year is more burdensome than the others,
The land is in confusion and is destroyed,
Made as ...

(11) Right is cast outside,
Wrong is in the council hall;[16]
The plans of the gods are violated,
Their ordinances neglected,[17]
The land is in turmoil,[18]
Mourning is in everyplace,
The towns (12), the districts are in grief.
Everybody alike is subjected to wrongs,
(As for) reverence, backs are turned to it,
The Lords of Silence[19] are disturbed;
(When) morning comes every day,
The faces shrink back from what has happened.

The Author Tries to Speak with His Heart about These Calamities (Recto 12 - Verso 1)
I cry out about it,
My limbs are weighed down;
I grieve in my heart,[20] [f]

c Eccl 1:11
d Eccl 1:9-10
e Eccl 1:16; 2:1, 15; 3:17-18
f Isa 21:3-4; Jer 23:9; cf. Jer 4:19

instrument to search out and to gain knowledge see: Scripture References *a* (cf. Sira 44:5) and *b*.

[6] Eg. *sbit r*. Alternative translation: "Transmitted (familiar) language."

[7] Khakheperre-sonb compares the act of giving voice to his troubles to a purgation "emptying the belly." This image, which is widespread in the Egyptian wisdom literature, derives from the belief that the belly is the seat of human thought and intelligence. Cf. "The Eloquent Peasant" B1 275-277, 280 and p. 103, n. 47; "The Instruction of Ptaḥhotep" 266-267. See also Shupak 1993:293-295.

[8] Lit., "There speaks one who will speak." Alternative translation: "But one who (at first time) speaks should speak."

[9] Cf. "The Prophecies of Neferti" where Neferti asks the king what he prefers: "Something that happened or something that is going to happen" (14).

[10] Khakheperre-sonb does not foretell of things to come but relies, rather, on the experience of the past: "I meditate on what has happened" (Recto 10); cf. "The Prophecies of Neferti": "I cannot foretell what has not yet come" (26). The Hebrew sages too drew on their own experience. The method of learning through personal experience is characteristic of Ecclesiastes (1:12-2:26;7:23-39; 8:16-17). And in the Book of Proverbs the sage learns a lesson by observing the fate of the slothful (24:30-32), or from his personal experience as a pupil (4:3-4).

[11] Eg. *sni*. See "The Admonitions" n. 39.

[12] The author cannot express himself since he knows only the traditional-conventional sayings. Yet he rejects the uttered repetitions of the past and thus deviates from the wisdom instructions based on the experience of previous generations.

[13] The formula of a man speaking to his heart or his soul is a literary pattern frequently used in the genre of speculative wisdom literature. Khakheperre-sonb seeks to share his troubles with his heart (Recto 7-9, Recto 12 - Verso 1), Neferti begins his speech with "Stir, my heart" etc. (8 cf. ibid. n.9), and "The Dispute between a Man and His *Ba*" (see *COS* 3) is conceived as a dialogue between a man and his soul. The same device is used by the authors of the Hebrew speculative wisdom literature; in Ecclesiastes the speaker addresses his heart six times; see Scripture References *e*.

[14] Eg. *sšr nf mnt mʿf* for which different readings have been suggested; cf. Kadish 1973:78, Lichtheim *AEL* 1:147.

[15] This section and Verso 1-5, which begin with the same phrase, "I meditate on what has happened," describe the troubled conditions of the country in a way similar to that of Ipuwer, Neferti and the Eloquent Peasant, at times even using the same words and phrases. Cf. Junge 1977:275 and Shupak 1990:91-92.

[16] The stylistic device of contrasts used here and in Verso 2-3 is aimed to describe the turbulent state of the land. This device is a dominant feature in the Egyptian as well as in the biblical wisdom literature. Cf. "The Eloquent Peasant" n. 32, "The Admonitions" n. 11, and "The Prophecies of Neferti n. 29. On the antonyms "right-wrong" (*mꜣʿt - isft*) see "The Prophecies of Neferti" 68-69 and p. 110, n. 39. See also "The Eloquent Peasant" n. 27.

[17] Cf. "The Admonitions of an Egyptian Sage," 10,12-11, 10.

[18] Eg. *sny mn*. Cf. "The Prophecies of Neferti" where the following refrain appears: "I show you the land in turmoil (*sny mn*)" (38,54).

[19] The "Lords of Silence" are the dead in the necropolis who are identified with Osiris, the god of the dead, whose epithet is the "Lord of Silence" in "The Eloquent Peasant" B1 27.

[20] The sense of anguish and physical suffering that accompanies Khakheperre-sonb's complaints (cf. also Recto 3) recalls the agonies

It is hard to keep silent[21] about it.
Another heart would bend,
(But) a stout heart in trouble,
It is companion to his master.

Would that I had (such) a heart (14) that knew how to suffer,
Then I would find relief in it,
I would load it with my words[22] of grief,
I would impose on it my malady.
(Verso 1) He said to his heart:
Come my heart, that I may speak to you —
Answer me my maxims,
And explain to me what is going on in the land,
Why those who were bright[23] have been cast down.

Description of the Bad State of the Land (cont.) and the Inability to Speak with the Heart about It (Verso 1-6)

I meditate about what has happened,
Misery enters in today,
Strange deeds[24] will not cease (also) tomorrow,
And all are silent about it.[25]
The whole land is in great confusion,
Nobody is free from wrong,
All people alike are doing it,
Hearts are greedy.[26]
He who used to give commands (3) is (now) one to whom commands are given,[27]
And the hearts of both of them are content.
One awakes to it every day,
And the hearts do not reject it,
The state of yesterday is like today;
And one passes over it because it (the bad) is much,[28]
(Thus) the faces (stay) solid.
None is wise (enough) to recognize it,
(4) None is angry (enough) to cry out,
One awakes to suffer every day.

Long and heavy is (my) malady,
There is no strength in the wretched man to save himself from one who overwhelms him.
It is painful to remain silent about what one hears,
It is misery to answer the ignorant.
To oppose speech makes enmity,
The heart does not accept the truth,
None endures contradiction,
Every man loves his own words.
Every man is lying[29] in crookedness,
Right speaking is abandoned.

I speak to you (6) my heart,
Answer me!
A heart that is approached does not keep silent,
Behold the affairs of the slave are like those of his master,[30]
There is much that weighs upon you!

associated with the vocation of the biblical prophets, see Scripture References *f.*

[21] Eg. *ḫ*ꜣ*p ẖt*. Lit., "to hide the belly" is a common expression denoting that the belly is man's innermost soul, the seat of his intelligence and thoughts which should be well guarded and wisely used. Cf. n. 7, above and see *Urk.* IV 47, 10; 971,2; 1198, 13 and *Wb.* III 357,3.

[22] Eg. *ḫnw* here may also mean "complaints"; see: Ockinga 1983:89-90.

[23] "Who were bright" refers to those wearing white garments.

[24] Eg. *ḏrḏr,* lit., "strange," is not suitable in this context; but since the word stands in parallelism with "misery" it might be understood as "strange deeds," "hostilities." Another suggestion proposed in research is instead of *ḏrḏrw* to read *ḏr ḏrtiw,* i.e., "since the ancestors" (Kadish 1973:83).

[25] Silence in response to the anarchy prevailing in the land is condemned see Verso 4,5 and cf. "The Prophecies of Neferti" 20; "The Admonitions" 6,5.

[26] Eg. *snm* may be also translated "sad."

[27] See n. 16, above.

[28] Difficult sentence. Alternative readings suggested in research are: "Because it is imitated by the masses, because of inflexibililty," Ockinga 1983:92; "Because of the transpiring of many things because of the cruelty (?)," Kadish 1973:78. The keyword is *sni* which can be explained as "to go beyond," "pass over," "miss" as well as "to imitate," "copy," see "The Admonitions" (p. 97 above) n. 39.

[29] Eg. *grg* has double meaning "to rely on," and "to lie" both of which may be suitable in this context.

[30] The word "slave" here relates to the heart.

REFERENCES

Urk. IV; *Wb.*; Junge 1977:275-284; Kadish 1973:77-90; Lichtheim *AEL* 1:145-149; Ockinga 1983:88-95; Shupak 1990:81-102; 1993.

THE PROPHECIES OF NEFERTI (1.45)

Nili Shupak

The single complete version of this composition is preserved on Pap. Petersburg 1116B which derives from the 18th Dynasty. This is augmented by fragments preserved on writing tablets and ostraca. "The Prophecies of Neferti" is a political document which was apparently composed in the court of the King Amenemhet I (1990-1960 BCE) who is here cast in the role of a redeemer-king. The text is introduced by a narrative frame, setting the work in the court of King Snefru of the Fourth Dynasty. The king wishing to be entertained, a lector-priest named Neferti is brought before him. Neferti is also a sage, able to utter "good words" and "choice maxims," qualities that place him in the same category as Khakheperre-sonb and the "Eloquent Peasant." His speech, which is presented as a prophecy, contains two main topics: The calamities of the time followed by redemption by a royal deliverer called Ameni; and social admonition concerning a variety of wrong-doings (murder, family rivalry, inversions of normal social hierarchies). But the pattern of prophecy is here only a literary disguise. The aim of the composition is to criticize the current government of the realm on the one hand, and to legitimize the monarchy of Amenemhet I on the other.

Frame-story: Introduction (1-18)

It happened when his majesty the King of Upper and Lower Egypt Snefru, the justified, was potent in this entire land. On one of these days it happened that the administrative council of the residence entered the palace l.p.h. to greet (the king). And they went out after they had greeted (him) according to their daily custom. Then his majesty l.p.h. said to the seal-bearer who was at his side: "Go and bring me back the administrative council of the residence who have gone from here after greeting (me) on this day."

They were brought to him (5) at once and they were on their bellies before his majesty l.p.h. once more. His majesty l.p.h. said to them: Fellows, behold I have caused you to be called that you seek for me a son of yours who is wise, a brother of yours who is excellent, a friend of yours who has done a good deed, who will tell me some good words, choice formulations,[1] which should entertain my majesty on hearing them.

Frame-Story (cont): The Summoning of Neferti (8-19)

They were on their bellies before his majesty once more. Then they said before his majesty l.p.h.: "There is a great lector priest of Bastet,[2] O sovereign, our lord, Neferti[3] is his name. He is a citizen valiant with his arm;[4] he is excellent with his fingers; he is a wealthy man, who has greater wealth (11) than any peer of his. Let him [be permitted] to see his majesty." Then said his majesty l.p.h. "Go and bring him to me." And he was brought to him immediately. And he was on his belly before his majesty l.p.h. Then his majesty l.p.h. said: "Come now Neferti (13) my friend, tell me some good words, choice formulations, which will entertain my majesty on hearing them. And the lector-priest Neferti said: "Something that happened or something that is going to happen, O sovereign l.p.h., my lord." (15) Then his majesty l.p.h. said "Something that is going to happen. It is (still) today and the passing of it already happens."[5] He stretched out his arm to a writing case and then he took for him a papyrus roll and a palette and put in writing what the lector-priest Neferti said;[6] A sage from the east he was, one belonging to Bastet when she appears, a child of the Heliopolitan[7] nome. He was concerned about what was happening in the land, calling to mind the state of the east with the Asiatics[8] travelling in their strength (19) upsetting those who were harvesting and grabbing the taxes (assigned) for the time of ploughing.

Neferti's Prophecies (20-71)

I. *Calamities* (20-57)

The Ruin of the Country (20-24)

He said:

Stir, my heart,[9]
Bemoan this land from which you derived.

[1] Mastery of the art of eloquence is a major attribute of the Egyptian sage (also see l. 13ff.). Neferti, like the Eloquent Peasant (see there n. 29) and Khakheperre-sonb (Recto 1-13), is distinguished by his accomplishments in rhetoric. In the Book of Proverbs too there is frequent praise of eloquence: cf. Prov 15:23; 24:26; 25:10 and Shupak 1993:334-336. On the connection of the Eg. word *ṯs*, formulation, maxim, with the image of knots and its Hebrew parallel *taḥbulôt*, see ibid., 313-317.

[2] Bastet. The cat-goddess of Bubastis in the eastern Delta.

[3] Neferti is mentioned among the eight great Egyptian scribes who are praised in Pap. Chester Beatty IV, dating from the period of the New Kingdom (Verso 3,6).

[4] "Valiant with his arm" - Eg. *ḳn n gꜣb.f* means a self-made official who rose to a high rank through his own efforts. See: Derchain 1972; cf. Westendorf 1973.

[5] Here the King declares his preference for hearing "something that is going to happen," i.e., the future, after which the verb *sr*, foretell, is employed in the text (see n. 16 below). Although the following words of Neferti are presented as prophecy it seems that they are a portrayal of contemporary or past events.

[6] Cf. "The Eloquent Peasant" (B1 80, B2 123ff.) where the words of the peasant are similarly written down at the king's command.

[7] "Heliopolitan nome." The northern derivation of Neferti is emphasized since Amenmehet I moved his seat from Thebes in the south, to the area of Memphis in the north.

[8] Also see 32-33, 63ff. On the phenomenon of Asiatics (*ʿꜣmw*) penetrating into Egypt cf. "Pap. Anastasi VI" 51ff.; for a detailed description of their land and way of life see: "The Instruction Addressed to Merikare" 92. In the light of ll. 32ff. one may assume that the *ʿꜣmw* were Palestinians who sought refuge in Egypt for economic reasons, as described in the patriarchs' stories in the book of Genesis; see: Scripture References *d;* Goedicke 1977:71.

[9] A literary pattern frequently used in works belonging to the speculative wisdom literature is the opening formula of a man speaking to his heart (*ib*) or to his soul (*ba*). Cf. "The Complaints of Khakheperre-sonb" Recto 7, Verso 1.5ff. and "The Dispute between a Man and His Ba" (see *COS* 3). The same device is used in the Hebrew speculative wisdom literature: Eccl 1:16; 2:1, 15-16; 3:17-18 and also ibid., 1:13,17; 2:20; 8,16, 19; 9,1. See also "The Complaints of Khakheperre-sonb" n. 13.

He who is silent is a wrongdoer.[10]
Behold, there was something of which one talks respectfully,[11]
Behold, he who was official is cast to the ground.[12]
Weary not of what is in front of you,
(22) Stand against that which is before you!
Behold, officials in the governance of the land are no more;
What is to be done is no (longer) done,
Re should begin to recreate.
(23) The land is entirely lost,[13] no remnant is left,
Without that the black of a nail (remains) from its taxes,[14]
(24) This land is destroyed, none cares about it,
None speaks and none sheds a tear: "How will this land be?"

Natural Disasters (25-29)

The sun is covered and does not shine for the people to see,[15] [a]
No one can live when the clouds cover (the sun),
Every face is numb from lack of it.
I shall say what is before me,
I cannot foretell what has not yet come.[16]
The river of Egypt is empty, [b]
One can cross the water on foot,
One will seek water for the ships to sail on.
Its course has become a riverbank,
A riverbank will be water,
What is in the water place will be riverbank.[17] [b]
Southwind will combat northwind,
So that sky will lack the single wind.[18]

Disasters Caused by Human Beings (29-57)

1. *Infiltration of Delta by Asiatics* (29-38)

Strange birds[19] will breed in the marshes of the Delta
After making a nest near the people.
The people let them approach because of the shortage,[20]
Perished indeed are those good things,[c]
Those fish ponds (where there were) those who clean fish,[21]
Overflowing with fish and fowl.
All good things have passed away,
(32) The land is burdened with misfortune
Because of those looking (?) for food,
Asiatics roaming the land.[22]
Foes (33) have arisen in the east,
Asiatics have descended into Egypt.[d]
The fortifications are destroyed ...
(34) When one will enter the fortifications,
When sleep will be banished from my eyes,
I spend the night wakeful.
The wild beasts of the desert will drink from the river (36) of Egypt,
They will be content on their banks by the absence of anyone to chase them away.[23]
For the land is seized and recovered (lit., brought)
And no one knows the result.
What will happen is hidden according to the saying,
(38) "When sight and hearing fail, the mute leads."[24]

2. *Civil Disasters* (38-54)

I show you the land in turmoil,[25]
(39) That which has never happened has happened.
One will seize the weapons of warfare, [e]
The land lives in (40) confusion.
One will make arrows of copper,
One will beg for bread with blood,

a Ezek 30:3, 17; 32:7-8
b-b Isa 19:5-7; Ezek 30:12; 31:15
c Isa 19:19-20
d Gen 12:10-20; 42:1-5; 43:1-2; 47:1-11
e Isa 19:2

[10] A difficult sentence. For different readings see: Barta 1971:37, Goedicke 1977:75-76, Helck 1970a:18 and Lichtheim *AEL* 1:140.

[11] The reading "respectfully" follows Helck 1970a:18.

[12] *Šᵓᶜ.n.k* probably crept in from l. 20 and should be deleted, as suggested by Helck 1970a:18.

[13] "Land" Eg. *tᵓ*, is one of the key terms in the composition. Synonymous formulas consisting of the word accompanied by phrases expressing loss, grief, or distress appear in ll. 23-24, 37. See also: 39,40; 45-46; 50 and cf. 20.

[14] "The black of the nail" is a metaphor for small measure and the phrase stresses the bad economic situation of the land. Alternative explanation: "The black of the nail" refers to Re's work of creation, meaning that everything that was created by him is now destroyed, even the black under the nail.

[15] The motif of the "hidden sun" returns in detail in ll. 51-54.

[16] "I cannot foretell (*sr*) what has not yet come." Cf. "foretelling by the ancestors," in "The Admonitions of an Egyptian Sage" 1,10.

[17] The metaphorical use of the image of the course of the Nile in reference to the fate of human beings appears in the wisdom literature. Cf. "The Instruction Addressed to Merikare" 125-126; "The Instruction of Amenemope" 6, 18-7,6; "The Instruction of Anii" 8,3-10.

[18] Another variation: "So that sky will consist of only one wind."

[19] The metaphor of "strange birds" refers to the foreign Asiatic tribes who were accustomed to settling down it the eastern Delta in order to survive the summer. For an alternative explanation see Blumenthal 1982:3 n. 24.

[20] Alternative reading: "After the weakened people let them come near."

[21] Lit., "Fish-slitting people."

[22] See n. 8 above.

[23] Another variation: "For lack of one to fear."

[24] Alternative reading: "Behold, when one who should hear is deaf the silent one is in front."

[25] This refrain reappears in l. 54. The phrase "the land is in turmoil" (Eg. *sny mny*) also comes in "The Complaints of Khakheperre-sonb" Recto 11 and *Urk.* IV 2027, 11; The introductory phrase "I show you ..." (lit., "I give you") is repeated five times in our text (38, 44, 48, 54, 55).

One will laugh[26] at distress;
None will weep over death,
None spends the night fasting because of death,
The heart of a man cares only for himself.
[f] Mourning is no (longer) carried out today,
Hearts have quite abandoned it.
A man sits with his back turned,
While one man kills another.
I show you a son as an enemy,
A brother as a foe,
A man (45) killing his (own) father.[27 f]

Every mouth is full of "love me,"
Everything good has disappeared.
The land has perished, laws are destined for it,
Deprived of produce, lacking in crops,[28]
What was done is (47) as if it were not done.
One will take the property of a man, and give it to a stranger,
[g] I show you a lord in worries, the stranger satisfied.
(48) He who has never filled up for himself is now empty.[29 g]
One will give something (only) out of hatred,
In order to silence the mouth that speaks;
One answers a complaint with an arm holding a stick
And says, Kill him!
The words fall on the heart like fire,
(50) None can endure a saying.
The land diminishes but its rulers are numerous,[h]
Bare, (but) its taxes are great.[30]
The grain is low (51) the measure is large,
One measures it in overflow.

Re separates himself (from) mankind [a]
If he shines the hour exists
(But now) none knows when noon comes;
None can discern his shadow,
None is dazzled by seeing (him),
Nor do the eyes fill with water.
As he is in the sky like the moon,
But his time of nightfall cannot be transgressed (i.e., remains unchanged),

f-f Isa 1:21, 23; 59:3-8; Prov 30:11-14; cf. ibid., 6:17-19

g Prov 30:22; Eccl 10:6-7

h Eccl 5:7

i Isa 11:1, 10; Jer 23:5; 30:9; Ezek 34:23; Hos 3:5

j Isa 11:12-13; Ezek 37:15-28; Mic 5:2;

k-k Isa 9:3-6, 11; Mic 5:3-5; Zech 9:10

(54) His rays will be on the face again as in former times.

3. *The World Upside Down: Inversion of Social Order* (54-57)

I show you the land in turmoil,[31]
The weak of arm is (now) the possessor of an arm,
[g] One salutes him who (formerly) saluted.
I show you the lowly as superior ...[g]
One lives in the necropolis.
[g] The poor man will make wealth,
The great one will [pray][32] to live.
The beggar will eat bread,
The slaves will be exalted (?).[33 g]
The Heliopolitan nome, the birthplace of every god, will not (longer) be.

II. *Redemption* (58-71)

The Redeemer King (58-62)

Then a king will come from the south,
Imeny,[34] the justified, is his name,
A son is he of a woman of the land of Nubia, [i]
A child is he of Upper Egypt.[35]
He will take the white crown,
He will wear the red crown;
(60) He will unite the Two Mighty Ones,[36 j]
He will appease the Two Lords with what they desire,
The field-encircler in his fist, the oar in motion.[37]
Rejoice, O people of his time,
The son of man will make his name forever and ever.

The Rehabilitation of the Country: Driving Away the Enemy and Restoring Order (62-71)

[k] They who incline toward evil,[k]
Who plot rebellion,
(63) They subdued their mouth in fear of him.
The Asiatics will fall to his slaughter,
The Libyans will fall to his flame,
The rebels to his wrath, the traitors to (65) his might,
The serpent which is on his forehead will still the traitors for him.

---

[26] A bitter laugh derives from a disturbed social order; cf. Blumenthal 1982:4 n. 33.

[27] Cf. "The Admonitions of an Egyptian Sage" 1.5.

[28] Cf. Lichtheim *AEL* 1:144 n. 11; alternative reading: "Damaging has been done, that which was lost is found."

[29] The stylistic device used in ll. 48, 54-57, i.e., presenting a series of contrasts to highlight absurdity, is common in the Egyptian as well as the Hebrew wisdom literature. See "The Eloquent Peasant" n. 32; "The Admonitions" n. 11; "The Complaints of Khakheperre-sonb" n. 16.

[30] Another variation: "While it dries up, its servants are rich."

[31] See n. 25 above.

[32] Obscure sentence; the reading above follows Goedicke's reconstruction: *wr(t) r [t]ri ḫpr*. Goedicke 1977:123-124.

[33] *Bhḳ*ꜣ an obscure word to which a variety of meanings have been given. It may derive from *bḥ* forced labour, and *ḳ*ꜣ, high.

[34] Ameny is a short name of Amenemhet I (1990-1960 BCE), the first King of the Twelfth Dynasty. The motif of a redeemer king also appears in "The Admonitions of an Egyptian Sage" (11.11-12.6) and see p. 97, n. 34, and has common features with the portrayal of the eschatological king in the Bible. See Shupak 1989-90:32-33.

[35] Eg. *H̱n - nḫn* designates the southern region of Egypt.

[36] "Two Mighty Ones" are the two goddesses, the vulture goddess Nekhebet of Upper Egypt and the cobra goddess Wadjet of Lower Egypt who preside over the double crown. These goddesses, like the "Two Lords" Horus and Seth, symbolize the unified Kingdom.

[37] Objects carried by the King during the coronation ceremony.

One will (66) build the Walls of the Ruler[38] l.p.h.,
To prevent Asiatics from descending to Egypt;
They will beg for water in the customary manner,
In order to let their herds drink.
Then order will come into its place
While wrongdoing is driven out.[39]

k-k see note on previous page

Joyful will be he who will observe and he who will serve the king.[k]
The wise man will pour out water for me,[40]
When he sees that what I have spoken comes to pass.

It has come to its end successfully by the scribe ...

[38] A series of fortresses built by Amenemhet I to protect the eastern frontier from penetration by foreign tribes. Cf. "The Story of Sinuhe" B17.

[39] The contrast pair *m*ᵓᶜ*t* — justice and *isft* — wrong symbolize order and chaos and play an important part in the Egyptian wisdom ideology, as shown by their common usage in the wisdom texts. See: "The Eloquent Peasant" B1 67, and ibid., n. 27; "The Admonitions of an Egyptian Sage," n. 20 (text 1.42); "The Complaints of Khakheperre-sonb," n. 16 (see text 1.44).

[40] The custom of the Egyptian scribes to bring libation for the sages of bygone times is alluded to here. Cf. Blumenthal 1982:11.

REFERENCES

Barta 1971; Blumenthal 1982; Derchain 1972; Goedicke 1977; Helck 1970a; Lichtheim *AEL* 1:139-145; Shupak 1989-90:1-40; 1993; Westendorf 1973.

3. INSTRUCTIONS

INSTRUCTION OF ANY (1.46)

Miriam Lichtheim

The Instruction of Any has long been known through a single manuscript: Papyrus Boulaq 4 of the Cairo Museum, which dates from the 21st or 22nd Dynasty. Of the first pages only small fragments have remained, and the copy as a whole abounds in textual corruptions due to incomprehension on the part of the copying scribe. The introductory sentence of the work is preserved on a tablet in the Berlin Museum (No. 8934), and small portions of the text are found in three papyrus fragments in the Musée Guimet, in Papyrus Chester Beatty V of the British Museum, and in four ostraca from Deir el Medina.

Given the corruption and lacunae of the main text copy and the absence of sizeable duplicate copies, the text has presented great difficulties to editors and translators. In the words of Gardiner: "The papyrus known as *P. Boulaq IV*, to the contents of which Chabas gave the name *Les Maximes du scribe Anii*, has long enjoyed the unenviable reputation of being the obscurest of all Egyptian wisdom texts" (1959a:12).

The work itself was composed in the New Kingdom, almost certainly in the 18th Dynasty. It combines traditional themes with a certain amount of innovation. Two aspects, in particular, distinguish it from most earlier Instructions. One is the fact that the Instruction of Any comes from the sphere of the middle class and is meant for the average man. The author presents himself as a minor official, and the advice he dispenses, in the usual form of a father instructing his son, is suited to the thinking of anyone who possessed a modicum of education and of material comforts. Thus there is nothing specifically aristocratic about the values that are taught. This is, of course, in keeping with the evolution of Egyptian society and with the growth of the middle class.

The other novel feature appears in the epilogue. In earlier Instructions the epilogue had consisted either in the grateful acceptance of the teaching by the listeners, or in the teacher's conclusion urging compliance. The epilogue of Any, however, is a debate between father and son in which the son makes the objection that the father's teachings are too difficult to be understood and obeyed. By making the son disinclined to learn and obey, the author of the work introduced a new dimension into the concept of didactic literature: the thought that instruction might fail to have an impact. The thought is introduced in order to be refuted. The father has the last word as well as the more telling arguments. Yet the expression of a negative point of view adds a fresh and realistic note to the Instruction genre by showing an awareness that the efficacy of teaching could be questioned and that the teachability of man had its limitations.

The page and line numbering used here is that of Suys's publication (1935) which was also employed by Volten (1937-38). My translation begins with page 3.1 preceded by the title of the work found on the Berlin tablet.

Beginning of the educational instruction made by the Scribe Any of the Palace of Queen Nefertari.[1]

(3.1) Take a wife while you're young,
That she make a son for you;
She should bear for you while you're youthful,
It is proper to make people.[2]
Happy the man whose people are many,
He is saluted on account of his progeny.[a]

Observe the feast of your god,[3]
And repeat its season,
God is angry if it is neglected.
Put up witnesses (3.5) when you offer,
The first time that you do it.
When one comes to seek your record,
Have them enter you in the roll;
When time comes to seek your purchase,[4]
It will extol the might of the god.
Song, dance, incense are his foods,
Receiving prostrations is his wealth;
The god does it to magnify his name,
But man it is who is inebriated.

Do not (3.10) enter the house of anyone,
Until he admits you and greets you;
Do not snoop around in his house,
Let your eye observe in silence.
Do not speak of him to another outside,
Who was not with you;
A great deadly crime
......

[b] Beware of a woman who is a stranger,
One not known in her town;
Don't stare at her when she goes by,
Do not know her carnally.
A deep water whose course is unknown,
Such is a woman away from her husband.
"I am pretty," she tells you daily,
When she has no witnesses;
She is ready to ensnare you,
A great deadly crime when it is heard.[b]
......[5]

Do not leave when the chiefs enter,
Lest your name stink;
In a quarrel (4.1) do not speak,
Your silence will serve you well.

Do not raise your voice in the house of god,
He abhors shouting;
Pray by yourself with a loving heart,
Whose every word is hidden.
He will grant your needs,
He will hear your words,
He will accept your offerings.
Libate for your father and mother,
Who are resting in the valley;
When the gods (4.5) witness your action,
They will say: "Accepted."
Do not forget the one outside,
Your son will act for you likewise.

[c] Don't indulge in drinking beer,
Lest you utter evil speech[6]
And don't know what you're saying.
If you fall and hurt your body,
None holds out a hand to you;
Your companions in the drinking
Stand up saying: "Out with the drunk!"
If one comes to seek you (4.10) and talk with you.
One finds you lying on the ground.
As if you were a little child.[c]

Do not go out of your house,
Without knowing your place of rest.
Let your chosen place be known,
Remember it and know it.
Set it before you as the path to take,
If you are straight you find it.
Furnish your station in the valley,
The grave that shall conceal your corpse;
Set it before you as your concern,
A thing that matters in your eyes.
Emulate the great departed,
Who are at rest within their tombs.
No blame accrues to him who does it,
It is well that you be ready too.
When your envoy[7] (5.1) comes to fetch you,
He shall find you ready to come
To your place of rest and saying:
"Here comes one prepared before you."

a Prov 17:6

b-b Prov 6:24-26; 7:6-27; 2:16-19

c-c Prov 20:1; 30:4-5

[1] Queen Ahmes-Nefertari, the wife of King Ahmose. The reading is due to Posener 1949:42 n. 2.

[2] Or: "Teach him to be a man" (Wilson *ANET* 420). There is no doubt that *iri rmṯ* sometimes means "to be a man"; but in this context a term denoting procreation seems more suitable. I can, however, not quote parallels.

[3] The understanding of this maxim was much advanced by Gardiner's rendering (1959a:12-14).

[4] Gardiner (1935b:143 n. 10) pointed out that *šsp* can have the meaning "purchase." This meaning suits here: the worshiper pays for offerings that are made in his name.

[5] Several obscure sentences.

[6] *Smi snw*, "evil speech," "noxious remarks," and the like.

[7] Death.

Do not say, "I am young to be taken,"
For you do not know your death.
When death comes he steals the infant
Who is in his mother's arms,
Just like him who reached old age.

Behold, I give you these useful counsels,
For you to ponder in your heart;
Do it (5.5) and you will be happy,
All evils will be far from you.
Guard against the crime of fraud,
Against words that are not <true>;
Conquer malice in your self,
A quarrelsome man does not rest on the morrow.
[d] Keep away from a hostile man,
Do not let him be your comrade; [d]
Befriend one who is straight and true,
One whose actions you have seen.
If your rightness matches his,
The friendship will be balanced.
Let your hand preserve what is in your house,
Wealth accrues to him who guards it;
Let your hand not scatter it to (5.10) strangers,
Lest it turn to loss for you.
If wealth is placed where it bears interest,
It comes back to you redoubled;
Make a storehouse for your own wealth,
Your people will find it on your way.
What is given small returns augmented,
⌜What is replaced brings abundance.⌝
The wise lives off the house of the fool,
Protect what is yours and you find it;
Keep your eye on what you own,
Lest you end as a beggar.
He who is slack amounts to nothing,[e]
Honored is the man who's active.
......[8]

(6.1) Learn about the way of a man
Who undertakes to found his household.
Make a garden, enclose a patch,
In addition to your plowland;
Set out trees within it,
As shelter about your house.
Fill your hand with all the flowers
That your eye can see;
One has need of all of them,
It is good fortune not to lose them.[9]

Do not rely on another's goods,
Guard what you acquire yourself;
Do not depend on another's wealth,
Lest he become master in your house.
Build a house or find and buy one,
Shun ⌜contention⌝
Don't say: "My mother's father has a house,
⌜'A house that lasts,'⌝ one calls it;"
When you come to share with your brothers,
Your portion may be a storeroom.
If your god lets you have children,
They'll say: "We are in our father's house."
Be a man hungry or sated in his house,
It is his walls (6.10) that enclose him.
Do not be a mindless person,
Then your god will give you wealth.

Do not sit when another is standing,
One who is older than you,
Or greater than you in his rank.
No good character is reproached,
An evil character is blamed.
Walk the accustomed path each day
Stand according to your rank.
"Who's there?" So one always says,
Rank creates its rules;
A woman is asked about (6.15) her husband
A man is asked about his rank.

Do not speak rudely to a brawler,
When you are attacked hold yourself back;
You will find this good (7.1) when your relations are friendly,
When trouble has come it will help you bear up,
And the aggressor will desist.
Deeds that are effective toward a stranger
Are very noxious to a brother.[10]
Your people will hail you when you are joyful,
They will weep freely <when you are sad>;
When you are happy the brave look to you,
When you are lonely you find your relations.

One will do all you say
If you are versed in writings;
Study the writings, put them in your heart,
(7.5) Then all your words will be effective.
Whatever office a scribe is given,
He should consult the writings;
The head of the treasury has no son,
The master of the seal has no heir.
The scribe is chosen for his hand,
His office has no children;
His pronouncements are his freemen,
His functions are his masters.

Do not reveal your heart to a stranger,
He might use your words against you;
The noxious speech that came from your mouth,
He repeats it and you make enemies.
A man may be ruined by his tongue,
Beware and you will do well.[11]
A man's belly is wider than a granary,
And full of all kinds of answers;
(7.10) Choose the good one and say it,

d-d Prov 22:24; 29:22

e Prov 6:6-11

[8] I do not understand the maxim in lines 5.15-17.
[9] The flowers are a metaphor for children.
[10] Parts of this maxim were rendered by Posener 1964:42-43.
[11] Read *ikr*.

While the bad is shut in your belly.
A rude answer brings a beating,
Speak sweetly and you will be loved.
Don't ever talk back to your attacker,
⌜Do not set a trap <for him>⌝;
It is the god who judges the righteous,
His fate comes and takes him away.[12] [f]

Offer to your god,
Beware of offending him.
Do not question his images,
Do not accost him when he appears.
Do not jostle him in order to carry him,
Do not disturb the oracles.[13]
Be careful, help to protect him,
Let your eye watch out (7.15) for his wrath,
And kiss the ground in his name.
He gives power in a million forms,
He who magnifies him is magnified.
God of this earth is the sun in the sky,
While his images are on earth;
When incense is given them as daily food,
The lord of risings is satisfied.

Double the food your mother gave you,
Support her as she supported you;
She had a heavy load in you,
But she did not abandon you.
When you were born after your months,
She was yet yoked <to you>,
Her breast in your mouth for three years.[g]
As you grew and your excrement disgusted,
She was not disgusted, saying: "What shall I do!"
When she sent you to school,
And you were taught to write,
She kept watching over you daily,
With bread (8.1) and beer in her house.
When as a youth you take a wife,
And you are settled in your house,
Pay attention to your offspring,
Bring him up as did your mother.
Do not give her cause to blame you,
Lest she raise her hands to god,
And he hears her cries.

Do not eat bread while another stands by
Without extending your hand to him.
As to food, it is here always,
It is man (8.5) who does not last;
One man is rich, another is poor,
But food remains for him ⌜who shares it.⌝
As to him who was rich last year,
He is a vagabond this year;
Don't be greedy to fill your belly,

f Prov 25:11
g 1 Sam 1:22-24

You don't know your end at all.
Should you come to be in want,
Another may do good to you.
When last year's watercourse is gone,
Another river is here today;
Great lakes become dry places,
Sandbanks turn into depths.
Man does not have a single (8.10) way,
The lord of life confounds him.[14]

Attend to your position,
Be it low or high;
It is not good to press forward,
Step according to rank.
Do not intrude on a man in his house,
Enter when you have been called;
He may say "Welcome" with his mouth,
Yet deride you in his thoughts.
One gives food to one who is hated,
Supplies to one who enters uninvited.

Don't rush to attack your attacker,
Leave him to the god;
Report him daily to the god,
(8.15) Tomorrow being like today,
And you will see what the god does,
When he injures him who injured you.

Do not enter into a crowd,
If you find it in an uproar
And about to come to blows.
Don't pass anywhere near by,
Keep away from their tumult,
Lest you be brought before the court,
When an inquiry is made.
Stay away from hostile people,
Keep your heart quiet among fighters;
An outsider is not brought to court,
One who knows nothing is not bound in fetters.

(9.1) It is useful to help one whom one loves,
⌜So as to cleanse him of his faults;⌝
⌜You will be sage from his errors,⌝
......
The first of the herd leads to the field.
......[15]

Do not control your wife in her house,
When you know she is efficient;
Don't say to her: "Where is it? Get it!"
When she has put it in the right place.
Let your eye observe in silence,
Then you recognize her (9.5) skill;
It is joy when your hand is with her,
There are many who don't know this.
If a man desists from strife at home,

[12] I.e., the aggressor will be punished.
[13] This passage was explained by Posener 1963a:98-102.
[14] The theme is the reversal of fortune, a topos that plays a considerable part in Eg. wisdom literature. Some of its aspects were studied by Volten 1941:371-379. A wide-ranging study of the theme in Mesopotamian literature is by Buccellati 1972:241-264.
[15] Several sentences which I do not understand. The whole maxim which occupies lines 9.1-3 is obscure to me.

He will not encounter its beginning.
Every man who founds a household
Should hold back the hasty heart.
Do not go after a woman,
Let her not steal your heart.[16]

Do not talk back to an angry superior,
Let him have his way;
Speak sweetly when he speaks sourly,[h]
It's the remedy that calms the heart.
Fighting answers carry sticks,
And your strength collapses;
......
Do not vex your heart.
He will return to praise you soon,
When his hour of rage has passed.
If your words please the heart,
(9.10) The heart tends to accept them;
Choose silence for yourself,
Submit to what he does.

Befriend the herald[17] of your quarter,
Do not make him angry with you.
Give him food from your house,
Do not slight his requests;
Say to him, "Welcome, welcome here,"
No blame accrues to him who does it.
......[18]

Epilogue

The scribe Khonshotep answered his father, the scribe Any:
I wish I were like (you),
As learned as you!
Then I would carry out your teachings,
And the son would be brought to his father's place.
Each man (9.15) is led by his nature,
You are a man who is a master,
Whose strivings are exalted,
Whose every word is chosen.
The son, he understands little
When he recites the words in the books.
But when your words please the heart,
The heart tends to accept them with joy.
Don't make your virtues too numerous,
That one may raise one's thoughts to you;
A boy does not follow the moral instructions,
Though the writings are on his tongue!

The scribe Any answered his son, the scribe Khonshotep:
Do not rely on such worthless thoughts,
Beware of what you do to yourself!
I judge your complaints to be wrong,
I shall set you right about them.

h Prov 15:1

There's nothing [superfluous in] our words,
Which you say you wished were reduced.
The fighting (10.1) bull who kills in the stable,
He forgets and abandons the arena;
He conquers his nature,
Remembers what he's learned,
And becomes the like of a fattened ox.
The savage lion abandons his wrath,
And comes to resemble the timid donkey.
The horse slips into its harness,
Obedient it goes outdoors.
The dog obeys the word,
And walks behind its master.
The monkey carries the stick,
Though its mother did not carry it.
(10.5) The goose returns from the pond,
When one comes to shut it in the yard.
One teaches the Nubian to speak Egyptian,
The Syrian and other strangers too.
Say: "I shall do like all the beasts,"
Listen and learn what they do.

The scribe Khonshotep answered his father, the scribe Any:
Do not proclaim your powers,
So as to force me to your ways;
⸢Does it not happen to a man to slacken his hand,⸣
So as to hear an answer in its place?
Man resembles the god in his way
If he listens to a man's answer.
⸢One (man) cannot know his fellow,⸣
If the masses are beasts;
⸢One (man) cannot know his teachings,⸣
And alone possess a mind,
If the multitudes are foolish.
All your sayings are excellent,
But doing them ⸢requires virtues⸣
Tell the god who gave you wisdom:
"Set them on your path!"

The scribe Any answered his son, the scribe Khonshotep:
Turn your back to these many words,
That are ⸢not worth⸣ being heard.
The crooked stick left on the ground,
With sun and shade attacking it,
If the carpenter takes it, he straightens it,
Makes of it a noble's staff,
And a straight stick makes a collar.[19]
You foolish heart,
Do you wish us to teach,
Or have you been corrupted?
"Look," said he,[20] "you ⸢my father,⸣

[16] If that is the meaning, the two lines are tacked on incongruously. Volten 1937-38:132 and 136, tried to obtain a different meaning.
[17] The policeman.
[18] The remainder of the maxim is obscure to me.
[19] *Ḏrt*, a horse collar; i.e., the crooked stick is made straight, and the straight one is rounded. On the passage see Posener 1973:130.
[20] The son speaks.

You who are wise and strong of hand: The infant in his mother's arms, His wish is for what nurses him."	"Look," said he,[21] "when he finds his speech, He says: 'Give me bread.'"

[21] The father answers. Any's concluding answer apparently means that when a child is old enough to speak he asks to be nourished materially and spiritually.

REFERENCES

Text: Mariette 1871 pls. 15-28; Suys 1935. Other fragments: Gardiner 1935a 2:50 and 2:27: P. Chester Beatty V, verso 2,6-11 (= P. Boulaq 4, 3,1-3 and 6,1-4); Posener 1935: nos. 1063, 1257, 1258, 1259. Translation: Volten 1937-38; Erman 1927:234-242. *ANET* 420-421 (excerpts); Volten 1941:373-374; Gardiner 1959a; Lichtheim *AEL* 2:135-146.

INSTRUCTION OF AMENEMOPE (1.47)

Miriam Lichtheim

With this long work, the Instruction genre reaches its culmination. Its worth lies not in any thematic richness, for its range is much narrower than, for example, that of the *Instruction of Ptahhotep*. Its worth lies in its quality of inwardness. Though it is still assumed that right thinking and right action will find their reward, worldly success, which had meant so much in the past, has receded into the background. Even poverty is no longer viewed as a misfortune.

The shift of emphasis, away from action and success, and toward contemplation and endurance, leads to an overall regrouping of values and a redefinition of the ideal man. As early as Ptahhotep, the ideal man lacked all martial values; he was a man of peace who strove for advancement and was generous with his wealth. The new ideal man is content with a humble position and a minimal amount of material possessions. His chief characteristic is modesty. He is self-controlled, quiet, and kind toward people, and he is humble before God. This ideal man is indeed not a perfect man, for perfection is now viewed as belonging only to God.

The style of Amenemope is rich in similes and metaphors which are sustained at length and with skill. The work as a whole is carefully composed and unified, both through the device of thirty numbered chapters and through a concentration on two basic themes: first, the depiction of the ideal man, the "silent man," and his adversary, the "heated man"; second, the exhortation to honesty and warnings against dishonesty. All other themes are subservient to these central ones.

The composition of the work is now usually assigned to the Ramesside period, although all the manuscript copies that have reached us are of later date. It was during the Ramesside age that the tribes of Israel became a nation, and much of Israelite knowledge of things Egyptian, as reflected in the Bible, resulted from contacts during this period. The most tangible literary evidence of these contacts is found in the chips from the Instruction of Amenemope that are embedded in the Book of Proverbs.[a] It can hardly be doubted that the author of Proverbs was acquainted with the Egyptian work and borrowed from it, for in addition to the similarities in thought and expression — especially close and striking in Proverbs 22 and 23 — the line in 22:20: "Have I not written for you thirty sayings of admonition and knowledge" derives its meaning from the author's acquaintance with the "thirty" chapters of Amenemope. Ever since Adolf Erman pointed this out there has been a consensus among scholars on a literary relationship, although some scholars have tried to interpret it in reverse by claiming priority for the Hebrew text, or have proposed to derive both works from a lost Semitic original.

The Instruction of Amenemope is completely preserved in the British Museum Papyrus 10474. Small portions of it are found on a papyrus in Stockholm, three writing tablets in Turin, Paris, and Moscow, respectively, and an ostracon in the Cairo Museum. In the British Museum papyrus and on the Turin and Louvre tablets the text is written stichically, that is to say, in lines that show the metrical scheme. This is unusual and important, for it allows us to see the metrical organization rather than having to guess it. And since the work is also divided into thirty numbered chapters, we are here precisely informed about two basic features of Egyptian prosody as applied to a particular work: the organization of the metrical line and the grouping of lines into sections or chapters.

The metrical line turns out to be exactly what one expects it to be. It consists of self-contained sentences or clauses. Through parallelism and related devices the lines are grouped loosely into distichs, tristichs, and quatrains. There is no indication that these groups of lines were further gathered into strophes or stanzas. Nor would such strophes be suited to the nature of instructional works. For the Instructions consist of thoughts developed freely over greater or lesser length, and the natural divisions occur when one topic is concluded and another taken up. In earlier Instructions such divisions were not marked by graphic or verbal devices; in Amenemope they are brought out clearly through the use of numbered chapters.

Amenemope is a difficult text. It abounds in rare words, elliptic phrases, and allusions whose meaning escapes us. Furthermore, the copying scribes introduced numerous errors. But we are fortunate to have the complete text preserved in the British Museum Papyrus, where it occupies all twenty-seven pages of the recto and the first line of the verso.

Prologue

I.1 Beginning of the teaching for life,
The instructions for well-being,
Every rule for relations with elders,
For conduct toward magistrates;
Knowing how to answer one who speaks,
To reply to one who sends a message.
So as to direct him on the paths of life,
To make him prosper upon earth;
To let his heart enter its shrine,[1]
Steering clear of evil;
To save him from the mouth of strangers,
To let (him) be praised in the mouth of people.
Made by the overseer of fields, experienced in his office,
The offspring of a scribe of Egypt,
The overseer of grains who controls the measure,
Who sets the harvest-dues for his lord,
Who registers the islands of new land,
In the great name of his majesty,
Who records the markers on the borders of fields,
II.1 Who acts for the king in his listing of taxes,
Who makes the land-register of Egypt;
The scribe who determines the offerings for all the gods.
Who gives land-leases to the people,
The overseer of grains, [provider of] foods,
Who supplies the granary with grains;
The truly silent in This of Ta-wer,
The justified in Ipu,
Who owns a tomb on the west of Senu,
Who has a chapel at Abydos,
Amenemope, the son of Kanakht,
The justified in Ta-wer.[2]
<For> his son, the youngest of his children,
The smallest of his family,
The devotee of Min-Kamutef,
The water-pourer of Wennofer,
Who places Horus on his father's throne,
Who guards him in his noble shrine,
Who -----
III.1 The guardian of the mother of god,
Inspector of the black cattle of the terrace of Min,
Who protects Min in his shrine:
Hor-em-maakher is his true name,
The child of a nobleman of Ipu,
The son of the sistrum-player of Shu and Tefnut,
And chief songstress of Horus, Tawosre.

Chapter 1

He says:
Give your ears, hear the sayings,
Give your heart to understand them;
It profits to put them in your heart,[a]
Woe to him who neglects them!
Let them rest in the casket of your belly,
May they be bolted in your heart;
When there rises a whirlwind of words,
They'll be a mooring post for your tongue.
If you make your life with these in your heart,
You will find it a success;
IV.1 You will find my words a storehouse for life,
Your being will prosper upon earth.

Chapter 2

Beware of robbing a wretch,[b]
Of attacking a cripple;
Don't stretch out your hand to touch an old man,
Nor ⌜open your mouth⌝[3] to an elder.
Don't let yourself be sent on a mischievous errand,
Nor be friends with him who does it.
Don't raise an outcry against one who attacks you,
Nor answer him yourself.
He who does evil, the shore rejects him,
Its floodwater carries him away.
The northwind descends to end his hour,
It mingles with the thunderstorm.
The storm cloud is tall, the crocodiles are vicious,

a Prov 22:17-24:22

b Prov 22:22-23

[1] The heart is viewed as the god who dwells in man. On this concept see Bonnet, *RÄRG* 225-228.

[2] Ipu and Senu are names for Akhmim (Panopolis); Ta-wer is the nome of Abydos. Amenemope identifies himself as a citizen of Akhmim who has built his tomb there and also owns a funerary monument at Abydos.

[3] The meaning of *ṯꜣi-r*, which recurs in 15.13, is not clear and it has been variously rendered. See Grumach 1972:31.

You heated man, how are you now?
He cries out, his voice reaches heaven,
It is the Moon[4] who declares his crime.
V.1 Steer, we will ferry the wicked,
We do not act like his kind;
Lift him up, give him your hand,
Leave him <in> the hands of the god;
Fill his belly with bread of your own,
That he be sated and weep.
Another thing good in the heart of the god:
To pause before speaking.

Chapter 3

Don't start a quarrel with a hot-mouthed man,
Nor needle him with words.
Pause before a foe, bend before an attacker,
Sleep (on it) before speaking.
A storm that bursts like fire in straw,
Such is the heated man in his hour.
Withdraw from him, leave him alone,
The god knows how to answer him.
If you make your life with these (words) in your heart,
Your children will observe them.

Chapter 4 [c]

As for the heated man in the temple,[5]
He is like a tree growing ⌈indoors⌉;
A moment lasts its growth of ⌈shoots⌉.
Its end comes about in the ⌈woodshed⌉;
VI.5 It is floated far from its place,
The flame is its burial shroud.
The truly silent, who keeps apart,
He is like a tree grown in a meadow.
It greens, it doubles its yield,
It stands in front of its lord.
Its fruit is sweet, its shade delightful,
Its end comes in the garden.

Chapter 5

Do not falsify[6] the temple rations,
Do not grasp and you'll find profit.
Do not remove a servant of the god,
So as to do favors to another.
Do not say: "Today is like tomorrow,"
How will this end?
VII.1 Comes tomorrow, today has vanished,
The deep has become the water's edge.
Crocodiles are bared, hippopotami stranded,
The fish crowded together.[7]
Jackals are sated, birds are in feast,
The fishnets have been drained.[8]
But all the silent in the temple,
They say: "Re's blessing is great."
Cling to the silent, then you find life.
Your being will prosper upon earth.

Chapter 6

Do not move the markers on the borders of fields,[d]
Nor shift the position of the measuring-cord.
Do not be greedy for a cubit of land,
Nor encroach on the boundaries of a widow.
The trodden furrow worn down by time,
He who disguises it in the fields,
When he has snared (it) by false oaths,
He will be caught by the might of the Moon.
VIII.1 Recognize him who does this on earth:
He is an oppressor of the weak,
A foe bent on destroying your being,
The taking of life is in his eye.
His house is an enemy to the town,
His storage bins will be destroyed
His wealth will be seized from his children's hands,
His possessions will be given to another.
Beware of destroying the borders of fields,
Lest a terror carry you away;
One pleases god with the might of the lord
When one discerns the borders of fields.[9]
Desire your being to be sound,
Beware of the Lord of All;
Do not erase another's furrow,
It profits you to keep it sound.
Plow your fields and you'll find what you need,
You'll receive bread from your threshing-floor.
Better is a bushel given you by the god,
Than five thousand through wrongdoing.
IX.1 They stay not a day in bin and barn,
They make no food for the beer jar,
A moment is their stay in the granary,
Comes morning they have vanished.
Better is poverty in the hand of the god,
Than wealth in the storehouse;
Better is bread with a happy heart
Than wealth with vexation.

Chapter 7

Do not set your heart on wealth,

c Ps 1:3-4

d Prov 22:8; 23:10

[4] The god Thoth.
[5] On this chapter see now Posener 1973:129-135.
[6] The verb ʿšg recurs in 7.17, 18.12, and 18.15. I follow Griffith in taking it to mean "overlay," "falsify," "disguise."
[7] So with Grumach 1972:50.
[8] The theme is the reversal of fortune; see the "Instruction of Any," text 1.46, n. 14 (above).
[9] Some translators take *wpt* as a participle referring to god: "He who determines the borders of fields." But then the meaning of the couplet is poor. I have followed Griffith.

There is no ignoring Fate and Destiny;
Do not let your heart go straying,
Every man comes to his hour.
[e] Do not strain to seek increase,
What you have, let it suffice you.
If riches come to you by theft,
They will not stay the night with you.
Comes day they are not in your house
Their place is seen but they're not there;
Earth opened its mouth, leveled them, swallowed them,
X.1 And made them sink into *dat*.
They made a hole as big as their size,
And sank into the netherworld;
They made themselves wings like geese,
And flew away to the sky.[e]
Do not rejoice in wealth from theft,
Nor complain of being poor.
If the leading archer presses forward,
His company abandons him;
The boat of the greedy is left (in) the mud,
While the bark of the silent sails with the Wind.
You shall pray to the Aten when he rises,
Saying: "Grant me well-being and health";
He will give you your needs for this life,
And you will be safe from fear.

Chapter 8

Set your goodness before people,
Then you are greeted by all;
One welcomes the Uraeus,
One spits upon Apopis. Guard your tongue from harmful speech,
XI.1 Then you will be loved by others.
You will find your place in the house of god,
You will share in the offerings of your lord.
When you're revered and your coffin conceals you
You will be safe from the power of god.[10]
Do not shout "crime" against a man,
When the cause of (his) flight is hidden.
Whether you hear something good or evil,
Do it outside where it is not heard.
Put the good remark on your tongue,
While the bad is concealed in your belly.

Chapter 9

Do not befriend the heated man,
Nor approach him for conversation.[f]
Keep your tongue from answering your superior,
And take care not to insult him.
Let him not cast his speech to catch you,
Nor give free rein to your answer.

e-e Prov 23:4-5

f Prov 23:24-25

Converse with a man of your own measure,
And take care not to ⌜offend⌝ him.
XII.1 Swift is the speech of one who is angered,
More than wind ⌜over⌝ water.
He tears down, he builds up with his tongue,
When he makes his hurtful speech.
He gives an answer worthy of a beating,
For its weight is harm.
He hauls freight like all the world,
But his load is falsehood.
He is the ferry-man of snaring words,
He goes and comes with quarrels.
When he eats and drinks inside,
His answer is (heard) outside.
The day he is charged with his crime is misfortune for his children.
If only Khnum came to him,
The Potter to the heated man,
So as to knead the ⌜faulty⌝ heart.
He is like a young wolf in the farmyard,
He turns one eye against the other,
XIII.1 He causes brothers to quarrel.
He runs before every wind like clouds,
He dims the radiance of the sun;
He flips his tail like the crocodile's young,
⌜He draws himself up so as to strike.⌝
His lips are sweet, his tongue is bitter,
A fire burns in his belly.
Don't leap to join such a one,
Lest a terror carry you away.

Chapter 10

Don't force yourself to greet the heated man,
For then you injure your own heart;
Do not say "greetings" to him falsely,
While there is terror in your belly.
Do not speak falsely to a man,
The god abhors it;
Do not sever your heart from your tongue,
That all your strivings may succeed.
You will be weighty before the others,
XIV.1 And secure in the hand of the god.
God hates the falsifier of words,
He greatly abhors the dissembler.

Chapter 11

Do not covet a poor man's goods,
Nor hunger for his bread;
A poor man's goods are a block in the throat,
It makes the gullet vomit.
He who makes gain by lying oaths,
His heart is misled by his belly;
Where there is fraud success is feeble,
The bad spoils the good.[11]

[10] "Power" here in the sense of "wrath."

[11] Assuming *whꜣ* to be transitive. The usual rendering, "good and bad fail," is not satisfactory.

You will be guilty before your superior,
And confused in your account;
Your pleas will be answered by a curse,
Your prostrations by a beating.
The big mouthful of bread — you swallow, you vomit it,
And you are emptied of your gain.[g]
Observe the overseer[12] of the poor,
XV.1 When the stick attains him;
All his people are bound in chains,
And he is led to the executioner.
If you are released before your superior,
You are yet hateful to your subordinates;
Steer away from the poor man on the road,
Look at him and keep clear of his goods.

Chapter 12

Do not desire a noble's wealth,
Nor make free with a big mouthful of bread;
If he sets you to manage his property,
Shun his, and yours will prosper.
Do not converse[13] with a heated man,
So as to befriend a hostile man.
If you are sent to transport straw,
Stay away from its container.
If a man is observed on a fraudulent errand,
He will not be sent on another occasion.

Chapter 13

Do not cheat a man <through> pen on scroll,
The god abhors it;
XVI.1 Do not bear witness with false words,
So as to brush aside a man by your tongue.
Do not assess a man who has nothing,
And thus falsify your pen.
If you find a large debt against a poor man,
Make it into three parts;
Forgive two, let one stand,
You will find it a path of life.
After sleep, when you wake in the morning,
You will find it as good news.
Better is praise with the love of men
Than wealth in the storehouse;
Better is bread with a happy heart
Than wealth with vexation.

Chapter 14

Do not recall yourself to a man,
Nor strain to seek his hand.
If he says to you: "Here is a gift.
⌜No have-not⌝ will refuse it,"[14]
Don't blink at him, nor bow your head,
Nor turn aside your gaze.
Salute him with your mouth, say, "Greetings,"
XVII.1 He will desist, and you succeed.
Do not rebuff him in his approach,
⌜Another time he'll be taken away.⌝

Chapter 15

Do the good and you will prosper,
Do not dip your pen to injure a man.
The finger of the scribe is the beak of the Ibis,
Beware of brushing it aside.
The Ape dwells in the House of Khmun,[15]
His eye encircles the Two Lands;
When he sees one who cheats with his finger,
He carries his livelihood off in the flood.
The scribe who cheats with his finger,
His son will not be enrolled.
If you make your life with these (words) in your heart,
Your children will observe them.

Chapter 16

Do not move the scales nor alter the weights,
Nor diminish the fractions of the measure;
Do not desire a measure of the fields,
Nor neglect those of the treasury.
The Ape sits by the balance,
XVIII.1 His heart is in the plummet;
Where is a god as great as Thoth,
Who invented these things and made them?
Do not make for yourself deficient weights,
They are rich in grief through the might of god.
If you see someone who cheats,
Keep your distance from him.
Do not covet copper,
Disdain beautiful linen;
What good is one dressed in finery,
If he cheats before the god?
Faience disguised as gold,
Comes day, it turns to lead.

Chapter 17

Beware of disguising the measure,
So as to falsify its fractions;
Do not force it to overflow,
Nor let its belly be empty.
Measure according to its true size,

[g] Prov 23:6-8

[12] The meaning of *ḥy* is not well established; the word recurs in 24.17 where the meaning "overseer," or "superior," is suitable. But here a negative connotation such as "oppressor" seems called for.

[13] See note 3.

[14] The verb $b^{c\supset}$ (or b^{c}) recurs in 21.2, 27.1, and 27.5. The meaning assigned in *Wb.* 1:446 "beachten, berücksichtigen," does not appear suitable here. The four occurrences in Amenemope suggest "rebuff," "refuse," as well as "pass up," "let pass."

[15] The ibis and the ape are the images or Thoth.

Your hand clearing exactly.
Do not make a bushel of twice its size,
For then you are headed for the abyss.
The bushel is the Eye of Re,
XIX.1 It abhors him who trims;
A measurer who indulges in cheating,
His Eye seals (the verdict) against him.
Do not accept a farmer's dues
And then assess him so as to injure him;
Do not conspire with the measurer,
So as to defraud the share of the Residence.
Greater is the might of the threshing floor
Than an oath by the great throne.

Chapter 18

Do not lie down in fear of tomorrow:
"Comes day, how will tomorrow be?"
Man ignores how tomorrow will be;
God is ever in his perfection,
Man is ever in his failure.[16]
The words men say are one thing,
The deeds of the god are another.
Do not say: "I have done no wrong,"
And then strain to seek a quarrel;
The wrong belongs to the god,
He seals (the verdict) with his finger.
There is no perfection before the god,
But there is failure before him;[17]
XX.1 If one strains to seek perfection,
In a moment he has marred it.
Keep firm your heart, steady your heart,
Do not steer with your tongue;
If a man's tongue is the boat's rudder,
The Lord of All is yet its pilot.

Chapter 19

Do not go to court before an official
In order to falsify your words;
Do not vacillate in your answers,
When your witnesses accuse.
Do not strain <with> oaths by your lord,
<With> speeches at the hearing;
Tell the truth before the official,
Lest he lay a hand on you.
If another day you come before him,
He will incline to all you say;
He will relate your speech to the Council of Thirty,
It will be observed on another occasion.

Chapter 20

Do not confound a man in the law court,
In order to brush aside one who is right.
XXI.1 Do not incline to the well-dressed man,
And rebuff the one in rags.
Don't accept the gift of a powerful man,
And deprive the weak for his sake.
Maat is a great gift of god,
He gives it to whom he wishes.
The might of him who resembles him,
It saves the poor from his tormentor.
Do not make for yourself false documents,
They are a deadly provocation;
They (mean) the great restraining oath,[18]
They (mean) a hearing by the herald.
Don't falsify the oracles in the scrolls,[19]
And thus disturb the plans of god;
Don't use for yourself the might of god,
As if there were no Fate and Destiny.
Hand over property to its owners,
Thus do you seek life for yourself;
Don't raise your desire in their house,
Or your bones belong to the execution-block.

Chapter 21

XXII.1 Do not say: "Find me a strong superior,
For a man in your town has injured me";
Do not say: "Find me a protector,
For one who hates me has injured me."
Indeed you do not know the plans of god,
And should not weep for tomorrow;
Settle in the arms of the god,
Your silence will overthrow them.[20]
The crocodile that makes no sound,[21]
Dread of it is ancient.
Do not empty your belly to everyone,
And thus destroy respect of you;
Broadcast not your words to others,
Nor join with one who bares his heart.
Better is one whose speech is in his belly
Than he who tells it to cause harm.
One does not run to reach success,
One does not move to spoil it.

Chapter 22

Do not provoke your adversary,
So as to <make> him tell his thoughts;
Do not leap to come before him,
XXIII.1 When you do not see his doings.
First gain insight from his answer,
Then keep still and you'll succeed.
Leave it to him to empty his belly,
Know how to sleep, he'll be found out.
⌜Grasp his legs,⌝[22] do not harm him,

[16] Lit., "the god," and "the man." Amenemope says "god" and "the god," interchangeably. The presence or absence of the definite article seems to be a matter of style.

[17] I emend *mn* to *wn*; otherwise the sentence contradicts all that has gone before.

[18] On the oath *sdfꜣ tr* see Baer 1964:179-180.

[19] The passage was explained by Posener 1963a.

[20] The adversaries.

[21] On this passage see Posener 1968.

[22] This meaning does not suit; I suspect a corruption.

Be wary of him, do not ignore him.
Indeed you do not know the plans of god,
And should not weep for tomorrow;
Settle in the arms of the god,
Your silence will overthrow them.

Chapter 23

Do not eat in the presence of an official
And then set your mouth before <him>;
If you are sated pretend to chew,
Content yourself with your saliva.[23]
Look at the bowl that is before you,
And let it serve your needs.
An official is great in his office,
As a well is rich in drawings of water.

Chapter 24

Do not listen to an official's reply indoors
XXIV.1 In order to repeat it to another outside.
Do not let your word be carried outside,
Lest your heart be aggrieved.
The heart of man is a gift[24] of god,
Beware of neglecting it.
The man at the side of an official,
His name should not be known.

Chapter 25

Do not laugh at a blind man,
Nor tease a dwarf,[25]
Nor cause hardship for the lame.
Don't tease a man who is in the hand of the god,[26]
Nor be angry with him for his failings.
Man is clay and straw,
The god is his builder.
He tears down, he builds up daily,
He makes a thousand poor by his will,
He makes a thousand men into chiefs,
When he is in his hour of life.[27]
Happy is he who reaches the west,
When he is safe in the hand of the god.

Chapter 26

Do not sit down in the beer-house
XXV.1 In order to join one greater than you,
Be he a youth great through his office,
Or be he an elder through birth.
Befriend a man of your own measure,
Re is helpful from afar.
If you see one greater than you outdoors,
Walk behind him respectfully;
Give a hand to an elder sated with beer,
Respect him as his children would.
The arm is not hurt by being bared,[28]
The back is not broken by bending it.
A man does not lose by speaking sweetly,
Nor does he gain if his speech bristles.
The pilot who sees from afar,
He will not wreck his boat.

Chapter 27

Do not revile one older than you,
He has seen Re before you;
Let <him> not report you to the Aten at his rising,
Saying: "A youth has reviled an old man."
Very painful before Pre
XXVI.1 Is a youth who reviles an elder.
Let him beat you while your hand is on your chest,
Let him revile you while you are silent;
If next day you come before him,
He will give you food in plenty.
A dog's food is from its master,
It barks to him who gives it.

Chapter 28

Do not pounce on a widow when you find her in the fields[29]
And then fail to be patient with her reply.
Do not refuse your oil jar to a stranger,
Double it before your brothers.
God prefers him who honors the poor
To him who worships the wealthy.

Chapter 29

Do not prevent people from crossing the river,
If you stride freely in the ferry.[30]
When you are given an oar in the midst of the deep,
Bend your arms and take it.
It is no crime before the god,
XXVII.1 ⌜If the passenger is not passed up⌝[31]
Don't make yourself a ferry on the river
And then strain to seek its fare;
Take the fare from him who is wealthy,
And let pass him who is poor.

Chapter 30

Look to these thirty chapters,[h]
They inform, they educate;

[h] Prov 22:20-21

[23] So following Polotsky 1973:140 n. 3.
[24] The Turin tablet has "gift" instead of the "nose" of the British Museum papyrus; see Posener 1966b:61-62.
[25] In the British Museum papyrus the two sentences appear as a single line but on the Turin tablet as two lines.
[26] Here in the special meaning of one who is ill or insane.
[27] Volten (1963:88) explained this to mean that the sun-god acts through the gods who are assigned to each hour of the day.
[28] I.e., stretching the arm out of the sleeve in a gesture of greeting. The same remark occurs in "Ptahhotep," line 445/448.
[29] I.e., when you find her gleaning in fields not her own.
[30] I.e., when there is ample room in the ferry.
[31] It is not clear whether *hwty* means "passenger" or "sailor"; in any case, the meaning is that the passenger should help with the rowing if asked to do so.

They are the foremost of all books,
They make the ignorant wise.
If they are read to the ignorant,
He is cleansed through them.
Be filled with them, put them in your heart,
And become a man who expounds them,
One who expounds as a teacher.
The scribe who is skilled in his office,[i]
He is found worthy to be a courtier.

i Prov 22:29

Colophon

That is its end.
XXVIII.1 Written by Senu, son of the divine father Pemu.

REFERENCES

Text: Budge 1923:9-18 and 41-51 and pls. 1-14; Lange 1925. Translation: Erman 1924b cols 241-252; Budge 1924:93-234; Griffith 1926:191-231; Lexa 1929:14-49; von Bissing 1955:80-90; *ANET* 421-424 (excerpts); Simpson, 1972:241-265; Grumach 1972; Lichtheim *AEL* 2:146-163. Discussion: Erman 1924 no.15; Simpson 1926:232-239; Humbert 1929 ch. 2; Williams 1961:100-106; Peterson 1966:120-128 and pls. xxxi-xxxiA (the Stockholm fragment); Posener 1966:45-62 and pls. 1-2 (the three tablets); Anthes 1970:9-18; Posener 1973:129-135; Loprieno 1980:47-76; Ruffle 1977:29-68.

DUA-KHETY OR THE SATIRE ON THE TRADES (1.48)

Miriam Lichtheim

Like the other Instructions, this work has a prologue and an epilogue which frame the actual teaching and set its stage. A father conducts his young son to the residence in order to place him in school, and during the journey he instructs him in the duties and rewards of the scribal profession. In order to stress the amenities and advantages that accrue to the successful scribe, he contrasts the scribal career with the hardships of other trades and professions, eighteen of which are described in the most unflattering terms.

Ever since Maspero called this Instruction "Satire des Métiers," scholars have understood it to be a satire, that is to say, a deliberately derisive characterization of all trades other than the scribal profession. Helck, however, in his new edition of the text has denied its satiric character and has claimed it to be a wholly serious, non-humorous work. I continue to think of it as a satire. What are the stylistic means of satire? Exaggeration and a lightness of tone designed to induce laughter and a mild contempt. Our text achieves its satirical effects by exaggerating the true hardships of the professions described, and by suppressing all their positive and rewarding aspects.

If it were argued that the exaggerations were meant to be taken seriously we would have to conclude that the scribal profession practiced deliberate deception out of a contempt for manual labor so profound as to be unrelieved by humor. Such a conclusion is, however, belied by all the literary and pictorial evidence. For tomb reliefs and texts alike breathe joy and pride in the accomplishments of labor. Moreover, the principal didactic works, such as Ptahhotep and the Eloquent Peasant, teach respect for all labor.

In short, the unrelievedly negative descriptions of the laboring professions are examples of humor in the service of literary satire. The result is obtained through unflattering comparisons and through exaggerations that rise to outright fabrications. What if not a fabrication for the sake of caricature is a bird-catcher who does not have a net — the very tool of his trade? What if not a caricature is a potter who is compared to a grubbing pig, a cobbler whose hides are termed "corpses," a courier terrorized out of his wits by the dangers of the road, and a fisherman blinded by his fear of crocodiles?

The text is preserved entirely in P. Sallier II, and partially in P. Anastasi VII (both in the British Museum), both of which were written by the same Nineteenth Dynasty scribe. Small portions are preserved on an Eighteenth Dynasty writing board in the Louvre, the Eighteenth Dynasty P. Amherst in the Pierpont Morgan Library, P. Chester Beatty XIX of the British Museum, and numerous, mostly Ramesside, ostraca.

Though ample, the textual transmission is exceedingly corrupt. Helck's comprehensive new edition has advanced the understanding considerably. But the corruptions are so numerous and so extreme that there remains much room for differing conjectures and interpretations.

(3.9) Beginning of the Instruction made by the man of Sile,[1] whose name is ⌜Dua-khety⌝,[2] for his son, called Pepi, as he journeyed south (4.1) to the residence, to place him in the school for scribes, among the sons of magistrates, with the elite of the residence. He said to him:

---

[1] *Ṯꜣrt*, or *Ṯꜣrw*, i.e., Sile, the border fortress in the eastern Delta.

[2] Three manuscripts write the name as "Khety, son of Duauf," two write "Dua-Khety"; a sixth gives yet another form. Helck has adopted Seibert's preference for "Dua-Khety." Brunner 1969:71, has reaffirmed his support for "Khety, son of Duauf."

I have seen many beatings —
Set your heart on books!
I watched those seized for labor —
There's nothing better than books!
It's like a boat on water.

Read the end of the *Kemit*-Book,[3]
You'll find this saying there:
A scribe at whatever post in town,
He will not suffer in it;
As he fills another's need,
He will ⌜not lack rewards⌝.
I don't see a calling like it
Of which this saying could be (5) said.

I'll make you love scribedom more than your mother,
I'll make its beauties stand before you;
It's the greatest of all callings,
There's none like it in the land.

Barely grown, still a child,
He is greeted, sent on errands,
Hardly returned he wears a gown.
I never saw a sculptor as envoy,
Nor is a goldsmith ever sent;
But I have seen the smith at work
At the opening of his furnace;
With fingers like claws of a crocodile
He stinks more than fish roe.

The carpenter who wields an adze,
He is wearier than a field-laborer;
His field is the timber, his hoe the adze.
There is no end to his labor,
He does more (5.1) than his arms can do,
Yet at night he kindles light.
The jewel-maker bores with his chisel[4]
In hard stone of all kinds;
When he has finished the inlay of the eye,
His arms are spent, he's weary;
Sitting down when the sun goes down,
His knees and back are cramped.

The barber barbers till nightfall,
He betakes himself to town,[5]
He sets himself up in his corner,
He moves from street to street,
Looking for someone to barber.
He strains his arms to fill his belly,
(5) Like the bee that eats as it works.

The reed-cutter travels to the Delta to get arrows;
When he has done more than his arms can do,
Mosquitoes have slain him,
Gnats have slaughtered him,
He is quite worn out.

The potter is under the soil,
Though as yet among the living;
He grubs in the mud more than a pig,
In order to fire his pots.
His clothes are stiff with clay,
His girdle is in shreds;
If air enters his nose,
It comes straight from the fire.
He makes a pounding with his feet,
And is himself crushed;[6]
He grubs the yard of every house
And roams the public places.

(6.1) I'll describe to you also the mason:
His loins give him pain;
Though he is out in the wind,
He works without a cloak;
His loincloth is a twisted rope
And a string in the rear.[7]
His arms are spent from exertion,
Having mixed all kinds of dirt;
When he eats bread [with] his fingers,
⌜He has washed at the same time⌝.

The carpenter also suffers much[8]
......
The room measures ten by six cubits.
A month passes after the beams are laid,
......
And all its work is done.
(5) The food which he gives to his household,
It does not ⌜suffice⌝ for his children.

The gardener carries a yoke,
His shoulders are bent as with age;
There's a swelling on his neck
And it festers.
In the morning he waters vegetables,
The evening he spends with the herbs,[9]

[3] A book of Instructions, the fragments of which were published by Posener 1972 2:pls. 1-25; see also Posener 1956:4-6.

[4] Eg. *Ms-ʿꜣt*. Brunner, "Steinmetz," Wilson, "fashioner of costly stones," Seibert, "Schmuckarbeiter," and Helck, "Juwelier." The activity of this craftsman is described by the verb *whb* in *DM* 1014, which means "to bore." The conjecture that mnh means "to string beads" lacks support, for in *Admonitions* 3.3 Gardiner merely took it to mean "to fasten."

[5] Emending *ʿmʿyt* to *dwyt*, as proposed by Vandier 1949:15.

[6] The pounding with the feet that occurred in pottery making was in the initial molding of the clay prior to its being shaped by hand. I see no occasion for the conjectured pounding tools.

[7] This seems to refer to the narrow strip of cloth tied in front, with its ends hanging down to cover the genitals, which was worn by some laborers. The dangling ends were sometimes tucked into the waistband or turned to the back. The resulting nudity may have aroused the derision of the well-dressed scribes.

[8] As Helck pointed out, this section deals with the carpenter. Unfortunately it is very obscure.

[9] A meaning broader than "coriander" is indicated for *šꜣw*. In the sun-temple of Ni-user-re, *šꜣw* is a water plant eaten by fish; see Edel 1961-1964:217.

While at noon he has toiled in the orchard.
He works himself to death
More than all other professions.

The farmer wails more than the guinea fowl,
His voice is louder than a raven's;
His fingers are swollen
And stink to excess.
He is weary ......
... (7.1) ...
He is well if one's well among lions.[10]
......
When he reaches home at night,
The march has worn him out.

The weaver[11] in the workshop,
He is worse off than a woman;
With knees against his chest,
He cannot breathe air.
If he skips a day of weaving,
He is beaten fifty strokes;
He gives food to the doorkeeper,
To let him see the light of day.

The arrow-maker suffers much
As he goes out (5) to the desert;
More is what he gives his donkey
Than the work it does for him.
Much is what he gives the herdsmen,
So they'll put him on his way.
When he reaches home at night,
The march has worn him out.

The courier[12] goes into the desert,
Leaving his goods to his children;
Fearful of lions and Asiatics,
He knows himself (only) when he's in Egypt.
When he reaches home at night,
The march has worn him out;
Be his home of cloth or brick,
His return is joyless.[13]

The ⌜stoker⌝, his fingers are foul,
Their smell is that of corpses;
His eyes are inflamed by much smoke,
(8.1) He cannot get rid of his dirt.
He spends the day cutting reeds,
His clothes are loathsome to him.

The cobbler suffers much
Among his vats of oil;
He is well if one's well with corpses,
What he bites is leather.

The washerman washes on the shore
With the crocodile as neighbor;
⌜"Father, leave the flowing water,"⌝
Say his son, his daughter,
⌜It is not a job that satisfies⌝
......
His food is mixed with dirt,
No limb of his is clean
⌜He is given⌝ (5) women's clothes,
......
He weeps as he spends the day at his washboard
......
One says to him, "Soiled linen for you,"
......

The bird-catcher suffers much
As he watches out for birds;
When the swarms pass over him,
He keeps saying, "Had I a net!"
But the god grants it not,
And he's angry with his lot.

I'll speak of the fisherman also,
His is the worst of all the jobs;
He labors on the river,
Mingling with crocodiles.
When the time of reckoning comes,
He is full of lamentations;
He does not say, "There's a (9.1) crocodile,"
Fear has made him blind.
⌜Coming from⌝ the flowing water
He says, "Mighty god!"

See, there's no profession without a boss,
Except for the scribe; he is the boss.
Hence if you know writing,
It will do better for you
Than those professions I've set before you,
Each more wretched than the other.[14]
A peasant is not called a man,
Beware of it!

Lo, what I do in journeying to the residence,
Lo,[15] I do it for love of you.
The day in school will profit you
Its works are for ever ...
......
I'll tell you also other things,
So as to teach you knowledge.
Such as: if a quarrel breaks out,

[10] This rendering, which is Brunner's, was rejected by Seibert and Helck but seems to me the right one. The sentences following it are extremely obscure.

[11] Or specifically, the "mat-weaver."

[12] Eg. *Sḫ*ᵓ*ḫ*ᵓ*ty*. Brunner, "Eilbote," Helck, "Karawanenträger." A member of a caravan would have much less reason to be frightened than a lone courier.

[13] This was Brunner's tentative rendering and seems to me the best guess.

[14] I emend to: *mk ky iry ḥwrw r iry.f.*

[15] Connective iterated *mk*, as also in the first poem of the "Dispute between a Man and His Ba," and in the "Prophecies of Neferti" (see there n. 2).

Do not approach the contenders!
If you are chided ......
And don't know how to repel the heat,
⸢Call the listeners to witness⸣,
And delay the answer.

When you walk behind officials,
Follow at a proper distance.
When you enter a man's house,
And he's busy with someone before you,
Sit with your hand over your mouth.
Do not ask him for anything,
Only do as he tells you,
Beware of rushing to the table!

Be weighty and very dignified,
Do not speak of (10.1) secret things,
Who hides his thought[16] shields himself.
Do not say things recklessly,
When you sit with one who's hostile.
If you leave the schoolhouse
When midday is called,
And go roaming in the streets,
⸢All will scold you in the end⸣.[17]
When an official sends you with a message,
Tell it as he told it,
Don't omit, don't add to it.[18]
He who neglects to praise,
His name will not endure;
He who is skilled in all his conduct,
From him nothing is hidden,
He is not ⸢opposed⸣ anywhere.

Do not tell lies (5) against your mother,
The magistrates abhor it.
The descendant who does what is good,
His actions all emulate the past.
Do not consort with a rowdy,
It harms you when one hears of it.
If you have eaten three loaves,
Drunk two jugs of beer,
And the belly is not sated, restrain it!
When another eats, don't stand there,
Beware of rushing to the table!
It is good if you are sent out often,
And hear the magistrates speak.
You should acquire the manner of the well-born,[19]
As you follow in their steps.
The scribe is regarded as one who hears,
For the hearer becomes a doer.
You should rise when you are addressed,
Your feet should hurry when you go;
⸢Do not⸣ (11.1) ⸢trust⸣.
Associate with men of distinction,
Befriend a man of your generation.

Lo, I have set you on god's path,
A scribe's Renenet[20] is on his shoulder
On the day he is born.
When he attains the council chamber,
The court ......
Lo, no scribe is short of food
And of riches from the palace.
The Meskhenet assigned to the scribe,
She promotes him in the council.
Praise god for your father, your mother,
Who set you on the path of life!
This is what I put before you,
Your children and their children.

Colophon
(5) It has come to a happy conclusion.

[16] Lit., "his belly."
[17] In this garbled passage I chose the reading of *DM* 1039, emending only *bw nk* to *bw nb*.
[18] Cp. the eighth maxim of the Instruction of Ptahhotep, see Lichtheim *AEL* 1:65.
[19] Lit., "the children of people," which is the plural counterpart of the term *sꜣ s*, "son of man."
[20] Renenet (Thermuthis) was a goddess of bounty and good luck. She was frequently associated with the goddess Meskhenet who presided over births.

REFERENCES

Text: Budge 1910:pls. 65-73. Brunner 1944; Helck 1970. Translation: Erman 1927:67-72; Van de Walle 1949:244-256; *ANET* 432-434; Lichtheim *AEL* 1:184-192; Studies: Piankoff 1933:51-74; Théodoridès 1958-1960:39-69; Van de Walle 1947:50-72;11; Seibert 1967:99-192.

4. LOVE POEMS

The extant Egyptian love song texts all date from the 19th dynasty (ca. 1305-1200 BCE) and the early 20th dynasty (ca. 1200-1150 BCE). The songs' composition too seems to date from the Ramesside period. They are collected on large papyri or inscribed on ostraca. They are sometimes labelled "Entertainment" (lit. "diverting the heart") and probably served to entertain guests at banquets. Numerous tomb murals show musicians singing to the guests and urging them to "divert" their hearts.

The sex of the speakers is indicated by grammatical gender. They all seem to be adolescents living under their parents' control. For a hieroglyphic transcription, translation, commentary, see Fox (1985). The numbering in the following is according to the numeration in Fox 1985 (see 5-7). Some of the following are stanzas extracted from longer songs. The translation below presupposes some minor emendations and supplies some pronouns and minor connectives.

PAPYRUS HARRIS 500 (1.49)

Michael V. Fox

BM 10060 (*HPBM 2*, pls. XLI-XLVI). The manuscript is a sort of literary anthology, containing two stories ("The Doomed Prince" and "The Capture of Joppa"), a mortuary song (the "Harper's Song") and three groups of love songs.

(*Girl*) (Number 4)
My heart is not yet done with your love,
my wolf cub![a]
Your liquor is your lovemaking.[1] [b]
I will not abandon it
until blows drive me away
to spend my days in the marshes, (or)
to the land of Syria with sticks and rods,
to the land of Nubia with palms,
to the highlands with switches,
to the lowlands with cudgels.
I will not listen to their advice.[2]

(*Boy*) (Number 6)
I will lie down inside,
and then I will feign illness.
Then my neighbors will enter to see,
and then my sister[3]
will come with them.
She'll put the doctors to shame
for she (alone) will understand my illness.[4] [c]

(*Girl*) (Number 10)
The voice of the goose cries out,
as he's trapped by the bait.
Your love restrains me,
so that I can't release it.
I'll take my nets[5],
but what shall I say to Mother,
to whom I go every day
laden down with birds?
I set no trap today —
your love captured me.[6]

(*Girl*) (Number 11)
The goose soars and alights:
while the ordinary birds circle,
he has disturbed the garden.[7]
...
I am excited (?) by your love[8] alone.
My heart is in balance with your heart.[9]
May I never be far from your beauty!

(*Girl*) (Number 12)
I have departed [from my brother].
[Now when I think of] your love,
my heart stands still within me.
When I behold sw[eet] cakes,
[they seem like] salt.
Pomegranate wine, (once) sweet in my mouth —
it is (now) like the gall of birds.
The scent of your nose alone[10] [d]
is what revives my heart.
I have obtained forever and ever
what Amun has granted me.[11]

(*Girl*) (Number 13)
The most beautiful thing has come to pass!
My heart [desires] (to tend)
your property (?)
as the mistress of your house,
while your arm rests on my arm,
for my love has surrounded you.
I say to my heart within me in prayer:

a Cant 2:15
b Cant 5:1; 8:2b
c Cant 2:5; 5:8
d Cant 7:9

[1] I.e., your lovemaking is what intoxicates me. The word for lovemaking, *dd*, with the phallus determinative, is a semiticism cognate to Hebrew *dodim*. It refers to acts of erotic love, from caresses to intercourse.

[2] "They" — her family, perhaps, or the society about her — try to separate the girl from her lover, but she defies them. For the motif of hostile surroundings compare the brothers in Cant 1:6 and (more severely) the watchmen in 5:7. For the maiden's defiance cf. Cant 8:5b-7.

[3] "Brother" (*sn*) and "sister" (*snt*) are common epithets of endearment. In the Song of Songs, only the latter is used.

[4] The boy plans a ruse to get his beloved to visit him. But his feigned sickness may be a reality: love-sickness, which cannot be cured by physicians; cf. numbers 21F, 32, 37. *Mr* "sickness" may be a pun on *mrwt* "love."

[5] The net is the girl's hair. *šnw* represents consonantal homonyms meaning "garden," "hair," and "net" (number 10); cf. Cant 7:6.

[6] The "love trap" theme. The girl has set out her bird traps (a favorite activity portrayed in tomb murals) and has caught a goose, yet she has no birds to take home that evening. The trapped goose is the youth, and she herself is ensnared in love. Several poems play on the love-trap theme; e.g. P. Chester Beatty I (text 1.51, no. 43 below).

[7] *šnw*; see n. 5. Here, the garden is the girl herself; cf. Cant 4:12-5:1a.

[8] "Your love" here and elsewhere may mean "you" or "your lovemaking" and well as "your love for me."

[9] That is, we feel the same way. The image of "balance" (*mḫꜣ*), used also in numbers 17 and 20A, suggests an equal and mutual emotion.

[10] Love paralyzes and confuses both in presence (Cant 2:5) and in absence (as here and in nos. 6, 34, and 37). "Scent of your nose" (as in Cant 7:9) may refer to the practice of nose kissing. The Eg. word for "kiss" is, in fact, written with a nose-determinative.

[11] I have obtained what the god Amun determined as my lot, namely your love.

["Give me] my prince tonight,[12]
or I am like one who lies in her grave!"
For are you not health and life itself?
The approach [of your face
will give me j]oy for your health,
for my heart seeks you.

The Beginning of the Song of Entertainment[13]
(*Girl*) (Number 17)
Mḫmḫ-flowers:
my heart is in balance[14] with yours.
For you I'll do what it wills,
when I'm in your embrace.
It is my prayer that paints my eyes.
Seeing you has brightened my eyes.
I've drawn near you to see your love,
O prince of my heart![15]
How lovely is my hour (with you)!
This hour flows forth for me forever —
it began when I lay with you.
In sorrow and in joy,
you have exalted my heart.
Do not [leave] me.

(*Girl*) (Number 18)
In it are *sꜥꜣm*-trees;
before them one is exalted[16]:
I am your favorite girl.[17]
I am yours like the field
planted with flowers
and with all sorts of fragrant plants.[18] [e]
Pleasant is the canal within it,
which your hand scooped out,
while we cooled ourselves in the north wind:
a lovely place for strolling about,
with your hand upon mine!
My body is satisfied,
and my heart rejoices
in our walking about together.
To hear your voice is pomegranate wine (to me):
I draw life from hearing it.
Could I see you with every glance,
it would be better for me
than to eat or to drink.

[e] Cant 4:12-5:1

[12] Lovers speak of themselves and each other as royal or noble because of the way they feel. The youth is a "prince" in her affections, a "prince of my heart" (number 17), while the maiden is the Mistress of the Two Lands, i.e. the queen of Egypt (number 8), when she is with her beloved. The references to royalty (1:4a, 12; 3:7-11) and nobility (7:2) in the Song of Songs can be understood similarly.

[13] This is the title given a song of three stanzas, each one opening with a pun on the name of a flower. "Entertainment" (*sḫmḫ ib*), cf. number 31, is lit., "making the heart forget" or "diverting the heart."

[14] Eg. *mḫꜣ*. See n. 9.

[15] See n. 12.

[16] Eg. *sꜥꜣ*, playing on *sꜥꜣm*.

[17] Lit. "foremost sister."

[18] The girl is likened to a garden; see n. 7. The flowers are, perhaps, her perfumes.

CAIRO LOVE SONGS (1.50)

(Deir el-Medineh 1266 + Cairo cat. 25218; Posener 1972)

Michael V. Fox

The following are stanzas from the second of two seven-stanza love songs (numbers 21A-21G) written on a vase, now shattered.[1]

(*Boy*) (Number 21A)
If only I were her Nubian maid,
her attendant in secret!
She brings her [a bowl of] mandragoras ...
It is in her hand,
while she gives pleasure.
In other words:
she would grant me
the hue of her whole body.

(*Boy*) (Number 21B)
If only I were the laundryman
of my sister's linen garment
even for one month!
I would be strengthened
by grasping [the clothes]
that touch her body.
For it would be I who washed out the moringa oils
that are in her kerchief.
Then I'd rub my body
with her cast-off garments,
and she ...
[Oh I would be in] joy and delight,
my [bo]dy vigorous!

[1] In each stanza of this song the youth expresses a wish to be something in close contact with the beloved, something that can touch and see her. The wish theme appears elsewhere in Eg. love poetry (numbers 7, 38-40) and in Cant 8:1-2.

(*Boy*) (Number 21C)
If only I were her little seal-ring,
the keeper of her finger![f]
I would see her love[2]
each and every day, ...
[and it would be I who] stole her heart ...

f Cant 8:6

[2] I.e., her.

PAPYRUS CHESTER BEATTY I (1.51)
(Gardiner 1931)

Michael V. Fox

A large papyrus containing three groups of love songs, the tale of "Horus and Seth," two hymns to the king, and a short business note.

From Pap. Chester Beatty I, C1,1-C5,2; the first group of love songs.

The Beginning of the Sayings of the Great Entertainer[1]
(*Boy*) (Number 31)
One alone is my sister, having no peer:
more gracious than all other women.
Behold her, like Sothis[2] rising
at the beginning of a good year:
shining, precious, white of skin,
lovely of eyes when gazing.
Sweet her lips when speaking:
she has no excess of words.
Long of neck, white of breast,
her hair true lapis lazuli.
Her arms surpass gold,
her fingers are like lotuses.
Full (?) her derrière, narrow (?) her waist,
her thighs carry on her beauties.
Lovely of walk when she strides on the ground,
she has captured my heart in her embrace.[g]
She makes the heads of all men
turn about when seeing her.
Fortunate is whoever embraces her —
he is like the foremost of lovers.
Her coming forth appears
like (that of) the one yonder — the Unique One.[3] [h]

g Cant 4:9

h Cant 4:1-7; 4:9-15; 5:10-16; 6:4-10; 7:2-10a

(*Girl*) (Number 32)
Second Stanza
My brother roils my heart with his voice,
making me take ill.
Though he is among the neighbors of my mother's house,
I cannot go to him.
Mother is right to command me thus:
"Avoid seeing him!"
Yet my heart is vexed when he comes to mind,
for love of him has captured me.
He is senseless of heart —
and I am just like him!
He does not know my desires to embrace him,
or he would send word to my mother.
O brother, I am decreed for you
by the Golden One.[4]
Come to me that I may see your beauty!
May father and mother be glad!
May all people rejoice in you together,
rejoice in you, my brother![5]

...

(*Girl*) (Number 34)
Fourth Stanza
My heart quickly scurries away[6]
when I think of your love.

[1] The feminine participle (*tꜣ sḫmḫt ib ʿꜣ*) suggests that the composer was a woman, a professional singer. In this song, each stanza after the first is labelled *ḥwt* (lit., "house") and numbered. Each stanza begins and ends with a word playing on the stanza-number. A similar device is used in a hymn to Amun from the same period.

The stanzas alternate between the boy and the girl, who are speaking to their hearts, not to each other. The underlying story is that the youth passed by the maiden's house and they fell in love with each other. Later, she passed by his house when walking with her mother. But the young lovers never got together to declare their love and make it public.

[2] The star Sirius, whose rising was supposed to occur in conjunction with the rise of the Nile and to bring fertility to the land.

[3] That is, Sothis-Sirius, who "goes forth" every year. The first stanza is a praise song enumerating the beloved's beauties approximately from head to foot.

[4] Hathor, goddess of love.

[5] Cf. numbers 36, 54. Compare the Shulammite's wish that her love will become public and accepted, Cant 8:1.

[6] The Egyptians often spoke of the heart as an independent entity and pictured it that way. The heart "goes forth" or "flees" to the object of its longing. In this stanza, the girl has a little argument with her heart.

It does not let me act like a (normal) person —
it has leapt from its place.
It does not let me don a tunic;
I cannot put on my cloak.
I cannot apply paint to my eyes;
I cannot anoint myself at all!
"Don't stop until you get inside" —
thus it says to me, whenever I think of him.
O my heart, don't make me foolish!
Why do you act crazy?
Sit still, cool down, until (my) brother comes to you,
when I shall do many such things (?).
Don't let people say about me:
"This woman has collapsed out of love."[7]
Stand firm whenever you think of him,
my heart, and scurry not away.
...

(Girl) (Number 36)
Sixth Stanza
I[8] passed close by his house,
and found his door ajar.
My brother was standing beside his mother,
and with him all his kin.
Love of him captures the heart
of all who stride upon the way —
a precious youth without peer!
A brother excellent of character!
He gazed at me when I passed by,
but I exult by myself.
How joyful my heart in rejoicing,
my brother, since I (first) beheld you!
If only mother knew my heart —
she would go inside for a while.
O Golden One, put that in her heart!

i Cant 8:1b

Then I could hurry to my brother
and kiss him before his company,
and not be ashamed because of anyone.[9] [i]
I would be happy to have them see
that you know me,
and I'd hold festival to my goddess.
My heart leaps up to go forth
to make me gaze on my brother tonight.
How lovely it is to pass by!

(Boy) (Number 37)
Seventh Stanza
Seven whole days I have not seen my sister.
Illness has invaded me,
my limbs have grown heavy,
and I barely sense my own body.
Should the master physicians come to me,
their medicines could not ease my heart.
The lector-priests have no (good) method,
because my illness cannot be diagnosed.
Telling me, "Here she is!" — that's what will revive me.
Her name — that's what will get me up.
The coming and going of her messengers —
that's what will revive my heart.
More potent than any medicine is my sister for me;
she is more powerful for me than the Compendium.[10]
Her coming in from outside is my amulet.
I see her — then I become healthy.
She opens her eyes — my limbs grow young.
She speaks — then I become strong.
I hug her — and she drives illness from me.
But she has left me for seven days.[11]

This song is from another group of seven independent songs on the Papyrus Chester Beatty I (ro. 16,9-17:13; nos. 41-47) that are ascribed to the scribe Nakhtsobek.

(Boy) (Number 43)
How skilled is she — my sister — at casting the lasso,
yet she'll draw in no cattle![12]
With her hair[13] she lassos me,
with her eye she pulls me in,
with her thighs she binds,
with her seal she sets the brand.[14]

[7] See P. Harris 500 (text 1.49, n. 4 above).
[8] The text has "he passed," an error.
[9] Cf. n. 5.
[10] A medical text.
[11] See P. Harris 500 (text 1.49, n. 4 above).
[12] A difficult line. This rendering takes *ms* as an aural error for *ms* "bring" and *irw* as a variant of *iryt* "cow."
[13] *šnw*; see P. Harris 500 (text 1.49, n. 5).
[14] The young lady lassoes not cattle but the youth. Cf. the "love trap" in P. Harris 500 (text 1.49, no. 10 above). The sexual allusions are transparent.

OSTRACON GARDINER 304 (1.52)
Recto (HO I, 38)

Michael V. Fox

A number of ostraca, mostly written as school exercises, hold love songs or phrases typical of love songs. This ostracon dates to the reign of Ramses III (ca. 1182-1151 BCE).

(*Boy*) (Number 54)
My sister's love is in the ...
Her necklace is of flowers;
her bones are reeds.
Her little seal-ring is [on her finger],
her lotus in her hand.
I kiss [her] before everyone,
that they may see my love.[1] [j]
Indeed it is she who captures my heart,[k]
when she looks at me,
I am refreshed.

j Cant 8:1
k Cant 4:9

[1] See P. Chester Beatty I (text 1.51, n. 5) above.

REFERENCES

Texts and translations: Fox 1985; Gardiner 1931; Schott 1950.

5. PSEUDEPIGRAPHA

THE FAMINE STELA (1.53)
(On Sehel Island)

Miriam Lichtheim

The inscription is carved in thirty-two columns on the face of a granite rock where it was given the shape of a rectangular stela. The rock face is split by a broad horizontal fissure, which already existed when the inscription was carved. After the carving, further ruptures occurred in the rock, and they have caused a number of textual lacunae. Above the text is a relief scene showing King Djoser offering to Khnum-Re, Satis, and Anukis, the gods of the cataract region.

The stela purports to be a decree by King Djoser of the Third Dynasty addressed to a "Governor of the South" at Elephantine. In it the king informs the governor that, distressed over the country's seven-year famine, he had consulted a priest of Imhotep. After a study of the sacred books, the priest had informed him in detail about the temple of Khnum at Elephantine, and how Khnum controlled the inundation. The priest had also named to him all the minerals, precious stones, and building stones found in the border region. In the following night the king had seen Khnum in his dream, and the god had promised him an end to the famine. In gratitude to the god, the king now issues a decree granting to the temple of Khnum of Elephantine a share of all the revenue derived from the region extending from Elephantine south to Takompso, a distance of "twelve *iter*." In addition, a share of all Nubian imports was to be given to the temple. The governor was charged with carrying out the decree.

In its present form, the text is undoubtedly a work of the Ptolemaic period. Some scholars have surmised that it was based on a genuine Old Kingdom decree from the time of Djoser. Others take it to be a complete fiction. In any case, the text puts forth a claim to revenue on behalf of the Khnum temple of Elephantine.

Who stood behind this claim? According to P. Barguet, it was Ptolemy V who issued the decree as a means of proclaiming Ptolemaic control of this Nubian region. H. de Meulenaere countered this suggestion by asking whether the "governor of the south," who bore the non-Egyptian name Mesir, may not have been a Nubian chief ruling the area in defiance of the Ptolemaic king. The most plausible hypothesis, it seems to me, is the one that sees the inscription as the work of the priesthood of the Khnum temple, who were anxious to strengthen their privileges in the face of the encroaching claims made by the clergy of Isis of Philae.

The extent of the "12-*iter* land" or, Dodekaschoinos, has also been much discussed, for the location of Takompso, its southern limit, is not known, and the length of the *iter* appears to have varied. The problem now seems to have been settled in favor of an *iter* usually averaging 10.5 km, except for a much shorter *iter* indicated by the boundary stelae of Akhenaten at El-Amarna. Thus, the "12-*iter* land" would designate the northern half of Lower Nubia, extending south from Elephantine for a length of about eighty miles.

Barguet's good edition has greatly advanced the understanding of this difficult text. There remain a number of problems and uncertainties.

(1) Year 18 of Horus: *Neterkhet*; the King of Upper and Lower Egypt: *Neterkhet*; Two Ladies: *Neterkhet*; Gold-Horus: *Djoser*; under the Count, Prince, Governor of the domains of the South, Chief of the Nubians in Yebu, Mesir.[1] There was brought to him this royal decree. To let you know:

I was in mourning on my throne,
Those of the palace were in grief,
My heart was in great affliction,
Because Hapy had failed to come in time
In a period of seven years.[2] [a]
Grain was scant,
Kernels were dried up,
Scarce was every kind of food.
Every man robbed (3) his twin,[3]
Those who entered did not go.[4]
Children cried,
Youngsters fell,
The hearts of the old were grieving;
Legs drawn up, they hugged the ground,
Their arms clasped about them.
Courtiers were needy,
Temples were shut,
Shrines covered with dust,
Everyone was in distress.

I directed my heart to turn to the past,
I consulted one of the staff of the Ibis,
The chief lector-priest of Imhotep,
Son of Ptah South-of-his-Wall;[5]
"In which place is Hapy born?
Which is the town of the Sinuous one?
Which god dwells there?
That he might join with (5) me."

a Gen 41:25-32

He stood "I shall go to Mansion-of-the-Net,[6]
⌈it is designed to support a man in his
deeds⌉;[7]
I shall enter the House of Life,
Unroll the Souls of Re,[8]
I shall be guided by them."

He departed, he returned to me quickly,
He let me know the flow of Hapy,
[His shores] and all the things they contain.
He disclosed to me the hidden wonders,
To which the ancestors had made their way,
And no king had equaled them since.
He said to me:
"There is a town in the midst of the deep,
Surrounded by Hapy, (7) Yebu by name;
It is first of the first,
First nome to Wawat,[9]
Earthly elevation, celestial hill,
Seat of Re when he prepares
To give life to every face.
Its temple's name is 'Joy-of-life,'
'Twin Caverns' is the water's name,
They are the breasts that nourish all.

It is the house of sleep of Hapy,[10]
He grows young in it in [his time],
[It is the place whence] he brings the flood:
Bounding up he copulates,
As man copulates with woman,
Renewing his manhood with joy;
Coursing twenty-eight cubits high,
He passes Sema-behdet (9) at seven.[11]
Khnum is the god [who rules] there,
[He is enthroned above the deep],[12]
His sandals resting on the flood;

[1] The reading of the name is not quite certain, and the name is probably not an Eg. one.

[2] When the inscription was first published, the description of a seven year famine was believed to be connected with the biblical story of a seven-year famine in Egypt (Gen 41). Since then it has been shown that a tradition of seven years of famine was widespread in the literatures of the ancient Near East; see Gordon 1953:79-81. Hapy is the deified Nile.

[3] Barguet 1953a:15, took *ḥtr* to be the word for "revenue," while I take it to be the word for "twin."

[4] The meaning seems to be that those who had entered a house were too weak to leave it again.

[5] The "staff of the Ibis" designates the corporation of scribes whose patron was Thoth. As Barguet (1953a:16) pointed out, the king consults a priest of Imhotep, not the god Imhotep himself, as previous translators had thought. The earlier view is argued by Wildung 1977:149-152.

[6] *Ḥwt-ibṯ.t*, the "Mansion of the Net," appears to have been a name for the temple of Thoth at Hermopolis Magna. The logic of the tale would seem to require that the king's consultation with the priest of Imhotep takes place in the capital, i.e., at Memphis, which was also the cult center of Imhotep. Since the priest is said to have returned "quickly," or "immediately," poetic license might stretch this to include a quick trip from Memphis to Hermopolis, but surely not a voyage to the Khnum temple of Elephantine. Hence the "Mansion of the Net," if it does not here refer to the temple of Hermopolis, could only designate a sanctuary in, or close to, Memphis.

[7] A somewhat obscure sentence which rendered literally would be: "gathered for the steadfastness of everyone for what they do," which I take to refer to the sanctuary, whereas Barguet construed it as referring to the priest.

[8] The "Souls of Re" are the sacred books kept in the temple's "House of Life."

[9] I.e., Elephantine, in the first nome of Upper Egypt, faces toward Lower Nubia (Wawat).

[10] The passage gives the traditional view that the inundation rose from twin caverns at Elephantine.

[11] I.e., by the time the inundation has reached the Delta town of Sema-behdet, the metropolis of the 17th nome of Lower Egypt, its height of twenty-eight cubits above low water has diminished to seven cubits.

[12] I have restored the lacuna merely to indicate that some such meaning is required. It is Khnum, the creator, who releases Hapy, the inundating Nile.

He holds the door bolt in his hand,
Opens the gate as he wishes.
He is eternal there as Shu,[13]
Bounty-giver, Lord-of-fields,
So his name is called.
He has reckoned the land of the South and the North,[14]
To give parts to every god;
It is he who governs barley, [emmer],
Fowl and fish and all one lives on.
Cord and scribal board are there,
The pole is there with its beam
......[15]
(11) His temple opens southeastward,
Re rises in its face every day;
Its water rages on its south for an *iter*,
A wall against the Nubians each day.[16]
There is a mountain massif in its eastern region,
With precious stones and quarry stones of all kinds,
All the things sought for building temples
In Egypt, South and North,[17]
And stalls for sacred animals,
And palaces for kings,
All statues too that stand in temples and in shrines."

"Their gathered products are set before the face of Khnum and around him; likewise (13) tall plants and flowers of all kinds that exist between Yebu and Senmut,[18] and are there on the east and the west."

"There is in the midst of the river — covered by water at its annual flood — a place of relaxation for every man who works the stones on its two sides."

"There is in the river, before this town of Yebu, a central elevation of difficult body which is called *grf-ꜣbw*."[19]

"Learn the names of the gods and goddesses of the temple of Khnum: Satis, Anukis, Hapy, Shu, Geb, Nut, Osiris, Horus, Isis, Nephthys."

"Learn the names of (15) the stones that are there, lying in the borderland:[20] those that are in the east and the west, those [on the shores] of Yebu's canal, those in Yebu, those in the east and west, and those in the river: *bḫn*,[21] *mtꜣy*,[22] *mḫtbtb*,[23] *rʿgs*, *wtšy*[24] in the east; *prḏn*[25] in the west; *tšy*[26] in the west and in the river."

"The names of the precious stones of the quarries that are in the upper region — some among them at a distance of four *iter* — are: gold, silver, copper, iron, lapis lazuli, turquoise, *ṯḥnt*,[27] red jasper, *ḳʿ*,[28] *mnw*,[29] emerald,[30] *tm-ꜣiḳr*.[31] In addition, *nšmt*,[32] *tꜣ-mḥy*,[33] *ḥmꜣgt*,[34] (17) *ibht*,[35] *bḳs-ʿnḫ*,[36] green eye-paint, black eye-paint, carnelian,[37] *shrt*,[38] *mm*,[39] and ochre[40] are within this township."

[13] The identification of Khnum with Shu also occurs in other texts of the Ptolemaic period, notably at Esna.

[14] Lit., "the land of Upper Egypt and Lower Egypt."

[15] Despite Barguet's explanation I fail to understand the words used to describe the instrument, its location, and its relation to Shu. Barguet 1953a:20-21 translated: "Il y a là un support de bois et sa croix faite de poutres *swt*, pour son poisson, qui sont sur la rive; à cela est affecté Chou, fils de Re, en tant que 'maître de largesse'," and he discussed the instrument further in *CdÉ* 28 1953:223-227.

[16] I.e., the first cataract of the Nile, which was an effective boundary throughout Egypt's history.

[17] Lit., "temples of Upper and Lower Egypt."

[18] The island of Biggah, south of Elephantine and opposite Philae.

[19] The two elevations described here, a pleasant one and a difficult one, have been identified with the "two mountains called Crophi and Mophi," mentioned in Herodotus 11,28. See Barguet 1953a:22, where Crophi is identified with *grf-ꜣbw*.

[20] Since many of the stones have not been identified, it is not clear to what extent the list may have been accurate.

[21] On the much discussed *bḫn* stone see now Harris 1961:78-82, where the translation "greywacke" is favored.

[22] Harris (1961:74) thinks it probable that *mṯꜣy* was merely another spelling of *mꜣṯ*, "granite."

[23] An unidentified material seemingly of golden color; see Harris 1961:88.

[24] The stones *rʿgs* and *wtšy* have not been identified; see Harris 1961:85 and 89.

[25] According to Harris (1961:105), this may be the Greek *prason*, "prase."

[26] An unidentified stone, see Harris 1961:92.

[27] This is both a precious stone and a term for faience, glass, and glaze, see Harris 1961:135-138.

[28] An unidentified stone, see Harris 1961:133 and 232.

[29] Harris (1961:110-111) thinks it probable that this is "quartz."

[30] Or perhaps "beryl," see Harris 1961:105.

[31] An unidentified stone, see Harris 1961:92.

[32] According to Harris (1961:115), this term usually designates "green felspar."

[33] According to Harris (1961:154), this is a writing of *ṯmḥy* and signifies a species of "red ochre."

[34] Harris (1961:118-120) thinks it probable that this is "garnet."

[35] An unidentified stone, see Harris 1961:96-97.

[36] Harris (1961:168 and 933-234) concludes that this stone, originally called *biꜣ ḳsy*, is haematite and possibly also magnetite.

[37] On *ḥrst*, "carnelian," see Harris 1961:120-121.

[38] Harris (1961:130-131) concludes that this was a semiprecious stone probably of green color.

[39] *Mm* or *mimi* is known as a word for seed-grain, but that does not suit here.

[40] On *sty* and *tꜣ-sty*, "ochre," see Harris 1961:150-152.

When I heard what was there my heart ⸢was guided⸣. Having heard of the flood <I> opened the wrapped books.[41] <I> made a purification; <I> conducted a procession of the hidden ones; <I> made a complete offering of bread, beer, oxen, and fowl, and all good things for the gods and goddesses in Yebu whose names had been pronounced.

As I slept in peace, I found the god standing before me. <I> propitiated him by adoring him and praying to him. He revealed himself to me with kindly face; he said:

"I am Khnum, your maker!
My arms are around you,
To steady your body,
To (19) safeguard your limbs.[42]
I bestow on you stones upon stones,
⸢That were not found⸣ before,
Of which no work was made,
For building temples,
Rebuilding ruins,
Inlaying statues' eyes.

For I am the master who makes,
I am he who made himself,
Exalted Nun, who first came forth,
Hapy who hurries at will;
Fashioner of everybody,
Guide of each in his hours,
Tatenen, father of gods,
Great Shu, high in heaven!

The shrine I dwell in has two lips,[43]
When I open up the well,[44]
I know Hapy hugs the field,
A hug that fills each nose with life,
(21) For when hugged the field is reborn!
I shall make Hapy gush for you,
No year of lack and want anywhere,
Plants will grow weighed down by their fruit;
With Renutet ordering all,
All things are supplied in millions!
I shall let your people fill up,
They shall grasp together with you!
Gone will be the hunger years,
Ended the dearth in their bins.
Egypt's people will come striding,
Shores will shine in the excellent flood,
Hearts will be happier than ever before!"

b Gen 14:20 etc.

The Donation

I awoke with speeding heart. Freed of fatigue I made (23) this decree on behalf of my father Khnum. A royal offering to Khnum, lord of the cataract region and chief of Nubia:

In return for what you have done for me, I offer you Manu as western border, Bakhu as eastern border,[45] from Yebu to Kemsat,[46] being twelve *iter* on the east and the west, consisting of fields and pastures, of the river, and of every place in these miles.

All tenants[47] who cultivate the fields, and the vivifiers who irrigate the shores and all the new lands that are in these miles, their harvests shall be taken to your granary, in addition to (25) your share which is in Yebu.[48]

All fishermen, all hunters, who catch fish and trap birds and all kinds of game, and all who trap lions in the desert — I exact from them one-tenth of the take of all of these, and all the young animals born of the females in these miles [in their totality].

One shall give the branded animals for all burnt offerings and daily sacrifices; and one shall give one-tenth[49] [b] of gold, ivory, ebony, carob wood, and ochre, carnelian, *shrt*, *diw*-plants, *nfw*-plants, all kinds of timber, (being) all the things brought by the Nubians of Khent-hen-nefer[50] (to) Egypt, and (by) every man (27) ⸢who comes with arrears from them.⸣

No officials are to issue orders in these places or take anything from them, for everything is to be protected for your sanctuary.

I grant you this domain with (its) stones and good soil. No person there ------- anything from it. But the scribes that belong to you and the overseers of the South shall dwell there as accountants, listing everything that the *kiry*-workers, and the smiths, and the master craftsmen, and the goldsmiths, and the ...,[51] (29) and the Nubians, and the crew of Apiru,[52] and all corvee labor who

[41] I.e., the king consulted the manuals that taught how to perform the temple ritual.
[42] The speech of the god abounds in assonances, which I have imitated whenever possible.
[43] The "lips" suggest some kind of gate or lid made of two sections which, when opened, releases the water.
[44] I take this to be the word for "well" rather than "sieve."
[45] Lit., "your west as Manu, your east as Bakhu," the two names for the mountain ranges bordering the Nile valley on the west and east.
[46] The Greek Takompso, the locality that marked the southern limit of the Dodekaschoinos.
[47] Barguet (1953a:29) read *imy s nb*; I wonder if it might be *iwy nḥb nb*, meaning the *nḥb* of Wb. 2:293.15.
[48] Barguet (1953a:29) read the name as "Ville du Piège" (Hermopolis). I think it is merely another writing of "Yebu."
[49] Barguet (1953a:30) read the signs as *ˁrf*, "sack," rather than *di r-10*. I have retained the reading *di r-10* and have discussed the problem of the whole donation in my article on the *Naucratis Stela* in Lichtheim 1977:142-144.
[50] A region of Nubia south of the second cataract; see Vandersleyen 1971:64-68.
[51] I wonder if the unread word might be *ḫnrw*, "prisoners"?
[52] On the Apiru, see Rowton 1976:13-20.

fashion the stones, shall give of gold, silver, copper, lead, baskets of ...,[53] firewood, the things that every man who works with them shall give as dues, namely one-tenth of all these. And there shall be given one-tenth of the precious stones and quarrying stones that are brought from the mountain side, being the stones of the east.

And there shall be an overseer who measures the quantities of gold, silver, copper, and genuine precious stones, the things which the sculptors shall assign to the gold house, (31) (to) fashion the sacred images and to refit the statues that were damaged, and any implements lacking there. Everything shall be placed in the storehouse until one fashions anew, when one knows everything that is lacking in your temple, so that it shall be as it was in the beginning.

Engrave this decree on a stela of the sanctuary in writing, for it happened as said, (and) on a tablet, so that the divine writings shall be on them in the temple twice.[54] He who spits (on it) deceitfully shall be given over to punishment.

The overseers of the priests and the chief of all the temple personnel shall make my name abide in the temple of Khnum-Re, lord of Yebu, ever-mighty.

[53] It is not clear what word is written, see Barguet 1953a:31. Since the edible produce has been listed separately, a species of grain is hardly suitable.

[54] What is written is: "in the temples twice on it."

REFERENCES

Text: Brugsch 1891; Barguet 1953a. Translation: Roeder 1915:177-184. Translation of excerpts: Vandier 1936:38-44 and 132-139; *ANET* 31-32. Studies: Sethe 1901; 1904:58-62; Schubart 1910:154-157; de Meulenaere 1957:33-34; Brunner 1967:cols. 2255-2256. Wildung, 1969:85-91; Schwab-Schlott 1969; 1972:109-113; 1975:cols. 1112-1113. Lichtheim 1977:142-144; *AEL* 3:94-103; Harris 1961.

THE LEGEND OF THE POSSESSED PRINCESS ("BENTRESH STELA") (1.54)
(From Karnak, Louvre C 284)

Miriam Lichtheim

A stela of black sandstone, 2.22 x 1.09 m, found in 1829 in a small, no longer extant, Ptolemaic sanctuary near the temple of Khons erected at Karnak by Ramses III. The stela was brought to Paris in 1844. The scene in the lunette shows King Ramses II offering incense before the bark of Khons-in-Thebes-Neferhotep. Behind the king, a priest offers incense before the smaller bark of Khons-the-Provider-in-Thebes. Below the scene is the text in twenty-eight horizontal lines.

Though made to appear as a monument of Ramses II, the stela is in fact a work of either the Persian or the Ptolemaic period. It tells a wondrous tale of healing performed by the Theban god Khons-the-Provider. If the tale had been written on papyrus it would rank with other stories told about the gods. But in the guise of a monument of Ramses II it possessed a propagandistic purpose. Just what the purpose was does not emerge very clearly. Was it meant to glorify the two principal manifestations of the Theban god Khons: Khons-the-Merciful (*nfr-ḥtp*) and Khons-the-Provider (*pꜣ ir sḫr*)? Or did it project a rivalry between their two priesthoods? Was it also designed to recall the glory of Egypt's native kings at a time of foreign — Persian or Ptolemaic — domination?

(1) Horus Mighty bull beautiful of crowns; Two Ladies abiding in kingship like Atum; Gold-Horus: Strong-armed smiter of the Nine Bows; the King of Upper and Lower Egypt, Lord of the Two Lands *Usermare-sotpenre*; the Son of Re, of his body: *Ramesses beloved of Amun*,[1] lord of Thrones-of-the-Two-Lands, and of the Ennead, mistress of Thebes.

Good god, Amun's son,
Offspring of Harakhti,
Glorious seed of the All-Lord,
Begotten by Kamutef,
King of Egypt, ruler of Red Lands,
Sovereign who seized the Nine Bows;
Whom victory was foretold as he came from the womb,
Whom valor was given while in the egg,
Bull firm of heart as he treads the arena,
Godly king going forth like Mont on victory day,
Great of strength like the Son of Nut!

When his majesty was in Nahrin according to his

[1] The two principal royal names are those of Ramses II, but the Horus, Two-Ladies, and Gold-Horus names are mistakenly composed, being derived from the titulary of Thutmosis IV.

annual custom,[2] the princes of every foreign land came bowing in peace to the might of his majesty from as far as the farthest marshlands. Their gifts of gold, silver, lapis lazuli, (5) turquoise, and every kind of plant of god's land[3] were on their backs, and each was outdoing his fellow. The prince of Bakhtan[4] had also sent his gifts and had placed his eldest daughter in front of them, worshiping his majesty and begging life from him. The woman pleased the heart of his majesty greatly and beyond anything. So her titulary was established as Great Royal Wife *Nefrure*.[5] When his majesty returned to Egypt, she did all that a queen does.

It happened in year 23,[6] second month of summer, day 22, while his majesty was in Thebes-the-victorious, the mistress of cities, performing the rites for his father Amun-Re, lord of Thrones-of-the-Two-Lands, at his beautiful feast of Southern Ipet, his favorite place since the beginning, that one came to say to his majesty: "A messenger of the prince of Bakhtan has come with many gifts for the queen." He was brought before his majesty with his gifts and said, saluting his majesty: "Hail to you, Sun of the Nine Bows! Truly, we live through you!" And kissing the ground before his majesty he spoke again before his majesty, saying "I have come to you, O King, my lord, on account of Bentresh,[7] the younger sister of Queen *Nefrure*. A malady has seized her body. May your majesty send a learned man to see her!"

His majesty said: "Bring me the personnel of the House of Life[8] and the council (10) of the residence." They were ushered in to him immediately. His majesty said: "You have been summoned in order to hear this matter: bring me one wise of heart with fingers skilled in writing from among you." Then the royal scribe Thothemheb came before his majesty, and his majesty ordered him to proceed to Bakhtan with the messenger.

The learned man reached Bakhtan. He found Bentresh to be possessed by a spirit; he found him to be an enemy whom one could fight.[9] Then the prince of Bakhtan sent again to his majesty, saying: "O King, my lord, may your majesty command to send a god [to fight against this spirit!" The message reached] his majesty in year 26, first month of summer, during the feast of Amun while his majesty was in Thebes. His majesty reported to Khons-in-Thebes-Neferhotep, saying: "My good lord, I report to you about the daughter of the prince of Bakhtan." Then Khons-in-Thebes-Neferhotep proceeded to Khons-the-Provider, the great god who expels disease demons.[10] His majesty spoke to Khons-in-Thebes-Neferhotep: "My good lord, if you turn your face to (15) Khons-the-Provider, the great god who expels disease demons, he shall be dispatched to Bakhtan." Strong approval twice.[11] His majesty said: "Give your magical protection to him, and I shall dispatch his majesty to Bakhtan to save the daughter of the prince of Bakhtan." Very strong approval by Khons-in-Thebes-Neferhotep. He made magical protection for Khons-the-Provider-in-Thebes four times. His majesty commanded to let Khons-the-Provider-in-Thebes proceed to the great bark with five boats and a chariot, and many horses from east and west.[12] This god arrived in Bakhtan at the end of one year and five months.[13] The prince of Bakhtan came with his soldiers and officials before Khons-the-Provider. He placed himself on his belly, saying: "You have come to us to be gracious to us, as commanded by the King of Upper and Lower Egypt, *Usermare-sotpenre*!" Then the god proceeded to the place where Bentresh was. He made magical protection for the daughter of the prince of Bakhtan, and she became well instantly.

Then spoke the spirit who was with her[14] to Khons-the-Provider-in-Thebes: "Welcome in

[2] The land of Mitanni on the Upper Euphrates had been reached by Thutmosis I and III, but Ramses II had never been there.

[3] On "god's land" meaning wooded regions see Lichtheim *AEL* 3:84, n. 105 and 86, n. 2.

[4] It has been surmised that the name "Bakhtan" is a corrupted Eg. version of the name of Bactria; see Lefebvre 1949:222.

[5] The historical marriage of Ramses II with a Hittite princess who was given the Egyptian name Maatnefrure is the basis for this fictional marriage.

[6] The scribe wrote "year 15," but the easy emendation to "year 23," first proposed by Erman, is very probable in view of the dates given later.

[7] This may be a Canaanite name; see Lefebvre 1949:222, n. 7.

[8] On the "House of Life" see Lichtheim *AEL* 3:36, n. 10.

[9] The learned scribe Thothemheb diagnosed the malady as one that might be cured, but he himself could not effect the cure, i.e., expel the demon.

[10] The Theban god Khons was worshiped under several distinct manifestations, with Khons-in-Thebes-Neferhotep occupying the leading position, while the most outstanding trait of Khons-*pꜣ-ir-sḫr* was that of a healer. The epithet *pꜣ ir sḫr* was been translated in various ways, including "he who determines fate." Bearing in mind that we do not know the exact shade of meaning, I have preferred "the Provider." See also Lichtheim *AEL* 3:33, n. 4.

[11] A movement on the part of the god's statue signifying approval.

[12] The chariot and horses were needed for the overland part of the journey.

[13] The remoteness of the land of Bakhtan is indicated in fairy-tale manner by the extreme length of the journey.

[14] I.e., "who had been in her."

peace, great god who expels disease demons! Bakhtan is your home, its people are your servants, I am your servant! (20) I shall go to the place from which I came, so as to set your heart at rest about that which you came for. May your majesty command to make a feast day with me and the prince of Bakhtan!" Then the god motioned approval to his priest, saying: "Let the prince of Bakhtan make a great offering before this spirit."

Now while this took place between Khons-the-Provider-in-Thebes and the spirit, the prince of Bakhtan stood by with his soldiers and was very frightened. Then he made a great offering to Khons-the-Provider-in-Thebes and the spirit; and the prince of Bakhtan made a feast day for them. Then the spirit went in peace to where he wished, as commanded by Khons-the-Provider-in-Thebes. The prince of Bakhtan rejoiced very greatly together with everyone in Bakhtan.

Then he schemed with his heart, saying: "I will make the god stay here in Bakhtan. I will not let him go to Egypt." So the god spent three years and nine months in Bakhtan. Then, as the prince of Bakhtan slept on his bed, he saw the god come out of his shrine as a falcon of gold and fly up to the sky toward Egypt. (25) He awoke in terror and said to the priest of Khons-the-Provider-in-Thebes: "The god is still here with us! He shall go to Thebes! His chariot shall go to Egypt!" Then the prince of Bakhtan let the god proceed to Egypt, having given him many gifts of every good thing and very many soldiers and horses.

They arrived in peace in Thebes. Khons-the-Provider-in-Thebes went to the house of Khons-in-Thebes-Neferhotep. He placed the gifts of every good thing which the prince of Bakhtan had given him before Khons-in-Thebes-Neferhotep, without giving anything to his (own) house.[15] Khons-the-Provider-in-Thebes arrived in his house in peace in year 33, second month of winter, day 19, of the King of Upper and Lower Egypt, *Usermare-sotpenre*, given eternal life like Re.

[15] I.e., Khons-the-Provider delivered all the presents to his superior, Khons-in-Thebes-Neferhotep, without keeping anything for his own temple.

REFERENCES

Text: Tresson 1933:57-78 and pl. i; de Buck 1948:106-109; Kitchen *KRI* 2:284-287. Translation: Lefebvre 1949:221-232; *ANET* 29-31; Brunner-Traut 1965:163-167; Bresciani 1969:533-536; Lichtheim *AEL* 3:90-94. Studies: Erman 1883:54-60; Spiegelberg 1906:181; Posener 1934:75-81; Lefebvre 1944:214-218; Donadoni 1957:47-50.

EGYPTIAN BIBLIOGRAPHY

ALBRIGHT, W. F.

1934 *The Vocalization of the Egyptian Syllabic Orthography*. New Haven: American Oriental Society.

ALLEN, T. G.

1974 *The Book of the Dead or Going Forth by Day*. SAOC 37. Chicago: The University of Chicago Press.

ALLEN, J. P.

1988a *Genesis in Egypt, the Philosophy of Ancient Egyptian Creation Accounts*. YES 2. New Haven: Yale Egyptological Seminar.

1988b "Funerary Texts and Their Meaning." Pp. 38-49 in *Mummies & Magic, the Funerary Arts of Ancient Egypt*. Ed. by S. D'Auria, P. Lacovara, and C. Roehrig. Boston: Museum of Fine Arts.

ALT, A.

1923 "Zwei Vermutungen zur Geschichte des Sinuhe." *ZÄS* 58:48-50.

1941 *PJ* 37:19ff.

ANTHES, R.

1957 "The Legal Aspect of the Instruction of Amenemhet." *JNES* 16:176-191.

1958 "A Further Remark on the Introduction to the Instruction of Amenemhet." *JNES* 17:208-209.

1970 Pp. 9-18 in *Studies Galling*.

ASSMANN, J.

1970 *Der König als Sonnenpriester*. ADAIK Ägyptologische Reihe, 7. Glückstadt: J. J. Augustin.

1975a *Zeit und Ewigkeit im alten Ägypten*. AHAW Phil.-hist. Kl. 1. Heidelberg: Karl Winter, Universitätsverlag.

1975b *Ägyptische Hymnen und Gebete*. Zürich: Artemis Verlag.

1990 *Ma^{c}at, Gerechtigkeit und Unsterblichkeit im Alten Ägypten*. Munich: C. H. Beck.

AUFFRET, P.

1981 *Hymnes d'Egypte et d'Israël: études de structure littéraires*. OBO 34. Freiburg: Universitätsverlag.

BAER, K.

1964 *JEA* 50:179-180.

BARGUET, P.

1953a *La stèle de la famine à Séhel*. Institut français d'archéologie orientale, Bibliothèque d'étude 34. Cairo.

1953b "Khnoum-Chou patron des arpenteurs." *CdÉ* 28:223-227.

1967 *Le Livre des Morts des anciens Égyptiens*. LAPO 1. Paris: Les Éditions du Cerf.

BARNS, J. W. B.

1952 *The Ashmolean Ostracon of Sinuhe*. London: Oxford University Press.

1967 "Sinuhe's Message to the King." *JEA* 53:6-14.

BARTA, W.

1971 "Zu einigen Textpassagen der Prophezeiung des Neferti." *MDAIK* 27:35-45.

1974 "Das Gespräch des Ipuwer mit dem Schöpfergott." *SÄK* 1:19-33.

1980 "Kult," *LdÄ* 3:cols. 839-848.

BARUCQ, A., and F. DAUMAS.

1980 *Hymnes et prieres de l'Egypte ancienne*. Paris: Cerf.

VON BECKERATH, J.

1966 "Die Dynastie der Herakleopoliten (9./10. Dynastie)." *ZÄS* 93:13-20.

1984 *Handbuch der ägyptischen Königsnamen*. MÄS 20. Munich: Deutscher Kunstverlag.

BERLEV, O. D.

1987 "The Date of the Eloquent Peasant." Pp. 78-83 in *Studies Fecht*.

VON BISSING, F. W.

1955 *Ältagyptische Lebensweisheit*. Die Bibliothek der alten Welt. Reihe der Alte Orient. Zürich: Artemis Verlag.

BLACKMAN, A. M.

1930 "Notes on Certain Passages in Various Middle Egyptian Texts." *JEA* 16:63-72.

1932 *Middle Egyptian Stories*. Bibliotheca Aegyptiaca 2. Brussels: Fondation égyptologique reine Elisabeth.

1936 "Some Notes on the Story of Sinuhe and Other Egyptian Texts." *JEA* 22:35-44.

BLUMENTHAL, E.

1973 "Die Erzählung des Papyrus d'Orbiney als Literaturwerk." *ZÄS* 99:1-17.

1982 "Die Prophezeiung des Neferti." *ZÄS* 109:1-27.

BORGHOUTS, J.

1978 *Ancient Egyptian Magical Texts*. Nisaba 9. Leiden: E. J. Brill.

1987 "Akhu and Hekau. Two Basic Notions of Ancient Egyptian Magic, and the Concept of the Divine Creative Word." Pp. 29-46 in *La Magia in Egitto ai Tempi dei Faraoni*. Ed. by A. Roccati and A. Siliotti. Milan: Ressegna internazionale di cinematografia archeologica.

BREASTED, J. H.

1902 "The Philosophy of a Memphite Priest." *ZÄS* 39: 39-54

1906-1907 *Ancient Records of Egypt*. 5 Vols. Chicago: The University of Chicago Press. Reprint, 1962.

1933 *The Dawn of Conscience*. New York.

BRESCIANI, E.

1969 *Letteratura e poesia dell' antico egitto*. Turin.

BRUGSCH, H. K.

1891 *Die biblischen sieben Jahre der Hungersnoth*. Leipzig: J. C. Hinrichs.

BRUNNER, H.

1944 *Die Lehre des Cheti, Sohnes des Duauf*. Ägyptologische Forschungen 13. Glückstadt: J. J. Augustin.

1955 *ZÄS* 80:5-11.

1964 *ZÄS* 91:139-140.
1967 "Die Hungersnotstele" in *Kindlers Literatur Lexikon*. Zürich: Kindler. 111:cols. 2255-2256.
1969 *BiOr* 26:71.

BRUNNER-TRAUT, E.
1963 *Altägyptische Märchen*. Märchen der Weltliteratur. Dusseldorf-Cologne: Diederichs. 2nd edition, 1965.

BUCCELLATI G.
1972 *BeO* 14:241-264.

DE BUCK, A.
1932 Pp. 57-60 in *Studies Griffith*.
1938 *The Egyptian Coffin Texts*. vol. 2. OIP 49. Chicago: The University of Chicago Press.
1939 Pp. 847-852 in *Orient Ancien*. Institut Français d'Archéologie Orientale. Mémoires 66. Cairo.
1946 *Le Muséon* 59:183-200.
1947 "Plaats en betekenis van Sjoe in de egyptische theologie." *Mededeelingen der Koninklijke Nederlandsche Akademie van Wetenschappen, afd. Letterkunde* 10: 215-249.
1948 *Egyptian Readingbook*. Leiden: Nederlandsh Archaeologisch-Philologisch Instituut voor het Nabije Oosten.

BUDGE, E. A. W.
1910 *Facsimiles of Egyptian Hieratic Papyri in the British Museum*. London.
1923 *Facsimiles of Egyptian Hieratic Papyri in the British Museum, Second Series*. London.
1924 *The Teaching of Amen-em-apt, Son of Kanekht*. London.

CAMINOS, R.
1954 *Late-Egyptian Miscellanies*. London: Oxford University.

CAULFEILD, A., and T. ST. GEORGE.
1902 *The Temple of the Kings at Abydos I*. London: B. Quaritch.

ČERNÝ, J.
1958 "Some Coptic Etymologies." *BIFAO* 57:203-215.

ČERNÝ, J., and A. H. Gardiner.
1957 *HO*.

CLÈRE, J.
1939a *JEA* 25:16-29.
1939b *Studies Dussaud* 2:829-832.

CLIFFORD, R. J.
1994 *Creation Accounts in the Ancient Near East and in the Bible*. CBQMS 26. Washington: Catholic Biblical Association.

DARBY, W. J., P. GHALIOUNGUI, and L. GRIVETTI.
1977 *Food: the Gift of Osiris*. London, New York and San Francisco: Academic Press.

DAUMAS, F.
1965 *La civilisation de l'Egypte pharaonique*. Collection les grandes civilisations 4. Paris: Arthaud.

DAVIES, N. de G.
1903-08 *The Rock Tombs of El Amarna*. 6 parts. Egypt Exploration Society, Archaeological Survey 13-18. London: Egypt Exploration Society.

VON DEINES, H. and W. WESTENDORF.
1961-62 *Wörterbuch der medizinischen Texte*. 7 volumes. Berlin: Akademie Verlag.

DERCHAIN, P.
1972 "Intelligenz als Karriere (Neferti 10-11)." *GM* 3:9-14.

DEROUSSEAUX, L.
1987 Editor. *La création dans l'orient ancien*. Paris: Cerf.

VAN DIJK, J.
1986 "Anat, Seth and the Seed of Pre." Pp. 31-51 in *Studies Hospers*.

DONADONI, S.
1957 *MDAIK* 15:47-50.

DRIOTON, E.
1960 *RdÉ* 12:90-91.

EDEL, E.
1955-1964 *Altägyptische Grammatik*. 2 volumes. AnOr 34/39. Rome: Pontificium Institutum Biblicum.
1961-1964 *Zu den Inschriften auf den Jahreszeitenreliefs der "Weltkammer" aus dem Sonnenheiligtum des Niuserre*. NAWG Phil.-hist. Kl., 1961 number 8 and 1963 numbers 4-5. Göttingen: Vandenhoeck & Ruprecht.
1968 Pp. 1-12 in *Textbuch zur Geschichte Israels*. Ed. by K. Galling. 2nd Edition. Tübingen: Mohr (Siebeck).

ENGLUND, G.
1978 *Akh — une notion religieuse dans l'Égypte pharaonique*. Boreas, 11. Uppsala: University of Uppsala.

ERMAN, A.
1883 *ZÄS* 21:54-60.
1900 *ZÄS* 38:1-14.
1906 *ZÄS* 43:1-26.
1911 *Ein Denkmal memphitischer Theologie*. SPAW Phil.-hist. Kl. 1. Berlin: Verlag der Königlichen Akademie der Wissenschaften.
1923 *Der Leidener Amonshymnus*. SPAW Phil.-hist. Kl. 11. Berlin: Verlag der Akademie der Wissenschaften.
1924 *OLZ* 27:241-252.
1927 *The Literature of the Ancient Egyptians*. Trans. by A. M. Blackman. London: Methuen & Co. Reprint New York, 1966 as *The Ancient Egyptians; A Sourcebook of Their Writings*. Original: *Die Literatur der Aegypter*. Leipzig, 1923.

FAULKNER, R. O.
1932 Pp. 69-73 in *Studies Griffith*.

1933 *The Papyrus Bremner-Rhind (British Museum No. 10188)*. Bibliotheca Aegyptiaca 3. Brussels: Édition de la Fondation Égyptologique Reine Élisabeth.
1937 "The Bremner-Rhind Papyrus — III." *JEA* 23:166-185.
1938 "The Bremner-Rhind Papyrus — IV." *JEA* 24:41-53.
1964 "Notes on 'The Admonitions of an Egyptian Sage'." *JEA* 50:24-36.
1969 *The Ancient Egyptian Pyramid Texts*. Oxford: Clarendon Press.
1964 "Some Notes on the God Shu." *JEOL* 18:266-71.
1973 *The Ancient Egyptian Coffin Texts*. Vol. 1: Spells 1-354. Warminster: Aris & Phillips.
1977 *The Ancient Egyptian Coffin Texts*. Vol. 2: Spells 355-787. Warminster: Aris & Phillips.
1985 *The Book of the Dead*. Rev. edition. London: The British Museum.

FECHT, G.
1964 "Die Form der altägyptischen Literatur: metrische und stylistische Analyse." *ZÄS* 91: 11-63.
1965 *Literarische Zeugnisse zur "Persönlichen Frömmigkeit" in Ägypten*. AHAW, Phil.-hist. Kl. 1965 no. 1. Heidelberg: Carl Winter.
1967 "Zur Frühform der Amarna-Theologie: Neubearbeitung der Stele der Architekten Suti und Hor." *ZÄS* 94:25-50.
1972 *Der Vorwurf an Gott in den "Mahnworten des Ipu-wer"*. Heidelberg: Carl Winter.

FENSHAM, F. C.
1962 "Widow, Orphan and the Poor in Ancient Near Eastern Legal Wisdom Literature." *JNES* 21:129-139.

FOX, M. V.
1985 *The Song of Songs and Ancient Egyptian Love Songs*. Madison: University of Wisconsin.

FEDERN, W.
1946 "The Opening Lines of the Antef Song." *JNES* 5:259.
1960 "The 'Transformations' in the Coffin Texts: A New Approach." *JNES* 19:241-257.

FOX, M. V.
1985 *The Song of Songs and the Ancient Egyptian Love Songs*. Madison: University of Wisconsin.

FRANKFORT, H.
1933 *The Cenotaph of Seti I at Abydos*. 2 vols. Egypt Exploration Society, 39th memoir. London: Egypt Exploration Society.

FRIEDMAN, F.
1984-85 "The Root Meaning of ꜣḫ: Effectiveness or Luminosity." *Serapis* 8:39-46.

GARDINER, A. H.
1905 "Hymns to Amon from a Leiden Papyrus." *ZÄS* 42: 12-42.
1908 "Notes on the Tale of the Shipwrecked Sailor." *ZÄS* 45:60-66.
1909a *Die Erzählung des Sinuhe und die Hirtengeschichte*. Literarische Texte des mittleren Reiches 2. HPKMB 5/2. Leipzig: J. C. Hinrichs.
1909b *Admonitions of an Egyptian Sage*. Leipzig: J. C. Hinrichs.
1913 "In Praise of Death: A Song from a Theban Tomb." *PSBA* 35:165-170.
1914 "New Literary Works from Ancient Egypt." *JEA* 1:20-36.
1916 *Notes on the Story of Sinuhe*. Paris: Libraire Honore Champion.
1923 "The Eloquent Peasant." *JEA* 9:5-23.
1931 *The Chester Beatty Papyri, No. I*. London: Oxford University Press.
1932a "The Astarte Papyrus." Pp. 74-85 in *Studies Griffith*.
1932b *Late-Egyptian Stories*. Bibliotheca Aegyptiaca 1. Brussels: La fondation égyptologique reine Élisabeth.
1935a *HPBM 3*.
1935b "A Lawsuit Arising from the Purchase of Two Slaves." *JEA* 21:143.
1937 *Late-Egyptian Miscellanies*. Bibliotheca Aegyptiaca 7. Brussels: La fondation égyptologique reine Élisabeth.
1939 Pp. 479-496 in *Orient Ancien*. Institut Français d'Archéologie Orientale. Mémoires 66. Cairo.
1959a "A Didactic Passage Re-Examined." *JEA* 45:12-15.
1959b *The Royal Canon of Turin*. Oxford: Oxford University Press.
1961 *Egypt of the Pharaohs*. Oxford: Oxford University Press.

GILULA, M.
1978 "Peasant B1 141-145." *JEA* 64:129-130.

GOEDICKE, H.
1957 "The Route of Sinuhe's Flight." *JEA* 43:77-85.
1965 "Sinuhe's Reply to the King's Letter." *JEA* 51:29-47.
1967 "Admonitions 3.6-10." *JARCE* 6:93-95.
1968 "The Beginning of the Instruction of King Amenemhet." *JARCE* 7:15-21.
1977 *The Protocol of Neferyt*. Baltimore: Johns Hopkins University Press.

GOLENISHCHEV, V. S.
1899 "Papyrus hiératique de la collection W. Golénischeff." *RT* 21:74-102.
1912 *Le conte du naufragé*. Bibliothèque d'étude 2. Cairo: Impr. de l'Institut français d'archéologie orientale.
1916 *Les papyrus hiératiques nos. 1115, 1116A et 1116B de l'Ermitage impériale à St-Petersbourg*. St. Petersburg.

GORDON, C. H.
1953 "Sabbatical Cycle or Seasonal Pattern? Reflections on a New Book." *Or* 22:79-81.
1982 "Khnum and El." Pp. 203-214 in *Egyptological Studies*. Ed. by S. Israelit-Groll. SH 28. Jerusalem: The Magnes Press.

GRAPOW, H.
1952 *Der stilistische Bau der Geschichte des Sinuhe*. Untersuchungen zur ägyptischen Stilistik 1. Berlin: Akademie Verlag.

GRDSELOFF, B.
1952 "Sur un passage de l'inscription de Shabaka." *ArOr* 20:484-486.

GRÉBAUT, E.
1874 *Hymne à Ammon-Ra*. Paris: A. Franck.

GRIFFITH, F. Ll.
1896 "The Millingen Papyrus." *ZÄS* 34:35-51.
1926 "The Teaching of Amenophis the Son of Kanakht." *JEA* 12:191-231.
GRIFFITHS, J. G.
1960 "Wisdom about Tomorrow." *HTR* 53:219-221.
GRUMACH, I.
1972 *Untersuchungen zur Lebenslehre des Amenope*. MÄS 23. Munich: Deutscher Kunstverlag.
HARRIS, J. R.
1961 *Lexicographical Studies in Ancient Egyptian Minerals*. Deutsche Akademie der Wissenschaften zu Berlin, Institut für Orientforschung, Veröffentlichung 54. Berlin: Akademie Verlag.
HASSAN, S.
1928 *Hymnes religieux du moyen empire*. Cairo: IFAO.
HELCK, W.
1961 *Urkunden der 18. Dynastie: Übersetzungen zu den Heften 17-22. Urk.* IV. Berlin: Akademie Verlag.
1961-1970 *Materialien zur Wirtschaftsgeschichte des neuen Reiches*. Teil 1-6 und Indices. Akademie der Wissenschaften und der Literatur, Mainz. Abhandlungen der geistes- und sozialwissenschaftlichen Klasse 1960, 10-11; 1963, 2-3; 1964, 4; 1969, 4; 1969, 13. Mainz: Akademie der Wissenschaften und der Literatur.
1969 *Der Text der "Lehre Amenemhets I. für seinen Sohn"*. Wiesbaden: Harrassowitz.
1970a *Die Prophezeiung des Nfr. tj*. Kleine ägyptische Texte. Wiesbaden: Harrassowitz.
1970b *Die Lehre des Dwꜣ-Ḫtjj*. Kleine ägyptische Texte. Wiesbaden: Harrassowitz.
1983 "Zur Herkunft der Erzählung des sog. 'Astartepapyrus.'" Pp. 215-223 in *Studies Brunner*.
HERMSEN, E.
1991 *Die zwei Wege des Jenseits*. OBO 112. Freiburg: Universitätsverlag.
HERRMANN, S.
1963 "Steuerruder, Waage, Herz und Zunge in ägyptischen Bildreden." *ZÄS* 79:106-115.
HOFFMEIER, J. K.
1983 "Some Thoughts on Genesis 1 & 2 and Egyptian Cosmology." *JANES* 15:39-49.
HOLWERDA, A. and P. BOESER.
1905-1932 *Beschreibung der aegyptischen Sammlung*. 14 Volumes. Leiden. Rijksmuseum van Oudheden. The Hague.
HORNUNG, E.
1963-67 *Das Amduat*. 3 parts. ÄA 7. Wiesbaden: Harrassowitz.
1972 *Ägyptische Unterweltsbücher*. Zürich: Artemis Verlag.
1973 *Der Eine und die Vielen*. Darmstadt: Wissenschaftliche Buchgesellschaft.
1975-76 *Das Buch der Anbetung des Re im Westen*. 2 vols. Aegyptiaca Helvetica, 2-3. Geneva: Ägyptologisches Seminar der Universität Basel and Centre d'études orientales de l'Université de Genève.
1979 *Das Totenbuch der Ägypter*. Zürich: Artemis Verlag.
1982 *The One and the Many*. Ithaca, NY: Cornell University Press.
HORNUNG, G.
1990 *Gesänge vom Nil. Dichtung am Hofe der Pharaonen*. Zürich: Artemis Verlag.
HUFFMON, H.
1965 *Amorite Personal Names in the Mari Texts*. Baltimore: Johns Hopkins University Press.
HUMBERT, P.
1929 *Recherches sur les sources égyptiennes de la littérature sapientiale d'Israel*. Mémoires de l'Université de Neuchatel 7. Neuchatel: Secrétariat de l'Université.
JESI, F.
1962 "Il tentato adulterio mitico in Grecia e in Egitto." *Aegyptus* 42:276-296.
JUNGE, F.
1973 "Zur Fehldatierung des sog. Denkmals memphitischer Theologie oder Der Beitrag der ägyptischen Theologie zur Geistesgeschichte der Spätzeit." *MDAIK* 29: 195-204.
1977 "Der Welt der Klagen." Pp. 275-284 in *Studies Otto*.
JUNKER, H.
1939 *Die Götterlehre von Memphis*. APAW 23. Berlin: Verlag der Akademie der Wissenschaften.
KADISH, G. E.
1973 "British Museum Writing Board 5645: The Complaints of Kha-kheper-Rēᶜ-senebu." *JEA* 59:77-90.
KEES, H.
1930 "Göttinger Totenbuchstudien. Ein Mythus von Köningtum des Osiris in Herakelopolis aus dem Totenbuch Kap. 175." *ZÄS* 65:65-83.
1956 *Totenglauben und Jenseitsvorstellungen der alten Ägypter*. Leipzig: J. C. Hinrichs. 4th ed., Berlin: Akademie Verlag, 1980.
1962 "Ein Handelsplatz des MR im Nordostdelta." *MDAIK* 18:1-13.
KEIMER, L.
1928a *ActOr* 6:288ff.
1928b "Sur quelques petits fruit en faience émaillée datant du Moyen Empire." *BIFAO* 28:50-97.
KITCHEN, K. A.
1979 "The Basic Literary Forms and Formulations of Ancient Instructional Writings in Egypt and Western Asia." Pp. 236-257 in *Studien zu altägyptischen Lebenslehren*. Ed. by E. Hornung and O. Keel.
1992 "Egypt, History of (Chronology)." *ABD* 2:321-331.
KOEFOED-PETERSEN, O.
1936 *Recueil des inscriptions hiéroglyphiques de la Glyptothèque Ny Carslberg*. Bibliotheca Aegyptiaca 6. Brussels: Édition de la Fondation Égyptologique Reine Élisabeth.
1948 *Les stèles égyptiennes*. Publications de la Glyptothèque Ny Carlsberg, 1. Copenhagen: Glyptothèque Ny Carlsberg.

KOENIG, Y.
1990 "Les textes d'envoûtement de Mirgissa." *RdÉ* 41:101-25.
KÖNIGLICHE MUSEEN ZU BERLIN.
1901 *Rituale für den Kultus des Amon und für den Kultus der Mut*. HPKMB 1. Leipzig: J. C. Hinrichs.
KOROSTOVTSEV, M. A.
1960 *Puteshestvie Un-Amuna v Biblos: Egipetskii ieraticheskii papirus no 120 Gosudarst. Muzeia im A. S. Pushkina*. Pamiatniki literatury narodov Vostoka. Teksty. Bol'shaia seriia, 4 Moscow: Akademia Nauk S.S.S.R. Institut Vostoknedemia.
KUHLMANN, K. P.
1992 "Bauernweisheiten." Pp. 191-207 in *Studies Brunner-Traut*.
LACAU, P., and H. CHEVRIER.
1977 *Une chapelle d'Hatshepsout à Karnak*, vol 1. Cairo: Institut français d'archéologie orientale.
LANCZKOWSKI, G.
1958 "Die Geschichte vom Riesen Goliath und der Kampf Sinuhes mit dem Starken von Retenu." *MDAIK* 16:214-218.
LANGE, H. O.
1925 *Das Weisheitsbuch des Amenemope, aus dem Papyrus 10,474 des British Museum*. Danske videnskabernes selskab, historisk-filologiske meddelelser 11/2 Copenhagen: A. F. Host & Son.
LEFEBVRE, G.
1944 "Encore la stèle de Bakhtan." *CdÉ* 19:214-218.
1949 *Romans et contes égyptiens de l'époque pharaonique*. Paris: A. Maisonneuve. Reprint 1988.
LEXA, F.
1929 *ArOr* 1:14-49.
LICHTHEIM, M.
1945 *JNES* 4:178-212.
1973-76 *AEL*. 1-2.
1977 "The Naucratis Stela Once Again." Pp. 142-144 in *Studies Hughes*.
1983 *Late Egyptian Wisdom Literature in the International Context: A Study of Demotic Instructions*. OBO 52. Freiburg: Universitätsverlag.
LIPIŃSKI, E.
1974 "'Anaq-Kiryat ᵓArba' — Hébron et ses sanctuaires tribaux." *VT* 24:41-48.
LOPEZ, J.
1963 "Le Papyrus Millingen." *RdÉ* 18:29-33 and pls. 4-8.
LORTON, D.
1968 "The Expression Šms-ᵓib." *JARCE* 7:41-54.
LÜDDECKENS, E.
1943 *Untersuchungen über religiösen Gehalt, Sprache und Form der ägyptischen Totenklagen*. MDAIK 11. Berlin: Akademie Verlag.
LUFT, U.
1977 "Das Totenbuch des Ptahmose." *ZÄS* 104:46-75.
MALININE, M.
1934 "Un fragment de l'enseignement d'Amenemhat Ier." *BIFAO* 34:63-74.
MARIETTE, A.
1871 *Les papyrus égyptiens du musée de Boulaq*. Vol. 1. Paris: A. Franck.
1872 *Les papyrus égyptiens du musée de Boulaq*. Vol. 2. Paris: A. Franck.
MASPERO, G.
1914 *Les enseignements d'Amenemhat Ier à son fils Sanouasrit Ier*. Cairo.
MAYSTRE, Ch.
1941 "Le livre de la vache du ciel." *BIFAO* 40:53-115.
DE MEULENAERE, H.
1957 "Review of Barquet 1953a." *BiOr* 14:33-34.
MILLER, R. L.
1990 "Hogs and Hygiene." *JEA* 76:125-140.
MÖLLER, G.
1905 *Hymnen an verschiedenen Götter*. HPKMB 2. Leipzig: J. C. Hinrichs.
1927 *Hieratische Lesestücke für den akademischen Gebrauch*. 3 fascicles. Leipzig: J. C. Hinrichs. Reprint, 1961.
MORET, A.
1902 *Le rituel du culte divin journalier en Égypte*. Paris: Ernest Leroux.
1931 *BIFAO* 30:725-750 and 3 plates.
MÜLLER, D.
1967 "Grabausstattung und Totengericht in der Lehre für König Merikare." *ZÄS* 94:117-124.
MÜLLER, W. M.
1899 *Die Liebespoesie der alten Ägypter*. Leipzig: J. C. Hinrichs.
NAVILLE, É.
1886 *Das aegyptische Todtenbuch der XVIII. bis XX. Dynastie aus verschiedenen Urkunden zusammengestellt und herausgegeben*. 2 vols. Berlin: A. Asher & Co.
NIMS, C. F.
1968 "Second Tenses in Wenamūn." *JEA* 54:161-164.
OCKINGA, B.
1983 "The Burden of Khaᶜkheperrēᶜ-sonbu." *JEA* 69:88-95.
OSING, J.
1976 *Die Nominalbildung des Ägyptischen*. 2 vols. Mainz/Rhein: Philipp von Zabern Verlag.

OTTO, E.
1951 *Der Vorwurf an Gott*. Hildesheim.
PARKER, R. A.
1960 *Egyptian Astronomical Texts*. Vol. 1. *The Early Decans*. BES 3. Providence: Brown University Press.
PARKER, R. A., J. LECLANT, and J.-C. GOYON.
1979 *The Edifice of Taharqa*. BES 8. Providence: Brown University Press.
PARKINSON, R. B.
1991a "The Date of the 'Tale of the Eloquent Peasant.'" *RdÉ* 42:171-181.
1991b *The Tale of the Eloquent Peasant*. Oxford: Oxford University Press.
PERRY, E.
1986 *A Critical Study of the Eloquent Peasant*. Ph.D. dissertation. Johns Hopkins University.
PESTMAN, P. W.
1982 "Who were the Owners, in the 'Community of Workmen', of the Chester Beatty Papyri." Pp. 155-172 in *Gleanings from Deir el-Medîna*. Ed. by R. Demarée and J. Janssen. Egyptologische Uitgaven 1. Leiden: Nederlands Instituut voor het Nabije Oosten.
PETERSON, B. J.
1966 "A New Fragment of *The Wisdom of Amenemope*." *JEA* 52:120-128.
PIANKOFF, A.
1933 "Quelques passages des 'Instructions de Douaf' sur une tablette du Musée du Louvre." *RdÉ* 1:51-74.
1955 *The Shrines of Tut-Ankh-Amon*. Bollingen Series 40. ERTR 2. New York: Pantheon Books. Reprint: Harper Torchbook.
PIERRET, P.
1874-1878 *Recueil d'inscriptions inédites du Musée Égyptien du Louvre*. 2 Volumes. Paris.
PLEYTE, W. and F. ROSSI.
1869-76 *Papyrus de Turin*. 2 vols. Leiden: E. J. Brill.
POLOTSKY, H. J.
1973 "Notre connaissance du néo-egyptien." Pp. 133-141 in *Textes et langages de l'Égypte Pharaonique: Hommage à Jean-François Champollion, 1*. BdÉ 64/1. Cairo.
POSENER, G.
1934 "A propos de la stèle de Bentresh." *BIFAO* 34:75-81.
1935 *Catalogue des ostraca hiératiques littéraires de Deir el Médineh*. Vol. 1. FIFAO 1. Cairo.
1949 "Les richesses inconnues de la littérature égyptienne (Recherches littéraires I)." *RdÉ* 6:27-48.
1950 "Trais passages de l'enseignement à Merikarê" *RdÉ* 7:176-180.
1956 *Littérature et politique dans l'Égypte de la xiie dynastie*. Bibliothèque de l'École des Hautes Études 307. Paris.
1962 "L'enseignement pour le roi Mérikarê." *ACF* 62:290-295.
1963a "Aménémopé 21,13 et *bjꜣj.t* au sens d'«oracle»." *ZÄS* 90:98-102.
1963b "L'enseignement pour le roi Mérikarê." *ACF* 63:303-305.
1964 "L'expression *bjꜣj.t ꜥꜣ.t* «mauvais caractère»." *RdÉ* 16:37-43.
1965 "L'enseignement pour le roi Mérikarê." *ACF* 65:305-307.
1966a "L'enseignement pour le roi Mérikarê." *ACF* 66:342-345.
1966b "Quatre tablettes scolaires de basse époque (Aménéopé et Hardjédef)." *RdÉ* 18:45-62 and pls. 1-2.
1968 Pp. 106-111 in *Studies Schott*.
1972 *Catalogue des ostraca hiératiques littéraires de Deir el Médineh*. Vol. 2. FIFAO 18. Cairo.
1973 "Le chapitre IV d'Aménémopé." *ZÄS* 99:129-135.
1977-80 *Catalogue des ostraca hiératiques littéraires de Deir el Médineh*. Vol. 3. FIFAO 20. Cairo.
REDFORD, D. B.
1986 *Pharaonic King-Lists, Annals and Day Books*. Mississauga: Benben.
RITNER, R. K.
1987 "Review of H. J. Thissen, *Die Lehre des Anchscheschonqi (P. BM 10508)*." *BiOr* 44:641-646.
1989 "Horus on the Crocodiles: A Juncture of Religion and Magic in Late Dynastic Egypt." Pp. 103-116 in *Religion and Philosophy in Ancient Egypt*. Ed. by W. K. Simpson. YES 3. New Haven, CT: Yale University Press.
1990 "O. Gardiner 363: A Spell Against Night Terrors." *JARCE* 27:25-41.
1993 *The Mechanics of Ancient Egyptian Magical Practice*. SAOC 54. Chicago: The Oriental Institute.
ROCCATI, A.
1984 "Lessico Meteorologico." Pp. 343-354 in *Studien zu Sprach und Religion Ägyptens zu Ehren von Wolfhart Westendorf*. Volume 1: *Sprache*. Ed. by F. Junge. Göttingen: Hubert & Co.
ROEDER, C.
1915 *Urkunden zur Religion des alten Ägypten*. Jena.
ROEDER, G.
1960 *Kulte, Orakel und Naturverehrung im alten Ägypten*. Zürich: Artemis Verlag.
RÖMER, M.
1987 "Der kairener Hymnus an Amun-Re zur Gliederung von pBoulaq 17." Pp. 405-428 in *Studies Fecht*.
RÖßLER-KÖHLER, U.
1979 *Kapitel 17 des ägyptischen Totenbuches*. Göttinger Orientforschungen, IV. Reihe: Ägypten, 10. Wiesbaden: Harrassowitz.
ROWTON, M. B.
1976 "Dimorphic Structure and the Problem of the ꜥApirû-ꜥIbrîm." *JNES* 35:13-20.
RUFFLE, J.
1977 "The Teaching of Amenemope and its Connection with the Book of Proverbs." *TynBul* 28:29-68.
SAINTE FARE GARNOT, J.
1948 *CRAIBL* 1948:543-549.
1949 "Notes on the Inscriptions of Suty and Ḥor (British Museum Stela No. 826)." *JEA* 35:63-68.

SANDMAN, M.

1938 *Texts from the Time of Akhenaten*. Bibliotheca Aegyptiaca 8. Brussels: Édition de la Fondation Égyptologique Reine Élisabeth.

SAUNERON, S.

1953 "L'Hymne au soleil levant des Papyrus de Berlin 3050, 3056, et 3048." *BIFAO* 53: 65-102.

1959 "La naissance du monde selon l'Égypte ancienne." in *Sources orientales 1: La naissance du monde*. Paris: Éditions du Seuil.

1960 "La différenciation des langages d'après la tradition égyptienne." *BIFAO* 60:31-41.

SCHARFF, A.

1936 *Der historische Abschnitt der Lehre für König Merikare*. SBAW 8. Munich: Bayerischen Akademie der Wissenschaften.

SCHLÖGL, H. A.

1980 *Der Gott Ta-tenen*. OBO 29. Freiburg: Universitätsverlag.

SCHOTT, S.

1938 "Die beiden Neunheiten als Ausdruck für 'Zähne' und 'Lippen'." *ZÄS* 74: 94-96.

1950 *Altägyptische Liebeslieder, mit Märchen und Liebesgeschichten*. Zürich: Artemis Verlag.

SCHUBART, W.

1910 "Dodekaschoinos." *ZÄS* 47:154-157.

SCHWAB-SCHLOTT, A.

1969 *Die Ausmasse Ägyptens nach altägyptischen Texten*. Dissertation, University of Tubingen.

1972 "Altägyptische Texte über die Ausmaße." *MDAIK* 28:109-113.

1975 "Dodekaschoinos" in *LdÄ*. 1:cols. 1112-1113.

SEIBERT, P.

1967 *Die Charakteristik. Untersuchungen zu einer altägyptischen Sprechsitte und ihren Auspragungen in Folklore und Literatur*. ÄA 17. Wiesbaden: Harrassowitz.

SETHE, K.

1901 *Dodekaschoinos das Zwölfmeilenland an der Grenze von Aegypten und Nubien*. Untersuchungen 2/3. Leipzig: J. C. Hinrichs. Reprint: Hildesheim, 1964.

1904 "Schoinos und Dodekaschoinos." *ZÄS* 41:58-62.

1924 *Ägyptische Lesestücke*. Leipzig: J. C. Hinrichs.

1926 *Die Ächtung feindlicher Fürsten, Völker und Dinge auf altägyptischen Tongefässscherben des Mittleren Reiches*. Berlin: Akademie der Wissenschaften.

1927 *Erläuterung zu den aegyptischen Lesestücken*. Leipzig: J. C. Hinrichs.

1928 *Dramatische Texte zu altaegyptischen Mysterienspielen*. Untersuchungen zur Geschichte und Altertumskunde Aegyptens 10. Leipzig: J.C. Hinrichs. Reprint: Hildesheim: Georg Olms Verlagsbuchhandlung, 1964.

SHUPAK, N.

1989-90 "Egyptian 'Prophecy' and Biblical Prophecy: Did the Phenomenom of Prophecy, in Biblical Sense, Exist in Ancient Egypt? *JEOL* 31:1-40.

1992 "A New Source for the Study of the Judiciary and Law of Ancient Egypt: 'The Tale of the Eloquent Peasant.'" *JNES* 51:1-18.

1993 *Where Can Wisdom Be Found? The Sage's Language in the Bible and in Ancient Egyptian Literature*. OBO 130. Freibourg: Universitätsverlag.

SIMPSON, D. C.

1926 "The Hebrew Book of Proverbs and the Teaching of Amenophis." *JEA* 12:232-239.

SIMPSON, W. K.

1973 Editor. *The Literature of Ancient Egypt: An Anthology of Stories, Instructions and Poetry*. 2nd edition. New Haven: Yale University Press.

1974 *The Terrace of the Great God at Abydos*. PPYEE 5. New Haven: Peabody Museum.

SPALINGER, A.

1984 "An Alarming Parallel to the End of the Shipwrecked Sailor." *GM* 73:91-95.

SPIEGELBERG, W.

1906 "Zu der Datierung der Bentresch-Stele." *RT* 28:181.

STADELMANN, R.

1975 "Astartepapyrus." *LdÄ* 1:cols. 509-511.

STERN, E.

1994 *Dor, Ruler of the Seas: Twelve Years of Excavations at the Israelite-Phoenician Harbor Town on the Carmel Coast*. Jerusalem: Israel Exploration Society.

STEWART, H. M.

1957 "A Possibly Contemporary Parallel to the Inscription of Suty and Ḥor." *JEA* 43:3-5.

SUYS, E.

1935 *La sagesse d'Ani: Texte, traduction et commentaire*. AnOr 11. Rome: Pontificium Institutum Biblicum.

SWELIM, N.

1983 *Some Problems on the History of the Third Dynasty*. The Archaeological Society of Alexandria, Archaeological & Historical Studies 7. Alexandria.

SZCZUDLOSKA, A.

1963 "The Fragment of the Chapter CLXXV of the Book of the Dead preserved in Sekoski's Papyrus." *Rocznik Orientalistyczny* 26:123-142.

TE VELDE, H.

1970 "The God Heka in Egyptian Theology." *JEOL* 21: 175-186.

THÉODORIDÈS, A.

1958-1960 *Bruxelles Annuaire* 15:39-69.

TRESSON, R.

1933 *RB* 42:57-78.

VAN SETERS, J.
1964 "A Date for the 'Admonitions' in the Second Intermediate Period." *JEA* 50:13-23.
VANDERSLEYEN, C.
1971 *Les guerres d'Amosis, fondateur de la XVIII dynastie*. Monographes reine Elisabeth 1. Brussels: Fondation égyptologique reine Elisabeth.
VANDIER, J.
1936 *La famine dans l'Egypte ancienne*. Institut français d'archéologie orientale, Recherches 7. Cairo.
1949 *BiOr* 6:15.
1962 *Le Papyrus Jumilhac*. Paris.
VARILLE, A.
1942 *BIFAO* 41:25-30.
VERNUS, P.
1978 *Athribis*. BdÉ 74. Cairo: Institut françyais d'archéologie orientale.
1986 "Traum." *LdÄ* 6:cols. 745-749.
VOLTEN, A. P. F.
1937-38 *Studien zum Weisheitsbuch des Anii*. Danske videnskabernes selskab, historisk-filologiske meddelelser, 23/3. Copenhagen: Levin & Munksgaard.
1941 "Ägyptische Nemesis-Gedanken." Pp. 371-379 in *Miscellanea Gregoriana: raccolta di scritti pubblicati nel i centenario dalla fondazione del Pont. Museo egizio*. Rome: Tipografia poliglotta vaticana.
1945 *Zwei altägyptische politische Schriften*. Analecta Aegyptiaca 4. Copenhagen: E. Munksgaard.
1963 *Les Sagesses du proche-orient ancien*. Colloque de Strasbourg 17-19 mai 1962. Paris.
VAN DE WALLE, B.
1947 "Le thème de la satire des métiers dans la littérature égyptienne." *CdÉ* 22:50-72.
1949 "Review of Brunner 1944." *CdÉ* 24:244-256.
1969 *L'Humour dans la littérature et dans l'art de l'ancienne Egypte*. Scholae Adriani de Buck memoriae dicatae 4. Leiden: Nederlands Instituut voor het Nabije Oosten.
WASHINGTON, H. C.
1994 *Wealth and poverty in the Instruction of Amenemope and the Hebrew Proverbs*. SBLDS 142. Atlanta: Scholars Press.
WENTE, E. F.
1973 Pp. 92-107 in Simpson, *Literature*.
WESTENDORF, W.
1968 Pp. 125-131 in *Studies Schott*.
1973 "Die Qualitäten des Weisen Neferti." *GM* 4:41-44.
WILDUNG, D.
1969 *Die Rolle ägyptischer Könige im Bewusstsein ihrer Nachwelt*. MÄS 17. Berlin: B. Hesslin.
1977 *Imhotep und Amenhotep. Gottwerdung im alten Ägypten*. MÄS 36. Munich: Deutscher Kunstverlag.
WILLIAMS, R. J.
1961 *JEA* 47:100-106.
1964 Pp. 16-19 in *Studies Meek*.
1969 "Some Egyptianisms in the Old Testament." Pp. 93-98 in *Studies Wilson*.
WILSON, J. A.
1969 *ANET*.
WOLF, W.
1929 "Der Berliner Ptah-Hymnus (P 3048, II-XII)." *ZÄS* 64: 17-44.
YOYOTTE, J.
1952 "Sur Bata, maître de Sako." *RdÉ* 9:157-159.
1962 "Processions géographiques mentionnant le Fayoum et ses localités." *BIFAO* 61:79-138 and pl. vii.
1964 "À propos du panthéon de Sinouhé (B 205-212)." *Kemi* 17:69-73.
ZABKAR, L.
1968 *A Study of the Ba Concept in Ancient Egyptian Texts*. SAOC 34. Chicago: University of Chicago Press.
ZANDEE, J.
1947 *Hymnen aan Amon van Pap. Leiden I 350*. Oudheidkundige Mededelingen uit het Rijksmuseum van Oudheiden te Leiden, Nieuwe Reeks 28. Leiden: E. J. Brill.
1971-72 "Sargtexte Spruch 75." *ZÄS* 97: 155-162; 98:149-155; 99:48-63.
1973a "Sargtexte Spruch 76." *ZÄS* 100:60-71.
1973b "Sargtexte Spruch 78." *ZÄS* 100:141-144.
1974 "Sargtexte Spruch 80." *ZÄS* 101:62-79.

HITTITE CANONICAL COMPOSITIONS

A. DIVINE FOCUS

1. MYTHS

ELKUNIRŠA AND AŠERTU (1.55)

Gary Beckman

Although the particular events of this tale are not known from the mythological tablets recovered at Ugarit, the story certainly belongs to the corpus of northern Syrian myths which they represent. This composition has come down to us in a number of fragments which originally belonged to two or three separate manuscripts, but only two portions of the text are well-enough preserved for connected translation. The Hittite translator has misunderstood the Canaanite phrase "El, Creator of Earth" as a simple divine name, which he has rendered as Elkuniršа.

Fragment 1

(A i 1´-7´) (Ašertu said to Baal:) "[Get behind me, and I will get behind] you. I will press [you] down with [my] word. I will pierce [you] with [my] little spindle(?). I will stimulate(?) you [...]" Baal heard (this) [and he] stood [up]. He came to the headwaters of the Euphrates River. [He came to] Elkuniršа, husband of Ašertu. He entered the tent [of] Elkuniršа.

(A i 8´-21´) [Elknuniršа] saw Baal and asked him, "[Why] have you come?" Baal said, "When I came into your house, [just then] Ašertu sent girls to me (with the message): 'Come sleep with me!' I refused. She ... me and said [as follows]: 'Get behind me, and I will get behind you. I will press you down with my [word. I will pierce] you [with] my [little spindle(?)].' On that account I have come, my father. I have not come to you [as] a messenger. I [have come] to you on my own behalf. Ašertu is rejecting your manhood. [...] your wife. She keeps sending to me: '[Sleep with me]!'" Elkuniršа [replied] to Baal: "Go, ... her! ... my [wife Ašertu]! Humiliate her!"

(A i 22´-27´) [Baal] heard the word [of Elkuniršа] and he [went] to Ašertu. Baal said to Ašertu: "I have slain your seventy-seven [sons]. I have slain eighty-eight." [When] Ašertu heard the humiliation, she was troubled in her soul and had mourning [women] take their places. She wailed for seven years. [The ...] ate and drank for them (the sons).

Fragment 2

(A ii 1´-3´) (Ašertu said to Elkuniršа:) "[...] I will press [down Baal with my word. I will pierce him with my little spindle(?). Then] I will sleep with you." [Elkuniršа] listened and said to his wife: "Come, [I will turn] Baal [over to you. Do] with him as you wish."

(A ii 4´-16´) Astarte overheard these words and became a goblet in the hand of Elkuniršа. She became an owl and perched on his wall. Astarte overheard the words which husband and wife spoke to one another. Elkuniršа and his wife went to her bed and they slept together. Astarte flew like a bird across the desert.[a] In the desert she found Baal, [and said] to him: "O Baal, [the husband(?)] of Ašertu [...] Do not drink wine together [... do not ...] against [...] she(?) will seek [...]"

[a] Ps 102:7

It seems that despite Astarte's warning Ašertu took her vengeance on Baal, for the remaining fragments of the text, which are very badly broken, discuss the treatment of various parts of Baal's body, including his penis, tendons, and muscles, as well as his ritual purification. Also mentioned are the "Dark Earth," the Hittite term for the Netherworld, and the Annunaki-deities, known from Mesopotamian texts as the rulers of this dismal portion of the universe. Thus it seems that Baal must have died and been brought back from the dead, an impression strengthened by the presence of the Mother-goddesses in this portion of the composition.

REFERENCES

Text: *CTH* 342; Fragment 1: A. KUB 36.35 i. B. KUB 36.34 i. Fragment 2: A. KUB 36.37 + KUB 31.118. B. KUB 12.61 ii. Literature: *ANET* 519; Bernabé 1987:127-29; Hoffner 1965; 1990:69-70; Laroche 1968b:25-30; Otten 1953.

THE STORM-GOD AND THE SERPENT (ILLUYANKA) (1.56)

Gary Beckman

The conflict between the Storm-god and the forces of chaos represented by the serpent (*illuyanka-* in Hittite) was the focus of two different tales known in second-millennium Anatolia, both of which served as etiological cult myths of the important Hittite festival called *purulli*, a term whose precise meaning remains unknown.

(A i 1-4) (This is) the text of the *purulli* (festival) for the [...] of the Storm-god of Heaven, according to Kella, [the "anointed priest"] of the Storm-god of (the town of) Nerik: When they speak thus —

(A i 5-8) "Let the land grow and thrive, and let the land be secure!" — and when it (indeed) grows and thrives, then they perform the festival of *purulli*.

(A i 9-11) When the Storm-god and the serpent came to grips in (the town of) Kiškilušša, the serpent smote the Storm-god.

(A i 12-14) (Thereafter) the Storm-god summoned all the gods (saying): "Come in! (The goddess) Inara has prepared a feast!"

(A i 15-18) She prepared everything in great quantity — vessels of wine, vessels of (the drink) *marnuwan*, and vessels of (the drink) *walḫi*. In the vessels [she made] an abundance.

(A i 19-20) Then [Inara] went [to] (the town of) Ziggarata and encountered Ḫupašiya, a mortal.

(A i 21-23) Inara spoke as follows to Ḫupašiya: "I am about to do such-and-such a thing — you join with me!"

(A i 24-26) Ḫupašiya replied as follows to Inara: "If I may sleep with you, then I will come and perform your heart's desire." [And] he slept with her.

(B i 3′-8′) Then Inara transported Ḫupašiya and concealed him. Inara dressed herself up and invited the serpent up from his hole (saying): "I'm preparing a feast — come eat and drink!"

(B i 9′-12′) Then the serpent came up together with [his progeny], and they ate and drank. They drank up every vessel and became intoxicated.

(B i 13′-16′) They were no longer able to go back down into (their) hole, (so that) Ḫupašiya came and tied up the serpent with a cord.

(B i 17′-18′) The Storm-god came and slew the serpent. The (other) gods were at his side.

(C i 14′-22′) Then Inara built a house on a rock (outcropping) in (the town of) Tarukka and settled Ḫupašiya in the house. Inara instructed him: "When I go out into the countryside, you must not look out the window. If you do look out, you will see your wife and your children."

(C i 23′-24′) When the twentieth day (after Inara's departure) had passed, he looked out the window and [saw] his wife and [his] children.

(C i 25′-27′) When Inara returned from the countryside, he began to whine: "Let me (go) back home!"

(A ii 9′-14′) Inara spoke as follows [to Ḫupašiya: " ...] away [... "] through an offense [...] the meadow of the Storm-god [...] she [... killed(?)] him.

(A ii 15′-20′) Inara [went] to Kiškilušša and how she set her(?) house and [the river(?)] of the watery abyss [into] the hand of the king — because (in commemoration thereof) we are (re-)performing the first *purulli* festival — the hand [of the king will hold(?) the house(?)] of Inara and the [river(?)] of the watery abyss.

(A ii 21′-24′) (The divine mountain) Zaliyanu is first (in rank) among all (the gods). When he has allotted rain in Nerik, then the herald brings forth a loaf of thick bread from Nerik.

(A ii 25′-29′) He had asked Zaliyanu for rain, and he brings it to him [on account of(?)] the bread ...

[Several badly damaged lines are followed by a break.]

(D iii 2′-5′) That which [Kella, the "anointed priest,"] spoke — [The serpent] defeated [the Storm-god] and took [(his) heart and eyes]. And the Storm-god [...] him.

(A iii 4′-8′) And he took as his wife the daughter of a poor man, and he sired a son. When he grew up, he took as his wife the daughter of the serpent.

(A iii 9′-12′) The Storm-god instructed (his) son: "When you go to the house of your wife, then demand from them (my) heart and eyes."

(A iii 13′-19′) When he went, he demanded from them the heart, and they gave it to him. Afterwards he demanded from them the eyes, and they gave these to him. And he carried them to the Storm-god, his father, and the Storm-god (thereby) took back his heart and his eyes.

(A iii 20′-28′) When he was again sound in body as of old, then he went once more to the sea for battle. When he gave battle to him and was beginning to smite the serpent, then the son of the Storm-god was with the serpent and shouted up to heaven, to his father:

(A iii 29′-33′) "Include me! Do not show me any mercy!" Then the Storm-god killed the serpent and his (own) son. And now this one, the Storm-god

[...]

(A iii 34´-35´) Thus says Kella, [the "anointed priest" of the Storm-god of Nerik: " ...] when the gods [...]"

[A break intervenes.]

(D iv 1´-4´) [Then] for the "anointed priest" they made the foremost gods the humblest, and the humblest they made the foremost gods.

(D iv 8´-10´) The cultic revenue of Zaliyanu is great. Zašḫapuna the wife of Zaliyanu is greater than the Storm-god of Nerik.

(D iv 8´-10´) The gods speak as follows to the "anointed priest" Taḫpurili: "When we go to the Storm-god of Nerik, where will we sit?"

(D iv 11´-16´) The "anointed priest" Taḫpurili speaks as follows: "When you sit on a diorite stool, and when the 'anointed priests' cast the lot,[a] then the 'anointed priest' who holds (the image of) Zaliyanu — a diorite stool will be set above the spring, and he will be seated there."

a Esth 4:7; 9:26

(A iv 14´-17´) "All the gods will arrive, and they will cast the lot.[a] Of all the gods of (the town of) Kaštama, Zašḫapuna will be the greatest."

(A iv 18´-21´) "Because she is the wife of Zaliyanu, and Tazzuwašši is his concubine, these three persons will remain in (the town of) Tanipiya."

(A iv 22´-23´) And thereafter in Tanipiya a field will be handed over from the royal (property) —

(A iv 24´-28´) Six *kapunu*-measures of field, one *kapunu*-measure of garden, a house together with a threshing floor, three buildings for the household personnel. It is recorded [on] a tablet. I am respectful [of the matter], and I have spoken these things (truly).

(A iv 29´-33´) Colophon: One tablet, complete, of the word of Kella, the "anointed priest." [The scribe] Piḫa-ziti wrote it under the supervision of the chief scribe Walwa-ziti.

REFERENCES

Text: *CTH* 321; A. KBo 3.7. B. KUB 17.5. C. KUB 17.6. D. KUB 12.66. E. KUB 36.54. F. KBo 12.83. G. KBo 12.84 (+) KBo 13.84. H. KBo 22.99. J. KUB 36.53. Bibliography: *ANET* 125-126; Beckman 1982; Bernabé 1987:29-37; Gonnet 1987; Hoffner 1990:10-14; Laroche 1968b:65-72; Pecchioli Daddi and Polvani 1990:39-55.

THE WRATH OF TELIPINU (1.57)

Gary Beckman

In the Hittite view, the operation of the universe required that each deity and human conscientiously perform his or her proper function within the whole. Calamity manifested in some sector of the cosmos was an indication that the god or goddess responsible for it had become angry and had abandoned his or her post. The remedy for this evil situation was the performance by both human and divine practitioners of an expiatory ritual which included a mythological account of the deity's displeasure, departure, and reconciliation. Such "disappearing god texts" (Parker 1989) are attested for at least a dozen Hittite divinities. The example translated here, the best preserved and consequently best known to non-specialists, is addressed to Telipinu, who belonged to the large class of Anatolian Storm-gods.[a]

[The beginning of the text has been lost.]

(A i 1´-4´) Telipinu [became angry and said]: "Do not practice intimidation!" He slipped(?) his right [shoe] on his left (foot). [He slipped(?)] his left [shoe] on his right.

(A i 5´-9´) Mist seized the windows. Smoke seized the house. On the hearth the logs were stifled. [On the altars] the gods were stifled. In the fold the sheep were stifled. In the corral the cows were stifled. The sheep refused her lamb. The cow refused her calf.

(A i 10´-15´) Telipinu went off and took away grain, the fertility of the herds, growth(?), plenty(?), and satiety into the wilderness, to the meadow and the moor. Telipinu proceeded to disappear into the moor. The *ḫalenzu*-plant spread over him. Barley and wheat no longer grow. Cows, sheep, and humans no longer conceive, and those who are (already) pregnant do not give birth in this time.

a 1 Kgs 17-18

(A i 16´-20´) The mountains dried up. The trees dried up, so that buds do not come forth. The pastures dried up. The springs dried up. Famine appeared in the land. Humans and gods perish from hunger. The great Sun-god prepared a feast and invited the Thousand Gods. They ate but were not sated; they drank but were not satisfied.

(A i 21´-25´) The Storm-god concerned himself for his son Telipinu: "My son Telipinu is not here. He became angry and took away for himself everything good." The great gods and the lesser gods began to search for Telipinu. The Sun-god dispatched the swift eagle: "Go search the high mountains!

(A i 26′-31′) Search the deep valleys! Search the blue sea!" The eagle went, but he did not find him. He brought back a report to the Sun-god: "I didn't find him, the honored god Telipinu." The Storm-god said to the Mother-goddess: "What will we do? We will perish from hunger!" The Mother-goddess said to the Storm-god: "Do something, Storm-god! *You* go search for Telipinu!"

(A i 32′-35′) The Storm-god set out and began to search for Telipinu. He [comes] to his city, to the city gate, but he is not able to open (it). He broke his mallet and wedge. The Storm-god [...], covered himself (with his garment), and sat down. The Mother-goddess [dispatched a bee]: "You go search for Telipinu!"

(A i 36′-39′) [The Storm-god] spoke [to the Mother-goddess]: "The great gods and the lesser gods repeatedly searched for him, but [they did not find] him. Now [will] this [bee] go [find] him? His wingspan is small, he himself is small, and furthermore they (the gods) ..."

[A break intervenes. Parallel texts inform us that despite the scepticism of the Storm-god, the bee indeed succeeded in finding the lost god, who was asleep in a meadow. The bee stung Telipinu on his hands and feet, awakening him and only increasing his rage. It is to placating this anger that the program of ritual action which constitutes the remainder of this text is directed. Here the actions of the human magical specialist and of Kamrušepa, goddess of magic, are inextricably intertwined.]

(A ii 3′-8′) And Telipinu [...] And she (the human practitioner) ground up(?) malt and beer-bread. [...] came forth(?). She cut off good [...] at the gate. [Let] the pleasant smell [summon(?) you], Telipinu. Choked (with rage), [may you be reconciled (with gods and humans)]!

(A ii 9′-11′) Here (before you) [lies] water of *walḫeššar*. [Let] your soul, O Telipinu, [be ... Turn] to the king in favor.

(A ii 12′-14′) Here lies *galaktar*. Let [your soul, O Telipinu], be pacified. Here [lies *parḫuena-*]. Let (its) form entice you(!), [O Telipinu].

(A ii 15′-18′) Here lie *šamama*-nuts. Let [your soul, O Telipinu], be sated with oil. Here [lie] figs. As [figs] are sweet, let [your soul, O Telipinu], likewise become sweet.

(A ii 19′-21′) As the olive [holds] its oil in its heart, [and as the grape] holds its wine in its heart, may you, Telipinu, likewise hold goodness in your soul and heart.

(A 22′-27′) Here lies *liti*-wood. Let it anoint [your soul(?)], O Telipinu. As the malt and beer-bread are joined in their essence, let your soul likewise [be] joined, [O Telipinu], to the words of the humans. [As ...] is pure, let Telipinu's soul likewise become pure. [As] honey is sweet and as ghee is mild, let [the soul] of Telipinu likewise become sweet and likewise become mild.

(A ii 28′-32′) I have now sprinkled the paths of Telipinu with fine oil. O Telipinu, tread the paths sprinkled with fine oil. Let boughs of *šaḫi-* and *ḫappuriya-* be your bed. As (stalks of) lemon grass(?) are intertwined, may you, O Telipinu, be reconciled (with gods and humans).

(A ii 33′-iii 2) In fury Telipinu came. He thunders with the lightning bolt. He smites the Dark Earth below. Kamrušepa saw him, [took] an eagle's wing (as an instrument of magic), and carried him off. She [brought] it, the displeasure, [to an end]. She brought it, the wrath, to an end. She brought [the offense] to an end. She brought the anger to an end.

(A iii 3-7) Kamrušepa speaks to the gods: "Go, O gods. Ḫapantali [is] now [herding] the sheep of the Sun-god. Cut out twelve rams so that I may treat the *karaš*-grain of Telipinu." I (the human practitioner) have taken for myself a sieve with a thousand 'eyes,' and I have sifted (in it) the *karaš*-grain, the rams of Kamrušepa.

(A iii 8-12) I have burned (a purificatory substance) over Telipinu on this side and that. I have taken his evil from Telipinu, from his body. I have taken his (perceived) offense. I have taken his displeasure. I have taken his wrath. I have taken his irritation. I have taken his anger.

(A iii 13-20) Telipinu is wrathful. His soul and [his] figure were stifled (like) kindling. As they have burned this kindling, let the displeasure, wrath, (perceived) offense, and anger of Telipinu likewise burn. As [malt] is meager (in fertility), and one does not take it to the field to use as seed, nor does one make it into bread, [nor] does one place [it] in the storehouse, so let the displeasure, [wrath], (perceived) offense, and anger of Telipinu likewise become meager (in effect).

(A iii 21-23) Telipinu is wrathful. His soul [and his figure] are a burning fire. As this fire [is extinguished], let (his) displeasure, wrath, and anger likewise [be extinguished].

(A iii 24-27) O Telipinu, let go of displeasure. [Let go of] wrath. Let go of anger. As a rain spout does not flow [backwards], so [let the displeasure, wrath], and anger of Telipinu not [come] back.

(A iii 28-34) The gods [take their seats in the place] of assembly beneath the hawthorn tree. Beneath the hawthorn tree [are set] long [...] All of the gods are seated (including): [Papaya], Ištuštaya, the Fate-deities, the Mother-goddesses, the Grain-deity, the Spirit of growth, Telipinu, the Tutelary Deity, Ḫapantali, [and ...] I have treated the deities for long years [and for ...] I have purified him (Telipinu).

(C 9′-12′) [I have taken] evil from Telipinu, [from his body]. I have taken his [displeasure. I have taken his] wrath. I have taken [his (perceived) offense. I have taken his] anger. I have taken [the evil] tongue. [I have taken] the evil [...]

[There is a break. The preserved text resumes with an address to the hawthorn tree.]

(A iv 1-3) [The ox goes beneath you, and] you pluck [his] coat(?). The sheep [goes] beneath you, and you pluck her fleece. Pluck from Telipinu (his) wrath, displeasure, (perceived) offense, and anger.

(A iv 4-7) In fury the Storm-god comes, and the man of the Storm-god (his priest) brings him to a halt. A pot comes to a boil, and the wooden spoon(?) brings it to a halt. Furthermore, let my words, those of the human, likewise bring displeasure, wrath, and anger to an end for Telipinu.

(A iv 8-13) Let them depart, the displeasure, wrath, (perceived) offense, and anger of Telipinu. Let the house release them. Let the central ... release them. Let the window release them. Let the door-pivot <release them>. Let the central courtyard release them. Let the city gate release them. Let the gate structure release them. Let the royal road release them. They shall not go to the fertile field, or garden, or grove. They shall go along the road of the Sun-goddess of the Earth.

(A iv 14-19) The doorkeeper opened the seven doors; he drew back the seven bolts. Below, in the Dark Earth, there stand bronze kettles. Their lids are of lead. Their latches are of iron. Whatever goes into (them) does not come up again, but perishes therein. Let them capture the displeasure, wrath, (perceived) offense, and anger of Telipinu, so that they do not come back.

(A iv 20-26) Telipinu came back home and concerned himself for his land. The mist released the window. The smoke released the house. The altars were reconciled with the gods. The hearth released the log. In the fold he (Telipinu) released the sheep. In the corral he released the cows. Then the mother tended her child. The sheep tended her lamb. The cow tended her calf. And Telipinu <tended> the king and queen. He concerned himself for them in regard to life, vigor, and future (existence).

(A iv 27-31) Telipinu concerned himself for the king. An *eya*-tree stands before Telipinu. From the *eya*-tree hangs a hunting bag (fashioned from the skin) of a sheep. In it is mutton fat. In it are grain, the fertility of the herds, and the grape. In it are cow and sheep. In it are long years and progeny.

(A iv 32-35) In it is the gentle bleating of the lamb. In it are ... and renown. In it is the ... In it is the right shank. In it [is growth(?), plenty(?), and satiety].

[The preserved text ends.]

REFERENCES

Text: *CTH* 324.1; A. KUB 17.10. B. KUB 33.2. C. KUB 33.1. D. KUB 33.3. E. KBo 24.84. Bibliography: *ANET* 126-128; Bernabé 1987:49-54; Hoffner 1990:14-17; Kellerman 1986; Laroche 1965b:89-98; Parker 1989; Pecchioli Daddi and Polvani 1990:71-84.

APPU AND HIS TWO SONS (1.58)

Harry A. Hoffner, Jr.

This text has been translated here as an independent story. According to Güterbock (1946), the text is continued in the tale of the Sun God, the Cow, and the Fisherman. Although the extant copies of the Appu story are New Hittite, archaic language indicates an archetype composed in the Old or Middle Hittite period. The story has a moral, which is stated in the *proemium*. The unnamed deity who is praised for always vindicating the just person will also thwart the evil son of Appu who attempts to defraud his honest brother. Only a little bit of the beginning is lost. Where the text becomes intelligible, a *proemium* is in progress.

He/she it is (i.e., some deity) who always exonerates just men, but chops down evil men like trees, repeatedly striking evil men on their skulls (like) ...s until he/she destroys them.

There was a city named Šudul. It was situated on the seacoast in the land of Lulluwa. Up there lived a man named Appu. He was the richest man in all the land. He had many cattle and sheep. He had amassed silver, gold and lapis lazuli like a huge heap of threshed grain. There was nothing which he lacked but one thing: he had neither son nor daughter.[1] [a]

The elders of Šudul sat eating in his presence. One gave bread and a piece of grilled meat to his son;

[a] Gen 15:2

[1] With the wealthy Appu, who had everything anyone might want, but was childless, cp. biblical Abraham (Gen 15:2).

another gave his son a drink. But Appu had no one to whom to give bread. The table was covered with a linen cloth and stood in front of the altar. Appu arose, went home, and lay down on his bed with his shoes on.

Appu's wife questioned their servants: "He has never had success before. You don't think he has now had success, do you?" The woman went and lay down with Appu with her clothes on. Appu awoke from his sleep, and his wife questioned him: "You have never had success before. Have you now had success?" When Appu heard this, he replied: "You are a woman and think like one. You know nothing at all."[2] [b]

Appu rose from his bed, took a white lamb, and set out to meet the Sun God. The Sun God looked down from the sky, changed himself into a young man, came to him, and questioned him: "What is your problem, that [I may solve] it for you?"

When [Appu] heard this, he replied to him: "[The gods] have given me wealth. They have given [me cattle and sheep]. I lack only one thing: I have neither son nor daughter." When the Sun God heard this, he said: "Get drunk, go home, and sleep with your wife. The gods will give you a son."

When Appu heard this, he went back home, but the Sun God went back up to the sky. Now Teššub (the Storm God) saw the Sun God coming three miles distant, and said to his vizier: "Look who's coming: the Sun God, Shepherd of the Lands! You don't suppose that somewhere the land is laid waste? Might not cities somewhere be devastated? Might not troops somewhere be put to rout? Tell the cook and cupbearer to provide him with food and drink."

[The Sun God] came, [...], and [Teššub ...ed] him there. Teššub [...ed] the Sun God, and began to question him: "Why [have you come, O Sun God of the Sky? ..."]

[Long break.]

[Beginning of column iii broken.]

Appu's wife became pregnant. The first month, the second month, the third month, the fourth month, the fifth month, the sixth month, the seventh month, the eighth month, the ninth month passed, and the tenth month arrived. Appu's wife bore a son. The nurse lifted the boy and placed him on Appu's knees. Appu began to amuse the boy and to clean him off(?). He put a fitting name upon him: "Since my ancestral gods didn't [take] the right way for him, but followed a wrong way, let his name be Wrong."[3]

b Job 2:9-10

c Gen 31:4-12

Again, a second time Appu's wife became pregnant. The [tenth] month arrived, and the woman bore a son. The nurse lifted [the boy] and (Appu) put the right name upon him, "Let them call him by a right name. Since my ancestral gods took the right way for him, let his name be Right."

[Appu's boys] grew up and matured and came into manhood. [When] Appu's boys had grown up [and matured] and come into manhood, they parted [from] Appu, and [divided up] the estate.

Brother Wrong said to Brother Right: "Let us separate and settle down in different places." Brother Right said [to Brother Wrong]: "Then who [...]?" Brother Wrong said to Brother Right: "Since the mountains dwell separately, since the rivers flow in separate courses, as the very gods dwell separately — I say these things to you: The Sun God dwells in Sippar. The Moon God dwells in Kuzina. Teššub dwells in Kummiya. And Šawuška dwells in Nineveh. Nanaya [dwells] in Kiššina. And Marduk dwells in Babylon. As the gods dwell separately, so let us also settle in different places."

Wrong and Right began to divide up (the estate), while the Sun God looked on from heaven. Brother Wrong took [a half] and gave the other half to his brother Right. They [...]ed among themselves. There was one plow ox and [one] cow. Wrong took the one healthy plow ox, and [gave] the unhealthy cow to his brother Right. The Sun God looked [on] from heaven (and said): "Let [Right's unhealthy] cow become healthy, and let her bear [...]"[4] [c]

(Colophon:) First tablet of Appu: incomplete.

[A separate fragment offers part of the continuation. Beginning broken away.]

[But when they] arrived in Sippar and took their stand before the Sun God for judgment, [the Sun God] awarded the judgment to Brother Right.

[Then Brother Wrong] began to curse. The Sun God heard the curses [and] said: "I will not [decide] it for you. Let Šawuška (a goddess), Nineveh's Queen, judge it for you."

[Wrong and Right] set out. And when they arrived

[2] For the wife who mocks the suffering of her righteous husband compare Job's wife (Job 2:9-10).

[3] For naming a child according to either circumstances at birth or its presumed destiny see Hoffner 1968a. This is a commonplace in the birth narratives of Genesis and Exodus.

[4] For a just deity's unseen frustration of fraud attempted against his worshiper compare Yahweh's protection of Jacob from Laban (Gen 31:4-12).

at Nineveh and stood before Šawuška [for judgment, ...] drew one acre in one direction [and ... in the other direction].

[Rest of the text lost.]

REFERENCES

Hoffner 1975a; 1990.

THE SUN GOD AND THE COW (1.59)

Harry A. Hoffner, Jr.

[Güterbock believes that this story is a continuation of Appu and his Two Sons. Beginning of the preserved portion is too broken for connected translation.]

The cow thrived and ...-ed. The Sun God looked down from the sky, and his desire leaped forward upon the cow. [He became] a young man, came down from the sky, and began to speak to the cow: "Who do you think you are, that you continually graze on our meadow [...]? When the grass is tender and young, [and you graze here], you destroy the meadow."

[The cow] replied: "Is [...] hire [...] in its [...]?" Then the Sun God responded: "[...] and it [is] in bloom [...] me [...]" [The Sun God] spoke [further] to the cow: "[...]"

[The rest of the column is broken away, as are the first lines of the next column.]

The Sun God drove the cow [...], and the Sun God [...] the cow, [and ...] cattle [...] [1]

[Most of three lines missing.]

... the second, third, [fourth, fifth, sixth, seventh, eighth], ninth and tenth month arrived, [and the cow gave birth]. The cow [called] back up to the sky [and] glowered [at the Sun God]. She said [to the Sun God]: "Now I ask you please: [My calf] should have four legs. Why have I borne this two-legged thing?" Like a lion, the cow opened her mouth and went toward the child to eat (it?). The cow made her ... as deep as the Deep Blue and set out toward the child [to ...].

The Sun God looked down from the sky. [He came down] and took his stand beside the cow. He began [to say to her:] "And who are you, [that you have approached ...] to gulp down [...]?"

The Sun God [...-ed] the cow [and ...]. And (s)he [...-ed ...]. When the child [...-ed, ...] grass [...] his eyes [...]. The Sun God [...] and him [...].

[Break of about 17 lines.]

"The great rivers [...] are troubled. The [...] are troubled for washing. [...] of blood [...] for washing. [...] let it keep on living." The day becomes warm [...]

When the Sun God had set out to go back up to the sky, he [...-ed] the child [...]. He strokes(?) its members along with [its head]. The Sun God spoke to [...]: [2] "Take a staff in hand, put the winds on [your feet as] winged [shoes]. Make the trip in one stage. Over the child [...] birds, ...-birds, [...] ... -birds, eagles [...] Let them ... their pegs away from over him. [...] snakes intertwined [...]"

[The rest of column iii and the beginning of column iv lost.]

[A fisherman] said [to ...]: "I will go see. [The ... -s] are standing in the mountains [..." The fisherman] arrived at the child. ... -birds [...] shelducks fly up. [...] are ascending(?) and they [...] to the sky.

[When the fisherman approached], the poisonous snakes retired to a distance. [...] strokes (the child's) members along with its head. He strokes [...] He strokes its eyes [...] The fisherman said to himself: "Somehow I have pleased(?) the gods, so that they have removed the unfavorable bread from the rock.[3] I have struck the Sun God's fancy, and he has led me out (here) for the sake of [the child]. Do you perhaps know about me, O Sun God, that I have no child, that you have led me out (here) for the sake of the child? Truly the Sun God puts [...] bread out for him who is dear to him!" The fisherman lifted the child up from the ground, tidied him up, rejoiced in him, held him close to his chest, and carried him back home.

The fisherman arrived at the city of Urma, went to his house, and sat down in a chair. The fisherman said to his wife: "Pay close attention to what I am about to say to you. Take this child, go into the bedroom, lie down on the bed, and wail. The whole city will hear and say: 'The fisherman's wife has borne a child!' And one will bring us bread, another will bring us beer, and still another will bring us fat. A(n ideal) woman's mind is clever. She has cut (herself) off from command(ing others).

[1] It appears that the Sun God copulated with the cow, since in the following context it gives birth to a two-legged being. Compare Baᶜal's copulating with a cow in Ugaritic myths.

[2] His messenger.

[3] This saying in the language of fishermen probably means: "Now the fish will take my bait."

She is dependent on the authority of the god. She stands in woman's subordination, and she does not disobey (her) husband's word."

(The fisherman's wife) heard the man's word, went into [the bedroom], lay down on the bed, [and began to wail]. When the men of the city heard, they said: "[The fisherman's] wife [has borne a child!"] The men of the city [said this] and began to bring [things to her. One] brought [bread, and another] fat [and beer].

[The colophon indicates that the story was continued on another tablet.]

REFERENCES

Hoffner 1975a; 1981; 1990.

2. PRAYERS

PLAGUE PRAYERS OF MURŠILI II (1.60)

Gary Beckman

When he came to the throne, the Great King Muršili II was confronted with both the fragmentation of the Hittite empire and the raging of an epidemic of uncertain character which had carried off in short succession both his father Šuppiluliuma I and his brother Arnuwanda II. Innumerable ordinary Hittites had perished as well. While Muršili mastered the political situation within the first decade of his rule, the plague continued unabated for many more years. To persuade the gods to bring the suffering to an end, the king (or his scribes) composed several prayers in which he confesses his own guilt and that of his land for various offenses, and details the reparations which have already been made. He also points out to the gods that they will only harm themselves by thinning out the ranks of their human servants. The order of the prayers is not indicated in the texts themselves but has been postulated by modern scholars on the basis of the development of Muršili's argumentation over the course of the series.

First Prayer

(A obv. 1-7) O [all of] you [male deities], all female deities, [all] male deities [of the oath], all female deities of the oath, [all] primeval [deities], all [male] deities and all female deities who were summoned to assembly for witnessing an oath in this [matter]! O mountains, rivers, springs, and underground watercourses! I, Muršili, your priest and servant, have now pled my case before you. O gods, my lords, [listen] for me to my concern about which I present you my justification.

(A obv. 8-15) O gods, [my] lords, a plague broke out in Ḫatti, and Ḫatti has been beaten down by the plague.[a] It [has been] very much [oppressed]. This is the twentieth year. Because Ḫatti is (still) experiencing many deaths, the affair of Tudḫaliya the Younger, son of Tudḫaliya, began to haunt [me]. I inquired of a god through an oracle, [and] the affair of Tudḫaliya the Younger was ascertained by the god (as a source of our suffering). Because Tudḫaliya the Younger was lord of Ḫatti, the princes, the noblemen, the commanders of the thousands, the officers, [the subalterns(?)], and all [the infantry] and chariotry of Ḫattuša swore an oath to him. My father also swore an oath to him.

(A obv. 16-22) [But when my father (Šuppiluliuma I)] mistreated Tudḫaliya, all [the princes, the noblemen], the commanders of the thousands, and the officers of Ḫattuša [went over] to my [father]. Although they had sworn an oath (to him), [they seized] Tudḫaliya, and they killed [Tudḫaliya]. Furthermore, they killed those of his brothers [who stood by] him. [...] they sent to Alašiya (Cyprus). [Whatever] was their [...] they [...] in regard to him. [Thus the ...] and the lords transgressed the oath.

(A obv. 23-40) [But] you, [O gods], my [lords], safeguarded my father. [...] And because Ḫattuša [had been burned down(?)] by the enemy, and the enemy had taken [borderlands] of Ḫatti, [my father repeatedly attacked the enemy lands] and repeatedly defeated them. He took back the borderlands of Ḫatti which [the enemy had taken]. He [settled] them anew (with Hittites). Furthermore, [he conquered] additional foreign lands [during] his reign. He sustained Ḫatti and [secured] its frontiers on every side. All of Ḫatti prospered in his time. [Humans], cows, and sheep became numerous in his time. The civilian captives who [were carried off] from the land of the enemy survived; none died. But later you came, O gods, [my lords], and have now taken vengeance on my father for this affair of Tudḫaliya the Younger. My father [died] because of the blood of Tudḫaliya. And the princes, the noblemen, the commanders of the thousands, and the officers who went over [to my father] also died because of [this] affair. This same affair also affected the (entire) land of Ḫatti, and

[a] 2 Sam 24

[Ḫatti] began to perish because of [this] affair. And Ḫatti [wasted(?)] away. Now the plague [has become] yet [worse]. Ḫatti has been [very much] oppressed by the plague and has become diminished. I, Muršili, [your servant], cannot [master] the turmoil [of my heart]. I cannot [master] the anguish of my body.

[The end of the obverse and the beginning of the reverse are too fragmentary for translation.]

(A rev. 8´-12´) [... Because] my father [killed] this Tudḫḫaliya, my father therefore later [performed] a ritual of (expiation of) bloodshed. But Ḫattuša did not [perform] anything. I came along, and I performed [a ritual of bloodshed], but the population did [not] perform anything. [No one] did anything [on behalf of] the land.

(A rev. 13´-20´) Now because Ḫatti has been very much beaten down by the plague, and Ḫatti continues to experience many deaths, the affair of Tudḫaliya has begun to trouble the land. It was ascertained for me (through an oracle) by [a god], and I made (further) oracular inquiries [about it]. They will perform before you, [the gods], my lords, the ritual of (transgressing of) the oath which was ascertained for you, [the gods], my lords, and for your temples in regard to the plague. They will purify [... before you]. And I will make restitution to you, the gods, my lords, with reparation and propitiatory gift on behalf of the land.

(A rev. 21´-40´) Because you, the gods, my lords, have taken vengeance for the blood of Tudḫḫaliya, those who killed Tudḫḫaliya have made restitution for the blood. This bloodshed has again ruined Ḫatti. Ḫatti has already made (sufficient) restitution for it. Because I have now come along, I and my household will make restitution for it through reparation and propitiatory gift. Let the souls of the gods, my lords, again be appeased. May you, the gods, my lords, be well-disposed toward me once more. Let me appear [before you]. May you listen to what I say to you. I have [not] done anything evil. (Of) those who sinned and did do evil, not one is still here today. They all died off previously. But because the affair implicating my father has devolved upon me, on behalf of the land I am now giving to you, the gods, my [lords], a propitiatory gift on account of the plague. I am making restitution. I am making restitution to you with propitiatory gift and reparation. May you, the gods, my lords, [be] well-disposed toward me once more. Let me appear before you. Because Ḫatti has been oppressed by the plague, [and] has been diminished, [they prepared] the offering bread and libation for you, the gods, my lords. He (the murderer?) is very much beaten down by the plague, and it (Ḫatti?) was [...] from the plague. Meanwhile, the aforementioned plague does not simply take it (Ḫatti) away, but people continue to die. These few bakers of offering bread and libation bearers who [are still here] — if they perish, no one will any longer give you offering bread or libation.

(A rev. 41´-51´) May you, [the gods, my lords], be [well-disposed toward me once more] because of the offering bread and libation which [they prepare]. Let me appear before you. Send the plague [out of Ḫatti]. Let (no one) beat down any further these few bakers of offering bread [and libation bearers] who [are still here] for you. Let them not [continue to die in great numbers]. They shall prepare [offering bread] and libation for you. [Come], O gods, my lords. Send the plague [away]. Whatever evils [...] to the enemy land, [or which] occurred in the midst of Ḫatti concerning [Tudḫaliya], send them [... away], O gods. Send them to the enemy land. May you be well-disposed toward Ḫatti. Let [the plague] abate once more. [Because] I am appearing before you as your priest and your servant, may you be well-disposed [toward me]. Send away the turmoil from my heart. Take away the anguish from my body.

(A Colophon): [One tablet], complete. When Muršili [pled] his case.

Second Prayer

(C i 1-18) O Storm-god of Ḫatti, my lord, [and gods], my [lords, King] Muršili, your servant, has sent me (saying): Go speak to the Storm-god of Ḫatti, my lord, and to the gods, my lords, as follows: What is this that you have done? You have allowed a plague into Ḫatti, so that Ḫatti has been beaten down severely by the plague. In the time of my father (Šuppiluliuma I) and of my brother (Arnuwanda II) people were dying, and since I have become priest of the gods, people are continuing to die in my time. This is the twentieth year that people have been dying in Ḫatti. By no means has the plague been removed from Ḫatti. I cannot master the turmoil of my heart. I can no longer master the anguish of my body.

(C i 19-28; A obv. 2´-5´) Furthermore, when I performed festivals, I paced back and forth (in worship) for all the gods. I did not privilege any single temple. I have pled my case concerning the plague to all the gods, and I have repeatedly offered [votive gifts to you (saying)]: "Listen [to me, O gods], my [lords, and send the plague out of Ḫatti. Hattuša simply cannot ...] master [the plague. Let the matter on account of which] people have been dying [in Ḫatti either be established through oracle], or [let me see] it [in a dream, or let a prophet (lit., 'man of god')] speak [of it]." But the gods [did not listen] to me, [and] the plague did not abate [in] Ḫatti. [Ḫatti has been beaten down severely].

(A obv. 6´-12´) The [few] bakers of offering bread

[and libation bearers] of the gods who [still] remained died off. [The affair of ...] continued to trouble [me. I sought (the cause of) the anger] of the gods, [and I found] two old tablets. One tablet [dealt with the ritual of the Euphrates River...] Earlier kings [performed] the ritual of the Euphrates [...], but since the time of my father (Šuppiluliuma I) [people have been dying] in Ḫatti, [and] we have never performed [the ritual] of the Euphrates.

(A obv. 13′-24′) The second tablet dealt with (the town of) Kuruštama — how the Storm-god of Ḫatti took the men of Kuruštama to Egyptian territory, and how the Storm-god of Ḫatti made a treaty concerning them with the Hittites. Furthermore, they were put under oath by the Storm-god of Ḫatti. And although the Hittites and the Egyptians had been put under oath by the Storm-god of Ḫatti, the Hittites came to repudiate (the agreement), and suddenly the Hittites transgressed the oath. My father sent infantry and chariotry, and they attacked the border region of Egyptian territory in the land of Amka. He sent (them) again, and they attacked again. When the Egyptians became frightened, they came and actually asked my father for his son for kingship. When my father gave them his son, and when they took him off, they killed him. My father became hostile, went to Egyptian territory, and attacked Egyptian territory. He killed the infantry and chariotry of Egypt.

(A obv. 25′-34′) And at that time the Storm-god of Ḫatti, my lord, gave my father the upper hand in the lawsuit (manifest in the armed conflict), so that he defeated the infantry and chariotry of Egypt. He killed them. When the prisoners of war who had been captured were brought back to Ḫatti, the plague broke out among the prisoners of war, and they [began] to die in great numbers. When the prisoners of war were carried off to Ḫatti, the prisoners of war introduced the plague into Ḫatti, and from that time people have been dying in Ḫatti. When I found the tablet mentioned earlier dealing with Egypt, I made an oracular inquiry of a god about it: "Has this matter discussed earlier been brought about by the Storm-god of Ḫatti because the Egyptians and the Hittites had been put under oath by the Storm-god of Ḫatti?"

(A obv. 35′-46′; C iii 3′-7′) It was ascertained (through an oracle) that the cause of the anger of the Storm-god of Ḫatti, my lord, was the fact that (although) the *damnaššara*-deities (guarantors of the oath?) were in the temple of the Storm-god of Ḫatti, my lord, the Hittites on their own suddenly transgressed the word (of the oath). Due to the plague I also made an oracular inquiry about the ritual of [the Euphrates], and at that point it was ascertained that I should appear before the Storm-god of Ḫatti, my lord. I have (therefore) now confessed (my) [sin before the Storm-god]: It is true. We have done [it. But the sin] did [not] take place in my time. [Rather, it took place] in the time of my father. [...] I am certainly aware. [...] The Storm-god [of Ḫatti, my lord], is angry about [...] If people have been dying in Ḫatti, I am [now] pleading my [case] concerning this [to] the Storm-god of Ḫatti, my lord. I kneel down to you and [cry out]: "Have mercy!" Listen to me, O Storm-god, my lord. Let the plague be removed from Ḫatti.

(C iii 8′-19′; B iii 16′-20′; A rev. 8′-9′) I will dispose of the matter which I thoroughly researched (through oracular inquiry) [and] of the affairs which were ascertained concerning the plague. I will make full restitution for them [...] In regard to the matter of [the oath] which was ascertained concerning the plague, I have offered the ritual [of] the oath for the Storm-god of Ḫatti, [my lord. For the gods, my lords], I have offered [it]. They have [... a ritual] for you, the Storm-god of Ḫatti, [my lord], and [they have ...] a ritual for you, [the gods, my lords]. Because [the ritual of the Euphrates] was ascertained for me [concerning the plague], and because I am now on my way [to] the Euphrates, O Storm-god [of Ḫatti], my lord, and gods, my lords, leave me alone concerning the ritual of the Euphrates. I shall perform the ritual of [the Euphrates], and I shall perform it fully. In regard to such matter as I will do it, namely the plague — may the gods, my lords, be well-disposed toward me. Let the plague abate in Ḫatti.

(A rev. 10′-19′) O Storm-god of Ḫatti, my lord, and gods, my lords — so it happens: People always sin.[b] My father sinned and transgressed the word of the Storm-god of Ḫatti, my lord. But I did not sin in any way. But so it happens: The sin of the father devolves upon his son.[c] The sin of my father has devolved upon me, and I have now confessed it to the Storm-god of Ḫatti, my lord, and to the gods, my lords: It is true. We have done it. Because I have confessed the sin of my father, let the souls of the Storm-god of Ḫatti, my lord, and of the gods, my lords, again be appeased. May you be well-disposed toward me once more. Send the plague away from Ḫatti again. Let those few bakers of offering bread and libation bearers who remain not die.

(A rev. 20′-36′) I am now pleading my case concerning the plague to the Storm-god, my lord. Listen to me, O Storm-god of Ḫatti, my lord, and save me! [I say] to you [as follows]: The bird takes refuge in the nest, and the nest [saves] it. Or if anything has become troublesome to some servant, and he pleads his case to his lord, his lord will listen to him and correct for him whatever had be-

b Gen 4:7; 6:5; 8:21; 1 Kgs 8:46; Eccl 7:20

c Deut 5:9; Jer 31:29; Ezek 18:2; 17-24

come troublesome [to him]. Or if a sin (hangs over) some servant, and he confesses the sin before his lord, then his lord may treat him however he wishes. But since he confesses his sin before his lord, the soul of his lord is appeased, and his [lord] does not call that servant to account. I have confessed the sin of my father: It is true. I did it. [If] there is any reparation (due), then there has indeed already been much because of this [plague introduced by] the prisoners of war whom they brought from the territory of Egypt and the civilian captives whom [they brought]. What is [this]? Ḫattuša has made restitution through the plague. It [has made restitution] twenty-fold.[d] So it happens. And the souls of the Storm-god of Ḫatti, my lord, [and of] the gods, my lords, are simply not appeased. Or if you wish to impose upon me some special restitution, tell me about it in a dream so that I can give it to you.

(A rev. 37′-40′) I repeatedly plead my case [to you], Storm-god of Ḫatti, my lord. Save me! [If] perhaps people have (indeed) been dying because of this matter, let those bakers of offering bread and libation bearers who remain not continue to die while I am correcting it.

(A rev. 41′-44′; C iv 14′-22′) [Or] if people have been dying because of some other matter, let me either see it in a dream, or [let] it [be discovered] by means of an oracle, or let a prophet speak of it.[e] Or the priests will sleep long and purely (in an incubation oracle) in regard to that which I convey to all of them. [...] Save me, O Storm-god of Ḫatti, my lord! Let the gods, my lords, reveal to me their providence. Let someone then see it in a dream. Let the matter on account of which people have been dying be discovered... Save me, O Storm-god of Ḫatti, my lord! Let the plague be removed from Ḫatti.

(C Colophon): One tablet, complete. [When] Muršili [...] because of the plague [... pled his case].

Third Prayer

(obv. 1-6) O Sun-goddess of (the town of) Arinna, my lady, and gods, my lords, what [have you done]? You have allowed a plague into Ḫatti, so that Ḫatti has been beaten down severely [by the plague]. In the time of my father (Šuppiluliuma I) and of my brother (Arnuwanda II), [people were dying]. Now I have become priest of the gods, [and] people are continuing to die [in my time]. This is the twentieth year [that] people have been dying [in great numbers in Ḫatti]. Ḫatti [has been very much oppressed] by the plague.

(obv. 7-13) Ḫatti has been very much beaten down by the plague. [If someone] produces a child, the [...] of plague [will ...] to him. He may attain adulthood, but he will not [grow old...] will remain for someone. He [will experience the plague(?)]. To [his] previous condition [he will] not [return]. If he should become old [...], he will not be warm.

[The bottom of the obverse and the upper portion of the reverse have been lost.]

(rev. 2′-14′) Now I, Muršili, [have pled my case. Listen] to me, O gods, my lords. [Send(?) away] the turmoil from my heart. [Let] the plague [be removed] from Ḫatti. Send [it] to the enemy lands. In Ḫatti [...] If you, the gods, my lords, [do not send] the plague [away] from Ḫatti, the bakers of offering bread and the libation bearers [will die]. And if they die off, [the offering bread] and the libation will be cut off for the gods, [my lords]. Then you will come to me, O gods, [my lords], and hold this (to be) a sin [on my part] (saying): "Why [don't you give] us offering bread and libation?" May you now be well-disposed to Ḫatti once more, O gods, my lords. Send the plague away again. [Let the plague abate] in Ḫatti. Let it (Ḫatti) thrive and grow. Let it [return] to its previous condition.

Fourth Prayer

(A i 1-16) O gods, my lords: Exalted Storm-god, the two lords of Landa, Iyarri, the deities of Ḫattuša, the deities of Arinna, the deities of Zippalanda, the deities of Tuwanuwa, the deities of Ḫupišna, the deities of Turmitta, the deities of Ankuwa, the deities of Šamuḫa, the deities of Šariššа, the deities of Ḫurma, the deities of Ḫanḫana, the deities of Karaḫna, the deities of Illaya, Kamrušepa of Taniwanda, the deities of Zarruiša, the Storm-god of Liḫzina, the Tutelary Deity of the Army Camp of the father of My Majesty which is in Maraššantiya, Uliliyašši of Parmanna, the deities of Kattila, the Storm-god of Ḫašuna, the deities of Muwanu(?), the deities of Zazziša, the Telipinus whose temples(?) in the land have been destroyed, the deities of Šalpa, and the Storm-god of [Arziya(?)].

(A i 17-20) O gods, my lords, I, Muršili, your priest, have now bowed down to you. Lend an ear and listen for me to the matter on account of which I have bowed down to you.

(A i 21-35) O gods, my lords, since earliest times you have been concerned with [humans], and you have [not] abandoned humankind. [You have] (rather) very much [safeguarded] humankind. Your divine servants [were] numerous, and they(!) set out for the gods, my lords, offering bread and libation. But now you have turned on humankind, so that it happened that in the time of [my] grandfather (Tudḫaliya III) Ḫatti was oppressed. [It was devastated] by the enemy. Then humankind [was diminished] by the plague; your [divine] servants [were reduced in number]. And of you, [the gods], my lords, [one had no] temple, and [the temple] of

d Isa 40:2

e 1 Sam 28:6

another [fell into ruin]. Whoever [served] before a god perished. [No] one performed for you the rites [which ...]

(A i 36-46) [But] when my [father] took his seat in kingship, [you], the gods, my lords, stood with him. He resettled once more the [depopulated] lands. [And for you], the gods, my lords, in whatever temple there were no [furnishings], or whatever divine image had been destroyed — my father made up that which he was able to do. He did not make up that which he was not able to do. O gods, [my] lords, you were never troublesome to my father, and you were never troublesome to me, but now you have troubled me.

(A i 47-55) When it happened that my father [went] to Egypt — since the time of (the campaign against) Egypt, the plague has persisted in [Ḫatti]. And from that [time] (the population of) Ḫatti has been dying. [My] father repeatedly made oracular inquiries, but he did not discover (the mind of) you, the gods, <my> lords, through the oracles. And I have repeatedly made oracular inquiries of you, but I have not discovered (the mind of) you, the gods, my lords, through the oracles.

[For the following section the scribe of the primary manuscript indicates that the tablet from which he was copying had been destroyed.]

(B ii 3′-11′) Because the gods, my lords, not [...] Because your eyes [...] I am already aware in regard to you [... I will make] up [everything(?) for you]. I will restore the [furnishings] for whatever [god] has [a temple] but no divine [furnishings]. I will rebuild a temple for whatever god [has no temple]. I will restore whatever divine image has been destroyed, [as] the image [had been] previously [...]

[A long break intervenes.]

(A iv 1-5) [...] Should I have restored it for [the gods], my lords, either with (the resources of) the land, or with the infantry and chariotry? If I should reestablish the gods — since my household, land, infantry, and chariotry continue to die, by what means should I reestablish you, O gods?

[Here the earlier tablet had once more been damaged.]

(A iv 16-28) And since they(!) died, by what means should I reestablish [you]? O gods, be well-disposed to me once more because of this [fact]. Bring me peace. Send the plague away from the land once more. Let it abate in the towns where people are dying. Let the plague not return to the towns in which it has (already) abated. [I have said] to myself(?) thus: "[If] the previously-mentioned matter concerning the god is true, my father [could not discover it (the mind of the gods)] through an oracle, nor could I discover it [through an oracle]. But Ḫatti [has made an oracular inquiry], and [has now discovered] it through an oracle." I have pled my case. [...]

[The final few lines are too fragmentary for translation.]

REFERENCES

Text: *CTH* 378; First Prayer: A. KUB 14.14 + KUB 19.1 + KUB 19.2 + KBo 3.47 + 1858/u + Bo 4229 + Bo 9433. B. KUB 23.3. Second Prayer: A. KUB 14.8. B. KUB 14.11 + 650/u. C. KUB 14.10 + KUB 26.86. Third Prayer: KUB 14.12. Fourth Prayer: A. KUB 14.13 + KUB 23.124. B. KBo 22.71. Bibliography: *ANET* 394-396 (Second Prayer only); *TUAT* 2/6:808-810 (First Prayer only); Malamat 1955; Bernabé 1987:279-284; Hoffner 1971b; Goetze 1930; Lebrun 1980:191-239.

3. RITUALS

THE "RITUAL BETWEEN THE PIECES" (1.61)

Billie Jean Collins

This ritual is written on a *Sammeltafel*, which, judging by the use of double paragraph dividers, contains at least ten separate compositions. The final composition is a lustration ritual to performed in the event of military defeat. It has been dated to the Middle Hittite period. The tablet itself, however, was copied in the Empire period.

If the troops are defeated by the enemy, then they prepare the "behind the river" ritual as follows: Behind the river they sever a human,[1] a billy-goat, a puppy[a] (and) a piglet. On one side they set halves and on the other side they set the (other) halves.[b] In front (of these) they make a gate of hawthorn and stretch a cord(?) up over (it). Then, before the gate, on one side they burn a fire and on the other

a Isa 66:3-4a
b Gen 15:7-18

[1] Possibly a prisoner of war.

side they burn a fire.[2] The troops go through,[c] but when they come alongside the river, they sprinkle water over them(selves). They perform the ritual again in the steppe. They celebrate the ritual of the steppe in the same way.[3]

c Jer 34:18-20

[2] A fire is not always required in such rituals.
[3] For other examples of the "ritual between the pieces" see Collins (1990).

REFERENCES

Text: *CTH* 426; KUB 17.28 iv 45-56. Editions: Collins 1990; Kümmel 1967:150-152; Masson 1950. Discussion: Eitrem 1947; Moyer 1983.

PULIŠA'S RITUAL AGAINST PLAGUE (1.62)

Billie Jean Collins

Puliša's Ritual [a] was recorded on a *Sammeltafel*. It is one of a handful of Hittite scapegoat rituals, all of which were performed to counteract plague. This particular ritual uses human beings as the scapegoats, both belonging to the enemy population and therefore expendible. They act as substitutes for the king, with whom responsibility for divine disfavor and the welfare of the population ultimately lay. Both a male and a female substitute were required to allow for a deity of either sex. The rituals with the man and the woman are followed immediately by identical rites involving a bull and a ewe.

§1 [T]hus says Puliša [... when the king] strikes an enemy [la]nd and marches [away from the border of the enemy land, if then ...] either some [male] deity [or female deity of the enemy land is angered(?) and (as a result) among] the people a plague occur[s, I do the following:]

§2 As he [is marching a]way from the border of the land of the enemy, they take one prisoner and one woman of the (enemy's) land. [On which(ever) road] the ki[ng] came from the land of the enemy, the king tr[avels] on that road. All of the lords travel with him. One prisoner and one woman they bring before him. He removes the garments from his body. They put them on the man. But on the woman [they p]ut the garments of a woman. To the man the king says as follows (if it is [not] convenient for the king, then he sen[ds] another and that one takes care of the ritual) that one [sa]ys [to] the man as follows: "If some male god of the enemy land has caused this plague, for him I have just given an adorned man as a substitute. This o[ne is gr]eat with respect to his head, this one is great with respect to his heart, and this [one is gr]eat with respect to his limb. You male god, be pacified with t[his ad]orned man. Turn [agai]n in friendship to the king, the [lords], the ar[my, and] to the land of Ḫatti. [...] but [let] this prisoner be[ar] the plague and transport (it) ba[ck into the land of the enemy.]"

§3 He speak[s t]o the woman also in the same way in case of a fema[le dei]ty.

§4 Afterward, [they drive up] one bull and one e[we and ...] of the la[nd] of the enemy. Th[ey ...] him, his ears, an earrin[g ...]. Red wool, yellow-green wool, bla[ck] wool, [white wool ...] he dra[ws] forth from the king's mouth. [He says as follows:] "Because the king kept becoming blood[-red, yellow-green, b]lack [and white ..., let t]hat [...] back to the land of the en[emy] and [for] the person of [the king], the lords, the inf[antry], the [cha]riotry [... do not] take notice, (but) take notice of it for the land of the enemy." ... The *ašušant-* bull [they bring before him(?) and] he [s]ays as follows: "The god [of]the enem[y] who [caused this plague], if he is a male god, to you I have gi[ven] an [ado]rned, *ašušant-*, and powerful(?) [bull]. You, O male god, be pacified. Let [th]is bull carry [this plague] back into the land of the enemy. [Turn again in friendship to the king, to the prin]ces, the lords, the army and to the la[nd of Ḫatti]."

§5 Afterwards, he speaks to the ado[rned] ewe [also in the same way] in case of a female deity.

§6 Then th[ey] send the *ašušant-* bull [and the ewe] to run in front [of the prisoner] and the woman.

§7 Then afterwards [...].

a Lev 16

REFERENCES

Text: *CTH* 407; Duplicates: A. KBo 15.1 i 1 - ii 4, B. KBo 21.9 (= A i 34-39); Edition: Kümmel 1967:111-125; Translation: Wright 1987:45-47. Discussions: Gurney 1977:47-58; Moyer 1983:35; Janowski and Wilhelm 1993.

UḪḪAMUWA'S RITUAL AGAINST PLAGUE (1.63) [a]

Billie Jean Collins

§1 Thus says Uḫḫamūwa, man of Arzawa. If in the land there is continual dying and if some god of the enemy has caused it, then I do as follows:

§2 They bring in one wether and they combine blue wool, red wool, yellow-green wool, black wool and white wool and they make it into a wreath and they wreathe the one wether and they drive the wether forth on the road to the enemy and they say to him (the god) as follows: "What god of the enemy has made this plague, now this wreathed wether we have brought for your pacification, O god! Just as a fortress is strong and (yet) is at peace with this wether, may you, the god who has made this plague, be at peace in the same way with the land of Ḫatti. Turn again in friendship to the land of Ḫatti." Then they drive the wreathed sheep into the enemy territory.

[a] Lev 16

§3 Afterward they bring fodder for the god's horses and sheep fat, and they recite as follows, "You have harnessed your horses. Let them eat this fodder and let them be satiated. Let your chariot be anointed with this sheep fat. Turn toward your land, O Storm God. Turn in friendship toward the land of Ḫatti."

§4 Afterward they bring one billy goat and two sheep. He consecrates the goat to the Ḫeptad, and one sheep he consecrates to the Sun God, but the other sheep they kill and (then) they cook it. Then they bring one cheese, one rennet, one *pulla*-vessel, a sour-bread, one *ḫūppar*-vessel of wine, one *ḫūppar*-vessel of beer, and fruit. They prepare these for the god of the journey.

REFERENCES

Text: *CTH* 410; Duplicates: A. HT 1 ii 17-47 (NS), B. KUB 9.31 ii 43-iii 13 (NH), C. KUB 41.17 ii 18-24. Translations: Friedrich 1925:10; *ANET* 347; Wright 1987:55-57. Discussions: Gurney 1977:47-58; Janowski and Wilhelm 1993:135 and passim.

ZARPIYA'S RITUAL (1.64)

Billie Jean Collins

The Ritual of Zarpiya [a] is the second of three scapegoat rituals contained on a single *Sammeltafel*. The author of the text is from Kizzuwatna and as a result the text is laden with Luwian words and incantations, often rendering translation difficult. The first half of the ritual involves an oath-taking on the part of the participants; the second half is a scapegoat ritual of sorts. The human scapegoats in this case are nine young boys. The theme of the number nine is repeated throughout the ritual. The gods at whom the ritual is directed are Šantaš and the Innarawanteš, a group of deities perhaps totalling nine.

§1 [Thus says Zarp]iya, physician of Kizzuwatna, (regarding) [when the year] is ruinous (and) in the land there is continual dying. [Then] in which(ever) city (there is) ruin as a result, [the master of (each)] house will do as follows:

§2 I hang up the *kelu*- [of the cli]ent. Its *ḫuppali*- is bronze. Its [*kariu*]*lli*-[cloth] is of a shaggy lion-skin. But its footstool is of basalt, and its (the footstool's) *ḫazziul* is a paw(?) of lapis, the strong paw(?) of a bear, [...] but he h[angs the ...] of a wild goat.

§3 And the *ali*-s are of black wool and red wool (and) the yellow wool of the town of Ḫarnuwašila. Before the sinew of a dog is ...ed, he [...] three [...s]. On one side he hangs one (piece) on a peg (made of) apricot(?)-wood,[1] while on the other side he hangs one (piece) on a peg (made of) cornel wood.

[a] Lev 16

§4 First and foremost, in front on that side he hits the apricot(?)-wood peg into the gate. He hangs a cooked *kuggulaš* of barley flour, a *kuggulaš* of *ḫariyanti*-barley flour, and one jug of wine. On this side, however, he hits [the peg] of cornel wood i[nto the gate], and from it (the peg) he hangs a cooked *kuggulaš* of barley flour, a *kuggulaš* of *ḫariyanti*-barley flour, and one jug of wine.

§5 With the pegs, a white bush is stuck in/planted. Downwards from the ground [...] downwards at the front. On either side he buries *waššiₓ*-, whose name is *ḫuwallari*. Furthermore, the gate behind the door of the courtyard on which he hangs the *kelu*-s — down in

[1] For the identification of [GIŠ]ŠENNUR see Postgate 1987:131.

front of the *kelu*-s he places a wicker table and on top of it he sets an ax[2] of bronze, one warm bread, thick bread (and) cheese. Thereon (he sets) a bronze ax, a bronze dagger, a strung bow, [and] one arrow.

§6 Down in front on the wicker table he places one *ḫuppar*-vessel of wine from the *puri*-stand, and from the *puri*-stand he places one pitcher of *PIḪU* drinking beer. Into the pitcher of *PIḪU* drinking beer he inserts one straw.

§7 They bring in one billy-goat and the master of the estate libates it with wine before the table for Šantaš. Then he holds out the bronze ax and says as follows: "Come Šantaš! Let the Innarawanteš-deities come with you, (they) who are wearing bloodied (clothes), who have bound on (themselves) the sashes(?) of the mountain dwellers,

§8 who are girt(?) with daggers, who hold strung bows and arrows. "Come and eat! We will swear (an oath)." When he is finished speaking, he places the bronze ax[3] down on the table and they slit (the throat of) the billy-goat.

§9 He takes the blood and the straw that was left in the mug — he anoints that with the blood. Then they bring the raw liver and the heart and the master of the estate holds them out for the gods. Further he takes a bite (and) they imitate (him).[4] He puts (his) lips on the straw and sips and says as follows:

§10 "O Šantaš and Innarawanteš-deities, we have just taken the oath.

§11 We have bitten from the raw liver; from a single straw we have drunk. O Šantaš and Innarawanteš-deities, do not approach my gate again." They cook the liver and heart on a fire and they butcher the entire goat "plain."

§12 Then, when the fat arrives, they bring out the liver and heart and the flesh — everything — to the god. With it they bring two times nine thick loaves (made) from wheat flour of one-half handful (of flour). He breaks nine loaves. Over these they place the liver and heart and he sets them back on the table and says as follows: "Eat, O Sun God of Heaven above and below. Let the gods of the father of the house eat! Let the thousand gods eat.

§13 And for this oath be witnesses." Next he libates the wine nine times before the table of the Innarawanteš-deities. He takes the shoulder and the breast (of the sacrifice) and breaks nine loaves of bread.

§14 He scatters them on the potstand and pours wine opposite. Then they bring (in) nine(!)[5] boys who have not yet gone to a woman. On one boy they put a goatskin and that one walks in front and calls (out) in the manner of a wolf. They surround the tables and devour the shoulder and breast.

§15 But [when they] wish to eat [...], he brings (them) in the same way and they devour the li[ver and heart]. They also drink. [He brings] the pitcher [of *PIḪU* drinking beer] and they drink the pitcher of *PIḪU* beer.

§16 The master of the house <holds> a staff/branch from a *šuruḫḫa*-tree, steps into the gate and in Luwian conjures as follows:

§§17-18 {Luwian incantation}

§19 He breaks a thick bread, while reciting as follows in Luwian:

§§20-21 {Luwian incantation}

§22 They take up the ritual implements and he closes the door. He anoints it with fine oil, and says:

§23 "Let (the door) shut out evil and let it keep in good."

§24 One tablet. Finished. The word of Zarpiya, physician from Kizzuwatna. If a year is ruinous and the land is dying, then the *kelu*-rituals he offers in this way.

[2]Hittite *ateš-* is unambiguously translated "ax" although how big this weapon was and what type of ax are matters of speculation. See Beal 1986.

[3]Presumably the bronze dagger in §5 was used for slitting the animal's throat, which prompts the question: what is the purpose of the ax here? I would suggest, based on Greek parallels, that the ax was used to stun the animal prior to killing it. This must have occurred in §7 during the recitation, which is when he is said to be holding the ax. The text fails to mention the act itself, we must assume, because it was taken for granted, as were so many other details of Hittite sacrifice.

[4]Hitt. *ḫimma-* "model, replica, imitation (of an object or animal)." The sense here seems to be that other participants in the ritual imitate the master of the house in biting from the liver and heart, since in §11 the text says that "we (plural) have bitten." Differently *HED* Ḫ 314.

[5]The text says eight.

REFERENCES

Text: *CTH* 757. Duplicates: A = KUB 9.31 i - ii 42 (MH/NS); B = HT 1 i - ii 16 (MH/NS); C = KUB 35.9; D = KUB 35.10; E = Bo 4809 (Otten and Rüster 1978:276, no. 68); F. KBo 34.243 (Rüster 1992:477f.). Edition: Schwartz 1938; Parital Translation: Starke 1985b:46-55. Discussion: Collins 1989:55f.

RITUAL AND PRAYER TO ISHTAR OF NINEVEH (1.65)

Billie Jean Collins

The beginning of this text, containing a ritual for the goddess, is broken. In §4, where the text becomes legible, the officiant is reciting an invocation.

§3 [...] they cover [her?] with a cloth [...] all the singers play [the ...-instruments] and sin[g]. [...] outside on seven paths [...] they go to [...] and [...]. The diviner [sets(?)] down a table. ... red, what are la[id] for soldier breads [...] he takes, and the singers pull [...] of the path (or: for the paths?).

§4 [...] He says as follows "... O Ištar [...] I will keep [...]ing and for you ... [If you are in Nineveh] then come from Nineveh. (But) if you are [in] R[imuši, then come from Rimuši]. If you are in Dunta, then come from Du[nta].

§5 (O Ištar,) [if you are] in [Mittanni], then come from Mittanni. [If you are in ..., then come from .... I]f you are in Dunippa then [come from] Duni[ppa. If you are in Ugarit] then com[e] from Ugarit. [If you are in ... then come from ...]. Come from Dunanapa. [Come from .... Come from .... Come] from Alalḫaz. [Come from .... Come from] A[murra.] Come from Zīduna. [Come from ....] Come from Nu[ḫašša]. Come from Kulzila. [Come from ....] Come from Zunzurḫa. Come from Aššur. [Come from ....] Come from Kašga. Come from every land. [Come from] Alašiya. Come from Ālziya. Come from Papanḫa. [Come from ....] Come from Ammaḫa. Come from Ḫayaša. [Come from ....] Come from Karkiya. [Come] from the lands of Arzauwa. [Come from ....] Come from the land of Maša. [Come] from Kuntara. [Come from ....] Come from Ura. Come from Luḫma. [Come from ...]. Come from Partaḫuina. Com[e] from Kašula. [Come from ....]

§6 If (you are) in the rivers and streams [then come from there.] If for the cowherd and shepherds [you ...] and (you are) among them, then come away. If (you are) among [the ...], if you are with the Sun Goddess of the Earth and the Primor[dial Gods] then come from those.

§7 Come away from these countries. For the king, the queen (and) the princes bring life, health, streng[th], longevity, contentment(?), obedience (and) vigor, (and) to the land of Ḫatti growth of crops (lit., grain), vines, cattle, sheep (and) humans, *šalḫitti-*, *mannitti-* and *annari-*.

§8 Take away from the (enemy) men manhood, courage, vigor and *māl*, maces, bows, arrows (and) dagger(s), and bring them into Ḫatti. For those (i.e., the enemy) place in the hand the distaff and spindle of a woman and dress them like women. Put the scarf[1] on them and take away from them your favor.[2] [a]

§9 But from the women take away motherliness, love (and) *mūšni-* and bring it into the Ḫattiland. Afterwards care for the king, the queen, the sons of the king (and) the grandsons of the king in wellbeing, life, health, vigor, (and) long years forever. Sustain it and make it rich. Let the land of Ḫatti, (which is) for you (both) bride and offspring, be a pure land.

§10 I have handed over to you the land of Ḫatti (which) again (has been) damaged. O Ištar of Nineveh, Lady, do you not know how the land of Ḫatti is damaged by this deadly plague?

§11 The diviner breaks one thin loaf for Ištar of Nineveh and crumbles it into the spring. Afterward he again breaks one thin loaf for Ištar of Nineveh and sets it down on the table. He sprinkles oatmeal before the table. Next he sprinkles meal into the spring.

§12 Further, before the table on the oatmeal he sprinkles sweet oil cake (and) meal. He libates wine three times into the spring and libates three times before the table.

§13 The diviner says these words, and when they attract (lit., pull) her with the thick loaf, they fill a KUKUB-vessel with water besides. Then in that place they open up ritual pits,[b] and the diviner pulls the deity up from there seven times with "ear" loaves. He says, "If the king, queen, or princes — anyone — has done something and has buried it, I am now pulling it from the earth." He recites the same words again, and they do the same in that place also.

§14 He cuts into one thin loaf and sets it on a pine cone. He pours fine oil on it and the diviner having taken the "ear" bread pulls the deity from the fire fourteen times and says as follows: "I have pulled it from the fire."

§15 He recites the same words again. He sets down the "ear" bread at the soldier loaves and buries one large bird for Ištar of Nineveh and *ḫūwalzi*-s. But they burn two birds for *unalzi*.

§16 When he is finished, the diviner takes up the table and in front of the red headband that lies

a Deut 18:9-12; 22:5

b 1 Sam 28:8-15; Isa 8:19; 29:4

[1] A garment associated with women.

[2] For Deut 18:9-12, see Hallo *BP* Sel. 53; for Deut 22:5, see Hoffner 1966:331.

on the table he holds another, and they bring (it) in to the goddess. The singers play the INANNA-instrument and the cymbals(?) and sing. They bring the god back into the temple.

[The remaining §§ are too fragmentary for translation.]

REFERENCES

Text: *CTH* 716. Duplicates: A = KUB 15.35 + KBo 2.9(MH/NS); B = KBo 2.36; C = KBo 21.48 (MH/NS). Discussions: Archi 1977; Bossert 1946:34f.; Ehelolf 1937:68; Hoffner 1966:331; 1967:391f.; Sommer 1921.

THE FIRST SOLDIERS' OATH (1.66)

Billie Jean Collins

The following is the second tablet[1] of a two-tablet text of a military oath, known as the first soldiers' oath. The language of the composition indicates that it was composed in the Middle Hittite period (late 15th century BCE), although the copies that survive were inscribed in the Empire period. The text is especially interesting for its parallels in the literature of other cultures, including Indian, Mesopotamian, Greek and Israelite.

§1 [...] he places [cedar in] their [hands]. [...] they [... it]. He [spread]s [out][2] a net [...] and he says to them, ["this ...] is it not [... in(?)] his house? Do the gods [not ...] them? Just as cedar [...] its fragrance [...].[3]

§2 [...[4] these oa]th d[eities ...].[5]

§3 [The diviner(?)[6] ...]s and says, ["Becaus]e [this person wa]s living and used to find heaven above, now they have blinded him in the place of the oath. [...] Who transgre[sses] these oaths and takes deceptive action against the king of Ḫatti, and sets (his) eyes upon the land of Ḫatti as an enemy, may these oath deities seize him and [may they] blind his army too, and further, may they deafen them. May comrade not see comrade. May this one not hear [that one]. May they give them a horrible d[eath]. May they fetter their feet with a wrapping below, and bind their hands above. Just as the oath deities bound the troops of the land of Arzawa by their hands and feet and set them in a heap, in the same way may they bind his troops too, and set them in a heap.

§4 He places yeast in their hands and they lick it. Then he says as follows[7]: "What is this? Is it not yeast? Just as they take a little of this yeast and mix it into the kneading bowl and (as) they let the bowl sit for one day, and it (i.e., the dough) rises, who transgresses these oaths and takes deceptive action against the king of Ḫatti and sets his eyes upon Ḫatti as an enemy, may these oath deities seize him. May he be completely broken up by diseases. May he carry off (i.e., suffer) a horrible death." They say, "(So) be it."[8]

§5 He places wax and sheep fat in their hands and he casts (some) on the flame and says, "Just as this wax melts [a] and just as the sheep fat is rendered,[9] who breaks the oath and takes deceptive action against the king of Ḫatti, may he melt like the wax and may he be rendered like the sheep fat." They say, "(So) be it."

§6 He places sinew (and) salt in their hands and he casts (some of) them into the flame. He says as follows: "Just as this sinew melts(?)[10] on the hearth, just as salt disintegrates on the hearth, so may he who transgresses these oaths and takes deceptive action against the

[a] Ps 68:2

[1] The first tablet of the First Soldiers' Oath survives in a fragmentary state only, making a coherent translation impossible. Duplicates to tablet one: A = KBo 21.10; B = KUB 40.13; C = KUB 48.75; D = KBo 27.12.

[2] This restoration has been proposed by H. A. Hoffner, Jr., personal communication. On the meaning of *ekt-* see Hoffner 1977.

[3] Three lines broken.

[4] Four lines broken.

[5] One line broken.

[6] The identity of the person administering the oath is not preserved. As suggested here, he may have been a diviner ([LÚ]ḪAL), one of a select number of professions qualified to carry out rituals of this kind.

[7] Text has KI.MIN "ditto."

[8] Oettinger 1976:73.

[9] English "render" refers to the extraction of the fat from the solid in the process of cooking, as for example, when bacon is fried. Cf. *CHD* L-N 180f.

[10] A *hapax legomenon*. Oettinger 1976:9 translates: "verschmoren" ("smeared").

king of Ḫatti and sets (his) eyes upon the land of Ḫatti as an enemy, may these oaths (var. oath deities) seize him and like the sinew may he melt(?) and like the salt may he disintegrate. Also, just as the salt does not (produce) its seed, for that man, may his name, his progeny, his household, his cattle, and his sheep perish in the same way."

§7 He places malt and beer seasoning in their hands and they lick it. He says to them as follows: "Just as they mill this beer seasoning with a millstone and mix it with water and cook it and mash it, who transgresses these oaths and takes part in evil against the king, the queen or against the princes or against the land of Ḫatti, may these oath deities seize him and in the same way may they mill his bones and in the same way may they heat him up and in the same way may they mash him. May he carry off a horrible death." They say, "(So) be it."

§8 "Just as this malt has no propagation, (and) they do not carry it to the field and make it (into) seed, and they do not make it (into) bread and store it in the storehouse, for him who transgresses these oaths and takes part in evil against the king, queen or against the princes, may the oath deities destroy his future in the same way, and may his wives not bear him a son or a daughter. In the plain, the field and the meadow may the vegetation not grow. May his cattle and sheep not bear calf or lamb."

§9[11] They bring a woman's garment, a distaff and a spindle and they break an arrow (lit., reed). You say to them as follows: "What are these? Are they not the dresses of a woman? We are holding them for the oath-taking. He who transgresses these oaths and takes part in evil against the king, queen and princes may these oath deities make (that) man (into) a woman. May they make his troops women. Let them dress them as women.[b] Let them put a scarf on them. Let them break the bows, arrows, and weapons in their hands and let them place the distaff and spindle in their hands (instead)."

b Deut 18:9-12; 22:5

c Num 5:16-28

§10 They lead before them a woman, a blind man and a deaf man and you say to them as follows: "Here (are) a woman, a blind man and a deaf man. Who takes part in evil against the king and queen, may the oath deities seize him and make (that) man (into) a woman. May they b[li]nd him like the blind man. May they d[eaf]en him like the deaf man. And may they utt[erly] destroy him, a mortal, together with his wives, his sons, and his clan."

§11[c] [12] He places [in] their hands a fig[urine of a man[13]] with its [in]sides full of water, and says as follows: "Who is this? Has he no[t] taken an oath? He took [an oath] before the gods, then he [tra]nsgressed the oath, and the oath deities seized him. His insides filled (with water). With his hands he holds his stomach lifted up in front. May these oath deities seize whoever transgresses these oaths. May his insides fill (with water). Within his insides may the child(ren?) of Išḫara[14] (i.e., disease) [dwell(?)] and may they devour him."[15]

§12 He holds out [a ...] and he [thro]ws it face (lit., eyes) down and they trample it with their foot. He says to them as follows: "Who breaks these oaths let it happen that the [troop]s of Ḫatti trample his city with (their) foot in the same way, and that they render the settlements deserted."

§13 They inflate a [bl]adder[16] and [tra]mple it with their foot, so that the air is [ex]pelled. He says, "As this has been emptied, let the house of who(ever) transgresses these oaths be emptied of people, his cattle and his sheep in the same way."

§14 You set an oven down before them and you set down before (them) models of a plow, a wagon and a chariot. They break them up. And he says as follows: "Who transgresses these oaths, for him may the Storm God break up (his) plow. Just as vegetation does not come up from an oven, may wheat and barley not come up in his field. Let cress (var. weeds)

[11] See Hoffner 1966 on the meaning of the magic used in this paragraph.

[12] The figurine has dropsy. Oettinger 1976:72 has suggested that dropsy as a punishment for oath-breaking and the practice of "Schwur beim Wasser" was a legacy of proto-Indo-European religion. See his discussion on pp. 71-73.

[13] Restoration suggested by H. A. Hoffner, Jr., personal communication. Such a figurine has been recovered; see Börker-Klähn 1992.

[14] Išḫara was a Netherworld goddess whose particular sphere was medicine and disease. See the discussion by Burde 1974:12-16. The "child" or "children(?)" of Išḫara could therefore be disease(s), an idea that seems to suit this context. Alternatively, Oettinger 1976:41 attributes her presence here to her role as "Königin des Eides," further suggesting that Išḫara together with the Moon God (who appears by name only in the second soldiers' oath, see below) are the the oath deities referred to in this text.

[15] Oettinger 1976:40f. offers an alternative possibility, restoring: *an-dur-za-ma-*[*aš-ši-*]*kán I-NA* ŠÀ-*ŠU* DUMU<*-an*> [d]*Iš-ḫa-a-ra*<*-aš*> [[d]*SIN ap-pa-an-d*]*u na-an ka-ri-pa-an-du* "drinnen aber in seinem Innern sollen [ihm] den Sohn Išḫara (und) [der Mondgott ergreifen] und ihn fressen!" solving the problem of the plural verb by adding an additional subject. There is room for his restoration, but the fact that the Moon God does not appear elsewhere in this text (although he does appear in the second soldiers' oath, see below) renders his restoration uncertain.

[16] [*nu* UZU]*ulan* is another possible restoration. *ula-* is a body part, but which one is not known. *walula-* may not be "bladder." Cf. *CHD* P *panduḫa-* "bladder(?)."

go up (instead)."

§15 You give to them a red pelt and he says, "Just as they make this red pelt blood colored and from it the bl[oo]d color does not leach out, in the same way may the oath deities seize you and may it (i.e., the blood color) not leave you."

§16 He sprinkles water on the fire and says to them as follows: "As this burning fire was extinguished, who[ever] breaks these oaths, let these oath deities seize him, and also may his life, his youth, (and) his prosperity in future — together with his wives and his sons — be extinguished in the same way. May the oath deities curse him cruelly. May the meadow not thrive for his herd, his flock (and) his livestock. And from his field and furrow may vegetation not come for him."

§17 Second Tablet. When they bring the troops for the oath.

REFERENCES

Text: *CTH* 427. Duplicates: A = KBo 6.34 + KUB 48.76; B = KUB 40.16 + KUB 7.59 (+) 342/u (+) 524/u (+) 1087/z + 797/v; C = KUB 40.13. Editions: Friedrich 1924; Oettinger 1976. Translations: *ANET* 353f.; Cornil 1994:102-108. Discussions: Börker-Klähn 1992; Burde 1974; Hoffner 1966; 1977.

THE SECOND SOLDIERS' OATH (1.67)

Billie Jean Collins

This text is of New Hittite date and shows many developments from the older example translated above. Among other things, there are marked Hurrian influences.[1]

§1´ [... If you transgress these oaths ...] may they [...], may they [...], may they [...].

§2´ But [if you keep them], for you (pl.). [...] he says: [...]

§3´ [He] h[olds] out torches [to them, and says,] "[...] these torches [...], if [you transgress] these [words,] may Umpa[2] and Šarruma[3] [destroy you along with your ...]."

§4´ "And as [the fire(?) ...] burns [the torches ...] again [he ...]s, (so) he who [transgresses] these wor[ds ... entir]ely(?) from the dark [netherworld ...] again to the dark netherworld [may he not(?) ...].

§5´ "[But if] you [keep them (i.e. the words), may it be] wel[l] with you."

§6´ [Afterwards] they extinguish [the torches], [and he says] to them [as follows: "...just as] the torches [...] and no one [...s] him/it, [... in the same way who transgresses these words may] no one [... him ...]."

§7´ "[Just as you have] extinguish[ed the torches, ...], may he [who transgresses] these wo[rds b]e extinguished [in the same way along with] his [progeny,] his house, his wife [...[4]] and to you (pl.) [...]."

§8´ [He places bowls in their hands and] they break [them] up [...] at the same time [saying] as follows: "[These are not bowls], they are your heads. [If] you do [not] keep [them (i.e., the words)] may the gods break [up your heads in the same way], and [may they ...] you in the [same way.]

§9´ "Bu[t if] you keep them may [the gods] break up [a horrible death] for [yo]u in the same way."

§10´ [Aft]erwards they pour out water [and simultaneously] he sa[ys as follows]: "Just as the earth [swallows down] this water and afterward no trace of it is visible, may the earth swallow [you] down in the same way, and, like the water, may no [trace] of you be visible afterward."

§11´ [Aft]erwards he pours out wine, and simultaneously [he says as follows:] "[This] is not w[ine], it is your blood. [Just as] the earth swallowed (this) dow[n], may the earth swallow down your [blood] and [...] in the same way."

§12´ [After]wards he pours water into the wine and [simultaneously] says as [follo]ws: "Just as this water [is mixed] with the wine, may these oath deities mix sick[ness] within your bodies in the same way."

§13´ (Concerning) t[his wh]ich is from the head, may the Moon God continually strike you.[5] May [...] flee from [your] insides and for you

---

[1] See Oettinger 1976:52f., 58, 94.

[2] This divine name, usually spelled Umbu, belongs firmly in the Hurrian pantheon. Umbu is a Moon God.

[3] Storm God and son of Tešub and Ḫebat, forming the third member of the Hurrian triad adopted by the Hittites in the period of the Empire.

[4] Two lines broken.

[5] I.e., give an astronomical omen portending evil? Cf. "[Whe]n the Moongod gives an omen, and in the portent he strikes [a per]son?, then I do as follows" KUB 17.28 i 1-2 (Incantation of the Moon, MH/NS).

[may] the inside [be ...], and may the Moon God make ..., and for you (pl.) ...[...], and may he [not] go to see the lands.

§14′ [Afterwards] they hold a rock with their hands underneath (it) and [simultaneously] they say [as fol]lows: "As this rock is h[eavy], [in the same way] may the oath and sickness become heavy [in your insides].

§15′ [If] you keep these oaths, [just as] they are [everla]sting for you, in the same way [may you be] everlasti[ng]."

§16′ If (it is) a *patili*-priest[6] then [...] him in [but if (it is) a ... then ... be]fore the gate [...].

[6] For the functions of the ^{LÚ}*patili-*, see Beckman 1983:235-238.

REFERENCES

Text: *CTH* 427; KUB 43.38. Edition: Oettinger 1976.

4. INCANTATIONS

PURIFYING A HOUSE: A RITUAL FOR THE INFERNAL DEITIES (1.68)

Billie Jean Collins

This text offers a tantalizing glimpse into Hurro-Hittite mythology. The underworld deities, referred to as the Primordial or Ancient Gods, are solicited on behalf of a house possessed of various types of uncleanness, to come up from below the earth and carry the uncleanness back down into the underworld with them.

The ritual is completed over two days, the location alternating between the house and various outdoor locales, including, at the end of the ritual, the steppe, where the ritual paraphernalia can be disposed of safely. The main recensions of this narrative were composed in the Middle Hittite period. The copies date to the Empire Period.

§1 When [they] cleanse a house of blood, impuri[ty], threat, (and) perjury, its treatment (is) as follows:

§2 In the morning the exorcist opens the house [and] he goes [in]. He holds a hoe, a spade and a shovel(?). He digs the ground (with) the hoe, (and) he [clears(?)[1]] the (resulting) pit[2] with the spade.

§3 He digs in this same way at the four corners (of the house) and he digs in this very same way [to the side of(?) the hea]rth. The (resulting) pit [he clears(?)[1] with] the shovel(?).

§4 He says as follows: "O Sun Goddess of the Earth, we are taking this m[atter ...]. Why is this house gasping? Why does it look upward to heaven?

§5 Either a human has perjured (himself), or he has [shed] blood and has turned [up] his *šeknu*-garment to these houses,[3] or someone has made a threat, or someone has spoken a curse, or someone having shed blood or having committed perjury has entered,

§6 or someone has practiced (witchcraft(?)[4]) and [has] en[tered], or bloodshed has occurred in the house. May this now release the evil, impurity, perjury, bloodshed, curse, threat, tears (and) sin of the house. May the floor (lit., earth), the floorboard, the bedroom, the hearth, the four corners, (and) the gates of the courtyard release (them).

§7 He goes forth to the courtyard. He takes mud in the courtyard and speaks in the same way. He takes mud in the gatehouse and speaks in the same way.

§8 He goes out. He cuts a reed off with an ax before the gate and says as follows: "Just as I cut this reed and it does not (re)attach (itself), now in the same way let it cut the evil bloodshed of the house, and let it not come back."

§9 [Then] at the top (lit., back) of the rain pipe they pour a *ḫanešša*-vessel of wine [and he says], "As water flows down [from the roof] and it does not go [back (up)] the rain pipe [again], may the evil, impurity, perjury, blood, tears, sin, curse, and threat of this house pour out and may they not come back again."

[1] Restoration of *liššaizzi* "to clear" suggested to me by H. A. Hoffner, Jr. and H. G. Güterbock, personal communication.

[2] The Hittite uses *patteššar* and *ḫatteššar* interchangeably in this text as a hole over which sacrifices are made. In contrast, an *āpi* is opened up in §31 as a hole through which to contact the Underworld Deities directly.

[3] The interpretation of this line follows *CHD* P sub *pippa-*, contra Otten 1961.

[4] So interpreted by Otten 1961:116f.

§10 He throws the *ḫanešša*-vessel down from the roof and smashes it. But the mud that he had taken,[5] that[6] he carries to (the place) where all the ritual paraphernalia[7] has been placed.

§11 He goes to the river bank and takes oil, beer, wine, *walḫi*-drink, *marnuan*-drink, a cupful (of) each in turn, sweet oil cake, meal, (and) porridge. He holds a lamb and he slaughters it down into a pit. He speaks as follows:

§12 "I, a human being, have now come! As Ḫannaḫanna takes children[8] from the river bank and I, a human being, have come to summon the Primordial Deities of the river bank[9], let the Sun Goddess of the Earth open the Gate and let the Primordial Deities and the Sun God(dess) of the Earth (var. the Lord of the Earth) up from the Underworld (lit., earth).

§13 Aduntarri the diviner, Zulki the dream interpretess, Irpitiga Lord of the Earth, Narā, Namšarā, Minki, Amunki, Ābi[10] — let them up! I, a human, have not come independently, nor have I come in quarrel. In a house, blood, tears, perjury, quarrel, (and) sin have occurred. Heaven above has been angered, and the Underworld below has been angered.

§14 The exorcist of the Storm God[11] sent[12] you, the Primordial Deities, from the underworld. He said this word to you:

§15 "[In this house] evil impurity, [blood, tears], quarrel, sin, (and) perjury [have occurred]. The exorcist[13] [has] summon[ed you,] the [Primord]ial Deities. [...] go back and go [...]. Cleanse [the house from] the evil, impurity, blood, [perjury, sin], quarrel, curses, tears, (and) [threat].

§16 "Bind [their (i.e., each evil's)] [fee]t (and) hands and carry them down to the Dark Underworld." He takes the clay of the river bank, but in its place he sets sweet oil cake, meal (and) porridge. He libates beer, wine, [*walḫi*]-drink, (and) [*m*]*arnuan*-drink. He takes [up] (what has) bubbled and binds it in.

§17 He stretches out a scarf along the ground [... and] walks along the scarf [...] and he goes in.

§18 He sprinkles the clay of the river bank with oil and honey. (With it) he fashions [the]se gods: Aduntarri the exorcist, Zulki the dream interpretess, Irpitiga, Narā, Namšara, Minki, Amunki, Ābi. He fashions them as (i.e., in the form of) daggers.[14] Then he spreads them along the ground and settles these gods there (*-šan*).

§19 He takes four jugs of wine, a thick loaf, meal, porridge, (and) *gangati*-vegetable soup and goes to the water and says as follows: "(Concerning) the matter for which I have come, let the spring, the water, ask me. With me the Lady (Ištar) has come from the vegetation.

§20 In her [le]ft ear they set earrings (in the form) of a *šuraššura*-(bird). It is important. But she does not [re]move[15] (her) cloak. She holds an empty vessel in her hand. [...] On her head was placed a wreath(?) of string.

§21 She spoke to the spring, and she spoke to the swamp, she spoke to the deity [of(?)] the *piten*[...] water, "The water for which I have come, give that water to me — the water of purification that cleanses bloodshed and perjury, that cleanses the gatehouse, that cleanses com[mon gossip, cur]se, sin, (and) threat."

§22 [The spring(?)] answered Ištar: "Draw the water seven times or draw the water eight times. Pour out [the water seven or eight times].[16] But on the ninth time what water you request, draw that [wa]ter and ta[ke] it."

§23 Her h[air fl]owed down from the throne to Kumarbi. Her hair flowed to [the under]-world, to the Sun Goddess of the Earth. While you are carrying [tha]t water, the falcon then brings other water from the sea. He holds the water in the right hand, while in the left hand he holds the words.

§24 Ištar is able to fly. She flew from Nineveh to

[5] In §7.

[6] The common accusative form *apūn* can only refer back to *purut* "mud" despite the fact that *purut* is a neuter noun. Cf. another case of gender disagreement in the following note and cf. *CHD* P *purut*.

[7] *aniyaz ḫuman* "all the ritual paraphernalia," is a case of gender disagreement between a common noun and its attributive, here in the neuter.

[8] KUB 41.8 i 20 has *i-tar*, 729/t i 3 has DUMU-*tar*. As the goddess of birth, Ḫannaḫanna fashions people from clay and gives fertility to women. See also Otten 1961:144.

[9] KUB 41.8 i 21 *wappuš*, KBo 10.45 i 37 [*wappu*]*waš*, 729/t i 4 *wappuw*[*aš*].

[10] ᵈĀbi is a divinization of the ritual pit and thus an underworld deity.

[11] Not the exorcist/diviner who is officiating in this ritual, but a mythological agent of the Storm God in an allusion to a mythological theomachy.

[12] Var. has "drove" in the sense of "transported" or "ferried".

[13] The titles ᴸᵁ́AZU and ᴸᵁ́ḪAL are used interchangeably for the officiant of this text. Note also that the god Aduntarri is called the ᴸᵁ́ḪAL in §13 but the ᴸᵁ́AZU in §18.

[14] Cf. the dagger god at Yazilikaya; see Akurgal n.d. plates 80-83.

[15] Restoration follows *CHD* L-N 366 (mng. 1 g).

[16] The main copy for this paragraph is KBo 10.45, restored from IBoT 2.128. The latter copy clearly contained more than was present in KBo 10.45. Cf. *CHD* L-N 4 which offers a translation based on a faulty transliteration.

meet the falcon. In her right hand she took water, while in her left hand she took the words. The water she sprinkles to the right, while the words she speaks toward the left:

§25 "May good enter the house. May it seek out the evil with (its) eyes and cast it out. May the pure water cleanse the evil tongue, impurity, bloodshed, sin, curse (var. adds: threat, [and] common gossip). Just as the wind blows away the chaff and carries it across to (var. into) the sea, let it likewise blow away the bloodshed and impurity of this house, and let it carry it across to (var. into) the sea.

§26 "Let it go into the sacred mountains. Let it go into the deep wells." He breaks a thick loaf and libates wine. He draws water seven times and pours (it) out. [On the eighth] time what he draws, that [he] k[eeps. Further,] two times seven stones he takes from the spring and he throws [them] in[to the ...]. Into a cup he throws two times seven *kappi*-measures. He takes red wool and binds it to <...>.

§27 He brings the water into the house and carries that also there where all the implements are placed, and puts it on the *pūriya*-stands. All the paraphernalia he places before the Anunnaki-deities.[17] He mingles(?) silver, gold, iron, tin, stone, oil, honey, baked clay implements, wicker implements, the mud of the house, (and) the mud of the gatehouse.

§28 He fashions it *(-an)* (into a figurine of) the Deity of Blood and seats it *(-an)* before the *taršanzipa-*.[18] He takes all the seeds and grinds them *(-at)* with the millstone.

§29[19] He pounds (them) with the basalt(?) of the millstone and wipes them off and they fashion it *(-an)* (into) a *kugulla*-vessel. What is left over they fashion it *(-at)* (into) a *kurtal*-container and he fills it *(-at)* with mud. He sets it with/below the God of Blood and seats the gods thereon. He places the *kugulla*-vessel before the deity.

§30 He washes his hands. He takes porridge and *gangati*-vegetable soup. The water that he had brought from the spring he libates into the water. Afterward he libates one lamb with the water and they slit it(s throat). The blood flows into a clay basin and he sets it down before the God of Blood and recites as follows: *āliš mammaš*, O Anunnaki-deities, I have invoked you in this matter. (So) decide the case of this house. What evil blood is present, you take it and give it to the God of Blood. Let him carry it down to the Dark Underworld, and there let him nail it down.

§31 Before the Anunnaki-deities he opens up a Pit[20] with a knife and into the Pit he libates oil, honey, wine, *walḫi*-drink, and *marnuwan*-drink. He also throws in one shekel of silver. Then he takes a hand towel and covers over the Pit.[a] He recites as follows: "O Pit, take the throne of purification and examine the paraphernalia of purification.

§32 "Examine the silver, gold, iron, tin, lapis lazuli, and carnelian with (your) scales.[21] What the God of Blood has said, the exorcist has set it all up. But since the exorcist set up the implements of the gods, ... the exorcist ... [...] broke, and he cast it into the hearth.

§33 "But if you (O Anunnaki) do not decide the case of this house fairly may the earth below you become the 'striker' and may the sky above become the 'crusher,'[22] and may the sky(?) crush [you(?)] therein.[23] May no one break a thick loaf for you and may you not taste the fragrance of cedar!"

§34 He takes three birds and offers two of them to the Anunnaki deities, but the other bird he offers to the Pit and he says as follows: "For you, O Primordial Deities, cattle and sheep will not be forthcoming. When the Stormgod drove you down to the Dark Underworld he established for you this offering."[24]

§35 He cooks the birds with fire (and) places them before the deity. He also places PIḪU-beer before the deity for drinking and provides four straws. He places assorted seeds before the deity: barley, wheat, *šeppit*-grain, *p[arḫ]uena*-grain, chick peas, broad beans, lentils, *karaš*-grain, malt, beer-bread, coriander, apr[ico]t(?), white cumin, black cumin, *titapala*-seed, salt, *lakkarwan*-plant, *šeniya*(?)-plant, a little (of) [ea]ch, and all these [he ...].

a 1 Sam 28:8-15; Isa 8:19; 29:4

[17] The Primordial Deities are sometimes referred to by the Akk. name for the group of deities with which they were identified.

[18] A part of a building.

[19] KBo 10.45 iii 3 (B) has no § divider here.

[20] Written with the divine determinative.

[21] The new duplicate KBo 39.12:7, kindly provided to me by H. Otten, offers a heretofore unknown syllabic reading of GIŠERÍN ZI.BA.NA, the beginning of which is, unfortunately, broken: *-]iš-wa-it*.

[22] *CHD* L-N 451 tr. mortar(?) and pestle(?).

[23] Following *CHD* P 59.

[24] Reference is made to a time when the Storm God exiled the Ancient Gods from the earth, and established that in their cult, as Underworld Deities, they would receive birds as their sacrifice rather than cattle or sheep. Cf. §14 which refers to the same mythological events.

§36 The priest[25] [ta]kes [...]. For the *PIḪU*-beer for drinking [...] he makes the offering rounds [for the god]s. Day one is finished.

§37 [In the morning(?)] the exorcist [tak]es one sheep, one container of *PIḪU*-beer, one thick loaf, wine, [...] and goes into the house. [...] he prepares. [...] he inscribes(?). The earth [...] he says as follows:

§38 "[Memešarti of Heaven] and [Earth],[26] Moon God, Išḫara, — gods [of perjury, curse, si]n, (and) bloodshed — I have [...]-ed [you ...] ... he(?) comes."

§39 [this § is too fragmentary for translation]

§40 "Push yourselves back! O Dark Underworld, restrain their inclination and swallow down the bloodshed, sin, impurity, perjury, evil step(?) (lit., "foot") and common gossip of the house (and) city."

§41 He[27] cooks the liver and cuts it (in half). He also breaks thick loaves and lays them upon the hole and upon the hearth. He also libates wine and pours *PIḪU*-beer for drinking and he provides straws. But no one drinks!

§42 He says, "Memešarti of Heaven and Earth, Moon God, Išḫara — gods of perjury, curse, and death — who(ever) is hungry, who(ever) is thirsty (among) the gods, come, eat and drink, and join with me. From the house and city may you cleanse the evil impurity, bloodshed, perjury, sin, and curse. He bound them, (each evil's) feet and hands, so let the Dark Underworld keep them in!"

§43 Those who are in the house, the guardians of the hearth, sit down and they eat the fat but they do not drink the *PIḪU*-beer. The exorcist comes back into the city and goes into the house and bows to the gods. He offers porridge, *gangati*-vegetable soup, beer, and wine to the gods.

§44 And he says as follows: "O Anunnaki-deities, I have just been on the steppe. ... [...] restrain! O Memešarti of He[av]en and Earth! For you (gods) *PIḪU*-beer (has been) poured out for drinking. Let them bind them (var. him) (with(?)) a *ḫaputri* to the evil impurity, perjury, sin, bloodshed (and) curse. Let it pull those forward, and may you push them from behind.

§45 The exorcist stands a ram and a ewe before the gods and says as follows: "The ram mounts the ewe and it becomes pregnant. Let this town and house become a ram, and in the steppe let it mount the dark earth and let the dark earth become pregnant with the blood, pollution, and sin. Just as the pregnant woman and ewe give birth, let this city and house bear evil blood in the same way, and let the Dark Underworld keep it in.

§46 "As the downpour washes urine and mud from the city, (as) the water washes the roof, and flows down the rain gutters, let this ritual likewise clean away the evil tongue of this city (and) house and let the downpour carry it into the sea."

§47 When he is finished, the exorcist sets the ritual paraphernalia on the copper vessel. He sets the gods thereon and picks it up and carries it to the steppe. He settles the deities where (the spot) is marked, and their ritual paraphernalia he sets before (them). He libates wine. He offers one lamb and eight birds to the Anunnaki-deities. On three hearths he burns (them) together with flat breads, cedar, oil and honey and he libates wine and says as follows:

§48 "O Anunnaki-deities, your tribute has just been set up. Accept these offerings to you. Chase out the bloodshed, impurity, sin, perjury, (and) threat of the house and carry them down (with you to the Dark Underworld).

§49 "You, O Primordial deities, who [...] come and [turn(?)] down from that [...]."

§50 Tablet One finished. [When they cleanse a house of] bloo[dshed, impurity, sin, perjury (and) threat, this is its treatment.]

[25] Even after collation, I cannot dismiss the completely the possibility that the sign is an AZU, and thus that the exorcist who is the main officiant of this text is the person referred to here. Cf. n. 27 below.

[26] The syntax does not follow Hittite rules of grammar, and one expects the translation "Memešarti, Moon God of Heaven and Earth, Išḫara ...," but see §44 where Memešarti appears alone with the epithet "of Heaven and Earth."

[27] Who is the officiant here? The activities of §§40-43 are taking place in the house, as the beginning §43 tells us. Although the exorcist was in the house in §37, he is said to return to the house again in §43 and so presumably had gone back out to the countryside somewhere in the fragmentary sections of §§38-39. This means that he cannot be officiating at the ritual meal described in §§41-43. If indeed another officiant is present, could it be the priest who is mentioned in §36?

REFERENCES

Text: *CTH* 446; Duplicates: A = KUB 7.41 (MH/NS), B = KBo 10.45 (MH/NS), C = KUB 41.8 + 251/w (MH/NS), D = KUB 12.56 (MH), E = IBoT 2.128 (MH/NS), F = KBo 7.57, G = 218/v, H = 427/t, I = 1112/u, J = 208/u, K = 1621/u, L = 729/t, M = KBo 39.12. Edition: Otten 1961:114-157. Discussion: Hoffner 1967:391; Moyer 1983:21-24.

THE STORM GOD AT LIḪZINA (1.69)[1]

Billie Jean Collins

This is a mythological text belonging to the group of Anatolian myths known as the missing deity myths. The original composition dates to the period of the Hittite Old Kingdom. The supreme Storm God is the deity whose absence is the focus of this particular narrative. Presumably the Storm God absented himself in the first column of the tablet, after which chaos ensued for man and livestock. When the text picks up in col. ii, a ritual incantation is underway that successfully contains the evils resulting from his absence in copper cauldrons lying beneath the sea, where they can no longer cause harm. Mankind is thus restored. What follows then is a resumption of the mythological portion of the narrative relating the Storm God's interlude in the town of Liḫzina, where he spent his time cultivating crops and fruit trees. He makes a triumphal return from Liḫzina, meeting nine divinities on the way, who inquire of his whereabouts. His supremacy is proclaimed and sacrificial animals are assembled for a celebration. Col. iv may have contained details of this celebration.

§2′[2] The palms [gave] it [to] the fingers, the fingers [gave] it to the nails, the nails gave it to the dark e[arth].

§3′ The dark earth [carried] it to the Sun God, and the Sun God carrie[d] it to the sea.

§4′ "In the sea are lying cauldrons of copper.[3] Their lids (are) of lead. [a] [Everything(?)] he put therein: he put a demon (*tarpin*),[4] [b] he put *par*[-...], he put bloodshed, he p[ut] *ḫapanzi*,

§5′ he put "red,"[5] he put tears, he put [...], he put ...,[6] [he put] fog, he put "white,"[7] he p[ut] disease.

§6′[8] It became luminous on the human's [entire(?)] body: On <his> head ditto (i.e., it became luminous), on the eyes ditto, on the *walulaša*-s ditto, on the white[s] of the eyes ditto, on his forehead ditto, [on] the eyebro[ws] ditto, and on the eyelashes [ditto]. As (he was) formerly, just so did he become [again(?)].

a Zech 5:5-11

b Gen 31:34-35; Judg 17:5 1 Sam 19:16; Ezek 21:21; Hos 3:4; Zech 10:2

§7′ The Storm God went and keeps striking t[hem(?)] and he kills him [...]. [In] Ziḫz[ina] he worked [the land(?)] and he harvested it.[9]

§8′ He planted an orchard[10] and [opened(?)[11] it]. He [came] back from Liḫzina.

§9′ The Storm God [met] nine lesser gods[12] on the road, and they bowed to him (saying), "O Storm God, [we were searching(??)] for you. Where were you?" (He replies,) "In Liḫzina [I worked the land(?)] and I harvested it. I planted an or[chard] and [I] ope[ned(?)] it."

§10′ (They reply,) "Leave (it). In the fallow land[13] the [...] of things/words is/are weak. W[e] are small, we are [...], we are in the land ...[...]." The Storm God their father [...] them/it and [he] conquered the lands

§11′ Down in the holes [...] them/it and they assembled an ox, [they assembled] sheep, they assembled human beings.

§12′ [...] Ziḫz[ina ...]

[1] The name of the town in this text is twice spelled Liḫzina and twice Ziḫzina. An explanation for this alternation of consonants is not easily forthcoming.

[2] The translation begins with col. ii; col. i is too fragmentary for connected translation.

[3] Cf. KUB 17.10 iv 15 (Tel. myth), the standard version of the missing deity myth, in which the cauldron is of bronze rather than copper and is located in the "dark earth." For a comparison of the Anatolian motif of the banishment of evil to a container in the underworld with Zech. 5:7, see Haas 1993:77-83.

[4] For Hitt. *tarpi-* = Akk. *šēdu* and a discussion of its possible range of meanings see Otten and von Soden 1968:27-32; Hoffner 1968b.

[5] Hoffner 1968b:65 n. 30 suggests reading the SA_5 sign as DIRI "sorrow, grief." In my opinion, this suggestion causes more problems than it solves. In view of the presence of *ḫarki* "white" two lines later, it seems simplest to give the Sumerogram its commonest value as SA_5, and to consider the two colors as symbolic of some specific kinds of evil, that is, as code words that would have been understood by the ancient audience.

[6] The signs are ŠI-PA-AN. Moore 1975:180 suggested a translation "sheaves" noting the form *še-e-pa-an* "sheaf" in §158 of the Hittite Laws, ed. Friedrich, *HG* 72f. In 1968 Hoffner suggested reading *lúm-pa-an* (1968b:65 n. 31). The value *lúm* for ŠI/IGI is not otherwise attested at Boğazköy, which makes his reading unlikely. Moreover, the parallel list transcribed KBo 23.4:5-11, not available in 1968, renders the reading *šipan* certain. Hoffner now reads *ši-pa-an* "daemon;" cf. divine names in *-z/šipa-*.

[7] For possible alternative readings see Hoffner 1968b:65 n. 32 and cf. n. 5 above.

[8] For this § cf. *CHD* L-N 28.

[9] Cf. KUB 33.34 obv. 8.

[10] For *tīēššar* as "orchard" (as opposed to *warḫueššar* "forest") see Košak 1993:112. The present text strongly supports Košak's supposition. I am grateful to R. Beal for bringing this reference to my attention.

[11] That is, he harvested the trees. This word is partially preserved in the following §, hence this restoration, suggested already by Moore 1975:181 with n. 6.

[12] Alternatively, "divine sons of the Storm God" (DUMU.MEŠ DINGIR.MEŠ ^{d}IM-*aš*). But since no enclitic object is indicated, but rather the reflexive particle *-za*, the former translation seems more likely.

[13] KI.KAL-*li* = Akk. *kankallu* seems likely here. The Hittite phonetic complement *-li* requires an underlying Hittite word with a stem ending in *-l-*.

REFERENCES

Text: *CTH* 331; KUB 33.66 (OH/MS). Discussions: Haas 1993:67-85; Hoffner 1968b:61-68; 1973a:197-228; Josephson 1979:177-184; Laroche 1965:70-71; Moore 1975:180-183; Moyer 1983:19-38; Otten and von Soden 1968:27-34.

ESTABLISHING A NEW TEMPLE FOR THE GODDESS OF THE NIGHT (1.70)

Billie Jean Collins

This is a four column tablet composed in the period of the Hittite Empire. It is the first of two tablets.[1] The second tablet is not preserved, although the first tablet has survived in four recensions. The main tablet describes the procedure for establishing a satellite temple for the Goddess of the Night. Her cult was centered in Kizzuwatna in southeastern Anatolia, and thus many Hurrian offering terms appear in this text. The nature of this deity is ambiguous.[2]

§1 Thus says the priest of the Deity of the Night (var. [Thus says ᵐNÍG.BA-ᵈU[3]] the Babylonian [scrib]e(?) and Ulippi, priest of the Deity of the Night).[4] If a person becomes associated with the Deity of the Night in some temple of the Deity of the Night and if it happens that, apart from that temple of the Deity of the Night, he builds still another temple of the Deity of the Night, and settles the deity separately, while he undertakes the construction in every respect:

§2 The smiths make a gold image of the deity. Just as her ritual (is prescribed) for the deity, they treat it (the new image) for celebrating in the same way. Just as (it is) inlaid(?)[5] (with) gems of silver, gold, lapis, carnelian, Babylon-stone, chalcedon(?), quartz(?), alabaster, sun disks, a neck(lace), and a comet(?) of silver and gold — these they proceed to make in the same way.

§3 One sun disk of gold of one shekel (weight), its name is Pirinkir.[6] One gold navel. One pair of gold *purka-* — they are set with Babylon stone. The priest assigns these to the smiths as their task. One (vessel) for "carrying forth" (made) of stone inlaid(?)[7] with silver, gold, lapis, carnelian, Babylon stone, quartz(?), NÍR-stone, (and) alabaster.

§4 Two broaches of iron inlaid with gold, two pegs of iron, two *ḫalwani*-vessels of silver, two cups of silver, two *ētmari-* of silver, two *ētmari-* of bronze (and) a potstand of bronze are included. Six sun disks of bronze, among them three inlaid with silver and three inlaid with gold. Two knives of bronze, two pairs of bronze GÌR.GÁN-vessels, one set of bronze cymbals(?),[8] one set of tambourines(?) either of boxwood or of ivory, one drum.

§5 One bull's horn (full of) fine oil, one set of cups either of boxwood or of ivory. One set of combs either of boxwood or ivory. Two wooden stands, two wooden tables, two wooden potstands. One set of *kišḫita*-chairs, six *šekan* in height — they are doubly *pazzanān*-ed. One set of *kišḫita*-chairs for sitting. One footstool, one set of wooden *tarmalla*.

§6 They take red wool, blue wool, black wool, green wool and white wool and they make two pair of *āzzalli-*. They again take blue

[1] A catalog text (KUB 30.64, *CTH* 282, ed. *CTH* p. 191) reveals that this ritual was complete on two tablets: "[First tablet not f]inished. Second tablet f[i]ni[sh]ed. [The word of NÍG.BA-ᵈU] and of Ulippi, pri[est of the Goddess of the Night. When] someone settles [the deit]y separately, [th]is is the ritual [for it]."

[2] For the possible identifications of this goddess see Lebrun 1976:30f., where three not necessarily mutually exclusive possibilities are offered. A deity named Išpanza, also spelled Išpanzašepa and GE_6-*za*-ᵈ*še-pa*, may be the phonetic spelling of DINGIR.GE_6. Carruba 1971 and Lebrun 1976 have proposed an identification with the Moon God, Arma. But the Moon God is male, while in our text DINGIR.GE_6 appears to be female (her cult statue wears the *kureššar*, a woman's headdress or scarf, see §31). Lebrun suggests that DINGIR.GE_6 is to be identified with Ištar/Šauška, an idea that might help to explain the presence of Pirinkir in this ritual as well, since Pirinkir seems herself to be an aspect of Šauška. For all these possibilities see Ünal 1993.

[3] Read Qišti-Adad?, or Ari-Tešub?

[4] Var. D, KBo 16.85 + KBo 15.29 i 1: [*UMMA* ᵐNÍG.BA-ᵈU ᴸᵁDUB.SA]R(?) ᵁᴿᵁKÁ.DINGIR.RA *Ù* ᵐ*U-li-ip-pí* ᴸᵁSANGA DINGIR-*LIM*. At the time of Kronasser's edition, KBo 16.85 had not been identified as belonging to this tablet. The restoration of the name ᵐNÍG.BA-ᵈU here and in note 2 above is based on KUB 29.4 i 39 (A).

[5] *appan išgarant-* lit., "back stuck" perhaps meaning that the back of the gems are stuck to the image, thus the meaning "inlaid." The alternative, that the back of the image was encrusted with precious stones, doesn't seem logical. I am indebted to Richard Beal for this suggestion.

[6] Present in the Temple of the Goddess of the Night apparently is a sun disk representing the goddess Pirinkir. An image of the goddess herself is not present (see Kronasser 1963:42). Kronasser attributes her presence here to the presumed similar nature and/or background of the two goddesses.

[7] See n. 5.

[8] *HAṢKALLATUM* is possibly the Akkadographic writing of *galgalturi-*, see Friedrich, *HW 3. Erg.* 18; Güterbock 1995:57-72.

wool, red wool, black wool, green wool and white wool and they make a *šuturiya*.[9] They nail two bronze pegs into the entryway of the courtyard of the (new) temple — one on one side and one on the other side. The *šuturiya* (is made to) hang down (from them). One basket(?) either of wicker or of *tamalata*.[10] One (bolt of[?]) *ḫūpara*-fabric, one red scarf, two bowls(?) of wine.

§7 These NÍG.BA-[d]U dispatched: One door, one [..., two ...] — one for setting down and one for carr[ying] forth [...] — one set of small bed(s) of boxwood [...], one bronze cutting implement, one bronze-handled pitcher for viewing, one bronze [...]-vessel, one small copper cauldron, seven *TAKITTUM* of bronze, one small bronze wash basin of one mina weight for the washing of the deity.

§8 One gathered garment,[11] one trimmed tunic, one hood, one cap, one *kaluppa*-garment, one set of belted tunics, one set of silver broaches — these are (the garments) of a woman. One garment, one set of tunics, one set of Hurrian tunics, one trimmed (and) ornamented cloth belt, one trimmed tunic, one set of robes, one set of *ŠATURRATU*-garments, one set of belted tunics, one bow, one quiver, one axe and one knife — these are (the garments) of a man. When they complete the making (of) the deity('s image), all this they arrange in (its) place. The officiant who is settling the goddess separately, the priest and the *katra*-priestesses wash on the following day. (Thus) that (first) day passes.

§9 When on the morning of the second day the Sun God has not yet risen, they take these things of his from the house of the officiant: One skein/strand of red wool, one skein/strand of blue wool, one plain (i.e. undyed) wool, one shekel of silver, one (bolt of[?]) *gazzarnul* fabric, a small amount of fine oil, three flat breads, one pitcher of wine. They go for drawing to the waters of purification and they draw the waters of purification. They carry them to the temple of the Deity of the Night from the temple of the Deity of the Night — (that is from) the temple of the Deity of the Night which is being built to that (old) temple of the Deity of the Night. They set it (the water) on the roof and it spends the night (lit., sleeps) beneath the stars. On the day on which they take the waters of purification, (they attract) the previous deity with with red wool and fine oil along seven roads and seven paths from the mountain, from the river, from the plain, from heaven and from the earth.

§10 On that day they attract (lit., pull) (the deity). They attract (lit. pull) her into the previous temple and bind the *uliḫi* to the deity('s image). The servants of the deity take these things: One skein/strand of red wool, one skein/strand of blue wool, one plain (i.e. undyed) wool, one white scarf, one gem, one *kirinni*-stone, one shekel of silver, a little fine oil, five flat breads, two *mūlati*-loaves of ½ handful (of flour), one small cheese, one pitcher of wine — these they take for the ritual of "pulling up." One skein/strand of red wool, one skein/strand of blue wool, one loop of white wool, two *mūlati*-loaves of ½ handful (of flour), five flat breads, a little fine oil — these they take for the ritual of *dupšaḫi*-.

§11 One white scarf, one skein/strand of blue wool, one skein/strand of red wool, one plain (i.e. undyed) wool, one set of blankets four layers thick, two shekels of silver of which one shekel is for the ritual pit and one shekel is for the *gangata*-, ten flat breads, two *mūlati*-loaves of ½ handful (of flour), one small cheese, a little fine oil, ½ handful of vegetable oil, ½ handful of honey, 1½ handfuls of butter, one *wakšur* of wine, and either a lamb or a kid — these they take for the ritual of blood. Five flat breads, three *mūlati*-loaves of ½ handful (of flour), one measure of wine and one sheep they take for the ritual of praise. Twenty flat breads, two *mūlati*-loaves of ½ handful, one measure of wine, ½ handful of vegetable oil, ½ handful of honey, ½ handful of butter, one handful of barley flour, one lamb — these they take for the *ambašši*- ritual. All this they arrange each in (its) place. The second day is finished.

§12 On the third day, at dawn, the officiant comes into the temple first thing in the morning. The stars are still standing (in the sky). Then they bring the waters of purification down from the roof and the officiant enters into the presence of the deity and bows to the deity. He then proceeds with[12] the ritual of "pulling up." The priest pulls the deity up from the pit seven times.[a] The officiant also pulls (the deity) up seven times.

§13 Furthermore, they come forth from the tem-

[a] 1 Sam 28:8-15; Isa 8:19; 29:4

[9] *HW*[2] I:638f. follows Kronasser 1963:43 in suggesting that both *āzzalli*- and *šuturiya* are types of weaves ("Gewebe") made of wool, such as gauze or netting.

[10] Hitt. *tamalata* occurs only in this text.

[11] Lit., "one garment pulled up" may refer to a pleated or gathered skirt or dress. Such are known for Hittite women in the iconography.

[12] The verb is *tiya*- "to step up, approach" etc. In this context it seems to denote getting on with the proceedings, hence the present translation.

ple into the storehouse. In the storehouse they perform the *dupšāḫi-* ritual. For the *dupšāḫi-* ritual they take one *mūlati*-loaf, but the single *mūlati*-loaf that remains they take later for the *dupšāḫi-* ritual (or) for the ritural of praise. Wher(ever) it is acceptable to the officiant, he goes thither.[13] But when on the evening of that day a star rises (lit., leaps), the officiant comes into the old temple. He does not bow to the deity. He proceeds with the ritual of blood. They offer the ritual of blood with a bird. Afterward they offer either a kid or a lamb. They ...[14] the officiant, and he stands up.

§14 He then proceeds with the ritual of praise. They make the sacrifice of praise with a sheep. Further, they purify the officiant along with the deity with silver and *gangati*-vegetable. Af[ter]ward, they burn the lamb for the *ambašši-* (ritual). The o[ffici]ant bows and goes back home to his house.

§15 During the [night on that da]y, while the Sun God is still standing (in the sky), the servants of the deity [take these (things): one skein/strand] of red wool, one skein/strand of blue wool, one plain (i.e. undyed) wool, [one shekel of silver, one (bolt of[?]) *gazza*]*rnul* fabric, three flat breads, one pitcher of wine, a [l]ittle fine oil. They go to the waters of [purif]ication and the waters of purifica[tio]n they bring to the old temple. They set it on the roof and it spends the night (lit., sleeps) [be]neath the stars. But those things (also they take): one sheep, one moist bread of ½ *ŠĀTU*, five loaves (made of) GÚG of a handful (of flour), three oil cakes of ½ handful, one *mūlati*-loaf of ½ handful, ten flat breads, three *ḫaršpauwant*-breads, their flour of ½ handful, *gangati*-soup, porridge, chick pea soup, broad bean soup, lentil soup, *euwan*-stew, stew of *ARSANNU*-meal, each of ½ handful, dried fruits, a small quantity of each, cress, ŠU.KIŠ-herb, a little fine oil, two skeins/strands of red wool, two skeins/strands of bl[ue] wool, one plain (i.e. undyed) wool, one jug of beer, one pitcher of wine — these they take up to the roof for the wellbeing (of) Pirinkir. One shekel of silver for the pit, two skeins/strands of red wool, two skeins/strands of blue wool, two plain (i.e. undyed) wools, a little fine oil, ½ handful of vegetable oil, ½ handful of butter, ½ handful of honey, one (bolt of[?]) *gazzarnul* fabric, one *mūlati*-loaf of ½ handful, three oil cakes of ½ handful, one loaf (made of) GÚG, one sweet bread of a handful, twenty flat breads, two *ḫutḫūtalla*-breads of ½ handful, three *ḫaršpauwant*-breads, their flour of ½ handful,

§16 *gangati*-vegetable soup, porridge, chick pea soup, broad bean soup, lentil soup, *euwan*-stew, stew of *ARSANNU*-meal, each of ½ handful, dried fruits, a small quantity of each, one *SŪTU*-measure of barley flour, one sheep, one jug of beer, one pitcher of wine, cress, ŠU.GÁN-herb — these they take inside before the deity (for the ritual) of wellbeing.[15] The officiant prepares a gift for the deity, either a neck(lace) of silver, or a "*wannuppaštalla*-star" of silver. Day three is finished.

§17 But when on the fourth day a star comes out (lit., leaps), the officiant comes into the temple and looks after Pirinkir. For Pirinkir they offer the ritual of wellbeing. But when they celebrate it, then they bring the deity down from the roof and for her they scatter dough balls and fruits and they bring her (i.e. the divine image) into the temple.

§18 Inside, before the deity they offer for wellbeing. The officiant rewards the deity, the priest and the *katra*-women. The officiant bows and goes out. Day four is finished.

§19 On the fifth day when it is morning, they take five flat breads, one *mūlati*-loaf of ½ handful, *gangati*-vegetable soup, cress, ŠU.KIŠ-herb, one pitcher of beer. They offer [to the deity for *tuḫal*]*zi*. The officiant [...] does not come again. The [ri]tual of the old temple is finished.

§20 The new temples which have been built [...] because they were turned in, and them [...]. They wave [...] and a lamb. Afterward [...] they wave. A new gold ⌈garment⌉ [...] together with her implements they carry into the new temple and set it down on the table from the basket(?) thusly.

§21 When those <perform> the *tuḫalzi* ritual in the temple of the old deity, they pour fine oil into the *tallai*-container and he speaks thus to the deity: "You, honored goddess, protect your person/body, divide your divinity, come to these new temples, take an honored place." When she goes and take<s> the aforementioned place, then they pull the deity out from the wall with red wool seven times and he sets the *uliḫi* in the *tallai*-container of fine oil.

§22 The *tallai*-container is stoppered, and they carry it into the new temple and set it down

[13] This sentence simply means that the officiant has the afternoon off.

[14] A Luwian verb.

[15] Unless we supply <*ANA* SISKUR> *keldiyaš*, the sentence makes no sense grammatically. The ritual of well-being is performed in the following paragraph. The proposed emendation follows the grammatical pattern established in earlier paragraphs.

apart. They do not put it with the deity.

§23 If it is acceptable to the officiant, on the day on which they offer *tuḫalzi* in(?) the old temple, on that day they also attract (lit., pull) the new deity into the new temples. If it is not acceptable to him, then they will attract (lit., pull) her on the second day. These (things) they will take for the attracting (lit., pulling): One skein/strand of red wool, one red scarf, a little fine oil, a *tallai*-container, twenty flat breads, two *mūlati*-loaves of ½ handful, one small cheese, one pitcher of wine. They go out to the river.

§24 They attract (lit., pull) the deity from Akkad, from Babylon, from Susa, from Elam, from Ḫursagkalamma to the city which she loves, from the mountain, from the river, from the sea, from the valley, from the meadow, from the *ušarunt-*, from the sky, from the earth by means of seven roads and by means of seven paths. The officiant goes behind.

§25 When they are finished attracting (lit., pulling) the deity, the tents have already been constructed before the river, and they carry the *uliḫi-* into the tents and set it on the wicker table. They (also) set (down) a little fine oil, a *naḫzi*-measure of vegetable oil, a *naḫzi-* of honey, a *naḫzi-* of fruit, twenty flat breads, three *mūlati*-loaves of ½ handful, three oil cakes of ½ handful, three small cheeses, one handful of barley flour, three pitchers of wine.

§26 They offer the ritual of blood with a kid. Afterward, they offer the ritual of praise with a lamb. Afterward the lamb is burned for the *ambašši-* (ritual). Afterward, with (the help of) a table man, they bring for the deity all the stews, one warm bread of ½ *ŠĀTI*, one loaf (made of) GÚG, one sweet bread of one handful, one jug of beer, one pitcher of wine and give to the deity to eat. Then they carry the *uliḫi-* into the house of the officiant with (the accompaniment of) a drum and cymbals(?). They scatter sour bread, crumbled cheese and fruits down for him/her.[16] Then they circle the deity with a *ḫūšti*-stone. Then they seat the deity in the storehouse.

§27 For the *ambašši-* (ritual): One lamb, twenty flat breads, one *mūlati*-loaf of ½ handful, one oil cake of ½ handful, one handful of barley meal, ½ handful of vegetable oil, ½ handful of ghee, ½ handful of honey, ½ handful of fruit are arranged. They dedicate the lamb to the deity for the *ambašši-* (ritual). Then they bring in the *uliḫi-* for the deity and they bind the *uliḫi-* to the new deity. There is no ritual of blood and no ritual of praise. The officiant leaves.

§28 Those take one skein/strand of red wool, one skein/strand of blue wool, one shekel of silver, one (bolt of[?]) *gazzarnul* fabric, one plain (i.e. undyed) wool, a little fine oil, three flat breads, one pitcher of wine and they go to the waters of purification. They carry the waters of purification to the new temple and set them on the roof and they spend the night (lit., sleep) beneath the stars. On that day they do nothing (more).

§29 Those ones take twenty flat breads, two *mūlati*-loaves of ½ handful, three oil cakes of ½ handful, three *ḫaršpauwant*-breads, their flour (is) a *tarna-* in weight, porridge, *gangati*-vegetable stew, *euwan*-stew, chick pea soup, broad bean soup, stew of *ARSANNU*-meal, each of ½ handful of flour, cress, ŠU.GÁN-herb, one jug of beer, one pitcher of wine, one moist bread of ½ *ŠĀTI*, one loaf (made of) GÚG, one sweet bread (of) one handful, and a little fruit.

§30 The *uliḫi-* which had been brought from the temple of the old (deity), they open that *tallai*-container and they wash the wall of the [tem]ple with this water. They mix that [in] with the old fine oil of the *tallai*-container and they wash the wall with that. The wall (is) pure. But the officiant does not come (in).

§31 The old *uliḫī-* they bind to the red [s]carf of the new deity.

§32 When at night on the second day (of the ritual)[17] a star comes out (lit., leaps), the officiant comes to the temple and bows to the deity. They take the two daggers that were made along with the (statue of) the new deity and (with them) dig a ritual pit for the deity in front of the table. They offer one sheep to the deity for *enumaššiya* and slaughter it down in the hole. However, there is no [pulling] from the wall. The table (that) had been built[18] they remove(?). They bloody the golden (image of the) deity, the wall and all the implements of the new [dei]ty. Then the [ne]w deity and the temple are pure. But the fat is burned up. No one eats it.

colophon: Tablet One. The word of the priest of the Deity of the Night. When someone set-

[16] Does the pronoun refer to the goddess or to the officiant in whose house this action takes place?

[17] That is, the second day of the ritual for the new temple, the ritual for the old one having been completed in §19 on day five.

[18] In §5.

tles the Deity of the Night separately, for her/ it this is the ritual. Not finished. Hand of Ziti, son of Mr. "Gardener"[19] written under the supervision of Anuwanza, the eunuch.

[19] The Hittite or Hurrian reading of this Sumerogram is unknown.

REFERENCES

Text: CTH 481. Duplicates: A = KUB 29.4 + KBo 24.86; B = KUB 29.5; C = KUB 12.23; D = KBo 16.85 + KBo 15.29 (+) KBo 8.90 (+) KUB 29.6 + KUB 32.68 + KBo 34.79 (edited as 102/f by Otten and Rüter 1981:123, 127f.). Edition: Kronasser 1963. Discussions: Beckman 1983:169; Carruba 1971:355; Haas 1993:74-76; Haas and Wegner 1979; Hoffner 1967; Lebrun 1976:28-31; Ünal 1993.

B. ROYAL FOCUS

1. EPIC

THE QUEEN OF KANESH AND THE TALE OF ZALPA (1.71)

Harry A. Hoffner, Jr.

The Queen of Kanesh

The Queen of Kanesh in the course of a single year gave birth to thirty sons. She said: "What a multitude(?)[1] [a] I have begotten!" She filled[2] (the interstices of) baskets with grease,[3] put her sons in them, and set them into the river.[4] [b] The river carried them down to the sea,[5] to the land of Zalpuwa.[6] The gods recovered the children from the sea and raised them.

After several years had passed, the queen gave birth again — (this time) to thirty daughters. These she raised herself. The sons are on their way back to Neša, driving a donkey. When they reached the city of Tamar[mara], they say: "Heat up an inner-chamber here, and the donkey will climb(?)." The men of the city replied: "Where we came,[7] a donkey [never(?)] climbs(?)." The sons said: "Where we came, a woman gives birth to [one or two] sons (at one time). Yet (our mother) begot us at one time!" The men of the city said: "Once our Queen of Kanesh[8] gave birth to thirty daughters at one time. (Her) sons had disappeared." The boys said to themselves: "We have found our mother, whom we have been seeking. Come, let us go to Neša (= Kanesh)." When they had gone to Neša, the gods made them look different(?), so that their mother [...] did not recognize them. She gave her daughters in marriage to her sons. The older sons did not recognize their sisters. But the youngest [said]: "Shall we take [th]ese our own sisters in marriage? You must not go near them. [It is certainly not] right, that [we should] sl[eep] with them. [...][9]

a Gen 25:22-23; Gen 30:11

b Exod 2

c Judg 11

When morning came, [they] wen[t] to the city of Zalpa. [...] thick bread to the Earth Goddess, the daughter of the Sungod [...] The Sungod strewed meal into her mouth [...], and she tasted it. The Sungod said: "[...] May it come about that the city of Zalpuwa prospers [...]."

When later on war broke out, [...] made peace with the grandfather of the king. [...] was the king of Zalpa, and to him in that same way [...] Allu[-... was] the chamberlain of the king of Zalpa. He put to death [...] daughter [...], and Tabarna's[10] [...] you put to death. And my daughter to/for ...[...] The [grand(?)]father of the king [went(?). Towards(?)] Zalpa, in Mt. Kapa[kapa], Alluwa died in that very defeat. [...] defeated [the allies(?) of] Zalpa. They [...] sixty houses [...] the "lord of his word(s)." And he brought them and settled them in Tawiniya. [...]ed.

Hittite King gives prince Ḫakkarpili to govern Zalpa.

The men of Zalpa heard, and they let him down from the city of [...-]pina. [...-ed] them in Ḫatti peacefully. The [grand]father of the king [...ed] the city Ḫurma to the old father of the king. [...] and Ḫatti. And the elders of Zalpa[11] [c] asked for a son from him. He [sent] them his son Ḫakkarpili.[12] [And] he instructed [him] as follows: "What separately [...] you place, in the same way [...] on

[1] Some translate this word as "monstrosity" or "bad omen." More likely it is related to Latin *vulgus* "crowd," as indicated by Hoffner 1980. Cp. Gen 25:22-23 ("two nations are in your womb") and Gen 30:11 (KJV "a troop cometh").

[2] Perhaps caulking or sealing is the idea.

[3] The Hittite word can be derived from either the word for "oil, fat, grease" or "dung." If waterproofing is intended, then "grease" is the preferred translation.

[4] The Maraššanta River (= classical Halys, Turkish Kizilirmak). The motif of setting an infant adrift in a basket on a river and its being found, raised by others, and becoming eminent has been often pointed out for Sargon and Moses (Lewis 1980). But it is often overlooked that the motive of the parent differs: the Queen of Kanesh wanted to get rid of her child. Jochebed, Moses' mother, wanted to save his life from the death decree of the Pharaoh (Exod 2). Moses' basket was placed in the reeds so that it would not flow with the Nile current.

[5] The Black Sea.

[6] Obviously, a region on the lowermost course of the Kizilirmak River, near to the coast of the Black Sea.

[7] Or: "Where we have seen," reading *a-ú-me-en* with the copy against the edition's *a-ru-me-en*.

[8] Tamarmara must have been under the control of Kanesh/Neša at this time.

[9] In the Hittite laws (§§187-200) brother-sister unions were prohibited as incest.

[10] This could be the name of a non-royal person here.

[11] Compare Judg 11. On Hittite elders see Klengel 1965.

[12] An otherwise unknown Hittite prince.

whose head [he ...s] a *tupalan*."

When Ḫakkarpili w[ent] to Zalpa, [he ...-ed] and he said to them: "The king gave this to me. He holds evil [in his heart(?)]. So make war. He sows(?) for himself [...]. So let the sword cut [...] down to the second and third generations."[13] [d] Now Kišwa said: "[...] defeated [them(?)] as far as Mt. Tapazzili. They defeated [...] So I will request a long weapon(?). Let him give [...], and indeed much." Ḫakkarpili replied: "I will request it from the king." Thus he said: "[...] we will [...], and [...] to us a weapon(?)." Kišwa came and [...]
(Continuation lost in large break in the text.)

Ḫappi and Tamnaššu Incite Zalpa to Revolt.
[...] my brother [...] was king [...] the king of the city Zi[-...] turned [...] Tamna[ššu ...] m[ade ...] king [...] a gold throne [...] this to you [...] ... [...] the gods [...]. Ḫappi [... "...] if [...] let me take [...] I will fill for you [...] with a shovel." He wrote (thus). He set out [...] and went back to Kummanni. But Zalpa made war. He went away [to/from] the city of [...] But Ḫappi [went(?)] to the city of Alḫiuta.

d 2 Sam 13-19

Ḫappi spoke to the men of Zalpa: "I am not loved by my father. I went to Ḫatti to die. Were there not 100 troops, men of Zalpa, with me? Yet they did not die."[14]

The Battle of Ḫaraḫšu.
The king (of Ḫatti) heard (about this). He set out (for Zalpa) and arrived at Ḫaraḫšu.[15] The troops of Zalpa came against him. The (Hittite) king defeated them, but Ḫappi escaped. They captured Tamnaššu alive and brought him to Ḫattuša.

The Siege and Destruction of Zalpa.
In the third year the king went and blockaded Zalpa. He remained there for two years. He demanded the extradition of Tabarna and Ḫappi, but the men of the city would not give them up. So (the Hittite troops) besieged them until they all died. The king returned to Ḫattuša to worship the gods, but he left the old king there. He went up against the city (saying) "I will become your king". Troops were with them. And he destroyed the city.
(The End)

[13] Compare the rebellious prince Ḫakkarpili with David's son Absalom (2 Sam 13-19).
[14] Ḫappi's point seems to be that the Zalpans need not be intimidated by the Hittites. Although, as a prince not in favor, he went to Ḫattuša expecting death, neither he nor his Zalpan accompaniment were harmed.
[15] On road North from Ḫattuša to Zalpa.

REFERENCES

Otten 1973; Tsevat 1983.

---

2. HISTORIOGRAPHY

PROCLAMATION OF ANITTA OF KUŠŠAR (1.72)

Harry A. Hoffner, Jr.

Reign of Pitḫana of Kuššar

§1 (lines 1-4) (Thus speaks) Anitta, son of Pitḫana, king of Kuššar. Say:[1] (Pitḫana) was dear to the Stormgod of the Sky.[2] When (Pithana) was dear to the Stormgod of the Sky, the king of Neša[3] was ...[4] to the king of Kuššar (= Pitḫana).

§2 (lines 5-9) The king of Kuššar ca[me] down out of the city (of Kuššar) with large numbers and to[ok] Neša during the night by storm. He captured the king of Neša but did no harm to any of the citizens of Neša. He treated [them] (all) as mothers and fathers.[5]

Reign of Anitta, son of Pitḫana

§3 (lines 10-15) After (the death of) [Pit]ḫana, my father, in the first year I suppressed a revolt. [Whate]ver land arose (in revolt) from the

[1] Forrer 1922, 1926:8, not seeing the *-MA* sign which the scribe inserted slightly below and to the right of the final sign in this line, read *QÍ-B*[*Í?-M*]*A?* "speak!". Figulla correctly copied that "extra" sign in KBo 3.22, making a reading *QÍ-B*[*Í?-M*]*A* likely. Steiner 1984 modified the reading to: *QÍ-B*[*Í?-Š*]*Ú?* "his utterance/command." Badalì's reading 1987 as a Hittite verb: *ki-ša-*[*a*]*t* "(Anitta, son of Pitḫana,) has become (king of Kuššara)" encounters too many paleographic and grammatical difficulties to be acceptable. Therefore we must retain the reading *QÍ-BÍ-MA* favored by the combination of Forrer's and Figulla's copies.
[2] See Starke 1977 #46.
[3] The modern site of Kaneš/Neša is Kültepe excavated by T. Özgüç.
[4] For possible readings and interpretation see Neu 1974.
[5] That is, he treated them mercifully. See Güterbock 1956; Archi 1979.

direction of the east,[6] I de[feated] them all.

§4 (lines 13-16) [...] the city of Ullamm[a[7] ...] the king of Ḫatti[8] c[ame(?) ...] back [...] in (the city of) [T]ešma[9] I defeated. Neša f[ire(??) ...].

§5 (lines 17-19) [I took] the city of Harkiuna in broad daylig[ht]. I took the city [Ullam]ma at night. [I took] the city Tenenda in broad daylight.

§6 (lines 20-26) I devoted[10] (them) to the Stormgod of Neša.[11] We [all]otted[12] (them) to the Stormgod [of Neša(?)] (as) a de[voted thing].[13] Whoever after me becomes king, whoever resettles [the cities of Ullamma, Tenend]a, and Harkiuna, [the enemies of] Neša, let him be enemy to [the Stormgod] of Neša.[14] [a] And he — let him be [...] of all the lands. Like a lion[15] the land [...].

§7 (lines 27-29) (If) he [doe]s (any other) [harm], (if) he settles [...] upon [...], and [...s] it to the Stormgod [...].

Year Two

§8 (lines 30-32) After (the death of) my father, [in the ... year, I proceeded(?)] to the s[ea] of the city of Zalpuwa.[16] The sea of [Zalp]uwa [was my boundary].[17]

§9 (lines 33-35) [I have copied] these [words] from the tablet(s) in my gate. Hereafter for all time [let no] one de[face] th[is tablet]. But whoever defaces[18] it, [let him] b[e] an enemy of [the Stor]mgod.[19]

Additions to the Original Monumental Inscription in the Gate

§10 (lines 36-37) A second time Piyušti, king of Ḫattuša, came. At the city Šalampa [I defeated(?)] his auxiliary troops[20] which he brought in (to aid him).

§11 (lines 38-48) [I ...ed] all the lands [...] this side of Zalpuwa by the sea. Previously Uḫna, king of Zalpuwa, had carried off (the cult statue of) our goddess[b] (Ḫalmaššuit) from Neša to Zalpuwa, and I brought [Hu]zziya, king of Zalpuwa, back alive to Neša. P[iyusti] had [f]ortified Ḫattuša. So I left it alone. But subsequently, when it became most acutely beset with famine(?),[21] their[22] goddess Ḫalmaššuit gave it over (to me),[c] and I took it at night by storm. In its place I sowed cress.[23] [d]

§12 (lines 49-51) Whoever after me becomes king and resettles Ḫattuša, [let] the Stormgod of the Sky strike him.

§13 (lines 52-54) Toward Šalatiwara [I] tur[ned] my face. šalatiwara drew out [its] ... [...] (and) troops to meet me. I carried them off to Neša.

§14 (lines 55-56) I built various city (fortifications) in Neša. Behind I built the temple of the Stormgod of the Sky and the temple of our goddess (Ḫalmaššuit).

§15 (lines 57-58) I built the temple of Halmaššuit,[24] the temple of the Stormgod my lord, [and the temple of ...].[25] And those goods which I had brought back from my campaign(s) I dedicated(?)[26] to that place.

a Deut 13:16; Josh 6:26; 1 Kgs 16:34; Isa 25:2; Ezek 26:14; Ezra 4:12-22

b 1 Sam 4-6

c Judg 6:1; 13:1; 2 Kgs 18-19; Isa 36-37; Jer 12:7; 21:10

d Judg 9:45

[6] Less likely because of the word order: "Whatever land arose, I defeated them all with (the help of) the Sungod"; so Neu 1974:11.

[7] To the SW of Neša. See del Monte and Tischler 1978:452.

[8] Cf. §10 ("the second time").

[9] Also written Taišama. Restoration according to Balkan, 1957:53. Neu 1974:10 considers the name [...]x-*te-e-eš-mi* to be incomplete. Del Monte and Tischler 1978:429 sub Tišama do not list this passage.

[10] Lit., "sold" (*ḫappariya-*). See Deut 32:30; Judg 2:14; 3:8 for God "selling" Israel "into the hands" of its enemies.

[11] So in the Old Script copy A; var. in C (KUB 36.98 obv. 11) "Stormgod of the Sky."

[12] [*ḫin*]*kuen* in dupl. C obv. 12.

[13] *ḫappar*. The following lines make it clear that this meant the permanent barring of human habitation from the site, i.e., its total annihilation. This is very much like the "ban" (Hebrew *ḥerem*) imposed on certain Canaanite cities by Joshua in the Hebrew Bible. See Deut 7:2; 13:16-18; Josh 6:17-18; 7:1, 11; 10:28-41. See Stern 1991.

[14] For the curse on one who resettles these cities see §12 below and Josh 6:26 (curse on rebuilder of Jericho).

[15] For the lion simile cf. Imparati and Saporetti 1965 (*CTH* 4) §§ 10 and 15. On the similes in the texts of Ḫattušili I see Hoffner 1980.

[16] Zalpuwa (also known as Zalpa) was located close to the Black Sea coast, near the mouth of the Marassanta River (Classical name Halys, Turkish name Kizil Irmak). Cf. del Monte and Tischler 1978:490f. and literature cited there.

[17] For subsequent Old Hittite kings making "the seas" their boundaries cf. Hoffmann 1984 (*CTH* 19) §§ 3, 6.

[18] *ḫulliezzi*, Neu 1974:12f.: "zerschlägt."

[19] Reading *ku-i-ša-at ḫu-ul-li-ez-zi-m[a* dIŠKUR-*un-n]a-aš*. Neu 1974:12f. reads *ku-i-ša-at ḫu-ul-li-ez-zi* U[RU*Ne-eš*]*a-aš* ("of Neša").

[20] *šardiyaššann-a*.

[21] Steiner 1993 (esp. p. 174) questions the validity of the accepted interpretation "beset by famine/hunger" and suggests instead that it means the city was left unprotected by troops who had gone elsewhere on campaign.

[22] Following Singer 1995, who reads: dḪal-ma-š[u-iz] / d Ši-i-uš-mi-iš and correctly notes the difference between *-šummiš* "our" and *-šmiš* "their." Neu 1974:12f. differently: "lieferte sie [i.e., die Stadt] mein Gott Šiu der Throngöttin Halmašuit aus."

[23] On cress (*saḫlû*) in Hittite texts see Hoffner 1974a:111. For sowing ruins with cress see *CAD* S sub *saḫlû* 2 b 3´ (p. 64). See also Judg 9:45, where a conqueror sows salt on a sacked city's ruins.

[24] The deified throne dais (see Starke 1979).

[25] The New Hittite duplicate reads here: "of our god(dess)." But, if this is taken to refer to Ḫalmaššuit, it would be redundant with the first part of the same sentence. There is, therefore, some reason to be skeptical about the accuracy of the late duplicate here.

[26] Hittite *ḫališšiya-* usually means "to plate (with silver or gold)."

§16 (lines 59-63) I made a vow. And [I went on] a hun[t].[27] On the first day (I captured): two lions, seventy boars, one boar of the cane-brake, and 120 (other) wild animals, whether leopards, lions, mountain sheep, wild sheep, or [...], and I brought this to my city Neša.[28]

Year Four

§17 (lines 64-67) In the following year I went to battle (again) a[gainst Šalatiwa]ra. The "man" (= ruler) of Salatiwara arose together with his sons and came against me. He left his land and his city behind and took up a position on the Hulanna River.

§18 (lines 68-72) [The army of] Neša came around behind him (stealthily) and set fire to his city.[f] Them in[side(?) ...] in the city [...] his [...], 1400 troops, chariots, horses, ...[...]...[...] he drew up and marched off.

f Josh 8:19

Year Five

§19 (lines 73-79) When I went on a campaign [to ...], the "man" of Purušḫanda [...] of his *ḫengur*-gift. He brought to me as a *ḫengur*-gift one iron throne and one iron crook.[29] But when I returned to Neša, I brought with me the "man" of Purušḫanda. When he goes to the inner chamber,[30] he shall sit before me on the right.[31]

[27] For this reading see Hoffner 1977.

[28] Many think that these were not dead animals "bagged" in a hunt, but rather animals captured alive to stock a royal zoo. For possible Middle Hittite evidence for the collecting of live animals for such a park see Hoffner 1995.

[29] Sumerian PA.GAM "bent staff," perhaps = Hittite *kalmuš*.

[30] Late duplicate has "to Zalpa" instead of "to the inner chamber."

[31] Imparati and Saporetti 1965 (*CTH* 4) §20, *CTH* 81 §12.

REFERENCES

Text: *CTH* 1. A= KBo 3.22, B = KUB 26.71 i 1-19, C = KUB 36.98 (+) 98a (+) 98b obv.-rev.6′. Bibliography: Edition Neu 1974. Discussions: Badalì 1987; Güterbock 1936:139ff.; 1983:23-25; Otten 1961:335-336; Hoffner 1980:291-293; Singer 1995; Steiner 1984; 1989; 1993.

CROSSING OF THE TAURUS (1.73)

Harry A. Hoffner, Jr.

§1 Thus (says) Puḫanu, the servant of Šarmaššu [...] A person to him [...] is dressed in a colorful tunic/garment. On his head a basket[1] has been placed. He holds his bow (variant: a bow). He has called for help, (saying:) "What have I done? What?"

§2 "I haven't taken anything from anyone. I haven't taken an ox from anyone.[a] I haven't taken a sheep from anyone.[2] I haven't taken anyone's male or female servants."

§3 "Why have you (plural) treated me so and bound this yoke[b] upon me? (Therefore) I must always bring ice[3] in this basket and keep fighting (until) I destroy the land(s) with these arrows. You, (O arrow,) will plunge into (i.e., penetrate) their heart(s)."[4]

a Num 16:15; 1 Sam 12:3

b Gen 27:40; Lev 26:13; Deut 28:48; 1 Kgs 12:4-14; Isa 14:25; Jer 27:8

c Jer 5:22

§4 "Isn't that opponent of mine whom you (plural) escorted to Arinna my donkey?[5] I will sit upon him,[6] and you (plural) shall escort *me* there!"

§5 "Who holds all the lands? Don't I fix in place the rivers, mountains and seas? I fix the mountain in place, so that it cannot move from its place. I fix the sea in place, so that it cannot flow back."[c]

§6 [Beh]ind them he became a bull, and its horns were a little bit bent. I ask [him:] "Why are its horns bent?" And he said: "[...] Whenever I went on campaigns/trips, the mountain was dif-

[1] Not "Korb in der Funktion als Köcher" (so Soysal 183f.), since the occurrence of *pattar* together with bow and/or arrows in ritual texts is no proof that the former is serving as a quiver to hold arrows. Nor is it likely that the quiver would be placed on the head(!) of the man, whereas both male and female workers regularly carry cargo in baskets on their heads. In Mesopotamia even kings are shown with baskets on their heads in which they (ceremonially) carry bricks for building temples, etc. See: *AHw* 1371 sub *tupšikku(m)*.

[2] See a similar statement in a quote inside a ritual: "He has committed no sin; he has not taken anything from anyone" KBo 10.37 i 59-60 (*CTH* 429.1).

[3] Not "Todeskälte" (so Soysal). Even if my earlier explanation (Hoffner 1971) as one of the duties of vassals is unprovable and might turn out to be wrong, one should not force the translation of the words for "basket" and "ice" in order to achieve the description of a military action. Acquiring ice is included among the "public works" (*luzzi* and *šaḫḫan*) in the Hittite laws (§56). Soysal's objections (233) and claim that *e-ki* in the OH copy A is a scribal error for *e-di* are unconvincing. One must first show that the emended reading is clearly preferable to explain the passage.

[4] With Starke 1985b:35 ("und du wirst in ihr Herz dringen") and contra Soysal 1987:174, 179 ("ihn [= den Pfeil] wirst du auch in ihr Herz schiessen").

[5] Or perhaps: "Whom did you bring to Arinna? That opponent of mine? Isn't he my donkey?"

[6] Not "Ich werde mich ihm widersetzen" (so Otten, followed by Soysal 1987:179), but with Neu apud Soysal 1987:252 (Nachträge).

ficult for us. But this bul[l] was [strong]. And when it came, it lifted that mountain and [m]oved it, so that we reached(?) the sea.[d] That is why its horns are bent."

d Deut 33:17; Pss 22:22; 92:11

§7 The Sungod(dess) of [...][7] is sitting [...], and he sends out messengers, (saying:) "Go to Aleppo." Say [...] to the troops: "Šuppiyaḫšu and Zidi are there. [...] The goddess Inara of Ḫatti and Zidi. [...] of Ḫatti [...]. [... g]o, say: 'Come (plural) to [Za]lpa! Come! [...] their/your land!'"

[The remainder of the tablet is too broken and disconnected for reliable translation.]

7 So Otten. Soysal "[Jetzt?] sitzt [e]r (auf dem Thron als) Majestät."

REFERENCES

Text: *CTH* 16a; A = KUB 31.4 + KBo 3.41, B = KBo 12.22 i 1-14, C = KBo 13.78 obv. 1-15. Editions: Otten 1963b; Soysal 1987:173-176, 179-180, 183-190. Bibliography: Hoffner 1971; Otten 1963b; Soysal 1987.

DEEDS OF ŠUPPILULIUMA (1.74)

Harry A. Hoffner, Jr.

Among the Hittite kings Šuppiluliuma I was the greatest conqueror. To him was due the destruction of the great and powerful rival kingdom of Mitanni and the eastward expansion of the Hittite state into North Syria during the first half of the 14th Century BCE. The story of his reign has often been told. Among the more recent attempts Güterbock 1960, Kitchen 1962, Bryce 1989, and Kempinski 1993 may be named. Letters from Šuppiluliuma to the Egyptian pharaoh Amenophis IV, which show the Hittite king's prestige and power, were found in the corpus of Akkadian tablets found at Amarna (Moran 1992). His reign was a long one, during which he established his sons as dynastic rulers in strategic Syrian urban centers such as Aleppo and Carchemish.

The Hittite text called "The Deeds of Šuppiluliuma" (*CTH* 40) was composed by one of his younger sons, who reigned as his second successor under the throne name of Muršili II. A first son and successor, Arnuwanda, was sickly and ruled only a few years. This composition was part of a large historiographic work by Muršili II comprising three compositions (Hoffner 1980, Güterbock 1983). The deeds of his father, the subject of the first part, served as a kind of prologue to the second and third parts: two sets of annals of his own reign, one a chronicle of his first ten regnal years, and the second a more detailed account of his entire reign. Muršili II's ten-year and extensive annals were edited by Goetze (1933). As might be expected, the Annals of Muršili II and the Deeds of Šuppliluliuma (abbreviated "DS"), since they are products of the same author, show many similarities in literary style.

In DS Muršili refers to Šuppiluliuma only as "my father," and Šuppiluliuma's father, Tudḫaliya, as "my grandfather." Even during the reign of his father, Šuppiluliuma was active as a battlefield commander, and on at least one occasion volunteered to lead campaigns when his father was ill (fragment 14, see also 11). Among the opponents faced by Tudḫaliya and Šuppiluliuma were armies from Ḫayaša and the Kaška, both located to the north or northeast of the Hittite capital. When campaigning in this region, the Hittite king used the city of Šamuḫa as a base of operations (fragment 10). Strategic maneuvers mentioned in this text included ambush (fragments 10, 14 and 17). Although usually the battles are described in a very general way, we occasionally meet with vivid details. In fragment 15 Šuppiluliuma fought Arzawan troops in the vicinity of Tuwanuwa and Tiwanzana. The text describes how he encountered them unexpectedly, while he was driving his own chariot in advance of his own supporting chariotry, and how the enemy assaulted him with arrows. In fragment 28 a plague broke out in the Hittite army, which must have been common enough in military encampments with so many people living together in close quarters. The glorification of the Hittite king as a warrior does not exclude the mention of the role of his commanders, Lupakki, Ḫimuili and Ḫannuti, or the activities of the corps of engineers (fragment 28), whose duties included the fortifying of towns and strong points along the way. Hittite princes, brothers of Muršili, such as Arnuwanda, Zita and "The Priest," are also mentioned by name. Rarely, even the name of an enemy commander — such as Takuḫli the Hurrian (fragment 28, A ii 15-20) — is mentioned. The author lays stress on the military organization of his father's various opponents, calling some of them "tribal groups" (see Güterbock 1956:62 note c and Hoffner 1979). This organization especially characterizes the Kaška people, who in Muršili's own annals are described as not being ruled by kings (Goetze 1933:88f., lines 73-75]). Such tribal fighting groups must have been quite elusive, since the author states that his father only defeated them when he was able to "catch" them (fragment 14). The Kaška enemy sometimes attacked by night (fragment 28, A i 21ff., ii 1ff.). Often the author indicates how many of such tribes or tribal groups were fighting in the confederation: nine in fragment 13, twelve in fragment 14, seven in fragment 15. This recalls the various groupings of the Israelite tribal confederacy involved in the localized wars of the Book of Judges. In one instance (fragment 13) an enemy surrenders to the Hittite army only to take up arms again behind its back and sabotage its recently built fortifications. Relocations of enemy population are also recorded. Both in this text (e.g., fragments 18, 19, 26) and in Muršili's own annals exchanges of messages by tablet are recorded, among which are several which challenge the enemy force to combat. Similar exchanges of messages prior to battle are recorded in Judg 11:12-28. The longest messages whose contents are recorded are those exchanged between Šuppiluliuma and the Egyptian queen in fragment 28.

The surviving colophons to the various tablets reveal not only that the native title of the work was "The Manly Deeds of Šuppiluliuma" (fragment 28, colophon of E_3), but also that the text of the Deeds was to be subsequently inscribed on a bronze tablet (fragment 28, colophon to copy A). Such a bronze tablet, although not containing this composition, was unearthed by Peter Neve in the 1986 season of excavations at Boğazköy (Otten 1988). It contained the full text of a state treaty between Tudḫaliya IV of Ḫatti and Kurunta of Tarḫuntašša.

A large part of the narrative is fragmentary, not lending itself to connected, easily understandable translation. We have limited ourselves therefore to the best preserved and most familiar parts. The full text with its many breaks and discontinuities may be found in Güterbock's edition.

This composition was first recognized by Emil Forrer, who collected all fragments he could identify in Forrer 1922, 1926) under numbers 31-37. These tablets were gradually republished in cuneiform, mostly by Goetze, in KUB 14 (1926: Nos. 22, 23), 19 (1927: Nos. 7, 10, 11, 13, 14, 18), 21 (1928: No. 10), 26 (1933: Nos. 73, 84), but some by Heinrich Otten and J. Sturm in KUB 31 (1939: Nos. 6, 7, 21, and 8). In addition, some fragments that Forrer had not recognized were published in cuneiform copies, in particular KUB 19: 4, 12, 47, 23: 2, 7, 8, 50, 31: 11, 25, 33 and 34. Excavations conducted by Kurt Bittel after 1931 added a large number of new fragments, almost all from Archive A in the south-east part of the acropolis. Hans Ehelolf made hand copies of some Šuppiluliuma fragments, which eventually appeared in two posthumous volumes, KUB 32 and 34.

An edition of the entire composition was published as Güterbock (1956). Further small fragments have continued to be identified since 1956, but none which adds appreciably to the text base used by Güterbock. Güterbock's numbering of the fragments has been retained. But since not all fragments are sufficiently well-preserved to allow coherent translation, there will be gaps in the numbering of fragments translated here.

Second and Third Tablets (Fragments 9-17)

(Fragment 10, D col. i) [beginning broken]

(2) When my father ma[rched on], he [did not] meet the Ḫayaša enemy in [the land of ...]. My father went [after the Ḫayaša] enemy, but again he did not [meet] him. (Instead) he met the Kaška enemy, all of their tribal troops,[a] in [the midst of the land]. The gods stood by him: [the Sun Goddess of Arinna], the Storm God of Ḫatti, the Storm God of the Army, and Ištar of the Battlefield, (so that) the en[emy] suffered many casualties. He also [took] ma[ny] prisoners and brought them back to Šamuḫa.

(11) Again [my] fa[ther] set out from [Šamuḫa]. And [in the land(?) of ...] which had been laid waste by i[ts] enemy, there stood the a[rmy(?)] of the enemy. [(Even) the ...] and the shepherds [had come to] help. [My father] laid an ambush[b] [for them] and [attacked] the Ka[ška men]. [He also attacked] the auxiliaries who had come, (so that) the Kaška troops and the au[xiliary] troops [suffered many casualties]. But the captives whom [he took were beyond counting].

(Fragment 11, A ii // B ii and C)

"[...] let him go. [...] There [...] because [... does not(?)] die, kill him [...]." — Thus (spoke) my father to my grandfather: "O my lord, send me on that [campai]gn. Then the gods will fulfill what is in my [heart]."

(8) So my grandfather sent forth my father from Šamuḫa. [And when he (my father)] arrived in the land of Ḫatti, since [the ... had been] burned down by the enemy, my father began to cast away the *kunzi*. And they cast it away [and] took [...]. ...

(Fragment 13, D iv // E i) [Beginning of the column in E is broken away.]

(end of D iii) [When my father] (iv 1) heard this, he set about [...].

(3) He proceeded to lay an ambush[b] in front of [... And] he [slew(?)] the enemy who(?)] had arrived [at ...]. [The Kaška men(?)] assembled nine tribal groups.[a] [My father took away] from him [what] he was holding. (8) And everyone [went away] to his own [town]. When my father [arrived with] l[arge numbers of troops], the Kaška enemy was afraid, and they put their weapons down.

(12) Si[nce] my father had built fortifications behind the empty towns of the whole land which had been emptied by the enemy, he brought the inhabitants back, everyone to his own town, and they occupied their towns again.

(E 7) My grandfather became well again and came down from the Upper Land. And since the troops of the lands of Maša and Kammala kept attacking the land of the Ḫulana River and the land of Kaššiya, my grandfather went to attack them. My father went along too on the campaign. (13) The

[a] Judg 1:3; 6:34-35; 7:24; 8:1-2

[b] Josh 8; Judg 9 and 20

gods went before my grandfather, (so that) he proceeded to destroy the land of Maša and Kammala. While my grandfather [was] in the land of Kammala, my father was with him. In the rear the Kaška enemy took up arms again; and the enemy for a second time destroyed the empty towns behind which my father had built fortifications.

(D 29) Now when my grandfather [came] back from the land of Maša — the lands of Katḫariya and Kazzapa which kept destroying [towns(?)] (as) the Kaška [troops] carried away their goods, silver, gold, bronze utensils and everything — my grandfather went to those towns in order to attack (the troops of Katḫariya and Kazzapa). [Then] the gods marched before my grandfather, (so that) he destroyed (the towns of) Katḫariya and Kazzapa and burned them down. The gods marched before my grandfather, (so that) he also defeated the Kaška troops who had come to help Katḫariya — and those Kaška troops [...] died en masse.

(40) When my grandfather came back from there, he went to the land of Ḫayaša. And my father was still with him. When my grandfather arrived in the land of Ḫa[yaša], Karanni (or: Lanni?), king of Ḫayaša, [came] to (meet him in) battle below (the town of) Kummaḫa. [... broken]

(Colophon of E) Third (tablet), (text) not complete, of the Deeds of Šuppiluliuma, the great king, the hero. [erasure]

(Fragment 14, F iii) [beginning broken]
(2) [... laid an] am[bush for the K]aška people. [... ... Piy]apili (nom.) [...........] they kill. [... Pi]yapili (nom.) ....[......] tr[eated] nothing [badly]. (7) But [when] my grandfather heard [of the ......of] Piy[apili] — since my grandfather was still [si]ck, my grandfather (spoke) thus: "[Who] will go?" My father answered: "I will go." [So] my grandfather sent my father out.

(12) When my father arrived in the land, (he found that) the Kaška enemy who had entered the land of Ḫatti had badly damaged the land. The Kaška enemy whom my father met inside the land consisted of twelve tribal groups.[a] The gods marched before my father, (so that) he defeated the aforementioned Kaška enemy, the tribal troops, wherever he caught them. My father took away from (the enemy) what he was holding, and gave it back to the Hittites. (22) My grandfather became well again and came down from the Upper Land. And when he arrived at (the town of) Zitḫara, he met a[ll] the troops of (the town of) [......] in Zitḫara. (26) The gods marched before my grandfather, (so that) he defeated [the enemy]. ...

(38) [My father said] to my grandfather: ["O my lord, send] me aga[inst the Arz]awa enemy." [So my grandfather sent my father(?)] aga[inst] the Arzawa enemy. (41) [And when] my father [had marched for] the first [day(?), he came(?) to (the town of?) K]asḫa. [The gods] — [the Sun Goddess of Arinna, the Storm God of] Ḫatti, the Storm God of the A[rmy, and Ištar of the Battlefield] — marched before [my father] (45) [(so that) my father defeated the] Arzawa [enemy ... ...] and the enemy troops [died in] lar[ge numbers ... [end of column, continuation of text lost]

(Fragment 15, F iv // G i) [beginning broken]
(1) [...on Mo]unt Allina [...l and [...] it with (its) goods; [......] bu[ilt ...] again. [But when(?)] he arrived [at ...], they brought [word to] my father below (the town of) [...]: "The enemy who had gone forth to (the town of) Aniša, is now below (the town of) [..]-išša." (So) my father went against him. And the gods — the Sun Goddess of Arinna, the Storm God of Ḫatti, the Storm God of the Army, and the Lady of the Battlefield — marched before my father (so that) he slew that whole tribal group, and the enemy troops died en masse.

(11) Furthermore again he met six tribes in (the town of) Ḫuwana[-...], and he (var: my father) defeated these, too, (so that) the enemy troops died en masse. He met still another seven tribal groups[a] in (the towns of) Ni[- ......] and Šapparanda and defeated them, (so that) the enemy troops died en masse. Still another Arzawa enemy was out in the land of Tupaziya and on Mount Ammuna in order to attack. Anna(?) was helping(?) as an ally(?), and he attacked Mount Ammuna, the land of Tupaziya and the [...] Lake, and kept its goods, along with the inhabitants, cattle and sheep. (21) When he arrived at (the town of) Tuwanuwa, he stopped below Tuwanuwa and fought against Tuwanuwa. My father defeated the enemy in (the towns of) [......], Naḫḫuriya and Šapparanda. Then he [we]nt back to (the town of) Tiwanzana to spend the night, and my father spent the night in Tiwanzana.

(26) In the morning my father drove down from Tiwanzana into the land, (while) in the rear his charioteers and six teams of horses were supporting him. And as my father was driving, he encountered(?) that whole enemy all at once, and my father engaged him in battle. Then the gods — the Sun Goddess of Arinna, the Storm God of Ḫatti, the Storm God of the Army, and [Ištar of the Battle-f]ield — marched before my father (so that) he (var.: my father) defeated that enemy. [And] because [the ......] was [v]ery(?) large, he cast away the civilian captives, cattle and sheep [which] they had taken. (36) [When the enemy had abandoned the boot[y](?), [he] fled and took to the moun[tain]. [And ... (?)] they attacked with arro[ws]. When my father saw the attack, he drove up to Tuwanuwa [and] bound the [...]. ... (end of tablet)

(Colophon of F) Second tablet, (text) not complete, of the [De]eds of Su[ppiluliuma ...]. [Hand of (?) ...]-su-ziti (?).

(Fragment 17, G iv) [beginning broken]
(1-2) ......(3) against my father [(4) Then the gods helped him, [(so that) he defeated the enemy, and the enemy] died [en masse]. The auxiliaries(?) [...-ed] Takkuri [and] Ḫimuili [......].

(7) And when he had slain the enemy, he defeated [...] and made it again [into Hittite land]. Then [he went] to (the town of Anz[iliya ......].

(10) And when Anzi[ilya ....]. But my father haste[ned ....]. And when my fa[ther ...., they brought word] to my father:

(14) "The enemy who was [...], now [attacked(?) (the towns of) ......] and Pargalla." (17) "But besides [he attacked(?) (the towns of) ......], Ḫattina, [and] Ha[-...] and holds [their goods, inhabitants], cattle and sheep, and [...]." (20) When my father he[ard (this), he ......] and [laid] an ambush[b] for the enemy. [And the gods] marched before [my father, (so that) he defeated] the en[e-my, and the enemy troops died] en masse.

(24) And the civilian captives, cattle, sheep and go[ods] which [the enemy held], he took away from him and ga[ve] them back [to the Hittites]. Then [......] forth [......] (end of tablet in G; continuation of text lost)

Fragments (18-27) Whose Tablet Numbers are Unknown

(Fragment 18, No. 4 i) (beginning of tablet) // No. 5 iv
(A i 1) The scout(?) troops of (the town(s) of) Peta [and Maḫuirašša who] had [gon]e [...] ... in the land of Arza[wa], tho[se] he brought back [and] settled [them again(?)] in their own lands.

(A i 4) Furthermore, while [my father(?)] was campaigning against the [...]-s, (the towns of) Maḫuirašš[a, ...,] and Peta rose u[p]. And he went [...into] the land of Arzawa to meet Anza-paḫḫ[addu.........]. (8) And for(?) them Anza-[paḫḫddu,...,] Alaltalli, Zapalli [.........] gov[ern-ed] these. (10) [And] my father [wrot]e [to Anza-paḫḫaddu]: [c] "These (are) m[y subjects... ....], but you [ha]ve [taken them away from(?)] me. And [...] [. 1...... (14) [...... for] struggle [........."] And [he......] to him [......: "...] my subjects up [in] the tow[n ...."] And it happened (that) my father [......] said: "Go to [the land] (of) [...and] give [me ba]ck [my subjects]. But if [you do not] deli[ver my] subjects, then be [my ene]my and be...[...]." (21) [...] my father [...] to the people of Arza[wa ....] and he [......] de-li[ver]ed nothing.

c Judg 11:12-28; 1 Sam 22:3; 2 Sam 14:32

(23) [Then] my father consequently sent [out Ḫimu-i]li, the commander, [and gave him(?) troops and ch]ariots. [And Ḫi]muili we[nt, and] attacked [the land of] Ma(ḫ)uirašša [... and] held [it. But] w[hen A]nzapaḫḫaddu [and (?) hea]rd [(this) thing], they [came] after (him) out of [...] and to[ok] him [by surpri]se on the way (28) [and defeated him]. When my father [heard] of the defeat o[f Ḫimu]ili, [his an]ger ro[se, and] he mobilized the troops and chariots [of Ḫatti at once and went into the land of Arzawa. [When] he [arri]ved [in the land of] Arzawa, he [...-ed] the land of Mira [...(broken)

(Fragment 19, KBo 14.6 i) [beginning broken]
(2) [......] defeated [.........]. But (the town of) Ma-(ḫ)uirašši [.] and al[l the inh]abitants of Arzawa took [Mount Tiwatassa, but ...] kept Mount Kuri-wanda apart and [turned] it into(?) three fortified c[amps. But] the enemy held [Mount Tiwatašša] with his force. [......] Alantalli [and] Zapalli [were......] below(?) Mount Tiwatašša. [...] (10) He surrounded it and [besieged(?)] it. [And] when [he] besieged it, [...] came [wi]th troops and chariots, and he [......].

(13) When my father heard [thi]s, [he... and] be-sieged the mountain. [And he wrote him:[c] "Come], let us fight." [But] Anzap[aḫḫaddu] did not [...] come to a battle and was [......]. Of the mounta[in ......] held, and he [......] spoke [...] [broken]

(Fragment 20, KBo 14.7 i) [beginning broken]
(1) [............ch]ariot[s......]. ... (2) [When] my father hear[d.........], he gave [troops and ch]ariots [to Mammali] and [......]. And [the enemy(?) over-took(?)] Mammali [on the] wa[y], and [captured] his troops, chariots, (and) depor[tees]. Mammali alone d[ied(?)...]. (7) My father (abandoned(?)] Mount Tiwa[tašša]. When Zapalli [and ...] were [no longer(?)] besieged, they went [......] into (the town of) Hapalla. [But] my father [..................], and so to his chariots [...] (end of column, continuation of text lost)

(Fragment 25, KUB 34.23 i) [beginning broken]
(1) [.........] to the troops [......the peop]le of Ḫul[-... had] gone over [.........] kept attacking [.........] in [som]e rich tow[n(?) the......of Ḫ]atti he took away and [......] their father(s), their mother(s) (and) their brothers [......] to his own father, mother, and portico [...] who [had gone] over to [...] (10) [...] (he) led (away? the popula-tion, cattle and sheep, [and] brought [them to ....]. And everyone took [.........]. But the people of Išuwa were [............], and to them, to (the things that had been) carried (away), they [...]-ed. But the Hittite civilian captives to them [..., ...] (he) took away. (16) [......] ......(he) left [......] ......(he) hrought. [...............] (he) was. But my father [...] revenge against [......] (20) [and]

went [into the land of] Zuḫḫapa and [burned] it down: [What] was around [the town, that] he burned down, and [all] of the town of Zuḫḫapa he burned [dow]n, (too). But the civilian captives went (sg. !) [.........in]to (the land of) Ḫayaša, [.........]-ed, and they [......]-ed them from Mount Laḫa.

(27) [The......] which [...] in the land of Išuwa, [............]; they belonged to Ḫatti. [............] something to someone [......] (30) [......] even in the winter (he) went [and] attacked [the land of ......]-šeni. And the civilian captives, [cattle, sheep, and bron]ze [utensils] which the army had left behind [in......, those bronze utensils] he brought from there. [...... ......] (he) came, and in the land of Išuwa [......] which [in(?)] Išuwa [.........] chariots [... [broken] [gap of about 25 lines]

(Fragment 26, KUB 34.2:3 ii) [beginning broken]
(2) from the battle [............]. And the civilian captives, cattle [and sheep.........] back to the army [...] whom they held back(?) [......]. Then in the land of Ha[tti ......] empty granaries(?) [.........] and him [......] broke(?) [..................] 370[+ ......]

(11) And when [my father........., he sent a message] to the k[ing of Mitanni and [wrote] him thus:[c] [" ....I] came before [...] (the town of) Carchemish (acc.), the to[wn............] I attacked, but to you [I wrote thus]: 'Come, let us fight.' But you] did not come [to battle]. So now [.........] and the land to you wi[th.........]. (20) So come and [let us] fight. [..."] But he stayed in (the town of) [Wašukanni], he did not [answer(?) ...] and did not [come] to a battle. [So my father went] there after [him]. (25) The harvest which was [......, ...] in Wašukanni ......] there was no water at all [......] the towns which (nom.) [......were] looted(?) [......] (30) around [...] with fru[it] ....]. And again [.........] to drink [...t]o my father [broken]

Tablet Seven (Fragment 28, KBo 5.6 and duplicates)
(A i 1) Then he went back to Mount Zukkuki and built (fortified) two towns: Atḫulišša and Tuḫupurpuna. While (the Hittite) built the towns, the enemy kept boasting: "Down into the land of Almina we shall never let him (come)." But when he had finished building the towns, he went into Almina, and none of the enemies could any longer resist him in battle.

(A i 9) So he set out to fortify (the town of) Almina. In the rear, in the army, a plague [d] broke out. Then my father took a stand on Mount Kuntiya. Ḫimuili, the commander, held the river Šariya, and Ḫannutti, the marshal, held a position in (the town of) Parparra. But the corps of engineers was still fortifying Almina. And because all Kaška-land was at peace, some of the Hittite people had inns behind Kaška towns, (while) some had again gone to the town.

[d] Num 11:33, 14:37; 16:46-49; 17:13; 25:8-9

(A i 18) But when the Kaška men saw that there was a plague [d] in the army, they seized the people who had again gone into their towns.

(A i 21) They killed some and seized others. Then the enemy came by night and deployed. They went to fight against all the fortified camps which the lords were holding. The gods of my father marched before the lords at whichever of the fortified camps they went for battle, so that they defeated them all, and the enemy died en masse. No one could resist the army of my father. When my father had killed the enemy, all the Kaška enemy feared him.

(A i 31) While he was fortifying Almina, he sent out Urawanni and Kuwalana-ziti, the Great Shepherd, to attack the land of Kašula. The gods of my father marched before them, so that they conquered all of the land of Kašula and brought its people, cattle and sheep before my father. There were one thousand civilian captives whom they brought. Then my father conquered all of the land of Tumanna and rebuilt it and reestablished it and made it again part of the Hittite land.

(A i 40) Afterwards he came back to Ḫattuša to spend the winter. When he had celebrated the year festival (in the spring), he went into the land of Ištaḫara. And since the Kaška enemy [had] taken Ištaḫara, Hittite territory, [my father] drove the enemy out of it and refortified the town of [...], Manaziya[na(?)], Kalimuna, and the town of [...] and reestablished them and made them again part of [the Hittite land]. And when he had reestablished [the land of Ištaḫara], he came back to Ḫattuša to spend the winter.

(A ii 1) Tribal troops came en masse and attacked his army by night. Then the gods of his father marched before my brother, so that he defeated the tribal troops of the enemy and [killed] them. And when he had defeated the tribal troops, [the land] of [the enemy] saw him, and they were afraid, and all the lands of Arziya and Carchemish made peace with him, and the town of Murmuriga made peace with him (too).

(A ii 9) In the land of Carchemish, Carchemish itself, as the one town, did not make peace with him. So the Priest, my brother, left six hundred men and chariots and Lupakki, the commander often of the army, in the land of Murmuriga, (while) the Priest came to Ḫatti to meet my father. And since my father was in the town of Uda performing festivals, he met him there. (A ii 15) When the Hurrians saw that the Priest was gone, the troops and chariots of the Hurrian land came — Takuḫli, the *amumikuni*, was among them — and surrounded Murmuriga. And they were superior to the troops and chariots of Ḫatti who were there.

(A ii 21) Egyptian troops and chariots came to the

land of Kinza, which my father had conquered, and attacked the land of Kinza (Kadesh). My father was informed: "The Hurrians have surrounded the troops and chariots that are up in Murmuriga." (A ii 26) So my father mobilized troops and chariots and marched against the Hurrians. When he arrived in the land of Tegarama,[e] he reviewed his troops and chariots in (the town of) Talpa. Then he sent his son Arnuwanda and Zita, the Chief of the Royal Guard, from Tegarama ahead into the Hurrian country. When Arnuwanda and Zita arrived in the country, (A ii 33) [the enemy] attacked them. Then the gods of my father marched before them, [(so that) they defeat]ed [the enemy]. But the enemy [...] below the town and went [down] from the town [in order to escape(?) ... the moun]tains of the land of Tegarama [...]. When [my father he]ard: "He [is trying to] escape from the town ahead of time" — (A ii 42) when my father came down into the land, he did not meet the enemy from the Hurrian land (variant adds: below the town). So he went down to (the town of) Carchemish and surrounded it and (E_2 6) [...]-ed [... on this side] and that side, (so that) he [surr]ounded it [completely]. The river [...] below the place [...] ships ...[...] (he) took, then [......] [broken]

(A iii 1) While my father was in the land of Carchemish, he sent Lupakki and Tarhunta(?)-zalma into the land of ᶜAmqa. They went to attack ᶜAmqa and brought civilian captives, cattle and sheep back to my father. (5) When the people of Egypt heard of the attack on ᶜAmqa, they were afraid. And since their lord Nibḫururiya (=Tutankhamun) had just died, the Queen of Egypt (=Ankhesenamun), who was the king's wife,[1] [f] sent a messenger to my father (10) saying: "My husband has died, and I have no son. They say you have many sons. If you will give me one of your sons, he will become my husband. I do not wish to choose a subject of mine and make him my husband ... I am afraid." (16) When my father heard this, he convened the Great Ones for council (saying): "Nothing like this has ever happened to me in my whole life." (20) My father sent Ḫattuša-ziti, the chamberlain, to Egypt (with this order): "Go bring back the true story to me. Maybe they are trying to deceive me. Maybe (in fact) they do have a son of their lord. Bring back the true story to me."

(A iii 26) (In the meantime) until Ḫattuša-ziti came back from Egypt, my father finally conquered the city of Carchemish. He had besieged it for seven days. Then on the eighth day he fought a battle against it for one day and [took(?)] it in a terrific battle on the eighth day, in [one] day. And when he had conquered the city — since [my father] fear[ed] the gods — on the upper citadel he let no one in[to the presence(?)] of (the deities) [Kubaba(?)] and LAMMA, and he did not intrude into any [of the temples]. (Rather,) he bowed (to them) and gave [...]. But from the lower town he removed the inh[abitants], the silver, gold, and bronze utensils and carried them to Ḫatti. (42) And the civilian captives whom he brought to the palace numbered three thousand three hundred and thirty, (E_3 iii 15) [whereas] those whom the Hitti[tes] brought (home) [were beyond counting] . Then [he ...] his son Šarri-Kušuḫ and [gave] him the land of Carchemish [and] the city of [Carchemish] to govern and ma[de] him a king in his own right.

(E_3 iii 21) When he had e[stablished] Carchemish, he [went] back into the land of Ḫatti and spe[nt] the winter in the land of Ḫatti.

(E_3 iii 24) When spring arrived, Ḫattuša-ziti [came back] from Egypt, (A iii 44) and the messenger of Egypt, Lord Ḫani, came with him. Now, since my father — when he sent Ḫattuša-ziti to Egypt — had given him these orders: "Maybe they have a son of their lord. Maybe they deceive me and do not want my son for the kingship." — therefore the queen of Egypt wrote back to my father as follows: "Why did you say 'they deceive me' in that way? If I had a son, would I (A iv 1) have written about my own and my land's embarrassing predicament to a foreign land? You did not believe me and have dared to speak this way to me. My husband has died, (6) and I have no son. I do not wish to take one of my subjects and make him my husband. I have written to no other land, only to you. They say you have many sons. Well then, give me one of them. To me he will be a husband, but in Egypt he will be king." (A iv 13) So, since my father was kindhearted, he granted the woman's wish and set about choosing the son he would send. (end of tablet in A)

(Colophon of A) Seventh tablet, (text) not complete. Not yet made into a bronze tablet.

[Gap of 6 to 12 lines. Šuppiluliuma speaks to ... Ḫani]
... [" ...] (E_3 iv 1) I [myself] was [...] friendly, but you, you suddenly did me evil. You [came (?)] and attacked the man of Kinza whom I had [taken away(?)] from the king of Hurri-land. (5) When I heard (this), I became angry and sent my own troops and chariots and the lords. They attacked your territory, the land of ᶜAmqa. And when they attacked ᶜAmqa, which is your territory, you were afraid. (10) (Therefore) you keep asking me for one of my sons (as if it were my) obligation. But [h]e will probably become a hostage, and you will not make him [king]." (13) Then Ḫani (replied) to my

e Gen 10:3

f 1 Kgs 11:19-20

[1] "The king's wife" is a literal translation of an Eg. expression *daḫamunzu* which is used here. See: Federn 1960:33. Cf. the personal name Tahpenes in 1 Kgs 11:19-20. See: Krauss 1978. For the personal name Takuhli (above, A ii 18) see Laroche 1966:170-171, no. 1215; Owen 1981.

father: "O my lord, this [is ...] our land's humiliation. If we had any [a son of the king] at all, would we have come to a foreign land and kept asking for a lord for ourselves? Nibḫururiya, who was our lord, has died. He had no son. Our lord's wife is childless. We are seeking a son of (you,) our lord, for the kingship of Egypt. And for the woman, our lady, we seek him as her husband. Furthermore, we went to no other land. We only came here. Now, O lord, (25) give us one of your sons." — So my father busied himself on their behalf with the matter of a son. Then my father asked for the tablet of the treaty again, (in which there was told) how formerly the Storm God took the people of Kuruštama, sons of Ḫatti, carried them to Egyptian territory, and made them Egyptian subjects, how the Storm God (30) concluded a treaty between the lands of Egypt and Ḫatti, and how they remained on friendly terms with each other.[2] And when they had read aloud the tablet before them, my father addressed them: (35) "Ḫatti and Egypt have been friends a long time. Now this too on our behalf has taken place between t[hem]. Thus Ḫatti and Egypt will keep on being friends." [End of tablet in E_3]

(Colophon of E_3) [... the table]t of the Deeds of Šuppilu[liuma]

Fragments Following "Seventh Tablet"

(Fragment 31, KUB 19.4) [beginning broken] (5) [When] they brought this tablet, they spoke thus: ["The people of Egypt(?)] killed (Šuppiluliuma's son) [Zannanza and brought word: 'Zannanza [died.'" And when] my father heard] of the slaying of Zannanza, (8) he began to lament [g] for [Zanna]nza, [and] to the god[s ...] he spoke [th]us: "O gods, I did [them no h]arm, [yet] the people of Egy[pt d]id [this to me], and they have (also) [attacked] the frontier of my land." [broken]

[g] 2 Sam 19:1

(Fragment 34, A. KUB 19.13 + KUB 19.14 i) [beginning broken]

(1) [...] before [... And the gods helped my father]: the Sun Goddess of Ari[nna, the Storm God of Ḫatti, the Storm God of the Army, and Ištar of the Battlefield, (so that)] he defeated the enemy. [... ... he burned down (the towns of) ...] and [Pa]lḫuišša [... ...]. And [ag]ain [he went] to (the town of) Kamm[ama and] burned] down the town of [Kamm]ama.

(7) [When my father] had burned down [these] lands, he went [from there into] the land of Istaḫara. [From Istaḫara] he went into (the town of) Ḫattena, (10) [and] ascended [Mount ...]-šu. And he proceeded to burn down [the land of ... ... and the land of] Teššita. [From there] he went into (the town of) Tuḫpiliša [and ref]ortified [it]. Furthermore, while my father was there, [the people of Zida]parḫa brought (him) word: "If you, O my Lord, (15) were to go [to ...] but not [to come] into the land of Zidaparḫa, [then] we would not hold out in front of the enemy." (17) [But my father] spoke [th]us: "If I from here I were [to march] along at the foot of [Mount ...]-mitta, [then I would] (have to) turn very much out [of my way." And he] (20) [marched on] from there and went into the land of T[ikukuwa. And he] spent the night [in T]ikukuwa. [From there he (went on and)] spent the night in Ḫurna [and] burned down [the land of Ḫurna. From there he ascended Mou]nt Tiḫšina and burned [down] the land of Ḫauri[- ... and came t]o the river Marass[anta]. (25) [Then he went] in[to the land of D]arittara. [And becau]se it [was at pe]ac[e(?), he did not destroy(?)] the land of Daritta[ra]. But [Pitak]katalli mobilized [... in] (the town of) Š[apidduwa(?) ...], and he [came(?) against my father(?)]. But when my father [saw(?)] h[im(?)], he did [no]t wait but [...

(31) My father [marched] away from there, as[cended] Mount Illuriya and spent the night in (the town of) Wašḫaya. He burned down the land of Zina[- ...]. From there he (went on and) spent the night in (the town of) Kaškilušša] (35) and burned down the lands of Kaškilušša and Tarukka. From there he (went on and) spent the night in (the town of) Ḫinariwanda and burned down the land of Ḫinariwanda and Iwatallišša. From there he (went on and) spent the night (in the town of) Šapidduwa and burned down the land of Šapidduwa.

(40) When he had burned down these lands, my father went into the land of Tumanna. And from [Tuma]nna he ascended Mount Kaššû and burned down [the land of ...]-naggara. And (the land of) the river Daḫara, [which] he had [con]quered, opened hostilities once again. (45) [So he] went into (the land of) the river Daḫara and burned down Daḫara and [the land of Ta]papinuwa. Then he came back [into (the town of) T]imuḫala. The town of Timuḫala was a place of pride [of the] Kaška men . He [would have] destroyed it, but they were afraid (50) [and] came to meet [him] and fell [down] to his feet; consequently, he did not destroy it, [but] made [it again part of the Hittite] land. [From there he marched away] and [went] into (the town of) [... , and from there he marched] into [the town of ...] [broken]

(Colophon) [. . the tablet] of the Deeds [of Šuppiluliuma]. (Text) not complete.

[2] The text of the mentioned treaty has never been recovered. But it fits what we know about Hittite treaties, which always contained a historical prologue.

REFERENCES

Bryce 1989; Federn 1960; Forrer 1922; 1926; Goetze 1933; Güterbock 1956; 1960; 1983; Hoffner 1979; 1980:283-332; Houwink ten Cate 1966; Kempinski 1992; Kitchen 1962; Krauss 1978; Malamat 1955; Moran 1992; Otten 1988; Owen 1981.

THE HITTITE CONQUEST OF CYPRUS: TWO INSCRIPTIONS OF SUPPILULIUMA II (1.75)

Harry A. Hoffner, Jr.

The present text derives from a single tablet found in the 1961 season of excavations at Boğazköy in the area of the House on the Slope. It was published in cuneiform copy by Heinrich Otten in 1963 in *Keilschrifttexte aus Boghazköi*, Heft XII, No. 38, and was partially transliterated and translated in the same year by Otten (1963a). The definitive edition was by Hans Güterbock in 1967 (see also Carruba 1968), who cites all anterior literature.

The tablet has four columns and contains two distinct compositions of related subject matter separated by a double horizontal rule near the bottom of column II, between lines 21 and 22. Both compositions describe Hittite military victories over the people of Cyprus, the first during the reign of the Hittite emperor Tudḫaliya IV (ca. 1239-1209) and the second under his direct successor Šuppiluliyama (=Šuppiluliuma II, ca. 1205-1175?), who was the last Hittite ruler reigning from Ḫattuša. Šuppiluliyama's own military operation included the first known Hittite sea battle, followed by disembarcation on Alašiya and a land battle.

Both compositions are by Šuppiluliyama, paralleling Muršili II's authoring of both the Deeds of his father Šuppiluliuma I and two sets of his own annals.[1] Šuppiluliyama tells us at the close of the first text (ii 4-21) that he made an image of his father Tudḫaliya, inscribed upon it his father's "true manly deeds," and installed it in a permanent royal mausoleum, called in Hittite ^{NA_4}*ḫegur* SAG.UŠ. Güterbock translated this expression as "Everlasting Peak." The determinative ^{NA_4} shows the structure was at least partly of stone, the verb "I built" (Hittite *wedaḫḫun*) shows it was man-made, and other texts inform us that it was reached by going "up," that it contained a shrine-like structure called the *kuntarra*, and that there was an inscription in it. But it is still unclear whether it was actually an entire hilltop or mountain top, or if it was a building or complex on an elevated part of the city. The most recently published Hittite textual reference to a ^{NA_4}*ḫegur* SAG.UŠ is found in the bronze tablet treaty between this same Tudḫaliya (IV) and King Kurunta of Tarḫuntašša.[2] The passage is difficult, and various translations and interpretations of the incident have been proposed.[3] But in it the above-mentioned characteristics of a ^{NA_4}*ḫegur* SAG.UŠ are confirmed.

The second text in KBo XII 38 tells of a Hittite victory over Alašiyan ships, followed by further operations on Alašiyan soil. Güterbock has suggested that the originals of both texts were display inscriptions in Hieroglyphic Luwian: the first inscribed on a lost statue of Tudḫaliya, and the second on a relief of Šuppiluliyama, perhaps the famous Nişantaş relief. The latter, which is so badly worn as to be virtually illegible, is being studied by J. David Hawkins with a view to editing it. Since Güterbock's edition of the present text, a monumental hieroglyphic text of this same Šuppiluliyama has been unearthed in the Upper City in the area known as the "Southern Citadel" (German *Südburg*) and published by Hawkins.[4] It is not only not the source of the present text, but Alašiya is not mentioned among the many geographical areas it lists where the king campaigned. This fact does not necessarily call into question the historicity of the Alašiya campaign, but it is somewhat disappointing that the newly discovered inscription does not confirm and elucidate our text. Although it is true that the opening words "I am (king so-and-so)" can be found on royal hieroglyphic display inscriptions, these inscriptions are sometimes accompanied by a relief or statue which actually depicts the king in battle dress. It is this which gives meaning to the words "I (the royal figure whom you see here) am PN." It is likely, therefore, that accompanying the second text which begins with these words was a relief or statue of Šuppiluliyama.

Since in ancient Israel it was forbidden to make an image representing God or a human ruler (see Exod 20), the mighty acts of Israelite kings were never inscribed on statues, as was the custom elsewhere in the ancient Near East. Instead the king's acts were commemorated in song (see the song about Saul and David in 1 Sam 18:6-7) and eventually in written records (2 Chr 32:32; 35:26). The mighty acts of Yahweh, Israel's true king, were similarly celebrated and remembered in song and story. But in addition certain artifacts associated with Yahweh's miraculous deeds

---

[1] For the former see: above, text 1.74; for the latter: Goetze 1933; Otten 1955.

[2] Otten 1988, col. I, lines 91ff.; see Otten's discussion on pages 42-46.

[3] Among recent interpretations of the Bronze Tablet are del Monte 1991-92; Heinhold-Krahmer 1991-92; Houwink ten Cate 1992; Stefanini 1992; Sürenhagen 1992; Beal 1993.

[4] Hawkins 1990.

were kept in the sacred ark: the manna, the stone tablets of the law, and Aaron's staff that budded (Exod 16:34; 25:16, 21; Deut 10:5; Num 17:25). In principle this corresponds to the commemoration of Tudḫaliya's mighty acts on an inscribed statue.

The First Text: About Tudḫaliya

[As an example of the nature of tribute imposed by an overlord on a vassal this text sheds light on many incidental references to paying tribute to overlords. In Num 31 the Mosaic laws governing the division of plunder and the share to be given to Yahweh's temple are regulated.]

(i 3-9) [...] I seized [...] with his wives, his children, [and ...]. I [re]moved all the goods, [including silver, go]ld, copper and all the captured people and [bro]ught them home to Ḫattuša. I [subjugated] the land of Alašiya and subjected it to tribute payment [a] on the spot. I imposed [the fol]lowing as tribute upon it:

(i 10-12) Let this tribute from the king of Alašiya and the *pidduri*-commissioner[5] be (owed) to the Sungoddess of Arinna and to the Tabarna, the Great King, priest [b] of the Sungoddess of Arinna:

(i 13-14) [...] of gold, one talent of copper, twenty-five liters of *gayatum*-grain for the Sungoddess of Arinna;

(i 15-16) [...] of gold, one talent of copper, twenty-five liters of *gayatum*-grain for the Stormgod of Zippalanda;

(i 17-18) [... of gold, one ta]lent of copper, three [*sūtu*-measures] of *gayatum*-grain [for the Stormgod] of Ḫatti;

(i 19-20) [... of gold, one ta]lent of copper, three *sūtu*-measures of *gayatum*-grain [for the Stormgod] of Nerik;

(i 21-23) [... mi]ll(?), utensils [...] in [Ḫattu]ša they shall present.

(i 24-25) [...] all [...] they shall [...].

(ii 1-3) [...] arises [...] reverent [...]

(ii 4-10) [My father,] Tudḫaliya, [did] not [make] this statue; [c] I, Šuppiluliyama, [Great King,] King of Ḫatti, son of Tudḫa[liya,] Great King, grandson of Ḫatt[ušili,] Great King, great-grandson of Muršili, Great King, made it.

(ii 11-16) And just as my father Tudḫaliya, Great King, was a true[6] king, so I have engraved upon it true exploits in the same way. What I have not accidentally omitted, I have also not deliberately suppressed.

(ii 17-21) I built a permanent mausoleum. I made the statue[c] and had it carried into the permanent mausoleum. I installed and appeased(?) [the statue representing the deceased king].

The Second Text: About Šuppiluliyama

(ii 22-26) I am Your Majesty, the Tabarna, Šuppiluliyama, Great King, King of Ḫatti, Hero, son of Tudḫaliya, Great King, King of Ḫatti, Hero, [gra]ndson of Ḫattušili, Great King, H[ero].

(ii 27-28) [My father,] Tudḫaliya, [...]

[The bottom of column II and the top of column III are broken away.]

(iii 1-4) And my father [...] I mobilized and I, Šuppiluliyama, Great King, immediately [crossed(?)] the sea.

(iii 5-9) Ships of the land of Alašiya met me in battle three times on the high seas. I defeated them. I captured the ships and set fire to them in the sea.

(iii 10-16) When I disembarked on the shore, a large number of enemy troops came against me for battle. [I defeated] them [in] b[attle ...] and to me [...] sent [...]

[The following badly broken paragraph mentions troops and the land of Ḫatti. The rest of column III and the beginning of IV are lost.)

(iv 1-4) [My father, Tudḫaliya, Great King,] did [not] make [this statue.] Nothing belonging to any [... did I ...] I, Šuppiluliyama, Great King, built for him this permanent mausoleum.[d]

(iv 5-8) I installed and app[ea]sed(?) the statue [...]. I gave ... (As for) villages (to support the mausoleum) they will designate seventy.

(iv 9-14) Whoever takes (the mausoleum) away from him or subjects it to feudal duty, [the gods] who recognized Tudḫaliya (as king) will [(punish) him (in some way)].

a Num 31; Judg 3; 2 Sam 8:2, 6; 1 Kgs 5:1; 17:3-4; Hos 10:6; Ps 72:10; Esth 10:1

b Ps 110:4

c Exod 20:4; Deut 5:8

d 2 Sam 18:18; 2 Kgs 13:13; 14:16; 2 Chr 21:20; 24:16, 25; 28:27

[5] Perhaps equivalent to the ^{LÚ}MAŠKIM = Akk. *rābiṣu* "royal commissioner" of Cyprus mentioned in the Amarna correspondence.

[6] Although the term used here, *ašant-*, is not the technical term for "legitimate," there is probably an intended contrast of Tudḫaliya IV with Kurunta of Tarḫuntašša who usurped the Hittite throne for a time in the middle of Tudhaliya's reign. See Hoffner 1992.

REFERENCES

Beal 1993; Carruba 1968; Del Monte 1991-92; Goetze 1933; Güterbock 1956; 1967; Hawkins 1990; Heinhold-Krahmer 1991-92; Hoffner 1992; Houwink ten Cate 1966; 1992; Otten 1955; 1963a; 1988; Stefanini 1992:143; Sürenhagen 1992.

3. BIOGRAPHY AND AUTOBIOGRAPHY

THE PROCLAMATION OF TELIPINU (1.76)

Th. P. J. van den Hout

The Proclamation or Decree of King Telipinu (ca. 1500 BCE) is an attempt to put an end to the inner-dynastic strife and bloodshed which seems to have held the Hittite Empire in its grip since Ḫattušili I (ca. 1600 BCE). In order to do so, Telipinu refrained from killing his own opponents, sending them away unharmed, and firmly established rules of succession (§28) and of how to deal with such offenders in the future (§§29-34). As is characteristic of Hittite literature and political thinking, the need is felt to justify this ruling by giving an historical account of the reasons that led up to this decision (§§1-27). This first part of the Decree of Telipinu, thereby, is the major source for our knowledge of the Old Hittite Empire; for an historical overview of the Old Hittite Kingdom see Gurney, *CAH* 2:1235-1255. The second part of the text (§§35-50) seems to deal "with an agricultural-administrative reform" (Singer 1984:103) but is much less well preserved. Being a "comparatively unreligious" document (Hoffner 1975b:53) as opposed to, for instance, the Apology of Ḫattušili (text 1.77 below) there are not as many possible links to the Old Testament as in the latter.

This originally Old Hittite composition has come down to us only in thirteenth century copies of which there may have been as many as at least seven exemplars (Starke 1985a:101). There also existed an Akkadian version of which we have fragments of two different manuscripts. Usually this Akkadian version is taken to be a translation of the Hittite original (cf. Beckman 1985:571; Starke 1985a:109-111 vs. Hoffmann 1984:8-9).

The translation basically follows the Hittite text as given by Hoffmann 1984; for criticism see the reviews by Beckman 1985 and Starke 1985a. Where relevant the Akkadian text is used and referred to in the footnotes.

Introduction

§1 (Column 1:1-4) [Thus] the Tabarna, Telipinu, Great King[1]:

Historical outline: Labarna

[Fo]rmerly, Labarna was Great King[2] and his [son]s, [brother]s, as well as his in-laws, his (further) family members and his troops were united.

§2 (1:5-6) The land was small but wherever he went[3] on campaign, he held the enemy country subdued by (his) might.

§3 (1:7-9) He destroyed the lands, one after another, stripped(?) the lands of their power and made them the borders of the sea.[4] When he came back from campaign, however, each (of) his sons went somewhere to a country:

§4 (1:10-12) The cities of Ḫupišna, Tuwanuwa, Nenašša, Landa, Zallara, Paršuḫanta (and) Lušna,[5] the(se) countries they each governed and the great cities made progress.[6]

Historical outline: Ḫattušili I

§5 (1:13-16) Afterwards Ḫattušili[7] was King and his sons, too, his brothers, his in-laws as well as his (further) family members and his troops were united. Wherever he went on campaign, however, he, too, held the enemy country subdued by (his) might.

§6 (1:17-20) He destroyed the lands one after the other, stripped(?) the lands of their power and made them the borders of the sea. When he came back from campaign, however, each (of) his sons went somewhere to a country, and in his hand the great cities[8] made progress.

§7 (1:21-23) When later on, however, the princes' servants became corrupt, they took to devouring their properties, they took to conspiring continually against their lords and they began to shed their[9] blood.[10]

[1] That Telipinu offers no genealogy may be due to the fact that he was not of royal descent himself or at any rate not directly a king's son (see below §22 and Hoffner 1975b:51, 53). For his name as a reference to the Ḫattian god Telipinu, who stands for nature's prosperity, see Hoffner 1975b:53.

[2] The existence of a separate Great King Labarna (first half 17th century BCE) prior to and different from Ḫattušili I (see below §5) is now confirmed by the so-called cruciform seal; see Dinçol et al. 1993:104.

[3] Lit., "goes." The historical present will be regularly translated as a past tense.

[4] I.e., he made the sea the border of his empire; the same phrase occurs in §§6 and 8.

[5] All to be located in southern Anatolia, just north of classical Cilicia.

[6] Similarly Beal 1988:277; differently Hoffmann 1984:15 with n. 1 ("were well looked after"). The same phrase occurs in §6.

[7] Ḫattušili I who reigned ca. 1650 BCE, and is known through several texts, among which his own annals describing his campaigns to eastern Anatolia and northern Syria.

[8] Var. "countries."

[9] Text: "our."

[10] Kümmel (*TUAT* 1/5:465) took only the last sentence as the main sentence with all preceding ones as still dependent on "when."

Historical outline: Muršili I

§8 (1:24-27) When Muršili[11] was King in Ḫattuša, his sons, too, his brothers, his in-laws, his (further) family members and his troops were united. The enemy country he held subdued by (his) might, he stripped(?) the lands of their power and made them the borders of the s[e]a.

§9 (1:28-34) He went to the city of Ḫalpa,[12] destroyed Ḫalpa and brought Ḫalpa's deportees (and) its goods to Ḫattuša. Now, later he went to Babylon, he destroyed Babylon[13] and fought the Hurrian [troops]. Babylon's deportees (and) its goods he kept in Ḫat[tuša[14]]. §10[15] And Ḫantil[i[16]] was cupbearer and he had Muršili's sister Ḫar[apši]li for his wife. §11[17] Zidanta,[18] <[the ...,[19] had ...] ..., the daughter of Ḫantili, for a wife, and he>[20] stole up to Ḫantili and they [committ]ed an evil dee[d]: they killed Muršili and shed (his) blood.

Historical outline: Ḫantili I

§12 (1:35-38) Ḫantili got afraid (saying): "Will I be pro[tected? The go]ds pr[ote]cted him. [...] ... wherever (he) went, the populatio[n ...] ... the cities of Aš[tat]a, [Šukzi]ya, Ḫurpana, Carchemi[sh[21] ...] ... [troops] they began to [giv]e and troo[ps ...].

§13 (1:39-42) And [when Ḫ]antili reac[hed] the city of Tegarama[22] [a] he began to sa]y: "What (is) [t]his (that) I have done? [Why] did I listen to [the words of] Zidan[ta, m]y(?) [son-in-law]? [As soon as] he (however) [reig]ned [as King],[23] the gods sough[t] (revenge for) the blood [of Muršili[24]].

a Gen 10:3

§14 (1:43-46) [... the H]urrian [tr]oops, chased (like) foxes[25] in the b[ushes,] they [c]alled. [When the Hurrian enemy(?)[26]] came [t]o Ḫatti-L[an]d, he [...-]ed [and ...] in(?) [the l]and he roamed(?). [...] ... they called and the[m ...].

§15 (1:47-52) (almost completed lost).

§16 (1:53-57) [... a]nd the Queen of the city of [Šukziy]a[27] [... The Que]en was dy[in]g. [... Ilal]iuma secretly s[e]n[t] out palace [attendant]s and [...-]ed: "May the Queen of Šukziya die!", so [they seized[28]] her [and ki]lled (her) [together with her children[28]].

§17 (1:58-62) When Ḫantili inquired into (the case of) the Queen of Šu[kziya and her children (saying:) "Who [has] ki[lled] them?", the Chief of the palace attendants brought word. They rounded up[29] h[er fam]ily and [drove] them to Tega[rama].[a] They chased them in the bushes and [they] d[ied(?)].

§18 (1:63-65) And when Ḫantili [gre]w ol[d] and began to become a god, Zidanta killed Ḫantili's son, [Pišeni[30]] together with his sons, [and] his [chie]f servants he killed.

Historical outline: Zidanta I

§19 (1:66-68) And Zidanta bec[a]me King. The gods sought (revenge for) the blood of Pišeni, so the gods made him Ammuna,[31] his begotten (son), his enemy[32] and he killed his father Zidanta.

Historical outline: Ammuna

§20 (1:69-71) And Ammuna became King. The gods sought (revenge for) the blood of his father Zidanta and [they did] no[t make] him,

[11] Grandson and adopted son of his predecessor Ḫattušili I, reigned ca. 1600 BCE.
[12] Aleppo.
[13] In 1594 BCE according to the middle chronology.
[14] Thus restored by Hoffmann 1984:18; in the handcopy there does not seem to be sufficient room for this restoration, however, so that a reading [KUR [UR]][U]*Ḫa-at*[*-ti*] "in Ḫat[ti-Land]" must be considered.
[15] Separate paragraph in manuscript B.
[16] Later successor to Muršili I.
[17] Separate paragraph in manuscript B.
[18] Later successor to Ḫantili I.
[19] Probably some title has to be restored here.
[20] Interpolation in B.
[21] All located in northern Syria.
[22] To the south-east of Ḫatti-Land proper, bordering on the Hurrian territory.
[23] Restoration after Kümmel *TUAT* 1/5:466.
[24] Preserved in the Akkadian version KBo III 89 i 3 (*ša* [m]*Muršil*[*i*]).
[25] The "donkeys" (ANŠE.ḪI.A KBo III 89 i 4) of the Akkadian version may be due to a confusion of the cuneiform signs for "donkeys" and "fox" (KA_5.A).
[26] Restoration after Hoffmann 1984:20 n. i.
[27] For a provocative but highly speculative reconstruction of this affair of a Queen and the city of Šukziya, involving the Akkadian version, see Helck 1984; see also Soysal 1990.
[28] Preserved in the Akkadian version KBo I 27 ii 4.
[29] The verb "to unite" is used here but the context and the Akkadian version KBo I 27 ii 8 (*iṣṣabbatušun*[*uti*] "they took them prisoner") suggest the above translation, cf. Starke 1985a:111.
[30] Also read Kaššeni (*Kaš-še-ni*).
[31] Later successor to Zidanta I.
[32] Var. "enemies."

the grain, wine, oxen (and) sheep [prosper(?)] in his hand [but it all ...] in (his) hand.

§21 (Column 2:1-7) Now, the land became his enemy: the cities of ...agga, [Mat]ila, Galmiya, Adaniy[a], Arzawiya,[33] Šallapa, Parduwata and Aḫḫula. But wherever (his) troops went[34] on campaign, they did not come back succesfully. When Ammuna, too, became god, Zuru, the Chief of the Royal Bodyguard, in those same days secretly sent, of his own offspring, his son Taḫurwaili,[35] Man of the Gold Spear, and he killed Titti(ya)'s family together with his sons.

Historical outline: Ḫuzziya I

§22 (2:8-12) He sent Taruḫšu, a courier, as well and he killed Ḫantili together with [his] sons. Now, Ḫuzziya became King and Telipinu had Ištapariya, his[36] sister of first rank, <as his wife>. When Ḫuzziya wanted to kill them, the matter came to light and Telipinu chased them away.

Historical outline: Telipinu

§23 (2:13-15) Five (were) his[37] br[ot]hers and he assigned houses to them (saying): "Let them go (and) live! Let them each eat (and) drink!" May nob[ody] do harm to them! And I declare: "They did evil to me, but I [will not do] evil to them."[b]

§24 (2:16-19) When I, Telipinu, had sat down on my father's throne,[38] I went on campaign to the city of Ḫaššuwa[39] and I destroyed Ḫaššuwa. My troops were in the city of Zizzilippa as well and in Zizzilippa a battle ensued.

b 1 Sam 24:5-15; 26:9

§25 (2:20-25) When I, the King, came to the city of Lawazantiya,[40] Laḫḫa[41] was [hostile to me] and made Lawazantiya rebellious. The gods put him at my mercy.[42] Of the Chiefs (there were) many: the Commander of Thousand, [...], Karruwa, the Commander of the Chamberlains, Inara, the Commander of the Cupbearers, Kill[a, the Commander of the ...], Tarḫumimma, the Commander of the Staffbearers, Zinwašeli and Lelli, and they secretly sent (a message) to Tanuwa, the Staffbearer.

§26 (2:26-30) I, [the Ki]ng, did not k[no]w [and he killed Ḫ]u[zzi]y[a] and his brothers as well. [W]hen I, the King, heard (of it), they brought Tanuwa, Taḫurwaili [and] Taruḫš[u] and the Council[43] sentenced them to death. And I, the King, said: "[Wh]y do they die? They will hide (their) eyes concerning them![44] I, the King, made them into tru[e[45]] farmers: I have taken their weapons from the shoulder and have given them a yok[e(?)[46]].

§27 (2:31-35) The blood of the whole royal family spread: Ištapari[y]a, the Queen, died, later it happened that Ammuna, the prince, died. The "Men of the Gods," too, each said: "Behold, blood(shed) is widespread in Ḫattuša." So I, Telipinu, summoned an assembly in Ḫattuša. From now on in Ḫattuša, let nobody do evil to a son[47] of the family and draw a dagger on him.

Succession rules

§28 (2:36-39)[48] King shall become a son (who is a) prince of first rank[49] only.[50] If there is no first

[33] Country located in south-western Anatolia. Reading according to B with Hoffmann 1984:26, Kümmel *TUAT* 1/5:467; A has *Ar-za-mi-ya*, cf. Beckman 1985:571.

[34] Lit., "goes" (present singular). In spite of the formal accusative plural of ÉRIN.MEŠ-*uš*, which could either be emended into a nominative (-*iš*!, cf. Starke 1985a:112) or taken as a modernization by a late thirteenth century scribe, this translation is preferred over the (formally possible) one offered by Hoffmann 1984:27 ("But wherever he went to the troops on campaign"); cf. *CHD* L-N 4 and Kümmel *TUAT* 1/5:467.

[35] For this Taḫurwaili see Carruba 1974. ("Became God" = died, said of kings and queens.)

[36] I.e., Ḫuzziya's; Telipinu's only explicit link to the royal family may thus have been his marriage to Ištapariya; see also §1 with note.

[37] I.e., Ḫuzziya's.

[38] In the case of Telipinu — not being a king's son himself — this clearly is a stock phrase, unless he was Ammuna's son; cf. Gurney *CAH* 2/1:663.

[39] In northern Syria.

[40] Near Ḫaššuwa in the Anti-Taurus.

[41] This same Laḫḫa occurs otherwise only in connection with Ḫuzziya in an historical fragment by Telipinu; see Carruba 1974:77-78 and Hoffmann 1984:63-67.

[42] Lit., "put him in my hand."

[43] Council to the Hittite king in mainly legal matters normally consisting of the highest authorities in the empire; most of these probably were members of the extended royal family.

[44] I.e., they will further ignore them completely; for this expression see Hoffmann 1984:120-122. For taking the two sentences as questions see the discussion in *CHD* L-N 331 with literature.

[45] Or "simp[le]"? The translation by Haase 1984:53 "I *castrated* them (and) made them into farmers" is a misinterpretation of the adj. *karš[auš]*.

[46] Reading suggested after the context by Forrer 1926:42 n. 8 and followed by most scholars, although noting that the traces rather favor ^{GIŠ}BA[LAG] (a musical instrument); differently Carruba 1974:75 ("And I gave them the hand(?) ... "), Hoffmann 1984:31 ("And I gave them shackles").

[47] Or "child."

[48] This paragraph states the actual rules for succession.

[49] I.e., a son of the main or first wife of the king.

[50] Translation with Hoffmann 1984:33 according to manuscript A; following the slightly differing manuscript G a translation "of the sons only the prince of first rank" is also feasible, cf. Starke 1985a:112.

rank prince, he who is a son of second rank shall become King. If there is no prince, (no) male, she who is a first rank princess, for her they shall take an in-marrying (son-in-law) and he shall become King.

§29 (2:40-45) Who will become king after me in future, let his brothers, his sons, his in-laws, his (further) family members and his troops be united! You will come (and) hold the country subdued with (your) might. And do not speak as follows: "I will clean (it) out," for you will not clean anything. On the contrary, you will get involved yourself.[51] Do not kill anybody of your![52] family. It (is) not right.

§30 (2:46-49) Furthermore, whoever becomes King and seeks evil for (his) brother (or) sister, you too are his Council and tell him straight: "This (is) a matter of blood." Look at the tablet (that says):[53] "Formerly, blood(shed) became excessive in Ḫattuša, and the gods took it out on the royal family."

§31 (2:50-58) If anyone does evil amongst both (his) brothers and sisters and lays eyes on the king's head,[54] summon the assembly and, if h[i]s testimony is dismissed,[55] he shall pay with his head. They shall not kill secretly, however, like Zuruwa, Tanuwa, Taḫurwaili and Taruḫšu. They shall not commit evil against his house, his wife (and) his children. So,[56] if a prince sins, he shall pay with (his) own head, while they shall not commit evil against his house and his children. For[57] the reason for which princes usually die (does) not (affect) their houses, their fields, their vineyards, their male (and) female servants, their oxen (and) their sheep.

§32 (2:59-65) So now, if some prince sins, he shall pay with (his) own head while you shall not commit evil against his house and his son. Giving (away) even a princes' blade of straw (or) a chip of wood[58] is not right. Those who commit these evil deeds, the [Chiefs of Staff(?)], (that is,) the Major-Domos, the Chief of the Palace Attendants, the Chief of the Royal Bodyguard and the Chief-of-the-Wine,[59] [if?] they want to take a prince's houses and [s]ay thus: "I wish that city to be mine," then he commits evil against the city lord.

§33 (2:66-73) But now, from this day onwards in Ḫattuša you, palace attendants, royal bodyguards, golden-chariot fighters, cupbearers, w[aite]rs, cooks, staff bearers, grooms, commanders of a [field] ba[ttalion], remember this word. Let Tanuwa, Taḫurwaili and Taruḫšu be a warning to you! [I]f someone commits evil again, either the Major Domo, the Chief of the [pala]ce attendants or the Chief of the Royal Bodyguard or the Chief of commanders of a field batallion — whether a lo[w]er (or) higher ranking one — you too, Council, seize (him) and devour him with your teeth!

§34 (Column 3:1-3) Now, in Ḫattuša they must take[60] the Chiefs of Staff, (that is,) the Major-Domos, the Chief of the Palace Attendants, the Chief-of-the-Wine, the Chief of the Royal Bodygu[ard], the Chief of the Chariot Fighters, the Commander of the Bailiffs, the troop[s], those who are grea[t(?)] in [the King's(?) h]ouse, [as well as furthe]rmore

[51] Lit., "you will close yourself in," that is, by killing someone else yourself you will not break the chain of murders in the royal family and you will end up dead yourself, whereas by sparing an opponent's life you will break the chain of murders. Normally, the verb *ḫatkišnuši* is taken in its literal sense as transitive with the object not expressed (cf. Sturtevant-Bechtel 1935:191 "(you pardon nothing) and actually order (his) arrest", Bryce n.d.:137 ("You must press him [i.e., the offender] all the more"), Kümmel *TUAT* 1/5:469 and Hoffmann 1984:33 "you will really oppress"), but the reflexive particle *-za* ("yourself"), not normally present with this verb, strongly suggests the above, more metaphorical interpretation.

[52] Lit., "his."

[53] Or "See this matter of bloodshed in the light of the tablet (which says): '....'"

[54] For the correct reading (*ḫar-aš-ša-na-a* "to the head") and interpretation (an offender, not identical to the king, plots against the king's life) see Melchert 1977:222-223 (cf. Bryce n.d.:157-158); for other interpretations based on the reading *ḫaraššanā* see Hoffner 1982 ("look to the person of the king" = have recourse to) and Kümmel *TUAT* 1/5:469 (the offender either claims immunity because of his close relationship with the king or — if the offender is king himself — points to his responsibilities as king). Some scholars (e.g., Sturtevant-Bechtel 1935:191; Hoffner 1982; Haase 1984:53) have assumed that the king is the implied subject of the first sentence and his victim the subject of the second. This then results in the unique stipulation that the king could be called to account and could be put to death. The unexpressed change of subject between the first two sentences resulting from such an interpretation, however, seems a major, although not unsurmountable, objection to it.

[55] Lit., "goes." This sentence has been interpreted variously, either referring to the verdict of the assembly ("when its word goes" i.e., when sentence is passed, cf. Haase 1984:53; Hoffmann 1984:35; Kümmel *TUAT* 1/5:469), to the plan of the offender ("If at that time he goes ahead with his plan(?)," cf. Sturtevant-Bechtel 1935:191 and Bryce n.d.:137), to the offender's case ("If his case goes against him," cf. Carruba 1964:421; Hoffner 1982:508) or to the offender's testimony ("If his speech fails him(?)" i.e., the accused stands silent, cf. Melchert 1977:223-224). The translation suggested here elaborates on the last one.

[56] The enclitic conjunction *-ma* is here taken as resumptive instead of adversative ("however"), thus avoiding a contrast which does not seem to be there.

[57] The enclitic conjunction *-ma* is here taken as marking an explanation.

[58] For the same phrase, see p. 204 §13 below. For the same phrase in Akk., see *CAD* s.v. *ḫuṣābu*.

[59] This title indicates one of the highest military officials.

[60] The exact meaning of "to take" here is unclear; Hoffmann 1984:39 n. 2 suggests "to respect."

their subordinates.

Administrative and other reforms

§35 (3:4-6) Now, [in (the territory of) Ḫat]tuša the fortified cities [must be] protected. Do not leave them! The fortified cities [... w]ater, but divert it 10 (to) 20 times to the grain.

§36 (3:7-16) (hardly anything is preserved here; line 7 mentions "T[e]lipinu, Great King"[61])

§37 (3:17-33) (fragmentarily preserved; contains a list of at least "60 [+ x?] cities (and their) storehouses"[62])[c]

§38 (3:34-42) (fragmentarily preserved; contains a list of "34 cities (and their) storehouses for (fodder) mix"[63])

§39 (3:43-48) I made the grain abundant again [...] the farmers those very fields ... [...] they must [s]eal. All those the population ... [..., but(?) let] them [not(?)] commit fraud! Beyond (their) ration(?) they kept binding either one or two cubits(?),[64] so they drank out the country's blood. But do not let them do (it) now! Whoever does it, may they give[65] him an evil death!

§40 (3:49-54) (You) who in future will bec[om]e king after me, always seal the gra[i]n with your[66] name. Behold, the administrators of the seal house will leave you and speak to you thus: "[... there (is) n]ot(?).[67] Do not seal it, however, for yourself(?), always [se]al [it ...") And, behold, the[y will] lift you up[68] ...

§41-43 (3:55-68) [except for a few traces not preserved]

§44 (3:69-75) [Who from n]ow on [will become king after] m[e and ...] ... humili[ates and] says thus [to yo]u: "[...]." Do not listen! [...]

c 1 Kgs 9:19; 2 Chr 8:6

d Exod 22:17; Deut 18:10-14

If you [have] harnesse[d] a deportee, you shall always compensate the equipment. The troops [...,] and [...] him to either your wife o[r ...].

§45-47 (Column 4:1-20) [partly lost, partly too fragmentarily preserved to be translated]

§48 (4:21-26) [Wh]en [lat]er on the *karpinattiš*(?)[69] of mortals took to div[id]ing ..., and [they were], oh so[70] disr[espectful] and therefore they[71] were struck by the god(s). But now, from no[w on, ...] if he somehow calls on them, (his) living parents because of (his) share, and whatever he calls on them with (his) mouth to share, they must throw him out of the house, and he must forfeit his own share.

§49 (4:27-29) And the procedure in case of bloodshed (is) as follows: whoever commits bloodshed, only (that) which the "lord of the blood" says (will happen): if he says "He shall die," let him die, but if he says "He shall pay" let him pay. For the king (there will be) nothing, however.

§50 (4:30-34) (The procedure in case) of witchcraft in Ḫattuša (is) as follows: You must clear all matters of (it). Whoever within the family knows witchcraft, you must seize him from the family and bring him to the palace gate. But [wh]oever does not bring him, for that man[72] a bad end will come.[d]

Colophon (4:35-36) First tablet of Telipinu. Finished.

[61] Singer 1984:103-104 suspects this paragraph might have contained a list of storehouse towns similar to the two following paragraphs, located in the central Hittite area.

[62] As far as attested in other texts, the geographical names "point to the northern ranges of the Antitaurus (... and) the region south of the Tuz Gölü," cf. Singer 1984:103. Singer (p. 104) also reminds of the "store cities, chariot cities and cities of the horsemen" in 1 Kgs 9:19; 2 Chr 8:6.

[63] None of the geographical names preserved in this list can be located with certainty.

[64] The meaning of this sentence remains problematic and unclear; cf. Singer 1984:104-105.

[65] The third person plural imperative was almost completely preserved according to Forrer 1926:45 ("*bi*[*-a*]*n-du*"), although not given in the hand copy by Figulla in KBo III p. 5.

[66] Although the verb is in the singular, the possessive pronoun is plural, possibly referring to the future kings. Hoffmann 1984:47 takes the possessive as a third person ("their").

[67] So Singer 1984:105 (NU.G]ÁL); differently Hoffmann 1984:47 (*zi-i*]*k*?).

[68] Singer 1984:105: "They will further lead you (astray)."

[69] Although a hapax of unknown meaning, may be better so than taken (with Hoffmann 1984:52) as two words (*karpina attiš*), cf. Starke 1985a:112.

[70] Cf. Beckman 1985:572.

[71] Text has singular verb form.

[72] C adds: "in his very own house."

REFERENCES

Text: *CTH* 19. Translation: *TUAT* 1/5:464-470; *CAH* 2/1:235-255; Discussion: Beal 1988; Beckman 1985; Bryce n.d.; Carruba 1964; 1974; Dinçol, Dinçol, Hawkins, and Wilhelm 1993; Forrer 1926; Haase 1984; Helck 1984; Hoffmann 1984; Hoffner 1975b; 1982:507-509; Melchert 1977; Singer 1984; Starke 1985a; Sturtevant and Bechtel 1935:182-200.

APOLOGY OF ḪATTUŠILI III (1.77)

Th. P. J. van den Hout

The so-called "Apology" of Ḫattušili III (1267-ca. 1240 BCE) is one of the major Hittite historical texts that have come down to us. At least eight different manuscripts must have existed among which were one-tablet and two-tablet versions, thus illustrating the relative importance the Hittites must have attached to it. All fragments have been found in the eastern storerooms of the Great Temple (Temple 1) in the Lower City of Ḫattuša/Boğazköy; this corresponds to the repeated mention of the deposition of historical texts "before the deity" (e.g. cf. below Apology §5 end). Since Götze (1925:113 n. 2), scholars have taken the peace treaty with Ramesses II in 1259 BCE as a *terminus post quem* for the composition of the text, because of §12b ("(Those) who had been enemies in the days of my fathers (and) grandfat[her]s, concluded peace with me"); for a late date towards the end of Ḫattušili's reign see Tadmor (1983:37-38, 54-57), and Houwink ten Cate (1992:265-267 n. 47).

The composition is notoriously difficult to categorize as to its genre, cf. the discussion in Wolf (1967:12-22); see further Archi (1971:186), Hoffner (1975b:49), Cancik (1976:41-44), Otten (1981:3 with n. 8 and 23 with n. *ad* IV 1f) Güterbock (1983:30). The designation "Apology" was first used by Sturtevant in 1935 in the heading of the relevant chapter, although he spoke of a "Justification" in the introduction (1935:84). The text may be described as a decree instituting the cult of the goddess Ištar, appointing Ḫattušili's son Tutḫaliya and future descendants as her priests, and granting tax freedom to her temple, all this more than amply justified by Ištar's divine providence which Ḫattušili claims to have experienced in his rise to power, so that the composition takes on the character of a eulogy to Ištar, but above all an apology as well as a religious legitimization of his usurpation. The text as a whole has often been compared with the story of David and Samuel in 1 Sam 15 - 2 Sam 8; for details see Wolf 1967. For an historical overview of Ḫattušili's life and times see Ünal 1974 and van den Hout 1995.[a]

The following translation is based on the edition by Otten 1981. The main manuscript is *KUB* I 1+ (A), restored where necessary by its duplicates. Only twice a reading from *KBo* III 6+ (B) is preferred: in ii 32 and 40 as indicated in the footnotes. Variants other than merely orthographic have been noted in the footnotes as well. The division into paragraphs also follows A except for the subdivisions in §§10(a-d) and 12(a-b) according to the manuscripts B and F.

Introduction: Genealogy

§1 (Column 1:1-4) Thus Tabarna Ḫattušili, Great King, King of Ḫatti, son of Muršili, Great King, King of Ḫatti, grandson of Šuppiluliuma, Great King, King of Ḫatti, descendant of Ḫattušili, King of Kuššar.[1]

Prooemium

§2 (1:5-8) Ištar's divine providence I will proclaim. Let man[2] hear it! And may in future His Majesty's son, his grandson (and further) offspring of His Majesty be respectful among the gods towards Ištar!

Ḫattušili's early youth; Ištar's first intervention

§3 (1:9-21) My father Muršili begot us four children: Ḫalpašulupi, Muwatalli, Ḫattušili and Maššanauzzi, a daughter. Of all these I was the youngest child.[3] As long as I was still a boy, I was a 'one-of-the reins.'[4] (Now,) Ištar, My Lady, sent Muwatalli, my brother to Muršili, my father, through a dream (saying): "For Ḫattušili the years (are) short, he is not to live (long). Hand him over to me, and let him be my priest, so he (will) live." My father took me up, (while still) a boy, and handed me (over) to the service of the goddess, and as a priest I brought offerings to the goddess. At the hand of Ištar, My Lady, I experienced prosperity, and Ištar, My Lady, took me by the hand[5] and provided for me.

a 1 Sam 15 - 2 Sam 8

Ḫattušili under Muwatalli; Armatarḫunta's first lawsuit

§4 (1:22-60) When my father Muršili became god,[6] my brother Muwatalli seated himself on the throne of his father, while I became army commander in front of my brother. My brother installed me as Chief of the Royal

[1] I.e., Ḫattušili I, ca. 1650 BCE.
[2] Var. "everybody."
[3] This sentence is omitted in B.
[4] Literal translation of the logograms *ŠA* KUŠ.KA.TAB ANŠE, possibly designating a "chariot driver."
[5] The king being taken by the hand of his personal deity is illustrated on many reliefs and seal impressions. Such representations are known for Muwatalli II, Muršili III/Urḫitešub and Tutḫaliya IV; for Ḫattušili III we only have the description of such a scene on the seal on the silver tablet containing the peace treaty with Ramesses II, cf. Edel *TUAT* 1/2:152.
[6] I.e., "died" in 1295 BCE.

Bodyguard[7] and gave me the Upper Country[8] to govern. So I was in command of the Upper Country. Prior to me, however, Armatarḫunta,[9] son of Zida, used to govern it. (Now,) since Ištar, My Lady, had shown me her recognition, and my brother Muwatalli had been benevolent towards me — when people saw the recognition of Ištar, My Lady, and my brother's benevolence towards me, they envied me. Armatarḫunta, son of Zida, and other people as well began to cause me harm, they were evil to me, and defeat hung over me. My brother, Muw[at]alli summoned me 'to the wheel'.[10] But Ištar, My Lady, appeared to me in a dream, and through the dream she said this to me: "To the deity (of the process)[11] I will leave you, so do not fear!" and through the deity I was acquitted.[12] Since the goddess, My Lady, held me by the hand, she never exposed me to an evil deity (nor) to an evil lawsuit, never did she let an enemy weapon sway over me: Ištar, My Lady, took me to her in every respect. Whenever illness befell[13] me, sick as I was, I looked on (it) as the goddess' providence. The goddess, My Lady, held me by the hand in every respect. But, since I was a man divinely provided for, since I walked before the gods in divine providence, I never did an evil thing against man.[14] You goddess, My Lady, always take me to you in every respect, wasn't it? The goddess, My Lady, never passed me over in time of fear, she never let me down before the enemy, nor did she ever let me down before my opponent in court (or) before (my) enviers: whether it (concerned) an enemy's word, or <the word> of an opponent or some word from the palace, it was Ištar, My Lady, who held (her) mantle over me in every respect, took me to her in every respect. Ištar, My Lady, put my enemies and enviers at my mercy[15] and I finished them off.[b]

b 2 Sam 8:6, 14

Ḫattušili's early military successes

§5 (1:61-74) Now, when my brother Muwatalli looked into the matter, not one evil thing was left against me. So he took me back and put me in charge of all[16] the troops (and) chariots of Ḫatti Land, and all the troops (and) chariots of Ḫatti Land I commanded. My brother Muwatalli kept sending me out, and now that Ištar, My Lady, had shown me (her) recognition, wherever I cast my glance towards enemy country, no enemy cast a glance back at me and each of the enemy countries I conquered: the recognition of Ištar, My Lady, was mine. And whoever was an enemy within the Lands of Ḫatti, I expelled him right out of the Lands of Ḫatti. Which enemy countries I conquered one after the other, while still young, these I will describe separately on a tablet and I will lay it down before the goddess.[17]

Muwatalli moves the capital to Tarḫuntašša; Ḫattušili suppresses the Kaškaeans

§6 (1:75-76) Now, when my brother Muwatalli at the behest of his own deity went down to the Lower Land,[18] he left (the city of) Ḫattuša behind.

(Column 2:1-30) He took up [the gods] of Ḫatti and the Manes[19] and [c]arried them to the land of [Tarḫuntašša]. Thereupon, however, (of) all the Kaška Lands Pišḫuru (and) Daištipašša revolted. The land of Išḫupi[tta], Marišta and the fortresses they destr[oye]d. The enemy crossed the Marašsanda[20] river and began to raid the land of Kaneš,[21] began to ra[i]d the cit[y of ...]. The cities of Ḫa[...], Kuruštama and Gazziura turned hostile on the spot. They began to raid the cities[22] of Ḫatti,

[7] This title, certainly exceeding its literal meaning, designates one of the highest ranking and most influential (military) officials at the Hittite court.

[8] I.e., the territory (north-)east of the capital Ḫattuša, bordering the northern Pontic area, home of the Kaška tribes.

[9] He was a cousin of Ḫattušili's father Muršili II.

[10] Whereas the sumerogram for "wheel" is written with the determinative for wooden objects in manuscript A (^{GIŠ}UMBIN), it is written with the divine determinative in B (^{d}UMBIN). Usually, this is taken to refer to some judicial procedure.

[11] It is not exactly clear to what deity is referred to here. Kümmel (*TUAT* 1/5:483 n.) assumes the deity is a personal, protective deity, although that should be Ištar herself. Some scholars (see Neumann 1985:290) have suggested taking this sentence as a rhetorical question: "Would I leave you to (some other) deity?" The interpretation here follows Götze (1925:69) who thought of a deity handling Ḫattušili's case in court. The variant writing of the "wheel" with the divine determinative may support this view.

[12] Lit., "I became clean."

[13] Lit., "befalls."

[14] Or "I never did the evil thing of man," thus Otten 1981:7.

[15] Lit., "in the hand."

[16] This word omitted in B.

[17] For the "laying down" of tablets in the temple see the introductory remarks to this text.

[18] I.e., the area south of the capital Ḫattuša, in the Konya plain.

[19] Lit., "Dead ones." These are the statues and bones of deceased royal ancestors.

[20] Formerly thought to be the classical Halys, nowadays Kızıl Irmak, but this equation has now become problematic, cf. *CHD* L-N 201.

[21] Nowadays Kültepe.

[22] Lit., "ruin mounds."

while the enemy of the land of Durmitta began to raid [T]uḫuppiya. [...] the land of Ippaššana, however, was uninhabited, [so the enemy troops] penetrated as far as the land of Šuwadara. Both the cities of [Ḫakpiš] and Ištaḫara,[23] however, escaped [but since the land] was cut off, they did not till their fields for ten years. Further, during the years that my brother Muwatalli was in Ḫatti, all Kaška Lands became hostile and they destroyed the lands of Šaddupa and Dankuwa. So he laid siege to the city of Pittiyariga. And my brother Muwatalli sent me, but gave me troops (and) chariots in small numbers. I took along auxiliary troops in small numbers from the country and went: I oppressed the enemy at the city of Ḫaḫḫa and fought him. The Lady,[24] My Lady, marched ahead of me, I defeated him and erected a monument(?).[25] What (population of the city of) Ḫattuša he held, that I took away and resettled it all. The (enemy) commanders, however, I seized and handed them to my brother. This, now, was my first manly deed[26] (and) Ištar, My Lady, for the first time proclaimed my name [c] on this campaign.

c 2 Sam 7:9

Ḫattušili's further successes against the Kaškaeans

§7 (2:31-47) It so happened, however, that the Pišḫurean enemy invaded (the country), and Karaḫna (and) Marišta [were] within the enemy country. On one side the country of Takkašta was its border,[27] on the other the city of Talmaliya was its border. Eight hundred teams of horses were (there) whereas the troops were innumerable. My brother Muwatalli sent me and he gave me one hundred and twenty teams of horses, but not even a single military man was with me. There too Ištar, My Lady, marched ahead of me, and there too, I personally conquered the enemy. When I killed the man who was in command,[28] the enemy fled. The cities of Ḫatti Land which had been cut off, they each fought and began to defeat the enemy. A monument(?) in the city of Wištawanda I erected. There, too, the recognition of Ištar, My Lady, was mine. The weapon that I held there, I had it inlaid and I deposited[29] it in front of the goddess, My Lady.

Ḫattušili becomes King of Ḫakpiš

§8 (2:48-68) My brother Muwatalli followed me and fortified the cities Anziliya and Tapiqqa,[30] (then) he went right off, did not come near me at all and he let[31] the troops (and) chariots of Ḫatti-Land march ahead and led them home. Then he gathered the gods of Ḫatti and the Manes on the spot, carried them down to the city of Tarḫuntašša and took (up residence in)[32] Tarḫuntašša. To Durmitta (and) Kuruštama, however, he did not go. In these countries he left me (behind), and these desolate countries he gave me to govern. The lands[33] of Išḫupitta, Marišta, Ḫiššašḫapa, Katapa, Ḫanḫana, Daraḫna, Ḫattena, Durmitta, Pala, Tumanna, Gaššiya, Šappa, the Ḫulana River (and their) chariots and 'golden' chariot fighters I commanded all. The lands of Ḫakpiš and Ištaḫara he gave me in vassalship and in Ḫakpiš he made me king. Concerning these desolate countries, which my brother had put me in charge of[34] — because Ištar, My Lady, held me by the hand, some enemies I defeated,[35] while others concluded peace with me.[36] Ištar, My Lady, sided with me and these desolate lands I resettled on my own and made them Hittite again.

The battle at Kadesh; Armatarḫunta's second attempt to bar Ḫattušili; Ḫattušili's marriage to Puduḫepa

§9 (2:69-82) Now, when it happened, that my brother went to Egypt,[37] I led for my brother

[23] All lands mentioned here were probably located in or near the "Upper Country," i.e., immediately east of Ḫattuša.

[24] Mistake for Ištar?

[25] Translation suggested by the context; the sumerogram + phonetic complement, if correctly identified as such, could be interpreted as the word for "hand," although in a special usage restricted to this text, thus matching one of the usages of the Hebrew word, cf. Wolf 1967:52-53.

[26] The Hittite word *pešnatar* (LÚ-*natar*) translated here by "manly deed" literally means "masculinity, manliness." Thus it matches the Heb. word *gᵉbûratô* (cf. 1 Kgs 15:23; 16:5 et passim) derived from *geber* "male, man."

[27] Manuscript A (*KUB* I 1 + ii 32) being corrupt here, the translation follows manuscript B (*KBo* III 6 + ii 16-17) at this point.

[28] Although manuscript A ii 40 is broken at this point, it seems to have had an extra sentence, possibly concerning the enemy commander, which was left out in B ii 23. Manuscript B is followed here. For the parallel with 1 Sam 17, see Hoffner 1968c.

[29] Present tense in B: "I (will) deposit;" cf. also the remark in the introduction to this text.

[30] B adds "for me."

[31] B adds "all."

[32] Var. "built/fortified." The site of Tarḫuntašša has not yet been located with certainty. The land of Tarḫuntašša must have comprised classical Cilicia Aspera and territory directly north of it.

[33] All the lands mentioned here are located in the northern half of Anatolia encircling Ḫattuša to its west, north and east.

[34] Lit., "had put in (my) hand."

[35] B adds "with the weapon."

[36] This sentence has mostly been interpreted to refer to the peace treaty between Ramesses II and Ḫattušili (1259 BCE), thus providing us with an important *terminus post quem* for the composition of the "Apology"; see the remarks above in the introduction to this text.

[37] This refers to the battle of Kadesh in 1275 BCE.

on campaign down to Egypt the troops (and) chariots of those lands which I had resettled, and I commanded the troops (and) chariots of Ḫatti-Land of which I was in charge in front of my brother. But when Armatarḫunta, son of Zida, saw the benevolence of Ištar, My Lady, and of my brother towards me, they (i.e. Armatarḫunta) with his wife (and) his son then began to cast spells over me, because they were not successful in any (other) way. Even Šamuḫa,[38] the city of the goddess, he filled with spells. When, however, I returned from Egypt, I marched to the city of Lawazantiya[39] to bring offerings to the goddess and worshipped the goddess.

(Column 3:1-13) [A]t the behest of the goddess I took Puduḫepa, the daughter of Pentipšarri, the priest, for my wife: we joined (in matrimony) [and] the goddess gave [u]s the love of husband (and) w[i]fe. We made ourselves sons (and) daughters.[40] Then the goddess, My Lady, appeared to me in a dream (saying): "Become my servant [with] (your) household!" so the goddess' [serv]ant with my household I became.[d] In the house which we made ourselves, the goddess was there with us and our house thrived: that was the recognition of Ištar, My Lady. [Then] I [w]ent and [fo]rtified the cities of Ḫawarkina and Dilmuna. Ḫakpiš, however, turned hostile. I sent Kaškaeans and on my own I set it straight again. I became King of Ḫakpiš while my wife became [Queen of] Ḫakpiš.[41]

Armatarḫunta's downfall; Muwatalli succeeded by Urḫitešub; Ḫattušili declares war on Urḫitešub

§10a (3:14-30) Now, when it happened, that the lawsuit[42] was somehow reopened by the palace, Ištar, My Lady, at that moment too showed (her) divine providence. The process resulted again in the verdict: They found witchcraft on Armatarḫunta, with his wife (and) his sons, and they charged him with it. He had filled Šamuḫa, the city of my goddess, with witch[craf]t, so the goddess, My Lady, made him succumb to me. And with his property, his wife (and) his son[43] my brother turned him over to me and my brother said to me: "Šippaziti (is) not in-(volved)." So, because my brother had made me triumph over [Arma]tarḫunta through the process, I did not fall back into further evil against him, and [be]cause Armatarḫunta was a blood relative of mine, (and because) moreover, he was an old man,[44] he provoked (feelings of) pity in me [a]nd I let him go. Šippaziti, to[o], his [son], I let go.[e] I did not harm them in any way.[45] Armatarḫunta's [wi]fe and his (other) son, however, I sent [t]o Alašiya[46] (in exile). I took half [(his) estate] and gave it back to Armatarḫunta. §10b (3:31-54) Because my [broth]er Muwatalli had [gi]ven [me the cities of ... -]ta, Durmitta, Zip[lanta, Ḫat]tena, Ḫakpiš (and) Išt[aḫar]a [in vassalship], I resettled [... the(se) deso]late (territories). [When] my [bro]ther became [go]d — because I [co]mmanded [Ḫatt]uša and (because) he had [...] me in lordship, I di[d] not [do] anything (evil) out of regard for [the love] for [m]y br[other. T]herefore, sin[ce] my brother did not have a [l]egitimate son, I took up Urḫitešub, son of a concubine. [I put] him into lordship over [Ḫa]tti Land and laid all of [Ḫattuša] in (his) hand,[47] so that he was Great King over the Ḫatti Lands, while I was king of Ḫakpiš. With the troops (and) chariots [...]. Because the city of Nerik had been destroyed since the days of (king) Ḫantili,[48] I rebu[il]t it and (of) the countries that surrounded Nerik, [I ma]de the cities of Nera (and) Ḫaštira the border. I [s]ubdued them completely and [made them m]y tributaries. [The mountain of] Ḫaḫarwa and the Maraššanda River [...], whatever they held in oppression towards Nerik (and) Ḫakpiš, I subdued them completely. §10c (3:54-79) However, when Urḫitešub thus saw the benevolence [o]f the goddess towards me, he became envious of me, he [beg]an to harm me:

d Josh 24:15

e 1 Sam 24:5-15; 26:9

[38] Ca. 200 km east of Ḫattuša.

[39] To the south-east of Ḫattuša in the vicinity of the Antitaurus.

[40] For these children, see van den Hout 1995.

[41] Both Otten 1981:17 and Kümmel *TUAT* 1/5:487 translate differently: "I became King of Ḫakpiš, you, the woman, however, became [Queen of] Ḫakpiš." For the above translation see Neumann 1985:292.

[42] I.e., the lawsuit of Armatarḫunta.

[43] Var. "sons."

[44] Armatarḫunta was of the generation of Ḫattušili's father.

[45] Var. "(And) I left them alone."

[46] Cyprus.

[47] Ḫattušili almost certainly gives himself too much credit here. According to the succession rules laid down by Telipinu, Urḫitešub was the sole legitimate heir, whom his father Muwatalli had kept to himself to raise him as his successor. Urḫitešub's brother Kurunta, however, was according to the Bronze Tablet (cf. Otten 1988:11) already as a boy entrusted by Muwatalli to Ḫattušili. A recently found bulla with the double sealing of both Muwatalli and Urḫitešub may point in the same direction.

[48] I.e., either Ḫantili I, the Old Hittite king and successor to Muršili I, shortly after 1600 BCE or Ḫantili II, the 15th century king.

he took away from me all those in my service,[49] and (all) the desolate countries which I had resettled, those too he took away from me. He humiliated me, but at the behest of the goddess he did not take away Ḫakpiš from me. Be[cau]se I was priest to the Stormgod of Nerik, he therefore did not take that (city) away from me (either). Out of regard for the love for my brother I did not react at all and during seven years I complied. He, however, sought my destruction at divine and human behest and he took away from me Ḫakpiš and Nerik. Now I no longer complied and I became hostile to him. But when I became hostile to him, I did not commit a moral offence[50] by revolting against him on the chariot or by revolting against him within (his) house. (No,) in a manly way I declared to him: "You opposed me. You (are) Great King, whereas I (am) king of the single fortress that you left me. So come! Ištar of Šamuḫa and the Stormgod of Nerik will judge us."[f] When I wrote thus to Urḫitešub — if someone speaks thus: "Why did you at first install him in kingship, but why do you now declare war on him in writing?" (I will answer:) "If he had in no way opposed me, would they (i.e. the gods) really have made a Great King succumb to a petty king?" Because he has now opposed me, the gods have made him succumb to me by (their) judgement.

§10d (Column 4:1-6) When I declared him these words: "Come!", he, however, hastened away from the city of Maraššantiya and went to the Upper Country, and Šippaziti, son of Armatarḫunta, was with him. He summoned him to the troops of the Upper Country. Since Šippaziti, however, was evil towards me, he did not ... towards me.

Downfall of Urḫitešub

§11 (4:7-40) Because Ištar, My Lady, had already early (fore)told kingship for me, Ištar, My Lady, appeared at that moment to my wife in a dream (saying): "I will march ahead of your husband and all of Ḫattuša will turn to (the side) of your husband. Since I elevated him, I never ever exposed him to an evil trial (or) an evil deity. Now, too, I will lift him and install him in priesthood for the Sungoddess of Arinna, and you must worship me as Ištar *parašši*!"[51] Ištar, My Lady, backed me, and as she promised me, it happened too.[52] Ištar, My Lady, provided for me there as well in abundance. To the generals whom Urḫitešub had dismissed to some place, Ištar[53] appeared in a dream, *while she strengthened them, the exhausted ones*[54] (saying): "All Ḫatti Lands I have turned over to[55] Ḫattušili." There, too, I experienced the divine providence of Ištar in abundance. When she had left Urḫitešub no other way whatsoever, she locked him up in Šamuḫa like a pig in a sty. The Kaškaeans, meanwhile, who had been hostile to me, backed me and all Ḫattuša backed me. Out of regard for the love of my brother I did not do anything (evil). I went back down to Urḫitešub[56] and brought him down like a prisoner. I gave him fortified cities in the country of Nuḫašše and there he lived. When he plotted another plot against me, and wanted to ride to Babylon — when I heard the matter, I seized him and sent him alongside the sea. They made Šippaziti cross the border as well, while I took away his property and gave it to Ištar, My Lady. That to Ištar, My Lady, I gave, while Ištar, My Lady, promoted me step by step.

Ḫattušili's career in retrospect; Kurunta King in Tarḫuntašša; transfer of properties to Ištar; Tutḫaliya priest of Ištar

§12a (4:41-48) I was a prince and became Chief of the Royal Bodyguard. As Chief of the Royal Bodyguard I became King of Ḫakpiš. As King of Ḫakpiš I then[57] became Great King. Finally, Ištar, My Lady, had put (my) enviers, enemies (and) my opponents in court at my mercy.[58] [g] Some died by the sword, others died on (their appointed) day:[h] all these I finished off. Ištar, My Lady, had given me kingship over Ḫatti Land.

f 1 Sam 24:15;

g 2 Sam 7:8-9

h 1 Sam 26:10

[49] Manuscripts B and E both add: "and he took Šamuḫa away from me."

[50] The Hittite word used here refers to religious impurity which normally has to be removed by magic ritual.

[51] Epithet of Ištar of uncertain provenance and meaning.

[52] B adds: "likewise exactly."

[53] B adds: "My Lady."

[54] The translation of this *crux* follows the solution offered by Nowicki (1985:26-35), although not all difficulties seem to be solved (*innarawaš* as 3rd sing. preterite of a verb **innarawae-*; the function of the sentence connective *-ma* in KUR.KUR$^{ME.EŠ}$ ^{URU}*Ḫatti-ma-wa-k*[*an*] introducing the direct speech of the goddess). Alternatively, one might suggest the possible analysis *innara-uwa-šmaš dariyanteš* "You (are) strongly urged (to come), (for I have turned over all Ḫatti Lands to Ḫattušili)" with *-šmaš* replacing the more usual reflexive *-za* in nominal sentences of this kind, and *innara* as the well known adverb.

[55] Var. "behind."

[56] B adds: "in Šamuḫa."

[57] This word is omitted in B.

[58] Lit., "in (my) hand."

§12b (4:48-80) I had become Great King: She took me as a prince and let me (rise)[59] to kingship. The kings (who were) my elders (and) who had been on good terms with me, they remained on just those good terms with me, and they began to send envoys to me. They began to send gifts to me, and the gifts they ke[ep] sending me, they never sent to any (of my) fathers and grandfathers.[60] The king supposed to respect me,[61] respected me, and the (countries) that had been my enemies, I conquered them. For the Ḫatti Lands I [a]nnexed territory upon territory. (Those) who had been enemies in the days of my fathers (and) grandfat[her]s concluded peace with me. Because the goddess, My Lady, had thus shown me (her) recognition, I did not do anything (evil) out of regard for the love for my brother. I took up my [nephew] Kurunta and installed him into kingship there on the spot[62] which my brother Muwatalli had built into the city of Tarḫuntašša. How often had Ištar, the Lady, taken me! She had installed me on 'the high place,' into kingship over Ḫatti Land! I, then, gave Ištar, My Lady, the property of Armatarḫunta: I withdrew it[63] and handed it over. What had been (there) formerly, that I handed over to her, and what I had had, that too I handed over. I withdrew it (all) and handed it over to the goddess.[i]

[i] 2 Sam 8:10-12

The property of Armatarḫunta which I gave to her and whatever settlements were Armatarḫunta's, behind every single cult monument they will erect her (statue) and they will pour a vessel. (For) Ištar (is) my goddess and they will worship her as Ištar the High. The mausoleum which I made myself, I handed it over to the goddess, (and) I handed over to you in subservience my son Tutḫaliya[64] as well. Let Tutḫaliya, my son, administer the house of Ištar! I (am) the servant of the goddess, let him be servant of the goddess as well! The property which I gave the goddess, let everyone strive and strain(?)[65] for the goddess.

Vindication clause

§13 (4:81-85) Whoever will take away in future the offspring of Ḫattušili (and) Puduḫepa from the service of Ištar (or) desires (so much as) a blade of straw from the storehouse (or) a chip of wood from the threshing floor of Ištar of Šamuḫa,[66] let him be Ištar of Šamuḫa's court opponent! Let no one take them for levy (and) corvée![67]

Curse

§14 (4:86-89) Whoever in future stands up against the son, grandson (or) offspring of Ḫattušili (and) Puduḫepa, may he among the gods be fearful of Ištar of Šamuḫa!

[59] Var. "recognized me in."
[60] In a letter to an Assyrian king Ḫattušili complains that until now he has not yet received any gift from him on the occasion of his enthronement, although this is customary; cf. Goetze 1940:28-29.
[61] Or "The king whom I was supposed to respect, (now) respected me" (see Neumann 1985:293-294).
[62] Var. "on that spot."
[63] The property which Ḫattušili once had assigned to Armatarḫunta, is now withdrawn and passed on to Ištar.
[64] Ḫattušili's son and successor, ca. 1240-1210 BCE.
[65] The Hittite uses two rhyme words *karnan marnan*, for which see Wegner 1989.
[66] On this expression here see von Schuler 1983:161-163 and above, p. 197 n. 58.
[67] This sentence is omitted in B and F.

REFERENCES

Text: *CTH* 81. Translation: *TUAT* 1/5:481-492. Discussion: Archi 1971; Cancik 1976; Götze 1925; 1940; Hoffner 1968c; 1975b; van den Hout 1995; Houwink ten Cate 1992; Neumann 1985; Nowicki 1985; Otten 1981a; 1988; von Schuler 1982; Sturtevant and Bechtel 1935; Tadmor 1983; Ünal 1974; Wegner 1989; Wolf 1967.

4. ORACLES

EXCERPT FROM AN ORACLE REPORT (1.78)

Gary Beckman

Since the Hittites believed that divine displeasure was the ultimate source of most evils, they developed a science of divination in order to communicate with their gods, ascertain the reasons for their anger, and bargain about required restitution. The Hittite diviners carefully researched the problems referred to them, making sure both to determine the exact aspect of a situation which had caused a deity's anger and to assure that no additional factors lay behind his or her rancor. Although the responses given by the gods to the questions put to them are characterized as "favorable" or "unfavorable," and indeed were probably originally held to portend in themselves good or ill fortune, they have become arbitrary signs in the later binary system documented in texts available to us. That is, in each particular instance the practitioner stipulates whether a "favorable" or an "unfavorable" response will constitute a "yes" answer to the query posed.[a] For essential bibliography concerning the Hittite practice of divination see REFERENCES below.

The inquiry documented in the text excerpted here was occasioned by the sickness of the Great King. Since the members of the royal family are referred to only by their titles, and most of the other individuals mentioned are not found elsewhere, the precise period to which this text should be assigned is uncertain. However, various linguistic and historical considerations suggest that it was composed early in the reign of Tudḫaliya IV (second half of the thirteenth century BCE).

The technical details of the extispicies and bird oracles have been omitted in this translation.

(obv. 1-3) In regard to the fact that His Majesty (Tudḫaliya IV?) became ill, [...] have not you, [O deity] of (the town of) Arušna, somehow been provoked [in connection with the illness of His Majesty? If you, O deity, are angry about this, let the first extispicy be favorable and the latter] unfavorable. First extispicy: favorable ... unfavorable. Latter [extispicy: ...] Unfavorable.

(obv. 4-5) In regard to the fact that in connection with the illness you, O deity of Arušna, were ascertained to be angry — are you, O god, angry in some way in your temple? (If so), let the extispicy be unfavorable ... Unfavorable.

(obv. 6) If you, O god, are angry only (about something) in your temple, but are not in any way angry with His Majesty, let the extispicy be favorable ... Unfavorable.

(obv. 7-10) In regard to the fact that you, O deity of Arušna, were ascertained to be angry with His Majesty, is this because the queen (Puduḫepa?) cursed Ammattalla before the deity of Arušna? Because Ammattalla began to concern herself with the deity, yet did not go back and forth (in service to the deity)? Because the son of Ammattalla has dressed himself in garments entrusted to his mother and was summoned to the palace? If you, O god, are angry about this, let the extispicy be unfavorable ... Unfavorable.

(obv. 11) If you, O god, are angry only about this, let the duck oracle be favorable. Unfavorable.

(obv. 12-27) In regard to the fact that it was once more unfavorable, is this because Mala spoke as follows: "The queen made for herself a crown of gold in the mausoleum of the Tutelary Deity. In a dream the deity of Arušna demanded it from the queen, but the queen did not give it. She set it aside in the storehouse of the treasurer, and in its place the queen made two other crowns of silver for the deity of Arušna. And as long as she had not sent it (the crown of gold) to the deity of Arušna, the matter brought trouble for the queen, and she was expelled from the palace. Then it happened that the queen wrote back to His Majesty from (the town of) Utruli: 'The crown of gold which the deity of Arušna demanded from me in a dream is now lying in the storehouse of the treasurer. The inlay pieces(?) and the precious stones which were left over (from its manufacture) are now lying in the container for *adupli*-garments. Send them off to the deity!'" They found that crown of gold, and with it lay a falcon of gold, a grape cluster (made up of) precious stones, eight rosettes, ten knobs(?), and eyebrow(s) and eyelid(s) of precious stones. Then they took them to the mausoleum of the Tutelary Deity, to the statue of the queen. But they did not find the inlay pieces(?) which (supposedly) lay in the container for *adupli*-garments. (Of) the two crowns of silver(!) which the queen made for the deity (in fulfillment) of (her) vow, they found (only) one crown of silver(!), and they sent it off to the deity. But they did not find the (other) crown of silver(!). Is it because they spoke as follows: "Whatever is found among the furnishings of the deity will certainly be given to the deity. It will not be exchanged (for something inferior)." Is it because we did not know about the single falcon of gold, the grape cluster (made up of) precious stones, the eight rosettes, the knobs(?), the eyebrow(s) and the eyelid(s), and because they were taken to the mausoleum of the Tutelary Deity, to the statue of the queen? (And because) they did not find the inlay pieces? If you, O god, are angry about this, let the extispicy be unfavorable ... Unfavorable.

(obv. 28) If you, O god, are angry only about this, but not in regard to anything else, let the extispicy be favorable ... Unfavorable.

(obv. 29-30) In regard to the fact that it was once more unfavorable, (is this) because the great princess (daughter of the king of Babylon and wife of Tudḫaliya IV?) secretly [brought] Ammattalla up into the palace? If you, O god, are angry about this, let the extispicy be unfavorable ... Unfavorable.

(obv. 31-32) We have not yet investigated what Ammattalla said — whether the testimony is true, or how (it is to be taken). It has not been included in an oracular inquiry. Now if the omen has occurred because of this, let the extispicy be unfavorable ...

[a] Exod 28:30, etc.

Unfavorable.

(obv. 33) If only this (is the cause of the divine anger), and (there is) nothing else in addition, let the first duck oracle be favorable and the latter unfavorable. The first duck oracle was unfavorable and the latter favorable.

(obv. 34-40) In regard to the fact that it was once more unfavorable, (is this) because the affair of Naru was postponed? Because Naru was brought and spoke of (the affair of the woman) Pattiya? Pattiya was expelled from the palace and will be given to the deity. Concerning the affair of Palla she said: "The queen said: 'May you, O deity, take cognizance of that which I gave to Palla, so that you will keep after Palla (about it).'" We interrogated the associates of Palla, and they said: "We do not know about that affair." And that affair will (therefore) be postponed, (but) we will make inquiries about it. If there is not anything in addition (as the cause of the divine anger), let the first extispicy be favorable and the latter unfavorable. The first extispicy: ... Unfavorable. The latter extispicy: ... Favorable.

(obv. 41-48) In regard to the fact that an omen of the deity of Arušna occurred once more, (is this) because the queen saw a dream? In the dream someone repeats: "Why will you give the furnishings which are in the mausoleum of the Tutelary Deity to the deity of Arušna? Leave something!" If this omen has occurred because of this, let the extispicy be unfavorable. The extispicy was favorable. ... In regard to the fact that it was once more unfavorable, (is this) because Naru [...] said: "Because Pattiya has stayed too long up in the palace, two women shall be included as reparation when she is given to the deity. They shall be clothed in palace garments. And although the queen might die because of that deity, they (still) have not put away (that is, satisfied?) the deity on her account." Because of [that, the reparation was determined upon]. Some [furnishings] will be left behind in the mausoleum of the Tutelary Deity. Those of the royal household will be kept separate. If [... In regard to the fact that] Pattiya has not (yet) been given [to the deity] of Arušna — if you, O deity, have given the omen in respect to this, ditto. Let it be kept separate from the [affair of the palace]. Let the extispicy be favorable ...

(obv. 49-50) In regard to the fact that it was once more unfavorable, (is it) because an offense remains in the mausoleum of the Tutelary Deity? We will make an oracular inquiry about it. Whatever is ascertained will be given to the deity. If you, O deity, have likewise approved, let the extispicy be favorable ... Favorable.

(obv. 51-52) In regard to the fact that that offense in the mausoleum of the Tutelary Deity was determined to remain, should they proceed to give it (that is, a present) with precious stones to the deity? Ditto (= If you, O deity, have approved), let the duck oracle be favorable. Unfavorable.

(obv. 53) Should they give it with gold to the deity? Ditto. Let the duck oracle be favorable. Unfavorable.

(obv. 54) Should they give it with gold and precious stones to the deity? Ditto. Let the duck oracle be favorable. Unfavorable.

(obv. 55) Have you, O deity, sought something with a sumptuous garment for yourself? (If so), let the duck oracle be favorable. Favorable.

(obv. 56) Should they proceed to give (a gift) with gold, precious stones, and a sumptuous garment to the deity? Ditto. Let the duck oracle be favorable. Unfavorable.

(obv. 57) Should they proceed to give (a gift) with a sumptuous garment and a person to the deity? Ditto. Let the duck oracle be favorable. Unfavorable.

(obv. 58) In regard to the fact that a (gift) with a sumptuous garment was ascertained — should they proceed to give one garment to the deity? Ditto. Let the duck oracle be favorable. Unfavorable.

(obv. 59) Should they give one garment and one cowl? Ditto. Let the duck oracle be favorable. Unfavorable.

(obv. 60) Should they give one garment, one cowl, and a woman's *kinanta*-garment? Ditto. Let the duck oracle be favorable. Favorable.

Thus after 60 lines of text, a preliminary conclusion has been reached about some causes of the deity's anger and the necessary compensatory gifts. The report continues, however, for a further 94 lines in which other matters displeasing to the deity and the means by which they might be put right are discussed.

REFERENCES

Text: *CTH* 566; KUB 22.70 obv. 1-60. Bibliography: Archi 1974; 1975; 1982; Hoffner 1987; Kammenhuber 1976; Laroche 1952; 1958; 1970; Ünal 1978; Ünal and Kammenhuber 1975; Schuol 1994:73-124.

ASSURING THE SAFETY OF THE KING DURING THE WINTER (1.79)
(KUB 5.4 + KUB 18.53 and KUB 5.3 + KUB 18.52)[1]

Richard H. Beal

The purpose of the texts comprising this selection is to assure the safety of the king while he is cooped up through the cold central Anatolian winter, by discovering ahead of time any problems that the gods foresee arising, and by ascertaining the correct method of correcting these. The selection is made up of two texts containing parallel sets of questions. The translation follows the better preserved tablet until the second tablet goes off on a tangent. Each section of the tablet not being translated at any one time can be followed in the footnotes.The texts date from the later part of the Hittite Empire period.

The texts, like other Hittite oracle texts, asks the gods a series of questions each phrased so that the gods can give a yes or no answer. If the validity of a good or optimistic statement is being ascertained, the deity is asked to give a "favorable" result. Conversely, if the validity of a bad or pessimistic statement is being ascertained, the deity is asked to give an "unfavorable" answer. A favorable answer to a request for a favorable response or an unfavorable answer to a request for an unfavorable confirms the statement. That is the answer is "yes." An unfavorable answer to a favorable request or vice versa indicates that the question is not true, that is, the answer is "no."

The primary method chosen by the questioner in these texts for the deity to indicate the answer is the "symbol"[2] oracles.[3] In this type of oracle the questions are presented to the deity by the female diviner/exorcist.[4] In this method, native to Anatolia, some symbolically named thing "takes" other symbolically named things and "gives" them to another symbolically named thing. There is no indication how this was performed in practice, but Archi's[5] idea of an animal running over or past certain marked spots on a large gameboard will fit the known evidence. This is particularly true since a rarer related type of oracle, the snake oracle, is clearly performed by having a symbolically named watersnake swim around past symbolically named places in a basin.[6]

The questioner in the second text also employs on occasion another type of oracle known as "flesh," "exta" or in earlier periods "liver" oracles. These questions are presented and interpreted by the male diviner/exorcist.[7] In this method, borrowed from the Mesopotamians via the Hurrians, he asks the god to reply via telltale marks to be found in the exta of sheep.[8]

(KUB 5.4 + KUB 18.53 i 1 - ii 42)

(i 1-10) [Thi]s y[ear His Majesty proposes to wi]nter [in Ḫattuša.] [He will celebrate the customa]ry [festivals,] the festival of the ye[ar], the thunder festival in Ḫattuša. [The birds of the neighborho]od(?)[9] will congregate in Ḫattuša for him. [If] we have nothing to fear[10] for the head of His Majesty up in Ḫattuša and you [O gods] have approved wintering in Ḫattuša for His Majesty, le[t the symbol oracle be favorab]le. 'The deity' took for himself 'the whole soul' and 'blood' and gave them to 'the king.' On the second 'day': 'The gods' arose and took 'well-being,' and gave it to 'the assembly.' One the third 'day': 'The dais' arose and took 'the ye[ar?].' Into 'good.' Favorable.

(11-15) We placed symbols of confirmation as a countercheck. Let the symbol oracle be favorable. 'Ḫannaḫanna'[11] arose and took 'the kindlinesses of

[1] The questions asked in KUB 5.3 + KUB 18.52 i 1-44 are transliterated and translated by Archi 1982:283-286.

[2] This is an attempt to fit a translation of the Sumerogram KIN, which is used to describe this method, to what happens in the course of the method. The Hittite for KIN may be *aniyatt-* which is known to have a translation "ritual gear." Alternatively, perhaps one should understand KIN as *aniur* "ritual" and call these "performance oracles." Both words use the Sumerogram KIN. The old translation "lot" is clearly wrong. The casting of lots (Hittite *pul*) was known, but there are no tablets of questions and answers using lots. For translations of passages involving the throwing of lots see the forthcoming articles in the *CHD pul* n. and *pulai-* v.

[3] See Archi 1974.

[4] Usually known by the literal translation of the Sumerogram MUNUS.ŠU.GI as "the old woman." However, the Hittite word for this profession, *ḫašawa-*, does not consist of "old" + "woman." The *ḫašawa-* performed symbol oracles and various healing/purificatory rituals. This profession is the female equivalent of the ^{LÚ}ḪAL/^{LÚ}AZU, who performed exta oracles, *ḪURRI*-bird oracles and various healing/purificatory rituals.

[5] 1974:130f. Cf. Hallo 1996:115 n. 269, 116 n. 278.

[6] See Laroche 1958.

[7] ^{LÚ}ḪAL/^{LÚ}AZU. Those of this profession performed exta oracles, *ḪURRI*-bird oracles and various healing/purificatory rituals. It is the male equivalent of the female *ḫašuwa*/MUNUS.ŠU.GI.

[8] "flesh" = SU and "exta" = TE. (for Akk. *terētu*), liver = ^{UZU}NÍG.GIG (see KBo 8.55:17). The first two signs are only one wedge apart and practically graphic variants. On this type see in general Laroche 1970, Schuol 1994; and footnotes below to specific words.

[9] MUŠEN.ḪI.A *meyanaš*. F. Starke, BiOr 46 (1989) 662 "die Vögel des Umkreises bzw. der Umgebung." *CHD* s.v. *meya(n)ni*, preferred "birds of the season," "birds of the cycle of the year," that is migratory birds being present only at a particular time of the year. Archi 1975:144 took the word from *miyatar* and translated "ucelli della prosperità." Archi's reasoning is dismissed by *CHD* L-N 233a.

[10] The reading ḪUŠ "fear" not LUL "lie" for this sign was established by H. G. Güterbock, *FsKraus* 83-89. See *CHD* s.v. *naḫ(ḫ)-*.

[11] The grandmother goddess (*ḫanna-* "grandmother"), i.e., the Stormgod's mother. She is one of the wisest of the gods, and very important in childbirth and the giving of fates. For a discussion see Beckman 1983:238-248.

the gods.' Into 'long life.'[12] On the second 'day,' 'the deity' took for himself 'hidden(?) anger.'[13] Into 'emptiness.'[14] On the third 'day': 'The assembly' to[ok] for itself 'rightness' and 'good of the house' and gave them to 'Tarḫunt.'[15] Favorable.

(16-25) This year His Majesty proposes to winter in Ḫattuša. He will celebrate the customary festivals, the festival of the year, the thunder festival in Ḫattuša. [The bird]s of the neighborhood(?) will congregate in Ḫattuša for him. If high fever will not find His Majesty while he is up in Ḫattuša, let the symbol oracle be favorable. 'The Sungod of Heaven'[16] arose and took 'thick-bread' and gave it to 'the assembly.' On the second 'day': 'The anger of the gods' was taken. To 'the lesser sickness.' On the third 'day': 'Good' took 'the kindlinesses of the Fates.'[17] 'To the Fates' whole soul.' Fourth track: 'The gods' arose and took 'the le[sser sickness(?)]' and gave it to 'the assembly.' Favorable.

(26-32) This year His Majesty proposes to winter in Ḫattuša. He will celebrate the customary festivals, the festival of the year, the thunder festival in Ḫattuša. The birds of the neighborhood(?) will congregate in Ḫattuša for him. If we have nothing to fear from revolt while His Majesty is up in Ḫattuša, let the symbol oracle be favorable. 'The king' took for himself 'rightness' and 'the word.' 'The revolt which they make' he placed in 'misbehavior' for them.[18] Unfavorable.

(33-34) Since the oracle was unfavorable, will someone inside revolt? Let the symbol-oracle be unfavorable. 'Evil' was taken and given to 'the assembly.' Unfavorable.

(35-36) Will someone outside revolt? Let the symbol-oracle be unfavorable. 'The deity' took for himself 'the whole soul' and 'fire.' They are placed to the right of the 'king.' Unfavorable.

(a blank paragraph follows)

(37-43) This year His Majesty proposes to winter in Ḫattuša. He will celebrate the customary festivals, the festival of the year, the thunder festival in Ḫattuša. The birds of the neighborhood(?) will congregate [in Ḫat]tuša [for him.] If we have nothing to fear from birds while [His Majesty] is up in Ḫattuša, let the symbol oracle be favorable. 'Tarḫunt' arose and took [...], 'vigor,' and 'the great misdeed' and [gave] them [to ... Favorable.]

(44-50) This year His Majesty proposes to w[inter] in Ḫattuša. He will celebrate the customary festivals, the festival of the year, the th[under] festival in Ḫattuša. The birds of the neighborho[od(?)] will congregate in Ḫattuša [for him]. If we have nothing to fear [from impurity while] His Majesty is up in Ḫattuša, let the symbol oracle be favorable.[...] took [...] and 'the hand.' To 'the gods.' Unfavorable.

(51-ii 1) They will go and give sworn instructions to the kitchen personnel[19] [...] and they will have them swear. If this will make the e[vil] disappear,[20] let the symbol oracle be favorable.'The dais' arose and took 'the king's [...].' To 'the gods.' On the second 'day': 'Ḫannaḫanna' arose and took 'the year' and 'the good of the land.' To 'the great sickness.' On the third 'day': 'The assembly' took for itself 'hidden(?) misdeed.'[21] Into 'emptiness.' Favorable.

(ii 2-7) This year [His Majesty] proposes to winter in Ḫattuša. He will celebrate the customary festivals, the festival of the year, the thunder festival in Ḫattuša. The birds of the neighborhood(?) will co[ngregate] in Ḫattuša for him. If we have nothing to fear from a downpour while His Majesty is up in Ḫattuša, let the symbol oracle be favorable. 'Evil' was taken. To 'the gods.' Unfavorable.

(8-13) This year His Majesty proposes to winter in Ḫattuša. He will celebrate the customary festivals, the festival of the year, the thunder festival in Ḫattuša. The birds of the neighborhood(?) will congregate in Ḫattuša for him. If we have nothing to fear from fire while His Majesty is up in Ḫattuša, let the symbol oracle be favorable. 'The assembly' took 'sinisterness' and 'fire.' Unfavorable.

(14-19) They will go and give sworn instructions concerning fire. If this will make the evil disappear, let the symbol oracle be favorable. 'The gods' arose and took 'life' and gave it to 'the assembly.' On the second 'day': The 'angers of the gods' were taken. To 'the lesser sickness.' On the third 'day': 'Ḫannaḫanna' arose and took 'life' and 'well-[being].' To 'the big sickness.' Favorable.

(20-26)[22] This year His Majesty proposes to winter

[12] Lit., "long years."

[13] *āppan arḫa karpin*. Cf. *āppan arḫa wašdul* below n. 21.

[14] SUD-*li*$_{12}$ = *šannapili*; see Archi 1974:140f., n. 102.

[15] The Stormgod, the chief male deity of the Hittite pantheon.

[16] God of justice, closely associated with the king.

[17] Gulšeš, on these deities see H. Otten and J. Siegelová, *AfO* 23 1970:32-38; Otten *RlA* 3:698; Beckman 1983:242-247.

[18] Or: in "their misdeed."

[19] EN.MEŠ TU$_7$ = *paršuraš išḫeš*. For the translation see *CHD* s.v. *paršur* 2 a.

[20] Lit., "If the evil will disappear on that account."

[21] *āppan arḫa wašdul*. Cf. *āppan arḫa karpin* above n. 13.

[22] This question is parallel to the first question in KUB 5.3 i 1-4.

in Ḫattuša. He will celebrate the customary festivals, the festival of the year, the thunder festival in Ḫattuša. The birds of the neighborhood(?) will congregate in Ḫattuša for him. If we have nothing to fear from accident[23] while His Majesty is up in Ḫattuša, let the symbol oracle be favorable. 'The assembly' took for itself 'rightness.' Into 'evil.' Unfavorable.[24]

(27-29)[25] They will go and give sworn instructions[26] concerning accidents. If this will make the evil disappear, let the symbol oracle be favorable.

(No answer is recorded in the blank lines provided.)[27]

(30-36b)[28] This year His Majesty proposes to wi[nter] in Ḫattuša. He will celebrate the customary festivals, the festival of the year, the thunder festival in Ḫattuša. The birds of the neighborhood(?) will congregate in Ḫattuša for him. If we have nothing to fear from road accident[29] while His Majesty is up in Ḫattuša, let the symbol oracle be favorable. 'The king' took for himself 'hidden(?) misdeed.' [...] Unfavorable.[30]

(37-42) [They will go and give sworn instructions] to the chariot-drivers concerning road accidents. [If] this will [make] the evil [disappear, let the symbol oracle be favorable. ...] took [...] 'life.' To 'the gods.' [... Int]o 'emptiness.' [... were tak]en. To the 'lesser sickness.' [...].[31]

(Another text as far as preserved gives the same series of questions.[32] In this second text, after discovering that road accidents will be a problem, it asks:)

(KUB 5.3 + KUB 18.54 i 23-iii)

(i 23-25) Since a road accident was ascertained for His Majesty, is this road accident due to the anger of some deity? Let the flesh oracle be unfavorable. The *nipašuri*,[33] *šintaḫi*,[34] and *keldi*.[35] The thing(?) took them inside itself.[36] The *zizaḫi*,[37] is placed. Twelve turns of the intestines. Favorable.

(26-29) The question by the female diviner/exorcist is the same. Let the symbol (oracle) be unfavorable. 'The deity' took for himself 'the whole soul,' 'the good of the house' and 'the good of the land.' Behind the 'dais.' On the second 'day': 'The angers of the gods' were taken from 'long life.' To 'the lesser sickness.' On the third 'day': 'The Sungod of Heaven' arose and took 'an evocation ritual' 'fire' and 'the great misdeed.' Into 'emptiness.' F[avorable].

---

[23] ŠU-*aš wašdul*, lit., "misbehavior of the hand." Differently Archi 1982:284f. "Beleidigung" ("insult"). For "the misbehavior of a hand" = "accidental" see Hittite Laws III, where three levels of homicide are mentioned: first degree is in the course of a robbery, second degree is "in a quarrel" and third degree is "(only) his hand misbehaved" (*keššar waštai*). See similarly in Laws 3, V, VI.

[24] In KUB 5.3 an answer is requested from a flesh oracle (i 4), but no answer is inscribed in the space provided. It is followed by the same question to a symbol oracle. The answer: "'The assembly' took for itself 'sinisterness' and 'evil.' To 'the whole soul' for 'the deity.' Unfavorable" (i 5-7).

[25] This question is paralleled by KUB 5.3 i 8-10.

[26] The parallel (i 9) text adds: "to the eunuchs and chariot-drivers."

[27] KUB 5.3 i 11-14 gives an answer to this question: "'The assembly' took for itself 'sinisterness' and 'evil.' Into 'emptiness.' On the second 'day': 'Ḫannaḫanna' arose and took 'well-being.' Behind 'the dais.' On the third 'day': 'The deity' took 'hidden(?) anger.' To 'small sickness.' Favorable."

[28] This question is paralleled by KUB 5.3 i 15-18.

[29] *ḪIṬṬUM* ANŠE.KUR.RA, lit., "misbehavior of a horse." Differently Otten, *HTR* 119 "Verlust an Pferden" ("damage to horses"), followed by Archi 1982:284f. Unlikely is Th. van den Hout's (*BiOr* 51 1994:125) "lack of horses," probably after Friedrich, *HW 2. Erg.* 33 "Mangel," (presumably thinking of Akk. *ḫiṭṭu* for which *CAD* does give a meaning "deficit" rather than Akk. *ḫīṭu*, for which such a meaning is not given (*CAD*: *ḫīṭu* A: "1. fault, harm, 2. act of negligence, 3. damage (OB only), 4. sin, offense, 5. crime, misdeed, 6. punishment"). Hittite *wašdul* is clearly synonomous with Akk. *ḫīṭu* and is probably the Hittite word underlying the Akkadogram. It seems silly to give such different interpretations to "misbehavior of a horse" and "misbehavior of the hand" (for which see above n. 21). If it were to be "damage to/lack of horses," why not then "damage to/lack of hands" in the latter?

[30] In KUB 5.3 a flesh oracle is first asked: "Let the first flesh oracle be favorable and the second unfavorable. The first flesh oracle: The *ḫiriḫi* reached the right/the border. Unfavorable. The second flesh oracle: The *nipašuri*, *šintaḫi*, the path, ten turns of the intestine. Favorable." Then the same question to the symbol oracles yields: "'the assembly' took for itself 'sinisterness.' To 'the whole soul' for 'the deity.' Unfavorable."

[31] The next paragraph in this text is parallel to KUB 5.3 + KUB 18.52 i 42-49, quoted below.

[32] KUB 5.3 + KUB 18.52 i 1-22 (see footnotes). A similar series of questions is found in KUB 18.12 i 1-58: "Have we nothing to fear for the head of His Majesty from death or difficult sickness; from [...]; from [...]; from revolt; from [...]; from road accident; from fire; from downpour; from [...]?" In KUB 18.12 i the questions are all asked of and answers received from bird oracles.

[33] Laroche 1970:131 equated this with the oracle liver (Akk. *amūtu*), but this is surely incorrect. See *CHD* s.v. *nipašuri-*.

[34] A part of the liver, probably equivalent to the Sum. KI.GUB = Akk. *manzazu* "emplacement" and/or *naplastum* "hatch"; see Goetze 1962:28.

[35] This Hurrian word seems to mean "well being" and is a translation of Akk. *šulmu*. Schuol 1994:253-255 takes it to be the pancreas. *AHw* 1269a s.v. *šulmu* C 2 takes no stand: "an der Leber unkl."

[36] NÍG-*aš-za andan* ME-*aš*. The subject could also be read NINDA "bread" or GAR "to be situated." The preverb *andan* occurs with *da-* only in this phrase. The *-aš* could, of course, be the nominative complement (see KBo 16.97 rev. 45 below) of the NÍG, but then the transitive verb *da-* would be left without an object. Laroche 1970:130 understands "un/le GAR s'est resserré/enveloppé," with *-aš* as the nominative complement and *-za* as reflexive object, but *-za da-* is a common combination meaning "to take for oneself" not "to take oneself." Outside of this phrase the NÍG is attested twice in two different phrases: GIŠTUKUL *ŠA* NÍG GÙB-*aš* "The 'weapon' of the 'thing(?)' is of the left" KUB 22.69:11 and NÍG-*aš-šan ANA* NÍG *šer* "A 'thing(?)' is over (another/the other) 'thing(?)' KBo 16.97 rev. 45. This last example appears to rule out NÍG being an abbreviation for NÍG.GIG "liver," unless an apparently healthy animal could have two livers. The "thing" appears to be an organ or large section thereof and of which there is more than one. Our whole sentence is entirely unclear.

[37] This word is translated "Bandwurmfinne" ("undeveloped tapeworm") by Schuol 1994:103, 108 obv 39, 281-284.

(30-31) Will the road accident happen to His Majesty due to the negligence of a person? Let the flesh oracle be unfavorable. The gallbladder was *ḫilipšiman*. Unfavorable.

(32-33) The question by the female diviner/exorcist is the same. Let the symbol (oracle) be unfavorable. 'The gods' arose and took 'an evocation ritual' and gave it to 'the assembly.' Unfavorable.

(34-37b) They will go and give sworn instructions to the c[hariot-drivers] concerning road accidents. If this will make the evil disappear, let the f[irst fle]sh oracle be favorable and the latter unfavorable. The first flesh: *nipašuri*-s [...] on the right and left. A 'bolt' is above them. The *šintaḫi*, *tanani*[38] (and) *keldi*. The *enti* of the left. [...] Favorable. The latter flesh: The SAG.ME. Unfavorable.

(38-41) The question by the female diviner/exorcist is the same. Let the symbol (oracle) be favorable. 'Tarḫunt' [arose and took ...] and gave them to 'the king.' On the second 'day': 'The Sungod of Heaven' arose and took 'the king's [...']. Behind 'the dais.' 'Ḫannaḫanna' arose (and) [took] 'life' [...] To 'the lesser sickness.' Favorable.

(42-49)[39] This year His Majesty proposes to winter in Ḫattuša. If, while His Majesty is up in Ḫattuša there will not be an epidemic among the standing army troops (i.e., the *šarikuwa* and UKU.UŠ)[40] — we are not concerned here if the day of death arrives this year for 10 or 20 soldiers —- if there will not be an epidemic up in Ḫattuša and if a general sudden death does not make us flee down from Ḫattuša, let the symbol oracle be favorable. 'The deity' [took] 'the whole soul' and gave it to 'the assembly.' Unfavorable.

(50-53) The question by the male diviner/exorcist is the same. Let the first flesh oracle be favorable and let the second be unfavorable. The first flesh oracle: The *nipašuri*, *šintaḫi*, *keldi* and the path. The thing(?) took them inside itself. Ten turns of the intestines. Favorable. The second flesh oracle: It is favorable, but behind it is *šuri*. Unfavorable.

(54-57) Concerning an epidemic that was ascertained to occur up in Ḫattuša among the standing army troops, is some deity going to cause the plague up in Ḫattuša? Let the symbol oracle be unfavorable. 'The gods' arose and took 'good.' They(!) placed it in 'anger' for 'the deity.' [Unfavorable.]

(58-63) [I]f the plague up in Ḫattuša within the year [...], let [the symbol oracle be u]nfavorable. 'The gods' arose and to[ok] 'life' and 'well-being.' [...] to 'the whole soul' for 'the deity.' [On the second 'day': ...] took 'evil of [...]' into 'emp[tiness.' On the third 'day': 'The Sungod] of Heaven' arose and took 'a long life' and pl]aced [it] [...]. Favorable.

(ii 1-4) Since the anger of a god was ascertained to be the cause of the plague, will some new deity be causing the plague up in Ḫattuša? Let the symbol oracle be unfavorable. 'The gods' arose and took 'life' and 'the great misdeed.' They gave them to 'the assembly.' Unfavorable.

(5-8) If only a new deity and not also some other deity will be causing the plague up in Ḫattuša, let the symbol oracle be favorable. 'Ḫannaḫanna' arose and took 'the kindlinesses of the gods' and gave them to 'the deity.' Unfavorable.

(9-12) Will it be some Hittite god also causing the plague up in Ḫattuša? Let the symbol oracle be unfavorable. 'The deity' took for himself 'the whole soul' and placed it in 'anger.' Unfavorable.

(13-18) If it will be only a new deity and the Hittite gods who will be causing the plague up in Ḫattuša, and further ditto (= not also some other deity causing it), let the symbol oracle be favorable. 'The deity' took 'the whole soul.' Into 'good.' On the second 'day': 'Evil' was taken. Into 'emptiness.' On the third 'day': 'The Sungod of Heaven' arose and took the 'angers of the gods.' Into 'the lesser sickness.' Favorable.

(19-22) Is the new deity who was determined to be causing the plague a new god of kingship? Let the symbol oracle be unfavorable. 'The deity' took for himself 'the whole soul.' Into 'good.' Unfavorable.

(23-26) If it will be only a new deity of kingship who will be causing the plague in Ḫattuša and not some further deity, let the symbol oracle be favorable. 'Ḫannaḫanna' arose and took 'good' and placed it 'in anger' for 'the deity.' Unfavorable.

(27-29) Is it a new deity (resident) in Ḫattuša who will be causing the plague in Ḫattuša? Let the symbol oracle be unfavorable. 'The assembly' took for itself 'sinisterness.' To the 'great sickness.' Unfavorable.

(30-34) Is the new deity of kingship who was ascertained a new deity of kingship wh[o lives] in a temple? Is that one somehow angry? Let the sym[bol oracle be unfavorable.] 'Ḫannaḫanna' arose and took 'good' and placed it 'in anger' for 'the deity.' Unfavorable.

(35-39) If it is the new deity of kingship who lives in a temple [...] and another new deity is in no way angry, let the [symbol oracle be fav]orable. 'The deity' took for himself 'the whole soul' (and) 'good.' To 'the lesser sickness.' Unfavorable.

---

[38] = Akk. *danānu* "strength."

[39] This paragraph is parallel to KUB 5.4 + KUB 18.53 ii 43-48. Apparently no reply was recorded in the space provided on the latter tablet.

[40] For $^{\text{ERÍN.MEŠ}}$UKU.UŠ and $^{\text{ERÍN.MEŠ}}$*šarikuwa*- comprising the standing army see Beal 1992:37-55.

(40-44) Is it a new deity of kingship who [...] among the gods [...] and that one also is somehow angry? Let the symbol oracle be unfavorable. 'The assembly' took for itself 'sinisterness' and 'the great sickness.' To the 'whole soul' for 'the deity.' Unfavorable.

(45-49b) Since concerning the plague, you, O new [de]ity of kingship, have been determined to be in anger, is it because you have not yet been put on the road (i.e., satisfied)? Let the symbol oracle be favorable. 'The angers of the gods' were taken from 'long life.' To 'Ḫannaḫanna.' Unfavorable.

(50-56) (The next section is too broken to translate, but seems to be asking if this is the only problem.) (Column iii preserves little more than traces. Presumably it contained questions on how to soothe the divine anger.)

(The top two-thirds of column iv are uninscribed. We return to the KUB 5.4 for its next question. KUB 5.3 resumes with a question parallel to the second question of KUB 5.4.)

(KUB 5.4 + KUB 18.53 iii)
(iii 1-2) His Majesty proposes to winter beside the Temple of Tarḫunt of Aleppo. Let the symbol oracle be favorable. (No answer is recorded in the space provided.)

(3-12)[41] This year His Majesty proposes to winter in Kātapa.[42] He will celebrate the customary festivals,[43] the festival of the year, the thunder festival in Kātapa. The birds of the neighborhood(?) will congregate in Kātapa for him. If we have nothing to fear for the head of His Majesty up in Kātapa[44] and if you O gods approved wintering in Kātapa for His Majesty, let the symbol oracle be favorable. 'The king' took for himself 'rightness' and 'the city.' To 'the whole soul' for 'the deity.' On the second 'day.' 'The dais' arose and took 'the year' and gave it to 'Ḫannaḫanna.' On the third 'day': 'Good' took 'the kindlinesses of the gods.' To 'long life.' Favorable.[45]

(uninscribed paragraph)

(13-14)[46] His Majesty proposes to winter[47] in Ānkuwa.[48] Let the symbol oracle be favorable. 'The gods' arose and took 'the city.' To 'the Sungod of Heaven.' Unfavorable.[49] (KUB 5.4 + KUB 18.53 ends here; KUB 5.3 + KUB 18.52 iv continues:)

(iv 13-15) This year His Majesty proposes to winter in Zitḫara.[50] Ditto. Let the symbol oracle be favorable. 'Tarḫunt' arose and took 'protection' and 'the great misdeed.' They are given to 'the assembly.' Unfavorable. (End of text).

[41] This question is paralleled by KUB 5.3 + KUB 18.54 iv 1-5, where it is somewhat abbreviated.
[42] For literature and guesses as to location see *RGTC* 6:197-201, *RGTC* 6/2:75f.
[43] The parallel question fails to mention the customary festivals.
[44] The first part of this sentence was omitted in KUB 5.3 + KUB 18.52.
[45] In the parallel text (iv 6-9) the answer is: "'Good' took 'the future.' To 'the gods.' On the second 'day': 'Ḫannaḫanna' arose and took 'fire.' Into 'emptiness.' On the third 'day': 'The Sungod of Heaven' arose and took 'well-being' and 'the year.' To 'the whole soul' for 'the deity.' [Favorable].
[46] This question is paralleled in the second text by iv 10-11.
[47] The parallel text adds "this year."
[48] Perhaps modern Alişar, see *RGTC* 6:19-23, *RGTC* 6/2:6f.
[49] The answer in the parallel text (iv 11-12) is: "'The gods' arose and took 'the city.' Into 'evil.' Unfavorable."
[50] For literature and guesses concerning the location see *RGTC* 6:513f.

REFERENCES

Archi 1974; 1975; 1982; Beal 1994; Berman 1982; Goetze 1962; Gurney 1981; Hoffner 1993; van den Hout 1991; Kammenhuber 1976; Laroche 1952; 1958; 1970; Lebrun 1994; Schuol 1994:73-124; 247-304; Ünal 1973; 1974; 1978; Ünal and Kammenhuber 1975.

C. INDIVIDUAL FOCUS

1. PROVERBS

HITTITE PROVERBS (1.80)

Gary Beckman

The sayings and generalizing anecdotes by which the Hittites expressed the received wisdom of their civilization were not collected for use in scribal instruction as was the practice in earlier Mesopotamia, but are rather to be found scattered throughout texts of various types. The following is a selection of proverbs and proverbial allusions:

1. [*In a prayer, a queen addresses the chief goddess of Ḫatti, asking her to cure her husband's illness, in return for service which she herself has rendered to the deity's child*:] Among humans one often speaks the proverb as follows: "A god is well-disposed to a midwife." I, Puduḫepa, am a midwife, (and since) I have devoted myself to your son (the Storm-god of Nerik), be well-disposed to me, O Sun-goddess of Arinna, my lady! Give to me [what I ask of you]; grant life to [Ḫattušili (III)], your servant.

2. [*It is probably the same queen who writes in irritation to a young man who had married into the royal family*:] Why does one speak thus: "The son-in-law whose wife has died remains in every sense a son-in-law?" You were my son-in-law, but you do not recognize my relationship(?).

3. [*A high Hittite authority in Syria addresses King Ammurapi of Ugarit concerning his impending divorce from the daughter of the Hittite Great King*:] A proverb of the Hittites: "A man was held in prison for five years. When they said to him, 'You will be released in the morning,' he was annoyed." Now you have acted in this manner. Did the daughter of His Majesty perhaps remove herself from her estate? (Or) [did] *you* somehow [do (it)? You removed her!]

4. [*A Hittite law reads*:] If someone elopes with a woman, and a rescuer goes after them — if two or three men die, there is no legal compensation. "You have become a wolf!"

5. The sin of the father devolves upon his son.[a]

6. Since humanity is depraved, rumors constantly circulate.

7. The will of the gods is severe! It does not hasten to seize, but when it does seize, it does not let go again!

8. (When) a bird takes refuge in its nest, the nest preserves its life.

9. The tongue is a bridge.

10. This one disappears, but that one's still here!

11. [Something] is on hand, (but) something (else) is not on hand.

a Jer 31:29; Ezek 18:2

REFERENCES

Texts: 1. KUB 21.27 ii 15-21; 2. KUB 23.85:7-9; 3. RS 20.216:5-19; 4. KBo 6.2 + ii 10-12; 5. KUB 14.8 rev. 13; 6. KBo 5.13 iv 8-9; 7. KUB 13.4 ii 22-24; 8. KUB 14.8 rev. 22; 9. KBo 11 iii 17; 10. KUB 13.35 iv 45-46; 11. KUB 40.88 iii 9; Bibliography: Beckman 1986; Nougayrol 1960.

2. OTHER WISDOM LITERATURE

FRAGMENT OF A WISDOM TEXT(?) (1.81)

Gary Beckman

The type of composition to which this small piece of a tablet belongs is uncertain.

[If a city is in ruins(?)], then [the builders] will build [it a second time]. If a rhyton [is cracked(?), then] the artisans [will cast] it a second time, [and] they will renew it a second time.

[If someone damages] a plated horse chariot, then its owner [will repair] it [a second time].

[If] a flood carries off an orchard(!), [then] its [owner will establish] the orchard a second time.

[You] are not a town, nor are you [the wall] of a structure, [so that] the builders will build you a second time.

You are not a rhyton, so that the artisans will cast you a second time. You are not a plated [horse chariot, so that] they will repair you a second time.

You are not an orchard, so that [they will establish] you a second time.

REFERENCES

Text: KUB 57.30: 1´-15´; Bibliography: van den Hout 1990:425-26.

EXCERPT FROM THE HURRO-HITTITE BILINGUAL WISDOM TEXT (1.82)

Gary Beckman

The recent discovery at Bogazköy/Ḫattuša of a multi-tablet composition in Hurrian with Hittite translation is very important for the study of the former language, which is still poorly understood. This text is also of significance because the genre of wisdom literature was previously only scantily represented at the Hittite capital. This translation is based primarily on the Hittite text.

(ii 1-15) A mountain expelled a deer from its expanse (lit., 'body'), and the deer went to another mountain. He became fat and he sought a confrontation. He began to curse the mountain: "If only fire would burn up the mountain on which I graze! If only the Storm-god would smite it (with lightning) and fire burn it up!" When the mountain heard, it became sick at heart, and in response the mountain cursed the deer: "The deer whom I fattened up now curses me in return. Let the hunters bring down the deer! Let the fowlers capture him! Let the hunters take his meat, and the fowlers take his skin!"

(ii 17-21) It is not a deer, but a human. A certain man who fled from his own town arrived in another land. When he sought confrontation, he began to undertake evil in return for the town (of his refuge), but the gods of the town have cursed him.

(ii 23-25) Leave that story. I will tell you another story. Listen to the message. I will speak wisdom to you.

(ii 26-30) There is a deer. He grazes the pastures which lie beside the streams. He always casts (his) [eyes] upon the pastures which are on the other side, but he does not reach the pastures of (the other) side. He does not catch sight of them.

(ii 31-38) It is not a deer, but a human. A certain man whom his lord made a district governor — although he was made governor of one district, he always cast (his) eyes upon a second district. Then the gods taught him a lesson, and he did not arrive at that (first) district, nor did he (even) catch sight of the second district.

(ii 39-41) Leave that story. I will tell you another story. Listen to the message. I will speak wisdom to you.

(ii 42-51) A smith cast a cup in a praiseworthy fashion. He cast and moulded it. He inlaid it with ornaments and engraved it. He put a shine on it with a woolen cloth. But the foolish piece of copper began to curse the one who had cast it: "If only the hand of the one who cast me were broken! If only his right forearm were palsied!" When the smith heard, he became sick at heart.

(ii 52-60) He began to say to himself: "Why has this piece of copper which I cast cursed me in return?" The smith uttered a curse against the cup: "Let the Storm-god smash the cup and rip off its ornaments! Let the cup fall into an irrigation ditch and the ornaments fall into a river!"

(iii 1-5) It is not a cup, but a human. A certain son who was hostile to his father became an adult and he moved to (a better) circle. He no longer looks after his father. The gods of his father have cursed him.

(iii 6-8) Leave that story. I will tell you another story. Listen to the message. I will speak wisdom to you.

(iii 9-12) A dog absconded with a loaf of bread from an oven. He pulled it out of the oven and dipped it in grease. He dipped it in grease, sat down, and set about eating it.

(iii 13-19) It is not a dog, but a human. <A certain man> whom his lord had made a district administrator later increased the tax payments in that town. He was very confrontational and no longer looked after the town. They managed to denounce him before his lord, and he began to disgorge before his lord the taxes which he had swallowed up.

(iii 20-22) Leave that story. I will tell you another story. Listen to the message. I will speak wisdom to you.

(iii 28-32) A rodent(?) dragged a loaf of bread from an oven. He pulled it out of the oven and dipped [it] in grease. He dipped it in grease, sat down, and set about eating it.

[It is not] a rodent(?), but a human. <A certain man> whom his lord had made a provincial governor later increased the tax payments in that [town]. He was very confrontational and no longer [looked] after the town. They managed to denounce him before his lord, and he began to disgorge before his lord the taxes which he had swallowed up.

(iii 34) Leave that story. I will tell you another story. Listen to the message. I will speak wisdom to you.

(iii 41-47) [A builder] built a tower in a praiseworthy fashion. He [sank] the foundation trenches down to the Sun-goddess of the Earth. He made the battlements(?) reach up nearly to heaven. Then the foolish [tower] began to curse the one who had built it: "If only the hand of the one who built me were broken! If only his [right] forearm were palsied!" The builder heard and he [became sick] at heart. [The builder] said to himself: "Why has the wall which I built cursed me?" Then the builder uttered a curse [against the tower]: "Let the Storm-god smash the tower and pull up the foundation blocks! Let its [...] fall down into an irrigation ditch and the brickwork fall down into a river!"

(iii 52) It is [not] a tower, but a human. A certain son who was an enemy of his father became an adult, and he attained [an honorable position(?)]. He no longer looks after his father. The gods of his father have cursed him.

REFERENCES

Text: KBo 32.14 ii 1-iii 52; Bibliography: Oettinger 1992; Otten 1984:54-60.

3. INSTRUCTIONS

INSTRUCTIONS TO PRIESTS AND TEMPLE OFFICIALS (1.83)

Gregory McMahon

This text is preserved in at least eight copies, several of which have been reconstructed through multiple joins of tablet fragments. The tablets are to be found in both the Istanbul and Ankara tablet collections. The copies date to the Empire period, but the text itself seems to go back to the pre-New Hittite period, before the reign of Šuppiluliuma I. The main text is KUB 13.4, a large well preserved four column tablet with the tops of columns i and ii broken away. Unless otherwise noted, line numbers given are for that tablet.

§1 (1´-13´) The first paragraph is too broken to translate meaningfully. An estimated twelve lines are missing completely, and lines x+1 through 12´ are only partially preserved. The preserved remnant includes allusions to measures (probably of grain), the palace, and a few prohibitions. Line 13´, although mostly preserved, is not intelligible without the context of previous lines.

§2 (i 14´-33´) Further: Let those who make the daily bread[a] be clean. Let them be washed and trimmed. Let (their) hair(?) and finger[nails] be trimmed.[1] Let them be clothed in clean garments I[f] (they are) [not], let them not prepare (them). Let those who normally [propit]iate the spirit and body of the gods prepare them. The baker's house in which they bake them must be swept and sprinkled down.

a Num 4:7; 1 Chr 9:31-32

Further, neither pig nor dog may come through the doors into the place where the bread is broken. (Are) the mind of man and god somehow different? No! In this which (is concerned)? No! The mind (is) one and the same. When the servant stands before his master, he (is) washed. He has clothed (himself) in clean (clothes). He gives him (his master) either to eat or to drink. Since the master eats and drinks, (in) his spirit he (is) relaxed. He is favorably inclined toward him (the servant). When he (is) solicitous(?), his master) does not find fault (with him). Is the mind of the god somehow different?[2] If the servant at some point angers his master, either

[1] Lit., "taken (off)."

[2] Sturtevant and Bechtel (1935:149), reading the text slightly differently, translate "If, however, he (the slave) is ever dilatory(?), and is not observant(?), he has a different disposition toward him." Goetze (*ANET* 207) translates with a sense similar to Sturtevant and Bechtel's. The passage is unclear because the word for solicitous(?)/dilatory(?) occurs (twice) only here.

they kill him, or they injure his nose, eyes, (and) ears. Or he (the master) [will sei]ze him, (and) his wife, his children, his brother, his sister, his in-laws, (and) his family, whether his (master's) male or female slave. They (may) only call (him) over. They (may) do nothing to him. If ever he dies, he does not die alone. His family (is) also included with him.

§3 (i 34′-38′) If, however, someone angers the mind of a god, does the god seek it (revenge) only from him alone? Does he not seek it from his wife, [his children,] his descendants, his family,[b] his male and female servants, his cattle, his sheep and his grain? He utterly destroys him with everything. Be very afraid of a god's word for your own sake.

§4[c] (i 39′-49′) Further: The festival of the month, the festival of the year, the festival of the stag, the festival of autumn, the festival of spring, the festival of thunder, the festival of *ḫiyara-*, the festival of *pudaḫa-*, the *išuwa-* festival, the festival of *šatlašša-*, the festival of the rhyton, the festivals of the holy priest, the festivals of the old men, the festivals of the *šiwanzanni-* priestesses, the festival of *daḫiya-*, the festivals of the *upati-* men, the festivals of *pula-*, the festivals of *ḫaḫratar*, or whatever festival (there is) up in Ḫattuša: If you do not perform them with all the cattle, sheep, bread, beer and wine set up, (or if) you officials of the temple make a deal with those who provide them (the offering materials), you will cause them (the offerings) to fall short of the will of the gods.[c]

§5 (i 50′-59′) Or if you take them (the offerings) when set up, and do not bring them forth for the pleasure of the gods, (but rather) carry them away to your own houses, and your wives, children, and servants eat them up, or a relative or some important(?) guest comes to you and you give them to him: You are taking them from the pleasure of the god. (If) you do not bring them straight in to him, (or if) you present them (divided) into several portions, that matter of dividing will be upon your head. Do not divide them. And he who does divide them shall die. Let there be no turning back for him.[d]

§6 (i 60′-66′, KUB 13.5+ ii 6-16) Keep all of the bread, beer, (and) wine up in the temple.[3] Let no one omit the thick bread or thin bread of the god.[4] [e] And let no one pour out beer (or) wine off the top of the cup. Render it all to the god. Then speak (this) word for yourselves before the god: "Whoever took from your divine bread (or) libation vessel, may the god my lord pursue him. May he seize his house from bottom to top." If [you are able] to eat (and) drink [everyth]ing on that day, eat and drink it. If, however, you are unable to do so, eat and drink [it within] three days. The *piyantalla-*[5] bread, however, [you may not give] to your wives, children, (or) female or male servants.[6] The beer and wine is not to [cross] the threshold of the gods. If a guest comes to anyone, if he (the host) in order to go up to the temple normally crosses the threshold of the god [or the king, that] one (the host) may [take] him up. He may eat and drink. If, however, he (is) a [forei]gner, (if) he (is) not a native of Ḫattuša (and) he approaches the gods, [he will die]. And it (is) a capital offence for whoever takes him (in).

§7[d] (KUB 13.5 ii 17-33) [If] some [ox or] sheep (is) driven in for the gods to eat, but you take away either the fattened ox or fattened sheep; and you substitute a thin one which you have slaughtered; (and) either you eat up that ox, or you put it into a pen, or you put it under a yoke; or you put the sheep into the fold, or you kill it for yourselves, (or) [you do] as you wish, or [you give] it in exchange to another man and you accept a payment: You are withholding [a morsel] from the mouth of the god. (If) [you give] it [for your own desire],[7] or you give it to another and you think thus: "Because he (is) a god, he will say nothing. He will do nothing to us:" Look at the man who grabs the morsel you desire from (before your) eyes! Afterwards, when it acts, the will of the gods (is) strong. It is not quick to seize. But once it seizes, it does not let go. Be very fearful of the will of the gods.

§8 (ii 25′-51′) Further: Whatever silver, gold, clothing, (and) bronze implements of the gods you hold, (you are) their guards (only).[f] (You have) no (right) to the silver, gold, clothing (or) bronze implements of the gods. What (is) in the house of the gods (is) not (for you).[8] It is for the god. Be very careful. There is to be no silver or gold for the temple official. Let

b Lev 20:5

c Exod 23:14-17; 34:18-24; Lev 23; Deut 16:1-17

d 1 Sam 2:12-17; Mal 1:6-13

e Lev 2:4

f Num 7; Josh 6:19, 24; 1 Chr 9:28-30; 26:20-22

[3] Or with Sturtevant and Bechtel (1935:151): "carry everything up into the temple."

[4] The sense of this is rendered freely by Goetze (*ANET* 208): "Let no one appropriate for himself a sacrificial loaf of the god (or) a thin loaf."

[5] Süel (1985:35) translates "bağış ekmeği," "gift bread", deriving *piyantalla-* from *pai-*, "to give."

[6] Sturtevant and Bechtel (1935:152-153) did not have the duplicate KUB 40.63 and therefore restored the text differently from Süel, whose restoration (p. 34) uses the new duplicate and is therefore more likely.

[7] Following Süel's restoration, p. 38.

[8] These two sentences in the original are difficult to translate exactly, although their sense seems clear. I have followed Goetze's sense (*ANET* 208).

him not carry it on his own body. Let him not make it into an adornment for his wife (or) child. If, however, they give him silver, gold, clothing, (or) implements of bronze as gifts from the palace, let them be listed: "The king gave it to him." As much as its weight (is), let it also be set down. Further, let it be set down as follows: "At this festival they gave it to him." And at the end let the witnesses be set down: "When they gave it to him, this one and this one were standing there." Further, let him not leave it in his house. Let him offer it for sale. When he sells it, he must not sell it in secret. Let the lords of Ḫatti be present and watch. Let them set down on a wooden tablet whatever he buys, and let them seal it. When the king comes up to Ḫattuša, let him take it (the tablet) into the palace. Let them seal it for him. If he sells it as he wishes, it (is) a capital offence for him. But whoever is not selling the gift of the king, on which the king's name (is) stamped, but is nevertheless selling silver, gold, clothing, (or) implements of bronze; whoever gets hold of him, and hides him, and does not bring him to the gate of the kings, it (is) a capital crime for both of them. Let them both die. There is no [...] from the god. There is to be no pardon for them.

§9 (ii 52´-72´) Further, you who (are) temple officials: If you do not perform the festivals at the time of the festivals; (if) you do the spring festival in fall, (or) the fall festival in spring, (or) if the right time for doing the festival (has) arrived, and he who is to do it comes to you, the priests, the "anointing priests," the *šiwanzanni-* priestesses, to you the temple officials, and he seizes your knees, (saying) "The harvests (are) before me," or a marriage or a journey or some other matter. "Let me off.[9] Let that matter finish for me, and when that matter is finished for me, I will do the festival thus": Do not do according to the wish of (that) man. He must not *persuade*[10] you. Do not conduct business concerning the will of the gods. (If) a man *persuades* you, and you take payment for yourselves, the gods will demand it of you at a later time. They will stand in evil against your spirit, wives, children, (and) servants. Work only for the will of the gods. You may eat bread, you may drink water, you may make a house. But do not do the will of a man. Do not sell death, neither buy it.

§10 (ii 73´-iii 20) Further: You who are temple officials, be very careful in the matter of the watch.[g] At nightfall go quickly down and eat and drink. And if anyone has thoughts of a woman, he may sleep with a woman. As soon as the s[un (is) up], let him [immediately bathe]. Let him come up pr[omp]tly into the temple to sleep. Whoever is a temple official — all [high] priests, lesser priests, anointing priests — whoever regularly crosses the threshhold of the gods: let each not neglect to sleep up in the temple. Further, let sentries be posted[11] at night, and let them continue to make the rounds all night. Outside, let the guards keep their watch. But inside the temples let the temple officials make the rounds all night. Let there be no sleep for them. Each night one high priest is to be in charge of the sentries. And further, of those who are priests, someone shall be (assigned) to the temple gate and shall guard the temple.[h] No one (with this duty) is to sleep with his wife in his own house. It (is) a capital offence for whoever they find down in his own house. Guard the temples very carefully, and let there be no sleep for you. Further, let the watch be divided among you. In whose watch a sin[12] occurs, he shall die. Let him not be pardoned.

§11 (iii 21-34) Whatever rite (there is) for someone up in Ḫattuša: If someone normally admits a priest, an anointing priest, or guards, let him admit them only. If there is a guard for anyone, he also must go into the precinct enclosure.[13] Let him not speak as follows: "I am protecting the temple of my god, but I will not go in there." If there is some enemy idea that someone will attempt to cause damage, and those on the outer wall do not see him, (but) the temple officials inside see him,[14] the guard must go after him. Let that (guard) not neglect to sleep next to his god. If, however, he does neglect (to do so), and they do not kill him, let them subject him to public humiliation. Naked — let there be no clothing on his body at all — let him carry water three times from the Labarna's spring into the temple of his

g 1 Chr 9:17-27; 26

h Num 3:6-7, 32, 38; 16:9; 18:2-4, 26-28; 2 Kgs 10:24

[9] Following the *CHD*, sub *memiya-*, p. 273. Lit., the Hittite phrase is "Step back for me." Goetze (*ANET* 209) translates "Do me a favor." Süel (1985:49) translates "Bana destek olunuz," "be a support to me."

[10] The verb is apparently a medio-passive form of the verb "to see." Thus perhaps lit., "He must not appear/show himself to you." Sturtevant and Bechtel (1935:157) translate "let him not be pitied by you." Goetze (*ANET* 209) translates "let him not *take precedence* (of the gods)." Süel (1985:51) translates "Size kötülük etmesin," "let him not do evil to you."

[11] Lit., "taken."

[12] That is, an oversight or mishap. For the parallel with Num 18:7, see Speiser 1963; Milgrom 1970:50-59.

[13] Or "he definitely must go on watch."

[14] Text: "them."

god. Let that be his humiliation.

§12 (iii 35-43) Furthermore you priests, anointing priests, *šiwanzanni-* priestesses (or) temple officials: [I]f some x[ ]-*tuḫmeyanza* person becomes drunk in the temple or another sacred building, and if he causes a disturbance or a quarrel in the temple and disrupts[15] a festival, let them beat him. [Furth]er, he must celebrate that festival as established with cattle, sheep, bread, (and) beer. He may not omit (even) the thin loaf. Whoever neglects it and does not celebrate the festival (as) established, let it be a great sin to that one. Let him make up the festival. Be very careful about quarrels.

§13 (iii 49-54) Further: In the matter of fire be very careful. If (there is) a festival (going on) in the temple, guard the fire well. When night falls, however, extinguish well with water any fire that remains on the hearth. If, however, (there is) in the matter of fire some (burning?)[16] dry wood here and there: Whoever is to extinguish it, even if only the temple in which (this) sin occurs is destroyed, while Ḫattuša and the king's goods are not destroyed, he who commits this sin will perish along with his descendants. Of those in the temple none will be left living. They will perish together with their descendants. Be extremely careful concerning the matter of fire.

§14 (iii 55-83) Furthermore: You who (are) kitchen attendants of all the gods: Cupbearers, tablemen, cooks, bakers, (or) vintners, be very respectful regarding the will of the gods for you. Maintain great respect for the sacrificial loaves (and) libation vessel(s) of the gods. The place for breaking bread must be swept and sprinkled by you. Neither pig nor dog is ever to cross the threshold. You yourselves are to be bathed. Wear clean clothes. In addition, your hair and fingernails are to be trimmed.[17] Let the will of the gods not find fault with you. If a pig or dog does somehow force its way to the utensils of wood or clay that you have, and the kitchen worker does not throw it out, but gives to the gods to eat from an unclean (vessel), to that one will the gods give excrement and urine to eat and drink. Whoever sleeps with a woman, as he performs a rite for the gods (and) gives them to eat and drink, let him go to the woman thus (clean). Furthermore, [break of 2-3 words].[18] As soon as the sun (is) up, he must immediately bathe, and arrive promptly at the time of the gods' eating in the morning. If, however, he neglects (this), it is a sin for him. Whoever sleeps with a woman and his superior (or) his supervisor presses (him), let him say so.[19] However, if he does not dare tell (his superior), let him tell a fellow servant. He still must bathe. However, if he intentionally delays, and without bathing he forces his way near the gods' sacrificial loaves (and) libation vessel (while) unclean,[i] and his fellow servant knows about him, and he appears to him(!)[20]: If he conceals (it), but afterward it becomes known, it (is) a capital offence for them and both must die.

§15 (iv 1-11) [Further: All you who (are) far]rm[ers of the god,] i[f ...] there is anything... Or a sacrific[ial l]oaf o[r...].[21] The first fruits[j] of animals which you, the farmers, present for the pleasure of the gods, present them promptly at the right time. Before anyone has eaten of them, bring them promptly for the pleasure of the gods. Let the gods not be kept waiting for them. If you delay them, it (is) a sin for you. They will consult an oracle about you, and as the gods your lords command, thus will they do to you. And they will fine you an ox and ten sheep and will (thus) calm the mind of the gods.

§16 (iv 12-24) Further: If you plant grain, and if the priest does not send you someone to sow the seed, (and if) he entrusts[22] it to you for sowing, and you sow much, but you declare before the priest that it (was) little, or (if) the god's field (is) productive, but the farmer's field (is) ruined, and you call the god's field yours and your field the god's field, or (if) while you are storing the grain, you declare half (of it), while half (of it) you hide, and you later come and divide it amongst yourselves, (if) it afterward becomes known: You may steal it from a man, but you cannot steal it from a god. It (is) a sin for you. They will take away all your grain and pour it onto the

i Num 19:13

j Exod 23:16, 19; 34:19-20, 22; Lev 2:14; Deut 15:19-21

[15] Lit., "beats."

[16] Süel (1985:65) suggests that the dry wood is wood which has not been completely extinguished.

[17] Lit., "taken."

[18] Süel (1985:71) translates based on her restoration "Sonra kadının yanında yatsın," "Then let him lie next to a woman." This fits the context but does not fit the traces on the tablet very well.

[19] The following lines indicate that the sense of this is that the superior is hurrying the kitchen worker along to his duties unaware that he is unclean.

[20] Text: "you."

[21] Following Süel's restoration (p. 74), which is possible based on my collation of the tablet.

[22] Sturtevant and Bechtel (1935:162) and Süel (1985:76) read a second person pl. verb, but see the *CHD* collation in volume L-N:164 *maniyaḫḫ-* 2.

threshing floor of the gods.

§17 (iv 25-33) Further: You who have the plow oxen of the threshing floor[23] (of the temple): If you sell a plow ox, or you kill and eat it, and you (thus) steal it for yourselves from the gods (saying) "It died of emaciation," or "It kept breaking (things)," or "It ran off," or "A steer gored it," but you yourselves eat it up, and it later becomes known, you will replace that ox. If, however, it does not become known, you will go (before) the god. If you are shown to be innocent, it (is due to) your protective deity. If, however, you are impure (guilty), it is a capital sin for you.

§18 (iv 34-55) Further: You who (are) cowherds (and) shepherds of the god. If (there is) a rite for any god at the time of bearing young, and you are to have either a calf, a lamb, a kid, or *ŠALLITE ḪAGGARATE*,[24] do not delay it. Present it at the appropriate time. Let the gods not be kept waiting for it. Before anyone eats from the first fruits, bring them promptly to the gods. Or if there is a festival of milk[25] for a god, while they are scraping (the cream off?) the milk, do not put it (the festival) off. Perform it for him. If you do not bring the first fruits of the gods promptly, but first eat of them yourselves, or you send them to your superiors, and it afterwards becomes known, it (is) a capital sin for you. If, however, it does not become known, whenever you bring them, you will bring them before the god (speaking) as follows: "If we have given these first fruits for our own desire first, or given them to our superiors, or to our wives (and) children, or to some other person, (then) we have offended the will of the gods." Then you will drain the rhyton of the god of life.[26] If you (are) innocent, (it is) your protective deity. If, however, you (are) guilty, you will perish together with your wives (and) children.

§19 (iv 56-77) Further: If you ever cut out a selection (of animals) and they drive them to the gods your lords, the cowherd and shepherd must go with the selected group. As it (was) selected from the enclosure (and) the fold, thus let them bring it in to the gods. They may not change it later on the road. If some cowherd or shepherd creates a deception while on the road, and turns aside either a fattened ox or fattened sheep, and receives a price (for it), or they kill it and consume it, and they put an emaciated one in its place: If it becomes known, it is a capital sin for them. They have taken the god's most desired portion. If, however, it does not become known, whenever they arrive, they must take the rhyton of the god of life from the offering stand and declare as follows: "If we have withheld the best portion from the mouth of the gods for ourselves and given it to ourselves for our own desire or (if) we have sold it or exchanged it, or accepted a payment for ourselves, (or) put an emaciated one in its place, you, O god, pursue us together with our wives (and) children for the sake of your special portion.

Colophon (iv 78-81) First tablet of the rules of all the temple officials, of the kitchen attendants of the gods, the farmers of the gods, and of the cowherds of the god and shepherds of the god. Completed.

[23] Süel (1985:78) restores DIN[GIR.MEŠ] instead of KIS[LAḪ] and translates "tanrı[ların] çift öküzlerini," "plow oxen of the gods."

[24] Read by Sturtevant and Bechtel (1935:164) as UZU*ša-li-ú(?)-eš ḫa-ag-g[a]-ra-te-(m)eš*. Süel (1985:80) reads UZU*ŠA-LI-T[E]*MEŠ *ḪA-AG-[GUR]-RA-TE*MEŠ. Both readings are possible; neither provides a recognizable phrase.

[25] Sturtevant and Bechtel (1935:164) read EZEN D[U]G, and both Sturtevant and Goetze translate "festival of the cup." Süel (1985:82, 150-151) follows Güterbock (*RHA* XXV/81:141f.) reading EZEN [G]A. She translates "süt bayramı," "festival of milk," which makes sense given that this passage concerns a festival at the time of bearing young. If the reading GA "milk" is correct, the verb probably means "to churn" (*CHD šap-*). It may refer to scraping the cream off the milk. Süel translates "sütü ne zaman yayıkta çalkalarsanız," "when you churn the milk in the churn."

[26] Apparently an ordeal or sealing of the oath.

REFERENCES

Text: *CTH* 264. Studies: Gurney 1967:94; Hoffner 1973a:220; Hulin 1970; Kühne 1978:179-184; Moyer 1983:35-37; Sturtevant and Bechtel 1935; Süel 1985.

INSTRUCTIONS TO COMMANDERS OF BORDER GARRISONS (*BEL MADGALTI*) (1.84)

Gregory McMahon

An essential element in Hittite administration of provinces was the *auriyaš išḫaš*, literally "lord of the watch tower/guard post,"[1] often written with the Akkadogram *BEL MADGALTI*. This was the officer in charge of garrisons and administration in sensitive frontier provinces of the empire. The Hittite term is often translated "border governor";

[1] Hebrew *mispāh*, "watchtower," is the name recorded in the Hebrew scriptures for a number of different cities in Palestine.

Hoffner has proposed "margrave," which implies the idea of governors assigned to frontier provinces. The very detailed instructions for these officials make it clear that they were responsible not only for military command and reconnaissance, but also for administering the city in which they were stationed. This text is perhaps the most important source we have for understanding the nature of the Hittite treatment of conquered territories.

The text is extant in many copies and fragments; the importance of the margraves and their proper understanding of their duties may be inferred from the great number of copies of their instructions. The critical edition of the text is found in von Schuler (1957), which must be supplemented by Goetze's edition of the first fifteen paragraphs in *JCS*.[2] The text is number 261 in Laroche's *CTH*. The main text is KUB 13.2. The first fifteen paragraphs are best preserved in KUB 13.1. Line numbers, unless otherwise noted, are for KUB 13.2.

§1 (KUB 13.1 i 1-3) Thus speaks His Maje[sty Arnuwanda the great king ...] Thus let the margra[ves] be [instructed].

§2 (KUB 13.1 i 4-5) Let [tho]se forward [cities] be [well guarded]. Let the enclosure [be] well guarded.

§3 (KUB 13.1 i 6-8) While the guards have not yet come down from (their) watch, let the scouts [com]e down from the city.

§4 (KUB 13.1 i 9-11) Let them thoroughly inspect the *kuranna*-[3] and bring back a report. The watchmen are to come down from (their) watch in the same way.

§5 (KUB 13.1 i 12-14) The main road scouts must take (their) posts.[4] [a] The sc[outs] must drive down from the city to in[spe]ct the *kuranna*-, and (then) inspect the *kuranna*-.

§6 (KUB 13.1 i 15-16) The scouts who [hold] the p[osts] on the main road, [whatever] they are to find, if [...]

§7 (KUB 13.1 i 17) (Then) they may let out the cattle, sheep, and workers from the city.

§8 (KUB 13.1 i 18-22) But when night falls let the scouts make [...] and take (their) posts. [... the roads(?)] which the scouts wa[tched] by day, they will [in the same way] watch [by night]. They must get the workers, cattle, sheep, horses, (and) donkeys moving and move [them] up [into the city].

§9 (KUB 13.1 i 23-28) Then let the scouts who [hold] po[sts] go up into the city. Let them bar the gates (and) posterns and shoot the bolts.[b] [Further] they must post troops behind the postern gates; they are to sleep behind the gate. Further, let them relieve the guards from (their) watch. They will keep (their) watch carefully.

§10 (KUB 13.1 i 29-32) But in the morning, the scouts [come out(?)] from the city. They must inspect the *kuranna*-s thoroughly [...] and take (their) posts. They may [the]n let the workers, cattle, sheep, horse(s) and donkey(s) down out of the city.

a 1 Sam 14:11-12

b Jer 49:31

§11 (KUB 13.1 i 33-34) Let the scouts hold (their) posts on the main road and let them keep [...] at a distance. Let the city be guarded.

§12 (KUB 13.1 i 35-36) The garrison which holds the posts [must] also [be] protected. The scouts must cover the roads carefully and watch for signs of the enemy.

§13 (KUB 13.1 i 37-38) Furthermore, let the margrave [keep] the garrison [together] at (their) posts. [The garrison] of the post [is to be] gone from the city for two days (maximum).[5]

§14 (i 5′-6′) Since the roads (are) covered, when the scouts see any sign of the enemy, they will send a message immediately.

§15 (i 7′-12′) Let them (then) close up the cities; they are not to let out the fieldworkers, cattle, sheep, horses (or) donkeys. Let them guard (them). The margrave must have kept account and written record of the posts which are most forward and of the enemy's routes. Further: Three scouts shall hold each road. Over the (whole system) three officers are to be in charge.

§16 (i 13′-19′) He (the margrave) must keep an account of the troops of the post and put it in writing. He will know the officers of second, third, and fourth rank in (each) place. And wherever the enemy attacks, the troops are to follow the enemy's track for three days. They are to hold the roads for two days. The margrave must arrest and send before His Majesty anyone who does not kill the enemy, (whether) officer of the second, third, (or) fourth rank.

§17 (i 20′-21′) If, however, His Majesty (is) nearby, the margrave must appear before His Majesty and bring the offenders (with him).

§18 (i 22′-29′) Let them keep an account of the supplies(?)[6] of the fortified cities which (are)

[2] Goetze 1960:69-73.

[3] A duplicate has "*kuranna*-s." Goetze (1960:73) suggests that the meaning of *kuranna*- can only be guessed at, as it only appears here. However, it also appears in the Instructions for the Royal Bodyguard (below, text 1.85). Goetze suggests "foreground." Güterbock and van den Hout 1991 do not translate, but on page 45 discuss the attestations of *kuranna*- and its general semantic range as a "closing device" on the city gates.

[4] Or "The scouts must take (their) posts on the main road."

[5] Duplicate has for the entire paragraph: "Further: the margrave, the troops, (and) the scouts are to be gone (from) the post for two days (maximum)."

[6] See Goetze 1959b:69.

in the province. Those posts (and) cities which (are) forward, into which the enemy can (most) quickly penetrate: When the [mar]grave [...] those cities, as long as [...], let him guard. Within, he [...] [Two lines of cuneiform missing.]

§19 (i 30´-?) [Too broken to translate: Bottom of column i broken away; uncertain how long §19 was, or how many more paragraphs are lost.]

§20´ (KUB 31.84 ii 1-4) ...the tower of ... should be x *gipeššar*[7] at the top, but around the bottom it should be six[8] *gipeššar*. Further, it must be encircled with a gutter and a wooden *mariyawanna*-.[9] The *mariyawanna*- is to be six *gippeššar* around the front, but let it (protrude?) five *šekan*.

§21´ (KUB 31.86 ii 6´-12´) [When] you fortify a [city],[c] let *ḫutanu*-s [of x] m[eters] be taken/removed. Up on top, let there be x [met]ers. Before you complete the fortifying of the city, the moat is to be three meters deep and two meters across. Before he *refills* [it] with water, let them pave [it] with stones.

§22´ (KUB 31.86 ii 13´-18´) Furthermore, let the gates, posterns, heads of stairways (and) windows of city-walls [b]e furnished with doors (and) bolts. Let nothing (of these) be lost.[10] [Do not neglect] to apply plaster to the city-wall. And let it be smoothed. A thatched roof may become leaky. Let it not (happen).

§23´ (KUB 31.86 ii 19´-25´) In the ... which you build, let the coppersmith make a [...] drain. Let the gates of the city-walls [be equipped with drains(?)] of stone inside and outside in the same way. Furthermore: allow no one to dig in the city wall or burn near it. The owners must not let (their) horses, mules, (or) donkeys near the plaster (of the city-wall).

§24´ (KUB 31.86 ii 26´-32´) No one is to put a torch on a wooden(?) [...] inside or outside. No one may take (part of) the city wall for an inn,[11] [d] nor may anyone start a fire near the wall. Allow no one to quarter their horses (or) m[ules there]. The city drains must not become clogged; they must be cleared out every year.

§25´ (ii 5´-10´) The margrave should organize the firewood for the fortified cities as follows: It should be twelve[12] fingers in diameter[13] and ⅔ meter in length. The diameter of the [x] wood is to be three fingers, with a length of ½ meter. The wood for the ... should also be (stored) in great quantity. [...] (and) *ḫardup-pi*-, all are to be (stored) in great quantity.

§26´ (ii 11´-15´) Let it (the wood(?)) be stored under seal. Every year he (the margrave) is to take account of it and deposit it with the *šaramna*-. Let them (the troops(?)) scrape the buildings of the king, cattle barns, storehouses and baths which are older. They must replaster them with new stucco and renew them.

§27´ (ii 16´-20´) Let them regularly remove from the (interior) walls the plaster which is crumbling. Let them uncover the foundation stones[e] (for inspection).[14] Furthermore, the threshing floor, the straw barn, the temple, the baths, (the buildings associated) with the orchards, the vegetable gardens, and the vineyards must be built properly.

§28´ (ii 21´-25´) The drains of the bath, the cupbearers' building, and the portico must flow freely; let (the men) regularly inspect them. Any that is stopped up with water they should clear out. And let the bird ponds which are in your district be well looked after.[15]

§29´ (ii 26´-31´) In a city through which the margrave drives, he shall take account of the elders, priests, anointing priests, (and) *šiwanzanni*- priestesses. He shall speak to them thus: "A temple which (is) in this city, either that of the Stormgod, or of some other god, is now neglected," or (")It (is) ruined.(")

§30´ (ii 32´-35´) (")It (is) not attended to with regard to priests, *šiwanzanni*- priestesses, (and) anointing priests. Now attend to it again.(") Let them restore it. As it was built before, let them rebuild it in the same way.

§31´ (ii 36´-41´) Furthermore: Reverence for the gods must be maintained, and special reverence for the Stormgod is to be established. If some temple (roof) leaks, the margrave and the city commander must repair it. Or (if) some rhyton of the Stormgod or any cultic implement of another god (is) ruined, the priests, anointing priests, and *šiwanzanni*-priestesses will renew it.

c 2 Sam 5:9

d Josh 2:15

e 1 Kgs 7:10; Ps 118:22

[7] A linear measurement, probably .5 meter; see Melchert 1980.
[8] Variant "three."
[9] This word occurs only in this passage; see *CHD* L-N 186 for discussion.
[10] Or "destroyed."
[11] Cf. Josh 2:15; see Hoffner 1974b.
[12] Variant: "five."
[13] Lit., "from the front."
[14] Variant adds: "They are not, however, to lift out the foundation stones."
[15] Or: "Let the birds which are on the ponds in your district be well looked after."

§32´ (ii 42´-46´) Furthermore: The margrave is to write down the cultic implements of the god and send it (the record) in to His Majesty. Further, they are to worship the gods at the (proper) times. Whatever is the (proper) time for any god, let them worship him at that time. (If) there is no priest, *šiwanzanni*-priestess, or anointing priest for any god, they must immediately assign one.

§33´ (KUB 40.56+31.88 iii 2, KUB 13.2 iii 1-3) Or whatever old cultic stela (there is), (if) it has not been kept track of, do an accounting of it now. Let them set it up, and furthermore whatever sacrifices (there were) for it formerly, let them provide for them.

§34´ (iii 4-8) Whatever springs (are) in the city, sacrifices are established for (those) springs: Let them celebrate them and attend to them. They must definitely attend (also) to those springs for which there is no sacrifice.[16] Let them not omit them. They must consistently sacrifice to the mountains and rivers for which there are rites.

§35´ (iii 9-16) Further: the margrave, the city commander (and) the elders must consistently judge cases properly, and carry out (their decisions), as the rule for serious crimes (has been) done from of old in the (particular) country: In a city in which they are accustomed to execute, let them continue to execute. In a city, however, in which they are accustomed to exile, let them continue to exile. Furthermore, afterward (the people) of the city must bathe, and further let it be announced: Let no one allow (the exile) back. Whoever does allow him back, they will keep him under observation(?).

§36´ (iii 17-21) And when they worship the gods, let no one cause a disturbance in the presence of the gods, and let no one cause a disturbance in the festival house. Furthermore, let reverence be established toward priests, temple workers, anointing priests, (and) *šiwanzanni*- priestesses. Let the priests, anointing priests, and *šiwanzanni*- priestesses be reverent to the gods. If, however, anyone brings a case (in the form of) a sealed wooden (or) clay tablet, the margrave must judge the case properly and make things right. If, however, the case is too great (for him), he is to send it before His Majesty.

§37´ (iii 25-28) Let him not, however, decide for (his) superior (or) for (his) brother, his wife, or his friend. Let no one take a bribe.[f] He is not to make the stronger case the weaker, or the weaker the stronger one. Do what (is) just.[g]

§38´ (iii 29-35) In whatever city you enter, call all the people of the city. Judge a case for anyone who has one and make things right. If a man's slave, or a man's female slave or a widow has a case, judge it for them and make things right. People of Kašiya, Ḫimmuwa, Tegara[ma][h] or Išuwa (may be) there. Supply them with everything.[17]

§39´ (iii 36-41) A deportee who (has been) settled on the land you must supply with winter food stores,[18] seed, cattle, (and) sheep. Provide him also with cheese, rennet (and) wool. Sow seed for whoever stays in the place of a deportee who leaves your province, and let him have sufficient fields. Let them promptly assign him a plot.

[§40´ (KUB 13.2 iii 42-44, KUB 31.84 iii 45´-46´) and §41´ (KUB 31.84 iii 47´-51´) are too fragmentary to translate. §40´ mentions field, orchard, garden, and the palace. § 41´ mentions horses and the palace.]

§42´ (KUB 31.84 iii 52´-56´) [...] ... [... Let] him build the walls [of the orchard]s well. In addition, irrigate them with water. Irrigate the meadow also with water. Let the meadow not be grazed.

§43´ (KUB 31.84 iii 57´-59´) Furthermore: Let the vine[yards] be well cultivated and constructed and the canals kept clean. Further, the word of the scout(?)[19] must be taken seriously.

§44´ (KUB 31.84 iii 60´-65´) When, however, they distribute the seed to the deportees, the margrave must keep an eye on all of them. If someone speaks in this way: "Give me seed. I will plant it in my field, and further I will add (it) to my food supply," then the margrave must keep an eye on (him). When harvest arrives, he (the margrave?) [is to] harvest that field.

§45´ (KUB 31.84 iii 66´-71´) All must be written down for you — the abandoned fields of a craftsman who has left, and those which (are) plots. When, however, they give out deportees, let them promptly assign places to them.[20] Keep an eye concerning the matter of building on those who (are) assigned(?) to the fields. Let (things) be built well.

[§§ 46´-51´ are too broken for connected translation.]

f 1 Sam 8:3; 12:3

g Lev 19:15

h Gen 10:3

[16] By establishing sacrifices for them.

[17] Or: "Pay attention to them in all things."

[18] Suggested translation of *išḫueššar* by Harry A. Hoffner, Jr. (personal communication).

[19] Or "inspector." See *CHD* L-N 369 sub *nakkiyaḫḫ*- 2.c for discussion and a collated reading of the text different from von Schuler.

[20] Text: "him."

§51´ (iv 13´-20´) Investigate thoroughly the palaces (and) dignitaries' houses which (are) in your province, whether someone has damaged anything or taken anything, or (if) someone has sold something, or (if) someone has broken into a granary or killed any of the king's cattle, or eaten (from) the granaries and then falsified the record tablets. Keep careful account of these (things).

§52´ (iv 21´-26´) Or (if) somone has taken something away from the servants, the margrave must arrest him and send him into His Majesty's presence. He must keep an eye on the king's cattle in winter. Support[21] the work of winter (and) of harvest. Let the soup-places[22] be well looked after. Let ice be collected, and let an ice storage house be built.[23]

§53´ (iv 27´-?) Keep account of the plantings of the vegetable garden(s) and fields. Let them be enclosed (with fences). The portion which (is) for the *pireš̮hanna-* cattle, let them eat that portion.

[The remainder of the paragraph is partially or completely broken away.]

§54´ [Only one sign remains of this paragraph. Uncertain how many more paragraphs are lost at the end of the tablet.]

[21] Lit., "stand behind."
[22] Variant: "and the soup-houses."
[23] See Hoffner 1971 for elucidation of this passage and the recognition that it had to do with collecting ice.

REFERENCES

Text: *CTH* 261. Translation: *ANET* 210-211; Goetze 1959a; 1959b; 1960; Hoffner 1971; 1973b; Melchert 1980; von Schuler 1957.

INSTRUCTIONS TO THE ROYAL GUARD (*MEŠEDI PROTOCOL*) (1.85)

Gregory McMahon

The royal bodyguard of the Hittite court are denoted by the Akkadogram MEŠEDI. One extant tablet contains instructions for them, primarily detailing their duties as they assume responsibility for the king's safety from the palace staff and as they escort him while he travels. Areas of responsibility are clearly delineated among the officials who see to guarding the palace and the king, primarily certain members of the palace staff, the MEŠEDI guard, the men of the golden spear and the gatekeepers. These last carefully monitor the movements of the guard.

The tablet, which is housed in Istanbul, is an unusual and difficult one, primarily because a number of additions in a smaller script were made to the text after its initial composition. Deciding how to fit these into the text of the instructions is a formidable problem. I have followed Güterbock and van den Hout's transliteration (1991), which included a good deal of reconstruction of the text in placing the additions. The text is full of technical terms for various ranks and offices within the Hittite army and bureaucracy, discussion of which continues among Hittitologists. I have in general followed Güterbock and van den Hout in their translation of these terms. These terms are discussed very thoroughly in Beal 1992. I have also in general followed Güterbock and van den Hout in their understanding of technical terms for various structures within the Hittite palace complex; a section of their work is devoted to commentary on architectural terms.

Column I

§1 (i 1-8b, 19b-21b) [The first line is broken away, the second partially broken.] [When] the guards [go] up [to the palace],[a] they [parade] before the gatekeepers[b] and courtyard sweepers. They go in and take their place at the courtyard's gates. Their eyes are turned outward, and they cover one courtyard of the palace.[1] [c] Then (the courtyard sweepers) sweep. *(added):* In the morning they raise the gate's bolts[2] on the outside, but they [...]. The guards [wa]lk in front; they lift them as well as the *kuranna-*. The bolt of the gatehouse, however, they do not raise. The [guar]ds, the gatekeepers, (and) the courtyard sweepers come out. However, if inside, on one side of a building, a bolt (has) not (been) raised, or they are going to open some storehouse and the key (?)[3] is lacking; if a low-ranking member of the palace staff comes out, the

a 2 Kgs 11:6
b 1 Chr 9:17-27
c 1 Kgs 7:9-12

[1] The architectural term [É]*halentu-* has long been debated as to the structure it denotes. Güterbock and van den Hout (1991:59-60) argue convincingly that the *halentu-* building is the palace.
[2] Or "bars;" see Goetze 1960:73.
[3] The word here is GI, the Sumerogram for "reed." Güterbock and van den Hout's translation "key" is based on context (1991:46, with discus-

man of the golden spear does not give it to him. (However), when an upper level member of the palace staff comes out, either a commander of ten or an army bailiff (or) a [gua]rd comes, they give the key (?) to that one. If [...] comes out, (then) either a guard or a man of the go[lden spear ...] comes and [...] [end of addition]

§2 (i 9-15) The guards take up (their) position in the courtyard of the guards.[d] At the wall which is on the inside, against the palace, twelve guards stand and hold spears. If twelve guards (can) not stand up — either someone (has been) sent on a journey, or someone (has been) given leave (to go) to his home — and there are too many spears, they take away the spears that remain and leave them with the gatekeepers.

§3 (i 16-19, B-C 1′, D-E 1′-5′) At the wall, however, which (is) on the gate side, the men of the golden spear are standing. One guard, however, stands near the gates on one side, against the wall of the guard. And one man of the golden spear stands near the gates on the other side, against the wall of the men of the golden spear. They stand the watch in the daytime.[e] [...] But in the courtyard of the guards only a comander of ten of the men of the golden spear is to command. If someone stands (at attention) poorly o[r ...] ... [...] Only the commander of ten of the men of the golden spear com[man]ds them. [...] ... One member [of the palace staff ...] If, however, (it is) a guard, each says [it] to the other. If [...] turns, once again [...] at the wall says the same to [...].

§4 (i 22-26) When the chief of the guard and the commander of ten of the guards come up: Because the chief of the guard has a staff, when he bows before the Tutelary Deity of the Spear, a guard who is high ranking takes the staff away from him. He places it on the altar. However, the staff which the commander of ten of the guard is holding he gives to a [...] guard, who holds it for him.

§5 (i 27-32) All the [guard]s, however, w[ho hav]e staffs: Whenever they come [u]p, the g[uards] surrender [the staffs to the g]atekeeper. If, however, the king [does not designate a man], he [does not send] out a palace attendant, guard, or man of the golden spear. [If,] however, the king does designate [him], he sen[ds] him out. If, [however,] it (is) the last man,[4] he does not sen[d] him out willingly.

§6 (i 33-38) The guard [does not go] to the gate at his own discretion. If he has only to urinate, he walks behind all the guards and says to the guard who is standing in front of him: "I (need to) go to the toilet." (That) guard will speak to the next guard, that one will speak to a man of third rank, and the man of third rank will speak to a man of second rank.

§7 (i 39-42) The man of second rank, however, will speak to the commander of ten of the guard. If a chief of the guard is in the formation, (that is) he is in the [court]yard of the guard, the commander of [ten of the guar]d brings it (before) the chief of the guard: "He (needs to) go to the toilet." The chief of the guard will say: "He may go."

§8 (i 43-47) If, however, a bowel movement presses someone, he will tell it one to another, (until) it reaches the chief of the guard: "He (needs to) go relieve himself." The chief of the guard will say, "He may go." However, (if) His Majesty notices the guard who is going to relieve himself, (then) the matter of relieving oneself has reached the palace. But he may not go at his own discretion.

§9 (i 48-52) A guard does not step into the portico[5] on his own. If, however, he does step (in) on his own, the gatekeeper will become angry at him (and say) "Either go up, or else go down." If, however, a guard goes out through the portico, he carries (his) spear through the portico, but (when) he arrives at the postern, he leaves the spear with the gatekeeper, and he goes on down.

§10 (i 53-59) If, however, a guard slips away and takes (his) spear down through the postern, the gatekeeper shall seize him in (his) offence, and shall loosen his shoes.[f] If however, the guard fools the gateman and takes (his) spear down, and the gatekeeper does not see him, the guard will seize the gatekeeper in (*his*) fault, (and say) "Since you did not see the spear, if some man tried to enter, how would you see him?" They will inform the palace about him, and they will question the gatekeeper. That (much) care regards the spears.

§11 (i 60-63) The guards (and) the palace staff do not go down through the main gate. They are to go down through the postern. One guard who is escorting a defendant, (or) someone whom the commander of messengers sends

d 2 Kgs 11:18b-19

e Judg 7:19

f Deut 25:5-10; Ruth 4:7-8

sion).

[4] Or with Güterbock and van den Hout (1991:9) "a [lowly(?)] man."

[5] The Hittite is ^{É}*ḫilammar*, which has been thought to be a gatehouse. Güterbock and van den Hout (1991:60) note that the ^{É}*ḫilammar* itself has a gate, and suggest that it is a pillared hall or portico.

out, he may go down through the main (gate). Lords and commanders of a thousand also may go down through the main (gate).

§12 (i 64-69) When, however, the king goes out, one palace attendant comes out of the palace and calls out "*Taḫaya*" in Ḫattic. *Taḫaya* (is what) they call the barber in Ḫattic. A guard, a man of the golden spear, and a gatekeeper go to the gatehouse. They lift off the doorbolt from the main gate. They open the doors inward, and the man of the [gold]en spear [...] ... The barber, however, holds a *galama-* and wipes off the doors.

§12a (i 69-74) The grooms turn the carriage, but the guards step next to the vestibule[6] on the right. If, however, in some city setting up on the right (is) not possible, they take their place on the left. What (is) constant (is) their setting up next to the vestibule. The guard who holds the stool [...] for the carriage lets no one in or out. They leave from the court of the guards.

§13 (i 75-77) Two *zinzinuil-* men stand (there). They hold maces [and ...] An officer of the army stands with them; he [holds] a staff.[g] Further, they are clothed in [go]od [clothes], like *ḫilammi-* men. They [...]

§14 (i 78-89) [After] that (there is) an interval of [one I]KU,[7] (then) two m[en... stand]. They hold [...] [Two more illegible lines to the bottom of the column.]

Column II

§15 (ii 1-4) After that (there is) again an int[erval of one IKU ...] Two men of a field army unit are standing. With them stand [a commander of a field unit] and an army bailiff. [They hold ... , and they] (are) walking before [the king].[h]

§16 (ii 5-8) After that again (there is) an interval of one IKU. [...] stand and hold spears. With them stand [a commander of a field unit] and an army bailiff. They hold sticks. They (are) walking before the king.

§17 (ii 9-14) Two officers of the spear-men, however, sta[nd] on the right opposite the king. They do not hold spears. A man of the golden spear [stands] wi[th them]. He holds a gold-plated [spe]ar. The palace attendant of the spear, however, holds a [...], a whip, and the sistrum[8] of the carriage. He (is) walking in front of [the king]. He goes and takes his place on the left of the carriage, next to the wheel.

§18 (ii 15-19) The guard sets up the stool. The king comes forth. The chief of the palace staff is holding him by the hand. The king sits in the carriage. The officers of the spear-men bow. Then they run (up) and walk in front. They march with the man of the [golden] spear.

§19 (ii 20-25) The man of the golden spear who stood with them, however, ... [...]. But the palace attendant of the spear gives the whip to the chief of the palace staff. The chief of the palace staff gives it to the king. The chief groom (is) walking in front of the carriage; he holds a staff. And when the carriage moves out, the chief of the palace staff bows after it, and gives over the king to the chief of the guards.

§20 (ii 26-31) The guard, however, who holds the stool, marches with the palace attendant of the spear at the wheel of the carriage on the left side. But when it reaches the gatehouse, he steps behind a *widuli-* . When the guards and palace staff are lined up with him, he gives the stool to the ma[n of the st]ool. He takes a spear and marches with the guards.

§21 (ii 32-38) While the guards march, two guards (are) walking in front. They hold spears, and they (are) in formation. [On] (their) left a palace attendant marches, carrying a lituus. He also (is) in formation with the two g[uard]s, so the three of them together (are) in formation. The guards (and) the [palace] attendants march in three groups: two groups of guards and one of palace attendants. They march one IKU behind the carriage.

§22 (ii 39-43) One palace attendant, however, goes; the supply officer gives him one strung bow, enclosed in a case, (and) one quiver (*added:* of a spear-man) filled with arrows.[i] He goes behind, and moves along separated from the guards and palace attendants. He goes and takes his place at the left wheel of the carriage.

§23 (ii 44-46) After that (there is) an interval of one IKU. (Then) a man of the golden spear holds a plated spear, and the physician holds a sistrum(?). They march together, and the physician recites spells.

§24 (ii 47-50) After that (there is) an interval of one IKU. (Then) two spear-men march. They (are) either high-ranking or low-ranking officers. They are clothed in good ceremonial garments (and) shoes like *ḫilammi-* officials. A chief of the spear-men and an army bailiff march with them. They hold staffs.

§25 (ii 51-55) After that (there is) again an interval of one IKU. Then two men of a field unit

g 2 Kgs 11:8, 11
h 1 Sam 8:11
i 2 Kgs 11:10

[6] The Hittite term ^{É}*arkiu-* denotes some kind of structure near the door. See Güterbock and van den Hout's discussion (1991:61-64).
[7] See Melchert (1980:50-56) for discussion of this procession and his use of it for determining the length of an IKU as fifteen meters.
[8] Güterbock and van den Hout (1991:50-51) discuss the evidence that a ^{GIŠ}*mukar* makes noise and the reasons for positing "sistrum."

march. They hold spears and (are) either high-ranking or low-ranking officers. They are clothed in good ceremonial garments (and) shoes like *ḫilammi-* officials. A field unit commander and an army bailiff march with them. They hold staffs.

§26 (ii 56-59) After that (there is) again an interval of one IKU. Then two men of a field unit march, holding spears. They are clothed in good ceremonial garments (and) shoes like *ḫilammi-* officials. A field unit commander (and) an army bailiff march with them. They hold staffs(?).

§27 (ii 60-63) The soldiers who (are) from a field unit keep the peaceful (crowd) lined up on the side.[j] The left (group) keep (it) lined up on the left, the right (group) keep (it) lined up on the right. They march three IKU apart. If, however, somewhere ahead of one the road (is) narrow, he moves in tighter.

§28 (ii 64-67) Then if someone of the first (two) allows something in — whether horses or an out of control ox, it (is) the fault of the first one. If, however, some one of the last (two) allows something in, it (is) the fault of the last one.

§29 (ii 68-75) [If], however, they bring in a defendant, ... [...] ... spears. Him ... [...] They set up [...] [Five lines lost at the end of column ii.]

j 2 Kgs 11:14

Column III

§30 (iii 1-5) [The gu]ard who [brings in] the defendants [takes his place] behind the man of the golden spear. [But when] the king requests a case, the guard [picks] it [out] and pl[aces] it in the hand of the chief of the guard. He tells the chief of the guard [what] the case (is), but the chief of the guard [tells the king].

§31 (iii 6-11) Then the chief of the guard goes, and two lo[rds stand[9]] behind him; whether chiefs of chariot-fighters or commanders of ten, they stand [behind] the chief of the guard. One (man) holds the outside, whether a gu[ard or] some official. The guard who brings in the defendants runs back. He goes and takes his place (next) to the man of the golden spear. Then they pick out one case.[10]

§32 (iii 12-16) The chief of the palace staff, however, stands with the palace staff. Behind him stand two members of the palace staff; they are three. When they release a defendant, however, the chief of the guard stays in (his) place, but the two lords who stand behind him (*added*: either lords o[r gu]ards,) they go back and rejoin the guards.

§33 (iii 17-22) But when the guard who holds the outside brings in another defendant, the two lords who stand behind the chief of the guard march beside the defendant on the inside. The guard who holds the outside, however, goes behind the defendant when they line up the defendant with the guards. He walks on the outside of the defendant, on (his) right.

§34 (iii 23-26) If, however, a palace attendant brings in a message later, he comes in on the left only, behind the palace attendants. But when he comes back, he comes the same way, but he comes across in front of the guards.

§35 (iii 27-30) The guard who goes behind (him) goes on the right behind the guard. He goes back the same way, on the right. However, he does not go in front of the guards. He goes with the palace attendant.

§36 (iii 31-34) If, however, a defendant is standing (there), but (there is) a case for a guard or for a palace attendant, he does not go in front of the defendant. He goes behind him, and takes his place with the guard who holds the outside.

§37 (iii 35-40) But if the king calls out some foreign soldiers,[11] either soldiers of the enemy Kaška, or soldiers of Kummaḫa or whatever soldiers, all the guards go behind (them). If, however, the spears prove to be too few for them, they take spears away from the spear-men and (then) go behind. They call that "encircling."

§38 (iii 41-46) Armed with staffs, however, they do not go behind, it (is) not proper for them. If someone among the guards who remain has no spear, because they (can) take (only) staffs, they are not to be formed up with the pal[ace] attendant of the lituus. Two different palace attendants step forward into for[ma]tion with him. The guards however who are holding staffs [wal]k [behind(?)] them.

§39 (iii 47-50) If however a *ḫazannu*[12] or commander of army bailiffs [is part of the for-m]ation, they[13] form up with them. For them it (is) proper. However, [if] they go behind the carriage, [they] may not go behind (it) armed (thus) with staffs; they take spears.

[9] Or "walk."

[10] That is, the next one.

[11] ERÍN.MEŠ, "soldiers," can also mean simply "people." Güterbock and van den Hout (1991:55) note that this may refer to foreign peoples being brought to court.

[12] See Güterbock and van den Hout (1991:55) for commentary on *ḪAZANNU* and the difficulties with the translation "mayor."

[13] The guards who were forced to walk behind because they only had staffs.

§40 (iii 51-54) When the defendants have been completed, when the last defendant whom they escort out goes in front, the guard who brings the defendants says to the chief of the guard (*added*: or to ... (or) to the guard who holds the inside): "It (the group of defendants) has been encircled." The chief of the guard, (*added*: or the commander of ten guards or the army bailiff) tells the king. "It is completed."

§41 (iii 55-59) If the king requests a chariot, a guard brings the stool and places it. The king grasps the chariot.[14] The guard (responsible) for finishing (the process) holds a staff and takes the right horse by the bit in (his) right hand. With (his) left, however, he holds a *kapur*[15] along with the staff. He holds the chariot down in front (so that) it does not tip.[16]

§42 (iii 60-62) The guards give the spears which they are holding to the groom [...]. When the carriage gets back home the groom gives the spears to the gatekeeper. He takes them up to the portico.

§42a (iii 63-65) If, however, (the king) returns by carriage, one guard waves with a spear to the guards and to the palace attendants and speaks thus in Hittite: "Over to the side."

§43 (iii 66-70) The guards and palace attendants run around to the rear, and the grooms [reach(?)] over the left mule and turn the carriage around. The spears, however, of the spear-men and field unit men turn around; (thus) the first becomes the last.

§44 (iii 71-75) He (the king) goes to the palace by carriage. [As] he draws near the gates, the chanters [and] the r[eciter fall in] behind the spears of the spear-men. When the chanters [come] within the gates they cry out "Welcome!" The reciter, however, does not [cry out].

§45 (iii 76-78) When, however, the carriage['s mules] reach [the gates,] the chanters [and the reciter] cry out.

Column IV

§46 (iv 1-7) [Men of] the city Ḫaḫḫa (are) walking behind. The spear[s] of the spear-men and [of the men] of the golden spear (are) walking in front, but the men of Ḫaḫḫa [ma]rch behind and sing. When however, the chanters come within the [gat]es of the portico, they cry out "Welcome!," although the reciter [sti]ll does not cry out. However, when the mules reach the gates, the chanters and the reciter cry out. They they go down through the postern.

§47 (iv 8-13) When just half [of] the spear-men has gone through the portico, it goes into that (place) where the spear-men (normally) go (after having) put down (their) spears. But a guard takes the stool and detaches himself from the palace attendants on the left. He walks to the wheel on the left side. When they turn the carriage, he sets up the stool.

§48 (iv 14-17) The men of Ḫaḫḫa (during this) are quiet. They do not come up to the gates [of the pal]ace. If (there are) two por[ticoes, however,] they come up to the lower gate. They do not, however, come up to the upper gate.

§49 (iv 18-24d) When the king steps down from the carriage, if a chief of the guard is standing (there), the chief of the guard prostrates himself behind (the king). He hands the king back over to the palace chief of staff. If, however, some other dignitary is lined up there in the front line, he (also) prostrates himself. But if no high dignitary is lined up there, the guard who is standing (there) prostrates himself. (*added*): Whenever he (the king) goes somewhere via chariot, however: When the king step[s] down from the chariot, [the chief of the gu]ard along with the guards prostrates himself behind the king. The guard (responsible) for finishing up prostrates himself opposite the right wheel of the chariot. The chariot driver, however, prostrates himself opposite the left wheel.

§50 (iv 25-27) The king goes [into] the palace. A guard, a man of the golden spear, (and) a gatekeeper g[o] in. They [come] up from the main gatehouse. They throw the doorbolt.

§51 (iv 29-30) The man of the golden spear leaves the plated spear which he holds in the courtyard where the guards normally step into the inne[r cha]mber.

§52 (iv 31-33) However, the guards who [hold] spears go out to the courtyard of the guards and take up (their) [position]. They stand there, hold[ing] spears. They do not put [them down].

§53 (iv 34-36) The guard, however, whom they [send(?)] goes out, holding a spear. He [comes down from(?)] the palace. But [when] he arrives at the postern, [he leaves] (his) spear with the gatekeeper [at the portico].

[14] Güterbock and van den Hout (1991:29) suggest "mounts," which is certainly the correct sense.

[15] Probably not the tongue of the chariot, for which the Hittite is *ḫišša-*. Güterbock and van den Hout (1991:74) suggest "yoke peg(?)."

[16] This paragraph contains a number of unusual or unique words. Güterbock and van den Hout (1991:56) comment on several of these words and give a good overview of evidence for their translation and the overall sense of the passage, much of which is translated on the basis of context.

Ditto (i.e. he goes [out].)

§54 (iv 37-39) As soon as [the food] is done[17] the footman [brings] from the ki[tchen ...] (and) one cooked joint. And from the creamery [he brings] one pitcher of [sweet milk]. He gives [it to] the guards, and they eat it.

§55 (iv 40-41) They give [...], one cooked joint, (and) one pitcher of sweet milk to the palace attendants also. And [they eat] it.

§56 (iv 42-44) But when [...] comes [into the] inn[er chamber]. He calls out as follows to the man [of the golden spear and (?) ... in Hitti]te: "[Let] them bring [it]."

§57 (iv 45-46) However, the man of the golden spear [...] calls out as follows to the spear-men in Luwian: ["..."]

§58 (iv 47-49) A spear-man, however, [takes] a spe[ar]. The bronze (blade) [of the sp]ear (is) tu[rned] down. He goes into the kitchen. [The spear-man(?)] speaks as follows: "To the inner chamber [...]."

§59 (iv 50-52) Then the spear-man [...]. The bronze (blade) of the spear, however, [is turned] up[ward ...] The [...] man [...] [of(?)] the palace [...]

Colophon (iv 53) First tablet of the Rules of the Guard. Not finished.

[17] Lit., "becomes good."

REFERENCES

Text: *CTH* 262; IBoT 1.36; Jakob-Rost 1965; Güterbock and van den Hout 1991. Discussion: Alp 1940; Beal 1992; Goetze 1960; Melchert 1980; von Schuler 1957.

HITTITE BIBLIOGRAPHY

AKURGAL, E.
n.d. *The Art of the Hittites*. New York: Harry N. Abrams.
ALP, S.
1940 *Untersuchungen zu den Beamtennamen im hethitischen Festzeremoniell*. Leipzig: Otto Harrassowitz.
ARCHI, A.
1971 "The Propaganda of Ḫattušiliš III." *SMEA* 14:185-215.
1974 "Il Sistema KIN della Divinazione Ittita." *OA* 13:113-144.
1975 "L'ornitomanzia ittita." *SMEA* 16:119-180.
1977 "I poteri della dea Ištar Ḫurrita-Ittita." *OA* 16:297-311.
1979 "L'humanité des hittites." in *Studies Laroche*.
1982 "Hethitische Mantik und ihre Beziehungen zur mesopotamischen Mantik." 25ième *RAI* (1978) = *BBVO* 1:279-293.
1987 *KUB*. Heft 57.
BADALÌ, E.
1987 "Eine neue Lesung im Anfang des Anitta-Textes." *WO* 18:43-44.
BALKAN, K.
1957 *Letter of King Anum-hirbi of Mama to King Warshama of Kanish*. Ankara: Türk Tarih Kurumu Basımevi.
BEAL, R. H.
1986 The Organization of the Hittite Military. Ph.D. Dissertation. University of Chicago.
1988 "The ^{GIŠ}TUKUL-institution in Second Millennium Ḫatti." *AoF* 15:269-305.
1992 *The Organisation of the Hittite Military*. THeth 20. Heidelberg: Carl Winter Verlag.
1993 "Kurunta of Tarḫuntašša and the Imperial Hittite Mausoleum." *AnSt* 43:29-39.
1994 "Hittite Oracles: Questions and Answers." in *Magic and Divination in the Ancient World, Proceedings of a Conference held Feb. 18, 1994 in Berkeley*. Ed. by L. Ciraolo and J. Seidel. Groningen: Styx.
BECKMAN, G. M.
1982 "The Anatolian Myth of Illuyanka." *JANES* 14:11-25.
1983 *Hittite Birth Rituals*. StBoT 29. Wiesbaden: Otto Harrassowitz.
1985 "Review of Hoffmann 1984." *JAOS* 106:570-572.
1986 "Proverbs and Proverbial Allusions in Hittite." *JNES* 45:19-30.
BERMAN, H.
1982 "Some Hittite Oracle Fragments." *JCS* 34:94-98.
BERNABÉ, A.
1987 *Textos literarios hetitas*. Madrid: Alianza.
BÖRKER-KLÄHN, J.
1992 "Illustration zum hethitischen Eidritual." Pp. 69-72 in *Studies Alp*.
BOSSERT, H. Th.
1946 *Asia*. Istanbul: Literarische Fakultät der Universität.
BRYCE, T. R.
1989 "Some Observations on the Chronology of Šuppiluliuma's Reign." *AnSt* 39:19-30.
n. d. *The Major Historical Texts of Early Hittite History*. Asian Studies Monograph 1. Brisbane: University of Queensland.
BURDE, C.
1974 *Hethitische medizinische Texte*. StBoT 19. Wiesbaden: Otto Harrassowitz.
CANCIK, H.
1976 *Grundzüge der hethitischen und alttestamentlichen Geschichtsschreibung*. Abhandlungen des Deutschen Palästinavereins. Wiesbaden: Otto Harrassowitz.
CARRUBA, O.
1964 "Hethitisch -*(a)sta*, -*(a)pa* und die anderen 'Ortsbezugspartikeln.'" *Or* 33:405-436.
1968 "Contributo alla storia di Cipro nel II millennio." *SCO* 17:5-29.
1971 "^{d}GI$_{6}$." *RlA* 3:355.
1974 "Tahurwaili von Hatti und die heth. Geschichte um 1500 v. Chr. G." Pp. 73-93 in *Studies Güterbock*.
COLLINS, B. J.
1989 *The Representation of Wild Animals in Hittite Texts*. Ph.D. Dissertation Yale University.
1990 "The Puppy in Hittite Ritual." *JCS* 42:211-226.
CORNIL, P.
1994 "Guerre et armé hittites." *RIDA* 41:99-109.
DEL MONTE, G. F.
1991-92 "Ulmitešub re di Tarhuntaša." *EVO* 14-15:123-148.
DEL MONTE, G. F., and J. TISCHLER.
1978 *Die Orts- und Gewässernamen der hethitischen Texte*. Ed. by W. Röllig. RGTC 6. Wiesbaden: Dr. Ludwig Reichert Verlag.
DINÇOL, A. M., B. DINÇOL, J. D. HAWKINS, and G. WILHELM.
1993 "The 'Cruciform Seal' from Boğazköy-Ḫattuša." *IM* 43:87-106 and Tafel 6.
EHELOLF, H.
1937 "Die Tontafeln." *MDOG* 75:61-70.
EITREM, S.
1947 "A Purificatory Rite and Some Allied *Rites de Passage*." *SO* 25:36-53.
FEDERN, W.
1960 "Dahamunzu (KBo V 6 iii 8)." *JCS* 14:33.

FORRER, E.

1922, 1926 *Die Boghazköi-Texte in Umschrift. Zweiter Band. Geschichtliche Texte.* WVDOG 42/1-2. Leipzig: J. C. Hinrichs'sche Buchhandlung.

FRIEDRICH, J.

1924 "Der hethitische Soldateneid." *ZA* 35:161-191.

1925 "Aus dem hethitischen Schrifttum." *Der Alte Orient* 25/2:1-32.

GOETZE, A.

1925 *Ḫattušiliš. Der Bericht über seine Thronbesteigung nebst den Paralleltexten.* MVAG 30. Leipzig: Hinrichs'sche Buchhandlung.

1930 "Die Pestgebete des Muršiliš." *KlF* 1:161-251.

1933 *Die Annalen des Muršiliš.* MVAG 38. Leipzig: J. C. Hinrichs'sche Buchhandlung.

1940 *Kizzuwatna and the Problem of Hittite Geography.* YOR 22. New Haven: Yale University Press.

1959a "Review of von Schuler 1957." *JCS* 13:65-70.

1959b "Remarks on the Lists from Alalaḫ IV." *JCS* 13:63-70.

1960 "The Beginning of the Hittite Instructions for the Commander of the Border Guards." *JCS* 14:69-73.

1962 "Review of H. G. Güterbock and H. Otten, *Keilschrifttexte aus Boghazköi* 10." *JCS* 16:24-30.

GONNET, H.

1987 "Institution d'un culte chez les hittites." *Anatolica* 14:89-100.

GURNEY, O.R.

1967 "VBoT. Nos. 95 and 97." *JCS* 21:94.

1977 *Some Aspects of Hittite Religion.* The Schweich Lectures 1976. Oxford: Oxford University Press.

1981 "The Babylonians and Hittites." Pp. 142-173 in *Oracles and Divination.* Ed. by M. Loewe and C. Blacker. Boulder: Shambhala.

GÜTERBOCK, H. G.

1936 "Die historische Tradition und ihre literarische Gestaltung bei Babyloniern und Hethitern bis 1200 (2. Teil)." *ZA* 44:45-149.

1946 *Kumarbi: Mythen vom churritischen Kronos.* Zürich: Europa Verlag.

1956 "The Deeds of Suppiluliuma I as Told by His Son, Mursili II." *JCS* 10:41-68, 75-98, 107-130.

1960 "Mursili's Accounts of Suppiluliuma's Dealings with Egypt." *RHA* XVIII/66:57-63.

1967 "The Hittite Conquest of Cyprus Reconsidered." *JNES* 26:73-81.

1983 "Hittite Historiography: A Survey." In *HHI* 21-35.

1995 "Reflections on the Musical Instruments *arkammi, galgalturi,* and *ḫuḫupal* in Hittite." Pp. 57-77 in *Studio Historiae Ardens. Ancient Near Eastern Studies Presented to Philo H. J. Houwink ten Cate on the Occasion of his 65th Birthday.* Ed. by Th. P. J. van den Hout and J. de Roos. PIHANS 74. Leiden: Nederlands Historisch-Archaeologisch Instituut te Istanbul.

GÜTERBOCK, H. G., and Th. P. J. VAN DEN HOUT.

1991 *The Hittite Instruction for the Royal Bodyguard.* AS 24. Chicago: The Oriental Institute of the University of Chicago.

HAAS, V.

1993 "Ein hurritischer Blutritus und die Deponierung der Ritualrückstände nach hethitischen Quellen." Pp. 67-85 in *RGBK.*

HAAS, V., and I. WEGNER.

1979 "Review of Lebrun 1976." *OLZ* 74:124-128.

HAASE, R.

1984 *Texte zum hethitischen Recht. Eine Auswahl.* Wiesbaden: Reichert.

HALLO, W. W.

1996 *Origins.* Leiden: E. J. Brill.

HAWKINS, J. D.

1990 "The New Inscription from the Südburg of Boğazköy-Hattuša." *AA* 1990 305-314.

HEINHOLD-KRAHMER, S.

1991-92 "Zur Bronzetafel aus Boğazköy und ihrem historischen Inhalt." *AfO* 38-39:138-158.

HELCK, W.

1984 "Die Šukzija-Episode im Dekret des Telipinu." *WO* 15:103-108.

HOFFMANN, I.

1984 *Der Erlaß Telipinus.* THeth 11. Heidelberg: Carl Winter Verlag.

HOFFNER, H. A., Jr.

1965 "The Elkunirsa Myth Reconsidered." *RHA* XXIII/76:5-16.

1966 "Symbols for Masculinity and Femininity: Their Use in Ancient Near Eastern Sympathetic Magic Rituals." *JBL* 85:326-334.

1967 "Second Millennium Antecedents to the Hebrew *ᵓôb.*" *JBL* 86:385-401.

1968a "Birth and Namegiving in Hittite Texts." *JNES* 27:198-203.

1968b "Hittite *tarpiš* and Hebrew *terāphim.*" *JNES* 27:61-68.

1968c "A Hittite Analogue to the David and Goliath Contest of Champions?" *CBQ* 30:220-225.

1971a "Hittite *ega-* and *egan-.*" *JCS* 24:31-36.

1971b *Or* 40:327-329.

1973 "The Hittites and Hurrians." In *POTT* 197-228.

1974a *Alimenta Hethaeorum.* AOS 55. New Haven: American Oriental Society.

1974b "The *Arzana* House." Pp. 113-122 in *Studies Güterbock.*

1975a "Hittite Mythological Texts: A Survey." Pp. 136-145 in *Unity and Diversity.*

1975b "Propaganda and Political Justification in Hittite Historiography." Pp. 49-62 in *Unity and Diversity.*

1977a "Hittite Lexicographic Studies, 1." Pp. 105-107 in *Studies Finkelstein.*

1977b "Review of E. Neu 1974." *BASOR* 219:78-79.

1979 "The Hittite Word for 'Tribe'." Pp. 261-266 in *Studia Mediterranea Piero Meriggi dicata.* Ed. by O. Carruba. Pavia: Aurora Edizioni.

1980 "Histories and Historians of the Ancient Near East: The Hittites." *Or* 49:283-332.

1981 "The Hurrian Story of the Sungod, the Cow and the Fisherman." Pp. 189-194 in *Studies on the Civilization and Culture of Nuzi and the Hurrians in Honor of E. R. Lacheman.* Ed. by M. Morrison and D. I. Owen. Winona Lake, IN: Eisenbrauns.

1982 "The Old Hittite Legal Idiom *šuwaye-* with the Allative." *JAOS* 102:507-509.
1987 "Ancient Views of Prophecy and Fulfillment: Mesopotamia and Asia Minor." *JETS* 30/3:257-265.
1990 *Hittite Myths*. Writings from the Ancient World 2. Atlanta: Scholars Press.
1992 "The Last Days of Khattusha." Pp. 46-52 in *The Crisis Years: The 12th Century B.C. From Beyond the Danube to the Tigris*. Ed. by W. A. Ward. Dubuque, Iowa: Kendall/Hunt Publishing Company.
1993 "Akkadian *šumma immeru* Texts and Their Hurro-Hittite Counterparts." Pp. 116-119 in *Studies Hallo*.
1995 "On Safari in Hittite Anatolia." *JIES* 23.

VAN DEN HOUT, Th. P. J.
1990 "Review of Archi 1989." *BiOr* 47:423-432.
1991 "Hethitische Thronbesteigungsorakel und die Inauguration Tudḫalijas IV." *ZA* 81:274-300.
1995 "Khattushili III, King of the Hittites." In *CANE* 2:1107-1120.

HOUWINK TEN CATE, Ph. H. J.
1966 "A New Fragment of the 'Deeds of Suppiluliuma as Told by his Son Mursili II'." *JNES* 25:27-31.
1992 "The Bronze Tablet of Tudhaliyas IV and its Geographical and Historical Relations." *ZA* 82:233-270.

HULIN, P.
1970 "A New Duplicate Fragment of the Hittite Instructions to Temple Officials." *AnSt* 20:155-157.

IMPARATI, F., AND C. SAPORETTI.
1965 "L'autobiografia di Hattusili I." *SCO* 14:40-85.

JAKOB-ROST, L.
1965 "Beiträge zum hethitischen Hofzeremoniell (IBoT I 36)." *MIO* 11:165-225.

JANOWSKI, B., and G. WILHELM.
1993 "Der Bock, der die Sünden hinausträgt. Zur Religionsgeschichte des Azazel-Ritus Lev 16,10.21f." Pp. 109-169 in *RGBK*.

JOSEPHSON, F.
1979 "Anatolien *tarpa/i-*, etc." Pp. 177-184 in *Studies Laroche*.

KAMMENHUBER, A.
1976 *Orakelpraxis, Träume und Vorzeichenschau bei den Hethitern*. THeth 7. Heidelberg: Carl Winter.

KELLERMAN, G.
1986 "The Telepinu Myth Reconsidered." Pp. 115-124 in *Studies Güterbock*[2].

KEMPINSKI, A.
1993 "Suppiluliuma I: The Early Years of His Career." Pp. 81-91 in *Studies Kutscher*.

KITCHEN, K. A.
1962 *Suppiluliuma and the Amarna Pharaohs*. LMAOS. Liverpool: Liverpool University Press.

KLENGEL, H.
1965 "Die Rolle der 'Ältesten' (LÚ.MEŠ ŠU.GI) im Kleinasien der Hethiterzeit." *ZA* 57:223-236.

KOŠAK, S.
1993 "Die Staatwerke von Ḫattuša." *Linguistica* 33:107-112.

KRAUSS, R.
1978 "Sōᵓ, König von Ägypten — ein Deutungsvorschlag." *MDOG* 110:49-54.

KRONASSER, H.
1963 *Die Umsiedelung der Schwarzen Gottheit: Das hethitische Ritual KUB XXIX 4 (des Ulippi)*. SÖAW 241.3. Vienna: Österreichische Akademie der Wissenschaften.

KÜHNE, C.
1978 "Instructions." Pp. 179-184 in *Near Eastern Religious Texts Relating to the Old Testament*. Ed. by W. Beyerlin. Philadelphia: Westminster.

KÜMMEL, H. M.
1967 *Ersatzrituale für den hethitischen König*. StBoT 3. Wiesbaden: Otto Harrassowitz.

LAROCHE, E.
1952 "Élements d'haruspicine hittite." *RHA* XII/54:19-48.
1958 "Lécanomancie hittite." *RA* 52:150-162.
1965 "Textes mythologiques hittites en transcription. Première Partie." *RHA* XXIII/77:63-178.
1966 *Les Noms des Hittites*. Études linguistiques 4. Paris: Klindsieck.
1968a "Textes mythologiques hittites en transcription. Deuxième Partie." *RHA* XXVI/82:7-90.
1968b *Textes mythologiques hittites en transcription*. Paris: Klincksieck.
1970 "Sur le vocabulaire de l'haruspicine hittite." *RA* 64:127-139.

LEBRUN, R.
1976 *Samuha. Foyer religieux de l'empire hittite*. Publications del'institut orientaliste 11. Louvain: Université Catholique de Louvain.
1980 *Hymnes et prières hittites*. Homo Religiosus 4. Louvain-la-Neuve: Centre d'Histoire des Religions.
1994 "Questions oraculaires concernant le nouveau déroulement de fêtes secondaires de printemps et d'automne = CTH 568." *Hethitica* 12:41-77.

LEWIS, B.
1980 *The Sargon Legend: a Study of the Akkadian Text and the Tale of the Hero who was Exposed at Birth*. ASORDS 4. Cambridge, MA: American Schools of Oriental Research.

MALAMAT, A.
1955 "Doctrines of Causality in Hittite and Biblical Historiography." *VT* 5:1-12.

MASSON, O.
1950 "A propos d'un rituel hittite pour la lustration d'une armée: Le rite de purification par le passage entre les deux parties d'une victime." *RHR* 137:5-25.

MELCHERT, H. C.
1977 *Ablative and Instrumental in Hittite*. Ph.D. Dissertation. Harvard University. Cambridge, MA.
1980 "The Use of IKU in Hittite Texts." *JCS* 32:50-56.

MILGROM, J.
1970 *Studies in Levitical Terminology*. Berkeley: University of California Press.
MOORE, G. C.
1975 *The Disappearing Deity Motif in Hittite Texts: A Study of Religious History*. B.A. Thesis. Oxford University.
MORAN, W. L.
1992 *The Amarna Letters*. Baltimore: The Johns Hopkins University Press.
MOYER, J. C.
1983 "Hittite and Israelite Cultic Practices: A Selected Comparison." In *SIC* 2:19-38.
NEU, E.
1974 *Der Anitta-Text*. Ed. by Otten. StBoT 18. Wiesbaden: Otto Harrassowitz.
NEUMANN, G.
1985 "Review of Otten 1981." *IF* 90:288-295.
NOUGAYROL, J.
1960 "Une fable hittite." *RHA* XVIII/67:117-19.
NOWICKI, H.
1985 "Ein Deutungsvorschlag zum "Großen Text" des Ḫattušili III." *KZ* 98:26-35.
OETTINGER, N.
1976 *Die Militärischen Eide der Hethiter*. StBoT 22. Wiesbaden: Otto Harrassowitz.
1992 "Achikars Weisheitssprüche im Lichte älterer Fabeldichtung." Pp. 3-22 in *Der Äsop-Roman. Motivgeschichte und Erzählstruktur*. Ed. by N. Holzberg. Tübingen: G. Narr.
OTTEN, H.
1953 "Ein kanaanäischer Mythus aus Boğazköy." *MIO* 1:125-50.
1955 "Neue Fragmente zu den annalen des Mursili." *MIO* 3:153-179.
1961a "Eine Beschwörung der Unterirdischen aus Boğazköy." *ZA* 54:114-157.
1961b "Das Hethiterreich." In *Kulturgeschichte des Alten Orient*. Ed. by H. Schmökel. Stuttgart: Alfred Kröner Verlag.
1963a "Neue Quellen zum Ausklang des Hethitischen Reiches." *MDOG* 94:1-23.
1963b "Aitiologische Erzählung von der Überquerung des Taurus." *ZA* 55:156-168.
1973 *Eine althethitische Erzählung um die Stadt Zalpa*. StBoT 17. Wiesbaden: Otto Harrassowitz.
1981 *Die Apologie Ḫattušilis III. Das Bild der Überlieferung*. StBoT 24. Wiesbaden: Otto Harrassowitz.
1984 "Blick in die altorientalische Geisteswelt. Neufund einer hethitischen Tempelbibliothek." *Jahrbuch der Akademie der Wissenschaften in Göttingen* 50-60.
1988 *Die Bronzetafel aus Boğazköy: Ein Staatsvertrag Tuthalijas IV*. StBoT Beiheft 1. Wiesbaden: Otto Harrassowitz.
OTTEN, H., and C. RÜSTER.
1978 "Textanschlüsse und Duplikate von Boğazköy-Tafeln (61-70)." *ZA* 68:270-279.
1981 "Textanschlüsse und Duplikate von Boğazköy-Tafeln (71-80)." *ZA* 71:122-134.
OTTEN, H., and W. VON SODEN.
1968 *Die akkadisch-hethitische Vokabular KBo I 44 + KBo XIII 1*. StBoT 7. Wiesbaden: Otto Harrassowitz.
OWEN, D.
1981 "An Akkadian Letter from Ugarit at Aphek." *Tel Aviv* 8:1-17.
PARKER, S. B.
1989 "*KTU* 1.16 III, the Myth of the Absent God and 1 Kings 18." *UF* 23:283-296.
PECCHIOLI DADDI, F., and A. M. POLVANI.
1990 *La mitologia ittita*. Testi del Vicino Oriente antico 4/1. Brescia: Paideia Editrice.
POPKO, M.
1978 *Kultobjekte in der hethitischen Religion*. Warsaw: Warsaw University.
POSTGATE, J. N.
1987 "Notes on Fruit in the Cuneiform Sources." *BSAg* 3:115-144.
RÜSTER, C.
1992 "Zu einem neuen Fragment des Telipinu-Mythos." Pp. 475-481 in *Studies Alp*.
VON SCHULER, E.
1957 *Hethitische Dienstanweisungen für höhere Hof- und Staatsbeamte*. Graz: Private. Reprint: Osnabrück: Biblio-Verlag, 1967.
1982 "Die Einleitung der "Autobiographie" Ḫattušilis." Pp. 389-400 in *Serta Indogermanica. Festschrift für Günter Neumann zum 60. Geburtstag*. Ed. by J. Tischler. IBS 40. Innsbruck.
SCHUOL, M.
1994 "Die Terminologie des hethitischen SU-Orakels. Eine Untersuchung auf der Grundlage des mittelhethitischen Textes KBo XVI 97 unter vergleichender Berücksichtigung akkadischer Orakeltexte und Lebermodelle, I." *AoF* 21:73-124, 247-304.
SCHWARTZ, B.
1938 "The Hittite and Luwian Ritual of Zarpiya of Kezzuwatna." *JAOS* 58:334-355.
SINGER, I.
1984 "The AGRIG in the Hittite Texts." *AnSt* 34:97-127.
1995 "'Our God' and 'Their God' in the Anitta Text." Pp. 471-480 in *Atti del II congresso internazionale di hittitolgia*. Ed. by O. Carruba, M. Giorgieri and C. Mora. Studia Mediterranea 9. Pavia: Gianni Iuculano.
SOMMER, F.
1921 "Ein hethitisches Gebet." *ZA* 33:85-102.
SOYSAL, O.
1987 "KUB XXXI 4 + KBo III 41 und 40 (Die Puḫanu-Chronik). Zum Thronstreit Ḫattušilis I." *Hethitica* 7:173-253.
1990 "Noch einmal zur Šukziya-Episode im Erlass Telipinus." *Or* 59:271-279.
SPEISER, E. A.
1963 "Unrecognized Dedication." *IEJ* 13:69-73, repr. in *Biblical and Oriental Studies*.

STARKE, F.
1977 *Die Funktionen der dimensionalen Kasus und Adverbien im Althethitischen.* StBoT 23. Wiesbaden: Otto Harrassowitz.
1979 "Halmasuit im Anitta-Texte und die hethitische Ideologie vom Königtum." *ZA* 69:47-120.
1985a "Der Erlaß Telipinus. Zur Beurteilung der Sprache des Textes anläßlich eines kürzlich erschienenen Buches." *WO* 16:100-113.
1985b *Die keilschrift-luwischen Texte in Umschrift.* StBoT 30. Wiesbaden: Otto Harrassowitz.
STEFANINI, R.
1992 "On the Tenth Paragraph of the Bronze Tablet (ii 91 - iii 1)." *AGI* 67:133-152.
STEINER, G.
1984 "Struktur und Bedeutung des sogenannten Anitta-Textes." *OA* 23:53-73.
1989 "Kültepe-Kaniš und der 'Anitta-Text.'" In *Anatolia and the Ancient Near East.* Ed. by K. Emre, B. Hrouda, M. Mellink and N. Özgüç. Ankara: Türk Tarih Kurumu Basımevi.
1993 "How Was the City of Hattusa Taken by 'Anitta'?" In *Uluslararasi 1. Hittitoji Kongresi Bildirileri (19-21 Temmuz 1990).* Çorum: Uluslararası Çorum Hitit Festivali Komitesi Başkanliğı.
STERN, P. D.
1991 *The Biblical Ḥerem.* BJS 211. Atlanta: Scholars Press.
STURTEVANT, E. H., and G. BECHTEL.
1935 *A Hittite Chrestomathy.* Philadelphia: University of Pennsylvania.
SÜEL, A.
1985 *Hitit Kaynaklarında Tapınak Görevlileri ile ilgili bir Direktif Metni.* Aüdtcfy 350. Ankara: Ankara Üniversitesi Dil ve Tarih-Çoğrafya Fakültesi Basımevi.
SÜRENHAGEN, D.
1992 "Untersuchungen zur Bronzetafel und weiteren Verträgen mit der Sekundogenitur in Tarḫuntašša." *OLZ* 87:341-371.
TADMOR, H.
1983 "Autobiographical Apology in the Royal Assyrian Literature." In *HHI* 36-57.
TSEVAT, M.
1983 "Two Old Testament Stories and Their Hittite Analogues." *JAOS* 103:35-42 = *Studies Kramer* 321-326.
ÜNAL, A.
1973 "Zum Status der 'Augures' bei den Hethitern." *RHA* XXXI:27-56.
1974 *Ḫattušili III. Teil I, Ḫattušili bis zu seiner Thronbesteigung. Band 1: Historischer Abriß.* THeth 3. *Band 2: Quellen und Indices.* THeth 4. Heidelberg: Carl Winter Verlag.
1978 *Ein Orakeltext über die Intrigen am hethitischen Hof. (KUB XXII 70 = Bo 2011).* THeth 6. Heidelberg: Carl Winter Verlag.
1993 "The Nature and Iconographical Traits of 'Goddess of Darkness.'" Pp. 639-644 in *Aspects of Art and Iconography: Anatolia and its Neighbors. Studies in Honor of Nimet Özgüç.* Ed. by M. J. Mellink, E. Porada and T. Özgüç. Ankara: Türk Tarih Kurumu Basımevi.
ÜNAL, A. and A. KAMMENHUBER.
1975 "Das althethitische Losorakel KBo 18.151." *KZ* 88:157-180.
WEGNER, I
1989 "*:karnan :marnan.* Eine hethitische Reduplikation." *AoF* 16:383-384.
WOLF, H.
1967 *The Apology of Ḫattušiliš Compared with Other Political Self-Justifications of the Ancient Near East.* Ph.D. Dissertation. Brandeis. Ann Arbor, Michigan: University Microfilms.
WRIGHT, D. P.
1987 *The Disposal of Impurity. Elimination Rites in the Bible and in Hittite and Mesopotamian Literature.* SBLDS 101. Atlanta, GA: Scholars Press.

WEST SEMITIC CANONICAL COMPOSITIONS

A. DIVINE FOCUS

1. UGARITIC MYTHS

THE BA^c^LU MYTH (1.86)

Dennis Pardee

The Ba^c^lu myth constitutes, by its length and relative completeness, the most important literary work preserved from those produced by the West Semitic peoples in the second millennium BCE. Before the discovery of this and related lesser works in the third and fourth decades of this century, virtually all our knowledge of West Semitic religious beliefs came from later descriptions emanating from cultures more or less alien to the one in which these myths were recounted, e.g., the Hebrew Bible or Philo of Byblos as preserved by the fourth-century (CE) Christian writer Eusebius. More recent discoveries show that the Ugaritic form of the Ba^c^lu myth had a long prehistory among the Amorite peoples (Durand 1993; Bordreuil and Pardee 1993). The presence in the Hebrew Bible of motifs similar to those in the Ugaritic myths indicates the existence of a Canaanite mythology very similar to the Amorite one, though determining the degree of similarity awaits the discovery of texts like the Ugaritic ones at a southern site.

The discovery of the Ugaritic mythological texts, in poetic form, has already demonstrated the high degree of similarity between second millennium poetic conventions in the northern part of the Syro-Palestinian area, surely descended from the old Amorite poetic tradition, and those of the Canaanite areas in the first millennium, visible in the poetic sections of the Hebrew Bible. The organization of a poem by parallel lines forming verses of two or three line-segments ("bicola" and "tricola") appears to be characteristic of poetry throughout the old Northwest Semitic area. Though meter in the strict sense of the term appears absent from all these traditions, the parallel lines are everywhere characterized by terseness and roughly comparable length.[1]

In spite of formal differences among them, the six tablets translated here are considered by most scholars to have originally belonged to a single work that would have consisted of some 2350 lines, approximately 1500 poetic verses.[2] At one evidential extreme is the fact that the text is manifestly continuous from the last line of *CTA* 5 to the first of *CTA* 6; at the other is the fragmentary nature of *CTA* 1 and *CTA* 2, the latter consisting of two fragments that are not even certainly from the same tablet. The principal formal dissimilarity is in the number of columns in which the text is written on the tablets: *CTA* 1, 3, 5, and 6 are arranged in three columns per side, while *CTA* 2 apparently was in two columns (judging from the width of the one well-preserved column), and *CTA* 4 was in four columns per side. On the other hand, a virtually certain point of similarity is the script: *CTA* 4 and 6 bear a colophon identifying the scribe as ^⊃^Ilīmilku, a very high priestly official in the court of one of the kings named Niqmaddu,[3] and the script of all six texts appears to be identical, making it highly probable that ^⊃^Ilīmilku inscribed them all. But did he write them and intend them as a sequence, or do some of these tablets belong to another sequence or to none at all? There is simply no empirical answer to that question,[4] and the approach to the problem is therefore usually a literary one, which can be rephrased as another question: Can the six tablets be organized into a meaningful narrative sequence? To this question most scholars have responded positively, though the form of the response and

[1] See the bibliography in Pardee 1988c, where one Ug. poem and one Heb. poem are analyzed in detail.

[2] From the epigraphic perspective, everything militates against the various hypotheses proposing that RS 24.245 be attached to *CTA* 3 (cf. Pardee 1988a:129, n. 20; Smith 1994:3-4). Whether, from a textual/literary perspective, RS 24.245 could be an extract from *CTA* 3, written by a different scribe in a different format, it is difficult to say.

[3] In *CTA* 4 the scribe's name is restored, but the restoration is likely because the end of the colophon corresponds to that of ^⊃^Ilīmilku. For a recent defense of the traditional dating of ^⊃^Ilīmilku, the most famous of Ug. scribes, to the time of Niqmaddu II (middle 14th century), see van Soldt 1991:27-29. As is clear from van Soldt's arguments on these pages in comparison with his analysis of the stratigraphy of and tablets found in the High Priest's house (pp. 213-20), where most of the tablets signed by ^⊃^Ilīmilku were found, the dating of the scribe who consigned to writing the Ug. myths is contingent on identifying him with another scribe, whose name appears to have been identical, responsible for three Akk. texts (in these texts his name is written logographically as ^m^AN.LUGAL). Should one wish, however, to dispute the identity of the two scribes, there is certainly nothing in the stratigraphy of the High Priest's house, which was in use until the destruction of the city in ca. 1186 BCE, to preclude that ^⊃^Ilīmilku may have served under a later Niqmaddu. Such an hypothesis may even be bolstered by the recent discovery in the house of Urtenu of a fragment of a tablet written by ^⊃^Ilīmilku, for Urtenu was an official in royal service at the end of the thirteenth century (Bordreuil and Pardee, forthcoming; the text, to be edited by A. Caquot and A.-S. Dalix, is RS 1992.2016). For Urtenu see also below, Text 1.100.

[4] The only obvious negative point is the matter of differences in number of columns per tablet already mentioned. The ^⊃^Aqhatu cycle seems to show that that is not a significant criterion, for one of the three tablets preserved of that cycle is in three columns per side (*CTA* 17), while the other two (*CTA* 18, 19) are arranged in two columns per side. Because the name ^⊃^Aqhatu appears on all three tablets, and in no other Ug. poem, it must be assumed that the three tablets recount, at the very least, episodes from the hero's life, and it is likely that the three tablets constitute a true narrative sequence (see text 1.103). Consistent use of an archival introduction (it would be *l b^c^l* on these tablets, as is shown

the related organization of the six tablets have varied.[5] The order most commonly accepted in recent years is followed here. It assumes that, for reasons not made clear in the text in its present state, ʾIlu, the head of the Ugaritic pantheon, at one time favors Yammu/Naharu, the god of bodies of water, but he allows Baʿlu to challenge Yammu; Baʿlu defeats his rival, then orders the construction of his own royal palace; Môtu, the god of death, challenges Baʿlu and eventually brings about his death; after a time in the underworld, Baʿlu returns to life. There appears to be a substantial qualitative difference between the kingship for which Baʿlu and Yammu vie and that of the other deities in this text who are ascribed kingship: each of these exercises kingship in his own way and in his own sphere (ʾIlu, Baʿlu, ʿAṯṯaru, and Môtu are the four others who are described as kings), whereas Yammu and Baʿlu appear to be in competition for the same kingship. We have information from these texts on the domains over which Baʿlu, ʿAṯṯaru, and Môtu rule (see notes 50, 98, 250), but no specific data on Yammu's sphere of kingship. From the projection that Baʿlu gives of his defeat of Yammu (*CTA* 2 iv, up to line 5), we may plausibly infer that Yammu's kingdom corresponded to his name, i.e., the sea. If so, how is it that he and Baʿlu are vying for the kingship in a sense that is not true of Baʿlu and ʿAṯṯaru or Baʿlu and Môtu? Two considerations for the formulation of a response: (1) Whatever the nature of ʿAṯṯaru's kingship, that deity is negligible as a world power (*CTA* 6 i 56-67), while Yammu is a powerful foe to be defeated in battle (*CTA* 2 iv); (2) Yammu has a palace, location unknown, though it is unlikely that it is on the 'heights of Ṣapānu' where Baʿlu eventually had his palace built (*CTA* 4). Plausibly, therefore, Yammu's palace was in the sea, while Baʿlu's dwelling was on the heights of Ṣapānu, and the question was which of these two features of the earth was the appropriate place from which to exercise executive authority over the entire earth.

Because the myth deals with Baʿlu, the principal weather god of the Levantine peoples, and his vicissitudes, most authorities have interpreted the cycle as somehow reflecting the vegetative cycle, though the approaches have varied considerably.[6] The symbolism apparent in the divine names appears to demand some form of naturalistic approach, though the precise interpretation of each element, as well as the overall interpretation of the myth, may be in doubt. Particularly problematic is the negative rôle, parallel to that of the god of death, of the watery elements, who are presented as enemies of Baʿlu, for in a naturalistic interpretation, such bodies of water might be seen as in cooperation with the god that produces rain, rather than inimical to him. Some scholars avoid the problem of conceptual origins and satisfy themselves with a description of the antiquity and broad spread of the motif; others consider that it is the superficial phenomenon of the effects of a storm on a body of water that is reflected in the mythological motif of animosity. Perhaps an appeal to the destructive aspect of the dual nature of water, beneficent in reasonable quantities, harmful when overly abundant or in turmoil, is in order. The explanation of the enmity of Baʿlu and Yammu/Naharu as reflecting the rôle of water in a cosmological myth (Smith 1994:84-87) deserves further attention, but Smith does not explain why the enemy is Yammu/Naharu rather than one of the entitites designated by the root *thm* (cf. Tiamat in the Mesopotamian version and *tᵉhôm* in the Hebrew one; on forms of *thm* in Ugaritic, see below, note 45). It, in any case, only pushes the question back a stage: one must still ask why these watery forces were seen as the enemy of the creator deity (probably ʾIlu at Ugarit, though no cosmological myth is yet attested). An explanation by social/agricultural systems, i.e. dry farming vs. irrigation, does not appear plausible, for the salt sea (*ym*), unsuitable for irrigation, is clearly the principal antagonist of Baʿlu (the opposition of dry farming and irrigation is more appropriately evoked to explain the contrasted rôles of Baʿlu and ʿAṯṯaru [see notes 48, 245, 250]).

---

by *CTA* 6 i 1) or of a colophon may be demonstrated by *CTA* 5 and 6 to be an invalid criterion for deciding whether a tablet belongs to a sequence or not, for *CTA* 6 has both, while *CTA* 5 has neither, though it is indubitable that the two tablets bore a single continuous text. The data on the other tablets are: *CTA* 4, 16, and 17 have a colophon on the left edge that identifies the scribe (none of these colophons is identical to the others); *CTA* 6 has a scribal colophon at the end of the text; *CTA* 19 has a sort of colophon at the end of the text, but it is textual in nature ("Here is where to resume the story") rather than scribal; *CTA* 5, 14, and 18 have no colophon, neither at the end of the text nor on the left edge; no colophon is visible on the extant left edge of *CTA* 2, 3, tablets from which the end of the tablet has disappeared. The facts that *CTA* 6 has the longest colophon of this series and that it is placed at the end of the tablet with some space to spare may indicate that this tablet constituted for ʾIlīmilku the last one in this cycle. The nature of the notation at the end of *CTA* 19 seems to indicate that that tablet was not considered to be the last of the ʾAqhatu cycle; the placement of the colophon on the left margin of *CTA* 16, its brevity, and the content of the text itself indicate that that tablet was not the last in the Kirta cycle. An element often omitted in the discussion of whether these six tablets constitute a literary unity is the indisputable fact that, up to the present, no single instance of a duplicate mythological text is known: there are clear instances of brief "quotations" from known texts (cf. Pardee 1988a:119-164, 257-260, 265) and there are clear instances of formulaic repetition in different texts (e.g., in CTA 7 as compared with *CTA* 3 ii-iii). But it nonetheless appears beyond the realm of plausibility that the six tablets known today of the Baʿlu cycle would come from "two versions of the Baal Cycle" (Smith 1994:12) and yet show no overlapping text.

[5] See the chart and detailed discussion in Smith 1994:2-15.

[6] Smith has provided useful overviews (1986; 1994:58-114). Contrast particularly the approach of de Moor 1971 — very precisely seasonal — as compared with Bordreuil 1991 and Yon 1989, 1990 — more broadly symbolic. See also the critique of the Frazerian approach by Walls 1992.

***CTA* 1**[7]

ʾIlu Sends Messengers to ʿAnatu (ii ?-13)[8]

[Now you shall head off
 to ʾInbubu,[9]
Through a thousand courts,
 ten thousand ....[10]
At the feet of ʿAnatu bow and fall,
 do homage and honor her.[a]

Say to Girl ʿAnatu,[11] [b]
 repeat to the sister-in-law[c] of Liʾmu:[12]
Message of the Bull, your father ʾIlu,[d]
 word of the Gracious One, your sire:[13]
Present bread offerings in the earth,
 place love-offerings[e] in the dust;
Pour well-being out into the earth,
 calmness[14] into the fields.[15]

a Pss 29:1-2; 86:9; 96:8-9; 1 Chr 16:28-29
b 2 Kgs 19:21; Jer 18:13; 31:4, 21; Amos 5:2 Lam 2:13
c Deut 25:7,9
d Deut 32:6,
e Gen 30:14; Cant 7:14

---

[7] *CTA* = Herdner 1963. See also *KTU* 1.1 = Dietrich, Loretz and Sanmartín 1976 (the other texts in this cycle are in the same order as in *CTA*). The *editio princeps* was by Virolleaud 1938:91-102. If this tablet belongs to the Baʿlu cycle, one may surmise that only a bit over a quarter of the original number of lines has been even partially preserved (about 120/400). On the problems of the relationship of this tablet to the others, see remarks above and Smith 1994:14-19. Portions of two columns are preserved in this fragment which the editor (Virolleaud 1938:91) described as coming from the center or lower right corner of the tablet; the first placement would imply a text arranged in two columns per side, the second, three columns per side, of which the first would have been totally lost. Herdner (1963:1) claimed that she could confirm that the text was originally in three columns, but left open the question of the recto/verso orientation. Smith (1994:20) followed Herdner. In fact, however, the recto/verso orientation should be easily verifiable by the curvature of the tablet, for the verso is usually more curved than the recto because the corners of the recto sag and the recto thus becomes flat during the time required to inscribe the verso (see, for example, the photograph of *CTA* 4 in Herdner 1963:pl. X). Unfortunately, I know of no published photograph of the tablet in side view. Given Virolleaud's unequivocal statement, I prefer to assume that he, a practiced epigrapher, had checked the curvature of the tablet (though this does not explain why he missed what should be the almost equally obvious indications provided by the thickness of the fragment at various points for its original number of columns). To make sense of the discussions of this question, the reader must be aware that multi-columned tablets were inscribed from left to right on the recto, the final column on the right side of the recto continued around the lower edge and onto the verso, then the additional columns on the verso proceeded from right to left. Thus, in a text written in three columns per side, cols. i and vi will be opposite each other on the left side of the tablet, recto and verso respectively, with the lower edge left uninscribed between them; cols. ii and v will be arranged in like manner in the center of the tablet; cols. iii and iv will be on the right side of the tablet, usually with the text inscribed continuously around the lower edge of the tablet, making the division between these two columns somewhat arbitrary.

[8] The first seven-plus verses have disappeared entirely, but may be plausibly reconstructed on the basis of lines 14-22 (and, more distantly, by comparison with *CTA* 3 iii 6-15 [lines 9-18 in my numbering]).

[9] The Liturgy against Venomous Reptiles (text 1.94 below) shows clearly that ʾInbubu is ʿAnatu's principal dwelling, for there (l. 20) the messenger is told to go to ʿAnatu in ʾInbubu, and, as we know from most of the addresses in that text, they represent the deities' principal seat of residence. Though ʾInbubu is known to be a mountain, its geographical location has not been identified. Below, in *CTA* 3 iv 78 (line 81 in my numbering), *ʾinbb* is in parallel with *ʾuǵr*, surely a further indication of where ʿAnatu's dwelling was located, but also presently unidentified.

[10] The attested formula for expressing the distance of a deity's journey is *ʾalp šd rbt kmn* (see note 21). In this case, the first elements are *ʾalp ḥẓr* (line 14), but the parallel phrase has disappeared.

[11] ʿAnatu's title *btlt* has elicited enormous discussion. The English word "virgin" is inappropriate as a translation because it emphasizes lack of sexual experience, while *btlt* refers rather to an age/maturity category and to the social norms and cultural overtones associated with that category. For a compact bibliography, see Pardee 1987:382 and 1989-90:464-466, and for a meaningful discussion, see Walls 1992.

[12] *ybmt lʾimm* is a much-discussed title of ʿAnatu. As in the title of the deity Môtu, *bn ʾilm*, "son of ʾIlu" (rather than "son of the gods"), the second element of this divine epithet bears the enclitic-*m* (*ybmt lʾimm*). This solution appears preferable to the nonsensical translation "sister-in-law of the peoples/thousand (gods)." Liʾmu is an old divinity of the Amorite world, poorly attested at Ugarit except in this title. For bibliography, see Pardee 1989-90:459, 464-466.

[13] The title of "Bull" (*ṯr*) is used principally of ʾIlu in Ug. texts and is usually linked explicitly with the concept of fatherhood (*ṯr ʾil ʾab*); the child may be either another deity or a semi-divine being such as Kirta (see note 13 to text 1.102). This is ʾIlu's principal title, with the widest attestations in the mythological texts (for some bibliographical elements, see Pardee 1987:456; 1989-90:434-436). *ltpn ḥtk* is a variant of the formula *ltpn ʾil d pʾid* (see below, note 28). *ltpn* denotes a quality of character, *ḥtk* a familial relationship, usually interpreted as belonging to the realm of fatherhood/sonship or daughtership because *ḥtk* is replaced in similar formulae by *bn* (as in *ḥtk dgn* [*CTA* 10 iii 35] for the usual *bn dgn*). Another noun from the same root is used in the Kirta text (*CTA* 15 i 10 [text 1.102]) for the "family" of Kirta. For bibliography on *ḥtk*, see Pardee 1987:398. ʾIlu is consistently depicted in these texts as an old man with grey hair and beard. Though he is consulted for the wisdom of his decisions (e.g. *CTA* 3 v 38-39 [here 29-30]; 4 iv 41-43, v 65-66), his old age also makes him vulnerable to the threats of ʿAnatu (*CTA* 3 v 9-11, 32-33 [here 1-3, 24-25]).

[14] The precise meaning of all four terms functioning as objects of the verbs has been debated: *mlḥmt* could have to do either with bread (*lḥm*) or with the verb "to fight" (now attested in RIH 78/12:9, 21), while *ddym* could be related to the Semitic word for "love" or have another etymology; *šlm* could mean "peace" in the narrow sense of the word (absence of warfare) or have its more common broader meaning of "well-being," while *ʾarbdd*, here translated "calmness," has been the object of multiple explanations, none of which may be judged certain. The function of antonymic parallelism in such an address would be difficult to explain, for, though the purpose of the plea is to convince ʿAnatu to leave off her war-like ways, the phrases "present war ... place love," can hardly mean "dispense with war and put love in its place." Moreover, in spite of the difficulty of *ʾarbdd*, most scholars have seen synonymous parallelism in the second verse; if *mlḥmt* denotes warfare, therefore, the macroparallelism would be ABBB. For a detailed discussion, see Smith 1994:202-208 (I find the explanation of *ddym* by Egyptian *ddyt* dubious because the narrative function of the word is different in the two literatures: in the Egyptian text cited *ddyt* is poured out by other deities with the purpose of tricking the goddess into leaving off warfare, whereas here she is asked to pour it out herself — if it is the same word, someone has misunderstood the function of the substance in the other story).

[15] Lit., "liver of the earth // liver of the fields." It is clear from the text below where ʿAnatu searches for Baʿlu at the borderland between the netherworld and the land of the living (*CTA* 5 vi 26-30) that the reference is to a particular point on the earth's surface, rather than to a descent into the earth. In that text the terms denote such a borderland and constitute perhaps something like a "navel of the earth" notion. Because the reference in *CTA* 5 vi is relatively specific when understood in conjunction with previous descriptions of the place of ingress to Môtu's domain (*CTA* 5 vi 3-9, with reference back to v 6-23 and to *CTA* 4 viii 1-14), one cannot help but wonder whether this text does not also refer to that particular location, i.e., whether these offerings are not depicted as being appropriately made at the "navel of the earth." It appears, in any case, difficult to deny the presence of at least a literary link between this message, which is repeated several times in *CTA* 1 and 3 (each time with appropriate

Hurry, press, hasten,
to] me let your feet [run,
to me let] your legs [hasten;
To Mount X[16] ...]
...[17]

The Envoys Go to ᶜAnatu and Deliver ᵓIlu's Message (ii 13-?)

Then [they head off
to] ᵓInbubu,
Through a thousand courts,
[ten thousand ....
At the feet] of ᶜAnatu [they bow and fall,
do] homage and [honor her.
They raise their voices and say] aloud:
Message of [the Bull, your father ᵓIlu,
word of the] Gracious One, your sire:
[Present bread] offerings [in the earth,]
place [love-offerings] in the dust;
[Pour well-being out] into the earth,
[calmness into the] fields.
Hurry, [press, hasten,
to me] let your [feet] run,
[to me let] your [legs hasten];
To Mount [X ...].
...[18]

ᵓIlu Sends for Kôṯaru-wa-Ḫasīsu (iii 1-16)

[Then they head off
to Memphis, (to) the god of it all,[19]
(To) Crete[f] (which is) the] throne [on which he sits, (to) Memphis (which is) the land of his own possession[20]],
Through a thousand yards,
ten [thousand furlongs.[21]
At the feet of Kôṯaru] they bow and fall,
they [do homage and honor him].
They say to Kôṯaru-[wa-Ḫasīsu,
repeat to Hayyinu[22]] the handicrafter:
[Message of the Bull, your father ᵓIlu],
word of the Gracious One [...]:
...[23]
Hurry, press, hasten,
[to me let your feet run,]
to me let [your] legs hasten;
[To Mount ?], the mountain of KS.[24]
For [I have something to tell you],
a matter to recount to you:
[Words regarding wood, whisperings regarding stone],[25]
conversings of heaven with [earth,
of the deep with the stars];
A matter (which) men cannot know,
[(which) the hordes of the earth cannot understand].[g]
Come and I will explain [it (for you)
in Mount X ...[26]].

f Deut 2:23; Jer 47:4; Amos 9:7
g Job 28:13

repetitions in the message-transmission structure), and the spot where Baᶜlu's body is eventually found. Note that the word *kbd*, "liver," is also used in the metaphor for death expressed as entering into the body of Môtu, god of death, where it expresses the end point after entry (*CTA* 5 ii 3-6).

16 The word *ḫršn* is actually extant in line 23 and partially so in iii 22, but broken in the other occurrences of the formula (here and iii 11). The immediately following word, on the other hand, has not been preserved in any of the passages. Below in iii 12, *ǵr ks*, "the mountain KS," functions as parallel to this formula. All the passages are, unfortunately, too broken to permit a decision as to the relationship between *ḫršn* and *ǵr*, apparently two words for "mountain," and as to the status of the word *ks*, whether a name or a qualifier. Unless one accept that *ḏd* also means "mountain" (see below, note 29), these four texts are the only ones in all of Ug. literature that place ᵓIlu's dwelling on a mountain. Other texts, including the liturgy against venomous reptiles, organized specifically according to the principal dwellings of the various deities invoked (RS 24.244:2-3 [text 1.94]), emphasize the watery aspect of ᵓIlu's abode. See Pope's attempt to locate ᵓIlu's home in a place characterized by mountain springs (1955) and Smith's detailed discussion (1994:225-230).

17 Lines 3b-13 are too broken to translate and there is no parallel text from which to propose a reconstruction. At the end of line 8 appears the verb "to die" (*ymtm*) and at the end of line 9 the expression *k ᵓiṯl*, which is only attested in expressions for the process of dying as provoked by ᶜAnatu (see *CTA* 18 iv 25, 36; 19 ii 88, 93 "like spittle" [text 1.103]).

18 If each column was 60-65 lines long, as is the case with the other tablets in this cycle, approximately 35-40 lines are missing between cols. ii and iii, though the distribution of these lines between the bottom of col. ii and the top of col. iii cannot be determined until the placement of the fragment within the outline of the original tablet is better defined.

19 The phrase *ᵓil klh* has been variously explained. Since interpretations based on analyses other than as *kl*, "all," + pronominal suffix, involve various grammatical, orthographic, or syntactic problems, it appears best to interpret the phrase as alluding to the ideological importance of Memphis during and after its decline from political power and as standing thus in a sense for all Egypt. The sacred name of Memphis, *Ḥ(w)t-kᵓ-ptḥ*, "the house of the ka of (the deity) Ptaḥ" (whence Ug. *ḥkpt*), became, through Greek, the modern name for Egypt. Because the Greek usage goes back at least to Homer, it does not appear implausible to posit the existence of a similar view at Ugarit. The reference, as is shown clearly by the continuation of this text and by other passages, is to the craftsman deity Kôṯaru-wa-Ḫasīsu. The double divine name Kôṯaru-wa-Ḫasīsu can appear in full form or just as Kôṯaru; in poetic structure it can either be split up in a bicolon or appear as a single unit, which then has as its parallel yet a third name, Hayyinu (as here below, line 4). The double deity can be treated either as a single deity or as a duality (as in *CTA* 17 v 18-21 [text 1.103]). The home of Kôṯaru-wa-Ḫasīsu is fixed either in Egypt (as in *CTA* 17 v 21-31 [text 1.103]), or in Crete (see RS 24.244:46 [text 1.94]), or in both places (as here and in *CTA* 3 vi 14-15).

20 Like Heb., *nḥlt* in Ug. denotes real property belonging to an individual, whether received by right of succession from one's father or not.

21 The words *šd*, "field" (cf. Akk. *šiddu*), and *kmn*, "(a land measure)," are here translated by terms denoting increasing lengths.

22 This name is explained by Arabic *hayyin^{un}*, "easy, light," which, coupled with following phrase *d ḥrš ydm*, lit., "who makes things by hand," denotes facility in craftsmanship.

23 The beginning of ᵓIlu's message, lines 7-9, does not correspond to known formulae and may not, therefore, be reconstructed.

24 See above, note 16.

25 Wood and stone here appear to be Kôṯaru-wa-Ḫasīsu's stock in trade as a craftsman deity. When the formulae are repeated by Baᶜlu below (*CTA* 3 iii 20-26), features characteristic of the weather deity are added, in particular, the thunder.

26 Where the passage like this one occurs in *CTA* 3 iii 26-28, the last invitation is followed by the descriptions of Baᶜlu's mountain. One would expect this text to have contained corresponding information for ᵓIlu.

Kôṯaru-wa-Ḫasīsu Obeys the Summons (iii 17-end)
Kôṯaru-wa-Ḫasīsu replies:
  [Come, come, attendants of the gods],
  you, you may tarry, but I'm [off
(From) Crete] for the most distant of gods,
  (from) Memphis [for the most distant of deities]:
By double stretches below [the springs of the earth,
  triple lengths] (in) the low places.[27]
So off he [heads,
  towards the Gracious One], the kindly god,[28]
  to Mount [?, the mountain of KS].
He penetrates Ilu's abode,
  [enters the dwelling[29] of the King], father of
  Šunama;[30]
At [ᵓIlu's feet he bows and falls],
  does homage [and honors him.
...]
the Bull ᵓIlu [...]
...[31]

ᵓIlu's Feast (iv)[32]
Unknown (v)[33]

CTA 2[34]
Yammu's Message (i 11-19)[35]
Yammu sends messengers,
  [Ruler Naharu[36] sends an embassy].[h]

h Ps 93:3-4

[27] The meaning and interpretation of these formulae expressing great distances are uncertain. They are used for distances both across land and, as here, across water, and they are descriptive of the travel of various deities. The terms "below/under the springs (or: furrows) of the earth" (*tḥt ᶜnt ᵓarṣ*) and "(in) the low places" (*ġyrm*) seem to indicate that the deities were thought capable of traveling the underground aquifers. One must either adopt this interpretation or else assume that formulae appropriate for travel across land (hence "down amongst the springs/furrows of the earth") were used conventionally for travel between two places separated by water (cf. Pardee 1980:278; Smith 1994:183-184).

[28] *lṭpn ᵓil d pᵓid* is one of the titles of ᵓIlu. The 1st element is etymologically related to Arabic *laṭīfᵘⁿ*, a title of Allah, while the 2nd has also an Arabic cognate, the root *fᵓd* denoting aspects of the heart as an organ and seat of various abstract concepts (mind, spirit, courage...). Without usages closer to Ug. it is impossible to know whether it there denoted primarily courage or generosity (cf. "big-hearted"), or some other notion.

[29] The terms here for ᵓIlu's dwellings are the standard ones, *ḏd* and *qrš* (to which may be added *ᵓahl*, "tent"). These terms have an archaic flavor about them (not *bt*, "house," *hkl*, "palace," *ḥẓr*, "court" — such terms are used elsewhere only rarely of ᵓIlu's dwelling) and apparently designate tent-like structures (see Clifford 1972:51-53, 124-125; bibliography in Pardee 1987:424). Though many believe that *ḏd* is simply a form of the word for "mountain" (by-forms *ṯd*, *ḏd*, *šd* are posited), its general semantic field seems to be indicated by the fact that the same word in the ᵓAqhatu text denotes YṮPN's encampment (*CTA* 19 iv 213, 220 [text 1.103]). Many have pointed out, as well, that *qrš* is the term used in the Torah for the moveable planks of which the desert sanctuary is constructed. The ideology of ᵓIlu's home appears, therefore, to be related to the semi-nomadic existence: though his home is comfortable, even palatial (see *CTA* 3 v 27-29 [my lines 19-21]), it may also have been portable.

[30] The title *ᵓab šnm* has been variously interpreted (for bibliography see Pardee 1987:367; 1988b:57-60; 1989-90:458). Because, according to RS 24.258:18-19 (text 1.97), the double deity Ṯukamuna-wa-Šunama do the duty of the good son by bearing ᵓIlu home when he is drunk (cf. note 9 to the ᵓAqhatu text 1.103), *šnm* may be taken as the divine name Šunama. Cf. also Text 1.95, passim.

[31] It is usually assumed that Kôṯaru-wa-Ḫasīsu is next asked to build a palace for Yammu. Unfortunately the entire reconstruction rests on the letter {b}, taken to be the first letter of the second word in the formula *ḥš bhtm tbnn* ..., "hurriedly build a palace" (the text reads {ḥš.b[...]}).

[32] Though over thirty lines of this column are partially preserved, not a single line is fully preserved and precious few are even restorable. There are motifs of a feast (*ṣḥ*, "to call, invite"; *yṯb*, "to sit"), of blessing (lines 9-10: "he takes [a cup in hand], a goblet in both hands"; cf. in the Kirta text *CTA* 15 ii 16-18 [text 1.102] and in the ᵓAqhatu text *CTA* 17 i 35ff. [text 1.103]), and of proclaiming the name (*pᶜr + šm*) of someone, perhaps Yammu (line 15: *w pᶜr šm ym*[...]; line 20: [...] *šmk mdd ᵓi*[*l*...]). The first twenty lines may, therefore, have to do with an installation and empowerment of Yammu, though the circumstances are unclear. For scholars who order the tablets as here translated, this section recounts an initial empowerment of Yammu by ᵓIlu, which would constitute the narrative origin of the conflict between Yammu and Baᶜlu. After these events, there is mention in lines 22-25 of an intervention by Baᶜlu and of someone being driven from a throne, but the object of the verb, the motivation, and the circumstances are all obscure. ᵓIlu's motivations in fostering the rivalry between Yammu and Baᶜlu are unknown, the tablet being too poorly preserved to provide such information, if indeed it was ever made explicit in the poem (cf. below, note 98). If Yammu was a son of ᵓIlu, according to the form of address Yammu uses in the next text ("the Bull, his father ᵓIlu"), then one can see a typical rivalry between sons, with the younger son eventually winning out over an arrogant and oppressive older brother. Moreover, Baᶜlu's title "Son of Dagan" may indicate that he, Baᶜlu, is not ᵓIlu's own son. Data on this problem are not available from Ug. sources, but various explanations based on comparative considerations have been given (see below, notes 163 and 190 and bibliography in Pardee 1989-90:442-445, 446-448).

[33] Col. v is even more fragmentary than col. iv, and no certain theme can be identified among the few sparse words.

[34] This tablet currently consists of two fragments that do not join — and the presumption that they belong to a single tablet is, therefore, based on physical and graphic similarities. Because of the width of the lines, it is assumed that the tablet originally bore only two columns per side, of which parts of cols. i and iv have been preserved on the larger fragment, as well as the beginnings of a few lines of col. ii. The smaller fragment was assigned by the editor (Virolleaud 1944-45:1) to col. iii of the original tablet, i.e., the right-hand column on the verso. Only one surface of this fragment has been preserved (not "inscribed," as Herdner claims 1963:5; cf. Virolleaud 1944-45:1). For arguments against considering this fragment as belonging to the same tablet as col. i, ii, iv, see Meier 1986; note that the argument from line length (i.e., the lines of col. iii are longer than those of cols. i and iv) is not convincing because this fragment is from the right side of the tablet and the lines wrap around the edge of the tablet (see the photograph in Smith 1994:pl. 26). Meier also argues that *CTA* 2 does not belong to the same cycle as *CTA* 3-6; physical characteristics of the tablets may not, however, play a role in such an argument, and the literary/formulaic arguments are inconclusive — Meier, and others who have had doubts on this score, may be correct, but data are presently insufficient for a clear decision. In any case, this tablet was part of a Baᶜlu cycle, almost certainly inscribed by ᵓIlīmilku; the real question, for a clear answer to which the data are also insufficient, is the relationship of this portion of the Baᶜlu story to the better-preserved portions, i.e., the tablet's relationship to the others in a single cycle, or the cycle's relationship to the other principal cycle known. The *editio princeps* of this tablet was more piecemeal than is usually the case: Virolleaud published cols. iv and iii in separate articles (1935 and 1944-45, respectively). Col. i appeared for the first time, in transcription only, in Gordon 1947:167-68 (text no. 137). Col. ii appeared for the first time in Herdner 1963, where hand copies of cols. i and ii also were first published.

[35] Lines 1-10 are poorly preserved and unrestorable. In line 6 one finds *ᵓaymr*, apparently a reference to the mace named ᵓAyyamurru with which Baᶜlu defeats Yammu according to col. iv, and in lines 7-8 a curse that makes appeal to the deity Ḥôrānu, one that is better preserved in *CTA* 16 vi 54-57, Kirta's curse on his upstart son (text 1.102) — unfortunately, here the crucial part is missing wherein the object of the curse is named, and we thus have no way of knowing who the protagonists are nor of fixing the curse into the narrative structure.

[36] One of Yammu's standard titles in these texts is *tpṭ nhr*, where the first word is the old West Semitic term *ṯāpiṭu*, denoting a tribal/clan ruler,

They rejoice...
Go, lads, [don't dally],
head for
the Great Assembly,[37]
for [Mount Lalu.
At the feet of ᵓIlu] do not fall,
do not prostrate yourself (to) the Great [Assembly.
Standing, say (your) speech],
repeat your information.
Say to the Bull, [my] father [ᵓIlu,
repeat to the Great] Assembly:
Message of Yammu, your master,
of your lord Ruler [Naharu]:
Give (up), O gods, the one whom you obey,
the one whom the hordes (of the earth) fear.[38]
Give (up) Baᶜlu [and his attendants],
(give up) the Son of Dagan,[39] that I might take possession of his gold.

At the Sight of the Approaching Messengers, the Gods Panic (i 19-29)
The lads head off, don't hesitate;
they head
for Mount Lalu,
for the Great Assembly.
The gods have sat down to eat,
the sons of the Holy One to dine,
Baᶜlu attending on ᵓIlu.
The gods see them,
see Yammu's messengers,
the embassy of Ruler [Naharu].
The gods lower their heads
onto their knees,
onto their princely thrones.
Baᶜlu rebukes them:
Why, gods, have your lowered (your) heads
even to your knees,
even to your princely thrones?
As one must the gods answer,
the tablet of Yammu's messengers,
the embassy of Ruler Naharu!
Lift, O gods, your heads[i]
off your knees,
off your princely thrones.

i Ps 24:7, 9

j Pss 57:5; 64:4

And let me answer Yammu's messengers,
the embassy of Ruler Naharu.
The gods then raise their heads
off their knees,
off their princely thrones.

The Messengers Arrive, Deliver Their Lines (i 30-35)
Thereafter the messengers of Yammu arrive,
the embassy of Ruler Naharu.
At the feet of ᵓIlu they [do not] fall,
they do not prostrate themselves (to) the Great Assembly.
Standing, they [say] (their) speech,
[repeat] their information.
They look like a fire, two fires,
their [tongue] like a sharpened sword.[j]
They say to the Bull, his father ᵓIlu:
Message of Yammu, your master,
of your [lord], Ruler Naharu:
Give (up), O gods, the one whom you obey,
the one whom the [hordes (of the earth)] fear.
Give (up) Baᶜlu and his attendants,
(give up) the Son of Dagan, that I might take possession of his gold.

ᵓIlu Declares That He Accedes to the Demand (i 36-38)
The Bull, his father ᵓIlu, [replies]:
Baᶜlu (is) your servant, O Yammu,
Baᶜlu (is) your servant, [O Naharu],
the Son of Dagan (is) your prisoner.
He will indeed bring you tribute,
like (one) of the gods he will bring [you a gift],
like one of the sons of the Holy One (he will bring you) presents.

Baᶜlu Defends Himself (i 38-end)
Then Prince Baᶜlu is sick (with rage),
[moreover he takes] in his hand a striking weapon,
in his right hand a smiting weapon,
the lads he [strikes].
[ᶜAnatu] grasps [his right hand],
ᶜAṯtartu grasps his left hand:
How could [you smite Yammu's messengers,
the] embassy of Ruler Naharu?

---

the second the standard Northwest Semitic word for "river." The conjunction of the names "Sea" and "River" seem to indicate that the deity in question does not personify the Mediterranean Sea alone, but all bodies of water — in opposition to Baᶜlu, the deity in charge of the rain (see above, introduction).

[37] "Great Assembly" is offered as a translation of the double formula *pḫr mᶜd*, each word of which means "assembly, council." The first word is the standard word for "assembly" in Akk. (*puḫru*), the second is cognate to Heb. *mōᶜēd*. In this text, the double formula refers to all the gods united, including Baᶜlu, whom we know to have had his own assembly (in the ritual texts we meet a composite deity *dr ᵓil w pḫr bᶜl*, "Circle of ᵓIlu and Assembly of Baᶜlu").

[38] Though the forms *tqh* and *tqyn* are often derived from the same root, the presence of /*h*/ in the first seems to indicate different roots, in consonance with the different subjects: the gods "obey" (allow themselves to be directed by) Baᶜlu (cf. Arabic *waqaha*, "obey," Heb. **yiqqāh*, "obedience"), while the human hordes (*hmlt*, taken here as an abbreviation of *hmlt ᵓarṣ*, attested above p. 244 [*CTA* 1 iii 15] and elsewhere [e.g., p. 251, *CTA* 3 iii 25]) "fear" and "reverence" Baᶜlu (cf. Arabic *waqâ*, "protect," but also "fear"). Alternatively, one could take the {*h*} on *tqh* as suffixal and derive both forms from the same root, interpreting, perhaps, *hmlt* as referring to the gods, rather than to humans.

[39] On this title of Baᶜlu, see notes 32 and 190.

...[40]

Then Prince Baᶜlu is (again) sick (with rage),
(to) the-field-of-a-man[41] ...
... Yammu's messengers
the embassy of Ruler Naharu.
...
I, for my part, hereby say to Yammu your master,
(to) [your] lord [Ruler Naharu]:
[...] the word of Haddu[42] the Avenger ...

Hostilities Continue (ii)[43]
Someone Sends Kôṯaru-wa-Ḫasīsu to ᵓIlu (iii 2-3)[44]
...
[(From) Crete] to the most distant [of gods,
(from) Memphis to the most distant of deities:
By double stretches below the springs of the earth,
triple lengths (in) the low places].

Off He Goes (iii 4-6)
[So] off he heads
to ᵓIlu at the source of [the double river,
midst the upspringings of the deeps.[45] [k]
He enters] ᵓIlu's dwelling,
goes into the home of the King, [father of Šunama;
At ᵓIlu's feet he bows] and falls,
does homage and honors [him].

k Ezek 47; Joel 4:18; Zech 14:8

ᵓIlu Enjoins the Building of Yammu's Palace (iii 6-11)
[Thereafter, the Bull, his father ᵓIlu, responds];
Kôṯaru-wa-Ḫasīsu be off:
(go) build a house[46] (for) Yammu,
raise a palace (for) Ruler Naharu,
...
Be off, Kôṯaru-wa[-Ḫasīsu:
you] are to (go) build a house (for) Prince Yammu
[you are to raise] a palace (for) [Ruler] Naharu,
...
[Hurry!] build the house,
Hurry! raise [the palace]:
A house [covering a thousand acres,
a palace (covering) ten thousand] hectares.[47]
...[48]

The Solar Deity Addresses ᶜAṯtaru (iii 15-18)
Šapšu, luminary of the gods, responds,
she raises her voice and [cries aloud]:
[Hear now, ᶜAṯtaru]:
The Bull, your father ᵓIlu, [will take blood] vengeance[49]

[40] Beginning with line 41, the text is progressively less well preserved. The goddesses' reproof apparently continues for about two lines, perhaps dealing with the diplomatic inviolability of messengers.

[41] *šdmt* as in *CTA* 23:10 (see note 17 to text 1.87).

[42] Haddu (Hadad in the "absolute" form) was the name of the old Amorite weather deity; Baᶜlu ("master") was a title of this deity, particularly in the coastal area, that came to function as a divine name.

[43] Only the first sign or signs of sixteen lines of col. ii have been preserved to the right of col. i. In line 8, one finds *ᵓimḫṣ*, "I will smite."

[44] On the placement of the fragment classified as col. iii of *CTA* 2, see above, note 34. Smith 1994, following various authors, places col. iii before cols. i and iv (see his discussion pp. 21-25, where he does not deal explicitly with the implications of this decision). Such a placement implies, of course, that col. iii comes from a tablet other than that represented by cols. i and iv (which would add some 250 lines to the cycle), for the latter two columns are from the left side of the tablet, hence from the beginning and end of the text, while col. iii is from the right side of the tablet, hence from somewhere in the middle of the text. (Caquot, Sznycer, Herdner 1974:108 do not discuss all the aspects of the problem, referring only to the discrepancy in line length between col. iii and cols. i/iv as an argument against placing the fragment labeled col. iii at the beginning of col. i.) According to the editor (Virolleaud 1944-45:1) this fragment should be placed near the end of col. iii, i.e., near the end of the right-hand column on the verso of the tablet. Including in the count the few heads of lines of col. ii, there would have been, assuming that col. iii belongs to the same tablet, approximately one hundred lines between the extant end of col. i and the beginning of col. iii as preserved.

[45] Though the parallel form *nhrm* is in all likelihood dual, expressing the cosmic river that encircles the earth in its two arms (cf. Caquot, Sznycer, Herdner 1974:109), one may question the common assumption that *thmtm* is also dual. Morphologically it could be either the dual (*tahāmatāma*) or the plural + "enclitic" *-m* (*tahāmātuma*). Because we know now that *thmt* in Ug. denotes the multiple waters of the underlying fresh-water ocean (see note 2 to text 1.94 [RS 24.244]), one might think that ᵓIlu dwells at the confluence of this plurality, rather than at the meeting place of two streams of the *thmt*, which are, in any case, as yet unidentified (an argument quite different from the one in Pardee 1980:270, where the form of *thmtm* was used as a basis for so interpreting *nhrm*). On attempts to locate ᵓIlu's dwelling place, see above note 16.

[46] The standard parallel pair in this text used to describe the dwellings of Yammu and Baᶜlu is *bhtm // hkl*, of which the first term is the standard Ug. plural of the word for "house," the second the technical term for the dwelling of a deity, corresponding to Heb. *hēkāl*, Akk. *ekallu*, Sum. É.GAL. I will everywhere translate *bhtm* by "house," though it is clear that the plural denotes the multiple constructions that make up a palace. In texts where *bhtm* is not in parallel with *hkl*, for example in the divine name *bᶜlt bhtm* that appears frequently in the ritual texts, *bhtm* may simply be translated by "palace" or "mansion."

[47] The terms designating the surface covered by the palace are *šd* and *kmn*, translated as length measures when used in the idiom for great distances (see above, note 21), are here translated as surface measures ("acre," "hectare").

[48] Lines 11b-15a are too damaged to translate. The deity ᶜAṯtaru, to whom Šapšu's message in lines 15-18 is addressed, first appears in line 12. Judging from what follows, his opposition to Yammu's hegemony may already have been mentioned there. Below, in *CTA* 6 i 53-67, we find an account of an unsuccessful attempt by ᶜAṯtaru to fill Baᶜlu's rôle when the latter is in the underworld; this is taken by those who interpret the name as signifying "irrigation" as meaning that irrigation cannot in the Levant fill the role of rain (cf. Caquot, Sznycer, Herdner 1974:233, who do not accept the hypothesis). There are also reasons to see ᶜAṯtaru as an astral deity: in Ug. religion, the morning and evening star may have been designated by masculine and feminine versions of the same name, ᶜAṯtaru functioning as the evening star, ᶜAṯtartu as the morning star (see note 58 to text 1.87). In terms of number of appearances and of dramatic roles in the mythological texts, ᶜAṯtaru is a relatively unimportant deity. This is equally true of the ritual texts where he appears in the so-called "pantheon" texts and in the sacrificial text dependent directly thereupon (RS 24.643) but otherwise very rarely. For bibliography, see Pardee 1989-90:466-70; for a recent overview, see Smith 1994:240-49.

[49] If the verb is correctly restored on the basis of line 21 as {[*yṯ*]*ᵓir*}, it denotes some form of reprisal based on consanguinity (*ṯᵓar* in Ug.;

for Prince Yammu,
for Ruler Naharu.
[Surely] he would not listen to you,
— the Bull, your father ʾIlu —
Surely he would pull up [the foundations of your] seat,
overturn [the throne of] your kingship,[l]
break the staff of your rulership.[50] [m]

ʿAṯtaru's Reply (iii 18-23)[51]
[ʿAṯtaru] responds [...]:
[...] in me,
the Bull, my father ʾIlu.
As for me, I [have] no house [as (do)] the (other) gods,
[nor] court [as (do) the sons of the Holy One].
X will go down my throat,
they will be washed ...[52]
In the house of [Prince] Yammu,
in the palace of Ruler Naharu.
The Bull, his father ʾIlu, may take blood vengeance
for Prince Yammu,
[for] Ruler [Naharu].
But I am king [...] am indeed king,[53]
whereas you [have] no wife as (do) [the (other) gods,
nor young bride as (do) the sons of the Holy One].

Yammu Responds (iii 23-24)
Prince Yammu [speaks up],
Ruler Naharu [replies]:
[...] will send.

ʿAṯtaru's Reply (iii 24-?)
ʿAṯtaru responds [...]

Baʿlu Swears the Destruction of His Enemies, Particularly Yammu (iv ?-5)
[...] I will indeed force them to leave,
moreover I will drive out [...].
And in Yammu I will indeed destroy the resting place,
in Yammu, at (his) very heart, (I will destroy) the [...],
[(as for) Ruler] Naharu, (I will destroy) (his) neck.
There with the sword I will lay waste,
I will assault (his) house:
The powerful one will fall to the earth,
the mighty one to the dust.

Yammu's Response (iv 6-7)
Hardly has the word left his mouth,
the utterance his lips,
When his voice is heard, there is a cry
(from) under the throne of Prince Yammu.[54]

Kôṯaru-wa-Ḫasīsu Prepares the Weapons Needed to Defeat Yammu (iv 7-27)[55]
Kôṯaru-wa-Ḫasīsu speaks up:
I hereby announce to you, Prince Baʿlu,
and I repeat, Cloud-Rider:[56] [n]
As for your enemy, O Baʿlu,
as for your enemy, you'll smite (him),
you'll destroy your adversary.[o]
You'll take your eternal kingship,
your sovereignty (that endures) from generation to generation.[p]

The First Mace (iv 11-18)
Kôṯaru prepares two maces[57]

l 2 Sam 7:13; Hag 2:22
m Ps 45:7
n Ps 68:5
o Ps 92:10
p Ps 145:13

see note 7 to the Kirta text [1.102] and the biblical references cited in note *e* to that text).

[50] The parallelism of *mlk* and *ṯpṭ* here is the standard one in Ug. to denote royal status. Because the very same threat is proffered against Môtu when he is on the verge of defeating Baʿlu *(CTA* 6 vi 27-29), we may assume that this passage dealt with a similar attack by ʿAṯtaru on Yammu. In the case of Môtu, it is clear that he has his own kingdom, separate from that of Baʿlu (see Bordreuil and Pardee 1993:66-67), with the loss of which Šapšu threatens him if he continues his attack on Baʿlu. As will become clear below *(CTA* 6 i 56-67; see note 250), ʿAṯtaru also has his own legitimate kingdom. Though this passage is too damaged to allow a solid decision as to whether the situations are similar, it is certainly plausible to see here a threat: if he continues to attack Yammu, ʿAṯtaru himself will suffer removal from his legitimate sphere of authority.

[51] ʿAṯtaru's reply seems first addressed to Šapšu, then directly to Yammu; it is the latter who in turn responds to ʿAṯtaru (lines 23-24). ʿAṯtaru's argument may be that he has already been named king (of his own domain — see preceding note) and has a wife, hence that he has a right to a palace.

[52] A most obscure verse. The "X" is a four-letter word {l⌜b-m⌝}, where the third sign is {*ʾu,d,b*}, giving the words meaning, respectively, "lions," "alone," and "hearts," none of which seems to make much sense. The verb is sometimes read {trd}, and taken as a third-person form, sometimes {ʾard}, a first-person form. After the verb "to wash" comes a phrase {kṯrm}, which has been variously interpreted. If it is a reference to bulls (*k ṯrm*), the washing in the second part of the verse makes one think that the reference is to sacrificial acts and "down my throat" to an act of devouring, but the formulae are without parallels in Ug. literature. Others have seen in {kṯrm} a reference to Kôṯaru or, as in the Kirta text, a reference to good health *(CTA* 14 i 16 [text 1.102]) or to skillfulness. See Smith's discussion (1994:217, 253-256).

[53] The reading in the middle of line 22 is unsure and it is difficult to know whether the formula *mlkt ... l mlkt* refers only to one or the other of the two deities, i.e., ʿAṯtaru and Yammu, or whether their status is being contrasted.

[54] Because the subject of the verb *yǵr* can hardly be Baʿlu, and because no other subject is stated explicitly, one must surmise that the actor is Yammu, who is either diving under his throne (hollow root *ǵr*) or crying out there (root *yǵr*) — see del Olmo Lete 1981:608. Why else would he be under his throne than for fear of Baʿlu? Note that, contrary to Môtu when he does battle with Baʿlu *(CTA* 6 vi 16-22), Yammu's rôle in the following "battle" is apparently entirely passive, i.e., there is no reference to his actions when Baʿlu attacks.

[55] In this episode, Kôṯaru-wa-Ḫasīsu has become the ally of Baʿlu against Yammu. What the connection between this episode and the previous one involving Kôṯaru-wa-Ḫasīsu, in which the latter was assigned the task of building Yammu's house (col. iii), cannot be determined because of the state of the text(s).

[56] *rkb ʿrpt*, lit., "he who mounts upon the clouds," is a direct reference to Baʿlu's function as bringer of rain.

[57] Dual forms are used in each of the two preparation episodes (*ṣmdm*, "two maces," *šmthm*, "the names of the two of them"), but each weapon

and proclaims[58] their names:
You, your name is Yagrušu;
Yagrušu, drive out[59] Yammu,
drive Yammu from his throne,
Naharu from his seat of sovereignty.
You'll whirl in Baᶜlu's hand,
like a hawk[60] in his fingers,
Strike Prince Yammu on the shoulder,
Ruler Naharu on the chest.
(So) the mace whirls in Baᶜlu's hand,
like a hawk in his fingers,
Strikes Prince Yammu on the shoulder,
Ruler Naharu on the chest.
(But) Yammu is strong,[q] he does not collapse,
his joints do not go slack,
his body does not slump.

The Second Mace (iv 18-27)
Kôṯaru prepares two maces
and proclaims their names:
You, your name is ᵓAyyamurru;
ᵓAyyamurru, expel[61] Yammu,
expel Yammu from his throne,
Naharu from his seat of sovereignty.
You'll whirl in Baᶜlu's hand,
like a hawk in his fingers,
Strike Prince Yammu on the head,
Ruler Naharu on the forehead.[r]
Yammu will go groggy
and will fall to the ground.
So the mace whirls in Baᶜlu's hand,
[like] a hawk in his fingers,
Strikes Prince [Yammu] on the head,
Ruler Naharu on the forehead.
Yammu goes groggy,
falls to the ground;
His joints go slack,
his body slumps.
Baᶜlu grabs Yammu and sets about dismembering (him),
sets about finishing Ruler Naharu off.

q Ps 74:13
r Exod 13:9; Dan 8:5

ᶜAṯtartu Intervenes (iv 28-30)[62]
By name ᶜAṯtartu reprimands (him):[63]
Scatter (him), O Mighty [Baᶜlu],[64]
scatter (him), O Cloud-Rider,
For Prince [Yammu] is our captive,
[for] Ruler Naharu is our captive.

Baᶜlu Carries Out the Order (iv 30-31)
...
Mighty Baᶜlu disperses him
...

Someone Announces Yammu's Death (iv 32)
Yammu is certainly dead, Baᶜlu,
Yammu is certainly [...]
...[65]

***CTA* 3**[66]
Baᶜlu's Feast (i)[67]
...[68]
He serves Mighty Baᶜlu,

is addressed in each episode as a singular (*šmk ᵓat*, "your name, you"). For a recent discussion of the weapons used in the various battle scenes in the Baᶜlu cycle, see Bordreuil and Pardee 1993; for the antiquity of the motif, see Durand 1993.

58 The same verb, *pᶜr*, is used here as in the proclamation of Yammu's (?) name in *CTA* 1 iv (see above, note 32).

59 Nomen omen: the name *ygrš* means "it will drive out" and Yagrušu is ordered to "drive out, expel" (*grš*) Yammu.

60 From the ᵓAqhatu story, *nšr* clearly denotes a raptor, rather than a bird whose diet consists primarily of carrion ("vulture") — see note 70 to text 1.103.

61 As in the case of Yagrušu, the name and the command correspond. Here the name includes an exclamatory element, *ᵓayya*, before the verbal element, *murr-*, apparently from a geminate root *mrr* II (*mrr* I = "be bitter" or, perhaps, from a root *mry*, "expel").

62 After line 30, the break at the end of each line becomes progressively larger, and the text can no longer be completely restored because there is no parallel text. It is, therefore, uncertain where the speeches begin and end and where the narration takes over.

63 The verb *gᶜr* clearly denotes a reprimand in both Ug. and Heb. Unfortunately, just what Baᶜlu is being reprimanded for doing is unclear. Because the verb incorporated in ᶜAṯtartu's speech (*bṯ*) differs from the ones used to describe Baᶜlu's preceding actions, one may surmise that he should have been doing *bṯ*, rather than *qṯ*, *št*, and *kly*. It has been pointed out (Caquot, Sznycer, Herdner 1974:139, n. b) that, if *bṯ* denotes "scatter, disperse," the net effect is the same as the scattering of Môtu's remains according to *CTA* 6 ii 30-37 (p. 270). One could surmise that the vocabulary differs in the two episodes because the nature of the deities is different: Yammu/Naharu is a watery entity, whatever Môtu may consist of. Judging from the Arabic verb *baṯṯa*, Baᶜlu is being commanded to disperse Yammu/Naharu by making the droplets of water fly in all directions. For those who see the origins of the myth in natural phenomena (see the introduction), the actions of a storm (Baᶜlu) on bodies of water (Yammu/ Naharu) would appear an apt parallel.

64 The second of Baᶜlu's principal titles, *ᵓalᵓiyn*, is derived from the root *lᵓy*, "to be strong, powerful" (on *rkb ᶜrpt*, "Cloud-Rider," see above, note 56). It is an *ᵓalif*-preformative noun, plausibly elative in character, used in apposition with *bᶜl*, lit., "the most mighty one, Baᶜlu."

65 The beginnings of eight more lines are extant, too fragmentary to be translated. Because of the presence of *ᵓibh*, "his enemy" in line 39 and of *[b]n ᶜnh*, "his forehead" (lit., "between his eyes") in line 40, one must assume either that this story is recounted again, perhaps as part of a proclamation or of a message to another deity, or that Baᶜlu takes on another enemy in battle.

66 This is the first of the tablets in this cycle that are relatively complete. Approximately the lower two thirds of this tablet are preserved, with the lower left corner missing. A very small fragment of the upper edge is preserved, from the upper right corner, containing remnants of the beginning of col. iii and the end of cols. iv and v. Because the beginning and end of the text have disappeared, there is no way of knowing whether it included the classification formula (*l bᶜl*) and/or a colophon. When ᵓIlīmilku ruled the columns on the recto, he made his first column considerably narrower than the other two (the three columns measure approximately 36/58/50 mm); this pattern is repeated on the verso, where the middle column is the widest and the one on the left, i.e., col. vi, the narrowest. The *editio princeps* was by Virolleaud (1938:1-90).

67 In addition to the missing upper third of the tablet, which would have contained some twenty lines, the lower corner has disappeared here, removing some fifteen complete lines and the beginnings of three others. Thus traces of only twenty-eight lines are preserved, of a probable total of sixty to sixty-five. For a detailed study of the poetic structure of the text preserved in this column, see Pardee 1988c.

68 It is generally assumed that the first five signs of line 2, {prdmn}, provide the name of Baᶜlu's head waiter, Pardamenni or Radmānu (if the

regales the Prince, master of the earth.

The Food (i 4-8)
He arises, prepares,
and gives him food:
He cuts the breast(-cut) before him,
with a salted knife (does he cut) a slice of fatling.

The Drink (i 8-17)
He arises, serves,
and gives him drink:
He puts a cup in his hand,
a goblet in his two hands,
A large vessel, mighty to look upon,
belonging to the furnishings of the heavens,
A holy cup (which) women may not see,
a goblet (which) ᵓAṯiratu (herself) may not eye;
One thousand *kd*-measures he takes from the new wine,
ten thousand he mixes into his mixture.[s]

The Entertainment (i 18-22)
He arises, chants, and sings,
cymbals (being) in the hands of the goodly one;
The good-voiced youth sings
for Baᶜlu in the heights of Ṣapānu.

Baᶜlu's Offspring (i 22-?)
Baᶜlu sees his daughters,
eyes Pidray, daughter of ᵓAru,
even Ṭallay, daughter of Rabbu.[69]
Pidar he recognizes [...]

ᶜAnatu Does Battle with Men (ii)[70]
... (with) henna (sufficient for) seven girls,
(with) scent of coriander and ᵓANHBM.[71]
The gate of ᶜAnatu's house is closed
and she meets the lads at the base of the mountain.[72]

s Ps 75:9
t Isa 22:18; cf. 2 Kgs 10:7
u Rev 14:20
v Hab 3:9, 14
w Ps 16:9

The First Battle (ii 5-16)
Thereupon ᶜAnatu's begins to smite (her adversaries) in the valley,
to attack (them) between the two cities.[73]
She smites the peoples (dwelling) on the seashore,
wreaks destruction on the humans (dwelling) to the east.[74]
Under her are heads like balls,[t]
above her are hands like locusts,
heaps of fighters' hands are like (heaps of) grasshoppers.[75]
She attaches heads around her neck,
ties hands at her waist.[76]
Up to her knees she wades in the blood of soldiers,
to her neck[u] in the gore of fighters.[77]
With (her) staff[v] she drives out the (potential) captors,
with her bowstring the opponents.

ᶜAnatu Goes Home, but is not Satisfied (ii 17-22)
Then ᶜAnatu goes to her house,
the goddess arrives at her palace.
But she is not sated with smiting (her adversaries) in the valley,
with attacking (them) between the two cities.
She prepares chairs for the fighter(s),
prepares tables for the armies,
footstools for the warriors.[78]

The Second Battle (ii 23-30)
Much she smites, then looks,
attacks and then gazes (on her handiwork), does ᶜAnatu.
Her liver swells with laughter,
her heart is filled with joy,[w]
ᶜAnatu's liver with success,
As to her knees she wades in the blood of soldier(s),

---

p be the conjunction).

[69] Baᶜlu's daughters and their mothers all have names associated with fertility: Pidray = "Fatty"; ᵓAru = a type of dew; Ṭallay = the regular Northwest Semitic word for "dew"; Rabbu = "showers" (cf. Heb. *r^ebîbîm*). One other daughter/mother pair is known from this text (iii 4-5), *ᵓarṣy bt yᶜbdr* ("Earthy," daughter of YᶜBDR, of which the meaning is disputed — see below, note 84), and another pair may be attested, *ᵓuzᶜrt bt ᶜlh* (for a possible interpretation, see Pardee 1988a:141-143). There seems to be a male counterpart to Pidray, the Pidar named in the next line (Ribichini, Xella 1984), but the relationship between the two divinities is unknown.

[70] This is one of the most controversial passages of Ug. literature, in no small part because the motivation for ᶜAnatu's slaughter is unclear owing to the state of the text. For a general discussion of ᶜAnatu's character, including its violent side, see Walls 1992.

[71] Below, iii 1-2, *ᵓanhb[m]*, fills the same slot as *ǵlp y[m]* in *CTA* 19 iv 204, of which the meaning is equally uncertain (see note 130 to 1.103).

[72] ᶜAnatu's home is on Mount ᵓInbubu (see above, note 9), and one would expect the *ǵr* here to refer to that mountain. The identification of the "lads" (*ǵlmm*), however, is lost in the preceding lacuna: were they messengers or more militarily oriented? It is to be noted that ᶜAnatu's adversaries in the following battle scenes are not termed *ǵlmm*.

[73] Without an identification of Mount ᵓInbubu, it is impossible to know to what cities reference is made here. The verbal forms in this verse are both infixed-*t* forms, without expressed objects; their function is plausibly a sort of middle: "she smites for her own benefit."

[74] The perspective is clearly that of the Levantine coast, with the totality of the region's inhabitants expressed by the merismus of "seashore" (*ḫp ym*) and "rising of the sun" (*ṣᵓat špš*). Strong emphasis is placed on the human nature of her adversaries, who are described as "peoples, tribes, clans" (*lᵓim*, probably plural construct in form) and "humankind" (*ᵓadm*, either singular collective or plural construct).

[75] This verse contains three distinct images of destruction: (1) severed heads rolling like balls at the goddess' feet, (2) severed hands flying through the air like locusts, then (3) being gathered together in heaps like grasshoppers after a plague.

[76] Lit., "to her upper back (*bmt*)/at her belt (*ḥbš*)"; the image is that of heads being strung together as a necklace and hung around the shoulders (see Pope 1977b:pl. IX, for a modern image of a goddess with heads around her neck and hands at her waist).

[77] The military terms in this passage (*mhr*, "fighter, serviceman," *ḏmr*, "soldier," lit., "guard"; *ṣbᵓu*, "army," appears below, as does *ǵzrm*, "warriors") overlap only partially with the military terminology used in the Kirta text (see notes 22 and 78 to text 1.102).

[78] Though an invitation is not mentioned, the preparations are appropriate for a feast. Apparently (unidentified) soldiers enter expecting a feast, only to be attacked.

to her neck in the gore of fighters.
Until she is satisfied, she smites (her adversaries) in the house,
attacks (them) between the tables.

The Peaceful Aftermath (ii 30 - iii 3)
They wipe up the blood of the soldiers in the house,
they pour out oil of peace in a bowl.
Girl ᶜAnatu bathes her hands,
the sister-in-law of Liᵓmu (bathes) her fingers.
She bathes her hands in the blood of the warriors,
her fingers in the gore of the fighters.
She prepares chairs (in addition) to chairs,
tables (in addition) to tables,
footstools she prepares (in addition) to footstools.[79]
She gathers water and washes,[80]
dew of heavens, oil of earth,
the showers of Cloud-Rider.
The dew (that) the heavens pour down,
the showers (that) the stars pour down.
She beautifies herself with ᵓANHBM,
that range [a thousand furlongs] in the sea.
...[81]

Someone Sings (iii 4-8)[82]
[She? will take lyre in hand],
pull[83] the harp to (her?) breast:
A song for the love of Mighty Baᶜlu (she? will sing),
the affection of Pidray, daughter of ᵓAru,
the love of Ṭallay, daughter of Rabbu,
the ardor of ᵓArṣay, daughter of Yaᶜibdarru.[84]

Baᶜlu's Message to ᶜAnatu (iii 8-31)
Then, lads, enter,
at ᶜAnatu's feet bow and fall,
do homage, honor her.
Say to Girl ᶜAnatu,
repeat to the sister-in-law[85] of Liᵓmu.
Message of Mighty Baᶜlu,
word of the mightiest of heroes:
Present bread offerings in the earth,
place love-offerings in the dust;
Pour well-being out into the earth,
calmness into the fields.
Hurry, press, hasten,
to me let your feet run,
to me let your legs hasten;
For I have something to tell you,
a matter to recount to you:
Words regarding wood, whisperings regarding stone,
conversings of heaven with earth,
of the deep with the stars;
I understand lightning which not even the heavens know,[86]
a matter (which) men do not know,
(which) the hordes of the earth do not understand.
Come and I will explain it (for you)
in my mountain, Divine Ṣapānu,[x]
in the holy place, in the mountain that is my personal possession,[y]
in the goodly place, the hill of my victory.[87]

═══════ [88]

x Cf. Ps 89:13

y Exod 15:17; Ps 78:54

[79] The formulation *ksᵓat l ksᵓat*, etc., is clearly in contrast with the previous preparation of chairs, tables, and footstools (lines 20-22). There they were prepared for the soldiers; here no group is mentioned.

[80] The text here plays on two usages of *rḥṣ* corresponding to "bathe" and "wash": above she bathes her hands in the the blood of the slain opponents, here she washes her hands in water to remove the blood of the previous bathing.

[81] Some twenty lines have disappeared between the small fragment containing the beginning of col. iii and the main text. My line numbering of the rest of col. iii differs from that in *CTA* (it is identical to that in *KTU*) because Herdner, following the original editor, ascribed the number "1" to the first line on the principal fragment of the tablet rather than to the first line of the column. On the other hand, I follow Herdner (and Virolleaud) in numbering the lines of cols. iii-iv continuously.

[82] On the indications that the message contained in lines 8-31 constitute Baᶜlu's entrusting of the message to his pages, see note 88. If that ascription be correct, lines 4-8, after which there is no obvious transition to lines 8-31, must constitute part of Baᶜlu's speech to his messengers, plausibly, though not certainly, describing what ᶜAnatu will be doing when they arrive.

[83] Collation of the tablet has confirmed the reading of {mšr} in the following line, and the word here translated as a verb, "pull," may also be spelled with {m} ({mšt}; see Pardee 1988a:150). The explanation of these forms is uncertain, though it may have something to do with the level of narrative embedding (see preceding note).

[84] There is general agreement that the first part of this name is related to Arabic *wᶜb*, "to be ample," but some analyze the second element as "generation" (*dr*) others as "copious flow" (*drr*). Either explanation is possible, though the latter appears more likely because more closely related to the other names having to do with various forms of precipitation (see above, note 69).

[85] The title is here spelled {ymmt}, apparently an error for *ybmt*.

[86] This line is additional as compared with the first occurrence of these formulae (*CTA* 1 iii) in a message of ᵓIlu addressed to Kôṯaru-wa-Ḫasīsu, here appropriately in the mouth of Baᶜlu the storm god. It appears probable that *šmm* here, ascribed powers of cognition, refers to the deity Šamūma, and not simply the sky. The Ug. pantheon texts contain a double-deity *ᵓarṣ w šmm*, "earth and heavens" (see Pardee [forthcoming] on RS 1.017:12). The claim is that, although the lightning and thunder appear in the heavens, their operation is the work of Baᶜlu.

[87] "Victory" here is *tlᵓiyt*, from the same root as Baᶜlu's title *ᵓalᵓiyn* (see above, note 64).

[88] The function of the double horizontal line drawn across the width of the column here has been much debated (see Rummel 1978:185-189). A plausible explanation is that it has to do with the omission of some part of the repetition that takes place when a message is sent from one party to another (for the narrative description of sending a message, see Ginsberg 1941:12-14). Such an explanation might imply that the preceding section relates the sending of the messengers, rather than their arrival, and that the journey and arrival of the messengers has been omitted from the narration. That hypothesis faces two problems, however: (1) Baᶜlu's speech to the messengers would include a description of ᶜAnatu's behavior (above, lines 4-8), not a common feature of the messenger-sending formulae; (2) there is no specific reference in the text to the omission, a feature sometimes present (see particularly the case in *CTA* 4 v [note 166]). In spite of these difficulties, I have translated as though the narrative

ᶜAnatu's Response (iii 32 - iv 51)

When ᶜAnatu sees the two deities,
her feet shake,
behind, her back muscles snap,
above, her face sweats,
her vertebrae rattle,
her spine goes weak.[89]
She raises her voice and says aloud:
How is it that Gupanu-wa-ᵓUgāru have come?[90]
What enemy has arisen against Baᶜlu,
(what) adversary against Cloud-Rider?
I have smitten ᵓIlu's beloved, Yammu,
have finished off the great god Naharu.[91]
I have bound the dragon's[z] jaws, have destroyed it,[92]
have smitten the twisting serpent,[aa]
the close-coiled one with seven heads.
I have smitten ᵓIlu's beloved ᵓArišu (Demander),[93]
have wreaked destruction on ᵓIlu's calf ᶜAtiku (Binder).
I have smitten ᵓIlu's bitch ᵓIšatu (Fire),
have finished off ᵓIlu's daughter D̠abibu (Flame).
I have smitten for silver, have (re)possessed the gold of
him who would have driven Baᶜlu from the heights of Ṣapānu,
him who would have caused (him) to flee like a bird (from) (the seat of) his power,
Him who would have banished him from his royal throne,
from (his) resting-place, from the seat of his dominion.
So, what enemy has arisen against Baᶜlu,
(what) adversary against Cloud-Rider?

z Ps 74:13

aa Isa 27:1

The Envoys Deliver Their Message (iv 52-67)

The lads answer up:
No enemy has arisen against Baᶜlu,
(no) adversary against Cloud-Rider.
(Rather we have a) message (from) Mighty Baᶜlu,
a word (from) the mightiest of warriors:[94]
Present bread offerings in the earth,
place love-offerings in the dust;
Pour well-being out into the earth,
calmness into the fields.
Hurry, press, hasten,
to me let your feet run,
to me let your legs hasten;
[For I have something] to tell you,
a matter [to recount to you]:
[Words regarding] wood, whisperings regarding [stone,
a matter (which)] men [do not] know,
[(which) the hordes of the] earth [do not] understand.
[Conversings of heaven with] earth,
of the deep [with the stars];
[I understand lightning] which not even the heavens [know].
[Come and] I will explain [it (for you)

has jumped from Baal's speech containing the message to ᶜAnatu's reaction when she sees the messengers, assuming the omission of the travel formulae (cf. de Moor 1971:4-5; 1987:8-10).

[89] These lines, which represent a formulaic and stylized reaction to unexpected visitors and bad news, are found in variant forms twice in the Baᶜlu epic (here and p. 257 in *CTA* 4 ii 16-20) and once in the ᵓAqhatu text (p. 352, *CTA* 19 ii 93-96 [text 1.103]). "Back muscles" is a somewhat free translation of *ksl*, which, with the adverbial phrase *bᶜdn*, should mean, lit., "the sinews (of the back)"; *ksl* also appears in *pnt kslh*, "vertebrae," lit., "the points of the sinews (of the back)" (for bibliography, see Pardee 1987:406).

[90] Baal's messenger, another double-deity, is here first identified by name, "Vineyard and Field," the latter term cognate to an Akk. word for field and apparently the root word behind the name of the city of Ugarit, plausibly a feminine form of the same root. As is the case with other double-deities, this one is sometimes referred to in the singular, sometimes in the dual.

[91] Because the cycle as extant does not contain an account of ᶜAnatu's defeat of Yammu/Naharu, these references and those that follow are enigmatic. One may surmise that ᶜAnatu intervened after Baᶜlu's battle with Yammu, and hence that this passage refers to a sequel to the narrative in *CTA* 2 iv, or that the mention of someone driving someone from a throne in *CTA* 1 iv (cf. note 32) was related to a defense by ᶜAnatu of Baᶜlu's rights (as described here below in her speech).

[92] On the reading behind this translation, see Pardee 1984. The word here translated "dragon" is *tnn* (cf. Heb. *tannīn*). The identification of the watery enemy with a reptilian one is well attested in Heb., but it is not so common in other sources (cf. Williams-Forte 1983). In Ug. sources, the *tnn* is once described as being "in the sea" (p. 273, *CTA* 6 vi 50), but the reptilian foes are not presented anywhere in this cycle as active allies of Yammu. I have, therefore, changed the poetic division (as compared with Pardee 1984:252-53) so as to place the *tnn* more closely in relation to the following reptilian terms. If *tnn* is not a sub-set of the watery deities, one wonders if it is possible to identify him with another known deity. Williams-Forte proposed Môtu, the god of death, a conclusion disputed by Lambert 1985. Perhaps it is best to see the reptilian terms here (to which must be added *ltn*, from p. 265, *CTA* 5 i 1) as a set structurally independent of the Yammu/Naharu set and representing a separate but related mythology, of which no lengthy cycle of myths has come down to us. The ubiquity of the snake in iconography (discussed at length by Williams-Forte and Lambert, among many others), the scattered references in Ug. texts, and the importance of the snake in the biblical fall and exodus stories may serve as bases for seeing the reptilian set of enemies as important in its own right and in some sense independent of, even though related to, the watery set.

[93] As in the case of Yammu, the following two sets of enemies are described in terms attaching them closely to ᵓIlu: two familial terms, *mdd* ("beloved") and *bt* ("daughter"), and two animal terms, *ᶜgl* ("calf") and *klbt* ("bitch"), these two sets arranged chiastically. The identities of the individuals and the import of their names are unknown. *ᵓarš*, apparently the "Demander," is found again in this cycle, associated with the dragon *tnn* (*CTA* 6 vi 50), and *ᶜgl ᵓil* is attested in one of the "para-mythological" texts, but in a broken passage (cf. Pardee 1988a:106-110). Because these beings are described as offspring of ᵓIlu, ᶜAnatu's (and Baᶜlu's) hostility to them may plausibly be explained by assuming that they have ᵓAt̠iratu for their mother. Indeed, in this cycle ᵓAt̠iratu's sons regularly occupy the camp opposed to Baᶜlu/ᶜAnatu (see below, note 190).

[94] Note the many variants, especially reshuffling of formulae, in this recital of the message as compared with the form entrusted to the messengers in col. iii.

in] my mountain, Divine Ṣapānu,
in the holy [place, in the mountain that is my personal] possession.

ᶜAnatu Agrees to Baᶜlu's Request (iv 68-83)
Girl ᶜAnatu replies,
yet again [the sister-in-law of] Liˀmu:
I will indeed present bread offerings [in the earth],
place love-offerings in the dust;
I will pour [well-being] out into the earth,
calmness into the fields.
May Baᶜlu place his watering devices in [the heavens],
may [Haddu] bring the [rain of] his X.[95]
(Then) I, for my part, will surely present bread offerings in the earth,
place love-offerings [in] the dust;
I will pour well-being out into the earth,
calmness into the fields.
Moreover, I say this:
Come, come, attendants of the gods,
you, you may tarry, but I'm off
(From) ˀUǵaru for the most distant of gods,
(from) ˀInbubu for the most distant of deities:
By double stretches below the springs of the earth,
triple lengths (in) the low places.

ᶜAnatu Visits Baᶜlu (iv 84-?)
So off she heads,
toward Baᶜlu in the heights of Ṣapānu.
(From) a thousand yards off,
ten thousand furlongs,
Baᶜlu sees his sister coming,
his father's daughter[96] striding along.
He shoos the (other) women away,
places beef in front of her,
a fatling before her.
She gathers water and washes,
dew of heavens, oil of earth.
The dew (that) the heavens pour down,
the showers (that) the stars pour down.
She beautifies herself with ˀANHBM,
that [range a thousand furlongs in the sea.]
...[97]

Baᶜlu's Claim to a Palace (iv 94-99)
[For Baᶜlu has no house as (do) the (other) gods,
(no) court] as (do) the sons of [ˀAṯiratu,
(No) dwelling (as does) ˀIlu, (no) shelter (as do)] his sons,
(no) dwelling (as does) [the Great Lady, ˀAṯiratu of the Sea[98]],
(No) dwelling (as does) Pidray, [daughter of ˀAru,
(no) shelter] (as does) Ṭallay, daughter of Rabbu,
[(no) dwelling (as does) ˀArṣay], daughter of Yaᶜibdarru,
[(no) dwelling (as do)] the honored [brides].[99]

ᶜAnatu's Reply (iv 99 - v 4)[100]
[Girl ᶜAnatu] replies:
The Bull, [my father] ˀIlu, will come around to

[95] Collation has provided the following plausible readings for this verse: {yšt ⌜b š⌝[mm.] bᶜl . mdlh . ybᶜr (line 74) [hd . mṭ] ⌜r⌝ [. -]rnh}. It is often assumed that *mdlh* means "his lightning," in no small part because of the parallelism with the last word, which is usually restored as {[q]rnh} and interpreted as meaning "lightning-flash." But there is no etymological basis for the interpretation of *mdl* as lightning (Pardee 1980:278) and no comparative basis for that of *qrn* as "lightning-flash." The traces of a sign with two horizontal wedges in the fifth slot in line 74 appears to rule out the usual restoration of *ˀil hd*, "the god Haddu" (a formula unattested in this cycle) and prompts the restoration there of *mṭr*, "rain," a word elsewhere attested in parallel with *mdl* (in Pardee 1980:278, before collating the tablet, I proposed reading {[mṭ]rnh} in place of {[q]rnh}). In such a context, *mdl* is plausibly explained as from the root *dly*, "draw water" and, therefore, as a different word from *mdl* denoting an element in the harnessing apparatus of an equid. On the various suggestions for interpreting *mdl*, see the bibliography in Pardee 1987:417.

[96] The meaning of *ybnt ˀabh* is unclear (cf. Pardee 1980:279). Among proposed emendations are: (1) *ybmt ˀabh*, "his father's sister-in-law" (i.e., his father's brother's wife); (2) *bt ˀabh*, "his father's daughter" (implying perhaps that they had a common father, but not a common mother); (3) *ybmt ˀaḫh*, "his brother's sister-in-law."

[97] Here approximately 15 lines are lost between the principal fragment of col. iv and the remnants of eight or nine lines preserved on the small fragment (see above, notes 66 and 81).

[98] The explanation of ˀAṯiratu's titles *rbt ˀaṯrt ym* has much exercised the minds of Ug. exegetes. Many have taken the name as derived from the title, i.e., "the great lady who treads upon the sea" (partial bibliography in Pardee 1989-90:440-441). None of the evidence for vocalization of the name ˀAṯiratu, however, favors the idea that the first vowel was ever long, as would be required of an active participial form. It appears more likely (1) that *rbt* is a title designating the goddess as queen (i.e., principal wife of ˀIlu) or queen mother (cf. Brooke 1979:86), (2) that ˀAṯiratu is the basic name of the goddess (this is the only form of the name that appears in the ritual texts), and (3) that *ym* is added as a supplemental titular element. Some of the factors to be considered in explaining the element *ym* are: (1) one passage seems to depict ˀAṯiratu's sons as waves of the sea (*CTA* 6 v 1-3); (2) the deity Qudšu(-wa)-ˀAmruru is called "the fisherman of ˀAṯiratu" (*dgy ˀaṯrt*) and this deity possesses a net that he apparently throws into the sea (*CTA* 4 ii 31-35); (3) the title must be taken into consideration in explaining ˀIlu's initial preference for Yammu (cf. above, note 32). But the mythological background of the title remains obscure.

[99] We are never told exactly why Baᶜlu's daughters have a house while he does not. The general structure of this passage (restored from similar passages below in v 38-44 and in *CTA* 4 i 10-19 and iv 50-57) and the specific presence of the term *klt*, which denotes in the narrow sense a father's son's bride, may indicate that Baᶜlu's daughters have married sons of ˀIlu by ˀAṯiratu and have become part of the sons' households. This hypothesis is supported by the placement of the reference to the "honored brides" at the head of the list of daughters in *CTA* 4 i 15-19; iv 54-57, rather than at the end as here. The adjective *knyt* by which the *klt* are described, appears to be related to Akk. *kunnû*, an epithet of deities, and *kanûtu*, an adjective used only for goddesses.

[100] Also in col. v (on col. iv, see above, note 81), my line numbering differs from that in *CTA* (and corresponds to that of *KTU*), for the same reason, i.e., Herdner, following Virolleaud, numbered the lines continuously beginning with the small fragment of col. iv through col. v. Thus, because the small fragment of col. iv contains eight lines, line 1 in col. v is numbered as the ninth line in *CTA*. (According to Herdner, the small fragment actually contains nine lines, but she did not include the first in her consecutive numbering, designating it as "1*"; when I collated the tablet, I did not find this line "1*.")

me,
he'll come around to me and to him [...].
...[101]
[I'll] trample him to the ground like a lamb,
[I'll cause] his gray hair [to flow] with blood,[bb]
the gray hairs of his beard [with gore],[cc]
That is if he does not give a house to Baᶜlu like (that of) the (other) gods,
[a court] like (that of) the sons of ᵓAṯiratu.

ᶜAnatu Is Off to Visit ᵓIlu (v 4-9)
[She digs in] (her) feet,
[takes off across] the earth;
She [heads] off
[towards ᵓIlu] at the source of the [double] river,
midst the [upspringings] of the [deeps].
She penetrates Ilu's abode,
enters the dwelling of the King, father of [Šunama],
She bends over[102] and enters the abode,
addresses the lord of the gods.[103]

ᵓIlu Responds (v 10-18?)[104]
The Bull, her father ᵓIlu, hears her voice,
[responds] (from) within seven rooms,
[(from) within] eight locked [chambers]:[105]
You [must cry] aloud to ᵓIlu [your lord]
...[106]
Šapšu, luminary of the gods, [glows hot],
the heavens are powerless under the control of [Môtu, the beloved of ᵓIlu].[107]

bb 1 Kgs 2:9
cc Cf. 2 Sam 20:10

ᶜAnatu Gets Tough (v 19-25)
Girl ᶜAnatu replies:
[In the grandeur of] your house, O ᵓIlu,
in the grandeur of [your] house do not rejoice,
do not rejoice in the height of [your] palace.[108]
Will I not seize them in my right hand,
squeeze [them][109] in my broad grasp?[110]
I'll [smite the ...] of your head,
I'll make your gray hair flow [with blood],
the gray hairs of your beard with gore.

ᵓIlu Reacts Placatingly (v 25-29)
ᵓIlu responds (from) within seven rooms,
(from) within eight locked chambers:
[I] know [you], (my) daughter, (I know) that [you] are a manly sort,
and that among goddesses there is none so emotional as you.[111]
What do you request, Girl ᶜAnatu?

ᶜAnatu Tries Flattery (v 29-34)
Girl ᶜAnatu replies:
Your decision(s), ᵓIlu, (are) wise,
your wisdom is forever,
your decision(s) (provide) a life of good fortune.
(Now,) our king is Mighty Baᶜlu,

[101] Several signs have disappeared from the end of the last line of col. iv and about four signs from the beginning of the first line of col. v, enough to make up a full line of text. Because of lack of parallels, it is impossible to determine whether the missing line continued the preceding verse or served as the first utterance in the following threats.

[102] The third sign from the end of line 8 appears to be {t}, rather than {m}, as in previous versions; thus (⸢t⸣ ṣr}, "she bends over" (cf. the hollow root *ṣr* in Arabic). On the words typically used to designate ᵓIlu's home, see above, note 29.

[103] Reading in line 9: {ṯtn⸢y⸣ [. l] ⸢ᵓa⸣dn [.] ⸢ᵓi⸣l⸢m⸣}.

[104] The damaged state of lines 13-16 leaves open the possibility that this section is not all one long speech from ᵓIlu.

[105] ᵓIlu, apparently afraid of ᶜAnatu's irascibility, declines to come out to speak with her.

[106] Only a few words are preserved in lines 13-16. It is at least possible that Šapšu, the sun deity, appears or is mentioned, for the adverb *ᶜln*, "on high," is present at the beginning of line 13 and this word is used elsewhere to describe Šapšu's position. See next note.

[107] This is the first occurrence of these formulae, repeated below *(CTA* 6 ii 24-25) to describe the ascendency of Môtu during Baᶜlu's demise. The principal terms in the formulae are *ṣḥrrt*, describing the blasting effect of the Šapšu, the sun (cf. Arabic *ṣḫr*, used to express sunstroke; below in text 1.87 the same verb is used for roasting a bird over a fire), and *lᵓa*, "to be weak," describing the inability of the heavens to produce precipitation (the form is apparently the infinitive, used absolutely, */laᵓâ/*). The state of the text precludes our knowing why reference is made at this point to Môtu's malefic action, but it is plausible that the formula is generally descriptive of Môtu, as here below in *CTA* 4 viii 21-24. Depending on whether or not Šapšu was mentioned in the previous passage (see preceding note), the reference here may have applied more or less directly to the sun deity's immediate presence. Below, *CTA* 6 v 4 and n. 268, an entity presented as *ṣḥr mt*, "Môtu's heat" is attacked right alongside the sons of ᵓAṯiratu, enemies of Baᶜlu. For a recent naturalistic interpretation of this motif, see Yon 1989. Môtu, "Death," is known both as the "beloved" *(mdd/ydd)* of ᵓIlu and as his "son," the last feature attested also by Philo of Byblos (Attridge and Oden 1981:57).

[108] Three principal lines of interpretation have been proposed for this passage and the parallel in the ᵓAqhatu text *(CTA* 18 i 6-10 [text 1.103]): (1) ᵓIlu is not to rejoice in the building (*bnt* < *bny*) of his house or (2) in the height (*bnt* < *nty/w*) of his house; (3) ᵓIlu's sons (read *bnt* as *bnm*) are not to rejoice (cf. Dijkstra and de Moor 1975:192-93; Margalit 1983:91-92). The first interpretation does not fit this context, the second is based on a rather shaky Arabic etymology (*ntw*, "to swell up [said of a limb of the body]"), while the third is based on emendation of an already damaged and uncertain text. More plausible variants of the third would be to restore *bnm // bnt*, "sons" // "daughters" (the first word is entirely absent in both passages) or *bnt // bnt*; "daughters" // "daughters." The last possibility is particularly appealing because it would constitute an example of the so-called "staircase" tricolon (Greenstein 1977): "May the daughters of your house, O ᵓIlu, /May the daughters of your house not rejoice, /May they not rejoice in the height of your palace." In this analysis, the masculine plural pronoun in the following verse ("seize them") would refer back to these references to the dwelling (*bhtk*, plural in form, "your house, mansion," and *hkl*, "palace"). Psychologically, however, it appears preferable to see here a direct threat to ᵓIlu himself and I tentatively adopt Margalit's proposal, though remaining dubious about the etymology.

[109] Traces of {šṣ} are visible near the end of line 22, suggesting the restoration {[ᵓa]⸢šṣ⸣[qhm]}, "I will squeeze them."

[110] Lit., "in the greatness of my length," apparently a reference to the length of the goddess' arms (cf. *gdl* + "arm" in Exod 15:16).

[111] Multiple interpretations of *ᵓnš//qlṣ* in this verse have been proposed, for it is difficult to establish the meaning of the terms by Ug. usage and various etymological explanations are possible (for bibliography see Pardee 1987:373, 445). The translation offered here assumes (1) that ᵓIlu is not speaking ironically (hence *ᵓnš* does not mean "gentle"), (2) that "sick" (another possible meaning of *ᵓnš*) is not used idiomatically in Ug. for immorality (viz. ᶜAnatu's violent behavior), and (3) that the /ṣ/ in *qlṣ* is genuine and hence that the root is not identical to Heb. *qls*

(he is) our ruler and there is none above him.[dd]
All of us (other gods) bear his vessel,
all of us bear his cup.[112]

Again, Baᶜlu's Claim to a Palace (v 35-44)
(But) groaning he does cry out to[113] the Bull, his father ᵓIlu,
to the king who established him,[114] [ee]
He cries out to ᵓAṯiratu and to her sons,
to the goddess and the host of her kin:
Baᶜlu has no house as (do) the (other) gods,
(no) court as (do) the sons of ᵓAṯiratu,
(No) dwelling (as does) ᵓIlu, (no) shelter (as do) [his sons],
(no) dwelling (as does) the Great Lady, ᵓAṯiratu of the Sea,
(No) dwelling (as does) Pidray, daughter of ᵓAru,
[(no) shelter] (as does) Ṭallay, [daughter of] Rabbu,
(no) dwelling [(as does) ᵓArṣay, daughter of Yaᶜibdarru],
(no) dwelling [(as do) the honored brides].
...[115]

The Summons to Kôṯaru-wa-Ḫasīsu (vi)[116]
Cross the mountain, cross the height,
cross the shores of heavenly Nupu.[117]
Have (your nets) drawn in,[118] O fisherman of ᵓAṯiratu,
come, O Qudšu-ᵓAmruru.

dd Isa 33:22; Ps 95:3
ee Deut 32:6

You must head off
to Memphis, (to) the god of it all,
(To) Crete (which is) the throne (on which) he sits,
(to) Memphis (which is) the land of his own possession,
Through a thousand yards,
ten thousand furlongs.
At the feet of Kôṯaru bow and fall,
do homage and honor him.
Say to Kôṯaru-wa-Ḫasīsu,
repeat to Hayyinu the handicrafter:
Message of Mighty [Baᶜlu],
word [of the mightiest of warriors:]
...[119]

***CTA* 4**[120]
...
Yet Again, Baᶜlu's Claim to a Palace (i 4-19)
[(But) groaning he does cry] out to the Bull, [his father ᵓIlu],
to ᵓIlu, the king [who established him],
[He cries] out to ᵓAṯiratu [and to her sons],
to the goddess [and the host of] her [kin]:
[Baᶜlu has no house as (do) the (other) gods,
(no) court as (do) the sons of] ᵓAṯiratu,
(No) dwelling (as does) ᵓIlu, (no) shelter (as do) his sons,
(no) dwelling (as does) the Great Lady, ᵓAṯiratu of the Sea.

"scorn" but cognate to Arabic *qlṣ*, "shrivel," and is used to express emotional turmoil. According to this interpretation, the verse describes two characteristics of ᶜAnatu: (1) that she fights like a man (cf. col. ii), (2) that she gives free vent to her emotions.

[112] The phrase "all of us" is in Ug. *klnyy*, which may be analyzed either as *kl* + *n* + *y* + *y*, where the *-n-* is the first person plural suffix and the twice-repeated *-y* is a so-called "emphatic" particle, or *kl* + *ny* + *y*, where *-ny* is analyzed as the 1st person dual suffix ("both of us") and the second *-y* the "emphatic" particle. In the parallel passage, *CTA* 4 iv 45, 46 (p. 259), where ᵓAṯiratu is the speaker, the form is *klnyn*, with the particle *-n* at the end instead of *-y*. The two analyses represent forms that are well attested elsewhere in Ug. According to the first analysis, ᶜAnatu (and ᵓAṯiratu) would be saying that all the gods serve Baᶜlu as cupbearers; in the second that she and ᵓIlu should be doing so, i.e., that ᵓIlu should join the procession. One might doubt that ᵓIlu, who occupies a higher position in the divine hierarchy than Baᶜlu (see below, note 114), would join the other gods in servitude to Baᶜlu. Because these formulae originate with ᶜAnatu, even if they are repeated below by ᵓAṯiratu, one may doubt to what extent they constitute a true "shift" of allegiance from Yammu to Baᶜlu (cf. Smith 1994:102 on *ṯpṭ*); they seem rather to reflect ᶜAnatu's position in the conflict (see below, note 190), adopted only half-heartedly by ᵓAṯiratu (see notes 190 and 244).

[113] The expression is taken to be *ṣḥ* + accusative (*l yṣḥ ṯr ᵓil ᵓabh*). Because the verb *ṣḥ* is sometimes followed by a *l*-complement, some interpret the formula here and in the parallel passages below with ᵓIlu, etc., as subject. Such an interpretation requires reinterpreting the sequence of speakers and requests — i.e., ᵓIlu, ᵓAṯiratu, and her sons would all be already in favor of Baᶜlu receiving a palace. A factor in favor of the interpretation adopted here is the following phrase, *yṣḥ ᵓaṯrt w bnh*: by comparison with *CTA* 6 i 39-40 (p. 269) *tšmḫ ht ᵓaṯrt w bnh*, one would expect *tṣḥ* in this text and it appears likely, therefore, that the subject of the verb *yṣḥ* is *bᶜl*. Unfortunately, the morphological criterion is not absolutely decisive, because *yṣḥ* could theoretically be 3m.pl. because of the compound subject of which one element is masculine plural.

[114] The relationship between ᵓIlu and Baᶜlu is well expressed in this verse and in this entire passage: ᵓIlu is chief executive king, Baᶜlu was appointed king over the earth by ᵓIlu. But even to acquire so apparently obvious a perquisite as a palace, Baᶜlu must have ᵓIlu's approval.

[115] Over twenty lines of text have disappeared at the bottom of col. v, of which just the ends of a few lines are visible on the small fragment (numbered as v 44-51, in *KTU*). The first ten lines of col. vi have also been entirely lost and the slanting break has taken the beginnings of seven more lines.

[116] ᶜAnatu's pleading has been successful, for ᵓAṯiratu's personal attendants, Qudšu(-wa)-ᵓAmruru (written without the *w* here but with it elsewhere), are sent as messengers to the craftsman deity Kôṯaru-wa-Ḫasīsu, and the message is indicated as originating with Baᶜlu.

[117] Some have seen in *np šmm* "the heights of the heavens" (≈Heb. *nôp* in Ps 48:3), others another name for Memphis (Heb. *nōp* and *mōp*). The presence of the word "shores" (*ᵓiht*) and the fact that Kôṯaru-wa-Ḫasīsu has an alternate dwelling in Egypt seem to favor the second interpretation (unless *ᵓiht* be given the specific sense of "islands," in which case the phrase *ᵓiht np šmm* could refer to the mountainous islands of the Mediterranean).

[118] Various explanations of the form *šmšr* have been given, but as it appears to be the Š-stem from the root *mšr* which, by comparative considerations, should mean "to draw, drag," a plausible interpretation would be to see the fisherman having his nets drawn in because he must leave on a trip.

[119] Approximately twenty lines have disappeared from the end of col. vi.

[120] Though made up of several fragments, this tablet as reconstituted contains the longest text of this cycle, inscribed in eight columns of sixty-five or more lines each, and it is the best-preserved of the tablets, cols. iv-v being almost completely extant for a continuous stretch of text of over 125 lines. The beginning and end of the text are lost, and we cannot know, therefore, whether this tablet bore the archival notation *l bᶜl*

(No) dwelling (as do) the honored brides:
(no) dwelling (as does) Pidray, daughter of ᵓAru,
(no) shelter (as does) Ṭallay, daughter of Rabbu,
(no) dwelling (as does) ᵓArṣay, daughter of Yaᶜibdarru.

Gifts Suggested and Prepared (i 20-44)[121]

I must also say this to you:
You really should prepare a gift for the Great Lady, ᵓAṯiratu of the Sea,
a present for the Progenitress[ff] of the Gods.[122]
Hayyinu steps up to the bellows,
in the hands of Ḫasīsu are the tongs.
He casts silver, causes gold to flow,[123]
he casts silver by the thousands (of shekels),
he casts gold by the ten thousands (of shekels).

ff Gen 4:1

He casts ḪYM and TBTḪ:[124]
A (throne-)stand for ᵓIlu[125] of twenty thousand (shekels' weight),
a (throne-)stand for ᵓIlu with silver decorations,
interspersed with[126] (decorations of) ruddy gold;
A chair for ᵓIlu, a seat of finest (gold),
a footstool for ᵓIlu (!)[127] covered with the brightest (metal);
A bed for ᵓIlu of the finest sort,
above, he places an engraving;[128]
A table for ᵓIlu filled with creatures,
creepy-crawlers[129] from the foundations of the earth;[130]
A bowl for ᵓIlu, hammered thin as (they do in) ᵓAmurru,
formed as (they do in) the land of YMᵓAN,
which has on it bulls by the ten thousands.[131]

at the beginning. The partially preserved colophon on the left edge of the tablet, apparently in a very brief form, may be taken as an indication that there was not a colophon at the end of the text. Approximately twenty lines are missing from the beginning of col. i; the several badly damaged lines after this lacuna may be restored quite plausibly on the basis of parallel texts. As in the case of *CTA* 3 (see above, note 66), the first and last columns of this text are narrower than the intervening columns. Virolleaud did the *editio princeps* of this text in a single article (1932).

[121] In spite of the fact that ᵓIlu has agreed to have Kôṯaru-wa-Ḫasīsu summoned, it would appear that ᵓAṯiratu and ᵓIlu must still be placated (baksheesh) to give their final permission for the palace to be built and for Kôṯaru-wa-Ḫasīsu to be signed on as contractor. The depth of ᵓAṯiratu's real hostility to Baᶜlu and ᶜAnatu's recognition of that hostility are both evident in the form of ᶜAnatu's announcement of Baᶜlu's death to ᵓIlu: "So now let ᵓAṯiratu and her sons rejoice, (let) the goddess (rejoice) and the host of her kin; for Mighty Baᶜlu is dead, perished the Prince, master of the earth" (*CTA* 6 i 39-43). The reasons for this hostility appear to reside in power struggles within ᵓIlu's family (see nn. 32, 163, 190).

[122] ᵓAṯiratu's title as mother goddess is *qnyt ᵓilm*, "she who produces gods," parallel to ᵓIlu's title as father god, *bny bnwt*, "he who builds offspring" (cf. *bn*, "son").

[123] The verb *yṣq* is used in Ug. and Heb. for working with metals, apparently for the artisan's casting work (< "to pour") rather than for the refiner's job. It belongs to the same semantic field as *nsk*, the standard word for "metal-worker," also related to a root meaning basically "to pour." The verb here translated "cause to flow" is *šlḥ*, lit., "to send"; it is not a standard term of metal working and hence has received various interpretations, among them "to beat flat," i.e. "extend."

[124] This line functions either as introduction to the list that follows or as the first items on the list. Unfortunately both terms are obscure. They are most commonly identified as meaning "tent" (≈ *ḥmt* in *CTA* 14 ii 65 and parallels [text 1.102]) and "resting place, bed" (≈ Akk. *tapšaḫu/tapšuḫtu*; cf., e.g., Dietrich and Loretz 1978b:59-60). The image, however, of "casting" a tent appears strange and the Ug. word *tbtḫ*, though it could be cognate to the Akk. term, cannot be a loan word (Akk. /ḫ/ would be written {ǵ}) and, in any case, the production of a bed is part of the list below. The other principal explanation is to take both terms as denoting metals and hence as belonging to the previous verse. For lack of other attestations in Ug. and reliable points of comparison, it appears best for the present to leave the words untranslated.

[125] This and the following occurrences of *ᵓil* are often taken as superlatives (*kt ᵓil* = "a divine stand," etc.). But given that ᵓAṯiratu is ᵓIlu's consort and that it is ᵓIlu who finally grants the sought-for permission, it appears more likely that the items in question are in fact intended in the end for ᵓAṯiratu's lord and master. The syntax is precisely the same as above in the statement regarding gifts for ᵓAṯiratu, i.e., the construct chain (*šskn mgn ᵓaṯrt*, "prepare the gift of ᵓAṯiratu" = "prepare a gift for" ≈ *yṣq kt ᵓil*, "cast the stand of ᵓIlu" = "cast a stand for"). This section may be taken, therefore, as prefiguring the section below where gifts are promised for ᵓIlu (iii 27-36).

[126] *šmrgt* appears to be a nominal or adjectival form based on the Š-stem of *mrg*. In Arabic that root can express notions of "mixing." One may surmise that the idea here is that the decorations (*nbt*, of which the precise meaning is uncertain) of the throne stand were in patterns produced by alternations of gold and silver.

[127] Written {ᵓid}.

[128] *ᶜln yblhm ḫrṣ* is, in this list of difficult phrases, one of the most difficult. I have chosen, because of the general context, to interpret the verse as a whole to refer to an article of furniture (*nᶜl* = "bed"), rather than to an item of clothing (cf. Heb. *naᶜᵃlayim*, "sandals"). This appears to be supported by the singular form at the end of the first line, *qblbl*, itself of uncertain meaning, perhaps lit., "very acceptable." *yblhm*, on the other hand, might be taken as bearing a dual/plural suffix — though no one has found a good explanation of the term as related to sandals. The key to the understanding of the verse may be to see in *ḫrṣ* not the standard word for "gold," but a form of *ḫrṣ* II, "cut, engrave," attested in the other West Semitic languages and in Akk. The reference would be, of course, to pictorial representations such as the ivory carvings from bed panels discovered in the palace at Ugarit, which were double-sided and hence intended for viewing from both sides and placed above (*ᶜln*, "above") the bed itself (Schaeffer 1954:51-59, pls. IX-X; Caubet and Poplin 1987:283-289, figs. 16, 17; Gachet 1992:72). *yblhm* is perhaps to be analyzed, therefore, as a verbal noun of *ybl*, with pronominal suffix indicating the subject, either singular with enclitic *-m* (/yabāluhuma/) or dual, reflecting the two names Hayyinu and Ḫasīsu (/yabāluhumā/).

[129] The word *dbbm* is attested in incantation texts with the sense of those who constitute the adversaries of the person for whom the incantation is devised (see note 6 to text 1.100). In those texts it can be explained as cognate to Akk. *dabābu*, basically "to speak" but with the derived notion of attacking verbally. In this context, the word is more plausibly compared with Arabic *dbb*, "walk slowly" (of certain animals), "to slither" (of reptiles) (Caquot, Sznycer and Herdner 1974:196, note q). I posit two separate words in Ug., with very different etymologies, though it is not impossible that the word in the incantation texts is etymologically identical to this one.

[130] The carved ivories discovered in the palace at Ras Shamra included elements of a table top, where sphinxes, among other things, were represented (Schaeffer 1954:59-61; Caubet and Poplin 1987:283-289, fig. 20; Gachet 1992:72-73). "Filled" (*mlᵓa*) in this description may refer to the fact that the representational friezes were set inside a plain raised border.

[131] The interpretation of *sknt*, here translated "formed," is much debated. Because the gender of *ṣᶜ*, "bowl," in Ug. is unknown, the words *dqt*

...[132]

ᵓAṯiratu at Home (ii 3-?)

She has taken her spindle [in hand],
a spindle befitting her high station in her right hand.
As her flesh has become soiled,
she puts her garments into the sea,
her twice-soiled (body) into the rivers.[133]
She places a pot on the fire,
a pan on top of the coals,
So as to prepare a (warm) drink for the Bull, the kindly god,[134]
so as to make a present[135] to the Creator of creatures.[136]

Baᶜlu and ᶜAnatu Arrive with ᵓAṯiratu's Gifts (ii 12-29)

When she looks up and sees Baᶜlu coming,
when ᵓAṯiratu (!)[137] sees Girl ᶜAnatu arriving,
the sister-in-law of [Liᵓmu] striding along,
Her feet [shake],
behind, her back muscles [snap,
above], her face sweats,
her [vertebrae] rattle,
[her] spine goes weak.
She raises her voice and says aloud:
How is it that Mighty Baᶜlu has come?
How is it that Girl ᶜAnatu has come?
Have those who would smite me smitten my sons,
or (have) [those who would finish me off] (smitten) the host of my kin?
(But) when ᵓAṯiratu spies the [works] of silver,
the works of silver and [the objects] of gold,[138]
they bring joy to the Great Lady, ᵓAṯiratu of the Sea.

ᵓAṯiratu Enjoins her Attendant to Complete an Unknown Task (ii 29-?)

Aloud [she cries] to her lad:
Look at the skillfully wrought thing(s) and [behold!]
O fisherman of the Great Lady, ᵓAṯiratu [of the Sea],
take the net in your hand,
the great [X] upon your two hands.
[...] in Yammu, the beloved of ᵓIlu,
...[139]

("hammered thin" in my translation) and *sknt* may be either adjectives (if *ṣᶜ* is feminine) or nouns used adverbially (if *ṣᶜ* is masculine). The discoveries at Ras Shamra have provided two magnificent examples of such bowls, both with charging bulls as part of the representations (Schaeffer 1949:1-48, pls. I-V, VII-VIII). One might expect that, if indeed the basic notion of *dqt* here is "thinness," *sknt* denotes the other principal technique, that of producing the figures in *repoussé*. Data are lacking to explain why the skill to make metal bowls with representations in relief is attributed to the polities of ᵓAmurru and YMᵓAN (the first is well known; the second appears for reasons as yet unknown in the Ug. ritual text RS 1.002:27′ — see Pardee forthcoming).

[132] About fifteen lines are missing from the beginning of col. ii and the first two extant lines are badly damaged. At the end of col. i a double line was drawn about a third of the way across the column width. As such lines are usually not used simply to mark the end of a column, one may surmise that this one again marks an omission of repetitive material (see above, note 88). Because, in the following text, ᶜAnatu and Baᶜlu arrive together at ᵓAṯiratu's house, they may arrive and have joined forces at some point for this visit to ᵓAṯiratu. Though Kôṯaru-wa-Ḫasīsu made the gift for ᵓAṯiratu (and for ᵓIlu — see note 125), he is apparently not here in the company of ᶜAnatu and Baᶜlu, for he is never mentioned and he must apparently be resummoned when the final permission is given to build the palace (p. 260, v 103).

[133] Because of the rare vocabulary in this verse, it has been interpreted in a multitude of ways. It appears difficult to explain *npynh* otherwise than as a derivative from *npy*, "sieve, winnow, expel," attested with various nuances from Akk. to Arabic (but not elsewhere in Ug., certainly not in RS 1.002 [n. 131]!). Particularly in Arabic, one finds derivatives denoting that which is sieved/winnowed out, i.e., "rubbish." Perhaps the noun here refers to the dusty state of someone who has been working with the spindle all day, lit., "her rubbish covering her flesh, she puts her garments into the sea, her double rubbish into the rivers."

[134] *ṯr ᵓil d pᵓid* is the title that ᵓAṯiratu uses for ᵓIlu (as opposed to *ṯr ᵓil ᵓab* — cf. notes 13 and 28) because their relationship is not that of father and daughter.

[135] Here also the precise sense of the verse is uncertain because of the rarity of the two verbs, *tᶜpp* and *tǵẓy*. Most take the second verb as related to the noun *mǵẓ*, "present," in i 23 (p. 256), of which the meaning is determined largely by the parallel with *mgn*, "gift"; this root is used again as a verb below, iii 24 and 31 (p. 258), in parallel with a verbal form of *mgn*. Because ᵓAṯiratu has just put a pot on the fire, one may think that she was preparing something comestible for ᵓIlu; hence I explain *tᶜpp* by the Arabic geminate root, which in the D-stem means "feed someone the type of milk called *ᶜuffatun*." The picture is that of ᵓAṯiratu expecting a visit from ᵓIlu, whose domicile, as is clear from the continuation of the story, is at a distance from ᵓAṯiratu's; after spinning, she cleanses herself, then prepares something warm to eat/drink. I have considered the option of seeing the entire passage as describing the preparation of cloth (spinning, immersing [the thread or the cloth?] in cold salt water, immersing in hot water, presenting as a gift to ᵓIlu), but the few relatively clear terms do not seem to lead in that direction.

[136] On the title *bny bnwt* ascribed to ᵓIlu, see above, note 122.

[137] Written {ᵓaṯṯrt}.

[138] The words used to describe the gifts are uncertain: the term for the objects of gold has almost entirely disappeared, while the one for the objects made of silver is apparently written {ẓl}, which normally denotes "shadow, shade," and for that reason is often read instead as {pᶜl}, "work" (the difference between the two readings is primarily a matter of spacing of sign elements — the {ᶜ} in this text is made somewhat differently from the third wedge of {ẓ}, however, and one should be able to determine at least what the scribe intended; unfortunately none of the published photographs is readable at this point). The general meaning of the verse appears clear, however: ᵓAṯiratu, at first frightened at the appearance of Baᶜlu and ᶜAnatu and expecting them to bring bad news about her sons (or expecting them to attack her sons), is reassured at the sight of the gifts they are bearing.

[139] Remnants of fourteen more lines are preserved, insufficient to allow an understanding of what is going on. This is unfortunate, for the presence of the various terms for fishing in the sea indicates that a fully preserved text might have helped us understand better ᵓAṯiratu's title "of the Sea" and her relationship to the deity Yammu. For example, the phrase *b mdd ᵓil y[m]* in line 34, after the order for the fisherman to take up his net, could indicate that a very naturalistic depiction of the deity Yammu is underway.

Baᶜlu Complains of His Treatment By the Other Gods (iii 10-22)[140]

Again Mighty Baᶜlu (speaks),
Cloud-Rider tells his story:
[...] they stood up and cast scorn upon me,[141]
they arose and spat upon me
in the assembly of the sons of the gods;[gg]
[X] was set upon my table,
mockery in the cup from which I drink.
Now there are two (kinds of) feasts[142] (that) Baᶜlu hates,
three (that) Cloud-Rider (hates):
An improper feast,
a low-quality feast,[143]
and a feast where the female servants misbehave.[144]
There, impropriety was certainly seen,
there, misbehavior of the female servants (was certainly seen).

Baᶜlu and ᶜAnatu Arrive chez ᵓAṯiratu, Present their Gifts, and Feast (iii 23-?)

Thereupon Mighty Baᶜlu arrives,
Girl ᶜAnatu arrives.[145]
They offer the gifts[hh] to the Great Lady, ᵓAṯiratu of the Sea,
the presents to the Progenitress of the Gods.
The Great Lady, ᵓAṯiratu of the Sea, responds:
How is it that you offer gifts to the Great Lady, ᵓAṯiratu of the Sea,
presents to the Progenitress of the Gods?
Have you offered gifts to the Bull, the kindly god,
presents to the Creator of creatures?
Girl ᶜAnatu replies:
We would (now) offer gifts to the Great Lady,
ᵓAṯiratu of the Sea,
presents to the Progenitress of the Gods.
[Afterwards] we will also present him with gifts.
[...] Mighty Baᶜlu
[...] the Great Lady, ᵓAṯiratu of the Sea,
[...] Girl ᶜAnatu.
[Thereupon the gods] eat and drink,
[they take] sucklings,[146]
[with] a salted [knife] cutlets from [a fatling].
[They drink] wine from goblets
[red] wine[ii] [from golden cups].
...[147]

ᵓAṯiratu Prepares to Visit ᵓIlu (iv 1-19)

[The Great Lady], ᵓAṯiratu of [the Sea, responds:
Listen, O Qudšu-]wa-ᵓAmruru,
[O fisherman of the Great Lady], ᵓAṯiratu of the Sea:
[Saddle the donkey], harness the ass,
[put (on it) trappings of] silver,
[decorations] of yellow (gold),
prepare the trappings of [my] jennet.[148]
Qudšu-wa-ᵓAmruru listens:
He saddles the donkey, harnesses the ass,
puts (on it) trappings of silver,
decorations of yellow (gold),
prepares the trappings of her jennet.
Qudšu-wa-ᵓAmruru grasps (her),
puts ᵓAṯiratu on the donkey's back,

gg Pss 29:1; 82:1; Job 1:6; 2:1; 38:7
hh Gen 14:20; Hos 11:8; Prov 4:9
ii Gen 49:11; Deut 32:14

[140] At least twelve lines have disappeared at the beginning of col. iii, then another ten lines are too damaged to permit translation. Because of this long break, it is uncertain where Baᶜlu's monologue takes place and to whom it is addressed. If the two arrivals mentioned in lines 23-24, Baᶜlu's and ᶜAnatu's, are coterminous (see note 145), then Baᶜlu would seem to be speaking to ᶜAnatu en route. If not, then Baᶜlu would be addressing his complaint to ᵓAṯiratu while waiting for ᶜAnatu to come.

[141] Lit., "shriveled me, treated me as a shriveled thing" (D-stem of *qlṣ* — see above, note 111). For the morpho-semantics, compare Heb. *qillēl*, "treat as a light thing, mock, curse" (*qlt*, "mockery," below in line 15, is from this root).

[142] The Akk. equivalent of Ug. *dabḥu* in one of the polyglot vocabularies is *isinnu*, "feast, festival (religious or secular)" (Nougayrol 1968 text 137 iii 6). The noun is derived from the verb *dbḥ* (< *ḏbḥ*), "to slit the throat (of the sacrificial beast)." The divine banquet is depicted in the same terms as are used for sacrificial feasts practiced by humans, though divinities would not, of course, "sacrifice" the beasts in the same sense as humans would (cf. Pardee 1988a:24-26).

[143] The phrase {w dbḥ} was erroneously written twice here.

[144] The three terms by which *dbḥ* is qualified in this list are *bṯt*, "shame, impropriety," *dnt*, "low quality," and *tdmm(t)*, "misbehavior" (there is disagreement about the precise meaning of the last two terms, depending on whether Arabic or Heb. etymologies are preferred). In the last case, if the meaning corresponds to the Arabic etymology ("misbehave"), it is uncertain whether the misbehavior consists of impertinence or debauchery. The three terms appear to cover three criteria for judging the quality of a feast: the appropriateness of the sacrificial victim, its quality, and the service.

[145] Because *ᵓaḫr* can function either as an adverb ("thereafter, thereupon") or as a subordinating conjunction ("after Baᶜlu arrives, ᶜAnatu arrives"), and because the text preceding Baᶜlu's monologue is lost, we cannot tell whether the two deities arrived together or one after the other.

[146] The phrase *mrġtm ṯd*, "those who suck upon the breast," is often taken as a parallel to *ᵓilm*, "the gods," and hence as a metaphor for the children of a goddess, in particular of ᵓAṯiratu. Because, however, the expression only occurs in dining scenes and because the syntax is difficult with that interpretation, de Moor's interpretation (1971:146) of the phrase as referring to the source of the meat, i.e., "suckling (beasts)," appears preferable.

[147] Seven lines are partially or completely destroyed at the end of col. iii, another dozen at the beginning of col. iv.

[148] Several of the words in this verse are uncertain of meaning. *mdl* is the standard verb for preparing a mount for travel, whether it refer to the harness or the (rudimentary) saddle (bibliography in Pardee 1987:417). *pḥl*, if we assume that the goddess followed the practices of women and because of the parallel terms (*ᶜr*, "donkey," and *ᵓatn*, "jennet"), designates an *Equus asinus*, rather than a horse, though the origin of the term seems to relate to the reproductive qualities of the male (bibliography and discussion in Pardee 1988a:205). *gpnm*, here translated "trappings," looks like the standard Northwest Semitic word for "vine(s)," but it is uncertain whether we have here that word used metaphorically or another word. Finally *nqbnm*, here translated "decorations," is of uncertain origin.

on the ass's beautiful back.[149]
Qudšu sets off, bright as fire,[150]
ʾAmruru like a star in front,
behind (came) Girl ʿAnatu.
As for Baʿlu, he went off to the heights of Ṣapānu.[151]

The Visit (iv 20 - v 81)
So off she goes
to ʾIlu at the source of the double river,
midst the upspringings of the deeps.
She penetrates ʾIlu's abode,
enters the dwelling of the King, father of Šunama;
At ʾIlu's feet she bows and falls,
does homage and honors him.

ʾIlu Expresses His Happiness at the Sight of ʾAṯiratu (iv 27-39)
When ʾIlu sees her,
his brow unfurrows[152] and he laughs;
He taps his feet on the footstool
and snaps his fingers.
He raises his voice and says aloud:
How is it that the Great Lady, ʾAṯiratu of the Sea, has come?
How is it that she has entered (here), the Progenitress of the Gods?
Are you really hungry (because) you've been wandering?
Are you really thirsty (because) [you've been] traveling all night?[153]
Eat or drink,
eat some bread at the table,
drink some wine from a goblet,
some red wine from golden cups.
Or is it the 'hand'[154] of ʾIlu the king that has excited thoughts in you,
the love of the Bull that has aroused you?

ʾAṯiratu Recites her Message, Including Baʿlu's Claim to a Palace (iv 40-57)
The Great Lady, ʾAṯiratu of the Sea, replies:
Your decision(s), ʾIlu, (are) wise,
(they are) eternal wisdom,
your decision(s) (provide) a life of good fortune.
(Now,) our king is Mighty Baʿlu,
(he is) our ruler and there is none above him.
All of us (other gods) [bear] his vessel,
all of us bear his cup.
(But) groaning he does cry out to the Bull, his father ʾIlu,
to ʾIlu the king who established him,
He cries out to ʾAṯiratu and to her sons,
to the goddess and the host of her kin:
Baʿlu has no house as (do) the (other) gods,
(no) court as (do) the sons of ʾAṯiratu,
(No) dwelling (as does) ʾIlu, (no) shelter (as do) his sons,
(no) dwelling (as does) the Great Lady, ʾAṯiratu of the Sea,
(No) dwelling (as do) the honored brides:
(no) dwelling (as does) Pidray, daughter of ʾAru,
(no) shelter (as does) Ṭallay, daughter of Rabbu,
(no) dwelling (as does) ʾArṣay, daughter of Yaʿibdarru.

ʾIlu Gives the Go-Ahead (iv 58 - v 63)
The Gracious One, the kindly god replies:
So I am a servant, an attendant on ʾAṯiratu!
So I am a servant, accustomed to tools!
And ʾAṯiratu is a servant-girl (who) will make the bricks![155] *jj*
Let a house be built for Baʿlu like the (other) gods' (houses),
a court like (the courts of) the sons of ʾAṯiratu.

jj Gen 11:3; Exod 5:7

ʾAṯiratu Congratulates ʾIlu on the Positive Results of his Decision (v 64-73)
The Great Lady, ʾAṯiratu of the Sea, replies:
Great indeed, ʾIlu, is (your) wisdom,
your gray beard surely instructs you,[156]
the respite that is yours alone (surely instructs

[149] The word for "back" (*bmt*) is the same as was used above for the part of her body around which ʿAnatu hung the human necklace (see above, note 76). It is debatable whether the donkey was beautiful in its own right, but it certainly was when its trappings were of gold and silver. The Ug. expression consists of a substantivized adjective preceding the nouns in question: *ysmsmt bmt pḥl*, lit., "the most beautiful (part[s] of) the thorax of the male equid."

[150] It is uncertain whether *šbʿr* is related to the verb for "burning" or the verb for "leading, taking, bringing" (as in Kirta, *CTA* 14 ii 101 [text 1.102 (p. 334)], there translated "entrusting"), i.e., whether the double-deity is being depicted simply as leading the donkey or whether he is also providing light. I choose the latter solution because of the explicit comparison with a star in the next line (*k kbkb*). Unfortunately, we do not know what it is about Qudšu-wa-ʾAmruru that links him/them particularly with light.

[151] This line illustrates the problems of deducing a narrative line in a badly damaged text: by means of this single line of text, Baʿlu is removed from the next scene and transported to his home. Had the text been damaged at this point, we could only have conjectured his whereabouts.

[152] For the meaning of *lṣb*, "forehead" rather than "rows of teeth," see discussion and bibliography in Pardee 1988a:69. For the interpretation of *prq*, see del Olmo Lete 1981:612.

[153] The last word in each line is partially damaged and of uncertain interpretation (cf. Gibson 1978:59, 154, 159).

[154] *yd* is either a euphemism for the male member (see note 48 to text 1.87) or a noun derived from a root *ydd* (<*wdd*), "to love."

[155] ʾIlu's reply appears ironic, accusing ʾAṯiratu in jest of proposing that he and she should themselves do the building.

[156] The motif is that of wisdom coming with old age (on ʾIlu as an old man, see above, note 13).

you).[157]
For now[158] Baᶜlu (can) send his rain in due season,
send the season of driving showers;[159]
(can) Baᶜlu shout aloud in the clouds,[160] [kk]
shoot (his) lightning-bolts to the earth; [ll]
A house of cedar[mm] he may complete,
Even a house of bricks he may raise.

ᵓAṯiratu Announces That He May Undertake Preparations (v 74-81) [nn]
Let them announce to Mighty Baᶜlu:
Summon an (entire) caravan to your house,
wares to your palace;
Let the mountains bring you massive amounts of silver,
(let) the hills (bring you) the choicest gold,
let them bring you magnificent gems.[161]
Then build a house of silver and gold,
a mansion of purest lapis-lazuli.

The Message is Borne by ᶜAnatu (v 82-97)[162]
(This) brings joy to Girl ᶜAnatu.
She digs in her feet,
takes off across the earth;
She heads off
toward Baᶜlu in the heights of Ṣapānu.
(While still) a thousand yards off,
ten thousand furlongs,
Girl ᶜAnatu laughs,
raises her voice and shouts aloud:
You have good news, Baᶜlu!
I bring you good news![oo]
They may build for you a house like (those of) your brothers,
a court like (those of) your kin.[163]

kk Jer 10:13; Joel 2:11; Pss 18:14; 46:7
ll Job 37:3
mm 2 Sam 7:2, 7
nn 1 Kgs 5:15-32
oo Isa 40:9; 41:27; 52:7

Summon an (entire) caravan to your house,
wares to your palace;
Let the mountains bring you massive amounts of silver,
(let) the hills (bring you) the choicest gold,
Then build a house of silver and gold,
a mansion of purest lapis-lazuli.

Baᶜlu Makes the Preparations (v 97-102)[164]
(This) brings joy to Mighty Baᶜlu:
He summons an (entire) caravan to his house,
wares to his palace;
The mountains bring him massive amounts of silver,
the hills (bring him) the choicest gold,
they bring him magnificent gems.

Then He Sends for Kôṯaru-wa-Ḫasīsu (v 103-105)
He sends a message[165] to Kôṯaru-wa-Ḫasīsu:

Go back to the recitation: "When the two lads take the message..."
__________[166]

Kôṯaru-wa-Ḫasīsu Arrives, Is Feted, and Urged to Work (v 106-119)
Thereafter Kôṯaru-wa-Ḫasīsu arrives.
They place beef in front of him,
a fatling before him.
A chair is prepared and they seat (him)
at the right hand of Mighty Baᶜlu,
while [the gods] eat and drink.
Mighty [Baᶜlu] speaks up:
...[167]
Hurry! (raise) a house, O Kôṯaru,

---

[157] The text reads {rḫn⌜-⌝t.d⌜-⌝.lᵓirtk} and has been interpreted in various ways. My translation implies that the first word is cognate with Arabic *rḫw*, which denotes softness and relaxation, that the second is the relative pronoun, and that *ᵓirtk* means "(belonging) to your chest, bosom." The "respite" would refer to ᵓIlu's old age.

[158] The cause-and-effect relationship between ᵓIlu's permission to allow Baᶜlu to have his own palace and Baᶜlu's exercise of his function as weather god is strongly marked in the Ug. text: the line begins with two particles, the first of which bears an extending morpheme (*wn ᵓap* = /wa-na ᵓapa/).

[159] The precise meaning of *ṯkt b glṯ* remains uncertain. If the second sign of the first word could be read as {r} rather than {k}, the word could be explained as from *ṯrr*, "be abundant (of water)" (Driver 1956:97, 151), a root that some believe to be already attested in Ug. (e.g., in text 1.94, line 64 (p. 298), on which see Pardee 1988a:215). The editor's copy (Virolleaud 1932:pl. xxvii) shows, however, the rather clear outline of {k} (subsequent editors have all indicated a damaged {k}).

[160] A common idiom for "to thunder" in Northwest Semitic is "to give the voice (in the clouds/in the heavens, etc.)." There is a striking parallel in one of the Amarna texts (*ša id-din ri-ig-ma-šu i-na sa-me ki-ma* ᵈIM, "who gives his voice in the heavens like the weather god" [EA 147:13-14]). The central part of Ps 29 (vss. 3-9), with the seven-fold repetition of *qōl*, "voice," is, of course, the depiction of YHWH as filling the rôle of the weather god.

[161] The word translated "gems," *ᵓilqṣm*, is of uncertain meaning. Other words for precious stones are attested in Ug. and in the Akk. of Ugarit which have /ᵓ/ as the first phoneme: *ᵓalgbṯ/alkabašu* and *algamišu*, to which may be compared Heb. *ᵓelgābīš* (Nougayrol 1968:101, n. 1).

[162] Either ᶜAnatu has accompanied ᵓAṯiratu to ᵓIlu's home or else the formulae for carrying ᵓAṯiratu's message to her have been omitted.

[163] Up to this point the houses to which comparison has been made have always been referred to as being those of "the gods" // "the sons of ᵓAṯiratu." The word for "kin" here, *ᵓary*, is the same as that used for ᵓAṯiratu's kin in several passages (*ṣbrt ᵓaryh*, "the host of her kin"), where the parallel phrase is *bnh*, "her sons." Below p. 262, vi 44-46, "his brothers // his kin" seem to be equated with "the seventy sons of ᵓAṯiratu." Has Baᶜlu been promoted to equality with the sons of ᵓAṯiratu, i.e., the terms are honorific, or has his rightful place simply been recognized? Perhaps a little of both if his parentage is complicated (see above, note 32, and below, note 190).

[164] In this section Baᶜlu gathers the materials, but the final verse of the preceding parallel passages is omitted, that concerning the actual construction. For this, he sends for Kôṯaru-wa-Ḫasīsu.

[165] The commonly adopted correction of {yᵓak} to {y<l>ᵓak} appears necessary.

[166] The disposal of the horizontal lines and the sense of the passage all indicate that the announcement of the message by Baᶜlu is omitted, as are its repetition by the messengers and all travel formulae.

[167] One line is almost totally destroyed.

hurry! raise a palace,
hurry! you must build a house.
Hurry! you must raise a palace
on the heights of Ṣapānu,
A house covering a thousand acres,
a palace (covering) ten thousand hectares.

Owner and Contractor Argue About a Window (v 120 - vi 15)[168]

Kôṯaru-wa-Ḫasīsu replies:
Listen, O Mighty Ba^{c}lu,
understand, O Cloud-Rider:
Must I not put a latticed window in the house,
a window-opening in the palace?
Mighty Ba^{c}lu replies:
You must not put a latticed window in [the house],
[no window-opening] in the palace![169]
Kôṯaru[-wa]-Ḫasīsu replies:
You'll come around, Ba^{c}lu, to [my view].[170]
Kôṯaru[-wa-]Ḫasīsu repeats (his) speech:
Listen, please,[171] O Mighty Ba^{c}lu:
Must I not put a latticed window in the house,
a window-opening in the palace?
Mighty Ba^{c}lu replies:
You must not put a latticed window in the house,
no window-opening in the palace!
Lest[172] Pidray, daughter of $^{\supset}$Aru, do [X],
[lest] Ṭallay, daughter of Rabbu, [do Y].
[...] $^{\supset}$Ilu's beloved, Yammu,
[...] cast scorn upon me,
and spit upon me [...].[173]
Kôṯaru-[wa-Ḫasīsu] replies:
You'll come around, Ba^{c}lu, to my view.

The Palace is Built (vi 16-40)

[Hurriedly] they build his house,
[hurriedly] they raise his palace.
(Some workers) [go] to Lebanon and its trees,
to Siryon[pp] (and) its choicest cedars;
[They X] Lebanon and its trees,
Siryon (and) its choicest cedars.
Fire is placed in the house,
flames in the palace.
For a day, two (days),
the fire consumes (fuel)[174] in the house,
the flames (consume fuel) in the palace;
For a third, a fourth day,
the fire consumes (fuel) in the house,
the flames (consume fuel) in the palace;
For a fifth, a sixth day,
the fire consumes (fuel) in the house,
the flames (consume fuel) in the palace;
Then on the seventh day,[175]
the fire is removed from the house,
the flames from the palace.
(Voilà!) the silver has turned into plaques,
the gold is turned into bricks.
(This) brings joy to Mighty Ba^{c}lu:
You have built my house of silver,
my palace of gold.
(Then) Ba^{c}lu completes the furnishing of [his] house,
Haddu completes the furnishing[176] of his palace.

pp Deut 3:9; Ps 29:6

The Inaugural Banquet (vi 40-?)

He slaughters bovids [and] caprovids,[177]
he fells bulls [and] fattened goats,

[168] Kôṯaru-wa-Ḫasīsu's motivation for wanting to put the disputed window in the palace is not stated: is it the simple fact that palaces had windows or is the contractor somehow in league with Môtu, whose defeat of Ba^{c}lu's follows the eventual opening of the window? Note that there is no parallel, as is often assumed, between the biblical passage according to which death comes in through a window (Jer 9:20) and this myth, according to which the contact between Ba^{c}lu and Môtu takes place at a series of feasts, while Ba^{c}lu's death takes place near Môtu's own domain (*CTA* 5 v - 6 i). Moreover, when below (vi 8-14) Ba^{c}lu raises specific objections, they are phrased in terms of his daughters and of Yammu (who is no longer a major player, at least in this arrangement of the tablets). The link between the window and Ba^{c}lu's demise appears to lie in the realm of hubris, rather than in means of access: once the window is in place, Ba^{c}lu is so impressed by his own abilities to make thunder and lightning pass through the window to earth that he presumes himself capable of taking on Môtu (vii 25 - *CTA* 5 ii). This rather clear link between the palace, the window, and Ba^{c}lu's eventual demise — so important to the overall struture of the myth — calls into question, it may appear, the interpretation of the palace motif as primarily cosmological in function (cf. Smith 1994:77, 105).

[169] The very end of col. v is broken away but it is uncertain whether there was any additional text there.

[170] Lit., "to my word," reconstructed on the basis of vi 15.

[171] As compared with the previous version of the speech, the particle *m^{c}* is added here after the verb *šm^{c}*, "listen." On the other hand, the second colon ("understand, O Cloud-Rider") is omitted here.

[172] The formulation here appears to be negative volitive: "Let Pidray not do [X]."

[173] The passage containing the reasons for Ba^{c}lu's refusal of a window is damaged and without parallels for reconstruction. If Ba^{c}lu's daughters were not described as having houses of their own, one might think that Ba^{c}lu here is worried about them going out through the windows of his house. In the case of Yammu, Ba^{c}lu is most plausibly worried about his enemy gaining entry by the window and treating him as is recounted above in col. iii, lines 10-22. Might the reference to spitting (cf. col. iii, line 13) be a reference to the foam of the sea? Might Ba^{c}lu be worried about his daughters somehow aiding Yammu, whether purposely or inadvertently? Might he be worried about the his daughters' husbands, who would be expected to be in league with Yammu (cf. notes 32, 98, 99, 190)?

[174] The image is probably not that of the fire burning freely throughout the palace, but of a giant casting process, in which the fire must constantly be fed.

[175] The seven-day sequence is a common literary motif in Ug. for expressing extended processes. Compare the use of the motif in connection with travel in the Kirta text (1.102).

[176] The words translated "complete the furnishing" constitute an etymological figure of speech (*^{c}dbt ... y^{c}db* // *^{c}db* [*^{c}d*]*bt*), using a root that is probably a developed form of the one that gave the word translated "wares" (*^{c}ḏbt*) above, v 76 and 92. Because of this connection and because of the generality of the formulation, it appears likely that the reference is to the general furnishing of the palace rather than to the specific preparations for the up-coming feast.

[177] Apologies for the semi-technical terms, used to express precisely the two Ug. terms: *$^{\supset}$alpm*, "(male) bovids" (specifically "male bovids"

yearling calves,
lambs (and) great numbers of kids.
He invites his brothers into his house,
his kin into his palace,
He invites the seventy sons of ᵓAṯiratu:
He provides the gods with rams (and) wine,[178]
he provides the goddesses with ewes (and) [wine];
He provides the gods with bulls (and) wine,
he provides the goddesses with cows (and) [wine];
He provides the gods with chairs (and) wine,
he provides the goddesses with seats (and) [wine];
He provides the gods with jars of wine,
he provides the goddesses with barrels of [wine].
So the gods eat and drink,
they take sucklings,
with a salted knife cutlets from [a fatling].
They drink wine from goblets,
red [wine from] golden cups.
...[179]

Baᶜlu Takes Possession of His Cities (vii 7-12)
He goes? from [city] to city,
goes again from town to town.[180]
He takes possession of[181] sixty-six cities,
of seventy-seven towns;
Eighty does Baᶜlu [X],
ninety does he [Y].

Baᶜlu Decides He Wants a Window After All (vii 13-25)
(Then) Baᶜlu [returns] to (his) house.
Mighty Baᶜlu speaks up:
I am going to charge Kôṯaru, this very day,
Kôṯaru, this very moment,[182]
With opening up a window in (my) house,
a latticed window in (my) palace,
With opening up a rift[183] in the clouds,
according to the pronouncement of Kôṯaru-wa-Ḫasīsu.
Kôṯaru-wa-Ḫasīsu breaks out laughing,
he raises his voice and says:
Didn't I tell you, O Mighty Baᶜlu,
(that) you, Baᶜlu, would come around to my word?

The Window Is Put to Immediate Use (vii 25-37)
(So) he he opens up a window in the house,
a latticed window in the palace.
Baᶜlu (himself)[184] opens up the rift in the clouds,
Baᶜlu emits his holy voice,
Baᶜlu makes the thunder roll over and over again.[185]
His [holy] voice [causes] the earth [to tremble],
[at his thunder] the mountains shake with fear.[186]

below in line 49 and specifically "domesticated bovids" in *CTA* 6 i 20, in opposition with *rᵓumm*, "wild bulls"), and *ṣᵓin* (≈Heb. *ṣō*(ᵓ)*n*), "mixed herd of sheep and goats."

178 The formulation of lines 47-54 consists of eight verses, in which masculine and feminine entities alternate, i.e., gods + masculine item // goddesses + feminine item. Because of this alternation and because of the ambiguity of the syntax, the formulae have often been understood as denoting simply a list of male and female deities (ram gods // ewe goddesses, etc.; e.g. de Moor 1987:60-61). This is plausible for the animal terms (lines 47-50), for representation of deities as animals is common, but it becomes less plausible in the cases of chairs and wine jars (lines 51-54), for such deified entities are virtually unknown in Ug. Because *špq* is the causative of the verb *pq*, attested here below at the end of the list (*pq*, "they take," in line 56) and in the Kirta text (*CTA* 14 i 12 [text 1.102, n. 5]) in the meaning "to obtain," hence "cause to obtain, give to, furnish with, provide for," there is no difficulty in interpreting *ᵓilm krm*, etc., as "double accusatives" (as in Heb., the Hiphil stem followed by two complements marked by *ᵓet*, the definite direct object marker). It is somewhat more problematic to see the end of the phrase, *krm yn*, etc., as an asyndetic accusative construction ("rams (and) wine"; e.g., Gibson 1977:63-64), but that solution appears preferable to denying the existence of *yn* at the end of every line but 53-54 (reading the form *yšql* in the other lines: Cassuto 1938:287-89; Caquot, Sznycer and Herdner 1974:214; Smith 1994:50), for a glance at the photograph and copy will show that there was no reason to separate the {y} from the rest of the form. Indeed, in line 51 all editors have seen another sign after the {y}, and the traces correspond perfectly to the beginning of {n}.

179 Of some six or seven lines at the end of col. vi only a few signs are preserved. At the beginning of col. vii, only the ends of the lines are preserved. Mighty Baᶜlu is certainly mentioned there and in all probability Yammu as well ({mdd ᵓil y[m]}, lines 3-4).

180 What is preserved as {ᶜdr} is usually interpreted as the first verb in this verse, though it is usually emended to {ᶜbr}, "cross (through), traverse"; the second verb is *ṯb*, "return," perhaps used to denote the repetition of the first act. The formulation of the complements is lit., "to city/cities of cities // to town(s) of towns."

181 The verb is *ᵓaḫd*, cognate with Heb. *ᵓāḥaz*. Because the preceding context is so broken, it is uncertain what degree of force is involved and to what extent these cites previously constituted holdings of Yammu.

182 In the absence of vocalization, the phrases *bn ym // bnm ᶜdt* are ambiguous and could also be translated "son of Yammu // son of the confluence (of the deeps)." Such an interpretation might help to explain Kôṯaru's willingness to build a house for Yammu (*CTA* 2 iii), but the difficulties are severe: (1) Kôṯaru is nowhere else designated the son of Yammu; (2) *ᶜdt* is not used elsewhere alone as the equivalent of *ᶜdt thmtm* (on which see note 4 to RS 24.244 [text 1.94]).

183 Etymologically *bdqt* should denote "a fissure, break, crack." The metaphorical juxtaposition of "window" and "rift," coupled with the description of what Baᶜlu does when the rift is opened up, indicates that the house he had built had become a form of confinement, keeping him from the proper exercise of his rain-making function. He, therefore, sees the rift as a liberation, though it will later be instrumental in his death.

184 Given the structure of this and the preceding verses, it appears that Kôṯaru-wa-Ḫasīsu, as he has proposed, opens the window, but that Baᶜlu himself takes over when it comes to opening up the rift in the clouds. Thus, in some sense, the window and the opening in the clouds were seen as separate entities. This distinction (a veritable rift!) between the window as an item of construction and the rift in the clouds as particular to Baᶜlu's divine status seems to indicate that the Ugaritians were well aware of the metaphors with which they were dealing (cf. Korpel 1990:375).

185 Lit., "Baᶜlu repeats the ut[terances of his li]ps."

186 The translations indicated as restorations are *ad sensum*; various restorations of the Ug. text have been proposed. The precise nuance of *ḫš*, here translated "shake with fear," is uncertain; my translation assumes the existence of a root *ḫš* II (which would, by comparison with Arabic, be derived from *ḫ*(*y*)*š́*) alongside *ḫš* I, used in ritual texts to describe a characteristic of ᵓIlu (on this root, see Pardee forthcoming on RS

...[187]
the high places of the earth totter.
Baᶜlu's enemies grasp hold of (the trees of) the forest,
Haddu's adversaries (grasp hold of) the flanks of the mountain(s).

Baᶜlu's Powers Incite Him to Hubris (vii 37 - *CTA* 5 ii)[188]

Mighty Baᶜlu speaks up:
Enemies of Haddu,[189] why do you shake with fear?
Why do you shake with fear, you who take up arms against Dimārānu?[190]
Baᶜlu looks ahead of (where) his hand (will strike) when the cedar (shaft) dances in his right hand.[191]
Since Baᶜlu has taken up residence[qq] in his house
is there or is there not a king
(who) can establish himself[rr] in the land of (Baᶜlu's) dominion?
Why don't I send a courier to Môtu, son of ˀIlu,
a messenger to the beloved warrior of ˀIlu?[192]

[qq] Pss 9:8; 29:10
[rr] Ps 68:17
[ss] Ps 95:3
[tt] Gen 27:28
[uu] Pss 103:5; 145:16; Isa 58:11
[vv] 2 Kgs 15:5

(For) Môtu is always proclaiming,
The beloved one (of ˀIlu) is always claiming:[193]
I am the only one who rules over the gods,[ss]
who fattens[tt] gods and men,
who satiates[uu] the hordes of the earth.

Baᶜlu Calls his Messengers (vii 52-?)

When Baᶜlu calls to his lads:
Look, [Gupanu-]wa-ˀUgāru:
The sea [is enveloped] in darkness,
in obscurity the [highest] peaks ....
...[194]

The Directions (viii 1-32)

So head off
for Mount Targ̀uziza,
for Mount Ṯarrummagi,
to the two ruin-mounds that mark the borders of the earth.[195]
Lift up (one) mountain on (your) hands,
(one) wooded hill on (your) palms.
Then go down to the place of seclusion[vv] (within) the earth,

---

4.474:9).

[187] The readings at the beginning of lines 33 and 34 are disputed.

[188] On the relationship between the window and Baᶜlu's eventual demise, see above note 168.

[189] The divine name is here spelled {hdt} — a mistake for {hdm}, i.e. *hd* + *-m*?

[190] Or: "Why do you fear the arm(s) of Dimārānu" (*n̲tq* could be either a concrete noun, "arm(s) of," or the participle of the corresponding verb or a nomen professionalis derived therefrom). Dimārānu is vocalized as a form of the root known elsewhere in Ug. under the form *d̲mr* (/d̲/ frequently is {d}). The epithet is usually identified with the theonym Demarous, who was the son of Ouranos though born only after the defeat of the latter at the hand of Kronos (= Elos [ˀIlu]) when his mistress, mother of Demarous, was given by Kronos to his brother Dagan (tradition according to Philo of Byblos: see, e.g., Attridge and Oden 1981:48-51). If the Ug. divine genealogy was anything like that transmitted by Philo of Byblos, Baᶜlu would have been the half-brother of both Dagan and ˀIlu/Kronos, who both were sons of Ouranos, and also the stepson of Dagan. Though deities corresponding to Ouranos and Ge (principal wife of Ouranos), i.e., ˀArṣu-wa-Šamûma, "Earth-and-Heaven," are known in Ug. from the pantheon and ritual texts, and though one pantheon text explicitly places ˀArṣu-wa-Šamûma before ˀIlu (see Pardee forthcoming on RS 24.643:23-25), Ug. mythology contains no story dealing with the generations preceding Dagan and ˀIlu. Another perspective, for which the data are closer in time to the Ug. texts, is that of the relationship between Kumarbi (≈ Dagan) and Tešub (≈ Baᶜlu) in Hurrian mythology (Niehr 1994). The problem with that set of comparisons is the absence of a clear correspondent to the larger group of Ug. divinities. Whatever the genealogical and ideological strata may be in these various relationships (and one would not expect the ideology perfectly to match the genealogy!), a broadly coherent picture emerges from this cycle itself: Baᶜlu and ᶜAnatu are on one side (below in *CTA* 6 ii 12 [p. 270] they are represented as siblings), perhaps along with Šapšu, while Yammu/Naharu, Môtu, Lôtan, and ˀAṯiratu and her sons are on the other (cf. notes 32, 93, 163, 254, 264). ˀIlu naturally favors his own son, Yammu, but does not intervene when Baᶜlu defeats Yammu and, under pressure, accepts Baᶜlu's claims — this is understandable if Baᶜlu is closely related to ˀIlu but not his own son. When Baᶜlu is temporarily defeated by Môtu, ˀIlu is represented as seeing for himself the negative effects of Môtu's reign (*CTA* 6 iii). ˀIlu's principal wife ˀAṯiratu is closely associated with the sea/Yammu, but is not said to be his mother. Perhaps this somewhat ambiguous relationship explains why she can be seduced by gifts to plead Baᶜlu's case (i 20 - v 81).

[191] This is one of the more difficult verses in the well-preserved parts of this myth and it has received multiple interpretations. The one offered here assumes that the motifs are (1) careful aim and (2) the weapon as a living tree (for a representation of such a weapon, see the "Baal aux foudres" stele from Ras Shamra, e.g., Yon 1991:no. 5; Bordreuil 1991). If *ktg̀d̲* in line 41 is indeed a verbal form (for a plausible interpretation as a noun, see Sanmartín 1978), it should be analyzed as a *t*-preformative form of a III-weak root related to Arabic *g̀dd/g̀dw/g̀dy/g̀d̲y/g̀d̲g̀d̲*, all of which have connotations of speed or hurrying, though whether the reference is to the weapon speeding from the deity's hand or dancing in his hand cannot be said.

[192] The standard form of Môtu's title as son of ˀIlu is *bn ˀilm mt*. The *-m* of *ˀilm* must, of course, be the so-called "enclitic" particle, not the plural morpheme. The second formulaic title in this verse is *ydd ˀil g̀zr*, lit., "the beloved one of ˀIlu, the warrior." I am not convinced that the fact that *g̀zr* is an epithet is sufficent evidence for taking the word as modifying ˀIlu rather than Môtu (Vaughn 1993). On the surface level, the structure of this phrase is precisely identical to *bn ˀilm mt*, the only difference being that *mt* is a proper name, *g̀zr* a nominal attribute. Mythologically, it is unlikely that *g̀zr* is an epithet of ˀIlu, for *g̀zr* describes relatively young and vigorous men (see note 78 to the Kirta text [1.102]), while ˀIlu is consistently described as an old man (see above, note 13) not at all interested in fighting.

[193] Lit., "Môtu calls out in his throat, the beloved one keeps saying within himself" (the second verb is *ystrn*, plausibly cognate with Arabic *srr*, "tell" — which would thus be historically distinct from *srr* denoting the umbilicus ≈ Heb. *šōr*).

[194] There are five partially preserved lines and about seven more totally broken away at the end of col. vii.

[195] The mountain names are unidentified and of uncertain vocalization; if the form of the names is Hurrian/Asianic as most commentators have thought, one may assume that they were considered to be situated at the northern extremes of the earth (for a summary discussion, see Astour 1980). Whether *tlm* denotes "ruin-mounds" (as "tell" is used in modern archaeological parlance) here or designates a particular type of hill (// *g̀r*, "mountain"), the use of the word, very rare in Ug. (cf. *CTA* 16 i 52 [text 1.102] "mound"), is surely meant to express a characteristic feature of these "delimiters" (*g̀ṣr*) between the land of the living and the land of the dead, a feature that is plausibly linked with the notion of ruin. In

you must be counted among those who go down
 into the earth.[196] [ww]
Once (down there) head
 for his city Hamray,[xx]
 (for) Mukku where his throne is established,[yy]
 (for) Ḫôḫu, the land of his own possession.[197]
But be careful, couriers of the gods:
 Don't get near Môtu, son of ʾIlu,
Lest he take you as (he would) a lamb in his mouth,
 lest you be destroyed as (would be) a kid in his crushing jaws.[198]
Šapšu, luminary of the gods, glows hot,
 the heavens are powerless under the control of Môtu, the beloved of ʾIlu.
(From) a thousand yards off,
 ten thousand furlongs,
At the feet of Môtu bow and fall,
 do homage and honor him.[199]

ww Pss 88:5; 143:7
xx Ps 140:11
yy Cf. Eccl 10:18
zz Isa 5:14; Hab 2:5
aaa Deut 33:20; Hos 13:8
bbb Deut 32:10; Ps 107:40; Job 6:18; 12:24
ccc Ps 42:2

Say to Môtu, son of ʾIlu,
 repeat to the beloved warrior of ʾIlu:

The Message (viii 32-47)
Message of Mighty Baʿlu
 word of the mightiest of heroes:
I have built my house [of silver],
 my [palace of gold].
...[200]

Môtu's Reply to Baʿlu (viii 48 - *CTA* 5 i 8)[201]
[Message of Môtu, son of ʾIlu,
 word of the beloved warrior of ʾIlu:
My throat[zz] is the throat of the lion[aaa] in the wasteland,[bbb]
 and[202] the gullet[203] of the 'snorter'[204] in the sea;
And it craves the pool (as do) the wild bulls,
 (craves) springs as (do) the herds of deer;[205] [ccc]
And, indeed, indeed,

the next verse it is *ḫlb* that is used parallel to *ǵr*, a better-attested parallelism in Ug., though the precise meaning of that term is also uncertain (in Akk. *ḫalbu* means "forest, wood, grove").

[196] The divine messengers' entry into the realm of the dead is described in the same terms as are used for the dying entering that realm.

[197] The three names (the vocalizations of which are hypothetical) denote aspects of the underworld: Hamray, "watery," Mukku, "sinking down, dilapidation," Ḫôḫu, "opening, hole, fault" (cf. Astour 1980:229). The last word is probably a different word from *ḫḫm* in *CTA* 17 vi 35 (see note 45 to text 1.103). It appears plausible to see in the description of Môtu by Philo of Byblos as "slime ... [or] the putrefaction of a watery mixture" at least a vague memory of the name Hamray ("watery") (Baumgarten 1981:97, 111-13), though the link is not as explicit as some have thought (Held 1973:188-190).

[198] The meaning of *qn* in *b ṯbrn qnh*, sometimes reread as *b ṯbr ntʿnh*, is uncertain (my translation "jaws" is primarily from context). These terms are repeated below, not for the messengers, but in Môtu's version of what happened to Baʿlu (*CTA* 6 ii 22-23 and note 256 — the narrator's version of this event has been lost in one of the earlier lacunae).

[199] The previous verse contains the standard formulae for travel over a long distance (see above, notes 10, 21). Because in at least some cases the distance formulae are used to designate separation between the traveler and the goal, it appears plausible, in the context of Baʿlu's warning for the messengers to maintain their distance, to interpret the juxtaposition of the distance formulae with the obeisance formulae here as denoting obeisance at a distance (see the similar formulae in Ug. letters [translated in *COS* 3]).

[200] The meat of Baʿlu's message is lost in the break, where only a few letters have been preserved in lines 38-47. Judging from the remnants of the messenger's name preserved in line 47 ([*gpn*] *w ʾugr*), we may surmise that the message and messenger formulae extended to there; the presence of a double line on the tablet at that point indicates that the complete repetition of Baʿlu's message to Môtu was omitted (see note 88) and that the rest of the column, some seventeen lines, contained Môtu's reply (see next note). The {t} at the end of line 48, the last sign visible, is plausibly the last sign of the introductory phrase *tḥm bn ʾilm mt* (as in *CTA* 5 i 12-13, p. 265).

[201] Simply in order to present in a coherent sequence what was at least the gist of Môtu's message as dictated to the messengers — though there are variations in reported messages, the basic content is reported faithfully — I restore here the beginning of the message as preserved below in lines *CTA* 5 i 12-27. Though quite well preserved in *CTA* 5, this section constitutes one of the most difficult and disputed passages of the Baʿlu cycle. In the cycle as preserved, the only explicit mention of the defeat of a reptilian adversary up to this point is that to which ʿAnatu has laid claim (*CTA* 3 iii 37-39 [here lines 40-42]). Here Môtu begins by describing his voracious appetite and challenges Baʿlu to invite him and his kinsmen for a meal, apparently in Baʿlu's new palace. At that point is inserted a challenge involving physical prowess, of which an important element is lost ("I can pierce you through..." — see note 208). The logic of the end of the message seems to be that when Baʿlu defeats Lôtan, Môtu dies also as a consequence, dies by being devoured (*spʾ//mt*). It is not stated why he dies. But then the message concludes by stating that Baʿlu must also die. The most logical explanation of this cause-and-effect sequence is to see Lôtan and his reptilian allies as the kinsmen of Môtu to which reference has already been made. If Baʿlu attacks them, Môtu must, as their kinsman, take up their cause. On the other hand, at least judging from the biblical materials, Baʿlu has no alternative to taking on the reptilian forces because they are also allies of Yammu (see above note 92). In spite of the damaged state of tablets 4 and 5, it is clear that, in Môtu's mind and hence for the plot line, the nub of the long exchange of messages between Baʿlu and Môtu is the latter's request for an invitation to take tea at the palace ("So invite me..."), for it is by the repetition of those terms that Môtu greets Baʿlu's eventual acquiescence (*CTA* 5 ii 21-23), which itself was not stated in anything approaching those terms (*CTA* 5 ii 12, 19-20: "Your servant am I, and forever (will be)!") (p. 266).

[202] "And" here and four more times in lines 15-21 reflects the particle *hm* that may mark either mutually exclusive alternatives or a list of open possibilities, the latter being the case here. I often do not translate the less strongly marked conjunction *w*, but do translate *hm* here each time it appears.

[203] As in *CTA* 5 i 7, *npš* is here the inner passage of the throat, the esophagus. The parallel term, *brlt*, is the regular parallel to *npš* in Ug. poetry, though its precise meaning is debated. Elsewhere in Ug., the two terms can denote not the physical apparatus of eating and breathing, but the vital life force.

[204] *ʾanḫr* is plausibly identical to Akk. *nāḫiru*, mentioned by Assyrian kings as the object of sea-hunts (*CAD N* 137). Because one of these texts mentions the "tusks" (*šinnê*) of the creature in question, doubt has been expressed as to the identification of the animal with the whale (some bibliography in Pardee 1987:373).

[205] Some have interpreted this verse as meaning that the sources of water attract the animals, rather than vice versa. The interpretation offered above appears preferable, however, because it is the animals that do the swallowing, not the sources. That the form *rʾumm* is adverbial is proven

my throat consumes[ddd] heaps (of things),[206]
yes indeed, I eat by double handfuls;
And my seven portions are in a bowl,
and they mix (into my) cup a (whole) river.[207]
So invite me, Baᶜlu, along with my brothers,
have me over, Haddu, along with my kin,
And eat bread with my brothers,
drink wine with my kin!
Have you forgotten, Baᶜlu, that I can pierce you through?
...[208]]

Colophon (left edge)
[The scribe: ᵓIlīmilku, *ṯāᶜi*]*yu*-official of Niqmaddu, king of Ugarit.[209]

***CTA* 5**[210]
When you smite Lôtan,[211] the fleeing serpent,
finish off the twisting serpent,[eee]
the close-coiling one with seven heads,
The heavens wither and go slack
like the folds (?) of your tunic.[212]
(Then) I, with groans, am devoured,
(like) a piece of dung I die.[213]
(So) you must (for your part) descend[214] into the throat of Môtu, son of ᵓIlu,
into the watery depths[215] [fff] of the beloved warrior of ᵓIlu.

ddd Ps 49:15

eee Isa 27:1; Ps 74:14

fff Ps 140:11

Môtu's Message is Delivered to Baᶜlu (i 9-?)
The gods do not hesitate;
they head off
for Baᶜlu on the heights of Ṣapānu.
Gupanu-wa-ᵓUgāru report:
Message of Môtu, son of ᵓIlu,
word of the beloved warrior of ᵓIlu:[216]
My throat is the throat of the lion in the wasteland,
and the gullet of the 'snorter' in the sea;
And it craves the pool (as do) the wild bulls,
(craves) springs as (do) the herds of deer;
And, indeed, indeed,
my throat consumes heaps (of things),
yes indeed, I eat by double handfuls;
And my seven portions are in a bowl,
and they mix (into my) cup a (whole) river.
So invite me, Baᶜlu, along with my brothers,
have me over, Haddu, along with my kin,
And eat bread with my brothers,
drink wine with my kin!
Have you forgotten, Baᶜlu, that I can pierce you through?
[...]
When you smite [Lôtan, the] fleeing [serpent],
finish off [the twisting serpent],
the close-coiling one [with seven heads],
[The heavens] wither [and go slack
like the folds (?) of] your [tunic].

by the quotation of this or a similar text in RS 24.293:7, where the word is preceded by the preposition *k*; that the form is plural seems to be proven by the same text, for marking a noun both prepositionally and with enclitic-*m* is not particularly common. For a comparison of the two texts, with previous bibliography, see Pardee 1988a:158-60.

[206] Most scholars have interpreted *ḥmr* as meaning "clay" and as a metaphor for "humankind" (cf. Job 4:19; 33:6, and the creation story in Genesis, where man is made from "dust from the soil," *ᶜāpār min-hāᵓᵃdāmāh*). It appears somewhat implausible, however, from a rhetorical perspective, that humankind would be introduced here, after a list of animals, under so obscure an image. The interpretation as meaning "heap(s)" finds etymological support in Heb. *ḥōmer* (used for heaps of frogs in Exod 8:10) and in Aram. and Arabic where forms of the root are used for heaping stones.

[207] Or: "And Naharu (himself) mixes (my) cup."

[208] The first part of *CTA* 5 i 27, from which the message up to this point is restored, has almost entirely disappeared; it is certain that only one line of this verse is missing there. Judging from the repetition of the message in *CTA* 5 i (lines 14 to the end of the column as preserved), this verse was the last on *CTA* 4 viii and the text continued immediately on *CTA* 5. Because of the varieties of semantic parallelism, from synonymous to none at all (for a presentation of the types of parallelism and their distributions in a poem, see Pardee 1988c), there is no way of knowing whether the line that has been lost from this verse restated Môtu's powers or provided a motivation or circumstances for their exercise. Because of this uncertainty, it is also uncertain whether the clause introduced by *k* in the following verse *(CTA* 5 i 1) is causal or temporal, and in the latter case whether the clause is dependent on this verse or on the verse following that containing the *k* clause (as I translate).

[209] On the title written *ṯᶜy*, see discussion and bibliography in Freilich 1992 and in Pardee forthcoming on RS 1.001:1. It is clear that the administrative title was also a religious one, for a *ṯᶜy*-priest is known from RS 24.266:8 (text 1.88) and from RIH 78/20:2 (text 1.96). On the possibility that the Niqmaddu of this colophon is Niqmaddu (III), who reigned at the end of the thirteenth century, see above, note 3. On the distribution of colophons in these tablets, see note 4.

[210] This six-column tablet consists of two primary fragments, found in different years (1930, 1931) but published together by Virolleaud 1934b. It is certain that this tablet bore neither introductory notation (*l bᶜl*) nor colophon, for the upper left corner fragment contains the beginning and end of the text and the left edge of the tablet is quite well preserved, with neither of those scribal formulae present. Unfortunately, about a third of the tablet was never found, a large portion of the upper right corner, where a major portion of cols. ii-v has disappeared. Moreover, the right half of cols. iii and iv, situated on the right side of this six-column tablet, has disappeared and the text partially preserved there is without parallels, making continuous translation impossible.

[211] On this divinity, corresponding to Leviathan in the Hebrew Bible, see Caquot 1992.

[212] {krs ᵓipdk} has received a great many explanations. I have analyzed the first three signs as the preposition *k* + a noun (or verbal noun?) *rs*, but my translation is a simple guess. The word translated "tunic" is *ᵓipd*, cognate with Heb. *ᵓēpōd* designating a garment.

[213] This interpretation is based primarily on the form *ᵓamtm*, analyzed as the first person singular of MT, "to die," plus enclitic-*m* (cf. note 201). Others see the verse as a threat on Môtu's part to devour Baᶜlu, "forearms" (*ᵓamtm*, dual of *ᵓamt*, cognate with Heb. *ᵓammāh*) and all.

[214] *l yrt* (< *yarad* + *ta*) = precative *l* + perfect, 2m.s., expresses the certitude of the event.

[215] *b mhmrt*, written across two lines, is here interpreted, as have many scholars before me, as a *m*-preformative noun from the same root as that from which the name of Môtu's city, Hamray, is derived (see above, note 197).

[216] The title is here written incorrectly: {ydd . bn . ᵓil (14) ǵzr} (*bn* is repeated from the previous formula).

[(Then) I, with groans, am devoured,
(like) a piece of dung I die.
(So) you must (for your part) descend the throat of Môtu, son of ᵓIlu,
into the watery depths of the beloved warrior of ᵓIlu].
...[217]

Baᶜlu Reflects on Môtu's Threat (ii ?-7)[218]

[He puts (one) lip to the] earth, (the other) lip to the heavens,
[he X] (his) tongue to the stars.[219] [ggg]
Baᶜlu will enter his insides,[220]
(will go down) his mouth like a roasted olive,
(like) the produce of the earth and the fruit of (its) trees.
Mighty Baᶜlu will fear him,
Cloud-Rider will be frightened of him.

Baᶜlu's Message, Very Brief, in Reply to Môtu's Threats (ii 8-13)

Go say to Môtu, son of ᵓIlu,
Repeat to the beloved warrior of ᵓIlu:
Message of Mighty Baᶜlu,
word of the mightiest of heroes:
Salutations, Môtu, son of ᵓIlu!
Your servant am I, and forever (will be)![hhh]
Be off and do not tarry, O gods.

ggg Ps 73:9
hhh Ps 116:16

The Message is Delivered (ii 13-20)

So they head off
toward Môtu, son of ᵓIlu,
to his city Hamray,
to Mukku where <his> throne is established,
to Ḫôḫu, the land of his own possession.
They raise their voices and say aloud:
Message of Mighty Baᶜlu,
word of the mightiest of heroes:
Salutations, Môtu, son of ᵓIlu!
Your servant am I, and forever (will be)!

Môtu's Reaction (ii 20-?)

(This) brings joy to Môtu, son of ᵓIlu:
[He raises] his voice and cries out:[221]
[Baᶜlu] will indeed invite me [along with my brothers],
Haddu will have me over [along with my kinsmen].
...[222]

Invitation and Preparations for the Feast in Honor of Môtu (iii)[223]

A Banquet (iv)[224]

Baᶜlu Receives the Final Invitation (v ?-17)

...[225]
and I will put him/it down amongst the gods of

[217] The end of the message, here restored in the form in which Môtu dictated it to Baᶜlu's messenger, has disappeared in the lacuna at the end of col. i, which the editor estimated to have caused the loss of some thirty lines (Virolleaud 1934b:306); the beginning of col. ii is also lost, about twelve lines by comparison with col. i.

[218] The precise context of these words from Baᶜlu is unclear because of the preceding lacuna and because there is no transition from the soliloquy to the messenger formulae introducing his return message to Môtu (line 13 "Be off..."). It is clear from this and the following section that Môtu's words have changed Baᶜlu's braggadocio into submission, but the missing text leaves us in the dark as to what it was that brought about the transformation. Note that the lacuna of forty-plus lines may have taken away a complete exchange of messages, either brief ones or longer ones with omission of repetition by the messengers (as has occurred above [see notes 88, 132, 200]).

[219] One finds a similar idiom in the myth Dawn and Dusk (text 1.87, lines 61-62), where the motif of a deity's mouth stretching from heaven to earth also expresses extreme voracity. The reference to the tongue here (partially restored in line 3: {[l]šn}) is not present in the other text and may or may not express that Môtu possessed powers unknown to Šaḥaru-wa-Šalimu.

[220] Lit., "his liver" (see above, note 15).

[221] The text reads here: {[...]gh w ᵓaṣḥ}, "[...] his voice and I will cry out"; Herdner assures us that there is only room in the lacuna for two wide signs or three narrow ones. Now the restoration {[yšᵓu]}, "he raises," would constitute three wide signs (1963:34, n. 4). Most scholars have adopted a similar restoration, nonetheless, and emended {ᵓaṣḥ} to {y!ṣḥ}, and I see no other solution (something like "I have heard his voice and I will cry out" would take even more space and is not, in any case, an attested idiom).

[222] Other than a few words and signs the rest of col. ii has disappeared. One of these words, *šmḫ*, seems to occur in RS 24.293:16, the text we have already presented as containing elements quoted from this or a similar text (see note 205), and another word is tantalizingly similar (*qẓb* in *CTA* 5 ii 24 vs. *qbẓ* in RS 24.293:13). Unfortunately, the interpretation of these words is not easy (see Pardee 1988a:160-64).

[223] As stated in note 210, the right half of cols. iii-iv has disappeared and no single line is completely restorable in col. iii. Moreover, there is a complete gap of thirty to forty lines between cols. ii and iii as preserved. The title ascribed to this column is based on some of the few complete words that have been preserved. In lines 9 and 18 is found the verbal form *ᵓaṣḥ*, "I will invite" (lit., "I will cry out to (to)," the same verb as was used in the first line of the two verses expressing Môtu's desire to be invited) and Môtu's name and title "beloved" are present both times. Also present are words for sheep and goats: *šgr* (cf. Heb. *šeger*), *ᵓiṯm* (which appears again in RS 24.252:14, but again in a badly broken context [Pardee 1988a:111]), and as a divine name in RS 24.643:31 [see Pardee forthcoming *ad loc.*), and *ṣᵓin* (cf. Heb. *ṣōᵓn*). These may be taken as constituting at least part of the beasts slaughtered for the feast.

[224] Col. iv being the continuation of col. iii, i.e., situated on the right side of the verso of the tablet, it has undergone damage symmetrical to that of col. iii. Also, because the bottom of the tablet is broken away, there is a gap of some forty or more lines between cols. iii and iv as preserved. Lines 12-18 certainly contain the terms characteristic of a banquet (as in *CTA* 4 iii 40-44 [see note 146]). Unfortunately, no characteristic term has been preserved by which to identify the feasting gods. The presence of the phrases *ᵓi ᵓap bᶜl* [...] *ᵓi hd*, "Where, then, is Baᶜlu [...] where is Haddu?" (lines 6, 7) seems to indicate, however, that a feast is depicted other than the one put on by Baᶜlu for Môtu. Because of these features and because in the next column Baᶜlu has not yet gone down to Môtu's domain, we may surmise that Baᶜlu's banquet for Môtu has already taken place, that at that banquet Môtu may have insisted again on Baᶜlu visiting the underworld, and that the banquet in col. iv represents another banquet of the gods from which Baᶜlu is absent, for reasons impossible to ascertain but which may have to do with his preparations for his descent (as in col. v).

[225] More than thirty-five lines have disappeared between cols. iv and v as preserved, and the first four lines of col. v are too broken to permit translation. The first partially translatable line is clearly the second segment of a verse.

the underworld.[226]
As for you, take your clouds, your wind,
your watering devices, your rain,[iii]
With you your seven lads,
your eight officers,
With you Pidray, daughter of ʾAru,
with you Ṭallay,[227] daughter of Rabbu.[228]
Head off
for the mountains of my covert;[229]
Lift up (one) mountain on (your) hands,
(one) wooded hill on (your) palms.
Then go down into the place of seclusion (within) the earth,
you must be counted among those who go down into the earth,
And the gods will know that you are dead.[230] [jjj]

Baʿlu Assures Himself a Form of Afterlife (v 17-?)
Hearing (this), Baʿlu loves a heifer in the pasture land,
a cow in a field on the edge of death's realm.[231]
Seventy-seven (times) he lies with her,
eighty-eight she bears him up.
She conceives and bears a male,
Mighty Baʿlu clothes him.[kkk]
...[232]

iii Ps 135:7
jjj Ps 82:7
kkk Gen 37;3
lll Ps 141:7
mmm Isa 47:1; Ezek 26:16
nnn Josh 7:6; Ezek 27:30; Lam 2:10

ʾIlu Learns of Baʿlu's Death (vi ?-25)
[Off they head
to ʾIlu at the source of the double river,
midst the upspringings of the deeps.
They enter ʾIlu's dwelling],
go into [the home of the King, father of] Šunama.
[They raise their voices and say aloud]:
We have done the rounds of [(some part) of the earth],
unto (its) well-watered portions.[233]
We arrived at the best part of the earth, the pasture land,
at the most beautiful field on the edge of death's realm.[234] [lll]
We arrived at where Baʿlu was fallen to the earth:
Dead was Mighty Baʿlu,
perished the Prince, master of the earth.[235]
Thereupon the Gracious One, the kindly god,
descends from the throne, sits on the footstool,
(descends) from the footstool, sits on the earth.[mmm]
He pours dirt[236] of mourning on his head,
dust of humiliation on his cranium,[nnn]

[226] Lit., "I will put him/it in the hole(s) of the gods, (in) the earth." The word for "hole(s)," *ḫrt*, is probably from the same root as the Ug. word for nostrils (*ḫr* in RS 24.247+:6 [text 1.90]) and as the Heb. word *ḥōr*, used once to describe the holes in the ground from which the Hebrews hid from the Philistines (1 Sam 14:11) and again for the dwelling-place of outcast people (Job 30:6), probably in both passages representing humans as living like animals. These usages indicate that the notion communicated by *ḫrt* in the phrase *ḫrt ʾilm* is probably not so much that of the grave, i.e., a hole dug in the ground, as that of the "caves, caverns, crevices, (geological) faults" that lead down into the earth, hence down to the dwelling-place of the deities of the netherworld. The "gods" in the Ug. expression probably include both the underworld deities, of whom Rašap and Milku were the leaders, and the divinized dead. Judging from the Ug. king list (RS 24.257; see Pardee 1988a:165-78; text 1.104 below), where each of the past king's names is preceded by the word *ʾil*, "god," the deceased, at least the royal deceased, were thought to be deified at death. Parallelism in other passages indicates that this phrase can be part of an idiom for burial (see here *CTA* 6 i 17-18 and the ʾAqhatu text *CTA* 19 iii 112, 126-27, 141 [text 1.103]). It is uncertain to whom reference is made here, for there is an explicit shift to Baʿlu in the next verse. For this reason and because here the line is missing that in the other texts refers explicitly to a tomb, it is not impossible that this verse was formulated differently from the parallel texts and that the phrase refers to descent into the underworld in a non-funerary context.

[227] Mistakenly written {tṭly}.

[228] This list of Baʿlu's suite shows that all manifestations of his powers are to go with him to the underworld, that drought must be the result of his descent. (The reason for the omission of ʾArṣay, daughter of Yaʿibdarru here, as in *CTA* 3 i 22-25, is unclear [cf. Smith 1994:72, n. 143].)

[229] The *-y* affixed to *knkny* indicates that it may well not be a toponym, as some have thought, but a common noun, as others have thought. Because it fills the slot of the two mountain names in *CTA* 5 viii 2-3, under which Môtu lives according to both accounts, the word is plausibly explained by Arabic *knn*, "cover, cover up, hide," and in reflexive stems "hide, find seclusion at home." According to the classical dictionaries, Arabic actually had a reduplicated stem like this one, *knkn*, that meant "stick around home, not go out (to battle, etc.), etc."

[230] In the text as it has been preserved the word "die" is here pronounced for the first time in the context of Baʿlu's descent into the netherworld. Môtu has previously used the verb only of himself (i 6, restored in i 33), while Baal's demise has been described as descending into Môtu's realm. In col. vi, Baʿlu is described as "dying" and in *CTA* 6 his corpse is described as in need of burial. Whether the intervening text, now lost, contained any narrative device functioning to lessen the dissonance of these two views of dying and of corpse disposal, it is impossible to know. It can be said, however, that the two views existed side-by-side in the case of human death: the dead were said to "descend into the earth" and this was accomplished for the corpse by placing it in a grave, along with the "forefathers" in the earth. At least in the case of kings, a special rite existed to ensure that the dead person joined the Rapaʾūma, the shades of the dead (see here RS 34.126 [text 1.105] and Pardee forthcoming on RS 34.126).

[231] "Death's realm" here is *mmt*, a *m*-preformative noun from the same root as that from which Môtu's name is formed.

[232] Another gap of more than forty lines separates cols. v and vi, more than ten lines here and another thirty or so lines in col. vi.

[233] This passage is similar, though not identical, to a passage in the Kirta text (1.102), *CTA* 16 iii 3-4. Unfortunately line 4 in the present text has almost entirely disappeared and there is no way to know precisely how it should be restored.

[234] It is to be noted that this passage, by repetition of the expression *šd šḥl mmt*, explicitly places the discovery of Baʿlu's body in the same place where he had loved the heifer (see v 18-23, and note 231), which in turn seems to be located near the spot where one descends into Môtu's realm. Therefore, however close the connections may be with death, the place described is earthly, not netherworldly, and there is no reason to interpret the terms "best" and "most beautiful" as euphemisms for the realm of death. Rather, because this place has mountains (*CTA* 4 viii 2-6; 5 v 12-14) and because "good" (*nʿmy*) is used to describe Baʿlu's mountain (*CTA* 3 iii 28 [here line 31]), one may see this use of *nʿm* and *ysm* as descriptive of mountainous areas associated with divinities.

[235] The title *zbl bʿl ʾarṣ* has not been used for Baʿlu, in the text as preserved, since he sat down at his own feast (*CTA* 3 i 3-4).

[236] It is disputed whether *ʿmr* here is to be explained by Heb. *ʾēper*, "soil, ashes," or by *ʿōmer/ʿāmīr*, words used to designate various forms

for clothing, he is covered with a girded garment.[237]
With a stone he scratches incisions on (his) skin,[ooo]
with a razor he cuts cheeks and chin.[ppp]
He harrows his upper arms,
plows (his) chest like a garden
harrows (his) back like a (garden in a) valley.[238]
He raises his voice and cries aloud:
Ba^{c}lu is dead, what (is to become of) the people,
the Son of Dagan (is dead), what (is to become of) the hordes (of the earth)?
After Ba^{c}lu, I also shall descend into the earth.

^{c}Anatu Finds and Buries Ba^{c}lu (vi 25 - *CTA* 6 i 32)
^{c}Anatu also goes and searches
every mountain to the heart of the earth,
every hill to the heart of the fields.[239]
She arrives at the best part of [the earth], the pasture land,
at the most beautiful field on [the edge of] death's realm.
She [arrives] at where Ba^{c}lu was fallen [to the] earth;
[for clothing], she is covered with a girded garment.[240]
***CTA* 6**[241]
(Belonging) to (the) Ba^{c}lu (cycle).
With a stone she scratches incisions on (her) skin,
[with a razor] she cuts cheeks and chin.
[She harrows] her upper arms,
plows (her) chest like a garden
harrows (her) back like a (garden in a) valley.
Ba^{c}lu is dead, what (is to become of) the people,
the Son of Dagan (is dead), what (is to become of) the hordes (of the earth)?
After Ba^{c}lu, we also shall descend into the earth,
with him Šapšu, luminary of the gods, shall descend.
She drinks (her) weeping until she is sated,
(she drinks her) tears like wine.[qqq]
(Then) she calls aloud to Šapšu, luminary of the gods:
Bear for me, please, Mighty Ba^{c}lu.
Šapšu, luminary of the gods, agrees:
She lifts Mighty Ba^{c}lu up onto ^{c}Anatu's shoulder.
Once (Šapšu) has placed him (on her shoulder), she takes him up
to the heights of Ṣapānu.
(There) she weeps for him and buries him,
places him down amongst the gods of the underworld.
She slaughters seventy wild bulls
as a GMN (for) Mighty Ba^{c}lu;[242]
She slaughters seventy domesticated bovids
[as] a GMN (for) Mighty Ba^{c}lu;
[She] slaughters seventy domesticated caprovids
[as a] GMN (for) Mighty Ba^{c}lu;
[She] slaughters seventy deer
[as a GMN] (for) Mighty Ba^{c}lu;

ooo 1 Kgs 18:28; Jer 16:6
ppp Isa 15:2; Jer 48:37
qqq Ps 80:6

of "grain," here taken as "straw." Del Olmo Lete (1981:601) observes that the latter meaning is inappropriate with a verb meaning "pour out."

237 The precise meaning of *m$^{\supset}$izrt*, here interpreted as from the root *$^{\supset}$zr*, "to gird," is uncertain. It and an apparently related word *$^{\supset}$uzr* are key terms in the first of the $^{\supset}$Aqhatu texts (see note 3 to text 1.103). A masculine form of the noun may appear in two economic texts in Akk. from Ras Shamra (Nougayrol 1970:99, 100), though that may be a different word.

238 For the interpretation of this verse, with some previous bibliography, see Dietrich and Loretz 1986c:109. Note that the word here translated "back" is *bmt*, the same as was used above for the part of the body where ^{c}Anatu hung the necklace of human heads (see notes 76, 149).

239 The formulation here, lit., "liver of the earth, liver of the fields," is precisely that of the passages in which ^{c}Anatu is requested to make peace offerings (see above, note 15). The second of these passages *(CTA* 3 iii) appears to be in a context of requesting ^{c}Anatu to abandon her bellicose ways — though the lacuna between cols. ii and iii renders that interpretation uncertain; the first occurrence is in a text too damaged to allow perception of the motivation for this form of address *(CTA* 1 ii).

240 The bicolon in which $^{\supset}$Ilu was described as pouring dirt and dust on his head *(CTA* 5 vi 14-16) is here absent; was this by haplography or does it reflect an intentionally different description of ^{c}Anatu's mourning?

241 The left third of this six-column tablet is well preserved, while the upper half of the columns to the right has disappeared. The bottom half of the tablet was discovered during the second campaign at Ras Shamra (1930), the fragment providing the upper part of the left column three years later (*editio princeps* by Virolleaud 1931, 1934a). As is the case with tablets belonging to the Kirta and $^{\supset}$Aqhatu cycles, this tablet bears as its first line the identification of the story cycle to which it belongs, viz. *l b^{c}l*. The preposition *l* plus the hero's name is so placed on *CTA* 14, 16, and 19. In the two other cycles the notation is present wherever the upper left corner of the tablet is preserved (the corner of *CTA* 15, 17, 18 is not preserved). In the Ba^{c}lu cycle, only two tablets have the upper left corner extant, *CTA* 5 and 6; the archival notation was not inscribed on *CTA* 5. The use of the preposition *l* in the archival notation is not to be confused with the *lamed auctoris* used in the (secondary) headings of several biblical psalms. *CTA* 6 also has the longest colophon of any tablet of the three cycles mentioned (see below, vi 53-57). On the use of colophons in these texts, see above note 4.

242 The signs {kgmn}, usually taken as the preposition *k* plus a noun *gmn*, are presently unexplained (for a summary, see Watson 1989b). Because equational phrases are frequently not marked prepositionally in Ug., leaving open the possibility that the four signs denote a single word, and because even *gmn* is open to several etymological explanations, we must await further evidence before we can hope to identify the meaning of the expression with some assurance. The relationship of this phrase to Ba^{c}lu is not marked lexically, probably indicating a construct chain, lit., "(as) the *(k)gmn* of Ba^{c}lu." The animals in the list constitute a mixture of wild and domesticated beasts (on *r$^{\supset}$um* and *$^{\supset}$alp*, the first two types mentioned here, see above, note 177). The total list is quite different from the repertory of sacrificial beasts characteristic of the prose ritual texts, and the difference is accentuated by the absence of the term *(k)gmn* in those texts. The terms for domesticated beasts here (*$^{\supset}$alp*, "bovid," *ṣ$^{\supset}$in*, "caprovid") are found in the ritual texts whereas the wild animals are absent (*r$^{\supset}$um*, "wild bull," *$^{\supset}$ayl*, "deer," *y^{c}l*, "wild goat"). If the correct reading in line 28 is {ḥmrm}, "donkeys" (rather than {[y]ḥmrm}, "roebucks," proposed by Ginsberg 1950:158), the word is not the same as that used in the ritual texts for a very particular type of donkey-sacrifice: there the word is *^{c}r* (see Pardee 1991 and forthcoming). Finally, the verb used in this passage is *ṭbḫ*, rather than *dbḥ*, the verb characteristic of the prose ritual texts and which appears in some mythological passages where a divine meal is depicted. (*ṭbḫ* also appears in descriptions of divine feasts, though more rarely, e.g., *CTA* 4 vi 40.) This passage varies

[She slaughters] seventy wild goats
  [as a GMN] (for) Mighty Baᶜlu;
[She slaughters seventy] asses
  [as a] GMN (for) Mighty Baᶜlu.
...[243]

ᶜAnat Informs ᵓIlu of Baᶜlu's Death (i 32-43)
Then off she goes
  to [ᵓIlu] at the source of the double river,
  midst the upspringings of the deeps.
She enters ᵓIlu's dwelling,
  goes into the home of the King, father of Šunama;
At ᵓIlu's feet she bows and falls,
  does homage and honors him.
She raises her voice and says aloud:
So now let ᵓAṯiratu and her sons rejoice,
  (let) the goddess (rejoice) and the host of her kin;
For Mighty Baᶜlu is dead,
  perished the Prince, master of the earth.[244]

ᵓIlu and ᵓAṯiratu Confer on a Replacement for Baᶜlu (i 43-55)
ᵓIlu cries aloud
  to the Great Lady, ᵓAṯiratu of the Sea:
Listen, O Great Lady, ᵓAṯiratu of the Sea:
  Give one of your sons that I might make him king.
The Great Lady, ᵓAṯiratu of the Sea, replies:
  Must we not appoint someone as king (who) knows (how) sap flows?[245]
The Gracious One, the kindly god answers:
One of meager strength cannot run (with Baᶜlu),
  with Baᶜlu cannot handle the lance,
  (for when he vies) with the son of Dagan, he falls prostrate.[246]
The Great Lady, ᵓAṯiratu of the Sea, replies:
  Must we not, then, appoint terrible ᶜAṯtaru as king?[247]
  Let terrible ᶜAṯtaru be king!

'Terrible' ᶜAṯtaru Attempts, Unsuccessfully, to Fill Baᶜlu's Rôle (i 56-?)
Thereupon terrible ᶜAṯtaru
  climbs the heights of Ṣapānu,[rrr]
  sits on Mighty Baᶜlu's seat.[248]
(But) his feet do not reach the footstool,
  his head does not reach the top (of the seat).[249]
(To this) terrible ᶜAṯtaru responds:
  I will not be king on the heights of Ṣapānu.
Terrible ᶜAṯtaru (then) descends,
  he descends from the seat of Might Baᶜlu,
And rules over the earth, god of it all,[250]
  [...] will draw in jars,

rrr Isa 14:13

considerably, therefore, from the ritual texts, most of which emanate from the royal sacrificial cult as actually practiced at Ugarit in ca. 1200 BCE. Such differences are surely owing to various historical and ideological factors that deserve more extensive treatment than can be given here. Comparing this text with the sacrificial use of game for ᵓIlu's table according to RS 24.258 (see n. 4 text 1.97), it appears that the gods were perceived as regularly dining on a combination of wild and domesticated beasts. The use of *ṭbḫ* here may be linked with the funerary nature of these sacrifices, though that can only be an hypothesis based on this passage. (*ṯᶜy* is used in the only certain funerary ritual presently known from Ugarit, RS 34.126 [Bordreuil and Pardee 1991:151-163 and here text 1.105].) It is very unfortunate that the precise meaning of *(k)gmn* escapes us.

243 Between the list of sacrifices and the following travel formulae there are two damaged lines that have no parallels to permit restoration.

244 ᵓAṯiratu's hostility to Baᶜlu is here assumed by all protagonists (see above, note 121).

245 Opinions are about evenly divided as to whether *ydᶜ ylḥn* means "he knows, he is intelligent" (*ydᶜ* + *lḥn*, the latter explained by Arabic *lḥn*, "be intelligent") or "he knows (how) sap flows," or "(how) to make the sap flow, cause moisture" (*ydᶜ* + *lḥ* [geminate root], the latter perhaps attested in a nominal form in the Ug. hippiatric texts, text 1.106). The first interpretation assumes that ᵓAṯiratu is proposing that the new king be wise, ᵓIlu (next verses) that the new king be strong; the second that the new king must be able to provide fertility as does Baᶜlu. A reference to intelligence would here be without resonance in the following text (ᶜAṯtaru is disqualified for physical reasons [lines 59-65], with no mention of intellectual inability), and the second explanation thus appears preferable. If ᶜAṯtaru is indeed linked with irrigation (see above, note 48), one might interpret this passage as meaning that in the hilly Levant irrigation is insufficient to make the sap flow everywhere; for that to happen, Baᶜlu's lance (*mrḥ* in ᵓIlu's speech that follows) that buds (see note 191) must be properly wielded in order that the rains may fall.

246 There seems to be agreement that the reading at the end line 52 is {ktmsm}, rather than {k . msm}, once proposed by Caquot, Sznycer and Herdner 1974:257, note l. The signs may be divided either as *kt msm*, "smitten, crushed as to beauty" (he who does not have the requisite beauty of form cannot vie with Baᶜlu), or as *ktms*, a form of *kms*, "fall prostrate" (parallel to *npl* in *CTA* 12 ii 54-55). The first solution is problematic lexically (*ktt* is not attested elsewhere in Ug. and is not attested in such a formula in Heb.), the second is problematic both morphologically (in *CTA* 12 ii 55 the form is *tkms*, not *ktms*; the form is here perf., whereas the two previous verbs are in the imperf.) and rhetorically (the two previous verbs denote forms of vying with Baᶜlu, this one would denote the result of vying with Baᶜlu but the prep. is still ᶜ*m*, "with, along with").

247 The interpretation of ᶜAṯtaru's title ᶜ*rẓ* is much debated. Most link the epithet with Heb. ᶜ*rṣ* (no root ᶜ*rẓ* is attested in Arabic), which denotes various aspects of inspiring fear, awe, and terror. If this is correct, ᵓAṯiratu is agreeing with ᵓIlu that the candidate should be someone who shares Baᶜlu's physical prowess and is claiming that ᶜAṯtaru qualifies. Also, if this interpretation of ᶜ*rẓ* is correct, it is difficult not to see in the repetition of the epithet in the following section, in which ᶜAṯtaru's disqualification is described, an ironic use of the title by the pro-Baᶜlu author/scribe.

248 The word used for the throne here is *kḥṯ*, which normally appears in second position, parallel to *ksᵓu*, "chair, throne."

249 A proper occupant of a throne, with feet on the footstool and tip of the cap touching the back of the throne, is illustrated by a stone statuette of a deity (perhaps ᵓIlu) discovered at Ras Shamra in 1988 (Yon 1991:347-348, 351).

250 The phrase here is ᵓ*il klh*, precisely the same as was used twice above with reference to Kôtaru-wa-Ḫasīsu's hegemony in Memphis (see note 19). Because they assume that Baᶜlu is king of the earth, some scholars have felt constrained to take ᵓ*arṣ* here as denoting a particular land (cf. Caquot, Sznycer and Herdner 1974:258, n. o). On the other hand, a formal claim to kingship of the earth is not to be found in the various statements regarding Baᶜlu's kingship. The closest one comes to the expression of such a concept is in one of his standard titles, *zbl b*ᶜ*l arṣ*, "the Prince, master of the earth," and in the phrase ᵓ*arṣ drkt*, "the land of (his) domain" [*CTA* 4 vii 44]). Because of the very specific terminology used in this passage, viz., that ᶜAṯtaru climbs (ᶜ*ly*) Mount Ṣapānu to take Baᶜlu's throne and descends (*yrd*) from there when he abandons that throne, it does not appear implausible to interpret ᶜAṯtaru's rôle as king of the earth as referring to the earth as flatlands. Such a limited kingship may already have been referred to in *CTA* 2 iii 17-18 (see above, note 50). This hegemony, though ultimately granted by ᵓIlu, may have been

[...] will draw in jugs.
...[251]

ᶜAnatu Punishes Môtu (ii 4-37)

A day, two days pass
and [Maid[252] ᶜAnatu] interrogates him.[253]
Like the heart of a cow for her calf,
like the heart of a ewe for her lamb,
so is the heart of ᶜAnatu after Baᶜlu.
She seizes Môtu by the hem of his clothes,
grasps [him] by the extremity of his garment.
She raises her voice and shouts aloud:
You, Môtu, give me my brother![254]
Môtu, son of ʾIlu, replies:
(You don't know) what you're asking, Girl ᶜAnatu.
I went searching
every mountain to the heart of the earth,
every hill to the heart of the fields.
There were no humans for me to swallow,
no hordes of the earth to swallow.[255]
I arrived at the best part of the earth, the pasture land,
at the most beautiful field on the edge of death's realm.
(There) I met up with Mighty Baᶜlu,
I took him as (I would) a lamb in my mouth,
he was destroyed as a kid (would be) in my crushing jaws.[256]
(Now) Šapšu, luminary of the gods, glows hot,
the heavens are powerless under the control of Môtu, the son of ʾIlu.
A day, two days pass,
the days become months,
(and) Maid ᶜAnatu interrogates him.
Like the heart of a cow for her calf,
like the heart of a ewe for her lamb,
so is the heart of ᶜAnatu after Baᶜlu.
She seizes Môtu, son of ʾIlu:[257]
with a knife she splits him,
with a winnowing-fork she winnows him,
with fire she burns him,
with grindstones she pulverizes him,
in the field she sows him;
The birds eat his flesh,
the fowl finish off his body parts,
flesh(-eaters) grow fat on flesh.[258]

seen as a vice-regency under Baᶜlu's control (in normal times, of course, when Baᶜlu is in control). The facts that (1) goddesses have claimed Baᶜlu as their king (*CTA* 3 v 40 [here line 32]; 4 iv 43); (2) Baᶜlu's kingship is stated in this and other passages to be "on the heights of Ṣapānu"; (3) the members of one of the so-called "pantheons," the best known, are described as "the gods of Ṣapānu" (RS 1.017:1 = *CTA* 29:1), lead to the conclusion that Baᶜlu was somehow seen as the king of the earth in the context of divine contact with the earth at Mount Ṣapānu. Descriptions of his activities also indicate that the link between mountain tops, storm clouds, and his function as provider of rain were inextricably linked (see particularly the link between the window in his palace and the phenomena of thunder and lightning, above *CTA* 4 vii 25-37). It appears plausible, therefore, to posit a Ug. conception of Baᶜlu as king of mountains and storms and ᶜAṯtaru as king of the flat earth, under Baᶜlu's control. Whether this concept was linked with the understanding of ᶜAṯtaru as god of irrigation (see above nn. 48, 245) or simply with the realities of flatland life, i.e., the need to draw water from wells and springs, cannot be determined from the following broken lines, which seem to contain references to drawing water.

[251] Approximately thirty-five lines are missing from the beginning of col. ii or too damaged to translate.

[252] The title *rḥm*, "girl, maid" (< "womb"?) is restored here from line 27; it is used of ᶜAnatu only in this passage (cf. note 22 to text 1.87).

[253] In line 27, where the same verbal form, *tngṯh*, appears, the antecedent of the suffixed pronoun is not clear from the preceding text; it is clear, however, that Môtu appears immediately before the phrase there. The pronoun is generally considered to refer to Baᶜlu, who is named at the end of the following section. One wonders why ᶜAnatu would be seeking him out, when she was the one who buried him (below, once Baᶜlu has given signs of life, the verb used for seeking him is *bqṯ* [iv 44]). In *CTA* 12 i 40 a perfect form of *ngṯ* appears, modified by the phrase *b pᶜnh*, usually interpreted as "seek on foot" — one wonders, however, why "foot/feet" bears the pronominal suffix. In none of these passages is there a parallel verb to *ngṯ*, which is often explained by Arabic *ngṯ*, which can mean "to seek, search, make inquiries." But that verb can also mean "search for information regarding someone," "scrutinize," "accuse," and even "cry out to someone for help." Perhaps we should take the antecedent as Môtu and interpret ᶜAnatu's act as somehow related to Môtu's confession in this passage and to her attack on him in the second passage (lines 27-37).

[254] For the first time in this text, the relationship between Baᶜlu and ᶜAnatu is expressed in terms reflecting a sibling relationship (see above, note 190). On the many facets of ᶜAnatu's character and on her relationship to Baᶜlu, see Pardee 1989-90:464-66 and, more recently, Walls 1992.

[255] Lit., "My throat lacked sons of mankind, my throat (lacked) the hordes of the earth."

[256] These terms were used by Baᶜlu in warning his messengers not to get too close to Môtu (*CTA* 4 viii 18-20 and note 198). The narrator's version of Baᶜlu's death has been lost in one of the lacunae above.

[257] See below v 11-19, where Môtu refers to the following treatment by ᶜAnat, but with an extended list of acts and significant variations. The problems that have faced the interpreters are: (1) Is the imagery entirely that of grain processing? (2) If so, why is this particular imagery used for Môtu, god of death? Although neither here nor above is a perfectly sequential depiction of how grain is processed, because some of the acts in this list are specifically related to grain processing, it is very likely that the rest of the expressions are so to be interpreted. For a cogent interpretation, esp. of the act of burning, as representing grain processing see Healey 1983b. In that context, "splitting with a knife/sword (*bqᶜ* + *ḥrb*)" refers to the process of cutting up by threshing, even though one might expect terminology closer to a description of threshing by a sledge that has sharp points fixed on its underside (Heb. *ḥārûṣ*). Because ᶜAnatu's acts, even with the exaggerated variants claimed by Môtu below in col. v, did not succeed in eradicating her victim, the explanation of the use of grain imagery is plausibly linked, as many scholars have thought, pointing out the similar idea in John 12:24, with the visible signs of death that accompany the planting of seed, followed by the reappearance of life. Because of several parallels, Moses' destruction of the golden calf (Exod 32:20) is often cited as parallel to these acts. The fact, however, that the objects destroyed and the literary presentations are quite different precludes an identical interpretation of the two passages — until the very end of the second account here (Môtu's version in v 11-19 [see n. 271]) the terms used to describe the destruction of a flesh-and-blood Môtu reflect agricultural realities, while the Exod passage describes the destruction of a metal object in terms more or less applicable to food preparation.

[258] Because the form *yṣḥ*, from the hollow root *ṣḥ*, "to cry out," is frequent in Ug., the word *yṣḥ* here in line 37 has usually been given the same interpretation. "Flesh crying out to flesh" hardly makes sense in this context, however, where we would expect the "flesh" in question to be Môtu's, and it appears likely, therefore, that we are dealing with a homograph. *nṣḥ* is attested in Syrian Arabic in the meaning "grow fat."

[259]

In a Dream ʾIlu Understands that Baʿlu has Revived (iii 1-21)[260]

[... that Mighty Baʿlu is dead,]
  that the Prince, [master of the earth], has perished.
And if Mighty [Baʿlu] is alive,
  if the Prince, lord of [the earth], exists (again),
In a dream of the Gracious One, the kindly god,
  in a vision of the Creator of creatures,
The heavens will rain down oil,
  the wadis will run with honey.[sss]
Then I'll know that Mighty Baʿlu is alive,
  that the Prince, master of the earth, exists (again).
In a dream of the Gracious One, the kindly god,
  in a vision of the Creator of creatures,
The heavens rain down oil,
  the wadis run with honey.
(This) brings joy to the Gracious One, the kindly god,
  he taps his feet on the footstool
  his brow unfurrows and he laughs.
He raises his voice and cries out:
(Now) I can again get some rest,
  my innermost being can get some rest,[261]
For Mighty Baʿlu is alive,
  the Prince, master of the earth, exists (again).

ʾIlu Seeks Confirmation of the Dream (iii 22 - iv)

ʾIlu calls aloud to Girl ʿAnatu:
  Listen, Girl ʿAnatu:
(Go) say to Šapšu, luminary of the gods:
Dried up are the furrows of the fields, O Šapšu,
  dried up are the furrows of ʾIlu's fields,
  Baʿlu is neglecting the furrows of the plowland.[262]
Where is Mighty Baʿlu?
  Where is the Prince, master of the earth?
(So) Girl ʿAnat leaves,
  she heads off
  for Šapšu, luminary of the gods.[263]
She raises her voice and says aloud:
Message of the Bull, your father ʾIlu,
  word of the Gracious One, your sire:[264]
Dried up are the furrows of the fields, O Šapšu,
  dried up are the furrows of ʾIlu's fields,
  Baʿlu is neglecting the furrows of the plowland.
Where is Mighty Baʿlu?
  Where is the Prince, master of the earth?
Šapšu, luminary of the gods, replies:
Pour sparkling wine in (your) tent,
  Put garlands on your kinfolk,[ttt]
For I will go looking for Baʿlu.[265]
Girl ʿAnatu replies:
Wherever you go, O Šapšu,
  wherever you go, ʾIlu will protect [you],
  [...] will protect you.
...[266]

Baʿlu Gets Revenge, Resumes His Kingly Estate (v 1-6)

Baʿlu seizes the sons of ʾAṯiratu,

sss Ezek 32:14; Joel 4:18; Job 20:17

ttt Prov 1:9

Perhaps the repetition of *šʾir*, "flesh," denotes the consumption of flesh and the resultant fattening of the consumers.

259 There is a short double horizontal line at the bottom of col. ii. Because the beginning of col. iii is lost (some forty lines), destroying the data for the sequence of the text from one column to the other, we have no way of determining the function of the double line here.

260 Apparently someone has claimed to ʾIlu (or ʾIlu is soliloquizing) that Baʿlu is alive. He responds that Baʿlu's death has been proven to him and he will only believe that Baʿlu is alive if in a dream he sees the effects of the weather deity's return, which indeed occurs. Though it appears clear that Môtu's demise has permitted Baʿlu's revival, the precise circumstances are lost in the lacuna at the beginning of col. iii (see preceding note), as are those attendant on the discovery of his whereabouts at the beginning of col. iv.

261 Lit., "and my gullet can rest in my chest" (see above, note 203).

262 This verse and the corresponding verse below in Šapšu's reply to this message (lines 42-44) have inspired extremely diverse interpretations. The translation offered here follows somewhat of a consensus; it reflects an interpretation according to which ʾIlu has seen signs of renewed fertility in a dream whereas reality on the ground has not yet changed. Hence his question in the following verse. The passage would be paraphrasable as: I have seen rain in a dream but the fields are still parched; so where is Baʿlu? Another form of interpretation, for which I have not been able to devise a credible philological analysis, is theoretically plausible, one that sees in ʾIlu's message an affirmation of the content of the dream rather than a contrast with the conditions viewed in the dream (paraphrased: I have seen fertility in a dream, something positive is happening in the fields, but Baʿlu hasn't shown up yet. Where is he?). Two negative factors in the consensus interpretation make one seek a better one: (1) The structure of this verse could be tighter — specifically: it starts off in a form appropriate for what has been called "staircase" parallelism (Greenstein 1977) but as here interpreted does not follow that pattern. (2) In Šapšu's reply there are several words that resemble (parts of) words in this verse (*šd*, *ʿn*, *ʿl*) but there is no semantic correspondence — are we missing something or do the correspondences operate solely on the phonetic level?

263 Note that Šapšu, here and in RS 24.244 (text 1.94), does not have a fixed domicile, like the other gods to whom messages are taken in both texts, not even so broad a one as the heavens (like Šaḥru-wa-Šalimu in RS 24.244:51-56), plausibly because she constantly circulates in the heavens and through the netherworld. In this context it is also to be noted that the solar deity in Ug. culture does not have a multiplicity of hypostases, each linked with a different place, and is thus unlike other major Ug. deities, such as Baʿlu and Rašap.

264 Previously, ʾIlu has only called himself "your sire" (*ḥtkk*) when addressing ʿAnatu (see above, note 13). Furthermore, it can be said that if Šapšu is considered in this story cycle to take sides (see above, note 190), it is on the side of Baʿlu and ʿAnatu. The use of *ḥtk* appears, therefore, to denote a relationship of these goddesses to ʾIlu that is different from his relationship to the sons of ʾAṯiratu, who are Baʿlu's enemies.

265 The first verse of Šapšu's reply, a bicolon, clearly corresponds to the first verse of ʾIlu's message, which was a tricolon, while her reply to ʾIlu's double question takes the form of a single utterance. As interpreted here, the reply offers reassurance in two forms, a command to relax and rejoice, motivated by the promise on Šapšu's part to seek (and hence to find) Baʿlu. The word "kinfolk" (*ʾumtk*), the same as is used for Kirta's family at the beginning of that story (*CTA* 14 i 6 [text 1.102]), is derived from the basic word *ʾum* ("mother"), hence "family, immediate kin, kin on the mother's side." The term seems to reflect ʾIlu's use above of the familial term *ḥtk* (see previous note). On the phonetic correspondences between ʾIlu's message and this reply, see note 262.

266 There are some forty lines at the end of col. iv that have either completely disappeared or are too broken to translate.

numerous (as they are) he smites them with the sword,
crushers (as they are) he smites them with the mace;[267]
Môtu's scorching heat he tramples to the ground.[268]
Ba^clu [takes his place] on his royal throne,
[on (his) resting-place], on the seat of his dominion.

Môtu Seeks His Own Form of Revenge (v 7-?)
The days turn into months,
the months into years.
In the seventh year,
Môtu, son of ᵓIlu, [comes]
to Mighty Baᶜlu.
He raises his voice and says aloud:
On account of you, Baᶜlu, I experienced abasement,
on account of you I experienced winnowing with <the winnowing-fork,
on account of you I experienced splitting with>[269] the knife,
on account of you I experienced burning in fire,
on account of you [I experienced] pulverization with grindstones,
on account of [you] I experienced [being strained] with a sieve,[270]
on account of you I experienced [scattering] in the fields,
on account of you I experienced sowing in the sea.[271]
(So) give one of your brothers (for) I would devour (him)
and the anger with which I (now) am sick would go away.
If one of your brothers [...]
then [...].
Now I eat [men],
I finish off the hordes [of the earth].[272]
...

The Final Battle (vi 10-22)[273]
Here now Baᶜlu has given (me) my own brothers to devour,
my own siblings to finish off.
He returned to Baᶜlu on the heights of Ṣapānu,
raised his voice and said aloud:
You have given (me), Baᶜlu, my own brothers to devour,
my own siblings to finish off.
They eye each other like finished (warriors),[274]
Môtu is strong, Baᶜlu is strong;
They butt each other like wild bulls,[uuu]
Môtu is strong, Baᶜlu is strong;
They bite each other like snakes,
Môtu is strong, Baᶜlu is strong;
They trample each other like running (animals),[275]
Môtu falls, Baᶜlu falls.

[uuu] Deut 33:17

[267] If the explanation of *dkym* (*dākiyūma*) by comparison with Heb. *dokyām* in Ps 93:3 is valid, the sons of ᵓAṯiratu are here being explicitly described as the innumerable waves of the sea, an important element in the explanation of ᵓAṯiratu's title (see above, note 98).

[268] A phenomenon similar to *ṣḫr mt*, with the first word taken either as singular, "Môtu's heat," or as plural, "the scorching/scorched ones of Môtu," has occurred previously in this cycle as extant only as a feature of the sun (see above, note 107). The state of the text does not allow us to determine whether this expression is a reference to that set of formulae or whether an expression closer to the form of this one occurred in a passage now lost. Because Šapšu, when active, has heretofore been an ally of Baᶜlu and ᶜAnatu, rather than of Môtu, it would appear more likely that the sun's scorching heat was viewed as involuntary, produced under coercion from Môtu, and to conclude that it is the scorching heat itself or some agents of heat (masculine in gender, while Šapšu is feminine) whom Baᶜlu treats here as allies of the sons of ᵓAṯiratu. The verb for Baᶜlu's treatment of the *ṣḫr mt* here is *mṣḫ*, the same as that by which ᶜAnatu threatens ᵓIlu in *CTA* 3 v 1, and as the one by which the fourth event of Baᶜlu's fight with Môtu is described here below in vi 20. The precise meaning of the verb is uncertain and a meaning associated with feet is based only on the simile "like runners" in vi 21.

[269] The picture of "winnowing with a knife/sword" does not make sense (one does indeed cut up the grain before winnowing, but that is a different process) and it appears necessary, therefore, to compare this passage with the description above of ᶜAnatu's acts (ii 30-37) and, in spite of the differences between the two passages, see here a case of haplography.

[270] Some, minimizing the difference between what a "sieve" (*kbrt*) does and what winnowing consists of, restore {[dr]y}, "to winnow," here. Because only the last consonant of the verb is extant ({[...]y}, another verb denoting the process of putting through a sieve, proper to grading flour by coarseness, should be restored.

[271] In the description of ᶜAnatu's acts (ii 34-35), Môtu was "sown" in the field (*drᶜ* + *šd*). Here the same verb is used, but the complement is *b ym*, "in the sea." That the root **ḏrᶜ* can be used metaphorically for acts similar to sowing seed in dirt is proven by Judg 9:45, where salt is sown (*zrᶜ*). There are three particularly interesting aspects to this assertion by Môtu: (1) that his claim is so blatantly different from ᶜAnatu's act described above; (2) that the act in the form here described would indeed, under normal circumstances, bring about the true death of the seed, which could not germinate in the sea; (3) that the sea (Yammu) has in this cycle consistently been linked with ᵓAṯiratu and her sons as an enemy of Baᶜlu. Is Môtu claiming here that even if he were chopped up and scattered in the sea, ᵓAṯiratu of the Sea would see that he survived?

[272] Lines 21-25 are badly damaged. This verse is plausibly restored on the basis of the word *hml[t]*, consistently used in this cycle to describe the human race. See esp. ii 17-19, where Môtu claims to have killed Baᶜlu because there were no humans available. The first word, *ᶜnt*, seems best taken as an adverb (cf. Heb. *ᶜattāh*). The previous verse cannot be restored, but seems to provide the link between Baᶜlu, one of his brothers, and the human race, the line of thought being that if Baᶜlu is willing to give up one of his brothers, Môtu will leave him, Baᶜlu, alone and return to his normal prey, human beings. After these lines, there are three more poorly preserved lines, then a lacuna of some twenty-five lines.

[273] The first nine lines of this column are too badly damaged to translate. There is a reference to "his/her seven lads" (*šbᶜt ǵlmh*) and Môtu is mentioned twice. Môtu is apparently addressing a message to someone regarding Baᶜlu's refusal to give up one of his brothers, an affront that is compounded by the proposal that Môtu should devour one of his own brothers. In lines 1-2 the two verbs *ṭrd* and *grš* are often restored in third person forms ({[yṭ]rdh} and {[yg]ršh}). One should envisage the possibility of this being part of a direct speech from Môtu and of restoring first person forms here: "I will expel... I will drive out," with Baᶜlu as the object.

[274] For differences between this battle and that between Baᶜlu and Yammu, see Bordreuil and Pardee 1993:66-67 (contrast Smith 1994:94, 101).

[275] On the meaning of *mṣḫ*, see above, note 268. In Akk. the verb *lasāmu*, "to run," is common and is frequently used for animals. Here the

Šapšu Intervenes (vi 22-29)
On high Šapšu cries out to Môtu:
Please listen, O Môtu, son of ᵓIlu:
How can you fight with Mighty Baᶜlu?
How can the Bull, your father ᵓIlu, continue to listen to you (if you do)?
Surely he would pull up the foundations of your seat,
overturn the throne of your kingship,
break the staff of your rulership.

Môtu Capitulates (vi 30-?)
Môtu, son of ᵓIlu, is afraid,
frightened, the beloved warrior of ᵓIlu.
Môtu arises at (the sound of) her voice,
he [lifts up his voice and says aloud]:[276]
Let them place Baᶜlu [on] his royal [throne],
on [(his) resting-place, on the seat of] his dominion.
...[277]

Praise to Šapšu and her Allies (vi 42-52)
Also, please eat the bread of oblation,
drink the wine that is presented (to you).[278]
Šapšu, you rule the Rapaᵓūma,
Šapšu, you rule the divine ones;[279]
In your entourage are the gods,
even the (divinized) dead.
In your entourage is Kôṯaru your companion,
and Ḫasīsu whom you know well.
In the sea are ᵓArišu (Demander) and the dragon;
may Kôṯaru-wa-Ḫasīsu drive (them) out!
may Kôṯaru-wa-Ḫasīsu drive (them) away![280]

Colophon (vi 53-57)[281]
The scribe: ᵓIlīmilku the Šubbanite, disciple of ᵓAttānu-purulini,[282] (who is) chief of the priests (and) chief of the cultic herdsmen; *ṯāᶜiyu*-official of Niqmaddu, (who is) king of Ugarit, lord (of) YRGB, (and) master (of) ṮRMN.[283]

image is apparently that of an animal such as a horse or bull inflicting damage with its feet.

[276] Hypothetical restoration, assuming that Môtu accedes and proclaims Baᶜlu's kingship.

[277] Some nine lines are badly preserved. In them is a reference to a corner (*pᵓit*), to womenfolk (*ᵓinšt*), and to someone arriving (*l tštql*).

[278] Judging from the following verses, this invitation is addressed to Šapšu. The word here translated "oblation" appears to be from the same root as Heb. *tᵉrūmāʰ*, though the form is different (*trmmt*), both from that form and from what appears to be the same word in a Ug. ritual text (*trmt* in RS 1.005:3). The phrase "that is presented (to you)" represents a nominal phrase, *tġẓyt*, a *t*-preformative noun from the same root as was used above for the gifts offered to ᵓAṯiratu (*CTA* 4 i 23, iii 26, 29, 35) and to ᵓIlu (*CTA* 4 ii 11, iii 31).

[279] *tḥtk* is often taken as the prepositional phrase "under you," but the presence here of the oblique form of the word for the shades of the dead (*rpᵓim*) indicates that the analysis as a verbal form, i.e. *ḥtk*, "exercise (parental) authority over," is preferable. Šapšu is presented here as in constant communication with the denizens of the underworld, into whose realm she enters every night, and with Kôṯaru-wa-Ḫasīsu, the craftsman deity, whose principal dwellings were earthly (Crete and Memphis [see above, note 19]) but whose workings with metals take him into the bowels of the earth. Her contact with the deified dead allows her to preside over ceremonies to which they are invited (RS 34.126 [text 1.105]) and, though no text presently known makes this explicit, may have allowed her to funnel blessings from the deified dead to the reigning king (cf. RS 24.252 [Pardee 1988a:75-118], which deals with such blessings, but without mention of Šapšu in its current, rather poor, state).

[280] There is no agreement on the interpretation of the two verbs in this verse, *yd* and *ytr*, some seeing here verbs denoting travel, others verbs of driving out. The latter interpretation provides a coherent interpretation of the passage, i.e., a motivation for the mention of ᵓArišu and the dragon between the two mentions of Kôṯaru-wa-Ḫasīsu, but it presents the narratological problem of introducing a new rôle for the craftsman deity, one that no previous text in this cycle led us to suspect, that of actively expelling the enemies of Baᶜlu. Both enemies have been mentioned above, in a speech by ᶜAnatu apparently referring to her own activities on behalf of Baᶜlu (*CTA* 3 iii 37, 40 [here lines 40, 43]).

[281] This is the longest of the colophons on the extant tablets from the three major cycles. One of the ᵓAqhatu tablets, *CTA* 17, bore a colophon limited to the beginning of this one, i.e., through "ᵓAttānu-purulini" (see note 53 to text 1.103). The only other colophon preserved on the tablets of the Baᶜlu cycle (*CTA* 4) identifies ᵓIlīmilku in terms of the royal affiliation rather than in these terms relating to his scribal training. The colophon to *CTA* 16, one of the Kirta tablets, identifies ᵓIlīmilku only as a *ṯāᶜiyu*-official.

[282] ᵓIlīmilku's hometown of Šubbanu has not been localized with certainty (for bibliography, see Pardee 1989-90:489). On the interpretation of ᵓIlīmilku's master's name, see van Soldt 1989.

[283] Because there are no explicit indicators of which titles belong to ᵓIlīmilku and which to his superiors, the attribution of the titles "chief of the priests (and) chief of the cultic herdsmen" (*rb khnm rb nqdm*) to ᵓAttānu-purulini, and "lord of YRGB, (and) master of ṮRMN" (*ᵓadn yrgb bᶜl ṯrmn*) to Niqmaddu is deduced from the variant forms of the ᵓIlīmilku colophons. Neither priests nor cultic herdsmen are mentioned in the ritual texts, but the terms are regular components in the lists of occupations, a genre of administrative document well attested at Ugarit. That the basic meaning of *khn* was "priest" seems certain from comparative considerations, but the precise status and the functions of the priests at Ugarit cannot be determined without additional textual material. The interpretation "cultic herdsmen" for *nqdm* is derived from Heb., where *nōqēd* denotes someone who raises cattle, and from the association with *khnm* in the Ug. lists of occupations. From this association, it may be assumed that they were in charge of the herds necessary for the royal sacrificial cult. Niqmaddu's titles "lord (of) YRGB, (and) master (of) ṮRMN" have inspired rather fantastic theories. For lack of data, no interpretation is certain. The most likely interpretations are that these terms are either geographical, with no presumption as to the thirteenth-century realities behind the ideological usage of the terms, or verbal/adjectival epithets, "lord (who) is/does RGB, master (who is) ṮRMN." The root *rgb* appears in two divine hypostases that are a part of a longer list of such hypostases, *yrgbbᶜl* and *yrgblᵓim* (RS 24.246:16, 22 [see Pardee forthcoming *ad loc.*]), where the verbal element plausibly means "he inspires awe." No such explanation is immediately obvious for *ṯrmn* (there is a divine name so spelled, but that deity corresponds to the Anatolian deity Šarrumannu).

REFERENCES

Astour 1980; Attridge and Oden 1981; Baumgarten 1981; Bordreuil 1991; Bordreuil and Pardee 1991; 1993; forthcoming; Brooke 1979; Caquot 1992; Caquot, Sznycer, and Herdner 1974; Cassuto 1938; Caubet and Poplin 1987; Clifford 1972; Dietrich and Loretz 1978b; 1986c; Dijkstra and de Moor 1975; Driver 1956; Durand 1993; Freilich 1992; Gachet 1992; Gibson 1978; Ginsberg 1941; 1950; Gordon 1947; Greenstein 1977; Healey 1983b; Held 1973; Herdner 1963; Korpel 1990; Lambert 1985; Margalit 1983; Meier 1986; de Moor 1968; 1971; 1987; Niehr 1994; Nougayrol 1968; 1970; del Olmo Lete 1981; Pardee 1980; 1984; 1987; 1988a; 1988b; 1988c; 1989-90; 1991; forthcoming; Pope 1955; 1977b; Ribichini and Xella 1984; Rummel 1978; Sanmartín 1978; Schaeffer 1949; 1954; Smith 1986; 1994; Van Soldt 1989; 1991; Vaughn 1993; Virolleaud 1931; 1932; 1934a; 1934b; 1935; 1938; 1944-45; Walls 1992; Watson 1980; 1989b; Williams-Forte 1983; Yon 1989; 1990; 1991.

DAWN AND DUSK (1.87)

(The Birth of the Gracious and Beautiful Gods)

Dennis Pardee

The text recounting the birth of the double deity Šaḥru-wa-Šalimu, "Dawn and Dusk," constitutes one of the most important of the texts discovered during the early years of excavations at Ras Shamra and which stand outside the principal cycles of texts (Baʿlu, Kirta, and ʾAqhatu). The text is inscribed on a single tablet, discovered during the second campaign in the building located between the two principal temples and which is known as the "High Priest's Library" (*editio princeps* by Virolleaud 1933). The tablet is relatively well preserved and the text on it appears to have been complete, for not only are both the upper and lower edges extant, with neither archival notation on the former nor colophon on the latter, but there is space for at least one more line of writing at the bottom of the *verso* which the scribe has left blank.

The text has two peculiar features: (1) it deals with the origin and characteristics of what must be judged, on the basis of other Ugaritic texts, to be a pair of relatively minor deities; (2) the text itself contains rubric indications which have been interpreted as reflecting a cultic usage of the text.

As regards the first point, there are two indications as to why the birth of Šaḥru-wa-Šalimu may be thought to have occupied a particular position in Ugaritic thought. The first is visible in the mythological narrative of this text, viz., that the mothers of these deities are not described with terms characteristic of divinity, indeed are termed simply *ʾaṯtm*, "two women." We seem to be dealing, therefore, with the motif of divine engenderment well known in classical literature, in this case the impregnation by the god ʾIlu of two human females, who each give birth to one of the deities who make up the pair Šaḥru-wa-Šalimu.[1] Though a text identifiable as a theogony has not appeared yet among the Ugaritic literature, the fact that the goddess ʾAṯiratu bears the title of *qnyt ʾilm*, "progenitress of the gods," has led most scholars to see her as the divine mother of ʾIlu's central family, known in the ritual texts as *bn ʾil, dr bn ʾil,* and *mpḫrt bn ʾil*, "the sons of ʾIlu," "the circle of the sons of ʾIlu," and "the assembly of the sons of ʾIlu." In one of these texts ʾIlu bears the title of *ʾab bn ʾil*, "the father of the sons of ʾIlu," and in the mythological texts he bears the name of *bny bnwt*, "the producer (lit. builder) of progeny (lit. that which is built)." Into this picture may be introduced the facts that the deity *Šalimu* is the last deity named in the two "pantheon" texts known at Ugarit up to the present (on RS 1.017 and RS 24.643, see Pardee forthcoming) and that he is the last deity named in a sacrificial sequence repeated in three texts (RS 1.001:8, RS 1.003:17, RS 18.056:18 — see Pardee forthcoming on RS 1.001:8). The identification of this deity with one member of the binomial Šaḥru-wa-Šalimu appears plausible, though not certain, and his place in the pantheon may be interpreted as indicating that he was seen as the deity who most appropriately brought up the rear of the procession of the gods. In the light of the present myth, the rank of the deity is perhaps best interpreted as reflecting his birth, not by ʾAṯiratu and perhaps, to the extent that time was a factor in divine genealogy, after ʾIlu's children by ʾAṯiratu. The double deity Šaḥru-wa-Šalimu also appears in a rather enigmatic ritual text of which the central part is a list of divine names (RS 24.271:11, see Virolleaud 1968:583-586). On these matters see the bibliographical data and discussions in Pardee 1989-90:456-458 and forthcoming.

These details concerning Šaḥru-wa-Šalimu may be of use in identifying the "gracious gods" (*ʾilm nʿmm*), mentioned in lines 1, 23, and 67 (in line 60 the text has *ʾilmy nʿmm*), who are sometimes identified with Šaḥru-wa-Šalimu, sometimes not. The sequence of the presentation requires either that they be seen as born after Šaḥru-wa-Šalimu or that they be identified with Šaḥru-wa-Šalimu whose birth would have been twice reported. The former solution appears narratologically the more plausible, but it requires that the description of the "gracious gods" as having "(one) lip to the earth, (the other) lip to the heavens" (lines 61-62) be applied to an unknown group of divinities, whereas that description and the following lines seem quite graphically to describe the gods of dawn and dusk. If Šaḥru-wa-Šalimu are indeed somehow identifiable with the single deity Šalimu, it is in any case unlikely that the "gracious gods" are to be indentified with the rest of the Ugaritic deities or even with the majority of ʾIlu's offspring, as many

[1] This motif appears again in Ugaritic but in a text even more difficult than this one, *CTA* 12 (Herdner 1963, text 12).

scholars have thought, for there is simply no reason to believe that the circumstances described by this poem correspond to the circumstances of the birth of the children of ᵓAṯiratu. It appears preferable, therefore, to see the double birth narrative simply as a narrative device expressing the birth by two women of two deities. This position is defended below in the note to lines 55-64. According to that interpretation, the text has as its central focus from beginning to end the deities Dawn and Dusk, who are, in this text, ascribed significant powers of blessing.

The second peculiarity, in comparison with the other mythological texts, is the organization of this text. The first twenty-nine lines are divided by horizontal lines across the tablet into nine sections, some of which seem to contain snippets of mythological texts, bearing motifs both familiar and unfamiliar, while others contain indications of liturgical activity, though the identity of the participants is not clear. Then the rest of the text, lines 30-76, relates, without a break by horizontal lines, the story of the birth of Šaḥru-wa-Šalimu, the "gracious gods" (lines 30-64), their characteristics and banishment to the desert (lines 64-67), and a final section dealing with the discovery by the "gracious gods" of agricultural products (lines 67-76). Beyond the basic problems of interpretation of the first nine sections, the matter of their relationship to the principal myth has exercised the minds of students of this text, with some seeing the short mythological texts as mere incipits, unrelated to the longer story, while others have attempted to discern an overarching story line. The intermingling of liturgical rubrics and mythological elements seems to favor the latter interpretation, for although one could without difficulty picture a tablet inscribed with a series of incipits, it is more difficult to posit the existence of an aleatory liturgical text from the ancient Near East. The motifs of agricultural plenty of the first sections may provide the pattern for the myth, according to which Šaḥru-wa-Šalimu are born voracious devourers of birds and fish who must be put in a situation where they will desire to live, like the other gods, from the produce of the fields (cf. Caquot, Sznycer and Herdner 1974:363-64). To the extent that this myth is reflected in the ritual prescriptions written in prose, one may assume the domestication of Šaḥru-wa-Šalimu to have succeeded, for, as mentioned above, Šalimu appears in those texts, and his diet is no different from that of any of the other deities. These facts regarding the divine diet may be interpreted as reflecting general Ugaritic sacrificial practice, where the deities normally receive the products of agricultural activity rather than of fishing and fowling;[2] this sacrificial practice would in turn reflect alimentary patterns in the ancient Levant (cf. Houston 1993). One could posit a view of the universe in which the alimentary world reflected by the sacrificial system is viewed as an improvement, because of the organized distribution of agricultural products that it implies, over a more primitive system, more dependent on nature's whims, presented here as one in which the voracity of certain spoiled children of ᵓIlu could provoke shortages and famine.

Is it possible to identify the ceremony at which this liturgical series would have been played out? There is one specific feature and one of a more general nature that may serve to fix this ceremony in the cultic cycle. The specific feature is the mention of "dwellings of the gods, eight ..." in line 19 (*mṯbt ᵓilm ṯmn*), for that phrase finds its closest parallel in a ritual text (RS 1.003:50-51, see text 1.95 below) where "dwellings (of the gods)" are distributed four by four on a roof, probably that of the temple of ᵓIlu, on the first day of an unnamed month that follows the month named Raᵓšu Yêni, "the beginning of the wine." Though most scholars have seen the text as referring to only one month and have assumed Raᵓšu Yêni to have been the first month of the year, the structure of RS 1.003 and a host of other arguments indicate that Raᵓšu Yêni was in all likelihood the last month of the year, the lunar month preceding the fall equinox, during which the grape harvest and vinification would have begun, and that the ceremony indicated in RS 1.003:50-55 is that of the first month of the new year[3]. As in the Hebrew system, where the feast of "booths" (*sukkōt*) began on the fifteenth day of the first month of the year (according to the calendar beginning in fall), the Ugaritic harvest festival would have taken place after the August-September harvest, though RS 1.003 indicates that at Ugarit it began on the first day of the new month/year, rather than the fifteenth. The more general feature of this text to which reference was made above is the mention of "wine" in lines 6 and 75 and the several allusions to viticultural activities, particularly appropriate for a harvest festival.

Because of the liturgical aspects of this text and the conception of Šaḥru-wa-Šalimu recounted in it, this text has been interpreted as reflecting the sacred marriage rite, the *hieros gamos*, at Ugarit (e.g., de Moor 1987:117-118). Though this interpretation appears plausible, to the extent that the first sections are interpreted liturgically and linked to the following myth, it must be stressed that this text provides no details whatever regarding the liturgical aspects of the *hieros gamos* itself, i.e., to what extent the various rôles were acted out and the specifics of the rite. On the *hieros gamos* in Mesopotamia, for which a greater number of details are known, see Cooper (1993).

---

[2] On birds as offerings in the Ug. ritual texts, see note 18 to RS 24.266 (text 1.88); fish appear extremely rarely in those texts (see Pardee forthcoming on RS 19.015:12 and RS 24.250+:22). In this text the products of the hunt occupy an intermediary position (the goddess Raḥmay hunts [line 16] and the "gracious gods" hunt during their stay in the steppe-land [line 68]). Game occupies an important place in the feast depicted in one of the "para-mythological" texts (Pardee 1988a:23-35 [text 1.97]), is mentioned in the Kirta text as a sacrificial item (*CTA* 14 ii 79 [text 1.102]), but appears rarely, if at all, in the prose ritual texts (Pardee forthcoming "Conclusions").

[3] See Pardee (forthcoming) for this interpretation of RS 1.003; for the interpretation of the present text as reflecting the New Year's festival, see de Moor 1987:117-118.

Invitation (lines 1-7)
I would call on[4] [a] the gr[acious][5] gods
[...] and beautiful,
sons of[6] [...],
Who have provided a city on high,[7]
[...] in the steppe-land, on the barren hilltops[8] [b]
[...]
[...] on their[9] heads,
and [...].

Eat the food, yes do,[c]
Drink the foaming wine,[d] yes do.[10]
Give well-being[e] to the king,[11]
give well-being to the queen,
to those who enter and to those who stand guard.[12]

Mutu-wa-Šarru Joins the Feast (lines 8-11)
Mutu-wa-Šarru takes a seat,[13]

a Deut 32:3
b Jer 4:11; 12:12
c Prov 4:17; 9:5; 23:6
d Ps 75:9; Prov 9:5
e Job 8:6

[4] The use of *qr*ᵓ here indicates an invitation, as in RS 34.126 (text 1.105; cf. Saracino 1982:196), rather than a purely lyrical invocation (cf. ᵓ*ašr*, "I would sing," first word in *CTA* 24). The entirety of lines 1-7 thus constitute an invitation to the "gracious gods," who are first described (lines 1-5), then explicitly invited (line 6), then urged to bless the main officials of the city (line 7). The "gracious gods" are invited again in line 23, their birth is mentioned in the main mythological section after that of Šaḥru-wa-Šalimu (either as identical to Šaḥru-wa-Šalimu or as separate entities — see the introduction), and they are then the principal protagonists until the end of the text.

[5] In English, this has become somewhat of a conventional translation of the phrase ᵓ*ilm n*ᶜ*mm*, though in Ug. it means simply "good gods," *n*ᶜ*m* being the primary adjective for expressing goodness, *ṭb* the secondary one, that is, the distribution is just the opposite of the one in biblical Heb.

[6] There is simply no way of knowing whether {bn š⌜-⌝[...]} is to be restored as *bn šrm* (cf. *šrm* in line 22), as *bn špm* (cf. *špm* in line 4), or with an entirely different word in second position (cf. Foley 1987 and Hettema 1989-90:82, n. 10).

[7] Given the state of the tablet, it appears improper to see as the subject of *ytnm* at the beginning of line 3 anyone but the ᵓ*ilm n*ᶜ*mm*, though the mythological reference is unknown. The last words of this line as preserved, {l ᶜly[...]}, may be interpreted either as a compound adverbial phrase, complete ("at the high place"), or as an indirect object phrase, of which the last letters have been lost, e.g., *l* ᶜ*ly*[*nm*], "for the exalted ones." Because there is no further reference in this text to a city and because the next line mentions the "steppe-land" (*mdbr*), itself an important feature in the *dénouement* of the drama, one may perhaps see here an opposition between the steppe-land, treated rather negatively in this text (see lines 64-76), and civilization, referred to in agricultural terms at the very end of the text. In such an interpretation, the "city" mentioned here would be a paragon of cultured civilization, hence, perhaps, Ugarit itself, and "on high" would refer to the imposing height of an earthly city on its mound, rather than to a heavenly city (the latter concept is, in any case, absent from Ug. literature).

[8] *mdbr špm* is plausibly a construct phrase, "in the steppe-land (consisting) of barren hill-tops." The translation "dunes" for *špm*, which one encounters too frequently, is entirely inappropriate, for *mdbr* does not denote a Sahara-like desert, generally absent in Syria-Palestine, but the scrub that lies beyond the arable land, which is usually suitable as pasture for the mixed herds of sheep and goats so typical of the area (Heb. *ṣō*ᵓ*n*, Ug. *ṣ*ᵓ*in*), and which may vary considerably in the amount of moisture received and hence in vegetation. *špm* will denote, therefore, the hilltops in the scrub land, which can themselves be either bare or covered with lower scrub than the valleys. On the other hand, because the damaged state of the tablet means that our division of the text into poetic lines is uncertain, *špm* could be a term further describing the "gracious gods," like *ytnm* a participle, though of what verb would be uncertain (cf. Gibson 1978:123). The "steppe-land" (*mdbr*), in any case, reappears below, both as the area to which the women and their offspring are temporarily banished (lines 64-67) and as marking the outer fringe of the arable land (*šd*//*p*ᵓ*at mdbr*, "field // edges of the steppe-land," line 68).

[9] The antecedent of the pronoun is probably the "gracious gods," still being referred to in the third person (cf. note 4).

[10] By etymology the word *ḥmr* may include a notion of bubbling and foaming, which de Moor (1987:119, n. 11) has interpreted as denoting wine still close to the process of fermentation. If the semantics of the word had not already moved beyond this sense (cf. Aram., where *ḥmr* is the standard word for "wine"), de Moor's appeal to it as proof that this text reflects a New Year's ceremony would be a valid one, for at the time of the autumn equinox in the third week of September the new wine would still be bubbling.

[11] In the phrases *šlm mlk*, etc., *šlm* may be parsed as imperative (D-stem), addressed to the "gracious gods," and thus parallel to *lḥm*, "eat," and *šty*, "drink," in the preceding verse. From the standard epistolary formula ᵓ*ilm tǵrk tšlmk*, "may the gods guard you and keep you well," it is clear that the effecting of *šlm* was considered to be a standard function of the deities. The syntax here is different from that of RS 34.126:31-34 (*šlm* ᶜ*mrp*ᵓ*i* ...), where *šlm* is a noun in construct with the following word (see Bordreuil and Pardee 1982:123, 128; Bordreuil and Pardee 1991:154-55, 162; Pardee 1993:209-210; Pardee forthcoming), though the active agents in both cases would be the deities invited to the ceremony (see the introduction and note 4). The usual translation of *šlm* here as a simple wish ("peace be with...") or greeting ("hail to ..."), besides the syntactic problem posed by the absence of a preposition in this context, leaves partially unmotivated the invitation tendered to the "gracious gods" in line 1. In this interpretation, the gods are not invited simply to feast but subsequently to bless the rulers of the city (the situation is thus very similar, though it is expressed differently, to that of RS 34.126).

[12] The "enterers" (ᶜ*rbm*) appear three times here below (lines 12, 18, 26) but not in other texts. The verb ᶜ*rb* is the standard verb denoting "to enter" in Ug. and is used in a variety of situations. The only common cultic use of the verb is with a deity as subject, entering the palace (*bt mlk*). Because there is no indication here that the ᶜ*rbm* are anything but human, there seems to be no basis on which to equate the two usages. Because the second category in this line is clearly military (on *ṯnn*(*m*), see note 18 to the Ug. birth omen texts [1.90] and note 22 to the Kirta text [1.102]), one may surmise that this line refers to two principal categories of personnel, those qualified to enter the sanctuary (or palace), comparable to the Akk. *ērib bīti*, "the one entering the house (of the deity)" (*CAD* E 290-92; cf. Caquot, Sznycer and Herdner 1974:370, n. e), and the guards, whose work would have ended at the gates. Because of our general ignorance regarding the details of societal structure at Ugarit, it must be left open whether the function of both categories concerns the sanctuaries or the palace or both (i.e., the privilege of entering the deity's presence or the king's presence and the exclusion therefrom).

[13] Because this is the only mention of *mt w šr* in Ug. (or any other literature), a good many explanations have been given of the name, of the nature of the double-deity, and of what he represents (see Pardee 1989-90:461-462; Wyatt 1992b). The presence here of the verb *yṯb*, "to sit," seems best explained as reflecting the context of the feast to which the gods have been invited, and *mt w šr*, as is to be expected from the double name, is to be seen as divine, rather than human, either, therefore, one of the "gracious gods" or a divine intruder in the feast (cf. *haśśāṭān* in the prologue to the Book of Job). The name has received two basic types of interpretation, reflecting whether the first element is interpreted as the word for "death" (*môtu*) or the word meaning "man, warrior" (*mutu*; a similar problem arises in the interpretation of the Ug. lung model inscription: see note 25 to texts 1.92). The second element has been generally seen as the Semitic word *šarr-*/*śarr-*, "king, prince, ruler," either with the positive connotation it has in the older languages or in the Arabic sense of "evil." Because this deity is presented formally as a single

in his hand the staff[14] of bereavement,[15]
in his hand the staff of widowhood.[f]
The pruners of the vine prune it,[16] [g]
the binders of the vine bind it,
they cause (it) to fall to the-field-of-a-man[17] [h] like a vine.

f Isa 47:8-9; Jer 15:7-8
g Lev 25:3, 4; Isa 5:6; Cant 2:12 (√*zmr*)
h Deut 32:32; 2 Kgs 23:4; Isa 16:8; 37:27; Jer 31:40 (*Qere*); Hab 3:17

deity with a double name, as is indicated by the singular suffix on the noun "hand(s)" in the following lines, it appears legitimate to interpret the two names as denoting two aspects of a single character. Thus the deity may be "Death-and-Ruler" (= "Death the Ruler"), "Death-and-Evil" (= "Evil Death"), "Warrior-and-Ruler" (= "The Ruler who is a Warrior," "The Warrior-Prince"), or "Warrior-and-Evil" (= "The Evil Warrior"). Because he holds in his hands the staffs of bereavement and widowhood, most interpreters have chosen to see the deity as malevolent. In this view "Death-and-Ruler" or "Death-and-Evil" (de Moor 1987:120, n. 15) would be the ultimate kill-joy at the feast, who is eliminated by means appropriate for a harvest festival, by being cut into pieces like a vine. Wyatt has recently proposed (1992b), as a new form of the interpretation of the deity as a positive entity, that the pruning image be taken as representing circumcision, necessary for reproduction, though he did not explain the motifs of bereavement and widowhood in that interpretation. This is indeed a problem, for those two motifs are normally associated with the slaying of children and husbands, not with male infertility. If Wyatt is correct, one might think that the two motifs are meant simply to express the absence of male fertility, the result of which is women without children and husbands. One might also doubt that *šdmt*, "shoots" in Wyatt's interpretation, i.e., a plural (1992a), would have been used to describe the singular foreskin (on this word, see note 17). I believe, moreover, even if Wyatt's interpretation be accepted, that he is going too far in formally identifying *mt w šr* with ᵓIlu; rather the double deity would be one of the "gracious gods" who exemplifies in this text the young male ready to enter the reproductive stage of his life. He would by his presence at the feast constitute, rather than a picture of ᵓIlu himself, a picture of what ᵓIlu would have been in his youth. Note, if this interpretation be correct, that circumcision is depicted here as taking place at maturity (*mutu wa šarru!*) rather than in infancy, a social situation that must have also existed in pre-Biblical Israel, judging from the words *ḥōtēn* and *ḥātān*, "father-in-law," "son-in-law," derived from a root meaning "to cut," i.e., "to circumcise."

Faced with the difficulties and ambiguities of any interpretation, I resort to a common-sense approach: (1) the two elements of double divine names are usually synonymous and such should be the *prima facie* interpretation of this one; (2) the common Northwest-Semitic meaning of *šr* is "king, prince, ruler," with a positive connotation, not "evil"; (3) because it prefigures ᵓIlu, who below is called *mt* by the two women, the first element is *mutu* rather than *môtu*; *ergo* (4) the name is best interpreted as Mutu-wa-Šarru, "Warrior-Prince"; *ergo* (5) the "staff of bereavement/widowhood" is so named because warriors slay sons and husbands in battle (cf. RS 24.277, Side 3, Inscription VIII [text 1.92]); (6) the pruning of the deity's staff represents, in imagery appropriate to a harvest festival, the pacification of the warrior and, very plausibly, his preparation for marriage by circumcision. The identification of this double deity remains, in any case, a problem: if the name is a title for another deity, single or double, which is it? If not, why does this deity enter and take a seat? On the narrative level, one can say that the appearance of Mutu-wa-Šarru here is comparable to that of the goddess Raḥmay in line 16 (cf. ᵓAṯiratu and Raḥm<ay> in line 13) and one can add that the identification of Mutu-wa-Šarru with a known god is just as difficult as is that of Raḥmay with a known goddess. It appears best at the moment to see in this deity a new figure who attends the feast and plays his role, perhaps depicting agricultural fertility through viticultural imagery. His rôle as a "man" prefigures that of ᵓIlu in the principal myth and the name/figure may represent a previously unknown hypostasis of ᵓIlu, elsewhere the picture of bearded old age, as a youth.

[14] There is certainly a literary connection between this staff (*ḫṭ*) and ᵓIlu's staff, designated by the same word in lines 43-44, though the literary function of the word need not be the same in each case. (The literary link in the "para-mythological" texts may be provided either by a pun [e.g., *ḏmr* in RS 24.252] or by a peculiar usage of a word [e.g., Yariḫu the dog, *klb*, in RS 24.258 (text 1.97)]; these literary devices are described briefly in Pardee 1988a:265). In Wyatt's interpretation of this text (1992b:426-427), the staff is the "penis," as in the Ug. incantation against male sexual dysfunction (RIH 78/20 [text 1.96]; Pardee 1993:211-213). As intimated in the previous note, however, an explanation of why the uncircumcised penis would have been described as the staff/penis of "bereavement/widowhood" would be in order, for though it may have been considered inept for procreation, it would not have itself directly slain children and husbands.

[15] The Ug. word is *ṯkl*. Given the viticultural imagery that follows, one must wonder if there is not here a play on words, with *ṯkl* (perhaps vocalized *ṯuklu*) recalling ᵓ*uṯkl*, "bunch of grapes" (probably vocalized ᵓ*uṯkalu* or ᵓ*uṯkālu*). If a similar explanation were available for the parallel word, ᵓ*ulmn*, "widowhood," one would be tempted to revamp the interpretation of this verse entirely, replacing the negative images with positive ones of vine-keeping.

[16] The antecedent of the pronominal suffix in the sentence *yzbrnn zbrm gpn* could theoretically be the deity or his staff, or even, proleptically, the vine (*gpn*). If the deity is a negative entity, the pruning might be effected on him, as most scholars have thought. Whatever interpretation is given to the deity and his staff, however, surely the staff, of vegetal origin, is more appropriate for pruning than is the deity himself. The motif of the living wood in a staff or weapon handle is known, for example, from "Aaron's rod that budded" (Num 17) and from the "Baal au foudre" stela from Ugarit (Yon 1991:294-299). In addition to the difficulty presented by the rarity of the syntactic construction, the third analysis of the pronominal suffix mentioned above seems ruled out by the form of the third line of the verse, where *gpn*, preceded by the preposition of comparison, cannot be the direct object of the verb *yšql*, "they cause to fall." The "pruners" and "binders" are unidentified here and the terms are taken as designations of the workers who would normally carry out these tasks in the vineyards, i.e., cutting the vines and binding them into bunches for easier removal. The third act, literally "causing to fall (to the ground)," is not depicted so specifically as typical of vineyard activity, i.e., by means of the participle of the verb denoting the activity (*yzbrnn zbrm*, *yṣmdnn ṣmdm*, but only *yšql*). Note finally that the "pruning" in question could be either the winter pruning, which promotes spring growth, or the summer pruning, which opens up the vine for better aeration and more direct access to the solar rays. The latter interpretation might be preferred here, because it would take place closer in time to the fall harvest festival and because the green leaves felled to the ground would provide a form of ground cover, not so necessarily removed as the dry cuttings of winter. On the other hand, the summer green pruning would not so plausibly be linked with circumcision (cf. Wyatt's interpretation cited in notes 13, 14).

[17] The word *šdmth* has usually been compared with biblical Heb. *šᵉdēmōt*, though interpretations of both terms have varied, in recent years crystalizing around two principal views, one in which *šdmt* is explained as parallel to *gpn* in a very narrow sense, denoting a form of growth (see, for discussion and bibliography, Wyatt 1992a), and one according to which the parallelism is broader, i.e., the "terrace(s)" on which the vine may grow, i.e., the agricultural terraces necessary for making hilly country productive (Stager 1982). A third principal interpretation is to see the word in both Heb. and Ug. as a compound noun, made up of the elements "field" and "death" (though the word is spelled with {š} in Heb., while the word for "field" is spelled with {ś}). In the interpretation of the present passage according to the first understanding of the word, the suffixed *-h* is explained as pronominal (e.g., "his/its shoots"), in the second (and third) as adverbial ("to the terraces/to the field of Môtu/death"). Whatever the implications may be for Heb., literary considerations surely indicate that the third interpretation must be given serious consideration

Recitation Rubric (line 12)

Seven times[i] they are to pronounce (these verses)[18] next to the ʿD-room[19] and those who enter respond.[20] [j]

The Field of the Gods and its Produce (lines 13-15)

The field is the field of the gods,[21]
the field of ʾAṯiratu and Raḥm<ay>.[22] [k]
Over the fire,[23] seven times the sweet-voiced
youths (chant):[24]
Coriander[25] in milk,[26] [l]

i Gen 33:3; Lev 4:6, etc. *j* Deut 27:14 *k* Judg 5:30 *l* Exod 3:8, etc.

---

in the present context, for a word *mt* appears at the beginning of this section (in the divine name) and in the principal myth (lines 40, 46), while the word *šd*, "field," appears at the beginning of the next mythological section (The Field of the Gods, lines 13-15) and again in the last section dealing explicitly with the "gracious gods" (line 68). The reference to a field in line 13 is an entirely new motif if it is not carrying forward a notion introduced in the word *šdmt*. As regards the matters of etymology and meaning, three remarks are necessary: (1) the word is certainly a single word in Ug., whether it be from a single root or a compound, for it is written without a word divider and the suffix *-h* comes at the end ("to the field of Môtu/death/a warrior," as separate words, would be written *šdh mt*; the translation of *šd mth* as "the field of his death/warrior" does not fit the context). (2) No plausible etymology has been proposed for the interpretation as a simple noun denoting "terraces," i.e., there is no root *šdm* susceptible of furnishing such an etymology. (3) If the Ug. and Heb. words are identical, as the similarity of the contexts in which they are used appears to indicate, and if the Ug. word contains the word for "field," then the Heb. word must be a loanword, not an inner-Heb. development, because of the writing with {š}. One anomaly indicates a foreign origin, i.e., the construct form *šadmōt*, in place of the expected *šidmōt* if the proto-Heb. form were *šadimāt*. The Heb. form favors neither of the two possible etymologies of the element *-mt*, for both /mawt/ and /mut/ could become /mōt/ in Heb., though the invariable ending *-mōt* favors the second derivation because the element /mawt/ when accented should become /māwet/, as in the Heb. common noun meaning "death." (This vocalization may be taken, of course, if one favors the first derivation, simply as another feature indicating the foreign origin of the word). Finally, it must be noted that the absence of an accusative suffix on the verb *yšql* in this line cannot be considered a serious argument against taking *šdmth* as a locative formula, as Wyatt avers (1992a:150), for the accusative suffix is often omitted in Ug., as in Heb., if apparent from context. Its absence here may indeed be explained as reflecting the ambiguity of the antecedent, the staff itself, singular, and the multiple cuttings removed from it.

18 As no object of the verb *yrgm* is expressed, and as this recitation rubric is set off by horizontal lines, it appears plausible to see the required recitations as being either of the preceding section or of the following section, as set off on the tablet, i.e., either the Mutu-wa-Šarru section or the Field of the Gods section. Because of the apparent lexical link between the two mythological sections (see preceding note), it appears preferable to see the reference in the recitation rubric to be to the preceding section.

19 From its appearances in both ritual texts and mythological texts, the word *ʿd* appears to denote a sort of inner sanctum, the king's throne room, which would correspond to the principal seat of the divine effigy in a sanctuary (see note 96 to the Kirta text [1.102] and note 10 to RS 24.266 [text 1.88]). Here the recitation is to take place *ʿl ʿd*, "next to" or even, if the architecture permitted it, "above" the ʿD-room.

20 The content of the response is no more indicated than was that of the recitation and may be thought to consist of the antiphonal recitation of the same verses.

21 The word *ʾilm* may be analyzed either as dual/plural, as I have done, or as the singular with enclitic *-m*, in which case the field would either be ascribed to Mutu-wa-Šarru, the only deity mentioned in the previous section, or to ʾIlu. Because the "gracious gods" visit a field in the last part of this text (lines 67-68) it appears plausible to see here a reference to that field, which would belong to "the gods" in general (the "gracious gods" come to the field from outside). The literary function of the field(s) mentioned in this section is open to dispute. If the text as a whole is interpreted as related to questions of agricultural and sexual fertility, the reference in this section to field(s) of male and female deities may connote sexual fertility. If such is the case, Wyatt's interpretation of the pruning episode in lines 8-11 as related to circumcision (see above, notes 13, 14) gains in plausibility. If the "field" here is somehow related to the *šdmt* in line 10, as well as to the field which the "gracious gods" visit (lines 67-76), it appears that the term denotes a field used for growing both grapes and grain, for lines 71-74 refer both to *lḥm*, "bread," and to wine. The description of a vineyard as part of a field is explicit in one of the Akk. documents describing *marziḫu* property (RS 18.001 [*PRU* iv 230] A.ŠÀ.MEŠ GIŠ.GEŠTIN), while the sowing of a grain crop between vines was (and still is to a certain extent) common practice.

22 The writing {rḥm} has caused no end of trouble: does it designate (1) a masculine deity named "Mercy" (the corresponding Heb. form is the pseudo-plural *raḥᵃmîm*), (2) a feminine deity named "Womb" (expressed in Heb. by *reḥem*/*raḥam*), or (3) the same feminine deity as is named *rḥmy* in line 16? The presence of the phrase *šd ʾaṯrt w rḥmy* in line 28 indicates the likelihood of a simple graphic error here. If the reading {rḥm} be accepted, the masculine deity would plausibly be ʾIlu, first because of the association with ʾAṯiratu, second because of the semantic similarity to ʾIlu's title of *ltpn ʾil d pʾid*, "the Gracious One, the god of kindness." The second and third options are usually taken as reflecting a title of one of the well-known goddesses of the Ug. pantheon, though there has been no consensus on the identity of that deity. The simple fact that ʿAnatu is once ascribed *rḥm* (*CTA* 6 ii 27; reconstructed in line 5) does not necessarily mean that she bore the same title. A brief bibliography on the various interpretations may be found in Pardee (1989-90:473) and in the various commentaries on this text. For a trenchant criticism of all identifications with known deities, see Day 1986:390. These two goddesses are sometimes identified with the two "women," the mothers of Šaḥru-wa-Šalimu in the major mythological section of this text. Without denying the possibility, one must ask why the two goddesses are so completely camouflaged as "women" in the myth.

23 The nature of the preposition *ʿl*, translatable as either "above, over" or "beside," according to context, is well illustrated in this verse, where the singers are probably not literally over the fire (smoke would get in their eyes), while the milk and butter would be.

24 The motif of the young singer with a nice voice is also attested in *CTA* 3 i 20-21 *ǵzr ṭb ql*, "the youth (who is) sweet of voice." The present text employs the other Ug. word for "voice" (*g*) in another syntax (the adjective modifies the word "voice" rather than the youths: *ǵzrm g ṭb*, "youth(s) (with) a sweet voice"). No verb of speech is present here but the reference to the "sweet voice" and the comparison with the text just cited from the Baʿlu cycle, where the sweet-voiced youth is said to sing (*yšr*), are taken as indicators of a speech act of some kind, as most commentators have thought since the reading of the text including *g*, "voice," was first proposed in Dietrich, Loretz and Sanmartín 1976:67. Because the word for "youth" appears in the singular in line 17, the word here has been interpreted also as the singular, with enclitic *-m* (cf. Watson 1994:5, 7). The state of the text in the next paragraph precludes any decision as to the identity of the *ǵzr(m)* in each passage. Here, one may surmise, after comparison with the text from the Baʿlu cycle cited above, that the singing youth(s) would correspond in the divine context to the musicians at an earthly feast.

25 The Ug. word is *gd*, long interpreted as "kid" (see following note) which, however, is attested in Ug. with the spelling *gdy*. As long ago as 1971 Caquot proposed translating here "coriander" or "safran" (cf. Heb. *gad*).

26 The rereading of this line by Herdner (1963:98), with further improvement by Dietrich, Loretz and Sanmartín (1976:67), has eliminated the interpretation of this passage, long a cornerstone of Ug.-Biblical parallels, by comparison with the biblical prohibition against cooking a kid in

mint[27] in butter.[m]
And over the jar[28] seven times again (they chant):
The *dǵ*[*t̲*-sacrifices have been sacri]ficed.[29]

The Hunt (lines 16-18)
Off goes Raḥmay and hunts,
[...] she/they gird;[30]
The goodly youth [...]
And those who enter pro[nounce] the name [...].[31]

Huts for the Gods (lines 19-20)
Dwellings[n] of the gods: eight [...][32]
Seven times [...].[33]

Holy Array (lines 21-22)
Purple, carnelian(-colored) [...]
scarlet;[o] singers[p] [...].[34]

Second Invitation (lines 23-27)
I would call on the gracious gods,
[who delimit[q] the day, sons of] a (single) day,[35]
who suck the nipples of the breasts of ᵓAt̲iratu.[36]
[...] Šapšu, who cares for their feebleness[37]
[(with) X] and (with) grapes.[38]
Give well-being to those who enter and to those who stand guard,
to those who form a procession with sacrifices of prosperity.[39]

The Field of the Gods Repeated (lines 28-29)
The field of the gods,
the field of ᵓAt̲iratu and Raḥm<ay>,

m 2 Sam 17:29; Isa 7:15, 22; Job 20:17
n Lev 23:34ff
o Exod25:4ff
p 2Sam 19:36; 1 Kgs 10:12
q Cf 1 Kgs 3:25; Ps 136:13

its mother's milk (Exod 23:19; 34:26; Deut 14:21). The comparison was always difficult because the verb would here have been *t̲bḫ*, "to slaughter," while in Heb. the verb is *bšl*, "boil, cook in a liquid" (cf. Pardee 1976:234; Ratner and Zuckerman 1986). The word for "milk" here is *ḥlb*, which could in theory be cognate either with Heb. *ḥālāb*, "milk," or with *ḥēleb*, "fat" (covering certain internal organs); the first meaning seems clear here from the parallelism with *ḫmᵓat*, for in Heb. *ḥemᵓāh*, "curdled milk, curds, butter, ghee," appears in association with *ḥālāb*.

27 The word ᵓ*annḫ* seems certainly to be related to words appearing in various Semitic languages, with and without prosthetic ᵓ*aleph* (e.g., Akk. *ananiḫu, naniḫu, nanaḫu*), identified as a form of mint or of ammi. Though the precise identification is uncertain, the existence of the cognates designating a plant for this word in parallel with *gd* provide an additional piece of evidence against translating the latter word as "kid."

28 The archaeological and epigraphic data seem to indicate that the ᵓ*agn*-vessel was of the crater type, i.e., a large, rather squat vessel with a large mouth (Amadasi Guzzo 1990:21-23). Others have seen here a word cognate to the Indo-European word for "fire" or a word for "coals" related to the Arabic root *gwn* that can denote the color "red." The word provides, in any case, one of the many literary links between the opening sections and the principal myth, for it plays an important part in the scene below in which ᵓIlu meets the two women who become his wives (lines 31-36).

29 The reading here of *dǵt̲*, a type of offering more clearly attested in the ᵓAqhatu text (see note 124 to text 1.103), was proposed with the {t̲} entirely restored by Caquot, Sznycer and Herdner (1974:371, note s), then as an actual reading but with a question mark on the {t̲}, by Dietrich, Loretz and Sanmartín (1976:67).

30 Many restore the divine name ᵓAt̲iratu after the verb "to hunt" in line 16, in imitation of line 13, where one finds {ᵓat̲rt w rḥm} (see above, note 22).

31 The damaged state of the text here makes any interpretation dubious. Because the word *šm*, "name," does not reappear in this text as preserved, it appears impossible to identify with any certainty the name to which this line refers.

32 In the ritual text RS 1.003 there is mention of dwellings made of cut branches, set up on the roof (apparently of the temple of ᵓIlu), and arranged in two groups of four: *b gg* ᵓ*a*⌈*r*⌉[*b*ᶜ] ᵓ*arb*ᶜ *mt̲bt* ᵓ*azmr bh*, "... (the king shall sacrifice) on the roof, four (and) four dwellings of cut (branches) on it" (lines 51-52). In an even more damaged and enigmatic passage in a ritual text (RS 24.248:21-23) there may again be a reference to dwellings set up for deities in groups of eight. The significance of the number eight is uncertain. However that may be, it appears legitimate to posit a connection between the *mt̲bt* ᵓ*azmr* in RS 1.003 and the *sukkōt* erected for the Israelite "feast of booths" (see above, introduction).

33 Whereas above the formula for a sevenfold repetition of a speech act was the multiplicative form *šb*ᶜ*d*(*m*), here a separate word for "times" is used (*p*ᵓ*amt šb*ᶜ), a formula common in the prose ritual texts. The term *p*ᵓ*amt* can, in theory, be used with any number (up to thirty repetitions are attested), expressing the repetition of various cultic acts, primarily sacrifices and processions.

34 The word ᵓ*iqn*ᵓ*u* denotes the color blue and is attested in two primary usages in Ug., viz., lapis lazuli stone, and blue-dyed textile (royal purple of the blue shade, as opposed to *pḫm*, which designates the redder shade). The word *šmt* is usually explained as denoting the stone "carnelian," but may designate a third shade of "purple" (Sanmartín 1992:102-103). Finally, the word *t̲n* could either be the number "two" or another noun denoting a color, corresponding to Heb. *šānī*, and designating a dye made from an insect as opposed to the "royal" purple dye, made from various sea mollusks. Because the damaged state of the text has left us without a context here, it is not possible to know for sure whether we are dealing with two types of stones and "two singers" or with three colors of textiles, hence, probably, of garments.

35 The restoration {[ᵓagzrym.bn] ym} is generally accepted, based on the same expression in a similar context in line 61. As is usual in this text, interpretations have varied widely, depending on whether *ym* is taken as meaning "day" or "sea," on whether the fifth and sixth letters constitute this word or are suffixal to {ᵓagzr}, and on the meaning of *gzr*. If one accepts that the "gracious gods" are Šaḥru-wa-Šalimu, then an interpretation reflecting their character appears most plausible, i.e., *gzr*, "to cut," denotes the separation of night from day (Gray 1965:98), i.e., cutting the day into two parts, while *bn ym*, literally "sons of a day," indicates that the two gods exercise their function within a single day.

36 As in the case of Yaṣṣubu, son of Kirta (*CTA* 15 ii 26-28 [text 1.102]), the suckling of an infant by a goddess here indicates divine adoption rather than biological motherhood. So the Ug. king is represented on the ivory panels from his bed as a youth suckled by the goddess (Schaeffer 1954: pl. 8).

37 On this interpretation, see del Olmo Lete 1981:442, 615; Hettema 1989-90:83. One might appeal to Arabic *ḍfr*, "help," for this interpretation of *mṣprt*. Because of the break at the end of line 24, it is uncertain precisely what Šapšu's role is here, though one would expect it somehow to be in relation with the fact that the dawn and dusk are directly related to the rising and setting of the celestial orb. According to the narrative of the birth of Šaḥru-wa-Šalimu (line 54), gifts are made to Šapšu and to the astral deities immediately after the birth of the "boys."

38 Here the word is *ǵnbm*, cognate with Heb. ᶜ*ēnāb*/ᶜᵃ*nābîm*, the word used for grapes as a fruit or as berries, rather than the bunch of grapes, which is ᵓ*eškōl* (Ug. ᵓ*ut̲kl*).

39 "Those who form a procession" are literally the "goers" (*hlkm*). The verb is used in RS 1.005 for a ritual procession in which the king participates (see Pardee forthcoming). "Sacrifices of prosperity" translates *dbḥ n*ᶜ*mt*. Note particularly that the second word is from the same root, *n*ᶜ*m*, as that by which the "gracious gods" are described (see above, note 5): the sacrifices are literally those of "goodness" or of "good things." Though the sacrifices would certainly consist of "good things," the phrase would appear to function primarily as an "objective genitive," i.e., the sacrifices, by placating the "goodly gods" will result in "goodness" for the offerer.

[...] s[i]ts/do[es ag]ain.[40]

The Myth (lines 30-31)

[ʾIlu goes][41] to the seashore,
strides along the shores of the Great Deep.[42]

ʾIlu Handpicks Two Women (lines 31-36)

ʾIlu [spies][43] two females presenting (him with) an offering,[44]
presenting (him with) an offering from the jar.[45]
One gets down low,[r]
the other up high.[46]
One cries out: "Father, father,"
the other cries out: "Mother, mother."[47]
"May ʾIlu's hand[s] stretch out as long as the sea,[48]
(may) ʾIlu's hand (stretch out as long) as the flowing waters;[49]
Stretch out, (O) hand of ʾIlu, as long as the sea,
(stretch out, O) hand of ʾIlu, (as long) as the flowing waters."
ʾIlu takes the two females presenting an offering,
presenting an offering from the jar;
he takes (them), estab<lish>es[50] (them) in his house.[t]

ʾIlu Tries His Hand at Shooting Birds (lines 37-39)

ʾIlu (first) lowers his staff,
(then) ʾIlu grasps his rod in his right hand.[51]
He raises (it), casts (it)[u] into the sky,

r Cf. Ezek 17:6, 24

s Num 11:23; Deut 4:34; Isa 9:11, 16, 20; 10:4; cf. Isa 57:8

t Gen 12:15; 20:2; cf. 26:10

u Cf. Exod 19:13ff

---

40 The verb *yṯb*, second sign uncertain, could be either from *yṯb*, "to sit," or from *ṯb*, "to return" or "to do again" when used with another verb. Because of the broken context we cannot know if the reference is to the sitting of gods or officials (as might be surmised from the form of the preceding formulae, i.e., not explicitly equational as the corresponding formulae were in line 13) or to the repetition of an act or of speech.

41 Any restoration here is entirely hypothetical, though it appears quite likely, as several scholars have seen, that the principal protagonist, ʾIlu, would have been introduced here along with a verb parallel to *ṣġd*, "to stride, walk," in the parallel line (cf. Wyatt 1987:381).

42 There are three principal water words in this section, *ym//thm* in this verse and *ym//mdb* in lines 33-35. *ym* denotes primarily the salt sea, *thm* the fresh-water sea thought to lie under the earth. Though *mdb* is much more rarely attested, it appears to function as the rough equivalent of *thm* (see Pardee 1988a:132-134). These water words reflect the concerns of this story and do their part to present ʾIlu as away from home when the encounter occurs, for though ʾIlu's dwelling place is presented in watery terms, only one of the terms overlaps and that one is in a different form (ʾIlu dwells at "the headwaters of the two rivers [*nhrm*], at the fountains/confluence of the deeps [*thmtm*]" — see on *CTA* 2 iii 4 [text 1.86, notes 145, 182], RS 24.244:2-7 [text 1.94, notes 2, 4]; cf. *CTA* 17 vi 48 [text 1.103]). In this story he is not, therefore, in a mountainous area where rivers begin, but at the seashore where rivers end.

43 Most scholars reconstruct the verb *lqḥ* here on the basis of line 35, but one might rather expect here a verb describing ʾIlu meeting the women (Hettema 1989-90:83).

44 "Two females presenting ... an offering" is an attempt at reflecting each element of the form *mštʿltm*, i.e., Št-participle, feminine, dual (perhaps /muštaʿlîtāma). After years in which various interpretations of this word were proffered (often based on the interpretation of *ʾagn* as meaning "fire" rather than "jar"), a certain consensus seems to have formed in recent years that we are dealing with a form of the verb *ʿly*, "to ascend, go up, mount." Even within that analysis, however, different interpretations exist. Seeking an interpretation based on Ug. usage, one sees that the simple Š-stem has three primary values: (1) the "literal" meaning, "cause to go up"; (2) a sexual meaning, "to be mounted," said of a cow mating with a bull (Baʿlu); and (3) "to present (as a gift/offering)," said of stelae and a vase in ritual texts. The infixed-*t* form may be thought to reflect one of these usages (Tropper 1990:51-53, 77-78), but which usage, and whether the function of the *-t-* is that of the reflexive or is closer to a middle (i.e., for one's own benefit) is uncertain. Because the form is participial, and ʾIlu does not "mount" these females until later in the story, it appears that the sexual sense is not at the surface level here, though it is plausibly an underlying one. Because these entities are below described as "two women" (*ʾaṯtm*) and because *šʿly* is used in the ritual texts for presenting a gift to a deity (not a burnt offering!), it appears plausible to interpret *mštʿltm* here as designating two women (i.e., human beings) either offering themselves as a gift to the divinity or as offering something else to the divinity for their own benefit. Because the phrase *l rʾiš ʾagn* is very difficult to interpret with the simple reflexive meaning of the participle (see next note), it does not appear that they are offering themselves to the divinity, and the interpretation as a middle becomes the more likely.

45 The "jar" can only be the jar already introduced in line 15. There we saw youths chanting about spiced milk being prepared "over a fire," "over a jar" (*ʿl ʾagn*), apparently as a *dġṯ*-offering. Here the "two women presenting a gift" are, literally, "at the head of the jar" (*l rʾiš ʾagn*). It is uncertain what this phrase means, for "jars" do not have heads and elsewhere *l rʾiš* does not seem to function as a complex preposition (Pardee 1976:309). Because the attested usages of *šʿly* in Ug. show it not to be the simple equivalent of Heb. *heʿĕlāh*, "to offer up (esp. as a burnt offering)," one doubts that the reference here is to a burnt offering of any kind, but rather to something presented to the divinity, presumably the spiced dairy products mentioned in line 14. In this interpretation, the phrase *l rʾiš* would denote the fact that the offering would have to be ladled out of the jar.

46 The verbs *tšpl* and *trm* apparently describe the women themselves, for the second form can only be intransitive. It is uncertain what the acts imply, perhaps nothing less banal than antics to get the god's attention (see next note).

47 I remain dubious that ʾIlu is here being addressed directly and wittingly as a mother (e.g., de Moor 1987:123, n. 37). Indeed below, lines 42-49, the possibility of the two women even addressing ʾIlu as "father" is considered and dropped. Because the encounter ends up with the women being taken to ʾIlu's house in view of marriage (the verb *trḫ* is actually used in line 64), we may surmise that the women were engaging in the activity with the express purpose of catching a male, indeed a divine one (the preparations seem to be described in line 15 as a type of offering to a deity, a *dġṯ*). If such be the case, the cries in lines 32-33 are addressed to their own parents, as in "Daddy, mommy, what do we do now?"

48 There is a general consensus that *yd*, "hand," here is a euphemism for "penis." There is not agreement, however, on whether (1) both verses are descriptive of ʾIlu's excitement at the sight of the women, (2) the first verse is a volitive formulation, the second descriptive, or (3) both verses are formulated volitively (*tʾirkm* = jussive, *ʾark* = imperative). I choose the last solution for morphological and literary reasons. The form *ʾark* in line 34 cannot be a perfect verb, for *yd* is a feminine noun and *ʾark* is not marked for feminine gender. The verb could, of course, always be parsed as an infinitive, used absolutely, as occurs rather frequently in Ug. poetry. But because the rhetoric of this poem seems usually to be allusive rather than direct in sexual matters, one may surmise that the sexual meaning here is at the level of paronomasia, and that the women are requesting, superficially, only that ʾIlu extend his hand to "take" them, as indeed he does in the following verse.

49 On *mdb*, see above, note 42.

50 There is general agreement to emend {yš} to {yš<t>}, i.e., the hollow verb *št*, "to put, place, establish."

51 Lit., "he grasps in his right hand the rod of his hand." *Ymnn* is taken, in agreement with many scholars, as the L-stem (the verbal stem

casts (it at) a bird in the sky.
He plucks (the bird), puts (it) on the coals,
(then) ᵓIlu sets about enticing[v] the women.[52]

ᵓIlu Comes Up With a Handy Test of the Women's Maturity (lines 39-49)[53]
"If," (says he,) "the two women cry out:
'O man, man,
you who prepare your staff,
who grasp your rod in your right hand,
you roast a bird[54] on the fire,
roast (it) on the coals,'
(then) the two women (will become) the wives of ᵓIlu,[55]
ᵓIlu's wives forever.
But if the two women cry out:
'O father, father,
you who prepare your staff,
who grasp your rod in your right hand,
you roast a bird on the fire,
roast (it) on the coals,'
(then) the two daughters (will become)[56] the daughters of ᵓIlu,
ᵓIlu's daughters forever."

v Exod 22:15; Judg 14:15; 16:5; Hos 2:16

w Prov 16:21; cf. Cant 4:11; 7:10

x Ps 8:4

The two women do (in fact) cry out:
"O man, man,
you who prepare your staff,
who grasp your rod in your right hand,
you roast a bird on the fire,
roast (it) on the coals."
(Then) the two women (become) the wives [of ᵓIlu],
ᵓIlu's wives forever.

The Birth of Šaḥru-wa-Šalimu (lines 49-54)
He bends down, kisses their lips,
their lips are sweet,[w]
sweet as pomegranates.
When he kisses, there is conception,
when he embraces, there is pregnancy.[57]
The two (women) squat and give birth
to Šaḥru-wa-Šalimu.
Word is brought to ᵓIlu:
"The two wives of ᵓIlu have given birth."
"What have they born?"
"The two boys Šaḥru-wa-Šalimu."[58]
"Take up, prepare (a gift) for great Šapšu
and for the immut[able] stars."[x]

characterized by a reduplicated final radical and having a factitive connotation similar to the D-stem) of a verb that is denominative from *ymn*, "right hand" (/yāmanana/ [pf.] or /yêmānin-/ [impf.] here, /mêmāninuma/ [participle plus enclitic *-m*] in lines 40 and 44). Because of the absence in this passage of a term for "bow" or "arrow" it may be doubted that the verbs denote the stringing of the bow (i.e., setting one end on the ground, bending it, and attaching the string with the right hand). Rather the image is that of killing a bird with a thrown stick (the verb *yry* in the following verse, though it can mean "shoot an arrow," means basically only "throw, cast") and the mention of preparing the staff (*ḫṭ*) and taking the rod (*mṭ*) in the right hand either refers to putting down the walking stick and picking up a throwing stick or, according to common usage in parallelistic poetry, simply to transferring a single stick from the left hand to the right. Though attempts have been made to see the sexual imagery carried forward consistently here (see especially Pope 1979), they appear strained. In particular, the attempt to see in the lowering of the staff (*nḥt* "descend") an image of impotency is closely linked with the preconception of ᵓIlu as a *deus otiosus*, and the "story line" here does not allow us to consider that aspect of the imagery a major one: the bird to which reference is made in the next line (the flesh of which is plausibly taken as a restorative, especially of male potency; cf. Caquot, Sznycer and Herdner 1974:374, note d) is shot down with the rod that has already been raised up. On the other hand, the conjunction of words elsewhere used as euphemisms for the male member with verbs of raising, lowering and shooting, and with the resultant use of bird flesh, roasted on hot coals, seems to indicate the presence of sexual allusions in keeping with the following explicitly indicated sexual activity. If the images were meant to express a consistent line of development, one is constrained to see in the bird flesh as much an aphrodisiac as a restorative, and meant as much to entice the women as to keep ᵓIlu's shooting apparatus in working order.

52 The use of *pt(y)* here, if correctly analyzed as cognate with Heb. *pth*, denotes the act of a male convincing a woman to engage in sexual activity, whether lawful ("attract, entice") or unlawful ("seduce"), or, more broadly, of enticing anyone into a path of action. The verb not being necessarily polarized negatively, and ᵓIlu's relationship being described below as that of marriage (line 64), this passage should be taken as introducing the following passage.

53 The function of this test seems to be to determine whether the women are mature enough to discern the sexual function of the roasting birds (see note 51) or whether they will simply see in ᵓIlu a father figure providing them with food.

54 On the place of the bird in the sequence of images here, see notes 51 and 53. It is important to point out the presence here, as in several cases already discussed, of a literary link between earlier and later parts of the text, in this case between this bird (ᶜṣr), instrumental in ᵓIlu's procurement of the two women as wives, and the recurrence of the word below (line 62) in the description of the voracious behavior of the offspring of this union.

55 The Ug. phrase is *ᵓaṯtm ᵓaṯt ᵓil*, lit., "the two women (will become) ᵓIlu's two women." The parallel passage indicates that the equational formulation is intended as a social classification: "the two girls (lit., daughters) (will become) ᵓIlu's two daughters" (*btm bt ᵓil*, line 45).

56 The formulation *btm bt ᵓil* is strictly parallel to *ᵓaṯtm ᵓaṯt ᵓil* in line 42, though the indication of change of status is less clear here: are the two "girls" to become his daughters (i.e., they will be adopted), or are they classified as belonging among his daughters (i.e., their status is recognized, rather than changed)? In either case, the term used to describe the two women who would have shown themselves by their address to be girls rather than women to be married is *btm*, "girls, daughters."

57 Judging from the parallel in the ᵓAqhatu story (*CTA* 17 i 41-42 [text 1.103]), this is the standard poetic idiom for intercourse and conception, with no variation in this formulation reflecting the divine status of the male partner. If there is a variation reflecting divine participation, it is expressed with regard to the women not the deity, i.e., in the description in the preceding verse of the women's lips being sweet, for the kissing motif is absent in the ᵓAqhatu version, where both partners are human. Compare Gen 6:2 where the "sons of the gods" are depicted as seeking after human wives because they were "good" (*ṭōbōt*).

58 There is general agreement that the two elements making up this double deity mean "Dawn" and "Dusk" (see bibliographical elements in the various studies of this text and in Pardee 1989-90:456-457). There is no apparent reason, however, for the subsequent identification with the morning and evening star, assumed by various scholars. The name Šaḥru, at least, is clearly linked with the concept of "dawn," not with a celestial body, and there is every reason to believe that the morning and evening manifestations of Venus were linked in Ug. thought with the deities ᶜAṯtaru and ᶜAṯtartu (bibliography in Pardee 1989-90:466-470; discussion in Pardee forthcoming on RS 1.009:4 and RS 1.017:18, 25).

The Second Birth Narrative (lines 55-64)[59]

He bends down, kisses their lips,
their lips are sweet.
When he kisses, there is conception,
[when] he embraces, there is pregnancy.
He sits down, he counts,
to five for the [bulge to appear],
[to t]en, the completed double.[60]
The two (women) squat and give birth,
they give birth to the gracious [gods],
who delimit the day, sons of a (single) day,
who suck the nipples of the breasts.
Word is brought to ᵓIlu:
"The two wives of ᵓIlu have given birth."
"What have they born?"
"The gracious gods,
who delimit the day, sons of a (single) day,
who suck the nipples of the breasts of the lady.[61]
(One) lip to the earth,
(the other) lip to the heavens,
Into their mouths enter
the birds of the heavens
and the fish in the sea.[y]
When they stand, delimitation to <deli>mitation,[62]
they prepare (food for themselves) on right and left,
into their mouth (it goes) but never are they satisfied."[63] [z]

ᵓIlu Temporarily Banishes Mothers and Sons (lines 64-67)

"O women whom I have wedded,
O sons whom I have begot,[64]
Take up (your belongings), prepare (yourselves a place)
in the holy steppe-land;[65] [aa]
There you must dwell as aliens[66]
among the stones and trees,
For seven full years,[bb]
eight revolutions of time."

y Zeph 1:3
z Isa 9:19
aa Ps 29:8
bb Gen 29:18

[59] This second narrative can be interpreted either as recounting the birth of additional children to ᵓIlu by the two women (so, e.g., Caquot, Sznycer and Herdner 1974:358-360) or as a second account of the birth of Šaḥru-wa-Šalimu. Two considerations lead me to adopt the latter hypothesis. (1) On the level of macrostructure and overall meaning of the text, one asks oneself why the "gracious gods" would appear early and late but Šaḥru-wa-Šalimu would occupy a mere five and a half lines, and those at the very center of the myth. Why speak at all of the birth of this double deity if the real concern of the text is with younger brothers? At the very least, one must assume a very close structural relationship between Šaḥru-wa-Šalimu and the "gracious gods" (e.g., the former "Dawn-and-Dusk," the latter the morning and evening star — rôles we have every reason to believe were already filled at Ugarit, see preceding note). (2) On the metaphorical level, the images of the "gracious gods" delimiting the day and standing with one lip in the heavens and the other on the earth, devouring birds and fish (see below), are perfectly appropriate for dawn and dusk, much less so for the morning and evening star. A possible indication that the two narratives refer to the birth of a single double deity may be found in the terms chosen to describe the offspring, i.e., *yldy*, "two boys," in line 53 (the explanation of the terminal *-y* is uncertain), as opposed to [ᵓ*ilm*] *n*ᶜ*mm*, "two good gods," in line 58. Given the assured divine status of Šaḥru-wa-Šalimu, it is striking that in their particular birth narrative they are described merely as "boys," while a following narrative describes the birth of two gods by the very same mothers. Was the second narrative understood as signifying a replacement of the "boys" by "gracious gods" or as a strong image for a process of maturation?

[60] Ginsberg (1945:4, n. 7; cf. Tsumura (1978; Hettema 1989-90:85, n. 29) was almost certainly right in seeing here a reference to the counting of the months of gestation. Compare the case of Dānīᵓilu, who also "sits down," explicitly to count the months of his wife's pregnancy (*CTA* 17 ii 43 [text 1.103]). Unfortunately the tablet is damaged here and the precise formulation is unclear. One can doubt, in any case, that *kl*ᵓ*at* in line 57 denotes "fullness" or that it is cognate to Akk. *kullatu*, as Tsumura proposed. The root *kl*ᵓ in Ug. regularly denotes doubleness, used for two hands and double gates. One would, therefore, expect it here to denote either the conception of two children or the simple fact that ten is five doubled. The presence of *pḫr* before *kl*ᵓ*at* seems to favor the latter interpretation, for the literal translation of the phrase, "the assembly of two (entities)," in which *pḫr* explicitly denotes the concept of bringing entities together, seems more fitting for expressing the notion of bringing two fives together than that of twins, who would always have been together. If Tsumura's reading {ṣ⌈b⌉[ᵓi]} is correct at the beginning of the lacuna, the verb would be *ṣb*ᵓ, which elsewhere in Ug. expresses various notions of "going forth," here the protrusion of the pregnant belly. Such an interpretation appears legitimate, for *ṣb*ᵓ is not a simple semantic equivalent to *yṣ*ᵓ, "exit," i.e., "pass from an enclosed space to the outside," which one would expect to be used to express the birth itself.

[61] *Št*, a general honorific term, apparently designates ᵓAṯiratu here, for this goddess was actually named in this formula above, line 24. On the use of the word in the ᵓAqhatu text, part of a title of the goddess ᶜAnatu's henchman *ytpn*, see note 64 to text 1.103. Unfortunately, the word *št* here is at the juncture between the two verses and the word may represent the verb *št*, "to put," of which the "lips" in the following verse would be the direct object (rather than standing as subjects in two nominal sentences as I have translated).

[62] The text reads {ndd gzr l zr}, usually emended to {ndd gzr l <g>zr}. With or without the emendation, there is certainly a reference here to the title of the "gracious gods" as ᵓ*agzr ym*. The use of *ndd*, "stand (up)" (N-stem of the hollow root *dd*), with the preposition *l* preceding the second word following the verb, seems to favor the interpretation of *gzr* as denoting the delimitation, rather than the "cut up pieces" upon which they would be feeding ("when they stand up piece to piece" is a rather odd formulation for "standing up to produce pieces" or "standing up to feed on pieces"). The image is that of "Dawn" and "Dusk," when they stand, filling the horizon, one in the east, the other in the west.

[63] The imagery in lines 61-64 seems particularly appropriate for dawn and dusk, which, on the horizontal axis, fill the horizon and, on the vertical axis, open and close like a mouth. The "fish in the sea" can in the Levantine context refer only to sunset; whether the "birds of the heaven" refers symmetrically to the realm of sunrise is less certain. Though the noisy activity of birds at sunrise would not be concentrated in the east to the same extent that the fish are concentrated in the west, perhaps the link of birdsong with sunrise was sufficient to engender the image.

[64] Unless the two women and the two sons have for reasons unknown become single, the forms ᵓ*aṯt* and *bn* are in construct with the following finite verbal forms.

[65] The interpretation of the phrase *mdbr qdš* is no easier here than in Ps 29:8, where the second element is vocalized as the geographical name Qadesh. Is this a generic statement about the divine characteristics of the *mdbr* or a reference to a specific *mdbr* in the vicinity of one of the several towns of which the names are derived from the root *qdš*? See also below, p. 304, n. 18.

[66] Though the motivation for the apparent reduplicated form (*tgrgr*) is not clear (should the signs be divided as *tgr gr*, in the familiar "infinitive absolute" construction?), the idea of banishment appears clear, and *gr* seems to have the notion of displacement from one's own ethnic group

The Gracious Gods Learn of Agriculture (lines 67-76)[67]

The gracious gods arrive at the field,
(while) hunting along the fringes of the steppe-land.
The guardian of the sown land[cc] meets them
and they call out to the guardian of the sown land:
"O guard, guard, open up!"
and he opens up.
He makes an opening (in the fence)[68] [dd] for them
and they enter.

"If [there is X-]bread,
then give (it to us)[ee] that we might eat;
If there is [X-wine,
then] give (it to us) that we might drink."
The guardian of the sown land answers them:
["There is bread that has ...]
There is wine that has arrived in/from[69] [...]."
[...] he approaches,
he serves a *luggu*-measure[ff] of his wine
[...]
And his companion fills with wine [...][70]

cc cf. Isa 27:3; Prov 27:18; Job 27:18
dd Isa 5:5; Pss 80:13; 89:41; Eccl 10:8; cf. Isa 58:12; Amos 9:11
ee 1 Sam 21:4
ff Cf. Lev 14:10, etc.

so familiar in Heb. and present in a Ug. ritual text (cf. Pardee forthcoming on RS 1.002:18′).

[67] Assuming that the gods have obeyed their father's order and have completed the banishment period, it is at the end of that period that, one day while hunting along the desert's edges, they meet the one in charge of protecting the sown land, request entry and become acquainted with the relative bounty of agricultural life. A classic case of the encounter of the Desert and the Sown, with the latter presented as the desirable state.

[68] The verb is *prṣ* which, though there is no expressed object, implies making a "breach" in some kind of protective construction, here plausibly a barrier of thornbush or a rough stone wall.

[69] The text reads {d ᶜrb b ṯk[...]}. There being no good parallel from which to deduce a restoration, it is uncertain whether the phrase beginning with *b* denotes the origin of the wine, the container in which it arrived, or some quality of the wine.

[70] The damaged state of the tablet precludes our knowing exactly how the text ended. It does not appear, however, that it indicated explicitly the effects of the bread and wine on the "gracious gods," and it is not impossible, therefore, that the text continued on another tablet, in spite of the arguments to the contrary. On these arguments, none of which is decisive, see the introduction.

REFERENCES

Amadasi Guzzo 1990:15-25; Bordreuil and Pardee 1982:121-128; 1991:139-172; Caquot 1971:168-170; 1979:Cols. 1367-1371; Cooper 1993:81-96; Cunchillos 1976; Cutler and Macdonald 1982:33-50; Day 1986:385-408; Dietrich and Loretz 1988; Dietrich, Loretz and Sanmartín 1976; Driver 1956; Foley 1987:61-74; Gaster 1946:49-76; Gibson 1978; Ginsberg 1935:45-72; 1945:3-10; Gordon 1977:5-133; Gray 1965; Herdner 1963; Hettema 1989-90:77-94; Houston 1993; del Olmo Lete 1981; de Moor 1987; Pardee 1976:215-322; 1987:366-471; 1988a; 1989-90:390-513; 1993a:207-218; forthcoming; Pope 1979:701-708; Ratner and Zuckerman 1986:15-60; Sanmartín 1992:95-103; Saracino 1982:191-199; Schaeffer 1954:14-67; Stager 1982:111-121; Tropper 1990; Tsumura 1978:387-395; Virolleaud 1933:128-151; 1968: 545-595; Watson 1994:3-8; Wyatt 1987:375-389; 1992a:149-153; 1992b:425-427; Xella 1973; Yon 1991: 273-344.

2. PRAYERS

UGARITIC PRAYER FOR A CITY UNDER SIEGE (1.88)
(RS 24.266)

Dennis Pardee

The sole clear example of a cultic prayer in the Ugaritic language is embedded in a ritual text, discovered in 1961 among a large quantity of ritually oriented texts (see the omen texts 1.90 and 1.92 below). The complete text is translated here to enable the reader to perceive the cultic context. The principal point of interest as regards the document as a whole is the degree to which the rituals prescribed here are accomplished in honor of various manifestations of Baᶜlu, to whom the prayer also is addressed. From a literary perspective, it is to be noted that the text of the ritual itself is in prose, as are most Ugaritic ritual texts, while that of the prayer is in poetic form.

The Ritual of the Month of ᵓIbaᶜlatu (lines 1-?)[1]

In the month of ᵓIbaᶜlatu,[2] on the seventh day:[a] a sheep[b] for Baᶜlu-RᶜKT[3] [...] and (in) the temple of

a Gen 2:3 etc. *b* Gen 22:7, 8; Exod 13:13; Lev 5:7; 12:8; Num 15:11; Deut 18:3; Isa 43:23; 66:3; Ezek 45:15

[1] The break at the bottom of the tablet prevents determining the temporal relationship between the texts on the *recto* and *verso* (see note 17).

[2] ᵓIbaᶜlatu corresponds perhaps to the month of December-January, during which, therefore, the winter solstice would have occurred. For this placement in the year, see Pardee (forthcoming) commentary on RS 1.003; for the placement of ᵓIbaᶜlatu in January-February, see de Jong and van Soldt 1987-88:69-71. This ritual may deal with events of two months; in this case the second month would have been Ḫiyyāru. The Ug. word *yrḫ* designates the celestial orb, the lunar deity, and the concept of month, the latter being determined by the phases of the moon. The "week" as one of a continuous sequence of seven-day weeks almost certainly did not exist at Ugarit, but the importance of the new-moon festival and of the full-moon festival, of which the primary celebration seems to have fallen on the fifteenth day of the month (see below, note 17), leads to the plausible conclusion that the lunar cycle was already divided into seven-day units, though the Ug. view of the last unit is unknown (a seven-day unit plus a variable number of days until the next new moon or a unit which was itself seen as being of variable length?).

[3] Baᶜlu-*rᶜkt* is apparently a hypostasis of Baᶜlu, but the second part of the theonym has not been satisfactorily explained. The principal deity

Baᶜlu-ᵓUgārīta [...].[4] At sunset[c] the king is clear (of further cultic obligations).[5] [d] On the seventeenth,[e] the king washes himself[f] clean.[6] [g] A cow[h] (in) the sanctuary of ᵓIlu, a cow for the Baᶜlu(-deities), a cow for ǴLM, two ewes and a cow for ǴLMTM;[7] at the house of the *ṯāᶜiyu*-priest[8] does one sacrifice (the preceding beasts). Next you[9] shall illumine[i] the ᶜD-room[10] of the temple of Baᶜlu-ᵓUgārīta: a lamb and a city-dove;[j] (these belong) to (the category) of the *ṯaᶜu*-sacrifice. On the eighteenth of ᵓIbaᶜlatu, a bull[k] for the MDGL[11] of Baᶜlu-ᵓUgārīta. A flame-sacrifice[12] and a presentation-sacrifice[13] [l] the king must offer (at) the temple of ᵓIlu: a "neck"[14] for ᵓI[...] a "neck" for Baᶜlu[...] and a donkey[15] for [...]...[16]

Another Festival, Perhaps of the Month of Ḫiyyāru[17] (lines 18′-25′)

[...] On the fourth:[m] birds.[18] [n] On the fifth:[o] birds and a liver[p] and a sheep (as) a burnt-offering for Baᶜlu-ᵓUgārīta in the temple. On the seventh: you shall bring the purifiers near. At sundown, the king is clear (of further cultic obligations). Behold the oil[q] of well-being of Baᶜlu, libation-offering (for the benefit) of the kings, of the first quality.[19] [r]

The prayer (lines 26′-36′)

When a strong (foe)[s] attacks[t] your gate,[u]
  a warrior your walls,[20] [v]
You shall lift your eyes to Baᶜlu[w] (and say):
O Baᶜlu, if you drive the strong one from[x] our

c Lev 23:32 *d* Deut 20:6; 28:30; Jer 31:5 *e* Gen 7:11; 8:4 *f* Job 9:30 *g* Zeph 3:9; Job 33:3 *h* Cf. Num 19:2 *i* Cf. Exod 25:37; 1 Sam 3:3; 1 Kgs 7:49 etc. *j* Lev 1:14 etc. *k* Cf. Exod 24:5ff *l* Exod 29:26 etc. *m* Gen 1:19 etc. *n* Lev 14:4 et passim in this chapter *o* Gen 1:23 etc. *p* Cf. Exod 29:13 etc. *q* Gen 28:18; 35:14 *r* Amos 6:6 *s* Isa 19:4 *t* Ps 140:3 *u* 1 Sam 17:52; Isa 28:6; Ezek 21:20, 27; Mic 1:9, 12 *v* Amos 1:7, 10, 14 *w* Ps 123:1; cf. 2 Kgs 19:22; Isa 51:6; Ps 121:1 *x* Cf. Exod 23:29 etc.

in the ritual sections of this text is Baᶜlu-ᵓUgārīta, the hypostasis of the weather god associated principally with the city itself. In the prayer and in the last cultic act leading up to the prayer (the oil libation in lines 24′-25′), the deity is simply Baᶜlu.

[4] In the first lacuna a term designating a further offering may have disappeared while in the second lacuna a specific offering to be made in the temple of Baᶜlu-ᵓUgārīta was probably indicated.

[5] The term denoting the passage from the state appropriate for cultic activity to that appropriate for secular activity is *ḥl*, which has received multiple explanations (for bibliography, see Pardee 1987:396 and forthcoming, commentary on RS 1.003:47). The passage was apparently effected by a rite entrusted to *mḥllm*, lit., "purifiers," attested here below in line 23′.

[6] The royal rite of lustration normally took place on the day before a major festival, sometimes on the first day of the festival. The ritual sequence outlined in this text is abnormal in that it includes neither the day of the new moon nor that of the full moon.

[7] The identification of the deities corresponding to the names *ǵlm*, "the lad," and *ǵlmtm*, "the two lasses," is unknown. On the use of *ǵlm/ǵlmt* in the Kirta text, see note 10 to that text (text 1.102).

[8] See note 103 to the Kirta text (1.102). The scribe of that text, ᵓIlīmilku, was a *ṯāᶜiyu*-priest.

[9] Ritual commmands either are expressed impersonally ("one shall do ...") or are addressed directly to the officiant, as here.

[10] In the Kirta text, the *ᶜd*-room is where the hero's throne is located (see note 96 to that text).

[11] This word is usually emended to {mgdl}, "tower" (or *mdgl* is given the same meaning). Because, however, the word *mgdl* is attested in Ug. meaning "tower," and because the reading {mdgl} here is quite clear, it is preferable to await further textual evidence before adopting one or the other of these solutions — Ug. may prove to have a word *mdgl* with a meaning distinct from *mgdl*.

[12] According to RS 1.001:8-9 (*CTA* 34) the heart of various beasts sacrificed according to one rite is roasted (*rmṣ*) in the flames (ᵓ*urm*).

[13] The Ug. *šnpt* corresponds etymologically to the Heb. *tᵉnūpāh*, but does not seem to function so narrowly as a subdivision of the *šlmm*-sacrifice as does the *tᵉnūpāh* with respect to the *šᵉlāmīm* (for bibliography, see Pardee 1987:411 and forthcoming, commentary on RS 1.001: 10).

[14] The word is *npš*, apparently denoting the portion of the body containing the breathing apparatus, i.e., the neck, as opposed to the inner throat/esophagus, the basis for most usages in poetry (see note 95 to the Kirta text [text 1.102] and notes 13 and 127 to the ᵓAqhatu text [text 1.103]). It is uncertain, however, exactly which part of the neck was offered, and the origin of the neck, i.e., from what particular animal, is usually not stated in the ritual texts.

[15] The sacrifice of the *ᶜr*, "donkey," is extremely rare in these texts, attested elsewhere only in the very peculiar ritual recorded in RS 1.002 (*CTA* 32). In the latter text a historical link with the old Amorite sacrifice of a donkey in association with various types of agreements and treaties appears plausible (for bibliography see Pardee forthcoming, commentary on RS 1.002).

[16] The bottom of the tablet is broken away, and approximately eight to twelve lines have been lost.

[17] It is uncertain whether the fourth day mentioned in the first completely preserved line on the *verso* is that of a festival beginning on a day named above (such a festival may have begun either on the eighteenth, named in line 11, or, more likely, another day named in the text lost in the lacuna) or the fourth day of a second month. Both interpretations have precedents in RS 1.003 (*CTA* 35) ≈ RS 18.056 (*CTA* Appendice II): the sequence "five" through "seven" in RS 1.003: 38-47 refers to the fifth through seventh days of the festival associated with the full moon, while lines 48-55 refer to events on the first day of the following month. Because festivals tended to begin on a day corresponding to a phase of the moon, particularly the new moon and the full moon, and because the days of the full-moon festival can be computed separately ("day one" = the first day of the festival = the fifteenth day of the month, etc.) one can postulate that the reference here is to the fourth and following days of the full-moon festival of the month of *Ḫiyyāru* (see above, note 2).

[18] The explanation of the anomalous form *ᶜṣrmm* here, and probably at the end of the line and into line 21′, is uncertain. It appears to be a dual or plural form of *ᶜṣr*, "bird," with enclitic *mem*. Because the form *ᶜṣrm* is usually a dual in these texts, *ᶜṣrmm* may be an emphatic form of the plural (*ᶜuṣṣurūmama*). *ᶜṣr* seems to function in the ritual texts as a generic word for "bird" (like *ṣpr* in the Punic sacrificial tariff [text 1.98]), while *ynt* (*qrt*), "(city)-dove," is the most common specifically designated species. ᵓ*uz*, "goose," appears rarely as do some other terms of which the meaning is less clear (see Pardee forthcoming).

[19] The genitival phrase *šmn šlm bᶜl* in lines 24′-25′ apparently denotes an offering of oil meant to induce well-being from Baᶜlu, while the *mtk mlkm*, "libation of the kings," is offered either by living kings (and the plural would be generic, since Ugarit apparently had one living king at a time) or for the benefit of dead kings, i.e., the kings named in RS 24.257 reverse (the Ug. king list; see Pardee 1988a:165-178) and those named in RS 34.126 (a connection with dead kings is favored by most scholars). See texts 1.104-105 below.

[20] The words designating the enemy here are *ᶜz*, an adjective used substantivally, "the strong (one)," and *qrd*, the old Semitic word for "warrior" (cf. Akk. *qarrādu*, "hero, warrior").

gate,
the warrior from our walls,
A bull,[21] [y] O Baʿlu, we shall sanctify,[z]
a vow, (O) Baʿlu,[22] we shall fulfill;[aa]
a firstborn,[23] [bb] (O) Baʿlu, we shall sanctify,
a *ḥtp*-offering,[24] (O) Baʿlu, we shall fulfill,
a *ʿšrt*-feast, (O) Baʿlu, we shall offer;

To the sanctuary, (O) Baʿlu, we shall ascend,[cc]
th(at) path,[25] [dd] (O) Baʿlu, we shall take.
And Baʿlu will hear [your] prayer:[ee]
He will drive the strong (foe) from your gate,
[the warrior] from your walls.[26]

y Isa 10:13 *z* Exod 28:38 etc. *aa* 1 Kgs 2:27; Jer 44:25; 2 Chr 36:21 Cf. 1 Kgs 8:15, 24; Ps 20:5, 6; 2 Chr 6:4, 15 *bb* Lev 27:26; Num 18:17; Deut 15:19; 33:17 *cc* Exod 34:24 etc. *dd* Prov 3:17ff *ee* Gen 21:17ff

[21] A poetic word is used here for "bull," *ʾibr* ("the powerful one"), instead of the usual word for "male bovine" in this and other ritual texts, *ʾalp*.

[22] Though the vocative marker *y* (probably *yā*, as in Arabic) appears on the first and second occurrences of the divine name (lines 28´, 29´), it is not used again. I have interpreted all the repetitions of *bʿl* as having a vocative function and the restoration of the end of line 33´ without *bt*, "house," makes the analysis of all occurrences of *bʿl* as vocatives easier (see below, note 25).

[23] The first letter of the second word in line 31´ has disappeared and the word has been restored by some as {[d]kr}, "male," by others as {[b]kr}, "firstborn." Space considerations actually favor the second restoration, but there is no reason to favor the interpretation of the term as denoting a human sacrifice as some have thought (e.g., Margalit 1986) over that of an animal firstborn.

[24] For bibliography on the interpretation of this word, see Pardee 1993:216, n. 33, and Pardee forthcoming, on this passage.

[25] Some restore here {*ntbt b[t bʿl]*}, "the path of Baʿlu's house," which would indicate a shift from the vocative formulation in line 28´ to a third-person formulation. The lacuna appears, however, a bit narrow for that restoration and I have restored simply {ntbt b[ʿl]}.

[26] This is certainly the last line of the text, but the corner of the tablet is broken away here and there could conceivably have been a very short conclusion of some kind.

REFERENCES

De Jong and van Soldt 1987-88; Herdner 1972:693-697; 1978; Margalit 1981; 1986; Miller 1988; de Moor 1983; 1987; del Olmo Lete 1989:27-35; 1992; Pardee 1987:366-471; 1988a; 1993a:207-218; forthcoming; Saracino 1983a:304-306; 1983b:263-269; Tarragon 1989:125-238; Xella 1978:127-136; 1981.

THE PRAYER OF NABONIDUS (*4QPrNab*) (1.89)

Baruch A. Levine, Anne Robertson

This Aramaic text from Qumran, Cave 4, which speaks of Nabonidus, the last king of Babylon, was first published by J. T. Milik (1956), who assembled it from separate fragments of a single manuscript. These fragments were later realigned by F. M. Cross (1984), who dated the inscription paleographically to ca. 75-50 BCE. Many large gaps remain, some of which can be restored on the basis of parallel statements occurring elsewhere in the inscription, itself. Other restorations can only be conjectured, mostly on the basis of thematic links with the Book of Daniel. Interpretations of *4QPrNab* have, as a consequence, varied greatly, although its overall thrust is quite clear.

While in Tema, a major oasis in northern Arabia, Nabonidus was stricken for seven years with an ailment inflicted on him by God, so that he became comparable with the beasts. When he prayed to God, his sin was forgiven. By way of recapitulation, the inscription explains in greater detail how Nabonidus was cured. It was a Jewish diviner of the exilic community who revealed to Nabonidus the cause of his ailment. He is quoted as saying that it was because the Babylonian king had continued to worship false gods, of silver and gold, thinking that they were true gods. The diviner instructed Nabonidus to give honor and praise to the true God, at which point his suffering ended.

In the biblical Book of Daniel, experiences similar to those associated with Nabonidus in this inscription are attributed to Nebuchadnezzar II, and in lesser degree to Belshazzar, Nabonidus' son, who ruled as co-regent for three years while his father was in Arabia. Quite possibly, the traditions of the Book of Daniel originated as tales about Nabonidus, whose fame was celebrated in Babylonian sources. His sojourn in Tema is recorded in the so-called Nabonidus Chronicle (*ANET* 305-307), and the Harran Inscriptions of Nabonidus (*ANET* 562-563) state that he had recourse to diviners, there identified as spokesmen of Sin, the chief god worshipped at Harran.

Biblical writers understandably focused on Nebuchadnezzar because he was, after all, the one who had destroyed Jerusalem and exiled masses of Judaeans to Babylonia. It is noteworthy, however, that at Qumran, other Jewish authors identified Nabonidus as the subject of legend, and credited him with ultimately acknowledging the God of Israel. See Meyer 1962; Sack 1992; and Garcia Martinez 1992:116-136.

Superscription: The Afflictions of Nabonidus (1-2a)
(Concerning) words of p[ra]yer[1] of Nabonidus[2], king of [Ba]bylon, [the Great] King[a], [when he was stricken] with a pernicious inflammation[3] by the decree[4] of G[o]d[5], in [the municipality of] Teman.[6] [b]

A First-Person Account of Nabonidus' Affliction and Healing (2b-4a)
I was stricken for seven years[7], and ever since [that time] I became comparable [with the beasts.[8] [c] Then I prayed before God][d], and (as for) my offense - he forgave it[9].

Recapitulation: It was a Jewish Diviner who Revealed to Nabonidus How He Could Be Healed (4b-8)
A diviner, [10] [e] who was himself a Jew fro[m among the exilic community of Judea],[11] [f] provided an interpretation,[12] [g] and wrote (instructions) to render honor and greatness to the name of G[od. And so did he write]: "You were stricken with a pernicious inflammation [by the decree of God in the municipality of Teman, but] you continued for seven years to pray [before] gods of silver and gold, [bronze and iron], wood and stone (and) clay,[h] because [you were of the opin]ion that t[hey were] (true) divinities." [13]

a Dan 2:10; Ezra 5:11
b Isa 21:14; Jer 25:21; Job 6:19
c Dan 4:21-22; 5:21
d Dan 6:11; Ezra 6:10
e Dan 2:27; 4:4; 5:7,11
f Dan 2:25; 5:13; 6:14
g Dan 2:4ff; 5:12ff
h Dan 5:4,23

[1] Since the inscription nowhere presents the actual text of Nabonidus' prayer, but only reports that he prayed to God in his affliction, we should understand "words of prayer" (*mly ṣlt*ʾ) as referring more generally to the subject of the inscription.

[2] The Aram. name, written *nbny*, is to be read *Nabônâi*, a shortened form of *Nabônāʾi[d]*, namely, Nabonidus, the last king of Babylon (556-539 BCE).

[3] The Aram. passive participle *ketîš* "stricken" is restored here from line 3 of the inscription, where it is clearly legible. The literal sense of *ktš* is "to crush, pound." Nabonidus was "stricken" with "a pernicious (=evil) inflammation" (*šḥnʾ bʾyšt*ʾ). Aram. *šḥn* is a cognate of Heb. *šeḥin* "boils, inflammation" (Exod 9:10), and cf. the Akk. verb *šaḫānu* "to become warm; to warm" (*CAD* Š 1:278). Sokoloff 1990:544.

[4] Aram. *pitgām* (Old Persian *patgam*) "word, report" has the meaning of "decree, edict." It is attested in Biblical Aram. (Dan 4:14), where it is parallel with *mēʾmar* "word, command" and enters into late BH (Esth 1:20; Josh 8:11; and cf. Sir 5:11; 8:9). It occurs regularly in most Aram. dialects, including Syriac. *KB*[1] 1114; Sokoloff 1990:454; Levy 1963 4:154; Brockelmann 1966:616.

[5] Following Cross we read simply *ʾlhʾ* "God" because of limitations of space, whereas Milik reads *ʾlhʾ ʿlyʾ* "the most high God" after Dan 3:26,32; 5:18,21.

[6] Reading *btymn* [*mdyntʾ*] "in the municipality of Teman" with Milik 1956:415, Addendum, who discovered this reading in an additional fragment belonging with the dream inscription. It accords with the conventional way of registering the names of cities and provinces in Aram. documents. Aram. *Tymn*, read *Têmān*, is to be identified with the oasis of Tema, in Arabia, where Nabonidus spent a considerable period of time between 553-543 BCE, during his prolonged absence from Babylon (Sack 1992; Collins 1992). This site, and its environs, are referred to in several biblical passages by the correct name, *Têmaʾ* (Isa 21:14; Jer 25:21; Job 6:19), whereas in this inscription that toponym is confused with *Têmān*, a more general name for "southern" areas.

[7] The duration of the ailment for seven years correlates with what is told of the seven seasons of Nebuchadnezzar's withdrawal from human habitation in Dan 4:21-22, and it is there that we read about his madness and habitation with the beasts of the field. Here, the translation follows the restoration suggested by Cross.

[8] Following Cross, it is best to read *wmn* [*dy*] šwy ʾ[*nh lḥywtʾ wṣlyt qdm ʾlhʾ*].

[9] Cross cites the Targum on Job from Qumran, cave 11 (11*QtgJob* 38:2-3) which reads: "And God harkened to Job's voice and forgave them their sins on his account" (*wšbq lhwn ḥṭʾyhwm bdylh*), referring to the sins of Job's friends. The sense of the verb *šbq*, frequent in most Aram. dialects, is "to release, abandon"; hence: "to forego punishment, forgive." *DNWSI* 1104-1105.

[10] Aram. *gzr* appears in the plural, *gāzerîn*, determined form: *gazerayyaʾ* "(the) diviners" in Dan 2:27; 4:4; 5:7,11 within a standard list of magical practitioners present at the Babylonian court. These included wise men, exorcists, and magicians, none of whom was able to interpret the royal dreams. With a degree of irony, this inscription has a Jewish diviner of the exilic communmity show concern for Nabonidus' plight and explain its cause to him, thereby allowing him to be cured.

[11] Since it is probable that the text goes on to identify the diviner's origin, both Milik and Cross fill in the gap with words to the effect that he was one of the Jewish exiles. Therefore, we read: *m*[*n bny glwtʾ dy yhwd*] after Dan 2:25; 5:13; 6:14. One could also read: *dy yhwdyʾ* "of the Judaeans," with the text of Daniel from Qumran, 4*Q*112.113.115 to Dan 2:25. Beyer 1994:150.

[12] Following Milik, we take the unclear reading *hḥwy* as a 3rd masculine perfect form *heḥewê* "he explained, interpreted." This verb is prominent in the biblical Daniel narratives, occurring no less than 10 times in the second chapter of Daniel (Dan 2:4ff) and 4 times in Dan 5. In every case it refers to the interpretation of dreams and signs.

[13] In line 8 of the inscription, Cross ingeniously restores *mn dy* [*hwyt śb*]*r*, which he takes to mean: "Because I was of the opinion," but which more likely means: "Since you were of the opinion." The Aram. form *hwyt* can represent either the 1st person masculine perfect, "I was," or the 2nd person masculine perfect, "You were," and the latter makes better sense here. The verb *sbr* "to think, intend" is attested in Dan 7:25.

REFERENCES

Beaulieu 1989; Beyer 1994; Brockelmann 1966; Collins 1992; Cross 1984; Garcia Martinez 1992; Levy 1963; R. Meyer 1962; Milik 1956; Sack 1992; Sokoloff 1990.

3. DIVINATION

UGARITIC BIRTH OMENS (1.90)
(RS 24.247 + RS 24.302)

Dennis Pardee

Recorded observations of the natural world in the Levantine and Mesopotamian areas of the ancient Near East had two primary foci, medical and divinatory. The two areas were probably thought to be equally empirical. In the case of a symptom, one applied a given remedy or remedies and the complaint was supposed to go away. Other natural phenomena were thought to be followed by events in man's world. Various forms of divination are well attested in the classical world and a lengthy introduction is therefore not necessary here. Many of these types of divination are known to have already been practiced in Mesopotamia, for which documentation exists from the beginning of the second millennium BCE on. A much less extensive documentation exists for the west, though forms of classical Mesopotamian divinatory texts have been discovered there, particularly at Emar (Tell Meskene on the Euphrates) and, in Hittite versions, at Boğazköy. Ugaritic texts exist for divination by misformed animal births (RS 24.247+), by misformed human births (RS 24.302), by lunar phenomena (RIH 78/14 [text 1.91]), by extispicy (RS 24.312 ... [texts 1.92]), and, perhaps, by dreams (RS 18.041 [text 1.93]). In the medical category, only hippiatric texts are attested to date (text 1.106). Though one suspects that these texts had a Mesopotamian origin, there is remarkably little evidence of direct Mesopotamian influence. For example, there are very few loanwords from Akkadian in the Ugaritic of these texts, and there is no instance of a Ugaritic text having been translated directly from a known Akkadian original. It appears, therefore, that there was a long native tradition of this type of text and that it may be necessary to rethink the role of the "Amorites" in the elaboration and spread of "science" in the Fertile Crescent.

Both birth-omen texts were discovered in the same archive, that of "le prêtre aux modèles de poumon et de foies," in the trench dubbed "ville sud," as were the lung and liver models translated in 1.92.

Because the omens are brief, consisting of one or two sentences per observation, the lines inscribed on the tablet by the scribe to set one omen off from another are indicated here and subheadings are omitted in the translation. RS 24.247+ was badly damaged in antiquity and has been incompletely pieced together from many fragments (*editio princeps* by Herdner 1978:44-60).[1] There is no set order of procedure from one anomaly to another and it is therefore usually impossible to reconstruct the beginning of the line when it is damaged. The interpretation of a given anomaly is not uniform in the various traditions, and it is usually difficult to reconstruct a missing prognostication. One can, however, observe one generality: the left side is negatively polarized, the right side positively. So a missing right organ or limb will generally be interpreted negatively, while the same abnormality on the left will have a positive interpretation. This is clearest in lines 35′-38′, mirror-image omens involving missing right and left ears. For parallels with the Mesopotamian tradition, termed *šumma izbu* after the first words of a typical entry ("if [there is] a misformed birth ..."), see particularly Xella and Capomacchia 1979, Pardee 1986, and Dietrich and Loretz 1990a.

A Text for Divining by Misformed Births of Sheep and Goats (RS 24.247+)

1) As for the ewes of the flock,[2] [when[3] t]hey give birth,[4] [a] (if it is a) stone,[5] many[6] will fall[b] in the land.[7]

a Gen 30:39; 31:8
b 2 Sam 1:4

2) (If it is a piece of) wood, behold [...] in place of the offspring/birth, its cattle will [...][8].

[1] Concerning the history of the fragment constituting the upper left corner of the tablet, all-important for the identification of the genre of the text, see Pardee 1986:117; Pardee forthcoming, on RS 24.247+.

[2] Ug. *ṣˀin* corresponds to Heb. *ṣōˀn*, and both designate a mixed herd of sheep and goats (the traditional translation "small cattle" is in opposition to bovids, "large cattle"). The word for "ewes" is *ṯˀatt*, which has clear cognates in Aram. and Akk. The second {t} of the form *ṯˀatt* either is a mistake or represents the plural morpheme added onto the singular *-t* (see Pardee 1986:126; 1989:80).

[3] The normal structure of a divinatory text is protasis, containing the observation, followed by apodosis, containing the interpretation. In the oldest Mesopotamian tradition, it was normal for protasis to have its complete form, i.e., with expressed hypothetical particle "if" (cf. Pardee 1986:127, n. 59). This seems also to have been the form in the Ug. texts for divining by misformed human births and by lunar observations (RS 24.302 here below and 1.91, respectively). In this text, however, the particle is absent below wherever the beginning of the line is preserved, though it is plausibly restored here in the lacuna, before the verb for birthing, not before the term designating the anomaly. (The hypothetical particle appears to be entirely absent in the text for divining by dreams, though that text is even more badly damaged than is this one).

[4] The form {tldˀat}, for which no satisfactory explanation has been found, is corrected to {tldn!}, which, in the Ug. script, is only a matter of spacing between wedges.

[5] Lit., "[when t]hey bear a stone."

[6] The final letter of *mˀadtn*, and frequently below, has been shown to be a particle attached to the first word of an apodosis, if that word is a singular noun in the absolute state (Hoftijzer 1982; Pardee 1986:126). As an apodosis marker, it is not translated. Note that some have translated it, incorrectly, as a first common plural pronominal suffix ("our").

[7] The use of "fall" (Ug. *ql*) in such a context normally implies warfare. "The land" in this text, unqualified, denotes the homeland, while "that land" designates the enemy's land. The Ug. term for the large political entity "land" (as opposed to the geological entity) is *ḥwt*, plausibly derived

3) (If the foetus) is smooth,[9] (without) h[air?],[c] there will be [...] in the land.

4) And (if) th[ere is no ...], the land will perish.[d]

5) [...], there will be famine in the land.[e]

6) [...] and (= nor) nostrils,[10] the land [...]; ditto.[11]

7) [And] (if) there is no [...], the king will seize the lan[d of his enemy and] the weapon of the king[12] will lay it (the land) low.[f]

8) [...] [...] cattle [...]

9) And (if) it has no [left] thigh, the king will [...] his enemy.

10) And (if) there is no lower left leg,[13] the king [will ...] his enemy.

11) And (if there is) a horn of flesh [in] its lef[t te]mple, [...].

12) (If) it has no spleen[14] [...] [...]; di[tto;]
13) the king will not obtain[15] offspring.[16]

14) [And] (if) it has no testicles,[g] the (seed-)gra[in[h] ...][17]

15) And (if) the middle part[i] of its [left?] foreleg[j] is missing, [...] will destroy the cattle[k] of [...].

16) [...], the enemy will destroy the cattle of the land.
17) [...], the mighty archers[18] will seize the enemy of the king.

18) [...]perish/destroy; ditto.

19) [...]famine, hard times[l] will disappear.

20) [...]will become strong/strengthen him.
21) [...]

22) [...]

23) [...]
..................[19]

24′) [...] [...]

25′) [...] [...]

26′) And (if) it has no right thigh [...]

27′) And (if) there is no tendon?[20] in [its?] K[...]

28′) And (if) it has no middle part of the [right] foreleg [...]
29′) will not obtain offspring.

30′) And (if) [it has] no nostrils [...]

31′) And (if) it has no tongue [...]

32′) (If) its lower lip (is) like [...]

33′) (If) its face (is) that of a ᵓIRN,[21] [...] will shorten
34′) the days[m] of the (= our) lord; behold, the catt[le? ...]

35′) And (if) [it] has no right ear, [the enemy will] devastate[n] the land
36′) [... and will] consume it.

37′) And (if) [it] has no left ear, the king [will] devastate the land of [his] enemy
38′) and will consume it.

39′) And (if) its (rear?) legs (are) short, the (= our) lord will confront the *ḫurādu*-troops[22] and

c Gen 27:11
d Jer 9:11
e Gen 12:10 etc.
f Cf. Pss 79:8; 116:6; 142:7(G-stem); Judg 6:6; Isa 17:4 (N-stem)
g Lev 21:20
h Gen 47:19, 23; Lev 26:16; 27:16; Num 24:7; Deut 28:38; Isa 5:10; 55:10
i Exod 12:9; Lev 1:9, 13; 8:21; 9:14; 11:21; Amos 3:12
j 1 Sam 17:37; Ps 22:21; cf. Gen 9:5
k Exod 9:1-6, 18-25
l Zeph 1:15; Pss 25:17; 107:6, 13, 19, 28; Job 15:24; cf. Deut 28:53, 55, 57; 1 Sam 22:2; Isa 8:22, 23; 30:6; Jer 19:9; Ps 119:143; Prov 1:27; Job 36:16 37:10;
m Pss 89:46; 102:24
n Jer 51:55 etc.

---

from *ḥwy*, "to live," and cognate to Heb. *ḥawwāh*, which designates a much smaller political entity, a "village." A paraphrase of this omen would thus be: the birth of a stone by a ewe or a nanny means that battle will occur in the homeland in the course of which many casualties will occur among the home troops.

[8] The word *bhmt*, translated here conventionally as "cattle," probably designates livestock in general, i.e., is neither so narrow as to designate only bovids nor so wide as to designate, as does *bᵉhēmāh* in some biblical texts, all creatures larger than the "creepers" (*remeś*, *šereṣ*). The restoration of ᶜ*br* at the end of this line proposed in Pardee 1986:129 must be abandoned; see Pardee forthcoming.

[9] The text is {gmš š[...]}, hypothetically restored as *ġmš š*[ᶜ*r*] and explained by Arabic *ġmš*, "shave," as meaning "smooth, devoid of hair" (Pardee 1986:129).

[10] The foetus is missing another organ in addition to the nostrils.

[11] The word *mṯn*, from *ṯny*, "do twice, repeat," denotes repetition of an element from the preceding entry.

[12] The phrase "weapon of the king" has excellent parallels in the Mesopotamian omen texts (GIŠ.TUKUL LUGAL = *kak šarri*), while the Ug. word here designating the weapon, viz. *mrḥy*, appears to be cognate to Arabic *marḥay* and, with metathesis, to Heb. *rōmaḥ*, "spear, lance." For the details of this interpretation, see Pardee 1986:130-131.

[13] The body part is the *qṣrt*, denoting perhaps the part of the animal's leg between the hoof and the "ankle" (Pardee 1986:132). This term appears also in the Punic sacrificial tariff text (1.98).

[14] Though not attested in Biblical Heb., *ṯḥl*, "spleen," has good cognates in the other Semitic languages.

[15] This passage has helped to explain the form *ypq* in the Kirta text (*CTA* 14 i 12; see note 5 to text 1.102) as from the hollow root *pq*, used several times in the Hiphil in Biblical Heb. as a parallel term to *māṣāᵓ*, "to find" (cf. Pardee 1989:84).

[16] The word for "offspring" in the omen texts is *špḥ*, "offspring (undifferentiated as to sex)" (see note 11 to the Kirta text [1.102]).

[17] Though the rest of the apodosis is missing, there appears to be a play on *ḏr*ᶜ, "seed(-grain)" and "semen," here and in line 55′ (see Pardee 1989:87-88).

[18] It is clear from the Kirta text that *ṯnn* (here) and *ḫpṯ* (line 57′) denote types of soldiers (see note 22 to text 1.102).

[19] Approximately one fourth to one third of the tablet has disappeared, and as few as fifteen and as many as thirty lines have been lost.

[20] The word *ḫrṣp* may denote a tendon or a ligament if the explanation by Heb. *ḥarṣubbôt*, "bonds" (Isa 58:6), is correct (for bibliography, see Pardee 1986:134).

[21] The term seems to denote either some reptile, perhaps a form of lizard, or a dog, particularly a puppy (for discussion with bibliography, see Pardee 1986:135-136).

[22] Like *ṯnn* (line 17) and *ḫpṯ* (line 57′), *ḫrd* denotes a military category (for bibliography, see Pardee 1987:387).

40′) Rašap will finish off[o] the posterity.[23]

41′) And (if) its nose (is) like the "nose" of a bird, the gods will destroy[24] [p] the land

42′) [...] and will fly (away[?]).[25]

43′) [...] to/on its head, the (seed-)grain of that king

44′) [...]

45′) [...] its [-]DR protrudes,[26] the Sun will abase[27] that land.

46′) [...], the king will lay low[28] the hand (= power)[q] of the *ḫurādu*-troops.

47′) [...] its penis,[29] the weapon of the king will be raised

48′) [...] his hand.

49′) [...] in place of its eyes and its eyes (are) in its forehead,[30]

50′) [the enemy will] tread the land under.[r]

51′) [And (if)] its [--]B protrudes from its mouth, the enemy will devour[s] the land.

52′) And (if) it has [no] feet, the *ḫurādu*-troops will turn[t] against the king.

53′) And if its tongue is [...], the land will be scattered.[u]

54′) (If) its [...]ḪR (is/are) in its temples, the king will make peace with[v] his enemy.

55′) And (if) it has n[o] [-]KB, the (seed-)grain of that land will be consumed.[w]

56′) And (if) [...], the gods will destroy that land.

57′) And (if) its eyes are [in] (its) forehead, the king will become more powerful[x] than his *ḫupṯu*-troops.

58′) And (if) it has ḤR and [-]R, the king will destroy his enemy.

59′) And (if) it has no left (fore[?])leg, the land of the enemy will perish.

A Text for Divining by Misformed Human Births (RS 24.302)[31]

1′) If [a woman] g[ives birth ...]
2′) the l[and ...]

3′) If [a woman] gives birth[...]
4′) will become more powerful than[...]

===========================

5′) If a wo[man] gives birth[...]
6′) the land of the enemy will [be destroyed.]
7′) If a wo[man] gives birth[...]
8′) help[32] will be [...]

9′) If a wo[man] gives birth[...]
10′) the weapon of[...]
11′) will not ob[tain offspring[?]...]

12′) BH[...]
13′) will[?] [...]

14′) I[f a woman gives birth ...]

o Josh 24:20ff
p Jer 4:4; Ezek 21:4; cf. Deut 13:6ff
q Josh 8:20ff
r Ezek 32:2; 34:18; Ps 68:31
s Cf. Gen 24:25, 32; 42:27; 43:24; Judg 19:19
t Est 9:1
u Ezek 17:21
v Josh 11:19; Job 5:23
w Deut 28:38
x Judg 3:10; 6:2; Ps 89:14

[23] "Posterity" is a hypothetical interpretation of ᵓ*uḫry*, "what comes after." A word with identical spelling is interpreted as an adverb, "thereafter," in the ᵓAqhatu text (see note 119 [text 1.103]), and a feminine form, ᵓ*uḫryt*, means "afterlife" in the same text (*CTA* 17 vi 35). The verb here is *kly*, D-stem, "bring to a state of depletion, bring to an end, finish off" (the same verb is used in the G-stem in the Kirta text [*CTA* 16 iii 13-15; text 1.102] to describe the disappearance of foodstuffs in time of famine), while the active agent here, the deity Rašap, is responsible for the disappearance of Kirta's fifth wife (*CTA* 14 i 18-19; the verb there is ᵓ*sp*, "gather in").

[24] On this meaning of *b*ᶜ*r*, see Dion 1980.

[25] The damaged state of the tablet prevents us from perceiving the precise form of the apparent play on "bird" and "fly" in this omen. On the verb *d*ᵓ*y*, see note 71 to the ᵓAqhatu text (1.103).

[26] By comparison with line 51′, this anomaly probably consisted of a body part protruding improperly from a bodily orifice.

[27] The form *tpšlt* is anomalous, but seems clearly to derive from a root *pšl*, hitherto unattested in Ug., explained as meaning "to be low, base, vile" by comparison with Arabic and Akk. It is uncertain whether *špš*, "the sun," denotes the celestial orb or one of the great kings of the time. In favor of the latter interpretation is the fact that the kings of both Hatti and Egypt were addressed as "the Sun" by Ug. kings in their correspondence; against it is the absence of mention elsewhere in this text of specific political figures on the international scene.

[28] Again, the verbal form is anomalous, written *yddll*, but seems clearly to derive from *dll*, "to be poor, humble, of low standing."

[29] The Ug. word is ᵓ*ušr*, cognate to Akk. *išaru* (*ušaru/mušaru* in late Babylonian). Because of the missing head of the line, it is impossible to say what the anatomical anomaly was.

[30] Though the beginning of the phrase designating the physical anomaly is lost, it appears to have consisted of some organ appearing in the place of (ᵓ*aṯr*) the eyes, while the eyes are to be found in the forehead. It is this text that clinched the meaning of "forehead" for the word *lṣb* (see note 18 to the ᵓAqhatu text [1.103]), for there are good parallels in the mantic literature for eyes in the forehead but none for eyes in the teeth (the previously most widely accepted interpretation of *lṣb*).

[31] This text consists of a small fragment from the lower left corner of the tablet. Though small, the fragment is precious, for it confirms the existence in Ug. of the genre corresponding to the Akk. *šumma sinništu* ("If a woman [gives birth] ..."), a subcategory of the texts dealing with divination by misformed births. Though it must be pieced together from the poorly-preserved beginnings of several lines, the all-important introductory phrase is indubitably present in the Ug. text: *k* ("if") *tld* ("gives birth") ᵓ*aṯt* ("woman"). Note the repetition of the hypothetical particle *k* at the beginning of each entry except the one beginning at line 12′, too damaged to permit an explanation of the omission. See note 3 above.

[32] The word ᶜ*ḏrt*, "help," is the only word present in the apodoses of this text that is not attested in the extant portions of RS 24.247+.

REFERENCES

Dietrich and Loretz 1986a; 1990a; 1990b:89-109; Dietrich, Loretz and Sanmartín 1975a; Dion 1980; Herdner 1978; Hoftijzer 1982; del Olmo Lete 1992; Pardee 1986; 1987; 1989; forthcoming; Xella 1981; Xella and Capomacchia 1979.

UGARITIC LUNAR OMENS (1.91)
(*RIH* 78/14)

Dennis Pardee

Like the texts for divination by misformed births, the Ugaritic collection of lunar omens corresponds directly to a Mesopotamian series, in this case *Sin*, the name of the Mesopotamian lunar deity. This text, which was discovered in 1978 at the site of Ras Ibn Hani, only a few kilometers from Ras Shamra, is badly damaged, only the upper portion having been preserved and that incompletely (*editio princeps* by Bordreuil and Caquot 1980:352-353). Like the tiny fragment attesting to the existence of the divinatory genre dealing with misformed human births, this incomplete text is precious, attesting to the transmission in Ugaritic of omens based on lunar phenomena. The text is too poorly preserved to permit a structural analysis, the only certain feature being that it begins with reference to the new moon and ends with a reference to the thirtieth day, that is, a full month as defined by consecutive sightings of the new moon. There seems, however, to be another reference to the new moon towards the end of the text (line 9′), and in line 11′ some have seen the Mesopotamian month name Kislimu. It appears unlikely, therefore, that the overall organization of the text consisted of a simple progression through the phases of the lunar month. As with the divination texts in the preceding section, no text from the Mesopotamian tradition can be identified as the original from which this one would have been translated, not even one of those from Emar (in eastern Syria) dating roughly to the same period as this one.

1) If[1] at the time of the new moon[2] [a] [...], there will be poverty.[3] [b]

2) If the moon,[c] when it rises,[4] is red,[5] [d]
3) there will be prosperity[6] [e] [during] (that month).

4) [If] the moon, when it rises, is yellow-green[7] [f]
5) [ ], the cattle will perish.[g]

6) [If the moon, when it ri]ses, is red,
7) [ ] assembly.
...[8]
8′) [will] perish.

9′) [ ] newness of the moon,[9] the personnel[10]
10′) [ ] and will be put down.[11]

11′) [ ]YM YH YRḪ KSLM,[12] the kings will keep an eye on each other.[13]

a Isa 47:13
b Prov 6:11ff
c Jer 8:2; Job 31:26
d Isa 54:16; Ps 11:6 (!)
e Ps 90:17
f Ps 68:14
g Exod 9:1-6, 18-25

[1] The hypothetical particle in this text is *hm*, corresponding closely to Heb. ᵓ*im*, rather than *k* as in the text dealing with misformed human births (and in the hippiatric text 1.106, below).

[2] This text uses two words for moon: *ḥdṯ*, literally "newness," designates the new moon, almost certainly the appearance of the new moon established by sighting, whereas *yrḫ* designates the celestial orb and the month (the month being determined by the phases of the moon at Ugarit — see on RS 24.266 [text 1.88], note 2). The first phrase here is *b ḥd*[*ṯ*], lit., "in the newness." It is unfortunately uncertain whether the next word is *yrḫ*, as in line 11′, the word *ym*, "day," or another.

[3] The phrase *ršn ykn* shows clearly that the standard expression of "to be" was by the hollow root *kn*, as in Phoenician and Arabic, rather than *h(w/y)h*, as in Aram. and Heb. The word *ršn* probably consists of *rš* + *-n* of apodosis (see note 6 to RS 24.247+, RS 24.302 [texts 1.90]); it may derive either from the hollow root *rš* denoting poverty (so translated here, as the better antonym to *n*ᶜ*m*(*n*) in line 3), or from *ršš*, "crush" (the state of Kirta's household at the beginning of that text was described by a form of this root [*CTA* 14 i 10, 22; text 1.102]).

[4] The structure is a familiar one in Semitic: the preposition meaning "in" (*b*) + the infinitive of the verb (ᶜ*ly*, "to ascend"). It is of interest that the term for the rising of the moon is different from that of the sun, which, when it rises, is said "to come forth (i.e., from its chamber and/or the netherworld)" (*yṣ*ᵓ) or to "shine forth, become visible" (*zrḥ* — though translated "to rise," this verb is not used to express the act of ascending for entities other than the sun). As a general parallel for this use of ᶜ*ly*, one can cite Neh 4:15 *mē*ᶜᵃ*lôt haššaḥar*, "from the rising of the dawn...."

[5] The word *pḥm* denotes a shade of red, never black, as its use here and for one of the shades of royal "purple" indicates (see note 130 to the ᵓAqhatu text [1.103]). (In Heb. *peḥām* denotes in all cases the "glowing coal," never the black lump of "coal"; only in later periods did the extension from "glowing coal" to "dead coal" to "black" occur.)

[6] As this omen is almost completely preserved, its structure is clear and *n*ᶜ*mn* can be said to consist, in all likelihood, of *n*ᶜ*m*, "goodness" + *-n* of apodosis (see note 3).

[7] Though the reading is not absolutely clear, the same word (*yrq*) was probably used here as was used in the Kirta text (1.102) to describe the color of gold (*CTA* 14 i 53 and parallels). The word *yrq* apparently covered a broad spectrum of colors, from leaf-green to golden yellow (see bibliography in Pardee 1987:402). The particularity here would be the relative darkness of the moon, with a greenish-gold cast, instead of its usual bright, clear color, normally perceived as white (√*lbn* in Heb.).

[8] If the shape of this tablet was typical, approximately half again as high as it is wide, as many as twenty-five to thirty lines have disappeared.

[9] Because the beginning of the line is missing, it is uncertain what the collocation of *ḥdṯ* with *yrḫ* here means (see above, note 2).

[10] *Bnš*, here in the plural (or singular with enclitic *-m*), is the standard Ug. word for free members of Ug. society (corresponding to *awīlum* in Akk.), often in one form or another of service to ranking members of the royal administration.

[11] The verb is *hbẓ*, probably the equivalent in other texts of *hbṭ*. The writing of etymological /ṭ/ by means of {ẓ} here and in the word for "rain" (line 13′) finds its best parallels in *CTA* 24. The precise meaning of *hbṭ* is difficult to determine in each of its occurrences, all others in epistolary texts, though it is usually explained by Arabic *hbṭ*, "to abase, to make low."

[12] The damaged state of the tablet means that we cannot be certain whether we have here a Ug. word (*ksl* normally denotes a tendon or a part of the back, as in the ᵓAqhatu text [1.103], *CTA* 19 ii 95) or the Mesopotamian month name Kislimu.

[13] See note 73 to the ᵓAqhatu text (1.103).

12′) [If] three times the moon is seen in the moon/month[14] (and) thereafter
13′) [...]LT, there will be rain.[15] [h]
14′) [If] a star falls[i] on the thirtieth day,[16] the king [...].

h Deut 32:2; Ps 72:6; Job 29:23
i Isa 14:12

[14] It is uncertain, for lack of clear parallels in the other collections of lunar omens, whether *yrḫ b yrḫ* refers to the apparent visibility of a second moon on the surface of the moon or to the reappearance of the moon three times during the month (because of apparent meteorological conditions or because the moon was thought actually to disappear during the month?).
[15] *mẓrn ylk* is apparently the entire apodosis, for the first word bears the *-n* of apodosis. The idiom consisting of the verb "to go" with a noun for "rain" as its subject is, to my knowledge, hitherto attested only in Akk. (*alāku* + a noun derived from *zanānu*). It is uncertain, however, whether the Ug. phrase is a calque on the Akk.
[16] The lunar cycle corresponds to approximately twenty-nine and a half solar days. Because of the difference between the lunar and solar cycles, the number of days between first visibility of the new lunar crescent can be either twenty-nine or thirty.

REFERENCES

Bordreuil and Caquot 1980; Dietrich and Loretz 1986a; 1990a; 1990b; Dietrich, Loretz and Sanmartín 1976; del Olmo Lete 1992; Pardee 1987; 1993b; forthcoming.

UGARITIC EXTISPICY (1.92)
(RS 24.312, RS 24.323, RS 24.326, RS 24.327, RS 24.654, RS 24.277)

Dennis Pardee

The practice of extispicy (the examination of the organs of a sacrificed animal for purposes of divination) is attested in the ancient Near East by collections of omens of the types encountered above ("if such-and-such a feature is present, such-and-such an event will occur") and by inscribed models of the organs themselves. Only the latter category is presently attested at Ugarit. There are several liver models and one lung model. The inscriptions can be either simple marks on the clay intended to replicate features present on the observed organ, or they can be such marks accompanied by actual texts describing the circumstances of the consultation. The leading authority on these objects, J.-W. Meyer, has deciphered the marks so as to be able to determine whether the response to the inquiry was positive or negative (Meyer 1987, 1990). The Ugaritic texts constitute a peculiarity in that other known inscriptions on organ models deal with the science of examination and interpretation, rather than with the circumstances of a particular consultation.

All the Ugaritic organ models come from a single archive, that found in the so-called "Maison du prêtre aux modèles de poumon et de foies," located to the south of the acropolis at Ras Shamra in the area dubbed "ville sud" by the excavator (Schaeffer 1978). The priest's name is unknown.

The texts on the liver models are set down on the flat surface of the model, arranged either as a single line winding around the curve of the model (RS 24.312) or as a series of lines beginning from one side (all others). The lung model has three large flat sides, each having roughly the shape of a flatiron, and the inscriptions are arranged in sections delimited by lines inscribed in the clay, either curved, forming small rough circles, or straight, running from one end to the other of the model. The delimiting lines sometimes cross each other, permitting a decision regarding the order of writing the inscriptions, but this is not always the case and, moreover, there is no way of determining the order in which the three sides were inscribed. The order in which the inscriptions are presented is, therefore, somewhat arbitrary, decided by what appears to the modern reader to be a logical sequence; I have for the most part followed the order proposed in the *editio princeps* (Dietrich and Loretz 1969).

A Consultation on the Buying of a Servant
(RS 24.312)

(This liver model is) for[1] ᵓAgapṯarri[2] when he was to buy[3] [a] the boy[4] of the Alashian.[5]

a Exod 21:2

[1] The text begins simply with *l*, "to, for," with the item ascribed to ᵓAgapṯarri unstated. It appears legitimate to conclude that the item in question was the liver model itself (see below, RS 24.326 and RS 24.654, which begin with the word *kbd*, "liver") and the consultation recorded on it. According to Meyer 1987:220; 1990:269, the response was positive.
[2] The name ᵓAgapṯarri, linguistically Hurrian, is also attested in a brief inscription on a vase in the form of lion's head found in the house adjacent to the one where the organ models were found: "*Binu ᵓAgapṯarri* — Lion's head that *Nūrānu* offered to *Rašap Guni*." Cf. Dietrich and Loretz 1978.
[3] *yqny*, imperfect of the verb *qny*, "buy, obtain, produce" (word used by Eve when recognizing Yahweh's part in the birth of Cain, Gen 4:1).
[4] The word is *ġzr*, on which see note 78 to the Kirta text (1.102).
[5] *ᵓalṯyy*, a person from *ᵓalṯy*, believed by most authorities to be Cyprus.

A Consultation at the Time of Sacrifice (RS 24.323)

Sacrificial (consultation)[6] of BṢY, so[n]/daught[er][7] of ṮRY, for the ᶜAṯtaru who is in ᶜAṯtartu.[8]

A Consultation at the Beginning of a Month (RS 24.326)

(This is) the liver[b] (pertaining to the consultation on behalf) of YPT, son of YKNᶜ, when this month was about to begin.[9]

A Consultation Regarding Military Service (?) (RS 24.327)

[...] of Yabnimilku with regard to *ḫpṯ*.[10]

A Consultation in Uncertain Circumstances (RS 24.654)

(This is) the liver (model)[11] for Ḥ[...] when [...] (on) a/the day of [...].

A Lung Model Bearing a Series of Inscriptions (RS 24.277)

(Side 1, Inscription I)

Sacrifices[12] of the entire month.[3] (First) a(n object) vow(ed)[c] and a sacrifice.

(Side 1, Inscription II)

Those (= the sacrifices) of (= offered by)[14] NᵓAT and gifts of (= for) Ṯarrummanni[15] and a sacrifice of (= offered by) all; all (will eat this) sacrifice (until) it is gone,[d] in accordance with the writings.[16]

(Side 1, Inscription III)

Those (= the sacrifices) of (= offered by) NᵓAT and Qurwanu; (these will be done) like the (preceding) sacrifice.

(Side 1, Inscription IV)

[...] personnel.[17]

(Side 2, Inscription V)

A ram [...][18]

(Side 2, Inscription VI)

YPY[...][19]

(Side 2, Inscription VII)

A bull[20] [e] of (= for) Dagan [...] in the house,[21] according to the wr[itings], and to/surely[22] the sacrifice [...].

(Side 3, Inscription VIII)[23]

If[24] the city is about to be seized,

b Ezek 21:26
c Jer 44:25
d Exod 12:8-10
e Lev 4:10; 9:4, 18; 22:23, 27; Num 15:11; Deut 17:1; 18:3; Judg 6:25; 2 Sam 6:13; Hos 12:12; Ps 69:32

[6] The first word of this text is *dbḥt*. Now, the normal word for "sacrifice" is the masculine form *dbḥ*. Perhaps the feminine form *dbḥt* was used particularly for the sacrificial act linked with extispicy. Because the end of the word for "son" is damaged leaving open the possibility of reading "daughter" (see next note), it is possible that the person in question is feminine and that *dbḥt* is a feminine verbal form.

[7] The last sign of this word is broken and could be either {n} (*bn*, "son") or {t} (*bt*, "daughter").

[8] ᶜAṯtartu is here a place name (rather than the divine name) of which two are known from the Ug. texts, a *gt* ᶜ*ṯtrt* within the kingdom, and ᶜ*ṯtrt*, known as the home of the deity *Milku* and located plausibly to the northeast of the Sea of Galilee (ᶜ*Aštᵉrōt Qarnayim* in the Hebrew Bible; for discussion and bibliography, see Pardee 1988:94-97). Male and female forms of the deity ᶜ*ṯtr* were known at Ugarit, corresponding probably to the evening and morning star, respectively (for bibliography, see Pardee 1989-90:466-470).

[9] *k yptḥ yrḫ hnd*, lit., "when this month was about to open" (taking *yptḥ* as N-stem).

[10] We have encountered *ḫpṯ* in two texts (Kirta [1.102, see note 22] and the Birth Omen text RS 24.247+ [1.90: see note 18]) where it clearly denotes a category of soldier. The state of this text does not allow a certain interpretation.

[11] Although fragmentary, this text is important for it and RS 24.326 are the only ones that bear inscriptions that include the word *kbd*, "liver."

[12] The genitive pronoun beginning "inscription II" is plural, an indication that *dbḥ* in "inscription I" is in fact a plural, in the construct state.

[13] Because Ug. does not have a definite article, it is difficult to determine if a phrase with *kl* means "every" or "all of." The phrase *kl yrḫ* in this text has been interpreted both ways. Given, though, the circumstantial nature of these organ-model inscriptions, the interpretation as sacrifices having to do with a particular month appears preferable to one that sees here a broader description. One can surmise, comparing the liver inscription RS 24.326 (see above), that the inscription reports a series of sacrifices carried out at the beginning of a month, one of which served divinatory purposes. The significance of the fact that the object on which the inscriptions were recorded is a lung model cannot be determined, nor can one know whether all the following inscriptions have to do with the condition indicated here. That all the inscriptions on sides 1 and 2 should be linked appears plausible, but the conditional formulation of inscriptions VIII-X does not to lend itself to so circumstantial a consultation.

[14] "Inscription II" begins with the relative/genitive pronoun *dt*, indicating that the sense of this inscription depends directly on that of the previous one. This syntactic indicator is corroborated by the delimiting lines, for the one around "inscription II" seems to have been inscribed after the one around "inscription I."

[15] Ṯarrummanni is known from other texts as a divine name (for bibliography, see Pardee 1989-90:478) while *nᵓat* appears to be the name of one of the persons presenting the sacrifices, Qurwanu ("inscription III") being the other.

[16] The verb for participating in the sacrificial meal is *kly*, lit., "devour, consume," apparently implying that the entire sacrifice is to be eaten at the sacral meal. Only one other ritual text states explicitly that all may eat of a sacrifice and there the verb is *lḥm* (RS 24.260:10 [*KTU* 1.115]) and the entire ritual context seems to be quite different. We do not know, therefore, what "the writings" were to which this text refers.

[17] The word is *bnš* (on which see note 10 to RS 78/14 [text 1.91]); the same word appears below in the inscriptions on "side 3."

[18] Only one sign is preserved in line 15′ after the letter {š}. I hypothesize that the structure of this inscription and that of "inscription VII" were similar and that the *š* denotes the animal sacrificed, while the next word would have qualified *š*, perhaps a divine name as in "inscription VII."

[19] This inscription is too poorly preserved to permit analysis of {ypy[...]}, either as to division of the letters or as to meaning.

[20] The word for "bull" here is *ṯr*, not the standard word in the sacrificial texts (usually *ᵓalp*).

[21] Again, the state of the inscription precludes a decision regarding whether *bt* here denotes the temple of Dagan or another house.

[22] *l* could be either the preposition or the "emphatic" particle.

[23] The inscriptions on "side 3" seem to form a single text, though the relationship between the three inscriptions is uncertain for three principal reasons: (1) the damage to the left side of this surface of the object has caused the loss of the beginnings of the lines in "inscription IX"; (2) though this surface is divided into four sections by straight lines in the clay, only three of the sections seem to have been inscribed (the traces of writing noted by the editors in one of the sections, their section "i," are in fact absent); (3) the scribe turned the model around and wrote "inscription X" in the opposite direction as compared with the two previous inscribed fields.

[24] The hypothetical particle *hm* is used twice in this line, though the state of the text means that we are uncertain as to where the second protasis ends and the apodosis begins. Note that the content of the protases has nothing to do with an observation of exta, and that this conditional formulation seems, therefore, to be dealing, not with the technique of extispicy, but with a hypothetical circumstance in which sacrifice (and extispicy?)

if the man (= warrior) attacks,[25] [f] the (male) personnel[26] (of the city)

(Side 3, Inscription IX)

[...] the women, they will take a goat [...][27]

(Side 3, Inscription X)

(in) (or: with regard to) the house, the (male) personnel will take[g] a goat[h] and see[i] afar.[28] [j]

f Num 13:31; Judg 1:1; 1 Sam 7:7; 1 Kgs 14:25; Isa 36:10 etc.

g Lev 12:8; 1 Kgs 19:21 *h* Exod 12:5; Lev 1:10; 3:12; 4:23; Num 7:16; 18:17; Ezek 43:22; 45:23 etc. *i* Ps 27:4; Job 36:25 *j* Isa 17:13; Jer 31:10

should be used.

[25] There are two verbs for the hostile act here, ˀḫd, "to seize," and ˁly, "to ascend (i.e., to go up against)." The word for "man" here is *mt*, which some have taken as the word for "death." Comparison with the prayer in RS 24.266 (text 1.88) leads rather to the conclusion that the word is *mutu*, "man," as a strong, fighting entity (cf. the same word in Akk.).

[26] The term here is *bnš*, denoting the free male citizen (see note 10 to RIH 78/14 [text 1.91]). We know from a letter (RS 1.018 [*CTA* 55]) that *bnš* could be appointed to transport statues of deities. It appears, therefore, that priests had at their disposal men to carry out the physical tasks involved in the cult and that these tasks extended to touching the holy and effecting divinatory sacrifices.

[27] The word *ˀaṯt* seems to set up an opposition between the males (*bnš*) in the city and the females; the same opposition is set up by the same two terms in RS 18.041:30´-31´ (text 1.93). The verb "to take" here is not marked for feminine gender, so the status of the women with regard to the actions of the men is unknown. The offering of a goat (*ˁz*) is not common, but the use of the verb *lqḥ* + *ˁz* here and of *lqḥ* + *gdy*, "kid" in a sacrificial context in RS 13.006 (*PRU* II 154; *KTU* 1.79) may be taken as an indication that we are dealing here with some form of sacrifice, though the precise term has disappeared in the lacuna. It is commonly believed that these lines deal with the offering of a goat in view of divination by extispicy, though it may be a matter of simple sacrifice. Any connection with the rite of atonement in Lev 16 and with the male goat used in that rite is dubious; the vocabulary and circumstances are too dissimilar to permit a close comparison.

[28] The expression *yḥdy mrḥqm* has inspired various interpretations. In this sacrificial context, perhaps one of extispicy, the interpretation of *ḥdy* as the verb meaning "to see" (which appears repeatedly in the section of the ˀAqhatu [text 1.103] where Dānīˀilu is looking for the birds in the heavens [*CTA* 19 ii 105 - iii 145]) appears plausible. *Mrḥqm*, probably an adverbial form of the noun *mrḥq*, "what is far off," will then denote either separation in time (the future) or in space (something located afar off). Because a *m-* preformative noun will usually denote a spatial relationship, rather than a temporal one, it appears plausible to see this phrase as denoting the retreat of the enemy. In line with this spatial interpretation of *mrḥqm*, others have interpreted the verb here by Arabic *ḥdw*, which means "to drive camels," and have proposed a comparison with Lev 16, where the scapegoat is driven out into the wilderness (*hammidbārāh*). For bibliography, see Pardee (forthcoming).

REFERENCES

Dietrich and Loretz 1969; 1978a; 1986a; 1990a; Loretz 1985; Meyer 1987; 1990; del Olmo Lete 1992; Pardee 1988a; 1989-90; forthcoming; Schaeffer 1978; Xella 1981.

UGARITIC DREAM OMENS (1.93)
(RS 18.041)

Dennis Pardee

This text, discovered in 1954 in the palace, is in a very poor state of preservation and its interpretation is uncertain (*editio princeps* by Virolleaud 1965, text 158). The presence of the word "dreams" in the first line and the variety of terms that have been preserved in the following lines make it at least plausible that we have here a rough catalogue of items that may be seen in dreams along with an interpretation by item or by category. The interpretation of dreams as a category of divination is well known from Mesopotamia (Oppenheim 1956). As with previous divinatory texts translated here, there is no Akkadian text that corresponds directly to this one, nor is there a single text that makes the attempt, as this one seems to do, to furnish a brief catalogue of the world as seen in dreams.

1) Document[a] of dreams.[1] [b] A year-old[c] bull[2] [d] and [...]
2) two years; the mature[e] bull:[3] the word (= interpretation?)[4] [...]
3) The bull:[f] the young bull of Baˁlu [...]
4) the heifer[g] (that?) will be slaughtered [...]
5) one year.

a Exod 17:14 etc. *b* Gen 31:10-12; 41:17-24; Dan 7-8

c Exod 12:5 etc. *d* Deut 7:13; 28:4, 18, 51 *e* Lev 1:3-10 etc. *f* Gen 32:16 *g* Gen 41:2, 3

[1] The various categories covered in this text seem to preclude the interpretation of *ḥlmm* as denoting "fattened animals" (for bibliography, see Pardee 1987:396). See also below, note 19 to "In a dream" (*b ḥlm*), line 28´.

[2] The term in this paragraph and at the beginning of the next is *ˀalp*, denoting the "bull" of various ages, while the "young bull" in line 3 is the *pr* ("heifer" is *prt*), apparently, as in Mari Akk., the immature bull, under a year in age. In Heb. *par* seems to fill the semantic slot of Ug. *ˀalp*, denoting the bull of various ages, for the age of the *par* can be defined, just as the age of the *ˀalp* is variously defined here.

[3] The Ug. phrase is *ˀalp dkr*, lit., "a male bovine." The point of the the qualifier *dkr* seems to be to indicate that the *ˀalp* has reached breeding age.

[4] The word *rgm* appears here near the end of the line. Because of the state of the text, it cannot be determined whether *rgm* here indicates that the interpretation follows. Because the ends of most lines have disappeared, it is also impossible to determine with what frequency *rgm* recurs. Its presence again in line 7, however, can be taken as an indication that it has a structural function in this text.

6) The horse[h] of ʿAṯtartu and the horse of Š[...][5]
7) and if the horse falls over:[6] [i] the word (= interpretation?) [...]
8) that arrives (where) the man[7] (is) [...].

9) And the donkey [...] donkey [...]
10) and ditto[8] [...]
11) and BN [...]
12) to the man, the donkey [...]
13) and that to the harness[9] [...]

14) And the flock:[j] the goat[k] [...]
15) the kid, offspring of [...]
16) the lamb [...][10]
17) son(s) of Baʿlu[11] [...]
...[12]
18′) [...] the servant-girl[13] [...]
19′) [...]

h 2 Kgs 23:11
i Judg 7:13; Jonah 3:4
j Gen 31:10
k Dan 8:5
l Deut 16:9; 23:26
m Gen 40:1 etc.

20′) The *nʾit*-tool[14] [...]
21′) then the *nʾit*-tool [...]
22′) spe[ak],[15] your servant [...]

23′) The worker (or: the work)[16] (with) the *ḫrmṯt*-tool[17] [l] [...]

24′) And the cups (of) ŠQYM/T[18] [...]
25′) the sons of the cup-bearers[m] [...]
26′) KBDT the personnel [...]

27′) The sandals [...]

28′) In a dream[19] [...]
29′) face of [...]

30′) The men (personnel) (and) the women [...][20]
31′) barley [...]

32′-34′) [...]

[5] It is now clear that the deities here are not ʿAṯtartu and ʿAnatu, as the original editor thought; unfortunately, all that can be said about the second phrase with *śśw*, "horse," is that it begins with the letter {š}. From an administrative text discovered in 1986 at Ras Shamra, we know that other deities at Ugarit had horses, living flesh-and-blood horses, for which rations of grain were issued (see Pardee 1988b; Bordreuil 1990). This omen seems, therefore, to deal with the appearance in a dream of a horse belonging to the goddess ʿAṯtartu and, plausibly, another deity whose name begins with {š}, such as šapšu. The sources are not of a kind to tell us whether particular types of horses went under the heading of "horses of X-deity" or whether the horse was identified simply by the presence of the deity in the dream. The association of ʿAṯtartu and the horse is particularly well attested in ancient Near Eastern iconography (Leclant 1960; for further bibliography, see Pardee 1989-90:468-70).

[6] One may surmise that the fall of the horse was a negatively polarized omen.

[7] The word for "man" here and in lines 12 and 26′ is *bnš*, which also appears in line 30′, along with *ʾaṯt*, "women," to designate one of the principal categories of entities covered by this text. On the usage of *bnš* in these divinatory texts, see note 10 to RIH 78/14 (text 1.91).

[8] As in RS 24.247:6, 12, 18, *mṯn* may mark the repetition of the entity whence the prognosis is drawn. See text 1.90 above.

[9] The same word for "harness," *mdl*, is used here as in the mythological texts (e.g., in the ʾAqhatu text, *CTA* 19 ii 52, 57 [text 1.103]), though the word for "donkey" here, *ḥmr*, is not the usual one (Dānīʾilu mounts a *ʿr*). The word *ḥmr* appears in the mythological texts only in the passage of the Kirta story where noisy animals keep the king of the besieged city from sleeping (*CTA* 14 iii 121, v 225 [text 1.102]).

[10] This paragraph opens with the generic term, *ṣʾin*, and three specific terms are extant, *ʿz*, "goat," *llʾu*, "kid," and *ʾimr*, "lamb."

[11] It is uncertain what the function of this phrase is in the text. It could mean "sons of the owner," but the presence of Baʿlu in line 3, where the presence of the deity is plausible because of the presence of deities in the following paragraph, leads me to prefer the same interpretation here.

[12] Some fifteen to twenty lines may have disappeared in the lacuna.

[13] Because of the state of the text, it is impossible to determine whether *ʾamt* constitutes the principal category of this paragraph, i.e., servants seen in dreams, or whether the appearance is incidental (like *bnš* in lines 8, 12, 26′, and, apparently *ʿbd*, "(male) servant," in line 22′). In any case the following paragraph initiates a sequence dealing with tools, not, primarily at least, persons.

[14] The word *nʾit* is attested in both Ug. and Akk. writing and denotes a type of tool that the sources do not allow us to define precisely (for bibliography, see Pardee 1987:425).

[15] The text reads {trg[-]}, perhaps to be restored as a form of the verb *rgm*, "to speak," though the subject cannot be determined.

[16] *mʿbd* could be either a *m*-preformative noun or a D-stem participle.

[17] Heb. *ḥermēš* seems to designate a type of sickle, but the Ug. term may denote a tool of similar shape but different function (Healey 1983a:50; Huehnergard 1987:130).

[18] The tablet is broken in such a fashion as to preclude determining whether the word here is the same as in the following line (*šqym*, "those who give drinks") or a feminine form from the same root.

[19] The phrase *b ḥlm* seems to support the interpretation of the text as dealing with dreams, and the repetition of the term here seems to indicate a shift in structure. The state of the text does not allow us to know, however, whether that shift was from the catalogue of entities to more general statements or, as some of the following vocabulary seems to indicate, from non-human to human entities.

[20] A similar expression of what appears to be the merismus "men – women" is found in RS 24.277: 23-26 (see notes 26, 27 to that text [1.92]).

REFERENCES

Bordreuil 1990; Healey 1983a; Huehnergard 1987; Leclant 1960; Oppenheim 1956:179-373; Pardee 1987; 1988b; 1989-90; forthcoming; Virolleaud 1965.

4. INCANTATIONS AND RITUALS

UGARITIC LITURGY AGAINST VENOMOUS REPTILES (1.94)
(RS 24.244)

Dennis Pardee

Three Ugaritic texts dealing specifically with the problem of venomous serpents have been discovered: this one, a very fragmentary text found along with this one (RS 24.251+), and RS 1992.2014 (translated below as text 1.100). The first two texts (*editio princeps* by Virolleaud 1968:564-580) were found in the archive of the "prêtre aux modèles de poumon et de foies" (on this building, see introduction to 1.92) and by their liturgical form reflect that person's interest in ritual (see on RS 24.266 [1.88]), whereas the third is an incantation in the narrower sense of the word.

This text consists of three major sections, of which the first is divided into twelve subsections. In these subsections the equine heroine, seeking a vanquisher of venomous serpents, sends a message to twelve deities. The first eleven, all important members of the Ugaritic pantheon, react with typical snake-charming gestures but go no further. Only the twelfth, Ḥôrānu, responds effectively and, in the second (or thirteenth) section, performs a ritual that renders the serpent venom powerless. The final section presents the negotiations between Ḥôrānu and the mare in view of marriage.

The text itself does not constitute a pure incantation, and in that respect is unlike RS 1992.2014 (text 1.100). Each of the pleas by the mare to a deity does contain, however, the recitation (*mnt*) of a brief incantation expressed in terms proper to a snake charmer (*mlḫš*). The quasi-narrative form of the text, its mythological features, and the dialogical form of the last paragraphs have led to the proposal that this text may constitute one of the few relatively clear examples in Ugaritic literature of a ritual in mythological form, that is, a ritual against venomous reptiles of which this text provides the libretto (Pardee 1978a:108; 1988a:225).

The Mare Seeks an Ally Capable of Vanquishing Venomous Serpents (lines 1-60)

The mother of the stallion, the mare,[1]
    the daughter of the spring, the daughter of the stone,[a]
    the daughter of the heavens and the abyss,[2] [b]
Calls to her mother, Šapšu:[3] [c]

Message to ʾIlu (lines 2-7)

Mother Šapšu, take a message
    to ʾIlu at the headwaters of the two rivers,[d]
    at the confluence of the deeps:[4] [e]
My incantation[5] for serpent bite,
    for the scaly serpent's[6] poison:[7]
From it, O charmer,[f] destroy,
    from it cast out the venom.[g]
Then he binds the serpent,
    feeds the scaly <serpent>,
    draws up a chair and sits.[8]

Message to Baʿlu (lines 8-13)

She again calls to her mother Šapšu:
Mother Šapšu, take a message

a Jer 2:27 *b* Gen 7:11; 8:2; 49:25; Deut 33:13; Ps 107:26; Prov 8:27-28 *c* 2 Kgs 23:11 *d* Cf. Gen 2:10-13; Ezek 47:1-12 *e* Cf. Deut 8:7 *f* Isa 3:3; Jer 8:17; Ps 58:6; Qoh 10:11 *g* Deut 32:33; Pss 58:5; 140:4; Job 6:4

[1] The Ug. phrase is *ʾum pḥl pḥlt*, the last two words being masculine and feminine nominal forms from the root *pḥl*. In the various Semitic languages, the root expresses primarily the reproductive capacities of males, be they human, animal, or vegetal. The terms used here do not necessarily denote a particular species. In Ug. *pḥl* seems, nonetheless, to be used primarily for equids (Pardee 1979:405-406; Dietrich and Loretz 1986b).

[2] Though the entities named here are certainly projected into the divine realm, the *ad hoc* nature of the list becomes evident by comparison with the mythological texts, on the one hand, and the rituals, on the other, for the entities named here are not attested as divinities in these other sources. Both "heavens" and "abyss" appear in these sources, but in combination with other entities: *ʾarṣ w šmm*, "earth and heavens," and *ǵrm w thmt*, "mountains and waters (of the abyss)," appear as double deities in the Ug. "pantheon" texts and rituals dependent thereupon (see Pardee forthcoming on RS 1.017 and RS 24.643). Note finally that vocalized forms of *šmm* and *thmt* (i.e., a feminine form of *thm*) appear in adjacent entries in one of the polyglot vocabularies (Nougayrol 1968 text 137 iii 33′ 34′). The root *thm* appears in three forms in Ug., *thm*, singular, designating the body of fresh waters lying under the earth, *thmt*, and *thmtm*, representing either the plural and the dual or the plural without and with "enclitic" *-m* (see below note 4). A fourth form, a singular form bearing the feminine morpheme *-at*, is also attested in syllabic script in the polyglot vocabulary just mentioned (cf. Huehnergard 1987:184-185).

[3] Šapšu, the sun deity, is feminine at Ugarit. On the link between the horse and the sun, see Delcor 1981:101-102.

[4] The address of each of the twelve deities is indicated in each commission. Some are well known from other texts, whereas some of the information provided by this text is new. Though similar to descriptions elsewhere of ʾIlu's abode (see note on *CTA* 2 iii 4 [text 1.86]; cf. *CTA* 17 vi 48 [text 1.103]), this one is unique in using the phrase *ʿdt thmtm*, "the meeting-place of the deeps," in place of *ʾapq thmtm*, "the fountains of the deeps."

[5] *mnt*, from *mny*, "to count," appears to have a semantic range similar to Akk. *minûtu*, "recitation," which can be used for the recitation of an incantation. If that is the correct interpretation of the word here (for discussion and bibliography see Pardee 1988a:206-208), the problem arises as to why the mare is sending a message containing the recitation of an incantation. I have explained the literary structure as consisting of a test sent by the mare to a series of deities, her real goal being marriage with the one who reacts most capably (1979:407-408).

[6] On the particular importance of the word *ʿqšr*, lit., "the one that sloughs its skin," see Bordreuil 1983.

[7] The word for "poison" here is *šmrr*, "that which produces bitterness" (on *mrr*, "bitter," see Pardee 1978b:249-288). The word for "venom" in the next verse is *ḥmt*, cognate to Heb. *ḥēmāh*, apparently from the root *yḥm*, a by-form of *ḥmm*, "be hot."

[8] For the interpretation of this verse as reflecting snake-charming devices, see Astour 1968:17-19, and for the interpretation of these devices

to Baᶜlu on the heights of Ṣapānu:[9]
My incantation for serpent bite,
for the scaly serpent's poison:
From it, O charmer, destroy,
from it cast out the venom.
Then he binds the serpent,
feeds the scaly serpent,
draws up a chair and sits.

Message to Dagan (lines 14-18)
She again calls to her mother Šapšu:
Mother Šapšu, take a message
to Dagan in Tuttul:[10]
My incantation for serpent bite,
for the scaly serpent's poison:
From it, O charmer, destroy,
from it cast out the venom.
Then he binds the serpent,
feeds the scaly serpent,
draws up a chair and sits.

Message to ᶜAnatu-wa-ᶜAṯtartu (lines 19-24)
She again calls to her mother Šapšu:
Mother Šapšu, take a message
to ᶜAnatu-wa-ᶜAṯtartu in ᵓInbubu:[11]
My incantation for serpent bite,
for the scaly serpent's poison:
From it, O charmer, destroy,
from it cast out the venom.
Then he[12] binds the serpent,
feeds the scaly serpent,
draws up a chair and sits.

Message to Yariḫu (lines 25-29)
She again calls to her mother Šapšu:
Mother Šapšu, take a message
to Yariḫu in Larugatu:[13]
My incantation for serpent bite,
for the scaly serpent's poison:
From it, O charmer, destroy,
from it cast out the venom.
Then he binds the serpent,
feeds the scaly serpent,
draws up a chair and sits.

Message to Rašap (lines 30-34)
She again calls to her mother Šapšu:
Mother Šapšu, take a message
to Rašap in Bibitta:[14]
My incantation for serpent bite,
for the scaly serpent's poison:
From it, O charmer, destroy,
from it cast out the venom.
Then he binds the serpent,
feeds the scaly serpent,
draws up a chair and sits.

Message to ᶜAṯtartu (lines 34a-e)[15]
<She again calls to her mother Šapšu:
Mother Šapšu, take a message
to ᶜAṯtartu in Mari:[16]
My incantation for serpent bite,
for the scaly serpent's poison:
From it, O charmer, destroy,
from it cast out the venom.

as falling short of the mare's expectations, Pardee 1978a:105-106. According to the latter interpretation, each of the first eleven deities is depicted as a simple snake charmer, capable of dealing with only a limited number of serpents, while Ḥôrānu acts on a grand scale, dissipating the venom in its entirety.

[9] Baᶜlu's home is consistently described as in the *mrym* (or, in other texts, the *ṣrrt*) *ṣpn*, terms denoting the heights and the recesses of Mount Ṣapānu. This was the West Semitic name for Mount Casius, modern Jabal al-Aqraᶜ, located on what is today the frontier between Syria and Turkey, some forty-five kilometers north of Ras Shamra as the crow flies. For bibliography, see Pardee 1987:442-443; 1988a:134-135; 1989-90:437, 445, 472, 494.

[10] Ancient Tuttul on the Baliḫ, modern Tell Bi'a, was particularly associated with Dagan in the high Amorite period. Dagan is a deity of fertility, particularly that of the grain (for bibliography, see Pardee 1989-90:446-448).

[11] In the Baᶜlu texts, *ᵓinbb* is attested as the home of ᶜAnatu (*CTA* 1 ii 14; 3 iv 78 [text 1.86]). Here we meet most acutely the problem of the relationship between ᶜAnatu and ᶜAṯtartu, for they appear in this section as a double deity, while ᶜAṯtartu appears again as an independent deity in line 34a (on the textual problem there, see note 15 below). For discussion and bibliography, see Pardee 1988a:48-50; 1989-90:464-466, 468-470.

[12] The verbal form does not reflect the gender of the deity addressed, indicating that the encapsulated incantation formula is presented as directed to a (male) serpent charmer, as is indicated in the preceding verse ("O charmer"). For this interpretation, see Pardee 1988a:209-210.

[13] The interpretation of *lrgt* was mysterious until the existence of a town named Larugatu was discovered in the texts from Ebla (bibliography in Pardee 1988a:211; 1989-90:490). The data are still too sparse to allow an explanation for the presence there of the principal West Semitic moon deity.

[14] The link between Rašap and the Anatolian town of Bibitta was established by Barré (1978) and this explanation supersedes all attempts at explanations of *bbt* based on Semitic etymology (bibliography in Pardee 1988a:211; 1989-90:473-475, 483).

[15] The paragraph dealing with ᶜAṯtartu of Mari was accidently omitted by the scribe, who noted his mistake on the left margin of the tablet as follows: *ᵓaṯr ršp ᶜṯtrt ᶜm ᶜṯtrt mrh mnt nṯk nḥš*, "After Rašap, ᶜAṯtartu: '... to ᶜAṯtartu in Mari: My incantation for serpent bite'" (in other words: "Insert after the paragraph on Rašap the one on ᶜAṯtartu, whose address is at Mari"). The neat abbreviation of an entire paragraph in a few words shows that the scribe was not only well aware of the repetitious nature of the text he was inscribing (how could he not be?), but had grasped perfectly well the distinctive features of each paragraph, i.e., the proper sequence in a list, the divine name, and the address. In the second serpent incantation text (see introduction), where essentially the same deities are mentioned according to different structural principals (i.e., by pairs, usually without address) but in essentially the same order, ᶜAṯtartu is replaced by a related double-deity, ᶜAṯtaru-wa-ᶜAṯtapir (RS 24.251:41′, cf. Pardee 1988a:242, 252-253). On this and other "haplographic marginalia" see Hallo 1977.

[16] Mari, modern Tell Hariri on the middle Euphrates, is one of the principal sources of information on life in upper Mesopotamia in ca. 1750 BCE, the heyday of the Amorites. On the identification of a temple of ᶜAṯtartu discovered there, see discussion and bibliography in Pardee 1988a:211; 1989-90:468-470.

Then he binds the serpent,
 feeds the scaly serpent,
 draws up a chair and sits. >

Message to Ẓiẓẓu-wa-Kamāṯu (lines 35-39)
She again calls to her mother Šapšu:
Mother Šapšu, take a message
 to Ẓiẓẓu-wa-Kamāṯu in Ḫurriyatu:[17]
My incantation for serpent bite,
 for the scaly serpent's poison:
From it, O charmer, destroy,
 from it cast out the venom.
Then he binds the serpent,
 feeds the scaly serpent,
 draws up a chair and sits.

Message to Milku (lines 40-44)
She again calls to her mother Šapšu:
Mother Šapšu, take a message
 to Milku in ^{c}Aṯtartu:[18] [h]
My incantation for serpent bite,
 for the scaly serpent's poison:
From it, O charmer, destroy,
 from it cast out the venom.
Then he binds the serpent,
 feeds the scaly serpent,
 draws up a chair and sits.

Message to Kôṯaru-wa-Ḫasīsu (lines 45-50)
She again calls to her mother Šapšu:
Mother Šapšu, take a message
 to Kôṯaru-wa-Ḫasīsu in Crete:[19]
My incantation for serpent bite,
 for the scaly serpent's poison:
From it, O charmer, destroy,
 from it cast out the venom.
Then he binds the serpent,
 feeds the scaly serpent,
 draws up a chair and sits.

Message to Šaḥru-wa-Šalimu (lines 51-56)
She again calls to her mother Šapšu:
Mother Šapšu, take a message
 to Šaḥru-wa-Šalimu in the heavens:[20]
My incantation for serpent bite,
 for the scaly serpent's poison:
From it, O charmer, destroy,
 from it cast out the venom.
Then he binds the serpent,
 feeds the scaly serpent,
 draws up a chair and sits.

Message to Ḥôrānu (lines 57-60)
She again calls to her mother Šapšu:
Mother Šapšu, take a message
 to Ḥôrānu in Maṣūdu:[21]
My incantation for serpent bite,
 for the scaly serpent's poison:
From it, O charmer, destroy,
 from it cast out the venom.[22]

Ḥôrānu Takes Care of the Problem (lines 61-69)
She (the mare)[23] turns (her) face to Ḥôrānu,
 for she is to be bereaved of her offspring.[i]
He (Ḥôrānu) returns to the city of the east,
 he heads

h Deut 1:4; Josh 12:4; 13:12, 31
i Gen 27:45; Isa 49:20

[17] Of the three proper names in this entry, only Kamāṯu, generally identified with the deity Kemōš known from the Hebrew Bible (bibliography in Pardee 1989-90:453), is known. The divine name's formation is that of the double divine name, but here the first element is unidentified, though one can say that its common explanation by Semitic *ṭīṭ*, "mud," is *prima facie* unlikely because of the name's writing with {ẓ} in Ug., in texts where {ṭ} and {ẓ} are not confused (Pardee 1988a:212, n. 64). The city where Ẓiẓẓu-wa-Kamāṯu dwelt has not been identified (Astour 1968:20).

[18] The geographical name is written like, and was plausibly identical with, the divine name ^{c}Aṯtartu, and the proper explanation of this entry and of the parallel entry in the second serpent incantation text (RS 24.251+) was first given by Astour 1968:19, 30. The importance of this datum for the interpretation of RS 24.252:2 was first understood by Margulis (1970:344; history of discussion in Pardee 1988a:94-97, 212, 252). Milku is poorly attested in the Ug. literature but is plausibly related to the deity Milkom, identified with the Ammonites in the Hebrew Bible. A connection with the Punic *molek*-sacrifice is disputed (Heider 1985) and unlikely. The home of Milku is situated in ^{c}Aṯtartu, the town located northeast of the Sea of Galilee (^{c}Aštārōt[-Qarnayim] in Heb.). This identification is rendered extremely likely by the parallelism of *^{c}ṯtrt* and *hdr^{c}y* in RS 24.252:2-3, essentially identical to ^{c}Aštārōt and ʾEdreʿī in Deut 1:4 and Josh 12:4; 13:12, 31, the two principal towns ruled by ^{c}Og, king of Bashan. Among recent discoveries at Ras Shamra is a text mentioning for the first time the deity and his home as a construct phrase, *mlk ^{c}ṯtrt*, providing evidence for the origin of the Phoenician deity Milk^{c}aštart (the text is RS 1986.2235:17′; see Pardee 1988b; Bordreuil 1990).

[19] In the case of the double-deity Kôṯaru-wa-Ḫasīsu, the first element corresponds to a deity well known from other ancient Near Eastern sources, while the second is basically an adjectival form meaning "wise," not known from other sources as an independent deity. Kôṯaru(-wa-Ḫasīsu) is the craftsman god at Ugarit, involved in building, manufacturing, and music-making. Here his home is fixed in Crete, while in the ʾAqhatu text (*CTA* 17 v 21, 31 [1.103]) it is in Egypt (Memphis). In the Ba^{c}lu cycle he is said to be domiciled both in Egypt and in Crete (*CTA* 1 iii 1-2, 18-19; 3 vi 14-15 [text 1.86]). This craftsman deity thus had shops in two of the principal centers of civilization and artisanship in the ancient Mediterranean world. In the syllabic versions of the "pantheon" texts from Ugarit, Kôṯaru is explicitly identified with Mesopotamian Ea; by inference from his home in Egypt, he is also identified with Egyptian Ptaḥ (see note 30 to the ʾAqhatu text [1.103]); and by inference from his other home further west in the Mediterranean world, with Hephaistos. For an overview with bibliography, see Pardee 1995.

[20] *CTA* 23 (1.87) deals primarily with the birth of this double-deity, the meaning of whose name is "Dawn-and-Dusk." It is debated whether these deities also represented the morning star and the evening star (Caquot, Sznycer and Herdner 1974:358, 361-363); one can doubt that such is the case because these rôles seem to fall specifically to ^{c}Aṯtaru and ^{c}Aṯtartu (see Pardee forthcoming on RS 1.009:4 and RS 1.017:18, 25).

[21] Ḥôrānu is closely associated with magic at Ugarit: he is invoked in the curse that Kirta calls down on his son's head (*CTA* 16 vi 55 [1.102]); here he is the only deity willing to vanquish venomous snakes; in the second serpent incantation (RS 24.251+ [see above, introduction]) he is ranked right alongside ʾIlu; and in RIH 78/20 [1.96] he works against sorcerers. For bibliography on this deity, see Pardee 1989-90:450-451. His domicile of *mṣd* is unidentified, except by etymological explanations. Theoretically, it could be either a proper noun designating a terrestrial cult place (such as Tuttul or Mari) or a common noun serving to designate his dwelling (such as "the heavens" in the case of Šaḥru-wa-Šalimu).

[22] The last tricolon of the previous sections is here omitted, the one in which the other deities were depicted as a snake-charmer. In its place is a long section depicting the mare appealing directly to Ḥôrānu and the latter carrying out a comprehensive program against serpent venom.

[23] That the subject here is *pḥlt* rather than *špš* seems to be indicated by the second clause, where *ṯkl* seems to indicate the worry of the equid,

for Great Araššiḫu,
for well-watered[j] Araššiḫu.[24]
He casts a tamarisk[25] [k] (from) among the trees,
the "tree of death"[l] (from) among the bushes.[m]
With the tamarisk he expels it (the venom),[n]
with the fruit stalk of a date palm he banishes it,
with the succulent part of a reed he makes it pass on,
with the "carrier" he carries it away.[26]
Then Ḥôrānu goes to his house,
arrives at his court.
The venom is weak as though (in) a stream,
is dispersed as though (in) a canal.[27] [o]

Ḥôrānu Weds the Mare (lines 70-76)
Behind her the house of incantation,[28]
behind her the house she has shut,
behind her she has set the bronze (bolt).

Ḥôrānu's Plea for Entry (lines 71-72)
Open the house of incantation,
open the house that I may enter,
the palace that I may come in.

The Mare's Requirements (lines 73-74)
Give as <my bride-price>[29] serpents,
give poisonous lizards as my bride-price,[p]
adders as my wife-price.[30] [q]

Ḥôrānu Assents (lines 75-76)
I hereby give serpents as your bride-price,
adders as your wife-price.

j 2 Sam 12:27
k Jer 48:6
l Cf. Gen 2:9
m Gen 2:5
n Exod 14:27
o Prov 5:16
p Gen 34:12; Exod 22:15, 16; 1 Sam 18:25
q Deut 23:19; Isa 23:17, 18; Ezek 16:31, 34, 41; Hos 9:1; Mic 1:7

rather than of the celestial orb.

[24] This name apparently reflects the Hurrian name for the Tigris (Astour 1968:23), though a city so named is unknown from presently available sources.

[25] The verb "to cast" here, i.e., *ydy*, is the same as that in the request to cast out the venom in the mare's message to the twelve deities. Though the verb is not used in this passage to express explicitly the requested casting out of the venom, its presence here at the beginning of the description of Ḥôrānu's acts may be interpreted as meaning that the following acts are intended to have the effect of carrying out the request. That is, by the act of casting pieces of wood in a particular fashion (see note 27) Ḥôrānu effectively casts out the venom. Just as this verse provides the explicit link with the mare's request by the repetition of the verb *ydy*, it also provides an explicit link with the ritual itself that Ḥôrānu performs in the following quadricolon, where the tamarisk (*ᶜrᶜr*) is the first of the plants mentioned. The identification of the "tree of death" (*ᶜṣ mt*) in the next line is unknown, however, and its function is thus unclear. Because the tamarisk is a desert tree, it appears plausible to see in "tree of death" an epithet of the tamarisk rather than the designation of a second type of plant. If such is the case, this verse mentions only the first of the four plants that appear in the following description of the ritual.

[26] As is appropriate in a magical rite, each of the acts is expressed by a punning formula (*ᶜrᶜr + ynᶜrn*!, *ssn + ysyn*, *ᶜdtm + yᶜdyn*, and *yblt + ybln*). For the identification of the plants in question, see Astour 1968:24-26. The last formula constitutes a *figura etymologica* based on the root *ybl*, "to bear, carry," but the plant designated as *yblt* has not been identified botanically (cf. Astour 1968:25).

[27] The entire preceding passage appears to reflect imitative magic: as the various types of wood float away, so the venom is dispersed, as though in water (Pardee 1978a:91-98, 105-106). Astour (1968:23-26) cited parallels in Mesopotamian magical literature for the use of various types of wood and plants in prophylactic rituals. The new Ug. incantation against serpents (RS 1992:2014 [text 1.100]) refers globally to wood so used as *ᶜṣ qdš*, "holy (pieces of) wood."

[28] Taking a clue from the fact that the only incantation mentioned in this text is the mare's (in each of the first twelve paragraphs — see above, note 5), I have interpreted this verse as marking a change of scene as compared with the preceding verses, i.e., a return to the mare's home (Pardee 1988a:219-220). She has, according to this view, shut herself up in her own house and will only open the door to a serious offer of marriage. Alternatively, one could consider the house in question to be Ḥôrānu's, the last mentioned in the text. That the following lines constitute a dialogue is clear from the change in persons (third to first); that one is female is indicated by the verbal forms in lines 70-71 ("she shut/set"). Because the content of the dialogue includes references to exchanges associated with marriage, it appears to be necessary to view the protagonists as male and female. Thus, though the subjects are not explicitly stated, it appears necessary to identify them as the primary male and female protagonists of this text, the mare and Ḥôrānu.

[29] The presence of the preposition *km* followed by *nḥšm* "serpents," whereas in the following line the same preposition is followed by *mhry*, "bride-price," has led many scholars to believe that the text here is faulty. Whether the word that fell out was also *mhry* or a synonym thereof cannot, of course, be known. I have surmised that the request for serpents as a bride-price, to make sense in context, should be interpreted as referring to the serpents with which Ḥôrānu has just dealt, i.e., devenomized serpents (Pardee 1978a:106). The terms for the reptiles in this passage are *nḥšm*, the generic word for "serpent" used up to this point in the text, *yḥr*, explained by Arabic *waḥrat*[un] as a type of poisonous lizard (Caquot 1969:252), and *bn bṯn*, "sons of the *bṯn*-serpent," where *bṯn* denotes some kind of asp or adder.

[30] The second word used to designate Ḥôrānu's contribution is *ᵓitnn*, meaning "gift" (derived from *ytn/ntn*). From context it may be interpreted as meaning "a gift (in view of marriage)." Given the rather transparent etymology of the noun, the biblical parallels for the word being used to designate a gift to a prostitute are not sufficient to prove that the mare in this Ug. text was of easy virtue (cf. Pardee 1978a:101).

REFERENCES

Astour 1968; Barré 1978; Bordreuil 1983; 1990; Caquot 1969; 1989; Caquot, Sznycer and Herdner 1974; Delcor 1981; Dietrich and Loretz 1980; 1986b; 1988; Gaster 1975; Heider 1985; Huehnergard 1987; Levine and Tarragon 1988; Margulis 1970; de Moor 1987; Nougayrol 1968; del Olmo Lete 1992; Pardee 1978a; 1978b; 1979; 1987; 1988a; 1988b; 1989-90; 1995; forthcoming; Tsevat 1979; Virolleaud 1961; 1962a; 1962b; 1968; Xella 1981.

UGARITIC RITES FOR THE VINTAGE (*KTU* 1.41//1.87) (1.95)

Baruch A. Levine, Jean-Michel de Tarragon, Anne Robertson

This is the most extensive Ugaritic temple ritual on record.[1] It describes the annual celebrations of the grape harvest at the Temple of Baal in Ugarit over the period of one month, in the autumn of the year. It highlights the New Moon, and other key days, especially the thirteenth and fourteenth of the month.

Two copies have been found, a fact which, in itself, indicates the canonical status of the ritual. In preparing the translation, *KTU* 1.41 :1-49 has been used as the base text, allowing for restorations from *KTU* 1.87: 1-53, a copy apparently made from *KTU* 1.41. *KTU* 1.41:50-55, which is appended to the principal ritual of *KTU* 1.41, will also be translated since it probably relates to the vintage festival.

KTU 1.41 was discovered during the campaign of 1929 in the residence of the High Priest, located not far from the Baal Temple, whereas *KTU* 1.87 was discovered during the campaign of 1954 in the Royal Palace of Ugarit. It was undoubtedly stored there for use by the king of Ugarit, who presided over the celebrations (Bordreuil and Pardee 1989:6, fig. 2.)

In listing sacrificial animals, the following abbreviations will be used: s.m. = small, male; s.f. = small, female; l.m. =large, male; l.f. = large, female.

Introduction: The Annual Time of the Vintage Rites (1a)
In the month of *Rišyn*.[2]

Dates of the Month for Celebration and Purification (1b-3)
On the New Moon[a] — cutting of the grape cluster.[3 b]
To Il[4 c] — 4 *šlmm* offerings.[5 d]
On the thirteenth — The pure king bathes himself.

The Main Event: The "First of the Tribute" Celebration (4-6a)
On the fourteenth: First of the tribute.[6]
And 2 s.m.[7] for the Lady of the temples,[8]
Birds for the staff of gods,
And 1 s.m. Elš,[9] the favored,
1 s.m., the gods.

The King Proclaims the Day (6b-12a)
The king is seated, the pure one.
And he clapped [his hands],[10 e]
And proclaimed the day.[f]
Then [the king] enters [the tem]ple
[with] a present[11] of [a cu]p and a chal[ice].
2 s.f.and a domestic pigeon[12] he prepares for Anat,[g]
and 1 l.m., 1 s.m. for Il.
And at the aperture:[13] [a libation] he pours.

Accompanying Burnt Offerings and Šlmm (12b-17a)
1 l.f. — the gods,
ṮKMN-w-ŠNM — 1 s.f.
Rashap — 1 s.f. — [all] as the burnt offering.[h]
And as *šlmm* offerings:
2 s.f. — the god,
1 l.m. and 1 s.m. — the gods,
1 l.f. — the gods.
Baal[i] — 1 s.m.
Athirat[j] — 1 s.m.
ṮKMN-w-ŠNM — 1 s.m.,

a Exod 40:2 *b* Judg 9:27 *c* Isa 14:13 *d* Lev 3; 7:11-18; Deut 27:7; 1 Kgs 3:15 *e* Isa 55:12; Ezek 25:6; Ps 98:8 *f* Lam 1:21 *g* Judg 3:31; 5:6 *h* Lev 1; 6:1-6; Jer 34:5 *i* Judg 6:25-32; 1 Kgs 16:31; 18:21-40; 2 Kgs 10:23-27 *j* 1 Kgs 15:13; 2 Kgs 23:4-7

[1] For the most recent treatment, see Levine and de Tarragon 1993.

[2] Ug. *Risyn* means "the first of the wine," and also "the best of the wine." This month fell in the autumn of the year: de Tarragon 1980:26.

[3] Ug. *šmtr* is taken as a Šafᶜel form of the root *mtr* "to cut," known in Arabic.

[4] Following is a list of gods and goddesses with their Heb. or other cognates for identification: Il = El, Akk. *ilu*; Anat = Anat; ṮKMN-w-ŠNM (identity unknown); Rashap = Resheph; Baal = Baal; Athirat = Asherah; Shalim = Shalem(?); [Baal] Ṣaphan = [Baal] Zaphon (see *m* below); Yariḫ, the moon god = Heb. *yarēaḥ* "moon"; Nikkal = Sum. NIN.GAL, the moon goddess; Shapash = Akk. *Šamaš*, the sun god; Yamm = Heb. *yam* "sea"; Ilib = "god of the father," or "Il is the father." (Cf. Gen 49:25, Heb. ᵓ*ēl* ᵓ*āb*); Athtart = Ashtoreth. Cf. 304, nn. 10 and 13.

[5] Ug. *šlmm* is taken as a cognate of Heb. *šelāmîm*, and both are seen as cognates of Akkadian *šulmānu* "gift of greeting" (see *d* above and Levine 1989:14-15). In the present ritual, *šlmm* contrasts with *šrp* "burnt offering," Heb. **miśrepôt* (see *h* above), suggesting that, like its biblical counterpart, the *šlmm* at Ugarit was mostly cooked, with some parts of the sacrificial animal burnt on the altar. A third kind of offering, "sacred meal" (Ug. *dbḥ*, cf. Heb. *zebaḥ*) was also prepared in this way. See *k* below.

[6] Ug. *argmn*, Heb. ᵓ*argaman* (also written ᵓ*argewān* in 2 Chr 2:6), may be an Anatolian-Hittite, or possibly a Hurrian word. In biblical usage it consistently designates royal purple but at Boğazköy it has the meaning "tribute," as it does here. It is unclear which connotation is primary. See *CAD* A 2:253.

[7] Most Ug. ritual texts distinguish between small and large sacrificial animals, and register their sex. Thus, male sheep and goats are listed as *s* (Heb. *śeh*, Akk. *šu*), and male cattle as *alp* (Heb. ᵓ*elep*, Akk. *alpu*). In a parallel fashion, small female animals are listed as *dqt* "small," and female cattle as *gdlt* "large" (Levine 1963).

[8] Ug. *bᶜlt bhtm* is one of several titles borne by goddesses who were in charge of temples. Cf. at Emar the title NIN.É.GAL-*li* "Lady of the Temple" (Arnaud 1985-86:372, no. 378, line 13).

[9] Elš (written *ilš*) is apparently a Hurrian divine name for the herald of the gods (Caquot 1978:573).

[10] The word for "his hands" is restored, producing *wmḥ* [*ydh*] "He clapped his hands." The same idiom occurs again in line 54.

[11] The reading of the word translated "present," Ug. *ṭgml*, is uncertain.

[12] The sense of "domestic pigeon" for Ug. *ynt qrt* assumes *qrt* to mean "town, city" as in Heb. and Phoen.

[13] The word translated "aperture," Ug. *urbt*, is taken as a cognate of Heb. ᵓ*arubbāh* "aperture, window, chimney" (Gen 7:11; 8:2; Hos 13:3).

Anat — 1 s.m.,
Rashap [k] — 1 s.m.
Circle of Il and Council of Baal — 1 l.f.
Shalim — 1 l.f.

The King Performs Rites at Midday (17b-24a)

And at midday,[14] inside the convening room[15] of the gods and the lords — goblets[16] and cups, thirty, fil[led].
And the entrance offering[17] that he brings to the royal chapel — a sacred meal [l] of myrrh oil, of blended oil; a gift of bee-honey, a domestic pigeon and two cages.[18]
And at the ledge(?)[19] — fourteen jugs of wine, ½ measure of flour.
At the steps of the altars of the chapel of the goddess — birds.

Two Series of Accompanying Burnt Offerings and Šlmm (24b-36a)

For Ṣaphan - 1 s.m.,
For "the Young Woman" — 1 s.m.,
and for [x] — [y],
[x] for Yariḫ,
1 l.f. for Nikkal,
1 l.f. for the Lady of the Temples,
birds for the staff of the gods,
1 l.f. — the gods,[20]
1 s.f. — Shapash,
1 l.f. — Rashap, [all] as the burnt offering.
And as *šlmm* offerings — same (as listed).

2 s.f. — the gods,
1 l.f. — the gods,
1 s.f. — ṮKMN-w-ŠNM,
1 s.f. — the Lady of the Temples,
2 s.f. — at the spring,[21] [all] as burnt offerings.
And as *šlmm* offerings — same (as listed).

The Regular Public Sacrifice: the Tamid of Ugarit (33b-38a)

1 l.f. for Baal Ṣaphan,[m]
1 s.f. for Ṣaphan,
1 l.f. for Baal of Ugarit,
1 s.m. for Ilib,
[x] [for Athi]rat,
And birds for [the staff of the gods].
Thirty times, and at the chapel of the Lady of the Exalted Temples, and atop the altars.

Special Rites for the First Quarter of the Month (38b-48a)

On the fifth, chapel of Il:
A shekel of silver, the *kubādu*[22] ceremony, and a sacred meal.
[x] for Athirat,
birds for the staff of the gods.
At the [pedestal] of the Baal altar:
1 l.f. for Baal,
1 s.f. for Ṣaphan,
And 1 s.f. for Baal of Ugarit, twenty-two times.
Elš, the favored — 1 s.m.
ŠMN, the favored, — 1 l.f.
And the pure king responds with a recitation.

On the sixth:
2 [s.m.] — ŠMN, the favored.
In addition to it: 1 l.f.
With a recitation he responds, the pure king.

On the seventh:
a) At the descent of the sun, the day is profane.[23]
At the setting of the sun, the king is profane.
b) The rising of Shapash, and the circuit of Yamm;
The setting of Shapash, and the circuit of 'the King.' [n]

k Exod 12:27; Judg 16:23; 1 Sam 9:12
m Exod 14:2, 9; Num 33:7
n Ps 113:3

[14] For the sense of "at midday; in the light of day" for Ug. *burm* see Levine 1983; de Tarragon 1989:137. This time-indicator contrasts with *wlll* "and at night," and *lpn ll* "before night" in other ritual texts (*KTU* 1.39, line 12; 1.49, line 9; 1.50, line 7).

[15] The sense of "inside the convening room" for Ug. *lbrmṣt* assumes the phonetic shift of *beth* to *mēm*, so that original *lbrbṣt* became *lbrmṣt*. If correct, **rbṣt*, like Ug. *trbṣ* "corral, sitting place" in the Kirtu epic (*KTU* 1.14, ii, 3; text 1.102) would refer to a meeting room, most likely for priests and others: Levine and de Tarragon 1993:86, 96, Fig. 1.

[16] Ug. *dṯt* is rendered "goblets" from context, and based on Egypto-Semitic *daši* "cup," in the Amarna vocabulary (*CAD D* 119).

[17] The word translated "entrance offering" is Ug. *mᶜrb*, lit., what is brought in. It is cognate with Heb. *maᶜărāb* "exchange" (Ezek 27:9), and Akk. *irbu* "offering (presented at the gate when entering a temple)" (*CAD I* 173, 175).

[18] Ug. *ḥṯm* is rendered "cages" from context, and based on Akk. *ḫīšu* "basket, nest" (*CAD H* 206).

[19] The translation "ledge" for Ug. *ǵr* is uncertain: Levine and de Tarragon 1993:96-97. Others have taken it to mean "cave," cognate with Heb. *meᶜārāh* (Blau and Greenfield 1970).

[20] On the tablet, this entry is written again, in error.

[21] Ug. *nbk* connotes a natural spring, but as used here it likely designates a metallic or stone basin, or reservoir, similar to Akkadian *apsû* "the deep" and Heb. *yām* "sea" (1 Kgs 6:23-26), both of which designate reservoirs located in temple courtyards. See Levine and Hallo 1967:51.

[22] The *kubādu* ceremony is known at Emar. As its name suggests, it served to "honor" the gods by offering them gifts. It was often part of larger, annual celebrations including processionals. Fleming 1992:167-169; Huehnergard 1987:135; Sivan 1984:237-238; Levine and de Tarragon 1993:98-102. Others have taken Ug. *kbd* merely to signify "honor, gift" and some have even translated it as "liver" (Heb. *kābēd*), a word attested in Ug. On that basis, it would merely designate part of a sacrificial animal. See text 1.122, n. 10 and text 1.124, n. 18, below (pp. 428, 437).

[23] Two alternative translations are provided for the record of the seventh day because there is genuine ambiguity about some of the terms of reference employed in this couplet. In Ug. it reads:
ṣbu špš wḥl ym
ᶜrb špš wḥl mlk
De Tarragon (translation a) takes the verb *ṣbu* to be synonymous with *ᶜrb* in describing the setting of the sun, and *ym* to mean "day." He further explains *ḥl* as cognate with Heb. *ḥol* "profane." On this basis, the text is recording that at the end of the sacred day the king (*mlk*) became profane once again.

An Addendum for the New Moon (48b-49)
On the New Moon:
2 s.m. for Athtart.

Rites Performed by the King on the Roof of the Baal Temple (50-55)
When the king offers sacrifice[o] to PRGL.ṢQRN[24] on the roof,[p]
there are f[our] and four stands bearing *azmr*[25] fruit [placed] on it.
1 s.m., as the burnt offering,
1 l.m, 1 s.m., as the *šlmm* offering.
Seven times, each, on it (=the roof).
The king offers a reci[tation].
a) At the setting of the sun, the king is profane.
b) The setting of Shapash, and the circuit of 'the King.'
[He wears] beautiful garments;[26]
He claps [his hands].
They are brought back[27] into the temple,
And when he is there,[28] he raises his ha[nds] to heaven.[q]

o Lev 3; 7:11-18; Deut 27:7; 1 Kgs 3:15 *p* 2 Kgs 23:12; Jer 19:13; 32:29,48:38; Zeph 1:5 *q* Exod 9:29; 1 Kgs 8:22; Ps 63:5; Lam 3:41; Ezra 9:5

Levine (translation b) understands the couplet to represent the actual words recited by the officiant, the opening lines of a liturgy. On this basis, it expresses a cosmic perception, from East to West, affirming that Il and his successor, Baal, ruled the entire universe, and had defeated Yamm, the sea god of the western horizon.

[24] The identity of PRGL.ṢQRN, a non-Semitic, probably Hurrian divine name is unknown.

[25] Ug. *azmr* is taken as a cognate of Neo-Assyrian *zamru* "a tree or shrub and its edible fruit" (*CAD* Z 40-41).

[26] The translation "[He wears] beautiful garments" is based on a restoration: *wl[bš] ypm*.

[27] The translation "They are brought back" reflects the partial restoration: *t[ṯ]ṯbn* = *tuṯaṯibūna*, a Šafel passive. Segert 1984:68, no. 54.46.

[28] "And when he is there" translates Ug. *wkm iṯ*. Existential *iṯ* (Heb. *yēš*, Aramaic *ˀîṯâi*) may convey the notion of presence. Gordon 1965:368-369, Glossary, no. 418.

REFERENCES

Text: *KTU*² 1.47; 1.87; Levine and de Tarragon 1993; de Moor 1987; del Olmo Lete 1987; 1989b:132; 1992:50-51, 73-87; de Tarragon 1980; 1989; Studies: Arnaud 1985-86; Blau and Greenfield 1970; Bordreuil and Pardee 1989; Caquot 1978; Fleming 1992; Huehnergard 1987; Levine 1963; 1989; Levine and Hallo 1967; Segert 1984; Sivan 1984.

UGARITIC INCANTATION AGAINST SORCERY (1.96)
(RIH 78/20)

Daniel Fleming

This Ugaritic magical text was found in 1978 not at Ras Shamra but at nearby Ras Ibn Hani, though it should be the same age.[1] The extant tablet is neatly inscribed but broken from the 16th line at the left edge across to the 22nd at the right. In spite of the good condition of the first 15 lines, interpretation is hindered by previously unknown terms. Clear references to sorcery and expulsion indicate an incantation, but the text lacks immediate literary counterparts at Ugarit or elsewhere to illuminate its focus or perspective. The two sections of the legible contents are introduced by repeated injunctions to drive off attack (lines 1, 9).[2]

Part I (lines 1-8)
(Baal) shall drive off the young man's accuser
— the affliction(?) of your staff, Rāpiˀu(?),
Baal, the affliction(?) of your staff.[3] [a]
So, you shall depart before the voice of the incantation priest,[4]
like[b] smoke through a chimney,[c]
like a snake up a pillar,
like goats to a rock,[d]
like lions to a lair.[5] [e]
Staff, attention!
Draw near, staff!

May it harm your back
and waste your figure.
May you eat the bread of fasting(?),[f]
may you drink without a cup(?), squeezing(?) (the water-skin),

a Exod 7:12; 8:1, 12; Num 17:23 *b* Deut 32:2; Hos 13:7-8; Ps 83:14-15 *c* Hos 13:3 *d* 1 Sam 29:3 *e* Jer 25:38; Ps 10:9 *f* Isa 30:20

[1] The first publication appears in Caquot 1978-79.

[2] See for recent discussion of the whole text, and the interpretation offered here, Fleming 1991:141-154.

[3] The awkward syntax that introduces each section is clarified by comparison of lines 1-2 with 9-10. Each leads with the pronouncement of expulsion and then elaborates on the divine actor, first Baal, then Horon. Horon is identified also as Ǵalmu, "Youth," and Baal by a broken title, perhaps Rāpiˀu as "Healer." The same parallel suggests that the attack comes from the human sorcerer (line 9), not some demons, *contra* the earlier studies by de Moor 1980b, Avishur 1981, Loretz and Xella 1982, and Caquot 1984. The malady is referred to as "the affliction(?) of your staff," with address to the magician who attacks by means of his staff (*ḫṭ*). A young man is the victim, though evidence is insufficient to diagnose impotence; so, Loretz and Xella 1982.

[4] The incantation priest (*ṯᶜy*) evidently pronounces the entire incantation, whose voice carries the power of the spell.

[5] Avishur (1981:18-20) discusses biblical comparisons for the assembled similes. For comparison of the Mesopotamian tradition with biblical use of simile, see Hillers 1983.

in the high country,
in the lowlands,
in the darkness,
in the sanctuary.[6]

Part II (lines 9-15)
Then (Horon) shall expel the sorcerer-accuser
— Horon, the magician,[g]
and Ǵalmu, the familiar.[7]
Go, you shall founder ...,
you shall find your tongue stammering,
you shall be tightly bound(?).[8]
The god clothed you,[h]
the god has stripped you.

O man, the one with the staff(s) is indeed gone to the underworld;
O human,[i] in weakness he is removed.

[Part III, lines 16 and following, increasingly damaged]

g Deut 18:10-11

h Gen 3:21; Isa 33:19

i Num 23:19; Jer 51:43; Job 25:6; 35:8

[6] The staff appears to be called on to turn against its holder. Shortage of drink is defined by obscure terms, here translated according to the suggestions of Watson 1992. Repetition reinforces the verbal force of the incantation, and the four points of reference iliminate all potential refuge from this curse.

[7] The root meanings "to unite" and "to know" for "magician" and "familiar" can produce nouns for either magic or friendship (see Smith 1984:377-380). As magician himself, Horon both empowers sorcery and can withdraw that power.

[8] All three curses have uncertain interpretation. The particle that introduces them allows either negative ("you shall not ...") or emphasis, and the command to "go" echoes "depart" of line 2, so likely addressed to the same attacker.

[9] This line shifts to the ailing man, now called "man"/"son of man" (human), with assurance of deliverance. The attacker is subjected to death, the very fate which threatened the young man.

REFERENCES

Avishur 1981; Caquot 1978-79; 1984; Fleming 1991; Hillers 1983; Loretz and Xella 1982; de Moor 1980b; Smith 1984; Watson 1992.

ᵓILU ON A TOOT (1.97)
(RS 24.258)

Dennis Pardee

Another text from the archive of the "prêtre aux modèles de poumon et de foies" presents the great god ᵓIlu as getting himself gloriously drunk and in need of a pick-me-up. This text provides one of the clearest examples of what I have termed a "para-mythological text," that is, one with mythological form or overtones but with a practical function (Pardee 1988a:265-266). The functional value of this text is evident not only from its content, that is, the passage from story to recipe, but also from its literary form, the myth being in poetic form while the recipe is in prose.

The structure of the first part of the myth follows ᵓIlu's progress from a feast to a drinking club to his private chambers. The drinking hall is the *mrzḥ* (Heb. *marzēaḥ*), a term used to describe a place, the group that meets there, and the socio-religious institution. Comparing the layout of the Baalshamin sanctuary at Palmyra, where there was a banqueting hall (indicated by the word *smk*ᵓ, literally "bench [for reclining while eating]"), dedicated by the members of a *mrzḥ*, located apart from the main sanctuary, I have suggested that the principal stages of ᵓIlu's progress correspond to the principal sections of his palace. (1) The feast would have taken place in a part of the palace (*b bth, b qrb hklh*, "in his house, within his palace," according to lines 1-2) corresponding to the position of the altar in a sanctuary and to a large room, relatively accessible to the public, in a palace such as the one at Ras Shamra; (2) the drinking club would have been located in a separate room or structure (*b mrzḥh*, "in his *mrzḥ*," according to line 15) corresponding to the banqueting area in the Baalshamin sanctuary and to a more intimate banqueting hall in a royal palace (a particular such room has not yet been identified in the palace at Ras Shamra);[1] (3) when ᵓIlu went home (*l bth, lḥẓrh*, "to his house, to his courts," according to lines 17-18) he would have gone to the private quarters of his palace, corresponding to the "holy of holies" in a sanctuary and to the living quarters of an earthly palace.

Once home ᵓIlu meets a "pink elephant," an apparition that has not yet been identified to everyone's satisfaction (see below, note 14). Whatever the form and nature of this mysterious being, ᵓIlu reacts by soiling himself and falling down in his refuse, a consequence of shock and inebriation. The goddesses ᶜAnatu and ᶜAṯtartu, who had already had a rôle to play at the feast, then go off, apparently to find the elements of a remedy for ᵓIlu, though the text breaks off here. When the text resumes, on the *verso* of the tablet, the goddesses are again mentioned, apparently bringing relief to the father of the gods.

[1] Research on the *mrzḥ* in later sources (summed up in O'Connor 1986:71-72) has indicated that membership normally did not exceed a dozen plus one, the head of the group (the latter was designated *rb* in both Ug. and the later dialects).

The last part of the text is marked off from what precedes by a horizontal line on the tablet and provides the prosaic cure for alcoholic collapse and hangover. In it is found the first known reference to "the hair of the dog" in the context of relief from the effects of alcohol.

Though some have seen in this text an example of ancient humor (bibliography in Pardee 1988a:41), it appears just as plausible to see here a serious attempt, even a scientific one, according to the science of the time, at dealing with the aftereffects of an evening spent on the benches of the *mrzḥ*. No single English term renders perfectly Northwest Semitic *mrzḥ*, but "drinking club" is chosen below because it expresses the common denominator of the textual sources, viz., the consumption of wine, as well as the social but non-cultic form and function of the institution. The written sources span at least two millennia, from Ugarit[2] to early Rabbinic texts, and nearly always refer to wine, its production, its provision by one party for others, or its effects. In spite of the widely held view that the *mrzḥ* was a theater for the cult of the dead, not a single text known to date explicitly links the two phenomena and I doubt, therefore, that such a connection was ever more than incidental (see Pardee 1996 for a more detailed argument along these lines, with some recent bibliography). Though each *mrzḥ* seems to have had a deity as patron, there is no evidence that sacrifice, the *sine qua non* of old Northwest Semitic cultic activity, took place in the *mrzḥ*. Indeed, the silence regarding sacrifice in the textual sources is corroborated by the meagre archaeological data, which appear to show that the sacrificial cult and the *mrzḥ* were very different institutions. Regarding the temple of Baalshamin at Palmyra, see above, and for a description of the building at Ras Shamra for which the best claim as a *mrzḥ* may be made, the so-called "Temple aux Rhytons," see Mallet 1987; Pardee 1996:280.

ʾIlu Throws a Banquet for the Gods (lines 1-13)
ʾIlu slaughters[3] [a] game[b] in his house,
  prey[4] [c] within his palace,
  (and) invites[d] the gods to partake.
The gods eat and drink,
  they drink wi<ne> to satiety,[e]
  new wine[5] [f] to drunkenness.[g]

Yariḫu Plays the Dog (lines 4-13)
Yariḫu prepares his cup,
  (then) like a dog he drags it
  under the tables.[6] [h]
Any god who knows him[i]
  gives him food;[7]
But one who does not know him
  strikes him with a stick
  under the table.
He goes up to ʿAṯtartu-wa-ʿAnatu;[8]
  ʿAṯtartu gives him a *nšb*-cut (of meat),
  ʿAnatu a shoulder-cut.[9] [j]
The doorman[k] of ʾIlu's house yells at them,[l]

a Deut 12:15, 21; 1 Sam 28:24; 1 Kgs 19:21; Ezek 34:3; 2 Chr 18:2 *b* Ezek 13:21 *c* Gen 25:28; 27:3; Lev 17:13 *d* Isa 42:11 *e* Isa 23:18; 55:2; Ezek 39:19 *f* Judg 9:13; Mic 6:15; Prov 3:10 *g* Gen 9:21; 1 Sam 1:14 *h* Judg 1:7 *i* 2 Sam 7:20; Hos 5:3; Job 11:11 *j* Ezek 24:4 *k* 2 Sam 4:6 (LXX); 2 Kgs 7:10, 11; 1 Chr 9:17 etc. *l* Gen 37:10; Jer 29:27; Zech 3:2; Ruth 2:16

[2] The institution may already be attested a millennium earlier at Ebla (Archi 1988:103-104, n. 2).

[3] The verb is *dbḥ*, "to slaughter, cut the throat, sacrifice, make a (sacrificial) feast." When a deity performs the act, it is depicted as an act of food procurement. In another sense, the deity is depicted as a priest/king, for in the Ug. ritual texts the king is usually the subject of the verb *dbḥ*.

[4] The Ug. words *mṣd* and *ṣd*, both from the root *ṣd*, "to hunt," are here translated by "game" and "prey," i.e., the fruits of the hunt. The same root appears below as the verb expressing what ʿAnatu-wa-ʿAṯtartu do in reaction to ʾIlu's collapse (see note 17 below). Some have taken *mṣd* and *ṣd* as meaning "provisions, food," rather than game. Related words in other Semitic languages designate specifically, however, "travel provisions," and such provisions are "prepared," not "slaughtered/sacrificed" (the verb here is *dbḥ* < *ḏbḥ* = Heb. *zbḥ*), and one concludes that ʾIlu is being depicted here as presenting a feast including non-domesticated animals.

[5] The standard parallelism of *yn* and *trṯ* assure that {y} in line 3 is a mistake for {yn}. The second term is cognate to Heb. *tîrôš* and, less directly, to the Mesopotamian beer-goddess *Sirish*. The precise meaning of *trṯ* is uncertain, but certain Heb. passages suggest "new wine."

[6] Yariḫu's role is mysterious in this text, as is the key word in this line, written *gb*, for which the most diverse explanations have been given (see Pardee 1988a:35-39). I have accepted the meaning "cup" because of the general context of drinking; the literary problem with that interpretation is the image of a dog dragging a cup, filled with wine, under the table (note, however, that the formula is *km klb*, i.e., Yariḫu is not a dog, he behaves like one). In the next section, when the hunting goddesses ʿAṯtartu and ʿAnatu give good cuts of meat to Yariḫu, they are rebuked for wasting them on a dog (lines 9-13). It appears plausible, therefore, for Yariḫu's meal, like that of the gods seated at the table, to consist of both meat and drink (presented in reverse order). It remains mysterious why the moon deity is depicted in this text as acting like and being treated like a dog. Though there is plausibly a connection between the fondness of hunting deities (e.g., Artemis [see below note 17]) for dogs and ʿAṯtartu-wa-ʿAnatu's treatment of Yariḫu in this text, that does not explain why Yariḫu was chosen to play the rôle of the dog in this vignette. Perhaps the choice was owing to nothing more than the link between hunting goddesses and the moon, i.e., two of the associations of a goddess such as Artemis (hunting dog and moon) would have been fused in the person of Yariḫu (cf. Pardee 1988a:39-40). See further below, note 24, on the literary function of the word *klb*, "dog," in this text.

[7] There are what appear to be explanatory additions between lines 7-8 and 8-9 (see copy in Pardee 1988a:15). The first, *d mṣd*, "of the game," seems to offer an explanation of the word *lḥm*, "food," in line 7, but the other additions are less well preserved and their interpretation is uncertain. In my edition of the text (Pardee 1988a:45-46) I gave my reasons, epigraphic in nature, for believing that these signs do not represent remains of an earlier text; the latter idea has been put forward again by Dietrich and Loretz 1993, without explicit refutation of the epigraphic arguments.

[8] One may surmise, on the basis of the switches back and forth between the forms ʿAṯtartu-wa-ʿAnatu (here and in line 26′) and ʿAnatu-wa-ʿAṯtartu (lines 22-23) that these two deities had not fused into a double-deity to the same extent as in RS 24.244:20 (text 1.94), where ʿAnatu-wa-ʿAṯtartu appears as a deity entirely separate from ʿAṯtartu (lines "34a-e"). This vacillation seems to be owing to a perception of this double-deity as consisting more clearly of two separate deities, as not having become an indissoluble unity to the extent that some other double-deities had so done.

[9] The word *ktp*, "shoulder," is well known in Ug., but the precise meaning of *nšb* remains unknown. From *PRU* II 128 it appears certain that *nšb*, like *ktp*, designates a particular anatomical part, for in that text *nšb* appears alongside other terms designating cuts of meat from a bull.

so they don't give a *nšb*-cut to a dog,[m]
(so) they (don't) give a shoulder-cut to a hound.

ˀIlu Moves on to the Marziḥu (lines 14-16)
He also yells at ˀIlu, his father;[10]
(at which point) ˀIlu calls together[n] his drinking [group],[11]
takes his seat in his drinking club.[12] [o]
He drinks wine to satiety,
new wine to drunkenness.

ˀIlu Goes Home (lines 17-22)
(Then) ˀIlu heads for home,[p]
arrives at his courts,
(But) Ṯukamuna-wa-Šunama
(have to) bear[q] him along.[13]
ḤBY meets him,[r]
he who has two horns and a tail,[14]
(and) he bowls him over in his feces and his urine.[s]
ˀIlu falls[15] [t] as though dead,[u]
ˀIlu himself (falls) like those who descend into the earth.[16] [v]

ᶜAnatu-wa-ᶜAṯtartu Seek a Remedy (lines 22-?)
ᶜAnatu-wa-ᶜAṯtartu go off on the hunt,[17] [w]
[...]QDŠ[18][...]
...[19]

ᶜAṯtartu-wa-ᶜAnatu Bring Back and Apply the Remedy (lines 26′-28′)
[...] ᶜAṯtartu-wa-ᶜAnatu [...]
And in them[20] she[21] brings back [...].
When she heals (him), he awakes.[22] [x]

The Recipe (lines 29′-31′)
What is to be put on his forehead:[23] hairs of a dog.[24] And the head of the PQQ[25] and its shoot

m Cf. Deut 23:19
n 2 Kgs 6:23
o Jer 16:5; Amos 6:7
p Gen 24:38; 2 Sam 13:7, 8; Ps 122:1
q Isa 46:1, 3
r 1 Sam 9:18; 30:21
s Isa 36:12
t 1 Sam 28:20
u Ps 143:3
v Ezek 26:20
w Gen 27:3, 5; Lev 17:13; Job 38:39; cf. Ezek 13:18
x Job 14:12

[10] Though the function of the rebuke (*gᶜr*) of the goddesses is clear from context, neither the specific identity of the "doorman" nor his motive for rebuking ˀIlu are made explicit. It is generally assumed that ˀIlu is rebuked for keeping a disorderly house, but the position of the line at the transition from the *dbḥ* to the *mrzḥ* may indicate that the rebuke is also for dawdling. As to the problem of identity, none of ˀIlu's sons is elsewhere identified as a *ṯǵr*, "doorman." Judging from this text alone, the doorman may be either the double-deity Ṯukamuna-wa-Šunama or one of the two (on the filial status of Ṯukamuna-wa-Šunama, see below, note 13). However that may be, one may surmise that the right to rebuke the patriarch ˀIlu was linked with the sonship of the doorman rather than with the job itself.

[11] Though the first sign of this word is clear, the next two are damaged, while the end of the word has totally disappeared. I have suggested restoring {ˀa⌜šk⌝[rh]} and have explained the word as a ˀ-preformative noun from *škr*, "drink, get drunk" (the noun *škr*, "drunkenness," occurs above, line 4, and below, line 16).

[12] For this translation of *mrzḥ*, see the introduction.

[13] The double-deity Ṯukamuna-wa-Šunama here do the duty of the good son (*ᶜms*, "to bear up," as in the ˀAqhatu text, *CTA* 17 i 31, etc. [1.103]). The title of ˀIlu, *ˀab šnm*, seems, therefore, to mean "father of Šunama" (see note 52 to the ˀAqhatu text).

[14] The origin of the name *ḥby* remains in dispute. I have preferred an identification with the Egyptian bull Apis, *ḥpy* in Egyptian (Liverani 1969:339), because a bull-figure appears more appropriate to the times than the devil-figure proposed by some and because Apis' role as psychopomp, bearing mummies to the underworld, appears in keeping with ˀIlu's reaction which is in imitation of someone dying (discussion and bibliography in Pardee 1988a:60-62).

[15] The verb is *ql*, the same as that which designates war casualties in the birth omens text RS 24.247+ (text 1.90).

[16] ˀIlu is depicted as "dead" drunk, a rather striking image for an immortal. It is to be carefully noted, as regards the structure and meaning of the text, that ˀIlu is depicted as collapsing only on sight of the apparition and under the immediate effect of it — unfortunately the precise meaning of *ylšn*, here translated "bowls him over," is uncertain, in particular whether *ḥby* actually knocks ˀIlu down or performs some other act that brings about ˀIlu's collapse. In any case, there can be little doubt that ˀIlu's drunkenness is depicted as instrumental in his abasement, though not the primary cause of the fall itself.

[17] Because of the following lacuna and the difficulty of the vocabulary in the text on the *verso*, it is impossible to say whether *ṣd* here denotes literal pursuit of game or a broader sense of "go in search of (items for the remedy)." The links between ᶜAnatu and the classical hunting goddess Artemis (bibliography in Pardee 1989-90:464-466) make a literal hunt plausible.

[18] Though the signs are reasonably clear (the first sign can be read only as {q}, the second only as {d}, {l}, or {ˀu}, the third only as {š}), the broken context precludes an analysis of the form, whether verbal or nominal, in the latter case whether it be a common noun or a proper noun, and in this latter case whether it be a geographical name or divine name. The restoration here of {[mdbr] qdš}, as in *CTA* 23:65, may be considered plausible because of the similarity of circumstances in the two texts (deities hunting). It would, however, be entirely hypothetical and not particularly enlightening because of the uncertainty regarding the meaning of the expression *mdbr qdš* (see note 65 to text 1.87).

[19] A dozen or so lines may have disappeared in the break at the bottom of the tablet (Pardee 1988a:13, 66, corroborating Virolleaud 1962a:52).

[20] The antecedent of this pronoun was a masculine plural noun, now lost in the lacuna.

[21] The verbal forms here do not bear the *-n* of the feminine dual forms in lines 12-13 and 23; it is uncertain, therefore, whether the subject is one or the other of the two goddesses just mentioned (as here translated) or whether the verb is dual without *-n* (for a discussion and a proposed partial reconstruction, see Pardee 1988a:66-67).

[22] The explicit subject of the verb *nᶜr* (N-stem of *ᶜr*, "awaken") is uncertain, because of the state of the text. If there has not been a significant shift in the narrative focus since the text on the *recto* broke off, one can surmise that it is ˀIlu here who is waking up from the swoon into which he fell just before the departure of ᶜAnatu-wa-ᶜAṯtartu.

[23] The word here is *lṣb*, on which see note 30 to RS 24.247+ (text 1.90). Again, the antecedent of the pronoun is not clear: is it ˀIlu or has the shift from poetry to prose entailed a shift from the hero of the myth to the person suffering from alcoholic collapse?

[24] The use of dog hair, as well as of various other body parts and by-products of the dog, was wide-spread in antiquity (for some bibliographical elements, see Pardee 1988a:69-70). The literary motivation for the appearance of the dog at the feast in the first part of the text is indicated by the presence of the dog here, for these "para-mythological" texts are characterized by various types of puns and recall words between the two or more principal parts of the text (summary in Pardee 1988a:265). This literary fact does not explain, however, why it is that the moon deity was chosen to play the rôle of the dog (see above, note 6).

[25] Several have identified *pqq* as designating a plant of some kind, though the botanical identification remains uncertain (perhaps a type of colocynth, widely used as a cathartic, though with that identification the reason for the use of the word *rˀiš*, "head," to describe a part of a member of the gourd family is not clear).

he is to drink (mixed) together[26] with fresh olive oil.[27] [y]

y Gen 49:11; Exod 27:20; 30:24; Lev 24:2; Deut 32:14

[26] The adverbial form ʾ*aḥdh*, lit., "as one," is a technical term in the only type of medical text that has reached us from ancient Ugarit, viz., the hippiatric type (1.106), where it denotes "together" in the process of mixing the ingredients of a medicine (bibliography in Pardee 1988a:72).

[27] Lit., "blood of the olive of autumn," i.e., freshly squeezed. The formulation indicates that the olive oil functions as a vehicle for the *pqq*. Given that the chosen vehicle is an oil, it is apparently also intended to amplify the effect of the *pqq* and to have its own soothing effect on the stomach lining.

REFERENCES

Archi 1988; Caquot 1989; Cathcart and Watson 1980; Dietrich and Loretz 1981; 1988; 1993; Dietrich, Loretz and Sanmartín 1975b; Liverani 1969; Loewenstamm 1969; 1980; Loretz 1988; Mallet 1987; de Moor 1969; 1987; O'Connor 1986; del Olmo Lete 1992; Pardee 1987; 1988a; 1989-90; 1996; Pope 1972; Virolleaud 1962a:51-52; 1962b; 1968; Watson 1990b; Xella 1977.

A PUNIC SACRIFICIAL TARIFF (1.98)

Dennis Pardee

The "Marseilles Tariff" was discovered in 1844 in the city after which it is named, where it was brought from Carthage, though at what date is unknown. Other examples of tariff inscriptions, even more fragmentary than this one, have since been found at Carthage. The heading of the inscription seems to indicate that it was originally affixed to the temple of Baᶜl-Ṣaphon in Carthage. It may be dated palaeographically to the late fourth or early third century BCE. Its purpose was to regulate distributions among priests and offerers of the items presented to the sanctuary as well as to set the fees that were attached to certain offerings.

The text was inscribed on a large block of stone, broken in two pieces when discovered (40 x 33 cm and 25 x 22.5 cm). In addition to various small lacunae, the left side of the stone has entirely disappeared, at an angle from left to right, and thus no single line is intact, while the preserved portion of each line becomes progressively shorter as one reads from top to bottom.

The text is tightly structured, with the body of the document organized according to size/age categories of animals offered, the supplementary fees and portions accorded to the priests decreasing proportionately as the size of the animals listed decreases.

Comparison with the Book of Leviticus is interesting, but the differences turn out to be greater than the similarities. As regards the Carthaginian cult itself, this text is entirely devoted to its economic aspects, with no explicit statements regarding the theory, ideology, or motivations of these offerings. Comparison with the Ugaritic ritual texts also reveals great differences. Though some of the vocabulary and many of the animals offered as sacrifices are the same, the Ugaritic ritual texts deal primarily with the cultic calendar and with the allocation of sacrifices to various deities, passing over almost entirely the matter of distribution of offerings among the cultic officials and the offerers. Moreover, the concept of fee associated with certain offerings in the Punic text is absent from the Ugaritic texts, either because the texts are not primarily economic in nature and therefore do not mention such fees or because the practice of attaching monetary fees to sacrificial beasts had not yet arisen.

Prologue (lines 1-2)

Temple of Baᶜl-Ṣaphon.[1] (This) tariff[2] of (priestly)

[1] The divinity Baᶜl-Ṣaphon is first attested in Ug. ritual texts. The Sumero-Akkadian versions of the so-called "pantheon" texts from Ugarit provide explicit evidence for the meaning of the compound divine name, for in them *bᶜl ṣpn* is translated as "the weather deity (lord/god) of the mountain Ḫazi" (ᵈIM be-el ḪUR.SAG ḫa-zi [RS 20.024:4]; ᵈX DINGIR ḪUR.SAG *ḫa-zi* [RS 26.142:19′]; ᵈX ḪUR.SAG ḫa-zi [RS 1992.2004:7]). Ḫazi is attested in Hittite and Akk. texts as the name of the mountain north of Ugarit, modern Jabal al-Aqraᶜ, known to the Ugaritians as Ṣapānu. These same "pantheon" texts also prove that *bᶜl ṣpn* is not identical with *ṣpn*, for the latter occurs elsewhere in the very same texts, rendered in the Sumero-Akkadian versions as ᵈḪUR.SAG ḫa-zi, "the divine mountain Ḫazi." In later periods, Baᶜl-Ṣaphon was particularly venerated in Egypt and was invoked in the treaty between Esarhaddon and Baal of Tyre (7th century) as a punisher of rebels. For an overview of the sources and bibliography, see Bonnet 1992. It is of interest that a temple of Baᶜl-Ṣaphon existed at Carthage, for he was not the principal manifestation of the weather god in the Punic world, that honor belonging to Baᶜl Ḥammon.

[2] The final letter of the word *bᶜt*, "tariff," is lost in the lacuna, but the restoration is assured by other attestations of the word (cf. in particular CIS i 167:1 *bᶜt hmšʾtt ʾš tnʾ* ... "Tariff of (priestly) revenues set up by ..."). The etymology of *bᶜt* is uncertain (Cooke 1903:115 suggested either the hollow root *bᶜ*, which in Arabic denotes various contractual notions in the economic sphere, or the III-Y root *bᶜh*, "to seek," well known in Arabic and in Aram., hence "demand, requirement"). For a summary treatment of the tariff texts discovered in North Africa, see Lipiński 1992c.

revenues[3] [a] (has been) set up (by)[4] [the thirty men[5] who are in charge of the revenues], in the time when Ḥilleṣbaʿl the mayor[6] [b] was [head],[7] [c] (he being) the son of Bodtinnit the son of Bod[ʾešmun, and (by)[8] Ḥilleṣbaʿl] the mayor, (he being) the son of Bodʾešmun the son of Ḥilleṣbaʿl, and (by) [their] colleagues.[d]

The Offering of a Mature Bovine (lines 3-4)

In (the case of)[9] a mature bovine:[10] [e] (whether it be) a whole offering,[11] [f] or a presentation-offering,[12] or a whole well-being offering,[13] [g] the priests receive

a Ezek 20:40; 2 Chr 24:6, 9 *b* Judg 2:16-19; Ruth 1:1 etc. *c* Jer 39:9; Jon 1:6; Dan 1:3 *d* Isa 44:11 *e* Deut 7:13; 28:4, 18, 51 *f* Lev 6:15, 16; Deut 33:10; Ps 51:21; cf. 1 Sam 7:9 *g* Amos 5:22 etc.

[3] *mšʾtt*, the plural of *mšʾt*, lit., "what is lifted, brought," could in theory mean simply "gifts, offerings." Below in this text, however, it sometimes designates explicitly the monetary fee accompanying a sacrifice (lines 3, 6, 10), while here and elsewhere in this text (lines 17, 18, 20, 21), as well as in CIS i 167:1 (and probably in CIS i 170:1, also, badly damaged), it designates both the portion of an offering that goes to the priest and the fee that accompanies certain offerings. The real function of the term, therefore, is to denote the revenue to the priests in the case of each offering, whether it be a part of the offering itself or a payment in cash. One may infer that any offering could have three possible destinations: (1) part or all of the sacrifice could be burned on the altar of the deity; (2) part could go to the priest, who was also entitled to a monetary fee in some cases; (3) part could go to the offerer. The word is attested three times in the plural, always with the double feminine ending *-tt* (here; CIS i 167:1; 170:1). The Heb. equivalent is *maśʾēt* (<*maśśē*(ʾ)*t* <*manśiʾt*), pl. *maśʾōt* (<*maśśᵉʾōt* <*manśiʾāt*), i.e., without the double feminine ending in the plural.

[4] The formulation in Punic is active (*ʾš ṭn*[*ʾ šlšm hʾš*], "which the thirty men set up") and is only rendered by the passive here because of the long subject phrase. The verb *ṭnʾ* is the standard Phoenician/Punic verb for "erecting" a statue or other object offered to a deity and is also used for "establishing" a person in a position.

[5] The restoration of this number is derived from CIS i 3917:1 *šlšm hʾš ʾš ʿl hmšʾ*[*tt*], "the thirty men who are over [= in charge of] the (priestly) revenues."

[6] The term *špṭ* designated an elective function, that of "mayor" of a city. From Latin transcriptions it is known to have been pronounced *sufeṭ* (cf. Heb. *šōpēṭ*). The office was shared by two (or three) persons and lasted for one year only, though the title could be kept for life; the year being named eponymically after its suphetes (Sznycer 1977:567-576; Lipiński 1992b). The usage of *špṭ* to designate a "leader" goes back to the earliest Semitic sources, where it denotes a clan or tribal leader. Among the functions of such a leader was that of deciding differences between members of the group, but the position included much beyond the strictly forensic and the usual translation "judge" is therefore inadequate. Because the title of "mayor" could be kept for life at Carthage, the mention here of two "mayors" does not necessarily mean that they were holding the office when the inscription was made, simply that out of the thirty, two were serving or had at one time served as chief executive officers of the city.

[7] The meaning of the term *rb* is clear when used in compound phrases, such as *rb sprm*, "head of the scribes," but when used alone, in the absolute state, it is unknown just what socio-political function it designates (Sznycer 1977:585; Lipiński 1992a). In a context such as this one, *rb* may simply indicate that Ḥilleṣbaʿl son of Bodtinnit was head of the governing body of the Temple of Baʿl-Ṣaphon, the group of thirty who set the tariffs. In the text from which the restoration here is taken, CIS i 170:1, as well as in CIS i 132:4 and 3919:4, one finds only {r}, which may be the abbreviation of an abstract form of *rb*, "leadership, headship" (*ʿt r ḥlṣbʿl*, "at the time of the headship of Ḥilleṣbaʿl").

[8] The syntax of the last part of this prologue is not straightforward. The two final phrases introduced by the conjunction *w* do not seem to depend logically on the phrase *ʿt*, "at the time of," a technical term designating the position of Ḥilleṣbaʿl son of Bodtinnit vis-à-vis the group for, at least in the case of "and their colleagues," the phrase cannot be linked either with the function of head or with that of mayor. It would seem, therefore, that Ḥilleṣbaʿl son of Bodtinnit was named particularly because he was head of the group, that Ḥilleṣbaʿl son of Bodʾešmun then had to be named because he also had been, or was currently, mayor, and that "their colleagues" was tacked on at the end by courtesy.

[9] The prepositional formula *b ʾlp ... l khnm ksp* seems to be based on the so-called *beth* of price (*beth pretii*), though it is clear that the ten shekels do not constitute a price *per se*. The idiom is repeated at the end of the first clause *l khnm ksp ʿšrt 10 b ʾḥd*, "to the priests (go) ten (shekels) of silver for each."

[10] This text is structured primarily according to the category of size/age of sacrificial beasts. Thus the young bovine and the mature deer are together in the next paragraph because they are approximately equal in size. *ʾlp* denotes here, therefore, any mature bovine, whether bull or cow.

[11] The three types of sacrifice in this text are designated by the terms *kll*, *ṣwʿt*, and *šlm kll*. The first is usually compared to Heb. *kālīl* and is identified as a "whole (burnt) offering" because in the Hebrew Bible the *kālīl* and the *ʿōlāh* may be identical. This identification appears correct and the fact that the priest gets a portion of the meat does not constitute a particular problem: the offerer does not receive any part of the animal, which is divided up between the deity and his employees, the priests (the deity's portion was burnt on the altar while the priests lived from theirs). On the correct syntactic analysis of *ʾm*, "whether, or," and the related correct analysis of *kll* as an offering type rather than a word meaning "general rule," see Creason 1992.

[12] The *ṣwʿt* is usually identified by process of elimination with one or the other of the Heb. sacrificial types (if *kll* = *ʿlh* and *šlm kll* = *šlmym*, *ṣwʿt* can be neither of these and must be one of the other types of sacrifice), with the choice usually falling on the *ḥṭʾt*, "sin-offering" (Ginsberg 1930-31). An etymology has been proposed, however, which points in the direction of the Heb. "wave-offering," Arabic *ḏwʿ*, "wave, agitate" (van den Branden 1965:116-117). This type of offering is well attested in Ug. and Heb., where it is designated by forms of the root *nwp* "raise, lift" (*šnpt* and *tᵉnūpāh*). It functions as a "presentation" offering (i.e., the emphasis is on the act of presenting to the deity, not on waving it in the air) and has good parallels in other sacrificial systems (Milgrom 1972; 1991:461-473). As in Ug., this offering was an independent one, rather than a portion of the well-being offering as could be the case in the Heb. system. If the etymological explanation is correct, the motion of "waving or moving back and forth in the air" of the offering may not have been as foreign to the act of presentation as Milgrom would have it.

[13] Because of the presence of *šlm*, the *šlm kll* is usually identified with the Ug./Heb. *šlmm*, "sacrifice of well-being," i.e., the communal sacrifice and meal which was believed to produce a state of well-being between the offerer and the deity. The lexico-syntactic basis for the interpretation of *kll* as linked with *šlm*, rather than as a term denoting "general rule," has been set forth clearly by Creason 1992. Though the use of *kll* in two sacrificial terms of precisely opposite destination, the one for the deity the other for the offerer, may appear to border on the ironic, if one keeps in mind that *kll* denotes only "entirety" one sees that the term itself has nothing to do with the direction in which the entirety is expedited. Because *šlm* is only used in conjunction with another term in Punic, one cannot know whether the relationship is adjectival, in which case *šlm* would be singular (e.g., *šelem kālīl*) or nominal, in which case *šlm* could be plural (e.g., *šalmê* + a nominal form of *kll*) as in Heb. and Ug. That the former analysis is plausible is shown by the use of the singular form *šelem* in Amos 5:22 and perhaps by a singular form of the same word in the Ug. royal funerary ritual (RS 34.126:31 [1.105]). This type of offering bears the least number of modifications in this text, i.e.,

ten (shekels)[h] of silver[14] for each (animal offered); in (the case of) the whole offering they receive in addition to this fee[15] [three-hundred (shekels)-weight of] meat;[16] in (the case of) the presentation-offering (they receive) the lower part of the legs[17] and the (leg-)joints,[18] [i] whereas the hide,[19] the ribs,[20] the feet and the rest of the flesh go to[21] the one who brought the sacrifice.[22] [j]

The Offering of an Immature Bovine or of a Mature Deer (lines 5-6)

In (the case of) the calf[k] whose horns are naturally missing[23] or in (the case of) the mature deer:[24] [l] (whether it be) a whole offering, or a presentation-offering, or a whole well-being offering, the priests receive five (shekels) of silver [for each (animal offered); in (the case of) the whole offering they receive in addition] to this fee one hundred and fifty (shekels-)weight of meat; in (the case of) the presentation-offering (they receive) the lower part of the legs and the (leg-)joints, whereas the hide, the ribs, the feet [and the rest of the flesh go to the one who brought the sacrifice].

The Offering of a Mature Sheep or Goat (lines 7-8)

In (the case of) a ram[m] or a goat:[25] [n] (whether it be) a whole offering, or a presentation-offering, or a whole well-being offering, the priests receive one shekel of silver (and) two *zr*[26] for each (animal offered); in (the case of) the presentation-offering [they] receive [in addition to this fee the lower part of the legs] and the (leg-)joints, whereas the hide, the ribs, the feet and the rest of the flesh go to the one who brought the sacrifice.

The Offering of an Immature Sheep, Goat, or Deer (lines 9-10)

In (the case of) a lamb,[o] or a kid,[p] or a young deer:[27] (whether it be) a whole offering, or a presentation-offering, or a whole well-being offering, the priests receive three-quarters (of a shekel) of silver (and) [two] *zr* [for each (animal offered); in (the case of) the presentation-offering they receive in addition] to this fee the lower part of the legs

h Lev 5:15; 27:5, 7
i Lev 7:31-32
j Lev 7:15-19; 19:5-6
k Lev 9:2, 3, 8; Jer 34:18, 19; Mic 6:6; cf. Gen 15:9; Deut 21:3, 4, 6; 1 Sam 16:2
l Cf. Deut 12:15, 22; 15:22
m Exod 29:1; Lev 5:15; Num 7:15; 23:1; 1 Sam 15:22; Mic 6:7 etc.
n Exod 12:5; Lev 1:10 etc.
o Ezra 6:9, 17; 7:17; cf. Exod 29:38; Lev 4:32; Num 7:15; Isa 1:11; Ezra 8:35 etc.
p Judg 6:19; 13:15, 19; 1 Sam 10:3; cf. Exod 23:19; 34:26; Deut 14:21

a monetary fee is attached to it when that is the case of all three sacrificial types, but beyond this fee no other stipulations are attached to the *šlm kll*.

14 *ksp ʿšrt 10*: the unit of silver is not indicated, while the number is given both as a word and as a symbol. The unit of measure is certainly the shekel, for below when the amount is a single shekel the formula is *šql 1* (line 7).

15 This is the singular form, *mšʾt*, of the word discussed above, note 3, translated "(priestly) revenues" in its plural form in line 1.

16 If the standard Carthaginian shekel weight of *ca.* 9.4 grams (Alexandropoulos 1992:323) applied here, the priests would have gotten a bit less than three kilograms of meat.

17 The word is *qṣrt*, which was used in the Ug. birth omen texts RS 24.247+:10, apparently to denote a part of the leg (see note 13 to 1.90).

18 Most authorities accept a link between the Punic *yṣlt* and biblical Heb. *ʾaṣṣīl*, attested only in the dual/plural and as part of the phrase *ʾaṣṣîlê/ʾaṣṣîlôt + yādayim*, meaning "elbows." Thus it either means "joint(s)" or, perhaps, the part of the leg above the "elbow," i.e., the thigh; if the latter is true, it would be the equivalent of Ug./Heb. *šq*, not attested in this text.

19 According to biblical law, the hide was either burned (Exod 29:14; Lev 4:11-12; 8:17; Num 19:5) or else went to the priest (Lev 7:8).

20 The meaning of *šlbm*, though apparently cognate to Heb. *šᵉlabbīm*, is uncertain, for the Heb. word is attested only as an architectural term: in 1 Kgs 7:28, 29, the word is used to designate parts of the framework in which the lavers of Solomon's temple were set.

21 The forms of the verb "to be" in the idiom "go to," i.e., "be to, belong to" in this text obey the rule of "*waw*-consecutive:" in line 3 the formula was *w b kll ykn lm*, "and in (the case of) the whole offering will be to them ...," whereas here the formula is *w kn hʿrt ... l bʿl hzbḥ*, "the hide ... will go to the one who brought the sacrifice."

22 Lit., "the owner of the sacrifice" (*bʿl hzbḥ*). The Heb. functional equivalent is *hammaqrīb*, lit, "the one who brings (the sacrifice) near" (Lev 7:18, 29, 33).

23 *ʾš qrny l m b mḥsr b ʾṭwmṭʾ*, lit., "which, its horns (are) for lack in *ʾṭwmṭʾ*. The last word does not have a plausible Semitic etymology and has been explained as Greek. Either a form of *automatos*, "natural," or an *alpha*-privative form of the verb *temnō*, "to cut" (the regular form being *atmētos*), seem most likely. In the latter case, the syntax of the phrase indicates that the reference would be to uncut horns, not to the calf being uncastrated. The point of the phrase in either case seems to be that the calf's horns have not grown yet — one cannot present an older calf whose horns have been polled and expect to pay a fee of only five shekels.

24 If the Punic vocabulary was similar to the Heb. here, the writing with /y/ ({ʾyl} < /ʾayyal/) indicates the meaning "deer," for "ram" would be written {ʾl} (/ʾayl/ > /ʾēl/) in Phoenician-Punic. This conclusion is borne out in the paragraph after next, where the three categories are "lamb," "kid" (i.e. young ram), and *ṣrb ʾyl*, apparently "young deer" (see below, note 27). According to Israelite law, the deer was not allowed as a sacrificial animal, though it could be eaten. In practice, however, at least at some sanctuaries, the offering of a deer seems to have been acceptable (Houston 1993:124-180).

25 The two terms are *ybl* and *ʿz*, the first denoting primarily the mature male ovid, the second the mature female of the caprids, with both apparently here including both sexes, as in the case of *ʾmr* and *gdʾ* in the next paragraph. The *ʿēz* is a common victim in biblical texts, for various types of sacrifice, whereas biblical *yōbēl* denotes only the "ram's horn," and the functional equivalent of the Punic ram-sacrifice is the *ʾayil*.

26 If *zr* is the name of a small coin, as is commonly believed, it should have weighed less than a quarter of a shekel, for in the next two paragraphs this word follows quarter divisions of the shekel, and more than the ʾGRT (see below, note 34).

27 The meaning of *ṣrb* in the phrase *ṣrb ʾyl* is unknown. Judging from the structure of the text, the expression should denote either the young of a deer or a small species of deer (if *ʾyl* was used generically for various species of Cervidae). Here, as above, the offering of a deer is in contrast with biblical legislation, whereas the offering of the young caprovids is unexceptional from the biblical perspective. The term for "lamb" here, *ʾmr*, has cognates that are common in Aram. and Akk. In biblical Heb. the term for "lamb" is *kebeś/kibśāh*, common in biblical legislation. The facts that (1) the offering of a kid (Heb. *gᵉdī*, Punic *gdʾ*) is not prescribed in biblical legislation (though the kid does feature as a sacrifice in biblical narratives) and that (2) *kebeś/kibśāh* is used not only for "lamb" but also to designate a "sheep" as opposed to a "goat" (as is shown by expressions such as *śeh bakkᵉbāśîm ʾô bāʿizzîm*, "a caprovid, either a sheep or a goat" [Num 15:11; cf. Deut 14:4]), seem to indicate that the preferred caprovid sacrifice in the eyes of the biblical legislators was that of an adult.

and the (leg-)joints, whereas the hide, the ribs, the feet and the rest of the flesh go to the one who brought [the sacrifice].

The Offering of a Bird (line 11)
[In (the case of) a] bird,[q] (whether it be) a fowl or a free-flying bird:[28] [r] (whether it be) a whole well-being offering or an extispicy offering or a divinatory offering,[29] [s] the priests receive three-quarters (of a shekel) of silver (and) two *zr* for each (bird offered) and the flesh goes [to the one who brought the sacrifice].

Other Bird Offerings (line 12)
[(In the case of) every (other)][30] bird (offering), (whether it be) holy first-born[t] (birds),[31] game-(bird) sacrifices,[32] or (bird-)fat[33] sacrifices, the priests receive ten ᵓ*grt*[34] [u] for each [...].

q Lev 14:4 *et passim* in this chapter; cf. Gen 15:9; Lev 1:14; 12:6, 8
r Cf. Jer 48:9
s Cf. Isa 28:15, 18
t Cf. Lev 2:12-13; Num 18:12; Deut 18:4 etc.
u Cf. 1 Sam 2:36
v Cf. Exod 23:19; 34:26; Deut 14:21
w Exod 23:18; 29:13; Lev 3:3; 1 Sam 2:15 etc.
x Gen 4:3 etc.

General Statement Regarding Presentation-Offerings (line 13)
[In] all (cases of) presentation offerings which (anyone) brings before the god, the priests shall receive the lower part of the legs and the (leg)-joints. And [in (the case of)] presentation-offerings [...]

The Gift-Offering (line 14)
In [addition] to any (flour-oil) mixture,[35] and in addition to milk,[36] [v] and in addition to fat,[37] [w] and in addition to any (other) sacrifice which a man may make as a gift-offering,[38] [x] [the priests] shall [receive ...].

Offerings Made by a Poor Person (line 15)
In (the case of) any sacrifice made by a man who

---

[28] The Punic terms are *ṣpr* for the generic designation (also used below, lines 12 and 15, as the generic term) and ᵓ*gnn* and *ṣṣ* for the two sub-categories. The first of the sub-categories is often explained by *gnn*, "to protect, surround," hence "bird of the poultry-yard," the second by various attestations in Northwest Semitic of a word *ṣīṣ* or *ṣēṣ* designating a type of bird or meaning "wing." Delcor (1990:89-91) suggests that this pair of terms reflects the distinction between the non-flying birds of the poultry-yard (cf. Dussaud 1921:141) and free-flying pigeons/doves (witness the fortune of the columbary from classical times to the recent past). The distinction could also be between domesticated and wild birds. In Heb., ᶜ*ōp* is the generic term for a bird offered for sacrifice (Lev 1:14), while *ṣippōr* is used only in the purification sacrifice for "leprosy" (Lev. 14). Pigeons and doves (*yōnāh* and *tōr*) are designated specifically. In Ug. ritual texts, the two primary designations of bird offerings are *ynt* (*qrt*), "(city) doves," and ᶜ*ṣr*(*m*), "bird(s)" (see note 18 to RS 24.266 [text 1.88]).

[29] Here we encounter the first change in sacrificial terminology, with *šlm kll* placed in the first slot and two new terms, *šṣp* and *ḥzt*, filling the second and third slots. It has been suggested that *šṣp* be explained by the Aram. verb *šṣp*, "cut," as denoting extispicy (van den Branden 1965:121) and that *ḥzt* be explained by the common Northwest Semitic verb *ḥzh*, "to see," as also denoting divination (Cooke 1903:120). Because the most common form of ornithomancy in the ancient world was by the observation of the flight of birds, these two terms could be directly related to the terms ᵓ*gnn* and *ṣṣ*, that is, the form of divination using poultry (ᵓ*gnn*) would be extispicy, while the free-flying birds (*ṣṣ*) would provide a source of divination by observation (*ḥzt*) of flight patterns (though the latter would involve a two-step process, first the observation, then the sacrifice).

[30] The first letter of this line has disappeared and it is uncertain whether {k} is to be restored, giving the word *kl*, as in line 13 ([*b*] *kl*), or {ᶜ}, giving the word ᶜ*l*, as in line 14. I have chosen the first solution for the principal reason that ᶜ*l* should denote supplementary offerings and the three types named seem inappropriate for supplements to a bird sacrifice. It seems, then, that this line is outlining specific types of bird offerings, other than the general ones named in the preceding line.

[31] Lit., "holy early ones" (*qdmt qdšt*). The form of the adjectives shows that *ṣpr* is, as in Ug. (ᶜ*ṣr*) and Heb., a feminine noun. The use of *qdš*, absent elsewhere in this text, seems to indicate a pre-existing state of holiness, i.e., a divine requirement to offer such birds. It is generally assumed that *qdm* here denotes a status equivalent to that indicated by *bikkūrīm* or *rēᵓšīt*, i.e., "first-born, first-fruits," in Heb.

[32] "Sacrifices of travel provisions" makes little sense as a translation of *zbḥ ṣd*, whereas, with the reconstruction suggested for the beginning of the line, "sacrifices of wild game-birds" is unexceptionable. On the use of *zbḥ* + *ṣd*, see above, note 4 to RS 24.258 (text 1.97).

[33] If this line does detail additional forms of bird offerings, then *zbḥ šmn* should designate a form of *šmn* coming from birds, rather than general "oil offerings" (as could be the case if this were a list of supplementary offerings). Because *ḥlb* appears below (line 14) to denote animal fat, one may surmise that *šmn* was used for the fat from poultry (the place of goose and duck fat in Mediterranean cuisine is well known, while the use of the goose as a sacrifice is attested, though rarely, at Ugarit).

[34] ᵓ*grt* is not well known as a fraction of a shekel and is usually explained as equivalent to Heb. *gērāh*, the smallest division of the shekel, i.e., one twentieth (about half a gram in the Carthaginian system).

[35] Forms of *bll* are used in Heb. for "mixing" (and secondarily for the "rubbing on" of a mixture), particularly in cultic contexts for a flour-oil mixture presented as a *minḥāh* in the form of cakes. The Punic term may, of course, have been used for another sort of mixture.

[36] Though the promised land was typified by an abundance of milk products and sources of syrup (ᵓ*ereṣ zābat ḥālāb ûdᵉbāš*, "a land flowing with milk and honey" [Exod 3:8ff]), neither of these types of products was considered appropriate sacrificial material: *ḥālāb* was ignored (except in the prohibition against eating a kid boiled in its mother's milk), while *dᵉbaš* was formally excluded, at least from the burnt offering (Lev 2:11). This discrepancy led Delcor (1990:93) to see here an influence of the Greco-Roman world on Carthaginian cult practice. In a warm climate with only primitive means of cooling, milk would, of course, either be drunk immediately or transformed into various secondary products (yogurt, butter, curds, ghee, cheese, etc.).

[37] In contrast with *ḥālāb*, "milk" (see preceding note), fat (*ḥēleb*) was an extremely important part of the Israelite sacrificial system, normally being removed from certain internal organs and offered as a burnt offering to the divinity. Though this Punic text is dealing with the economic side of the cult rather than with sacrificial practice *per se*, the organization of the text, where fat is mentioned only in association with birds (line 12) and with the gift-offering (see next note), seems to indicate that the proper disposal of the fat did not have the same ideological significance as in the Israelite cult.

[38] This offering, the *mnḥt*, is often described in Heb. terms as a "meal-offering" (e.g., Cooke 1903:114), but in point of fact only one of the terms used in the preceding list may designate an entity including flour (*bll*), two of the other three being animal-derived (milk and fat), and the fourth potentially so (*zbḥ* need not designate a bloody sacrifice, but usually does). It seems better, therefore, to translate *mnḥt* here as designating a particular type of offering, which can range in content from a small cake to a sacrificial animal (*kl zbḥ*). One may judge from the preceding rather exhaustive list of sacrificial animals that *kl zbḥ* refers to a part of a sacrificial animal which the offerer had the right to keep but desired to offer to the deity or, perhaps, to types of domesticated animals or game not covered in the preceding normative list that may have been offerable in certain situations. We know nothing, for example, about the cultic status in the Punic world of beasts that in Heb. terms would be "unclean,"

is poor[y] as regards beasts[39] or birds, the priests shall not receive anything [at all].

Offerings Made by a Group (lines 16-17)
Any citizens' association,[40] any clan,[41] [z] any drinking club[aa] (devoted to) a god,[42] or any (other group of) men who sacrifice [...], these men [must pay] a fee in addition to each sacrifice in accordance with what is set down in the writs[bb] [...].

Cases Not Covered in this Document (lines 18-19)
Any fee that is not set down in (the text on) this plaque shall be tendered according to the writs[43] that [were written (by) the thirty men who are in charge of the revenues, in the time when Ḥilleṣbaᶜl was head, (he being) the son of Bodtinn]it, and (by) Ḥilleṣbaᶜl the son of Bodᵓešmun, and (by) their colleagues.[44]

The Oppressive Priest (line 20)
Any priest who requires[cc] a fee deviating from what is set down in (the text on) this plaque shall be fined[dd] [...].

The Recalcitrant Offerer (line 21)
Any offerer who does not tender with [whatever he brings][45] the fee that [is set down in (the text on) this plaque ...].

y Lev 5:7, 11; 12:8; 14:21
z Exod 12:21; 1 Sam 20:6, 29
aa Jer 16:5; Amos 6:7
bb Dan 10:21; 1 Chr 28:19
cc 1 Sam 2:16
dd Exod 21:22; Deut 22:19

e.g., the donkey (offered in very particular circumstances among the Amorites and at Ugarit), the camel, the pig, or the dog.

[39] The term used here as generic for sacrificial animals as opposed to birds is *mqn*ᵓ, cognate with Heb. *miqneh*, also a generic term for "livestock."

[40] Punic *mzrḥ* is usually compared to Heb. ᵓ*ezrāḥ*, "native," and explained as a council of common citizens.

[41] The Punic term is *šph*, cognate to Ug. *šph*, "offspring" (see note 11 on the Kirta text [text 1.102] and note 16 on RS 24.247+ [text 1.90]), and to Heb. *mišpāḥāh*, "clan, tribe, lineage."

[42] On the *mrzḥ* institution in general, see introduction to RS 24.258 (text 1.97). As regards the expression *mrzḥ* ᵓ*lm* here, it is a commonplace of the *mrzḥ* to have a patron deity (note that ᵓ*lm* functions in Phoencian-Punic as a singular, not a plural). The *mrzḥ* of Šatrana is known from Ugarit (and there is indirect evidence for others devoted to ᶜAṯtartu Ḫurri and ᶜAnatu), Šamaš is attested as patron of a *mrzḥ* in a Phoenician inscription, and Obodat and Dušara are known as patrons from Nabataean sources. When the meeting place of the *mrzḥ* was located next to the sanctuary of a deity (as in the case of the sanctuary of Baalshamin at Palmyra), or when the priests of a given deity formed a *mrzḥ* (as in the case of the priests of Bol at Palmyra), it appears likely that in these cases also the *mrzḥ* in question was devoted to the deity mentioned, even if the relationship is not stated explicitly. And when there is a myth regarding a deity who has "his" *mrzḥ* (as in the case of ᵓIlu in RS 24.258), it is not illegitimate to posit the existence of a *mrzḥ* devoted to that deity in the real world, in this case twelfth-century Ugarit. One may find documentation on and discussion of these data in Pardee 1988a:55-56.

[43] The word used here for the present inscription is *ps*, a "tablet or plaque" (Cooke 1903:122), while the word for "writs" is *ktbt*.

[44] Because of the lacuna and because of the repetitive nature of Punic onomastics, it is not possible to know whether the reference here is to a more extensive documentation prepared by the same men who set up this inscription or to a document prepared by an earlier group. The first solution seems the more likely, for the extant name is identical to the second *sufeṭ* named in the introduction while the two words described in the preceding note clearly refer to different forms of documentation. If the two persons mentioned correspond to the two named in the introduction, the grandfather was not named here in either case (the {t} at the beginning of line 19 would be the last letter of Bodtinnit) and working backwards from the second name, the title of *sufeṭ* would not have been given either time. This gives a restoration of 35 to 38 letters, about right to fit the lacuna at the end of line 18 ({ᵓš [ktb šlšm hᵓš(m) ᵓš ᶜl hmšᵓtt ᶜt r(bt) ḥlṣbᶜl bn bdtn]t}. *Ktbt* would in this hypothesis designate a more complete document than the *ps*, of which this inscription represents only a digest.

[45] Because the definite direct object marker is ᵓ*yt* in Phoenician and usually so in Punic (as opposed to Neo-Punic), it appears best to take ᵓ*t* here before the lacuna as the preposition meaning "with." The reconstruction of the phrase as {ᵓt k[l yb]l}, lit., "with everything he brings," then appears plausible.

REFERENCES

Alexandropoulos 1992; Baker 1987; Bonnet 1992; van den Branden 1965; Cooke 1903; Creason 1992; Delcor 1983; 1990; *KAI* 69; Dussaud 1921; Ginsberg 1930-31; Houston 1993; Lipiński 1992a; 1992b; 1992c; Milgrom 1972; 1991; Pardee 1988a; Sznycer 1977.

THE ARAMAIC TEXT IN DEMOTIC SCRIPT (1.99)

Richard C. Steiner

The Aramaic Text in Demotic Script[1] is a text written on both sides of a twelve-foot-long papyrus in the Pierpont Morgan Library (Amherst Egyptian 63), originally joined by a few fragments which are now at the University of Michigan (Michigan-Amherst 43b). It was acquired by Lord Amherst of Hackney at the end of the nineteenth century.

The decipherment of the text has been a long and painful process of trial and error, which began in the early decades of this century and will no doubt continue well into the next millennium. The translation given here should be viewed

[1] I would like to thank the Texts Program of the National Endowment for the Humanities (an independent federal agency of the United States Government), the Littauer Foundation, and Yeshiva University for their generous support of my work on this text.

as an interim progress report, building on the work of many scholars but with many uncertain and controversial elements. Steiner and Moshavi (1995) can be used as a guide to what the author considers reasonably reliable in the translation; however, considerable progress has been made since that selective glossary was completed, and it will need to be expanded.

This largely poetic text is the liturgy of the New Year's festival of an Aramaic-speaking community in Upper Egypt, perhaps in Syene. It seems to have been dictated by a priest of the community, possibly at the beginning of the third century BCE, to an Egyptian scribe trained in the fourth century BCE.

The original homeland of these people, called *rš* and *ᵓrš* in the papyrus, is the subject of controversy. The present writer has suggested that it is the land between Babylonia and Elam which the Assyrians called Rashu and Arashu and that Assurbanipal, who captured Rashu in his campaign against Elam, deported its inhabitants to the Assyrian province of Samaria, like the Elamites from Susa mentioned in Ezra 4:9-10. There is reason to believe that most or all of them wound up in Bethel, joining the foreign colonists settled there by earlier Assyrian kings. Their subsequent migration to Egypt may be recorded in the text's account of the arrival of soldiers from Judah and Samaria (XVI.1-6).

The text shows how the groups deported by the Assyrians to Samaria "would venerate the Lord but serve their own gods according to the practices of the nations from which they had been exiled" (2 Kgs 17:33).

Veneration of the Lord is represented by prayers in cols. XI-XII that contain Hebrew words and Israelite divine names (Adonai, 7 times, Yaho, once). Among these prayers is one which parallels Ps 20 (XI.11-19). Phrases like "Yaho, our bull" (XI.17; cf. "let them kiss [your] bull[s], ⌜let them de⌝sire your calves" in V.12), "lord of Bethel" (XI.18, cf. VIII.13), and "a city full of ivory houses" (XI.9, immediately before the prayer), if correctly deciphered, suggest that this prayer is a descendant of one used in Jeroboam's temple in Bethel. There may even be echoes of this prayer (XI.17) in Abijah's battlefield condemnation of Jeroboam and his calf-cult (2 Chr 13:8, 10, 12).

Service of other gods is the main thrust of the text, which allows us to follow the progress of a pagan New Year's festival from morning until night. The rituals have counterparts at Babylon, Emar, and Sumer. The wait in the courtyard (III.9-11) and the declaration of innocence (VI.3, 9) followed by a *Heilsorakel* (VI.12-18) are paralleled in the ritual for the fifth day of the New Year's festival at Babylon. The selection by the god of a maiden from among the "daughters of Arash" to be "elevated" to the status of priestess (VIII.13-16) resembles the rite in which "the daughter of any son of Emar" was chosen by the god and "elevated" to the status of *entu*-priestess (text 1.122 below). The laying of the priestess on a bed of perfumed rushes (V.9, XVI.7) covered with an embroidered bedspread (XVI.13-14) made of flax (XV.15-16) has parallels in Sumerian sacred marriage rites.

The chief gods of the community are referred to as *mr* "lord" (a back-formation from *mry* < *mrᵓy* "my lord" attested already in Old Aramaic) and *mrh* "lady." These epithets are rendered below as Mar and Marah, because their usage in the text (e.g., IVB.3 *lmrty mrh* "to my lady, Marah") suggests that they have taken on the status of names, much like their Canaanite counterpart *bᶜl* "lord," the epithet of Hadad.

Marah appears to be identified with Nanai in the text (except in VII.2, 6, where they are listed separately). She is depicted as a cow (II.19; XIII.5, 7, 18, 19; XVI.16) that suckles (exceptional) human infants (I.19; II.7-8, 16-17; III.5, 16; IVA.5). Each year, after feasting, she falls asleep in the pit, in the waters of fertility (*bšwḥh bmy pryh*), where she brings forth sweet fruit for Mar, her consort (II.8-11).

Nanai's consort, Nebo, appears frequently in the text, as does the god Bethel. The latter is called Resident of Hamath in VIII.6, 10 and Ashi(m)-Bethel in XV.1, 14, 15. This takes us back once again to the Assyrian province of Samaria, where "the men of Hamath made Ashima" (2 Kgs 17:30).

The text concludes with a story about Assurbanipal, the king who destroyed Rashu, and his brother, Shamash-shum-ukin (XVII.5-XXII.9). This story is, in all likelihood, an ancestor of the Sardanapalus legend known from Greek and Latin sources. The original kernel of the story is a piece of pro-Assurbanipal propaganda, similar to the editions of Assurbanipal's Annals which postdate the civil war, intended presumably to win the hearts and minds of the defeated Babylonians (648-c.620 BCE) or to counter claims by the resurgent Babylonians that the Assyrians had committed aggression against them and deserved to be punished (627-612 BCE). However, there are indications that it was revised at a later date and reused, possibly as a weapon in the propaganda war waged against Nabonidus by Cyrus' priestly backers (third quarter of the sixth century BCE).

Introduction (I.1-15)

Mar dwells
... mighty
... your ⌜in⌝timates
... on papyrus
... ⌜in⌝ the gate
... you shall wri⌜te⌝
... the king, Mar, with
... [h]arp and lyre
... Rash
... ⌜let us⌝ ex⌜al⌝[t]
...

all the go⌈d⌉[s] …
is ⌈exa⌉[lted];
exalted is Mar[ah],
…
Marah.

A Plea to Marah to Accept the Morning Sacrifice (I.16-17)
Your ⌈nour⌉ishment
[we have] sac⌈rif⌉[iced],
[Ma]rah,
and may [your] e⌈ye⌉[s]
[glance at]
our sacrifice

Marah's Contemptuous Rebuff (I.17-19)
[M]an!
… outside,
[and hear me!]
[I am exa]lted.
I rea⌈r⌉ed you,
you [sucked my breast,]
[the sap of Marah]
[nourished you,]
[she strengthens,]
[she empowers]
with [her] [po]wer.

A Prayer to Marah Who Sustains Mankind from her Grave (II.1-11)
Come out and make
[your] g⌈ra⌉[ve] …
we will make your grave …
My wis[e] ⌈one⌉ carries you / for you;[a]
⌈she⌉ carries your burden and your l[oa]d,[b]
creating
at your decr[ee].
She builds
and *upro⌈ot⌉s*;
⌈her⌉ breast
[su]⌈ck⌉les ⌈y⌉ou.
My Princess ea[t]s [and is s]ated ⌈and⌉ sleeps.[c]
And she ⌈lies⌉
⌈in⌉ the pit,
in the waters of fertility,
[bringi]ng forth ⌈fr⌉uit
for Mar,
and it is sweet
like you.

Another Plea to Accept the Offering (II.11-13)
Marah,
[in] heaven
[you] [re]side;
you dwell *on hi⌈gh⌉*,
⌈Mar⌉(ah).
Your [nour]ishment
we have [sac]⌈ri⌉ficed,
Marah,
and may [your] eye[s]
g[lan]ce

a Isa 46:7
b Ps 55:23
c 1 Kgs 18:27; Ps 121:3-4
d Dan 10:11; Neh 9:3; 2 Chr 34:31; 35:10

at our sacrifice.

More Rebuffs (II.14-III.6)
Man!
… outside
⌈and⌉ [hea]r me!
I am exalted.
[I] reared [you],
you sucked my [bre]ast,
the sap of Marah
nourished [you].
[She streng]thens,
she empowers
with her power.
To …
you call
Hear …
I am the Co[w]
… outside
… out[side]
…

Col. III
[*M*]*an*!
… outside,
and hear me!
I am exalted.
I reared you,
you sucked my breast,
the sap of Marah
nourished you.
⌈She⌉ strengthens,
she empowers
with her power.

The King Denied Entrance (III.6-12)
Our judge
comes/came to the ga⌈te⌉
and stands/stood still.
"Mar ⌈is⌉ blessed
seven times
all ⌈that which⌉
my mouth ⌈s⌉ays."
And he (=Mar) [c]ries/[c]ried out:
"You may cert⌈ain⌉ly not enter,
king.
[Wa]it outside.
Stay at your station."[d]
He washes/washed
his hands
inside the courtyard.
"Mar,
[bri]ng our ⌈lord⌉ near to you;
Nebo
…."

More Rebuffs (III.14-IVA.6)
[Man!]
… outside,
[and] hear me!

I am exa⌜lted⌝.
I [reared you]
You sucked my ⌜bre⌝ast,
the sap of Marah
[nourished you.]
[She strengthens,]
[she empowers]
with her power.

Col. IVA

Man!
... [outside,]
and hear me!
I am exalted.
[I] reared you,
you sucked my breast,
the sap of Marah
nourished you.
She strengthens,
she empowers
with her power.

The Enthronement of Marah-Nanai (IVA.6-21)

Kings saw yo[u]
and they were afraid,
Nanai;
you frighten them
in front of their officials
...
exalted.
But we saw/see
the [quee]n,
the queen of Ra[sh]
brought in,
Marah, among the [go]⌜d⌝s.
And they rise
⌜from⌝ their thro⌜ne⌝s:
"Let Marah be enthr[on]ed
among the gods;
let her [th]rone
be glo⌜ri⌝ous;
in Rash
let [her] footstool
[be] glor⌜ious⌝."
...
that Mar[ah] was enthroned /
of the enthronement of Mar[ah]
...
allow our king to come up,
Mar[ah]
... may he bless
... Marah, ⌜b⌝le⌜ss⌝
... may he bless you
... [b]less(,) *Shamash*
... ble[ss]
...

Col. IVB

New Year's Delights (IVB.1-9)

to Marah ... ⌜ca⌝ll
... to my lady, Marah
the he⌜aven⌝s
...
...
on the earth.
...
come, walk before ⌜me⌝
on every
... those who call upon you,
⌜mig⌝hty one
...
mighty one,
we pu⌜t⌝
in your cou⌜rty⌝ard
fr[*uit*]
from the vin⌜eya⌝rds
[we brin]g out
on New Years
...
which delight my heart and your heart,
my Fire
...
in El's heart

Col. V

The Destruction of Rash (V.1-11)

You, Mar, ⌜p⌝ut
te[rror in the land];
Terror [fi]lled
the country
...
They [de]stroyed for you
all your cit⌜ies⌝;
in the land
trembling dwells.
...
belittles you,
your entire assembly
of princes.
He ⌜re⌝viled
your sons and your mothers;
with shackles
he clothed their hands.
He hunted the chiefs;
he treated them all with contempt.
He stoned your baker
who used to present b<re>ad
and make
all your loaves;
your ⌜bu⌝tcher
who used to present a ram —
he would ⌜str⌝ike the *neck*,
he would strike the *windpipe*,
he would make all
the c<o>ws of your ...;
your priest{s}
who used to pr⌜es⌝ent
the devotee — / meal offering —
he would lay down for you
fragrances and rushes;

⌈your⌉ ⌈mus⌉[ici]an{s}
who used to present
joyous music —
he would carry the harp,
he would carry the lyre.
…
they pour
the ⌈d⌉ri⌈nk⌉ of his belly.

Kissing the Calves of Bethel (V.12-22)

…
let them kiss [your] bull[s],[e]
⌈let them de⌉sire your calves,[e]
Exalted One,
the ⌈c⌉[alves]
of your …s
my m⌈outh⌉
… and shake
…
…
⌈he will⌉ find
…
…
Resident of Rash
…
…
⌈B⌉[e]⌈th⌉el

Col. VI

A Lament to Mar (VI.1-12)

…
…
…
…
⌈Mar⌉.
Mar, good god —
my god, what
should I do/have you done?
let me know … my god.
No evil is in my hands,[f]
my god;
no duplicity/slander in my mouth.[g]
(But) you have made me
a lamb in their flocks,
a ram in their folds.
They constantly feel me
(saying) "Let us kill him
that we may become fat and corpulent.[h]
Let us eat his flesh [i]
and become fat;
let us drink his blood [i]
and become inebriated.
Lord, god of Rash, Mar —
Make my body[j]
…
in their mouths,
bitters
under their tongues.[k]
Mar, good god —
my god, what
should I do / have you done?
Let me know … my god.
No evil is in my hands,
our god;
no duplicity/slander in my mouth.
(But) you have made me
a date in their mouths,
sweets
under their tongues.[k]
Lord, god of Rash, Mar —
Make my body
ve⌈nom⌉ in their mouths,
poison under their tongues.[l]

A Reassuring Reply (VI.12-18)

Mar speaks up
and says to me:
"[Be] ⌈stro⌉ng,
my ⌈se⌉rvant, fear not. I will ⌈save⌉ [m]
your ….
To Marah,
if you will …,
to Mar
from your shrine and Rash,
[I shall destroy]
[your] ⌈en⌉[emy in] your days
and during your year⌈s⌉
[your] advers[ary]
will be smitten.
[Your foes]
I shall destroy
in front of you;
your foot on their necks [you will place].[n]
[I shall suppo]⌈rt⌉ your ⌈r⌉ight (hand)[o]
I shall ⌈cro⌉wn ⌈you⌉
with prosperity;
your house
…
…
⌈u⌉p⌈o⌉n you
your cup …
…
…

Col. VII

The Blessings of the Gods (VII.1-7)

your blessings
…
may they bless you.
May Mar from Rash
bl⌈ess you⌉;
Marah from Shur —
[she] should bless you.
May Baal from Zephon bless you;[p]
Pidra[i]/<i> from Raphia —
she should bless you.
May Bel from Babylon
bless you;
Belit from Esangila —
she should bless you.

e Hos 13:2
f 1 Sam 24:12 (11); Job 16:17
g Isa 53:9
h Deut 32:15
i Ezek 39:17; Ps 50:13
j Isa 51:23
k Ps 10:7; 66:17; Cant 4:11; Job 20:12
l Ps 140:4
m Jer 1:8; 30:10; 42:11, 46:27
n Josh 10:24
o Isa 41:8-13
p Ps 128:5 (different syntax!)

May Nebo from Borsippa
bless you;
Nanai from Ayakku —
she should bless you.
May the Throne of *Horus*
and *Osiris* from the *Negeb*
bless you.

Offerings to the Gods (VII.7-19)
Give the fire-offerings
and offer (them) up
in fire.
Pick up, send
a lamb, a young sheep;
send a lamb.
Make abundant
holocaust-aroma
for Mar;
may he bless you
abundantly.
Bow down to Anat
and *Mami*;
to Nebo
send
the consecrated animals.
Let there be remembered
as a remembrance,
Mar,
sixty singers.
Let them lift
their voices, Mar;
Mar, let them bless you.
Let there be remembered
as a remembrance,
Mar,
six⌈ty⌉
temple ser⌈vit⌉ors —
their (lit., his) handfuls
of myrrh (and) frankincense
for the nostril[s]
of Bethel.
Let there be remembered
as a remembrance,
Mar,
sixty sheep.
Favor your loved ones,
Mar,
favor your loved ones
and Rash.
Favor your loved ones
(and) Rash.
The blood
of the *dead* sheep
is a sea.
The sheep
floats
to you,
lord of heaven;
wheat
{of} barley
comes near to you.
...
the dust
... lord,
may you se⌈t⌉ a hand,
snatch them.

A Hymn to Mar (VII.20-VIII.3)
Your going out, Mar
...
your coming in
...
on ...
on the path ...
the ⌈w⌉all
⌈your⌉ window⌈s⌉ ...
[your] pal⌈ace⌉,
Mar
...
Col. VIII
[Al]l the blessings
...
until eternity.
your sons,
and with your daughters
he dealt kindly ...
⌈was brought low⌉
and the god of Rash
was victorious over all of them.

An Enticing Invitation (VIII.3-8)
I have taken out
your box, my god —
open (it),
and your mouth
...
Your table
will be covered
with the fat of stags.
Butchers will wait
on it.
All of them,
with skillful hands,
will tremble.
Every bull
you will snatch,
Resident of Hamath.[q]
Your krater
you will pour out
and it will be filled;
and butlers will wait
on it,
each of them standing
and speaking up:
"You are at a banquet.
Look, see!
Drink it!"

q 2 Kgs 17:30

A Hymn to Mar (VIII.8-10)
Mar, from your snorts
all the <ea>rth perishes;
like smoke, lord,
from your breaths.[r]
You fly
to your followers;
you spread the wing
like an eagle,
and they arise.
The beams of your house,
Bethel,
are from Lebanon;
from Lebanon,
{and} your garden,
are they.
And Resident of Hamath
...

The Selection of Mar's Bride (VIII.10-11)
Elevate a lass.
Who is the lass?
All of your manifestations
are concealed.

A Hymn to Mar (VIII.11-13)
Mar is/se<t>s like the *sun*
and rises like the moon,
like the moon
along the length of his heavens.
Oh, let them build,
in heaven,
your house,
concealed, with stars;
let your bed
be brought down in Epiph.
In your temples
let them build,
lord of Bethel,
a thousand *new* altars.

The Selection of Mar's Bride (VIII.13-16)
A beautiful priestess
elevate,
and the burnt offer⌜ing⌝s of the city
let her offer;
in Rash
...
"This one here
is ⌜beauti⌝ful;
in *the shape of* her face
she is love⌜ly⌝."
Elevate a lass.
Who is the lass?
All of your manifestations
are concealed.

The Diadem of Prosperity for Mar's Bride (VIII.16-22)
Our Prince has ⌜been good⌝ to
the daughters of Arash:
Mar has ⌜gi⌝ven
the diadem of prosperity;
the god of <Ra>sh
has crowned her
in his hou[se],
and he makes her rule in his palaces.[s]
He rai⌜se⌝s her up
like the sea
in his hou[se],
in ...
⌜his⌝ hor⌜ns⌝
...
like the river.
⌜And⌝ our Prince,
the god of <Ra>[sh],
has done good with his water;
the god of <Ra>sh,
with the sea.
...
⌜Your⌝ shrine, Mar,
is perfect;
...
who has improved?
All of it, Mar, my god
...
a diadem of prosperity
...
...
...
...
our yearly harv[est] (lit., ingathering),
because your peo⌜ple⌝
...
He
... Glean wheat
and glean ...
Glean
...

Col. IX

A Prayer for Rain (IX.1-13)
⌜Answer me⌝
...
from Rash;
⌜to⌝ my ...
....
The river is disappearing,
it is worn out.
and my lord —
the river
is not rising.
Your mind
is sealed, Mar.
Send to me
your cloud.
Exalted One,
awake for me, awake.
Marah,

r Ps 18:16; Job 4:9
s Esth 1:22

lift up the bucket for me;
inspect the canals for me,
Marah.
Inspect,
my g<o>d, my queen,
the pool;
lift up,
the bucket.
In every generation
you rule {in her palaces} in your palaces,[s]
{and} and you/come
…
…
…
and my wife.
I shall bring a ram
to my lord;
…
…
Oh, Bethel,
nourishing god / god of the world,
who causes the sea to rise
generation after generation —
all the clouds of moisture[t]
offspring of the primeval mist[u]
are hidden away for you
Make it rain, Mar;
baths of rain
send down.
Our silver is yours and our gold;[v]
our possessions are yours,
our mature cattle are yours,
like our heifers
(and) *yearling calves*.

Chorus (IX.13-17)
He will help us.
We shall be raised up in safety.
He will guard our rear.
The god of Rash will help us.
Let us ponder his mysteries.
Mar is my father
and my bull/shepherd.
He will raise me up.
Let me vaunt
his mighty deeds.
…
…
…
…
let the throng say
Amen, Amen.

A hymn to Mar (IX.17-20)
Mar, my god —
father of the orphan, champion of the widow.[w]
She who has lifted up her h⌜a⌝nds
to you,
you calm
in her *sobbing*.
She has lifted up her hands —
⌜you⌝ ca⌜lm⌝
her *sob⌜bin⌝g*.
Mar humbles the *haughty*.
May you exalt him
with the …
of your …;
[your] catt⌜le⌝
[and] ⌜all⌝ your bounty.

Chorus (IX.20-23)
[And he will] ⌜help me⌝.
I shall be raised up ⌜in safety⌝.
He will guard [our] r[ear].
The god of R⌜ash⌝ will
hel⌜p⌝ us.
Mar is ⌜my⌝ father
and my bull/shepherd.
He will ra[ise me up].
Let me ⌜va⌝unt
his migh⌜ty⌝ deeds
…
…
…
…
let the throng say
Amen, Amen.

Col. X

A Prayer for the Rising of the Nile (X.1-6)
Ret⌜urn⌝, our father,
Mar of ⌜A⌝rash;
…
You stretched out the heavens,[x]
Mar,
⌜you⌝ s⌜et⌝ the stars in place,
you dwell throughout
the land of Rash,
our god.
Let canal (and) pool[y]
rise through its waves.
Let canal (and) pool
rise through its waves.
The river is poor in floodwater.
The river will die
and it will be bitter.
They will become thin again, Mar;
as thin, god of Rash,
as splinters of flint.[z]

Chorus (X.6-8)
Mar is my father
and my bull/shepherd.
He will raise me/us up.
Let us vaunt
his mighty deeds.
…

s Esth 1:22
t Job 37:11
u Job 36:27
v Hag 2:8
w Ps 68:6
x Isa 40:22
y Exod 7:19, 8:1
z Jer 23:29

…
…
…
let the throng say
Amen, Amen.

A Dream about Rash (X.8-13)
In my dream,
I was in my youth;
I was in the land of Rash.
I was building a city,
in Rash
I was *erecting it*;
its name was
Ellipi Pait.
Rash was supported;
my lord
watched over
Ellipi Pait:
He would beat
her troublemakers
in her stocks;
he would break (them)
in corporal punishment.
The righteous man
he would help,
escorting him
in the face of his troubles,
him whom the oppression
of the creditor
has filled/embittered.

Chorus (X.13-16)
And he will h<el>p me;
I shall be raised up in safety.
He will guard our rear.
The god of Rash will help me.
Let us ponder his mysteries.
Mar is my father
and my bull/shepherd.
He will raise us up.
Let me vaunt
his mighty deeds.
…
…
…
…
let the throng say
Amen, Amen.

A Prayer for the Destruction of Rash's Enemies (X.16-20)
Mar who goes ⸢out⸣
from Rash,
who is like you,
who is more for⸢bea⸣ring than you?
⸢Ta⸣ke away, destroy the enemy.
Arise, Mar,
take away, destroy
our enemy
…
⸢that⸣ the Kassites and
Ela⸢m⸣ites not destroy us.
May ⸢you⸣ heal,
⸢O⸣ Mar,
your int⸢imate⸣s,
⸢that⸣ they not *per⸢ish⸣*,
and sate
their ⸢en⸣emi⸢es⸣
with all that
with ⸢which⸣
your oppressed ones
[were sated.]

Col. XI
The Bridal Chamber for the Sacred Marriage (XI.1-3)
A …
in …
erect;
on a height [aa]
construct it.
Er⸢ect⸣ ⸢i⸣t
under lofty ced[ar]s; [aa]
there, my powe⸢rful⸣ one,
may you construct [it],
may you … it.

Father not Old, Brothers not Frail (XI.3-6)
Satu[rate], invigorate (lit., oil) [bb]
your father.
Your father
is a disabled old man,
your brothers
are frail.
My father
is not a disabled old man,
my brothers
are not frail,
for my father
is like a stable (full) of steeds;
my brothers,
like eagles
and <wi>ld asses.

Drought in Bethel (XI.6-11)
"You are poor,
my brother.
Why has the flow of the spring
dis⸢app⸣eared?"
"It flowed
and was lost,
and its flow disappeared.
The well flowed,
its water was lost;
our faces
wasted away / *dried out*.
Stricken is a city
full of ivory houses[cc]
⸢and⸣ with linen

aa 1 Kgs 14:23; 2 Kgs 17:10; Jer 2:20; Ezek 6:13; 20:28

bb Ps 23:5

cc Amos 3:14-15

and lapis lazuli
on her windows;
her insides/windows
a mountain of ma⸢rb⸣le,
her walls iron and bron⸢ze⸣." [dd]

A Psalm from Bethel (XI.11-19)
May *Horus* answer us in our troubles;
may Adonai answer us in our troubles.[ee]
O crescent (lit., bow) / bowman
in heaven,
Sahar / shine forth;
send your emissary from the temple of Arash,[ff]
and from Zephon may Horus help us.[ff]
May *Horus* grant us what is in our hearts;
may Mar grant us what is in our hearts.[gg]
All <our> plans may *Horus* fulfill.[gg]
May *Horus* fulfill — [hh]
may Adonai not fall short in satisfying —
every request of our hearts.[hh]
Some with the bow, some with the spear; [ii]
but (lit., behold) as for us — Mar is our god; [jj]
Horus-Yaho, our bull, is with us.[kk]
May the lord of Bethel answer us[ll]
on the morrow.
May Baal of Heaven Mar
grant a blessing / bless you;
to your pious ones, your blessings.[mm]

Col. XII
Lambs for Adonai (XII.1-3)
⸢H⸣ear me,
my ⸢go⸣[d], my king.
Choice ⸢lamb⸣s,[nn]
sh[ee]p,
we sacrifice
to you (alone)
among the gods;
our banquet
is for you (alone)
out of all the supreme beings /
from the shepherds/chiefs
of the people,
Adonai, for you (alone)
out of all the supreme beings /
from the shepherds/chiefs
of the ⸢peo⸣ple.

Wine and music for Adonai (XII.4-10)
Adonai,
the people bless you;
accept your yearly liturgy.
From the pitcher
saturate yourself,
my god;
I will fill (it) with
the juice of the winepress.
Tower,
mercif⸢ul⸣ father,
Horus
benefactor of the lowly —
they have mixed wine
in *goblets*,
in *goblets*
at our *wedding*.
Drink, *Horus*,
from the bounty
of a thousand basins;
saturate yourself, Adonai,
from the bounty of men.
Musicians stand
in attendance upon Mar:
a player of the harp,
a player of the lyre.
Here is the music
of the har<p>,
the music of
a Sidonian lyre
and sweet things
in his ear
at the banquets of men.

A prayer to Adonai (XII.11-17)
Who among gods,
among men, *Horus*?
Who among gods,
among royalty,
(among)/among non-royalty.
Who is like you, *Horus*, among gods?[oo]
Come from Shur,
take vengeance
for those who call upon you,
a peo⸢ple⸣ dwelling
among the crooked.
And make us strong again,
beneath you, *Horus*;
beneath you,
Adonai,
Resident of Heaven;
like *the phoenix*,
Horus,
Resident of Heaven.
Call out
to us your words
among the crooked;
and make ⸢us⸣ strong again,
Baal from Ze⸢ph⸣on.
May *Horus* grant a blessing.
Arise, *Horus*,
to our aid / help us.
May Adonai
give heed to my prayer.[pp]
Mar, ari⸢se⸣!
Horus, may you grant protection,
just as you protect
your ey⸢e⸣ from degeneration.[qq]

dd Jer 1:18
ee Ps 20:2
ff Ps 20:3
gg Ps 20:5
hh Ps 20:6
ii Pss 20:8; 46:10
jj Ps 20:8; 2 Chr 13:10
kk Ps 46:12; 2 Chr 13:8, 12
ll Ps 20:10
mm Ps 3:9
nn Gen 49:21
oo Exod 15:11
pp Prov 1:23
qq Ps 6:8

Col. XIII

A Hymn to Marah-Nanai (XIII.1-9)
⸢B⸣[le]ssed are you,
O Marah,
more than all
blessed ones.
You are my commander
...
You are my queen
and you are a hawk;
Marah from Rash
are you,
queen over all.
Raise the crowns
...
You had mercy on
him who did not finish
the crowns
of your house.
Merciful one, / Beloved,
the summit of your sanctuary
who can build?
Who can build,
merciful one, / beloved,
the tower
by its side?
Nana, Cow,
the niche for your statue
may you build;
may you ⸢carve⸣,
my goddess,
the pedestal
of your testimony.
The *sun* of
blinding light
shines through your windows,
your windows, divine Cow,
over the gate of men.
The men, Dove,
I shall watch for you,
the watch of the portal for you
so that I may satiate myself
from your abundance,
saturate myself,
my si<s>ter,
from your *baths*
in the sea.

Nanai's Statue Trampled in the Sack of Rash (XIII.9-17)
The one who rebels (lit., raises a hand)
against Mar/Mar<ah> —
on Nana's hands
he trampled
and went (away).
He stretc<hed> forth his hand
against the merciful one / beloved,
against the one who nourishes.
He threw down
the one who proclaimed to us
and taught.
He threw down, trampled
the proclaimer
who proclaimed
(and) taught.
He came,
threw down, trampled.
He threw down
the Dove,
threw down my treasure.
For Na⸢nai⸣
take up the harp,
(for) Baalat
loosen the tongue.
Your metal is *shattered*;
on my floor
you lie.
Quickly we entered.
We shake it.
Get up
...
that we may exalt you.
Our <str>ength has fallen,
our holy one has fallen,
the teacher of wisdom.
I ran to you.
...
Get up,
watch over the orphan;
over me,
Foster-mother!
The merciful one / beloved was cast;[rr]
it was from metal plates.
...
Its feet he smashed,
its hand he smashed.
Against the merciful one / beloved
he came;
its feet he smashed.
Appoint an idol-maker
from Tyre.

A Prayer to Nanai (XIII.17-XIV.4)
Who are you?
You are
my powerful goddess.
From our *desolation*
grant me rest.
....
Over the king's ⸢s⸣eat,
⸢C⸣ow-head —
appoint lookouts
over the throne;
over the throne,
Cow of Babylon(ia),
guards.

rr Isa 40:19; 44:10

Col. XIV
Who are you?
You are
our mighty goddess.
Your mer[cy]
for my people —
for my people,
like the gods,
establish, Na⌜n⌝ai.
Let them become intoxi⌜cated⌝
with casks of wine;
may you intox⌜icate⌝
with its intoxication,
Nanai.
Who are you?
You are my power⌜ful⌝ godd⌜ess⌝.
From *our desolation*
grant me rest.
....

The Tramplers Stricken by Nanai's Venom (XIV.4-6)
On my back horses *have walked*; [ss]
I am the viper at their heel. [tt]
Horses *have walked*
⌜on⌝ my belly;
from my poison they grew old,
they were sickened
by my venom,
their hide rotted
from my *venomous bite*.
Drink an *antidote*,
...
pick up a remedy,
fill the vessels
with drugs,
load the ⌜anti⌝dote
with balm.
...
...
...
...
fashion it.
...
Nebo
...
...

Col. XV
Blessings and Prayers (XV.1-9)
...
...
Ashim-Bethel
⌜Nebo⌝
...
...
⌜you⌝ entered;
⌜with goats⌝
you came before
your ...
man,

ss Ps 129:3
tt Gen 49:17
uu Ps 78:69
vv Obad 4

who grants
pea⌜ce⌝ everlasting.
In the month
of ⌜Epiph⌝,
may Nebo remember you;
may he put you in mind
on earth and on high.[uu]
Blessed are you, Hadad;
Had, with a blessing
fit for El.
Blessed are you,
Baal of Heaven.
The holder of your fort
is the Bull,
Nebo is your ⌜gu⌝ard,
⌜Pid⌝rai is
your sturdy beam.
Great Baal!
Tip a pitcher of must
and drink with me.
Spend the night in my house;
come to the threshold,
en⌜ter⌝.
I have placed
on your tray/crown
...
Bull,
in your memory
whom do you leave?
(Whom) do you regard
in <you>r mind,
Nebo?
A nest among golden stars he sets (for) you.[vv]
Into gold,
divine Sheep,
⌜let⌝ the goldbeaters
⌜b⌝eat lapis lazuli.
My god, much plunder
I have carried off:
I shall give you
the silver;
the gold will be added to yours.
...
with the foster-fathers
of the orphan,
speak (saying):
"Exalt Mar El,
may you ascribe to him
supremacy."
They exal<t> me (saying):
"To whom would you liken El,
among foster-fathers
of the orphan?"

Spoon-Stuffed Ducks Brought to the Table (XV.9-12)
I/you/she spoke (saying):
"Come up to me.
Bring near to me
and my *dovecote(s)*

a *dovelet* grain.
Bring near to me
and *my dovecote(s)*
a vessel ⌜of cha⌝rm,
a vessel of beauty.
⌜*On*⌝ *an ivory* ⌜*tray*⌝
bring to the table
of Bel, the king /
of the King's son (= Nebo son of Bel)
the ducks,
the ducks
placed on ivory.
Stuff the ducks
with a spoon;
make the wine abundant,
increase the fat tenfold."

Jackal and Hare (XV.12-13)
Jackal, jackal!
Here, in front of you
is a hare!
Moon-howler,
jackal!
Rove,
go out and look!
Rove
away from my wilds!
Hare!
Here, a hunter is hunting you
assiduously,
with skillful hands.

A Prayer to Ashim-Bethel (XV.13-17)
The force of
the divine bull
is your force,
Horus.
Ashim-Bethel,
the force of
the divine bulls
is your force;
your ⌜venom⌝ is like that of ⌜se⌝rpents.[ww]
Your bow in heaven
you, Mar, ⌜sho⌝ot;
draw it, Ashim-Bethel,
at your enemies.
My mighty one,
may your hammer be good;
my ⌜*bro*⌝*ther, for me*
against Elam
may ⌜*you*⌝ *raise it*.
My mighty one,
may my linen be good,
my linen
which will touch your couch.
Why does your enemy carry off
...
...
...

ww Deut 32:33; Ps 58:5

He *fills* his hand
with ... and vessel
taking out
from your shrine and Rash
...
that I/you did not see.

Jackal and Hare (XV.17-19)
Jackal, jackal!
⌜Here⌝, ⌜in⌝ front of you
is a hare!
Moon-howler,
jackal!
⌜R⌝ove,
go out and look!
Rove
away from my wilds!
Hare!
Here, a hunter is hunting you
assiduously,
with skillful hands.

Col. XVI
Soldiers from Judah and Samaria (XVI.1-6)
[With] my (own) two eyes
I watched a tr⌜oo⌝[p]
...
a b[and] of
Samari⌜tan⌝s
sounded out
my lord, the king.
"Who / From where
are y⌜ou⌝, lad?
Who / From where
is your...?"
"I come from ⌜J⌝udah,
my brother
has been br⌜ought⌝ from Samaria
and now
a man ⌜is⌝ bring⌜ing⌝ up
my sister
from J⌜er⌝usalem."
"Enter, lad;
we will give you lodging.
A kab of ⌜wh⌝eat
pick up
on your sho⌜ul⌝der,
boy;
...
...
...
On your table
will be placed
lap⌜is la⌝zuli —
from every
dovelet grain,
lapis lazuli;
and from every mina
a vessel of beauty."

The Sacred Marriage Ceremony (XVI.7-19)
Nana, y⌈o⌉u are my wife.
The *bed of rushes*
they have ⌈laid⌉ down,
perfumed fragrances
for ⌈you⌉r nostril<s>.
Our goddess,
may you be carried,
escorted ⌈t⌉o your dear one;
let them bear you
to the dear one.
In your bridal chamber
a priest sings.
Nanai,
bring near to me
your lips.
We dwelled (here)
in the morning;
we shall dwell (here)
in the evening.
I have stayed wi⌈th⌉ you until evening.
The chosen lad too
has come.
A sound keeps you awake in the ⌈evening⌉;
into our ⌈sh⌉rine,
my ...,
who is coming?
<A sound of> harps
keeps you awake in the evening;
in the grave
of my ancestor,
a dirge.
A sound of lyres from
the grave keep⌈s⌉ you awake in the evening.[xx]
My beloved,
enter the doo⌈r⌉
into our house.
With my mouth,
consort of our lord,
let me kiss you.
⌈And⌉ I go
and enter.
In my nostrils
it is sweet;
Come, enter
the perfumed hideaway.
Horus-Bethel will lay you
on a bedspread;
El, on embroidered covers.
In his heavens,
Mar from Rash blesses;
Mar, a bless⌈ing⌉
before Bethel
everlasting:
"My sister, Marah —
blessed are you,
O Cow, our lady."
"Blessed are you,

xx Isa 65:4

yy Isa 1:29; 65:3; 66:17

zz Nah 2:9

O Had,
with a blessing
fit for El.
Blessed are you,
Baal of Heaven."
"Rebuild, man, Ellipi.
A cursed land rebuild,
a city of ruins rebui⌈ld⌉;
by the side
of the Hambanites.
a great land.
Keep alive the pauper;
...
the poor [m]an.

Col. XVII

A Lament for Nineveh After the Wedding (XVII.1-5)
O ⌈my⌉ godd⌈ess⌉ / "Woe," ⌈I⌉ lamented
... the king
...
you/I have come
here;
indeed
you were / I was brou⌈ght⌉ up
to my garden.[yy]
You/I have perfumed
my scent
amo⌈ng⌉ cedars;
you/I have played music
on a l⌈y⌉re;
you/I have put down
perfume.
Baal of Heaven
has come up,
ascended to my/your bower.
O ⌈my⌉ goddess, / "Woe," I lamented,
...
O my goddess, / "Woe," I lamented,
I wailed.
Ni<ne>veh is (nothing but) swamps; /
There are swamps in Ni<ne>veh;[zz]
it [has tur]⌈ned⌉ into mud.
T<o> (lit., dow<n to>) the ground
it has been razed (lit., thrown down).

A Tale of Two Brothers in Two Cities (XVII.5-XXII.9)
Omens When the Princes Were Born (XVII.5-XVII.13)
The year in which was born
our lord, King Sar⌈ba⌉nabal,
the land was prosperous
the thin, *the split*
grew thick.
A man would find
its gatekeepers
in good health
(and be told):
"You, my brother,
enter this gate.
From our house

let us fetch (lit., take) for you
a morsel (of bread)[aaa]
and *let me roast* a goat
on ... onions."
(Then came) days
which had not been,
years which had not
passed / been spent / been turned.
The year in which was born
our lord, our brother,
Sarmuge,
the earth was bronze, the heavens, of iron,[bbb]
the soil,
in a bad/<a>rid state,
the heavens,
in poor/droughty condition,
A ma<n> would find its gatekeepers
very greatly
in distress / in need of food
(and be told): "Get away <from> this gate."
They (lit., he) would be wary of him
as of spies.

Sarmuge Sent to Babylonia as Governor to Collect Tribute (XVII.14-18)
(Then came) ⸢da⸣ys
which had not been,
years which had not
passed / been spent / been turned.
The king
spoke up and said,
addressing
Sar[mu]ge:
"Go
to (!) the land
of Babylonia.
Eat ⸢its⸣ bread
(as good) ⸢as *la*⸣*mb*
Dri⸢nk⸣ its wine
(as good) as the finest imported wine.
Devo<te> yourself
to its payment
of tribute
to [A]⸢ssy⸣ria."
Sarmuge went
⸢to⸣ the land
of Ba⸢by⸣lonia.
He (!) ⸢a⸣te its bread
(as good) as [*lamb*].
He [d]⸢ra⸣nk its wine
(as good) as the finest import⸢ed wine⸣.
He *devoted himself*
to ⸢its⸣ p[ay]me⸢nt⸣
of tribu⸢te⸣
[to] [A]ssy[ria].

Col. XVIII
A Defiant Message Instead of Tribute from Sarmuge's Emissaries (XVIII.1-4)
(Then came) days
which had not [b]⸢e⸣en,
years which had not
passed / been spent / been turned.
The emissaries went out
from <Ba>bylon
until they were ushered
into Nineveh.
They longed to (lit., for) rest
and to satiate themselves, (lit., and satiation)
dressed in their tunics.
"From Sarmuge
to Sarbanabal.
I am the king
of (!) / in (!) Babylon,
and you are
the/a governor
of/in Ni<ne>veh.
Pay tribute to me! [ccc]
Why should I show you respect?"

The Emissaries Imprisoned and Released (XVIII.5-15)
The king became angry
at the emissaries.
"Let them be brought down
from the dining hall, / to (!) the dungeon,
allotted bread and water." [ddd]
The *sun* shone (and) rose.
The general sent up ⸢ser⸣vants
to (!) the palace / from his palace.
"The word of our lord
to the king:
'O lord of kings, hear! [eee]
From the days of your father, [fff]
from the days of
your father's fathers,
emissaries
have not been imprisoned,
allotted bread and water.
Take out the emissaries
from the dungeon.
Let them be brought
to the bathhouse.
Dress them in embroidered garments.[ggg]
Go to *the prince*;
be gracious to him.
Count their sin against me.'"[hhh]
The advice was pleasing to the king.[iii]
The king
spoke up and said:
"I will take out the
emissaries

aaa Gen 18:5; 1 Kgs 17:10-11
bbb Lev 26:19; Deut 28:23; Jer 20:14
ccc 2 Sam 8:2, 6
ddd 2 Sam 10:4; 1 Kgs 22:27
eee Jer 37:20; Dan 2:47
fff Dan 5:11; Ezra 9:7
ggg Gen 41:14; Ezek 16:10
hhh Gen 27:13; 2 Sam 14:9
iii Ps 104:34

from the dungeon.
Let them be ⸢brought⸣
to the ba⸢t⸣h house.
I will dress them
in embroi⸢dered⸣ garments.
I shall go to the *prince*;
I shall be gracious to him.
Go out, emissaries, <from> the dungeon.[jjj]
Be brought
to the ⸢ba⸣th house.
Pu⸢t⸣ on
embroidered garments.
I shall go ⸢to⸣ [*the prince*];
[*I sha*]⸢*ll be grac*⸣*ious to* ⸢*hi*⸣*m*."

Saritrah Sent to Reason With an Ungrateful Brother (XVIII.15-XIX.8)

The king
⸢spo⸣[ke up] and [sai]d:
"Let them call
[S]aritrah,
my sister.
⸢Let⸣ Saritrah ⸢be⸣ ⸢br⸣[ought].[kkk]
⸢Let her (!)⸣ be caused
to [st]and
in the ga[te]
of the [p]ala⸢ce⸣
of the king ...."
The ⸢ki⸣[ng]
[spoke up and said,]
Col. XIX
add[re]⸢ss⸣ing
Saritrah:
You ...
The rotten fellow
who has sinned against me —
I made him the/a governor [lll]
of (!) / in (!) Babylon,
while I am king
in/of Nineveh.
A mighty horse
from (!) Media —
it was brought
to Sarmuge.
{Mighty} linen from (!) Egypt [mmm] —
we brought (it)
to our brother.
Daggers / *Purple (wool)*
from .../*Ty*<*re*>
we brought <to> Sarmuge.
A mighty bow from Elam [nnn]
we brought to our brother.
Go to the rotten fellow.
Speak,
say (it) to him.
Let him know,
listening to your words [ooo]
and giving heed
to your remarks."

jjj Isa 49:9
kkk Ps 45:15
lll Ezra 5:14
mmm Ezek 27:7
nnn Jer 49:35
ooo Job 33:1
ppp Gen 41:43
qqq Gen 31:21
rrr 2 Sam 18:24
sss 2 Kgs 13:7; Isa 41:2; Ps 83:14
ttt Prov 1:23
uuu Gen 29:1

Saritrah's Journey to Babylon (XIX.8-12)

Sarit(ah) went out
from the palace.
They seated her in the chariot. [ppp]
She set her fac⸢e⸣ toward Babylon. [qqq]
The lookouts went up on the wall [rrr]
of Babylon.
The lookouts
spoke up (and) said:
"The troop which
is coming / has come
is too large
to consist of emissaries,
too small
to consist of warriors."
Saritrah beckoned
from the city gate.
"Who here
is this / are you?"
"I am Saritrah,
sister of
the twins / the equal brothers."

An Attempt to Persuade Sarmuge to Return to Nineveh (XIX.12-XX.2)

Sarmuge
spoke up and said:
"*Nikkal is now*
between me and Sarit(ah):
She (=Nikkal) will not
let her (! = Saritrah)
see my face."
Saritrah
spoke up (and) said:
"Who made us/me
like ⸢stub⸣ble
<for> her feet? [sss]
Sarmuge, my brother!
Fortune has con<fou>nded you
and smiled upon (lit., been good to)
your brother.
Do listen to my words,
and may you give heed ⸢to⸣ my remarks. [ttt]
Act like (lit., make yourself) a governor /
Put your hands / (in) fetters.
Lift up ⸢your⸣ feet from here. [uuu]
Come to the king,
your bro⸢ther⸣.
He is fo⸢rbea⸣ring.
⸢He⸣ will not del<ay>
in <re>⸢ce⸣iving you."
Col. XX
Sarmuge
spoke up and said:
"Have [you] rubbed down
⸢and rested⸣
your hor⸢se⸣?
Why so swift
your riding?

A Second Unsuccessful Attempt at Persuasion (XX.2-6)
Sarit[rah]
spoke up (and) said:
"Listen / hear me, lord,
listen / hear me!
Truly, truly —
two kings
are being overturned
on account of
one of (!) *them*;
a man (lit., a brother)
and ⌜his⌝ brother
are quarreling
on account of
one of (!) *them.*
If my advice may be heard — /
If my king will listen to me —
disregard the tribute
<which> they did not pay you.
Act like (lit., make yourself) a governor/
Put your hands (in) fetters.
Lift up your feet from here.
Come to the king,
your brother."
Sarmuge
did not listen to her,
and did not give <heed>
to her remarks.

Saritrah's Parting Advice (XX.6-11)
Sarit(ah) spoke up (and) said:
"If you will not listen
to my words,
and *if* you will not give heed
to my remarks,
go from the house of Bel,
away from the house of Marduk.[vvv]
Let there be built for you
a bower (lit., a house of boughs);
a booth (lit., a house of sticks)
do constr<uct>.
Throw down tar and pitch [www]
and sweet-smelling/Arabian perfumes.[xxx]
Bring in your sons
and your daughters
and your doctors
who have made you act brashly.
When you see
how (low) they have sunk
on you (= to your detriment),
let fire burn you
together with your sons
and your daughters
and your doctors
who have made you act ⌜bra⌝shly."

Saritrah's Return and Report to the King (XX.11-15)
Sarit(ah) went out
from Babylon.
She set her face (toward) Nineveh.
She turned ⌜her⌝ ha⌜nd⌝ (and) her foot [yyy]
to go out from Babylon
until she(!) was ushered
into Nineveh.
The king
spoke up (and) said,
addressing Saritrah:
"What said to you
the rotten fellow
to ⌜who⌝m I sent you?" [zzz]
"The mee⌜ti⌝ng was
stormy (lit., like a blazing fur⌜nace⌝).[aaaa]
He contemned me."

The General Sent to Bring Sarmuge Back Alive
(XX.15-18)
The king
spoke up and said,
addressing the general:
"*I shall call up*
the <*t*>*roops*
in(to) the rank<*s*> *of*
the Ninevites.
You appoint a scribe [bbbb]
for ⌜*ba*⌝*tt*<*le*>,/ *Ca*⌜*ll*⌝ *up*
a war-scribe,
and polish all of your ⌜*swo*⌝*rds* and your spea⌜rs⌝. [cccc]
Furthermore,/Afterwards,
to Babylon you shall go,
general,
at the head
of a det⌜achment⌝."
The ⌜k⌝in⌜g⌝
spoke up and said,
addre⌜ss⌝ing
the general:
"Furthermore,/Afterwards,
let them smite Babylon
(but) let them keep my brother alive."

An Appeal and a Warning from the General (XX.18-XXI.7)
The ge⌜ne⌝ral went ⌜out⌝
from (!) the pala⌜ce⌝.
They seated him
in the cha[ri]ot.
He [se]⌜t⌝ h⌜is⌝ face
[toward] [Ba]bylon.

Col. XXI
The loo⌜kouts⌝ went up
to the wall of Babylon.
The look[out]⌜s⌝
spoke up (and) said:
"The troop [which]
⌜is coming / has come⌝ is
too large
to consist of emissaries,
too small

vvv Jer 50:2
www Isa 34:9
xxx 2 Chr 16:14
yyy 1 Kgs 22:34
zzz Jer 42:9
aaaa Dan 3:6
bbbb Jer 51:27; 52:25
cccc Jer 46:4

to be the army of the king."
The general
spoke up and said,
addressing Sarmuge:
"Listen / hear me, lord,
listen / hear me!
Truly — two kings
are being overturned
on account of (!)
one of them.
If my advice may be heard — /
If my king will listen to me —
disregard the tribute
which they did not pay you
Act like (lit., make yourself) a governor/
Put your hand (in) fetters.
Lift up your feet from here.
Come to the king, your brother.
He is forbearing.
He will not del<ay>
in receiving you."
Sarmuge
spoke up and said:
"So he (= the king) decreed
upon his governor,
your servant,
and so it is decreed."
"Then if so,
listen to your words
and may you give <heed>
to your remarks.
Begone,
for the wall of Babylon
in three days / after a day
we shall capture;
for the wall
I shall breach
af<t>er a day."

Sarmuge's Suicidal Response (XXI.7-11)
Sarmuge went
from the house of Bel,
away from the house of Marduk.
He {will have} built for himself
a bower (lit., a house of boughs);
a boot⸢h⸣ (lit., house of stic⸢ks⸣)
he did con⸢stru⸣ct.
He threw down tar and pitch
[and] sweet-smel⸢ling⸣ / Ara⸢bian⸣
[pe]rfumes.
He brou⸢ght⸣ in
his sons
and ⸢his⸣ daughters
⸢and⸣ [hi]⸢s⸣ doc⸢tors⸣
⸢who⸣ had made him act brashly.
Wh⸢en⸣ he [s]aw
⸢how⸣ (low) they had sunk
on h⸢im⸣ (= to his detriment),
... ⸢burned h⸣im ... [dddd]

dddd 1 Kgs 16:18
eeee Ps 41:4
ffff 2 Sam 1:24; Ezek 32:16

with hi[s] sons
[and his daughters]
and his doc[tor]s
who had made h⸢im⸣ act brashly.

A Desperate Attempt to Bring Sarmuge Back Alive (XXI.11-15)
The g⸢en⸣[er]al
keeps al⸢ive⸣ ...
y[ou]ng <and> old.
He ⸢we⸣[nt] ⸢out⸣
[from the palace].
They seated him
in the chari[ot].
He (!) ⸢se⸣t
⸢hi⸣[s] fa⸢c⸣[e]
toward <Ba>⸢bylon⸣. (*sic*!?)
Sarmuge
[he took] ⸢with⸣ [him].
Away they hu⸢rr⸣ied,
and they [*ca*]*me*
...
...
men
...
The doctor pounds
balm [and] [cas]sia;
(with) fran⸢kinc⸣[ense]
and lau⸢da⸣[num].
He bandages
...
He supports ... on ... a be⸢d⸣. [eeee]
⸢He ga⸣ve
...
and ⸢he hurried⸣
... ⸢up⸣ to the wall
...

Reactions to Sarmuge's Death (XXI.16-XXII.9)
...
The daughters of As⸢sy⸣[ria] ... ⸢mou⸣[rned] ⸢and⸣ ⸢wa⸣[iled]. [ffff]
...
...
...
⸢to⸣ <Ba>bylon
...
⸢to perish⸣
... ⸢and on⸣
...

Col. XXII
⸢my⸣ [ha]⸢nds⸣
in/with his blood."
...
to ...
to which of (lit., to whom out of all of)
...
one ... bring near.
⸢To⸣ my ⸢sist⸣er
let him be sent

⌜and let him⌝ say:
... the ...s
who overturned him
I shall bani⌜sh⌝.
They rebelled against me (lit., their hand
they lifted up against me), [gggg]
the one who nourished him
...
Saritrah
urged the king.
She sent (and)
urged the king
to ⌜wr⌝ite his wo[r]⌜d⌝
"Let them
⌜take away⌝ ... haughtiness from my presence. [hhhh]
I shall break
...
⌜r⌝ope
...
To the ⌜he⌝[ig]ht⌜s⌝ of
his temple
[I shall] ascend,
[I shall] go."

gggg 2 Sam 18:28; 20:21; 1 Kgs 11:26, 27

hhhh Dan 5:20

iiii 2 Sam 18:5, 12

Remember
how he perished (lit., his perishing),
(and) you shall bea⌜r⌝
your yo[ke],
refraining from ⌜go⌝ing up
to the hou[se] of
the one who holds
⌜h⌝[eav]⌜en⌝ and earth.
The king
⌜spo⌝[ke up] and said
⌜ad⌝[dress]ing the gener⌜al⌝:
"[Leave] the ⌜pa⌝lace,
get out.
Your sentence
I [pronounce]
on behalf of my god
...
Your ⌜fa⌝ce
he will not let [me] ⌜see⌝,
[for] ⌜I⌝ said [to you]:
'Let them smite Babylon
(but) let them keep my brother al⌜ive⌝.'" [iiii]

REFERENCES

Bowman 1944; Kottsieper 1988; 1992; Nims and Steiner 1983; Segert 1986; Smelik 1983; Steiner and Nims 1984; 1985; Steiner 1991; 1995; Steiner and Moshavi 1995; Vleeming and Wesselius 1982; 1983-84; 1985; 1990; Weinfeld 1985a; 1985b; Zevit 1990.

A UGARITIC INCANTATION AGAINST SERPENTS AND SORCERERS (1.100) (1992.2014)

Dennis Pardee

A new Ugaritic incantation text, similar in many respects to RIH 78/20 (text 1.96), was discovered in 1992 in the archive that has since been identified as belonging to Urtenu (Bordreuil and Pardee 1995), a high official in the city shortly before its demise (Arnaud 1982:106). The incantation was prepared especially for Urtenu (see lines 14-15) and shows a concern for venomous reptiles reminiscent of that visible in the "para-mythological" text RS 24.244 (text 1.94). We learn from this text that especially to be feared was the joining of forces between sorcerers and serpents. The text is expressed in the first person, the incantation priest speaking to the individual who fears attack.

Incantation Against Serpents (lines 1-8)
(When) the unknown one[1] [a] calls you and begins foaming,[2]

a Deut 11:28; 13:3, 7, 14; 28:64; 29:25; 32:17; Jer 7:9; 9:15; 14:18; 16:13; 17:4; 19:4; 22:28; 44:3

I, for my part, will call you.
I will shake[3] bits of sacred wood,
So that the serpent[4] not come up

[1] The Ug. formula is *dy l yd*^{c}, "the one not known." Because neither this text nor RIH 78/20, where the term *d*^{c}*tm* designates a category of sorcerer, deals with necromancy, one may conclude that the "knowledge" in question was not linked in any particular way with necromancy. The same conclusion is probably applicable to the *yidd*$^{e c}$*ōnīm* of the Hebrew Bible. Necromancy would, therefore, have been one form of divination among others practiced by sorcerers. The formulation of this text, in spite of the fact that the *d*^{c}*tm* are not mentioned in it, may indicate that the name of this group arose from their ability to deal with the unknown.

[2] The vocabulary of line 1 is non-problematic except for the last phrase, *ʾu zb*, taken here as cognate to Arabic *zabba*, which can mean "to foam." If this analysis is correct, it seems to indicate that the "unknown one" earlier in the line is the serpent, for the motif of serpent venom as foam or spittle is well known from Mesopotamian literature (see *CAD* I-J 139-141), while the ability of the serpent to speak is known from biblical sources (Gen 3) and its general cunning from various Mesopotamian sources (Lipiński 1983:40-43).

[3] The form is *ʾamrmrn*, a reduplicated verbal form either from the root meaning "pass on" (i.e., "make pass back and forth") or from the one meaning "to bless" (Pardee 1978b). Though either solution is plausible, the former is chosen here because moving the bits of wood back and forth shows more similarity to the acts described in more detail in RS 24.244:64-67 (text 1.94).

[4] The word for "serpent" here is *bṯn*, which appears only near the end of the Ug. liturgy against serpent venom, RS 24.244 (see note 28 to

against you,[b]
So that the scorpion[c] not stand up under you.[5]
The serpent will indeed not come up against you,
The scorpion will indeed not stand up under you!

Incantation Against Sorcerers (lines 8-13)
In like manner, may the tormenters, the sorcerers[6] not give ear[7] [d]

To the word of the evil man,[e]
To the word of any man:[8]
When it sounds forth[9] in their mouth, on their lips,
May the sorcerers, the tormenters, then[10] pour it to the earth.

Dedication to Urtenu (lines 14-15)
For *Urtenu*,[11] for his body, for his members.[12]

b Cf. Prov 30:19 *c* Deut 8:15; Ezek 2:6 *d* Deut 1:45; Ps 135:17 *e* Pss 1:1; 55:4; 119:1-10; Prov 11:18; 12:5, 6; 19:28; Job 10:3; 21:16; 22:18

text 1.94).

[5] The verb used for the movement of the serpent is the common *ᶜly*, "to ascend, go/come up, attack," while the scorpion is described by a verb previously unattested in Ug. (root *qnn*), perhaps best explained as geminate and compared with Arabic *qanna*, one meaning of which is "to stand on top of something," for the latter meaning is reminiscent of the stance taken by a scorpion when threatened.

[6] The two words used in this text to designate the enemies of ᵓUrtenu are *dbbm* and *kšpm*. Both occur in RIH 78/20 (text 1.96), where they also designate the adversaries of the person in need of the incantation (Pardee 1993a; forthcoming). The first is derived from a root meaning basically "to speak," secondarily "to attack verbally," while the second is cognate with Akk. *kaššāpu*, "sorcerer."

[7] Because the verbal form *tᵓudn* is followed by *hwt*, "word," it appears best to analyze it as denominative from *ᵓudn*, "ear," meaning "give ear to, listen to" (cf. Heb. *heᵓᵉzīn*).

[8] The terms designating the enemies of Urtenu who hire the sorcerers are *ršᶜ*, "the evil man" (cf. Heb. *rāšāᶜ*) and *bn nšm*, previously unattested in Ug., apparently similar in formation to Heb. *ben ᵓādām/ᵓīš* and to Aram. *bar ᵓᵉnōš*, "son of man." *Nšm* in Ug. is masculine, not feminine as in Heb.

[9] The root *ghr* is previously unattested in Ug. In Syriac it denotes weakness, especially of the eyes, while in Arabic, it denotes strength, especially of the voice and of the sun's rays. Because of the context of speaking here, the semantic field of the Ug. verb seems to be closer to that of Arabic.

[10] *kmm* is here taken as correlative with *km*, "in like manner," in line 8. It may also be analyzed, in proximity with the verb *špk*, "to pour," as consisting of the preposition *k* + a rare form of the word *my/mym*, "water."

[11] See the introduction to this text.

[12] "Body" and "members" represent another pair of words that occur also in RIH 78/20, *gb* and *tmnt*, designating the trunk and the extremities, i.e., the entirety of the body. In the text from Ras Ibn Hani, they also designate the body of the person in whose favor the incantation is made (there nameless), but in the context of that person potentially committing evil deeds against his own body, probably of a sexual nature (Pardee 1993a; forthcoming). Here the terms designate what Urtenu wants to be protected from serpent bite.

REFERENCES

Arnaud 1982; Bordreuil and Pardee 1996; Lipiński 1983; Pardee 1978b; 1993a; forthcoming.

THE LONDON MEDICAL PAPYRUS (1.101)

Richard C. Steiner

The London Medical Papyrus, usually dated to the late 18th dynasty (fourteenth century BCE), contains a number of short Semitic magical texts transcribed into hieratic syllabic script (Wreszinski 1912:150-152). Like magical texts of later periods, they are written in a *Mischsprache*, reflecting their transmission from one group to another. As befits a period when Canaanite vassals wrote to their Egyptian suzerain in Akkadian colored by their own dialects, we appear to be dealing with a mixture of Northwest Semitic dialects (Canaanite and Aramaic), with Egyptian phrases (rendered below in bold letters) and a few Akkadian terms thrown in for good measure. The determinatives used by the scribe show that he understood the texts and provide invaluable guidance to the decipherer. It appears that in these texts, Egyptian *k* renders Semitic *ḳ*, and Egyptian *s* renders Semitic *š* and *s* (as well as *ś* and *ṯ*), against the norm for this period. The notes given below are meant to supplement those of Steiner (1992);[1] they are fullest for those phrases which were not yet deciphered in that article.

(Number 27) **[Another] incantation against** ḥ-m-k-tu-**sickness in the language of those who dwell beyond the desert edge (= foreigners):**

[Hea]ler, **hidden one (= Amun), honor your spirit ...**
... spittle of our lord,[2] spittle ...
... spittle of our father.[3] Ishtar, mother[4] ...

[1] That article was written under the guidance of two outstanding Egyptologists: S. G. J. Quirke and R. K. Ritner.

[2] So Helck (1971:528). For the use of divine spittle as a remedy, see Ritner (1993:78-82).

[3] *Bu-n* = *būnā* < *ᵓabūnā* "our father" by apheresis. Cf. *bā* < *ᵓabbā* "father" in Targum Onkelos and the Galilean Aram. name *Būn*, derived from the word for "our father" (Dalman 1905:97). No. 28 has the full form, *ᵓ-bu-[n]*.

[4] So, approximately, Helck (1971:528). According to one interpretation of Amarna letter 23, Ishtar was a goddess of healing for the Egyptians

(Number 28)

...

⌜E⌝shmun,[5] [our] father

Ishtar and ...

(Number 29)

... physician ...

...

... healing

(Number 30) **An incantation against the fnṯ-snake/-worm:**

"⌜L⌝eave us," I say, "l<ea>ve us." **(Twice.)**

We have said our incantation.

(Number 31)

It is not so-and-so but I, the daughter of Spr.tw-n.s,[6] the daughter of my lord,[7] the governess.[8]

(Number 33) **An incantation against** s-mu-n-**sickness.**[9]

And ⌜through⌝ the vomiting up of the drunken demon,[10]

let ḥ-m-k-tu[11] go out, (O) my healer, **great one,** mother.[12]

(Helck 1971:459), but this interpretation has been disputed by Moran (1992:62).

[5] So Bossert (1946:114), noting that the Phoenician god Eshmun is equated with Asklepios, the Greek god of healing, in a trilingual inscription from Sardinia commemorating the healing of a certain Kleon.

[6] A scorpion goddess, the wife of Horus and daughter of Re. A daughter of this goddess would be a scorpion, for which the Eg. words (*wḥᶜ.t*, *ḏ*ᵓ*r.t*) are feminine. The patient proclaims, "It is not so-and-so but I, the daughter of Spr.tw-n.s," by which he/she means that he/she is no longer so-and-so but rather a scorpion. The declaration is designed to establish kinship with the scorpion whose venom is attacking him/her. I am indebted to R. K. Ritner for this entire interpretation and to S. G. J. Quirke for correcting Helck's reading of this spell.

[7] This Semitic phrase describes *Spr.tw-n.s* as the daughter of Re (personal communication from R. K. Ritner).

[8] This epithet of *Spr.tw-n.s* seems to be the feminine of *rābiṣu* "governor," an Akk. word common in the Amarna letters, which can be used of officials in the world of the demons.

[9] For this disease, see Massart (1954:50-52). For the Mesopotamian *samana/sāmānu* disease, which Massart believes may be identical, see now Kinnier Wilson (1994). I am indebted to R. D. Biggs for this reference.

[10] *W⌜b⌝-ḳi st s-bu-*ᵓ = *wa-⌜ba⌝-ḳī*(ᵓ) *šēdi sabū*ᵓ*i*. The word for "vomiting" is followed, appropriately, by the dirt-sickness determinative. For the widespread use of beer (Akk. *sību*) as an emetic, see Ritner (1993:81). The pathogenic demon is intoxicated and then regurgitated.

[11] The word *ḥ-m-k-tu*, written with the disease determinative in the introduction to no. 27, is written here with the seated-person determinative, suggesting that the disease is personified as a demon. In Steiner (1992:198), I compared it with the two strangling goddesses (ᵓ*iltm ḫnḳtm*) of Ug. and the strangling-demon (*ḥnḳt*) of the first Arslan Tash incantation. I subsequently learned from Hoch (1994:227-228) that Ebbell (1924:149) had equated it with Arabic *ḥumāq* "smallpox." Ritner informs me that "papular eruptions" indicative of smallpox have been found in the mummy of Ramses V (Smith and Dawson 1924:105-106; Harris and Weeks 1973:166). Ebbell's theory is phonetically simpler than mine, but is based on far later sources.

[12] The Aram. ending of ᵓ*-m-*ᵓ = ᵓ*imma*ᵓ "(the) mother," in a text which is otherwise Canaanite, and its position following an Eg. phrase at the end mark it as a later addition. This is further evidence for the theory that these texts are Phoen. spells which were borrowed and adapted by Arameans (Steiner 1992:199-200).

REFERENCES

Bossert 1946:114; von Deines, Grapow, and Westendorf 1958:254-259; Ebbell 1924:149; Helck 1971:528-529; Massart 1954:50-52; Steiner 1992; Wreszinski 1912.

B. ROYAL FOCUS

1. EPIC

THE KIRTA EPIC (1.102)

Dennis Pardee

The Kirta story was recorded on three tablets that were discovered during the second and third campaigns at Ras Shamra (1930-1931). Lacunae prevent a complete understanding of the story, which must have been longer, recorded on tablets never discovered. On the other hand, the high degree of poetic narrative repetition permit the comparatively certain restoration of some important lacunae. The story turns around the difficulties encountered by Kirta, king of a city designated only as Bêtu-Ḫubur, in obtaining an heir to his throne and in maintaining his hold on life after the birth of the son. The absence of reference to Ugarit may indicate that the story had its origin elsewhere, though that origin is uncertain, both in time and in place. The reference to Tyre and Sidon indicates an origin not far from Phoenicia and the mention of horses indicates a version dating after the introduction of the horse into the area (early second millennium). The story may have served a didactic role at Ugarit, teaching proper relationships between kings and deities, between people and king, and between royal offspring and their parents.

***CTA* 14**[1]

Classification of Tablet (i 1)

[Belonging to[2] (the)] Kirta[3] (text).

...

The Loss of Kirta's Brothers and Wives (i 7-25)

The house of the king perished,[a]
  who had seven brothers,
  eight siblings.[4] [b]
Kirta—(his) family was crushed,[c]
  Kirta—(his) home was destroyed.
His rightful wife he never obtained,[5]
  even his legitimate spouse.[6] [d]
A(nother) woman he married and she disappeared,
  even the kinswoman[e] who had become his.[7]
A third spouse[8] died in good health,[f]
  a fourth in illness;[9]
A fifth Rašap[g] gathered in,
  a sixth the lad(s) of Yammu,[10]
  the seventh of them fell by the sword.[h]
Kirta saw[i] his family,
  he saw his family crushed,
  his dwelling utterly destroyed.
Completely did the family perish,
  in their entirety the heirs.[11]

Kirta Mourns, Sleeps, Has a Dream (i 26 - iii 153)

He entered his room, he wept
  as he spoke (his) grief, he shed tears.
His tears poured forth
  like shekel(-weights) to the earth,
  like five(-shekel-weights) to the bed.
As he wept, he fell asleep,
  as he shed tears, he slumbered.[j]

a 2 Kgs 9:8
b Judg 8:19; Ps 69:9
c Mal 1:4
d Prov 18:22
e Lev 18:6, etc.
f Job 21:23
g Job 5:7
h Joel 2:8
i 1 Sam 18:9
j Job 33:15

[1] See also *KTU* 1.14.

[2] The archival classification is indicated by the preposition *l*, also known from tablets belonging to the Baʿlu (see notes 4 and 241 to text 1.86) and ʾAqhatu cycles; not to be confused with the *lamed auctoris* used in the (secondary) headings of several biblical psalms.

[3] Several other vocalizations of the name are possible, e.g., Karrate, Kuriti, Kurti, Karta. Since there is no evidence of Ug. having a vowel corresponding to Heb. *seghol*, the traditional vocalization "Keret" is the least likely.

[4] Lit., "sons of a mother" (*bn ʾum*).

[5] The meaning of *ypq* (from the hollow root *pq*), is established by the omen apodosis *mlkn l ypq špḥ*, "the king will not obtain offspring" (RS 24.247+:13; text 1.90).

[6] The meaning of *mtrḫt* is established by usages of the verb *trḫ*, "to marry," D-stem "to marry off," in Ug., by *terḫatu*, "bride-price," in Akk., and by *mtrḥ*, a priestly title, "spouse," in Punic.

[7] *t̲ʾar ʾum*, probably his first cousin on his mother's side, less desirable than the first cousin on the father's side, the first projected bride.

[8] *mt̲lt̲t* (and similar forms for the numbers "four" through "seven") are D-stem passive participles ("she who is made three/third," etc.), formed in imitation of *mtrḫt*, line 13, "she who is married off," i.e., "she who was the third (to be espoused to Kirta)." Lines 12-21 thus refer to seven wives that Kirta married or should have married, none of whom bore him a son.

[9] See: Held 1968.

[10] Rašap is the lord of the underworld, Yammu the sea-god. The reference to the "lad(s) of Yammu" is obscure; perhaps a metaphor for waves and hence a reference to death by drowning? The word *ǵlm* is used below as an epithet of Kirta with respect to ʾIlu (*nʿmn ǵlm ʾil*, "the goodly lad of ʾIlu") and as an epithet of Kirta's son Yaṣṣubu (see below, note 47). The feminine form *ǵlmt* is used of Kirta's nubile bride, whereas *pǵt*, "girl," is used to designate his female daughters (see below, note 51).

[11] It is uncertain whether *yrt̲* refers to Kirta's brothers mentioned above, to children who died at birth, or is simply the abstract notion, used in parallel with *špḥ*, "family, offspring" (from the same root as *mišpāḥāh* in Heb.), referring to the children the wives should have born him. The word *špḥ* reappears again only at the very end of Kirta's dream to designate his offspring (lines 152, 298). In *CTA* 16 it is used as a title of Kirta himself, identifying him as *špḥ ltpn w qdš*, "offspring of the Gracious and Holy One." Judging from the usage here and in lines 152,

Sleep overcame him and he lay down,
slumber and he curled up.[12]
In a dream ᵓIlu descended,
in a vision, the father of mankind.
He came near, asking Kirta:
Who is Kirta that he should weep?
should shed tears, the goodly lad of ᵓIlu?
Would he request the kingship of the Bull,[13] his father,
or dominion like (that of) the father of mankind?

Kirta Claims No Desire for Wealth, Preferring Children (i 52 - ii 58)[14]

[What need have I of silver
and of yellow gold][k]
along with its place;[l]
Of a perpetual [servant],[m]
of three [horses],
of a chariot in a courtyard,
of the son of a handmaid?[n]
[Permit] me to acquire sons,[o]
[Permit] me to multiply [children].

ᵓIlu's Reply: How to Obtain the Child-Bearing Wife (ii 59 - iii 153)

The Bull, his father ᵓIlu, [answered]
[(with) goodly (words)][15] as Kirta wept,
as the goodly lad of ᵓIlu shed tears:

Sacrifice (ii 62-79)

Wash and rouge yourself,
wash your hands to the elbow,
your fingers to the shoulder.
Enter [the shade of (your) tent],[p]
take a lamb [in your hand],[q]
a sacrificial lamb [in] (your) right hand,
a kid in both hands,
all your best food.
Take a fowl, a sacrificial bird,
pour wine into a silver cup
honey into a golden bowl.

k Ps 68:14
l Job 28:1
m Deut 15:17; Job 40:28
n Ps 86:16
o Gen 4:1
p 2 Sam 6:17
q 1 Sam 16:2
r 2 Kgs 23:12; Jer 19:13; Zeph 1:5
s Ps 73:4
t Exod 21:2; 1 Sam 17:25
u Jer 4:13; Zech 10:1; Job 28:26; 38:25
v Deut 20:7; 24:5
w Judg 6:5; 7:12; Nah 3:15-17

Climb to the summit of the tower,
yes, climb to the summit of the tower,[16]
mount the top[17] of the wall.
Raise your hands heavenward,
sacrifice to the Bull, your father ᵓIlu.
Bring down Baᶜlu with your sacrifice,
the Son of Dagan[18] with your game.

Preparation for the Campaign (ii 79-84)

Then Kirta must descend from the rooftops,[r]
must prepare food for the city,
grain for Bêtu-Ḫubur.[19]
He must bake bread for the fifth (month),
fine foods for the sixth month.[20]

Description of the Army (ii 85-103)

A throng will be provisioned and march forth,
a mighty throng will be provisioned,
a throng will indeed go forth.
Your army will be a numerous host,[s]
three hundred myriads,[21]
soldiers[t] without number,
archers without count.[22]
They will go by thousands like storm-clouds,[u]
by myriads like rain.
After two, two go,
after three, all of them.

Even Those Normally Excused from Military Service Will Go (ii 96-103)

The only son must shut up his house,
the widow hire someone (to go).
The invalid must take up his bed,
the blind man grope his way along.[23]
The newly-wed must go forth,[v]
entrusting his wife to someone else,
his beloved to someone unrelated.

The Campaign (ii 103 - iii 123)

Like grasshoppers you will invade the field,
like locusts the edges of the steppe-land.[w]

298, and from the formula *l ypq špḥ* in the birth-omen texts (e.g., RS 24.247+: 13 [text 1.90]), one can surmise that the word *špḥ* denoted offspring undifferentiated as to sex. For the latest of many interpretations of i 15-20, see Sasson 1988.

[12] See: Greenfield 1969:61-62.

[13] ᵓIlu is referred to below as *ṯr ᵓabk/h ᵓil*, "the Bull, your/his father ᵓIlu."

[14] The text containing the end of ᵓIlu's speech and the beginning of Kirta's reply is lost in the lacuna of about eight lines at the end of column i. The complete list that follows is restorable because it serves as a *Leitmotif* in this story, being offered also below by the father of the bride Kirta seeks, in place of the girl.

[15] {d[mq]t} hypothetically restored.

[16] This repetition may be a scribal error.

[17] Lit., "mount the shoulders of the wall."

[18] *bn dgn*, "Son of Dagan," is a standard title of Baᶜlu (see note 32 to the Baᶜlu text 1.86).

[19] The origin of this name is uncertain: perhaps an unknown place name or a circumstantial title for Kirta's city, "the house of union."

[20] Lit., "for the fifth ... for the sixth of months." Though the chronological indications in the following text do not indicate a campaign lasting six months, it appears unlikely that the reference here is to the fifth and sixth months of the year, for these would fall in winter (roughly January 21 to March 21). One may surmise that the formulation is hyperbolic for a long campaign.

[21] The significance of "three" here and in line 95 ("after three, all of them") is unclear, though in the second case, the term after "two" is expected to be "three" in standard parallelistic usage. Perhaps in both instances "three" is meant to underscore the vast number by virtue of its status as the first of the plural numbers (Ug. has a productive dual for expression of two entities, so plural expression begins with "three").

[22] The terms *ḥpṯ* and *ṯnn* denote two categories of military forces in Ug. (for bibliography, see Pardee 1987:385, 387, 454). Both these types, as well as the *ḫrd*-troops, are mentioned in one of the birth-omen texts (RS 24.247+ [text 1.90]).

[23] The meaning of *mzl ymzl* is disputed. Some see it as parallel to the second line of the preceding verse, i.e., the blind man does not go with the army (e.g., he puts out a sum of money, understood as meant to hire an able-bodied person to go in his place). Others see it as parallel to the preceding verse segment, i.e., the blind man, like the invalid, does go (as translated here above).

Go a day, a second,
  a third, a fourth day,
  a fifth, a sixth day.
Then at sunset on the seventh (day)
  you will arrive at ᵓUdmu[24] the great (city),
  at ᵓUdmu the well-watered (city).
Occupy the cities,
  invest the towns.[25]
The women gathering wood[26] will flee from the fields,
  from the threshing-floors the women gathering straw;
The women drawing water will flee from the spring,
  from the fountain the women filling (jugs).[x]
Then for a day, a second,
  a third, a fourth day,
  a fifth, a sixth day,
Do not shoot your arrows at the city,
  your sling-stones[y] at the towers.[27]
Then at sunset on the seventh (day of the siege)
  Pabil the king (of that city) will not (be able to) sleep
For the sound of the roaring of his bulls,
  for the noise of the braying of his donkeys,[z]
  for the lowing of his plough-oxen,[aa]
  the howling of his hunting dogs.

Reaction of the King of ᵓUdmu to the Siege (iii 123-136)

He will send messengers to you,
  to Kirta at his camp:
Message of Pabil the king:
Take silver
  and yellow gold
  along with its place;
A perpetual servant,
  three horses,
  a chariot in a courtyard,
  the son of a handmaid.
Take, Kirta, many gifts of peace,[28]
  leave, king, my house,
  go away, Kirta, from my court.
Do not besiege ᵓUdmu the great (city),
  ᵓUdmu the well-watered (city).
ᵓUdmu was given of ᵓIlu,
  (it is) a present of the father of mankind.[bb]

x Gen 24:11; 1 Sam 9:11
y Num 35:17
z Job 6:5
aa Job 6:5; 1 Sam 6:12
bb Deut 32:8; Eccl 3:13
cc Cant 7:5
dd Ps 11:4

Kirta's Reply (iii 136-53)

Send the messengers back to him (with the message):
What need have I of silver
  and of yellow gold
  along with its place;
Of a perpetual servant,
  of three horses,
  of a chariot in a courtyard,
  of the son of a handmaid?
Rather, you must give what my house lacks:
  give me maid Ḥurraya,
  the best girl of your firstborn offspring;
Whose goodness is like that of ᶜAnatu,
  whose beauty is like that of ᵓAṯiratu;
The pupils (of whose eyes) are of pure lapis-lazuli,[cc]
  whose eyes[dd] are like alabaster bowls,
  who is girded with ruby;
That I might repose in the gaze of her eyes,
  whom ᵓIlu gave in my dream,
  even in my vision, the father of mankind;
That she might bear a scion for Kirta,
  a lad for the servant of ᵓIlu.

Kirta Awakes, Carries Out the Instructions (iii 154 - end of tablet)[29]

Kirta looked about and it had been a dream,
  the servant of ᵓIlu, and it had been a vision.
He washed and rouged himself,
  washed his hands to the elbow,
  his fingers to the shoulder.
He entered the shade of (his) tent,
  took a sacrificial lamb in his hand,
  a kid in both hands,
  all his best food.
He took a fowl, a sacrificial bird,
  poured wine into a silver cup
  honey into a golden bowl.
He climbed to the summit of the tower,
  mounted the top of the wall.
He raised his hands heavenward,
  sacrificed to the Bull, his father ᵓIlu.
He brought down [Baᶜlu] with his sacrifice,
  the Son of Dagan with his game.
Kirta descended from the [rooftops],
  he prepared food for the city,

---

[24] As with Kirta's city, so the object of his campaign is unidentified, though the root letters are the same as those of Edom.

[25] The forms and meanings of the verbs are disputed. It appears possible to interpret this passage, in comparison with the passage below where Pabil is not attacked, as referring to the occupation of the towns surrounding Pabil's capital.

[26] The word for "female gatherers of wood" is problematic in each occurrence, here written *ḥṭbh* (corrected to *ḥṭbt* in *KTU*) in col. iv, line 214, *ḥṭb*, the verbal form being each time feminine (*sᶜt*).

[27] The passage is interpreted as prescribing a passive siege. The negative particle *ᵓal* sometimes appears in contexts where a positive meaning is expected, perhaps as a negative interrogative, i.e., a rhetorical question. If that were the case here, the reference would be to an active siege. In either case, those persons who normally provide provisions for the animals kept in the city (to which have been plausibly added those of persons fleeing the surrounding towns) are kept from their duties and the animals suffer (see the following lines).

[28] The text has here ***šlmm šlmm***, a plural noun repeated. Without vocalization, it is impossible to know whether the form of this noun is precisely the same as the sacrificial term ***šlmm***, "offering of well-being" (cf. Heb. *šᵉlāmîm*), or only etymologically related to it.

[29] There is much narrative repetition in this account, but with variants and additions.

grain for Bêtu-Ḫubur.
He baked bread for the fifth (month),
[fine foods] for the sixth month.
A throng was provisioned and [marched forth],
[a mighty] throng was provisioned,
[a throng did] indeed [go forth].
His army was a [numerous] host,
three hundred myriads.
They went by thousands like storm-clouds,
by myriads like rain.
After two, two went,
after three, all of them.
The only (son)[30] shut up his house,
the widow hired someone (to go).
The invalid took up his bed,
the blind man groped his way along.
The newly-wed conducted (his bride),[31]
entrusted his wife to someone else,
his beloved to someone unrelated.
Like grasshoppers they invaded the field,
like locusts the edges of the steppe-land.

Kirta Takes a Vow (iv 194-206)[32]

They went a day, a second;
at sundown on the third (day)
He arrived at the sanctuary of ʾAṯiratu of Tyre,
at (the sanctuary of) the goddess of Sidon.[33]
There noble[ee] Kirta took a vow:
The gift of ʾAṯiratu of Tyre,[34]
the goddess of Sidon (is this):
If I (successfully) take Ḥurraya to my house,[ff]
Bring the girl[gg] into my courts,
Double her (weight) in silver I will give,
triple her (weight) in gold.
(Then) he went a day, a second,
a third, a fourth day.
At sundown on the fourth (day)
he arrived at ʾUdmu the great (city),
at ʾUdmu the well-watered (city).
He occupied the cities,
invested the towns.
The women[35] gathering wood fled from the fields,
from the threshing-floors the women gathering straw;
The women drawing water fled from the spring,
from the fountain the women filling (jugs).
Then for a day, a second,
a third, a fourth day,
a fifth, a sixth day,
<They did not shoot their arrows at the city,
their sling-stones at the towers.>[36]
Then at sundown on the seventh (day)
Pabil the king (of that city could) not sleep
[For the sound of] the roaring of his bulls,
for the noise of the braying of his donkeys,
[for the lowing] of his plough-oxen,
the howling of his hunting dogs.
Thereupon Pabil [the king]
cried aloud to his wife:
Hear ...[37]
Now [head] off
towards [Kirta in (his)] camp
and say to noble [Kirta]:
Message [of Pabil the king]:
Take [silver
and yellow] gold
[along with its place];
A [perpetual] servant,
[three] horses,
[a chariot] in [a courtyard,
the son of a handmaid.
Take, Kirta, many gifts of peace,
do not besiege ʾUdmu the great (city),
ʾUdmu the well-watered (city).
ʾUdmu was given of ʾIlu,
(it is) a present of the father of mankind.
Leave, king, my house,
go away, Kirta,] from my courts.[38]
...[39]
[Then the messengers left without hesitation,
They headed off
Towards Kirta in his camp].
They raised [their voices and said aloud]:

ee Isa 32:5; Job 34:19
ff Gen 24:67; Ruth 4:11, 13
gg Isa 7:14

[30] ʾaḥd, "one," here in place of *yḥd*, "the solitary one," col. ii, line 96.
[31] *ybl*, "to bear, to carry," here in place of *yṣʾi*, "he must go forth," col. ii, line 100.
[32] This section breaks quite obviously into the sequence of seven days that was unbroken in the section of instructions (col. iii, lines 106-108). As there is no record in the text as preserved of Kirta's having carried out his vow, many believe that the woes he suffered after the birth of his children arose from his failure to carry out this duty.
[33] The form *ṣdynm*, which I take as the city name, is apparently archaic, preserving the original third radical. The form may be singular with enclitic *-m*, dual (*ṣidyānāma*), or plural (*ṣidyānūma*). In favor of the interpretation as a dual or a plural, note the references to different quarters of the city in the Eshmunazar inscription (*KAI* 14).
[34] The meaning of the phrase *ʾi ʾiṯt* is in doubt. Two principal explanations have been given: (1) a form of the particle of existence *ʾiṯ*, meaning "by the life of" or "as she lives;" (2) a noun meaning "gift" (from the hollow root *ʾṯ*) and referring to the silver and gold promised in lines 205-206.
[35] The form of the word meaning "gather" is not marked for feminine gender, though the verb "to flee" is (see above, note 26).
[36] This bicolon is absent here, apparently a true omission rather than a simple variant, for the preceding section is marked off by a particle (*dm ym w ṯn*), making it difficult to see the sequence of days as a description of the absence of the women workers, while the following section is not only introduced by a particle (*mk špšm b šbʿ*), making a syntactic link between the two difficult, but the timing (*špšm*) and the logic of the story seems to go against the link (i.e., Pabil is not at an end of his resources from the first day on).
[37] Col. v lines 230-243 are damaged and not repetitive of a previous section and thus cannot be restored. Because the next restorable section contains Pabil's words to his messengers, there has clearly been a change of address somewhere in the unrestorable portion.
[38] Space considerations seem to indicate the presence of this bicolon here rather than after "gifts of peace" as above, lines 131-133.
[39] The five-line lacuna at the beginning of col. vi is only partially filled by the restoration of the initial messenger formulae.

Message [of Pabil the king]:
Take [silver
  and yellow] gold
  [along with its place];
A [perpetual] servant,
  [three] horses,
  [a chariot] in a courtyard,
  [the son of a handmaid.]
Take, Kirta, many [gifts of peace],
  do not besiege ʾUdmu the great (city),
  ʾUdmu the well-watered (city).
ʾUdmu was given of ʾIlu,
  (it is) a present of the father of mankind.
Go away, king, from my house,
  Leave, Kirta, my courts.
Noble Kirta replied:
What need have I of silver
  and of yellow [gold]
  along with its place;
Of a perpetual servant,
  of three horses,
  of a chariot in a courtyard,
  of the son of a handmaid?
Rather, you must give what my house lacks,
  give me maid Ḥurraya,
  the best girl of your firstborn offspring;
Whose goodness is like that of ʿAnatu,
  whose beauty is like that of ʾAṯiratu;
The pupils (of whose eyes) are of pure lapis-lazuli,
  whose eyes are like alabaster bowls;
Whom ʾIlu gave in my dream,
  even in my vision, the father of mankind;
That she might bear a scion for Kirta,
  a lad for the servant of ʾIlu.
The messengers left without hesitation,
  They headed off
  Towards Pabil the king.
They raised their voices and said aloud:
Message of noble Kirta,
  word of the goodly [lad of ʾIlu...]

hh Ps 82:1

CTA 15[40]

Praise of Ḥurraya (i 1-7)
With her hand [she raises the hungry one,]
  with her hand she raises the thirsty one.
[...][41]
  to Kirta in his camp,
(As) the cow lows for her calf,
  the young nurslings[42] for their mother,
  so the ʾUdmites will lament for her.[43]

Kirta's Reply (i 8 - ii broken section)[44]
Noble Kirta replied:
...

Banquet for the Gods (ii 1-11)[45]
...
Noble Kirta prepared [a banquet] in his house
...
[Thereafter] the assembly of the gods[hh] arrived.

Blessing of ʾIlu (ii 12 - iii 19)
Mighty Baʿlu spoke:
Must you not depart, Gracious One, kindly [god],[46]
  must you not (go to) bless noble [Kirta],
  must you not pronounce a benediction upon the goodly [lad] of ʾIlu?
[ʾIlu] took a cup [in] (his) hand,
  a goblet in [(his) right hand].
He did indeed bless [his servant,]
  ʾIlu blessed [noble] Kirta,
  [pronounced a benediction] upon the goodly lad of ʾIlu:
The woman you take, Kirta,
  the woman you take into your house,
  the girl who enters your courts,
She shall bear you seven sons,
  even eight shall she produce for you.
She shall bear the lad Yaṣṣubu,[47]
  who will drink the milk of ʾAṯiratu,
  shall suckle at the breasts of Girl [ʿAnatu].
Suckling...

[40] This tablet is less well preserved than the preceding one; some forty lines are missing from the beginning of col. i. Judging from col. i, line 8, indicating a response from Kirta, the first part of the missing text contained portions of three speeches: (1) Kirta's refusal of wealth as recounted by the messengers to Pabil, (2) Pabil's entrusting of a new message for Kirta to his messengers, and (3) in the preserved portion of the column, the end of this message as recounted by the messengers to Kirta.

[41] Partially broken and uncertain; from context the passage should mean: "If Ḥurraya goes to Kirta, the following will be the situation."

[42] The meaning of *bn ḥpṯ* is uncertain; translated from context.

[43] *tnḫn* may be derived from the hollow root *nḫ*, "to lament," or from *nḫy*, "to lead." In the former case, the structure is comparative and similar to *CTA* 6 ii 6-9 (if that text be interpreted like this one). In the second case, the final clause is temporal: "... when the ʾUdmites lead her off."

[44] The formula of reply is preserved as the last line of column i. After the lacuna, Kirta is already offering what is apparently a feast for the gods in his house. One must assume rather typical narrative brevity, therefore, i.e., that Kirta has made his speech, obtained Ḥurraya, and returned home in the some twenty lines missing at the beginning of column ii.

[45] This is a badly damaged section, containing several divine names and a term for the gods viewed as a group, i.e., *ʿdt*, "assembly." The crucial words for what it is that Kirta prepared for the gods having disappeared from lines 8-10, the assumption of a type of banquet or feast is based on the fact that in the following section drinking vessels are mentioned.

[46] On these titles of ʾIlu, see note 46 to the Baʿlu text (1.86).

[47] On the name Yaṣṣubu, see the bibliography in Pardee 1989-90:407. His epithet *ǵlm* is the same as that applied to Kirta with respect to ʾIlu (see above, note 10).

…[48]
[Greatly uplifted] is Kirta,
  [amongst the Shades] of the earth,
  [in the gathering of] the assembly of Ditānu.[49]
Her time will come[50] and she will bear daughters for you:
  she shall bear girl […][51]
  she shall bear girl […]
  she shall bear girl […]
  she shall bear girl […]
  she shall bear girl […]
  she shall bear girl […]
Greatly uplifted is [Kirta],
  amongst the Shades of the earth,
  in the gathering of the assembly of Ditānu.
The youngest of these girls, I shall treat as the firstborn.[ii]
The gods bless, then depart,
  the gods depart to their tents,
  the circle of gods to their dwellings.

Birth of Kirta's Children (iii 20-25)
Her time came and she bore a son for him,
  her time came and she bore (two) sons for him.[52]
In seven years' time
  Kirta's sons were as they had been vowed (by ʾIlu),
  and so also were Ḥurraya's daughters.

ʾAṯiratu Claims the Vow (iii 25-?)
Then ʾAṯiratu thinks of his vow,
  the goddess […].
She raises her voice and [cries out]:
  O Kirta […]
  Or has repeated[53] the vow […]?
I'll annul[jj] […][54]
…

Kirta Sets a Feast (iv 1-13)[55]
Aloud to [his wife he cries out]:
Listen, [lady Ḥurraya]:
Slaughter the best [of your fatlings],
  open jars of wine;
Invite my seventy bulls,[kk]
  my eighty gazelles,[56] [ll]
  the bulls of Ḫubur the great,
  of Ḫubur [the well-watered].
…

Ḥurraya Obeys (iv 14 - vi)
Lady Ḥurraya listened:
She slaughtered the best of her fatlings,
  she opened jars of wine.
She brings in to him his bulls,
  she brings in to him his gazelles,
  the bulls of Ḫubur the great,
  of Ḫubur the well-watered.

ii Deut 21:16; Ps 89:28; 1 Sam 16:11
jj Ps 89:34
kk Jer 50:27
ll Isa 23:9

[48] Some fifteen lines are missing at the beginning of col. iii. Judging from col. iii, lines 7-12 where the daughters' names were set, part of this section may have been devoted to prescribing the younger sons' names.

[49] Standard formulae describing the ancestors of Kirta as well as of the Ug. dynasty (see RS 34.126, text 1.105). Ditānu, etymologically denoting a large ruminant of some kind ("bison"?), is probably the eponymous ancestor of an Amorite clan (see bibliography in Pardee 1989-90:448, to which should be added Lipiński 1978). We know from RS 24.252 (Pardee 1988a:75-118) that the Rapaʾūma (Heb. *rʿpāʾīm*, "the shades of the dead") served as conduits for divine blessing. Kirta's high status among them is not meant, therefore, to imply that he is dead, but that he is highly regarded and blessed by them.

[50] Here and in lines 20-21, the inception of the birth process is indicated by a form of the root *qrb*, "to be near, to approach," of which the precise explanation is uncertain, referring either to conception itself or to the end of gestation, as in our translation. The feminine form of the verb indicates that the wife is the subject, and the translation with "her time" is purely for ease of expression.

[51] It appears that lines 7-12 contained an enumeration of the names to be given to the daughters, though these may have been descriptive, rather than representing genuine proper names (the first and last signs of the first name are preserved, in both cases *t*, perhaps an adjectival form). Though six girls are named here, one of Kirta's daughters is below called Ṯitmanatu ("Octavia" < *ṯmn* "eight"). The word for the infant female daughters here is *pǵt*, not the same as the word *ǵlmt* used above to designate Kirta's nubile bride. *Pǵt* is the name of ʾAqhatu's sister (see text 1.103) and, in its proper Heb. form, that of one of the Heb. midwives in the Exodus story (Exod 1:15 Pūʿāh). For bibliography, see Pardee 1987:440-41.

[52] For reasons of logic, some emend "son" and "sons" to "sons" and "daughters," but the perceived importance of male offspring seems adequate explanation for the text dwelling here on the sons. The form *bnm* in line 21 could be either dual, referring to the second son or to twins, or plural, referring to the sum of sons born.

[53] The root *ṯny* does not denote active "change," as most translators have thought, for it is not cognate with the root *šnh* known from later WS languages, but is the verb derived from the number "two" and thus means "do twice," with various semantic developments. Kirta is not, therefore, being accused *here* of having altered his vow. Perhaps the sentence once contained a question regarding either his initial statement of the vow (*ṯny* can refer to a simple speech) or a later repetition of the verbal vow at a time corresponding to when he should have carried it out. The subject is uncertain as well, the form being *ʾuṯn*, though it appears likely that *ʾu* is the conjunction and *ṯn* therefore not an imperfect.

[54] It is tempting to follow most of the commentators in taking *ʾapr* as cognate with Heb. *prr*, which means "annul" in the Hiphil, in spite of the weakening of the semantic link with the preceding line produced by a correct analysis of *ṯn*. The following lacuna, a total of some twelve lines, leaves unknown, however, just what the goddess may have been annulling. It is also necessary to note that the Ug. form does not correspond to the Heb. Hiphil, for the causative stem in Ug. is marked by *š*-.

[55] Because Ḥurraya, in one of her speeches to the invitees, refers to Kirta's demise (col. v, lines 18-21), it appears that the divine punishment of Kirta must have been announced before that moment. It is unclear, however, where that was described in the text, whether in the text that has disappeared between columns iii and iv or in the lacuna between columns iv and v (or in both places, once as the initial announcement by the goddess, once as a repetition). In favor of the second placement, one might think that Kirta's behavior as depicted in column iv is hardly that of someone who has just been condemned by a goddess. In favor of the first, one can interpret the entirety of the banquet scene as some sort of a measure to deal with the problem of the condemnation.

[56] The two primary hypotheses for explaining the reference to bulls and gazelles are: (1) metaphors for magnates of the kingdom; (2) priestly and/or divinatory officiants who may have been wearing masks of the animals named.

The house of Kirta they enter,
 to the dwelling [...]
 to the tent of myrrh[57] they proceed.
She puts forth (her) hand to the bowl,[mm]
 puts the knife to the meat.
Lady Ḥurraya announces:
 To eat, to drink have I invited you,
 [...][58] Kirta your master.
...[59]
She puts forth (her) hand to the bowl,
 puts [the knife to] the meat.
Lady Ḥurraya [announces]:
 To eat, to drink have I invited you,
 ...
[For] Kirta you will weep,
...[60]
Kirta will go to where the sun sets,
 our master to where the sun rises.[61]
Then Yaṣṣubu will reign over us,
...[62]
Listen [...]:
 Again eat and drink
Lady Ḥurraya announces:
To eat, to drink have I invited you,
 (to) the sacrificial feast [of Kirta] your lord.
They weep over[63] Kirta,
 Like the voice of bulls is their voice.
In a dream [...] Kirta ...[64]

CTA 16

[Belonging to] (the) Kirta (text).

ʾIluḥaʾu Deals with the Prospect of His Father's Death (i 2-23)[65]

Like a dog we grow old in[66] your house,
 like a hound in your court;
Must you also, father, die like mortal men,[nn]
 must your court pass to mourning,[oo]
 to the control of women,[67] beloved father?
Will the mountain of Baʿlu weep for you, father,
 Ṣapānu, the holy citadel,
 Nannaya the mighty citadel,
 the broad-spread[pp] citadel?
For Kirta is the son of ʾIlu,[qq]
 the offspring of the Gracious and Holy One.
Unto his father he entered,
 he wept, gnashed his teeth,
 raised his voice in weeping.
In your life, father, we! rejoice,[68]
 In your not dying do we find happiness.
Like a dog we grow old in your house,
 like a hound in your court;
Must you also, father, die like mortal men,
 must your court pass to mourning,
 to the control of women, beloved father?
How can (that be when) they say:
Kirta is the son of ʾIlu,
 the offspring of the Gracious and Holy One.
Do gods die,[rr]
 Does the offspring of the Gracious One not live?

Kirta Replies, Requesting That Ṯitmanatu Be Summoned (i 24-45)

Noble Kirta replied;
Do not weep, my son,
 do not lament[ss] for me.
Do not empty out, my son, the fountain of your eyes,
 the water[69] from your head, your tears.[tt]
Summon your sister Ṯitmanatu,

mm Judg 5:26; Job 28:9
nn Num 16:29; Ps 82:6-7
oo Gen 45:2
pp Ezek 17:3, 7
qq 2 Sam 7:14; Pss 2:7; 89:27-28
rr Gen 3:22; Ps 82:6-7
ss Isa 23:2; Ezek 24:17; Lam 2:10
tt Jer 8:23

[57] In spite of some damage, there is general agreement to read the signs here as {wlḫmmr}, the best division of which seems to be *w l ḫm mr*, explained as an idiom for a banqueting hall, where myrrh-scented oil was used copiously.

[58] Restoration is not possible here, for the parallel versions in col v, lines 10-11, and col. vi, lines 4-5, seem to show variation in the second colon of the verse.

[59] About fifteen lines are lost from the end of col. iv and the first six partially preserved lines of col. v are too damaged to restore. It is thus uncertain whether we are dealing with multiple references to a single feast or to multiple feasts.

[60] After the order to "weep," i.e., to mourn for Kirta, there are five lines too damaged to translate. Line 13 (and col. vi, line 7) may contain a reference to "the voice of bulls" (in the second passage the expression takes the form of a comparison, for there, apparently, the family is weeping as loudly as bulls). Lines 14 and 16 may contain a reference to "the dead" (*mtm*), though the *-m* could be enclitic and *mt* could mean "man."

[61] The interpretation of these lines has been much discussed, the essential problem lying in the word *ṣbʾiʾa* (root *ṣbʾ*). The parallel terms *ʿrb* and *ṣbʾiʾa* have been best explained as a merismus, expressing the extent of the underworld to which Kirta must go (Garbini 1983:56). The order "west-east" reflects the progression of the sun through the underworld.

[62] Some eight lines are too damaged to translate at the end of column v. The shift from *bʿl*, "master," in col. iv, line 28, and col. v, line 20, to *ʾadn*, "lord," here in col. vi, line 5, may indicate that the family is being addressed here. In Ug. letters, *ʾadn* is used for one's natural father, while *bʿl* is used with reference to someone who is socially/politically superior (the only exception to this usage of which I am aware is in *PRU* v 60, where both *ʾadn* and *bʿl* are used of a political superior, perhaps implying the existence of a family relationship, whether real or fictional). See Ug. letters translated in *COS* 3.

[63] According to Caquot, Sznycer, Herdner (1974:548, n. *p*) the tablet is in bad enough shape here to allow for the reading *tbkn*, "they weep," though Herdner first read *tbʾun* (1963:71).

[64] Most of the end of col. vi is lost, for the few preserved lines are from the beginning. The bottom of the tablet having disappeared across the width of the tablet, it is impossible to calculate the exact number of missing lines, but one can estimate the loss at between forty and fifty lines. There is, therefore, no reason to be surprised that text 16 opens on what is apparently an entirely different scene.

[65] The first part of this passage contains someone's speech to ʾIluḥaʾu (or a self-address), then ʾIluḥaʾu repeats the gist of the speech.

[66] Or: "pass from," in the sense of "die."

[67] Mourning women.

[68] Written {ʾašmḫ}, rather than the expected {nšmḫ}.

[69] Correcting *mḫ*, "brain," to *my*, "water" (Gevirtz 1961), as is indicated by *mmh* in line 34.

the daughter whose ...[70] is strong,
that she may weep, may lament for me.
(My) boy, no need[71] to tell your sister (right away),
no need to tell your sister to mourn.
I know that she is compassionate;
so let's not have her pour forth her tears[72] in the fields,
her utterances on the heights.
[...] the rising of the great one, the sun,
the shining[73] of the great light.
Say to your sister Ṯitmanatu:
Kirta has prepared a sacrificial feast,
the king has set a banquet.
Take your tambourine in (your) hand,
your [...] in (your) right hand.
Go stay on the heights[74] (where) your lord[75] (lives);
take [silver] as your gift,
gold for all.[76]

ᵓIluḫaᵓu Complies (i 46 - ii ?)[77]

Thereupon, valiant[78] ᵓIluḫaᵓu,[79]
took his spear in hand,
his ...[80] in (his) right hand.
He approached (the place called) TRẒẒ;
when he arrived it was getting dark.
His sister had come out to draw water;
he planted his spear in a mound.
Her face came out the door,
then she saw her brother.
Her [...] broke on the ground,
[...] her brother, she wept.
[Is he] sick, the king,
[...] Kirta your lord?
Valiant ᵓIluḫaᵓu [replied]:
[Not?] sick is the king,
[...] Kirta your lord.
[...] has prepared a sacrificial feast,
[...] has set a banquet.
...

Ṯitmanatu Learns the Truth (ii 79-?)[81]

She approached her brother [and said]:
Why are you leading me [to ...]?
How many months has he [been sick],
how long has Kirta been ill?
Valiant [ᵓIluḫaᵓu] replied:
Three months has he [been sick],
Even four has Kirta been ill.[uu]
Perhaps Kirta has already departed.
A tomb you will ...

Ṯitmanatu Mourns the Prospect of Losing Her Father (ii 97-111)

She wept, gnashed her teeth,
raised her voice in weeping.
In your life, father, we rejoice,
In your not dying do we find happiness.
Like a dog we grow old in your house,
like a hound in your court;
Must you also, father, die like mortal men,
must your court pass to weeping,
to the control of women, beloved father?
Do gods die,
Does the offspring of the Gracious One not live?
Will the mountain of Baᶜlu weep for you, father,
Ṣapānu, the holy citadel,
Nannaya the mighty citadel,
the broad-spread citadel?
For Kirta is the son of [ᵓIlu],

uu Amos 1:3; Prov 30:15

[70] The meaning of *ḥmḥ* is unknown.

[71] The verbs in this section are preceded by ᵓ*al* or *l*. Because there is an emphatic *l* and because ᵓ*al* appears in phrases that must be interpreted positively (whether as a separate particle or in negative rhetorical questions is uncertain), some interpret negatively, some positively. Overall it appears best to interpret the forms as orders not to inform Ṯitmanatu of her father's illness, but to leave that news for later.

[72] Lit., "her water."

[73] The form *tgh* does not, unfortunately, provide a certain solution for the interpretation of *ṣb*ᵓ, with which it is in parallel here (see note 61), for it could be derived either from a root *ghy*, "depart" (and refer to the setting of the sun) of from a root *ngh*, "shine" (and refer to the rising of the sun). For bibliography on *ṣb*ᵓ, see Pardee 1987:441. *Nyr rbt* is, in any case, an epithet of the sun, not of the moon as some have thought, as is proven by RS 34.126:18-19 (text 1.105).

[74] If *ṣrrt* is the same word as is used in the description of Baᶜlu's dwelling, the reference is to mountain recesses.

[75] The word here is ᵓ*adn* (see above, note 62).

[76] The restoration at the end of line 44 and the interpretation of the two lines are uncertain.

[77] The beginning of col. ii is so damaged as to preclude a precise delineation of the speech(es) recorded there.

[78] The word *ǵzr* is difficult to translate into English (for bibliography see Pardee 1987:457-458). In this text it is used as an epithet of ᵓIluḫaᵓu, but not of Kirta, and some have for that reason translated "boy, lad." In the ᵓAqhatu text (1.103), however, it is used for both father (Dānīᵓilu) and son (ᵓAqhatu). In the Baᶜlu cycle the god Môtu is called a *ǵzr*. In administrative texts it appears to designate a son still living with his parents (*//pǵt*, "girl"). Finally, it appears in one of the Baᶜlu texts (*CTA* 3 ii 22) in parallel with other terms designating military personnel. The etymology usually cited, Arabic *ǵzr*, denotes abundance and generosity. From the Ug. usages, the term appears to designate a young man in full possession of his forces, able to do battle and to father sons. Because of the usage to designate both father and son, an English term denoting "youth" appears improper, while "hero" is too general and stilted. To translate the word *ǵzr* when used as an appositional title, the most frequent usage in these texts, the English adjective "valiant" seems to sum up reasonably well the connotations of the Ug. noun. When *ǵzr* appears alone, I have preferred "warrior."

[79] From this text, ᵓIluḫaᵓu is the son of Kirta and the brother of Ṯitmanatu. Since this story makes a point of all Kirta's children being from a single wife, one must assume that ᵓIluḫaᵓu was full brother to Yaṣṣubu, though this is not stated in the text as preserved. The form and "meaning" of the name remain obscure (the vocalization is a guess).

[80] The word at the beginning of line 48 is usually restored as {[g]⸢r⸣grh}, though that word is elsewhere unattested in Ug. and of uncertain etymology (cf. Sanmartín 1980:336).

[81] After the word *qbr* in line 87, the text is broken and obscure for nine lines.

the offspring of the Gracious [and Holy] One.

Ṯitmanatu Visits Her Father (ii 112-?)[82]

Weeping she entered [unto her father],
She entered the …

The Earth Does Not Produce (iii)[83]

Oil was poured [from a bowl].
(Someone) saw[84] the quaking of earth and heaven,
did the rounds to the extremities of the earth,[vv]
of (its) well-watered portions.
A spring for the earth is the rain of Baᶜlu,
even for the field(s) the rain[ww] of the High One;[xx]
Good[yy] for the earth is the rain of Baᶜlu,
even for the field(s) the rain of the High One.
Good is it for the wheat in the garden(s),
in the tilled land (for) the emmer,
upon the mounds (for) the ….[85]
The ploughmen lifted (their) heads,
on high those who work the grain,
(For) the bread was depleted [from] their bins,
the wine was depleted from their skins,
the oil was depleted from [their jars].[86] [zz]
…

The Divine Machinery is Set in Motion for Healing Kirta (iv)[87]

…
Like ᵓIlu are you wise,
like the Bull, the Gracious One.
Summon the herald of ᵓIlu, ᵓIlšu,
ᵓIlšu, <the herald of the house of Baᶜlu>,[88]
and his wife, the herald of the goddesses.
…
He summoned the herald of ᵓIlu, ᵓIlšu,
ᵓIlšu, the herald of the house of Baᶜlu,
and his wife, the herald of the goddesses.

vv Ps 48:11; 65:6
ww Ps 147:8; Job 5:10
xx 1 Sam 2:10; Ps 7:11; 68:35
yy Gen 49:15
zz 1 Kgs 17:14; Hab 3:17; Ps 104:15
aaa Exod 15:11
bbb 1 Kgs 18:29; Job 5:1
ccc Job 33:6

The Gracious One, the kindly god, responds:
Listen, herald of ᵓIlu, ᵓIlšu,
ᵓIlšu, herald of the house of Baᶜlu,
and your wife, the herald of the goddesses:
Climb to the summit of the edifice,
to the high terrace…

ᵓIlu Seeks a Healer Among the Gods (v 10-22)

…[89]
The Gracious One, [the kindly god, asked]:
[Who] among the gods[aaa] [will expel the sickness],
banish the illness?
[None of the gods] responded to him.[bbb]
A [second time, a third time] he spoke:[90]
Who among [the gods will expel] the sickness,
banish [the illness]?
None of the gods responded [to him].
[A fourth], a fifth time he spoke.
[Who among the gods] will expel the sickness,
banish [the illness]?
None of the gods responded [to him].
A sixth, a seventh time he spoke:
[Who] among the gods will expel the sickness,
banish the illness?
None of the gods responded to him.

Finding No Takers, ᵓIlu Fashions a Healer (v 23-?)

So the Gracious One, the kindly god, said in response:
Go sit down, my sons, on your seats,
on your princely thrones.
I will personally fashion and establish,
will establish a female expeller of the sickness,
a female banisher of the illness.
He filled [his hand] with clay,
[his right hand] with the very best clay.
He pinched off … [91] [ccc]

---

[82] The state of the tablet prevents us from knowing whether Ṯitmanatu's trip home took place earlier or is dispensed with in the narrative. Col. iii contains a very different set of motifs and, unless they are part of a speech made by Ṯitmanatu in her father's presence, these indicate a major narrative shift. There are about eleven lines partially or totally destroyed at the end of col. ii and another thirty from the beginning of col. iii.

[83] Though it is isolated from its context by breaks, one can judge from general parallels in other texts that this passage presents agricultural fertility as having waned because of Kirta's illness. If this interpretation is correct, the divine aspect of Kirta's nature is thereby emphasized.

[84] Space does not appear sufficient to read the divine name ᶜAnatu here, as some have proposed on the basis of parallels in the Baᶜlu cycle.

[85] The signs *ᶜṭrṭrm*, apparently parallel to *ḥṭṭ*, "wheat," and *ksmm*, "emmer-wheat," in the preceding lines, are enigmatic. If divided as *ᶜṭr ṭrm* the words may reflect a vision of rows (*ṭrm*) of grain constituting a crown (*ᶜṭr*) upon the tells (Caquot, Sznycer, Herdner 1974:561, n. *n*). Or the signs may represent a single word, showing partial reduplication of the root *ᶜṭr*, which in Arabic denotes various notions of "fragrance," though it is unclear what crop would be designated as the "fragrant ones."

[86] The precise meaning of the word here translated from context as "bins" (*ᶜdn*) is uncertain, the word denoting "skin (for wine)" (*ḥmt*) is attested in Biblical Heb. only as a container for water, while only the first sign is preserved of the word for the oil containers, i.e., {q}, which does not permit restoration, for no word for oil containers is attested with {q} as its first letter (*dd* and *kd* are the two best-attested words).

[87] The remains of this column also are separated from the context by major breaks, with more than thirty lines missing between this text and the preceding and nearly thirty between this text and the following.

[88] Emended after lines 8 and 12.

[89] The first nine lines are too broken to translate. In lines 8, 9 one finds the words *ṯnnth* and *ṯlṯth*, the second certainly a form of the number "three," the first perhaps derived from *ṯny*, the root whence the number "two" is derived. The similarities between these forms and those used by Kirta in his vow (*CTA* 14 col. iv, lines 205, 206, *ṯnh*, *ṯlṯh*) indicate the possibility of a literary connection between the two passages, though this one is too damaged to allow meaningful comparison.

[90] All the numerically designated repetitions are expressed verbally: "He duplicated, he triplicated the word," etc.

[91] *qrṣ* denotes the potter's act of taking from a large piece of prepared clay the amount needed to fashion the specific object he has in mind. Some thirty lines are damaged or missing at the end of col. v. The act of creation of a healer seems to be completed quickly, for in lines 40-41 one finds *ks* and *kr[pn]*, the usual terms for drinking vessels used at feasts and in blessings, followed by an apparent address to the healer (*ᵓat š[ᶜtqt]* in line 42), and in lines 50-51 a reference to the illness she is to dispel (*mr[ṣ]*, *zb[ln]*). It is tempting to see in the word *tnn* appearing after lacunae in lines 31 and 32 (plausibly cognate with Heb. *tannîn*, "dragon") a parallel to the Mesopotamian creation story which refers to the blood of another creature used in the creation of man (De Moor 1980a:181-82; cf. del Olmo Lete 1981:318).

End of ʾIlu's Address to Šaᶜtiqatu [92]the Healer (vi 1-2)

O death, be shattered,
  O Šaᶜtiqatu, be powerful.

Šaᶜtiqatu Does Her Job (vi 2-14)

Off went Šaᶜtiqatu:
  she entered Kirta's house,
  amongst weeping did she arrive and enter,
  amongst distress did she go on in.
She overflew cities...
  overflew towns...[93]
...
  the sickness (from ?) upon his head.[94]
She comes back (or: sits down), washes him of his perspiration,
  opens up his throat so he can eat,
  his gullet so he can dine.[95]
Death is shattered,
  Šaᶜtiqatu is powerful.

Kirta Recovers (vi 14-24)

Noble Kirta gave orders,
  he raised his voice and said aloud:
Listen, lady Ḥurraya:
Slaughter a lamb that I might eat,
  a fatling that I might dine.
Lady Ḥurraya listened:
She slaughtered a lamb and he ate,
  a fatling and he dined.
Then for a day, even two,
  Kirta returned to his (throne-)room,[96]
  he sat on the royal throne,
  on the dais, on the seat of dominion.

Yaṣṣubu, Impatient, Wishes to Rule (vi 25-end)

Yaṣṣubu also returned to the palace,
  where his inner self instructed[ddd] him:[97]
Go to your father, Yaṣṣubu,
  go to your father and speak,
  say to Kirta [your lord]:
Listen closely and tend [(your) ear:
When raiders] lead [raids],
  and creditors [detain (debtors)],[98]
You let your hands fall slack:
  you do not judge the widow's case,[eee]
  you do not make a decision regarding the oppressed.[99]
Illness has become as it were (your) bedfellow,[fff]
  sickness (your) constant companion in bed.
So descend from your kingship, I will reign,
  from your dominion, I, yes I, will sit (on your throne).
Yaṣṣubu the lad went off,
  entered his father's presence.
He raised his voice and said aloud:
Listen, noble Kirta,
  listen closely and tend (your) ear:
When raiders lead raids,
  and creditors detain (debtors),
You let your hands fall slack:
  you do not judge the widow's case,
  you do not make a decision regarding the oppressed
  you do not cast out those who prey upon the poor.[ggg]
Before you, you do not feed the orphan,
  behind your back the widow.[hhh]
Illness has become at it were (your) bedfellow,
  sickness (your) constant companion in bed.
So descend from your kingship, I will reign,
  from your dominion, I, yes I, will sit (on your throne).

Kirta, Not Liking That Idea at All, Curses Yaṣṣubu (vi 54-58)

Noble Kirta responded:
May Ḥôrānu[100] break, my son,

ddd Ps 16:7

eee Deut 10:18; Isa 1:17; Job 29:12-13

fff Ps 41:4; Job 17:14

ggg Amos 5:11

hhh Isa 10:2; Ps 82:2-4; Job 22:9; 31:16-17

---

[92] The name means "She who causes to pass on," a feminine nominal formation of the causative stem of the root ᶜ*tq*, "pass on." This is the root that designated old age and/or death in the opening lines of the text on this tablet.

[93] Because of the uncertainty of the following units, it is difficult to determine whether the reference to Šaᶜtiqatu's aerial travels describes a departure from Kirta's house or, retrospectively, her arrival there. Unfortunately, the verbal form *t*ṯ*b* in line 10 does not help, for it can be derived either from the hollow root ṯ*b*, "return," or from *y*ṯ*b*, "sit down."

[94] The obscurity of line 8 leaves uncertain the function of the reference to the illness.

[95] On *npš* and *brlt*, see note 203 to the Baᶜlu text (1.86 above). The use of the verb *ptḥ*, "open," makes it clear that the words in question denote the body part(s), not an abstract notion such as "appetite." The means by which the throat is opened, physical, chemical, or magical, being uncertain, it is equally uncertain how the fact of opening is related to the illness.

[96] The word ᶜ*d* seems also to be attested as designating a room in the temple of Baᶜlu ʾUgārīta (RS 24.266:9 [text 1.88]).

[97] *ggn*, apparently another word for "throat" (< "tube") is here the active agent of the verb "instruct." The translation is literal, though the modern equivalent would seem to be "he said to himself."

[98] Lines 30-31 have inspired the most divergent interpretations: a description of Kirta's illness, a rhetorical question regarding his ability to lead, an accusation of duplicity, etc. The translation proposed here is no surer than several of those already made, but it takes into account the one reasonably sure thing that can be stated, though that only negatively: ṯ*wy* does not mean "be like," as some have thought, for it cannot be cognate with Heb. and Aram. *šwh*. As the G-stem of the root takes a mono-consonantal form in Ug. (*t*ṯ *lḥmy* "she furnishes my food" [RS 17.117:6]), *t*ṯ*wy* in line 31 (restored on the basis of line 44) is probably a D-stem form, which means "detain" in Arabic. The retention of the final root consonant may indicate a following long vowel, indicating a plural form. Thus the subject of this (and the preceding) verb is not Kirta, but the perpetrators of the violence and oppression that he is accused of being unable to quell.

[99] See: Haak 1982.

[100] Ḥôrānu is a chthonic deity best known from Ug. sources for his power over serpents and sorcerers (see here RS 24.244 [text 1.94] and RIH 78/20 [text 1.96]).

may Ḥôrānu break your head,
Aṯtartu "name" of Baᶜlu[101] your skull.
You will surely fall...
...[102] and be humbled.

Colophon
The scribe: ᵓIlīmilku the *ṯāᶜiyu*-official.[103]

[101] Though the title *šm bᶜl* appears once again some seven centuries later as a title of Astarte in Sidon (in the Eshmunazar inscription, *KAI* 14:18, the two occurrences do not provide sufficient data for an explanation.

[102] The parallel phrases *b gbl šntk* and *b ḥpnk* have not been satisfactorily explained.

[103] The *ṯāᶜiyu*-official exercised what was basically a cultic function, as is shown by various nominal forms of the root *ṯᶜy* used in the ritual texts to denote a type of sacrifice and the priest in charge of that sacrifice, while the verb is used to denote the offering of that sacrifice.

REFERENCES

Text: *CTA* 14-16; *KTU* 1.14. Translations and studies: Caquot, Sznycer and Herdner 1974; Driver 1956; Garbini 1983; Gevirtz 1961; Gibson 1978; Ginsberg 1946; Gordon 1977; Greenfield 1969; Haak 1982; Held 1968; Herdner 1963; Lipiński 1978; de Moor 1980a; 1987; del Olmo Lete 1981; Pardee 1987; 1988a; 1989-90; Parker 1989; Sanmartín 1980; Virolleaud 1936a; 1941a; 1941b; 1942-43a; 1942-43b.

THE ᵓAQHATU LEGEND (1.103)

Dennis Pardee

The ᵓAqhatu story was recorded on three tablets that were discovered during the second and third campaigns at Ras Shamra (1930-1931). Lacunae prevent a complete understanding of the story, which must have been longer, recorded on tablets never discovered. Like the story of Kirta, this one tells how a father obtained a son, here Dānīᵓilu and his son ᵓAqhatu, but from that point the two stories diverge: Here the son assumes the primary role instead of the father. The kernel of the story is ᵓAqhatu's confrontation with a deity, the goddess ᶜAnatu, whose overtures to obtain his favorite bow he repels, with the result that the goddess has him put to death. After his death, his sister Pūġatu comes to the center of the stage, a heroine who attempts to avenge her brother's death. She is apparently on the point of doing so when the text breaks off.

CTA 17

Dānīᵓilu Seeks a Son (i 1-34)

[Thereupon, as for Dānīᵓilu the man of Rapaᵓu],
thereupon, as for the valiant [Harnamite man],[1]
Girded, he gave the gods food,
[girded, he gave] the Holy Ones [drink].[2]
He cast down [his cloak, went up],[a] and lay down,
cast down [his girded garment[3]] so as to pass the night (there).[b]
A day, [even two,
girded,] Dānīᵓilu (gave) the gods (food),
[girded,] he gave [the gods] food,
girded, [he gave] the Holy Ones [drink].
A third, even a fourth day,
[girded,] Dānīᵓilu (gave) the gods (food),
girded, he gave [the gods] food,
girded, he gave the [Holy] Ones drink.
A fifth, even a sixth day,
girded, Dānīᵓilu (gave) [the gods] (food),
girded, he gave the gods food,

a Gen 49:4; 2 Kgs 1:4, 16
b 1 Sam 3; Ps 17:3, 15

[1] Dānīᵓilu's two titles have elicited a great deal of discussion. Judging from the writing of the first, it is a genitive expression, as translated above, not a gentilic (i.e. not "the Rapaᵓite man," as some have translated), and it appears to be related to the term Rephaim, well known in the Bible, in Phoenician inscriptions, and in Ug., perhaps even to the eponymous ancestor of the Rephaim, known in the Bible as *hārāpāᵓ*. The second title, *hrnmy*, bears the gentilic suffix and has often been explained as geographical in origin (Albright 1953). Dānīᵓilu's name is derived from the hollow root *dn* "to judge" (in the forensic sense, rather than the sense of a tribal leader, the latter being *ṯpṭ*), which is the only social occupation ascribed to him in the story (col. v, lines 5-8). His wife's name, Dānatay, seems to be built off the same root.

[2] There is no consensus regarding the interpretation of this verse, of which the restoration is supplied by repetitions below. It presents two primary difficulties, (1) the meaning of *ᵓuzr* and (2) the proper analysis of the verbs *lḥm* and *šqy*, whether simply transitive ("he ate/drank") or factitive/causative ("he gave food/drink"). The verbs are here analyzed as factitive ("give to eat/drink"). Though such a usage cannot be shown to exist elsewhere for *lḥm*, Tropper (1989) has demonstrated that *šqy* is used factitively (he does not, however, adopt that interpretation in this passage), and it appears plausible on that basis to posit such a usage of *lḥm*. This conclusion is based primarily on the fact that the interpretation of the verbs as simple transitives entails the acceptance of an aberrant syntactic structure, i.e., the breaking up of the construct chain "*ᵓuzr* of the Holy Ones," for the verb is placed between *ᵓuzr* and *bn qdš*. Though the meaning of *ᵓuzr* is unknown, it appears more plausible to see the word as modifying the subject (as translated here) or as an adverbial ("with X did he ...") than to take it as a noun denoting what is eaten and drunk (why would the same word be used for both the food and the drink?). Tied up with the interpretation of the terms is that of the passage as a whole: does it describe an incubation scene? That interpretation appears more likely if Dānīᵓilu is feeding the gods than if he is himself eating high-class food.

[3] The precise meaning of *mᵓizrt*, here taken from the same root as *ᵓuzr*, is uncertain. A masculine form of the noun may appear in two economic texts in Akk. from Ras Shamra (Nougayrol 1970:99-100), though that may be a different word. The basic question here is whether the garment is only a loin-cloth, which would imply that he served the gods half naked (as some have argued) and that he lay down naked, or whether it implies a full garment held in place by a belt.

[girded,] he gave the Holy Ones drink.
Dānīʾilu cast down his cloak, went up, and lay down,
[cast down] his girded garment so as to pass the night (there).

Baʿlu Appears, Intercedes on Dānīʾilu's Behalf (i 16-27)

Then on the seventh day,
Baʿlu approached, having had mercy on
The lamenting of Dānīʾilu the man of Rapaʾu,
the groaning of the valiant Harnamite [man],
Who had no son like his brothers,
no scion[c] like his kinsmen.[d]
May he, like his brothers, have a son,
like his kinsmen, a scion.
For, girded, he has given the gods food,
girded, he has given the Holy Ones drink.
O Bull ʾIlu, my father, please bless him
please pronounce a benediction upon him, O creator of creatures,
So that he may have a son in his house,[4]
a scion within his palace:

The Duties of a Son (i 27-34)[5]

Someone to raise up the stela of his father's god,[6]
in the sanctuary the votive emblem of his clan;[7]
To send up from the earth his incense,
from the dust the song of his place;[8]
To shut up the jaws of his detractors,[e]
to drive out anyone who would do him in;
To take his hand[f] when (he is) drunk,
to bear him up [when] (he is) full of wine;[9]
To eat his grain(-offering) in the temple of Baʿlu,
his portion in the temple of ʾIlu;[g]
To re-surface his roof when rain softens it up,[10]
to wash his outfit[11] on a muddy day.

ʾIlu Blesses Dānīʾilu (i 35-?)[12]

[A cup] ʾIlu took <in his hand,
a goblet in his right hand,
He did indeed bless> his servant,
blessed Dānīʾilu the man of Rapaʾu,
pronounced a benediction upon the valiant Harnamite [man]:
May Dānīʾilu, [the man] of Rapaʾu, live indeed,
may the valiant Harnamite man live to the fullest.[13]
[...] may he be successful:[14]
to his bed he shall mount [and lie down];
As he kisses his wife [there will be conception],
as he embraces her there will be pregnancy;
[...] she who was about to bear,
pregnancy [for the man of] Rapaʾu.
He will have a son [in his house,
a scion] within his palace:
[Someone to raise up the stela of] his father's god,
in the sanctuary [the votive emblem of his clan];
To send up from the earth [his incense,
from the dust the] song of his place;
[To shut up the jaws of his detractors],
to drive out anyone who would do [him] in;
...[15]

ʾIlu's Promise is Recounted to Dānīʾilu (ii 1-8)

...
[Someone to raise up the stela of your father's god,
in the sanctuary the] votive [emblem of your

c Isa 11:1, 10; Amos 2:9; Dan 11:7
d Num 27:4; 2 Sam 11:10
e Ps 63:12
f Isa 51:18
g 1 Sam 1:4

[4] Lit., "so that his son may be in the house."

[5] This unit constitutes a set piece within the larger drama, being repeated three times below. As is shown by the verbal forms from derived stems, each attribute is expressed as a participle, "the one who does such-and-such," here translated as "someone to ...."

[6] At the head of the Ug. "pantheon" lists stands ʾIluʾibī, "the god of the father," apparently the generic designation of the special deity of a clan, tribe, or other ethnic group. The *ʾilʾib* in this text is the same formulation in the form of a common noun, probably a true compound noun, with the same shift of /a/ to /i/ in the first syllable of the second element under the influence of the long case vowel (nominative /ʾabū/, genitive /ʾabī / > /ʾibī/). It must be noted carefully that this deity, like the directly related common noun, does not, according to this explanation, represent the "deified ancestor," but the "deity of the ancestor." The veneration of the deity ʾIluʾibī in the sacrificial cult betrays no particular characteristics of a cult of dead and deified ancestors. In this text that type of cult is referred to, if at all, in the next verse.

[7] *ztr* ≈ Hittite *sittar-* "votive (sun) disk" (Tsevat 1971:351-352).

[8] A much discussed verse, as regards both individual words and over-all interpretation, here taken as referring to the cult of the ancestors at the family vault, which was at Ugarit located under the house. Though recent archaeological work has shown the unlikelihood of frequent incursions into the vault itself (Pitard 1994a), one may expect there to have been some regular, formal recognition of the presence of the dearly departed, as well as a funerary cult in the narrow sense of the term whenever a new inhumation occurred. The outline of the funeral service for a dead king of Ugarit, Niqmaddu (III), has been recorded in RS 34.126 (here text 1.105).

[9] RS 24.258:18-19 (here text 1.97) depicts the double deity Ṯukamuna-wa-Šunama doing this for their father ʾIlu.

[10] Lit., "... on a day of mud." Every house at Ugarit had its roof-roller (Elliott 1991:85) to reconsolidate the clay surface of the roofs and terraces after moisture had loosened the surface bonding.

[11] *npṣ* is a generic term, apparently denoting a combination of garments and equipment.

[12] Col. i breaks off in the middle of ʾIlu's speech. On the restored and emended text at the beginning of this section, see Pardee 1977, with previous bibliography.

[13] The Ug. formulation is difficult to render in English: "As to (his) throat, may Dānīʾilu, the man of Rapaʾu, live, as to (his) gullet, the valiant Harnamite man." The words *npš* and *brlt*, already encountered in the Kirta text (text 1.102; see note 95 to that text and here below, note 127), here denote metonymically the life forces.

[14] The beginnings of lines 39-43 are broken and unreconstructable with certainty because the formulae seem to vary as compared with other examples of the conception/pregnancy/birth motif. The reconstruction and explanation of the first line in part follow Dijkstra, De Moor 1975:178.

[15] Col. i breaks off here; ʾIlu certainly included in his blessing the remainder of the ideal son's duties. The text missing between the remains of cols. i and ii contained the narrative framework for transmitting the message of ʾIlu's blessing to Dānīʾilu, for the end of that message is found at the beginning of col. ii, as preserved. Note that in the recounted form, Dānīʾilu is addressed directly, whereas in ʾIlu's blessing he was referred to in the third person.

clan;
To send up from the earth your incense,]
from the dust the song [of your place;
To shut up] the jaws of your detractors,
to drive out [anyone who would do you in;][16]
To eat your grain(-offering) in the temple of [Baᶜlu,
your portion] in the temple of ᵓIlu;
To take your hand when [(you are) drunk],
to bear you up when (you are) full of wine;
To roll your roof when rain softens it up,
to wash your outfit on a muddy day.

Dānīᵓilu Rejoices in the Prospect of a Son (ii 8-23)
Dānīᵓilu's face lit up with joy,
His countenance[h] glowed.[17]
Signs of worry disappeared from his forehead[18] as he laughed,
he (relaxed as he) put his feet on the footstool.
He cried aloud:
I can sit and be at rest,
my innermost being[19] can rest,
For a son will be born to me,[i] as (to) my brothers,
a scion, as (to) my kinsmen:
Someone to raise up the stela of my father's god,
in the sanctuary the votive emblem of my clan;
<To send up from the earth my incense>,
from the dust the song of [my] place;
To shut up the jaws of my detractors,
to drive out anyone who would do me in;
To take my hand when (I am) drunk,
to bear me up when (I am) full of wine;
To eat my grain(-offering) in the temple of Baᶜlu,
my portion in the temple of ᵓIlu;
To roll my roof when rain softens it up,
to wash my outfit on a muddy day.

h Ps 104:15
i Isa 9:5

Dānīᵓilu Does His Part (ii 24-?)
Dānīᵓilu arrived at his house,
Dānīᵓilu entered his palace.
The Kôṯarātu[20] entered his house,
the daughters of brightness,[21] the pure ones.
Thereupon, as for Dānīᵓilu the man of Rapaᵓu,
thereafter, as for the valiant Harnamite man,
A bull he slaughtered for the Kôṯarātu,
he fed the Kôṯarātu,
provided the daughters of brightness, the pure ones, with drink.
A day, even two,
he fed the Kôṯarātu,
provided the daughters of brightness, the pure ones, with drink.
A third, even a fourth day,
he fed the Kôṯarātu,
provided the daughters of brightness, the pure ones, with drink.
A fifth, even a sixth day,
he fed the Kôṯarātu,
provided the daughters of brightness, the pure ones, with drink.
Then, on the seventh day,
the Kôṯarātu left his house,
(as did) the daughters of brightness, the pure ones.
... the lovely bed ...[22]
... the beautiful bed ...
Dānīᵓilu sat down to count the months ...[23]
...

The Bow is Promised (v 2-3)
I will bring the bow there,
I'll bring arrows in multiples of four.[24]

---

[16] This and the following verse are inverted as compared with the first and fourth recitals of the list (this section has disappeared from the second recital, end col. i).

[17] Lit., "In Dānīᵓilu, (his) face rejoices, above, he shines in (his) temples."

[18] For the meaning of *lṣb*, "forehead" rather than "rows of teeth," see discussion and bibliography in Pardee 1988a:69. For the interpretation of *prq*, see del Olmo Lete 1981:612.

[19] Another usage of *npš*, lit., "my throat (*npš*) within my chest (*ᵓirt*)."

[20] The Kôṯarātu are known from the Ug. texts primarily as goddesses of conception (see Pardee 1995). If the damaged passage at the end of this column has been correctly interpreted, the Kôṯarātu are present at conception, then leave. If the goddesses also functioned as midwives, as many scholars believe, one may surmise that their return at the time of birth was recounted in the text of columns iii-iv, now lost.

[21] *hll* is either an abstract term denoting brightness and purity or the name of a goddess Hulel, known from Emar (see references in Pardee 1995).

[22] Lines 41-42 are damaged and it is uncertain exactly what the phrases *nᶜmy ᶜrš* and *ysmsmt ᶜrš* denote. The words denoting "beauty" being placed before the word for "bed," they can either modify another entity or, as translated here, they can be taken as modifying *ᶜrš* genitivally.

[23] The word for "months" bears a third person pronominal suffix (*yrḫh*), but the antecedent is uncertain, whether referring to Dānīᵓilu, his wife, or even, least likely in my estimation, to the child who, according to this hypothesis, has already been born. In line 45 one finds the numbers "three" and "four," indicating that the count progresses, but the surrounding text is too damaged to allow us to perceive the context of the counting. Most scholars believe that the months of gestation are being counted (cf. Job 39:2). According to this interpretation, the birth and infancy of ᵓAqhatu would have been recounted in the missing columns iii and iv, which originally ran to over one hundred lines.

[24] The identity of the speaker is lost in the preceding lacuna. Below, it is the double deity Kôṯaru-wa-Ḫasīsu who brings the bow (lines 10-13). The formulae in this verse are partially repeated below, but several terms are dubious: is *ṯmn* the noun meaning "eight" (referring perhaps to the multiple elements of which the composite bow is made) or the adverb meaning "there"? What is the precise meaning of *ᵓašrbᶜ*, "I shall quadruplicate," applied to arrows; is the derivation from *rbᶜ*, "four," even correct? (Square-shafted darts [a possible interpretation of *rbᶜ*], such as were used in pre-modern Europe, have not been discovered, to my knowledge, in the ancient Near East.) Does the word *qṣᶜt*, of unclear etymology, denote the bow or the arrow? If one accepts the derivation of *ᵓašrbᶜ* from the root denoting "four," it is unlikely that *ṯmn* is here the word for "eight" because decreasing number parallelism is not common. Also against the numerical interpretation of *ṯmn* is its absence in the parallel passage (line 12). In its favor, perhaps, is the use of *ṯmn*, "eight," plausibly referring to arrows, in *CTA* 19 i 5 (below, p. 350).

Kôṯaru-wa-Ḫasīsu Arrives and Presents the Bow to Dānīˀilu (v 3-33)
Then, on the seventh day,
Dānīˀilu the man of Rapaˀu,
the valiant Harnamite man,
Arose and sat at the entrance to the (city-)gate,[j]
among the leaders (sitting) at the threshing floor.[k]
He judged the widow's case,
made decisions regarding the orphan.[l]
Looking up he perceived
a thousand yards off,
ten thousand furlongs off,[25]
He saw Kôṯaru coming,
saw Ḫasīsu striding along.[26]
He was bringing the bow,
bringing the arrows in multiples of four.
Then Dānīˀilu the man of Rapaˀu,
then the valiant Harnamite man,
Aloud to his wife did call:
Listen, Lady Dānatay:[27]
prepare a lamb from the flock
For the throat of Kôṯaru-wa-Ḫasīsu,
for the gullet[28] of Hayyinu[29] the handicrafter.
Give the gods something to eat, something to drink,
serve, honor them,[m]
the lords of Memphis, the gods of all of it.[30]
Lady Dānatay listened,
she prepared a lamb from the flock
For the throat of Kôṯaru-wa-Ḫasīsu,
for the gullet of Hayyinu the handicrafter.
When Kôṯaru-wa-Ḫasīsu arrive,
they place in Dānīˀilu's hand the bow,
set upon his knees the arrows.
Then Lady Dānatay
gave the gods something to eat, something to drink,
served, honored them,
the lords of Memphis, the gods of all of it.
Kôṯaru left for his tent,
Hayyinu left for his dwelling place.

Dānīˀilu Presents the Bow to ˀAqhatu (v 33-end)
Thereupon, Dānīˀilu the man of Rapaˀu,
thereupon, the valiant Harnamite man,
The bow he ...[31]
[...] upon/unto ˀAqhatu[32] he ...[33]
The best[34] of your game, O [my] son [...]
[...] the best of your game [...]
[...] game in his temple/palace [...]

ᶜAnatu Demands of ˀAqhatu His Bow (vi 16-19)[35]
[She raised her voice] and shouted:
Listen, [valiant ˀAqhatu]:
Ask for silver and I'll give (it to) you,
[for gold and I'll] present (it to) you.
Just give your bow [to ᶜAnatu],
let the sister-in-law of Liˀmu[36] [take] your arrows.

Aqhatu Isn't Interested (vi 20-25)
Valiant ˀAqhatu replied:
I'll vow[37] ash wood from Lebanon,

j Deut 21:19; Amos 5:10, 12, 15
k 1 Kgs 22:10
l Exod 22:21; Deut 10:18; Isa 1:17; Ps 68:6; Job 29:12-13
m Gen 18:5-8

[25] On *šd // kmn*, see note 21 to the Baᶜlu text (1.86).

[26] The double divine name Kôṯaru-wa-Ḫasīsu can either be split up in a bicolon as here, or appear as a single unit, which then has as its parallel yet a third name, Hayyinu (line 18). This complex of names can be treated as plural (so in lines 18-21). The home of Kôṯaru-wa-Ḫasīsu is fixed either in Egypt, or in Crete (see RS 24.244:46 [text 1.94]), or in both places (*CTA* 1 III 1, 18; 3 VI 14 [text 1.86]).

[27] Dānīˀilu's wife seems to bear a name derived from the same root as her husband's (see above, note 1).

[28] On *npš//brlt*, see note 13.

[29] This name is explained by Arabic *hayyin*[un], "easy, light," see note 22 to the Baᶜlu text (1.86).

[30] On *bᶜl ḥkpt ˀil klh*, see note 19 to the Baᶜlu text (1.86).

[31] The verb *yqb* is uncertain both as to reading (some take the following vertical wedge not as a word divider but as the first wedge of {l} or {ṣ}) and as to interpretation. One wonders if it could not be cognate to Heb. *qbb*, "to curse," but without the negative connotation of that verb, meaning rather "to pronounce a spell upon." In the present case, the spell pronounced by a second party (Dānīˀilu) would be equivalent to a vow pronounced by a first party (ˀAqhatu), and its purpose/content would be that ˀAqhatu must offer to the gods the first-fruits of the game killed with the bow. Perhaps, therefore, this text also contained a motif similar to the vow-to-a-god motif in the Kirta text.

[32] In the story as preserved, this is the first occurrence of the name ˀAqhatu, the explanation of which is uncertain, though it appears to be related to the Heb. name Qᵉhāt.

[33] This verb begins {yq} and is thus plausibly, though not certainly, the same as in the preceding line.

[34] The word is *prᶜm* (the root *prᶜ* expresses "firstness" and "topness," as in "the top of the head"), apparently semantically similar to *rˀiš* and *rˀišyt*, "best (part)" (< *rˀš* "head"), both corresponding to the Biblical notion of offering first-fruits and first-born to God. In Heb., forms of the root *bkr* are more common in this usage (*bikkûrîm*, "first-fruits").

[35] The first fifteen lines of this column are too badly damaged for even an approximate translation, though certain words and phrases are well enough preserved to allow a general interpretation. Judging from some of the standard words and phrases for eating and drinking, ᶜAnatu is at a feast where she first spies ˀAqhatu's bow. The text is too damaged, however, for us to learn the circumstances under which ˀAqhatu would be present at such a feast.

[36] On *ybmt lˀimm*, see note 12 to the Baᶜlu text (1.86).

[37] This interpretation of *ˀadr* is based on the assumption that ˀAqhatu is offering to the goddess personally to provide her with the materials necessary to have a bow made for herself just like his; *ndr* is thus appropriate, expressing the human-divine relationship. Others take *ˀadr* as the adjective "mighty, powerful," in which case the entire list functions as the direct object of *tn*, "give," in line 24; here the goddess is expected to find the materials herself. The basic study of this passage is Albright and Mendenhall 1942.

I'll vow sinews from wild bulls,
I'll vow horns from rams,
tendons from the hocks of a bull,
I'll vow reeds from ǴLᵓIL.[38]
Give (these) to Kôṯaru-wa-Ḫasīsu,
and he'll make a bow for ᶜAnatu,
arrows for the sister-in-law of Liᵓmu.

ᶜAnatu Ups the Ante (vi 25-33)
Girl[39] ᶜAnatu replied:
Ask for life, O valiant ᵓAqhatu,
ask for life and I'll give (it to) you,[n]
for immortality[40] and I'll make it yours;
I'll make you count years with Baᶜlu,
with the son of ᵓIlu will you count months;
(You will be) like Baᶜlu (who), when he comes (back) to life, feasts:
they give a feast[41] to the living one, give him drink,
the goodly one[42] chants and sings in his honor.
So I, for my part, will answer (the request),[43]
I will give life[o] to valiant ᵓAqhatu.[44]

n Ps 21:5
o 2 Kgs 5:7
p Num 23:10; Eccl 6:12
q Num 16:29; Ps 82:7

Aqhatu, Still Not Interested, Shows Little Tact (vi 33-40)
Valiant ᵓAqhatu replied:
Don't lie to me, girl,
your lies are despicable[45] to a real man;
What after(life)[p] can one obtain?
what can a man obtain hereafter?
(For) they will pour glaze [on] (my) head,
white stuff over my cranium.[46]
[And] I'll die the death of every man,[q]
I also must surely die.
[Moreover], I've something else to say:
The bow is a fighting man's [weapon];[47]
Shall womankind now go hunting?

ᶜAnatu Takes Umbrage, Threatens ᵓAqhatu (vi 41-45)
[Outwardly] ᶜAnatu laughs,
But within she hatches [a plot].
Reconsider,[48] valiant ᵓAqhatu,
reconsider for your own sake [...].
(Otherwise) I'll meet you on the path of rebellion,

---

[38] From context *ǵlᵓil* is a geographical term, but it is uncertain whether it is a proper or a common noun.

[39] ᶜAnatu's title *btlt* refers to an age/maturity category and to the social norms and cultural overtones associated with that category. See note 11 to the Baᶜlu text (1.86).

[40] Ug. *bl mt*, "not dying."

[41] The repetition of *ᶜšr* has been seen as a problem. It appears plausible to see in the first form a usage for receiving a feast (perhaps intransitive, or even passive), the second as denoting the presenting of a feast. This interpretation sees the passage as reflecting a feast in honor of Baᶜlu's seasonal return to life. Others interpret the verbal forms in line 30 as active/transitive and see here a feast offered by Baᶜlu to the one receiving life from him. The first interpretation appears preferable because it fits better into Ug. mythology as we know it.

[42] Whatever the correct restoration of line 32 may be (see following note), it appears difficult to avoid interpreting this passage in light of *CTA* 3 i 18-21 (text 1.86), where someone designated *nᶜm* sings in honor of Baᶜlu.

[43] {ᶜnynn} is clearly from the root *ᶜny*, "to answer, respond, speak up," apparently with accusative pronominal suffix (*-nn*). Unfortunately, the absence of the preformative element means that the subject is uncertain. Some restore *t* and see a narrative indicator of the following conclusion of ᶜAnatu's speech ("she responded to him"), others a continued reference to the singing (note that this should not be a reference to the singing designated in Heb. by *ᶜny*, of which the Arabic cognate is *ǵny*), others to another aspect of the feast. Examination of the original hand copy and of the photograph leads me to believe that the generally accepted restoration of three signs in the lacuna is too generous and that two signs (Dijkstra and De Moor 1975:187) correspond better to the available space. Read perhaps {nᶜm[. w ᵓa]ᶜnynn}. The verb *ᶜny* is not usually used with an accusative complement in Ug., and it is difficult to know if the suffix here refers to ᵓAqhatu or to the thing requested, i.e., immortality. Given the rarity of the accusatival usage, the suffix could even refer to Baᶜlu: "I ᶜAnatu will answer him (=act correspondingly to him, i.e., Baᶜlu)."

[44] The nature of the proffered immortality has been much discussed: maintenance of human life, repeated restoration to life after dying, or joining with divine immortals after death? The present formulation seems to indicate the second option, i.e., the Baᶜlu model, but ᵓAqhatu in any case refuses the offer of any form of immortality as being fraudulent, in keeping with general thinking in the ancient Near East on the possibility of human immortality (cf. Gilgamesh, Adapa ...).

[45] The precise meaning of *ḫḫm* is disputed, some comparing with Heb. *ḥōᵃḥ*, "briar, thorn, hook," others with Akk. *ḫaḫḫu*, "slime, spittle."

[46] A much-debated passage: *spsg* is also attested in an administrative text (*PRU* II 106:8) alongside terms designating semi-precious stones and has been identified with a Hurrian word that may denote a type of glaze (also attested in a Sumero-Akkadian lexical text: *CAD Z* 10). See bibliography in Pardee 1987:432. Many scholars have accepted the specificity of the term *spsg* and have endeavored to explain the second word, *ḥrṣ*, on the basis of the first, but with less obvious success, for no Semitic language provides an etymology clearly in the same semantic field as *spsg* (cf. the *tour de force* in Albright 1945:24-25, with its jump from alkali to "(molten) glass"). Watson (1990:423) proposed a new Akk. etymology, "*ḫuriẓu* or *urīẓu*," which designates "a stone or mineral of as yet undetermined meaning." The proposal to see in this passage a reference to the Neolithic practice of plastering the skulls of the deceased encounters severe difficulties (Rainey 1971:154). From a literary perspective, one must note that this bicolon is placed before the explicit statement of death and could constitute a metaphor for the white hair of old age rather than for a procedure practiced on the dead.

[47] The restorations at the beginnings of lines 40-44 are uncertain.

[48] The precise meaning of the idiom *ṯb l* is uncertain, though something like the above translation appears preferable to "go away," which does not work in all contexts and which might, in any case, be expressed by a verb other than "return."

[...] on the path of pride,
I'll personally bring you down and [trample] you,[49]
(however) good and strong (you may be) among men.

ᶜAnatu Departs, Seeks Permission from ᵓIlu to Attack ᵓAqhatu (vi 46-end)[50]

[She dug in] her feet,
took off across the earth;
She [headed off]
towards ᵓIlu at the source of the two rivers,
[amidst the fountains] of the deeps.
She penetrated Ilu's abode,
[entered the] dwelling[51] of the king, father of Šunama.[52]
[At ᵓIlu's feet] she bowed and fell,
she did homage [and honored] him.
She heaped slander[r] on valiant ᵓAqhatu,
[... the child of] Dānīᵓilu the man of Rapaᵓu.
[Girl ᶜAnatu] spoke,
[she raised] her [voice]
and cried out the word [...]

Colophon (left edge)

[The scribe: ᵓIlīmilku the Šubbanite, disciple of ᵓAttānu-]purulini.[53]

CTA 18

ᶜAnatu Threatens ᵓIlu (i 1-14)[54]

...
[Girl ᶜAnatu] replied:
[In the grandeur of] your [house], O ᵓIlu,
[in the grandeur of your house do not rejoice],
do not rejoice [in the height of your palace].
Will I [not] seize them [in my right hand],
[... in my] broad grasp?[55]
[I'll smite the ...] of your head,
I'll make [your gray hair] flow [with blood],
your [gray] beard with gore.
(If) [you (appeal to)[56]] ᵓAqhatu, will he (be able to) save you?
will the son of [Dānīᵓilu] (be able to) help you (when you're) in the grasp of Girl [ᶜAnatu]?

ᵓIlu Caves In (i 15-19)

The Gracious One, the kindly god, replied:
I know you, (my) daughter, (I know) that you are a manly sort,
and that [among goddesses] there is none so emotional as you.[57]
(So) let anger (against me) depart (from) [your] heart, (my) daughter;
[(so then) go ahead and] lay hold of what you desire,[s]
carry out what you wish:[58]
The one who gets in your way[t] may be struck down.

ᶜAnatu Leaves, Addresses ᵓAqhatu (i 19-end)[59]

Girl ᶜAnatu [left],
headed [off
towards] valiant ᵓAqhatu,
A thousand yards away,
[ten thousand] furlongs.
Girl [ᶜAnatu] laughed,
[raised] her voice and cried out:
Hear, valiant [ᵓAqhatu],
You are (my) brother and I am [your] sister,[u]

r Prov 30:10
s 2 Sam 7:3
t Job 37:4
u Cant 4:9, 10

[49] Lit., "I'll cause you to fall under [my feet]."

[50] The beginning of this passage contains a series of formulae, attested elsewhere in variant forms, for divine travel and arrival at ᵓIlu's abode.

[51] The two terms for ᵓIlu's dwelling place, *ḏd* and *qrš*, apparently designate a tent-like structure. See note 29 to the Baᶜlu text (p. 245, 1.86).

[52] On the title *ᵓab šnm*, see note 30 to the Baᶜlu text (1.86).

[53] Considerations of space make the restoration of this form of ᵓIlīmilku's titulary plausible. ᵓIlīmilku's hometown of Šubbanu has not been localized with certainty (for bibliography, see Pardee 1989-90:489). On the interpretation of ᵓIlīmilku's master's name, see van Soldt 1989.

[54] The proper restoration of lines 1-9 is uncertain; these lines show close parallels with *CTA* 3 V 27-33 (p. 254), also damaged though less so than here. See note 108 to the Baᶜlu text (p. 254, 1.86).

[55] Lit., "in the greatness of my length," apparently a reference to the length of the goddess' arms (cf. *gdl* + "arm" in Exod 15:16). The restoration of *ymn*, "right hand," appears plausible from the parallel text in *CTA* 3 V 30 ({b y[--]y}). It is uncertain whether another word for "hand" or a verb parallel to "seize" should be restored in the intervening lacuna.

[56] The proper restoration here is unknown, though something along the lines of this translation is suggested by the following reference to helping and rescuing. The concept of ᵓIlu, father of the gods, appealing to a mortal for help is nonetheless a striking one.

[57] Various interpretations of *ᵓnš//qlṣ* in this verse have been proposed (for bibliography see Pardee 1987:373, 445). On ᵓIlu's description of ᶜAnatu here, see note 111 to the Baᶜlu text (1.86).

[58] Lit., "you may seize what is in your heart, you may place/put/establish what is in your breast." The damaged state of the passage and the fact that *ḫnp* is only attested here have made the meaning obscure. As translated, the "anger" in the first line is ᶜAnatu's anger directed against ᵓIlu, not against ᵓAqhatu. ᵓIlu is apparently telling ᶜAnatu that she can do whatever she wishes to ᵓAqhatu, as long as she leaves him, ᵓIlu, alone.

[59] After the stereotyped formulae in lines 19-23, the text becomes so damaged as to be uninterpretable. From the first line of ᶜAnatu's speech, it would appear that the goddess has chosen to approach ᵓAqhatu in a friendly fashion. Because, in addition to the loss of the end of this column and the beginning of col. iv, all of columns ii and iii have disappeared, we have no idea as to how the duel between ᵓAqhatu and ᶜAnatu continued. According to col. iv, line 5, ᶜAnatu goes off to put her plan of attack into motion, but the previous lines are too damaged for us to know with whom she was talking before her departure.

[...] seven of your kin[60] [...]
[...] of my father [...]
[...] you'll go hunting [...]
[...] I'll teach you [...]
[...] the city of ʾAbilūma,
ʾAbilūma [the city of Prince] Yariḫu,[61]
Of which the tower [...]
...

ʿAnatu and YṬPN Devise a Plan of Attack (iv 5-27)[62]
Girl ʿAnatu left,
[headed off]
towards YṬPN,[63] the soldier of the Lady.[64]
Girl ʿAnatu cried [aloud]:
YṬP sit/return[65] [...]
(to) the city of ʾAbilūma,
ʾAbilūma [the city of Prince Yariḫu].
How can Yariḫu not be renewed?[66]
[...] on his right horn,[67]
on the ?[68] [...] of his head?

YṬPN, [the soldier of the Lady], replied:
Listen Girl ʿAnatu:
You are the one who will strike him [for his bow]
(for) his arrows, you will not [let] him [live].
The goodly warrior has prepared a meal,
and [...] he has stayed on in tents,
and he has settled [...].[69]
Girl ʿAnatu replied:
Sit down, YṬP, and [I'll tell] you (what we'll do):
I'll put you like a hawk[70] under [my] belt,[v]
like a bird[71] in my bag.[72]
[When] ʾAqhatu [sits down] to eat,
the son of Dānīʾilu for a meal,
[Above him] the hawks will soar,[w]
[the flock of] birds will survey the scene.[73]
I myself will soar amongst the hawks,
above ʾAqhatu (I'll) position you.
Strike him twice on the head,

v Isa 46:11
w Gen 1:2; Deut 32:11

[60] Given the presence of the word for "father" in the following line, one can surmise that *ṯʾirk* is related to *ṯʾar*, the word designating a relation of kinship in the Kirta text (*CTA* 14 I 15, here text 1.102), instead of guessing a meaning on the basis of Arabic usage.

[61] This is the common formula in the following text for the spot where ʾAqhatu was struck down. To the extent that the name of the city reflects onomastic reality, it seems to be based on *ʾabil-*, a common formative element in Northwest Semitic place names. In this text, however, the name could correspond less to geographical reality than to a *topos* of the story, that of mourning (*ʾbl*). In the latter interpretation, the literary function of the link between the city of mourners and the moon deity Yariḫu would not be clear.

[62] The few words extant in the first four lines seem to indicate acts of violence (*yṯbr*, "he will break," and *ʾuṭm ḏr[qm]*, a phrase of uncertain meaning appearing only here and in *CTA* 5 i 5-6, a passage dealing with Môtu, god of death).

[63] No etymology and, hence, vocalization have been generally accepted for this name. In two passages the shorter form *yṭp* appears (here following line and line 16), generally taken as a variant of the name, but the context is each time broken and the form in question could be verbal (cf. Watson 1976:373; further bibliography in Pardee 1989-90:406).

[64] The second term in the formulaic title of *yṭpn*, *mhr št*, has given rise to various interpretations, the most commonly accepted of which are (1) "lady," cognate with Arabic *sittᵘⁿ*, an apparent reference to ʿAnatu herself, and (2) "Sutaean" (for which meaning one might expect a gentilic form, since *sutû* is identified as a geographical entity in the cuneiform sources). For bibliography, see Pardee 1987:413; 1989-90:490.

[65] *yṭp* may be the subject, or the word lost in the following lacuna may supply the subject. Hence we do not know whether *yṯb* refers to sitting (root *yṯb*) or to returning (hollow root *ṯb*).

[66] In Ug. Yariḫu designates the "moon" as celestial orb and as lunar deity and also means "month." The verb "renew," *ḥdṯ*, is from the same root as the commonly attested word for "new moon." The meaning of the entire passage is, however, unclear, especially as regards YṬPN's appointed task. Since his answer shows him to be already aware of the task, we may surmise that in the broken text of columns ii and iii ʿAnatu was presented as engaging YṬPN and, consequently, that in the present passage she and YṬPN devise the details of the attack.

[67] If the referent is still Yariḫu, the words *qrn ymn* may be thought to refer to the right point of the crescent moon.

[68] Similar questions arise here as for the use of *ʾnš* by ʾIlu in reference to ʿAnatu (see above, note 57 and note 111 to the Baʿlu text [1.86]). Here, however, the context is too damaged to attempt an explanation.

[69] Lines 14-15 are obscure and lacunary (at least three signs are missing at the end of each line) and have been interpreted variously. I take *ṯrm* as from the root *ṯrm*, denoting an act of eating, as here below lines 19 and 30 (rather than as the plural of *ṯr*, "bull"), *ḏdm* as the same word used above for ʾIlu's abode (see note 51 and note 29 to the Baʿlu text [1.86]), and *nʿrs* as cognate with Arabic *ʿrs*, which denotes "binding" and hence various forms of "settling down" (the form is thus more plausibly N-stem, with ʾAqhatu as subject, than G-stem, 1st plural, "we will *ʿrs*," though, because of the following lacuna, the latter interpretation cannot be ruled out). The precise nuance of *ʾištʾir*, normally "remain behind/after," is not clear.

[70] As one can see from this passage, *nšr* denotes in Ug., as in Heb., a raptor rather than a carrion bird ("hawk" is here intended as generic).

[71] The root *dʾy* means "to fly" in Ug.; the precise type of bird denoted by *dʾiy* is uncertain, though it seems to belong to the raptor class (for bibliography, see Pardee 1988:104-105). The form here may be simply that of the G-stem participle, *dāʾiyūma*, "flyers"; below, in *CTA* 19 iii 115, etc., *dʾiy* denotes the "pinions" of the hawks.

[72] The precise meaning of the terms *ḥbš* and *ṯʿrt* is unclear. *ṯʿrt* is elsewhere attested in the meaning "scabbard" (*CTA* 19 iv 207), and is used here either metaphorically (i.e., the hawk is to function as a sword) or as a designation of any kind of hunting bag, holding weapons, knives, game, etc. *ḥbš* can only, for the present, be explained etymologically, i.e., by the Semitic verb *ḥbš*, "to bind" (the noun *ḥbš* is also attested in *CTA* 3 ii 13, where a meaning similar to "belt" also appears plausible). In any case, the general meaning of the terms indicates that the motivation is concealment, and this general context and the absence of any motifs characteristic of falconry (i.e., the use by humans of trained falcons as hunters) rule out the latter interpretation here.

[73] The meaning "look at, keep an eye on" for *bṣr* is now confirmed by RIH 78/14:11′ (text 1.91), a lunar omen of which the prognosis is *mlkm tbṣrn*, "the kings (of the various lands) will keep an eye on each other," paralleled in the *Sin* omens from Emar by the verb *innaṭṭalū*, with the same meaning (Arnaud 1985-86 text 651:37).

three times above the ear,
Pour out (his) blood like one emptying (a bucket),[74]
(pour it out) on his knees like one slaughtering (an animal),
So that his life force rushes out like wind,[x]
like spittle his vitality,
like smoke from his nostrils.
Thus I'll not let the soldier live on![75]

The Plan is Carried Out (iv 27-37)
She took YṬPN, the soldier of the Lady,
put him like a hawk under her belt,
like a bird in her bag.
When ʾAqhatu sat down to eat,
the son of Dānīʾilu for a meal,
The hawks soared above him,
the flock of birds surveyed the scene.
ʿAnatu soared [amongst] the hawks,
above [ʾAqhatu] she positioned him.
He struck him twice [on the head],
three times above the ear,
Poured out his blood [like] one emptying (a bucket),
(poured it out) [on his knees] like one slaughtering (an animal),

x Ps 146:4

[His] life force rushed out like wind,
[like spittle] his vitality,
like smoke [from his nostrils].

ʿAnatu Expresses Sorrow (iv 37-end)
[Moreover,] ʿAnatu, as she smote the soldier,[76]
[...] ʾAqhatu,
She wept [...]
I would have made[77] [...]
But on account of [your bow ...],
[on account of] your arrows you have ceased [to live].[78]
...
... perished ...

CTA 19

Classification of Tablet (i 1)
[Belonging to[79] (the)] ʾAqhatu (text).

Something Happens to the Coveted Bow (i 2-5)
...
... the bow was broken ...
... the eight [...] were broken ... [80]

Another Account of ʾAqhatu's Death (i 5-19)[81]
Girl ʿAnatu returned [...]
[...] took[82] weapons[83] as (does) [... in] his hand,

[74] The meaning of *šʾy* is uncertain. One of the possible corresponding roots in Arabic means "to draw up mud from the bottom of a well/spring (in the process of cleaning it out)." Perhaps the verb denoted in Ug. the accompanying act of pouring out the sludge. The writing with {ʾi} shows the form plausibly to be a participle (*šāʾiyu*).

[75] The conclusion to ʿAnatu's speech is a monocolon, hence without parallelism to help elucidate its meaning. The first sign seems from the photograph to be a cross between {b} and {ʾu} (one does not see three clear vertical wedges). The word written {mprh} is, on the basis of line 38, to be corrected to {mhrh}. The most likely form of this concluding line thus appears to be, in vocalized form: *ʾū ʾapa muhrahu lā ʾaḥawwiyu*, literally "And moreover I'll not allow his soldiership (i.e., the abstract expression of the qualities making him a soldier) to continue living."

[76] The structure is similar to that of lines 26-27 (see preceding note), lit., "as she smote his soldiership."

[77] Lit., "built," though there is not unanimous agreement on this identification, the context being broken. Moreover, it is impossible to ascertain the object of this verb, though the phrase plausibly has to do with rewards ʾAqhatu would have received if he had been more receptive of ʿAnatu's offers. The verb "to build" could refer, for example, to quasi-creative maintenance of life or to building for ʾAqhatu a house or dynasty.

[78] The letters {lḥ[...]} may be restored as {l ḥ[wt]}, lit., "you did not live."

[79] See note 2 to the Kirta text above (text 1.102).

[80] Because of the state of the text here, it is impossible to determine whether *qšt*, "bow" is subject or object of the verb (*ṯṯ[b]r*) in lines 3-4. In line 4 the verb is apparently repeated again, this time differently marked for gender (y[ṯ]br). On that basis alone, I assume that *qšt* is the subject in the first case and that the partially destroyed phrase {ṯmn [...]} is the subject in the second. Given the standard parallelism of *qšt* and *qṣʿt*, both above and below (lines 14, 15), and given the use of the verb "quadruplicate" above for the arrows (see above, note 24), it appears likely, as many commentators have believed, that *ṯmn* here in line 5 is the number "eight" and that it modifies a word with similar meaning to *qṣʿt*. Though opinion varies widely as to the meaning of the passage, it is generally thought that it refers somehow to a loss suffered by ʿAnatu (or by YṬPN) of the weapon that the goddess has killed to obtain.

[81] Lines 5-19 constitute one of the most difficult texts of the ʾAqhatu story: several lines have undergone various degrees of damage and even in the well-preserved sections the vocabulary is so difficult that multiple, wildly varying, interpretations have been proposed. (If the scientific credibility of Ugaritology depended on a consensus in the interpretation of this passage, the discipline would be in deep trouble!) The translation here proposed can only be considered, therefore, as a new attempt at understanding. The principal problem in determining the structure and overall interpretation of the passage lies in determining the actor(s). Indeed, in the present state of conservation of the text, this is not easily done, neither from explicitly indicated subjects nor from grammatical markers of gender and number. Judging from the phrase *ʿl qṣʿth hwt l ʾaḥw*, "on account of his arrows I did not let him live" (lines 15-16) the speaker at that point is ʾAqhatu's killer, either ʿAnatu/YṬPN or a party who is here presented as having committed the act. The name ʿAnatu, with her normal title, "girl," is extant in line 5. Is the goddess the speaker/actor in the intervening lines? The fact that the verbal forms are not all clearly marked as 3rd feminine singular seems to indicate that, if ʿAnatu's involvement continues to the end of the passage, she is the speaker rather than the actor. In such a hypothesis, she is explaining to someone how ʾAqhatu died as well as the fact that the bow has disappeared. Judging from the new vocabulary in this passage, if ʿAnatu is the speaker (as I surmise), she is presenting a fanciful account of ʾAqhatu's death, one in which the death occurred in a different fashion from that indicated above in the narrative. In the present state of the text, there is no way to know whether YṬP(N) here bears the blame, being represented by ʿAnatu as a fierce being who acted on his own, or whether the blame is entirely shifted to another party.

[82] According to *CTA*, the lacuna in line 6 is long enough to have contained six signs, perhaps one word designating the complement of the verb "return," another the subject of the verb *nšʾ*.

[83] The meaning of *tlm* is very uncertain; here taken as cognate to Heb. *tᵉlî* with a broader meaning than that of "quiver" usually ascribed to the Heb. word in its one occurrence in Gen. 27:3.

as (does) a singer the lyre (in) his fingers.[84]
The "stones of his mouth"[85] tore,
his teeth seized,
they put food in his devouring (maw).[86]
He tore according to the wishes of the gods,[87]
then he told the exploits,
the prince recounted his exploits:[88]
ᵓAqhatu has been put down like a veritable fugitive,
like a vicious viper in a wall,
(like) a dog on its stake did I smite him.
For on account of his bow I smote him,
on account of his arrows I did not let him live.
His bow, however, was not given to me,
and in death [...].[89]
The first growth of summer has/will [...],
the ear in the stalk.[90]

The Father Learns of ᵓAqhatu's Death (i 19 - ii 93)
Thereupon, Dānīᵓilu the man of Rapaᵓu,
thereupon, the valiant Harnamite [man],
Arose [and sat at the entrance] to the (city-)gate,
among [the leaders (sitting) at the threshing floor].
He judged [the widow's case],
made decisions [regarding the orphan].

y Job 8:12
z Hos 8:1; Jer 12:9; Job 39:26-30
aa Lam 2:11
bb Gen 37:34; Judg 11:35; 1 Kgs 11:30
cc Gen 41:26; 2 Kgs 8:1
dd Ps 68:5
ee 1 Kgs 17:1
ff Gen 7:11; 2 Sam 1:21; Prov 3:20

...[91]
... the coming of ...
Looking up, she sees ...[92]
On the threshing floor [...] is dried up
bends over, droops, do the young ears[y] [...].
Above her father's house hawks were soaring,
a flock of birds were surveying the scene.[z]
Pūġatu[93] began to weep inwardly,
to shed tears silently.[aa]
She tore the garment[bb] of Dānīᵓilu the man of Rapaᵓu,[94]
the cloak of the valiant Harnamite man.

Dānīᵓilu Seeks to Counter the Effects of the Drought (i 38-46)
Thereupon, Dānīᵓilu the man of Rapaᵓu,
uttered a spell[95] upon clouds in the heat of the season,[96]
upon the rain that the clouds pour down on the summer fruits,
upon the dew that falls on the grapes.
Seven years[cc] has Baᶜlu failed,
eight (years) he who rides upon the clouds:[dd]
No dew, no showers,[ee]
no upsurging (of water) from the deeps,[ff]
no goodly voice of Baᶜlu.[97]

---

[84] Because of the breaks in the middle of lines 6 and 7, it is uncertain whether ᶜAnatu is the actor here and precisely what the form of the comparison is in lines 6-7. The suffixes of the third person singular being undifferentiated for gender in the writing system ({h} = either *-hu* or *-ha*), it is also uncertain whether the suffix on "hand//fingers" refers to the subject of the sentence or to the elements in the comparative phrases.

[85] Apparently an idiom for "teeth, fangs."

[86] In Arabic, the root *qmm* denotes various verbal notions of devouring, particularly like a ravenous beast.

[87] The signs {klb ᵓilnm} can be interpreted either as "the hound of (*klb*) the gods" or "according to the wishes of (*k lb*) the gods." Were there, in the absence of an explicit statement, clear parallels for a divine canine bearing the blame for ᵓAqhatu's death, the former interpretation could be embraced.

[88] The forms *gprm* and *gprh* have received multiple explanations. No convincing etymology having presented itself other than the comparison with *gbr*, denoting various forms of "might" and "greatness," I interpret the words in question as containing the subject's self-description (as represented by ᶜAnatu!) of the killer's deed.

[89] The end of line 17 is damaged and of uncertain interpretation.

[90] Below, consequences of drought on plant life function as signs of broader misfortune. Because of the lacuna in line 18, the link between this verse and the subsequent text cannot be ascertained. In *CTA* the lacuna is said to have contained two signs, an assessment that observation of the published photograph seems to uphold; in a note the restoration of *y[bl]*, "it will bear," accepted by several scholars, is preferred. In *KTU* a single sign is read and presented as partially visible (the reading is *yḥ**, "may it live"). Whatever the correct reading, it appears plausible to interpret the statement, following as it does upon the fallacious account of ᵓAqhatu's death, either, as a fallacious assurance that this death will not perturb the patterns of life elsewhere, or as an observation that the process of drying up has already begun.

[91] Approximately two and a half lines are missing, wherein were contained plausibly a reference to the arrival of Dānīᵓilu's daughter.

[92] The verb "to see" here has the form *tphn*, precluding that the subject be Dānīᵓilu. The subject may be (1) "eyes," (2) a plurality of human beings (Dānīᵓilu and the judges, Dānīᵓilu and whoever has arrived in lines 25-28?), or (3) ᵓAqhatu's sister Pūġatu, who plays an increasingly important rôle in the story. The same problem arises below, col. ii, line 76, where a group is not present (apparently ruling out the second possibility here).

[93] Judging from the use of *pġt* as a common noun in Ug., the name should mean simply "Girl." See note 51 to the Kirta text (text 1.102).

[94] The obvious subject of the verb *tmzᶜ* is Pūġatu, though others take *kst*, "garment," as subject of the verb in a passive formulation. In the context, as preserved, Dānīᵓilu is unaware of ᵓAqhatu's death and the tearing of the garment should, therefore, be seen as a reaction to the effects of drought.

[95] The meaning of the following speech depends largely on the interpretation of the verb *yṣly*, variously taken to mean "to pray" or "to curse." If a strong connotation of "cursing" is intended, then Dānīᵓilu is apparently in the following lines calling down seven years of drought, whereas if the meaning is "pray" then he is praying for relief from drought. The previous text, as preserved, has made no reference to seven years of drought already having occurred. On the other hand, no motivation for Dānīᵓilu cursing the land with a drought is immediately ascertainable, if one assumes, as the following sections seem to say, that he is unaware of ᵓAqhatu's death. The interpretation of the text as referring to the effects of a multiple-year drought assumes some sort of telescoping of time, for though years of drought have occurred, ᵓAqhatu's remains are still to be found inside the birds of prey who devoured him. Could the drought have been proleptic, beginning before ᵓAqhatu's death and becoming life-threatening only after this death?

[96] The elements of the phrase *ḥm ᵓun* are interpreted as from *ḥmm*, "be hot," and from *ᵓny*, "meet, be opportune," which gives nouns meaning "occasion, appropriate time."

[97] The voice of the weather god functions as a metaphor for thunder and hence, by metonymy, for rain.

Dānīˀilu Inspects the Effects of the Drought
(i 46 - ii 74)

When she had torn the garment of Dānīˀilu the man of Rapaˀu,
the cloak of the valiant Harnamite man,
Aloud [Dānīˀilu called] to [his] daughter:
Listen Pūġatu, you who bear [water] on (your) shoulders,
who gather dew for barley,
who know the paths of the stars:[98]
Saddle the donkey, harness the ass,
put (on it) trappings of silver,
decorations of yellow (gold).
Pūġatu listened, she who bore water on (her) shoulders,
who gathered dew for barley,
who knew the paths of the stars:
Weeping she saddled the donkey,
weeping she harnessed the ass,
Weeping she lifted her father,
placed him on the back of the donkey,
on the beautiful back of the ass.
Dānīˀilu approached,[99] circulated through his cracked fields,[100]
he spied something green[gg] (growing) in the cracked field,
he spied something green (growing) among the weak (sprouts).
He hugged the green growth (to himself), he kissed (it and said):
Oh that the green growth would grow tall in the cracked field,
(Oh that) the green growth would grow tall among the weak (sprouts).
O plant,[hh] may the hand of valiant ˀAqhatu gather you,
put you in the storehouse.[101]
He approached thereunto, circulated through his desolate fields,
he spied an ear of grain[ii] (growing) in the desolate field,
he spied an ear of grain (growing) among the dried-up (sprouts).
He hugged the ear of grain (to himself), he kissed (it and said):
Oh that the ear of grain would grow tall in the desolate field,
(Oh that) the ear of grain would grow tall [among] the dried-up (sprouts).
O plant, may the hand of valiant ˀAqhatu gather you,
put you in the storehouse.

gg 2Kgs 4:42
hh 2Kgs 4:39
ii Gen 41:5-7; Isa 17:5; Ruth 2:2
jj Ps 139:4
kk Ezek 21:11

The Message of Death (ii 75-93)

Hardly had the words left his mouth,
[the utterance] his lips,[jj]
When, raising her eyes, she (Pūġatu) sees
(and) there is no [... in] the arrival of two pages, ...[102]
He/they struck [twice] on the head,
three times above the ear.[103]
...[104]
They arrive [and say] aloud:
Listen, Dānīˀilu, [man of Rapaˀu]:
Valiant ˀAqhatu is dead.
Girl ˁAnatu [caused his life force to go out] like [wind]
like spittle his vitality.

Dānīˀilu's Reaction (ii 93 - iv 189)

[His (Dānīˀilu's) feet] totter,
above, [his face perspires,
behind], his back muscles [snap,[kk]
his vertebrae rattle,
his spine] goes weak.[105]
[Aloud] he cries [...]
has smitten ...
[...][106]

Dānīˀilu's Rather Unorthodox, Though Empirically Sound, Search for ˀAqhatu's Remains (ii 105 - iii 145)

When he raised [his eyes and looked, he saw

[98] Pūġatu's standard epithets make of her a specialist in agricultural matters.

[99] Reading, with many scholars, {ydn <dn> ˀil}.

[100] Of the terms in the following lines that designate the areas inspected by Dānīˀilu, *pˀalt* and *ˀaklt*, only the second is reasonably clear and the first is translated from context. It is assumed that the passage describes the effects of the drought to which Dānīˀilu has just referred and *ˀakl* is explained, therefore, by the root *ˀkl*, "eat, devour" (the common comparison with Akk. *akkullātu* is of dubious value, as it denotes something like clods in a field). The words *yǵlm* and *ḥmdrt*, used to describe the two types of fields (lines 63/65 and 70/72), also pose problems, though the identification of the second with Akk. *ḫamadīrūtu*, "desiccated," is generally accepted (Greenfield 1967:89-90). *Yǵlm* is usually compared with Arabic *wǵl*, and legitimately so, but the range of meanings available from the Arabic dictionary is too broad (from "thick green growth" to "parasite") to be of much real help.

[101] This passage is one that indicates that Dānīˀilu is unaware of ˀAqhatu's death. (The text as preserved provides no warrant for seeing in Dānīˀilu's reference to ˀAqhatu an expression of hope in the deceased son's resurrection.)

[102] The root *yṣˀ* appears twice in line 78 and is plausibly restored at the end of line 77, but the subject is each time uncertain.

[103] Most interpret this as an explicit reference to ˀAqhatu's death, but it may be an imitative gesture on the part of the messengers (Margalit 1989:383). In any case, their actual arrival and the transmission of the message is not stated explicitly until lines 89-93.

[104] Lines 80-88 are damaged and obscure. The only relatively clear line of verse contains a reference to weeping that is similar to the account of Kirta's weeping (lines 82-83: "he/they pour(s) out tears like quarter-shekel pieces"). If this section is still preparatory to the actual transmission of the message, it is the messengers themselves who weep.

[105] These lines, which represent a formulaic and stylized reaction to bad news, are found in variant forms twice in the Baˁlu epic (*CTA* 3 iii (D) 29-32; 4 II 16-20 [text 1.86]).

[106] Six-line lacuna.

[hawks] in the clouds.
He cried out [aloud]:
May Baᶜlu break [the wings of the hawks],
may Baᶜlu break [their pinions],
So that they fall down at my feet,[ll]
so that I may open up [their innards],[107]
[And] see whether there be (there) any fat,
whether there be (there) any bone,
So that I may weep,[108] so that I may bury him,
so that I may put (him) in a grave (with) the gods of the earth.[109]

Baᶜlu Responds (iii 113-120)
Hardly had the words left his mouth,
the utterance his lips,
When Baᶜlu broke the wings of the hawks,
Baᶜlu broke their pinions.
They fell down at his feet;
he opened up their innards and [looked]:
no fat, no bone.
He cried out aloud:
May <Baᶜlu> rebuild[mm] the wings of the hawks,
may Baᶜlu rebuild their pinions.
May the hawks escape and fly away!

Another Try (iii 120-134)
When he raised his eyes and looked, he saw
Hirgabu,[110] father of the hawks.
He cried out aloud:
May Baᶜlu break Hirgabu's wings,
may Baᶜlu break his pinions,
So that he fall down at my feet,
so that I may open up [his] innards,
And see whether there be (there) any fat,
whether there be (there) any [bone],
So that I may weep, so that I may bury him,
so that I may put (him) in a grave (with) the gods [of the earth].

Again Baᶜlu Responds (iii 127-134)
[Hardly had the words left his mouth],
the utterance his lips,
When Baᶜlu broke Hirgabu's wings,
Baᶜlu broke his pinions.

ll 2 Sam 22:39

mm Josh 6:26; cf. Gen 2:22; Jer 24:6

He fell down at his feet;
he opened up his innards and looked:
no fat, no bone.
He cried out aloud:
May Baᶜlu rebuild Hirgabu's wings,
may Baᶜlu rebuild his pinions,
May Hirgabu escape and fly away!

The Third Time's the Charm (iii 134-145)
When he raised his eyes [and] looked, he saw
Ṣamlu,[111] mother of the hawks.
He cried out aloud:
May Baᶜlu break Ṣamlu's wings,
may Baᶜlu break her pinions,
So that she fall down at my feet,
so that I may open up her innards,
And see whether there be (there) any fat,
(whether) there be (there) any [bone],
So that I may weep, so that I may bury him,
so that I may put him in a grave (with) the gods [of the earth].

Yet Again Baᶜlu Responds (iii 141-144)
Hardly had the words left his mouth,
the utterance his lips,
When Baᶜlu <broke> Ṣamlu's wings,
Baᶜlu broke her pinions,
She fell down [at] his feet.

Dāniʾilu Finds ʾAqhatu's Remains and Buries Them (iii 144-147)
He opened up her innards and looked:
there was fat, there was bone.
He took from them ʾAqhatu;
he wailed,[112] slept not a wink,[113]
He wept and buried (him),
buried him in a dark place, in KNKT/KNRT.[114]

Dāniʾilu Warns Off the Hawks (iii 148-151)
He cried out aloud:
May Baᶜlu break the wings of the hawks,
may Baᶜlu break their pinions,
If they fly over the grave of my son,
if they do him harm as he sleeps.

---

[107] Lit., "split their liver."

[108] In this context, and given the regular Ug. strategy of omitting object pronouns, the verb here and below may be in the D-stem, which would be translated "beweep (him)."

[109] Lit., "in the hole of the gods of the earth." Judging from the Ug. king list (RS 24.257; see Pardee 1988:165-178), where each of the past king's names is preceded by the word *ʾil*, "god," the deceased, at least the royal deceased, were thought to be deified at death.

[110] It can hardly be a coincidence that Arabic *hirġab*[un] means "tall" when said of a man and "rapid" when said of a camel.

[111] Again, it can hardly be a coincidence that *ṣml* in Arabic denotes both "hit (with a stick)" and "be hard, solid." Because the name is not marked for feminine gender, it is not purely descriptive in form, consisting plausibly of a verbal noun, though the form is uncertain.

[112] The text has {yb}; either emend to {yb<ky>} or interpret as from the root *ybb*, that denotes a loud cry or wail in several Semitic languages. Alternatively, instead of taking the *l* before the following word, *yqẓ*, as "emphatic," one could consider taking the word divider after *yb* as misplaced and read *ybl*, "he bore (him)."

[113] The reading here is disputed. Rather than *CTA*'s {lqẓ}, the authors of *KTU* suggest {yqẓ}, best explained in context as from *yqẓ* (Heb. *yqṣ*), "awake, be awake, stay awake," i.e., "observe a wake."

[114] The reading of this word, which constitutes the principal point of attachment in the text for the "Kinneret" interpretation of the ʾAqhatu text (Margalit 1989), remains in dispute. For a recent epigraphic study, where the reading {knrt} is accepted, see Pitard 1994b.

Dānīʾilu Curses the Environs of ʾAqhatu's Murder
(iii 151 - iv 168)

Spring of [water], may what pertains to you[115] be destroyed,
Woe to you, spring of water,
for you must bear the responsibility for[116] valiant ʾAqhatu's murder:
(May you) constantly (be) an alien residing (as a refugee)[nn] in a temple,[117]
now, for a long time,[118] and forever more,
now and for all generations.[oo]
He took thereafter[119] (his) staff (in) his hand,[pp]
traveled to MRRT TǴLL BNR.[120]
(There) he cried out aloud:
Woe to you, MRRT TǴLL BNR,
for you must bear the responsibility for valiant ʾAqhatu's murder:
May your root not grow in the earth,
may (your) top be lowered into the hand of him who would pull you up;[121]
now, for a long time, and forever more,
now and for all generations.
He took thereafter (his) staff (in) his hand,
traveled to the city of ʾAbilūma,
ʾAbilūma, city of Prince Yariḫu.
(There) he cried out aloud:
Woe to you, city of ʾAbilūma,
for you must bear the responsibility for valiant ʾAqhatu's murder:
May Baʿlu make you blind,[qq]
at this very moment and forever more,
now and for all generations.

Dānīʾilu Goes Home and Mourns His Son
(iv 169-179)

He took thereafter (his) staff (in) his hand,
Dānīʾilu traveled to his house,
Dānīʾilu arrived at his palace.
The wailing women entered <his house>,[122]
the mourning women his palace,[rr]
those who rend their[ss] skin his court.[123]
They (all) wept for valiant ʾAqhatu,
shed tears for the child of Dānīʾilu the man of Rapaʾu.
For days, for months,
for months, for years,
even for seven years
Did they (all) weep for valiant ʾAqhatu,
shed tears for the child of Dānīʾilu the man of Rapaʾu.

Dānīʾilu Halts the Mourning and Sacrifices
(iv 179-189)

[Then] after seven years
[Dānīʾilu the man of] Rapaʾu spoke up,
The valiant [Harnamite] man responded.
He cried aloud:
Leave [my house], wailing women,
my palace, mourning women,
my court, you who rend your skin.
Then he offered the sacrifice of the gods,
caused his DǴṮ-sacrifice[124] to ascend (as smoke) to the heavens,
the Harnamite DǴṮ-sacrifice [of] the stars.
...[125]

nn Ps 61:5; cf. Exod 21:13-14
oo Exod 3:15; Ps 33:11
pp Gen 38:18; Exod 12:11
qq Deut 28:28
rr Jer 9:16-17
ss 1 Kgs 18:28; cf. Deut 14:1; Jer 16:6

[115] Since Dānīʾilu is not elsewhere designated as a king, it is unlikely that *mlk* here has that meaning. In comparison with *mhy* in the phrase *mhy rgmt*, "What did she say" (RS [Varia] 4:9 = *KTU* 2.14), *mlk* is interpreted as meaning "what is yours" (Renfroe 1986:70), i.e., a compound relative phrase rather than an interrogative one. As the following verse indicates, the reference here is to the humans who depend on the spring. Cp. Deut 21:1-9.

[116] *d ʿlk*, lit., "who upon you." The same formula recurs below in reference to the city, showing that *ʿl* need not denote "upon, above" in this formula. It can be interpreted either spatially ("near, next to") or causally ("on your account").

[117] Others have seen in the signs {grbtʾil} a reference to "leprosy" (see Watson 1989:47-48).

[118] The phrase *brḥ* is usually identified as a single word, meaning either "fleeing" or "evil" (bibliography in Pardee 1987:381). The first of these meanings would be parallel to *gr*, "resident alien," in the preceding line, and may well be correct. The phrase in the slot of *ʿnt brḥ* in col. iv, line 167, however, is *lht*, a prepositional phrase meaning "for now." {brḥ} may be analyzed, therefore, as *b rḥ*, with the second word interpreted as from the hollow root *rḥ*, "be wide, spacious" (used for a spatial interval in Gen 32:17).

[119] The word *ʾuḫry* has received multiple translations (cf. Renfro 1986:71). A word written like this one means "posterity" in the birth omens text RS 24.247+:39′-40′ (text 1.90)—without vowels we cannot know whether they were pronounced alike. Seeing no interpretation of this passage that admits such a meaning here, I translate as an adverb. One could also translate "he prepared the extremity of the staff in his hand," but one wonders why this word was used for so banal a statement if it refers to simple "taking" and what a more complicated "preparing" would involve.

[120] From context, this long name is that of the nearest settlement, perhaps, judging from the following metaphor for loss of progeny within a lineage (see next note), a tribal center. The name is unknown in administrative texts and etymological interpretations vary. Assuming that the function of the name is literary rather than geographical, one can interpret the first word as a form of the root *mrr* "be bitter," for "the bitterness of death" is a known idiom.

[121] That the use of tree imagery does not require that *mrrt tǵll bnr* be interpreted as the name of a tree is shown by the use of similar imagery in the Bible and in the Eshmunazar inscription (*KAI* 14) to denote descendants.

[122] *b bth*, "in his house," is restored on the basis of the plausible restoration of line 183.

[123] This verse refers to tribal or professional wailing women who put on a proper public show of grief, weeping and wailing (*bky*) and mourning aloud (*spd*), while the men cut their skin (*pẓǵ ǵr*), like the prophets of Baal in 1 Kgs 18:28 (*wayyitgōdᵉdû*).

[124] *Dǵṯ* is plausibly one of very few Indo-European loanwords in Ug. (Hoffner 1964:66-68; some subsequent bibliography in Pardee 1987:391).

[125] Lines 187-189 are damaged and, though they deal certainly with music (the words *[mṣ]ltm*, "cymbals," and *mrqdm d š[n]*, "ivory clappers," are present), it is uncertain who the musicians are and how close the formulae are to those attested later in RS 24.252:3-5 (see Pardee 1988:97-101).

Pūġatu Sets out to Avenge her Brother (iv 190-end)
Pūġatu, she who bore water on (her) shoulders, responded:
My father has offered sacrifice to the gods,
has caused his DĠṮ-sacrifice to ascend (as smoke) to the heavens,
the Harnamite DĠṮ-sacrifice of the stars.

Pūġatu Seeks and Receives her Father's Blessing (iv 194-202)
Now bless me so that I may go in a state of blessedness,[tt]
pronounce a benediction upon me so that I may go beatified,
So that I may strike down him who struck down my brother,
so that I may finish off him who finished off the (most important) child of my family.[126]
Dānīʾilu the man of Rapaʾu responded:
May [Pūġatu] live (long and prosper),[127] she who bears water on (her) shoulders,
who gathers dew for barley,
who knows the paths of the stars.
[...] she will be successful:[128]
She will strike down the one who struck down [her brother],
she will finish off him who finished off the (most important) child of [her] family.

tt Gen 24:60

Under the Disguise of a Woman, Pūġatu Dresses as a Warrior (iv 202-208)
[...] that falls in the sea,
she washed herself, [hand] and shoulder;[129]
She rouged herself with 'husk of the sea',[130]
which ranges a thousand furlongs in the sea.[131]
She [...], she puts on the outfit[132] of a warrior,
she put [a knife in] her NŠG,[133]
a sword she put in [her] sheath;
Then over (these) she put on women's garb.

Pūġatu Meets her Brother's Assassin (iv 208-224)
[At] the going forth of the Divine Light, the Sun,
Pūġatu [...] the MʾINŠ of the fields;
At the setting-place of the Divine Light, the Sun,
Pūġatu arrived at the tents.[134]
Word is brought to YṬPN:
Our hireling[135] has come to your dwelling,
[the girl] has come to the tents.
YṬPN, [the soldier of] the Lady, responded:[136]
Take, give me wine to drink,
take (this) cup in my hand,
(this) goblet in my right hand.
So Pūġatu took, gave him wine to drink,
took [the cup] from his hand,
the goblet from his right hand.
YṬPN, the soldier of the Lady, responded:
From (this very) wine does ʾILʾA[137] drink, the god

---

[126] In the phrase *ʿl ʾumty*, the second word may be either a by-form of *ʾum*, "mother," or, as one would expect, the word for "tribe, clan" (< "mother's lineage"). In the latter case, *ʿl*, which *strictu sensu* means "suckling," would denote "child."

[127] The idiom here is the same as above addressed to Dānīʾilu (see note 13), "as to (her) throat, may she live."

[128] The reading and interpretation of this line are uncertain; this version is based on a comparison with *CTA* 17 i 39 (*hw* there and *hy* here seem to mark the gender distinction).

[129] *KTU* read, hesitantly, *w ṯkm* at the beginning of line 204, a formula different from that found in the Kirta text (*ʿd ṯkm*), which makes reconstruction difficult at the end of line 203. The restoration of *yd* at the end of line 203 produces a formula similar to that attested in the Kirta text, while translating *trtḥṣ* reflexively makes the explanation of the singular form *ṯkm* easier (cf. Margalit 1989:165).

[130] It has been commonly accepted since De Moor 1968 that the reference is to purple dye, produced from several species of sea mollusk. It is uncertain, however, (1) whether the mollusk would be designated as "husk/envelope of the sea" (the ancients knew well that the actual color came from the organism living inside the shell); (2) whether an idiom used elsewhere for great distances (*ʾalp šd*—see above, note 25 and note 21 to the Baʿlu text [1.86]) would be used for the range (see following note) of the mollusk; (3) whether Pūġatu would be depicted as putting royal purple dye on her skin, and (4) whether that act would be expressed by the root *ʾdm*, "red" (various aspects of dying and the two principal shades of "purple" are designated by *ʾiqnʾu* and *pḥm* in Ug.).

[131] Lit., "which a thousand *šd* is its exiting (*ẓʾuh*) in the sea." It is possible, as others have proposed, that a noun parallel to *ġlp* is to be reconstructed at the end of line 204; the antecedent of the relative pronoun would have in that case been this noun.

[132] The word here and for women's garb below is *npṣ*, the same as designated the father's outfit needing washing in the list of the duties of the good son (see above, note 11).

[133] Because *nšg* denotes a specific accoutrement, it is impossible to do more than guess at this meaning. Arabic *nsg*, "to weave," may indicate that the item in question was woven, but that generality could apply to a type of garment or to a type of carrier (cf. the parallel term *tʿrt*, "sheath").

[134] The structure of the formula *ṣbʾ//ʿrb* is that of the merismus, rather than of parallelism (for bibliography see Pardee 1987:441). Unfortunately the obscurity of the second line of these two verses makes it difficult to determine how the merismus is set up. Judging from *mʿrb*, the basic type of reference should be spatial ("east ... west") rather than temporal ("morning ... evening"). This is corroborated by the parallelism of "fields" and "tents." The meaning of *mʾinš* is, however, uncertain and the verb in that line has disappeared. From the other indicators, one can posit that Pūġatu was traveling from east to west, through fields towards a settlement or encampment. The solar imagery may imply a day's journey as well.

[135] For lack of vowels it is uncertain whether Pūġatu is being described as the one who does the hiring or as the one who is hired. The distinction is important, for in the following line some restore *ʿnt*, assuming on the basis of the interpretation of *ʾagrtn* as "she who hired us," that Pūġatu has been mistaken for the goddess, while others restore *pġt*, interpreting *ʾagrtn* as "she whom we have hired," perhaps a reference to the girl as a camp follower. The verse, in the latter interpretation, may have contained a double reversal of expectations: *ʾgr* used passively rather than actively, *pġt* meaning "girl" rather than "Pūġatu" (i.e., the common noun rather than the name of ʾAqhatu's sister).

[136] Because of the ambiguities inherent in the Ug. writing system, it is uncertain whether the following speech is addressed to the ones who announced Pūġatu's coming or to the girl herself (the translation proposed).

[137] Most authorities emend to {ʾiln}, a divine name attested elsewhere.

of the [lady],
the god who created tent-dwellings.
The hand that struck down valiant ʾAqhatu
shall strike down by the thousands the enemies of the lady.
[He who] assigned workmen (to make) tents[138]
[...]

[...] his/her heart like a serpent [...][139]
A second time she served the mixture,
served him drink [...]

Colophon
Here is where to resume the story.[140]

[138] The resemblance between *ḥršm l ʾahlm* (line 222) and *yqny ḏdm* (line 220) is too great to be ignored.
[139] Perhaps a reference to Pūġatu taking a crafty line of behavior.
[140] The form of the colophon here is not that in which the scribe identifies himself, but an indication of how the story is to be taken up on the next tablet (Margalit 1984:178-179).

REFERENCES

Text: *CTA* 17-19; *KTU* 1.17-19. Translations and studies: Aitken 1990; Albright 1945; 1953; Albright and Mendenhall 1942; Arnaud 1985-86; Caquot 1985; Caquot, Sznycer, and Herdner 1974; Clifford 1972; Dijkstra and de Moor 1975; Dressler 1984; Driver 1956; Elliott 1991; Gibson 1977; Gordon 1977; Greenfield 1967; Herdner 1963; Hillers 1973; Hoffner 1964; Margalit 1983; 1984; 1989; de Moor 1968; 1987; Nougayrol 1970; del Olmo Lete 1981; Pardee 1977:53-56; 1987; 1988a; 1989-90; 1995; Parker 1989; Pitard 1994a; 1994b; Rainey 1971; Renfroe 1986; van Soldt 1989; Tropper 1989; Tsevat 1971; Virolleaud 1936b; Walls 1992; Watson 1976; 1989a; 1990a; Xella 1976:61-91.

2. HISTORIOGRAPHY

UGARITIC KING LIST (1.104)

K. Lawson Younger, Jr.

This poorly preserved, enigmatic tablet (RS 24.257 = *Ugaritica* 5.5 = *KTU* 1.113) contains a retrograde[1] list of the kings of Ugarit in two columns on its verso. The very broken recto seems to preserve some sort of ritual, consistently alternating between two musical instruments (*tp* "a tambourine/drum" and *ṯlb* "a flute) and the word *lnʿm* "for the Pleasant One."

What the exact relationship is (if any) between the recto and the verso has fueled debate over the tablet's genre. Moreover, the use of the divine determinative *ilu* before each royal name in the verso has also caused some scholars to see affiliations with a cult of the royal ancestors at Ugarit. For the most recent discussions see Lewis 1989:47-52; del Olmo Lete 1986; Pardee 1988a:165-178; 1996:276; and Schmidt 1994:67-71.

RECTO

[...] and his tambourine is high
[...] the peoples, for the Pleasant One

[...] and the flutes are high
[...] for the Pleasant One.

[...] and his tambourine is high
[...] for the Pleasant One.
[...] arrive

[...] the flutes are high
[... for the Pl]easant One.
[...] the Pleasant One.

[ ]x[ ]
...

[1] Kitchen (1977) cites Assyrian and Egyptian evidence of retrograde king lists. Also see most recently Schmidt 1994:67-71.

VERSO

	Left	*Right*
(12′)	[	] [ ]
(13′)	[	the divine[3] ᶜAmmiṯtamru[4]
(14′)	[	the divine Ni]qmepaᶜ
(15′)	[	the divine ᶜAmmu<rā>piᵓ
(16′)	[[2]]	the divine ᵓIbirānu
(17′)	[ ]	the divine Yaᶜḏuraddu
(18′)	[ ]	the divine Niqmepaᶜ
(19′)	[ ]⌜p⌝	the divine ᵓIbirānu
(20′)	[ ]d[	the divine ᶜAmmurāpiᵓ
(21′)	[the divine Niq]mepaᶜ*	[the divine] Niqmepaᶜ
(22′)	[the divine ᶜAmmi]ṯtamru	the divine ᵓIbirā[nu]
(23′)	[ ]	the divine Niqmepaᶜ
(24′)	[ ]	the divine ᵓIbirānu
(25′)	[ ]	the divine Niqmaddu
(26′)	[ ]⌜q⌝	the divine Yaqaru

[2] From line 16 to line 19 there is a double vertical line between the columns.

[3] Lewis suggests that "it is safe to say that, upon death, a ruler was not deified in the full sense of becoming one of the gods who made up the Ug. pantheon ... upon death a ruler was grouped with his deceased ancestors and was referred to as an *ilu*. These *ilu*'s were not worshipped in the same way that El or Baal were and we find no elaborate cult attempting to make them into high gods ... former rulers are singled out and 'honored' much in the same way as they were in life (compare the proper burial accorded to Jezebel in 2 Kings 9:34 'because she was a king's daughter')" (1989:49-51).

[4] For a recent discussion of the identification of each king in the list see Aboud 1994:11-26, 40.

REFERENCES

*KTU*²:128-129; *TUAT* 1985 1:496-497; Aboud 1994:3-4; Kitchen 1977; Lewis 1989:47-52; del Olmo Lete 1986a; Pardee 1988a:165-178; 1996; Schmidt 1994:67-71; de Tarragon 1980; Virolleaud 1968; Wilson 1977; Xella 1981.

---

3. REPHAᵓIM TEXTS

THE PATRONS OF THE UGARITIC DYNASTY (KTU 1.161) (1.105)

Baruch A. Levine, Jean-Michel de Tarragon, Anne Robertson

KTU 1.161 is a canonical liturgy, commemorating the accession of the last king of Ugarit, Ammurapi (III), and his queen, Tharyelli. It was first published by Caquot (1975), working only from a cast of the uncleaned tablet. Subsequently, six photographs appeared in *Ugaritica* 7, plates VII-IX. Bordeuil and Pardee (1982) prepared a new edition of *KTU* 1.161 based, for the first time, on a careful exanination of the tablet in Aleppo. It is this version that serves as the basis for the translation presented here.

INTRODUCTION: The Title (line 1)
The written record of the sacred celebration[1] [in honor] of the Patrons:[a] [2]

The Invitation to the Rephaim (lines 2-10)
You have summoned[3] the Rephaim[b] of the nether-world;[4]

a Num 14:9; Jer 48:45; Ps 121:5-6; Lam 4:20
b Isa 14:9; 26:14; Ps 88:11

[1] Ug. *dbḥ*, like Heb. *zebaḥ*, may designate a sacred celebration of many parts. Cf. *KTU* 1.148:1: *dbḥ ṣpn* "the sacred celebration in honor of Saphan." See Exod 12:27; 1 Sam 9:12; 20:29; 2 Kgs 10:19.

[2] Ug. *ẓlm*, written with the variant *-ẓ-*, instead of the usual *Ṣade*. Pitard 1978 was the first to translate *ẓlm* "protectors," an interpretation that yielded "Patrons." Thus, the Israelites are told that the Canaanites can be defeated, because "their protector (*ṣillam*) has departed from them, but YHWH remains with us" (Num 14:9b). Similar meanings occur in Akk. (*CAD* Ṣ 189, s.v. *ṣillu*, meaning 5). In Aram., the cognate *ṭll* "shadow," also connotes "protection" (Greenfield-Porten 1982:30, 61, Word List, s.v. *ṭll*). Thus, "shade" from the scorching sun became a metaphor for the shelter and protection provided by gods and kings. On the same basis, the long departed ancestors of the Ug. kings were their "Patrons," the guarantors of kingship and succession.

[3] The given translation follows Caquot 1975, and Pope 1977:177 in taking the form *qritm* as a perfect, second person plural "You have summoned," whereas Pitard 1978 takes it as a perfect, first person singular "I have summoned," with enclitic *mem*. The same of uncertainty remains as to the precise form represented by *qbitm* "You have commanded." The verb *qba* is cognate with Akk. *qabû* "to speak, command" (*CAD* Q, 34, s.v. *qabû*, meaning 4).

[4] The translation "the Rephaim of the netherworld" for Ug. *rpi arṣ*, takes the singular, oblique form, *rpi*, as a collective. The nominative

You have commanded the the Council of the Didanites![5]
Summon ULKN, Raph[a!
Summon TRMN, Raph[a!
Summon SDN-w-RDN, [Rapha!][6]
Summon ṮR-^{c}LLMN, [Rapha!]
[All] summon the most ancient Rephaim!
You have summoned the Rephaim of the netherworld!
You have commanded the Council of the Didanites!

The Invitation to Departed Kings (lines 11-12)
Summon Ammishtramru, the King!
Summon, as well, Niqmaddu, the King![7]

The Lamentation (lines 13-17)
O, throne of Niqmaddu — weep!
Let his footstool shed tears!
It front of it[8] — let the royal table weep;
Let it swallow its tears.
Tears, and [more] tears; many tears![9]

Shapash is Sent to Locate the Departed Kings in the Netherworld (lines 18-26),
Shine bright,[10] O Shapash!
Shine bright, O great luminary!
On high Shapash cries out:
After your lord, from the throne;[11]
After your lord, to the netherworld descend![c]
To the netherworld descend;
And go down low into the earth.
Below is SDN-w-RDN;[12]
Below is ṮR-KLLMN;
Below are the the most ancient Rephaim.
Below is Ammishtamru, the King;
Below is Niqmaddu, the King, as well.

Sacrifices in Honor of the New King (lines 27-30)
Once — offer a benefaction.[13]
A second time — offer a benefaction.
A third time — offer a benefaction.
A fourth time — offer a benefaction.
A fifth time — offer a benefaction.
A sixth time — offer a benefaction.
A seventh time — offer a benefaction.
You shall present a bird.

Blessings (lines 31-34)
Hail![d]
Hail, Ammurapi!
And hail to his household![14]
Hail, [Tha]ryelli![15]
Hail to her household!
Hail, Ugarit!
Hail to her gates!

c Gen 37:35
d 1 Sam 25:6; 1 Kgs 2:33; Isa 57:19; 1 Chr 12:19

singular form is *rpu*, here taken to be in the accusative, *rp[a]*. Kings and heroes buried in the earth were eventually beatified. For a discussion of this theme at Ugarit and in biblical literature see de Moor 1976; Pope 1977; Levine and de Tarrgon 1984.

[5] Ug. *qbṣ ddn* "the council of the Didanites" parallels *pḫr qbṣ dtn* "the assembled council of the Ditanites" in the Keret epic (*KTU* 1.15, iii 4,15). Both entities are associated with the Rephaim. The word *Didānu*, also written *Ditānu* and *Tidānu(m)*, refers to a tribe, or large group, perhaps composed of Amorites or neighbors of the Amorites, who inhabited Northeastern Syria in earlier times. To judge from our text and from the Keret epic, the Ugaritians traced their origins to the Didanum people, and thus desired the presence of the Council of Didanites at the accession of their kings. Levine-de Tarragon 1984:654-656; Buccellati 1966:243ff; and Astour 1973.

[6] The identities of the divine, dead kings, ULKN, TRMN, SDN-w-RDN, and ṮR-^{c}LLMN are unknown, except that they are numbered among the Rephaim.

[7] Reference is to Niqmaddu III, the father of Ammurapi III, the last king of Ugarit. In the Ug. king list, Niqmaddu III was immediately preceded by a certain Ibiranu, not by Ammistamru II, the king named in the present text. It is likely that our text is summoning only the major kings of the Ug. dynasty to the coronation of Ammurapi III. Another possibility is that Ibiranu and Niqmaddu III were brothers, or co-regents. Kitchen 1977; Healey 1978.

[8] Ug. *lpnh* could alternatively be taken to mean "in front of him," namely, in front of Niqmaddu, himself.

[9] Ug. ^{c}*dmt* may represent a metathesis of *dm*^{c}*t* "tears," resonating the prothetic form *udm*^{c}*t* "tears" in the previous line. Others have derived it from a cognate of Arabic ^{c}*adima* "to be lacking, without vegetation," hence: "desolation" Lane 1874 Book 1/5:1975-1976.

[10] Ug. *išḫn* is to be read *iššaḫīnī* "be warming, bright", an N-stem imperative, fem. sing., addressed to the goddess Shapash. Akk. attests a cognate *šaḫānu* "to become warm, to warm — the earth" (*CAD Š* 1:78, s.v. *šaḫānu*).

[11] The Ug. text reads *l ksh*, a scribal error, to be corrected to *l ksi* "from the throne."

[12] Ug. *tḥt* is taken as a cognate of Heb. *taḥat* "below, underneath."

[13] Ug. *ṯ*^{c}*y* "offer a benefaction" is a verbal form, denominative of *ṯ*^{c} a type of sacrificial offering, listed in *KTU* 1.39, line 1. The sense of "benefaction" derives from the epithet *ṯ*^{c} "noble, gracious" as in *krt ṯ*^{c} "Keret, the noble" in *KTU* 1.14, IV, 37, a cognate of Heb. *šô*^{c}*a* "a generous, noble person" (Job 30:24). A noble person offers a benefaction, just as, in Heb. usage, the *nādîb* "generous, noble person," offers a sacrifice called *nedābāh* "free-will offering" (Isa 32:5). In form, *ṯ*^{c}*y* may be read as a D-stem, plural imperative, *ṯa*^{cc}*āyū*, or as an infinitive absolute, *ṯa*^{cc}*āyu,* with essentially the same meaning.

[14] The text actually reads *ba(!)h,* corrected with considerable certainty to *bth* "his household."

[15] The name Tharyelli, Ug. *[ṯ]ryl* ,is partially restored, but fairly certain. It is clearly written and complete in *KTU* 2.14, line 8, an official letter. One would expect it to be the name of Ammurapi's queen. It occurs as the name of a donor of a stele to Dagan in *KTU* 6.13, restored *[ṯ]ryl*, as here, and this name has been equated with Akk. *Šarelli*, a queen of Ugarit named in an Akk. business document from Ugarit, *Ugaritica* 5:159. The same identification is probable in *Ugaritica* 5:161. Laroche 1976.

REFERENCES

Text: *KTU* 1.161; *Ugaritica* 5 vii; Studies: Astour 1973; Bordreuil and Pardee 1982; Buccellati 1966; Caquot 1975; Greenfield and Porten 1982; Healey 1978; Kitchen 1977; Lane 1874; Laroche 1976-77; Levine and de Tarragon 1984; de Moor 1976; Pitard 1978; Pope 1977a.

C. INDIVIDUAL FOCUS

1. INSTRUCTIONS

HIPPIATRIC TEXTS (1.106)

Chaim Cohen

The Ugaritic hippiatric texts, dating from the fourteenth to the twelfth centuries BCE, have been known to the scholarly world since 1934, when the first two fragmentary copies (here referred to as B,C) were published by C. Virolleaud. Only in 1968, however, when the best preserved copy (here referred to as A) was first published in *Ugaritica* V, did it become clear that all three texts were in fact copies of the same veterinary procedural (or professional instruction) text, dealing with the therapeutic treatment of sick horses and consisting of a title and ten (copies B and C: nine) structurally parallel sections, demarcated by the underscoring of the last line of each division.[1] Since then, a fourth fragmentary text (here referred to as D) was published in *KTU*[1] in 1976 and this has been followed by two modern critical editions of all four texts by Cohen and Sivan (1983) and Pardee (1985).[2] Methodologically, these texts are among the most difficult of the Ugaritic texts to interpret since the language is highly technical and many of the terms are nowhere else extant in Ugaritic.[3] On the other hand, the very clear tripartite structure of each of the ten sections (Symptoms, Remedy-Components and Their Preparation, The Administering of the Remedy [constant for all ten sections]) as well as the existence of four copies of the same text, provide much more textual and structural evidence than is usually available. A major comparative tool is provided by the occurrence of many of these technical terms (both symptoms and remedy-components) in Akkadian medical texts and plant and drug lists. The few extant Akkadian hippiatric passages and the classical Greek and Latin hippiatric texts have also been consulted.

The following translation refers to the "new revised composite text of UHT" established by C. Cohen which will appear in *UF* 28 together with extensive commentary (Cohen 1997).

Commas have been used in this translation *only* to separate the three parts of each section according to the formal tripartite structure of this text (see Cohen and Sivan 1983:10, 48-51).

Title (1)
Treatise[a] concerning the well-being[b] (health) of horses:
____

Section One (2-4)
If[c] a horse roars,[d] a *št*-measure of the scorpion-like

a Exod 24:7; Num 21:14; Josh 10:13; 2 Sam 1:18; 1 Kgs 8:13 (LXX); 11:41; 14:19,29; Nah 1:1; Esth 2:23; 6:1; 10:2; Neh 7:5; 1 Chr 9:1; 2 Chr 16:11; 25:26 *b* e.g., Prov 3:17 (contrast 2:18); 24:25; Job 36:11 *c*) e.g., Exod 21:2,7; Lev 2:1,4 *d* 2 Sam 22:14-16 = Ps 18:14-16; 104:5-9; Job 26:11

[1] For the importance of Copy A (= RS 17.120; *KTU* 1.85; Cohen and Sivan 1983:Text A; Pardee 1985:Tablette 1) in restoring the other three texts and in demonstrating that all four are copies of the same hippiatric text, see already *CTA* 1:245 and esp. Fronzaroli 1975:38; Cohen and Sivan 1983:1; Pardee 1985:14-16. For the typology, see especially Cohen and Sivan 1983:1-2; Pardee 1985:13-14; Mack-Fisher 1990. Here it should be emphasized that seven Akk. hippiatric sections and related references have also been found, in some cases embedded in between the "regular human" sections of various Akk. medical texts (see Pardee 1985:appendix III; Stol 1986:174). For a full edition and translation of the two most important Akk. hippiatric sections (*BAM* 159:V:33-36,37-47) see Cohen 1983. See also Köcher *BAM* xiv-xvi; Fronzaroli 1975:44 and n. 40; Stol 1986:174; and most recently Biggs 1990:629b. Regarding the underscored lines see Fronzaroli 1975:41 and nn. 22-27; Cohen and Sivan 1983:8, 11; Pardee 1985:15, 26, n.39. Section eight was omitted from copies B and C and contains somewhat different symptom formulations in A and D (Pardee 1985:15, 27, n. 41). Thus, the four copies reflect divergent traditions only concerning section eight in this otherwise canonical Ug. hippiatric text. See in general Hallo 1991.

[2] Besides the many different interpretations of individual technical terms, the two main differences in these two critical editions are as follows: a) In Cohen and Sivan, the readings of *KTU*[1] were used (in almost all cases) as the basis for establishing a composite text of paragraphs 1-7 and 10, with an apparatus listing all significant variants in the four copies and with a provisional translation of that text. The Pardee edition contains what appear to be far superior readings of paragraphs 8-9 together with collations undertaken by Prof. Pardee of all four copies. The readings of all four texts are presented individually with RS 17.120 being considered the main standard text, which is also the only one translated. See Pardee 1985:12-13, 20-37. b) In Cohen and Sivan, much more emphasis was placed on utilizing the formal structure of the composite text as crucial evidence for determining the approximate usage and meaning of individual terms. See Cohen and Sivan 1983:48-51. Neither of these two critical editions took the other into consideration. The present translation is of an unpublished "new revised composite text of UHT" incorporating virtually all of Pardee's new readings and most of his restorations in accordance with the formal structure of the composite text as established in the Cohen-Sivan edition. See now Cohen 1997.

[3] See Fronzaroli 1975:40, 45-46; Cohen and Sivan 1983:1-3; Pardee 1985:13-14.

plant should be pulverized[e] and liquified[f] either in a solution[g] of *dalīqātu*-groats or of *mundû*-groats, and it (the remedy) should (then) be poured into his nose.

Section Two (5-6)
If a horse discharges/d a putrid liquid, the *mēmētu*-plant and a *bṣql*-measure [h] of the ᶜ*rgz*-tree/plant should be pulverized together, [i] and it (the remedy) should (then) be poured into his nose.

Section Three (7-8)
Or if a horse discharges/d a putrid liquid, grain and bitter almond should be pulverized together, and it (the remedy) should (then) be poured into his nose.

Section Four (9-11)
If a horse does not defecate or urinate,[j] the sap of a *št*-measure of the *qulqulliānu*-tree/plant and a *št*-measure of the ᶜ*rgz*-tree/plant should be pulverized together, and it (the remedy) should (then) be poured into his nose.

Section Five (12-14)
If a horse is seized[k] with "pain," a *št*-measure of average quality *mkšr* and a *št*-measure of the *šakirû*-plant and the "fruit" of the lettuce plant should be pulverized together, and it (the remedy) should (then) be poured into his nose.

Section Six (15-17)
Or if a horse is seized with "pain," the *nīnû*-plant and a *št*-measure of average quality *mkšr* and a *št*-measure of the *urânu*-plant of *ḥmr*-quality should be pulverized together, and it (the remedy) should (then) be poured into his nose.

Section Seven (18-19)
If a horse *yr*ᵓ*aš*, a *št*-measure of the *pillû*/*billû*-plant of *qṭ*-quality should be pulverized, and it (the remedy) should (then) be poured into his nose.

{*Section Eight* (20-22)
Or if a horse [discharges/d a putrid liquid and is/was leth]argic(?), coriander[l] from the hills {and a *š*[*t*-measure of ... and] the leaves[m] of [...] should be pulverized [together, and it (the remedy) should (then) be po]ured [into his nose.]}

Section Nine (23-29)
Or if a horse roars, [...] of the juniper-tree [and] the "fruit" of the ᶜ*ṯrb*-tree/plant <and> the seed [l] of the [bitter al]mond similar to [l] coriander [and(?) sim]ilar to fennel(?) [and] the *mēmētu*-plant and a *št*-measure of the *nīnû*-plant and the "fruit" of the *abukkatu*-plant and a *š*[*t*-measure of the sc]orpi[on-like plant] <<(and) the *mēmētu* plant>>(?) and the "fruit" of the lettuce-plant and a [*bṣq*]*l*-measure of the *urânu*-plant of *ḥmr*-quality should be pulverized togeth[er], and it (the remedy) should (then) be poured into his nose.

Section Ten (30-32)
<Or> if <a horse> *yr*ᵓ*aš* and *ykhp* incessantly, old fig-cakes[n] and old raisins[o] and flour of groats should be pulverized together, and it (the remedy) should (then) be poured into his nose.

e Num 11:7-8
f Exod 16:21
g Isa 5:22; Ps 102:10; Prov 9:2,5
h 2 Kgs 4:42
i Deut 22:11; Isa 41:19; 60:13
j 1 Sam 25:22, 34; 1 Kgs 14:10; 16:11; 21:21; 2 Kgs 9:8; 18:27 = Isa 36:12
k Exod 15:14, 15; 2 Sam 1:9; Isa 21:3; 33:14; Jer 13:21; 49:24; Ps 48:7; 119:53; Job 21:6; 30:16.
l Exod 16:31; Num 11:7
m Ezek 47:12
n 1 Sam 30:12; 2 Kgs 20:7; Isa 38:21
o 1 Sam 30:12

REFERENCES

Text: *CTA* 160-161 (B,C including copies and photos); *UT* 55-56 (B,C); *Ugaritica* 5:625-627 - figures 16, 16A, 16B (Photo of A); *KTU*² 1.85; 1.71; 1.72; 1.97 (A,B,C,D); Cohen and Sivan 1983 - composite edition of lines 1-19, 30-32; Pardee 1985 - latest readings, copies and photos (A,B,C,D). Studies: Biggs 1990; Cohen 1983; 1997; Cohen and Sivan 1983; Fronzaroli 1975; Hallo 1991; Köcher *BAM* xiv-xvi; Mack-Fisher 1990; Pardee 1985; Stol 1979.

2. SCHOOL TEXTS

ABECEDARIES (1.107)

Aaron Demsky

The alphabet was invented in Canaan ca. 1700 BCE, during the Middle Bronze IIB period, a time of increased urbanization and cross cultural fertilization. This invention was probably the result of reflective thought of a local Canaanite scribe familiar with the scripts of the major powers, i.e., Akkadian cuneiform and most likely Egyptian hieroglyphic and hieratic writing. These latter scripts were logo-syllabic in nature, so that each sign represented a word/idea and/or a syllable thus creating a writing system of hundreds of signs. The alphabetic revolution was the radical reduction of graphemes to less than thirty in number. Once the consonantal signs could be memorized in a standard order this revolution in visual communication would have resounding effects on all aspects of society, religion and education in the ancient world. It would not be far-fetched to say that the abecedary, i.e., the conventional order of the letters, is the fundamental building block of western literacy.

There is a difference of opinion among scholars regarding the nature of the Semitic alphabet prior to its adoption by the Greeks who gave letter form to the vowels. There are those who argue the novelty of a true alphabet having reduced writing to a pure consonantal system (e.g., A. H. Gardiner, W. F. Albright, F. M. Cross, J. Naveh,

A. R. Millard, A. Demsky). On the other hand, other maintain that the Semitic alphabet is actually a syllabic system of consonant plus any vowel (I. J. Gelb, G. R. Driver, S. Yeivin, W. W. Hallo). Whatever the case, the basic letter order is documented from Ugarit of the 14th century BCE, which probably indicates also the antiquity of the letter names and method of instruction.

1. *The Order of the Letters*
There are two basic systems for ordering the letters of the alphabet. The first and most familiar is generally called the Northwest Semitic order. It is found already in Ugaritic cuneiform and in the linear scripts used for Canaanite and Aramaic from which were derived the Greek, Latin and Etruscan forms in the west and classical Arabic in the south. It is this basic sequence which has given us the terms *aleph-bet* in Hebrew, *alpha beta* in Greek, *abecedarium* in Latin and *abgedhawa* in Arabic.

The second system is the so-called South Semitic order known from South Arabic inscriptions (5th century BCE) and from medieval Ethiopic (Geez) manuscripts. However, recent research has shown that this too was an alternate sequence known and practiced in the scribal schools of ancient Canaan. A. G. Lundin (1987b) deciphered this order on a 13th century BCE alphabetic cuneiform tablet discovered in the 1930's at Tel Beth Shemesh. With the stabilization of the alphabet at the beginning of the Iron Age, the *ABC* order dominated and caused the second *HLḤM* sequence to be displaced to the periphery of the Semitic world, though there might have been some later contact between the two (Knauf 1985:204-206).

The Ugaritic abecedary with twenty-seven individual signs represents the full phonetic range of that language, which may have been also the original Proto-Canaanite alphabet (Lundin 1987a). Local scribes probably added three more signs at the end for greater clarity in writing other languages in use at Ugarit. Many complete and incomplete abecedaria have been found in Israel from the Iron Age down to the Roman period; they were written by professional writers as well as by semi-literates. Sometimes they were engraved on stone, even in the negative by seal cutters practicing their trade, sometimes they were written in ink on shards. For some it was a learning exercise and for others it was a way to pass time.

The Izbet Sartah ostracon (ca. 1200) is worth special attention for it is the oldest reduced twenty-two letter alphabet inscribed in the Proto-Canaanite script (Demsky 1977; 1986). This beginner's exercise tablet, written from left to right, is also peculiar in that some of the letters are transposed: the *heth* precedes the *zayin* and the *pe* comes before the *ᶜain*. While one might assume this to be a child's sloppiness, the *pe-ᶜain* sequence is found in the alphabetic acrostics of Lamentations 2, 3 and 4, as well as in the triple abecedary in the Hebrew script found at Kuntillet Ajrud (early 8th century BCE) indicating a contemporary secondary Israelite scribal tradition of ordering the letters.

The Greek alphabet reflects the conservative nature of a literate education in that it preserves the basic order of the Canaanite alphabet as well as the traditional (and the unintelligible) Semitic names. At the same time, it also demonstrates the ability of a recipient culture, especially a geographically distant, non-dependent one, to deviate from the norm in adapting the alphabet to its own phonetic stock, which in this case probably led to the innovative visualization of the vowels. As in the Ugaritic alphabet, the Greeks added additional letters at the end of the list.

The classical Arabic alphabet, derived from the twenty-two letter Aramaic through the Nabataean script (Healey 1990-91), was six letters short of its phonemic range. This difficulty was resolved by adding diacritical points to the available forms, similar to the *shin/sin* distinction in Hebrew. The Arabic alphabet was then reordered according to the external shape of the letters. Still one can discern the underlying influence of the traditional Aramaic abecedary when new forms appear, e.g., *alf*, *ba*, *gim*, *dal* ... *ᶜyn*, *fa* ... *kaf*, *lam*, *mim*, *nun* ... *he*, *waw*, *ya* and the use of the *abgedhawa* sequence to represent numerals.

The North Semitic abecedary and its derivatives

Ugaritic: ᵓa b g ḫ d h w z ḥ ṭ y k š l m ḏ n ẓ s ᶜ p ṣ q r ṯ ǵ t + ᵓi ᵓu s̀

Standard Canaanite: ᵓ b g d h w z ḥ ṭ y k l m n s ᶜ p ṣ q r š t

Izbet Sartah: ᵓ b g d h w ḥ z ṭ y k l m n s p ᶜ ṣ q r š t

Greek: A B Γ Δ E Z H Θ I K Λ M N Ξ O Π P Σ T + Y Φ X Ψ Ω

Arabic: ᵓ b t ṯ g ḥ ḫ d ḏ r z s š ṣ ḍ ṭ ẓ ᶜ ġ f q k l m n h w y

The South Semitic abecedaries

South Arabic: h l ḥ m q w š r ġ/b t s k n ḫ ś f ᵓ ᶜ ḍ g d b/ġ ṭ z ḏ y ṯ ṣ/ẓ

Ethiopic: h l ḥ m š r s q b t ḫ n ᵓ k w ᶜ z y d g ṭ p ṣ ḍ f ps

2. *The Letter Names*
The names of the letters seem to be an integral part of the abecedary, preserving through a mnemonic ditty the traditional order. The letter sequence was not determined in antiquity by either similarity of shape or phonetic origins. In his decipherment of the Proto-Sinaitic script, A. H. Gardiner (1916) proposed the *acrophonic principle*

where the pictographic form of the letter was chosen because it represented an object whose name began with the desired consonant, e.g., "house," in Canaanite *bet*, represents the phoneme *b*. This would mean that the names go back to the very invention of the alphabet. Cross and Lambdin (1960) published an exercise tablet from Ugarit which gives the initial syllable in Akkadian cuneiform for the names of the alphabet. As they have shown these initial syllables correspond to the Canaanite letter names.

This observation has been challenged by W. W. Hallo (1958), who has argued on the basis of Isa 28:9-13 that the names were actually the consonant plus a helping sound like *aw*, e.g., *waw*, *ṣaw*, *qaw*, *taw* (cf. Greek mu, nu). Following this possibility, we might suggest that in certain scribal schools some of the names were composed by adding a *t* to the initial consonant, e.g., *bet*, *ḥet*, *ṭet* and Greek *zeta* or by seeking words that begin and end in the same consonant, e.g., *waw*, *mem*, *nun* and possibly **gag*, **ṭiṭ* **ṣiṣ* (cf. in rabbinic literature the late names *hehin*, *pepin*, *b. Šabb*. 103b). It seems therefore that letter names were somewhat fluid, especially as the form of the signs became simplified and chronologically removed from the original pictograph.

The letter names of the Hebrew alphabet are first recorded in the Greek Septuagint of the alphabetic acrostic Psalm 119, reflecting the nomenclature of the third century BCE at the latest. An examination of the names will show two linguistic sources that probably reflect the adoption of the Aramaic script by the Jews no later than this century. We can determine the late non-Canaanite names either by the pronunciation of the diphthong (*ᶜain*, *zain*) or by the choice of an Aramaic word instead of the Canaanite form preserved in the Greek alphabet, e.g., *zain* instead of *zet* or *resh* instead of *ro(sh)* and *nun* instead of *nahash* as in Ethiopic.

3. *Exercises*

Since learning the alphabet was a function of a formal curriculum, we can assume that there were different exercises for memorizing the order of the letters already at an early period. An exercise that is already documented in the sixth century BCE is the *ATBaSh* exercise which is based on the equal division of the twenty-two letters of the alphabet, correlating the first and last letter, the second and 21st letter and so on. Jeremiah (25:25,26; 51:1,41) uses this elementary school exercise to create audience participation in comprehending the intent of his prophesy by substituting the corresponding letters: *ššk* ⇔ *bbl*; *lbkmy* ⇔ *kśdym*; *zmry* for *zmky* ⇔ *ᶜylm* (i.e., Elam).

For variety, the teachers devised the *ALBaM* exercise, where the first and twelfth letters, etc. were matched, e.g., *ᵓbg* ⇔ *lmn*. In the Latin primary school one could therefore learn his *abecedarium* or the *elementum*, which gave rise to the term elementary (school) (Coogan 1974). Further variations and combinations were devised and are noted in the classical period for Hebrew (*b. Šabb*. 104), Greek (Jerome) and Latin (Quintilian).

4. *Application of the Abecedary*

In antiquity, the fixed abecedary created new opportunities for literary expression and memory aids especially in three areas:

a) the organization of information and the placing of objects in their proper order according to the alphabet. E. Puech (1980) has published a second century CE document that contains an abecedary in addition to an incomplete alphabetized list of personal names. It seems from Zech 6:10, 14 that the prophet and his audience also were using the alphabet to order and remember pertinent data already in the late 6th century BCE (Demsky 1981). Occasional inscriptions of letters of the alphabet found on the back of ivory pieces from Samaria or on stone gutters or pillars show that the alphabet had become knowledge of joiners and masons and their tool for facilitating their work.

b) aesthetics as expressed in writing alphabetic acrostic poetry. This literary technique allows the biblical poet to strive for completeness and totality (cf. *meᵓalef veᵓad taw*, *b. Šabb* 55a; *b. ᶜAbod. Zar.*), as well as challenging the poet's ability to express himself within the structural demands of the alphabet, which would be similar to composing a haiku or a sonnet. There is variation in the limited number of acrostic poems, for instance some are complete or partially incomplete and others are fragmentary (Nah 1:1-11; Pss 9-10). Furthermore, Lam 3 is a triple acrostic while Ps 119 is eightfold. It is possible that this literary form influenced the length of other compositions, limiting them to twenty-two verses, the number of the letters in the alphabet, as in Lam 5 (Brug 1990:290). The alphabetic acrostic might have been popular among learned members of the Wisdom School not only as a didactic method but also as a literary device to conclude their works as in Prov 31:10-31 and Sir 51 or to express the comprehensive nature of Torah (Ps 119). In this context, note Ceresko's observations (1985) that the additional pe at the end of Pss 25 and 34 creates a subtle acrostic pattern *alp*, with the first and middle letters of these psalms, which spells not only the name of the first letter but also the verb "to teach" (see Job 33:33), or perhaps "to alphabetize." Garsiel (1994) has shown another literary development in the biblical poets' predilection to play on the conventional letter names.

c) express the mysterious and the magical or a reference to the divine, e.g., *Alpha-Omega* (Rev 1:8; 22:13) or the rabbinic statement (*y. Sanh*. 18a) that God's personal seal reads *ᵓEmet*, i.e., "truth," which is composed of the first, last and (almost) middle letters of the alphabet (see Dornseiff 1925).

In a very perceptive proverb found at the end of the Syriac version of Ahiqar (Conybeare 1913:127), the author juxtaposed the school lesson in learning the alphabet with its potential for popular literacy. An unlikely but intuitively intelligent student — the wolf — is brought into the formal educational system including the teacher/master (*rab*), the school house (*bet sfr*ᵓ*a*) and elementary curriculum ᵓ*alf bet*. The result of this meeting is that the wolf quickly recognizes the potential of the alphabet as a means of achieving his own goals, in this case in having a good meal of kid. While the teacher is still on the opening lesson of the first two letters, the wolf anticipates the next lesson by providing a word which includes the following two letters and one that indicates his personal aim in life.

"They brought him (the wolf) into the school house. His master said to him, 'ᵓ*Aleph-Beth*.' The wolf said, '*Gady*ᵓ*a*'" ("the kid," here used for the name of the third letter).

REFERENCES

Brug 1990; Ceresko 1985; Coogan 1974; Cross and Lambdin 1960; Demsky 1977; 1981; 1986; Dornseiff 1925; Gardiner 1916; Garsiel 1994; Hallo 1958; Healey 1990-91; Knauf 1985; Lundin 1987a; 1987b; Puech 1980.

WEST SEMITIC BIBLIOGRAPHY

ABOUD, J.
1994 *Die Rolle des Königs und seiner Familie nach den Texten von Ugarit.* Forschungen zur Anthropologie und Religionsgeschichte = FARG 27. Münster: Ugarit-Verlag.

AITKEN, K. T.
1990 *The Aqhat Narrative. A Study in the Narrative Structure and Composition of an Ugaritic Tale.* JSS Monograph 13. Manchester: University of Manchester.

ALBRIGHT, W. F.
1945 "A New Hebrew Word for 'Glaze' in Proverbs 26:23." *BASOR* 98:24-25.
1953 "The Traditional Home of the Syrian Daniel." *BASOR* 130:26-27.

ALBRIGHT, W. F., and G. E. MENDENHALL.
1942 "The Creation of the Composite Bow in Canaanite Mythology." *JNES* 1:227-229.

ALEXANDROPOULOS, J.
1992 "Numismatique." In *DCPP,* 320-327.

AMADASI GUZZO, M. G.
1990 "Noms de vases en phénicien." *Semitica* 38:15-25.

ARCHI, A.
1988 "The Cult of the Ancestors and the Tutelary God at Ebla." Pp. 103-112 in *Studies Ehrman.*

ARNAUD, D.
1982 "Une lettre du roi de Tyr au roi d'Ougarit: milieux d'affaires et de culture en Syrie à la fin de l'Âge du Bronze récent." *Syria* 59:101-107.
1985-86 *Recherches au pays d'Aštata. Textes sumériens et accadiens.* Emar VI/1-3. Paris: Éditions Recherche sur les Civilisations.

ASTOUR, M. C.
1968 "Two Ugaritic Serpent Charms." *JNES* 27:13-36.
1973 "A North Mesopotamian Locale of the Keret Epic?" *UF* 5:29-39.
1980 "The Nether World and its Denizens at Ugarit." Pp. 227-238 in *RAI* 26.

ATTRIDGE, H. W., and R. A. ODEN, Jr.
1981 *Philo of Byblos, The Phoenician History. Introduction, Critical Text, Translation, Notes.* CBQMS 9. Washington, DC: The Catholic Biblical Association of America.

AVISHUR, Y.
1981 "The Ghost-Expelling Incantation from Ugarit." *UF* 13:13-25.

BAKER, D. W.
1987 "Leviticus 1-7 and the Punic Tariffs: A Form Critical Comparison." *ZAW* 99:188-197.

BARRÉ, M. L.
1978 "^{d}LAMMA and Rešep at Ugarit: The Hittite Connection." *JAOS* 98:465-467.

BAUMGARTEN, A. I.
1981 *The Phoenician History of Philo of Byblos.* EPRO 89. Leiden: Brill.

BEAULIEU, P.-A.
1989 *The Reign of Nabonidus, King of Babylon 556-539 BC.* YNER 10. New Haven and London: Yale University Press.

BEYER, K.
1984 *Die Aramäischen Texte vom Toten Meer.* Göttingen: Vandenhoeck & Ruprecht, *Ergänzungsband.*

BIGGS, R. D.
1990 "Medizin. A. In Mesopotamien." *RlA* 7/7-8:623-629.

BLAU, J., and J. C. GREENFIELD.
1970 "Ugaritic Glosses." *BASOR* 200:11-17.

BONNET, C.
1992 "Baal Saphon." In *DCPP,* 60-61.

BORDREUIL, P.
1983 "'Venin de printemps, venin foudroyant:' À propos de RS 24.244 l.5." *UF* 15:299-300.
1990 " À propos de Milkou, Milqart et Milk^{c}ashtart." *Maarav* 5-6:11-21.
1991 "Recherches ougaritiques. I. Où Baal a-t-il remporté la victoire contre Yam?" *Semitica* 40:17-27.

BORDREUIL, P., and A. CAQUOT.
1980 "Les textes en cunéiformes alphabétiques découverts en 1978 à Ibn Hani." *Syria* 57:343-373.

BORDREUIL, P., and D. PARDEE.
1982 "Le rituel funéraire ougaritique RS 34.126." *Syria* 59:121-128.
1989 *La trouvaille épigraphique de l'Ougarit. I. Concordance.* RSOu 5/1.
1991 "Les textes ougaritiques." Pp. 139-172 in RSOu 7.
1993 "Le combat de *Ba^{c}lu* avec *Yammu* d'après les textes ougaritiques." *MARI* 7:63-70.
1995 "L'épigraphie ougaritique: 1973-1993." Pp. 27-32 in RSOu 11.

BOSSERT, H. T.
1946 *Asia.* Istanbul: Universität Istanbul.

BOWMAN, R. A.
1944 "An Aramaic Religious Text in Demotic Script." *JNES* 3:219-231.

VAN DEN BRANDEN, A.
1965 "Lévitique 1-7 et le tarif de Marseille, *CIS* I. 165." *RSO* 40:107-130.

BROCKELMANN, K.
1966 *Lexicon Syriacum.* Hildesheim: Georg Olms.

BROOKE, G. J.
1979 "The Textual, Formal and Historical Significance of Ugaritic Letter RS 34.124 (=*KTU* 2.72)." *UF* 11:69-87.
BRUG, J. F.
1990 "Biblical Acrostics and Their Relationship to Other Ancient Near Eastern Acrostics." Pp. 283-304 in *SIC* 3.
BUCCELLATI, G.
1966 *The Amorites of the Ur III Period*. Naples.
CAQUOT, A.
1969 "Nouveaux documents ougaritiens." *Syria* 46:241-265.
1971 Review. *RHR* 180:168-170.
1975 "Hébreu et Araméen." *ACF* 75:423-432.
1978 "Textes ougaritiques de Ras Ibn Hani." *ACF* 78:570-577.
1978-79 "Ras Ibn Hani 78/20." *ACF* 79:188-190.
1979 "La naissance des dieux (SS = *CTA* 23 = *UT* 52)." Cols. 1367-1371 in *SDB* 9. Paris: Letouzey & Ané.
1984 "Une nouvelle interprétation de la tablette ougaritique de Ras Ibn Hani 78/20." *Or* 53:163-176.
1985 "Une nouvelle interprétation de KTU 1.19 I 1-19." *SEL* 2:93-114.
1989 "Textes religieux." Pp. 7-123 in *Textes ougaritiques*. Tome II: *Textes religieux, rituels, correspondance*. LAPO 14. Paris: Cerf.
1992 "Le Léviathan de Job 40,25 - 41,26." *RB* 99:40-69.
CAQUOT, A., M. SZNYCER, and A. HERDNER.
1974 *Textes ougaritiques*. Tome I: *Mythes et légendes*. LAPO 7. Paris: Cerf.
CASSUTO, U.
1938 "Il palazzo di Baᶜal nella tavola II AB di Ras Shamra." *Or* 7:265-290.
CATHCART, K. J., and W. G. E. WATSON.
1980 "Weathering a Wake: A Cure for a Carousal. A Revised Translation of *Ugaritica* 5. Text 1." *PIBA* 4:35-58.
CAUBET, A., and F. POPLIN.
1987 "Les objets de matière dure animale. Étude du matériel." Pp. 273-306 inRSOu 3.
CERESKO, A. R.
1985 "The ABCs of Wisdom in Psalm XXXIV." *VT* 35:99-104.
CLIFFORD, R. J.
1972 *The Cosmic Mountain in Canaan and the Old Testament*. HSM 4. Cambridge, MA: Harvard University Press.
COHEN, C.
1983 "The Ugaritic Hippiatric Texts and BAM 159." *JANES* [appeared 1986] 15:1-12.
1997 "The Ugaritic Hippiatric Texts: Revised Composite Text, Translation and Commentary." *UF* 28 (forthcoming).
COHEN, C., and D. SIVAN.
1983 *The Ugaritic Hippiatric Texts: A Critical Edition*. AOS 9. New Haven: AOS.
COLLINS, J. J.
1992 "Nabonidus, Prayer of." In *ABD* 4:976-978.
CONYBEARE, F. C., J. R. HARRIS and A. SMITH LEWIS
1913 *The Story of Ahikar*. 2nd Edition. Cambridge: Cambridge University Press.
COOGAN, M. D.
1974 "Alphabets and Elements." *BASOR* 216:61-63.
COOKE, G. A.
1903 *A Text-Book of North-Semitic Inscriptions: Moabite, Hebrew, Phoenician, Aramaic: Nabataean, Palmyrene, Jewish*. Oxford: Clarendon Press.
COOPER, J. S.
1993 "Sacred Marriage and Popular Cult in Early Mesopotamia." Pp. 81-96 in *OCPR*.
CREASON, S.
1992 "The syntax of אם and the structure of the Marseille Tariff." *RSF* 20:143-159.
CROSS, F. M.
1984 "Fragments of the Prayer of Nabonidus." *IEJ* 34:260-264.
CROSS, F. M., and T. O. LAMBDIN.
1960 "A Ugaritic Abecedary and the Origins of the Proto-Canaanite Alphabet." *BASOR* 160:21-26.
CUNCHILLOS, J.- L.
1976 *Cuando los angeles eran dioses*. Bibliotheca Salmanticensis 14, Estudios 12. Salamanca: Universidad Pontificia.
CUTLER, B., and J. MACDONALD.
1982 "On the Origin of the Ugaritic Text KTU 1.23." *UF* 14:33-50.
DALMAN, G.
1905 *Grammatik des jüdisch-palästinischen Aramäisch*. 2nd Edition. Leipzig: J. C. Hinrichs.
DAY, J.
1986 "Asherah in the Hebrew Bible and Northwest Semitic Literature." *JBL* 105:385-408.
VON DEINES, H., H. GRAPOW, and W. WESTENDORF.
1958 *Übersetzung der Medizinischen Texte. Grundriss der Medizin der Alten Ägypter*. Vol. 4, Part 1. Berlin: Akademie Verlag.
DELCOR, M.
1981 "Les cultes étrangers en Israël au moment de la réforme de Josias d'après 2R 23. Étude de religions sémitiques comparées." Pp. 91-123 in *Mélanges Cazelles*.
1983 "A propos du sens de *ṣpr* dans le tarif sacrificiel de Marseille (*CIS* I, 165, 12): parfum d'origine végétale ou parfum d'origine animale?" *Semitica* 33:33-39.
1990 "Le tarif dit de Marseille (*CIS* I, 165). Aspects du système sacrificiel punique." *Semitica* 38:87-93, pl. XVI.
DEMSKY, A.
1977 "A Proto-Canaanite Abecedary Dating from the Period of the Judges and its Implications for the History of the Alphabet." *Tel Aviv* 4:14-27.

1981 "The Temple Steward Josiah ben Zephaniah." *IEJ* 31:100-102.
1986 "The ᶜIzbet Sartah Ostracon — Ten Years Later." Pp. 186-197 in *ᶜIzbet Sartah. An Early Iron Age Site Near Rosh Haᶜayin, Israel.* Ed. by I. Finkelstein. Oxford: Oxford University Press.

DIETRICH, M., and O. LORETZ.
1969 "Beschriftete Lungen- und Lebermodelle aus Ugarit." Pp. 165-179 in *Ugaritica* 6.
1978a "Die keilalphabetische Krugaufschrift RS 25.318." Pp. 147-148 in *Ugaritica* 7.
1978b "Die sieben Kunstwerke des Schmiedegottes in *KTU* 1.4 I 23-43." *UF* 10: 57-63.
1980 "Die Bannung von Schlangengift (KTU 1.100 und KTU 1.107: 7b-13a 19b-20)." *UF* 12:153-170.
1981 "Neue Studien zu den Ritualtexten aus Ugarit (I)." *UF* 13:63-100.
1986a "Ugaritische Omentexte." *TUAT* 2/1:94-101.
1986b "Die akkadischen Tierbezeichnungen *immeru, puḫādu* und *puḫālu* im Ugaritischen und Hebräischen." *UF* 17:99-103.
1986c "Die Trauer Els und Anats (*KTU* 1.5 VI 11-22. 31 - 1.6 I 5)." *UF* 18:101-10.
1988 "Ugaritische Rituale und Beschwrungen." *TUAT* 2/3:299-357.
1990a ALASP 3.
1990b "The Syntax of Omens in Ugaritic." *Maarav* 5-6:89-109.
1993 "KTU 1.114, ein 'Palimpsest'." *UF* 25:133-136.

DIETRICH, M., O. LORETZ, AND J. SANMARTÍN.
1975a "Der keilalphabetische *šumma izbu*-Text RS 24.247+265+268+328." *UF* 7:133-140.
1975b "Der stichometrische Aufbau von RS 24.258 (= Ug. 5, S. 545 Nr. 1)." *UF* 7:109-114.
1976 *KTU.*
1995 *KTU.*[2]

DIJKSTRA, M., AND J. C. DE MOOR.
1975 "Problematical Passages in the Legend of Aqhâtu." *UF* 7:171-215.

DION, P.-E.
1980 "Tu feras disparaître le mal du milieu de toi." *RB* 87:321-349.

DORNSEIFF, F.
1925 *Das Alphabet in Mystik und Magie*. Berlin: Teubner.

DRESSLER, H. H. P.
1984 "Reading and Interpreting the Aqht Text." *VT* 34:78-82.

DRIVER, G. R.
1956 *Canaanite Myths and Legends*. OTS 3. Edinburgh: T. & T. Clark.

DURAND, J.-M.
1993 "Le mythologème du combat entre le dieu de l'orage et la mer en Mésopotamie." *MARI* 7:41-61.

DUSSAUD, R.
1921 *Les origines cananéennes du sacrifice israélite*. Paris: Ernest Leroux.

EBBELL, B.
1924 "Die ägyptischen Krankheitsnamen." *ZÄS* 59:144-149.

ELLIOTT, C.
1991 "The Ground Stone Industry." Pp. 9-99 in RSOu 6.

FLEMING, D. E.
1991 "The Voice of the Incantation Priest (RIH 78/20)." *UF* 23:141-154.
1992 *The Installation of Baal's High Priestess at Emar*. HSS 42. Atlanta: Scholars Press.

FOLEY, C. M.
1987 "Are the 'Gracious Gods' *bn šrm*? A Suggested Restoration for KTU 1.23:1-2." *UF* 19:61-74.

FREILICH, D.
1992 "Ili-malku the *ṯᶜy*." *SEL* 9:21-26.

FRONZAROLI, P.
1975 "La lingua dei testi ippiatrici di Ugarit." *AGI* 60:34-46.

GACHET, J.
1992 "Ugarit Ivories: Typology and Distribution." Pp. 67-89 in *Ivory in Greece and the Eastern Mediterranean from the Bronze Age to the Hellenistic Period*. Ed. by J. L. Fitton. BMOP 85. London.

GARBINI, G.
1983 "Note sui testi rituali ugaritici." *OA* 22:53-60.

GARCIA MARTINEZ, F.
1992 *Qumran and Apocalyptic: Studies on the Aramaic Texts from Qumran*. Leiden: E. J. Brill.

GARDINER, A. H.
1916 "The Egyptian Origin of the Semitic Alphabet." *JEA* 3:1-16.

GARSIEL, M.
1994 "Playing on the Names of the Letters of the Alphabet in Acrostic Literary Compositions in the Bible." *Beth Miqra* 139:313-334 (Hebrew).

GASTER, T. H.
1946 "A Canaanite Ritual Drama. The Spring Festival at Ugarit." *JAOS* 66:49-76.
1975 "Sharper Than a Serpent's Tooth: A Canaanite Charm Against Snakebite." *JANES* 7:33-51.

GEVIRTZ, S.
1961 "The Ugaritic Parallel to Jeremiah 8:23." *JNES* 20:41-46.

GIBSON, J. C. L.
1978 *Canaanite Myths and Legends*. Second edition. Edinburgh: T. & T. Clark.

GINSBERG, H. L.
1930-31 "A Punic Note: צועת." *AJSL* 47:52-53.
1935 "Notes on "The Birth of the Gracious and Beautiful Gods'." *JRAS* 1935:45-72.

1941 "Did Anath Fight the Dragon?" *BASOR* 84:12-14.
1945 "The North-Canaanite Myth of Anath and Aqhat." *BASOR* 97:3-10.
1946 *The Legend of King Keret: A Canaanite Epic of the Bronze Age*. BASORSup 2-3. New Haven: ASOR.
1950 "Interpreting Ugaritic Texts." *JAOS* 70:156-160.

GORDON, C. H.
1947 *Ugaritic Handbook*. AnOr 25. Rome: Pontifical Biblical Institute.
1965 *Ugaritic Textbook*. AcOr 38. Rome: Pontifical Biblical Institute.
1977 "Poetic Legends and Myths from Ugarit." *Berytus* 25:5-133.

GRAY, J.
1965 *The Legacy of Canaan. The Ras Shamra Texts and Their Relevance to the Old Testament*. VTSup 5. 2nd Rev. Edition. Leiden: Brill.

GREENFIELD, J. C.
1967 "Ugaritic Lexicographical Notes." *JCS* 21:89-93.
1969 "Some Glosses on the Keret Epic." *EI* 9:60-65.

GREENFIELD, J. C., and B. PORTEN.
1982 *The Bisitun Inscription of Darius the Great, Aramaic Version*. London: Lund Humphries.

GREENSTEIN, E. L.
1977 "One More Step on the Staircase." *UF* 9:77-86.

HAAK, R. D.
1982 "A Study and New Interpretation of *QṢR NPŠ*." *JBL* 101:161-167.

HALLO, W. W.
1958 "Isaiah 28:9-13 and the Ugaritic Abecedaries." *JBL* 77:324-338.
1977 "Haplographic Marginalia." Pp. 101-103 in *Studies Finkelstein*.
1991 "The Concept of Canonicity in Cuneiform and Biblical Literature: A Comparative Appraisal." *SIC* 4:1-19.

HARRIS, J. E., and K. R. WEEKS.
1973 *X-Raying the Pharaohs*. New York: Charles Scribner's Sons.

HEALEY, J. F.
1978 "Ritual Text *KTU* 1.161 — Translation and Notes." *UF* 10:83-88.
1983a "Swords and Ploughshares: Some Ugaritic Terminology." *UF* 15:47-52.
1983b "Burning the Corn: New Light on the Killing of Mōtu." *Or* 52:248-251.
1990-91 "Nabataean to Arabic: Calligraphy and Script Development among the Pre-Islamic Arabs." *Manuscripts of the Middle East* 5:41-52.

HEIDER, G. C.
1985 *The Cult of Molek: A Reassessment*. JSOTSup 43. Sheffield: JSOT Press.

HELCK, W.
1971 *Die Beziehungen Ägyptens zu Vorderasien im 3. und 2. Jahrtausend v. Chr*. 2nd Edition. Wiesbaden: Otto Harrassowitz.

HELD, M.
1968 "The Root *ZBL/SBL* in Akkadian, Ugaritic and Biblical Hebrew." *JAOS* 88:90-96.
1973 "Pits and Pitfalls in Akkadian and Biblical Hebrew." *JANES* 5:173-190.

HERDNER, A.
1963 *CTA*.
1972 "Une prière à Baal des ugaritains en danger." *CRAIBL* 1972:693-697.
1978 "Nouveaux textes alphabétiques de Ras Shamra - XXIVe campagne, 1961." Pp. 1-74 in *Ugaritica* 7.

HETTEMA, T. L.
1989-90 "'That it be Repeated'. A Narrative Analysis of *KTU* 1.23." *JEOL* 31:77-94.

HILLERS, D. R.
1973 "The Bow of Aqhat: The Meaning of a Mythological Theme." Pp. 71-80 in *Studies Gordon*.
1983 "The Effective Simile in Biblical Literature." *JAOS* 103:181-185.

HOCH, J. E.
1994 *Semitic Words in Egyptian Texts of the New Kingdom and Third Intermediate Period*. Princeton: Princeton University Press.

HOFFNER, H. A., Jr.
1964 "An Anatolian Cult Term in Ugaritic." *JNES* 23:66-68.

HOFTIJZER, J.
1982 "Quodlibet Ugariticum." Pp. 121-127 in *Studies Kraus*.

HOUSTON, W.
1993 *Purity and Monotheism. Clean and Unclean Animals in Biblical Law*. JSOTSup 140. Sheffield: JSOT Press.

HUEHNERGARD, J.
1987 *Ugaritic Vocabulary in Syllabic Transcription*. HSS 32. Atlanta: Scholars Press.

DE JONG, T., and W. H. VAN SOLDT.
1987-88 "Redating an Early Solar Eclipse Record (KTU 1.78). Implications for the Ugaritic Calendar and for the Secular Accelerations of the Earth and Moon." *JEOL* 30:65-77.

KINNIER WILSON, J. V.
1994 "The *Sāmānu* Disease in Babylonian Medicine." *JNES* 53:111-115.

KITCHEN, K. A.
1977 "The King List of Ugarit." *UF* 9:131-142.

KNAUF, E. A.
1985 "A South Safaitic Alphabet from Khirbet Es-Samrāʾ." *Levant* 17:204-206.

KÖCHER, F.
1963 *BAM*. Vol. 1. Berlin.

KORPEL, M. C. A.
1990 *A Rift in the Clouds. Ugaritic and Hebrew Descriptions of the Divine*. UBL 8. Münster: Ugarit-Verlag.

KOTTSIEPER, I.
1988 "Anmerkungen zu Pap. Amherst 63." *ZAW* 100:217-244.
1992 "Die literarische Aufnahme assyrischer Begebenheiten in frühen aramäischen Texten." Pp. 283-289 in *RAI* 38.

LAMBERT, W. G.
1985 "Trees, Snakes and Gods in Ancient Syria and Anatolia." *BSOAS* 48:435-451.

LANE, E. W.
1863-93 *An Arabic-English Lexicon*. London.

LAROCHE, E.
1976-77 "Glossaire de la Langue Hourite." *RHA* 34-35.

LECLANT, J.
1960 "Astarté à cheval d'après les représentations égyptiennes." *Syria* 37:1-67.

LEVINE, B. A.
1963 "Ugaritic Descriptive Rituals." *JCS* 17:105-111.
1989 *Leviticus*. JPS Torah Commentary. Philadelphia: Jewish Publication Society.

LEVINE, B. A., and W. W. HALLO.
1967 "Offerings to the Temple Gates at Ur." *HUCA* 38:17-58.

LEVINE, B. A., and J.-M. DE TARRAGON.
1984 "Dead Kings and Rephaim: The Patrons of the Ugaritic Dynasty." *JAOS* 104:649-659.
1988 "'Shapshu Cries out in Heaven:' Dealing with Snake-Bites at Ugarit (*KTU* 1.100, 1.107)." *RB* 95:481-518.
1993 "The King Proclaims the Day: Ugaritic Rites for the Vintage (*KTU* 1.41//1.87)" *RB* 100:76-115.

LEVY, J.
1963 *Wörterbuch über die Talmudim und Midraschim*. 4 Vols. Darmstadt: Wissenschaftliche Buchgesellschaft.

LEWIS, T.
1989 *Cults of the Dead in Ancient Israel and Ugarit*. Atlanta: Scholars Press.

LIPIŃSKI, E.
1978 "Ditanu." Pp. 91-110 in *Studies Loewenstamm*.
1983 "Ancient Types of Wisdom Literature in Biblical Narrative." Pp. 39-55 in *Studies Seeligmann*.
1992a "Rab." In *DCPP*, 369.
1992b "Suffète." In *DCPP*, 429.
1992c "Tarifs sacrificiels." In *DCPP*, 439-440.

LIVERANI, M.
1969 "Recensione." *OA* 8:338-340.

LOEWENSTAMM, S. E.
1969 "Eine lehrhafte ugaritische Trinkburleske." *UF* 1:71-77.
1980 "A Didactic Ugaritic Drinkers' Burlesque." Pp. 369-381 in *Comparative Studies in Biblical and Ancient Oriental Literatures*. AOAT 204. Kevelaer: Butzon & Bercker; Neukirchen-Vluyn: Neukirchener Verlag.

LORETZ, O.
1985 *Leberschau, Sündenbock, Asasel in Ugarit und Israel*. UBL 3. Soest: CIS-Verlag.
1988 "The Ancient Syro-Palestinian Institution of the *Marziḥu* 'Thiasos, Symposium' According to the Ugaritic Text KTU 1.114." Pp. 171-174 in *Studies in the History and Archaeology of Palestine (Proceedings of the First International Symposium on Palestine Antiquities)* III. Aleppo: Aleppo University Press.

LORETZ, O., and P. XELLA.
1982 "Beschwörung und Krankenheilung in RIH 78/20." *MLE* 1:37-46.

LUNDIN (LOUNDINE), A. G.
1987a "Ugartic Writing and the Origin of the Semitic Consonantal Alphabet." *AO* 5:91-99.
1987b "L'abecedaire de Beth Shemesh." *Le Muséon* 100:243-250.

MACK-FISHER, L.
1990 "From Ugarit to Gades: Mediterranean Veterinary Medicine." *Maarav* 5-6:207-220 [= *Studies Segert*].

MALLET, J.
1987 "Le temple aux rhytons." Pp. 213-248 in RSOu 3.

MARGALIT, B.
1981 "(RS 24.266) תפילה אוגריתית לעת מצור." *WCJS* 7/2:63-83.
1983 "Lexicographical Notes on the *Aqht* Epic (Part I: KTU 1.17-18)." *UF* 15:65-103.
1984 "Lexicographical Notes on the *Aqht* Epic (Part II: KTU 1.19)." *UF* 16:119-179.
1986 "Why King Mesha of Moab Sacrificed His Oldest Son." *BAR* 12/6:62-63, 76.
1989 *The Ugaritic Poem of AQHT*. BZAW 182. Berlin: Walter de Gruyter.

MARGULIS, B.
1970 "The Canaanite Origin of Psalm 29 Reconsidered." *Biblica* 51:332-348.

MASSART, A.
1954 *The Leiden Magical Papyrus I 343 + I 345. Oudheidekunde Mededelingen*. New Series, Supplement 34. Leiden: Brill.

MEIER, S.
1986 "Baal's Fight With Yam (*KTU* 1.2.I, IV). A Part of the Baal Myth as Known in *KTU* 1.1, 3-6?" *UF* 18:241-254.

MEYER, R.
1962 *Das Gebet des Nabonid*. Berlin: Akademie Verlag.

MEYER, J.-W.
1987 *Untersuchungen zu den Tonlebermodellen aus dem Alten Orient*. AOAT 39. Kevelaer: Butzon & Bercker; Neukirchen-Vluyn: Neukirchener Verlag.
1990 "Zur Interpretation der Leber- und Lungenmodelle aus Ugarit." In Dietrich and Loretz 1990a:241-280.

MILGROM, J.
1972 "The Alleged Wave-Offering in Israel and in the Ancient Near East." *IEJ* 22:33-38.
1991 *Leviticus 1-16. A New Translation with Introduction and Commentary*. AB 3. Garden City, NY: Doubleday.
MILIK, J. T.
1956 "Prière de Nabonide' et autres écrits d'un cycle de Daniel: fragments araméens de Qumran 4." *RB* 63:407-415.
MILLER, P. D., Jr.
1988 "Prayer and Sacrifice in Ugarit and Israel." Pp. 139-155 in *Studies Fensham*.
DE MOOR, J. C.
1968 "Murices in Ugaritic Mythology." *Or* 37:212-215.
1969 "Studies in the New Alphabetic Texts from Ras Shamra I." *UF* 1:167-188.
1971 *The Seasonal Pattern in the Ugaritic Myth of Baᶜlu According to the Version of Ilimilku*. AOAT 16. Kevelaer: Butzon & Bercker; Neukirchen-Vluyn: Neukirchener Verlag.
1976 "*Rāpiʾūma* — Rephaim." *ZAW* 88:323-345.
1980a "El, the Creator." Pp. 171-187 in *Studies Gordon*.[2]
1980b "An Incantation Against Evil Spirits (Ras Ibn Hani 78/20)." *UF* 12:429-432.
1983 "Enkele liturgische teksten uit Ugarit." Pp. 247-252 in *Schrijvend Verleden. Documenten uit het oude nabije oosten vertaald en toegelicht*. Ed. by K. R. Veenhof. Mededelingen en Verhandelingen van het vooraziatisch-egyptisch Genootschap "Ex Oriente Lux" 24. Leiden: Zutphen.
1987 *An Anthology of Religious Texts from Ugarit*. Nisaba: Religious Texts Translation Series 16. Leiden: Brill.
MORAN, W. L.
1992 *The Amarna Letters*. Baltimore: Johns Hopkins University Press.
NIEHR, H.
1994 "Zur Frage der Filiation des Gottes Baᶜal in Ugarit." *JNSL* 20/2:165-177.
NIMS, C. F., and R. C. STEINER.
1983 "A Paganized Version of Ps 20:2-6 from the Aramaic Text in Demotic Script." *JAOS* 103:261-274.
NOUGAYROL, J.
1968 "Textes suméro-accadiens des archives et bibliothèques privées d'Ugarit." Pp. 1-446 in *Ugaritica* 5.
1970 *PRU* VI. MRS 12.
O'CONNOR, M.
1986 "Northwest Semitic Designations for Elective Social Affinities." *JANES* 18:67-80.
DEL OLMO LETE, G.
1981 *Mitos y leyendas de Canaan segun la tradicion de Ugarit*. Madrid: Ediciones Cristiandad.
1986 "The 'Divine' Names of the Ugaritic Kings." *UF* 18:83-95.
1987 "Liturgia ugarítica del primer mes (*KTU* 1.41//1.87)." *AO* 5:257-270.
1989a "Liturgia sacrificial y salmodia en Ugarit (KTU 1.119)." *AO* 7:27-35.
1989b "Addenda." *AO* 7:132.
1992 *La religión cananea según la litúrgia de Ugarit*. Estudio textual. AOSup 3. Barcelona: Editorial AUSA.
OPPENHEIM, A. L.
1956 *Dreams*.
PARDEE, D.
1976 "The Preposition in Ugaritic." *UF* 8:215-322.
1977 "An Emendation in the Ugaritic Aqht Text." *JNES* 36:53-56.
1978a "A Philological and Prosodic Analysis of the Ugaritic Serpent Incantation *UT* 607." *JANES* 10:73-108.
1978b "The Semitic Root *mrr* and the Etymology of Ugaritic *mr(r) // brk*." *UF* 10:249-288.
1979 "*mᵉrōrăt-pᵉtanîm* 'Venom' in Job 20:14." *ZAW* 91:401-416.
1980 "The New Canaanite Myths and Legends." *BiOr* 37:269-291.
1984 "Will the Dragon Never Be Muzzled?" *UF* 16:251-255.
1985 *Les Textes Hippiatriques*. Editions Recherche sur les Civilizations, Mémoire nº 53. Paris.
1986 "Ugaritic: The Ugaritic *šumma izbu* Text." *AfO* 33:117-147.
1987 "Ugaritic Bibliography." *AfO* 34:366-471.
1988a RSOu 4.
1988b "A New Datum for the Meaning of the Divine Name Milkashtart." Pp. 55-68 in *Studies Craigie*.
1988c *Ugaritic and Hebrew Poetic Parallelism. A Trial Cut (ᶜnt I and Proverbs 2)*. VTSup 39. Leiden: Brill.
1989 "(Rather Dim but Nevertheless Appreciable) Light from (a Very Obscure) Ugaritic (Text) on (the) Hebrew (Bible)." Pp. 79-89 in *Studies Fitzmyer*.
1989-90 "Ugaritic Proper Nouns." *AfO* 36-37:390-513.
1991 "The Structure of RS 1.002." Pp. 1181-1196 in *Studies Leslau*.
1993a "Poetry in Ugaritic Ritual Texts." Pp. 207-218 in *Verse in Ancient Near Eastern Prose*. Ed. by J. C. de Moor and W. G. E. Watson. AOAT 42. Kevelaer: Butzon & Bercker; Neukirchen-Vluyn: Neukirchener Verlag.
1993b "Review of Dietrich and Loretz (1990a)." *JAOS* 113:614-617.
1995 "Koshar, Kosharot." Pp. 913-917 in *DDD*.
1996 "*Marziḥu*, *Kispu*, and the Ugaritic Funerary Cult: A Minimalist View." Pp. 273-287 in *Studies Gibson*.
Forthcoming *Les Textes Rituels*. Paris: Éditions Recherche sur les Civilisations.
PARKER, S. B.
1989 *The Pre-Biblical Narrative Tradition*. SBLRBS 24. Atlanta: Scholars Press.
PITARD, W. T.
1978 "The Ugaritic Funerary Text RS 34.126." *BASOR* 232:65-75.
1994a "The 'Libation Installations' of the Tombs at Ugarit." *BA* 57/1:20-37.
1994b "The Reading of *KTU* 1.19:III:41: The Burial of Aqhat." *BASOR* 293:31-38.

POPE, M. H.
1955 *El in the Ugaritic Texts*. VTSup 2. Leiden: Brill.
1972 "A Divine Banquet at Ugarit." Pp. 170-203 in *Studies Stinespring*.
1977a "Notes on the Rephaim Texts from Ugarit." Pp. 163-182 in *Studies Finkelstein*.
1977b *Song of Songs: A New Translation with Introduction and Commentary*. AB 7C. Garden City, NY: Doubleday.
1979 "Ups and Downs in El's Amours." *UF* 11:701-708.
PUECH, E.
1980 "Abécédaire et liste alphabétique de noms hébreux du début du IIe s. A.D." *RB* 87:118-126.
RAINEY, A. F.
1971 "Observations on Ugaritic Grammar." *UF* 3:151-172.
RATNER, R., and B. ZUCKERMAN.
1986 "'A Kid in Milk?': New Photographs of *KTU* 1.23, Line 14." *HUCA* 57:15-60.
RENFROE, F.
1986 "Methodological Considerations Regarding the Use of Arabic in Ugaritic Philology." *UF* 18:33-74.
RIBICHINI, S., and P. XELLA.
1984 "Il dio *pdr*." *UF* 16:267-272.
RITNER, R. K.
1993 *The Mechanics of Ancient Egyptian Medical Practice*. SAOC 54. Chicago: Oriental Institute.
RUMMEL, T. S.
1978 *The ᶜNT Text: A Critical Translation*. Dissertation, Claremont Graduate School. Ann Arbor: University Microfilms.
SACK, R. H.
1992 "Nabonidus." In *ABD* 4:973-976.
SANMARTÍN, J.
1978 "Die Lanze (*ktǵd̲*) des Bᶜl." *UF* 10:447-448.
1980 "Glossen zum ugaritischen Lexikon (IV)." *UF* 12:335-339.
1992 "Tejidos y ropas en ugarítico: apuntes lexicográficos." *AO* 10:95-103.
SARACINO, F.
1982 "Il letto di Pidray." *UF* 14:191-199.
1983a "Un parallelo elegiaco a KTU 1.119:26-36." *UF* 15:304-306.
1983b "A State of Siege: Mi 5 4-5 and an Ugaritic Prayer." *ZAW* 95:263-269.
SASSON, J. M.
1988 "The Numeric Progression in Keret 1:15-20. Yet Another Suggestion." *SEL* 5:181-188.
SCHAEFFER, C. F. A.
1949 *Ugaritica 2. Nouvelles études relatives aux découvertes de Ras Shamra*. MRS 5. Paris: Geuthner.
1954 "Les fouilles de Ras Shamra-Ugarit. Quinzième, seizième et dix-septième campagnes (1951, 1952 et 1953)." *Syria* 31:14-67.
1978 "Contexte archéologique et date du rhyton léontocéphale de la maison d'Agaptarri (RS 25.318)." Pp. 149-154 in *Ugaritica* 7.
SCHMIDT, B.
1994 *Israel's Beneficent Dead. Ancestor Cult and Necromancy in Ancient Israelite Religion and Tradition*. FAT 11. Tübingen: J. C. B. Mohr.
SEGERT, S.
1984 *A Basic Grammar of the Ugaritic Language*. Berkeley: University of California.
1986 "Preliminary Notes on the Structure of the Aramaic Poems in the Papyrus Amherst 63." *UF* 18:271-299.
SIVAN, D.
1984 *Grammatical Analysis and Glossary of the North-west Semitic Vocables in Akkadian Texts of the 15th-13th Centuries B.C. from Canaan and Syria*. AOAT 214. Kevelaer: Butzon & Bercker; Neukirchen-Vluyn: Neukirchener Verlag.
SMELIK, K. A. D.
1983 "Een Aramese parallel voor psalm 20." *Nederlands Theologisch Tijdschrift* 37:89-103.
SMITH, G. E., and W. R. DAWSON.
1924 *Egyptian Mummies*. New York: The Dial Press.
SMITH, M. S.
1984 "The Magic of Kothar, the Ugaritic Craftsman God, in *KTU* 1.6 VI 49-50." *RB* 91:377-380.
1986 "Interpreting the Baal Cycle." *UF* 18:313-339.
1994 *The Ugaritic Baal Cycle*. Volume 1: *Introduction with Text, Translation & Commentary of KTU 1.1-1.2*. VTSup 55. Leiden: Brill.
SOKOLOFF, M.
1990 *A Dictionary of Jewish Palestinian Aramaic of the Byzantine Period*. Ramat Gan: Bar Ilan University.
VAN SOLDT, W. H.
1989 "ᵓ*Atn prln*, 'ᵓAttā/ēnu the Diviner.'" *UF* 21:365-368.
1991 *Studies in the Akkadian of Ugarit: Dating and Grammar*. AOAT 40. Kevelaer: Butzon & Bercker; Neukirchen-Vluyn: Neukirchener.
STAGER, L. E.
1982 "The Archaeology of the East Slope of Jerusalem and the Terraces of the Kidron." *JNES* 41:111-121.
STEINER, R. C.
1991 "The Aramaic Text in Demotic Script: The Liturgy of a New Year's Festival Imported from Bethel to Syene by Exiles from Rash." *JAOS* 111:362-363.
1992 "Northwest Semitic Incantations in an Egyptian Medical Papyrus of the Fourteenth Century B.C.E." *JNES* 51:191-200.
1995 "Papyrus Amherst 63: A New Source for the Language, Literature, Religion, and History of the Arameans." Pp. 199-207 in *Studia Aramaica*.
STEINER R. C., and A. MOSAK MOSHAVI.
1995 "A Selective Glossary of Northwest Semitic Texts in Egyptian Script." Pp. 1249-1266 in *DNWSI*.

STEINER, R. C., and C. F. NIMS.
1984 "You Can't Offer Your Sacrifice and Eat It Too: A Polemical Poem from the Aramaic Text in Demotic Script." *JNES* 43:89-114.
1985 "Ashurbanipal and Shamash-shum-ukin: A Tale of Two Brothers from the Aramaic Text in Demotic Script." *RB* 92:60-81.
STOL, M.
1986 "Review of Cohen and Sivan 1983." *BiOr* 43:172-174.
SZNYCER, M.
1977 "Carthage et la civilisation punique." Pp. 473-483, 545-593 in *Rome et la conquête du monde méditerranéen 264-27 avant J.-C.* Tome II. *Genèse d'un empire*. Ed. by Claude Nicolet. Nouvelle Clio 8bis. Paris: Presses Universitaires de France.
DE TARRGON, J.-M.
1980 *Le culte à Ougarit: d'après les textes de la pratique en cunéiformes alphabétiques*. Cahiers de la Revue Biblique 19. Paris: Gabalda.
1989 "Les rituels." Pp. 125-238 in *Textes ougaritiques. Tome II: Textes religieux, rituels, correspondance*. LAPO 14. Paris: Cerf.
TROPPER, J.
1989 "Ugaritisch *šqy*: 'trinken' oder 'tränken'?" *Or* 58:233-242.
1990 ALASP 2.
TSEVAT, M.
1971 "Traces of Hittite at the Beginning of the Ugaritic Epic of AQHT." *UF* 3:351-352.
1979 "Der Schlangentext von Ugarit. UT 607 — KTU 1.100 — Ug V, 564ff. — RS 24.244." *UF* 11:759-778.
TSUMURA, D. T.
1978 "A Problem of Myth and Ritual Relationship — CTA 23 (UT 52):56-57 Reconsidered —." *UF* 10:387-395.
VAUGHN, A. G.
1993 "*Il ǵzr* — An Explicit Epithet of El as a Hero/Warrior." *UF* 25:423-430.
VIROLLEAUD, Ch.
1931 "Un poème phénicien de Ras-Shamra-La lutte de Môt, fils des dieux, et d'Aleïn, fils de Baal." *Syria* 12:193-224.
1932 "Un nouveau chant du poème d'Aleïn-Baal." *Syria* 13:113-163.
1933 "La naissance des dieux gracieux et beaux. Poème phénicien de Ras-Shamra." *Syria* 14:128-151.
1934a "Fragment nouveau du poème de Môt et Aleyn-Baal." *Syria* 15:226-243.
1934b "La mort de Baal. Poème de Ras-Shamra (I* AB)." *Syria* 15:305-336.
1935 "La révolte de Košer contre Baal. Poème de Ras-Shamra (III AB,A)." *Syria* 16:29-45.
1936a *La légende de Keret roi des Sidoniens publiée d'après une tablette de Ras-Shamra*. MRS 2. Paris: Geuthner.
1936b *La légende phénicienne de Danel*. MRS 1. Paris: Geuthner.
1938 *La déesse ᶜAnat*. MRS 4. Paris: Geuthner.
1941a "Le roi Kéret et son fils (II K), 1re partie. Poème de Ras-Shamra." *Syria* 22:105-136.
1941b "Le roi Kéret et son fils (II K) (Deuxième partie)." *Syria* 22:197-217.
1942-43a "Le roi Kéret et son fils (II K) (Troisième partie)." *Syria* 23:1-20.
1942-43b "Le mariage du roi Kéret (III K). Poème de Ras-Shamra." *Syria* 23:137-172.
1944-45 "Fragments mythologiques de Ras-Shamra." *Syria* 24:1-23.
1961 "Les nouveaux textes alphabétiques découverts à Ras-Shamra." *Groupe linguistique des études chamito-sémitiques, comptes rendus* 9:41-42.
1962a "Les assesseurs de la déesse-soleil à Ras-Shamra." *Groupe linguistique des études chamito-sémitiques, comptes rendus* 9:50-52.
1962b "Les nouveaux textes mythologiques de Ras-Shamra." *CRAIBL* 105-113.
1965 *PRU* V. MRS 11. Paris: Imprimerie Nationale; Klincksieck.
1968 "Les nouveaux textes mythologiques et liturgiques de Ras Shamra (XXIVe Campagne, 1961)." Pp. 545-595. In *Ugaritica* 5.
VLEEMING, S. P., and J. W. WESSELIUS.
1982 "An Aramaic Hymn from the Fourth Century B.C." *BiOr* 39:501-509.
1983-84 "Betel the Saviour." *JEOL* 28:110-140.
1985 *Studies in Papyrus Amherst 63*. vol. 1. Amsterdam.
1990 *Studies in Papyrus Amherst 63*. vol. 2. Amsterdam.
WALLS, N. H.
1992 *The Goddess Anat in Ugaritic Myth*. SBLDS 135. Atlanta: Scholars Press.
WATSON, W. G. E.
1976 "Puzzling Passages in the Tale of Aqhat." *UF* 8:371-378.
1980 "An Example of Multiple Wordplay in Ugaritic." *UF* 12:443-444.
1989a "Notes on Some Ugaritic Words." *SEL* 6:47-52.
1989b "What Does Ugaritic *gmn* Mean?" *AO* 7:129-131.
1990a "Sundry Ugaritic Notes." *UF* 22:421-423.
1990b "Comments on KTU 1.114: 29′-31′." *AO* 8:265-267.
1992 "Imagery in a Ugaritic Incantation." *UF* 24:367-368.
1994 "Aspects of Style in KTU 1.23." *SEL* 11:3-8.
WEINFELD, M.
1985a "The Pagan Version of Psalm 20:2-6—Vicissitudes of a Psalmodic Creation in Israel and its Neighbors." *EI* 18:130-140.
1985b "The Aramaic Text (in Demotic Script) from Egypt on Sacrifice and Morality and its Relationship to Biblical Texts." *Shnaton* 9:179-189. (Hebrew).
WILLIAMS-FORTE, E.
1983 "The Snake and the Tree in the Iconography and Texts of Syria During the Bronze Age." Pp. 18-43 in *Ancient Seals and the Bible*. Ed. by L. Gorelick and E. Williams-Forte. Malibu: Undena.
WILSON, R. R.
1977 *Genealogy and History in the Biblical World*. New Haven: Yale University Press.
WRESZINSKI, W.
1912 *Der Londoner Medizinische Papyrus (Brit. Museum Nr. 10059) und der Papyrus Hearst*. Die Medizin der Alten Ägypter 2. Leipzig: J. C. Hinrichs.

WYATT, N.
1987 "Sea and Desert: Symbolic Geography in West Semitic Religious Thought." *UF* 19:375-389.
1992a "A New Look at Ugaritic *šdmt*." *JSS* 37:149-153.
1992b "The Pruning of the Vine in *KTU* 1.23." *UF* 24:425-427.
XELLA, P.
1973 *Il mito di ŠḤR e ŠLM. Saggio sulla mitologia ugaritica*. Studi Semitici 44. Rome: Istituto di Studi del Vicino Oriente.
1976 *Problemi del mito nel Vicino Oriente Antico*. AIONSup 7. Naples: Istituto Orientale di Napoli.
1977 "Studi sulla religione della Siria antica. I. El e il vino (RS 24.258)." *Studi Storico-Religiosi* 1:229-261.
1978 "Un testo ugaritico recente (RS 24.266, Verso, 9-19) e il 'sacrificio dei primi nati'." *RSF* 6:127-136.
1981 *I testi rituali di Ugarit*. I. *Testi*. Studi Semitici 54. Rome: Consiglio Nazionale delle Ricerche.
XELLA, P., and A.-M. G. CAPOMACCHIA.
1979 "Tre testi ugaritici relativi a presagi di nascite." *OA* 18:41-58.
YON, M.
1989 "*Šḥr mt*, la chaleur de Mot." *UF* 21:461-466.
1990 "Ougarit et ses dieux (travaux 1978-1988)." Pp. 325-343 in *Studies Bounni*.
1991 "Stèles de Pierre" and "Note sur la sculpture de pierre." Pp. 273-344, 345-353 in RSOu 6.
ZEVIT, Z.
1990 "The Common Origin of the Aramaicized Prayer to Horus and of Psalm 20." *JAOS* 110:213-228.

AKKADIAN CANONICAL COMPOSITIONS

A. DIVINE FOCUS

1. MYTHS

THE DESCENT OF ISHTAR TO THE UNDERWORLD (1.108)

Stephanie Dalley

The Akkadian story is first attested in Late Bronze Age texts, in both Babylonia and Assyria, and later from the palace library at Nineveh. It is a short composition of some 140 lines, and seems to end with ritual instructions for the *taklimtu*, an annual ritual known from Assyrian texts, which took place in the month of Dumuzi (Tammuz = June/July) and featured the bathing, anointing, and lying-in-state of a statue of Dumuzi in Nineveh, Arbela, Assur and Kalah.[1] Weeping for Tammuz was observed in Jerusalem in the 6th century BCE according to Ezek 8:14.

The Sumerian version, *The Descent of Inanna*, is attested earlier, and is much longer, consisting of some 410 lines. It is a fuller, more detailed account, and shows clearly that Dumuzi periodically died and rose, causing seasonal fertility, a fact which had been doubted until 1963, when a newly published fragment disclosed the crucial evidence. This version contains no ritual or incantation. However, like the Akkadian story, it seems to represent the goddess as a cult statue, and it has been suggested that the goddess's statue makes a ritual journey from Uruk, her home town, to Kutha, seat of Underworld deities.

There is an obvious similarity in basic theme to the Greek myth of Persephone, who was abducted by Hades. He periodically released her to her mother Demeter, thus causing fertility on earth to be seasonal, but of course there are many major differences between the Greek and the Akkadian myths.

Certain lines of text in *The Descent of Ishtar* are also found in *Nergal and Ereshkigal* and in *Gilgamesh*.

To Kurnugi, land of [no return],[2]
Ishtar daughter of Sin was [determined] to go;[3]
The daughter of Sin was determined to go
To the dark house, dwelling of Erkalla's god,
To the house which those who enter cannot leave,
On the road where travelling is one-way only,
To the house where those who enter are deprived of light,
Where dust is their food, clay their bread.
They see no light, they dwell in darkness,
They are clothed like birds, with feathers.[4]
Over the door and the bolt, dust has settled.
Ishtar, when she arrived at the gate of Kurnugi,
Addressed here words to the keeper of the gate,
"Here gatekeeper, open your gate for me,
Open your gate for me to come in!
If you do not open the gate for me to come in,
I shall smash the door and shatter the bolt,
I shall smash the doorpost and overturn the doors,[5]
I shall raise up the dead and they shall eat the living:
The dead shall outnumber the living!"[6]
The gatekeeper made his voice heard and spoke,
He said to great Ishtar,
"Stop, lady, do not break it down!
Let me go and report your words to queen Ereshkigal."
The gatekeeper went in and spoke to [Ereshkigal],
"Here she is, your sister Ishtar [...]
Who holds the great *keppū*-toy,[7]
Stirs up the Apsu in Ea's presence [...]?"
When Ereshkigal heard this,
Her face grew livid as cut tamarisk,
Her lips grew dark as the rim of a *kunīnu*-vessel.[8]
"What brings her to me? What has incited her against me?

[1] Farber 1977:122-123; Stol 1988:127-128.

[2] This passage occurs almost verbatim in *Nergal and Ereshkigal* (see text 1.109 below).

[3] Ishtar is named as daughter of Sin rather than daughter of Anu, as she is in Gilgamesh. This may imply that the story is not closely associated with the literary traditions of Uruk.

[4] Underworld creatures are often represented with feathers in Mesopotamian iconography.

[5] The tablet from Assur adds an extra line: "I shall break the hinges(?) and tear out the knob(?)."

[6] The same threat is made by Ereshkigal in *Nergal and Ereshkigal* if the sky gods do not send Nergal back down to the Underworld, and by Ishtar in Gilgamesh.

[7] *keppū*-toy: perhaps a whipping top. The old interpretation of *keppū* as a skipping rope was based on a misinterpretation of a glyptic scene, and should be abandoned. It may be a whipping-top (a spinning top lashed into faster gyrations with a cord) which is shown in action at Carchemish on a mural sculpture in relief, dating to the early first millennium BCE.

[8] Namtar's reactions in Nergal and Ereshkigal, when he saw Nergal at the gate, are expressed in identical similes. The *kunīnu* was a particular kind of vessel often made of reeds, of which the rim was coated with bitumen, thus black-lipped.

Surely not because I drink water with the Anunnaki,
I eat clay for bread, I drink muddy water for beer?
I have to weep for young men forced to abandon sweethearts.[9]
I have to weep for girls wrenched from their lovers' laps.[9]
For the infant child I have to weep, expelled before its time.[9]
Go, gatekeeper, open your gate to her.
Treat her according to the ancient rites."
The gatekeeper went. He opened the gate to her.
"Enter, my lady: may Kutha give you joy,[10]
May the palace of Kurnugi be glad to see you."
He let her in through the first door, but stripped off (and) took away the great crown on her head.
"Gatekeeper, why have you taken away the great crown on my head?"
"Go in, my lady. Such are the rites of the Mistress of Earth."
He let her in through the second door, but stripped off (and) took away the rings in her ears.
"Gatekeeper, why have you taken away the rings in my ears?"
"Go in, my lady. Such are the rites of the Mistress of Earth."
He let her in through the third door, but stripped off (and) took away the beads around her neck.
"Gatekeeper, why have you taken away the beads around my neck?"
"Go in, my lady. Such are the rites of the Mistress of Earth."
He let her in through the fourth door, but stripped off (and) took away the toggle-pins at her breast.[11]
"Gatekeeper, why have you taken away the toggle-pins at my breast?"
"Go in, my lady. Such are the rites of the Mistress of Earth."
He let her in through the fifth door, but stripped off (and) took away the girdle of birth-stones[12] around her waist.
"Gatekeeper, why have you taken away the girdle of birthstones[12] around my waist?"
"Go in, my lady. Such are the rites of the Mistress of Earth."
He let her in through the sixth door, but stripped off (and) took away the bangles on her wrists and ankles.
"Gatekeeper, why have you taken away the bangles on my wrists and ankles?"
"Go in, my lady. Such are the rites of the Mistress of Earth."
He let her in through the seventh door, but stripped off (and) took away the proud garment of her body.
"Gatekeeper, why have you taken away the proud garment of my body?"
"Go in, my lady. Such are the rites of the Mistress of Earth."
As soon as Ishtar went down to Kurnugi,[13]
Ereshkigal looked at her and trembled before her.
Ishtar did not deliberate (?), but threatened her.
Ereshkigal made her voice heard and spoke,
Addressed her words to Namtar her vizier,
"Go, Namtar [ ] of my [ ]
Send out against her sixty diseases [ ] Ishtar;
Disease of the eyes to her [eyes],
Disease of the arms to her [arms],
Disease of the feet to her [feet],
Disease of the heart to her [heart],
Disease of the head [to her head],
To every part of her and to [ ]."
After Ishtar the mistress of (?) [had gone down to Kurnugi],
No bull mounted a cow, [no donkey impregnated a jenny],
No young man impregnated a girl [in the street (?)],
The young man slept in his private room,
The girl slept in the company of her friends.
Then Papsukkal, vizier of the great gods, hung his head, his face [became gloomy];
He wore mourning clothes, his hair was unkempt.
Dejected (?), he went and wept before Sin his father,
His tears flowed freely before king Ea.
"Ishtar has gone down to the Earth and has not come up again.
As soon as Ishtar went down to Kurnugi
No bull mounted a cow, no donkey impregnated a jenny,
No young man impregnated a girl in the street,
The young man slept in his private room,
The girl slept in the company of her friends."
Ea, in his wise heart, created a person.[14]

---

[9] Alternatively these lines may be interpreted as rhetorical questions.

[10] Buccellati suggested that the Sum. *Descent of Inanna* is based on the ritual journey made by a statue of the goddess from Uruk to Kutha (Buccellati 1982), and George remarked that the goddess is described as if she were a statue in this version. The reference to Kutha here may be a relic of the journey theme in the Sum. version; or since Kutha had Nergal as patron god, the city name may be used as a name for the Underworld as Nergal's dwelling (George 1985:109-113).

[11] The identification of *tudittu* as "toggle-pin" rather than "pectoral" was made by Klein 1983.

[12] Or: "the girdle with the birthstone."

[13] Note that Ishtar does not cross the river in order to reach the Underworld, nor does Nergal in *Nergal and Ereshkigal*.

[14] Pun on *zikru*, "word, name" and *zikaru/zikru*, "man, male," as also in Gilgamesh, II.

He created Good-looks the playboy.[15]
"Come, Good-looks, set your face towards the gate of Kurnugi.
The seven gates of Kurnugi shall be opened before you.
Ereshkigal shall look at you and be glad to see you.
When she is relaxed, her mood will lighten.
Get her to swear the oath by the great gods.
Raise your head, pay attention to the water-skin,[16]
Saying, 'Hey, my lady, let them give me the waterskin, that I may drink water from it.'"

(And so it happened. But)

When Ereshkigal heard this,
She struck her thigh and bit her finger.
"You have made a request of me that should not have been made!
Come, Good-looks, I shall curse you with a great curse.[17]
I shall decree for you a fate that shall never be forgotten.
Bread (gleaned [?]) from the city's ploughs shall be your food,[18]
The city drains shall be your only drinking place,
The shade of a city wall your only standing place,
Threshold steps your only sitting place,
The drunkard and the thirsty shall slap your cheek."
Ereshkigal made her voice heard and spoke;
She addressed her words to Namtar her vizier,
"Go, Namtar, knock (?) at Egalgina,
Decorate the threshold steps with coral,[19]
Bring the Anunnaki out and seat (them) on golden thrones,[20]
Sprinkle Ishtar with the waters of life[21] and conduct her into my presence."
Namtar went, knocked at Egalgina,
Decorated the threshold steps with coral,
Brought out the Anunnaki, seated (them) on golden thrones,
Sprinkled Ishtar with the waters of life and brought her to her (sister).
He let her out through the first door, and gave back to her the proud garment of her body.[22]
He let her out through the second door, and gave back to her the bangles for her wrists and ankles.
He let her out through the third door, and gave back to her the girdle of birth stones[12] around her waist.
He let her out through the fourth door, and gave back to her the toggle pins at her breast.
He let her out through the fifth door, and gave back to her the beads around her neck.
He let her out through the sixth door, and gave back to her the rings for her ears.
He let her out through the seventh door, and gave back to her the great crown for her head.
"Swear that (?) she has paid you her ransom, and give her back (in exchange) for him.[23]
For Dumuzi, the lover of her youth.
Wash (him) with pure water, anoint him with sweet oil,
Clothe him in a red robe, let the lapis lazuli pipe play (?).[24]
Let party-girls raise a loud lament (?)."[25]
Then Belili tore off (?) her jewelry,
Her lap was filled with eyestones.
Belili heard the lament for her brother, she struck the jewelry [from her body],
The eyestones with which the front of the wild cow was filled.[26]
"You shall not rob me (forever) of my only brother!
On the day when Dumuzi comes back up, (and) the lapis lazuli pipe and the carnelian ring

[15] Lit., "His appearance is bright." he may have been a boy castrated as an act of devotion. Such a practice is described by Lucian, The Syrian Goddess (see Attridge and Oden 1976). The name may be an intentional play on a name of the moon-god, who like the boy could travel to and from the Underworld without being harmed. In the Sum. version of the story, two impotent creatures are sent down to the Underworld and they take a plant of life and water of life with them.

[16] Kilmer suggests this is a cryptic reference to Ishtar's corpse. *halziqqu* is a very rare word for a waterskin, and a pun may be intended on the two words *alû*, "ghost" and *ziqqu*, "gust" (1971:229-311); I suggest this to support her idea.

[17] The same line is used in *Gilgamesh*, VII.i.

[18] Similar formulation of the curse, and two identical lines, are found in Enkidu's curse of Shamhat in *Gilgamesh*, VII.i. The Sum. version does not include any cursing. "City's ploughs": the variant, "city's bakers," may be due to mis-hearing by oral tradition, since "bakers" and "plough" are both Akk. words beginning *epi*.

[19] "Coral" or "cowries"; the meaning of the noun is not quite certain.

[20] Possibly a reference to a ritual against seizure by ghosts. See Introduction to Nergal and Ereshkigal. Akk. *kussû* is both a chair and a throne. In the Sum. story the Anunnaki seize the goddess, demand a substitute for her, and send her out of the Underworld with demons who are to bring her back if their demand is not met.

[21] Waters of life also feature in the myth of Adapa; and in John 4:10.

[22] Either Namtar or the doorkeeper is the subject.

[23] Equivalent instructions are given to the demons in the Sum. story. A variant Akk. text gives the information that Ereshkigal is speaking to Namtar.

[24] Corpses were wrapped in red cloth for burial; traces have occasionally been recovered by excavations.

[25] "Party girls": attached to the staff of Ishtar's temples.

[26] Probably beads of banded agate and similar stones, which were often inscribed with the name of the donor; see Lambert 1969b:65-71.

come up with him,[27]
(When) male and female mourners come up
with him,

The dead shall come up and smell the incense
offering."
(3 lines missing)

[27] In the Sum. story Dumuzi's sister Geshtin-anna pleads for his periodic release. Also in the Sum. story, Inanna took the "rod and ring," emblems of kingship, down to the Underworld; this may be a reference to those emblems.

REFERENCES

Text: Borger *BAL*[2] 1:95-104, 2:340-343. Studies: Buccellati 1982; Dalley 1989:154-162; Ebeling 1949; George 1985; Klein 1983; Attridge and Oden 1976; Kilmer 1971; Lambert 1969b.

NERGAL AND ERESHKIGAL
(Standard Babylonian Version) (1.109)

Stephanie Dalley

Two very different versions of this story are extant. The earlier one was found at Tell el-Amarna in Egypt, dating from the fifteenth or fourteenth centuries BCE, and is told in a highly abbreviated manner in about ninety lines. Nergal visits the Underworld accompanied by demons, seizes the throne of Ereshkigal, queen of the Underworld, by force, and remains thereafter as king.

The version known from Sultantepe of the seventh century BCE and from Uruk in the Late Babylonian period is much longer, consisting of perhaps 750 lines. In this story Nergal makes two visits to the Underworld, and takes down with him not demons but a special chair or throne. The meaning of the chair may be explained by reference to a particular piece of furniture called a "ghost's chair" in lexical texts; its purpose is explained in a ritual text as preventing seizure by ghosts:

> If a man is chosen for death, and a ghost has seized him, you must purify everything, ... place a bread ration before Shamash, Ea, and Marduk, threefold; scatter dates, flour, set up three *adagurru*-vessels; set up three censers with aromatics, scatter all kinds of cereals. You must put down a chair to the left of the offerings for the ghost of his kin, ...

Thus, Nergal takes the chair down in an attempt to ensure that he can escape from the Underworld and elude death.

Both myths share the same basic theme: that the gods hold a banquet and, since Ereshkigal as queen of the Underworld cannot come up to join them, she sends her vizier to fetch a portion for her. Nergal behaves disrespectfully to the vizier, and for the insult to Ereshkigal he must be punished by her. He ends up as her husband.

It might appear that this myth records the transition of rule in the Underworld from a solitary female deity to a pair. However, Nergal is called "the Ellil of the Netherworld" in a composition from the late third or early second millennium, so it may be preferable to ascribe to the myth a different purpose, such as harmonizing two separate traditions. No Sumerian version of the story is known.

Nergal's ability to travel between heaven and the Underworld may be related to a major event in Phoenician religion. The name of Melqart, chief god of Tyre, is a Phoenician translation of the Sumerian name Nergal, and they are thus very closely assimilated. There is now evidence that Melqart was a dying and rising god, although the precise timing of events during the ritual of his death and resurrection has still to be established. Possible Phoenician influence upon Nergal and Ereshkigal is found in the use of the "plural of majesty," in referring to Nergal as "gods."

(SBV i) [About 4 lines missing?][1]
[Anu made his voice heard and spoke, he
addressed his words to Kakka],
["Kakka, I shall send you to Kurnugi].
You must speak thus to Ereshkigal [...],
Saying 'It is impossible for you to come up].
[In your year you cannot come up to see us]
[And it is impossible for us to go down].
[In our month(s) we cannot go down to see
you].
[Let your messenger come]
[And take from the table, let him accept a
present for you].
[I shall give something to him to present to
you].'"
[Kakka went down the long stairway of heaven].
[When he reached the gate of Ereshkigal (he said)],
["Gatekeeper, open] the gate to me!"
["Kakka, come] in, and may the gate bless
you."
He let the god Kakka in through the first gate,
He let the god Kakka in through the second gate,

[1] The opening of the myth as suggested by Gurney 1960 was wrongly assigned to this composition, and is now joined to a different tablet.

He let the god Kakka in through the third gate,
He let the god Kakka in through the fourth gate,
He let the god Kakka in through the fifth gate,
He let the god Kakka in through the sixth gate,
He let the god Kakka in through the seventh gate.
He entered into her spacious courtyard,
He knelt down and kissed the ground in front of her.
He straightened up, stood and addressed her,
"Anu your father sent me
To say, 'It is impossible for you to go up;
In your year you cannot go up to see us,
And it is impossible for us to go down;
In our month we cannot go down to see you.
Let your messenger come
And take from the table, let him accept a present for you.
I shall give something to him to present to you.'"
Ereshkigal made her voice heard and spoke, she addressed her words to Kakka,
"O messenger of Anu our father, you who have come to us,
May peace be with Anu, Ellil, and Ea, the great gods.
May peace be with Nammu and Nash, the pure god(desse)s.[2]
May peace be with the husband of the Lady of Heaven.[3]
May peace be with Ninurta, [champion] in the land."
Kakka made his voice heard and spoke, he addressed his words to Ereshkigal
"Peace is indeed with Anu, Ellil, and Ea, the great gods.
Peace is indeed with Nammu and Nash the pure.
Peace is indeed with the husband of the Lady of Heaven.
Peace is indeed with Ninurta, champion in the land."
Kakka made his voice heard and spoke, he addressed his words to Ereshkigal,[4]
"[ ] may be well with you."
Ereshkigal made her voice heard and spoke, she addressed her words to her vizier Namtar,
"O Namtar my vizier, I shall send you to the heaven of our father Anu.
Namtar, go up the long stairway of heaven.
Take from the table and accept a present (for me).
Whatever Anu gives to you, you must present to me."

[about 16 lines missing]

(ii) [about 10 lines missing]

Ea addresses Nergal

[...]
"[When he arrived [...]
[...] path [...]
The gods are kneeling together before him.
The great gods, the lords of destiny.
For it is he who controls the rites, controls the rites of [...]
The gods who dwell within Erkalla.
Why do you not kneel down before him?
I keep winking at you,
But you pretend not to realize,
And ...

[6 lines missing]

(Nergal addresses Ea)

[...] I will rise to my feet[5]
[...] you said.
[...] will double it."
When Ea heard this he said to himself,
"..........."
(Then) Ea made his voice heard and spoke, he addressed his words to Nergal.
"My son, you shall go on the journey you want (to make), ... grasp (?) a sword in your hand.
Go down to the forest of *mēsu*-trees.
Cut down *mēsu*-trees, *tiāru*-trees, and juniper!
Break off *kanaktu*-trees and *simberru*-trees."[6]
When [Nergal] heard this, he took an axe up in his hand,
Drew the sword from his belt,
Went down to the forest of *mēsu*-trees,
Cut down *mēsu*-trees, *tiāru*-trees, and juniper,
Broke off *kanaktu*-trees and *simberru*-trees,
[ ] and Ningišzida.[7]
He painted it with gypsum [... as a substitute for silver],[8]
Painted it with yellow paste and red paste as a substitute for gold,
Painted it with blue glaze as a substitute for lapis lazuli.

---

[2] Nash is an abbreviated and assimilated form of the name Nanshe. Nammu and Nanshe are the mother and daughter of Ea.

[3] Possibly a reference to Dumuzi.

[4] This line appears to be an unnecessary addition.

[5] Or, "Should I rise to my feet?"

[6] *mēšu*-wood: a dark wood used in making divine statues, probably a form of rosewood (Dalbergia). *tiāru*: described as "white pine" in explanatory texts. *kanaktu*: an aromatic timber, not identified. *simberru*: an aromatic fruit tree; maybe Umbrella pine/pine-nuts, Arabic *ṣnōbar*; the Uruk text established this reading, replacing Gurney's restoration of the Sultantepe text, which was damaged at that point, as "staff."

[7] Uruk version has "[...] he made a throne for far-sighted Ea."

[8] The Sultantepe version has "lapis lazuli" here, perhaps as a scribal confusion because it is a school exercise tablet; so the Uruk version is preferred here.

The work was finished, the chair complete.

Then he (Ea) called out and laid down instructions for him,
"My son, (about) the journey which you want to make: from the moment you arrive,
[Follow whatever instructions [I give you].
From the moment they bring a chair to you,
Do not go to it, do not sit upon it.
(When) the baker brings you bread, do not go to it, do not eat the bread.
(When) the butcher brings you meat, do not go to it, do not eat the meat.
(When) the brewer brings you beer, do not go to it, do not drink the beer.
(When they) bring you a foot bath, do not go to it, do not wash your feet.
(When) she (Ereshkigal) has been to the bath
And dressed herself in a fine dress,[9]
Allowing you to glimpse her body ...
You must not [do that which] men and women [do]"
Nergal [...]

[about 12 lines missing]

Nergal set his face towards Kurnugi,
To the dark house, dwelling of Erkalla's god,
To the house which those who enter cannot leave,
(iii) On the road where travelling is one way only,
To the house where those who enter are deprived of light,
Where dust is their food, clay their bread.
They are clothed, like birds, with feathers.
They see no light, they dwell in darkness.
[...]
[... they moan](?) like doves.
[...]
[The gatekeeper opened his mouth and addressed his words to Nergal,
"I must take back a report about the [god(?) standing] at the door."

The gatekeeper entered and addressed his words to Ereshkigal,
"My lady, a [...] has come to see us.
[...] who will identify him."

[a few lines missing]

Ereshkigal made her voice heard and spoke to Namtar.

[3 lines missing, comprising Ereshkigal's speech]

[Namtar replies:]
"Let me identify him [...]
Let me ... him at the outer gate.
Let me bring back to my lord [a description of him."
Namtar went and looked at Erra in the shadow of the door.
Namtar's face went as livid as cut tamarisk.
His lips grew dark as the rim of a *kunīnu*-vessel.[10]
Namtar went and addressed his lady,
"My lady, when you sent me to your father,
When I entered the courtyard of Anu
All the gods were kneeling, humbled [before him(?)]
All the gods of the land were kneeling [humbled before him.]
'The gods' rose to their feet in my presence.[11]
Now 'they' have gone down to Kurnugi."
Ereshkigal made her voice heard and spoke, she addressed her words to Namtar,
"My dear Namtar, you should not seek Ellil-power
Nor should you desire to do heroic deeds.
(What,) come up and sit on the throne of the royal dais?
You, perform the judgments of the broad Earth?
Should I go up to the heaven of Anu my father?[12]
Should I eat the bread of the Anunnaki?
Should I drink the water of the Anunnaki?
Go and bring the god [into my presence!]"
Namtar went and let in 'the gods,' Erra.
He let Nergal in through the first, the gate of Nedu.[13]
He let Nergal in through the second, the gate of Kishar.
He let Nergal in through the third, the gate of Endashurimma.
He let Nergal in through the fourth, the gate of Enuralla.
He let Nergal in through the fifth, the gate of Endukuga.
He let Nergal in through the sixth, the gate of Endushuba.
He let Nergal in through the seventh, the gate of Ennugigi.
He came into the broad courtyard,
And he knelt down, kissed the ground in front of her.
He straightened up, stood and addressed her,
"Anu your father sent me [to see you],
Saying, 'Sit down on [that] throne,
Judge the cases [of the great gods],

[9] "Fine robe": restoring the broken signs to give *lamaḫuššu*.
[10] *kunīnu*-vessel: see to the Descent of Ishtar above (text 1.108, note 8).
[11] "The gods" is used to refer to Nergal. This is a Phoenician and Punic usage, also found in the Old Testament when Yahweh is called *Elohim* "gods," and in Amarna letters from Phoenician cities where Pharaoh is addressed as "my gods" (*RlA*, s.v. *Elohim*).
[12] These three questions should probably be taken as sarcastic and rhetorical, emphasizing that each deity has a separate and appropriate sphere.
[13] The Uruk version names the gates as: Nedu, Enkishar, Endashurimma, Nerulla, Nerubanda, Endukuga, and Ennugigi, which are all Sumerian names or epithets. The cuneiform text uses ditto signs for the main areas of repetition here.

The great gods who live within Erkalla!'"
As soon as they brought him a throne
(He said to himself) "Don't go to it!" and did not sit on it.[14]
(When) the baker brought him bread, "Don't go to it!" and did not eat the bread.
(When) the butcher brought him meat, "Don't go to it!" and did not eat his meat.
(When) the brewer brought him beer, "Don't go to it!" and did not drink his beer.[15]
(When) they brought him a footbath, "Don't go to it!" and did not wash his feet.[16]
(When) she went to the bath
And dressed herself in a fine dress
And allowed him to catch a glimpse of her body,
He [resisted] his heart's [desire to do what] men and women [do].

[about 10 lines missing]

(iv) [3 lines fragmentary]
Nergal [...]
She went to the bath
And dressed herself in a fine dress
And allowed him to catch a glimpse of her body.
He [gave in to] his heart's [desire to do what men and women do].
The two embraced each other[17]
And went passionately to bed.
They lay there, queen Ereshkigal and Erra, for a first day and a second day.
They lay there, queen Ereshkigal and Erra, for a third day and a fourth day.[18]
They lay there, queen Ereshkigal and Erra, for a fifth day and a sixth day.
When the seventh day arrived,
Nergal, without [...]
Took away after him [...]
"Let me go, and my sister [...]
Do not make tremble [...]
Let me go now, and I will return to Kurnugi [(later)]."
Her mouth turned dark (?) (with rage) [...]
Nergal went [...][19]
[...] addressed his speech to the gatekeeper,
"Ereshkigal your lady sent me,
Saying, 'I am sending you to the heaven of Anu our father,'
So let me be allowed out! The message [...]."
Nergal came up the long stairway of heaven.
When he arrived at the gate of Anu, Ellil, and Ea,
Anu, Ellil, and Ea saw him and (said),
"The son of Ishtar has come back to us,[20]
She (Ereshkigal) will search for him and [...].
Ea his father must sprinkle him with spring water, and bareheaded,
Blinking and cringing let him sit in the assembly of all gods."[21]
Ereshkigal [...]
To the bath [...]
[...]
Her body [...]
[...]
She called out [...]
"The chair [...]
Sprinkle the room with the water [of]
Sprinkle the room with the water [of]
Sprinkle the room with the water [of]
The [...] of the two daughters of Lamaštu (?) and Enmešarra,
Sprinkle with the waters of [...]
The messenger of Anu our father who came to see us
Shall eat our bread and drink our water."
Namtar made his voice heard and spoke,
Addressed his words to Ereshkigal his lady,
"The messenger of Anu our father who came to see us —
Before daylight he disappeared!"
Ereshkigal cried out aloud, grievously,
Fell from the throne to the ground,
Then straightened up from the ground.
Her tears flowed down her cheeks.
"Erra, the lover of my delight —
I did not have enough delight with him before he left!
Erra, the lover of my delight —
I did not have enough delight with him before he left."
Namtar made his voice heard and spoke, addressed his words to Ereshkigal,
"Send me to Anu your father, and let me arrest that god!
[Let me take him to you,] that he may kiss you again!"
(v) Ereshkigal made her voice heard and spoke,
Addressed her words to Namtar her vizier,
"Go, Namtar, [you must speak to Anu, Ellil, and Ea!]
Set your face towards the gate of Anu, Ellil, and Ea,

[14] Uruk version has: "He did not go to it" instead of "Don't go to it."
[15] Uruk version has: "cupbearer" instead of "brewer."
[16] Uruk version has: "The foot-washer brought him water."
[17] Reading *aḫa-meš*, "together" rather than logographically "brothers."
[18] Dittos are again used.
[19] Later in this column the story implies that he departed without her realizing.
[20] "son of Ishtar" implies that he is a lover with the capacity for fertility.
[21] Either Nergal exhibits apparent congenital deformities through Ea's magic, or (as translated) the disguise is momentary.

To say, ever since I was a child and a daughter,
I have not known the playing of other girls,
I have not known the romping of children.
That god whom you sent to me and who has impregnated me — let him sleep with me again!
Send that god to us, and let him spend the night with me as my lover!
I am unclean, and I am not pure enough to perform the judging of the great gods,
The great gods who dwell within Erkalla.
If you do not send that god to me
According to the rites of Erkalla and the great Earth
I shall raise up the dead, and they will eat the living.
I shall make the dead outnumber the living!"[22]
Namtar came up the long stairway of heaven.
When he arrived at the gate of Anu, Ellil, and Ea,
Anu, Ellil, and Ea saw him, and (said),
"What have you come for, Namtar?"
"Your daughter sent me,
To say, 'Ever since I was a child and a daughter,
I have not known the playing of other girls,
I have not known the romping of children.
That god whom you sent to me and who has impregnated me — let him sleep with me again!
Send that god to us, and let him spend the night with me as my lover!
I am unclean, and I am not pure enough to perform the judging of the great gods,
The great gods who dwell within Erkalla.
If you do not send that god to me,
I shall raise up the dead, and they will eat the living!
I shall make the dead outnumber the living!'"
Ea made his voice heard and spoke, addressed his words to Namtar,
"Enter, Namtar, the court of Anu,
[Search out your wrongdoer and bring him!]."[23]
When he entered the court of Anu,
All the gods were kneeling humbled [before him],
[All] the gods of the land were kneeling [humbled before him].
He went straight up to one, but did not recognize that god,
Went straight up to a second and a third, but did not recognize that god either.
Namtar went (away), and addressed his words to his lady,
"My lady, about your sending me up to the heaven of Anu your father:
My lady, there was only one god who sat bareheaded, blinking and cringing at the assembly of all the gods."
"Go, seize that god and bring him to me!
(I expect) Ea his father sprinkled him with spring water,
And he is sitting in the assembly of all the gods bareheaded, blinking and cringing."
Namtar came up the long stairway of heaven.
When he reached the gate of Anu, Ellil, and Ea,
Anu, Ellil, and Ea saw him and (said),
"What have you come for, Namtar?"
"Your daughter sent me,
To say, 'Seize that god and bring him to me.'"
"Then enter, Namtar, the courtyard of Anu, and
Search out your wrongdoer and take him."
He went straight up to one god, but did not recognize him,
Went straight up to a second and third, but did not recognize him either.
[Then X] made his voice heard and spoke,
[addressed his words] to Ea,
"Let Namtar, the messenger who has come to us,
Drink our water, wash, and anoint himself."

[break of about 15 lines]

(vi) "He is not to strip off [...]
Erra, [...]
I shall [...]."
Namtar [made his voice heard and addressed his words to Erra],
"Erra, [...]
All the rites of the great Underworld [...]
When you go from [...]
You shall carry the chair [...]
You shall carry [...]
You shall carry [...]
You shall carry [...]
You shall carry [...]
You shall carry [...][24]
[...]
[Do not grapple with him (?) lest] he bind (?) your chest."
[Erra to]ok to heart [the speech of Namtar].
He [...] oiled his strap and slung his bow.
Nergal went down the long stairway of heaven.
When he arrived at the gate of Ereshkigal (he said (?)),
"Gatekeeper, open [the gate for me (?)]!"
He struck down Nedu, the doorman [of the first] gate, and did not let him gr[apple with him (?)].[25]

[22] This is identical to Ishtar's threat in the Descent of Ishtar.
[23] Line restored from a presumed repeat eighteen lines later.
[24] Several entirely different refrains are possible.
[25] Read ^{lú}*atû ša* KÁ *[ina l-en]* KÁ *i-nar-šu-ma ana ti-[iṣ-bu-ti?] ul i-din*.

He struck down the second [doorman] (and did not let him grapple with him).
He struck down the third [doorman] (and did not let him grapple with him).
He struck down the fourth [doorman] (and did not let him grapple with him).
He struck down the fifth [doorman] (and did not let him grapple with him).
He struck down the sixth [doorman] (and did not let him grapple with him).
He struck down the seventh [doorman] (and did not let him grapple with him).
He entered her wide courtyard,
And went up to her and laughed.
He seized her by her hairdo,
And [pull]ed (?) her from [the throne].
He seized her by her tresses
[...]
The two embraced each other
And went passionately to bed.
They lay there, queen Ereshkigal and Erra, for a first day and a second day.
They lay there, queen Ereshkigal and Erra for a third day.[26]
They lay there, queen Ereshkigal and Erra, for a fourth day.
They lay there, queen Ereshkigal and Erra, for a fifth day.
They lay there, queen Ereshkigal and Erra, for a sixth day
When the seventh day arrived,
Anu made his voice heard and spoke,
Addressed his words to Kakka, his vizier,
"Kakka, I shall send you to Kurnugi,
To the home of Ereshkigal who dwells within Erkalla,
To say, 'That god, whom I sent to you,
Forever [...]
Those above [...]
Those below [...]

[break, about 20-25 lines missing to end]

[26] The text has dittos again.

REFERENCES

Gurney 1960; Hunger 1976: no. 1; Dalley 1989:163-177.

NERGAL AND ERESHKIGAL
(Amarna Version) (1.110)

Stephanie Dalley

When the gods organized a banquet,[1]
They sent a messenger
To their sister Ereshkigal.
"We cannot come down to you,
And you cannot come up to us.
So send someone to fetch a share of the food for you!"
Ereshkigal sent Namtar her vizier,
"Go up, Namtar, to high heaven!"
He went into [where] the gods were [sitting],
And they [bowed (?)] and greeted Namtar,
The messenger of their eldest sister.
They bowed respectfully (?) when they saw him and ...
The high gods [...]
[...] food for the goddess his mistress.
[...] wept and was overcome.
[...] the journey (?)

[about 6 lines missing]

Ea [...]
Went [to Namtar and] sent (him) back.
"Go and [tell] my words to [our] sister.
She will say, 'Where (?) is the one who did not rise to his feet in the presence of my messenger?
Bring him to me for his death (?), that I may kill him!'"[2]

[And so it happened]

Namtar came (back) and spoke to the gods,
The gods summoned him and discussed the death with him.
"Look for the god who did not rise to his feet in your presence,
And take him before your mistress!"
Namtar counted them. The last god was crouching down.
"That god who did not rise to his feet in your presence — he is not here!"

[1] Some confusion is caused in this text by the arrangement of lines. Probably a tablet with very short lines was badly copied on to one with longer lines so that ends of lines do not always correspond to ends of sentences as would be normal.
[2] Pun: *mutu*, "husband" and *mūtu*, "death."

Then Namtar went and gave his report, (saying):
"[My mistress, I went and counted] them.
The last god [was crouching down].
[The god who did not rise to his feet in my presence] was not there."
[Ereshkigal made her voice heard],
[And addressed Namtar] her messenger,
"[...] month."
[...] Ea, honored lord.
"Identify the one," [...] to the hand of [Ea].[3]
"Take (him) to Ereshkigal!" He was wee[ping]
Before his father Ea: "He will see me!
"He will not let me stay alive!" "Don't be afraid [...]
I shall give to you seven and seven [demons]
To go with you: ..., ..., ..., Flashes-of-Light ning,
Bailiff, Croucher, Expulsion, Wind,
Fits, Staggers, Stroke, Lord-of-the-Roof, Feverhot, Scab [...]
With you [...] door
Ereshkigal will call out: 'Doorkeeper, [...] your door.'
[You must say]
'Loosen the thong, that I may enter into the presence of your mistress,
Ereshkigal. I have been sent!'" The doorkeeper went
And said to Namtar: "One god is standing at the entrance of the door,
Come, inspect him and let him enter." Namtar came out
And saw him and gladly: "[Wait (?)] here!" He said
To his mistress: "My lady, here is the god who in previous
Months had vanished (?), and who did not rise to his feet in my presence!"[4]
"Bring him in. As soon as he comes, I shall kill him!"
Namtar came out and [...], "Come in, my lord,
To your sister's house and ... ."
Nergal [said], "You should be glad to see me.
[...] Nergal [...]

[2 lines missing]

... at the third, Flashes-of-Lightning at the fourth.[5]
Bailiff at the fifth, Croucher at the sixth, Expulsion
At the seventh, Wind at the eighth, Fits
At the ninth, Staggers at the tenth, Stroke
At the eleventh, Lord-of-the-Roof at the twelfth,
Feverhot at the thirteenth, Scab at the fourteenth
Door, he managed to seal her in (?). In the forecourt he cut off[6]
Namtar. He gave his troops orders: "Let the doors
Be opened! Now I shall race past (?) you!"
Inside the house, he seized Ereshkigal
By her hair, pulled her from the throne
To the ground, intending to cut off her head.
"Don't kill me, my brother! Let me tell you something."
Nergal listened to her and relaxed his grip, he wept and was overcome (when she said),
"You can be my husband, and I can be your wife.
I will let you seize[7]
Kingship over the wide Earth! I will put the tablet
Of wisdom in your hand! You can be master,
I can be mistress." Nergal listened to this speech of hers,
And seized her and kissed her. He wiped away her tears.
"What have you asked of me? After so many months,
It shall certainly be so!"[8]

[3] "Identify": reading as imperative of *wussûm*.
[4] Rituals and customs for honoring and placating the dead were carried out on a monthly schedule linked to the phases of the moon.
[5] Ishtar/Inanna has similar shamanistic control of demons in the Sumerian story, The Descent of Inanna. In the cult of Ishtar at Nineveh, the goddess controlled demons who formed her entourage (Haas 1979:397-401).
[6] Tentatively reading *ḫuṭṭumaša*, "to seal her in."
[7] Exactly the same words are used by Ishtar in Gilgamesh, VI. i.
[8] Some scholars think this ending is too cryptic and abrupt to be intentional, and that the story would have continued.

REFERENCES

Knudtzon 1915; Dalley 1989:178-181.

EPIC OF CREATION (1.111)
(*Enūma Elish*)

Benjamin R. Foster

The so-called epic of Creation preserves a relatively late Babylonian conception of the creation of the physical world (including humanity), but its real focus is on the elevation of Marduk to the top of the pantheon in return for taking up the cause of the embattled gods, who build his great temple of Esagila in Babylon in recognition of his leadership.

The composition could therefore be as readily called "The Exaltation of Marduk." As such it provides a parallel of sorts to the exaltation of Yahweh as celebrated by Moses and Miriam in the Song of the Sea (Exodus 15), and the subsequent erection of the Tabernacle in the Wilderness (Hallo and van Dijk 1968 ch. 6; Mann 1977; Hurowitz 1992). Unique to the epic is its denouement, in which Marduk is acclaimed by fifty names and these are given learned explanations or etymologies (Bottéro 1977). [WWH]

Tablet I

When on high no name was given to heaven,
Nor below was the netherworld called by name,
Primeval Apsu was their progenitor,
And matrix-Tiamat was she who bore them all,
They were mingling their waters together,
No cane brake was intertwined nor thicket matted close.
When no gods at all had been brought forth,
None called by names, none destinies ordained,
Then were the gods formed within the(se two).
Lahmu and Lahamu were brought forth, were called by name.
When they had waxed great, had grown up tall,
Anshar and Kishar were formed, greater than they,
They grew lengthy of days, added years to years.
Anu their firstborn was like his forebears,
Anshar made Anu, his offspring, his equal.
Then Anu begot his own image Nudimmud,
Nudimmud was he who dominated(?) his forebears:
Profound in wisdom, acute of sense, he was massively strong,
Much mightier than his grandfather Anshar,
No rival had he among the gods his brethren.[1]
The divine brethren banded together,
Confusing Tiamat as they moved about in their stir,
Roiling the vitals of Tiamat,
By their uproar distressing the interior of the Divine Abode.[2]
Apsu could not reduce their clamor,
But Tiamat was silent before them.
Their actions were noisome to her,
Their behavior was offensive, (but) she was indulgent.
Thereupon Apsu, begettor of the great gods,
Summoned Mummu his vizier, saying to him,
"Mummu, vizier who contents me,
Come, let us go to Tiamat."
They went, took their places facing Tiamat,
They took counsel concerning the gods their offspring.
Apsu made ready to speak,
Saying to her, Tiamat, in a loud voice,
"Their behavior is noisome to me!
By day I have no rest, at night I do not sleep!
I wish to put an end to their behavior, to do away with it!
Let silence reign that we may sleep."
When Tiamat had heard this,
She grew angry and cried out to her spouse,
She cried out bitterly, outraged that she stood alone,
(For) he had urged evil upon her,
"What? Shall we put an end to what we created?
Their behavior may be most noisome,
but we should bear it in good part."
It was Mummu who answered, counselling Apsu,
Like a dissenting vizier's was the counsel of his Mummu,
"Put an end here and now, father, to their troublesome ways!
By day you should have rest, at night you should sleep."
Apsu was delighted with him, he beamed.
On account of the evils he plotted against the gods his children,
He embraced Mummu, around his neck,
He sat on his knees so he could kiss him.
Whatever they plotted between them,
Was repeated to the gods their offspring.
The gods heard it as they stirred about,
They were stunned, they sat down in silence.
Surpassing in wisdom, ingenious, resourceful,
Ea was aware of all, recognized their stratagem.
He fashioned it, he established it, a master plan,
He made it artful, his superb magic spell.
He recited it and brought (him)
to rest in the waters,
He put him in deep slumber, he was fast asleep,
He made Apsu sleep, he was drenched with slumber,
Mummu the advisor was drowsy with languor.
He untied his sash, he stripped off his tiara,
He took away his aura, he himself put it on.
He tied up Apsu, he killed him,
Mummu he bound, he locked him securely.
He founded his dwelling upon Apsu,
He secured Mummu, held (him) firm by a lead-rope.
After Ea had captured and vanquished his foes,

[1] This elaborate theogony, or genealogy of the gods, builds on Sum. precedent. It finds a parallel in Hesiod's version of Greek mythology, and is perhaps its ultimate source (Walcot 1966), but is absent in the Bible.

[2] For the perennial theme of noise disturbing the gods, cf. the Atra-hasis Epic (below, Text 1.130). But here it is the (younger) deities themselves who make the noise. See Finkelstein 1956:328-331.

Had won the victory over his opponents,
In his chamber, in profound quiet, he rested.
He called it "Apsu," (meaning) "They Recognize Sanctuaries."
He established therein his chamber,
Ea and Damkina his wife dwelt there in splendor.
In the cella of destinies, the abode of designs,
The most capable, the sage of the gods, the Lord was begotten,
In the midst of Apsu Marduk was formed,
In the midst of holy Apsu was Marduk formed!
Ea his father begot him,
Damkina his mother was confined with him.
He suckled at the breasts of goddesses,
The attendant who raised him endowed him well with glories.
His body was splendid, fiery his glance,
He was a hero at birth, he was a mighty one from the beginning!
When Anu his grandfather saw him,
He was happy, he beamed, his heart was filled with joy.
He perfected him, so that his divinity was strange,
He was much greater, he surpassed them in every way.
His members were fashioned with cunning beyond comprehension,
Impossible to conceive, too difficult to visualize:
Fourfold his vision, fourfold his hearing,[3]
When he moved his lips a fire broke out.
Formidable his fourfold perception,
And his eyes, in like number, saw in every direction.
He was tallest of the gods, surpassing in form,
His limbs enormous, he was surpassing at birth.
"The son Utu, the son Utu,
The son, the sun, the sunlight of the gods!"
He wore (on his body) the auras of ten gods, had (them) wrapped around his head too,
Fifty glories were heaped upon him.
Anu formed and produced the four winds,
He put them in his hand, "Let my son play!"
He fashioned dust, he made a storm bear it up,
He caused a wave and it roiled Tiamat,
Tiamat was roiled, churning day and night,
The gods, finding no rest, bore the brunt of each wind.
They plotted evil in their hearts,
They said to Tiamat their mother,
"When he killed Apsu your husband,
You did nothing to save him but sat by, silent.
Now he has made four terrible winds,
They are roiling your vitals so we cannot sleep.
You had no care for Apsu your husband,
As for Mummu, who was captured, you remained aloof.
Now you churn back and forth, confused.
As for us, who cannot lie down to rest, you do not love us!
Think of our burden, our eyes are pinched,
Lift this unremitting yoke, let us sleep!
Battle has begun, give them what they deserve,
[Ma]ke a [tempest], turn them into nothingness."
When Tiamat [heard] these words, they pleased her,
"[As y]ou have counselled, we will make a tempest,
[We will] the gods within it,
(For) they have been adopting [wicked ways] against the gods [thei]r parents."
[They clo]sed ranks and drew up at Tiamat's side,
Angry, scheming, never lying down night and day,
[Ma]king warfare, rumbling, raging,
Convening in assembly, that they might start hostilities.
Mother Hubur, who can form everything,
Added countless invincible weapons, gave birth to monster serpents,
Pointed of fang, with merciless incisors(?),
She filled their bodies with venom for blood.
Fierce dragons she clad with glories,
Causing them to bear auras like gods, (saying)
"Whoever sees them shall collapse from weakness!
Wherever their bodies make onslaught, they shall not turn back!"
She deployed serpents, dragons, and hairy hero-men,
Lion monsters, lion men, scorpion men,
Mighty demons, fish men, bull men,
Bearing unsparing arms, fearing no battle.
Her commands were absolute, no one opposed them,
Eleven indeed on this wise she crea[ted].
From among the gods her offspring, who composed her assembly,
She raised up Qingu[4] from among them, it was he she made greatest!
Leadership of the army, command of the assembly,
Arming, contact, advance of the melee,
Supreme command in warfare,
(All) she entrusted to him, made him sit on the dais.
"I cast your spell. I make you the greatest in the assembly of the gods,

[3] See the statue of a god with four heads possibly illustrating this conception in Jacobsen 1976:166.

[4] Others read Kingu, and take it as a pun on the Sum. name of Sumer, i.e., Kengir, and Tiamat (lit., "Sea," cognate with Heb. *tehom*) similarly as standing for the Sealand (Akk. *māt tamtim*). See Jacobsen 1975:76.

Kingship of all the gods I put in your power.
You are the greatest, my husband, you are illustrious,
Your command shall always be greatest, over all the Anunna-gods."
She gave him the tablet of destinies, had him hold it to his chest, (saying)
"As for you, your command will not be changed, your utterance will be eternal.
Now that Qingu is the highest and has taken [supremacy],
And has [ordained] destinies for his divine children,
Whatever you (gods) say shall cause fire to [subside],
Your concentrated venom shall make the mighty one yield."

Tablet II

Tiamat assembled her creatures,
Drew up for battle against the gods her brood.
Thereafter Tiamat, more than(?) Apsu, was become an evildoer.
She informed Ea that she was ready for battle.
When Ea heard this,
He was struck dumb with horror and sat stock still.
After he had thought and his distress had calmed,
He made straight his way to Anshar his grandfather.
He came in before his grandfather, Anshar,
All that Tiamat plotted he recounted to him,
"My father, Tiamat our mother has grown angry with us,
She has convened an assembly, furious with rage.
All the gods rallied around her,
Even those you created are going over to her side,
They are massing around her, ready at Tiamat's side.
Angry, scheming, never lying down night and day,
Making warfare, rumbling, raging,
Convening in assembly, that they might start hostilities.
Mother Hubur, who can form everything,
Added countless invincible weapons,
gave birth to monster serpents,
Pointed of fang, with merciless incisors(?),
She filled their bodies with venom for blood.
Fierce dragons she clad with glories,
Causing them to bear auras like gods, (saying)
'Whoever sees them shall collapse from weakness!
Wherever their bodies make onslaught,
they shall not turn back!'
She deployed serpents, dragons, and hairy hero-men,
Lion monsters, lion men, scorpion men,
Mighty demons, fish men, bull men,
Bearing unsparing arms, fearing no battle.
Her commands were absolute, no one opposed them,
Eleven indeed on this wise she created.
From among the gods her offspring, who composed her assembly,
She raised up Qingu from among them, it was he she made greatest!
Leadership of the army, command of the assembly,
Arming, contact, advance of the melee,
Supreme command in warfare,
(All) she entrusted to him, made him sit on the dais.
'I cast your spell. I make you the greatest in the assembly of the gods,
Kingship of all the gods I put in your power.
You are the greatest, my husband, you are illustrious.
Your command shall always be greatest,
over all the Anunna-gods.'
She gave him the tablet of destinies,
had him hold it to his chest, (saying)
'As for you, your command will not be changed, your utterance will be eternal.
Now that Qingu is the highest and has taken [supremacy],
And has [ordained] destinies for his divine children,
Whatever you (gods) say shall cause fire to [subside],
Your concentrated venom shall make the mighty one yield.'"
[When Anshar heard] the speech, the affair was confused,
He cried out "Woe!"; he bit his lip,
His spirits were angry, his mind was uneasy,
His cries to Ea his offspring grew choked,
"My son, you yourself were instigator of battle!
Do you bear the consequences of your own handiwork!
You went forth and killed Apsu,
So Tiamat, whom you have enraged,
where is one who can face her?"
The sage counsellor, wise prince,
Producer of wisdom, divine Nudimmud,
Answered his father Anshar gently,
With soothing words, calming speech,
"My father, inscrutable, ordainer of destinies,
Who has power to create and destroy,
O Anshar, inscrutable, ordainer of destinies,
Who has power to create and destroy,
I will declare my thoughts to you, relent for a moment,
Recall in your heart that I made a good plan.

Before I undertook to kill Apsu,
Who had foreseen what is happening now?
Ere I was the one who moved quickly to snuff out his life,
I indeed, for it was I who destroyed him,
[wh]at was occurring?"
When Anshar heard this, it pleased him,
He calmed down, saying to Ea,
"Your deeds are worthy of a god,
You can(?) [ ] a fierce, irresistible stroke,
Ea, your deeds are worthy of a god,
You can(?) [ ] a fierce, irresistible stroke,
Go then to Tiamat, sub[due] her onslaught,
May her anger [be pacified] by [your] magic spell."
When he heard the command [of his father] A[n-shar],
He set off, making straight his way,
Ea went to seek out Tiamat's stratagem.
He stopped, horror-stricken, then turned back.
He came before Anshar the sovereign,
He beseeched him with entreaties, saying,
"[My father], Tiamat has carried her actions beyond me,
I sought out her course, but my spell cannot counter it.
Her strength is enormous, she is utterly terrifying,
She is reinforced with a host, none can come out against her.
Her challenge was in no way reduced, it was so loud(?) against me,
I became afraid at her clamor, I turned back.
My father, do not despair, send another to her,
A woman's force may be very great, but it cannot match a man's.
Do you scatter her ranks, thwart her intentions,
Before she lays her hands on all of us."
Anshar was shouting, in a passion,
To Anu his son he said these words,
"Stalwart son, valiant warrior,
Whose strength is enormous, whose onslaught is irresistible,
Hurry, take a stand before Tiamat,
Soothe her feelings, let her heart be eased.
If she will not listen to what you say,
Say something by way of entreaty to her,
so that she be pacified."
When he heard what his father Anshar said,
He set off, [made str]aight his way,
Anu went to seek out Tiamat's stratagem.
He stopped, horror-stricken, then turned back.
He came before [Ansha]r, [his father who begot him],
He beseeched him with entreaties, s[aying],
"My father, Tiamat has carried her actions beyond me,
I sought out her course, but my s[pell cannot counter it].
Her strength is enormous, she is utterly terrifying,
She is reinforced with a host, none can [come out against] her.
Her challenge was in no way reduced, it was so loud(?) against me,
I became afraid at her clamor, I turned back.
My father, do not despair, send another to her,
A woman's strength may be very great, but it cannot match a man's.
Do you scatter her ranks, thwart her intentions,
Before she lays her hands on all of us."
Anshar fell silent, gazing at the ground,
Nodding towards Ea, he shook his head.
The Igigi-gods and Anunna-gods were all assembled,
With lips closed tight, they sat in silence.
Would no god go out [at his] command?
Against Tiamat would none go as [he] ordered?
Then Anshar, father of the great gods,
His heart was angry, he [would not summon] anyone!
The mighty firstborn, champion of his father,
Hastener to battle, the warrior Marduk
Did Ea summon to his secret place,
Told him his secret words,
"O Marduk, think, heed your father,
You are my son who can relieve his heart!
Draw nigh, approach Anshar,
Make ready to speak. He was angry,
seeing you he will be calm."
The Lord was delighted at his father's words,
He drew near and waited upon Anshar.
When Anshar saw him, his heart was filled with joyful feelings,
He kissed his lips, he banished his gloom.
"My father, let not your lips be silent but speak,
Let me go, let me accomplish your heart's desire.
[O Anshar], let not your lips be silent but speak,
Let me go, let me accomplish your heart's desire!
What man is it who has sent forth his battle against you?"
Why, Tiamat, a woman, comes out against you to arms.
[My father], creator, rejoice and be glad,
Soon you will trample the neck of Tiamat.
[Anshar], creator, rejoice and be glad,
Soon you will trample [the neck] of Tiamat!"
"[Go], son, knower of all wisdom,
Bring Tiamat to rest with your sacral spell.
Make straight, quickly, with the storm chariot,
Let it not veer from its [course], turn (it) back!"
The Lord was delighted at his grandfather's words,

His heart was overjoyed as he said to his grandfather,
"Lord of the gods, of the destiny of the great gods,
If indeed I am to champion you,
Subdue Tiamat and save your lives,
Convene the assembly, nominate me for supreme destiny!
Take your places in the Assembly Place of the Gods,
all of you, in joyful mood.
When I speak, let me ordain destinies instead of you.
Let nothing that I shall bring about be altered,
Nor what I say be revoked or changed."[5]

Tablet III

Anshar made ready to speak,
Saying to Kakka his vizier these words,
"Kakka, vizier who contents me,
Let it be you that I send off towards Lahmu and Lahamu.
You know how [to find a way], you can make a fine speech.
Send over to my presence the gods my ancestors,
Let them bring all the gods before me.
Let them converse, sit down at a feast,
On produce of the field let them feed, imbibe of the vine.
Let them ordain destiny for Marduk, their champion.
Be off, Kakka, wait upon them,
All that I tell you, repeat to them:
'It is Anshar your son who has ordered me to come,
He has bade me speak in full the command of his heart,
To wit: "Tiamat our mother has grown angry with us,
She has convened an assembly, furious with rage.
All the gods rallied around her,
Even those you created are going over to her side.
They are massing around her, ready at Tiamat's side.
Angry, scheming, never lying down night and day,
Making warfare, rumbling, raging,
Convening in assembly, that they might start hostilities.
Mother Hubur, who can form everything,
Added countless invincible weapons,
gave birth to monster serpents,
Pointed of fang, with merciless incisors(?),
She filled their bodies with venom for blood.
Fierce dragons she clad with glories,
Causing them to bear auras like gods, (saying)
'Whoever sees them shall collapse from weakness!
Wherever their bodies make onslaught,
they shall not turn back.'
She deployed serpents, dragons, and hairy hero-men,
Lion monsters, lion men, scorpion men,
Mighty demons, fish men, bull men,
Bearing unsparing arms, fearing no battle.
Her commands were absolute, no one opposed them.
Eleven indeed on this wise she created.
From among the gods her offspring, who composed her assembly,
She raised up Qingu from among them, it was he she made greatest!
Leadership of the army, command of the assembly,
Arming, contact, advance of the melee,
Supreme command in warfare:
All she entrusted to him, made him sit on the dais.
'I cast your spell, I make you the greatest in the assembly of the gods,
Kingship of all the gods I put in your power.
You are greatest, my husband, you are illustrious,
Your command shall always be greatest, over all the Anunna-gods.'
She gave him the tablet of destinies, had him hold it to his chest, (saying)
'As for you, your command will not be changed,
your utterance will be eternal.
Now that Qingu is the highest and has taken over [supremacy],
And has [ordained] destinies for his divine children,
Whatever you (gods) say shall cause fire to [subside],
Your concentrated venom shall make the mighty one yield.'
I sent Anu, he could not confront her,
Nudimmud was afraid and turned back.
Marduk came forward, the sage of the gods, your son,
He has resolved to go against Tiamat.
When he spoke, he said to me,
'If indeed I am to champion you,
Subdue Tiamat and save your lives,
Convene the assembly, nominate me for supreme destiny!
Take your places in the Assembly Place of the Gods,
all of you, in joyful mood,
When I speak, let me ordain destinies instead of you.

[5] Marduk demands supremacy in the pantheon as the price of defending it against the older generation of gods led by Tiamat. This can be seen as a metaphor for the rise of Babylon, Marduk's city, perhaps under Nebuchadnezar I; see Lambert 1964.

Let nothing that I shall bring about be altered,
Nor what I say be revoked or changed.'
Come quickly to me, straightaway ordain him your destinies,
Let him go and confront your powerful enemy."
Kakka went and made straight his way
Towards Lahmu and Lahamu the gods his ancestors.
He prostrated, kissed the ground before them.
He stood up straight and said to them,
"It is Anshar your son who has ordered me to come,
He has bade me speak in full the command of his heart:
'Tiamat our mother has grown angry with us,
She has convened an assembly, furious with rage.
All the gods rallied around her,
Even those you created are going over to her side.
They are massing around her, ready at Tiamat's side.
Angry, scheming, never lying down night and day,
Making warfare, rumbling, raging,
Convening in assembly, that they might begin hostilities.
Mother Hubur, who can form everything,
Added countless invincible weapons,
gave birth to monster serpents,
Pointed of fang, with merciless incisors(?),
She filled their bodies with venom for blood.
Fierce dragons she clad with glories,
Causing them to bear auras like gods, (saying)
"Whoever sees them shall collapse from weakness!
Wherever their bodies make onslaught
they shall not turn back!"
She deployed serpents, dragons, and hairy hero-men,
Lion monsters, lion men, scorpion men,
Mighty demons, fish men, bull men,
Bearing unsparing arms, fearing no battle.
Her commands were absolute, no one opposed them.
Eleven indeed on this wise she created!
From among the gods her offspring who composed her assembly,
She raised up Qingu from among them, it was he she made greatest!
Leadership of the army, command of the assembly,
Arming, contact, advance of the melee,
Supreme command in warfare:
(All) she entrusted to him, made him sit on the dais.
"I cast your spell and make you the greatest in the assembly of the gods,
Kingship of all the gods I put in your power.
You shall be the greatest, you are my only spouse,
Your name shall always be greatest, over all the Anunna-gods."
'She gave him the tablet of destinies, had him hold it to his chest, (saying)
"As for you, your command will not be changed, your utterance will be eternal.
Now that Qingu is the highest and has taken over [supremacy],
And has [ordained] destinies for his divine children,
Whatever you (gods) say shall cause fire to [subside],
Your concentrated venom will make the mighty one yield."
'I sent Anu, he could not confront her,
Nudimmud was afraid and turned back.
Marduk came forward, the sage of the gods, your son,
He has resolved to go against Tiamat.
When he spoke, he said to me,
"If indeed I am to champion you,
Subdue Tiamat and save your lives,
Convene the assembly, nominate me for supreme destiny!
In the Assembly Place of the Gods take your places,
all of you, in joyful mood.
When I speak, let me ordain destinies instead of you.
Let nothing that I shall bring about be altered,
Nor what I say be revoked nor changed."
'Hurry to me, straightaway ordain him your destinies,
Let him go and confront your powerful enemy.'
When Lahmu and Lahamu heard, they cried aloud,
All of the Igigi-gods wailed bitterly,
"What (is our) hostility, that she has taken a[ct]ion (against) us?
We scarcely know what Tiamat might do!"
They swarmed together and came.
All the great gods, ordainers of [destinies],
Came before Anshar and were filled with [joy].
One kissed the other in the assembly [ ],
They conversed, sat down at a feast,
On produce of the field they fed, imbibed of the vine,
With sweet liquor they made their gullets run,
They felt good from drinking the beer.
Most carefree, their spirits rose,
To Marduk their champion they ordained destiny.

Tablet IV

(1) They set out for him a princely dais,
He took his place before his fathers for sovereignty.
"You are the most important among the great gods,

Your destiny is unrivalled, your command is supreme.

(5) O Marduk, you are the most important among the great gods,

Your destiny is unrivalled, your command is supreme!

Henceforth your command cannot be changed,

To raise high, to bring low, this shall be your power.

Your command shall be truth, your word shall not be misleading.

(10) Not one of the gods shall go beyond the limits you set.

Support is wanted for the gods' sanctuaries,

Wherever their shrines shall be, your own shall be established.

O Marduk, you are our champion,

We bestow upon you kingship of all and everything.

(15) Take your place in the assembly, your word shall be supreme.

May your weapon never strike wide but dispatch your foes.

O Lord, spare his life who trusts in you,

But the god who has taken up evil, snuff out his life!"

They set up among them a certain constellation,

(20) To Marduk their firstborn said they (these words),

"Your destiny, O Lord, shall be foremost of the gods',

Command destruction or creation, they shall take place.

At your word the constellation shall be destroyed,

Command again, the constellation shall be intact."

(25) He commanded and at his word the constellation was destroyed,

He commanded again and the constellation was created anew.[6]

When the gods his fathers saw what he had commanded,

Joyfully they hailed, "Marduk is king!" [a]

They bestowed in full measure scepter, throne, and staff,

(30) They gave him unopposable weaponry that vanquishes enemies.

"Go, cut off the life of Tiamat,

Let the winds bear her blood away as glad tidings!"

The gods, his fathers, ordained the Lord's destiny,

On the path to success and authority
did they set him marching.

(35) He made the bow, appointed it his weapon,

He mounted the arrow, set it on the string.

He took up the mace, held it in his right hand,

a Pss 93:1; 96:10; 97:1; 99:1; 1 Chr 16:31

Bow and quiver he slung on his arm.

Thunderbolts he set before his face,

(40) With raging fire he covered his body.

Then he made a net to enclose Tiamat within,

He deployed the four winds that none of her might escape:

South Wind, North Wind, East Wind, West Wind,

Gift of his grandfather Anu;
he fastened the net at his side.

(45) He made ill wind, whirlwind, cyclone,

Four-ways wind, seven-ways wind, destructive wind, irresistible wind:

He released the winds which he had made, the seven of them,

Mounting in readiness behind him to roil inside Tiamat.

Then the Lord raised the Deluge, his great weapon.

(50) He mounted the terrible chariot, the unopposable Storm Demon,

He hitched to it the four-steed team, he tied them at his side:

"Slaughterer," "Merciless," "Overwhelmer," "Soaring."

Their lips are curled back, their teeth bear venom,

They know not fatigue, they are trained to trample down.

(55) He stationed at his right gruesome battle and strife,

At his left the fray that overthrows all formations.

He was garbed in a ghastly armored garment,

On his head he was covered with terrifying auras.

The Lord made straight and pursued his way,

(60) Toward raging Tiamat he set his face.

He was holding a spell ready upon his lips,

A plant, antidote to venom, he was grasping in his hand.

At that moment the gods were stirring, stirring about him,

The gods his fathers were stirring about him, the gods stirring about him.

(65) The Lord drew near, to see the battle of Tiamat,

He was looking for the stratagem of Qingu her spouse.

As he looked, his tactic turned to confusion,

His reason was overthrown, his actions panicky,

And as for the gods his allies, who went at his side,

(70) When they saw the valiant vanguard,
their sight failed them.

Tiamat cast her spell pointblank,

Falsehood, lies she held ready on her lips.

"...... lord, the gods rise against you,

They assembled [where] they are,

---

[6] The ability to destroy or create by fiat is the test of divine supremacy.

(but) are they on your side?"
The Lord [raised] the Deluge, his great weapon,
To Tiamat, who acted conciliatory, sent he (this word),
"Why outwardly do you assume a friendly attitude,
While your heart is plotting to open attack?
Children cried out, they oppress their parents,
But you, their own mother, spurned all natural feeling.
You named Qingu to be spouse for you,
Though he had no right to be, you set him up for chief god.
You attempted wicked deeds against Anshar, sovereign of the gods,
And you have perpetrated your evil against the gods my fathers.
Though main force is drawn up,
though these your weapons are in array,
Come within range, let us duel, you and I!"
When Tiamat heard this,
She was beside herself, she turned into a maniac.
Tiamat shrieked loud, in a passion,
Her frame shook all over, down to the ground.
He was reciting the incantation, casting his spell,
While the gods of battle were whetting their blades.
Tiamat and Marduk, sage of the gods, drew close for battle,
They locked in single combat, joining for the fray.
The Lord spread out his net, encircled her,
The ill wind he had held behind him he released in her face.
Tiamat opened her mouth to swallow,
He thrust in the ill wind so she could not close her lips.
The raging winds bloated her belly,
Her insides were stopped up, she gaped her mouth wide.
He shot off the arrow, it broke open her belly,
It cut to her innards, it pierced the heart.[7]
He subdued her and snuffed out her life,
He flung down her carcass, he took his stand upon it.
After the vanguard had slain Tiamat,
He scattered her forces, he dispersed her host.
As for the gods her allies, who had come to her aid,
They trembled, terrified, they ran in all directions,
They tried to make a way out(?) to save their lives,
There was no escaping the grasp that held (them)!

b Gen 1:1-8

He drew them in and smashed their weapons.
They were cast in the net and sat in a heap,
They were heaped up in the corners, full of woe,
They were bearing his punishment, to prison confined.
As for the eleven creatures, the ones adorned with glories,
And the demonic horde(?), which all went at her side,
He put on lead ropes, he bound their arms.
He trampled them under, together with their belligerence.
As for Qingu, who was trying to be great among them,
He captured him and reckoned him among the doomed.
He took away from him the tablet of destinies
that he had no right to,
He sealed it with a seal and affixed it to his chest.
Having captured his enemies and triumphed,
Having shown the mighty(?) foe subservient(?),
Having fully achieved Anshar's victory over his enemies,
Valiant Marduk having attained what Nudimmud desired,
He made firm his hold over the captured gods,
Then turned back to Tiamat whom he had captured.
The Lord trampled upon the frame of Tiamat,
With his merciless mace he crushed her skull.
He cut open the arteries of her blood,
He let the North Wind bear (it) away as glad tidings.
When his fathers saw, they rejoiced and were glad,
They brought him gifts and presents.
He calmed down. Then the Lord was inspecting her carcass,
That he might divide(?) the monstrous lump and fashion artful things.
He split her in two, like a fish for drying,
Half of her he set up and made as a cover, heaven.
He stretched out the hide and assigned watchmen,
And ordered them not to let her waters escape.[b]
He crossed heaven and inspected (its) firmament,
He made a counterpart to Apsu, the dwelling of Nudimmud.
The Lord measured the construction of Apsu,
He founded the Great Sanctuary, the likeness of Esharra.[8]
(In) the Great Sanctuary, (in) Esharra, which he built, (and in) heaven,

[7] Technically, Marduk conquers Tiamat by forcing her body open with the wind as with a bellows, then shooting an arrow into her innards. Symbolically, there may be here an allusion to the military triumph of Kassite Babylonia over the First Sealand Dynasty in the 15th century BCE; cf. above, n. 4.

[8] The creation of heaven and earth here and in the next tablet (chapter) serves as a way of disposing of the defeated Tiamat rather than as the main focus of the epic.

He made Ea, Enlil, and Anu dwell in their holy places.

Tablet V

(1) He made the position(s) for the great gods,
He established (in) constellations the stars, their likenesses.
He marked the year, described its boundaries,
He set up twelve months of three stars each.
(5) After he had patterned the days of the year,
He fixed the position of Neberu[9] to mark the (stars') relationships.
Lest any make an error or go astray,
He established the position(s) of Enlil and Ea in relation to it.
He opened up gates on both (sides of her) ribs,
(10) He made strong bolts to left and right.
In her liver he established the zenith.
He made the moon appear, entrusted (to him) the night.
He assigned to him the crown jewel of nighttime to mark the day (of the month):
Every month, without ceasing, he exalted him with a crown.
(15) "At the beginning of the month, waxing over the land,
You shine with horns to mark six days,
At the seventh day, the disk as [ha]lf.
At the fifteenth day, you shall be in opposition, at the midpoint of each [month].[10]
When the sun f[ac]es you from the horizon of heaven,
(20) Wane at the same pace and form in reverse.
At the day of di[sappeara]nce, approach the sun's course,
On the [ ] of the thirtieth day, you shall be in conjunction with the sun a second time.
I d[efined]? the celestial signs, proceed on their path,
[ ] approach each other and render (oracular) judgment.
(50) To raise the wind, to cause rainfall,
To make mists steam, to pile up her spittle (as snow?),
He assigned to himself, put under his control.
He set down her head and piled [ ] upon it,
He opened underground springs, a flood was let flow(?).
(55) From her eyes he undammed the Euph[rates] and Tigris,[c]
He stopped up her nostrils, he left ...
He heaped up high-peaked mo[unt]ains from(?) her dugs.
He drilled through her waterholes to carry off the catchwater.

c Gen 2:14

He coiled up her tail and tied it as(?) "The Great Bond."
(60) [ ] Apsu beneath, at his feet.
He set her crotch as the brace of heaven,
Spreading [half of] her as a cover, he established the netherworld.
[After he had completed his task inside Tiamat,
[He spre]ad his net, let all (within) escape.
[...]
After he had designed his prerogatives and devised his responsibilities,
He put on leadlines, entrusted (those) to Ea.
[The tablet] of destinies, which he took from Qingu and brought away,
(70) As the foremost gift he took away, he presented (it) to Anu.
The [ ] of battle, which he had fastened on and set on his head,
[ ] he led before his fathers.
[And as for] the eleven creatures which Tiamat created ...
He smashed their [wea]pons, he tied them to his feet.
(75) He made images [of them] and set them up at the [Gate of] Apsu:
"Lest ever after they be forgotten, let this be the sign."
When [the gods] saw, they rejoiced and were glad,
Lahmu, Lahamu, and all his fathers.
Anshar [embra]ced him, proclaimed (his) salutation (to be) "king."
(80) [A]nu, Enlil, and Ea gave him gifts,
[ ] Damkina his mother made cries of joy over him,
She(?) made his face glow with (cries of) "Good ...!"
To Usmu, who brought (Damkina's) gift at the glad tidings,
[He en]trusted the ministry of Apsu and care of the sanctuaries.
(85) All the Igigi-gods together prostrated themselves before him,
[And] the Anunna-gods, all there are, were doing him homage,
The whole of them joined together to pay him reverence,
[Before him] they stood, they prostrated themselves, "This is the king!"
[After] his fathers had celebrated him in due measure,
(90) [ ] covered with the dust of battle.
[ ] ...
With cedar [oil] and [ ] he anoi[nted] his body,
He clothed himself in [his] princely [gar]ment,
The kingly aura, the awe-inspiring tiara,

[9] Lit., "the passage," i.e. the Milky Way.
[10] Cf. Atra-hasis (below, Text 1.130) I 206 and n. 5.

He picked up the mace, he held it in his right hand,
[ ] he held in his left hand.
[ ]
[ ] he made firm at his feet.
He set over [ ]
The staff of success and authority [he hung] at his side.
After he [had put on] the aura of [his kingship],
His netted sack, the Apsu [ ] awesomeness.
He was seated like [ ]
In [his] throne room [ ]
In his cella [ ]
The gods, all there are, [ ]
Lahmu and Lahamu [ ]
Made ready to speak and [said to] the Igigi-gods:
"Formerly [Mar]duk was 'our beloved son,'
Now he is your king, pay heed to his command."
Next all of them spoke and said:
"'Lugaldimmerankia' is his name, trust in him!"
When they had given kingship over to Marduk,
They said to him expressions of good will and obedience,
"Henceforth you shall be provider for our sanctuaries,
Whatever you shall command, we will do."
Marduk made ready to speak and said
(These) words to the gods his fathers,
"Above Apsu, the azure dwelling,
As counterpart to Esharra, which I built for you,
Below the firmament, whose grounding I made firm,
A house I shall build, let it be the abode of my pleasure.
Within it I shall establish its holy place,
I shall appoint my (holy) chambers,
I shall establish my kingship.
When you go up from Apsu to assembly,
Let your stopping places be there to receive you.
When you come down from heaven to [assembly],
Let your stopping places be there to receive all of you.
I shall call [its] name [Babylon], (meaning) "Houses of the Great Gods,"
We shall all hold fe[stival]s with[in] it."
When the gods his fathers heard what he commanded,
They ... [ ]
"Over all things which your hands have created,
Who has [authority, save for you]?
Over the earth that you have created,
Who has [authority, save for] you?
Babylon, to which you have given name,
Make our [stopping place] there forever.
Let them bring us our daily portions,
[ ] our [ ].
Whosoever shall [ ] our task which we [ ],
In his place [ ] his toil [ ]."
[...]
The gods prostrated themselves before him, saying,
To Lugaldimmeran[ki]a their lord they [said],
"Formerly [we called you] 'The Lord, [our beloved] son,'
Now 'Our King' ... [shall be your name],
He whose [sacral] sp[ell] saved our lives,"
[au]ra, ma[ce], and ne[t],
[Ea(?), ev]ery [sk]ill.
Let him make the plans, we ... [ ]."

Tablet VI

When [Mar]duk heard the speech of the gods,
He was resolving to make artful things:
He would tell his idea to Ea,
What he thought of in his heart he proposes,
"I shall compact blood, I shall cause bones to be,
I shall make stand a human being, let 'Man' be its name.
I shall create humankind,
They shall bear the gods' burden that those may rest.
I shall artfully double the ways of the gods:
Let them be honored as one but divided in twain."
Ea answered him, saying these words,
He told him a plan to let the gods rest,
"Let one, their brother, be given to me,
Let him be destroyed so that people can be fashioned.
Let the great gods convene in assembly,
Let the guilty one be given up that they may abide."
Marduk convened the great gods in assembly,
He spoke to them magnanimously as he gave the command,
The gods heeded his utterance,
As the king spoke to the Anunna-gods (these) words,
"Let your first reply be the truth!
Do you speak with me truthful words!
Who was it that made war,
Suborned Tiamat and drew up for battle?
Let him be given over to me, the one who made war,
I shall make him bear his punishment, you shall be released."
The Igigi, the great gods answered him,
To Lugaldimmerankia, sovereign of all the gods, their lord,
"It was Qingu who made war,

Suborned Tiamat and drew up for battle."
They bound and held him before Ea,
They imposed the punishment on him and shed his blood.
From his blood he made mankind,
He imposed the burden of the gods and exempted the gods.
After Ea the wise had made mankind,
They imposed the burden of the gods on them![11]
That deed is beyond comprehension,
By the artifices of Marduk did Nudimmud create!
Marduk the king divided the gods,
The Anunna-gods, all of them, above and below,
He assigned to Anu for duty at his command.
He set three hundred in heaven for (their) duty,
A like number he designated for the ways of the netherworld:
He made six hundred dwell in heaven and netherworld.
After he had given all the commands,
And had divided the shares of the Anunna-gods of heaven and netherworld,
The Anunna-gods made ready to speak,
To Marduk their lord they said,
"Now, Lord, you who have liberated us,
What courtesy may we do you?
We will make a shrine, whose name will be a byword,
Your chamber that shall be our stopping place, we shall find rest therein.[12]
We shall lay out the shrine, let us set up its emplacement,
When we come (to visit you), we shall find rest therein."
When Marduk heard this,
His features glowed brightly, like the day,
"Then make Babylon the task that you requested,
Let its brickwork be formed, build high the shrine."
The Anunna-gods set to with hoes,
One (full) year they made its bricks.
When the second year came,
They raised up Esagila, the counterpart to Apsu,
They built the high ziggurat of (counterpart-)Apsu,
For Anu-Enlil-Ea they founded his ... and dwelling.
Majestically he took his seat before them,
Its pinnacles were facing toward the base of Esharra.
After they had done the work of Esagila,
All the Anunna-gods devised their own shrines.
The three hundred Igigi-gods of heaven
and the six hundred of Apsu all convened.
The Lord, on the Exalted Dais, which they built as his dwelling,
Seated the gods his fathers for a banquet,
"This is Babylon, your place of dwelling.
Take your pleasure there, seat yourselves in its delights!"
The great gods sat down,
They set out cups, they sat down at the feast.[13]
After they had taken their enjoyment inside it,
And in awe-inspiring Esagila had conducted the offering,
All the orders and designs had been made permanent,
All the gods had divided the stations of heaven and netherworld,
The fifty great gods took their thrones,
The seven gods of destinies were confirmed forever for rendering judgment.
The Lord took the bow, his weapon, and set it before them,
The gods his fathers looked upon the net he had made.
They saw how artfully the bow was fashioned,
His fathers were praising what he had brought to pass,
Anu raised (it), speaking to the assembly of the gods,
He kissed the bow, "This be my daughter!"
He named the bow, these are its names:
"'Longwood' shall be the first, 'Conqueror' shall be the second."
The third name, 'Bow Star,' he made visible in heaven.
He established its position with respect to the gods his brethren.
After Anu had ordained the destinies of the bow,
He set out the royal throne which stood highest among the gods,
Anu had him sit there, in the assembly of the gods.
Then the great gods convened,
They made Marduk's destiny highest, they prostrated themselves.
They laid upon themselves a curse (if they broke the oath),
With water and oil they swore, they touched their throats.
They granted him exercise of kingship over the gods,
They established him forever for lordship of heaven and earth.
Anshar gave him an additional name, Asalluhi,
"When he speaks, we shall all do obeisance,
At his command the gods shall pay heed.

[11] Though the motivation for the creation of humanity is the same here as in Atra-hasis (below, Text 1.130), i.e., to relieve the gods of their labors, it is stated here much more briefly, the creator is Ea, not the mother-goddess, and his method of creation is quite different.

[12] The physical symbol of Marduk's exaltation is the construction of his temple in Babylon by all the other deities.

[13] A banquet marks the formal inauguration of the temple (Hurowitz 1992b).

His word shall be supreme above and below,
The son, our champion, shall be the highest.
His lordship shall be supreme, he shall have no rival,
He shall be the shepherd of the black-headed folk,[14] his creatures.
They shall tell of his ways, without forgetting, in the future.
He shall establish for his fathers great food offerings,
He shall provide for them, he shall take care of their sanctuaries.
He shall cause incense burners to be savored, he shall make their chambers rejoice.
He shall make on earth the counterpart of what he brought to pass in heaven,
He shall appoint the black-headed folk to serve him.
Let the subject peoples be mindful that their gods should be invoked,
At his command let them heed their goddess(es).
Let their gods, their goddesses be brought food offerings;
Let (these) not be forgotten, let them sustain their gods.
Let their holy places be apparent(?),
let them build their sanctuaries.
Let the black-headed folk be divided as to gods,
(But) by whatever name we call him, let him be our god.[15]

Tablet VII

The Igigi-gods pronounced all the names.
When Ea heard (them), he was joyful of heart,
He said, "He whose name his fathers have glorified,
His name, like mine, shall be 'Ea.'
He shall provide the procedures for all my offices,
He shall take charge of all my commands."
With the name "Fifty" the great gods
Pronounced his fifty names, they made his position supreme.
They must be grasped: the "first one" should reveal (them),
The wise and knowledgable should ponder (them) together,
The master should repeat, and make the pupil understand.
The "shepherd," the "herdsman" should pay attention,
He must not neglect the Enlil of the gods, Marduk,
So his land may prosper and he himself be safe.
His word is truth, what he says is not changed,
Not one god can annul his utterance.
If he frowns, he will not relent,
If he is angry, no god can face his rage.
His heart is remote, his feelings all encompassing,
He before whom crime and sin must appear for judgment.
The revelation (of the names) which the "first one" discoursed before him (Marduk),
He wrote down and preserved for the future to hear,
The [wo]rd of Marduk who created the Igigi-gods,
[His/Its] let them [ ], his name let them invoke.
Let them sound abroad the song of Marduk,
How he defeated Tiamat and took kingship.

[14] The expression "black-headed folk" is a poetic term for mankind in general. It may also imply contrast with fair-haired people living beyond the bounds of ancient Mesopotamia.

[15] The rest of Tablet VI and the beginning of Tablet VII are given over to the proclamation and elucidation of the fifty names of Marduk (not included here).

REFERENCES

Text: Lambert and Parker 1966. Translations and studies: *ANET* 60-72, 501-503; Heidel 1951; Foster *BM* 1:351-402; *FDD* 9-51.

THE THEOGONY OF DUNNU (1.112)

William W. Hallo

The city of Dunnu(m), whose name is a generic term for "fort, fortress," is equated in a lexical text with the "pristine heavenly city" (URU-SAG-AN-NA), and in a date formula with the "ancient capital city" or rather perhaps the "bolt" (URU-SAG-MAH) of the kingdom of Isin. Its fall in 1795 BCE ushered in the fall of Isin to Larsa in the following year. In the present text, it is even called an "eternal city" (*ālu ṣâtu*; line 6), built by Heaven and Earth themselves "in the beginning." It is their third and climactic creation and is followed by a complicated theogony set in the primordial past.

In the beginning,[1] [a] [Haʾrab[2] married Earth.]
Family[3] [b] and lord[ship he founded.]
[Saying: "A]rable land we will carve out (of) the plowed land of the country."
[With the p]lowing of their *harbu*-plows they caused the creation of Sea.[4] [c]
[The lands plowed with the *mayaru*-pl]ow by thems[elves] gave birth to Sumuqan.[5]
His str[onghold,] Dunnu, the eternal city, they created, both of them.
Harab gave himself clear title to the lordship in Dunnu, but
[Earth] lifted (her) face to Sumuqan, his son, and
"Come here and let me make love to you!" she said to him.
Sumuqan married his mother Earth and
Hara[b his fat]her he killed (and)
In Dunnu which he loved he laid him to rest.
Moreover Sumuqan took over the lordship of his father.
Sea, his older sister, he married.
Gaiu,[6] the son of Sumuqan, came [and]
Sumuqan he killed and in Dunnu
in the g[rave] of his father he laid him to rest.
Sea, his mother, he married.
Moreover Sea murde[red] Earth, her mother.
In the month Kislimu, the 16th day, he took over lordship and kingship.[7]

[Gaiu], son of Gaiu, married Ida (River), his own sister.
[Gaiu], (his) father, and Sea, his mother, he killed and
[In the gra]ve he laid them to rest together.
In the month Tebitu, the 1st day, he [seize]d kingship and lordship for himself.
[Kush,[8] son of G]aiu, married Ua-ildak,[9] his sister, and
[the verdure] of the earth he made abundant.
He put it at the [disposal of sheepfold and] cattle-pen,
[for the cosumpt]ion of wildlife and herds of wild animals.[10]
[Moreover the necessitie]s he put at the [disposal] of the needs of the gods.
[Gaiu and] Idu (River), his mother, he kille[d and]
[in a grave] he caused them to dwell.
[In the month Shabatu, the xth day,] he took over lordship and kingship for himself.

[Haharnum,[11] son of Ku]sh, married Belit-seri,[12] his sister, [and]
[Kush and] Ua-ildak, his mother, he [killed and]
[in a grave] he caused them to dwell.
[In the month Addar]u, the 16th day (var.: the 29th day), [he took over] kingship and lordship.
[Hayyashum,] the child of Hahaharnum,
Married [...,] his own sister.
[At the New Year] he took over the lordship of his father.
[He did not] kill him but a[live]
[he seized him and to the city of Shupat-[... he brought him.]

(Approximately 40 lines largely destroyed.)

At the *akitu*-festival of the month Ayaru
the Song of the Plowing Oxen in the country [let him declaim] sweetly.[13]
(Colophon) [According to the wording] of a tablet
which is a copy from Babylon and Assur, written and checked.
(Composition called) Harab.[14] Complete.

a Gen 1:1
b Num 3:24 *et passim*
c Gen 1:2

[1] Jacobsen restored ᵈHa-rab at the beginning of the line based, perhaps, on the colophon (see below) but there is hardly room enough for that; moreover, *ina rēš* occurs as an *incipit* (twice) in a literary catalogue (van Dijk 1980:90:3f.).

[2] Jacobsen read ᵈHa-rab based on the absolute form of *ḫarbu* = "plow" (cf. lines 4f.) and the Kassite deity Harbe, equated variously with Anu (Heaven) and Enlil, the two chief deities of the Sumero-Akkadian pantheon. Earlier scholars read ᵈ*Ḫa-in*, not to be confused with the divine name *ḥyn* in Ug., equated there with the third ranking deity, Ea (Lipiński 1988).

[3] Lit., "a father's house." For the comparable biblical idiom, see Weinberg 1973.

[4] Written ᵈA.AB.BA, read ᵈ*T(i)amtu*, cognate with Heb. *tehom*.

[5] For the equation of ᵈAMA.GAN.DU with Sumuqan, the embodiment of wildlife, see Jacobsen 1984:24; previously *apud* Cross 1976:330.

[6] Earlier scholars read Lahar. Both Gaiu and Lahar are readings of the sign in question when serving as a divine name. As a generic term it stands for "ewe." It is the embodiment of domesticated cattle, as in the disputation between Lahar and Ashnan, conventionally known as "Cattle and Grain" or "Ewe and Wheat" (below, text 1.180).

[7] A double dividing line here and after lines 24 and 32 identifies the beginning of a new section.

[8] I.e., the divine herdsman (*kizû*).

[9] I.e., the divine pasture (*rītu*) and poplar (*ildakku*).

[10] Alternatively: vermin and creeping things (cf. Gen 1:20).

[11] Haharnum and his son Hayyashum, recur otherwise only in broken context in KAR 339a and at the beginning of the "Marduk Prophecy," last edited by Longman (1991:233-235). See text 1.149 below.

[12] I.e., the lady (goddess) of the open country, equated with the Sum. "lady of the vine."

[13] The *akitu*-festival of the first month (Nisannu) was part of the New Year's rites, but here it is observed in the second month, named (in Sum.) for the ceremonial inauguration of the plowing, to the accompaniment of the "Song of the Plowing Oxen" which begins E-EL-LU MA-AL-LU in Sum. (Civil 1976) and *alali* (as here) in Akk. (Livingstone 1980).

[14] This need not be the *incipit* (opening word/words) of the composition (Jacobsen) since some colophons identify their composition by its protagonist or otherwise (Leichty 1964:148, n. 4).

REFERENCES

Text: CT 46:43. Translations and studies: Lambert and Walcot 1965; Grayson in *ANET* 517f.; Hallo 1970:66; Jacobsen 1984 (largely followed here); Dalley 1989:278-281.

ERRA AND ISHUM (1.113)

Stephanie Dalley

In the extant text known to us at present, Erra and Ishum may date no earlier than the eighth century BCE, but it almost certainly incorporates older elements. It consists of five tablets comprising some 750 lines; the final tablet is shorter than the others. Tablets with the text come from both Assyria (Nineveh, Assur, Sultantepe) and Babylonia (Babylon, Ur, Tell Haddad). The main tablet, from Assur, takes the form of an amulet.

The introductory lines belong to the genre associated with oral narrative in Standard Babylonian compositions, in which the poet in the first person declares the main theme of his subject; similar introductions are found in the Standard versions of Anzu and of Gilgamesh.

A few quotations have been found in the inscriptions of Sargon II and his contemporary in Babylon, the notorious Merodach-Baladan II, of the late eighth century, but those kings may have been quoting from the work because it was popular then, and not necessarily because it was composed at that time. Although the various tablets show very little textual variation, much more variation is exhibited in extracts, which were written commonly on amulets, and they show that different versions did indeed exist, perhaps due to oral tradition. Certain evidence of older associations has been noted, particularly with reference to the Suteans, traditionally nomadic enemies who damaged Babylonian cities in the eleventh century BCE, but they may have been incorporated deliberately to lend an air of antiquity and thus authority to the poem. Such a possibility is reinforced by an apparent element of pseudo-prophecy, which is expressed in Tablet IV, when Erra proclaims: "But afterwards a man of Akkad shall rise up." So a date in the ninth or eighth century BCE seems likely. Erra and Ishum are quite similarly depicted in the Crown Prince's Vision of the Nether World, which was probably composed in the early seventh century BCE.

Erra, also known as Nergal, one main subject of the poem, is a great god in the Mesopotamian pantheon whose aspects as a god of plague and lord of the Underworld made him particularly unpredictable and awesome. Partially assimilated with Gilgamesh on the one hand and with Heracles on the other, he was a fertility god, patron of copper smelting, controller of both wild and domesticated animals, and his weapon was floods and mountain torrents. As consort of the great fertility goddess Mami he had succeeded the Sumerian god Shulpae. As a heroic warrior of sudden and uncertain changes of mood, the poem presents him as an effective challenge to Marduk, now represented as the disgruntled and senile god of Babylon. The other main subject of the poem is Ishum, whose essential nature as god of fire and as leader in battle is tempered by his skill as a wise counsellor and cunning placator of Erra.

The poem does not describe a clear narrative of specific events, but rather consists of direct discourse in which the poet, Erra, Ishum, and Marduk all make speeches, mostly in a rhetorical and declamatory style. War threatens Babylonia because of Marduk's impotence and Erra's aggression, but total disaster is narrowly averted thanks to the soothing flattery of Erra by Ishum. There is no real enemy, no rivalry, no dangers faced and overcome, no failure. An element of ridicule and satire spices the characterization of both Erra and Marduk. Possibly the poem shows features of ritual drama: the poet speaks to the gods who are sometimes addressed in the second person, sometimes he speaks for them in the first person; at other times the narrative is in the third person. At times direct speech is given without preamble, as in the Epic of Creation; at times an epic type of formulaic introduction to direct speech is given in full. Thus the composition may offer information on the ancestry of true drama, which is thought to have arisen in Greece from a dithyrambic chorus that began a dialogue, in which a single actor played the god.

As for the purpose and form of the work, it is generally reckoned that it refers to the recent past history and tribulations of Babylonia which will now be put to right by the new "man of Akkad," perhaps Nabonassar or Merodach-Baladan II, and the poem relates the events in a didactic manner. The ending of the work, and its use in extracts on amulets, makes it clear that certain passages served to ward off danger and illness. There is no clear evidence that the poem was used in the cult in specific circumstances, and there is no reason to connect its author with worship of Erra, whose main cult center at Kutha plays no part in the poem.

The ending of the poem is unusual, for the scribe is named as Kabti-ilani-Marduk of the Dabibi clan, a family first attested around 765 BCE and associated with high temple office in both Babylon and Uruk. A dream is the express source of his inspiration. In the final lines Erra in the first person exhorts the people to praise him. The destructive prophecies of Erra have been compared in general with the Oracles against the Nations in Ezekiel 24-32.

Although an epic formula to introduce direct speech is sometimes used, many of the speeches in this work occur abruptly. In some cases, especially where there are breaks in the text, the precise points at which a speech begins and ends are not certain.

Tablet I

[I sing of the son of] the king of all populated lands, creator of the world,[1]
Of Hendursanga, Ellil's heir,
Holder of the lofty scepter, herder of the black-headed people, shepherd of [populations],
Of Ishum, pious slaughterer whose hands are adept at carrying his furious weapons
And making his fierce axes flash! Erra, warrior of gods was stirring at home;[2]
His heart urged him to make war.
He spoke to his weapons, "Rub yourselves with deadly poison!"
To the Sebitti, unrivalled warrior, "Arm yourselves with your weapons!"
He said to you (Ishum), "I shall go out into the open country — [3]
You will be the torch, people can see your light.
You are to march in front, and the gods [will follow you].
You are the sword that slaughters [...]."
"O Erra, rise up, and in overwhelming the land
How happy your mood, how joyous your heart!"[4]
Yet Erra himself felt as weak as a man short of sleep,
Saying to himself, "Should I rise or sleep?"
He told his weapons, "Stay propped in the cupboard!"
To the Sebitti, unrivalled warrior, "Go back to your home."
Until you (Ishum) rouse him, he will stay asleep in bed,
Enjoy himself with Mami his lover!
For he is Engidudu, lord who prowls by night, leader of princes,
Who leads on youths and girls and makes (night) as bright as day.
Different is the divine nature of the Sebitti, unrivalled warrior;
Their birth was strange and full of terrible portents.
Anyone who sees them is smitten with terror, for their breath is lethal;
People are petrified and cannot approach them.[5]
Ishum is the door bolted before them.
When Anu, king of the gods, impregnated Earth,
She bore the Seven Gods for him and he named them Sebitti.
When they stood before him, he decreed their destiny.
He summoned the first and gave him orders,
"Wherever you band together and march out, you shall have no rival."[6]
He spoke to the second, "Ignite like Gerra and blaze like a flame!"
He said to the third, "You must put on the face of a lion, so that anyone seeing you will crumble in terror."
He spoke to the fourth, "Let the mountain flee before the one who bears your fierce weapons!"[7]
He ordered the fifth, "Blow like the wind, and seek out the rim of the world!"
He commanded the sixth, "Go through above and below, and do not spare anyone!"
The seventh he filled with dragon's venom, and "Lay low living things!"
When Anu had decreed the destinies of all the Sebitti,
He gave them to Erra, warrior of the gods,
"Let them march at your side!
Whenever the hubbub of settled people becomes unbearable to you,[8]
And you want to wreak destruction,
To kill off some black-headed people and lay low Shakkan's cattle.[9]
These shall act as your fierce weapons, and

[1] The opening lines are modelled on the opening of Anzu. Some commentators would restore the name of Marduk or of Erra/Nergal at the end of the line, but it is very doubtful whether there is a lacuna at the ends of lines 1 or 2, and Hendursanga is definitely a name for Ishum. Therefore I have followed Edzard, *RlA*, s.v. Irra; the prologue, like the epilogue, is addressed to Ishum and Erra. The epilogue shows that Erra and Nergal are two names for the one god.

[2] Unusual vocabulary for the phrase "fierce axes" is also found in the letter describing Sargon's eighth campaign, line 122 (Thureau-Dangin 1912).

[3] The second person address, only briefly maintained, perhaps implies that the dialogue within the poem was a hymn sung around a statue of Ishum.

[4] These two lines read like the exclamation of a chorus, tinged with sarcasm.

[5] Lit., "him." The Sebitti, "The Seven Gods," can be regarded both as a singular and as a plural deity.

[6] Reading *[te-n]e-di-ru*, from *edēru* N, "band together."

[7] Cagni translated "be razed to the ground" rather than "flee."

[8] This speech echoes Atrahasis, I-II in which the gods recommend that overpopulation be curbed by plague, although the idea comes from Ellil, not Anu, in the version known to us.

[9] "Black-headed people"; see the Epic of Creation, text 1.111, n. 14 above (p. 402).

march at your side!"
They were indeed fierce, and their weapons rose up.
They said to Erra, "Rise! Stand up!
Why do you stay in town like a feeble old man?
How can you stay at home like a lisping child?
Are we to eat women's bread, like one who has never marched on to the battlefield?
Are we to be fearful and nervous as if we had no experience of war?
To go on to the battlefield is as good as a festival for young men!
Anyone who stays in town, be he a prince, will not be satisfied with bread alone;
He will be vilified in the mouths of his own people, and dishonored.
How can he raise his hand against one who goes to the battlefield?
However great the strength of one who stays in town,
How can he prevail over one who has been on the battlefield?
City food, however fancy, cannot compare with what is cooked on the embers.
Best beer, however sweet, cannot compare with water from a water-skin.
A palace built on a platform cannot compare with the shelters of [a camp.]
Go out to the battlefield, warrior Erra, make your weapons resound!
Make your noise so loud that those above and below quake,
So that the Igigi hear and glorify your name,
So that the Anunnaki hear and fear your word,
So that the gods hear and submit to your yoke,
So that kings hear and kneel beneath you,
So that countries hear and bring you their tribute,
So that demons hear and avoid (?) you,
So that the powerful hear and bite their lips,
So that mountain peaks hear and bow their heads in terror,
So that the rolling seas hear and are stirred up and destroy their produce,
So that tree trunks are lopped in a mighty grove,
So that the reeds of an impenetrable reed-bed are cut down,
So that people are frightened into controlling their noise,
So that cattle tremble and turn to clay,
So that the gods your fathers see and praise your valor!
Warrior Erra, why did you abandon the battlefield and stay in town?
Even Shakkan's cattle and wild beasts despise us.
Warrior Erra, we must tell you, and our words will surely be harsh for you,
As long as the whole land is too much for us,
Surely you will listen to our words!
Do a favor for the Anunnaki who love silence!
Sleep no longer pours over the Anunnaki, because of people's noise.[10]
Cattle are trampling down the pasture land, the life of the country.
The farmer weeps bitterly over his [yield].
The lion and the wolf lay low Shakkan's cattle.
The shepherd prays to you for his sheep, he cannot sleep by day nor by night.
And we, who know the mountain passes, we have quite forgotten the road!
Spiders' webs are spun over our campaign gear.
Our trusty bows have rebelled and become too tough for our strength.
The points of our sharp arrows are blunt.
Our daggers are corroded with verdigris for lack of butchery."
Warrior Erra listened to them.
The speech which the Sebitti made was as pleasing to him as the best oil.
He made his voice heard and spoke to Ishum,
"How can you listen and stay silent?
Open up a path, and let me take the road!
Let me appoint the Sebitti, unrivalled warrior, [to][11]
Make them march at my side as my fierce weapons.
And as for you, go ahead of me, go behind me."
When Ishum heard this,
He made his voice heard and spoke to the warrior Erra,[12]
"Lord Erra, why have you planned evil for the gods?
You have plotted to overthrow countries and to destroy their people, but will you not turn back?"
Erra made his voice heard and spoke,
Addressed his words to Ishum who marches before him,
"Ishum, be silent, and listen to my speech
About settled people whom you say I should spare!
Wise Ishum, who marches in front of the gods, whose advice is good,

[10] Another use of the overpopulation theme from Atrahasis.
[11] Reading *lupqi[d]*, "appoint," rather than *luppi[t]*, "draw (them)" (Cagni).
[12] Var. "He felt compassion and ..."

In heaven I am a wild bull, on earth I am a lion.
In the country I am king, among the gods I am fierce.
Among the Igigi I am the warrior, among the Anunnaki I am powerful.
Among cattle I am the smiter, in the mountains I am a wild ram.[13]
In the reed-thicket I am Gerra, in the grove I am the *magšaru*-axe.
In the course of a campaign I am the standard.
I blow like the wind, I rumble like Adad,
I can see the rim of everything like Shamash.
I go out on to the battlefield, and I am a wild sheep.
I go into sheepfolds (?), and I make my dwelling there.[14]
All the (other) gods are afraid of battle,
So that the black-headed people despise (them).
But I, because they no longer fear my name,
And since prince Marduk has neglected his word and does as he pleases,
I shall make prince Marduk angry, and I shall summon him from his dwelling, and I shall overwhelm (his) people."
Warrior Erra set his face towards Shuanna, city of the king of gods.
He entered Esagila, palace of heaven and earth, and stood in front of him (Marduk),
He made his voice heard and spoke (to) the king of gods,
"Why does the finery, your lordship's adornment which is full of splendor like the stars of heaven, grow dirty?
The crown of your lordship which made E-halanki shine like E-temen-anki — its surface is tarnished!"
The king of gods made his voice heard and spoke,
Addressed his words to Erra, warrior of gods,
"Warrior Erra, concerning that deed which you have said you will do:
A long time ago, when I was angry and rose up from my dwelling and arranged for the Flood,[15]
I rose up from my dwelling, and the control of heaven and earth was undone.
The very heavens I made to tremble, the positions of the stars of heaven changed, and I did not return them to their places.
Even Erkalla quaked; the furrow's yield diminished, and forever after (?) it was hard to extract (a yield).
Even the control of heaven and earth was undone, the springs diminished, the floodwater receded. I went back, and looked and looked; it was very grievous.
The (remaining) offspring of living things was tiny, and I did not return them to their (former) state,
To the extent that I was like a farmer who can hold (all) his seed-corn in his hand.[16]
I made a house and settled into it.
As for the finery which had been pushed aside by the Flood, its surface dulled:
I directed Gerra to make my features radiant, and to cleanse my robes.[17]
When he had made the finery bright, and finished the work,
I put on my crown of lordship and went back to my place.
My features were splendid, and my gaze was awesome!
(As for) the people who were left from the Flood and saw the result of my action,
Should I raise my weapons and destroy the remnant?[18]
I made those (original) Craftsmen go down to the Apsu, and I said they were not to come back up.[19]
I changed the location of the *mēsu*-tree (and of) the *elmešu*-stone, and did not reveal it to anyone.[20]
Now, concerning that deed which you have said you will do, Warrior Erra,
Where is the *mēsu*-wood, the flesh of the gods, the proper insignia of the King of the World,[21]
The pure timber, tall youth, who is made into a lord,[22]
Whose roots reach down into the vast ocean through a hundred miles of water, to the base of Arallu,[23]

[13] The word for "smiter," *māḫiṣu*, can also be translated "hunter."
[14] "Sheepfolds" or "pasture land."
[15] Here Marduk takes responsibility for the Flood; in Atrahasis it was Ellil's idea.
[16] Lit., "To the extent that I held their seed in my hand like a plowman."
[17] In this speech Marduk refers to himself as a cult statue made of precious metals, gems, and timbers.
[18] Var. has: "Should you raise your weapons ..." The line may equally be taken as an affirmative statement, not as interrogative.
[19] These Craftsmen are the Seven Sages.
[20] Or, "of the *mēsu*-tree (which bears) *elmešu*-stone." Although a translation "amber" has been suggested for *elmešu*, amber seems not to have been used in ancient Mesopotamia. The word is sometimes used with *būṣu*, "glass," and may perhaps be rock crystal. *mēsu* may have been a rosewood (Dalbergia) with wider mythical connotations.
[21] I.e., the wood was used to make the gods' basic statues, which were then adorned with inlay etc.
[22] This is a pun on *mes* as a logographic value for *eṭlu*, "youth," and *mēsu*-timber (Cagni 1969:194). The same pun occurs in a late third millennium poem known as *Shulgi King of Abundance* (Klein 1981:11).
[23] Lit., "a hundred double hours."

Whose topknot above rests on the heaven of Anu?
Where is the pure *zagindurû*-stone which [...] threw away?[24]
Where is Nin-ildu the great carpenter-god of my Anu-power,
Who carries the pure axe of the sun, and knows ... timbers,
Who makes [the night (?)] as radiant as day and makes [people (?)] bow down beneath me?
Where is Kusig-banda, creator of god and man, whose hands are pure?
Where is Ninagal, who carries the hammer and anvil,
Who chews hard copper like hide and manufactures tools?
Where are the precious stones, produce of the vast ocean, fitting ornament for crowns?
Where are the Seven Sages of the Apsu, the holy carp, who are perfect in lofty wisdom like Ea their lord, who can make my body holy?"[25]
The warrior Erra listened to him as he stood (?) there.
He made his voice heard and spoke to prince Marduk,
"[...]
[...]
The holy *elmešu*-stone [...]."
When Marduk heard this,
He made his voice heard and spoke to warrior Erra,
"I shall rise up from my dwelling, and the control of heaven and earth will be undone.
The waters will rise and go over the land.
Bright day will turn into darkness.
A storm will rise up and cover the stars of heaven.
An evil wind will blow, and the vision of people and living things will [be obscured (?)].
Gallu-demons will come up and seize [...]
Those who are undressed will [...] who opposes them.
The Anunnaki will come up and trample on living things.
Until I gird myself with weapons, who can make them go back?"
When Erra heard this,
He made his voice heard and spoke to prince Marduk,
"Prince Marduk, until you re-enter that house and Gerra cleanses your robes, and you return to your place,
Until then shall I rule and keep firm control of heaven and earth.
I shall go up into heaven, and give orders to the Igigi;
I shall go down to the Apsu and direct the Anunnaki.
I shall send ferocious *gallu*-demons to Kurnugi,
And I shall set my fierce weapons over them.
I shall tie the wings of the wicked wind like a bird.
At that house which you shall enter, prince Marduk,
I shall make Anu and Ellil lie down like bulls, to right and left of your gate."
Prince Marduk listened to him,
And the speech that Erra made was pleasing to him.

(*Catchline*)

He rose up from his inaccessible dwelling and set his face towards the dwelling of the Anunnaki.

Tablet II

He rose up from his inaccessible dwelling and set his face towards the dwelling of the Anunnaki.
He entered ... and sto[od before them,]
[Discarded] his radi[ance] and let his rays fall [...][26]
[Because (?)] he had set his face towards another place and no longer [...] the earth,
[The winds (?)] rose up, and bright day was turned into darkness.
[...] of the land together [...]
[...] went up [...]
[...] and the bottom of [...]
[...] all of the rim of [...]

(gap of 7 lines)

The crown [...]
His heart [...]
"The mantle of radiance [...]
Let Ea in the Apsu [...]
Let Shamash see [...] and let the people [...]
Let Sin look, and at his sign [...] to the land
Concerning that work Ea [...] is expert (?)."
The warrior Erra was filled with anger,[27]
Why, because of foam on the surface of water, did Marduk
Give the [...] of mankind, whom I myself

[24] A blue stone, possibly top-quality lapis lazuli.

[25] When a divine statue was made or repaired, rituals known as "washing the mouth" and "opening the mouth" were carried out with incantations, Ea's speciality, to bring the statue to "life." In an inscription of Esarhaddon (680-669 BCE) "(the newly fashioned statues) entered the city with rituals by sages, with 'washing the mouth' and 'opening the mouth'" (Borger *Asarh.* 89).

[26] The idea that a god is made powerless when divested of his rays or mantle of radiance is also found in the episode of Humbaba in *Gilgamesh*.

[27] This restoration and those which follow are based on a new, fragmentary tablet from Tell Haddad, kindly made available by Dr. Farouk al-Rawi and Dr. Jeremy Black. That tablet shows that Tablet II had about 160 lines.

created
To bring promptly the *taklīmu*-offerings of the Anunnaki,
At the wrong time?
He plotted evil, to devastate the land, to destroy people [...]"
Ea-sharru considered, and then he said,
"Now, (it was) prince Marduk who rose up, who told those Craftsmen that they were not to come back up.
Statues of them, which I made among the people, for [his great divinity]
Which no god goes and approaches [(?) ...]"[28]
He gave to the Craftsmen a generous heart, and [...]-ed their base.
He bestowed on them wisdom and made their work beautiful.
They made that finery radiant, and more choice (?) than before.
The warrior Erra stood before him night and day without cease;
Whatever (?) was placed there to make the finery radiant for the king of kings, he would say:
"You can't come near the work!
[...] I shall cut off his life, I shall stretch out his ...
[...] hasten to the work.
[...] has no rival.
[...] ...
[...] shall rival princes." (?)
[...] his head
[made his finery radiant]
[...] ...
[...] at his door.
[...] king Shamash was clothed.
[...] set down his dwelling
[...] light was established
[...] assembled.
[...] Marduk

(8 lines fragmentary)

The king of gods made his voice heard and spoke
"[...] and they will go up to heaven.
[...] return to your dwelling.
[...] ...
[...] upon your cheek
[...] their people
[...] you did not turn back."
[...] spoke to the king of gods,
"[...] of the day

(gap of about 17 lines)

[...] father of the gods [...]
Ellil [...]
The gods, all of them in [...]
Among Shakkan's cattle, all of them [...]
Erra among all the gods [...]
Among the stars of heaven the Fox Star [...][29]
Was twinkling and its rays [...] to him.
The stars of all the gods were dazzling [...]
Because they were angry with each other and Prince Marduk [...] put [...].
"The star of Erra is twinkling and carries rays, [...] of Anunitu.
His mantle of radiance will be activated (?) and all people will perish.
As for (?) the dazzling stars of heaven that carry a sword (?),
As for (?) the titch (?) of creation, the ant, it does not ... [...].
Among Shakkan's cattle, their astral image is that of the Fox [...]
Endowed with strength, a fierce (?) lion [...]
Ellil is the father of populations (?) and he has made the final [decision (?)]."
Innina replied from the gods' assembly, gave advice [...],
[Addressed] her words to Anu and Dagan [...],
"Pay attention, all of you, go into your private quarters;
Cover your lips. Did you not smell the inc[ense-offering (?)]
In the presence of Prince Marduk, nor give advice, nor bese[ech him (?)]?
Until the time is fulfilled, the [hour] is passed,
The word Marduk spoke is like a mountain where trees (?) [grow]; he does not change it (?) [...]
Erra [...]

(gap of 4 lines)

Ishtar went and they entered the private quarters.
She urged Erra, but he would not agree [...][30]
Ishum [made his voice heard and spoke],
Addressed [his words to Innina],[31]
"He has ill-treated (?) [...]
Erra is angry and will not be silent [...].
Let the mountains be at peace, [...] to him."
Ellil's lofty son, who does not take the road without the leader Ishum,
Entered Emeslam and made his dwelling there.
He deliberated (?) with himself concerning that work.[32]
But his heart [...]; it gave him no reply.
He asked himself, "How can you sit still? (?)[33]
Open up a path, and let me take the road!

[28] Cagni translates: "Where the god does not go, they draw near."
[29] The Fox Star was equated with Erra.
[30] The main restorations using the Tell Haddad tablet end here.
[31] The new passage shows that Innina, not Erra, should be restored here.
[32] Tentatively reading *išâlma ramānuš*.
[33] Tentatively reading *tuš-bi mìn-su*.

The time has elapsed, the hour has passed.
I promise that I shall destroy the rays of the Sun;
I shall cover the face of the Moon in the middle of the night.
I shall say to Adad, 'Hold back [your] well-springs,
Drive away the clouds and cut out snow and rain.'
To Marduk (?) and to Ea I shall bring a reminder:
He who grows up in times of plenty shall be buried in times of deprivation.
He who travels out on a path with water shall return along a way of dust-storms.
I shall say to the king of gods, 'Stay in Esagila!'
They will do as you have told them, they will carry out your command in full.
The black-headed people will revile you, and you will not accept their prayers.
I shall finish off the land and count it as ruins.
I shall devastate cities and make of them a wilderness.
I shall destroy mountains and fell their cattle.
I shall stir up oceans and destroy their produce.
I shall dig out reed-thickets and graves and I shall burn them like Gerra.
I shall fell people and [I shall leave no] life
I shall not keep a single one back!
I shall not leave out any of the cattle of Shakkan nor any wild beasts [whatsoever].
From city to city I shall seize the one who governs.
A son will not ask after the health of his father, nor the father of his son.
A mother will happily plot harm for her daughter.
I shall let a [barbarian] enter a god's shrine where evil men should not go.
I shall let a rogue sit down in the dwelling of princes.
I shall let a wild beast of ... enter [cult centers].
I shall stop anyone entering any city which he encounters.
I shall let wild beasts of the mountains go down (into cities).
I shall devastate public places, wherever people tread.
I shall let wild beasts of the countryside which are not ... come into the public square.
I shall let a bad omen occur to devastate a city.
I shall let the demon 'Supporter of Evil' enter the gods' [inaccessible] dwelling.
I shall devastate the royal palace and make it into a ruin [( )].
I shall cut off the noise of mankind and deprive him of joy,
Like [...] like fire where there was once peace.
[...] I shall let evil enter."

(Catchline)

[...] he would pay attention to nobody.

Tablet III

[...] he would pay attention to nobody,
The words of caution that they spoke [...]
Lions [...]
[...]
To [...]
"I shall make them take [...] and I shall shorten their lifetime,
I shall sever the life of the just man who takes on paternal responsibility,
I shall set up [at the head (?)] the wicked man who cuts off life.
I shall change the minds of people, so that the father will not listen to the son:
The daughter will speak words of rejection to the mother.
I shall make their words wicked, and they will forget their god,
Will speak great insolence to their goddess.
I shall muster the bandit and cut off the highway.
They will even plunder each other's property in the city center.
The lion and the wolf will fell Shakkan's cattle.
[...] I shall cause to rage and he will cut off offspring.
I shall deprive the nurse of the baby's cry and toddler's prattle.
I shall make Alala leave the pasture.
Shepherd and herdsman will forget the shelter.
I shall cut off the garment from a man's body
And I shall make the young man walk naked in the city square.
I shall make the young man go down into the Earth unshrouded.
The young man — his supply of sacrificial sheep will be interrupted and endanger his own life.
The prince — his supply of lambs will become too scarce to obtain oracles from Shamash.[34]
The sick man will demand roast meat (perversely) to satisfy his craving.
He will not free for ... he will go.
[...] I shall stop the steeds of princes.
[...] I shall cut off.
[...] I shall cause to seize.

[34] Shamash and Adad were gods of extispicy (the reading of entrails) and other omens.

(gap of uncertain length)[35]

Rain [...]
Evil winds [...]

(gap of uncertain length)[35]

"You have (?) set up the weapons of *kidinnu*-men as an abomination to Anu and Dagan.[36]
You have made their blood flow like water in the drains of public squares.
You have opened their veins and let the river carry off (their blood).
Ellil has cried "Woe!" and clutched at his heart
[He has risen up from] his dwelling.
An irredeemable curse is set in his mouth,
He has sworn not to drink the river's waters,
He shuns their blood and will not enter into Ekur."
Erra addressed his words to Ishum, who marches before him,
"The Sebitti, unrivalled warrior [...]
All of them [...]
Who [...]
Who marches before [...]
Who [...]
Who like Gerra [...]
In front of the house [...]
Who like [...]
Who [...]
Whom Erra [...]
The face of a lion [...]
In my rage [...]
Open the path, let me take the road!
Let me appoint the Sebitti, unrivalled warrior [...].
Make them march at my side as my fierce weapons.
And as for you, go ahead of me, go behind me!"
Ishum listened to this speech of his;
He felt compassion and said to himself,
"Woe to my people against whom Erra rages and [...]
Whom the warrior Nergal, as in the moment of battle, [...] Asakku.[37]
His arms, like those which (slew (?)) the ruined god, are not too weak to slay them,[38]
His net, like that (which overwhelmed) wicked Anzu, is spread to overwhelm them."[39]
Ishum made his voice heard and spoke,
Addressed his words to the warrior Erra,
"How could you plot evil for gods and men?
Even though you have plotted evil against the black-headed people, will you not turn back?"
Erra made his voice heard and spoke,
Addressed his words to Ishum who marches before him,
"You know the decisions of the Igigi, the counsels of the Anunnaki.
You give the command for the black-headed people, and gain their attention (?).
How can you speak like one who is ignorant,
Advise me as if you did not know of Marduk's words to me!
The king of gods has risen up from his dwelling
So how can all the lands stay firm?
He has taken off his lordly crown:
King and princes [...] will forget their rites.
He has undone his girdle:
The belt of god and man is loosened and cannot be retied.
Furious Gerra has made his finery bright as day, and has displayed his radiance.
He holds a mace in his right hand, the great weapon
Of Prince Marduk; his glance is terrifying.
Yet to me you speak [...]
Leader of the gods, wise Ishum, whose counsel is good,
How can you now sit and [...]
Was Marduk's word not pleasing to you?"
Ishum made his voice heard and spoke to warrior Erra,
"Warrior Erra, [...]
Trample on the people and [...]
Where the cattle [...]
The reed-thicket and grove which [...]
Now, as for what you say, warrior Erra,
One was put in charge, but you [...]
You killed seven and did not spare one.

[35] If the total number of lines for this tablet should be about 160 as indicated by the tablet from Tell Haddad, this and the following gap represent about forty-three missing lines.

[36] Certain cities were accorded the privileged status of protection called *kidinnūtu* in which its citizens were exempted from military service, and professional soldiers were forbidden to bear arms within the city walls. Such places proclaimed their status with standards set up at the gates of the city. They may in return have supported permanent encampments of professional soldiers. In Babylonia the cities Sippar, Nippur, Babylon, and Borsippa, in Assyria the cities Assur and Harran enjoyed the status, at least in the early first millennium, although not without interruption. *kidinnu*-men in such cities appear to have had a special relationship with the two gods Anu and Dagan. It is not certain whether the *kidinnu*-men were citizens exempt from military service or the soldiery stationed in those cities.

[37] Or, "storm," rather than "moment." This line assimilates Nergal with Ninurta, who defeated Asakku in the Sum. story Lugal-e (Van Dijk 1983).

[38] This literary allusion is not understood. According to one text "the ruined gods were in the sea," and the Epic of Creation, VI may allude to the same event. It is possible that a feat of Ninurta is involved.

[39] The reference is to the myth of Anzu, but a different version from the one known to us in which no net is used. As in previous lines here assimilation with Ningirsu and Ninurta is implied. However, the text may be corrupt; cf. Etana, text 1.131, note 18 below.

Cattle [...]
Erra, you clash your weapons together
And the mountains shake, the seas surge
At the flashing of your sword [...] they look towards the mountain.
The palace [...]"

(gap of uncertain length)

Ishum made his voice heard and spoke to warrior Erra,
"Warrior Erra, you hold the nose-rope of heaven,[40]
You control the whole earth, and you rule the land.
You made the sea rough and encompass mountains,
You govern people and herd cattle.
Esharra is at your disposal; E-engurra in your hands.
You look after Shuanna and rule Esagila,
You control all the rites and the gods respect you.
When you give counsel, even Anu listens.
The Igigi revere you, the Anunnaki fear you,
Ellil agrees with you. Does conflict happen without you,
Or warfare take place in your absence?
The armory of war belongs to you
And yet you say to yourself, 'They despise me!'

(Catchline)

O warrior Erra, did you not fear prince Marduk's name?

Tablet IV

O warrior Erra, did you not fear prince Marduk's name ?
You have untied the bond of Dimkurkurra, city of the king of gods, the bond of lands!
You have changed your divine nature and become like a human![41]
You have donned your weapons and entered in,
Into the heart of Babylon, and have spoken like a braggart (?), that you would seize the city.
The sons of Babylon, who have none to take charge of them, like reeds in a reed-thicket, have all gathered about you.
He who is ignorant of weapons is unsheathing his dagger,
He who is ignorant of bows is stringing his bow,
He who is ignorant of battle is making war,
He who is ignorant of wings is flying like a bird.
The weakling covers the master of force;[42]
The fatty is overtaking the sprinter.
To the governor in charge of their shrines they utter great blasphemies.
Their hands have dammed up the city gate of Babylon, the artery of their wealth.
They have thrown firebrands into the shrines of Babylon like looters of the country.
You are the one who marches at the head, and you take the lead for them.
You press down arrows upon Imgur-Ellil until he says 'Woe is me!'
You have founded a dwelling for Muhra, keeper of its city-gate, in the blood of young men and women.
You are the decoy for the inhabitants of Babylon, and they are the bird;
You ensnared them in your net and caught and destroyed them, warrior Erra.
You left the city and went off elsewhere;
You put on the face of a lion and entered the palace.
The army saw you and donned their weapons.
The governor, who had treated Babylon well, became enraged,
Directed his troops to loot like enemy looters,
Incited the leader of the army to crime,
'You are the man whom I shall send to that city!
You shall respect neither god nor man.
Put young and old alike to death.
You shall not leave any child, even if he still sucks milk.
You shall pillage the accumulated wealth of Babylon.'
The royal troops were put into units and entered the city.
The bow twanged, the dagger pricked.
You set up the weapons of *kidinnu*-men as an abomination to Anu and Dagan.
You have made their blood flow like water in the drains of public squares.
You have opened their veins and let the river carry off (their blood).
The great lord Marduk saw and cried 'Woe!' and clutched at his heart.
An irredeemable curse is set in his mouth.
He has sworn not to drink the river's waters.
He shuns their blood and will not enter into Esagila,
'Woe to Babylon, which I made as lofty as

[40] This speech is quoted on plague amulets (Reiner 1960).

[41] Erra/Nergal may have been equated with Heracles, whose ambivalent nature as a god and as a mortal hero is stressed by Herodotus (Dalley 1987).

[42] For "wings" see Tsevat 1987. The second phrase probably implies a wrestler's strength, arm muscles.

a date-palm's crown, but the wind shrivelled it.
Woe to Babylon, which I filled with seeds like a pine-cone, but whose abundance I did not bring to fruition.
Woe to Babylon, which I planted like a luxuriant orchard, but never tasted its fruit.
Woe to Babylon, which I have thrown on to the neck of Anu like a cylinder seal of *elmešu*-stone.
Woe to Babylon, which I have taken in my hands like the Tablet of Destinies and will not deliver to anyone else.'"
Then prince Marduk spoke thus,
"[...] which from time immemorial [...]
Henceforth he who would cross from the quayside shall cross on foot.
Henceforth the rope which would go down into the cistern shall not save the life of a single man.
Henceforth they shall drive out the deep-sea fisherman's boat a hundred leagues into the vast expanse of sea-water with a pole.
Even Sippar, the eternal city, which the Lord of Lands did not allow the Flood to overwhelm, because it was so dear to him;
You destroyed its wall without Shamash's permission and dismantled its parapet.[43]
Even Uruk, the dwelling of Anu and Ishtar, city of prostitutes, courtesans, and call-girls,
Whom Ishtar deprived of husbands and kept in her (lit. their) power:
Sutean men and women hurl their abuse;
They rouse Eanna, the party-boys and festival people
Who changed their masculinity into femininity to make the people of Ishtar revere her.
The dagger-bearer, bearers of razors, pruning-knives, and flint blades
Who frequently do abominable acts to please the heart of Ishtar:
You set over them an insolent governor who will not treat them kindly.
He persecuted them and violated their rites.
Ishtar was enraged and became angry with Uruk.
She summoned an enemy and despoiled the land like (standing) corn before (flood-) water.
The inhabitants of Parsa would not cease ritual wailing because of E-ugal, which had been contaminated.
The enemy whom you had summoned would not agree to stop."
Angal replied,
You have made the city of Der into a wilderness;
You have snapped the people within it like reeds!
Like scum (?) on the surface of water you have stopped their hubbub,
And you did not spare me; you delivered me up to the Suteans.[44]
So I, because of my city Der,[45]
Shall not give fair justice, I shall not make decisions for the land.
I shall not give any orders, nor will I open my ear.
The people abandoned justice and took to atrocities.
They deserted righteousness and planned wickedness.
I made the seven winds rise up against the one country.
Anyone who has not died in battle will die in an epidemic.
Anyone who has not died in the epidemic, the enemy will carry off as spoil.
Anyone whom the enemy has not carried off as spoil, thieves will murder.
Anyone whom thieves have not murdered, the king's weapon will overcome.[46]
Anyone whom the king's weapon has not overcome, a prince will fell.
Anyone whom a prince did not fell, Adad will wash away.
Anyone whom Adad has not washed away, Shamash will parch.[47]
Anyone who goes out on to the land, the wind will infect.
Anyone who enters his own home, the Croucher will hit.
Anyone who goes up into the heights will die of thirst,
Anyone who goes down into the depths will die by water,
For you encompass the heights and the depths alike.
The city governor will say thus to his mother,

[43] The historical event to which this line alludes cannot be pinpointed.

[44] The Suteans were traditional enemies of Assyria and had raided Der, Nippur, and Parsa in the eleventh century (Heltzer 1981:90-94); they are attested again on the fringes of Babylonia in the eighth and early seventh centuries; Sargon II in the late eighth century claimed to have driven Sutean bandits from Babylonian countryside.

[45] This allusion to Der is not clear. The Assyrians were defeated there by Elam in 720 BCE, perhaps with Babylonian help (Brinkman 1984:48) but retained control of the city.

[46] Probably a reference to the winged disk, symbol of royalty on which oaths of loyalty to the king were sworn under threat of horrific penalties for perjury. Such symbols were regularly referred to as weapons because of their power to harm and kill.

[47] Or, "will take away" rather than "will parch."

'Would that I had been obstructed in your womb on the day you bore me,
Would that my life had ended and that we had died together,
Because you delivered me to a city whose walls were to be demolished,
Its people treated like cattle, their god turned smiter,[48]
And because his net is of such fine mesh, even picked men could not draw (their swords), but died by the sword.'[49]
He who sired a son will say, 'This is my son
And I reared him and he does good in return,' —
Yet shall I put the son to death and his father shall bury him.
Afterwards I shall put the father to death, and he shall have nobody to bury him.
He who builds a house and says, 'This is my home,
I have built it and I shall find peace within it,
And when Fate carries me off I shall rest there (forever)' —[50]
Yet shall I put him to death and vandalize his home.
Afterwards it will be wrecked, and I shall give it to someone else"

(Ishum answers)

"O warrior Erra, you have put the just to death,
You have put the unjust to death.
You have put to death the man who sinned against you,
You have put to death the man who did not sin against you.
You have put to death the *en*-priest who made *taklīmu*-offerings promptly,
You have put to death the courtier who served the king,
You have put old men to death on the porch,
You have put young girls to death in their bedrooms.
Yet you will not rest at all,
Yet you say to yourself, 'They despise me!'
Yet this is what you tell yourself, Warrior Erra,
'I shall smite the strong and terrify the weak.
I shall murder the leader of the army and rout the army,
I shall ruin the shrine on top of the temple-(tower) and the wall's crenellations, and destroy the city's vitality.
I shall tear out the mooring poles and let boats drift downstream,
I shall break the rudder, so that it cannot reach the bank,
I shall rip out the mast and tear out its rigging.
I shall dry out the breast so that the baby cannot live,
I shall block springs, so that small channels cannot bring the waters of fertility.
I shall make Erkalla quake, so that the skies billow,
I shall fell the rays of Shulpae and throw away the stars of heaven,
The roots of trees shall be cut through so that their new growth will not flourish,
I shall destroy the base of the wall so that the top of it sways.
To the dwelling of the king of gods I shall go, so that counsel shall not prevail.'"
Warrior Erra listened to him,
And the words that Ishum spoke to him were as pleasing as the best oil.
And Warrior Erra spoke thus,
"Sealanders shall not spare Sealanders, nor Subartian (spare) Subartian, nor Assyrian Assyrian,[51]
Nor shall Elamite spare Elamite, nor Kassite Kassite,
Nor Sutean spare Sutean, nor Gutian Gutian,
Nor shall Lullubean spare Lullubean, nor country country, nor city city,
Nor shall tribe spare tribe, nor man man, nor brother brother, and they shall slay one another.
But afterwards a man of Akkad shall rise up and fell them all and shepherd all (the rest) of them."[52]
Warrior Erra addressed his words to Ishum, who marches before him,
"Go, Ishum! Take full discretion for the words you spoke!"
Ishum set his face towards the mountain Hehe.
The Sebitti, unrivalled warrior, stormed (?) behind him.
The warrior arrived at the mountain Hehe,
Raised his hand and destroyed the mountain,
Counted the mountain Hehe as (flat) ground.
He lopped the tree trunks in the forest of *hašūru*-trees[53]

---

[48] Or, "hunter" rather than "smiter," both meanings of *māḫiṣu*.
[49] The word *haʾīru*, "chosen one," normally means a lover, bridegroom, first husband. A widower was often obliged to marry the widow of a relative, and had little choice upon remarriage.
[50] People were commonly buried under the floors of their houses.
[51] The Sealand probably refers to southern Mesopotamia, where the marsh-lands were inhabited by several different tribes or "houses."
[52] "Man of Akkad" probably refers to an urban Babylonian as opposed to a nomad or a foreigner. This line indicates that there is an important element of pseudo-prophecy in the epic. Cf. below, texts 1.149-150 for this genre.
[53] *hašūru*: a kind of cypress.

Like [...]
He finished off the cities and made of them a wilderness,
Destroyed mountains and struck down their cattle,
Stirred up the seas and destroyed their produce,
Devastated reed-beds and groves, and burnt them like Gerra
Cursed the cattle and turned them into clay.

(Catchline)

When Erra had rested and settled in his dwelling,

Tablet V

When Erra had rested and settled in his dwelling,
All the gods began to look at his face.
The Igigi and the Anunnaki, all of them, were standing in awe.
Erra made his voice heard and spoke to all the gods,
"Keep quiet, all of you, and learn what I have to say!
What if I did intend the harm of the wrong I have just done?
When I am enraged, I devastate people!
Like a hired man among the flocks, I let the leading sheep out of the pen.
Like one who does not plant the orchard, I am not slow to cut it down.
Like one who plunders a country, I do not distinguish just from unjust, I fell (them both).
One does not snatch a corpse from the mouth of a marauding lion,
And where one man is beside himself, another man cannot give him advice !
What would happen if Ishum, who goes before me, were not there?
Where would your provider be, wherever would your *en*-priest be?
Where would your *nindabû*-offerings be? You would not (even) smell the incense-offering!"
Ishum made his voice heard and spoke,
Addressed his words to warrior Erra,
"Warrior, be still and listen to my words!
What if you were to rest now, and we would serve you?
We all know that nobody can stand up to you in your day of wrath!"
Erra heard him and his face brightened;
His features lit up like the dawning of a (new) day.
He entered into Emeslam and settled in his dwelling.
Ishum called out and said the key word,
Began to confirm the decision concerning the scattered people of Akkad.
"May the reduced people of the land become numerous again,
May the short man and the tall man go along its paths,
May the weak man of Akkad fell the strong Sutean,
May one man drive away seven (of them) as if they were flocks!
You shall make *their* towns into ruins and *their* hills into wildernesses,
You shall bring their heavy spoils into Shuanna,[54]
You shall put the country's gods who were angry safely back into their dwellings,
You shall let Shakkan and Nissaba (i.e., cattle and grain) go down into the country,
You shall let the mountains bear their wealth and the sea its produce,
You shall let the meadowlands, which you allowed to be devastated, bear their produce!
Then let the governors of all cities, every one of them, haul their heavy tribute into Shuanna,
Let the temples, which were allowed to become damaged, lift their heads (up) as high as the rising sun,
Let the Tigris and Euphrates bring the waters of abundance,
Let the governors of all cities, every one of them, deliver up to the provider of Esagila and Babylon!"
For countless years shall the praises of the great lord Nergal and the warrior Ishum (be sung):
How Erra became angry and set his face towards overwhelming countries and destroying their people,
But Ishum his counsellor placated him so that he let a remnant!

The one who put together the composition about him was Kabti-ilani-Marduk son of Dabibi.
(Some god) revealed it to him in the middle of the night, and when he recited it upon waking, he did not miss anything out,
Nor add a single word to it.
Erra heard and approved it,
And it was pleasing also to Ishum who marches in front of him.
All the other gods gave praise with him.
And the warrior Erra spoke, saying,
"Wealth shall be piled up in the shrine of the god who praises this song![55]
But whoever discards it shall never smell the incense-offering!
The king who magnifies my name shall rule the world,
The prince who recites the praise of my valiant

[54] Veenhof has pointed out an identical phrase used in an inscription of Merodach-Baladan II, who ruled Babylon in 721-710 and 703 BCE. See Brinkman 1984:49, n. 230.

[55] This and the following lines are paraphrased in the subscripts of plague amulets (Reiner 1960).

deeds shall have no rival,
The musician who sings it shall not die in an epidemic.
The words of it will find favor with kings and princes.
The scribe who learns it will survive even in enemy country, and will be honored in his own.
In the shrine of craftsmen where they ever proclaim my name, I shall make them wise,[56]
In the house where this tablet is placed, even if Erra becomes angry and the Sebitti storm,
The sword of judgement shall not come near him, but peace is ordained for him.
Let this song endure forever, let it last for eternity!
Let all countries listen to it and praise my valor!
Let settled people see and magnify my name!"

(Colophon)

Fifth tablet, series "Erra."
I, Assurbanipal, great king, mighty king, king of the world, king of Assyria,
Son of Esarhaddon king of Assyria, son of Sennacherib king of Assyria,
Wrote, checked, and collated this tablet in the company of scholars
In accordance with clay tablets and wooden writing boards, exemplars from Assyria, Sumer, and Akkad,
And put it in my palace for royal reading.
Whoever erases my written name and writes his own name,
May Nabu, the scribe of all, erase his name.

[56] Lit., "I shall make them open their ears."

REFERENCES

Text: Cagni 1969 and 1977. Translation: Dalley 1989:282-315; Foster *BM* 2:771-805; *FDD* 132-163.

2. HYMNS AND PRAYERS

PRAYER TO MARDUK (1.114)

Benjamin R. Foster

The harmony and effectiveness of this composition set it apart as a masterpiece.

O warrior Marduk, whose anger is the deluge,
Whose relenting is that of a merciful father,
I am left anxious by speech unheeded,
My hopes are deceived by outcry unanswered,
Such as has sapped my courage,
And hunched me over like an aged man.
O great lord Marduk, merciful lord!
Men, by whatever name,
What can they understand by their own efforts?
Who has not been negligent, which one has committed no sin?
Who can understand a god's behavior?
I would fain be obedient and incur no sin,
Yes, I would frequent the haunts of health!
Men are commanded by the gods to act under curse,
Divine affliction is for mankind to bear.
I am surely responsible for some neglect of you,
I have surely trespassed the limits set by the god.
Forget what I did in my youth, whatever it was,
Let your heart not well up against me!
Absolve my guilt, remit my punishment,
Clear me of confusion, free me of uncertainty,
Let no guilt of my father, my grandfather, my mother, my grandmother, my brother, my sister, my family, kith, or kin
Approach my own self, but let it be gone!
If my god has commanded (it) for me, let him purify me as with medicaments.
Commend me into the hands of my (personal) god and my (personal) goddess for well-being and life,
Let me stand before you always in prayer, supplication, and entreaty,
Let the fruitful peoples of a well-ordered land praise you.
Absolve my guilt, remit my guilt!
O warrior Marduk, absolve my guilt, remit my guilt!
O great lady Erua-Sarpanitu, absolve my guilt,
O Nabu of the good name, absolve my guilt,
O great lady, Tashmetu, absolve my guilt,
O warrior Nergal, absolve my guilt,
O gods who dwell <in> Anu's <heaven>, absolve my guilt!
The monstrous guilt that I have built up from my youth,
Scatter it hence, absolve it sevenfold.

Like my real father and my real mother,
Let your heart be reconciled to me.

(40) O warrior Marduk, let me sound your praises!

REFERENCES

Text: Ebeling 1953: No. 61, and duplicates. Translations and studies: Foster *BM* 2:591-593; *FDD* 247f.

PRAYER TO GODS OF THE NIGHT (1.115)

Benjamin R. Foster

The short prayers to the "gods of the night" (i.e., the stars) are among the less stereotypical and more creative liturgical poems of the Akkadian canon. Their individualized variations on a common theme may have been inspired by the setting: typically they were recited (and perhaps composed) at night while praying on the roof of the house and with the surrounding city or countryside asleep; see Oppenheim 1959. [WWH]

The noble ones are safely guarded(?), doorbolts drawn, rings in place,
The noisy people are fallen silent, the doors are barred that were open.
Gods of the land, goddesses of the land,
Shamash, Sin, Adad, and Ishtar are gone off to the lap of heaven.[1]
They will give no judgment, they will decide no cases:
The veil is drawn for the night, the palace is hushed, the open land is deathly still,
The wayfarer cries out to a god, even the petitioner (of this omen) keeps on sleeping!
The true judge, father to the orphaned,
Shamash has gone off to his bedchamber.
May the princely ones of the gods of the night: brilliant Girra, warrior Erra,
The "Bow," the "Yoke," Orion, the "Dragon,"
The Great Bear, the Lyre, the "Bison," the "Horned Serpent,"[2]
Stand by! In the extispicy I perform,
in the lamb I offer, place the truth![3] [a]

[a] 1 Sam 14:41

[1] I.e., sun, moon, (storm) and evening-star have all set.
[2] Various constellations, in many cases still called by their Babylonian names. But Orion is a Greek equivalent for the constellation which the Babylonians called "the true shepherd of Heaven" (SIPA-ZI-AN-NA).
[3] In divination it was crucial that a true answer be obtained, whether by the inspection of the entrails of sacrificial sheep or goats (extispicy) as here, or by the use of the Urim and Thummim as in the Bible (1 Sam 14:41). See Horowitz and Hurowitz 1992.

REFERENCES

Text: Dossin 1935. Translations and studies: *ANET* 390f.; Oppenheim 1959:295f.; Foster *BM* 1:146f.

DIURNAL PRAYERS OF DIVINERS (1.116)

Benjamin R. Foster

As with the immediately preceding selection (above, Text 1.115, note 3), divination (here again by means of the entrails) demanded and relied on a "truthful" answer from the deity. To secure such an answer, the divination priest invoked Shamash and Adad, patrons of divination, here in the company of other great deities. [WWH]

O Shamash, I hold up to you seven and seven sweet loaves,[a]
The rows of which are ranged before you.
O Shamash, lord of judgment, O Adad, lord of divination,
Seated on thrones of [gold], dining from a tray of lapis,
Come [down to me] that you may eat,
That you may sit on the throne and render judgment.
In the ritual I perform, in the extispicy I perform, place the truth!

O Shamash, I hold up to you the plentiful yield of the gods, the radiance of the grain goddess.
O Shamash, lord of judgment, O Adad, lord of divination,
In the ritual I perform, in the extispicy I perform, place the truth!

[a] Exod 40:23; Lev 24:5f.

O Shamash, I have laid out for you the plentiful yield of the gods, the radiance of the grain goddess,
O Shamash, lord of judgment, O Adad, lord of prayer and divination,
In the ritual I perform, in the extispicy I perform, place the truth!
Take your seat, O valiant Shamash,
Let there be seated with you the great gods,
Let Anu, father of heaven, Sin, king of the tiara,
Nergal, lord of weaponry, Ishtar, lady of battle
Be seated with you.
In the ritual I perform, in the extispicy I perform, place the truth![b]

b 1 Sam 14:41

REFERENCES

Text: YOS 11:22. Translations and studies: Goetze 1968; Hallo 1991:144f.; Foster *BM* 1:148-150, *FDD* 288-290.

THE SHAMASH HYMN (1.117)

Benjamin R. Foster

This "preceptive hymn" is one of the "literary prayers" of the Babylonians which rise above the level of standard religious texts by their artful poetic construction and diction. Even the length of the composition (precisely 200 lines) seems carefully and deliberately contrived. The object of the poet's attention is Shamash who, as the all-seeing eye in the daytime sky, plays the role of guardian of justice in Akkadian (as the goddess Nanshe did in Sumerian). In particular he keeps an eye on the merchant travelling far from home and seemingly free of constraints. In the section reproduced here, he is particularly concerned with the merchant's use of honest weights and measures, a perennial theme in ancient Near Eastern literature. [WWH]

Illuminator of all, the whole of heaven,
Who makes light the d[arkness for mankind] above and below,
Shamash, illuminator of all, the whole of heaven,
Who makes light the dark[ness for mankind a]bove and below,
Your radiance [spre]ads out like a net [over the world],
You brighten the g[loo]m of the distant mountains.
Gods and netherworld gods rejoiced when you appeared,
All the Igigi-gods rejoice in you.
Your beams are ever mastering secrets,
At the brightness of your light, humankind's footprints become vis[ible].
You blunt the horns of a scheming villain,
The perpetrator of a cunning deal is undermined.
You show the roguish judge the (inside of) a jail,
He who takes the fee but does not carry through, you make him bear the punishment.
The one who receives no fee but takes up the case of the weak,
Is pleasing to Shamash, he will make long his life.
The careful judge who gives just verdicts,[a]
Controls the government, lives like a prince.
What return is there for the investor in dishonest dealings?
His profits are illusory, and he loses his capital.
He who invests in long-range enterprises(?), who returns (even?) one shekel to the ... [...],
Is pleasing to Shamash, he will make long his life.
He who [commits] fra[ud as he holds the ba]lances,
Who switches weights, who lowers the [...],[b]
(His) profits are illusory, and he lo[ses the capital].
The one who is honest in holding the balance,[c] [...] plenty of [...],
Whatever (he weighs) will be given to him in plenty [...].
He who commits fra[ud] as he holds the dry measure,
Who pays loans by the smaller standard, demands repayment by the extra standard,
Before his time, the people's curse will take effect on him,
Before his due, he will be called to account, he will bear the consequence(?).
No heir will (there be) to take over his property,
Nor will (there be) kin to succeed to his estate.
The honest merchant who pays loans by the [ex]tra(?) standard, thereby to make extra virtue,
Is pleasing to Shamash, he will grant him extra life,
He will make (his) family numerous, he will acquire wealth,
[His] seed will be perpetual as the waters of a perpetual Spring.
For the man who does virtuous deeds, who knows not fraud,
The man who always says what he really means, there will be [...],
The seed of evil-doers wi[ll not be perpetual].
The nay-sayers' speeches are before you,
You quickly analyze what they say.

a Lev 19:15
b Deut 25:13-16; Amos 8:5
c Lev 19:35-36

You hear and examine them, you see through the trumped-up lawsuit.
Each and every one is entrusted to your hands,
You make their omens the right ones for them, you resolve what perplexes.
You heed, O Shamash, prayer, supplication, and blessing,
Obeisance, kneeling, whispered prayer, and prostration.[1]
The feeble one calls you as much as his speech allows him,
The meek, the weak, the oppressed, the submissive,
Daily, ever, and always come before you.
He whose family is far off, whose city is distant,
The shepherd [in] the afflictions of the wilderness,
The herdsman in trouble, the keeper of sheep among the enemy, come before you.
O Shamash, there comes before you the caravan, passing in fear,
The travelling merchant, the agent carrying capital.
O Shamash, there comes before you the fisherman with his net,
The hunter, the archer, the driver of the game,
The fowler among his snares comes before you,
The skulking thief comes before Shamash,
The bandit on the wilderness paths comes before you,
The wandering dead, the vagrant spirit come before you,
O Shamash, you have listened to them all.
You did not hold back(?) those who came before you, you heeded them,
For my sake, O Shamash, do not despise them!
You grant wisdom, O Shamash, to humankind,
You grant those seeking you your raging, fierce light.
[You make] their omens [the rig]ht ones for them, you preside over sacrifices.
You probe their future in every way.[1]
You grant wisdom to the limits of the inhabited world.
The heavens are too puny to be the glass of your gazing,
The world is too puny to be (your) seer's bowl.[d]

d 1 Kgs 8:27

On the twentieth of the month you rejoice with mirth and joy,
You dine, you drink fine brew, the tavernkeep's beer at wharfside.
They pour barkeep's beer for you, you accept it.
You are the one who saved them, surrounded by mighty waves,
You accept from them in return their fine, clear libations.
You drink their sweet beer and brew,
You are the one who makes them achieve the goals they strive for.
You release the ranks of those who kneel to you,
You accept prayers from those who are wont to pray to you.
They revere you, they extol your name,
They(?) praise your greatness(?) forever.

[1] As patron deity of divination, Shamash was the object of the prayers of all who sought to divine the future by one of the numerous techniques developed in Mesopotamia.

REFERENCES

Text: Lambert *BWL* pls. 33-36 and duplicates. Translations and studies: *ANET* 387-389; Lambert *BWL* 121-137; Reiner 1985:68-84; Foster *BM* 2:531-539; *FDD* 254-261.

3. LAMENTATIONS AND ELEGIES

A NEO-BABYLONIAN LAMENT FOR TAMMUZ (1.118)

William W. Hallo

This text, of Seleucid date, laments the destruction of the cities of Sumer and Akkad at the hand of the Gutians, a theme strangely out of place two millennia after their historic incursions. So it either represents a late version of a much earlier original or, more likely, a case of deliberate archaizing.

"Oh grieving women of Uruk, (a) oh grieving women of Akkad,[a] I am laid to rest!"

a Gen 10:10

The goddess of Uruk[1] wept, whose female chair-bearer had departed, (ditto), who has been stripped (even) of her loincloth.
The daughter of Uruk wept, the daughter of Akkad

[1] Both Uruk (Erech) and Akkad appear as cities in the "Table of Nations" (Gen 10). "The goddess of Uruk" is an attempt to render Akk. *urukaītu*, *arkaītu*, "Our Lady of Uruk," which like all the other "goddess of GN" names in the text, refers to local manifestations of Ishtar, whose consort was Tammuz.

was lamenting.
Of the daughter of Larak[2] — her face was shrouded by (her garment down to) its very fringes.
(5) The goddess of Hursag-kalamma wept, who was deprived of her husband.[3]
The goddess of Hulhudhul[4] wept, she who had set up her staff.
The goddess of Siptu[5] wept, whose seven brothers were killed, whose eight brothers-in-law have been laid to rest.[b]
The goddess of Akkad wept, whose shoe-soles were torn, whose lord in whom she delighted was killed.
The goddess of Kesh[6] wept, sitting in the alleyway, she the lord of whose house a lynx had put and end to.
10) The goddess of Dunnu[7] wept: "For whom the couch, for whom the coverlet?
For whom are guarded by me the coverlets, (now) deathly still?"
The daughter of Nippur wept: "It is for the Gutians to finish the task!"[8]
Her cheeks were sore (from weeping), she was deprived of her husband in whom she delighted.
The goddess of Der[9] (wept): "It is for the Gutians to finish (the task!")
(15) She whose city was toppled, whose family broken and violated, (wept):
"(Oh women,) weep on account of Uruk, my headband caught in a thornbush.
As for me, I do not know where I stepped in the tempest.
(Oh women,) weep on account of Larak, I am deprived of my saltier[10] (and) cloak.
My eyes cannot look upon my [...], the ripping of mothers' wombs. (20) (Oh women,) weep on account of Nippur. Silence abides with me.
The heavens have covered me.
My throne has been overturned on me.
Bel has deprived me of my consort, the husband in whom I delighted!"[11]
(A lengthy colophon follows.)[12]

b Mic 5:4; Eccl 11:2

[2] An antediluvian city in Sum. tradition (Hallo 1970:64f. and n. 94).
[3] The reference is to Ishtar of Kish and her consort Tammuz.
[4] Perhaps identical with Hulhullu north of Uruk (Zadok 1985:165).
[5] For Siptu and various toponyms beginning with Siptu, cf. Zadok 1985:279. For the numerical sequence "x/x+1" in ancient Near Eastern literature, see Roth 1962.
[6] Different from Kish (see n. 3).
[7] For Dunnu see above, text 1.112.
[8] Nippur is the ancient religious capital of Sumer and Akkad. For the Gutians as stereotypes of destructive mountaineers from the eastern frontier in first millennium texts, see Hallo 1971b:717-719.
[9] A major city east of the Tigris (Zadok 1985:117f.).
[10] Restoring *lubari* with Lambert. For the translation by "saltier" cf. Hallo and Hoffner *apud* Pope 1970:193. *CAD* E 66d restores *aḫtallup buri* and translates "I am wrapped in a reed mat(?)."
[11] Bel = Marduk, chief deity of Babylon; that city here appears to receive the blame for the misfortunes that have befallen Uruk and the other cities of the south.
[12] See for the colophon Lambert 1983:213; previously Oelsner 1964:263f., n. 7, 268; Hunger 1968:57 No. 146.

REFERENCES

Text: Pinches 1901. Translations and studies: Pinches 1901; Oppert 1901:830ff.; Pinches 1902:477f.; Langdon 1909:263ff., No. XXV; Hallo 1971:718; Lambert 1983; Foster *BM* 2:838f. (largely followed here).

AN ASSYRIAN ELEGY (1.119)

William W. Hallo

Akkadian poets rarely speak of themselves in the first person (for a notable exception see Foster 1983), so it is doubly curious that in this short poetic dialogue, the chief speaker is a woman who has died in childbirth - from all indications a young bride experiencing her first delivery. Her interlocutor is also apparently a woman, perhaps her mother, perhaps a midwife. Their speeches are here indicated by (Mother) and (Bride) respectively; in the original they are at most implied by a change in intonation, a rising inflection elsewhere associated with interrogative sentences.

(Mother:) Why are you cast adrift like a boat in the middle of a river,
Your thwarts in pieces, your mooring rope cut,
Your face shrouded (as) you cross the river of Inner City?
(Bride:) How could I not be cast adrift, my

mooring rope not be cut?
On the day that I bore fruit, how happy I was!
Happy was I, even I, happy my chosen husband![1]
On the day of my labor-pains, did my face grow overcast?
On the day I gave birth, were my eyes prevented (from seeing)?
With opened fists I prayed to Belet-ili:[2]
"You are the mother of women who give birth — save my life!"
When Belit-ili heard this, she shrouded her face, (saying)
"You are [...], why do you keep praying to me?"
[My husband, who lov]ed me, kept uttering his complaint:
["Why do you leave] me, the wife in whom I delight?
[...] in the course of the years
[Have you haunted] a terrain full of ruins?
[In the In]ner City, have you piteously[3] declaimed a lament?"
[All] those days with my chosen husband[1] was I!
I lived with him who was my lover.
(But) death slunk stealthily into my bedroom.
It has driven me out of my house.
It has separated me, even me, from the presence of my chosen husband[1]
It has set my feet into my terrain-of-no-return.

[1] Or: "husband of the preferred wife"; cf. Hallo 1973:167f.
[2] Lit., "lady of the gods," a name for the Mother Goddess, who pleads for her human children in face of the Flood (see Text 1.132 XI 122, below).
[3] Reading *re-miš*, an otherwise unattested adverb from *rêmu*, "to take pity" etc.

REFERENCES

Text: Strong 1894:634. Translations and studies: Albertz 1978:54; Reiner 1978:186f.; 1985:85-93; Livingstone 1989:37-39; Foster *BM* 2:905; *FDD* 329.

4. DIVINATION

Ann K. Guinan

According to a first millennium text from Assurbanipal's library, Enmedurannki, an antediluvian king of Sippar, learned oil and liver divination — the secrets of heaven and earth — directly from Shamash and Adad. He in turn taught these arts to learned men in the cities of Sippar, Nippur, and Babylon.[1] While the sources that attest to Mesopotamian divinatory practices span three millennia, it was not until the second millennium that a written Akkadian literature developed around the observation of omens. Once the recording of omens was instituted, divination began to evolve into a complex, literate, and highly venerated discipline. By the first millennium Mesopotamian scholars applied much of their intellectual energy to the practice of divination and the scholarship associated with the omen collections. They produced a vast written record consisting of lengthy omen compendia,[2] commentaries, instruction manuals, reports, correspondence related to divination, rituals and prayers.[3]

Although typologies of divinatory practices are notoriously difficult to establish (with one form blending into another),[4] it is useful to distinguish three basic types: 1.) *omina oblativa* observation of freely offered or unsolicited omens. 2.) Impetrated divination — various techniques for asking a question and directly evoking a response. There is a conceptual difference between techniques designed to elicit omens (*omina impetrativa*) and the manipulation of divinatory objects such as lots. 3.) mediumistic divination — various practices which utilize a human being as a divinatory vehicle and produce a message in speech or written language. It can involve altered states of consciousness and divine intervention in human cognition. Necromancy, consultation with the dead, is also a form of mediumistic divination. *In all cases, a divinatory vehicle in the material world mediates communication between a sensory and suprasensory realm. Divination operates on a case by case basis to address specific situations.*

Documents from the Old Babylonian period preserve evidence for a variety of different forms of impetrated divination: observing oil as it is dropped into water (lecanomancy),[5] smoke as it rises from a censer (libanomancy),[6] flour

[1] Lambert 1967:132; Vanstiphout and Veldhuis 1995.
[2] An individual omen was formulated as a conditional sentence: the ominous sign recorded in the protasis of the sentence, and the prognostication in the apodosis. Paradigmatic distinctions between contrasts such as right/left; up/down; front/back; top/middle/base; white, black, red, yellow/green characterize the genre.
[3] For a survey of Mesopotamian divination see: Bottero 1974:70-197; Oppenheim 1977:213-227; and most recently, Cryer 1994:124-338.
[4] Peek 1991:11-12.
[5] For bibliography see Cryer 1994:145-147.
[6] For bibliography see Cryer 1994:148.

scattered on water (aleuromancy),[7] and examination of entrails (extispicy).[8] As the tradition developed, scholars increasingly turned to the investigation of unsolicited omens and, except for extispicy, impetrated omens ceased to be part of the standard repertoire.[9] The diviners were attentive to sudden ruptures in pattern, deviations in nature, and to whatever was noteworthy or unusual. While prodigies such as eclipses and monstrous births may have formed the core of divinatory observations, the diviner's attention inevitably extended to lesser details and minutiae of related events. Celestial and meteorological events, abnormal births, behavior of animals, features of the human habitat, attributes of human physiognomy and behavior were studied not as events to be understood for their own sake, but for their cryptic power to signify.

On the surface, none of the divinatory techniques practiced in Israel whether licit, illicit, or falling somewhere in between, bear strong resemblances to the Mesopotamian divinatory traditions. Fully legitimate forms include divining by Urim and Thummim (Num 27:21; Exod 28:15-30), ephod (1 Sam 14:41; 23:6-12) and "inquiring of YHWH" (1 Sam 14:35-37; 22:10-17; 23:1-12; 30:7-8; 2 Sam 2:1). Dreams could be a legitimate means of obtaining knowledge (Gen 28:10-22; Judg 7:13; 1 Sam 28:6; 1 Kgs 3) or they could be misleading and false (Deut 13:2-6; Jer 29:8). The elusive teraphim, household idols or apotropaic figurines, could also have a divinatory function (Hos 3:4; Ezek 21:21; Zech 10). The prohibitions against foreign divination, *qesem*[10] and *naḥaš* in particular (Lev 19:26, 31; 20:6 and Deut 18:10-11, 14), cannot be clearly identified with or connected in any substantial way to specific Mesopotamian forms.

The liver models found at Hazor, Megiddo, Ebla, and Ugarit and the corpus of omen texts recovered from Ugarit[11] clearly attest to a pre-Israelite transmission of Mesopotamian practices to the Levant.[12] While the biblical record preserves clear evidence of familiarity with Mesopotamian practices, there is no biblical corollary to the divinatory texts produced in Mesopotamia.[13] There are a few direct references to Mesopotamian practices (Ezek 21:21; Isa 47:12-13; Dan 5:11). Echoes of, or, perhaps, direct references to Mesopotamian texts,[14] find their way into other conceptually very different genres.[15]

In contrast with Mesopotamia, there was no scholarly tradition associated with divination nor any systematic observation of omens. The signs sent by God (2 Sam 5:24; Judg 7:13-15; 2 Kgs 3:22-23) are significant only in the moment — they never accumulate meaning that carries over from one context to another. All authorized practices are characterized by simplicity and the near presence of God. The divinatory apparatus never becomes disassociated from the divine, it never operates independently, nor does any form take on the artificial quality that long standing practices tend to acquire. Descriptions of specific techniques and paraphernalia are often omitted from the narrative.

Various biblical practices have been explored for a common ancient Near Eastern background or for Mesopotamian parallels. Strong parallels do connect Mesopotamian and biblical accounts of dream interpretation.[16] The texts from Mari provide a rich body of source material for the study of mediated divination.[17] Various scholars have argued a parallel to Mesopotamian extispicy.[18] There are references to necromancy in both the Mesopotamian[19] and the biblical record (1 Sam 28:3-25; Isa 29:4). While they may share a common cultural context, the evidence on both sides is far too limited to make a determination and consulting the dead is such a basic form of divination that ethnographic parallels may be equally valid. Recent scholarship has sought a general Near Eastern background for divinatory forms, such as teraphim, the Balaam Story (Num 22:7) and aspects of the book of Daniel.[20]

A Mesopotamian psephomancy ritual, *LKA* 137 (see text 1.127 below), provides the clearest parallel to biblical divination. The technique of casting stones in a ritual context is a marginal practice in Mesopotamia and represented by a single text. Although there is much to be gained by examining the broader Near Eastern background behind various forms of divination, the contrasts between Mesopotamian and biblical divination are more telling than the parallels.

[7] Nougayrol 1963.
[8] For a discussion of the types of documents relating to extispicy, see: Cryer 1994:168-180.
[9] See: *STT* 73, Reiner 1960 for an unusual first millennium text referring to impetrated practices.
[10] See: Hurowitz 1992a and Sasson 1994.
[11] Meyer 1987.
[12] Dietrich and Loretz 1990.
[13] Hallo 1966:231-232.
[14] Cryer 1994:306-323.
[15] See for example Porter 1983 and Meier 1989.
[16] See: Oppenheim 1956:186-211 and more recently for discussion and bibliography see: Cryer 263-272.
[17] *ARM* 10, AEM 1/1, Ellis 1989:133-140.
[18] Although it is never explicitly described, several scholars have argued that divination by means of animal sacrifice (extispicy) is an implicit part of the repertoire of priestly divination. For bibliography and reevaluation of the sources see Cryer 1994:286-305.
[19] Finkel 1983-1984.
[20] van der Toorn 1990; Horowitz 1992a; Wolters 1993; and Porter 1983.

MESOPOTAMIAN OMENS (1.120)

Extispicy[21] [a]

1. If there is a *Hal* sign at the emplacement of "the well-being" the reign of Akkad is over.[22]
2. If the entire liver is anomalous — Omen of the king of Akkad regarding catastrophe.[23]
3. Omen of Ibbi-Sin when Elam reduced Ur to tell and rubble.[24]
4. If the "rise of the head of the bird" is dark on the left and the right there will be *pitrusta*.[25]
5. When you make an extispicy and in a favorable result there is one *pitrustu* (the extispicy is) unfavorable; in an unfavorable result (the extispicy is favorable).[26]

Behavior of the Sacrificial Sheep[27]

6. If a sheep bites his right foot — raids of the enemy will be constant against my land.[28]

Lecanomancy[29]

7. If (I throw oil (in)to water and) the oil divides itself into two — the sick person will die; for the campaign: the army will not return.[30] [b]

Anomalous Births: šumma izbu[31]

8. If an anomaly has no right ear — the reign of the king will come to an end; his palace will be scattered; overthrow of the elders of the city; the king will have no advisors; the mood of the land will change; the herds of the land will decrease; you will make a promise to the enemy.[32]
9. If an anomaly has no left ear — the god has heard the prayer of the king, the king will take the land of his enemy, the palace of the enemy will be scattered, the enemy will have no advisors, you will decrease the herd of the enemy, he will make a promise you.[33]
10. If an anomaly's right ear is cleft — that ox-fold will be scattered.[34]
11. If an anomaly's left ear is split — that ox-fold will expand; the ox-fold of the enemy will be scattered.[35]
12. If an anomaly has two ears on the left and none on the right — the enemy will take your border city, your adversary will prevail over you.[36]
13. If an anomaly's horns are on the right — the prince will have auxiliary troops.[37]
14. If an anomaly's horns are on the left — the enemy: the equivalent.[38]
15. If a ram's horns protrude from its forehead — that ox-fold will be scattered.[39] [c]

Celestial Divination[40] [d]

16. If there is an eclipse of the moon in Nisannu

a Ezek 21:26; Dan 2:4; 2 Kgs 16:15

b Gen 44:5, 15

c Dan 8:3

d Dan 5:11; Isa 47:12-13; Jer 10:2; Nah 3:16

[21] Extispicy, divination from the examination of entrails, derives from the ritual of animal sacrifice. The offering provides a mode for soliciting the gods and a medium on which they could respond. The practice had a complex and lengthy tradition developed over three millennia and was widely disseminated throughout the ancient Near East. It produced a voluminous and varied textual record consisting of reports, clay models, prayers, and queries. Starr 1990:xiii - lv; Meyer 1987. The process of compiling systematic collections of extispicy omens culminated in the production of the great first millennium series, *Bārûtu*. Jeyes 1989:8-14.

[22] Note the use of a cuneiform sign as an ominous mark. YOS X 61:7; Jeyes 1989:114; The zone of the liver called the *šulmum*, "the well-being," has been identified as a groove running between the umbilical fissure and the gall bladder, see Jeyes 1978. Cf. Lieberman 1977.

[23] TCL 6 1:18. For a discussion of "historical" omens, see Cooper 1980:100; Cryer 1994; Hallo 1991c:160.

[24] *RA* 35 43 no. 8A. The text is inscribed on a liver model from Mari. The model represents the anomaly. For a depiction and discussion, see: Meyer 1987:195; Hurowitz 1992a:5-15.

[25] YOS X 53:17. The term *pitrus/štu* refers to a negative feature occurring in both left and right contexts. In OB omens a *pitrus/štu* renders the omen inconclusive.

[26] CT 20 47:53. In the first millennium series *Multābiltu*, the 10th Tablet of *Bārûtu pitrus/štu* is paired with another ambiguous sign, *nipḫu*, and both terms systematically presented. A *pitrus/štu* is unfavorable in a particular zone, but it will also reverse the reading of a final tally. CT 20 43-48: Jeyes 1989:111; Starr 1976:244.

[27] See Leichty 1993 for a discussion of omen collections dealing with the behavior of a lamb before sacrifice.

[28] Arnaud 1987:320:41-42.

[29] Cryer 1994:145-147.

[30] CT V 4:18; Pettinato 1966 vol 2 17:18; each version has slightly different wording: B: "the army will go on a campaign and not return." D: "the army will not return from a campaign." Cf. Lambert 1967:132.

[31] For biblical parallels from Daniel, see: Porter 1983 and Cryer 1994:320.

[32] CT 27 37:1, Leichty 1970:131:1.

[33] CT 27 37:2, Leichty 1970:131:2.

[34] CT 27 37:3, Leichty 1970:131:3.

[35] CT 27 37:4, Leichty 1970:131:4.

[36] Leichty 1970:139:116′.

[37] Leichty 1970:118:49′.

[38] Leichty 1970:119:50′.

[39] Leichty 1970:171:87′ K3823+.

[40] The celestial omens were systematically collected and compiled into the series *Enūma Anu Enlil*, "When Anu Enlil ..." The most comprehensive and best preserved version of the series come from Assurbanipal's library at Nineveh. Unlike extispicy, this form of divination is not well documented in the Old Babylonian period. The growth of the discipline and its increasing importance at the Neo-Assyrian court occurred as part of the shift to observational forms of divination, Rochberg-Halton 1988:5-29; Van Soldt 1995. See Walker, Galter and Scholz 1993 for bibliography.

and it is red — prosperity for the people.[41]

17. If Venus wears a black tiara (it means) Sa-[turn(?)] stands in front of her.
If Venus wears a white tiara (it means) J[upiter] stands in front of her. ...
If Venus wears a green tiara (it means) Mars stands in front of her.
If Venus wears a red tiara (it means) Mercury stands in front of her.
[Co]mmentary to the 61st Tablet of Enuma Anu Enlil.[42]

The Human Habitat: šumma ālu[43]

18. If a city lifts its head to the heaven — that city will be abandoned[44] [e]
19. If a city's garbage pit is green — that city will be prosperous, variant: go to ruin.[45]
20. If there are many messengers in the city — dispersal [of the city.] [46]
21. If a man repairs a moon-disk — his god wil[l always shepherd him] steadfastly.
22. If there are bearded women in a city — hardship will seize the land.[47]
23. If in a man's house a dog is inscribed on the wall — worry [...] [48] [f]
24. If everything for a banquet in the temple is regularly provided — the house will have regular good fortune.[49]
25. If a god enters a man's house for a banquet — constant uprising and contention will be constant for the man's house.[50]
26. If syrup is seen in a house or on the walls of a house — the house will be devastated.[51]
27. If the house makes the sound of a kettle-drum — [...][52]
28. If a man repairs a moon-disk — his god wil[l always shepherd him] steadfastly.[53]
29. If a man repairs a sun-disk — his god wil[l always shepherd him] steadfastly.[54]
30. If a king repairs (the statue) of the god — the god will [...] [55]
31. If a man sees the body of a king — t[hat] man [...] [56]
32. If there is black fungus in a man's house — there will be brisk trade in the man's house; the man's house will be rich.[57]
33. If there is green and red fungus in a man's house — the master of the house will die, dispersal of the man's house.[58] [g]
37. If a snake crosses from the right of a man to the left of a man — he will have a good name.[59]
38. If a snake crosses from the left of a man to the right of a man — he will have a bad name.[60]
39. If a white cat is seen in a man's house — (for) that land hardship will seize it.
If a black cat is seen in a man's house — that land will experience good fortune.
If a red cat is seen in a man's house — that land will be rich.
If a multicolored cat is seen in a man's house — that land will not prosper.
If a yellow cat is seen in a man's house — that land will have a year of good fortune.[61]
40. If "mountain grass" is seen [in a fie]ld inside the city — the field will become fallow, that man will die.[62]
41. If the linen curtain of a temple (in front of the cult statue) looks like a figure — those who have entered that temple will go out and never (re)enter the door.[63] [h]

e Gen 11:1-9
f Dan 5:5
g Lev 14:33

[41] Labat 1965:70 144; ACh Sin 25:10, 12, 17. Cf. Stol 1992:157. The series, *Iqqur īpuš*, uses signs that parallel *Šumma ālu* and *Enūma Anu Enlil* but organizes them according to a calendar of auspicious and inauspicious dates. Tablet 17 and 18 of *Enūma Anu Enlil* and *Iqqur īppus* 70-74 preserve parallel lunar eclipse omens, the former organized by phenomena and the latter by month; see: Rochberg-Halton 1988:139.

[42] K148 r 8-12, 30; *Ach Supp*. Ištar 36:8-12; Pingree 1993:265-266.

[43] The omen series *Šumma ālu* is a collection of terrestrial omens observed against the background of the human environment. At the present time, the only sources are Gadd's copies (CT 38-41) and the text edition based on them by Nötscher 1928-1930. There is, in addition, a general introduction to the series by Moren 1978. See also: Guinan 1989.

[44] CT 38 1:15: for discussion see: Guinan 1989:234.

[45] CT 38 2:38; Note that the var. gives an inauspicious meaning.

[46] CT 38 4:80.

[47] CT 38 5:124, cf. CT 29 48 53; note that the goddess Ishtar can be bearded; see: Reiner 1995:6. Cf. *ACh Supp*. 33:41.

[48] CT 38 16 83; CT 40 1:18.

[49] CT 40 11:86 plus joins to K2685+.

[50] CT 40 5:38 plus joins to K268+

[51] CT 40 2:27.

[52] K268+ 8.

[53] CT 40 11 ii 76. Cf. Stol 1992:247.

[54] CT 40 11 ii 77.

[55] CT 40 8:1; CT 40 10:ii 57.

[56] CT 40 9; Rm.136:13.

[57] CT 40 16:43.

[58] CT 40 18 83; Caplice *Or* 40 (1971) 144-146; Cryer 1994:317-319; *ABL* 367; Oppenheim 1967:167; *JEOL* 32 (1991-92) 65 n. 157.

[59] KAR 386 10.

[60] KAR 386 11.

[61] CT 39 48:5-9.

[62] CT 39 3:20, cf. CT 38 5:140. Cf. Veldhuis 1990; Reiner 1985:94-100.

Cledonomancy (from šumma ālu)[64]

42. If a kledon (a divinatory sound) answers a man yes twice — deferment (of meaning).[65]
If a kledon answers yes three times — it is a firm yes.[66]
If a kledon answers no to a man two times — attainment of desire
If a kledon answers no to a man 4 times — *nipḫu* (indeterminate meaning).[67]
If a kledon answers a man on his right — deferment (of meaning)[68]
If a kledon as a pig answers a man to his face — no attainment of desire.[69]
If a kledon (as) a bird answers a man to his face — yes, truly, his prayer will be g[ranted].[70] [i]
43. If a man scrapes dirt from his nose — his adversary will submit [to him.][71]
44. If a man breaks a drinking vessel from which he is drinking — for three days lamentations [will befall him].
So that (the evil) not approach: he should throw its shards in the river and then [it will] not [approach him.][72]
45. If a woman, her husband dies and a son of her fat[her-in-law marries her — that man will be rich][73]
46. If a man "goes" (i.e., has intercourse) to a woman lying on (her) back and her feet go around the back of his neck — wherever he goes god, king, and noble will be agreeable.[74]
47. If a man "goes" (i.e., has intercourse) to his brother's daughter — wherever he goes [there will be] sh[ortages].
So that (the evil) does not approach: Say thus, "God, my strength!" [and then it will not approach him.][75]
48. If a man "goes" to the daughter of his brother's daughter — [he will lay his hand] on whatever is not his; he will have profit; the family [will be rich].[76]
49. If a man has sexual relations with an old woman — he will quarrel daily.[77]
50. If a man ejaculates in his dream and is spattered with his semen — that man will find riches; he will have financial gain.[78] [i]
51. If a man has anal sex with a man of equal status — that man will be foremost among his brothers and colleagues.[79] [k]
52. If a man divorces his first-ranking wife — unhappiness (until) the end of days, quarrelling will be constant for him, his days will be short.[80]
53. If in a man's house, a ghost enters the ear of the mistress of the house — mourning will take place in the man's house.[81]
54. If a severed head laughs — conquest of the army [...].[82]
55. If a man laughs in his sleep — he will become very sick.[83]
56. If a man grinds his teeth (while sleeping) — he will experience troubles.[84] [l]

h Exod 26:1

i 1 Sam 14:8-12; 1 Kgs 20:30-35; Judg 7:13f

j Lev 15:16-17

k Lev 18:22; Lev 20:13

l Deut 18:10-11; Lev 19:31; 20:6-7, 1 Sam 28:6-14; Isa 8:19; 2 Kgs 21:6; 1 Sam 3

[63] CT 39 33:51, 40 46:11.
[64] Oppenheim 1954-1956; 1956:210-211; Finet 1982.
[65] CT 39 41:4.
[66] CT 39 41:5.
[67] *CAD* N/2 s.v. *nipḫu* 3.a. "unreliable, false prediction" A divinatory response that cannot be resolved and leaves the inquirer without guidance can in itself be a negative omen (cf. Starr 1983; Jeyes 1989:88-89). See above, n. 26, for a discussion of the terms *nipḫu* and *pitrus/štu* in the series *Multābiltu*.
[68] CT 39 41:15.
[69] CT 39 42:30 (plus unpubl. dups.).
[70] CT 39 42:32 (plus unpubl dups.).
[71] CT 37 47:17.
[72] CT 37 48:7.
[73] CT 39 43 K3677 4-5′.
[74] K8268+, AMT 65:3. From Tablet 103. The coital positions recorded in Tablet 103 correspond to the positions represented on erotic plaques, figurines, and seals; see: Cooper *RlA* 4:259-270. Cf. Scurlock, 1993 "Lead Plaques and Other Obscenities," *NABU* 1993/1:15.
[75] CT 39 43 K3134 3′-4. Omens in this group deal with intercourse with a female relative and her daughter.
[76] CT 39 43 K3134 6′.
[77] CT 39 43 K3134 10′; CT 39 44:1.
[78] CT 39 45:26; cf. 45:25; 44:9-10; 38 r.13; van der Toorn 1985:32.
[79] CT 39 44:13; MAL A 19/20; Olyan 1994.
[80] CT 39 45:39. *LU* 9, *LH* 137-141, MAL A 37.
[81] CT 38 26:33: Abusch 1995.
[82] K6229 8′ (unpublished); CT 29 48:2, CT 40 46:51, CT 41 22:19. Communication with the dead could also be impetrated. See Finkel 1983:1-17. Whether apparitions of the dead are taken as omens or contact is deliberately sought, it is not uncommon to look to the dead for divinatory information. Mesopotamian necromancy rituals attest to the practice of deliberately provoked communication for the purposes of divination. The ritual produces a vision which allows the inquirer to see and speak with a ghost. Another type of ritual enables a skull to be used as a medium of speech; Finkel 1983-84.
[83] Cf. K9739+ 9 (and dupls); CT 37 49:9; Köcher and Oppenheim 1957-58:74:9 The belief that laughing in one's sleep is a sign of sorrow is widespread and occurs in a variety of historical contexts. For a discussion see, Köcher and Oppenheim 1957-58:62 n. 13 and Guinan 1990:12.
[84] K9537+ 10′. See "If a sheep grinds his teeth ..." Arnaud 1987:321:4. Omens from human behavior share many parallels with omens derived from the behavior of a sheep before sacrifice. See note 27 above.

Oneiromancy[85] [m]

56. [If] (he dreams) that a dog rips his [garment] — he will experience losses.[86]
57. If a man (dreams) he kisses his penis — what he says will find acceptance; whatever he desires will not be withheld from him.[87]

Physiognomic Omens[88] [n]

58. If a mole is very white — that man will become poor, very [...]

m Jer 23:25; 1 Sam 28:6; Gen 40:1-23; Dan 2:1-49; Judg 7:13f.; Deut 13:2-6

n Lev 13

59. If a mole is very green — ditto [...]
60. If a mole is very red — he will be ri[ch][89]
61. If his garment hangs down and is marked with white blemishes — garment of deprivations.[90]
62. If the walls of a house are dotted with very white (spots) — the master of that house will die a death of violence.[91]
63. If a man (while speaking) bites his lower lip — (his word?) will find acceptance.[92]

[85] Oppenheim following Artemidorus, the Roman dream interpreter, distinguishes between message dreams and symbolic dreams. Both types can be divinatory. Message dreams in which a deity is solicited (often in a sanctuary) and speaks in response is a form of mediumistic divination. Mediumistic dreaming was practiced at Mari; see: Sasson 1983; and in later at the sanctuary of Arbela; see: Oppenheim 1956:188, 200, 249; for more recent bibliography see: Ellis 1989:147. Oblated dream omens are collected in the canonical series, *[d]Zaqiqu*; see Oppenheim 1956. The text, named for the god of dreams, is a divinatory interpretation of dream symbols. In some cases the omens are similar to observations made while awake and in other cases they have a fantastic quality befitting of dreams. There is also evidence for the practice of impetrating symbolic dream omens, but this form of dream incubation was peripheral and rare, see: Reiner 1960:27,33:61-70, 34:82-84.

[86] This omen comes from a poorly preserved sequence of omens in the Series, *[d]Zaqiqu*, which concern dreams about clothing. K9812+ 10862 Oppenheim 1956:292, 336; Oppenheim 1969:158-159.

[87] From the Susa version of dream omens, MDP 14 55 4. i 20-22; Oppenheim 1956:258.

[88] Omens dealing with human physiognomy were collected in the series *Šumma alamdimmû* which concerns,according to the ancient scribe, Esagil-kin-Apli, "external form and appearance and they imply the fate of man," Finkel 1988:149:29. There are various subseries such as *Šumma kataduggû* which reads outer traits and body language for clues to deeper aspects of personality and *Šumma liptu* which collects omens related to moles.

[89] Kraus, *AfO* Beiheft 3:53: r.26-28. Cf. Köcher and Oppenheim 1956-1957:66:42-45.

[90] Köcher and Oppenheim 1956-1957:6-7; for a discussion of the term *pūṣu*, "a white patch," see: Jeyes 1989:91.

[91] CT 38 15:49.

[92] CBS 4501 r 53, Kraus 1937:233, Cf. Bryce 1975. See also: If a sheep bites his upper lip ... CT 31 33:10.

REFERENCES

Abusch 1995:588-593; Arnaud 1987; Biggs 1969:73-74; Bottero 1974:70-197; Bryce 1975:19-37; Cooper *RlA* 4:259-270; 1980; Cryer 1994; Deitrich and Loretz 1990; Ellis 1989:127-186; Finet 1982:48-55; Finkel 1983:50-57; 1983-84:1-17; Goetze 1968:25-29; Greenberg 1991:267-271; Greenfield and Sokoloff 1989:201-214; Guinan 1989:227-235; 1990:9-14; 1996a:61-68; 1996b; Hallo 1966:231-242; 1991:267-271; Horowitz and Hurowitz 1992:95-115; Hurowitz 1992a:5-15; Huffmon 1983:355-359; Kraus 1936-37:219-230; 1939; Köcher and Oppenheim 1957-58:62-77; Jeyes 1980:13-32; 1989; Labat 1965; Lambert 1967:126-139; Leichty 1970; 1977:147-154; 1993:238-242; Leiderer 1990; Lieberman 1977:147-154; Long 1973:489-497; Meier 1989:184-192; Meyer 1987; Moren 1980:53-70; Notscher 1928-30:39-42, 51-54; Nougayrol 1963:318-384; Olyan 1994:179-206; Oppenheim 1954-56:49-55; 1956; 1967; 1969:153-165; 1977; Pettinato 1966; Pingree 1993:259-273; Porter 1983; Reiner 1960:23-35; 1995; Rochberg-Halton 1988; Sasson 1983:283-293; 1994:39-40; van Soldt 1995; Starr 1976:241-247; 1983; 1990; Stol 1992:245-276; van der Toorn 1990:203-222; 1985; Vanstiphout and Veldhuis 1995:30-33; Veldhuis 1991:28-44; Walker, Galter, and Scholz 1993; Wolters 1993:291-306.

5. INCANTATIONS

OLD BABYLONIAN INCANTATION AGAINST CATTLE DISEASE (1.121)

D. O. Edzard

(1) There was a whirl[wind] in the sky,
(2) A fire was kindled,
(3) And the "peg"[1] fell
(4) On all the cattle.
(5) It was infected with heat
(6) The kids and the lambs
(7) And also the small ones on the nurse's shoulder.[2]
(8-9) Address my mother Ningirim.[3]
(10) Let the face of the cattle be bright again,
(11) Let Sumuqan rejoice,[4]
(12) Let the herbs rejoice,
(13) Let the trail resound[5] with merry bleating —
(14-16) (Then) I will most carefully apply lots of little sun disks to the seats of the great gods.
(17) Incantation of sheep infected with the "peg."

[1] The illness called "peg" (*sikkatum*) has not yet been identified beyond doubt; "constipation" has been suggested.

[2] As in the modern Middle East, children sat astride on their mother's or nurse's shoulders.

[3] This is an abbreviation of the formula describing how a messenger is sent to a deity who is an expert in matters of incantation.

[4] God of cattle.

[5] Lit., "let the trail jubilate."

REFERENCES

van Dijk, Goetze, and Hussey 1985:Number 7.

---

6. RITUALS

RITUALS FROM EMAR[1]

Daniel Fleming

THE INSTALLATION OF THE STORM GOD'S HIGH PRIESTESS[2] (1.122)

This text combines length and variety with minimal loss by tablet breaks to provide the best point of entry for reading Emar rituals. The translation offered here follows the principal tablet, which is large and neatly inscribed, with only one major break on the front side. Four further copies are represented by other fragments, so it is evident that the text had attracted special interest in the diviner's training system, along with the collected *kissu* festivals.[3] Sections of the text are marked by horizontal lines drawn across the tablet, though these vary in position from copy to copy. The whole festival centers on the installation itself, which begins on the third day and continues through a seven-day feast, with the priestess settled in her new residence on the last day. A distinct preparatory rite of shaving occupies a day to itself before the installation, and the priestess is designated by lot on the opening day. This unique installation text combines wedding imagery with more widely applied rites for consecration to temple service, but it does not display the sexual aspect attributed to the *hieros gamos* or sacred marriage. For the sake of simplicity, the text presented here draws from multiple copies with bias toward the fuller version (text A), usually without comment.

Heading (line 1)
Tablet of rites for the high priestess of Emar's storm god.[4] [a]

Day 1: The Day of Selection (lines 1-6)
When the sons of Emar[b] elevate the high priestess to the storm god, the sons of Emar[b] take lots[c] from the temple of NINURTA and grasp them before the storm god.[5]
The daughter of any son of Emar may be designated.
On the same day they take fragrant oil from the palace and from NINKUR's temple and place it on her head.[6] [d]

a Exod 29; Lev 8
b Ezek 23:1-5; Joel 4:6
c Lev 16:8; Num 26:55, 34:13; Josh 14:2; 18:6; Esth 3:7;9:24
d Exod 29:7; Lev 8:12; 1 Sam 10:1; 16:13
e Deut 32:51; Isa 30:29
f Num 6:9, 18
g Ezek 46:4, 6; Neh 5:18

They offer before the storm god one sheep, one quart jar, and one standard vessel of wine.[7]
They give the diviner one shekel of silver.
They send back to NINURTA's temple eight dried cakes and one standard vessel along with the lots.[c]
During the consecration of the shaving ceremony they consecrate all the gods[e] of Emar with bread and beer.[8]

Day 2: The Day of Shaving (lines 7-21)
The shaving[f] of the high priestess falls on the next day.
One ox and six sheep[g] proceed to the storm god's temple as the sacrifice of the high priestess. The

---

[1] The following translations take considerable liberties with Emar vocabulary in order to provide a rendition not continually burdened with transliterated terms of unknown or uncertain meaning. Notes to the text provide brief rationale for many of the choices made, some of which cannot be close to literal, especially for the multitude of vessels and breads presented for offerings. Lineation likewise is less precise than strict adherence to the Akk. word order would allow, for the sake of clarity.

[2] See Arnaud 1986 no. 369 (Hereafter *Emar*); Dietrich 1989; Fleming 1992.

[3] In addition to Fleming 1992, Dietrich 1989 examines the copying of this text at some length. On the *kissu* festivals, see below.

[4] The "high priestess" is written with the Sum. NIN.DINGIR, read in one lexical text as *ittu*, evidently derived from the Akk. high priestess *entu* (Fleming 1990). This figure occupies the highest position in a Mesopotamian temple, originally the human wife of a god, as the *ēnu* priest was husband of a goddess. Emar's storm god is rendered by the Sum. ^{d}IM, which in different settings may have been read as Baal (Baʿlu) or Addu.

[5] The god written by Sum. ^{d}NIN.URTA serves as divine authority in conduct of local legal affairs, alongside human elders. This defines him as "city god," like the original Ninurta of Nippur, but some native divine name is likely covered by the Sum. writing. It is not clear what specific divinatory technique is indicated by "grasping" the lots.

[6] The goddess ^{d}NIN.KUR is prominent in Emar ritual though not so in wider Mesopotamia. Again, the Sum. writing likely covers a native Semitic name.

[7] The "quart" refers to the size of the *quʾû* vessel, and the "standard" recalls the fact that the *ḫizzibu* vessel serves one meal for one person in the feasts, below, just as the *naptanu* provides one serving of bread for one meal. The derivation of the word *ḫizzibu* remains uncertain.

[8] The usual term for consecration (root *qdš*) here refers not to preparation of new statues for sacred use but only the more immediate preparation for participation in one sacred event.

[9] The divine weapon is specified elsewhere as the divine axe, lit., "the axe of the god(s)." No particular deity is associated with this sacred implement, which seems to serve the divine sphere more generally.

divine weapon and the high priestess follow them, while the singers walk in front.[9] [h]
When they reach the storm god's temple, they shave the high priestess at the entrance of the courtyard gate.[i]

[...] they perform a sacrificial homage[j] before the storm god.[10] Her father carries the divine weapon for the sacrificial homage on her behalf.

After they finish the Greater Sacrificial Homage, they give the diviner (one?) shekel of silver, and they sacrifice the one ox and the six sheep before the storm god.

They set before the gods the ritual portion of beef and the ritual portion of mutton.[11]
They set before the gods seven standard loaves,[12] seven dried cakes, and two dried cakes with fruit.
They fill goblets with wine.[k]

The officials who give the consecration-gift(?), the heralds(?), and seven [and seven Hamšaʾu-men] eat and drink at the storm god's temple.[13] [l] The men of the consecration-gift(?) receive one standard loaf and one standard vessel of barley-beer each.

The clan head[14] [m] slaughters one sheep at his house. Once he cooks it, they set five tables with three standard loaves each at the gate of the storm god's temple, in the room of the high priestess.

One[n] table is for the previous high priestess.[15]
One table is for the high priestess of Šumi.
One table is for the war-priestess.[16]
One table is for the king of the land of Emar.
One table is [for the king of Šatappi].

On them they set out the mutton and one dried cake with fruit each.
(The tables) receive one jar of barley-beer each and one presentation vessel of barley-beer each.[17]

They offer to all the gods of Emar one standard loaf each, one standard vessel of barley-beer, thick bread,[18] cedar oil, and fruit, which they distribute among the gods.

Just before evening,[o] they take fragrant oil of NINKUR's temple and of the palace, and the diviner pours it on the head of the high priestess[d] at the gate of the storm god.
When the men of the consecration-gift(?) leave the storm god's temple, they bring her [into the house of her father].

The Consecration of the Installation Proper
(lines 22-28)[19]
On the consecration day of the installation, they consecrate all the gods of Emar [with bread and beer].
They lay NINKUR in the house of (the high priestess's) father, [take] the red wool[p] vestment of [NINKUR's] temple, and put it on NINKUR.
They set four tables before the gods.[q]

They set one table for the storm god,
one table for [...],
and [two tables] on the ground for the underworld gods.[20]
On them they set out twelve fat loaves, [...], and standard loaves, four dried cakes each, and four dried cakes with fruit each.[21]

For seven days ...

h Josh 6:4, 8; Ps 68:26
i Lev 8:4
j 2 Chr 32:33
k Exod 29:40; Lev 23:13; Isa 65:11
l Exod 24:11
m Exod 22:7; Judg 19:22-23
n 1 Sam 20:5, 25, 29
o Exod 12:6; Lev 23:5
p Exod 25:5
q Exod 25:23, etc.; Isa 65:11

[10] The "sacrificial homage" is a *kubadu*, which usually designates a combination of offerings more generally, but here is focused at the moment of presentation, before actual slaughter of the animals. The *kubadu* offering is evidently characterized by this presentation ceremony, which only happens to be detailed here because of responsibilities that shift from the father to the new priestess.

[11] The noun *parṣu* (GARZA) means "ritual," but in this context refers to a specific portion of sacrificed meat, apparently determined by ritual standard.

[12] Just as the *ḫizzibu* represents a standard allotment of drink for one person at one meal, so the *naptanu* provides one portion of bread at a single "meal."

[13] These participants are all unique to Emar ritual. "The officials who give the consecration-gift(?)" (*šarrū nādinū(ti) qidaši*) include at least the diviner and the singers, perhaps along with the king (lines 54-55, 83). Use of the verb *nadānu* need not suggest that these figures fund the festival; on the contrary, they are described only as recipients of payments. Instead, the role may relate to the statements from the administrative sections of other festival texts that the king, the diviner, and the chief scribe consecrate the gods with bread and beer; see Fleming 1992:160; and Dagan's *kissu* festival, *Emar* 385:25-26, (text 1.126) below. The "consecration-gift" would then be the *qidašu*. The "heralds" are *ḫussū*, from the root *ḫss* "to bring to mind," associated with oath-taking in Mari letters.

[14] Lit., "lord of the house." This is not a sacred profession, and may instead identify a one-time festival sponsor.

[15] If the installation takes place at the death of a high priestess, this offering is then posthumous. No calendar indicates any annual occasion, and the text ends with arrangements at time of death.

[16] The *mašʾartu* is not known outside Emar. Her installation text places her in service of Aštart-of-Battle, and a rare verb *šaʾāru* means "to conquer," from which the noun may be derived.

[17] The *maḫḫaru* vessel is derived from the verb *maḫāru*, "to face," which can refer to both presentation and reception of offerings. This translation adopts "presentation" to distinguish it from the common Emar offering verb *naqû* (originally, "to libate").

[18] "Thick bread" is the Hittite sense of NINDA.GUR$_4$.RA, whose Emar reading is not certain.

[19] Advance "consecration" for the installation begins the day before the installation proper just as consecration for the shaving began one day prior to that ceremony. Apparently because NINKUR stays in the father's house through the whole installation feast, this text section anticipates the seven days which begin on the installation day itself.

[20] Lit., "the gods below."

[21] The fat loaves, *aklu ebû*, appear to be distinct from the NINDA.GUR$_4$.RA, "thick bread," unless the first represents a syllabic equivalent of the second.

They fill goblets with wine.
[They offer] one ox, one sheep, seven standard vessels of wine, and two bushels [of barley to ...].[22]

They set before the gods the ritual portions of the ox and of the sheep, the heads[r] of the ox and one sheep, and seven standard vessels of barley-beer.

Day 3: The Installation (lines 29-48)
The installation[s] of the high priestess falls on the next day.[23]
One ox [and six sheep[g] proceed to the storm god's temple as the sacrifice of the high priestess]. The divine weapon and the high priestess follow them, while the singers walk in front.[h]
They perform the Greater Sacrificial Homage[j] [before the storm god]. The high priestess (herself) carries the divine weapon for the sacrificial homage.
After [they finish the sacrificial homage], they purify the ... and bring (the priestess) into the storm god's temple.

[They sacrifice] the one ox and the six sheep [to the storm god, and ...].
The high priestess travels in procession with the divine weapon and the singers.

[They enter the House of Trust, and (provide) one lamb] for Adammatera.[24]
After they leave the House of Trust they go to the House of Fortune.[t] (There,) they [sacrifice one lamb to the storm god] and one lamb for the upright stone of Hebat.[25]
The high priestess pours fragrant oil on the top of Hebat's upright stone.[u] On that day (the stone) enters the House of Fortune, but (the high priestess) must not do so.[v]

They return, and at the storm god's temple they set before him the ritual portions of the ox and of the six sheep.[26]

They set before the storm god seven standard loaves, seven dried cakes, and two dried cakes with fruit.
They fill goblets with wine and barley-beer.[k]

Since the men of the consecration-gift(?) and heralds(?) (act as) the servers and the attendants, they may eat and drink as (the storm god's) servers and attendants.
They set up five tables in the room of the high priestess('s mourning).[27]
Just as for the Day of Shaving.[28]
Just before evening, they seat the high priestess on her throne,[w] set before her a new table from her father's house, and set bread on it.

They put on her ears two gold earrings[x] from her father's house, put on her right hand the storm god's gold ring,[y] and wrap her head with a red wool headdress.
They offer fragrant oil for the storm god.
They put in the diviner's hand a ten-shekel silver coil.[29]

Two of her brothers[30] carry her on their shoulders as she proceeds to the house of her father.

The town elders fall at her feet and present her a seven-shekel silver clasp as her (official) gift.
Her brothers likewise present her lavish gifts.
The divine axe follows her, while the singers walk in front.[h]

Then once she has entered her father's house, they set the divine axe on NINKUR for seven days.
On the same day, they offer one standard loaf each, one standard vessel of barley-beer each, thick bread, and the meat of NINKUR's ox,[31] and distribute them among all the gods of Emar.
On the third day of the high priestess' ... festival, the wailing woman gives forth her cry.[32] [z]

Days 3-9: The Seven-Day Feast (lines 49-58)
For seven days[aa] they sacrifice daily two sheep to the gods on behalf of Hebat in the (temple) room (of the high priestess).[33]

r Lev 1:8, 12
s 2 Kgs 11:12 = 2 Chr 23:11; 2 Kgs 23:30
t Gen 30:11; Isa 65:11
u Gen 28:18; 31:13; 35:14
v Lev 9:23
w 1 Sam 1:9; 4:13
x Ezek 16:12
y Gen 24:22; 41:42; Ezek 16:11, 42
z Judg 11:40; Jer 9:16, 19; Ezek 32:16
aa Lev 8:33-35; 9:1, 23

[22] The *parīsu* is a large dry measure, translated roughly as "bushel," without intending equivalent size.
[23] The word translated "installation" is *malluku*, lit. "to make rule." This use of the common Semitic root neither assumes kingship as in West Semitic nor counsel as in East Semitic Akkadian. It should be noted that enthronement is central to the installation (lines 40, 51, 84), a possible point of contact with kingship.
[24] The *bīt tukli* is associated with the domain of the city-god NINURTA and may serve some administrative function.
[25] The "House of Fortune" is the *bīt Gadda*, a term that may anticipate the Gad from Roman Syria. Hebat's stone is a *sikkānu*, also attested at Ugarit and elsewhere in early Syria.
[26] Text B diverges through the sacrificial homage and the processions to the House of Trust and the House of Fortune. Essentially, B reverses the homage and the processions, which allows the homage to serve as direct preparation for sacrifice, as it did on the Day of Shaving.
[27] Text B repeats "the room of the high priestess" from the Day of Shaving, but text A adds a further detail, *bīt bukki* NIN.DINGIR, where *bukki* might be understood as "weeping," in reference to mourning for the previous priestess. The priestess's room in the temple is still given to mourning until the end of the festival transition, when the new priestess takes up residence.
[28] This abbreviation indicates completion of the feast according to the pattern above.
[29] Or in text B, two gold *lamassu*-figurines of one gold shekel weight. The *lamassu* is a Mesopotamian protective spirit.
[30] Brothers may allow a wider range of male kin, as would the sister below.
[31] Texts B and D mention oils and cedar.
[32] This installation day does represent the third day of the festival counted so far, but the term *datnātu* (*tadnātu*?) remains obscure; perhaps, from *nadānu*, "to give?"
[33] Lit., this line reads, "to the gods to her house to Hebat." The translation offered here locates the offering in the priestess's room, and conceives sacrifice divided between the primary recipient Hebat and the collective gods, as is performed for the storm god and the gods, above.

Every day they set before the gods a ritual portion of the meat and the two heads of the sheep.[r]

For seven days[aa] they offer daily at the storm god's temple the heart and the lungs of one sheep, one large standard loaf, one dried cake with fruit, one pot of barley-beer, and one presentation vessel of wine.

When the high priestess is enthroned at her feast, she must present to the storm god and Hebat two gold figurines of one shekel weight.

They sacrifice one lamb to Šaḫru.[bb]

The seven and seven Hamšaʾu-men[cc] eat and drink for two days in the room of the high priestess, and give her one bushel of barley-flour each with one jug of malt beer.[34]

In addition, the men of the consecration-gift(?) eat and drink for seven days in her room, receiving seven standard loaves and seven standard vessels of barley-beer each.

The previous high priestess, the high priestess of Dagan Lord of Šumi, the war-priestess, the king of the land of Emar, and the king of Šatappi — their tables, together with beef, mutton, seven dried cakes with fruit, seven pots of barley-beer, and (seven) presentation vessels of barley-beer supply the seven days.

The haunch is for the (past) high priestess of the storm god.

The hock is for the high priestess of Dagan Lord of Šumi.

The boiled meat[dd] is for the war-priestess.

The kidney[ee] is for the king of the land of Emar.

The kidney is (also) for the king of Šatappi.

Day 9: The Final Day (lines 59-75)

[Text disturbed at lower edge of tablet.][35]

... They raise up NINKUR and send NINKUR's red wool vestment back to her temple along with bread and beer.

When the high priestess leaves the (family) house, they cover her head like a bride[ff] with a bright sash from her father's house.

Her two maids[gg] embrace her like a bride.[hh]

bb Isa 14:12
cc 1 Sam 8:12; cf. 2 Kgs 1:9
dd Num 6:19
ee Lev 3:4-5, etc.
ff Gen 24:65
gg Judg 11:37; Ps 45:15;
hh Isa 49:18; 61:10
ii Gen 15:17
jj 2 Kgs 4:10
kk Gen 47:31
ll Gen 19:2; 1 Sam 25:41; 2 Sam 11:8

Just before evening, one ox, seven sheep, three lambs, along with a torch[ii] and the singers proceed in front of her, while the divine axe follows behind.

She enters the House of Trust to sacrifice one lamb for Adammatera.

After she leaves the House of Trust she proceeds to NINKUR's temple. (There,) she sacrifices one lamb to NINKUR and sets out three standard loaves for the gods.

After she leaves NINKUR's temple she proceeds to the temple of the storm god.

(There,) she sacrifices one lamb to the storm god, sets seven standard loaves before the gods, and fills goblets with wine.[k]

The men of the consecration-gift(?) and the town elders follow, to eat and drink at the storm god's temple.[l]

They send back to the house of the clan head[m] the above ox and seven sheep which proceeded in front of the high priestess.

After the town elders have eaten and drunk, they give one fine robe as her garment, as well as one bed, one chair, and one footstool.[jj]

On this bed they spread one Akkadian blanket from her sacred wardrobe.[36]

They set up Hulelu's table at the entrance to its head[37] [kk] and set on this table three standard loaves each, one dried cake with fruit, one standard vessel of wine, and a woven garment.

The singers chant for Hulelu and perform the rites of this table.[38]

Then her sister washes her feet,[ll] and they place one silver ring of half-shekel weight in the water that washed her feet, which her sister receives.

The high priestess ascends her bed to lie down.

Administration (lines 76-94)

On the seventh day, the men of the consecration-gift(?) slaughter at her father's house the one ox that proceeded in front of the high priestess and divide it among themselves.[39]

The representative of the king of the land receives the kidneys of the ox plus his share.[40]

---

[34] The Hamšaʾu-men remain obscure; the root *ḫmš* recalls the leaders of "fifty" in the Bible, as well as the Old Assyrian *ḫamištum*, an administrative body — though Emar ritual excludes the possibility of five members. The "jug" is called *anatu*, and may be sizeable, to match the large volume of barley.

[35] Text B mentions a "last day" (*ūmi arki*), and this entire section deals with a single closing day. Line 59 combines broken elements of separate idioms: offering, filling chalices, and feasting, without clear sense. Line 60 resumes the legible text.

[36] Lit., "of the pure house/room of her bed."

[37] This picture might envision a bed with a screen, which would have an opening.

[38] The idiom *parṣī leqû* can mean "to perform a ritual." Otherwise, the statement could be translated, "and receive the ritual portion of this table." See also Dagan's *kissu* festival, *Emar* 385:23 (text 1.126) below.

[39] This number seven counts the days of the feast, so that the seventh day is the final day of the last procession, when the ox was still left alive. Text C reads "eight," either counting the Day of Shaving or locating this slaughter one day after the proper end of the festival in line 75, unless the scribe was simply in error.

[40] Text A has "the man of the king" rather than the king directly.

The diviner receives the half-cut[41] plus his share, the head, the intestines, the fat, and the hide.
The singers receive the lungs plus their share.
The men of the consecration-gift(?) eat half of its intestines.

Among the four tables which they set up for the gods, two of them are pure tables and two impure.

The diviner and the singers divide among themselves (as follows):
The diviner and the singers also divide among themselves the hides of all the sheep.[mm]
The diviner receives the three ox hides.
For the seven days, the diviner and the singers receive one standard loaf and one pot of barley-beer each.

The diviner receives the half-cut of the oxen and the sheep for all the days.
The singers receive the lungs of all the oxen and the sheep.
They distribute the meat of the ox sacrifice among the gods.

When the high priestess is enthroned at her banquet, five shekels are the gift for the diviner and one shekel is the gift for the singers.
In a good year, they give her from the House of Trust thirty bushels of barley. In a bad year, she receives fifteen bushels of barley.
From the House of the Gods they give her six hundred (shekels) of wool, two jars of oil, one juglet of oil, four hundred (shekels) of aromatics, five store-jars of wine,[42] two racks of grapes, two racks of apples, two racks of apricots, one pot of milk, one large (pot) of soured milk, one bushel of emmer, one bushel of aromatics, three quart jars of malt beer, two pairs of sandals, two pairs of boots, two gazelles, two fish, and four pigeons — per annum.

When the high priestess goes to her fate,[43] they slaughter one ox and one sheep at the temple.[44]
They offer to Šaḫru[bb] one sheep, one juglet of oil, a standard vessel, and two ...

The diviner receives the hide of the above ox.
One sheep ...

These items belong to the house of her father. The town (gets) nothing.

[mm] Lev 4:11; Exod 29:14

[41] The meat *ḫaṣītu* might be related to the Hebrew words for "half."
[42] "Store-jars" translates *ḫubu*, probably a larger vessel for wine.
[43] That is, she dies.
[44] It is not certain which location is in view; the larger temple would be the appropriate place of sacrifice, rather than the residence ("room") of the priestess.

THE *ZUKRU* FESTIVAL (1.123) [1]

In a culture that generally observed two axes in the turn of the year, at spring and autumn, the term "new year" is often too loosely applied. Nevertheless, the Israelite feasts of Unleavened Bread and Booths and the Mesopotamian *akītu* festival do occupy these key turning points in the annual cycle, with special significance for public religious commitments. Emar's *zukru* festival provides a first early Syrian representative of this practice, attested in one primary tablet, with a badly broken alternative text, and various related fragments of indeterminate relation to these two tablets.

The shorter, broken *zukru* tablet displays a simpler, perhaps older annual event, which the large tablet translated here has magnified into by far the most lavish rite in the Emar collection. In this expanded form the *zukru* is celebrated every seventh year, with one year's preparation, under a "festival" rubric omitted from the short text. This *zukru* festival is divided into two parts, one focused on offering and the second focused on procession. They repeat the same calendar, which allows restoration of missing dates. Whereas the shorter form shows provision only from "town" supplies evidently administered outside the palace, the long *zukru* festival introduces extensive royal sponsorship. In spite of this evidence of the king's ambition, the festival itself gives him no active role, and the event preserves an ancient dedication of the town to its chief god Dagan at a shrine of stones outside the city walls that recalls Dagan's rule before construction of the town and its temples.

This large *zukru* tablet is composed in four columns, neatly inscribed.

[1] See *Emar* 373.

Part I, Offerings (lines 1-173)
Column I

First Month of 6th Year (lines 1-6)
[8-10 lines missing at top][2]
... one pure lamb ...
... from its midst ...

24th Day of Niqali (Second Month), 6th Year (lines 7-13)
[During the month of Niqali] on the 24th day, they distribute to all the gods from the king one(?) gallon of barley bread, two store jugs of ...[3]
They enclose [one sheep for Dagan Lord of the] Firstborn;[a]
likewise one sheep for the storm god, one sheep for the Sun, [one sheep for Dagan,[4] one] sheep for Ea, one sheep for the Moon,[5] one sheep for NINURTA,[6] [one sheep for Nergal] Lord of Trade, one sheep for the Lord of the Horns,[7] one sheep for NINKUR,[8] [one sheep for Bēlet-ekalli], one sheep for Aštart of the Warrior — these sheep ... they enclose.[9]

25th Day of Niqali, 6th Year (lines 14-34)
[During the month of Niqali on] the 25th [day], all the gods and the Šaššabēyānātu-spirits [go out (in procession).][10]
... Dagan Lord of the Brickwork goes out, his face covered.
Two calves and six sheep from the king, with [two(?) sheep] from the town, proceed in front of Dagan.
They offer to Dagan from the king one gallon and one quart of (barley-)mash bread, [one quart] of barley bread, one flagon and one bowl(?) of wine.[11]
(Additionally,) one gallon and one quart of (barley)-mash bread, [one quart] of barley bread, one flagon, and one jar are provided by the House of the Gods.
One gallon of (barley-)mash bread, four gallons of [barley bread, and four] store jugs are provided for the people.
They sacrifice to Dagan one calf and one pure lamb.
Among them, from precious stones ...[12]
They offer to NINURTA:
two sheep from the king and one from the town;
one gallon and one quart of (barley-)mash bread, one quart of barley bread, one flagon and [one] bowl from the king;
one quart of (barley-)mash bread and one jar from the House of the Gods.
Šaššabētu of NINURTA's temple goes out (in procession) to the Gate of the Upright Stones.[13]
They offer to Šaššabētu:
one calf and six sheep[b] from the king, and one sheep from the town;
one gallon and one one quart of (barley-)mash bread, one quart of barley bread, one flagon and one bowl of wine from the king;
one gallon and one quart of (barley-)mash bread, one quart of barley bread, and one flagon from the House of the Gods.

a 1 Sam 6:10, 14
b Ezek 46:4, 6; Neh 5:18

[2] This section is almost entirely lost, with the date restored by comparison to Part II. The "first month" is written SAG.MU, "the head of the year."

[3] The BÁN equals something more than a gallon, and the QA (cf. *quʾû*, previous text, note 7 above) roughly a quart. Translation is not intended to capture precise amounts but general effect. Measures appear to derive from the grain required to produce the stated breads, so liquid measures are appropriate for the pots that served such accounting. The "store jug" is a large vessel for beer, the *pīḫu*.

[4] The offering to "Dagan" without title should be addressed to his primary temple, distinct from the special festival cult as "Lord of the Firstborn." Identification of Syrian Dagan as the mountain Šadû (^{d}KUR) makes suggested connection with the Hebrew Šadday more attractive. Note that this offering list is restored from the near-equivalents in lines 66-78 and the god list *Emar* 378.

[5] The moon god is written ^{d}30, and has unknown reading. Equation with Šaggar occurs in seals with Hittite hieroglyphs, but in ritual texts that god is spelled syllabically or by ^{d}ḪAR. Mesopotamian Sîn and Canaanite Yariḫ are alternatives. The sun god is rendered ^{d}UTU, also with uncertain local reading; "Sun" and "Moon" reflect this ambiguity.

[6] NINURTA is Emar's city god (see the installation of the storm god's high priestess, [text 1.122] above).

[7] This title reflects another cult of Nergal.

[8] See text 1.122, note 6 above for NINKUR.

[9] Provision of these animals is described by the term *paʾādu*, "to enclose," not usually used for offering. In the text for six months' rites (below), the *paʾādu* offerings precede the principal event by one day, in some kind of preparation. Enclosure may have originally represented consignment for sacrifice rather than the slaughter itself.

[10] The Šaššabēyānātu-spirits are female divine beings collectively associated with the city god NINURTA via the single goddess Šaššabētu. Both titles may derive from the verb *wašābu*, "to sit, reside," so that these are spirits separate from the pantheon of gods and perhaps inhabit the city for its care, like the later Syrian Tyche.

[11] This translation attempts a variety of English terms for diverse breads or confections from grains and various vessels for drink. In many cases, the true character of the item remains obscure, with only a hint of size or status. In this text the ḪA (flagon), *ḫubbar* (jar), and *kurkurru* (bowl) are the common vessels, entirely unlike the high priestess installation. The *ḫubbar* is the one vessel in this set clearly derived from Hittite ritual practice. Likewise the (barley-)mash bread (*pappāsu*) and barley bread represent a completely different set of foodstuffs.

[12] The "precious stones" occur in one other Emar fragment, not evidently for tools, monuments, or identification with divine presence. This translation guesses a smaller scale, with function entirely unclear.

[13] One upright stone (*sikkānu*) is associated with the storm god's consort Hebat in the installation of his high priestess.

They bring out Bēlet-ekalli, and the Moon and Sun of the palace in procession to the Gate of the Upright Stones.[14]

One calf and ten sheep from the king proceed in front.

They offer before (these gods) three gallons and three quarts of (barley-)mash bread, three quarts of barley bread, three jars and three bowls of wine.

One gallon of (barley-)mash bread, four gallons of barley bread, and four store jugs (of drink) from the palace are provided for the people.[c]

Total: four calves and forty sheep for the consecration.[15]

After eating and drinking they rub all the stones[d] with oil and blood.[e]

In front of the Battle Gate they perform a sacrificial homage[f] for all the gods with a ewe,[g] two pair of thick loaves made of (barley-)mash bread, and one jar from the king.

That one ewe is to be burnt for all the gods.

The breads, the beverages, and the meat go back up into the town.[h]

14th Day of First Month, 7th Year (lines 35-40)

During the next year they perform the *zukru* festival.

During the First Month, on the 14th day,[i] they enclose for all the seventy[j] gods[a] of Emar seventy pure lambs from the king, ..., thick bread, oil, and three store jugs.

They give seven of those sheep to the seven sowing-men of the palace.[16]

They enclose one calf and one lamb for Dagan Lord of the Firstborn.[a]

Also the people and the gods go out in procession a second time on the later day of the *zukru* festival.[17]

They enclose the same (for) the others.[18] [a]

15th Day of First Month, 7th Year — Start of zukru (lines 41-60)

They perform (the *zukru* festival) on the next day, the 15th[k] or Šaggar-day.[19]

They bring out Dagan Lord of the Firstborn, NINURTA, Šaššabētu of NINURTA's temple, Bēlet-ekalli, the Moon and Sun of the palace, all the gods and the Šaššabēyānātu-spirits ... in procession to the Gate of the Upright Stones.

[(A number of calves and pure lambs)] from the king and ten lambs from the town proceed in front of Dagan.

They offer to Dagan:

[one gallon and quart] of (barley-)mash bread, one quart of barley bread, one flagon and one bowl of wine from the king;

[one gallon and one quart of (barley-)mash bread, one quart of] barley bread, and one flagon from the House of the Gods.

[One gallon of (barley-)mash bread, four gallons of barley bread,] and four store jugs from the House of the Gods are provided for the people.[c]

(They offer to NINURTA:)

[(a number of calves and lambs) from] the king, and two lambs from the town;

one gallon and one quart of (barley-)mash bread, one quart of barley bread, [one flagon, and one] bowl from the king;

one quart of (barley-)mash bread and [one] jar from the House of the Gods.

They offer to Šaššabētu:

[(a number of calves and lambs)] from the king, and two lambs from the town;

[one gallon and one quart] of (barley-)mash bread, [one quart of barley bread, one] flagon and one bowl of wine from the king;

one gallon and one quart of [(barley-)mash bread], one quart of barley bread, and [one flagon] from the House of the Gods.

They offer to Bēlet-ekalli, and the Moon and Sun of the palace:[14]

[(a number of calves and)] lambs from the king;

three gallons and three quarts of (barley-)mash bread, [three quarts] of barley bread, three jars, and [three bowls] of wine from the king.

After eating and drinking they anoint the upright stones[d] with oil and blood.[e]

Just before evening,[l] they bring the gods back up into the town.[h]

[In front] of the Battle Gate they perform the Lesser Sacrificial Homage.[f] They burn for all the gods one ewe,[g] one jar, and [two] pairs of (barley-) mash breads from the king.

[The breads, the beverages], and the meat go back up [into the town].[h]

c Exod 32:6
d Gen 28:18; 31:13; 35:14
e Exod 29:21; Lev 8:30
f 2 Chr 32:33
g Num 6:14
h Exod 9:29, 33; Josh 6:16, 20; 2 Sam 15:24-25
i Exod 12:6, 18; Lev 23:5; Josh 5:10; Ezra 6:19; 2 Chr 30:15
j Exod 1:5; 24:1, 9; Num 11:16, 24, 25; 2 Kgs 10:1, 6, 7; Ezek 8:11
k Lev 23:6, 34; 1 Kgs 12:32-33
l Exod 12:6; Lev 23:5

[14] The name Bēlet-ekalli here parallels the Moon and Sun "of the palace" as Lady of the Palace, all associated with a purely royal donation.

[15] The consecration (*qaddušu*) usually occupies one day directly before a ritual event. This consecration counts the sheep for both the 24th and 25th of Niqali, and the whole preparation is separated from the *zukru* proper by nearly a year.

[16] "The men of the sowing" (so, *zirʾatu*) appear only in a ritual role, but an autumn setting might make sense of this interpretation as time for planting preparations.

[17] The enclosure suggests equivalence with the sixth day of the *zukru* festival proper (line 200), not the last and seventh day.

[18] The "others" appear to be the rest of the pantheon represented by the idealized figure "seventy," after Dagan is specified first.

[19] Šaggar is equated with the writing ᵈ30 for the moon god in Hittite hieroglyphic seals, but Emar rituals associate Šaggar more narrowly with the full moon, and the autumn (September/October) full moon in particular.

15th-21st, First Month, 7th Year — Seven-Day Feast (lines 61-151, 168-173)[20]

Column II

[13-15 lines missing]

... they perform.

... of the eight sacrificial homages ...

... jar(s), pomegranates, birds from the king ...

For the seven days[m] of the *zukru* festival they serve all the gods of Emar.[21]

[They offer] to Dagan Lord of the Firstborn:

one calf and ten pure lambs, one gallon and one quart of (barley-)mash bread, one quart of barley bread, one [flagon], and one bowl from the palace.

To the storm god, just as to Dagan [Lord of the Firstborn];
To Dagan — ditto;
To Ea — ditto;
To the Moon and Sun — ditto;
To NINURTA — ditto;
To Alal [and Amaza — ditto];[22]
To Nergal [Lord of Trade — ditto];
To Nergal [Lord of Horns — ditto];
To NINKUR, [Šaggar, and Ḫalma — ditto];
To Bēlet-ekalli — [ditto];
To Aštart of the Š[ubu(?) — ditto]
To the Moon of the Palace [— ditto]
To the Sun of the Palace [— ditto]
To Dagan of the Palace [— ditto]
To Aštart of [...];
To Aštart of [...];
To Aštart of [...];
To ....

Five lambs from the king; one quart of (barley)-mash bread, one quart of barley bread, and [one flagon from the palace]:

To Dagan Lord of ... — ditto;
To two Dagan Lord of Creation,[23] [n] two pairs — [ditto];
To Anna of ... [— ditto];
To Dagan Lord of the Camp, just as for Dagan Lord of ... [— ditto];
To Dagan Lord of Habitations — ditto;
To Aštart of the Abi and Yāmu, two pair — ditto;
To ...;
To Aštart of ... — ditto;
To Išḫara Lady of the Town — ditto;
To Išḫara of the King — ditto;
To Išḫara of the Prophetesses[o] [— ditto];
To Hanana of the Palace — ditto;
To Hanana of the city — ditto;
To Udḫa — ditto;
To Aštar — ditto;
also to all these gods, vessels....[24]

Two lambs from the king; one quart of (barley)-mash bread, one quart of barley bread, and one jar [from the palace]:

To the Lord of the Hill-Country — ditto;[25]
To Dagan Lord of the Valley — ditto;[26]
To Dagan Lord of Šumi — ditto;[27]
To Dagan Lord of Buzqa — ditto;
To Dagan Lord of Yabur — ditto;
To Aštart of ... — ditto;
To ... of the House of Trust — ditto;
To ...;
To ...;
To two ...;
To Mu- ...;
To Šaggar ...;
To the Lord of Akka ...;[28]
To the Lord of Imar;[29]
To the Storm God Lord of ...;
To Gašru ...;
To the Lord of Shade and Protection [p] ...;[30]
To the Lord of Buzqa ...;
To the Lord of Yabur ...;
To the Lord of the Fortress(?) [q] ...;[31]

Column III

[To the Seven Couns]elors of the Seven Gates — ditto;[32]
To ... — ditto;
To the Seven — ditto;
To Halaba — ditto;
To the Lord of Šagma — ditto;
To the Storm God of Mount Bašima — ditto;
To Nawarni — ditto;

m Exod 23:15; Lev 23:6, 34, etc.; Deut 16:3, 13, etc.

n Gen 14:19; Exod 15:16; Deut 32:6

o Exod 15:20; Judg 4:4

p Ps 121:5

q Deut 32:10

[20] My revised text omits lines 152-167 based on combination of fragments from the original edition. Column IV is left to begin with line 168, by the original numbering.

[21] The verb *palāḫu*, "to fear," is used to define obligation of service in Emar contracts, and the offerings listed here represent a similar concrete service to the gods, rather than worship or reverence simply as attitudes of the mind.

[22] The beginning of this list can be restored by comparison to lines 9-12 at the opening of the *zukru* festival text (above p. 432) and to the start of the god list *Emar* 378.

[23] Dagan *bēl qūni* may be related to the El title "Creator of the earth" (*qn ʾrṣ*, as in the biblical citations).

[24] Some otherwise unattested vessel is indicated: ^{dug}*ḫar-de-e-x*.

[25] Bēl Gabʾa, cf. Hebrew *gibʿâ*?

[26] Bēl Amqi, cf. Hebrew *ʿēmeq*?

[27] Šumi, Buzqa, and Yabur are villages in the Emar region, attested elsewhere in the rituals and beyond.

[28] Cp. *Emar* 452:54, but the reading here is uncertain.

[29] This title is restored by comparison with the god list *Emar* 378:25, though the reading remains uncertain. Imar appears to be the older vocalization for the town of Emar, as found in the early second millennium and before.

[30] This name is restored by comparison with line 138, below.

[31] Cp. line 139, below.

[32] This name appears in the god list *Emar* 378:41.

To two pair of Baliḫ-River Deities of the Palace Garden — ditto;
To NINURTA of the Burnt Offerings — ditto;[33]
To the Storm God Lord of Imar — ditto;
To NINURTA Lord of … — ditto;[34]
To Aštart Lady of Ani — ditto;[35]
To the Baliḫ-River Deities of … — ditto;
To NINKUR Lady of the Wadi — ditto;
To NINKUR Lady of the Circle — [ditto];
To Dagan Lord of Shade and Protection [p] — ditto;
To Dagan Lord of the Fortress [q] — ditto;
To the Balih-River Deities of … — ditto;
To the Lord of Rabbâ — ditto;[36]
To NINKUR Lady of the Quiver — ditto;
To Dagan Lord of the Quiver — ditto;
To Dagan Lord of … — ditto;
To the Sarta clan deity — ditto;
To NINKUR of the Gate of the Sarta clan — [ditto];
To the Storm God of the House of Fortune — ditto;
To the Upright Stone of Hebat [d] — ditto;[37]
To the Lord of …;
To …;
To …;
[26-30 lines broken, to end of column]

Column IV

21st Day, First Month, 7th Year — Day 7 of Seven-Day Feast (lines 168-173)[38]

…the wagon [of Dagan [r] passes] between [the upright] stones, his [face] uncovered.
He proceeds [to] NINURTA, whom they have mount (the wagon) [with] him.
The divine [weapon] follows him.[39]
When they reach the Battle [Gate], they perform the Lesser Sacrificial Homage. [f]
They burn for all the gods [one ewe, two] pair of thick loaves, and [one] jar from the king.
They anoint the stones [d] [with oil and blood]. [e]
… tamarisk to the gods …

Part II, Procession[40]

Heading (lines 174-175)

When the sons of Emar [s] give the *zukru* festival [to] Dagan Lord of the Firstborn during the seventh year:[41] [t]

15th Day, First Month, 6th Year (lines 175-184)

During the sixth year, in the First Month, on the 15th [day],[k] the Šaggar-day, they bring out Dagan Lord of the Firstborn in procession, his face uncovered.
They perform the Lesser Sacrificial Homage [f] before [him] at the Gate of the Upright Stones.[u]
After they sacrifice, eat, and drink, they cover his face.
The wagon of Dagan passes between the upright stones.[u]
He proceeds to [NINURTA], whom they have mount (the wagon) with him, their faces covered.

[On] the same day, they purify all the oxen and the sheep.
On the same day, once they bring out [all the] gods, just before evening they bring out Šaggar … from NINURTA's temple, from the House of Trust.[42]
Also, the [breads and the meat which were before (all) the gods] go back up into the midst of Emar.[43]

25th Day of Niqali, 6th Year (lines 185-190)

During the month of Niqali, [on the 25th day,] they bring out [Dagan] Lord of the Firstborn and all the gods in procession to the Gate of the Upright Stones.[44]
His [face] is covered for both his departure and his return.
From that day, the calves, the pure lambs, …
The wagon of Dagan passes between the upright stones.
He proceeds to NINURTA;
also the breads and the meat which were before the gods go back up into the midst of the town.

14th and 15th Days of First Month, 7th Year (lines 191-199)

During the next year, in the First Month, on the 14th day,[i] they distribute the enclosed lambs [a] to the gods.
On the next day, the 15th [k] or Šaggar(-day), they

r 1 Sam 6:7, etc.; 2 Sam 6:3
s Ezek 23:15; Joel 4:6
t Deut 31:10; cf. Lev 25:4, etc.; Deut 15:1, etc.
u Ps 24:7-10

[33] [d]NIN.URTA *ša ma-qa-li*, where the last element may be related to *maqlû*, "burning."
[34] Arnaud (1986) set a fragment below the main tablet from lines 151-167 to produce additional material for the list, but this fragment joins the main tablet for lines 133-151. This translation simply skips lines 152 to 167 in order to join Arnaud's enumeration at line 168, for clarity of comparison.
[35] Compare Eni, in the god list *Emar* 378:44.
[36] Rabbâ(n) is the home village of the royal family.
[37] The Storm God of the House of Fortune (*bēt Gadda*) and the Upright Stone (*sikkānu*) of Hebat reflect the installation of the high priestess, with the stone she anoints.
[38] Lines 168-173, rejoining Arnaud's lineation (1986), conclude Part I at the top of column IV.
[39] There is room for a word or two after this sentence, though no addition makes good sense.
[40] The impression of two distinct parts of the text is confirmed by a space of approximately 8 lines left uninscribed before resumption of what follows.
[41] Compare the first line of the high priestess installation and Dagan's *kissu* festival.
[42] Perhaps another deity is brought out with Šaggar. There is room for one name.
[43] This line is restored from the 25th of the month of Niqali, below.
[44] Restoration follows the parallel to Part I for the sixth year, above.

bring out Dagan Lord of the Firstborn along with all the gods and the Šaššabēyānātu-spirits in procession to the Gate of the Upright Stones.[u]

Dagan's face is covered for his departure.

They give to the gods the offerings as prescribed on the tablet.

They bring out in procession Dagan the very father [v] and Šaggar on the same day.

Also, the Šaggar(-day) breads for all Emar go back up.

Just before evening,[l] Dagan passes between the upright stones.[u]

They cover his face.

In the Battle Gate they perform the rites just as for the consecration day.[45]

The breads and the meat which were before the gods go back up into the town.

20th Day, First Month, 7th Year — Day 6 of Seven-Day Feast (lines 200-201)

On the sixth day they distribute the enclosed lambs[a] to the gods, just as (mentioned) previously.[46]

21st Day, First Month, 7th Year — Day 7 of Seven-Day Feast (lines 202-209)

On the seventh day Dagan, along with all the gods and the Šaššabēyānātu-spirits, goes out in procession, his face covered.

They give the ritual requirements[47] to the gods just as for the day (mentioned) previously.

All the meat and breads, everything which they eat, from the [seven] days and from between the upright stones they take up and [place] in return.[48]

Nothing goes back up into the midst of the town.

After the fire,[w] just [before evening] ...

They uncover Dagan's face.

The wagon of Dagan passes between the upright stones.

He proceeds to NINURTA, [whom they have mount (the wagon) with him.]

They perform the rites just as for the day (mentioned) previously.

Part III, Administration

Heading (line 210)

... they consecrate[x] the *zukru* festival ...

[14-16 lines missing to bottom of column IV]

Summary Statement (lines 211-212)

Left edge

Total: 700 lambs, 50 calves.

Twelve calves to the gods ...

v Deut 32:6; Isa 63:16; 64:7; Jer 3:4, 19; 31:9; Mal 1:6; 2:10

w Gen 15:17

x Exod 20:8; Deut 5:12; Joel 1:14; 2:15

[45] This statement should refer to the description in lines 31-34 for the 25th of the month of Niqali.

[46] This reference seems to be to the last preparation day when lambs were enclosed, the 14th of the First Month.

[47] Lit., "rites."

[48] "Return," *tūrtu*, is a technical term for treatment of ritual provisions at the end of the festival, not attested in this use outside Emar.

SIX MONTHS OF RITUAL SUPERVISION BY THE DIVINER (1.124) [1]

This tablet belongs to a separate type entirely from the previous two festivals. It is much smaller, especially relative to the material squeezed onto it, and is written in a cramped script with distinct sign forms. Instead of treating one ritual event, this text gathers diverse rites for unrelated cults, apparently united by involvement of the official who calls himself the diviner.

The tablet is divided into four columns. The first treats one month and the last covers four; the third touches two months, the earlier one evidently completed on the same day left at the end of column I. Although certainty remains elusive, the text most likely was created to address six months from fall to spring, one half-year between the major ritual axes of the calendar. The full moon of the first month, defined as autumn by preparation for sowing at the top of column III, dominates the text with several concurrent events, likely including a simpler annual observance of the *zukru* (lines 8-10, for Dagan).

Column I

Heading (line 1)

[Tablet of the] rites of the town.

Month of Zarati, 8th Day (lines 2-6)

[The month of Zarati:]

[On] the 8th day, ...[2]

... one sheep

... from ...

... at the temple ...

... they gather.

[1] See *Emar* 446.

[2] Zarati is the month for celebration of the *zukru* in annual form, rather than SAG.MU, "the head of the year," in the seventh-year festival. The unusual scribal hand of the six-month tablet matches that annual *zukru* text, and column III of this text alludes to autumn sowing and the god Šaggar, who is associated specifically with the *zukru* full moon.

Month of Zarati, 14th Day? (lines 6-7)

On the [14th] day, [they enclose a lamb for Dagan].[3] ...

Month of Zarati, 15th Day (lines 8-57)[4]

On the 15th day,[a] Dagan [goes out in procession ...][5]

They give ... a sheep from the fire-lighters ...[6]
The ...-men [feast].[7]

On the same day, [NINURTA of the] Amit [Gate] goes out in procession.[8]

They give ... (to someone, some provision) from the House of the Gods.
... a sheep from the fire-lighters [proceeds in front of him].
The divine axe [follows him], and the whole populace ...
They place the ...

On (a day ...), they enclose (a lamb) ...
On the [same] day ...[9]

... goes into the great gate of (some god's) temple ...[10]
... two sheep in the temple ...
(Some participants) feast on bread and beer from the House [of the Gods].

On the day ..., they enclose[b] [a lamb at] the temple of NINURTA.

[NINURTA] goes out in procession to the great gate.
An ox [(and sheep?)...] proceed in front of him.[11]
...
[The diviner][12] receives the right breast[c] for ...
The hide, the head, ... belong to the diviner.
The chiefs and the men of the countryside eat [and drink] (some food).[13]

In the temple of (NINURTA or Išḫara) ... they slaughter the ox.

[They give (some parts) to] NINURTA of Išḫara's temple.
They offer (some part).
The ...-meat and the hocks are for the leaders, and they give [the ...-meat] to the slaughterer.[14]
The kinsmen of Udḫa's temple receive (some part).
The leaders and the whole populace eat the breast before Išḫara.
The diviner receives the head.[d]
They place ...
The divine axe ...

Column II [40 lines, only some traces at right edge]

Column III

... they slaughter these sheep.
He offers their ..., along with the breast-meats.[15]
The divine axe follows them.
Also, the hides of the sacrificed (animals) belong to the diviner.

On the 15th day,[a] they bring Šaggar down to the cattle barn, and (perform) sacrifice.

They slaughter one sheep at the horse stables.

On the same day,[16] in the evening, they bring out (a procession).

They slaughter one sheep for the fire-lighters, one sheep for the Garden of the Storm God's Pool, and a sheep for Dagan Lord of the Seed.
The diviner casts down seed.
...-bread from the House of the Gods, cups (of drink), and the meat of the right breast belong to the diviner.

On the next day at dawn[17] ... they slaughter (a sacrifice) for Dagan and perform sacrificial homages[e] for lasting days(?) and difficulty(?).[18]

Until they finish the sacrificial homages, no one may go out to plant.[19]

Month of NINKUR (lines 58-74)

The month of NINKUR:

a Lev 23:6, 34; 1 Kgs 12:32-33
b 1 Sam 6:10, 14
c Lev 7:31, 34
d Exod 12:9
e 2 Chr 32:33

[3] This speculative restoration follows the common preparation by "enclosure" through this text, sometimes one day in advance of the main rite.
[4] The numbering system follows the first edition's count of legible lines and omits the 40 lines of column II.
[5] This would match the time for the *zukru*, and should represent the same event.
[6] The noun *nuppuḫannu* appears to derive from a verb "to kindle." Some keepers of flocks are intended, and the title might refer to nighttime responsibilities.
[7] Lit., "eat." This would fit the likely function of human participants in other parts of the tablet.
[8] The deity can be restored from the offering list *Emar* 274:6.
[9] This does not begin a new line, and appears to represent the same day.
[10] The subject is some single figure.
[11] Compare line 107, below.
[12] The diviner receives this portion in lines 52-53.
[13] The leaders are "great men" (lúGAL, LÚmeš GAL, see line 38), and appear to be associated with the people of the countryside.
[14] Several words for sacrifice occur in the Emar rituals. The common western root *zbḥ*, "to slaughter for sacrifice," appears only in this noun.
[15] "Their *nību*-meat" represents an unknown portion.
[16] Lit., "the same month," but the idiom and context indicate a day, and this should reflect scribal error.
[17] This movement to the next day is not treated here as a new calendar definition, but an extension of the 15th. The statement is not set at the start of the line.
[18] These are the *kubadu* ceremonies found in the installation and the *zukru* festival, above. The homages are not for gods but for some result, possibly as translated (text: *a-na* UŠ-*ma da-ri-ia u a-na da-na-ni*(?)).
[19] Lit., "no planter may go out."

On the 17th day they enclose [b] a lamb for NINKUR.

On the 18th day NINKUR goes out in procession.

One fine white sheep (comes) from the fire-lighters.

Bread and beer from (some person) the men of the consecration-gift ... [eat and] drink.[20]

Contract-bread[21] ... ghee,

in the contract-bread ...

the diviner ...

the diviner ...

a lamb ...

[on the] 19th [day] ...[22]

... [proceeds] in front.

[The divine axe follows] behind.[23]

...

[5-7 lines missing]

...

... a sheep to (some god) ...

... a sheep to (another god) ...

... one sheep to ...

...

Column IV[24]

Month of Anna (lines 77-82)

The month of Anna:[25]

The fire-lighters, along with the Hamšaʾu-men[f] give [bread] and beer to Adammatera.[26]

One sheep for the Abi[27] of the House of the Gods, one sheep for the temple of Dagan, and one sheep for the town — these sheep (come) from the fire-lighters.

The diviner receives these hides.

Month of Adamma (lines 83-85)

The month of Adamma:

The return-ceremony of Illila falls on the 7th day.[28]

The return-ceremony for all the gods falls on the 8th day.

Month of Marzaḫāni (lines 86-95)

The month of Marzaḫāni: [g]

The Buqaratu fall on the 14th day.[29]

On the 16th day she goes out in procession from the crossroads.[30]

A sheep (comes) from the town.

Also, the divine axe follows from the crossroads.

The Hunt of Aštart falls on the same day.[31]

The Hunt of the Storm God falls on the 17th day.

They burn at the Hurrian(?) temple one sheep from the fire-lighters.[32]

The Marzaḫu-men [g] of the fellowship(?) bring a standard loaf to the gods.[33]

Half of the one sheep belongs to the diviner.

Month of Halma (lines 96-119)

The month of Halma:

On the second day they perform sacrificial homages at the temple of Dagan.[34]

In the evening they fill goblets with wine and burn a bird.[35]

The New Moon[h] of Dagan falls on the third day.[36]

One sheep (comes) from the town.

The divine axe takes up residence in the temple.

The sheep's hide belongs to the diviner.

On the 8th day Halma goes out in procession.

The divine axe follows after him.

One sheep (comes) from the town.

The men of the consecration-gift(?) feast.

The bread and the beer belong to the diviner.

On the same day, they enclose[b] a lamb at the temple of the Storm God.

f 1 Sam 8:12; cf. 2 Kgs 1:9

g Jer 16:5; Amos 6:7

h 1 Sam 20:5, 18, 24, 27, 34; cf. 2 Kgs 4:23; Isa 1:13; Hos 2:13; Amos 8:5

[20] The broken text prevents certain determination of the relationship between these players, the sheep, and the bread and beer.

[21] In contracts, a table is anointed and *ḫukku*-bread is broken. This association offers the basis for translation here, though the actual identity of *ḫukku*-bread is unknown.

[22] The number 19 begins line 67, which would fit a sequence to another day, but no more is visible.

[23] The axe consistently follows at the back of processions.

[24] There are no further missing lines between the end of column III and the beginning of column IV.

[25] Anna appears to be the Sumerian sky god An (= Anu), like Illila for Enlil, the Sumerian pantheon head, below, note 28.

[26] The items offered are not certain; bread and beer would be unusual. Adammatera appears also in the installation of the storm god's high priestess.

[27] The *a-bi* appear repeatedly in the text for the month of Abî, which in spite of alternatives for similar ritual terms appears to be read as "fathers" at Emar, based on one spelling with double *-bb-*, *abbī*.

[28] This is evidently Enlil as Anna is An(u), above, both major Sumerian deities from earlier southern Mesopotamia. The return-ceremony is the *tūrtu*, also found on the last day of the *zukru* festival.

[29] The meaning of this term is unknown. But see below note 33.

[30] The subject of the procession is not mentioned, though the goddess Aštart is the only deity active on this day (below).

[31] The verb *ṣâdu* means "to roam, hunt."

[32] The "Hurrian" temple is uncertain.

[33] See McLaughlin (1991) for recent treatment of evidence for this group at Ugarit. The "standard" loaf is the *naptanu*. The verb "to bring" (*wašābu*) is unique in Emar ritual, though in inheritance documents it can refer to responsibility for continued sustenance. The modifier *mi-di* appears to mean "acquaintance."

[34] Here the homages are rendered *kibadu*, not *kubadu*.

[35] Burning of birds constitutes a particularly Hurrian ritual act, performed for purification, especially for contact with the underworld or death; see Haas and Wilhelm 1974:50-54, 137-142.

[36] The New Moon is the *ḫidašu*, a word not previously attested. The climax of this annual celebration falls on the third day, once the new moon is established, rather than at first visibility as expected for this term.

On the 9th day the Storm God of Canaan[37] [i] goes out in procession.

An ox and six sheep proceed to his temple.
Among them, ...
... the temple of Dagan Lord ...[38]
... the servers ... he receives ...
...
The hides, the intestines, the fat ... belong to the diviner.

i Exod 15:15; Judg 5:19; etc.

... the kidneys ... belong to the king of the land.

(Left Edge)

The Hiyaru of the Storm God falls on the 18th day.[39]

They slaughter an ox and two sheep.
The men of the consecration-gift(?) eat and drink.

[37] The storm god of "Kina᾿u" is most easily explained by reference to the coastal region to the west, which several Amarna letters render Kinaḫḫu. In his pairing with the goddess Aštart at Emar's western temples, the storm god is called Baal and reflects a Canaanite or western coastal association.

[38] This line is not clear.

[39] The Hiyaru is a Syrian and Hurrian rite of uncertain derivation. Durand (1988) suggests that the word is the same as the Mesopotamian month Ayaru, with both ultimately derived from the word for "donkey," as a sacrifice.

TWO MONTHS JOINED BY THE UNDERWORLD, WITH BARRING AND OPENING OF DOORS (1.125) [1]

Emar's tablet of rites for the month of Abî focuses on observances at the middle and end of the moon's cycle, set in a frame of offerings through the remaining intervals. The largest section of the text addresses rites at various *abû* shrines, with a central event on the 26th day, when "they bar the doors." This act is carried out with the last visibility of the lunar crescent and has its complement in the first line of a second tablet, which begins on "the day of opening the doors." Although the second tablet does not name a month, comparison of these two tablets with the fifth and sixth of the diviner's six-month collection confirms the sequence. Rites following the opening of doors therefore belong to the New Moon celebration for Dagan which is identified in the six-month tablet during the month of Halma. Both tablets are presented together in order to display both parts of the event which links them, through the waning and then the new appearance of the moon.

First Tablet

Frame Part 1 (lines 1-8)

During the month of Abî on the day of declaration,[2] they distribute among the gods:

two gallons and two quarts of second quality flour, one store jug, ten doves, one juglet of oil, and one quart of raisins.

On the 3rd day, they offer to Aštart of the Abî:

one quart of second quality flour, barley, ..., (one) flagon, and one jar from the House of the Gods;
one female kid from the fire-lighters;
... cedar oil, barley, ghee, one hundred (shekels) of aromatics, one standard vessel, one brick of figs, ten pomegranates, and raisins from the palace.[3]

On the same day, as the offering to Mount Šinapši:[4]

one quart of (barley-)mash, two quarts of second quality flour, (one) standard vessel, one dove, fruit, and oil.

On the 8th day, they distribute among the gods:

two gallons and two quarts of second quality flour, one store jug, ten [doves, one] juglet of oil, and one quart of raisins.

Also on the 8th day, as the offering for Mount Šinapši:

one quart of (barley-)mash, two quarts of second quality flour, a store jug, ... [one] standard vessel, fruit, oil, and one dove.[5]

Mid-Month Observance (lines 9-26)

On the 14th day, they offer to Aštart of the Šubu:

two gallons and one quart of (barley-)mash, one flagon, one standard vessel, ... [one brick of figs,] and ten pomegranates.
With bread and beer, ...

On the same day, (as the offering to ...):

one gallon and one quart of (barley-)mash, one flagon, one standard vessel ... [from the House

[1] See *Emar* 452 and 463.

[2] The noun *ḫussu* was encountered as a name for feasting personnel in the installation, above ("heralds(?)"). Here, it should refer to identification and perhaps accompanying proclamation of the new lunar crescent, so the first of the month.

[3] In the *zukru* festival text, the given source evidently refers to the entire list that precedes, but in the initial offering of the 25th day (lines 31-32), the single source is moved forward into the middle of the list, so that it must be considered possible that only the immediately prior item is thus defined. The translation offered here preserves this ambiguity.

[4] This location is known from Hurrian texts found at Ḫattuša, the Hittite capital, and is not part of the local Emar terrain.

[5] The word for "offering" is moved ahead of the last item, the dove, an apparent scribal slip.

of the Gods(?)];
one gallon and one quart of (barley-)mash, one ...-vessel from the king(?);
one gallon and one quart of (barley-)mash, one ... [from ...].[6]

They offer to Aštart of the Šubu:
...

During the days of the sacrificial homages, they offer to Aštart of the Pools:
...

They give to them:
... one gallon of breads, barley flour, and one flagon.

They offer to Aštart of the Abî:
... from the House of the Gods;
one sheep from the fire-lighters.[7]

[On the 16th day,] they offer (to ...):
... one flagon, and sweet cakes.[8]

They bring in with her with wailing cries ...
They bring in ...
The Hunt is on the same day.
They bring out from the storehouse, ... the crossroads ...
The Hunt of Aštart is on the 16th day.[9]
[On the 17th day, (they offer ...)]:
... a jar, and one standard vessel from the House of the Gods;
...

On the same day, (they offer ...):
... one standard vessel from the House of the Gods.

They bring out the divine weapon ...
They make offering behind the temple of NINURTA.
They perform ...

Frame Part 2 (lines 27-30)
[On the 19th] day, [... gallons and ... quarts] of (barley-)mash, three standard vessels, one brick of figs, ten pomegranates, and one hundred (shekels) of aromatics — on the 19th day these go out in procession.[10]

On the 20th day they offer them.
... offering ...
They offer to Mount Ṣuparatu:[11]
... sheep from the king;
two quarts of (barley-)mash, two quarts of second quality flour, one gallon of barley flour, and one store jug from the House of the Gods;
one sheep from the fire-lighters;
one [quart(?)] of *abluṣu*-flour.[12]

On the 20th day, as the offering for Mount Šinapši:
one quart of (barley-)mash, one quart of second quality flour, one standard vessel, one dove, fruit, and oils.

Barring the Doors at the Last Lunar Crescent (lines 31-52)
On the 25th day, they offer to the *abû* of the House of Trust:
one half gallon of (barley-)mash, two gallons of barley flour, one store jug from the House of the Gods;
one standard vessel, one brick of figs, ten pomegranates, one sheep from the fire-lighters, and one dove.

On the same day, they give to the *abû* of NINKUR's temple:
two grasping loaves,[13] second quality flour, one dove, and fruit.

On the same day, they perform the Greater Sacrificial Homage [a] at the Cemetery Gate,[b] with:
one gallon of barley flour, two quarts of second quality flour, one flagon, two sheep from the king, one standard vessel, and twenty-five Hurrian(?) birds.[14]

On the 26th day, up to the time of barring the doors [c] of the Gate[15] they offer to all the gods:
two gallons of barley flour, two store jugs, twelve sheep from the fire-lighters, five sheep from the shepherds,[16] and one juglet of oil.

Then they bar the doors.[c]
On the same day, they offer to the *abû* of the palace:
one gallon and one quart of (barley-)mash, one

[a] 2 Chr 32:33
[b] Deut 26:14; Isa 38:10; 65:4
[c] Mal 1:10; Neh 6:10; 7:3; 13:19; 2 Chr 28:24

[6] The tablet preserves less and less at the left edge, until it breaks off after this last line. Based on the proportions of the tablet, however, there should be only one line missing at most.
[7] It is not clear whether the above lines belong to the 14th day or move to the full moon (15th). Comparison with the text for six months suggests this may still belong to the 14th day, called there the Buqaratu. Full moon rites are only attested at Emar for the first month, SAG.MU ("The Head of the Year") or Zarati.
[8] This line begins a new section separated by a horizontal line, and comparison with the text for six months indicates location on day 16.
[9] See the month of Marzaḫāni in the text for six months for the same event, one indication that Abî and Marzaḫāni are equivalent months.
[10] The repeated day references appear to be redundant.
[11] This location is not known, but like Mount Šinapši may be at some distance from Emar and the Euphrates River.
[12] This word is unique at Emar, as well as unknown elsewhere.
[13] This attempts to derive the *ṣabbuttu* bread from the verb *ṣabātu*, "to grasp, hold." This action describes manipulation of lots before the storm god in confirmation of the high priestess selection.
[14] The MUŠEN *ḫur-ri* may be understood as Hurrian, in connection to Hurrian practice of offering birds for purification in contacts with death and the underworld; see Haas and Wilhelm 1974:50-54, 137-142.
[15] The "Gate" may be the Cemetery Gate ("gate of the grave") mentioned at the end of day 25.
[16] The "shepherds" appear only here at Emar, lit., "men of the sheep."

gallon of second quality flour, two gallons of barley flour, two store jugs, and one standard vessel of wine from the palace;
one ox, one sheep, one gazelle, one bird, honey, oil, ghee, and fruit.

On the same day,
for the *abû* of Dagan's temple: two grasping breads, second quality flour, one dove, and fruit;
for Alal's temple: two grasping breads, second quality flour, one dove, and fruit;
for (Dagan) Lord of Habitations: two grasping breads, one dove, and fruit;
for Išḫara's temple: two grasping breads, second quality flour, and one bird.

On the 27th day, they offer the Lesser Sacrificial Homage [a] before the *abû* of Dagan's temple, with:
one gallon and one quart of (barley-)mash, a jar, one presentation vessel of barley beer, one presentation vessel of wine, one sheep, one dove, honey, oil, ghee, beef, venison, fish, apricots, soured milk, figs, all kinds of fruits, and four Hurrian birds.

For the *abû* of the temple of ...:
one half gallon of (barley-)mash, one half gallon of second quality flour, ... gallon of barley flour, and two store jugs from the House of the Gods.

They perform the song of the gods.
On the same day,
for the *abû* of Alal's temple: one gallon and one quart of (barley-)mash, one [jar, one] presentation vessel of barley beer, one presentation vessel of wine, honey, oil, ghee, one dove, beef, venison, one lamb, and all kinds of fruits.

On the same day,
they give to the *abû* of the House of Trust, for the *abû* from ...: honey, oil, ghee, beef, venison, fish, and all kinds of fruits.

Frame Part 3 (lines 53-55)
At the head of the month, on the day of (the moon's) disappearance (until?) ... it shines (again), they purify the city.[d]
They offer to the Lord of Akka:
one half quart of barley flour, one jar from the House of the Gods, and ... sheep from the fire-lighters.
They bring out Latarak for three days.[17]

d Neh 12:30

e 1 Sam3:15; 2 Chr 29:3

Second Tablet
The New Moon of Dagan (lines 1-14)[18]
On the day of opening the doors,[e]
they distribute among the gods: one sheep, one gallon of ...
one quart of barley flour, one standard vessel of wine, one ...-vessel ... from the king are provided for Dagan.
One dove ...

On the next day, [they perform] the Greater Sacrificial Homage [a] for ...
They distribute among the gods:
one hundred thick breads, two store jugs, one ...-vessel, ..., and seventy doves.

In the evening, they sacrifice one dove to Dagan.
They fill chalices from the city.

At night, they burn one water-bird, honey, and ghee.
One gallon of (barley-)mash is for the chalices.
One <quart> of (barley-)mash is for the breads.
One quart of [(barley-)mash] is for the thick breads.
(Also,) one sheep and one standard vessel of wine.

On the same day, after the sun is lit,
One sheep is from the fire-lighters.
One gallon of (barley-)mash, one quart of (barley-)mash, three standard vessels for the chalices, ten [figs], pomegranates, and the breads and the beers are from the House of the Gods.

[break]

Celebration for Halma (lines 15-18)[19]
...
... they offer oil ... ... on the day of the Hiyaru,[20] to Halma.

The Hiyaru *of the Storm God* (lines 19-25)
On the 18th day,
for the Hiyaru of the storm god: two sheep from the king, one for(?) the *ambašši*,[21] two birds, one calf from the town ... of ... of the *ambašši*, one ox and one sheep from the town ..., beer, one gallon and one quart of barley flour, one ...-vessel, one standard vessel of wine, one quart of (barley)-mash, and one jar from the House of the Gods.
The breads and the beers are from the ...-men.

[17] Latarak is a Mesopotamian god associated with Ištar. The Lord of Akka is not otherwise known.

[18] This title is taken from the rite for six months, where it covers the second and third days of the month of Halma. The procedure for the second day of this tablet corresponds to that for the six-month collection.

[19] The divine name reads *Ḫal-ba*, but Emar displays frequent interchange of /b/ and /m/ in the place name Halab (Aleppo), from which the divine name may derive. Rites for Halma occur on the 8th day of the month named for him in the text for six months.

[20] See the note for the last two lines of the text for six months, p. 439, note 39 (above).

[21] Hurrian *ambašši* refers to some kind of cult place or object; see Laroche 1976-77:46.

Celebration for the Storm God and Hebat (lines 26-30)
On the 20th day, (they offer):
to the Storm God: one (ox);
to Hebat: one ox and one sheep.
[They offer] to Hebat one gallon and three quarts of (barley-)mash and one quart of barley flour.
They distribute among the gods: ... from the king, one quart of barley flour, two flagons, a juglet, and ...

TWO *KISSU* FESTIVALS (1.126) [1]

The most often copied ritual texts from the diviner's collection are also among the most mysterious. Emar's *kissu* festivals serve a cluster of deities at the nearby village of Šatappi, though the language and procedure share the common stock of the larger center, especially of the installations for the storm god's high priestess and for the *maš*ʾ*artu*. The festivals are found in several combinations on individual tablets, gathered once as a full set for Dagan, EREŠKIGAL, Ea, Išḫara and NINURTA, and a final rite for all *kissu*'s. No further gods are addressed in the separate fragments.

In their simplest form (EREŠKIGAL, Ea, Išḫara and NINURTA), the *kissu* festivals do no more than devote one day to offering and feasting for a single god (or pair). Association of a *kissu* rite with the *maš*ʾ*artu* priestess installation shows that this act of devotion may even be piggy-backed onto another event. The word *kissu* itself represents some local form, most easily accounted for as "throne," elsewhere *kussu* and *kissû* at Emar. A *kissu* would perhaps then celebrate the dominion of each god over his or her proper sphere.

Two of the most interesting *kissu* festivals are presented here. The rite for Išḫara and NINURTA includes a new attestation of personnel called *nābû*, evidently related to the Hebrew word for "prophet."

Dagan[2]

Heading for all Šatappi kissu rites (line 1)
Tablet of rites for the *kissu* festival of Šatappi.

The Consecration Day (lines 2-9)
When the sons of Šatappi [a] perform the *kissu* [b] festival for Dagan,
on the consecration day of aromatics before the tables[3] they consecrate the gods of the town with bread and beer.[4] [c]
They lay NINKUR in (Dagan's) temple, (and) sacrifice one ox and one sheep to NINKUR.
The wailing woman gives forth her cry.[d]
They set before NINKUR the ritual portion of the ox and of the sheep.
They set four tables.[e] Among them,
they set one table for Dagan,
one table for Išḫara and NINURTA,
(and) two tables on the ground for Alal and Amaza.[5]

The Festival Proper (lines 10-20)
On the next day, they offer meats and thick breads, and distribute one standard loaf each to the (aforesaid) gods of Šatappi.
They sacrifice two sheep to ...[6] and set before the gods their ritual portion.
The men of the consecration-gift(?) eat and drink for three days in his temple. Also, they sacrifice two sheep regularly for each of the aforesaid three days. The high priestess of the storm god,[7] the high priestess of Šumi, (and) the high priestess of Šatappi ... their tables [f] receive regularly one presentation vessel ...
Also, daily they set before the gods four standard loaves and four dried cakes with fruit.
They regularly set one standard loaf and one dried cake with fruit (for each god).[8]

Day 4: The Final Day (lines 21-24)
On the fourth day they raise up NINKUR. In the evening[g] they send the two brides (who) gave gifts on the second day back to the temple of Udḫa along with bread and beer.[9]
The singers enter and chant for Šuwala and Ugur,

a Ezek 23:15; Joel 4:6
b 1 Kgs 22:19; Isa 6:1; Jer 3:17; 17:12; Ezek 1:26; 10:1; 43:7; Ps 11:4
c Deut 32:51; Isa 30:29
d Judg 11:40; Jer 9:16, 19; Ezek 32:16
e Exod 25:23, etc.; Isa 65:11
f 1 Sam 20:5, 25, 29
g Exod 12:6; Lev 23:5

---

[1] See *Emar* 385 and 387.
[2] Dagan's *kissu* festival is found on six separate tablets, and possibly a seventh small fragment (tablets A - G). These attest the following combinations: A (Dagan and EREŠKIGAL), B (Dagan — a splinter), C (Dagan and EREŠKIGAL), D (Dagan), E (Dagan), F (Dagan, EREŠKIGAL, Ea, Išḫara and NINURTA, all *kissu*'s), G (Dagan, another rite). Lineation here follows text A, which is by far most complete.
[3] This qualification for the consecration day is unique and awkward. The text may be corrupt.
[4] The broken tablets D and E specify particular types of bread. Text E adds an obscure reference to the diviner and (chief) scribe.
[5] Tablet E lists various breads for the tables, but the broken tablet prevents full reading.
[6] The text of A is confused, while tablet E introduces the goddess Šaššabētu, encountered in the *zukru* festival (above Text 1.123 and note 10).
[7] This is the same figure known from the installation festival (above, Text 1.122).
[8] These offerings appear to recall the four tables set for four gods on the consecration day.
[9] Comparing the last day of the installation for the storm god's high priestess, this act should somehow relate to raising up the goddess NINKUR. Unlike that text, however, the objects of the return are not described earlier. It appears that either these two "brides" (not clear whose) or their gifts are intended. Since no gifts are specified, the girls seem the more likely, though both their role and their evident origin in the temple

and perform their rites.[10]
The musicians of the gods enter to perform.[11]

Administration (lines 25-27)
Also, the officials who give the consecration-gift(?) receive three standard loaves each.
The king of the land, the diviner, and the chief scribe consecrate them (the gods) with contract-bread and a pot of barley beer.[12]
They give thirty *gurtu* of silver to EREŠKIGAL.[13]

Išḫara and NINURTA[14]
The Consecration Day (lines 1-8)
On the consecration day of the festival, they consecrate Išḫara and NINURTA with contract-bread, a dried cake with fruit, and a pot of barley beer.[15] [c]
They bathe them, and then they bake seventeen bushels of fine flour for the contract-bread, and bake fifteen bushels of bright(?) flour for the bread-rings.[16]
They beat with their hands all thirty-two bushels of flour together.
They give to Išḫara and NINURTA a bucket of bitter flavor,[h] a sweet bucket,[i] a bucket of barley-beer, an offering of two sheep, two ewes(?) — that is(?) two *sirtu*-sheep.[17]

h Exod 12:8; Num 9:11

i Neh 8:10

j 1 Sam 10:5, 10; 19:20; 1 Kgs 20:35; 2 Kgs 2:3

The Festival Proper (lines 9-14)
[On the next] day, they sacrifice those two sheep to Išḫara and NINURTA at the house of the Nābû.[18] [j]
They set out for the gods the ritual portion of the sheep.
They set out one dried cake with fruit and one rack of bread for Išḫara and one rack of bread for NINURTA.
[They set out] two standard loaves and one pot of barley beer for Išḫara [and NINURTA].[19]

Administration (lines 15-21)
Also, each and every man and woman of the town receives a due portion[20] from the loaves (baked from) the above thirty bushels of flour and from the buckets.
Also, they confine[21] a slave-woman so as to have her bake with the sweet (bucket).[22]
She receives the contract-bread and the pots of barley beer.

Also, the officials who give the consecration-gift(?) eat and drink [in the temple of Dagan/Išḫara(?)].[23]
They take away the pure bread from the tables.
[They ...] Išḫara and NINURTA in Dagan's temple.[24]

of a local god Udḫa are obscure.
[10] See *Emar* 369:73, on the last day of the high priestess installation (above, p. 430).
[11] It is not clear what difference in performance distinguishes the *zammārū* (verb *zamāru*) from the (collective) *ḫarrūta* (verb *ḫarāru*), here translated "singers" and "musicians" respectively.
[12] This administrative description evidently displays who provides the consecration offerings which begin the festival; see Fleming 1992:158-160, and above.
[13] The term *gur-tu₄* represents an alternative to the expected shekel measure.
[14] This festival is attested in only two copies: the full *kissu* set of tablet F, and a second tablet J. Lineation follows F, which offers a longer text.
[15] Text J does not mention the deities, but only "the consecration."
[16] Emar *zarḫu* is uncertain, and this translation compares Hebrew *zrḥ*, "to be bright." The *kakkaru* is a round loaf. Consider also *ṣarḫu*, "roasted flour" (Akk. *ṣarāḫu*).
[17] Text J mentions only Išḫara.
[18] A second new attestation of this plural noun at Mari indicates that they are indeed identified with prophecy; see for complete discussion of the data, Fleming (1993a, 1993b). Text J sacrifices only to Išḫara and locates the event at "the temple of Išḫara." In text F, *all* the *kissu* festivals take place in Dagan's temple, and "the house of the *nābû*" seems to provide a comparable setting within this alternative temple site. The connection with Išḫara's cult is nevertheless preserved.
[19] Only text F contains this last offering.
[20] Lit., "before him."
[21] Lit., "seize."
[22] The verb appears to be *epû*, "to bake," but the form is not expected Akk. for an evident causative meaning.
[23] One expects the feast to take place in the same location as the main offering. Dagan's temple appears in Ea's *kissu* festival, however, and serves as a general center for the set. Perhaps this is the temple of Dagan in text F and of Išḫara in J.
[24] This appears only in text F.

REFERENCES

Arnaud 1986; Dietrich 1989; Durand 1988; Fleming 1990; 1992; 1993a; 1993b; Haas and Wilhelm 1974; Laroche 1976-77; McLaughlin 1991.

A PSEPHOMANCY RITUAL FROM ASSUR (1.127)
(*LKA* 137)

Victor Hurowitz

This text was found by the German excavations at Assur.[1] It is an incantation recited while performing a ritual for divination by use of black (hematite) and white (alabaster) stones (psephomancy). The ritualist, while pronouncing the liturgy, tells which cultic manipulations he is performing, thus permitting the reader to follow his actions. The type of divination described has general similarities to other types of divination practiced in Mesopotamia. But it may provide a specific parallel to the enigmatic Urim and Thumim, the only type of mechanical divination legitimized by the Bible in general and by the Priestly source (P) in particular.[2] [a]

Invocation (lines 1-2)

(1) Incantation: I have called upon you O Shamash[3] [...]
(2) In the midst of the [pure (?)] heavens [...]

Description of Ritual (lines 3-8)

(3) I am carrying a star; [...] you (?) [...]
(4) I am carrying a star; I am touching my head [...]
(5) x [...] offering, *masḫatu*-flour ... [...]
(6) The pure grain, in its body, a stone [...]
(7) I offer bread, pure water, fine oil.
(8) There is a star. According to the written tablet I incant.

Performance of Psephomancy and Request for Oracle (lines 9-28)

(9) Judgement is nigh, O pu[re] Shamash,
(10) The word hastens, hear the ut[terance of my mouth(?)].
(11) You will judge me, O Bel. Reveal to me secrets!
(12) Day and night [show] me secret lore.
(13) [broken]
(14) In the hem of my garment [...],
(15) In the pure hem of my garment [...],
(16) "Draw on the ground (the names of) seven god[s ...]
(17) Sin, Shamash, Adad, Marduk, Urash-g[ub-ba],
(18) Dagan and Nab[u]."
(19) I have drawn them, and now I am lifting up a st[one(?)].
(20) If (your) judgement is nigh, and my plea is accepted,
(21) If, Bel, in your heart, there is judge[ment],
(22) If, Shamash, in your heart, there is revela[tion],
(23) May a stone of desire jump up and may the hands cat[ch (it)].
(24) If (your) judgement is not nigh, (and my) plea is not accepted,
(25) (If) Bel, in your heart, there is no judg[ment],
(26) (If) Shamash, in your heart, there is no revela[tion],
(27) May a stone of no desire jump up and may the hands cat[ch it].
(28) A second time for judgement, a third time for decis[ion].

Title (line 29)

(29) Incantation for (achieving) oracular decisions with alabaster[4] and hematite.[5]

Reverse

(1) Its ritual: On an appropriate day, you draw these [seven] gods on the ground and you intone the incantation ["I have called upon you O Shamash ...] in the midst of the pure heaven" [three] times, over the white and black stones. Afterwards, you shall inquire of the gods and it (the answer) will be reliable.

Diagram [Here are the names of seven deities (ll. 17-18) written perpendicular to the direction of writing of the text.]

---

(5) [t]his[xxx]

Colophon

(1) According to the long tablet of Nabu-[...]
(2) ... like the old one.
(3) An excerpt tablet of Kisir-[Assur, the exorcist of the Assur temple,]
(4) son of Nabu-bessunu, the exorcist [of the Assur temple,]
(5) son of Baba-shuma-ibni, the *zabar*[*dabbû*[6] official of Esharra.]

a Exod 28:30; Lev 8:8; Num 27:21; Deut 33:8; 1 Sam 14:4 (LXX); 1 Sam 28:6; Ezra 2:67; Neh 7:65

---

[1] For an edition, commentary and discussion of this text see Horowitz and Hurowitz 1992; Finkel 1995.

[2] For the identification see Reiner 1960; Lipiński 1970; Horowitz and Hurowitz 1992. Reservations are expressed by Milgrom 1991 and Finkel 1995.

[3] Shamash, the sun god, is the Mesopotamian deity responsible for divination and oracles. As purveyor of divine decisions he is also referred to as the judge of the gods.

[4] The Akk. word for alabaster, *gišnugallu*, means "great lamp" and corresponds with a possible meaning of *ʾûrîm*.

[5] An Akk. nickname of hematite is "truth stone," corresponding with a possible meaning of *tummîm*.

[6] Lit., "bearer of the bronze implements." The function of this official is totally obscure.

REFERENCES

LKA 137; Finkel 1995; Horowitz and Hurowitz 1992; Lipiński 1970; Milgrom 1991:507-511; Reiner 1960b; Van Dam 1993.

---

6. LOVE POEMS

LOVE LYRICS OF NABU AND TASHMETU (1.128)

Alasdair Livingstone

(1) Let anyone trust in whom he trusts; as for us we trust in Nabu, are filled with awe by Tashmetu!
(4) What belongs to us is ours; Nabu is our lord and Tashmetu the mountain of our trust! Ditto.

(6) Say to the one of the wall, to the one of the wall, to Tashmetu: "Grant safety from disaster! Settle down in the cella!"
(8) Let the pure scent of juniper incense circulate in the sanctuary! Ditto.

(9) O the shade of the cedar, the shade of the cedar, the shelter of kings! O the cypress shade of the magnates! The shade of a sprig of juniper is shelter for my darling Nabu and for my fun and games! Ditto.

(12) Tashmetu dangles a golden ... in the lap of Nabu. Ditto.
(13) My lord, put an earring on me and I'll give you pleasure in the garden!
(15) [Nabu], my lord, put an earring on me and I'll make you rejoice in the Edubba!

(17) O my [Tashmetu], I will put bracelets of carnelian on you!
(18) [...] your bracelets of carnelian!
(19) I will open [...]. Ditto.

(20) [...] out came the goddess.
(21) [...] like a mural crown
(22) [...] ... [...] them
(23) [...] Ditto.

(At this point there is a lacuna of several lines in the text, followed by three poorly preserved lines.)

Reverse
(4) Let me give you a new chariot [...]!
(5) Ditto, [whose] thighs are a gazelle in the plain! [Refrain.][1]
Ditto, [whose] ankle bones are an apple of the month of Siman! [Refrain.]
Ditto, whose heels are obsidian! [Refrain.]
Ditto, any part of whom is as fine as a tablet of lapis lazuli. Refrain.
Looking blossoming, Tashmetu entered the nuptial chamber.
(10) She shut the door, putting in place the lapis lazuli lock.
She rinsed herself, climbed up, got onto the bed. Refrain.
Into a bowl of lapis lazuli, into a bowl of lapis lazuli, her tears flow. Refrain.
With a flock of scarlet wool he wipes away her tears. Refrain.
Thither ask, ask, question, question! Refrain.
(15) "Why, O why are you adorned, O my own Tashmetu?"
"So that I may [go] to the garden with you, my Nabu! [a]
Let me go the the garden and [to the lord! Refrain].
Let me go alone to the most exceedingly beautiful garden! Refrain.
They did not place my throne among the counsellors. Refrain.
(20) May my eyes see the plucking of your fruit! Refrain.
May my ears hear the twittering of your birds! Refrain.
Bind and harness thither! Refrain.
Bind your days to the garden and to the lord! Refrain.
Bind your nights to the beautiful garden! Refrain.
(25) Let my own Tashmetu come with me to the garden! Refrain.
Among the counsellors, her throne is foremost! Refrain.[2]

(At this point there is a lacuna of three lines after which the text continues on the edge of the tablet.)

(30) May her eyes behold the plucking of my fruit! [Refrain.]
May her ears listen to the twittering of my birds! [Refrain].
May her eyes behold, her ears listen! [Refrain.]

a Cant 6:11; 7:13

---

[1] The imagery here is of a type well known in both Sumerian and Babylonian poetry. The subject and what it is to be compared with are simply juxtaposed in a nominal sentence, rather than being construed in the manner of a simile.

[2] The point is that she is not accompanied by her ladies in waiting; cf. line 19, which draws attention to the fact that this is not a day for temple business.

(A colophon concludes the tablet, but does not give any information apart from the name of the scribe, Budilu, and his title LÚ.A.BA.)

REFERENCES

Matsushima 1987:143-149; Livingstone 1989:35-37; Foster *BM* 2:902-904.

B. ROYAL FOCUS

1. EPIC

THE ADAPA STORY (1.129)

Benjamin R. Foster

In Mesopotamian tradition, Adapa was the first of the semi-divine sages (*apkallu*) who served as counselors (*ummānu*) to the ante-diluvian kings, bringing the arts of civilization to humanity. In a late formulation of this tradition, each of these kings had his own counselor, and Adapa served Alulim, the first king. He was identified as Oannes in the Greek version of the tradition as preserved by Josephus in the name of Berossos. In addition, Adapa was the protagonist of a myth known from a tablet found at El Amarna in Egypt and dating to the 14th century BCE, as well as from first millennium exemplars found in the royal libraries of Nineveh. This myth provides an aetiology of death and thus a parallel to the story of Adam in the Bible. [WWH]

Anu's messenger reached him,
"'Adapa, who fractured the wing of the south wind,
Send him to me!'"
He brought him along the [ro]ad to heaven,
He went up to heaven.
When he went up to heaven,
And drew near Anu's door,
Tammuz and Gizzida were standing at Anu's door.[1]
When they saw Adapa, they cried, "(Heaven) help (us)!
"Fellow, for whom are you like this?
Adapa, why are you dressed in mourning?"
"Two gods have disappeared from the land,
So I am dressed in mourning."
"Who are the two gods who have disappeared from the land?"
"Tammuz and Gizzida."
They looked at each other and laughed and laughed.
When Adapa made his approach to Anu the king,
Anu saw him and cried,
"Come now, Adapa, why did you fracture the wing of the south wind?"
Adapa answered Anu,
"My Lord, I was fishing in the depths of the sea,
For my master's temple.[2]
The sea was like a mirror,
Then the south wind blew upon me and capsized me.
I spent the rest of the day in the home of the fish.
In my fury, I cursed the [win]d."
There spoke up for [him Tammuz] and Gizzida,
Saying a favorable word about him to Anu.
His heart grew calm, he became quiet.
"Why did Ea disclose what pertains to heaven and earth
To an uncouth mortal,
And give him a violent temper?
Since he has so treated him,
What, for our part, shall we do for him?
Bring him food of life, let him eat."[3] [a]
They brought him food of life, he did not eat.
They brought him waters of life, he did not drink.
They brought him a garment, he put it on.
They brought him oil, he anointed himself.
Anu stared and burst out laughing at him,
"Come now, Adapa, why did you not eat or drink?
Won't you live? Are not people to be im[mor]tal?"
Ea my lord told me,
'You must not eat, you must not drink.'"
"Let them take him and [ret]urn him to his earth."

a Gen 2:16

[1] Tammuz (Sum. Dumuzi) and (Nin-)gizzida (lit., "lord of the right-hand tree") here serve as doorkeepers of heaven. There are indications that deceased kings ascended to heaven to serve as stand-ins for these divine doorkeepers for seven days; see below, text 1.132 and n. 3.

[2] His master is Ea (Sum. Enki), on whose advice he refuses the proffered food and water, thus forfeiting once and for all the chance to make humanity immortal.

[3] Like the divine command to Adam to eat from all the trees of the garden of Eden including, implicitly, the tree of (eternal) life) (Gen 2:16), the offer of the food of life (and the waters of life) to Adapa implied an offer of eternal life. See Buccellati 1973; differently Michalowski 1980.

REFERENCES

Text: BRM 4:3 and duplicates. Translations and studies: Picchioni 1981; Dalley 1989:182-188; Foster *BM* 1:429-434; *FDD* 97-101.

ATRA-ḪASIS (1.130)

Benjamin R. Foster

The "primeval history" of humanity, which occupies the first eleven chapters of Genesis, also exercised the Mesopotamian imagination. In Akkadian, the Epic of Atra-hasis constitutes its earliest and most systematic formulation. This epic explains the creation of man as intended to relieve the (lesser) deities of their toil, and the attempted destruction of humanity as divine response to the noise of the expanding human population which threatened the very rest that their creation had sought to provide for the gods. This destruction, decreed by Enlil, took several successive forms, culminating in the Deluge but, as in other flood-stories, its purpose was frustrated by the survival of the flood-hero, here called Atra-hasis ("exceeding wise"), through the intervention of Ea, the divine friend of humanity. The problem of over-population is resolved by other means in a concluding aetiology. The composition is nearly complete in a Late Old Babylonian recension in three tablets (chapters), and is known as well in various fragmentary later recensions. [WWH]

When gods were man,[1]
They did forced labor, they bore drudgery.
Great indeed was the drudgery of the gods,
The forced labor was heavy, the misery too much:
The seven(?) great Anunna-gods were burdening
The Igigi-gods with forced labor.
...
[The gods] were digging watercourses,
[Canals they opened, the] life of the land.
[The Igigi-gods] were digging watercourses,
[Canals they opened, the] life of the land.
[The Igigi-gods dug the Ti]gris river,
[And the Euphrates there]after.
[Springs they opened up from] the depths,
[Wells ...] they established.[a]
...
[They heaped up] all the mountains.
[ ]
[years] of drudgery,
[ ] the vast marsh.
They [cou]nted years of drudgery,
[and] forty years, too much!
[ ] forced labor they bore night and day.
[They were com]plaining, denouncing,
[Mut]tering down in the ditch:
"Let us face up to our [foreman] the prefect,
He must take off (this) our [he]avy burden upon us!
[ ], counsellor of the gods, the warrior,
Come, let us remove (him) from his dwelling;
Enlil, counsellor of the gods, the warrior,
Come, let us remove (him) from his dwelling!"
...
"Now then, call for battle!
Battle let us join, warfare!"
The gods heard his words:
They set fire to their tools,
They put fire to their spaces,
And flame to their workbaskets.[2]
Off they went, one and all,
To the gate of the warrior Enlil's abode.
[ ]
It was night, half-way through the watch,
The house was surrounded, but the god did not know.
It was night, half-way through the watch,
Ekur[3] was surrounded, but Enlil did not know!

(The gods awake, convene and send a messenger to the rebels.)

[Nusku opened] his gate,
[Took his weapons] and w[ent] ... Enlil.
[In the assembly of a]ll the gods,
[He knelt, s]tood up, expounded the c[omm]and,
"Anu, your father,
[Your counsellor, the] warrior Enlil,
[Your prefect], Ninurta,
And [your bailiff] Ennugi [have sent me (to say)]:
'Who is [instigator of] battle?
Who is [instigator of] hostilities?
Who [declared] war,
[(That) battle has run up to the gate of Enlil]?
In [ ]
He trans[gressed the command of] Enlil.'
"Every [one of us gods has declared] war;
...
We have set [ ] in the e[xcavation].
[Excessive] drudgery [has killed us],
[Our] forced labor was heavy, [the misery too much]!
Now, every [one of us gods]
Has resolved on [a reckoning(?)] with Enlil."
...

(When the gods learn the reason, they decide to create man to relieve them from labor.)

(a) Ea made ready to speak,
And said to the gods [his brothers]:
"What calumny do we lay to their charge?
Their forced labor was heavy, [their misery too

a Gen 4:5f.

[1] The opening line of the epic has sparked a lengthy debate as to its each meaning; see Lambert 1969a.
[2] In effect, the first work stoppage in world history, or at least in world literature; see Komoróczy 1976.
[3] Enlil's temple in Nippur; later, any temple.

much]!
(e) Every day [ ]
The outcry [was loud, we could hear the clamor].
There is [ ]
[Belet-ili, the midwife], is present.
Let her create, then, a hum[an, a man],
(j) Let him bear the yoke [ ],
Let him bear the yoke [ ]!
[Let man assume the drud]gery of god ..."

"[Belet-ili, the midwife], is present,
Let the midwife create a human being,
Let man assume the drudgery of god."
They summoned and asked the goddess,
The midwife of the gods, wise Mami:
"Will you be the birth goddess, creatress of mankind?
Create a human being that he bear the yoke,
Let him bear the yoke, the task of Enlil,
Let man assume the drudgery of god."
Nintu[4] made ready to speak,
And said to the great gods:
"It is not for me to do it,
The task is Enki's.
He it is that cleanses all,
Let him provide me the clay so I can do the making."
Enki made ready to speak,
And said to the great gods:
"On the first, seventh, and fifteenth days of the month,[5] [b]
Let me establish a purification, a bath.
Let one god be slaughtered,
Then let the gods be cleansed by immersion.
Let Nintu mix clay with his flesh and blood.
Let that same god and man be thoroughly mixed in the clay.
Let us hear the drum for the rest of time,
From the flesh of the god let a spirit remain,
Let it make the living know its sign,
Lest he be allowed to be forgotten, let the spirit remain."
The great Anunna-gods, who administer destinies,
Answered "yes!" in the assembly.
On the first, seventh, and fifteenth days of the month,
He established a purification, a bath.
They slaughtered Aw-ilu, who had the inspiration, in their assembly.
Nintu mixed clay with his flesh and blood.
<That same god and man were thoroughly mixed in the clay.>

b 2 Kgs 4:23; Isa 1:13; 66:23

For the rest [of time they would hear the drum],
From the flesh of the god [the] apt[rit remained].
It would make the living know its sign,
Lest he be allowed to be forgotten, [the] spirit remained.
After she had mixed that clay,
She summoned the Anunna, the great gods.
The Igigi, the great gods, spat upon the clay.
Mami made ready to speak,
And said to the great gods:
"You ordered me the task and I have completed (it)!
You have slaughtered the god, along with his inspiration.
I have done away with your heavy forced labor,
I have imposed your drudgery on man.
You have bestowed(?) clamor upon mankind.
I have released the yoke, I have [made] restoration."
They heard this speech of hers,
They ran, free of care, and kissed her feet, (saying):
"Formerly [we used to call] you Mami,
Now let your n[am]e be "Mistress-of-All-the Gods (Belet-kala-ili)"

[The population increases until their noise disturbs the gods. They try to reduce humanity with disease and starvation, but Enki saves the human race through advising a wise man, Atrahasis, what to do. The gods resolve on a flood to wipe out all humans. Enki warns Atrahasis in a dream.]

E[nlil] committed an evil deed against the peoples.

Atrahasis made ready to speak,
And said to his lord:
"Make me know the meaning [of the dream],
[ ] let me know, that I may look out for its consequence."
[Enki] made ready to speak,
And said to his servant:
"You might say, 'Am I to be looking out while in the bedroom?'
Do you pay attention to message that I speak for you:
'Wall, listen to me!
Reed wall, pay attention to all my words!
Flee the house, build a boat,
Forsake possessions, and save life.[6]
The boat which you build,
[ ] be equal [ ]

[4] Nin-tu, whose very name means "lady who gives birth," is the mother-goddess par excellence. Belit-ili, "the mistress of the gods," Mami, "the mother?" and Aruru are other manifestations of the same goddess.

[5] I.e, the new moon, the first quarter, and the full moon, the principal lunar festivals of Old Babylonian times. The last was called *šapattu* in Akk., and it is possible that the original meaning of Heb. *šabbat* was the same; see Hallo 1977 and Epic of Creation (above, text 1.111) V 14-18 and n. 10.

[6] For the play on words involved, see Gilgamesh Epic XI (below, text 1.132) 24-26 and n. 2.

[gap]

Roof her over like the depth,
(30) So that the sun shall not see inside her,
Let her be roofed over fore and aft.
The gear should be very strong,
The pitch should be firm, and so give (the boat) strength.
I will shower down upon you later
(35) A windfall of birds, a spate(?) of fishes.'
He opened the water clock[7] and filled it,
He told it of the coming of the seven-day deluge.[c]
Atrahasis received the command,
He assembled the elders at his gate.
(40) Atrahasis made ready to speak,
And said to the elders:
"My god [does not agree] with your god,
Enki and [Enlil] are constantly angry with each other.
They have expelled me from [the land(?)].
(45) Since I have always reverenced [Enki],
[He told me] this.
I can[not] live in [ ]
Nor can I [set my feet on] the earth of Enlil.
[I will dwell(?)] with <my> god in(?) the depths."
(50) "[This] he told me [ ] ..."

[gap of four or five lines]

(ii)

[gap]

(ii 10) The elders [ ]
The carpenter [carried his axe],
The reed-worker [carried his stone].
[The rich man? carried] the pitch,
The poor man [brought the materials needed].

[gap]

Atrahasis [ ]

[gap]

Bringing [ ]
(ii 30) Whatever he [had]
Whatever he had [ ]
Pure (animals) he sl[aughtered, cattle] ...
Fat (animals) [he killed, sheep(?)] ...
He chose tand brought on] board.
(ii 35) The [birds] flying in the heavens,
The cattle(?) [and of the cat]tle god,
The [creatures(?)] of the steppe,
[ ] he brought on board
[ ] ...
(ii 40) [ ] he invited his people

c Gen 7:4, 10

[ ] to a feast.
[ ] his family he brought on board.
While one was eating and another was drinking,
(ii 45) He went in and out; he could not sit, could not kneel,
For his heart was broken, he was retching gall.
The outlook of the weather changed,
Adad began to roar in the clouds.
(ii 50) The god they heard, his clamor.
He brought pitch to seal his door.
By the time he had bolted his door,
Adad was roaring in the clouds.
The winds were furious as he set forth,
(ii 55) He cut the mooring rope and released the boat.

[four lines lost]

(iii 5) [ ] the storm
[ ] were yoked
[Anzu rent] the sky with his talons,
[He] the land
(iii 10) And broke its clamor [like a pot].
[ ] the flood [came forth],
Its power came upon the peoples [like a battle].
One person did [not] see another,
They could [not] recognize each other in the catastrophe.
(iii 15) [The deluge] bellowed like a bull,
The wind [resound]ed like a screaming eagle.
The darkness [was dense], the sun was gone,
[ ] ... like flies[8]
(iii 20) [the clamor(?)] of the deluge

[The gods regret their hasty action when they find themselves hungry and thirsty. When they find that Atrahasis has survived, they agree to a proposal that certain classes of humanity not reproduce.]

(iii 45) [Enki] made ready to speak,
And [said to] Nintu the birth goddess:
"[You], birth goddess, creatress of destinies,
[Establish death] for all peoples!

...

(1) "Now then, let there be a third (woman) among the people,
Among the people are the woman who has borne and the woman who has not borne.
Let there be (also) among the people the (she) — demon,
(5) Let her snatch the baby from the lap of her who bore it,
Establish high priestesses and priestesses,[9]
Let them be taboo, and so cut down childbirth.

[7] For the water clock in Mesopotamia, see Neugebauer 1947.
[8] For the role of the flies in the aftermath lof the Deluge, cf. Gilgamesh Epic XI (below, text 1.132) 161-163 and n. 6.
[9] The high priestess and certain other classes of priestesses were forbidden to have children (except perhaps by the king). See below, 1.133 and note 2.

REFERENCES

Text: Lambert and Millard 1969. Translations and studies: Dalley 1989:1-38; Foster *BM* 1:160-185; *FDD* 52-77.

ETANA (1.131)

Stephanie Dalley

The story centers on a king of Kish who is attested in the Sumerian king list as a quasi-historical character. Presumably the legend had its origin in Kish, although the patron deities of Kish, Zababa and Ishtar, play no part, for the sun-god Shamash alone is involved. The length and ending of the story are still disputed; if it was a three-tablet composition in its "Standard" form, it should consist of about 450 lines in all.

Tablets of the Old Babylonian version come from Susa in Elam and from Tell Harmal; a Middle Assyrian version comes from Assur, and the "Standard" version from Nineveh, to which may be added unprovenanced tablets in museum collections. But the story is certainly much older, for Lu-Nanna, the demi-sage of Shulgi, king of Ur (21st century), is credited as the author, and the ascent of Etana on an eagle's back is shown on cylinder seals of the Akkadian period (ca. 23rd century). The late version omits some episodes which are quite crucial to the understanding of the story although in other ways the versions seem close, with mainly rephrasing of individual lines or passages.

The bare motif, of a man's ascent to heaven on an eagle's back, is also found in the Greek myth of Ganymede; it was incorporated into the Alexander Romance, and is also found in Iranian stories and Islamic legends. The motif of a tree inhabited by a snake and a bird also occurs in the Sumerian text *Gilgamesh and the Halub Tree*, (see Dalley 1989:134, n. 147).

Etana is the only Mesopotamian tale to have been identified unequivocally on ancient cylinder seals (see Baudot 1982).

The different versions were almost certainly divided into tablets at different points in the text. SBV is followed here.

(SBV) (**Tablet I**)
[The great gods, the Igigi] designed a city,
[The Igigi] laid its foundation.
[The Anunnaki] designed the city of Kish,
[The Anunnaki] laid its foundation,
The Igigi made its brickwork firm
[ ].
"Let [ ] be their shepherd [ ]
Let Etana be their builder (?) [ ] the staff of [ ]."
The great Anunnaki who decree destinies
Sat and conferred their counsel on the land.
They were creating the four quarters (of the world) and establishing the form (of it).
The Igigi [ ] decreed names (?) for them all.[1]
They had not established a king over all the teeming people.[2]
At that time the headband and crown had not been put together,[3]
And the lapis lazuli sceptre had not been brandished (?),[4]
At the same time (?) the throne-dais had not been made.[5]
The Sebitti barred the gates against armies (?),
[The] barred them against (other) settled peoples.
The Igigi would patrol the city [ ].[6]
Ishtar [was looking for] a shepherd
And searching high and low for a king.
Inninna [was looking for] a shepherd
And searching high and low for a king.
Ellil was looking for a throne-dais for Etana.
"The young man for whom Ishtar [is looking so dilige]ntly
And searches endlessly [ ].
A king is hereby affirmed for the land, and in Kish [it is established (?)]"
He brought kingship [ ]
[ ]
The gods of the lands [ ][7]

(about 120 lines missing)

---

[1] OBV has "festival" for "names(?)."

[2] "Teeming," *apâti*, used to be translated "beclouded" owing to an incorrect etymology.

[3] Early crowns consisted of two parts: a rigid conical or high oval cap, and a band encircling its edge.

[4] Taking the verb as *ṣabāru* II, not *ṣapāru*. Alternatively, "The sceptre had not been inlaid with lapis lazuli."

[5] This line is taken from OBV, since it connects with a subsequent line, eight lines later.

[6] OBV adds: "Sceptre and crown, headband and staffs, Were set before Anum in heaven. There was no advice for its people, (Until) kingship came down from heaven."

(Tablet II)
He named him [ ]-man [ ][8]
He built a fort (?) [ ][9]
In the shade of that throne-dais a poplar sprouted [ ]
On its crown an eagle crouched, [and a serpent lay at its base].
Every day they would keep watch [for their prey (?)].
The eagle made its voice heard and said to the serpent,
"Come, let us be friends,
Let us be comrades, you and I."
The serpent made its voice heard and spoke to the eagle,
"[You are not fit for] friendship [in the sight of Shamash!]
You are wicked and you have grieved his heart.
You have done unforgivable deeds, an abomination to the gods.[10]
(But) come, let us stand up and [make a pledge (?)]"[11]
In the presence of Shamash the warrior they swore an oath,
"Whoever oversteps the limit set by Shamash,
Shamash shall deliver into the hands of the Smiter for harm.[12]
Whoever oversteps the limit set by Shamash,
May the mountain keep its pass far away from him,
May the prowling weapon make straight for him,
May the snares (on which) the oath to Shamash (is sworn) overturn him and ensnare him!"[13]
When they had sworn the oath on [the net of Shamash (?)],
They stood up (?) and went up the mountain.[14]
Each day they kept watch [for their prey (?).]
The eagle would catch a wild bull or wild ass,
And the serpent would eat, (then) turn away so that its young could eat.
The serpent would catch mountain goats or gazelles,[15]
And the eagle would eat, (then) turn away so that its young could eat.
The eagle would catch wild boar and wild sheep.
And the serpent would eat, (then) turn away so that its your could eat.
The serpent would catch cattle from the plains and wild beasts from the countryside,
And the eagle would eat, (then) turn away so that its young could eat.
The young of the serpent [had an abundance] of food.
The eagle's young grew large and flourished.
When the eagle's young had grown large and flourished,
The eagle plotted evil in its heart,
And in its heart it plotted evil,
And made up its mind to eat its friend's young ones.
The eagle made its voice heard and spoke to its young,
"I am going to eat the serpent's young ones,
The serpent [is sure to be an]gry
So I shall go up and abide in the sky.
I shall come down from the tree top only to eat the fruit!"
A small fledgling, especially wise, addressed its words to the eagle, its father,
"Father, don't eat! The net of Shamash will ensnare you.
The snares (on which) the oath of Shamash (is sworn) will overturn you and ensnare you.
(Remember:) Whoever oversteps the limit set by Shamash,
Shamash shall deliver into the hands of the Smiter for harm."
It would not listen to them, and would not listen to the word of its sons.
It went down and ate the serpent's young.
In the evening at the close of day,
The serpent came and was carrying its load,
Laid the meat down at the entrance to its nest,
Stared, for its nest was not there.
Morning came (?), but [the eagle] did not [appear]
For with its talons it had [clawed at] the ground,
And its dust cloud [covered] the heavens on high.
The serpent lay down and wept,
Its tears flowed before Shamash.
"I trusted in you, Shamash the warrior.
And I was helpful (?) to the eagle who lives on the branches.[16]

[7] In the following gap, Kinnier Wilson inserted a fragment that may better be placed in Tablet III. It is too fragmentary for translation here.
[8] Perhaps "They" instead of "He."
[9] "Throne-dais" may be used here to mean a whole shrine.
[10] "You have done ... an abomination": lit., "You ate *asakku*-food." When pacts were made, ritual food was eaten which would "turn against" the one who broke the pact.
[11] Oaths were sworn while touching an appurtenance or symbol of a deity, which then could act as a weapon enforcing retribution upon a perjurer. The net thus may be referred to as a "prowling weapon" six lines later.
[12] Or, "hunter" rather than "smiter."
[13] MAV adds: "May Shamash lift his head for the slaughterer, May Shamash deliver the evil one into the hands of the smiter, May he station an evil *gallu*-demon over him."
[14] OBV inserts a perfunctory line: "All conceived, all gave birth," which MAV elaborates to: "In the crown of the tree the Eagle gave birth, And at the base of the poplar the serpent gave birth, In the shade of that poplar The Eagle and the Serpent became friends, They swore an oath together, they were partners, They confided their worries to each other."
[15] OBV has: "The serpent would catch a leopard (or) a tiger."
[16] Reading: *ana erî tumanî anāku ašrum* (SMD).

Now the serpent's nest [is grief-stricken].[17]
My own nest is not there, while its nest is safe.
My young ones are scattered and its young ones are safe.
It came down and ate my young ones!
You know the wrong which it has done me, Shamash!
Truly, O Shamash, your net is as wide as earth,
Your snare is as broad as the sky!
The eagle should not escape from your net,
As criminal as Anzu, who wronged his comrade."[18]
[When he heard] the serpent's plea,
Shamash made his voice heard and spoke to the serpent,
"Go along the path, cross the mountain
Where a wild bull [ ] has been bound for you.[19]
Open up its innards, slit open its stomach,
Make a place to sit inside its stomach.
All kinds of birds will come down from the sky and eat the flesh.
The eagle too [will come down] with them.
[Since] it will not be aware of danger to itself,
It will search out the tenderest morsels, will comb the area (?),
Penetrate to the lining of the innards.
When it enters the innards, you must seize it by the wing,
Cut its wings, feather and pinion,
Pluck it and throw it into a bottomless pit,
Let it die there of hunger and thirst!"
At the command of the warrior Shamash,
The serpent went, it crossed the mountain.
The serpent came upon the wild bull,
And opened up its innards and slit open its stomach,
And made a place to sit inside its stomach.
All kinds of birds came down from the sky and began to eat the flesh.
But the eagle was aware of the danger to itself
And would not eat the flesh with the other birds.
The eagle made its voice heard and spoke to its son,
"Come, let us go down and let us eat the flesh of this wild bull!"
But the young fledgling was exceptionally wise, and said to the eagle its father,
"Don't go down, father; perhaps the serpent is lying in wait inside this wild bull!"
The eagle reasoned thus to itself:
"If the birds felt any fear,
How would they be eating the flesh so peacefully?"
It did not pay heed to them, did not listen to the words of its sons,
Came down and stood upon the wild bull.
The eagle inspected the flesh,
But kept scanning ahead of it and behind it.
It inspected the flesh again,
But kept scanning ahead of it and behind it.
It kept going further in (?) until it penetrated to the lining of the innards.
As it went right in, the serpent seized it by the wing.
"You robbed (?) my nest, you robbed my nest!"[20]
The eagle made its voice heard and began to speak to the serpent,
"Spare me, and I shall give you, as one betrothed, a *nudunnû*-payment."[21]
The serpent made its voice heard and spoke to the eagle,
"If I were to free you, how would I answer Shamash the Most High?
The punishment due to you would revert to me,
The punishment that I now inflict on you!"
It cut its wings, pinion and feather,
Plucked it and threw it into a pit,
To die of hunger and thirst.
[The eagle]
Every day it prayed repeatedly to Shamash,
"Am I to die in the pit?
Who realizes that it is your punishment I bear?
Save my life for me, the eagle,
So that I may broadcast your fame for eternity!"
Shamash made his voice heard and spoke to the eagle,
"You are wicked, and you have grieved my heart.
You did an unforgivable deed, an abomination to the gods.
You were under oath, and I shall not go near you!
But a man, whom I am sending to you, is coming — let him help you."
Every day, Etana prayed repeatedly to Shamash,
"O Shamash, you have enjoyed the best cuts of my sheep,
Earth has drunk the blood of my lambs,
I have honored the gods and respected the spirits

[17] Restored from OBV.
[18] As it stands in SBV, this line alludes to Anzu's betrayal of Ellil while acting as his trusted doorkeeper. However, MAV has the similar-sounding word *anzillu*, "abomination," at the same point, so the allusion to Anzu may derive from a corrupt text. Cf. also Erra and Ishum, note 39 Text 1.113 above.
[19] Or, "Where [Shakkan] has bound a wild bull for you" or: "Where [I, Shamash,] have bound a wild bull for you."
[20] Very uncertain; von Soden reads as: "you entered and changed my nest"; Kinnier Wilson "You entered upon my nestlings." Edzard 1986:137 suggests a serpentine tongue-twister.
[21] The word implies payment to a bride before marriage which ensured her livelihood after her husband's death.

of the dead.
The dream-interpreters have made full use of my incense.
The gods have made full use of my lambs at the slaughter.
O Lord, let the word go forth from your mouth
And give me the plant of birth,
Show me the plant of birth,
Remove my shame and provide me with a son!"[22]
Shamash made his voice heard and spoke to Etana,
"Go along the road, cross the mountain,
Find a pit and look carefully at what is inside it.
An eagle is abandoned down there.
It will show you the plant of birth."
At the command of Shamash the warrior,
Etana went, crossed the mountain,
Found the pit and looked at what was inside it.
An eagle was abandoned down there.
The eagle raised itself up at once.

(Tablet III)

(LV) The eagle made its voice heard and spoke to Shamash,[23]
"O Lord, [ ]
The offspring (?) of a bird [ ]
I am [ ]
Whatever he says [ ]
Whatever I say, [ ]."
At the command of Shamash, [ ]
The offspring (?) of the bird [ ].
The eagle made its voice heard and spoke to Etana,
"Why have you come to me? Tell me!"
Etana made his voice heard and spoke to the eagle,
"O my friend, glve me the plant of blrth,
Show me the plant of birth!
Remove my shame and provide me with a son!
Leave [...]
When you get out (?) [...]
Then the eagle said [to Etana (?)],
"All alone I shall [search the mountains (?)].[24]
Let me bring [the plant of birth (?)] to you."
(MAV) When Etana heard this,[25]
He covered the front of the pit with juniper,
Made for it and threw down [...]
And kept [...]
Thus he kept (?) the eagle alive in the pit.
He began to teach it to fly again.
For one [month], then a second [month]
He kept (?) the eagle alive in the pit
And began to teach it to fly again.
For a third [month], then a fourth mo[nth]
He kept (?) the eagle alive in the pit
And began to teach it to fly again.
(OBV) [Etana] helped it for seven months.
In the eighth month he helped it out of its pit.[26]
The eagle, now well fed, was as strong as a fierce lion.
The eagle made its voice heard and spoke to Etana,
"My friend, we really are friends, you and I!
Tell me what you wish from me, that I may give it to you."
Etana made his voice heard and spoke to the eagle,
"Change my destiny (?) and disclose what is concealed!"

(Gap of about 6 lines?)

(SBV) Etana (?) went and [helped the eagle out (?)].[27]
The eagle hunted around [in the mountains (?)]
But [the plant of birth] was not [to be found there].
"Come, my friend, let me carry you up [to the sky],
[Let us meet] with Ishtar, the mistress [of birth].
Beside Ishtar the mistress [of birth let us].
Put your arms over my sides,
Put your hands over the quills of my wings."
He put his arms over its sides,
Put his hands over the quills of its wings.
[The eagle] took him upwards for a mile.
"My friend, look at the country! How does it seem ?"
"The affairs of the country buzz (?) [like flies (?)][28]
And the wide sea is no bigger than a sheepfold!"
[The eagle took him] up a second mile,
"My friend, look at the country! How does it seem ?"
"The country has turned into a garden [...],
And the wide sea is no bigger than a bucket!"
It took him up a third mile.
"My friend, look at the country! How does it seem ?"
"I am looking for the country, but I can't see it!
And my eyes cannot even pick out the wide sea!
My friend, I cannot go any further towards heaven.

[22] Reading *piltu* (from *pištu*) rather than *biltu*, "load, burden," which is the traditional translation, but inappropriate (SMD).

[23] Kinnier Wilson's IV c (p. 112) is taken here as a better-preserved variant of III A (p. 104) in his edition. His fragment III/B on p. 106 may not belong to this myth. I am indebted to Dr. Jeremy Hughes for the observation that Kinnier Wilson and others had assigned obverse and reverse to his Text M (plates 24-25) incorrectly (collated).

[24] Restorations are based on line endings preserved in III A, p. 104 of Kinnier Wilson's edition.

[25] The translation differs from that of Kinnier Wilson here, rejecting the restoration of a ladder with rungs, and taking the phrase *ṣabābu* + *kappu* in its attested sense of "to teach to fly."

[26] Taking the verb as *ṣâdu*.

[27] Kinnier Wilson would place this episode in a hypothetical fourth table (see his IV/A on p. 108). The present reconstruction supposes that line 8 of OBV in Kinnier Wilson p. 40 is a version of line 13 of SBV on p. 114, but this is far from certain.

[28] Reading *ihambuba* instead of *ihammuš*.

Retrace the way, and let me go back to my city!"
The eagle shrugged him off for one mile,
Then dropped down and retrieved him on its wings.
The eagle shrugged him off for a second mile,
Then dropped down and retrieved him on its wings.
The eagle shrugged him off for a third mile,
Then dropped down and retrieved him on its wings.
A metre from the ground, the eagle shrugged him off,
Then dropped down and retrieved him on its wings.

(Gap of uncertain length)

(They go back to Kish. Etana has a series of three (?) dreams which encourage him to make a second attempt to reach heaven.)

Etana said to the eagle,
"[My friend, I saw a first (?) dream.]
The city of Kish was sobbing [...]
Within it [the people were in mourning (?)]
I sang [a song of lamentation (?)].
'O Kish, giver of life!
Etana [cannot give you an heir (?)]
O Kish, giver of life,
[...]
Etana [cannot give you an heir (?)] ...'"

(Gap of uncertain length)

His wife said to Etana,[29]
"[The god] showed me a dream.
Like Etana my husband [I have had a dream (?)],
Like you [the god has shown me a dream (?)].
Etana was king [of Kish for x years (?)]
And his ghost [ ]

(Gap of uncertain length)

(Tablet IV)

Etana opened his mouth and spoke to the eagle,
"My friend, that god showed me [another dream (?)].[30]
We were going through the entrance of the gate of Anu, Ellil, and Ea.
We bowed down together, you and I.
We were going through the entrance of the gate of Sin, Shamash, Adad, and Ishtar,
We bowed down together, you and I.
I saw a house with a window that was not sealed.
I pushed it open and went inside.
Sitting in there was a girl
(10) Adorned with a crown, fair of face.
A throne was set in place, and [...]
Beneath the throne crouched snarling lions.
I came up and the lions sprang at me.
I woke up terrified."
The eagle said to Etana,
"My friend, [the significance of the dreams] is quite clear!
Come, let me carry you up to the heaven of Anu.
Put your chest over my breast,
Put your hands over the quills of my wings.
(20) Put your arms over my sides."
He put his chest over its breast,
Put his hands over its feathers,
Put his arms over its sides.
The eagle tied its load on securely,
Took him up a mile
And spoke to him, to Etana,
"See, my friend, how the country seems!
Inspect the sea, look carefully for its features!
The country is only the edge (?) of (?) a mountain!
(30) And whatever has become of the sea?"[31]
The eagle took him up a second mile
And spoke to Etana,
"See, my friend, how the country seems!
Whatever [has become of (?)] the country?"
The eagle took him up a third mile
And spoke to Etana,
"See, my friend, how the country seems!
The sea has turned into a gardener's ditch!"
When they came up to the heaven of Anu,
They went through the gate of Anu, Ellil, and Ea.
(40) The eagle and Etana bowed down together.
They went through the gate of Sin, Shamash, Adad, and Ishtar.[32]
The eagle and Etana bowed down together.
[...]
He pushed it open [and went inside].

(The rest of the text is missing)

(According to the Sumerian King List, Etana was succeeded by his son Balih.)

---

[29] This fragment, given by Kinnier Wilson, p. 125 as LV, V, may come as the second in the preceding sequence of three dreams. Both in Etana and in Gilgamesh the reconstructions given here allow for a sequence of threes for confirmation. The dream may have indicated that Etana would have a son to carry out his funerary rites.

[30] For the phrase *ana mimmê tuāru* see *AHw*, s.v. *mimmû* B_2 (SMD).

[31] The text has "ditto" at the repetitions.

[32] The text has "ditto" at the repetitions.

REFERENCES

Text: Kinnier Wilson 1985. Translations: Dalley 1989:189-202; Foster *BM* 1:437-460; *FDD* 132-163.

GILGAMESH (1.132)

Benjamin R. Foster

The Gilgamesh Epic is deservedly the most famous literary relic of ancient Mesopotamia. Its evolution can be traced from episodic Sumerian beginnings ("The Tale of Ziusudra") through successive Akkadian translations and adaptations to a final canonical version in twelve tablets (chapters) (see Tigay 1982), and serves as an empirical model for testing hypotheses about the evolution of the Biblical canon (Tigay 1985). Its recovery began early and helped spark interest in the further exploration of Assyria and, later, of Babylonia; the recovery is still not complete, and new discoveries continue to complete our knowledge of the text in its successive recensions. The overall theme of the integrated epic is the (doomed) quest for eternal life and the "consolation-prize" of enduring fame which, in the case of Gilgamesh, has actually been achieved. Of the many translations into English, those of Speiser in *ANET* (1956), Gallery Kovacs (1989) and Dalley (1989) can be singled out for accuracy, that of Gardner and Maier (1984) for its poetry. Note also two important new translations into French by Bottéro (1992) and Tournay and Shaffer (1994) respectively.

Of the many Biblical parallels featured in the Epic, none are more numerous or more familiar than those of Tablet XI with its version of the Mesopotamian story of the Deluge. It is the most elaborate version of a story that had been told in briefer compass already in other contexts, both Sumerian and Akkadian. Here it is put into the mouth of the Flood-hero himself, known in different versions by different names but here as Utnapishtim, (Uta-napishtam, "I have/he has found life"). At one stage of its evolution, Tablet XI was the last tablet of the epic, and concluded with the return of Gilgamesh to Uruk (omitted here). Subsequently a twelfth tablet was added by straight translation from a Sumerian prototype; it included a vision of the netherworld over which Gilgamesh presided as a deity. [WWH]

Gilgamesh said to him, to Utnapishtim the far-off,
"As I look upon you, Utnapishtim,
Your limbs are not strange, you are just as I am,
You are not strange at all, you are just as I am!
I imagined you ready for battle,
Yet my arm [ ] and you lie on your back.
[Tell me], how did you join the ranks of the gods when you sought life?"
Utnapishtim said to him, to Gilgamesh,
"Let me reveal to you, O Gilgamesh, a hidden matter,
And a secret of the gods let me tell you.
Shuruppak, a city you know of,
[And which on] Euphrates [bank] is situate,
That city was ancient and the gods were within it.
The great gods resolved to send the deluge.[1]
They [sw]ore their father Anu,
Their counsellor the warrior Enlil,
Their throne-bearer Ninurta,
Their canal-officer Ennugi,
The leader Ea was under oath with them.
He repeated their plans to the reed hut,
'Reed hut, reed hut, wall, wall!
Listen reed hut, be mindful, wall!
Man of Shuruppak, son of Ubartutu,
Destroy this house, build a ship,
Forsake possessions, seek life,
Build an ark and save life.[2]
Take aboard ship seed of all living things.
The ship which you shall build,
Let her dimensions be measured off.
Let her width and length be equal,
Roof her over like a hidden depth.'
I undestood full well, I said to Ea my lord,
'[Your command], my lord, which you spoke just so,
I shall faithfully execute.
What shall I answer to the city, the multitude, and the elders?'
Ea made ready to speak,
Saying to me, his servant,
"Young man, do you speak to them thus,
'It seems that Enlil dislikes me,
I cannot dwell in your city,
I may not set my foot on the dry land of Enlil,
I shall go down to the depths and dwell with my lord Ea.
[Upon] you shall he shower down in abundance,
[ ] of birds, a surprise of fishes,
[ ], harvest riches,
[In the morning] spate of cakes,
[In the evening] rain of grain.
[With the fir]st glimmer of dawn in the land,
The land was assembling [around me].
The carpenter carried his ax[e],
The [reedcutter] carried his kn[ife],
[ ] the workmen [ ],
The houses [made rope],

[1] Akk. *abūbu*. But in Sum., the word for flood is *amaru* (*amatu, marru*) and a near homonym with the native name for the Amorites who overran the lower valley of Tigris and Euphrates early in the third millennium, probably by descending the river courses "like a flood." It can therefore be suggested that, for the Sumerians, the "flood" was a metaphor for the Amorite incursions while the Akkadians and Akkadian-speaking Amorites who succeeded them in the rule of Mesopotamia "resolved" the metaphor by treating it literally; see Hallo 1990:194-197.

[2] There is a double-entendre in the original, for the words for "ship" and "possessions" are virtual homonyms in Akk.; for the corresponding passage in Atra-hasis, see above, Text 1.130 I 23-25 and note 6; for both see Hoffner 1976. For the alleged Janus parallelism of the passage (i.e. looking both forwards and backwards) see Noegel 1991.

The wealthy carried the pitch,
The poor brought ... what was needful.
On the fifth day I laid her framework,
One full acre was her floorspace,
Ten dozen cubits each was the height of her walls,
Ten dozen cubits each were the edges around her.
I laid out her contours, I sketched out her lines,
I decked her in six,
I divided her in seven,
Her interior I divided nine ways.
I drove the waterplugs into her,
I saw to the spars and laid in what was needful.
Thrice 3600 measures of pitch I poured in the oven,
Thrice 3600 measures of tar did [I pour out] inside her.
Thrice 3600 measures of oil for the workers who carried the baskets,
Aside from the 300 measures of oil that the caulking consumed,
And twice 3600 measures of oil that the boatmen stored away.
For the [builders] bullocks were slaughtered,
And I killed sheep every day,
Fine beer, [grape] wine, oil and date wine,
[Did I give] the workers [to drink] like drinking water,
They made a feast as on New Year's Day.
[I opened(?)] ointment, dispensed (it) with my own hand.
On the seventh day(?) the ship was completed,[3] [a]
[ ] were very difficult.
They brought on gang planks(?), fore and aft,
[They ca]me [up] her (side?) two thirds (of her height?).
[Whatever I had] I loaded upon her:
What silver I had I loaded upon her,
What gold I had I loaded upon her,
What living creatures I had I loaded upon her.
I made go aboard all my family and kin,
Beasts of the steppe, wild animals of the steppe,
all skilled craftsmen I made go on board.
Shamash set for me an appointed time:
'In the morning when it spates in cakes,
In the evening when it rains in grain,
Go into your ship, batten the door!'
That appointed time arrived,
In the morning spates in cakes,
In the evening rain in grain,
I gazed upon the appearance of the storm,
The storm was frightful to behold!
I went into the ship and battened my door,
To the caulker of the ship, to Puzur-Amurri, the boatman,

a Gen 7:4, 10

b Gen 3:19

I gave (away my) palace, with all its possessions.
At the first glimmer of dawn,
A black cloud rose up from the horizon,
Inside [the cloud] Adad was thundering.[4]
While Shullat and Hanish went on before,
Moving as a retinue over hill and plain,
Erragal tore out the dike posts,
Ninurta came and brought with him the dikes.
The Anunna-gods held torches aloft,
Setting the land ablaze with their glow.
Adad's awesome power passed over the heavens,
Whatever was light he turned into darkness.
[He smote ...] the land, it shattered like a pot!
For one day the storm wind [ ],
Swiftly it blew, [the flood cam]e forth,
It was passing over the people like a battle.
No one could see his neighbor,
Nor could the people see each other in the downpour.
The gods became frightened of the deluge,
They shrank back and went up to Anu's highest heaven.
The gods cowered like dogs, crouching outside,
Ishtar screamed like a woman in childbirth,
And sweet-voiced Belet-[ili] moaned aloud:
'Would that day had turned to nought,
When I spoke up for evil in the assembly of the gods!'
'How could I have spoken up for evil in the assembly of the gods,
'And spoken up for an assault to the death against my people?
It was I myself who bore my people!
(Now) like fish spawn they choke up the sea!'
The Anunna-gods were weeping with her,
The gods sat where they were(?), weeping.
Their lips were parched(?), taking on a crust.
Six days and [seven] nights
The wind continued, the deluge and windstorm levelled the land.
When the seventh day arrived, the windstorm and deluge left off their assault,
Which they had launched, like a fight to the death.
The sea grew calm, the tempest grew still, the deluge ceased.
I looked at the weather, stillness reigned,
And all of mankind had turned into clay.[b]
The landscape was flat as a terrace.
I opened the hatch, daylight fell upon my face.
Crumpling over, I sat down and wept,
Tears running down my face.
I beheld the edges of the world, bordering the sea,
At twelve times sixty leagues a mountain rose up.
The boat rested on Mount Nimush,

[3] For the significance of the seven-day motif in the various versions of the Flood-story, see Hallo 1991a:178-181.
[4] Adad represented the storm, while the other deities mentioned in the next five lines represented other natural phenomena.

Mount Nimush held the boat fast, not allowing it to move.[5] [c]
One day, a second day Mount Nimush held the boat fast, not allowing it to move.
A third day, a fourth day Mount Nimush held the boat fast, not allowing it to move.
A fifth day, a sixth day Mount Nimush held the boat fast, not allowing it to move.
When the seventh day arrived,
I released a dove to go free,
The dove went and returned,
No landing place came to view, it turned back.
I released a swallow to go free,
The swallow went and returned,
No landing place came to view, it turned back.
I sent a raven to go free,
The raven went forth, saw the ebbing of the waters,
It ate, circled, left droppings, did not turn back.[d]
I released (all) to the four cardinal points,
I set up an offering stand on the top of the mountain.
Seven and seven cult vessels I set out,
I heaped reeds, cedar, and myrtle in their bowls.
The gods smelled the savor,
The gods smelled the sweet savor,[e]
The gods crowded around the sacrificer like flies.
As soon as Belet-ili arrived,
She held up the great fly-ornaments that Anu had made her in his infatuation,[6]
'O these gods here, as surely as I shall not forget this lapis on my neck,[7]
I shall be mindful of these days, and not forget, forever!
Let the gods come to the offering,
But Enlil must not come to the offering,
For he, unreasoning, brought on the deluge,
And reckoned my people for destruction!'
Suddenly, as Enlil arrived,
He saw the boat, Enlil became angry,
He was filled with fury at the gods.
'Who came out alive? No man was to survive destruction!'
Ninurta made ready to speak, and said to the warrior Enlil,
'Who but Ea could devise such a thing?
For Ea alone knows every craft.'
Ea made ready to speak, and said to the warrior Enlil,
'You, O warrior, are the sage of the gods,
How could you, unreasoning, have brought on the deluge?
Impose punishment on the sinner for his sin,
On the transgressor for his transgression,
(But) be lenient, lest he be cut off, bear with him, lest he fall.
Instead of your bringing on the flood, would a lion had risen up to diminish mankind!
Instead of your bringing on the flood, would a wolf had risen up to diminish mankind!
Instead of your bringing on the flood, would a famine
had risen up for the land to undergo,
Instead of your bringing on the flood, would pestilence
had risen up for mankind to undergo!
I was not the one who disclosed the secret of the great gods,
I made Atra-hasis see a dream, he heard a secret of the gods.[8]
Now then, make some plan for him.'
Then Enlil came up into the ship,
Leading me by the hand, he brought me up too.
He took my wife up and made her kneel beside me,
He touched our brows, stood between us and blessed us,
"Hitherto Utnapishtim has been a human being,
Now Utnapishtim and his wife shall become like us gods,
Utnapishtim shall dwell afar-off at the source of the rivers."
Thus it was they took me afar-off and made me dwell at the source of the rivers.

c Gen 8:4
d Gen 8:6-12
e Gen 8:21

[5] Others read Nisir. The mountain is elsewhere located "in the land of Gutium," presumably somewhere in the Zagros highlands east of the Tigris not, as in the Bible, in Urartu (Ararat, i.e., eastern Turkey); see Hallo 1971b:718f.

[6] The fly-ornaments may have been suggested by the simile of line 161 (or vice versa); for their significance see Kilmer 1987. For flies in the Atra-hasis version of the flood-story, see above, Text 1.130 III 19 and n. 9.

[7] The reference may be to a cylinder-seal made of lapis and typically mounted on a pin attached to a necklace worn around the neck; see Hallo 1985.

[8] Atra-hasis is the hero of an earlier version of the Flood-story in which famine and pestilence actually precede the Deluge as a means of stemming the growth of population; see above, Text 1.130.

REFERENCES

Text: Borger *BAL*[2] 1:105-111, 2:344-350. Translations and studies: see introductory note.

THE BIRTH LEGEND OF SARGON OF AKKAD (1.133)

Benjamin R. Foster

Sargon of Akkad erected the first world empire on Asiatic soil around 2300 BCE, and his exploits almost immediately became the stuff of legend. His (throne) name, in Akkadian *šarru-kēn(u)*, means "the king is legitimate," "the legitimate king," and served to make up for his usurpation of the claims of the ancient dynasty of Kish. The name was assumed again by an early king of Assyria (Sargon I, 20th century BCE) and by the more famous Sargon II (8th century BCE). "Sargon" is the biblical rendering of the last-named king (Isa 20:1). It was presumably also this king who commissioned a number of texts intended to glorify his old namesake, including the following legend of the latter's birth and rise to power, which shares features with the Moses narrative and with later treatments of the theme of the hero exposed at birth who nevertheless grows up to claim his birthright including, in this case, kingship. [WWH]

I am Sargon the great king, king of Agade.[1] [a]
My mother was a high priestess, I did not know my father.
My father's brothers dwell in the uplands.
My city is Azupiranu, which lies on Euphrates bank.
My mother, the high priestess, conceived me, she bore me in secret.[2]
She placed me in a reed basket, she sealed my hatch with pitch.
She left me to the river, whence I could not come up.[b]
The river carried me off, it brought me to Aqqi, drawer of water.
Aqqi, drawer of water, brought me up as he dipped his bucket.
Aqqi, drawer of water, raised me as his adopted son.
Aqqi, drawer of water, set (me) to his orchard work.
During my orchard work, Ishtar loved me,[3]
Fifty-five years I ruled as king.
I became lord over and ruled the black-headed folk,
I ... [ ] hard mountains with picks of copper,
I was wont to ascend high mountains,
I was wont to cross over low mountains.
The [la]nd of the sea I sieged three times,
I conquered Dilmun.
I went up to great Der, I [ ],
I destroyed [Ka]zallu and [ ].
Whatsoever king who shall arise after me,
[Let him rule as king fifty-five years],
Let him become lo[rd over and rule] the black-headed folk.
Let him [ ] hard mountains with picks [of copper].
Let him be wont to ascend high mountains,
[Let him be wont to cross over low mountains].
Let him siege the [la]nd of the sea three times,
[Let him conquer Dilmun].
Let him go up [to] great Der and [ ].
... from my city Agade
[breaks off]

a Gen 10:10
b Exod 2:2f.

[1] Agade, the capital newly constructed by Sargon, also known as Akkad after its spelling in the Biblical "Table of Nations" (Gen 10), where it is associated with the semi-legendary Nimrod, perhaps a reflex of Naram-Sin, the grandson of Sargon; see Hallo 1971a.

[2] As explained at the end of the Atra-hasis Epic (above, Text 1.130 and n. 9), the high priestess (*entu*) was forbidden to bear children perhaps, on one theory, because her child-bearing capacities were reserved for the king.

[3] The infatuation between Ishtar (or her Sum. equivalent Inanna) and a gardener, or vice versa, is the theme of several myths; see Hallo 1980a; Abusch 1985:161-173.

REFERENCES

Text: CT 13:42f. and duplicates. Translations and studies: *ANET* 119; Lewis 1980; Hallo 1991b:130f.; Foster *BM* 2:803-804; *FDD* 165-166.

2. HISTORIOGRAPHY

BABYLONIAN KING LISTS (1.134)

Alan Millard

Lists of rulers with lengths of reign were needed by scribes for calculating how long ago legal deeds had been concluded. They also enabled kings to learn when their predecessors had built temples or palaces which they were rebuilding. For a royal family they could supply a genealogy and justification for kingship although in Babylonia there were many changes of dynasty, in contrast to Assyria (compare the continuity of David's line contrasted with the changes in Israel). Lists of kings were read in religious ceremonies commemorating the dead. It is likely that they were also used in historical discussion; see the Weidner Chronicle (Text 1.138).

There are several lists of Babylonian kings. Two tablets give the lengths of reign and names of the kings of the Third Dynasty of Ur and the Dynasty of Isin, from ca. 2112 to about 1812 BCE, when they were written (Ur-Isin King List). Another tablet, clearly a practice or note tablet, lists kings of the Dynasty of Larsa, ca. 2025-1738 BCE twice (Larsa King List). A similar one gives the Second Dynasty of Isin, ca. 1157-1069 BCE (King List C). Kings of the First Dynasty of Babylon and the Dynasty of the Sea-Land, ca. 1894-1500 BCE, are listed on another of Neo-Babylonian date (King List B). The "Genealogy of the Hammurabi Dynasty" was created for a funerary cult at which the spirits of the dead were pacified with offerings and the recitation of their names in order to prevent them from harming the living. This tablet lists nineteen names, then the kings of the First Dynasty of Babylon (Hammurabi Dynasty, ca. 1894-1595 BCE), titled "Dynasty of the Amorites," followed by references to other ruling families and an attempt to ensure that all the dead were covered; see Finkelstein 1966, Lambert 1968. The principal Babylonian King List (A) gives all the rulers from the First Dynasty of Babylon until the end of Assyrian rule, with a note identifying each dynasty (*palû*), the number of its kings and its span. Regrettably, the tablet is damaged. Another composition, which is known in Akkadian and in bilingual Akkadian and Sumerian versions, begins in parallel with the Sumerian King List at the institution of monarchy and continues to the mid-eighth century BCE, with narrative passages that have led to its being called the "Dynastic Chronicle." Two texts, both incomplete, cover later periods, one commencing with Kandalanu and reaching to Seleucus II, ca. 647-226 BCE (Uruk King List), the other running from Alexander to Demetrius II, ca. 330-125 BCE, with each entry set beside the appropriate year of the Seleucid era (Seleucid King List). Each of these texts was drawn from more extensive sources. All the texts, except the Genealogy of the Hammurabi Dynasty, are set out by Grayson 1980.

Genealogy of the Hammurabi Dynasty

Arammadara, Tubtiyamuta, Yamquzuhalamma, Heana, Namzû, Ditana, Zummabu, Namhû,[1] Amnanu, Yahrurum, Iptiyamuta, Buzahum, Sumalika, Ashmadu, Abiyamuta, Abiditan, Mam[ ], Shu[ ], Dad[b]a[nâ], Sum[uabum],[2] Sumula[el], Zabium, Apil-Sin, Sin-muballit, Hammurabi, Samsuiluna, Abieshuh, Ammidita[na];

---

dynasty of Amorites, dynasty of Haneans, dynasty of Gutium;
any dynasty which is not written on this tablet and any soldier who fell in his master's service;
royal sons, royal daughters, all mankind from sunrise to sunset,
who have no one to care for them or celebrate them,
come, eat this, drink this,
bless Ammisaduqa, king of Babylon!

King List A (col. iv)

[ ] Nabu-shum-ishkun, [his son]
[ ] Nabu-na[sir][3]
2 years Nabu-nadin-zeri, his son
1 month, 13 days Nabu-shum-ishkun, his son

22[?] dynasty of Babylon

---

3 years Ukin-zer, dynasty of Shapi[4]
2 Pulu[5] [a]
5 Ululayu,[6] [b] dynasty of Ashur
12 Marduk-apla-iddin,[7] [c] dynasty of the Sea-Land
5 Sargon[d]
2 Sennacherib,[e] dynasty of Habigal[8]
1 month Marduk-zakir-shumi, son of Ardu
9 months Marduk-apla-iddin, Habi soldier[9]
3 years Bel-ibni, dynasty of Babylon
6 Ashur-nadin-shumi, dynasty of Habigal
1 Nergal-ushezib
5 Mushezib-Marduk, dynasty of Babylon
8 Sennacherib[10]
[ ] Esarha[11] [f]
[ ] Shamash-shum[12]
[ ] Kandal[13]

Seleucid King List

[ ] Alexander (III, the Great) [ ], Philip (III), brother of Alexander [ ]. For [x]1 years there

a 2 Kgs 15:19; 1 Chr 5:26
b 2 Kgs 17:3; 18:9
c 2 Kgs 20:12; Isa 39:1
d Isa 20:1
e 2 Kgs 18:13 et passim
f 2 Kgs 19:37; Isa 37:38; Ezra 4:2

---

[1] The names up to this one have some similarities with the first entries in the Assyrian King List (see below text 1.135) and may reflect a common tradition; see Finkelstein 1966; Malamat 1968; Hallo 1978; Glassner 1993:88-89; Chavalas 1994.

[2] Sumuabum was the first king of the First Dynasty of Babylon, ca. 1894-1881 BCE.

[3] Nabu-nasir: known from Greek sources as Nabonassar.

[4] Shapi is probably an abbreviation for Shapi-Bel, a stronghold in south-east Babylonia.

[5] Pulu: apparently a short name for Tiglath-pileser III, not found in documents contemporary with him, but in this King List, in 2 Kgs 15:19; 1 Chr 5:26 (where it is equated with Tiglath-pileser) and in Hellenistic Greek sources; see Brinkman 1968:61-62, 240-241.

[6] Ululaya: apparently the private name of Shalmaneser V (2 Kgs 17:3; 18:9), found also in the Assur Ostracon of the mid-seventh century BCE and in the Ptolemaic Canon of Babylonian kings; see Brinkman 1968:62, 243.

[7] Marduk-apla-iddin: biblical Merodach-baladan, see text 1.137, n. 4. He occurs twice because for a time he was chased from his throne by Sargon II.

[8] Habigal: probably a form of Hanigalbat, a term for Upper Mesopotamia current from the mid-second millennium BCE.

[9] Habi soldier: the meaning is unknown.

[10] Sennacherib occurs twice because the upheavals in Babylonia brought a number of short-lived rulers to the throne, both local and Assyrian nominees, before he finally brought the city under his direct control.

[11] Esarha: an abbreviation for Esarhaddon.

[12] Shamash-shum: an abbreviation for Shamash-shum-ukin, 667-648 BCE.

[13] Kandal: an abbreviation for Kandalanu, 647-627 BCE.

was no king in the land; Antigonus (the One-eyed), the general, was in control]. Alexander (IV) son of Alexander (III), [ruled until] year 6 (of the Seleucid Era). Year 7 is the year Seleucus became king; he ruled for 25 years. Year 31, month of Elul, king Seleucus was killed in the north-west. ...

[Year] 90, Antiochus (III, the Great) became king; he ruled for 35 [years. From year] 102 to year 119 Antiochus [ ] and Antiochus sons of the king. Year 125, month of Siwan, it was heard in Babylon that Antiochus (III) was killed on the 25th in Elam.

g Dan 8:9-14; 11:21-45

The same year Seleucus (IV, Philipator), his son, became king; he ruled for 12 years. Year 137, month of Elul, 10th day, king Seleucus died x x. The same month Antiochus (IV),[14] [g] his son, became king; he ruled for 11 years. The sa[me year], in Arahsamna, Antiochus and Antiochus, his son, became kings. [Year 1]42, in Ab, king Antiochus, son of Antiochus, was executed at the command of king Antiochus (IV). [Year 14]3, Antiochus was king alone. [Year 148] in Kislev, it was reported that king Antiochus [had died]. ...

[14] Antiochus IV, Epiphanes (175-164 BCE), the "little horn" of Daniel 8:9-14, the "despicable creature" of 11:21-45; cf. 1 Macc 1-6; 2 Macc 4-9.

REFERENCES

ANET 271 (King List B), 272 (King List A), 566-567 ("Seleucid" King List); Studies: Chavalas 1994; Finkelstein 1966; Glassner 1993:145-146; Grayson 1980; Hallo 1978; Lambert 1968; Malamat 1968.

ASSYRIAN KING LISTS (1.135)

Alan Millard

Lists of Assyrian kings have been found at Assur, Nineveh and Dur-Sharrukin (Khorsabad). The 'Assyrian King List' is known in five copies, none complete, two being only small fragments; there are slight variants between them. It begins with names of nomadic kings who lived about 2000 BCE, which some scholars think may be names of tribes rather than persons because there are similarities between them and names in the Genealogy of the Hammurabi Dynasty (see Babylonian King Lists, Text 1.134 above); however, tribes may also be named after their progenitors (cf. the tribes of Israel). The scheme of the List is simple: royal name, father's name, length of reign; each entry is separated from the next by a ruling. All copies share various short narrative passages and these are clearly part of the composition, not insertions by later hands, although it is clear that the opening sections were drawn from different sources. The purpose of the List was apparently to show continuity by collecting the names of all known rulers of Asshur considered to be "kings" (at least one is known today who is absent from the List; see Grayson *ARI* 1:29-30) and to supply relationships between them as far as possible. While there are evident links with the Eponym Canon (Text 1.136 below), the King List contains extra information, implying the existence of a more extensive record. Variant numbers of years and damage to the texts prevent construction of a complete chronology for Assyrian kings. There are small textual variations, given as alternatives in the translation, or mentioned in the footnotes. Two of the tablets, at least, had a tab at the top, pierced horizontally so that they could be fixed to a wall in such a way that someone could read the front, then lift up the tablet to read the back.

Fragments of two slightly different versions of the King List were found at Assur, and also five pieces of Synchronistic King Lists which set the names of the kings of Assyria in parallel with the kings of Babylon and vice-versa (cf. the synchronisms in Kings and Chronicles, e.g. 1 Kgs 15:1,9), one adding the names of the viziers (*ummânu*) who served many of the kings (*ANET* 272-274). All the Assyrian King Lists are set out by Grayson 1980.

Tudiya, Adamu, Yangi, Suhlamu, Harharu, Mandaru, Imsu, Harsu, Didanu, Hanu, Zuabu, Nuabu,[1] Abazu, Belu, Azarah, Ushpia, Apiashal.

Total: 17 kings who lived in tents.

Aminu was son of Ilu-kabkabu, Ilu-kabkabu of Yazkur-el, Yazkur-el of Yakmeni, Yakmeni of Yakmesi, Yakmesi of Ilu-Mer, Ilu-Mer of Hayani, Hayani of Samani, Samani of Hale, Hale of Apiashal, Apiashal of Ushpia.[2]

Total: 10 kings who are their ancestors?.

Sulili son of Aminu; Kikkiya; Akiya; Puzur-Ashur (I); Shalim-ahhe; Ilu-shuma.[3]
Total: 6 kings [named? on] brick, whose [number?] of eponyms is [unknown?].

Erishu (I), son of Ilu-shuma, [whose x?], ruled for

[1] The occurrence of similar sounding names may be compared with examples in Gen 36: 21,35; 46:21; etc.

[2] The names in this section are in reverse order and may have been taken from a ritual text for commemorating dead ancestors, cf. the King List of Ugarit (Text 1.104).

30/40 years.

Ikunu, son of Erishu, ruled for [x years].

Sargon (I), son of Ikunu, ruled for [x years].

Puzur-Ashur (II), son of Sargon, ruled for [x years].

Naram-Sin, son of Puzur-Ashur, ruled for [x]4 years.

Erishu (II), son of Naram-Sin, ruled for [x] years.

Shamshi-Adad (I), son of Ilu-kabkabu,[4] [a] went to Karduniash[5] [in the t]ime of Naram-Sin. In the eponymate of Ibni-Adad, [Shamshi]-Adad [went up] from Karduniash. He took Ekallatum where he stayed three years. In the eponymate of Atamar-Ishtar, Shamshi-Adad went up from Ekallatum. He ousted Erishu (II), son of Naram-Sin, from the throne and took it. He ruled for 33 years.

a 1 Kgs 15:11, etc.

Ishme-Dagan (I), son of Shamshi-Adad, ruled for 40 years.

Ashur-dugul, of no lineage, who had no title to the throne, ruled for 6 years.

In the time of Ashur-dugul, of no lineage, Ashur-apla-idi, Nasir-Sin, Sin-namir, Ipqi-Ishtar, Adad-salulu, Adasi, six kings of no lineage, ruled briefly.[6]

Bel-bani, son of Adasi,[7] ruled for 10 years.

Libaya, son of Bel-bani, ruled for 17 years.

Sharma-Adad (I), son of Libaya, ruled for 12 years.

Iptar-Sin, son of Sharma-Adad, ruled for 12 years.

Bazaya, son of Iptar-Sin, ruled for 28 years.

Lullaya, of no lineage, ruled for 6 years.

Shu-Ninua, son of Bazaya, ruled for 14 years.

Sharma-Adad (II), son of Shu-Ninua, ruled for 3 years.

Erishu (III), son of Shu-Ninua, ruled for 13 years.

Shamshi-Adad (II), son of Erishu, ruled for 6 years.

Ishme-Dagan (II), son of Shamshi-Adad, ruled for 16 years.

Shamshi-Adad (III), son of Ishme-Dagan, brother of Sharma-Adad, son of Shu-Ninua, ruled for 16 years.

Ashur-nerari (I), son of Ishme-Dagan, ruled for 26 years.

Puzur-Ashur (III), son of Ashur-nerari, ruled for 24/14 years.

Enlil-nasir (I), son of Puzur-Ashur, ruled for 13 years.

Nur-ili, son of Enlil-nasir, ruled for 12 years.

Ashur-shaduni, son of Nur-ili, ruled for 1 month.

Ashur-rabi (I), son of Enlil-nasir, ousted [Ashur-shaduni], seized the throne; [he ruled for x years.]

Ashur-nadin-ahhe (I), son of Ashur-rabi, [ruled for x years.]

Enlil-nasir (II), his brother, [ousted] him; he ruled for 6 years.

Ashur-nerari (II), son of Enlil-nasir, ruled for 7 years.

Ashur-bel-nisheshu, son of Ashur-nerari, ruled for 9 years.

Ashur-rem-nisheshu, son of Ashur-bel-nisheshu, ruled for 8 years.

Ashur-nadin-ahhe (II), son of Ashur-rem-nisheshu, ruled for 10 years.

Eriba-Adad (I), son of Ashur-bel-nisheshu[8], ruled for 27 years.

Ashur-uballit (I), son of Eriba-Adad, ruled for 36 years.

Enlil-nerari, son of Ashur-uballit, ruled for 10 years.

Arik-den-ili, son of Enlil-nerari, ruled for 12 years.

Adad-nerari (I), son[9] of Arik-den-ili, ruled for 32 years.

Shalmaneser (I), son of Adad-nerari, ruled for 30 years.

Tukulti-Ninurta (I), son of Shalmaneser, ruled for 37 years.

Tukulti-Ninurta.... Ashur-nadin[10]-apli, his son, seized the throne and ruled for 3/4 years.

---

[3] Contemporary inscriptions name Shalim-ahu son of Puzur-Ashur and Ilu-shumma son of Shalim-ahu (see Grayson *ARI* 1:6-8); assuming these are the rulers named here, each of the names in this section may be set in a father-son relationship.

[4] If this is the Ilu-kabkabu listed earlier as father of Aminu, he was more likely the ancestor rather than father of Shamshi-Adad, given the number of generations and lengths of reign intervening, a recognised use of the word "father" (cf. 1 Kgs 15:11, etc.).

[5] Karduniash is a name for Babylon current from the fifteenth century BCE onwards.

[6] The meaning of the Akk. word translated "briefly," *ṭuppišu*, is uncertain; it seems to denote a very short period.

[7] Esarhaddon (680-669 BCE) claimed descent from Bel-bani, evincing belief in the line of descent traced for over one thousand years (cf. the line of David); see Borger 1956:35, etc.

[8] One copy has Ashur-rem-nisheshu, but Eriba-Adad's own inscriptions prove that to be an error; see Grayson *ARI* 1:41.

[9] Two copies have "brother," again proved erroneous by Adad-nerari's own inscriptions; see Grayson *ARI* 1:78.

[10] In both cases there are variant readings Ashur-nasir-apli, but contemporary texts show they are mistaken; see Grayson *ARI* 1:136, 138.

Ashur-nerari (III), son of Ashur-nadin[10]-apli, ruled for 6 years.

Enlil-kudurri-usur, son of Tukulti-Ninurta, ruled for 5 years.

Ninurta-apil-Ekur, son of Ili-hadda, a descendant of Eriba-Adad, went to Karduniash. He came up from Karduniash, seized the throne and ruled for 3/13 years.

Ashur-dan (I), son of Ninurta-apil-Ekur, ruled for 46 years.

Ninurta-tukulti-Ashur, son of Ashur-dan, ruled briefly.[6]

Mutakkil-Nusku, his brother, fought him and took him to Karduniash. Mutakkil-Nusku held the throne briefly,[6] then died.

Ashur-resh-ishi (I), son of Mutakkil-Nusku, ruled for 18 years.

Tiglath-pileser (I), son of Ashur-resh-ishi, ruled for 39 years.

Ashared-apil-Ekur, son of Tiglath-pileser, ruled for 2 years.

Ashur-bel-kala, son of Tiglath-pileser, ruled for 18 years.

Eriba-Adad (II), son of Ashur-bel-kala, ruled for 2 years.

Shamshi-Adad (IV), son of Tiglath-pileser, came up from Karduniash. He ousted Eriba-Adad, son of Ashur-bel-kala, seized the throne and ruled for 4 years.

Ashur[nasirpal (I), son of] Shamshi-Adad, ruled for 19 years.

Shalmaneser (II), son of Ashurnasirpal, ruled for [x]2 years.[11]

Ashur-nerari (IV), son of Shalmaneser, ruled for 6 years.

Ashur-rabi (II), son of Ashurnasirpal, ruled for 41 years.

Ashur-resh-ishi (II), son of Ashur-rabi, ruled for 5 years.

Tiglath-pileser (II), son of Ashur-resh-ishi, ruled for 32 years.

Ashur-dan (II), son of Tiglath-pileser, ruled for 23 years.

Adad-nerari (II), son of Ashur-dan, ruled for 21 years.

Tukulti-Ninurta (II), son of Adad-nerari, ruled for 7 years.

Ashurnasirpal (II), son of Tukulti-Ninurta, ruled for 25 years.

Shalmaneser (III), son of Ashurnasirpal, ruled for 35 years.[b]

Shamshi-Adad (V), son of Shalmaneser, ruled for 13 years.

Adad-nerari (III), son of Shamshi-Adad, ruled for 28 years.

Shalmaneser (IV), son of Adad-nerari, ruled for 10 years.

Ashur-dan (III), brother of Shalmaneser, ruled for 18 years.

Ashur-nerari (V), son of Adad-nerari, ruled for 10 years.

Tiglath-pileser (III), son of Ashur-nerari, ruled for 18 years.[c]

Shalmaneser (V), son of Tiglath-pileser, ruled for 5 years.[d]

b Hos 10:14
c 2 Kgs 15:29 et passim
d 2 Kgs 17:3; 18:9

[11] One of the two copies available at this point omits this entry.

REFERENCES

ANET 564-566; Borger, *Asarh.*; Glassner 1993:146-151; Grayson *ARI.* 1:6-8; 1980:101-125.

ASSYRIAN EPONYM CANON (1.136)

Alan Millard

From the nineteenth century BCE onwards, Assyrian documents bear dates in the form "day X, month Y, *līmu* Personal Name." The *līmu*, "eponym," was an official who gave his name to the year. Little is known about the operation of the system before the first millennium BCE and nothing of its origin. (It may be compared with the systems of *archons* in Greece and *consuls* in Rome.) For the system to operate, scribes had to have lists of the officials in their sequence in order to be able to calculate how long ago a deed of loan, for example, had been written. No simple lists from the earliest period have been found, but from Mari has come an "Eponym Chronicle" in five fragmentary copies, listing over sixty names with a note of a significant event beside many of them, for the years about 1850-1775 BCE (for translation see Glassner 1993:157-160). This anticipates by a thousand years the

Eponym Chronicle for the Neo-Assyrian period. Whatever the purpose of these chronicles was — and, as for the Babylonian Chronicles (text 1.137), it is unknown — they prove a concern for recording precisely the dates of important happenings and so give a basis for exploring the past. From Assur there is a damaged list of eponyms' names which began about 1200 BCE, but the sequence can only be restored completely from 910 down to 649, thanks to the Eponym Lists, simple lists of the names from Assur, Nineveh and Sultantepe, and the Eponym Chronicles from Nineveh and Sultantepe. The kings in the later period held the office in the second full year of their reigns, until Sennacherib broke the custom, their appearances in the sequence giving a helpful link with the King Lists (texts 1.134 and 1.135). The key date in the Eponym Chronicle is the entry for 763 BCE, reporting a solar eclipse. The eponym dates were used to pin-point when military campaigns were undertaken and royal monuments erected, and so provide invaluable aid in computing the chronologies of various surrounding states whose records are meagre or imprecise and, in particular, the chronology of the kingdoms of Israel and Judah. The texts covering 910-612 BCE are edited in Millard 1994. Extracts only are given here.

805 BCE In the eponymate of Ashur-taklak, chamberlain, against Arpad.[a]

804 BCE In the eponymate of Ilu-issiya, governor of Assur, against Hazaz.[1]

803 BCE In the eponymate of Nergal-eresh, governor of Rasappa,[b] against Baᵓal.[2]

773 BCE In the eponymate of Mannu-ki-Adad, governor of Raqmat, against Damascus.[3]

765 BCE In the eponymate of Ninurta-mukin-nishi, of Habruri, against Hatarikka[c]; plague.

763 BCE In the eponymate of Bur-sagale, of Guzan, revolt in the citadel of Assur; in the month of Siwan there was an eclipse of the sun.[4]

755 BCE In the eponymate of Iqisu, of Shibhinish, against Hatarikka.

754 BCE In the eponymate of Ninurta-shezibanni, of Talmush, against Arpad;[5] return from Assur.

745 BCE In the eponymate of Nabu-belu-usur, of Arrapha, in Ayar on the 13th day, Tiglath-pileser (III) sat himself on the throne[6]; in Teshrit he went to the land at the river's bend.[7]

743 BCE In the eponymate of Tiglath-pileser, king of Assyria, against Arpad,[8] defeat inflicted on Urartu.

742 BCE In the eponymate of Nabu-daᵓᵓinanni, commander in chief,[9] [d] against Arpad.

741 BCE In the eponymate of Bel-Harran-belu-uṣur, palace herald,[10] [e] against Arpad, conquered after 3 years.

738 BCE In the eponymate of Adad-belu-kaᵓᵓin, governor of Ashur, Kullani[f] conquered.

734 BCE In the eponymate of Bel-dan, of Kalah, against Philistia.[11]

733 BCE In the eponymate of Ashur-daᵓᵓinanni, of Mazamua, against Damascus.[12] [g]

732 BCE In the eponymate of Nabu-belu-uṣur, of Siᵓmê, against Damascus.

a 2 Kgs 18:34, 19:13 (= Isa 36:19, 37-:13); Isa 10:9; Jer 49:23

b 2 Kgs 19:12 (= Isa 37:12)

c Zech 9:1

d 2 Kgs 18:17; Isa 20:1

e 2 Sam 8:16; 20:24; 1 Kgs 4:3; 2 Kgs 18;18, 37 (=Isa 36:3, 22); 1 Chr 18:15; 2 Chr 34:8

f Isa 10:9; Amos 6:2

g 2 Kgs 16:5-9; Isa 7:1-9

[1] Hazaz, modern Azaz, lies north of Arpad.

[2] The place Baᵓal has been identified with Baᵓali-rasi, the promontory south of Tyre, but is more likely to be Baᵓal-ṣaphon, Mount Casius, on the Syrian coast, north of Ugarit.

[3] This campaign against Damascus, when its king Hadianu paid tribute to Assyria, may have led to the weakening of the kingdom which allowed Jeroboam II of Israel to extend his realm; see 2 Kgs 14:25-28.

[4] The eclipse is dated astronomically 15th-16th June, 763 BCE. Setting out the names for each year before and after that date yields good equations with Babylonian and Greek records.

[5] A fragmentary treaty, found at Nineveh, was imposed upon Matiᵓel, king of Arpad, by Ashur-nirari V (754-745 BCE) at this time (see *COS* volume 2).

[6] Tiglath-pileser's accession was irregular in some way. His three predecessors were all sons of Adad-nirari III (810-783 BCE) and he may have been a member of the royal family who gained power in the revolt the Eponym Chronicle reports for the previous year. His name as written in Hebrew reflects accurately the Assyrian pronunciation of his day (Millard 1976).

[7] The Akk. term *bīrit nāri* seems to mean "land at the bend of the river" and is comparable with Heb. Aram-naharaim and Greek Meso-potamia; see Finkelstein 1962.

[8] The determined campaign against Arpad may have resulted from the local king, Matiᵓel, breaking the oath of loyalty he swore to the Assyrian Ashur-nirari V and making promises to a different overlord, recorded in the Aram. Sefire treaty texts (see *COS* volume 2).

[9] The commander in chief (*turtānu*) usually held office as eponym immediately after the king, emphasizing his high position, corresponding to the positon "over the army" in Israel (2 Sam 8:16; 17:25; 1 Kgs 4:4 etc.).

[10] The palace herald was also one of the highest officials in the court and may be compared with the biblical *mazkîr*; see Mettinger 1971:52-62.

[11] This Assyrian attack probably aimed to secure the route to Egypt's frontier, making the local kings vassals, an activity which had to be continued in following years.

[12] The major campaign against Damascus reduced it to a provincial capital. During the fighting, one of Tiglath-pileser's loyal vassals was killed, as the vassal's son recorded with pride (see the inscription of Bar-Rakib, *COS* volume 2). The assault on Damascus owed part of its impetus to Ahaz of Judah's plea to Tiglath-pileser for help against his enemies, Rezin of Damascus and Pekah of Samaria.

REFERENCES

Finkelstein 1962; Glassner 1993:161-170; Mettinger 1971; Millard 1976; 1994.

THE BABYLONIAN CHRONICLE (1.137)

Alan Millard

The series of cuneiform tablets known as The Babylonian Chronicle covers the years from 745 BCE into the late Seleucid period (2nd century BCE). Entries follow a chronological order, introduced by the year of reign of the king of Babylon, although not every year is included. Warfare is the most common topic, within Babylonia and beyond, the accessions and deaths of kings are noted, the celebration or lapse of the New Year Festival in Babylon and a variety of other subjects. Some years have single, short entries, some longer, more detailed ones, or reports of several events. All the Babylonian Chronicle tablets appear to be excerpts from more extensive compositions, for where some overlap they do not give identical information. Perhaps a form of diary[a] was kept on wax-covered wooden writing boards (Millard 1980). Although this type of chronicle is only known from the 6th century and later in Babylonia, some tablets report events from earlier centuries, indicating that older records remained available (cf. Assyrian Eponym Canon 1.136 above). One, commencing at the start of history, notes the burial places of various kings[b] from about 1000 BCE, another lists market prices in various reigns. Most of the texts were re-edited by Grayson *ABC*, whose numbering is followed here. All known examples were translated by Glassner 1993. Extracts only are given here.

(Chronicle 1 i 27-32)

727 BCE On 27th Tebet Shalmaneser (V)[1] [c] ascended the throne in Assyria and Babylonia. He shattered Samaria (*šá-ma-ra-ᵓ-in*).[2] [d]

722 BCE Year 5: Shalmaneser died in Tebet. Five years Shalmaneser ruled Babylonia and Assyria. On 12th Tebet Sargon[3] [e] ascended the throne in Assyria. In Nisan Merodach-baladan[4] [f] ascended the throne in Babylon.

(Chronicle 1 iii 34-38)

681 BCE On 20th Tebet Sennacherib[5] [g] king of Assyria - his son killed him in a revolt.[6] [h] For [24] years Sennacherib ruled over Assyria. From 20th Tebet until 2nd Adar the revolt continued in Assyria. On [1/2]8th Adar Esarhaddon[7] [j], his son, ascended the throne of Assyria.

(Chronicle 5 1-11)

605 BCE [Year 21:] the king of Babylon[8] was in his country. Nebuchadrezzar[9] [k], his eldest son, the crown prince, [called] out the [army of Babylon], took the van and went to Carchemish[10] [l] on the bank of the Euphrates. He crossed the river [to face the army of Egypt] which was camped at Carchemish. [...] they fought together and the army of Egypt fled

a Esth 2:21-23; 6:1, 2 *b* 1 Kgs 2:10; 11:43; 14:20, 31, etc. *c* 2 Kgs 17:3-6; 18:9 *d* 2 Kgs 18:9-12 *e* Isa 20:1 *f* 2 Kgs 20:12; Isa 39:1 *g* 2 Kgs 18:13; 19:9, 16, 20, 36; 2 Chr 32:1, 2, 9, 10, 16, 22; Isa 36:1; 37:9, 17, 21, 37 *h* 2 Kgs 19:37; Isa 37:38 *j* 2 Kgs 19:37; Isa 37:38 *k* Jer 21:2 etc.; 2 Kgs 24:1 etc. *l* 2 Chr 35:20; Jer 46:2

[1] The reign of Shalmaneser V (727-722 BCE) is little known as no monuments of his survive. The Babylonian Chronicle, damaged entries in the Eponym Canon, a few references in other texts and the biblical verses are the only sources.

[2] The reading of the place name has been disputed because the signs for *ba* and *ma* are very similar in the cuneiform script; however, identification with Samaria is now accepted (Tadmor 1958:39).

[3] Sargon, king of Assyria 721-705 BCE, was not in the direct line of succession, hence his throne name, meaning "legitimate king." (The Heb. form in Isa 20:1 reflects the name accurately as it appeared in the Assyrian dialect of his time, see Millard 1976:8.) The death of Shalmaneser was the signal for a general revolt by subject states, including recently conquered Samaria, but Sargon quickly re-asserted control in the west.

[4] Merodach-baladan was a Chaldaean from Bit-Yakin in southern Babylonia whose family sought to control the country. He ruled from Babylon until Sargon took the city in 710 BCE, thereafter constantly fighting Assyria, regaining the throne in 703 but losing it after nine months and eventually being ousted from Babylonia to die in exile in Elam (Brinkman 1964; 1991). His embassy to Hezekiah of Judah is to be set in 703. The Heb. form of his name reflects well the Babylonian Marduk-apla-iddina (Millard 1976).

[5] Sennacherib, 704-681 BCE, son of Sargon, acceded upon his father's death in battle in 705 and, like him, faced revolt around the edges of the empire, the most famous being Judah's, led by Hezekiah, but the Chronicle does not mention that. For the Heb. rendering of his name see Millard 1976:8, 13.

[6] The Bible names two assassins, Adrammelech and Sharezer in 2 Kgs 19:37; Isa 37:38, and Esarhaddon reports that "his brothers went mad" (see *ANET* 289). Their identity is uncertain (Parpola, 1980). The dreadful deed was remembered in Assyria by Ashurbanipal, over a century later in Babylonia by Nabonidus, and echoed by Berossus and Josephus (Grayson 1991:120, n. 73).

[7] Esarhaddon, 680-669 BCE, defeated his brothers to gain the throne his father had promised to him and strengthened Assyrian power, even penetrating Egypt. The Assyrian form of his name, "Ashur has given a brother," is well-rendered in Heb., Millard 1976.

[8] The king is Nabopolassar, a Chaldaean, perhaps a descendant of Merodach-baladan, who wrested control of Babylon from the Assyrians in 626 BCE. At this time he was elderly or ill, hence the campaign was led by his son.

[9] The famous Nebuchadnezzar ruled for forty-three years (605-562 BCE), but only the first eleven years are covered in surviving tablets of the Chronicle and there are few other Babylonian historical accounts from his reign to set beside the biblical and Greek sources.

[10] The forces of Necho II of Egypt had made their way through Israel and Syria and camped at Carchemish, the major crossing of the Euphrates, in league with the last remnants of Assyrian power. Nabopolassar advanced into the area in 607, but retreated in 606, then in 605 Nebuchadnezzar routed the Egyptians as described here.

before him. He defeated them utterly. The rest of the army of [Egypt, which] had escaped from the defeat and which the army of Babylon had not conquered, the army defeated in the district of Hamath so that [not] a single man [returned] to his country. At that time Nebuchadrezzar conquered the whole of Hamath. Nabopolassar ruled Babylon for 21 years. On 8th Ab he died. In Elul Nebuchadrezzar returned to Babylon and on 1st Elul he ascended the throne in Babylon.

(rev. 11-13)

598/597 BCE Year 7: in Kislev the king of Babylonia called out his army and marched to Hattu.[11] He set his camp against the city of Judah [*Ya-a-ḫu-du*] and on 2nd Adar he took the city and captured the king.[12] [m] He appointed a king of his choosing there[n], took heavy tribute[o] and returned to Babylon.

(Chronicle 7 iii 12-16)

539 BCE In Tishri when Cyrus[13] fought with the army of Babylon at Opis on the bank of the Tigris, the people of Babylon retreated. He took booty and killed people. On 14th Sippar was taken without battle. Nabonidus fled. On 16th Ugbaru, governor of Gutium, and the army of Cyrus entered Babylon without battle. Afterwards, after Nabonidus had retreated, he was taken in Babylon.

(Chronicle 7 iii 18)

539 BCE On 3rd Marcheswan Cyrus entered Babylon.[14] [p]

m 2 Kgs 23:33; Jer 29:2

n 2 Kgs 24:17; 2 Chr 36:10

o 2 Kgs 24:13; 2 Chr 36:10

p Dan 5:30; 6:28

[11] Hattu is a general term for the west in the Chronicle.

[12] Biblical sources make it clear the king captured was Jehoiachin, who ruled only three months in Jerusalem and spent most of his life in prison in Babylon.

[13] After becoming king of Persia in 559 BCE, Cyrus gradually built up his power, conquering Media (550), Lydia (547) and finally Babylon. There he continued many of the old customs, restoring the traditional cults neglected by Nabonidus.

[14] All the Babylonian sources make it clear that Cyrus was the conqueror of Babylon, so Darius the Mede of Dan 5:30; 6:28 is a mystery. Unless dismissed as an error or fiction, he may be identified with Ugbaru, mentioned here, who became governor of Babylon, see Whitcomb 1959, or with Cyrus himself under a Median name as Wiseman proposed 1965.

REFERENCES

ANET 301-307; Brinkman 1964; 1991; Glassner 1993:179-204; Grayson *ABC* 8-126; 1991; Millard 1976; 1980; Parpola 1980; Tadmor 1958; Whitcomb 1959; Wiseman 1965:9-16.

THE WEIDNER CHRONICLE (1.138)

Alan Millard

Excavations at Ashur yielded a damaged tablet which was announced by E. F. Weidner in 1926 and so is called after him. Since then four smaller pieces of other copies have been identified and recently an almost complete tablet was recovered from Sippar, adding greatly to the interpretation of the text, although many uncertainties and gaps remain. The composition is set in the form of a letter from a king of Babylon to a king of Isin in the 19th century BCE, but probably composed centuries later. The propagandist aim is clear from the outset: the offerings for the god Marduk in his temple Esagila in Babylon were decreed by the gods, so the writer recounts the fate of various kings who brought, or failed to bring, offerings to Esagila or respect for it. Thus their attitudes to the god affected his treatment of the kings.

"Say to [Apil-S]in[?], ki[ng of Babyl]on[?], thus says Damiq-ilishu[?], king of Isin:
'[ ] like [ ] his reign. I [mys]elf have written to you a matter to be pondered, a matter [ ], but you have not considered them. You have not listened or paid attention to the advice I gave you, nor heeded the special advice that [ ], you have been looking for something else. To do you a good turn [I have] you, but it is not in your mind. For your own good I have advised you to reinforce the training[?] of your army, but you have not put your hand to it. His sh[rines] where I sought advice [ ] has ceased. Now I shall tell you my experience [ ] learn from it speedily!

I offered a sacrifice to my lady Ninkarrak,[1] mistress of Egalmah; I prayed and implored her, I told her the matter that I was constantly considering, and I spoke like this: "Entrust to me the people of Sumer and Akkad [ ] all the lands.

[1] Ninkarak was a title of Gula, goddess of healing, whose temple, Egalmah, stood in Isin.

Let the people of the Upper and the Lower lands bring their weighty tribute into Egalmah." In the night-time, holy Gula, the exalted lady, stood before me, she heard my speech, spoke to me clearly and blessed me. "You shall set a place in the underground water, in the ocean beneath the earth, [ ] you shall raise the top to the distant sky, in x [ ] above, a state of privilege. [Aft]erwards, Marduk, the king of the gods, who [ ] the whole of heaven and earth, [will the peop]le of Sumer and Akkad to his city Babylon x x x. He went quickly to his father, Ea, the craftsman, the counsellor of heaven and earth. "[May Bab]ylon, the city chosen in my heart, be exalted among all people! May Esagila, the majestic shrine, be [ ] to the limits of heaven and earth! May the lord of lords, who dwells in the shrine, from east to west, x x x x! May he shepherd human beings like sheep! May the city be famous x x x!" The lord Nudimmud[2] [carried out] all he had said. Throughout heaven he honored him [ ].

Then Anu and Enlil, the great gods, favored him and [decreed?]. "May he be the leader of the Upper and the Lower lands. May the great gods of heaven and earth tremble before his shrine. Raise up to the sky the top of Esagila, of Ekua, the palace of heaven and earth [ ]. May its foundation be fixed like sky and earth forever! By your sacrifice I understood what you said and [I have given to you?] long life [ ]. Apart from the order announced in the dream, good advice for [ ]. For the gods of that city, the great gods of heaven and earth, x x for daily, monthly and yearly purification/ renewal of life? x x x no god shall oppose it x x whose mind x x x at his command they are bound, the hostile gods clad in dirty clothes x x x whoever sins against the gods of that city, his star shall not stand in the sky x x x his kingship will end, his scepter will be taken away, his treasury will become a heap of [ruins] x x x his x x and the king of the whole of heaven and earth (said) thus?, "The gods of heaven and earth x [ ] the behavior of each former king of which I hear to x x x [ ].

Akka, son of Enmebaragesi x x x x [ ]. Enmekar, king of Uruk, destroyed the people x x x x. The sage Adapa, son of x x x heard in his holy sanctuary and cursed Enmekar. [ ] he/I gave to him rule over all lands and his rites [ ] he/I beautified like the heavenly writing (the constellations) and in Esagila the king who controls the whole of heaven and earth for his 3,020 years x x x. In the reign of Puzur-Nirah, king of Akshak, the freshwater fishermen of Esagila [ ] were catching fish for the meal of the great lord Marduk; the officers of the king took away the fish. The fisherman was fishing when 7/8 days had passed [ ] in the house of Kubaba, the tavern-keeper, x x x they brought to [Esag]ila. (At that time BROKEN[3] anew for Esagila x x x) Kubaba gave bread to the fisherman and gave water, she [made him offer?] the fish to Esagila. Marduk, the king, prince of the Apsû,[4] favored her and said, "Let it be so !' He entrusted to Kubaba, the tavern-keeper, sovereignty over the whole world. Ur-Zababa [ordered] Sargon, his cupbearer, to change the wine libations of Esagila. Sargon did not change but was careful to offer [ ] quickly to Esagila. Marduk, king of the world/ son of the prince of the Apsu, favored him and gave him rule of the four corners of the world. He took care of Esagila. Everyone who sat on a throne [brought] his tribute to Babylon. Yet he [ignored] the command Bel had given him.[a] He dug soil from its pit and in front of Akkad he built a city which he named Babylon.[5] Enlil changed the order he had given and from east to west (people) opposed him. He could not sleep. Naram-Sin destroyed the people of Babylon, so twice (Marduk) summoned the forces of Gutium[6] against him. They [maltreated?] his people with a goad. He (Marduk) gave his kingship to the Gutian force. The Gutians were unhappy people unaware how to revere the gods, ignorant of the right cultic practices.[b] Utu-hegal, the fisherman, caught a fish at the edge of the sea for an offering. That fish should not be offered to another god until it had been offered to Marduk, but the Guti took the boiled fish from his hand before it was offered, so by his august command, he (Marduk) removed the Guti force from the rule of his land and gave (it) to Utu-hegal. Utu-hegal, the fisherman, carried out criminal acts against his (Marduk's) city, so the river carried off his corpse.[7] Then he (Marduk) gave sovereignty over the whole world to Shulgi, son of Ur-Nammu, but he did not perform his rites to the letter, he defiled his purification rituals and his sin x x body? x [was s]et?. Amar-Sin, his son, changed the offerings of large ox[en] and sheep of the New Year festival in Esagila. It was foretold (he would die) from goring by an ox, but he died from the "bite' of his shoe.[8] Shu-Sin made Esagila like the constellations for his

a 2Kgs 15:3-6
b 2Kgs 17:26

[2] Nudimmud was a name or title of Ea.

[3] This translates an ancient copyist's note indicating that his exemplar was damaged.

[4] Apsu was the freshwater ocean beneath the earth, source of rivers and wells, ruled by Ea and so home to his son Marduk.

[5] Sargon's sin was, apparently, to treat Babylon as a conquered city, taking soil to symbolize his rule over it in his new capital, Akkad. His action is reported in other Babylonian traditions. One copy reverses the names.

[6] The Guti were mountain people from the east, a long-term threat to the urban settlements of lower Mesopotamia.

[7] Another tradition reports that Utu-hegal, king of Uruk about 2100 BCE, who re-established Babylonian rule after the Guti, was drowned while inspecting a dam.

well-being. BROKEN what Shulgi did, his sin his son, Ibbi-Sin,[9] [ ]. BROKEN a former king who preceded x x x x your desire and over his father Ea, the heaven and earth x x he did not create. Anu and Ishtar x x his majestic son, the great lord Marduk, [king?] of the gods, whom the gods x x, his (Ea's) grandson Nabu, who x x x he will name the king.

To his descendant Sumu-la-El,[10] the king, whose name Anu pro[nounced], for your well-being and x x all of it a pea[ceful?] dwelling place, a lasting rule? in your hand.

[8] The fate of Amar-Sin of Ur (ca. 2046-2038 BCE), also known from other sources, may have been gangrene resulting from too tight a shoe, seen as a reflection of an ominous forecast that an ox would gore him.

[9] Ibbi-Sin, the last king of Ur (ca. 2028-2004 BCE), was captured by the Elamites who sacked his city.

[10] Sumu-la-El was second king of the First Dynasty of Babylon (ca. 1880-1845 BCE).

REFERENCES

Al-Rawi 1990; Arnold 1994; Glassner 1993:215-218; Grayson *ABC*, 43-45, 147-151.

3. ROYAL HYMNS

A HYMN CELEBRATING ASSURNASIRPAL II'S CAMPAIGNS TO THE WEST (1.139)
(*LKA* 64)

Victor Hurowitz

This text was found by the German excavations at Assur in the house of a *nargallu* (chief singer).[1] It begins as a hymn to Enlil (Assur),[2] but then praises Assurnasirpal II (883-859 BCE) for his campaigns to the mountains in the west and for contributing to various temples the wood taken on the campaigns. It ends with a blessing of the king.[3] The events referred to are described in detail in the king's annals and mentioned briefly in his royal titles.[4]

Invocation (obv. lines 1-3)
I[5] will sing to the king of the ends of the earth
 the prince of the gods may I praise;[6]
Of Enlil[7] who dwells in Esharra,[8]
 may I glorify his divinity.

Presentation of King Assurnasirpal II (obv. lines 4-6)
Aššur-nāṣir-apli the obstinate,[9]
 the desire of the great gods;[10]
(5) The son of Tukulti-Ninurta,
in fame is glorified.[11]
By the lances(?) of his battle,
 (he is) king of the huntsmen,
 (who) knocks over all foreign rulers.[12] [a]

a Ps 140:12

[1] See Pedersén 1986:38 text 24. For the library of the *nargallu* see Pedersén 1986:34-41. Groneberg 1987:189-190 states that *LKA* 64 mentions Assurnasirpal I, son of Tiglathpilesar I. This remark is unexplainable and obviously a total error.

[2] Schramm, *EAK* 2:58 calls it "Ein Loblied auf Ellil und Anp." *CAD* passim cites the text as a "NA hymn to Assurnasirpal."

[3] For other Assyrian hymns poetically relating individual military campaigns described in prose in the royal inscriptions see Livingstone 1989:43-53; Reade 1989; Hurowitz and Westenholtz 1992.

[4] See *AKA* iii 56-91 = *ANET* 276 = *ARI* 2 para. 584-586 = *RIMA* 2:216-219 column 3 lines 56-91; Schramm *EAK* 2 58 11; Ikeda 1984-1985. Brinkman *PHPKB* 393-394, Schramm, *EAK* 2:58, di Fillipi 1977:27-30, and Conradie 1989 discuss the number and extent of Assurnasirpal's campaigns to the west but make no mention of *LKA* 64 or its content. In fact, the author of *LKA* 64 seems to be of the opinion that there was more than one campaign but he lumps them all together as a trip to the Lebanon. If the sea was mentioned explicitly, it would have been in the broken lines.

[5] See Groneberg 1987:114.

[6] See Groneberg 1987:113.

[7] dBAD/BE, read Enlil, is the chief of the traditional Mesopotamian pantheon. By this time he has been syncretistically assimilated to Assur so that the name is simply a synonym for the chief god of Assyria. Groneberg 1987:190 identifies the god as Bēl, following a neo-Assyrian practice (cf. Parpola, *Iraq* 34 [1972] 25). This identification disregards the fact that the god in question resides in Esharra, which was Assur's temple and not Marduk's.

[8] The god Assur's temple in the city Assur.

[9] See Lambert 1957-58:43 n. 35 for the reading and meaning of the title *par-ri-ku*. Seux *ER* 221 translates "chef(?)" and *AHw* s.v. *parriku* gives "eigenwillig." Groneberg 1987:44 "KN der widersetzliche, Wunsch der grossen Götter." The title is obviously to be understood positively.

[10] Seux *ER* 104 s.v. *ḫišiḫtu* translates "réclamé par les grands dieux."

[11] Taking *šurruḫ* to be a D stative of *šarāḫu*. It may, however, be an imperative, in which case the line is addressed to Assur and means "of the son of Tukulti-Ninurta, glorify (his) fame!" Cf. *AHw* 1318b s.v. *tanattu*.

[12] Following *CAD* N 1:7 s.v. *na'āpu*, taking the verb as derived from *da'āpu*, "to knock down." The line is a tricolon, with AB//BA parallelism in the second and third cola: *šar bajjarī // utta'ipu kal mālikī*. For the combination of *bajāru* (to hunt) and *da'āpu* (to knock down) cp. Ps 140:12 "... as for a wicked man of violence — they shall hunt him down in fall-pits (*yᵉṣûdennû lᵉmadhēpōt*)."

The Campaign to Lebanon (obv. line 7 - rev. line 11)
He left[13] the city of Kalhu,[14] [b]
to the mountain of Lebanon he took the road.
To wage his war,
(10) the city of Carchemish he approached —
which is in the land of Hatti.[15]

In order to (show the) strength of my rule,[16]
the possesions of his[17] palace I plundered;[18]

A valuable image of my likeness,[19]
for his temples I glorified.[20]

The Kummuheans[21] and Patinians,[22]
radiance overwhelmed them.[23]
(15) [They brought][24] to him possessions,
ebony[25] and lapis lazuli he constantly received.[26]
The daughter of the king of the [Pat]inians[27]
for making merry are your [...].

All the [en]ds of the earth I roamed,[28]
(20) to the Amanus mountains[29] I ascended over and over again.[30]
[Tw]o times[31] ...] pure sacrifices to [the gods]
[I sacrificed] to [...]

b Gen 10:11, 12

c 2 Kgs 19:23; Isa 14:8; 37:24

Reverse (rev. lines 1-6)[32]
...] ... [...
his [...] all the land [of ...]
...] ... [...
[...] wood ...[...]
(5) ... the l]and (?) of Ha-ra-[[33] ...]
sacrifices [...] ... [...]

Presentation of the Wood in the Temples (rev. lines 7-12)
Beams of cedar from the Aman[us...] [c]
[he carried off] and took to Eshar[ra][34]
[to the temple, the shr]i[ne, to the temple of happiness, to the temple
of Sin] and Shamash [great/holy gods.]

They entered into Esharra; [verb]
by the lifting of his eyes.[35]

Divine Blessing for Assurnasirpal (rev. lines 13-14)
"The king is beloved of my heart,
Aššur-nāṣir-apli the governor."[36]

Colophon (rev. line 15)
(15) Acc]ording to Sukuja it was written.[37]

[13] The copy seems to show a slightly broken and unintelligible IZ TA(?) ZIZ. The translation given here assumes the regular expression *GN ittamuš* ... *ḫarran GN iṣbat* as found in the parallel passage in the annals which reads TA URU *kal-ḫi at-ta-muš*, "I set forth from Kalhu" (*RIMA* 2:219 column 3 line 56). Collation is necessary.

[14] Gen 10:11, 12. Present day Nimrud.

[15] Cf. Groneberg 1987:114 "um (seinen Kampf) zu führen, prüfte er (die Stadt)." But see the annals, *RIMA* 2:216 line 57; 217 line 65. *issiniqi* in *LKA* 64 is a synonym of *iqterib* in the annals. Cf. de Filippi 1977:151:101.

[16] The poem continues here in the voice of the king.

[17] The possesive pronominal suffix has no antecedent.

[18] See *CAD* N 1:233 s.v. *namkūru* d).

[19] Groneberg 1987:44 *ma-aq-ru*, "die kostbare Abbildung meiner Gestalt." See *CAD* A 2:209 s.v. *aqru* c 5′ and *CAD* M 1:47 s.v. *magru* d) for *maqru*= (*w*)*aqru*.

[20] Placing a royal statue in temples, including those of conquered peoples, was a common practice. See *CAD* Ṣ 80b s.v. *ṣalmu* a2′ a′-c′.

[21] The Kummuheans are not mentioned in the annals' account of the western campaigns (*RIMA* 2:216-219 column 3 lines 56-92). They do occur, however, in the next campaign (*RIMA* 2:216 column 3 line 96).

[22] I.e., people of Patina, formerly read Hattina. For Kummuheans and Patinians see Hawkins 1972-1975, 1980-1983.

[23] See *CAD* S 33a s.v. *saḫāpu* 1e).

[24] Restoring [*i-šu*]-*ṭu-ni*, "they brought," from *šâṭu*.

[25] See annals *RIMA* 2:219 column 3 line 88 for receipt of ebony.

[26] Cf. *CAD* N 1:233 s.v. *namkūru* d).

[27] See annals *RIMA* 2:218 column 3 line 76 where the king receives the daughter of the brother of Labarna, king of Patinu, along with her rich dowry.

[28] See *CAD* A 1:324-325 s.v. *alāku* 6 (Gtn) for other uses of this verb. It is frequent in Assurnasirpal's inscriptions as well as in some epic texts and texts of Sargon I.

[29] *Ḫa-ma-nu* is the Amanus range in western Syria and not the Amanah of the Bible (2 Kgs 5:12; Song 4:6) which is parallel to Akk. Ammananum (Anti-Lebanon.) See Cogan 1984.

[30] See annals *RIMA* 2:219 column 3 line 88. *e-ta-ta-li* is Gtn perfect of *elû* (*AHw* 208a s.v. *elû* Gtn 1a); cf. Sargon Birth Legend lines 16, 26 (see text 1.133 above). The verbs used here and in the next line indicate numerous campaigns.

[31] Line 21 begins [x]-*ú* KÁM, probably to be restored [2]-*ú* KÁM, "twice."

[32] The upper right corner of the tablet is destroyed and many of the preserved lines are effaced, making continuous translation impossible.

[33] Harran would be a possible restoration geographically and orthographically (cf. KUR KASKAL-*ni* in Tiglath-pilesar I's annals: *RIMA* 1:26 line 71) but it is not otherwise mentioned in Assurnasirpal II's inscriptions.

[34] Reverse lines 7-11 are restored according to the annals *RIMA* 2:219 column 3 line 90. The restoration is meant to be suggestive of content rather than an exact reconstruction of the text.

[35] See *CAD* N 2:295a s.v. *nīšu* B 3a1′ for *nīš īni* meaning "look, glance, chosen person or object, choice, discretion."

[36] See *AHw* 1140a s.v. *šakkanakkum*; *CAD* Š 1:175b s.v. *šakkanakku* 2c).

[37] See Hunger *BAK* 262.

REFERENCES

Text *LKA* 64. No previous editions, translations or studies. Brinkman 1968:393-394; Cogan 1984; Conradie 1989; de Filippi 1977; Groneberg 1987; Hawkins 1972-1975; 1980-1983. Hurowitz and Westenholtz 1992; Ikeda 1978; 1984-1985; Lambert 1957-58:43; Livingstone 1989; Pedersén 1986; Reade 1989.

A PRAYER FROM A CORONATION RITUAL OF THE TIME OF TUKULTI-NINURTA I (1.140)

Alasdair Livingstone

(1) May Assur and Ninlil, the lords of your crown, set your crown on your head for a hundred years!

(3) May your foot in Ekur and your hands stretched toward the breast of Assur, your god, be agreeable!

(4) May your priesthood and the priesthood of your sons be agreeable to Assur, your god! With your straight scepter widen your land! May Assur give you authority, obedience, concord, justice and peace!

REFERENCES

Müller 1937:4-89 and obv. col. ii.30-36.

A HYMN TO NANAYA WITH A BLESSING FOR SARGON II (1.141)

Alasdair Livingstone

Obverse

I.1′ [... *she grasps in her hand*] the naked sword, [the emblem of Nergal], and the pointed axe,
appropriate to the [Pleiades].
Right and left, battle is set in lines.
I.5′ She is the foremost of the gods, whose play is combat, she who leads the coalition of the seven demons.
Musicians of wide repertoire are seated before her, performers on the lyre, the harpsichord, the clappers, the flute, the oboe, the long pipes.
I.10′ The jesters calm her heart with spindles, whiplashes and with sweet [...]s.
[...] ... of loveliness of ...
They wear armbands ... [...]
[...] a bunch of grapes [......]
I.15′ [their] hands are weighed down with [...] of the finest gold
[...] their noses [......]
Their [....
II.1′ [...] Nanaya [......]
The daughter-in-law of Esagil ... [...], the wife of Muati, the darling of Bel, [his] father, whom Belet-ili honored among the goddesses.
II.3′ Go forth, depart, female warrior of the goddesses, capable one who adorns the function of the warrior,
II.7′ [...] of the unmerciful, belligerent heart(?),
II.8′ [......] to the end of days perform their [......]!

Reverse

I.3′ [O world, hearken to the praise of the queen], Nanaya!
[Exalt the beautiful one, magnify the] resonant one!
I.5′ [Extol the exalted one, adore with praise] the powerful one!
[Beseech her and pray to her constantly!]
II.1′ Even a capable [...] whom [she does not guide], [......] a gift [...];
The bridal gift of an open [...] , whom she [does not guide], is [......];
II.5′ Even a wise exorcist, whom she does not guide, where is his expertise? His perambulations [...]
The hand of even an erudite physician, whom she does not guide, is powerless before his patients!
Without her, who can achieve anything?
II.10′ Journey far, hasten, learn how she is praised!
Honor the merciful one monthly, for ever,
she who can make rich the destitute, bring abundance to the poor! [a]
Hear, O world, the praise of the queen, Nanaya!
Exalt the beautiful one, magnify the resonant one!
II.15′ Extol the exalted one, adore with praise the powerful one!
Beseech and pray to her constantly!

Calm down, daughter of Sin, settle in your sanctuary!
Bless Sargon, who holds fast to the hem of your garment, the shepherd of Assyria, who walks behind you!
II.20′ Decree for him as his fate a life of long days! Make firm the foundations of his throne, prolong his reign!

[a] 1 Sam 2:8; Ps 113:7

Protect the stallions harnessed to [his] yoke!
Keep affliction and weakness distant from his body!
II.24′ The evil locust which ravages the grain, the malignant grasshopper which dries up the orchards, which would cut off the regular offerings of god and goddess, — Enlil listens to you, Tutu obeys you — may it (the grasshopper) be counted as nought!
The genie and protective spirit which stand before you [...]
II.30′ [...] plains, mountains [...]

REFERENCES

Foster *BM* 709-711; Livingstone 1989:13-16; Martin 1903:196ff.; MacMillan 1906:564.

ASSURBANIPAL'S CORONATION HYMN (1.142)

Alasdair Livingstone

This text should be read together with the Middle Assyrian Coronation Ritual Prayer and the Late Piece of Constructed Mythology (see text 1.146 below).

(1) May Shamash, king of heaven and earth, raise you to shepherdship over the four regions!
May Assur, who gave you the [scepter], prolong your days and years!
Spread your land wide at your feet!
May Sherua extol your name to your personal god![1]
(5) Just as grain and silver, oil, the cattle of Shakan[2] and the salt of Bariku[3] are good, so may Assurbanipal be favored by the gods of his land!
May eloquence, understanding, truth and justice be granted him as a gift!
(9) May the [population] of Assur buy thirty kor of grain for one shekel of silver! May the [population] of Assur buy three seah of oil for one shekel of silver! May the [population] of Assur buy thirty minas of wool for one shekel of silver!
(12) May the lesser speak and the [greater] listen! May the greater speak and the [lesser] listen! May concord and peace be established in Assyria!
(15) Assur is king — indeed Assur is king! Assurbanipal is the [representative] of Assur, the creation of his hands!
May the great gods make his reign firmly established! May they guard the life of Assurbanipal, king of Assyria!
May they give him a straight scepter to widen his land and peoples!
May his reign be renewed and may they firmly establish his royal throne for ever!
Daily, monthly and yearly may they bless him and guard his reign!
(20) During his years may rains from heaven and floods from the underground source be steady!
Give our lord, Assurbanipal, long [days], copious years, great strength, a long reign, years of abundance, good repute and fame, health and well-being, a propitious oracle and leadership over other kings!

At this point there is the following instruction to a priest:

Reverse

(3) Having pronounced this blessing, he turns round and pronounces a further blessing at the opening of the censer in front of Shamash:
(5) Anu gave his crown,[4] Enlil his throne; Ninurta gave his weapon; Nergal gave his awesome luminance. Nusku made a deputation and placed advisers before him.
(9) Anyone who speaks with the king deceitfully or falsely, if a notable, will be killed with a weapon, if a rich man, will become impoverished.
As for him who privately plots evil against the king, Erra will call him to account with murderous plague.

---

[1] By personal god is meant Assur and the idea is that Assurbanipal intercedes through the medium of the god's consort Sherua.
[2] God of cattle; cf. in a hemerology "On the first of the month Kislim he should libate water before the returning herds; he should prostrate himself before Shakan!" (CT 51 161 // STT 302).
[3] A locality fabled for its salt.
[4] The donations agree with the character and symbolism of the gods. Cf. the reference to a crown of "Anu-ship" in a Late Babylonian New Year's festival text, where the donning of the tiara of Anu is brought into a logical relationship with the taking over of the "kingship of Anu" (*SBH* VIII obv. col. i 24-25).

He who privately utters malicious talk against the king, his property is wind and his garment hem litter.
(15) Gather round, all gods of heaven and earth, and bless Assurbanipal, the circumspect king!
Place in his hand the weapon of combat and battle and give him the black-headed people, that he may rule as their shepherd!

REFERENCES

Foster *BM* 2:713-714; Livingstone 1989:26-27; Weidner 1939-41:210ff.

AN ASSURBANIPAL HYMN FOR SHAMASH (1.143)

Alasdair Livingstone

(1) Light of the great gods, resplendent illuminator of the universe,
Lofty judge, shepherd of the celestial and earthly regions,
As if they were cuneiform signs you watch over all lands with your light!
You are one who does not become tired by divination, daily making the decisions for the denizens of heaven and earth!
(5) At your coming out, blazing fire, all the stars of heaven become invisible!
You alone are supremely brilliant, no one among the gods can rival with you!
You consult with Sîn, your father, and then give instructions.
Anu and Enlil cannot give counsel without you!
Ea, who decides cases, looks up to you from the Apsu!
(10) All the gods pay attention at your bright appearance!
They smell the incense and accept the pure offerings!
Beneath you [kneel] the exorcists, to avert omens of evil!
The diviners stand at attention before you, to make their hands fit to receive oracular commands!
[I am] your [servant], Assurbanipal, whom by means of divination you commanded to exercise kingship,
(15) who praises your bright divinity, honors the symbol of your divinity,
[who proclaims] your greatness, makes manifest your praise to the far-flung peoples!

Reverse

(1) Judge his case, make the decision for him for well-being!
May it be appointed for him, that he walk safely in the light of your rising!
May he constantly shepherd over your peoples, whom you gave him, in justice.
[In the temple] which he set up — and in which he caused you to dwell in joyousness — [1]
(5) may his heart be elated, his spirit rejoice, be sated with life!
Whoever gives praise, sings this, and names the name of Assurbanipal,
may he shepherd the peoples of Enlil in abundance and justice!
Whoever learns this text by heart and honors the judge of the gods, Shamash,
may he bring into esteem his [words], make good his command over the people!
(10) Whoever should nullify this song, or not praise Shamash, the light of the great gods,
or who should change the name of Assurbanipal, whom by means of divination Shamash appointed to exercise his kingship,
or who names the name of another king,
(13) may his string music be painful to those who listen, his exultation as the thorn of a bush.

[1] This line brings the hymn into a definite relationship with actual building activities of Assurbanipal, whether in Assur or elsewhere.

REFERENCES

SAHG 5; *ANET* 386; Foster, *BM* 2:725f.

AN ASSURBANIPAL PRAYER FOR MULLISSU (1.144)

Alasdair Livingstone

(1) [......] ... [......]
[...] she provides [......]
[...] ... she is in authority, does not ... [...]
[...], who grants scepter, throne, and a long reign,
(5) [who makes] their offspring abundant, fashions totality,
[...]. at its mention the Igigi tremble.
[At its ...] who made the Anunnaki tremble.
[Humanity], — mankind, the black-headed people, beseech you for their lives!
Merciful, sparing [sovereign], who grants clemency,
(10) [who makes joyful] the wandering vagrant, takes the hand of the one in extremity,
[who looks to] the wronged and the one in mortal danger, who restores life to the one on his deathbed,
she who can alter the status of the weak and the lowly,
that is you, queen, lady of clemency and peace!
You establish clemency, cause peace to come into being!
(15) Mullissu is the one who give peace and life to whoever enters her shrine!
I am your servant, Assurbanipal, whom your hands created,
whom without father and mother you brought up and raised to greatness.
Your [...] ... you blossom constantly with life, and you protected my life!
[...] I recite your glorification, I rejoice in your concord!
(20) [......] greatly, one who values [...]...
[......] her [...] is praised.

Reverse

(1) [......] lady of kind deeds, the city [...]
[......] and you made me rejoice!
[Mullissu, lady] of the gods, it is to you that I have turned!
You know both to [save from disaster] and to spare; I have seized the hem of your garment![1]
(5) I have been enduring [...], I cannot bear it!
[Through a misdeed] which I am or am not aware of, I have become weak!
[Through an offense, which] I am or am not aware of, may I not come to an end, lady!
[Through any crime] which I may have committed since the time of my youth
[or] the mentioning of a god, whether knowingly or unknowingly, I express great regret!
(10) May evil be driven away daily, lady!
May your pleasant [breeze] waft and the darkness be illuminated!
In the distress and extremity which oppress me, take my hand!
May any detractor of mine who exults over me not prosper!
[May I have life and prosperity], that I may constantly praise the deeds of your divinity!

---

(15) [...] a spontaneous wish, a prayer for Mullissu, the merciful queen, by one who stands attentively before her.

(Colophon)

(i) [Palace] of Assurbanipal, king of the universe, king of Assyria, son of Esarhaddon, king of Assyria, grandson of Sennacherib, king of Assyria, who trusts in Assur and Mullissu. [He who] trusts in you will not come to shame, O Assur, king of the gods!
(v) [He who erases my written name or the name of my favorite brother] by any devious action, [... or] they destroy, are hostile to his land, [may Assur] and Mullissu [with rage and fury overthrow him]!

[1] The fact that the hem of a garment could be used for sealing documents with statements under oath gives greater force to this metaphor.

REFERENCES

OECT 6:pl. xiii 72ff.

DIALOGUE BETWEEN ASSURBANIPAL AND NABU (1.145)

Alasdair Livingstone

(1) In the assembly of the great gods [I constantly] speak in your adulation, Nabu!
May the [assembly] of my detractors not take control of me!
(3) [In the temple of the Queen of] Nineveh I approach you, hero among the gods, his

gods, his brothers. You are the eternal trust of Assurbanipal!

(5) [Since I was a small] child I have lain at the feet of Nabu! Nabu, do not leave me to the assembly of my detractors!

(7) Please listen, Assurbanipal! I am Nabu! Until the end of time your feet shall not falter nor your hands tremble. Your lips shall not tire in praying to me, nor your tongue be twisted on your lips, for I shall give you pleasant speech. I will raise your head and give you great stature in É.MAŠ.MAŠ.[1]

---

(13) Nabu continues to speak: Your pleasant mouth, which prays ever to Ishtar of Uruk! Your figure, which I created, prays for ever to me in É.MAŠ.MAŠ!

(16) Your fate, which I created, prays ever to me thus: "Bring order into É.GAŠAN.KALAM.MA!"[2] "The breath of your life prays ever to me: 'Give long life to Assurbanipal!'"

---

(19) Assurbanipal is kneeling on his knees and prays ever to Nabu, his lord: "Listen please, do not leave me! My life is spelt out before you, my soul safe kept in the lap of Mullissu. Listen please, mighty Nabu, do not leave me amongst my detractors!"

---

(23) There answered a dream god from the presence of Nabu, his lord: "Fear not, Assurbanipal, I will give you long life! I will entrust favorable winds with the breath of your life! My pleasant mouth shall ever bless you in the assembly of the great gods!"

Reverse

(1) Assurbanipal opened his fists, ever praying to Nabu, his lord: "May he who grasps the feet of the Queen of Nineveh not come to shame in the assembly of the great gods! May he who kneels by the hem of Ishtar of Uruk not come to shame in the assembly of his detractors. Do not leave me in the assembly of my detractors, O Nabu! Do not leave the breath of my life to the assembly of those who would take issue against me!"

---

(6) "You were a child, Assurbanipal, when I left you with the Queen of Nineveh; you were a baby, Assurbanipal, when you sat on the lap of the Queen of Nineveh! Her four teats were placed in your mouth: two you would suckle and two you would milk before you!"

---

(9) Your detractors, Assurbanipal, will fly away like pollen(?) on the surface of the water! They will be squashed before your feet like fat spring insects! You, Assurbanipal, will stand before the great gods and praise Nabu!

---

[1] É.MAŠ.MAŠ was the Ishtar temple at Nineveh. Its history reaches back to the Akkad period and major building activity was carried out around 1800 BCE by Shamshi-Adad I. The temple was given attention by Hammurabi who claimed in the prologue to his code of laws (*CH* iv 61) to have promulgated the rites of Ishtar in É.MAŠ.MAŠ. Its fabric and cult was enhanced by numerous Assyrian kings, not least Esarhaddon and Assurbanipal. In the late period, due to religious syncretism, Ninlil or Mullissu was also worshipped in this temple.

[2] É.GAŠAN.KALAM.MA was the temple of Ishtar at Arbela. For an edition and translation of and commentary on a tablet describing its cult see *MMEW* p. 116ff.

REFERENCES

Livingstone 1989:13; *SAHG* 39:292.

A LATE PIECE OF CONSTRUCTED MYTHOLOGY RELEVANT TO THE NEO-ASSYRIAN AND MIDDLE ASSYRIAN CORONATION HYMN AND PRAYER (1.146)

Alasdair Livingstone

(1) [...] ... [...
Their faces were turned away [...
Bēlet-ilī, their lady, was frightened by their silence;
she spoke out to Ea, the exorcist:
(5) "The toil of the gods has become wearisome to them!
... [...] . belt . [...]
Their faces are turned away, and enmity has broken out!
Let us create a figure of clay and impose the toil on it
and relieve them from their exertions for ever."
(10) Ea began to speak, addressing Bēlet-ilī:
"You are Bēlet-ilī, the lady of the great

gods.
[...] ... later
[...] ...... [...] ... his hands."
Bēlet-ilī pinched off clay for him.
Craftily she made clever things.
[...] she purified and mixed clay to create him.
[...] she decorated his body,
[...] his whole stature.
She put a ... [......]
She put a ... [......]
She put a ... [......]
[......] she placed on [his] body.
Enlil, hero of the great gods, [...]
[as soon as he saw him] his own features beamed!
[...] took a comprehensive view of [...] in the assembly of the great gods.
his [...], he gave final perfection to the created being.
Enlil, the hero of the great gods [...]
Let me determine his name as [*lullū*-man],[1]
and gave the order to make him bear the toil of the gods.
Ea began to speak, addressing Bēlet-ilī:[2]
"You are Bēlet-ilī, lady of the great gods!
It is you who have created *lullû-man,*
now create a king, a man to be in control!
Encircle the whole of his body with something fine.
Finish perfectly his appearance, make his body beautiful!
So Bēlet-ilī created the king, the man to be in control.
The great gods gave to the king the power of battle.
Anu gave his crown, Enlil his [throne].[3]
Nergal gave his weapons, Ninurta his [terrifying splendor].
Bēlet-ilī gave [his] beautiful countenance.
Nusku gave directions, gave counsel and stood in service [before him].
Anyone who speaks with the king [deceitfully or falsely],
if a notable [...]

[1] This word *lullû* is used in the Epic of Atrahasis to described the first human created by the mother goddess from clay and spittle. It is used in the Babylonian Epic of Creation (*Enuma Elish*) to describe the first human before he is given the name "man" (*amēlu*), while in the Epic of Gilgamesh it describes Enkidu before he is initiated into the habits of civilization.

[2] Up to this point the mythological story line agrees closely with that in the Epic of Atrahasis and similar stories or poems of creation. What follows, however, adds a completely new dimension. After man had been created to free the gods from toil, a king is to be created to organize them. Textually, the material in this latter section is evidently based on the Assurbanipal Coronation Hymn or, as is far more likely, on other older material on which this part of the Assurbanipal Coronation Hymn itself was based.

[3] The donations made by the individual gods agree broadly with their known attributes and iconography; see the corresponding section in the Coronation Hymn (text 1.142 and note 4).

REFERENCES

Mayer 1987:55ff.

4. FICTIONAL ROYAL AUTOBIOGRAPHY

THE ADAD-GUPPI AUTOBIOGRAPHY (1.147)

Tremper Longman III

In 1906 H. Pognon discovered a much-broken stela at Eski Harran (Nab. H 1, A). The text left many questions unanswered but was identified as composed for either the mother or grandmother of Nabonidus. Happily, D. S. Rice discovered a duplicate in the pavement steps of the northern entrance to the Great Mosque at Harran (Nab. H 2, A). Both texts had been used to construct the steps leading to the mosque. The text has been transliterated and translated by Gadd, but no copy has yet been made.

Introduction (Column I, lines 1-5)

I am [a] Adad-guppi, mother of Nabunaid, king of Babylon, a worshipper[1] of Sin, Ningal, Nusku, and Sadarnunna, my gods, for whose divinity I have cared since my youth.

a Prov 8:12; Eccl 1:12

[1] Akk. *paliḫtu* is a lay term, cf. von Voightlander 1964:222-223.

Autobiographical Narrative (Column 1, line 5 to column III, line 43' [the following extract is through Column II, line 11])

Whereas[2] in the sixteenth year of Nabopolassar, king of Babylon, Sin, the king of the gods, became angry with his city and his house, and went up to heaven (with the result that) the city and its people were transformed into a ruin.[b] During that time I cared for the sanctuaries of Sin, Ningal, Nusku, and Sadarnunna, since I revered their deity. Sin, the king of the gods,[c] I was constantly[3] beseeching. I daily, without fail, cared for his great deity. I was a worshipper of Sin, Shamash, Ishtar, and Adad all of my life (whether) in heaven or on earth. My fine possessions that they gave to me,[4] I gave back to them, daily, nightly, monthly, yearly. I was continually beseeching Sin. Gazing at him[5] prayerfully and in humility, I knelt before them.[d] Thus (I said): "May your return to your city take place.[e] May the black-headed people worship your great divinity." In order to appease the heart of my god and my goddess, I did not put on a garment of excellent wool,[6] silver, gold, a fresh garment; I did not allow perfumes (or) fine oil to touch my body. I was clothed in a torn garment. My fabric was sackcloth.[7] [f] I proclaimed their praises.[g] The fame of my god and goddess were set (firmly) in my heart. I stood their watch.[h] I served them food.[8] [i]

From the twentieth year of Assurbanipal, king of Assur, in which I was born, until the forty-second year of Assurbanipal, the third year of Assur-etillu-ili, his son, the twenty-first year of Nabopolasser, the forty-third year of Nebuchadnezzar,[j] the second year of Awel-Marduk,[k] the fourth year of Neriglissar — for ninety-five years I cared for Sin, the king of the gods of heaven and earth,[l] and for the sanctuaries of his great divinity. He looked upon me and my good deeds with joy. Having heard my prayers[m] and agreeing to my request, the wrath of his heart calmed. He was reconciled with Eḫulḫul, Sin's house, located in the midst of Harran, his favorite dwelling.

Sin, the king of the gods, looked upon me. He called Nabunaid, my only son, my offspring, to kingship.[n] He personally delivered[9] the kingship of Sumer and Akkad, from the border of Egypt and the upper sea, to the lower sea, all the land.

I lifted my hands to Sin,[o] the king of the gods, reverently in prayer[p]: [Thus (I said): "Nabunaid is (my) son, my offspring, beloved of his mother]. II:1 You are the one who called him to kingship and have spoken his name by your own divine utterance. (Now) may the great gods go at his side.[q] May they fell his enemies. Do not forget Eḫulḫul but complete and restore its rites."

When, in my dream, Sin, the king of the gods, had set his hands (on me), he said thus: "Through you I will bring about the return of the gods (to) the dwelling in Harran, by means of Nabunaid your son. He will construct Eḫulḫul; he will complete its work. He will complete the city Harran greater than it was before and restore it. He will bring Sin, Ningal, Nusku, and Sadarnunna in procession[r] back into[10] the Eḫulḫul."

The narrative continues with only minor breaks. The text concludes with an exhortation to observe the worship of Sin.

Final Exhortation (Column III:44´-56´)

[Whoever] you are — whether king, prince [ ] in the land. [Continually stand watch] for Sin, the king [of the gods], the lord of the gods of heaven and earth, his great divinity and reverence [the divinities of heaven and] earth who [ ] dwell in Esagil and Eḫulḫul and pray (to the divinities) in heaven and earth and [ ] the command of Sin and Ishtar who saves [ ] keep your seed safe forever and ever.

b Lam 2:4-8
c Ps 95:3
d Pss 22:30; 95:6
e 1 Sam 6:1-7:1
f Isa 22:12; 32:11; Pss 35:13; 69:12
g Gen 29:35; Exod 15:2; Deut 10:21; Ps 48:2
h Pss 63:6; 119:148
i Lev 21:6,8, 17,22; Ps 50:12-15
j 2 Kgs 24:1ff; Dan 1:1,18, etc.
k 2 Kgs 25:27; Jer 52:31
l Pss 115:15; 121:2
m Pss 34:7; 66:19
n 1 Kgs 11:34; Ps 78:70
o Lev 9:22; Ps 141:2
p Ps 5:8
q Ps 124:1-5
r Pss 42:5; 68:25; 118:27

[2] The use of the relative pronoun *ša* at the beginning of the Adad-guppi text is difficult. Cf. *CT* 34, 27:41ff.; see Moran 1959:135-136.

[3] Idiomatic rendering of *mūši u urra*; lit., "night and day."

[4] Taking the second *-nu* as a first person singular possessive suffix; cf. von Soden, *GAG* 42 j and k.

[5] Lit., "my two eyes were with him."

[6] According to Oppenheim, however, this is "wool of a specific color," *ANET* 311, n. 3.

[7] Contra Gadd who translates "my goings-out were noiseless," see *CAD* M 2:245 for *muṣû* as a type of woven fabric. This translation more clearly fits into the context which is a description of Adad-guppi's mourning the departure of the gods from Harran.

[8] For feeding the gods, see Oppenheim 1964:183-198.

[9] "Personally deliver" translates the idiomatic expression *mullû qātussu*, lit., "fill into his hand"; cf. *CAD* M 1:187. Also, cf. Moran 1959:136: "G(add)'s *u-ták-la-a* is morphologically very difficult, conventional idiom demands some form of *mullû*, and epigraphically there is no difficulty with *mal...*"

[10] Akk. *šūrubu* is a technical term for bringing the divine statue into a temple.

REFERENCES

Gadd 1958; Longman 1991:97-103, 225-228.

THE AUTOBIOGRAPHY OF IDRIMI (1.148)

Tremper Longman III

The text is preserved on a statue of Idrimi, discovered by Sir Leonard Woolley in 1939 during his excavations at Tell Atshana (Alalaḫ). Although found in the debris of Level IB (ca. 1200 BCE), the statue was dated by most scholars back to Level IV (1500 BCE). Presently, the statue is housed at the British Museum.

The short statue (1.07 m) represents the king sitting on a throne (which has since been found). It was fashioned from magnesite and dolorite and covered on the front by an inscription of 104 lines. The last few lines run down Idrimi's cheek to his mouth, giving the impression that these words were uttered by the figure represented by the statue.

Introduction (lines 1-2)

(1) I am Idrimi,[a] the son of Ilimilimma, the servant of Adad,[b] Ḫepat, and Ishtar, the lady of Alalaḫ, my ladies.

Personal Narration (lines 3-91)

(3) An act of hostility occurred in Aleppo, my ancestral home, and we fled to the people of Emar, my mother's relatives, and we lived in Emar.[c] My older brothers lived (there) with me, but none of them were thinking of the matters of which I was thinking.

(10) Thus I (said): "Whoever possesses his father's house is indeed the foremost heir and whoever [does not] is a servant of the citizens of Emar." I [to]ok my horse, my chariot, and my groom and I went into the desert.[d] I [en]tered into the midst of Sutean warriors. I spent the night with him (?) in the midst of ...

(17b) I set out the next day. I went to the land of Canaan. The town of Ammiya is situated in the land of Canaan. In the town of Ammiya lived citizens of Ḫalab, Mukiš, Niya, and Amae. (When) they saw that I was their lord's son, they gathered around me. "I have become chief; I have been appointed."[1]

(27b) I dwelt in the midst of the Ḫapiru warriors for seven years. I released birds and examined sheep entrails. The weather god turned to me in the seventh year and I built ships. Soldiers ...[2] I caused them to board the ships and proceed by sea to the land of Mukiš. I landed at Mount Ḫazi. I went up, and my land heard of me. They brought oxen and sheep before me. In one day, like one man, Niya, Amae, Mukiš, and Alalaḫ, my city, turned to me. My allies heard and came before me. When they made a treaty with me,[3] [e] I established them as my allies.

(42b) Now for seven years Barrattarna, the strong king, the king of the Hurrian troops, was hostile toward me. In the seventh year I sent (a message) to Barrattarna, the king of the Umman-manda, and I informed (him) of the vassal service of my ancestors when my ancestors made a treaty with them. And our words were pleasing to the (former) kings of the Hurrian troops and a strong agreement existed between them. The mighty king heard of the vassal service of our predecessors and the agreement between them, and he had respect for the oath because of the words of the agreement and because of our vassal service. My greeting he accepted and I increased the sacrifices and returned to him his lost estate. I swore a binding oath[f] to him concerning my position as a loyal vassal and I was king in Alalaḫ.

(59) Kings on my right and left rose up against me. And like them ...[4] which my ancestors piled up on the ground and I also heaped up on the ground. Thus I put an end to their warfare.

(64) I took troops and went against Ḫatti. I destroyed cities under their sovereignty,[5] [g] (including) Paššaḫe, Damrut-rēʾî, Ḫulaḫḫan, Zise, Ie, Uluzila, and Zarana, these cities were (under) their treaty protection. The land of Hatti did not assemble and come against me. So I did as I pleased: I took them as captives; I took their goods, their possessions and their valuables and divided (them) among my auxiliaries. I took my brothers and my comrades together with them and returned to Mukiš. I entered my city Alalaḫ with captives.[h]

(79) I constructed a house with the property, goods, possessions, and valuables that I had brought down from Ḫatti. I made my throne like the throne of

a Prov 8:12; Eccl 1:12

b Deut 12:7; 2 Sam 7:5; Job 42:5

c 1 Sam 22:3-4

d Judg 11:1-11; 1 Sam 20-30 [David's wilderness wandering]

e Gen 21:32; Jos 9:15

f Gen 21:31; 24:7; 50:5; Jos 6:26; Neh 5:12

g Judg 9:5; Pss 57:1; 63:7; 91:1; Isa 51:16; Lam 4:20

h Num 21:29; Ps 68:18; Jer 40:1; Ezek 12:11

[1] This line is extremely difficult. All suggestions are subject to problems. Detailed discussions of this line may be found in Oller 1977a:36-38 and Greenstein and Marcus 1976:75-77.

[2] The text is not broken, but the word(s) is/are so problematical that it is best to leave the rest of the sentence untranslated. For discussion and suggestions, see Oller 1977a:45-47 and Greenstein and Marcus 1976:79-80.

[3] *Innaḫu* from *nâḫu*. This is difficult because the N of *nâḫu* only occurs once. For this reason Greenstein and Marcus posit an "orthographic doubling of the *n*," and regard the form as a G. Oller's translation based on an N of *anāḫu* ("My brothers labored with me") is a possible alternative. Dietrich and Loretz (1981:215) assert that it is an N ptc 3rd pl. from *aḫû* II, a denominative verb. If true, this would be (along with line 48) the only occurrence of the N form.

[4] This is the most difficult line in the whole composition. Greenstein and Marcus argue for a reading *ku-um-ta el ku-[uk]-ma-ti-su-nu*, but Oller's collation does not substantiate their transliteration. We leave it untranslated.

[5] *Ṣalulu* (*ṣululu*) may signify (like the biblical *ṣel*) the protection offered a vassal by a sovereign in a treaty arrangement.

kings. I made my brothers like the brothers of kings, my sons like their sons and my friends like their friends. I made my inhabitants who were in the midst of my land dwell in better dwellings. Those who (formerly) did not dwell in dwellings, I made them dwell (so). I established my land. I made my cities as they were previously with our fathers. (In accord with?) the signs that the gods of Alalaḫ established and the sacrifices of our father who repeatedly performed them, I repeatedly performed them. I performed them and entrusted them to my son Adad-nirari.

Blessing/Curse Formulas (lines 92-104)

(92) Whoever...this my statue, may his progeny be destroyed. May the heaven-god curse him.[i] May the earth below destroy his progeny. May the gods of heaven and earth measure out his kingdom. Whoever changes it..., may IM the lord of heaven and earth and the great gods extirpate his name, his seed in his land.

(98b) Šarruwa is the scribe, the servant of IM, UTU, Kušuḫ, and ANŠUR.[6] Šarruwa is the scribe who inscribed this statue. May the gods of heaven and earth give him good health, protect him, and favor him. May Shamash, the lord of the upper and lower worlds, the lord of the spirits, give him life.

(102) I reigned as king for 30 years. I have inscribed my labors on a statue. Let one look on them and continually bless me.[7]

i Deut 4:2; 12:32; Prov 30:6; Ezra 6:11-12

[6] See the translation and the discussion of these lines in Sasson 1981:310ff.

[7] See Oller 1977b.

REFERENCES

Dietrich and Loretz 1981; Greenstein and Marcus 1976; Kempinski and Naʾaman 1973; Longman 1991:60-66, 216-218; Oller 1977a; 1977b; Sasson 1981; Smith 1949.

THE MARDUK PROPHECY (1.149)

Tremper Longman III

The Marduk Prophecy is the most complete and clearest example of fictional autobiography which ends with a prophecy. R. Borger has provided a copy, transliteration, translation into German, and commentary on the text.

(i 1) O Ḫarḫarnum, Ḫayyašum,[1] Anum, Enlil, Nudim[mud], Ea, ⸢Muati⸣, Nabium! Let the great gods learn my secrets.[a] After I gird my loins, I will give my speech.

(i 7) I am Marduk[b] the Great Lord. I am always watching,[2] walking watchfully over the mountains, I watch, a watchman[c] roaming the lands. I am he, who in all the lands — from sunrise to sunset — am constantly roaming.

(i 13) I gave the command that I go to Hatti.[d] I inquired into Ḫatti. I set up the throne of my Anu-power in its midst. I dwelt in its midst for ⸢24⸣ years. I established [the tr]ade of the citizens of Babylon [in] its midst. I oversaw its [...], its goods, and its valuables [in] Sippar, Nippur, [and Baby]lon.

(i 23) [A king of Babylon] arose[e] and ⸢led me⸣ [3] [f] [to] Babylon. [...] were in order (?). Fair was the processional way[g] of Ba[bylon.] [...] the crown of my Anu-power [...] and the statue [...] water, winds [...]. Three days [...] the crown of my Anu-power [...] and statue [...] to my body [did I ...] I went home. [With reference to Babylon, I said:] "Bring [your tribute, O you] la[nds, to Babylon ...]."

[gap]

(i 1′) [...] Assur was good [...] Ekur, Assur [...]. [Make its temples shine] like a *zalāqu*-stone. Abounding [...] I gave [it. Monthly, daily, and ye]arly [I blessed it]. I girded [the loins] of the people of Enlil with it. I gave [it] wings like a bird.[h] I filled all [the lands]. I filled [...]. I blessed Assur. I gave it fates [...]. I gave it strong approval [...]. I went home. With reference to Babylon I said: "Bring your tribute, O you lands, to Babylon [...]."

(i 18′) I am Marduk, the great prince. I am Lord of fate[i] and oracle.[j] Who has undertaken this campaign? As I have gone away, I will come back — I have commanded it. I went to Elam — all the

a Deut 29:29; Ps 44:21; Isa 45:19; 48:16
b Prov 8:12; Eccl 1:12
c Hos 9:8
d 1 Sam 4:1b-11
e Dan 11:7
f Gen 19:16
g Pss 42:4; 68:24
h Exod 19:4; Ps 55:6
i Job 20:29; 21:17
j Jer 23:33-40

[1] Two rarely mentioned gods. It is surprising that the Marduk text begins with an invocation to such rarely attested deities.

[2] LAL.MEŠ is translated as a Gtn of *ḫâtu* (*aḫtanatta*); see *CAD* Ḫ 159b. Cf. Borger who translates LAL.MEŠ as "der Wanderer," connecting LAL with the root *ṣûd*. The *tan* form is translated as iterative. The use of logograms is frequent in the Marduk Prophecy and imparts an esoteric cast to the composition.

[3] Lit., "grasped my hand," which is an idiom for leading the god's statue (*ṣalmu*) back to the temple.

gods went — I commanded it. I myself cut off the *nindabû*-offering of the temples. Shakkan and Nisaba[4] I caused to go away to heaven. (ii 1) Sirish[5] made the midst of the land sick.[6] [k] The corpses of the people block the gates.[7] [l] Brother consumes brother. Friend strikes his friend with a weapon. Aristocrats stretch out their hands (to beg) from the commoner. The scepter grows short.[8] Evil lies across the land. [...] kings diminish the land. Lions block off the way.[m] Dogs go mad and bite people.[n] ⌜As many as⌝ they bite do not live; they die.[9] I fulfilled my ⌜days⌝; I fulfilled my years. Then I carried myself back to my city Babylon and to the Ekursagil.[o] I called all the goddesses together. I commanded: "Bring your tribute, O you lands, to Babylon [...]."

(ii 19) A king of Babylon will arise,[p] and he will renew the house of announcement, the Ekur-sagil. He will draw the plans of heaven and earth in the Ekur-sagil. He will change its height. He will establish tax exemptions for my city Babylon. He will lead me and bring me into my city Babylon and the Ekur-sagil forever. He will renew the ship Matush. He will inlay its rudder with *ṣāriru*-metal. He will [cover] its walls with *pašallu*-metal. He will let sailors who serve on it embark on it. They will face each other on the ⌜right⌝ and left. ⌜A king⌝ who like (?) the star (?) of the Ekur-sagil [...].

[gap, then some fragmentary lines]

(iii 1′) [gap, some fragmentary signs] ⌜Ningirsu⌝ will rule. The rivers will carry fish.[q] The fields and plains will be full of yield. The grass of winter (will last) to summer. The grass of summer will last to winter. The harvest of the land will thrive.[r] The marketplace will prosper. He will set evil aright. He will clear up the disturbed. He will illumine evil. The clouds will be continually present. Brother will love his brother. A son will fear his father as if he were a god.[s] Mother [...] daughter. The bride will marry. She will fear her husband. He will be compassionate toward the people. The man will regularly pay his taxes. That prince will [rule all] the lands.

(iii 21′) And I, the god of all, will befriend him. He will destroy Elam. He will destroy its cities. The city and its swamps he will turn away. He causes the great king of Der to arise in his doorframe. He will change its deathly silence. His evil [...]. His hand he will seize. He will ever cause him to enter Der and the Ugal-kalama.

[Break]

k Joel 1:9
l Nah 3:3
m 1 Kgs 13:24-28; Prov 26:23
n Pss 22:16; 59:6, 14
o 1 Sam 6:1-7:2
p Dan 11:7
q Ezek 47:9, 10
r Pss 67:6; 85:12
s Exod 20:12

[4] These are gods of cattle and grain respectively, thus the reference is to famine.

[5] A beer goddess.

[6] The verbs in this section are explicitly present/future when they are not written in logograms. Borger translates them in the past and wonders why they are written in the present. It may be a case of the "historical" present utilized in order to make the description more vivid.

[7] The following section describes a situation of total social disorder. A similar theme is found in the Shulgi Prophecy IV, 9′ff.

[8] See Borger, *BiOr* 14 (1957) 120b for *ḫattu* with *arāku*. *Ḫattu* "scepter" is a metonym for "reign."

[9] Dogs were vicious in Near Eastern towns, and during times of calamity were major problems. Thus the motif of dogs wandering the streets became a literary motif, see "The Curse of Agade."

REFERENCES

Borger 1971; Foster *BM* 1:304-307; Longman 1991:132-142; 233-235.

THE DYNASTIC PROPHECY (1.150)

Tremper Longman III

The Dynastic Prophecy is the most recent addition to the growing corpus of Akkadian prophecy texts. A. K. Grayson provided an edition of the text in 1975. The text is in a poor state of preservation, not having a single complete line. The Dynastic Prophecy has only one certain exemplar although, as Grayson points out, BM 34903 (= CT 51:122) could possibly be part of the text. The following excerpt excludes the fragmentary introduction which preserves indications of first-person speech. It also omits the fragmentary fourth column. Generically and stylistically, this prophecy bears close resemblance to Daniel 11:2-45.

[Break][1]

i 1′ [...] me. [...] me.[2] [...] left. [...] great. [...] seed. [...] he sees.

(i 7′) [...] a later day. [...] will be overthrown. [...]

[1] There is a lacuna of uncertain length before the first line.

[2] Lines 1 and 2 end [ ]-*in-n*[*i*] and [ ]-*ni-in-ni* respectively. The interpretation adopted in this translation is that they are ventive endings on verbs. This is an indication that the complete Dynastic Prophecy would have begun with an autobiographical introduction, see Longman 1991:151-152.

will be annihilated. [...] Assyria. [...] silver (?) and [...] will attack and [...] Babylon, will attack and [...] will be overthrown. [...] will lift up and [...] will come/go [...] will seize [...] he will destroy [...] will shroud [...] he will bring ext[ensive booty][a] into Babylon. [...] he will decorate the Esagil and the Ezida.[b] [...] he will build the palace of Babylon. [...] Nippur to Babylon. He will exercise kingship [for x year]s.

[Break]

(ii 1′) [...] he will go up. [...] he will overthrow [...]. [He will exercise kingship] for three years. Borders and [...]. For his people [...]. After him his son will [sit] on the throne. [...] not [...].

(ii 11′) A ⸢rebel⸣ prince will arise.[c] [He will establish] the dynasty of Harran. [He will exercise kingship] for seventeen years. He will oppress the land and [he will cancel?] the festival of ⸢Esagil⸣. [He will build] a fortress in Babylon. He will plot evil against Akkad.[3]

(ii 17′) A king of Elam will arise. The scepter [...]. He will remove him from his throne [...]. He will seize the throne and the king who arose from the throne [...]. The king of Elam will change his place [...]. He will cause him to dwell in another land [...]. That king will oppress the land and [...]. All the lands [will bring] tribute [to him].[d] During his reign Akkad [will not enjoy] a peaceful abode.[4]

(iii 1) [...] kings [...] of his father [...]. [He will exercise kingship] for two years. A eunuch [will murder] that king. Any prince [will arise]. He will attack and [will seize the thron]e. He will [exercise kingship] for five years. [...] army of the Hanaeans [...] will attack [...]. His army [...] will plunder and ro[b him]. Afterward [his ar]my will regroup and ⸢raise⸣ their weapons.[e] Enlil, Shamash, and [Marduk] will go at the side of his ar[my]. He will bring about the overthrow of the Hanaean army. He will [carry] off his extensive booty [and bring] it into his palace. The people who had ex[perienced] misfortune [will enjoy] well-being. The mood of the land [...] tax exemption [...].[5]

[Break]

a Gen 34:29; Exod 3:22; Deut 13:16; Jer 20:5; Dan 11:24

b 1 Kgs 7:13-51

c Dan 11:7

d Judg 3:15-18; 2 Sam 8:2; 2 Kgs 17:3

e Exod 15:3; 2 Sam 5:22-25

[3] This section clearly alludes to Nabonidus (Harran).

[4] This section alludes to the Achaemenids (Elam).

[5] This section alludes to the Greeks (Hanaeans; cf. Ionians).

REFERENCES

Grayson 1975:24-37; Longman 1991:149-152; 239-240.

C. INDIVIDUAL FOCUS

1. JUST SUFFERER COMPOSITIONS

DIALOGUE BETWEEN A MAN AND HIS GOD (1.151)

Benjamin R. Foster

This is the earliest Akkadian treatment of the problem of theodicy, the theme of the just sufferer that reaches a literary climax of sorts in the biblical book of Job. The present treatment is known from a single text of Old Babylonian date. Like later ones, it is primarily concerned with suffering in the form of illness, assumed to be punishment for sins known or unknown, and it concludes with restoration to divine favor, i.e., to health. [WWH]

(i) A young man was imploring his god as a friend,
He was constantly supplicating, he was [praying to(?)] him.
His heart was seared, he was sickened with his burden,
His feelings were sombre from misery.
He weakened, fell to the ground, prostrated himself.
His burden had grown too heavy for him, he drew near to weep.
He was moaning like a donkey foal separated (from its mother),[a]
He cried out before his god, his master.
His mouth a wild bull, his clamor two mourners,
[His] lips bear a lament to his lord.

(ii) He recounts the burdens he suffered to his lord,
The young man expounds the misery he is suffering:
"My Lord, I have debated with myself, and in my feelings
[...] of heart: the wrong I did I do not know! [b]
Have I [...] a vile forbidden act?
Brother does not de[sp]ise his brother,
Friend is not calumniator of his friend!"
The [...] does not [...]

[large gap]

(iv) [4 lines lost or fragmentary]

"[From] when I was a child until I grew up, (the days?) have been long, when [...]?
How much you have been kind to me, how much I have blasphemed you,
I have not forgotten.
In[stead(?)] of good you revealed evil, O my lord,] you made glow ...
My bad repute is grown excessive, it ...to (my) feet.
It [rains] blows on my skull(?).
Its [...] turned my mouth ... to gall."

a 1 Sam 6:12

b Job 9;20f.; 13:23

c Prov 25:21

d Ps 107:18; Job 38:17

[large gap]

(vii) [4 lines lost]

[...] he brought him to earth,
[...] he has anointed him with medicinal oil,
[...] food, and covered his blotch,
He attended him and gladdened his heart,
He ordered the restoration of his good health to him:

(viii) "Your disease is under control,
let your heart not be despondent!
The years and days you were filled with misery are over.
Were you not ordered to live,
How could you have lasted the whole of this grievous illness?
You have seen distress, ... is (now) held back.
You have borne its massive load to the end.
They have you, (but) the way is open to you,
The path is straight for you, mercy is granted you.
You must never, till the end of time, forget [your] god
Your creator, now that you are favored."

(ix) "I am your god, your creator, your trust,
My guardians are strong and alert on your behalf.
The field will open [to you] its refuge.
I will see to it that you have long life.
So, without qualms, do you anoint the parched,
Feed the hungry, water the thirsty,[c]
But he who sits there with burning e[yes],
Let him look upon your food, melt, flow down, and dis[solve].
The gate of life and well-being is open to you! [d]
Going away(?), drawing near, coming in, going out: may you be well!"

Make straight his way, open his path:
May your servant's supplication reach your heart!

REFERENCES

Text: Nougayrol 1952. Translations and studies: Nougayrol 1952; Lambert 1987; Foster *BM* 1:75-77, *FDD* 295-297.

A SUFFERER'S SALVATION (1.152)

Benjamin R. Foster

This treatment of the theme of theodicy bridges the gap between the Old Babylonian ones (in Sumerian and Akkadian) and those of neo-Assyrian date. It comes from Ugarit, where scribal schools adopted and adapted the Mesopotamian curriculum in the Late Bronze Age. It is preserved in a single fragmentary exemplar. [WWH]

[Gap of about 15 lines]
Evil [portents?] were continually set against me [...]
My omens were obscure, they became like [...]
The diviner could not reach a ruling concerning me,
The "Judge" would give no sign.
The omens were confused the oracles mixed up.
Dream interpreters used up the incense, diviners the lambs,
Learned men debated the tablets (about my case),
They could not say when my affliction would run its course.[a]
My family gathered round to bend over me before my time,
My next of kin stood by ready for the wake.
My brothers were bathed in blood like men possessed,
My sisters sprinkled me with fine(?) oil from the press.
Until the Lord raised my head,
And brought me back to life from the dead,
Until Marduk raised my head
And brought me back to life from the dead,
I could eat scant bread,
I took for my] drink bilge(?) and salt pools.
[When I lay down], sleep would not overcome me,
[I would lie aw]ake my whole night through.
My heart [...] me, my(!) mind ...,
I was wasting away(?) from the sickness I suffered.
[... I] was made most anxious [...]
My [te]ars [had to serve] as my sustenance.[b]
[Lest] Marduk be forgotten,
That Marduk be praised:
Were it not for Marduk, breath had gone from me,
Would not (?) [the mour]ner have cried out 'alas for him!'
I praise, I praise, what the lord Marduk has done I praise!
[I praise, I praise], what the angry (personal) god [has done] I praise!
[I praise, I praise], what the (personal) goddess [has done] I praise!
Praise, praise, do not be bashful, but praise!
[He it] is, Marduk, I entreat(?) him, I entreat(?) him,
[He it] was who smote me, then was merciful to me.
He scuttled(?) me, then moored me,
He dashed me down, then grabbed me (as I fell),
He scattered me wide, then garnered me,
He thrust me away, then gathered me in,
He threw me down, then lifted me high.[c]
He snatched the jaw of death,
He raised me up from hell.
He smashed my smiter's weapon,
He wrested the shovel from the digger of my grave.
He opened my shrouded eyes,
He made my [sp]eech intelligible,
He [...] my ears.
(Text breaks off)

a 1 Sam 28:6, 15
b Pss 42:4, 80:6
c Ps 113:5f.

REFERENCES

Text: Nougayrol *Ugaritica* 5:435 No. 162. Translations and studies: Nougayrol 1968:265-273; Dietrich 1993; Foster *BM* 1:324f., *FDD* 314f.

THE POEM OF THE RIGHTEOUS SUFFERER (1.153)

Benjamin R. Foster

This is the most elaborate treatment of the theme of theodicy. It includes a veritable thesaurus of medical symptoms (Tablet II) and their cure (Tablet III). Because the sufferer protests not so much innocence as ignorance of his sins, his modern designation could well be "pious sufferer" rather than "just sufferer."[1] He is identified by name in the text (Tablet III, line 43) and was possibly its author. The ancient name of the composition is, as usual, taken from its opening words or incipit.[2] When complete, the poem had four tablets (chapters) of presumably 120 lines each, for a total of 480 lines. [WWH]

[1] Mattingly 1990.
[2] *Ludlul bel nemeqi*, "I will praise the lord of wisdom," sometimes further abbreviated to *Ludlul*.

Tablet I

I will praise the lord of wisdom, solicitous god,[3]
[Fur]ious in the night, growing in the day:
Marduk! lord of wisdom, solicitous god,
[Fur]ious in the night, growing in the day:
Whose anger is like a raging tempest,
But whose breeze is sweet as the breath of morn.
In his fury not to be withstood, his rage the deluge,
Merciful in his feelings, his emotions relenting.
The skies cannot sustain the weight of his hand,
His gentle palm rescues the moribund.
Marduk! The skies cannot sustain the weight of his hand,
His gentle palm rescues the moribund.
He it is, in brunt of whose anger, graves are dug,
At the same moment, raised the fallen from disaster.
He glowers, protective spirits take flight,
He regards, the one whose god forsook him returns.
His severe punishment is harsh and speedy,
He stops short and quickly returns to his natural state.
He is bull-headed in his love of mercy,
Like a cow with a calf, he keeps turning around watchfully.
His scourge is barbed and punctures the body,
His bandages are soothing, they heal the doomed.
He speaks and makes one incur many sins,
On the day of his justice sin and guilt are dispelled.
He is the one who afflicts with demons of shaking-disease,
Through his sacral spell chills and shivering are driven away.
Who ... the flood of Adad, the blow of Erra,
Who reconciles the wrathful god [and god]dess,
The lord divines the gods' inmost thoughts,
(But) no [god] understands his behavior.
Marduk divines the gods' inmost thoughts,
Which god understands his mind?
As heavy his hand, so compassionate his heart,
As brutal his weapons, so life-sustaining his feelings.
Without his consent, who could cure his blow?
Against his will, who could sin and [escape]?
I, who touched bottom like a fish, will proclaim his anger,
He quickly granted me favor, as if reviving the dead.
I will teach the people that his kindness is nigh,
May his favorable thought take away their [guilt?].
From the day the Lord punished me,
And the warrior Marduk became furious with me,
My own god threw me over(?) and disap[peared],
My goddess broke rank and vanished.
He cut off the benevolent angel who (walked) beside [me],
My protecting spirit was frightened off, to seek out someone else.
My vigor was taken away, my manly appearance became gloomy,
My dignity escaped and lit on the roof.
Terrifying signs beset me:
I was forced out of my house, I wandered outside.
My omens were confused, they were contradictory every day,
The prognostication of diviner and dream interpreter could not explain what I was undergoing.
What was said in the street portended ill for me,
When I lay down at night, my dream was terrifying.
The king, incarnation of the gods, sun of his peoples,
His heart hardened against me and appeasing him was impossible.
Courtiers were plotting hostile action against me,
They gathered themselves to instigate base deeds:
If the first "I will make him end his life"
Says the second "I ousted (him) from his command!"
So likewise the third "I will get my hands on his post!"
"I'll come into property!" vows the fourth
As the fifth subverts the mind of fifty,
Sixth and seventh follow on his heels!
The clique of seven have massed their forces,
Merciless as fiends, the likeness to demons.
So one is their body, (but seven) their mouths.
Their hearts fulminate against me, ablaze like fire.
Slander and lies they try to lend credence against me.
My eloquent mouth they checked, as with reins,
My lips, which used to discourse, became those of a deaf man.
My resounding call struck dumb,
My proud head bent earthward,
My stout heart turned feeble for terror,
My broad breast brushed aside by a novice,
My far-reaching arms pinned by my clothing,
I, who walked proudly, learned slinking,
I, so grand, became servile.
To my vast family I became a loner,
As I went through the streets, I was pointed at,
I would enter the palace, eyes would squint at me,
My city was glowering at me like an enemy,
Belligerent and hostile would seem my land!
My brother became my foe,
My friend became a malignant demon,
My comrade would denounce me savagely,

[3] I.e., Marduk (line 3). Withholding the precise identity of the (human or divine) protagonist until the second or a subsequent line is a traditional device taken over from Sumerian poetry.

My colleague kept the taint to(?) his weapons for bloodshed,
My best friend made my life an aspersion.
My slave cursed me openly in the assembly (of gentlefolk),
My slave girl defamed me before the rabble.
An acquaintance would see me and make himself scarce,
My family disowned me.
A pit awaited anyone speaking well of me,
While he who was uttering defamation of me forged ahead.
One who relayed base things about me had a god for his help,
For the one who said "What a pity about him!" death came early,
The one of no help, his life became charmed,
I had no one to go at my side, nor saw I a champion.
They parceled my possessions among the riffraff,
The sources of my watercourses they blocked with muck,
They chased the harvest song from my fields,
They left my community deathly still, like that of a (ravaged) foe.
They let another assume my duties,
And appointed an outsider to my prerogatives.
By day sighing, by night lamentation,
Monthly, trepidation, despair the year.
I moaned like a dove all my days,
Like a singer, I moan out my dirge.
My eyes endure(?) constant crying,
My cheeks scald from tears, as if eroded(?).
My face is darkened from the apprehensions of my heart,
Terror and panic have jaundiced my face.
The wellsprings of my heart quaked for unremitting anxiety,
I was changeable(?) as a flickering fire,
Prayer was disorder, like an exploding flame,
My entreaty was like the fracas of a brawl.
My sweet-lipped discourse was murky, obscure,
When I turned a biting comment, my gambit was stifled.
"Surely in daylight good will come upon me!
The new moon will appear, the sun will shine!"

Tablet II
One whole year to the next! The (normal) time passed.
As I turned around, it was more and more terrible.
My ill luck was on the increase, I could find no good fortune.
I called to my god, he did not show his face,
I prayed to my goddess, she did not raise her head.
The diviner with his inspection did not get to the bottom of it,
Nor did the dream interpreter with his incense clear up my case,
I beseeched a dream spirit, but it did not enlighten me,
The exorcist with his ritual did not appease divine wrath.[a]
What bizarre actions everywhere!
I looked behind: persecution, harrassment!
Like one who had not made libations to his god,
Nor invoked his goddess with a food offering,
Who was not wont to prostrate, nor seen to bow down,
From whose mouth supplication and prayer were wanting,
Who skipped holy days, despised festivals,
Who was neglectful, omitted the gods' rites,
Who had not taught his people reverence and worship,
Who did not invoke his god, but ate his food offering,
Who snubbed his goddess, brought (her) no flour offering,
Like one possessed(?), who forgot his lord,
Who casually swore a solemn oath by his god:[b]
I, indeed, seemed (such a one)!
I, for my part, was mindful of supplication and prayer,
Prayer to me was the natural recourse, sacrifice my rule.
The day for reverencing the gods was a source of satisfaction to me,
The goddess's procession day was my profit and return.[c]
Praying for the king, that was my joy,
His sennet was as if for (my own) good omen.
I instructed my land to observe the god's rites,
The goddess's name did I drill my people to esteem.
I made my praises of the king like a god's,
And taught the populace reverence for the palace.
I wish I knew that these things were pleasing to a god!
What seems good to one's self could be an offense to a god,
What in one's own heart seems abominable could be good to one's god![4]
Who could learn the reasoning of the gods in heaven?
Who could grasp the intentions of the gods of the depths?
Where might human beings have learned the way of a god?[5] [d]
He who lived by (his) brawn died in confinement.

a 1 Sam 28:6, 15
b Ex 20:7; Deut 5:11
c Ps 68:25
d Deut 30:11-14

[4] This couplet sums up the dilemma posed by the poet.
[5] Contrast the biblical view as expressed, e.g., in Deut 30:11-14.

Suddenly one is downcast, in a trice full of cheer,
One moment he sings in exaltation,
In a trice he groans like a professional mourner.
People's motivations change in a twinkling!
Starving, they become like corpses,
Full, they would rival their gods.
In good times, they speak of scaling heaven,
When it goes badly, they complain of going down to hell.
I have ponde[red] these things; I have made no sense of them.
But as for me, in despair, a whirlwind is driving(?) me!
Debilitating disease is let loose upon me:
An evil vapor has blown against me [from the] ends of the earth,
Head pain has surged up upon me from the breast of hell,
A malignant spectre has come forth from its hidden depth,
A relentless [ghost] came out of its dwelling place.
[A she-demon came] down from the mountain,
Ague set forth [with the] flood [and sea?],
Debility broke through the ground with the plants.
[They assembled] their host, together they came upon me:
[They struck my he]ad, they closed around my pate,
[My features] were gloomy, my eyes ran a flood,
They wrenched my muscles, made my neck limp,
They thwacked [my chest], pounded(?) my breast,
They affected my flesh, threw (me) into convulsions,
They kindled a fire in my epigastrium,
They churned up my bowels, they tw[isted] my entrails(?),
Coughing and hacking infected my lungs,
They infected(?) my limbs, made my flesh pasty,
My lofty stature they toppled like a wall,
My robust figure they flattened like a bulrush,
I was dropped like a dried fig, I was tossed on my face.
A demon has clothed himself in my body for a garment,
Drowsiness smothers me like a net,
My eyes stare, they cannot see,
My ears prick up, they cannot hear.
Numbness has spread over my whole body,
Paralysis has fallen upon my flesh.
Stiffness has seized my arms,
Debility has fallen upon my loins,
My feet forgot how to move.
[A stroke] has overcome me, I choke like one fallen,
Signs of death have shrouded my face!
[If someone th]inks of me, I can't respond to the inquirer,
"[Ala]s!" they weep, I have lost consciousness.
A snare is laid on my mouth,
And a bolt bars my lips.
My way in is barred, my point of slaking blocked,
My hunger is chronic, my gullet is constricted.
If it be of grain, I choke it down like stink weed,
Beer, the sustenance of mankind, is sickening to me.
Indeed, the malady drags on!
For lack of food my features are unrecognizable,
My flesh is waste, my blood has run dry,
My bones are loose, covered (only) with skin,
My tissues are inflamed, afflicted with gangrene(?).
I took to bed, confined, going out was exhaustion,
My house turned into my prison.
My flesh was a shackle, my arms being useless,
My person was a fetter, my feet having given way.
My afflictions were grievous, the blow was severe!
(ii 100) A scourge full of barbs thrashed me,
A crop lacerated me, cruel with thorns.
All day long tormentor would torment [me],
Nor at night would he let me breathe freely a moment.
From writhing, my joints were separated,
My limbs were splayed and thrust apart.
I spent the night in my dung like an ox,
I wallowed in my excrement like a sheep.
The exorcist recoiled from my symptoms,
While my omens have perplexed the diviner.
The exorcist did not clarify the nature of my complaint,
While the diviner put no time limit on my illness.
No god came to the rescue, nor lent me a hand,
No goddess took pity on me, nor went at my side.
My grave was open, my funerary goods ready,
Before I had died, lamentation for me was done.
All my country said, "How wretched he was!"
When my ill-wisher heard, his face lit up,
When the tidings reached her, my ill-wisher, her mood became radiant.
The day grew dim for my whole family,
For those who knew me, their sun grew dark.

Tablet III

Heavy was his hand upon me, I could not bear it!
Dread of him was oppressive, it [me].
His fierce [pun]ishment [ ], the deluge,
His stride was ..., it ... [ ].
[Ha]rsh, severe illness does not ... [ ] my person,
I lost sight of [aler]tness, [ ] make my mind stray.
I gro[an] day and night alike,
Dreaming and waking [I am] equally wretched.
A remarkable young man of extraordinary physique,
Magnificent in body, clothed in new garments,
Because I was only half awake, his features lacked form.

He was clad in splendor, robed in dread —
He came in upon me, he stood over me.[6]
[When I saw him, my] flesh grew numb.
[ ] "The Lady(?) has sent [me],
[ ]."
[ ] I tried to tell [my people],
"[ ] sent [for me]."
They were silent and did not [speak],
They heard me [in silence and did not answer].
A second time [I saw a dream].
In the dream I saw [at night],
A remarkable purifier [ ],
Holding in his hand a tamarisk rod of purification,
"Laluralimma, resident of Nippur,
Has sent me to cleanse you."
He was carrying water, he po[ured it] over me,
He pronounced the resuscitating incantation, he massaged [my] bo[dy].
A third time I saw a dream.
In my dream I saw at night:
A remarkable young woman of shining countenance,
Clothed like a person(?), being li[ke] a god,
A queen among peoples [ ],
She entered upon me and [sat down] ... [ ]
She ordered my deliverance [ ]
"Fear not!" she said, I [will]
Whatever one sees(?) of a dream [ ]."
She ordered my deliverance, "Most wre[tched] indeed is he,
Whoever he might be, the one who saw the vision at niqht."
In the dream (was) Ur-Nindinugga, a Babylonian(?)
A bearded young man wearing a tiara,
He was an exorcist, carrying a tablet,
"Marduk has sent me!
To Shubshi-meshre-Shakkan I have brought a sw[athe],
From his pure hands I have brought a sw[athe]."
He has entru[sted] me into the hands of my ministrant.
[In] waking hours he sent a message,
He reve[aled] his favorable sign to my people.
I was awake in my sickness, a (healing) serpent slithered by.
My illness was quickly over, [my fetters] were broken.
After my lord's heart had quiet[ed],
(And) the feelings of merciful Marduk were ap[peased],
[And he had] accepted my prayers [ ],
His sweet [relen]ting [ ],
[He ordered] my deliverance!: "He is g[reatly trie]d!"
[ ] to extol [ ]
[ ] to worship and [ ]
[ ] my guilt [ ]
[ ] my iniquity [ ]
[ ] my transgression [ ]
He made the wind bear away my offenses.

[The exact placement of the following lines is unknown.]

[He applied] to me his spell which binds [debilitating disease],
[He drove] back the evil vapor to the ends of the earth,
He bore off [the head pain] to the breast of hell,
[He sent] down the malignant spectre to its hidden depth,
The relentless ghost he returned [to] its dwelling,
He overthrew the she-demon, sending if off to a mountain,
He replaced the ague in flood and sea.
He eradicated debility like a plant,
Uneasy sleep, excessive drowsiness,
He dissipated like smoke filling the sky.
The turning towards people(?) with "woe!" and "alas!" he drove away like a cloud, earth ... [ ]
The tenacious disease in the head, which was [heavy] as a [mill]stone,
He raised like dew of night, he removed it from me.
My beclouded eyes, which were wrapped in the shroud of death,
He drove (the cloud) a thousand leagues away, he brightened [my] vision,
My ears, which were stopped and clogged like a deaf man's,
He removed their blockage, he opened my hearing.
My nose, whose [bre]athing was choked by symptoms of fever,
He soothed its affliction so I could breathe [freely].
My babbling lips, which had taken on a h[ard crust?],
He wiped away their distress(?) and und[id] their deformation.
My mouth, which was muffled, so that proper speech was diffi[cult],
He scoured like copper and r[emoved] its filth.
My teeth, which were clenched and locked together firmly,
[He op]ened their fastening, fre[ed?] the jaws(?).
My tongue, which was tied and [could] not converse,
[He] wiped off its coating and [its] speech became fluent(?).
My windpipe, which was tight and choking, as though on a gobbet,
He made well and let it si[ng] its songs like a flute.
My [gul]let, which was swollen so it could not take

[6] This is the typical form in which dream reports are cast in cuneiform literature; see Oppenheim 1956:187-190, 250. The allusion may be to the dream-god himself, called Zaqar. See Kutscher 1988.

[food],
Its swelling went down and he opened its blockage.
My [ ], which [ ]
[ ] above [ ]
[which] was darkened like [ ]

[three damaged lines, then gap]

[The following lines are known only from the ancient commentary, but must go in the gap here, in sequence but not necessarily seriatim.]

(a) My intestine, which was ever empty for want, and was coiled (tight) like basketry,
(b) Accepts nourishment, holds drink.
(c) My neck, which was limp and twisted at the base,
(d) He shored up, a hillock, he planted upright like a tree(?).
(e) He made my body that of a perfect athlete.
(f) He pared my nails as if to drive out a "vengeance."
(g) He drove out their illness and made their upper parts well.
(h) My knees, which were tied and b[ound] like a ... bird's
(i) The shape of my bo[d]y [he made] remarkable(?)
(j) He wiped off the grime, he cleansed its filth
(k) My gloomy mien began to glow (=120?)

Tablet IV (Episode A)
The Lord [ ] me,
The Lord took hold of me,
The Lord set me on my feet,
The Lord revived me,
He rescued me [from the p]it,
He summoned me [from destruc]tion,
[ ] he pulled me from the river of death.
[ ] he took my hand.
[He who] smote me,
Marduk, he restored me!
He smote the hand of my smiter,
It was Marduk who made him drop his weapon.
[He] the attack of my foe,
It was Marduk who [ ]

[Two fragmentary lines, then gap. Insert here, perhaps, two lines known only from the ancient commentary]:

(l) At the place of the river ordeal, where people's fates are decided,
(m) I was struck on the forehead, my slave mark removed.

(Fragment B)
[ ] which in my prayers [ ]
[With] prostration and supplication [ ] to Esagila
[ ]
[I who went] down to the grave have returned to the "Gate of [Sunrise]."
[In the] "Gate of Prosperity" prosperity was [given me].
[In the] "Gate of the Guardian Spirit" a guardian spirit [drew nigh to me].
[In the] "Gate of Well-being" I beheld well-being.
In the "Gate of Life" I was granted life.
In the "Gate of Sunrise" I was reckoned among the living.
In the "Gate of Splendid Wonderment" my signs were plain to see.
In the "Gate of Release from Guilt"[7]
I was released from my bond.
In the "Gate of Praise(?)" my mouth made inquiry.
In the "Gate of Release from Sighing" my sighs were released.
In the "Gate of Pure Water" I was sprinkled with purifying water.
In the "Gate of Conciliation" I appeared with Marduk,
In the "Gate of Joy" I kissed the foot of Sarpanitum.
I was consistent in supplication and prayer before them,
I placed fragrant incense before them,
An offering, a gift, sundry donations I presented,
Many fatted oxen I slaughtered, butchered many [sheep?].[8]
Honey-sweet beer and pure wine I repeatedly libated.
The protecting genius, the guardian spirit, divine attendants of the fabric of Esagila,[9]
I made their feelings glow with libation,
I made them exultant [with] lavish [meals].
[To the threshhold, the bolt] socket, the bolt, the doors
[I offered] oil, butterfat, and choicest grain.[10]
[ ] the rites of the temple.

[large gap]

[insert here?]

(o) I proceeded along Kunush-kadru Street in a state of redemption.
(p) He who has done wrong by Esagil, let him learn from me.
(q) It was Marduk who put a muzzle on the mouth of the lion that was devouring me.
(r) Marduk took away the sling of my pursuer and deflected his slingstone.

(Fragment C)
[ ] golden grain [ ]

[7] For a similarly designated gate in a Sum. letter-prayer, see Hallo 1968:86:49.
[8] This topos, or literary cliche, goes back to Sum. precedent and recurs in the Akk. Gilgamesh Epic (above Text 1.132, lines 70f.).
[9] *E-sag-ila*, lit., "house that lifts the head (i.e. to heaven)," the great temple tower (ziggurrat) of Marduk at Babylon.
[10] For archival texts recording offerings to temple gates see Levine and Hallo 1967.

[He?] anointed himself with sweet cedar perfume,
upon him [ ]
A feast for the Babylonian(s?) [ ]
His tomb he(?) had made [was set up] for a feast!
The Babylonians saw how [Marduk] can restore to life,
And all mouths proclaimed [his] greatness,
"Who (would have) said he would see his sun?
Who (would have) imagined that he would pass through his street?
Who but Marduk revived him as was dying?
Besides Sarpanitum, which goddess bestowed his breath of life?
Marduk can restore to life from the grave,[11]
Sarpanitum knows how to rescue from annihilation.
Wherever earth is founded, heavens are stretched wide,
Wherever sun shines, fire blazes,
Wherever water runs, wind blows,
Those whose bits of clay Aruru pinched off (to form them),[12]
Those endowed with life, who walk upright,
[Tee]ming mankind, as many as they be, give praise to Marduk!
[ ] those who can speak,
[ ] may he rule all the peoples
[ ] shepherd of all habi[tations]
[ ] floods from the deep
[ ] the gods [ ]
[ ] the extent of heaven and netherworld,
[ ]
[ ] was getting darker and darker for him."

[11] Sarpanitum (or Zer-banitum), the consort of Marduk.
[12] Aruru, (a manifestation of) the mother goddess, who created humankind from clay.

REFERENCES

Text: Lambert *BWL* pls. 1-18 and duplicates. Translations and studies: Lambert *BWL* 21-62; *ANET* 596-600; Foster *BM* 1:306-323, *FDD* 298-313.

THE BABYLONIAN THEODICY (1.154)

Benjamin R. Foster

Formally, this classic statement of the theme of theodicy comes closest to the biblical book of Job, for it is cast in the form of a dialogue, albeit the sufferer has only one "friend" to put up with as interlocutor, and that friend is unnamed. A further formal parallel to biblical poetry in general is provided by the strophic structure which, like Ps. 119, features successive stanzas of equal length whose initial signs spell out a message of their own.[1] In the biblical case, such "acrostics" are exclusively alphabetic, i.e., they list the letters of the alphabet in their traditional order.[2] Babylonian acrostics cannot be alphabetic, since Mesopotamian cuneiform is involved. The present acrostic reveals (or conceals) the name of the author and his protestation of religious and political correctness — as if to head off any criticism of the rather daring views expressed in his poem.[3] [WWH]

I. *Sufferer*
O sage, [...], come, [let] me speak to you,
[...], let me recount to you,
[...],
[I ...], who have suffered greatly, let me always praise you,
Where is one whose reflective capacity is as great as yours?
Who is he whose knowledge could rival yours?
Wh[ere] is the counsellor to whom I can tell of woe?
I am without recourse, heartache has come upon me.
I was the youngest child when fate claimed (my) father,
My mother who bore me departed to the land of no return,
My father and mother left me, and with no one my guardian!

II. *Friend*
Considerate friend, what you tell is a sorrowful tale,
My dear friend, you have let your mind harbor ill.
You make your estimable discretion feeble-minded,
You alter your bright expression to a scowl.
Of course our fathers pay passage to go death's way,
I too will cross the river of the dead,
as is commanded from of old.
When you survey teeming mankind all together,
The poor man's son advanced, someone helped him get rich,

[1] On the assumption of 27 stanzas of 11 lines each, the composition when complete comprised a total of 297 lines.
[2] On this order see above, text 1.107 (abecedaries) and Brug 1990.
[3] He says in effect: "I am Saggil-kinam-ubbib the exorcist, a worshipper of god and king." For this individual see Finkel 1988:144f.

Who did favors for the sleek and wealthy?
He who looks to his god has a protector,
The humble man who reveres his goddess will garner wealth.

III. *Sufferer*
My friend, your mind is a wellspring of depth unplumbed,
The upsurging swell of the ocean that brooks no inadequacy.
To you, then, let me pose a question, learn [what I would say].
Hearken to me but for a moment, hear my declaration.
My body is shrouded, craving wears me do[wn],
My assets have vanished, my res[ources?] dwindled.
My energies have turned feeble, my prosperity is at a standstill,
Moaning and woe have clouded [my] features.
The grain of my mead is nowhere near satisfying [me],
Beer, the sustenance of mankind, is far from being enough.
Can a happy life be a certainty? I wish I knew how that might come about!

IV. *Friend*
My well-thought-out speech is the ulti[mate] in good advice,
But you [make?] your well-ordered insight [sound] like babble.
You force [your ...] to be [sca]tter-brained, irrational,
You render your choicest offerings without conviction.
As to your [ever]lasting, unremitting desire [...],
The [fore]most protection [...] in prayer:
The reconciled goddess returns to [...]
The re[conciled gods] will take pity on the fool(?), the wrong-doer.
Seek constantly after the [rites?] of justice.
Your miqhty [...] will surely show kindness,
[...] ... will surely grant mercy.

V. *Sufferer*
I bow down before you, my [comrade],
I apprehend your w[isdom],[a]
[...] what you say.
Come, let me [tell you],
The on[ager], the wild ass, that had its fill of [...],
Did it pay attention [to] ca[rry out?] a god's intentions?
The savage lion that devoured the choicest meat,
Did it bring its offerings to appease a goddess's anger?
The parvenu who multiplies his wealth,
Did he weigh out precious gold to the mother goddess for a family?
[Have I] withheld my offerings? I prayed to my god,
[I] said the blessing over my goddess, my speech [...].

a Job 12:2 etc.

b Job 21:7-16 etc.

VI. *Friend*
O date palm, wealth-giving tree, my precious brother,
Perfect in all wisdom, O gem of wis[dom],
You are a mere child, the purpose of the gods is remote as the netherworld.
Consider that magnificent wild ass on the [plain],
The arrow will gash that headstrong trampler of the leas!
Come, look at that lion you called to mind, the enemy of livestock,
For the atrocity that lion committed, the pit yawns for him.
The well-heeled parvenu who treasured up possessions,
The king will put him to the flames before his time.
Would you wish to go the way these have gone?
Seek after the lasting reward of (your) god.

VII. *Sufferer*
Your reasoning is a cool breeze, a breath of fresh air for mankind,
Most particular friend, your advice is e[xcellent].
Let me [put] but one matter before you:
Those who seek not after a god can go the road of favor,[b]
Those who pray to a goddess have grown poor and destitute.
Indeed, in my youth I tried to find out the will of (my) god,
With prayer and supplication I besought my goddess.
I bore a yoke of profitless servitude:
(My) god decreed (for me) poverty instead of wealth.
A cripple rises above me, a fool is ahead of me,
Rogues are in the ascendant, I am demoted.

VIII. *Friend*
O just, knowledgeable one, your logic is perverse,
You have cast off justice, you have scorned divine design.
In your emotional state you have an urge to disregard divine ordinances,
[...] the sound rules of your goddess.
The strategy of a god is [as remote as] innermost heaven,
The command of a goddess cannot be dr[awn out].
Teeming humanity well understands trouble,

[fragmentary lines, then large gap]

XIII. *Sufferer*
I will forsake home [...]
I will crave no property [...]

I will ignore (my) god's regulations, [I will] trample on his rites.
I will slaughter a calf, I will [...] the food,
I will go on the road, I will learn my way around distant places.
I will open a well, I will let loose a fl[ood?],
I will roam about the far outdoors like a bandit.
I will stave off hunger by forcing entry into one house after another,
I will prowl the streets, casting about, ravenous.
Like a beggar I will [...] inside [...],
Good fortune lies afar off [...].

XIV. *Friend*
My friend, [you have] resolved [upon ...]
The transactions of mankind, which you had no urge to [...],
[...] are in your mind,
Your discretion has forsaken [you ...]

[fragmentary lines]

XV. *Sufferer*
[four lines lost]

Daughter says [unjust words] to her mother,
The fowler who casts [his net] is fallen (into it):
All in all, which one [will find] profit?
Many are the wild creatures that [...],
Which among them has gotten [...]?
Shall I seek son and daughter [...]?
Shall I not leave behind what I find [...]?

XVI. *Friend*
O modest, submissive one, who [...] all [...],
Your mind is always receptive, most precious one [...],

[fragmentary lines, then gap]

XVII. *Sufferer*
The son of a king is clad [in rags?],
The son of the destitute and naked is dressed in [fine raiment?].
The maltster [can pay in] finest gold,
While he who counted red gold bears a [debt?].
He who made do with vegetables [sates himself] at a princely banquet,
While the son of the eminent and wealthy (has only) carob to eat.
The man of substance is fallen, [his income] is removed.

[fragmentary lines, gap]

XX. *Friend*
You have let your subtle mind wander,
[...] you have overthrown wisdom.
You have spurned propriety, you have besmirched (every) code.
Far will be the workman's basket from him who ...
[...] is established as a person of importance,
[...] he is called a scholar,
He is well served, he gets what he wants.
Follow in the way of a god, observe his rites,
[...] be ready for good fortune!

[gap]

XXII. *Friend*
As for the rascal whose good will you wanted,
The ... of his feet will soon disappear.
The godless swindler who acquires wealth,
A deadly weapon is in pursuit of him.
Unless you serve the will of a god, what will be your profit?
He who bears a god's yoke shall never want for food, though it may be meager.
Seek after the favorable breeze of the gods,
What you lost for a year you will recoup in a moment.

XXIII. *Sufferer*
I have looked around in society, indications are the contrary:
God does not block the progress of a demon.
A father hauls a boat up a channel,
While his first-born sprawls in bed.
The eldest son makes his way like a lion,
The second son is content to drive a donkey.
The heir struts the street like a peddler,
The younger son makes provision for the destitute.
What has it profited me that I knelt before my god?
It is I who must (now) bow before my inferior!
The riffraff despise me as much as the rich and proud.

XXIV. *Friend*
Adept scholar, master of erudition,
You blaspheme in the anguish of your thoughts.
Divine purpose is as remote as innermost heaven,
It is too difficult to understand, people cannot understand it.[c]
Among all creatures the birth goddess formed,
Why should offspring be completely unmatched(?)?
The cow's first calf is inferior,
Her subsequent offspring is twice as big.
The first child is born a weakling,
The second is called a capable warrior.
Even if one (tries to) apprehend divine intention, people cannot understand it.

XXV. *Sufferer*
Pay attention, my friend, learn my (next) parry,
Consider the well-chosen diction of my speech.
They extol the words of an important man who is accomplished in murder,
They denigrate the powerless who has committed no crime.
They esteem truthful the wicked to whom tr[uth] is abhorrent,
They reject the truthful man who he[eds] the will of god.

c Deut 30:11-14

They fill the oppressor's st[rongroom] with refined gold,
They empty the beggar's larder of [his] provisions.
They shore up the tyrant whose all is crime,
They ruin the weak, they oppress the powerless.
And as for me, without means, a parvenu harasses me.

XXVI. *Friend*
Enlil, king of the gods, who created teeming mankind,
Majestic Ea, who pinched off their clay,
The queen who fashioned them, mistress Mami,
Gave twisted words to the human race,
They endowed them in perpetuity with lies and falsehood.
Solemnly they speak well of a rich man,
"He's the king," they say, "he has much wealth."
They malign a poor man as a thief,
They lavish mischief upon him, they conspire to kill him.
They make him suffer every evil because he has no wherewithal(?).
They bring him to a horrible end, they snuff him out like an ember.

XXVII. *Sufferer*
You are sympathetic, my friend, be considerate of (my) misfortune.
Help me, see (my) distress, you should be cognizant of it.
Though I am humble, learned, suppliant,
I have not seen help or succor for an instant.
I would pass unobtrusively through the streets of my city,
My voice was not raised, I kept my speaking low.
I did not hold my head high, I would look at the ground.
I was not given to servile praise among my associates.
May the god who has cast me off grant help,
May the goddess who has [forsaken me] take pity,
The shepherd Shamash will past[ure] people as a god should.

REFERENCES

Text: Lambert *BWL* pls. 19-26. Translations and studies: Lambert *BWL* 63-89; *ANET* 438-440, 601-604; Foster *BM* 2:790-798, *FDD* 316-323.

2. DIALOGUE

DIALOGUE OF PESSIMISM OR THE OBLIGING SLAVE (1.155)

Alasdair Livingstone

["Slave, oblige me again!"] "Here, master! Here!"
["Get a move on and get ready] the chariot and harness up so I can go driving to the palace!"
["Go driving, master, go driving!] You'll achieve your goal!"
["...] will show you preference!"
["No, slave,] I will not go driving to the palace!"
["Do not go driving, master, do not go driving!"]
[The palace n]otable will send you off on his business
and will make you take a [route] you don't know;
day and night he'll expose you to miseries."

"Slave, [oblige] me [again]! "Here, master! Here!"
"Get a move on and get ready for me some hand ablution water and give it to me
so I can sup!"
"Sup, master, sup! Having supper regularly makes one content.
[Even ...]. the supper of his god; Shamash approves of clean hands."
"No [slave], I definitely won't sup."
"Don't sup, master, don't sup!
To be hungry, or to eat, to be thirsty, or to drink, are but human."

"Slave, oblige me again! " "Here, master! Here!"
"Get a move on and get ready the chariot and harness it up so I can drive off to the steppe!"
"Drive off master, drive off! The roving man has a full stomach.
Even a prowling dog has a bone to crunch,
and the roving raven finds a place to nest.
The roaming wild ass finds its fill in the steppe."
"No, slave I will definitely not [drive off] to the steppe."
"Do not drive off, master, do not drive off!
The roving man may become insane,
the prowling dog may break its teeth,
as for the dwelling of the raven, it is but in

the [crack] of a wall,
while the roaming wild ass has its resting place in the wastes."

"Slave, oblige me again!" ["Here, master! Here!"]
"I want to build a [house] and found a family!"
"Found one, [master], found one. [The man who builds] a house [...].

(Lines 32 to 38 contain textual disorder and substantial lacunae)

"Slave, oblige me again!" "Here, master! Here!"
"See here, I'll go in for skulduggery!" "So go in for it, master, go in for it!
If you don't go in for skulduggery, what will be your finery?
Who will just give you handouts so you can fill your stomach?"
"No, slave, I will definitely not go in for skulduggery!"
"The man who goes in for skulduggery is killed, flayed,
blinded, arrested or thrown in jail."

"Slave, oblige me again!" "Here, master! Here!"
"I'm going to fall in love with a woman!" "Fall in love, master, fall in love!
The man who falls in love with a woman forgets depression and melancholy."
"No way, slave, I will not fall in love with a woman."
"Don't fall in love, master, don't fall in love.
Woman is a well, she's a well, a pit, a hole.
Woman is a whetted iron dagger that cuts the throat of a fine man."

"Slave, oblige me again!" "Here, master! Here!"
"Get a move on and get water for my hands and give it to me
so that I can make a sacrifice to my personal god!" "Make a sacrifice, master, make a sacrifice!
A man who makes a sacrifice to his personal god will be content.
On trust he is making loan upon loan."
"No way, slave. I will not make a sacrifice to my personal god."
"Don't do it, master, don't do it.
Can you teach your personal god to run after you like a dog?
He'll just demand of you rites, a votive statue, and many other things."

"Slave, oblige me again!" "Here, master! Here!"
"I will act as a guarantor!" "So act as one, master, act as one!
The man who acts as a guarantor: his grain remains his grain but his
return is manifold."
"No way, slave, I will not act as a guarantor."
"Do not make loans, master, do not make loans.
The giving is like love-making, but the return is like childbirth.
They will eat your grain while cursing you again and again
and then make you do without the interest on your grain."

"Slave, oblige me again!" "Here, master! Here!"
"I will carry out a good service for my country!" "So carry one out, master, carry one out.
The man who carries out a good service for his country,
his deeds are placed in the carrying basket of Marduk."
"No way, slave, I will not carry out a good service for my country."
"Don't carry one out, master, don't carry one out.
Go up onto the ancient ruin heaps and walk about!
Search out the skulls of high and low!
Which was a crook and which did good services?"

"Slave, oblige me again!" "Here, master! Here!"
"Now then, what is good?"
"What's good is to break my neck and your neck
and to be thrown in the river.
Who is tall enough to ascend to the heavens?
Who is broad enough to encompass the earth?"
"No way, slave, I'll kill you and send you in advance."
"But my master wouldn't even survive me three days!"

REFERENCES

BWL 139-149; *ANET* 600-601; *TUAT* 3/1:157-163.

3. HUMOROUS TEXTS

"AT THE CLEANERS" (1.156)

Alasdair Livingstone

"Come on fuller, let me give you instructions! Wash my garment!
Don't ignore my instructions and
don't carry out your own methods!
You should set the hem and the lining in place;
you should stitch the front to the inside;
you should pick the thread of the border;
you should soak the thin part in beer;
you should carry out a filtering operation with a sieve;
you should loosen the hem of the lining;
you should ... it in clean water;
you should purify it as if it were a fine cloth.
To the part ... like ...
to the edge bit ...
You should mix alkali and gypsum ...
You should slap it on a washing-board.
You should stir it in a beer jug and you should ...
Yes indeed, you should stretch it over a ...,
you ... it and you should comb it out.
You should tap it with a wand of hardwood.
You should ... the fleecy part which has become flattened nap.
The web, the work with the needle ...
You should squeeze the hem ... and let it cool down.
In the early evening, when the web has not yet
become dry, you should take it and place it in a receptacle, in a container.
Then let it cool down! Carry this out and I'll reward you right away!
You will bring it to the house and ten liters of grain will be poured in your lap!"
The fuller answers him: "By Ea, Lord of
Wisdom, who keeps me alive!
Cut it out! Not me. As to all you say, it's only the guys who lend me money and collect my taxes
that have a nerve like you! And
there's no-one whose hand can achieve the work.
What you instructed me I cannot even repeat, speak,
say, or reiterate.
Come, somewhere upstream from the city, at the outskirts of the city,
let me show you a washing place. And then
carry out yourself the great exertions which are on you hands!
But dinnertime mustn't go by! Go on in and
undo all the many threads done by the fuller!
If you don't compose yourself
there's no fuller who'll pay attention to you!
They'll have contempt for you, you'll get
all heated up and
give yourself a fit!"

REFERENCES

Gadd 1963:181-188; Livingstone 1988; George 1993:73 (collations after the tablet had been baked and cleaned); Foster 1992.

AKKADIAN BIBLIOGRAPHY

ABUSCH, T.
1985 "Ishtar's Proposal and Gilgamesh's Refusal." *History of Religions* 26:143-187.
1995 "Etemmu." Pp. 588-593 in *DDD*.

ALBERTZ, R.
1978 *Persönliche Frömmigkeit und offizielle Religion*. Stuttgart: Calwar.

AL-RAWI, F. N. H.
1990 "Tablet from the Sippar Library, I: The 'Weidner Chronicle." *Iraq* 52:1-14.

ARNAUD, D.
1986 *Emar* 6/3.
1987 *Emar* 6/4.

ARNOLD, B. T.
1994 "The Weidner Chronicle and the Idea of History in Israel and Mesopotamia." Pp. 129-148 in *FTH*.

ATTRIDGE, H. W., and R. A. ODEN.
1976 *The Syrian Goddess*. Missoula, MT: Scholars Press.

BAUDOT, M.-P.
1982 "Representations in Glyptic Art of a Preserved Legend: Etana ..." *Studies Naster* 2:1-10.

BIGGS, R.
1969 "A propos des textes de libanomancie." *RA* 63:73-74.

BORGER, R.
1956 *Asarh*.
1971 "Gott Marduk und Gott-König Šulgi als Propheten." *BiOr* 28:3-24.
1979 *BAL* ².

BOTTÉRO, J.
1974 "Symptômes, signes, écritures en mesopotamie ancienne." Pp. 70-197 in *Divination et Rationalité*. Ed. by J. P. Vernant. Paris: Editions du Seuil.
1977 "Les noms de Marduk ...." Pp. 5-28 in *Studies Finkelstein*.
1992 *L'Épopée de Gilgameš*. Paris: Gallimard.

BRINKMAN, J. A.
1964 "Merodach-Baladan II." Pp. 6-53 in *Studies Oppenheim*.
1968 *A Political History of Post-Kassite Babylonia, 1158-722 B.C.* AnOr 43. Rome.
1984 *Prelude to Empire: Babylonian Society and Politics 747-626 BC*. BFOP 7. Philadelphia: University Museum.
1990 "The Babylonian Chronicle Revisited." Pp. 73-104 in *Studies Moran*.
1991 "The Chaldaean Struggle for Independence." In *CAH*² 3/2:26-38.

BRUG, J. F.
1990 "Biblical Acrostics and their Relationship to Other Ancient Near Eastern Acrostics." Pp. 283-304 in *SIC* 3.

BRYCE, G.
1975 "Omen Wisdom in Ancient Israel." *JBL* 94:19-37.

BUCCELLATI, G.
1973 "Adapa, Genesis, and the Notion of Faith." *UF* 5:61-66.
1982 "The Descent of Inanna as a Ritual Journey to Kutha?" *Syro-Mesopotamian Studies* 4/3. Malibu.

CAGNI, L
1969 "L'Epopea di Erra." *Studi Semitici* 34. Rome.
1977 *The Poem of Erra*. Sources and Monographs, SANE 1/3. Malibu: Undena.

CHAVALAS, M.
1994 "Genealogical History as 'Charter': A Study of Old Babylonian Period Historiography and the Old Testament." Pp. 103-128 in *FTH*.

CIVIL, M.
1976 "The Song of the Plowing Oxen." *Studies Kramer* 83-95.

COGAN, M.
1984 "... From the Peak of Amanah." *IEJ* 34:255-259.

CONRADIE, A. F.
1989 "The Calah Wall Inscriptions." *JNSL* 15:31-38.

COOPER, J.
1972-75 "Heilige Hochzeit. B. Archäologisch." *RlA* 4:259-270.
1980 "Apodotic Death and the Historicity of 'Historical' Omens." Pp. 99-105 in *RAI* 26.

CROSS, F. M.
1976 "The Olden Gods in Ancient Near Eastern Creation Myths." Pp. 329-338 in *Studies Wright*.

CRYER, F.
1994 *Divination in Ancient Israel and its Near Eastern Environment: A Socio-Historical Investigation*. JSOTSup 142. Sheffield: Sheffield Academic Press.

DALLEY, S.
1987 *Near Eastern Patron Deities of Mining and Smelting*. Reports of the Department of Antiquities in Cyprus.
1989 *Myths from Mesopotamia*. Oxford: Oxford University Press.

DE FILIPPI
1977 "The Royal Inscriptions of Aššur-Nāṣir-Apli II (883-859 B.C.): A Study of the Chronology of the Calah Inscriptions Together with an Edition of Two of These Texts." *Assur* 1/7:123-169. Malibu: Undena.

DIETRICH, M.
1989 "Das Einsetzungsritual der Entu von Emar (Emar VI/3, 369)." *UF* 21:47-100.
1993 "The Hymn to Marduk from Ugarit." Pp. 62-67 in *Verse in Ancient Near Eastern Prose*. Ed. by J. C. de Moor and W. G. E. Watson. AOAT 42. Neukirchen-Vluyn: Neukirchener Verlag.
DIETRICH, M., and O. LORETZ.
1981 "Die Inschrift der Statue des Königs Idrimi von Alalah." *UF* 13:201-268.
1990 ALASP 3.
VAN DIJK, J.
1980 *Texte aus dem Rēš-Heiligtum in Uruk-Warka*. *BaM* Beiheft 2. Berlin: Gebr. Mann.
1983 *Lugal ud me-lám-bi nir-gál, le récit épique et didactique des Travaux de Ninurta, du Déluge et de la Nouvelle Création*. Leiden: E. J. Brill.
VAN DIJK, J., A. GOETZE, and M. I. HUSSEY.
1985 *Early Mesopotamian Incantations and Rituals*. YOS. Babylonian Texts 11. New Haven and London: Yale University Press.
DOSSIN, G.
1935 "Prières aux 'dieux de la nuit'." *RA* 32:179-187.
DURAND, J.-M.
1988 *Archives épistolaires de Mari* I/1. Paris: Éditions Recherche sur les Civilisations.
EBELING, E.
1949 "Ein Heldenlied auf Tiglatpileser I und der Anfang einer neuer Version von 'Ištar's Höllenfahrt' nach einer Schülertafel aus Assur." *Or* 18:30-39.
1953 *LKA*.
EDZARD, D.-O.
1986 "Review of Kinnier Wilson 1985." *ZA* 76:134-137.
ELLIS, M. de Jong
1989 "Observations on Mesopotamian Oracles and Prophetic Texts: Literary and Historiographic Considerations." *JCS* 41:127-186.
FARBER, W.
1977 *Beschwörungsrituale an Ištar und Dumuzi*. Wiesbaden: Harrassowitz.
FINET, A.
1982 "Un cas de clédonomancie à Mari (ARM X, 4)." Pp. 48-55 in *Studies Kraus*.
FINKEL, I. L.
1983 "A New Piece of Libanomancy." *AfO* 29:50-57.
1983-84 "Necromancy in Ancient Mesopotamia." *AfO* 29-30:1-17.
1988 "Adad-apla-iddina, Esagil-kin-apli, and the Series SA.GIG." Pp. 143-159 in *Studies Sachs*.
1995 "In Black and White, Remarks on the Assyrian Psephomancy Ritual." *ZA* 85:271-276.
FINKELSTEIN, J. J.
1956 "Hebrew *ḥbr* and Semitic *HBR." JBL 75:328-331.
1962 "Mesopotamia." *JNES* 21:73-92.
1966 "The Genealogy of the Hammurapi Dynasty." *JCS* 20:95-118.
FLEMING, D. E.
1990 "The NIN.DINGIR/*ittu* at Emar." *NABU* 8:5.
1992 *The Installation of Baal's High Priestess at Emar*. Atlanta: Scholars Press.
1993a "*Nābû* and *munabbiātu*: Two New Syrian Religious Personnel." *JAOS* 113:175-183.
1993b "The Etymological Origins of the Hebrew *nābîʾ*: The One Who Invokes God." *CBQ* 55:217-224.
FOSTER, B. R.
1983 "Self-Reference of an Akkadian Poet." *JAOS* 103:123-130 = *Studies Kramer*².
1992 "Humor and Wit in Mesopotamia." *ABD* 3:328-330.
1995 *FDD*.
1996 *BM*.
GADD, C. J.
1958 "The Harran Inscriptions of Nabonidus." *AnSt* 8:35-92.
1963 "Two Sketches from the Life of Ur." *Iraq* 25:177-188.
GALLERY KOVACS, M.
1989 *The Epic of Gilgamesh*. Stanford, CA: Stanford University Press.
GARDNER, J., and J. Maier.
1984 *Gilgamesh*. New York: Knopf.
GEORGE, A. R.
1985 "Observations on a passage of 'Inanna's Descent.'" *JCS* 37:109-113.
1993 "Ninurta-Paqidāt's Dog Bite, and Notes on Other Comic Tales." *Iraq* 55:73.
GLASSNER, J.-J.
1993 *Chroniques mésopotamiennes*. La roue à livres 19. Paris: Les Belles Lettres.
GOETZE, A.
1968 "An Old Babylonian Prayer of the Divination Priest." *JCS* 22:12-29.
GRAYSON, A. K.
1972 *ARI*.
1975 *Babylonian Historical-Literary Texts*. Toronto: University of Toronto.
1975 *ABC*.
1980 "Königslisten und Chroniken. B. Akkadisch." *RlA* 6:89-101.
1991 "Sennacherib." In *CAH*² 3/2:103-22.
GREENBERG, M.
1991 "Parting of the Ways." Pp. 267-271 in *Studies Tadmor*.

GREENFIELD, J., and M. SOKOLOFF.
1989 "Astrological and Related Texts in Jewish Palestinian Aramaic." *JNES* 48:201-214.
GREENSTEIN, E. L., and D. MARCUS.
1976 "The Akkadian Inscription of Idrimi." *JANES* 8:59-96.
GRONEBERG, B. R. M.
1987 *Syntax, Morphologie und Stil der jungbabylonischen "hymnischen" Literatur*. 2. Belegsammlung und Textkatalog. FAOS 14/2. Wiesbaden and Stuttgart: Franz Steiner Verlag.
GUINAN, A.
1989 "The Perils of High Living." Pp. 227-235 in *Studies Sjoberg*.
1990 "The Human Behavioral Omens: On the Threshold of Psychological Inquiry." *BCSMS* 19:9-14.
1996a "Social Constructions and Private Designs." Pp. 61-68 in *Houses and Households in Ancient Mesopotamia*. RAI 40. Ed. by K. R. Veenhof. *PIHANS* 78. Istanbul.
1996b "Right/Left Symbolism in Mesopotamian Divination." *SAAB* 9 in press.
GURNEY, O. R.
1960 "The Sultantepe Tablets." *AnSt* 10:105-131.
HAAS, V.
1979 "Remarks on Hurrian Ištar-Sawuska of Nineveh in the Second Millennium BC." *Sumer* 35:397-401.
HAAS, V., and G. WILHELM.
1974 *Hurritische und luwische Riten aus Kizzuwatna*. Neukirchen-Vluyn: Neukirchener Verlag.
HALLO, W. W.
1957-71 "Gutium." *RlA* 3:708-720.
1990 "The Limits of Skepticism." *JAOS* 110:187-199.
1966 "Akkadian Apocalypses." *IEJ* 16:231-242.
1968 "Individual Prayer in Sumerian: the Continuity of a Tradition." *JAOS* (= *Studies Speiser*) 88:71-89.
1970 "Antediluvian Cities." *JCS* 23:57-67.
1971a "Akkad." *Encyclopaedia Judaica* 16:493f.
1971b "Gutium." *RlA* 3/9:708-720.
1973 "Choice in Sumerian." *JANES* 5:165-172.
1977 "New Moons and Sabbaths." *HUCA* 48:1-18.
1978 "Assyrian Historiography Revisited." *E-I* 14:1*-7*.
1980a "Šullanu." *RA* 74:94.
1985 "'As the Seal upon thy Heart'." *Bible Review* 1/1:19-27.
1991a "Information from Before the Flood." *Maarav* 7:173-181.
1991b *BP*.
1991c "Death of Kings." Pp. 148-165 in *Studies Tadmor*.
HALLO, W. W., and J. J. A. VAN DIJK
1968 *The Exaltation of Inanna*. YNER 3. New Haven and London: Yale University Press.
HAWKINS, J. D.
1972-1975 "Hattin." *RlA* 4:160b-162a.
1980-1983 "Kummuh." *RlA* 6:338-340.
HELTZER, M.
1981 *The Suteans*. Istituto Universitario Orientale, seminario di studi asiatici, series minor 13. Naples.
HOFFNER, H. A.
1976 "Enki's command to Atrahasis." Pp. 241-245 in *Studies Kramer*.
HOROWITZ, W., and V. HUROWITZ.
1992 "Urim and Thummim in Light of a Psephomancy Ritual from Assur (*LKA* 137)." *JANES* 21:95-115.
HUFFMON, H.
1983 "Priestly Divination in Israel." Pp. 355-359 in *Studies Freedman*.
HUNGER, H.
1968 *Babylonische und assyrische Kolophone*. AOAT 2. Neukirchen-Vluyn: Neukirchener Verlag.
1976 *Spätbabylonische Texte aus Uruk I*. Berlin: Mann.
HUROWITZ, V.
1992a "The Expression *ûqᶜsāmîm bᵉyādām* (Numbers 22:7) in Light of Divinatory Practices from Mari." *HS* 33:5-15.
1992b *I Have Built You an Exalted House*. JSOTSup 115. Sheffield: Sheffield Academic Press.
HUROWITZ, V., and J. G. WESTENHOLTZ.
1992 "*LKA* 63. A Heroic Poem in Celebration of Tiglath-Pilesar I's Muṣru-Qumanu Campaign." *JCS* 42:1-50.
IKEDA, Y.
1978 "Hermon, Sirion and Senir." *AJBI* 4:32-43.
1984-1985 "Assyrian Kings and the Mediterranean Sea — The Twelfth to Ninth Centuries B.C." *Abr-Nahrain* 23:22-31.
JACOBSEN, T.
1975 "Religious Drama in Ancient Mesopotamia." Pp. 65-97 in *Unity and Diversity*.
1976 *The Treasures of Darkness*. New Haven and London: Yale University Press.
1984 "The Harab Myth." *SANE* 2/3:99-120.
JEYES, U.
1978 "The 'Palace Gate' of the Liver: A Study of Terminology and Methods in Babylonian Extispicy." *JCS* 30:209-233.
1980 "The Act of Extispicy in Ancient Mesopotamia: An Outline." *Assyriological Miscellanies* 1:13-32. Copenhagen.
1989 *Old Babylonian Extispicy: Omen Texts in the British Museum*. PIHANS 64. Istanbul.
KEMPINSKI, A., and N. NA᾿AMAN.
1973 "The Idrimi Inscription Reconsidered." Pp. 211-220 in *Excavations and Studies: Essays in Honor of Shemuel Yeivin*. Ed. by Y. Aharoni. Tel Aviv: Carta [Hebrew].

KILMER, A. D.
1971 "How Was Queen Ereshkigal Tricked?" *UF* 3:229-311.
1987 "The Symbolism of the Flies in the Mesopotamian Flood Myth...." Pp. 175-180 in *Studies Reiner*.
KINNIER WILSON, J. V.
1985 *The Legend of Etana*. Warminster: Aris & Phillips.
KLEIN, J.
1981 "The Royal Hymns of Shulgi, King of Ur." *Transactions of the American Philosophical Society*. 71/7.
KLEIN, H.
1983 "Tudittum." *ZA* 73:255-284.
KNUDTZON, J. A.
1915 *EA*.
KÖCHER, F., and A. L. OPPENHEIM.
1957-58 "The Old-Babylonian Omen Text VAT 7525." *AfO* 18:62-77.
KOMORÓCZY, G.
1976 "Work and Strike of the Gods." *Oikumene* 1:9-37.
KRAUS, F.
1936-37 "Babylonische Omina mit Ausdeutung der Begleiterscheinungen des Sprechens." *AfO* 11:219-230.
1939 *Texte zur babylonischen Physiognomatik*. AfO Beiheft 3. Berlin.
KUTSCHER, R.
1988 "The Mesopotamian God Zaqar and Jacob's *Maṣṣēbāh*." *Beer-Sheva* 3:125-130 (in Hebrew).
LABAT, R.
1965 *Un Calendrier Babylonien des Travaux des Signes et des Mois*. Paris.
LAMBERT, W. G.
1957-58 "Three Unpublished Fragments of the Tukulti-Ninurta Epic." *AfO* 18:38-51.
1964 "The Reign of Nebuchadnezzar I." *Studies Meek* 3-13.
1967 "Enmedurannki and Related Matters." *JCS* 21:126-139.
1968 "Another Look at Hammurabi's Ancestors." *JCS* 22:1-2.
1969a "New Evidence for the First Line of *Atra-hasis*." *Or* 38:533-538.
1969b "An Eyestone of Esarhaddon's Queen and Other, Similar Gems." *RA* 63:65-71.
1983 "A Neo-Babylonian Tammuz Lament." *JAOS* 103:211-215; rep. in *Studies Kramer* 2 (1984) 211-215.
1987 A further attempt at the Babylonian 'Man and his God'." Pp. 187-202 in *Studies Reiner*.
LAMBERT, W. G., and A. R. MILLARD.
1969 *Atra-ḫasīs: the Babylonian Story of the Flood*. Oxford: Clarendon Press.
LAMBERT, W. G., and S. B. PARKER.
1966 *Enuma Elish: The Babylonian Epic of Creation*. Oxford: Oxford University Press.
LAMBERT, W. G., and P. WALCOT.
1965 *A New Babylonian Theogony and Hesiod*. Offprint of Kadmos 4/1. Berlin: W. de Gruyter.
LANGDON, S. H.
1909 *Sumerian and Babylonian Psalms*. Paris, P. Geuthner.
LAROCHE, E.
1976-77 *Glossaire de la langue hourrite*. *RHA* 34-35. Paris: Éditions Klincksieck.
LEICHTY, E.
1964 "The Colophon." Pp. 147-154 in *Studies Oppenheim*.
1970 *The Omen Series Šumma Izbu*. TCS 4. Locust Valley, New York: J. J. Augustin.
1977 "Literary Notes." Pp. 147-154 in *Studies Finkelstein*.
1993 "Ritual, 'Sacrifice', and Divination in Mesopotamia." Pp. 238-242 in *Ritual and Sacrifice in the Ancient Near East*. Ed. by J. Quaegebeur. OLA 55. Leuven.
LEIDERER, R.
1990 *Anatomie der Schafsleber im babylonischen Leberorakel: eine makroskopisch-analytische Studie*. Bern and San Francisco: W. Zuckschwerdt.
LEVINE, B. A., and W. W. HALLO.
1967 "Offerings to the Temple Gates at Ur." *HUCA* 38:17-58.
LEWIS, B.
1980 *The Sargon Legend*. ASORDS 4.
LIEBERMAN, S.
1977 "The Names of Cuneiform Graphemes in Old Babylonian Akkadian." Pp. 147-154 in *Studies Finkelstein*.
LIPIŃSKI, E.
1970 "Urim and Tummim." *VT* 20:495-496.
1988 "Ea, Kothar et El." *UF* 20:137-143.
LIVERANI, M.
1982 "Adapa ospite degli dei." Pp. 55-67 in *Religioni e Civiltà. Scritti in memoria di Angelo Brelich*. Ed. by V. Lanternari, et al. Bari: Edizione Dedalo.
LIVINGSTONE, A.
1980 "A Fragment of a Work Song." *ZA* 70:55-57.
1988 "'At the Cleaners' and Notes on Humorous Literature." Pp. 175-187 in *Ad bene et fideliter seminandum. Festschrift für Karlheinz Deller*. Ed. by G. Mauer and U. Magen. AOAT 220. Neukirchen-Vluyn: Neukirchener Verlag.
1989 *Court Poetry and Literary Miscellanea*. SAA 3. Helsinki: Helsinki University Press.
LONG, B.
1973 "The Effect of Divination upon Israelite Literature." *JBL* 92:489-497.

LONGMAN, T., III.
1991 *Fictional Akkadian Autobiography*. Winona Lake, IN: Eisenbrauns.
MCLAUGHLIN, J. L.
1991 "The *marzēaḥ* at Ugarit: A Textual and Contextual Study." *UF* 23:265-281.
MACMILLAN, K.
1906 "Some Cuneiform Tablets Bearing on the Religion of Babylonia and Assyria." *Beiträge zur Assyriologie* 5/5:531-712.
MALAMAT, A.
1968 "King Lists of the Old Babylonian Period and Biblical Genealogies." *JAOS* 88:163-173 (= *Studies Speiser*).
MANN, T. W.
1977 *Divine Presence and Guidance in Israelite Tradition: the Typology of Exaltation*. Johns Hopkins Near Eastern Studies. Baltimore: Johns Hopkins University Press.
MARTIN, F.
1903 *Textes religieux assyriens et babyloniens, première série*. Paris.
MATSUSHIMA, E.
1987 "Le rituel hiérogamique de Nabû." *ActSum* 9:131-175.
MATTINGLY, G. L.
1990 "The Pious Sufferer: Mesopotamia's Traditional; Theodicy and Job's Counselors." Pp. 305-348 in *SIC* 3.
MAYER, W.
1987 "Ein Mythos von der Erschaffung des Menschens und des Königs." *Or* 56:55ff.
MEIER, S.
1989 "House Fungus: Mesopotamia and Israel (Lev 14:33-53)." *RB* 96:184-192.
MEYER, J.-W.
1987 *Untersuchungen zu den Tonlebermodellen aus dem Alten Orient*. AOAT 39. Neukirchen-Vluyn: Neukirchener Verlag.
MICHALOWSKI, P.
1980 "Adapa and the ritual process." *Rocznik Orientalistsyczny* 41:77-82.
MILGROM, J.
1991 *Leviticus 1-16. A New Translation with Introduction and Commentary*. AB 3. New York: Doubleday.
MILLARD, A. R.
1976 "Assyrian Royal Names in Biblical Hebrew." *JSS* 21:1-14.
1980 "Review of *ABC*." *JAOS* 100:364-68.
1994 *The Eponyms of the Assyrian Empire 910-612 BC*. SAAS 2. Helsinki: University of Helsinki, Neo-Assyrian Text Corpus Project.
MORAN, W. L.
1959 "Notes on the New Nabonidus Inscriptions." *Or* 28:135-136.
MOREN, S. M.
1978 *The Omen Series Šumma Ālu: A Preliminary Investigation*. Ph.D. Dissertation. University of Pennsylvania. Ann Arbor: University Microfilms.
1980 "*Šumma Izbu* XIX: New Light on the Animal Omens." *AfO* 27:53-70.
MUELLER, H.-P.
1983-84 "Mythus als Gattung archaischen Erzählens und die Geschichte von Adapa." *AfO* 29-30:75-89.
MÜLLER, K. Fr.
1937 "Das assyrische Ritual, Teil I." *MVAG* 41/3:4-89.
NEUGEBAUER, O.
1947 "The Water Clock in Babylonian Astronomy." *Isis* 37:37-43; repr. *Astronomy and History*. New York: Springer, 1983, 239-245.
NOEGEL, S. B.
1991 "A Janus Parallelism in the Gilgamesh Flood Story." *ActSum* 13:419-421.
NÖTSCHER, F.
1928-30 "Die Omen-Serie *šumma âlu ina mêlê šakin*." *Or* 31:39-42, 51-54.
NOUGAYROL, J.
1952 "Un version ancienne du 'juste souffrant'." *RB* 59:239-250.
1963 "Aleuromancie babylonien." *Or* 32:318-384.
1968 "Textes suméro-accadiens des archives et bibliothèques privées d'Ugarit." *Ugaritica* 5:1-446.
OELSNER,
1964 "Ein Beitrag zu keilschriftlichen Königstitulaturen in hellenistischer Zeit." *ZA* 56:262-274.
OLLER, G. H.
1977a *The Autobiography of Idrimi: A New Text Edition with Philological and Historical Commentary*. Ph.D. diss. University of Pennsylvania.
1977b "A Note on Lines 102-104 of the Idrimi Inscription." *JCS* 29:167-168.
OLYAN, S.
1994 "'And With a Male You Shall Not Lie the Lying Down of a Woman': On the Meaning and Significance of Leviticus 18:22 and 20:13." *Journal of the History of Sexuality* 5/2:179-206.
OPPENHEIM, A. L.
1954-56 "Sumerian: inim.gar, Akkadian: egirrû = Greek: kledon." *AfO* 17:49-55.
1956 *The Interpretation of Dreams in the Ancient Near East*. Transactions of the American Philosophical Society 46/3. Philadelphia.
1959 "A New Prayer to the 'Gods of the Night'." AnBib 12:282-301.
1964 *Ancient Mesopotamia*. Chicago: The University of Chicago Press.
1967 *Letters from Mesopotamia*. Chicago: University of Chicago Press.
1969 "New Fragments of the Assyrian Dream-Book." *Iraq* 31:153-165.
1977 *Ancient Mesopotamia*. 2nd ed. Chicago: University of Chicago Press.

OPPERT, J.
1901 "Une complainte des villes chaldéennes sur la suprématie de Babylone, de l'époque des successeurs d'Alexandre." *CRAIB* 1901:830-846.
PARPOLA, S.
1980 "The Murderer of Sennacherib." Pp. 171-182 in *RAI* 26.
PEDERSÉN, O.
1986 *Archives and Libraries in the City of Assur. A Survey of the Material from the German Excavations*. 2. Acta Universitatis Upsaliensis. SSU 8. Uppsala: Almqvist & Wiksel.
PEEK, P. Editor.
1991 *African Divination Systems: Ways of Knowing*. Bloomington: Indiana University Press.
PETTINATO, G.
1966 *Die Ölwahrsagung bei den Babyloniern*. 2 Vols. Studia Semitica 22-23. Rome.
PICCHIONI, S. A.
1981 *Il Poemetto di Adapa*. Assyriologia 6. Budapest: Az Eötvös Loránd Tudományegyetem.
PINCHES, T. G.
1901 "Assyriological Gleanings, II." *PSBA* 23:188-210.
1902 *The Old Testament in the Light of Historical Records and Legends of Assyria and Babylonia*. 2nd Edition. London, S.P.C.K.
PINGREE, D.
1993 "Venus Phenomenon in *Enūma Anu Enlil*." Pp. 259-273 in *RAKM*.
POPE, M.
1970 "The Saltier of Atargatis Reconsidered." Pp. 178-196 in *Studies Glueck*.
PORTER, P.
1983 *Metaphors and Monsters: A Literary-Critical Study of Daniel 6-7*. Coniectanea Biblica. OT series 20. Uppsala.
READE, J.
1989 "Shalmaneser or Ashurnasirpal in Ararat." *SAAB* 3:93-97.
REINER, E.
1960a "Plague Amulets and House Blessings." *JNES* 19:148-155.
1960b "Fortune-Telling in Mesopotamia." *JNES* 19:23-35.
1978 "Die akkadische Literatur." Pp. 151-210 in *Altorientalische Literaturen*. Neues Handbuch der Literaturwissenschaft 1. Ed. by W. Röllig. Wiesbaden: Akademische Verlagsgesellschaft Athenaion.
1985 *Your Thwarts in Pieces Your Mooring Rope Cut: Poetry from Babylonia and Assyria*. Michigan Studies in the Humanities 5. Ann Arbor: University of Michigan.
1995 *Astral Magic in Babylonia*. Philadelphia: The American Philosophical Society.
ROCHBERG-HALTON, F.
1988 *Aspects of Babylonian Celestial Divination: Lunar Eclipse Tablets of Enūma Anu Enlil*. AfO Beiheft 22. Horn, Austria: Ferdinand Berger.
ROTH, W. M. W.
1962 "The Numerical Sequence x/x+1 in the Old Testament." *VT* 12:301-311.
SASSON, J.
1981 "On Idrimi and Šarruwa, the Scribe." Pp. 309-324 in *Nuzi and the Hurrians*. Ed. by M. A. Morrison and D. I. Owen. Winona Lake, IN: Eisenbrauns.
1983 "Mari Dreams." *JAOS* 103:283-293.
1994 "Divine divide: re FM 2:71:5." *NABU* 1994:39-40.
SMITH, S.
1949 *The Statue of Idri-mi*. London: British Institute of Archaeology in Ankara.
VAN SOLDT, W.
1995 *Solar Omens of Enuma Anu Enlil: Tablets 23(24)-29 (30)*. PIHANS 73. Istanbul.
STARR, I.
1976 "Notes on Some Technical Terms in Extispicy." *JCS* 27:241-247.
1983 *The Rituals of the Diviner*. BiMes 12. Malibu: Undena Publications.
1990 *Queries to the Sun God: Divination and Politics in Sargonid Assyria*. SAA 4. Helsinki: Helsinki University Press.
STOL, M.
1988 "Greek Deikterion: the Lying-in-state of Adonis." Pp. 127-128 in *Funerary Symbols and Religion. Essays Dedicated to Professor M. S. H. G. Heerma van Voss*. Ed. by J. H. Kamstra, H. Milde, and K. Wagtendonk. Kampen.
1992 "The Moon as Seen by the Babylonians." Pp. 245-276 in *Natural Phenomena: Their Meaning, Depiction, and Description in the Ancient Near East. Proceedings of the Colloquium, Amsterdam, 6-8 July 1989*. Ed. by D. J. W. Meijer. Amsterdam and New York: North-Holland.
STRONG, S. A.
1894 "On Some Oracles of Esarhaddon and Ašurbanipal." *BA* 2:627-645.
TADMOR, H.
1958 "The Campaigns of Sargon II of Assur: a Chronological-Historical Study." *JCS* 12:22-40.
THUREAU-DANGIN, F.
1912 *Une relation de la huitième campagne de Sargon*. TCL 3. Paris.
TIGAY, J. H.
1982 *The Evolution of the Gilgamesh Epic*. Philadelphia: University of Pennsylvania Press.
1985 Editor. *Empirical Models for Biblical Criticism*. Philadelphia:University of Pennsylvania Press.
VAN DER TOORN, K.
1985 *Sin and Sanction in Israel and Mesopotamia*. Assen-Maastricht. The Netherlands: van Gorcum.
1990 "The Nature of the Biblical Teraphim in the Light of the Cuneiform Evidence." *CBQ* 52:203-222.

TOURNAY, R. J., and A. SHAFFER.
1994 *L'Epopée de Gilgamesh*. LAPO 15. Paris: Cerf.
TSEVAT, M.
1987 "Note brève, Erra IV, 7-10." *RA* 81:184.
VAN DAM, C.
1993 *The Urim and Thummim. An Old Testament Means of Revelation*. Winona Lake, IN: Eisenbrauns.
VANSTIPHOUT, H., and N. VELDHUIS.
1995 "*ṭuppi ilāni takāltu pirišti šamê u erṣetim*." *Annali* 55/1:30-33. Napoli.
VELDHUIS, N. C.
1990 "The Heart Grass and Related Matters." *OLP* 21:28-44.
VON VOIGTLANDER, E. N.
1964 *Survery of Neo-Babylonian History*. Ann Arbor: University Microfilms.
WALCOT, P.
1966 *Hesiod and the Near East*. Cardiff: Wales University Press.
WALKER, C. B. F., H. GALTER, and B. SCHOLZ.
1993 "Bibliography of Babylonian Astronomy and Astrology." Pp. 274-290 in *RAKM*.
WEIDNER, E.
1939-41 "Assurbânipal in Assur." *AfO* 13:204-218.
WEINBERG, J. P.
1973 "Das *beit ᵓabot* im 6.-4. Jh. v.u.Z.." *VT* 23:400-414.
WHITCOMB, J. C.
1959 *Darius the Mede*. Nutley, NJ: Presbyterian and Reformed Publishing Co.
WISEMAN, D. J.
1965 "Some Historical Problems in the Book of Daniel: A. Darius the Mede." Pp. 9-16 in *Notes on Some Problems in the Book of Daniel*. Ed. by D. J. Wiseman, et al. London: Tyndale Press.
WOLTERS, A.
1993 "An Allusion to Libra in Daniel 5." Pp. 291-306 in *RAKM*.
ZADOK, R.
1985 *Geographical Names According to New- and Late-Babylonian Texts*. RG 8.

SUMERIAN CANONICAL COMPOSITIONS

A. DIVINE FOCUS

1. MYTHS

THE SONG OF THE HOE (1.157)

Gertrud Farber

The ancient scribe seemingly had a humorous purpose in mind when composing this text. It should probably be categorized as a satirical school text composed for use in the Edubba (= school) and for other learned people.[1] The composition has no coherent topic or theme. The thread winding through the whole text is the syllable /al/ which is a Sumerian logogram meaning hoe but which also occurs as part of other words or as a grammatical element. Thus the text contains sections in which the hoe is the main topic: a mythological section on creation, a hymnical praise of the hoe, or the description of the hoe's use in agriculture or when building temples. These sections are only loosely connected as if they had been examples of scholastic exercises. In addition to that, however, /al/ has been abstracted as a syllable and is used throughout the composition in quite imaginative alliterations and puns, some of which still resist all our attempts of understanding. Such poetic devices unfortunately get completely lost when translated literally. The following translation will try therefore to mark them by adding short explanations in parentheses or in the notes, and by marking all words which contain the syllable /al/ (or sometimes /ar/) with an asterisk.

The text has 109 lines of which 92 have been included here. (....) marks abridged text. So far this text has been preserved in 70 copies from Nippur, 6 from Ur and 13 from other cities. About 12 originally contained the complete composition; all others are excerpts. All sources are from the Old Babylonian period. The exact date of the origin of the text is not known.[2] But the presence of the goddess Nininsina points to the Isin period and the clearly astral aspect of the god Shulpaea[3] does not allow an earlier date.[4]

Creation of the World (lines 1-7)

Not only did the lord who never *changes his promises for the future make the world appear in its correct form,
— Enlil who will make the seed of *mankind rise from the earth —
not only did he hasten to separate heaven from earth,
(....) and earth from heaven,
but, in order to make it possible for humans to grow "where the flesh sprouts,"
he first affixed the axis of the world in Duranki.[5]

Introducing the Hoe (lines 8-17)

He did this with the help of the *hoe and (as a result) daylight *broke forth.
By distributing the shares of duty he established daily tasks
and for the *hoe and the (carrying) basket even wages were *established.[6]
Then Enlil praised his *hoe:
his *hoe, wrought in gold,[7] with a top inlaid with lapis lazuli,
his *hoe whose blade was tied (to the handle) with a string, which was adorned with silver and gold,
whose blade was like a battering ram standing up against a *wall.
The lord evaluated the *hoe. (....)

Creation of Mankind (lines 18-27)

Here, "where the flesh sprouts," he set this very *hoe to work:
he had it place the first model of mankind in the brickmold.[8]
And (according to this model) his *people started to break through the soil towards Enlil,[9]

[1] For the humorous aspect of this text, see Wilcke 1972:37, and Farber forthcoming, with additional bibliography.

[2] See Wilcke 1972:37. Wilcke compares the irregularities and the many variants of the grammatical elements with those of compositions which are known from older periods. I rather think that the arbitrary use of grammatical elements as well as the high sophistication of the text suggests a later date. It is quite clear, however, that the poet was mainly thinking in the Sum. language, even though some puns and allusions rather fit Akk. words, a fact that also would date this composition into a period after the collapse of the Sum. empire.

[3] Falkenstein 1963:21, 33.

[4] No complete edition of the text has been published yet. For the sources see *HKL* 1:155; 2:84 ad *TCL* 16:72. For partial translations and discussion of the text see Kramer 1944:51-53; Jacobsen 1946:134; Civil 1969:70; Wilcke 1972:36-38; Pettinato 1971:82-85.

[5] "Where the flesh sprouts" is the name of a sacred site in Nippur. Duranki is located in the middle of Enlil's temple complex in Nippur.

[6] Hoe and basket are tools used for brick making and processing. The hoe stirs the clay and puts it in brick molds. The dried bricks are carried in baskets; see lines 35-58 and line 98.

[7] The ordinary hoe was made of wood, even with a wooden blade. What is described here is Enlil's hoe.

[8] The hoe works here (creation) just as it does in brick making; see lines 10 and 96.

[9] Two different traditions of creation are intertwined here, the creation from seeds where mankind grows like a weed and breaks through the

and he looked approvingly at his "blackheaded people."[10]
Now the Anuna-gods[11] stepped up to him: (....)
they wanted to demand the "blackheaded people" from him.
The lady who (once upon a time) had given birth to the ruler, who had given birth to the king,
Ninmena now *set the human reproduction going.

Assignment of Tasks to the Human Race (lines 28-34)

The foremost of heaven and earth, the lord Nunamnir (= Enlil),
named the strong and *important leaders (....)
and recruited them for the gods to provide (for them).
Now Enki praised (Enlil's) *hoe,
and the girl Nidaba was made responsible for (keeping a record of) the decision.
And so (the people) *took the shining *hoes, the pure *hoes into their hands (and started to work):

Building of Temples (lines 35-58)[12]

(The Ekur in Nippur: 35-41; the Abzu in Eridu: 42-45; Ninḫursaĝa's temple in Keš: 46-48; the Eanna in Uruk: 49-51; Inanna's temple in Zabalam: 52-55; Nidaba's "equal temple": 56-58)

The Ekur, the temple of Enlil, was founded with the hoe,
during the day it *was building, during the night it *caused (the temple) to grow.
Into Nippur, the well founded, (....)
into the innermost chamber of the *Tummal entered the hero Ninurta
with regular food deliveries into the presence of Enlil, (....)
and so did the pure Nininsina with black kids and fruit offerings for the lord.
(Next comes) the Abzu, the one with the lion face (= its gate), where the divine offices *may not be claimed:[13]
The *hoe wielder (= builder), (....), the lord Nudimmud (= Enki),
*was building the Abzu, Eridu having been chosen as a *construction site.
The mother of the gods, Ninḫursaĝa,
had the *"mighty light of the lord" live with her in Kesh,
had Shulpaea indeed help her with the *construction work.
The temple Eanna was cleaned up by the *hoe.
— (For) the lady of Eanna (= Inanna), the noble *cow,
the *hoe stands for (cleaning up) ruins; the *hoe means (removing) weeds. —
Concerning the city of *Zabalam the *hoe is Inanna's work force.(....)
With (her) *building project Utu was ready to help her.
(....)
The lady with the *intelligent mind, Nidaba, ordered the measuring of the Eanna as (part of) a *construction project
and (according to the result) designed (her own) "Equal Temple" for *construction.

Other Gods and their Relationship with the Hoe or the Syllable /al/ (lines 59-70)

The *king who has measured (or: counted) the *hoe(s), who has *spent the day in the tracks (made by the hoe),
the hero Ninurta has introduced working with the *hoe in the *rebellious land:
he *subdues[14] the city that does not obey (its) lord.
Towards heaven he *roars like a storm,
earthwards he *strikes like a *dragon.
Shara sat down on Enlil's knees,[15]
and (Enlil) gave him what he had *desired:
mace, weapon, arrow, quiver, and the *hoe he had mentioned.
Dumuzi is the one who makes the "upper land" *fertile.
Gibil made his *hoe lift its head towards heaven,
the *hoe, the pure one indeed, he had refined with fire.
The Anuna were *rejoicing.

The Syllable /al/ Occurs in Sumerian Words in all Aspects of Life (lines 71-93)

The temple of Ĝeshtinanna resembled an **alĝarsur*-instrument,
(....) which had a beautiful sound.
The lord (= Enlil) bellowed at his *hoe like a bull.[16]
(Concerning) the *grave: the *hoe buries people,
but the dead body is also brought up from the earth by the *hoe.[17]
The hero honored by An, the younger brother of *Nergal,

soil, and the creation through the molding of a clay model.

[10] The blackheaded people are the Sumerians.

[11] Anuna gods refers to all senior gods, here excluding Enlil who is the highest Anuna.

[12] As explained above, see note 6, the hoe was an important tool in the brick making process and therefore was used in the building of temples.

[13] This refers to the composition "Inanna and Enki" (see text 1.161 below), in which the goddess Inanna takes the ME (= divine offices) from Enki, in front of the lion gate of the Abzu.

[14] The hoe is here used either as a weapon (see also line 97), or as a stirring tool (see note 6), thus creating chaos in the enemy country.

[15] This denotes a begging position.

[16] Enlil's bellowing must be understood as affectionate.

[17] Digging up a dead body may refer to the composition "Gilgamesh, Enkidu, and the Netherworld" where the shadow of the dead Enkidu is brought up through a hole to bring news about the underworld, see Civil 1969:70.

the warrior Gilgamesh: with the *hoe he is (as powerful as) a hunting net.
The son of Ninsun: with the *oars he is foremost,
with the hoe he is the great *barber of the river.[18]
(....)
In the sky (/al/) is the *ALTIRIKU-bird, the bird of the god,
for the earth (/al/) is the *hoe, in the canebrake it is a *dog, in the forest it is a *dragon.
On the battle field it is the *DURALLUL-ax.
At the city wall it is the *warfare net.
At the dining table it is the *maltum-bowl.
At the carriage it is the *majaltum-sledge.
In the donkey stable it is the *ARGIBIL-structure.
It is the *hoe! Its name (= the sound of this word) which is sweet, also *occurs in the mountains:
the wood of the mountains is the *allānum-oak,
the fragrance of the mountains is the *argānum-balm,
the rock of the mountains is the *ALGAMEŠUM-steatite.

The Practical Use of the Hoe (lines 94-106)
The *hoe makes (everything) prosper, the *hoe makes (everything) grow lush,
the *hoe (means) good barley, the *hoe (works like) a hunting net.[19]
The *hoe (has to do with) the brickmold, the *hoe has made mankind *appear.[20]
It is the *hoe that is the arm of young manhood.[21]
The *hoe and the basket are the tools for building cities.[22]
It *builds the right kind of house, it *cultivates the right kind of field.
You (oh hoe!) are the one who *makes the good field fertile.
The field that has *rebelled against its *owner,
the field that has not submitted to its *owner,
the *hoe makes it subdue to its *master:
it smashes off the heads from the halfa-grass,
at its roots it extracts it, it tears off its stalks,
the *hoe (also) *subdues the ḪURIN-weed.
Doxology to the Hoe and Nidaba Follows.

[18] This refers to the cutting of weeds in the waterways for better boating.
[19] The hoe is compared to the net as a means of chasing birds away from the crop.
[20] For this see notes 6 and 8.
[21] Is the hoe thought of as a weapon in this case? See note 14.
[22] See note 6.

REFERENCES

HKL 1:155; 2:84 ad *TCL* 16:72 = de Genouillac 1930; Civil 1969; Falkenstein 1963; Farber forthcoming; Jacobsen 1946; Kramer 1944:51-53; Pettinato 1971:82-85; Wilcke 1972.

THE ERIDU GENESIS (1.158)

Thorkild Jacobsen

The fragment here translated was written at some time around 1600 B.C. It constitutes the lower third of a six-column tablet, the upper part of which, containing roughly some 36 lines per column, is lost. The content of the lost sections can be restored to some extent from other versions of the same tradition, most of which are of later date. By the time of the Assyrian Empire the tradition in somewhat shortened form had been included in the so-called Babylonian Chronicle (cf. Text 1.137 above), heading it.

The story, which has a structure much like that of the biblical stories in Genesis, dealt with the creation of men and animals, the antediluvian cities and their rulers, and finally the Deluge, paralleling in order the creation, the antediluvian patriarchs, and the story of the Deluge in the Bible. It may conceivably have served as model or inspiration for the biblical account.

(long lacuna)

Mother Goddess Pities the Nomad Existence of Man
[Nintur[1]] was paying [attention:]
"Let me bethink myself of my humankind, (all) forgotten as they are;
and mind[ful] of mine, Nintur's, creatures let me bring them back,
let me lead the people back from their trails."
"May they come and build cities and cult places, that I may cool myself in their shade;
may they lay the bricks for the cult cities in pure spots, and
may they found places for divination in pure spots!"
She gave directions for purification, and cries for clemency, the things that cool (divine) wrath,

[1] Goddess of birth and creatrix of man.

perfected the divine service and the august offices,
said to the (surrounding) regions: "Let me institute peace there!"
When An, Enlil, Enki, and Ninḫursaga[2]
fashioned the dark-headed (people),[3]
they had made the small animals (that come up) from (out of) the earth
come from the earth in abundance
and had let there be, as befits (it), gazelles, (wild) donkeys, and four-footed beasts in the desert.
[...]

(Lost account of first attempt at city-building failing for lack of leadership[?])

Mother Goddess Institutes Kingship

["...] and let me have [*h*]*im* [a]dvise;
let me have *him* overse[e] their [la]bor,
and let *him* t[each] the nation to follow along unerringly like [cat]tle!"

When the royal [sce]pter was com[ing] down from heaven,
the august [cr]own and the royal [th]rone being already down from heaven,
he (the king) [regularly] performed to perfection
the august divine services and offices,
laid [the bricks] of those cities [in pure spots.]
They were [n]amed by name and [allotted [ha]lf-bushel baskets.[4]

First Cities

The firstling of those cities, Eridu, she gave to the leader Nudimmud,[5]
the second, Bad-Tibira,[6] she gave to the prince and the sacred one[7]
the third, Larak, she gave to Pahilsag,[8]
the fourth, Sippar, she gave to the gallant, Utu.[9]
the fifth, Shuruppak, she gave to Ansud.[10]

These cities, which had been named by names, and had been allotted half-bushel baskets,
dredged the canals, which were blocked with purplish
(wind-borne) clay, and they carried water.
Their cleaning of the smaller canals
established abundant growth.
[...]

(Lost account of the antediluvian rulers,[11] and of how human noises vexed the chief god Enlil so much that he persuaded the divine assembly to vote the destruction of man by the deluge.)

That day Nin[tur] wept over her creatures
and holy Inanna[12] [was full] of grief over their people;
but Enki to[ok] counsel with his own heart.
An, Enlil, Enki,[13] and Ninḫursaga
had the gods of heaven and earth [swear[14]] by the names An and Enlil.

Ziusudra's Vision of the Gods Assembling

At that time Ziusudra was king
and lustration priest.
He fashioned, being a seer,
the god of giddiness[15]
and [stood] in awe beside it, wording his wishes humbly.

[As he] stood there regularly day after day
something that was not a dream was appearing: conversa[tion]

---

[2] The triad An, Enlil, and Ninḫursaga constituted originally the highest deities. Ninḫursaga, "mistress of the foothills," who was normally considered identical with Nintur, is here apparently seen as a different goddess.

[3] A standing epithet for mankind, specifically for the Sumerians themselves.

[4] Half-bushel baskets seem to have been used to pay workers the grain rations that constituted their wages. Apparently they serve here as symbols of the major centers of the economy. The word for them was also used to denote a standard measure used as a check.

[5] A name for Enki.

[6] The present mound Medinah.

[7] "The prince" is presumably the god Dumuzi. "The sacred one" is an epithet of Inanna's.

[8] Larak has not yet been located. Its city god Pabilsag is a god of trees.

[9] Sippar is the present mound of Abu-Habba. Its city god, Utu — Akkadian Shamash — was god of the sun and of righteousness.

[10] Shuruppak is the present mound Fara. Its city goddess Sud or Ansud "the lush ear of grain" was a grain goddess. As consort of Enlil she was known as Ninlil.

[11] The list as found in parallel accounts differs on minor points. The form in which it appeared in the Dynastic Chronicle probably read "in Eridu Alulim reigned 36,000 years, Alalgar ruled 10,800 years. Two kings reigned 46,000 years, Eridu's term. Eridu's term was commuted. In Bad-Tibira Enmenluanna reigned 46,800 years, Enmengalanna reigned 64,800 years. Dumuzi, the shepherd, reigned 36,000 years. Three kings reigned 147,600 years, Bad-Tibira's term. Bad-Tibira's term was commuted. In Sippar Enmeduranki reigned 64,800 years. One king reigned 64,800 years. Sippar's term. Sippar's term was commuted. In Larak Ensipadzianna reigned 36,000 years. One king reigned 36,000 years, Larak's term. Larak's term was commuted. In Shuruppak Ubaratutu reigned 28,800 years. Ziusudra reigned 64,800 years. Two kings reigned 93,600 years, Shuruppak's term. Five individual cities, nine kings reigned 352,800 years, their terms. Enlil took a dislike to mankind, the clamor they made kept him sleepless."

The reigns were extraordinarily long. A similar feature is the long life of the biblical antediluvian patriarchs. For Mesopotamia, a document called "The Lagash King List" indicates that these early people were thought to have developed very slowly. The idea is also found in Greece, where the childhood of the people of Hesiod's silver age lasted a hundred years.

[12] A many-sided deity, among other things goddess of love and war.

[13] God of the waters in rivers and marshes and god of practical wisdom.

[14] The oath was one of abiding by the decisions of the assembly.

[15] Ecstasy was apparently induced — as in the modern dancing dervishes — by giddiness, which was why Ziusudra made a statue of the god inducing it. The ancient rulers combined administrative, military, and priestly functions. To the last mentioned belonged divination, because it

a swearing (of) oaths by heaven and earth,
[a touching of throats[16]]
and the gods [bringing their] thwar[ts] (up) to [K]iur.[17]

Enki's Advice

And as Ziusudra stood there beside it, he [went on he]aring:
"Step up to the wall to my left and listen!
Let me speak a word to you at the wall
[and may you grasp] what [I] say,
May you he[ed] my advice!
By our hand a flood will sweep over
(the cities of) the half-bushel bas[kets, and the country;]
[the decision,] that mankind is to be destroyed, has been made.
a verdict, a command of the assemb[ly cannot be revoked,]
(100′) an order of An and En[lil is not known ever to have been countermanded,]
their kingship, their term, [has been uprooted they must bethink themselves of that]
Now [...]
What I ha[ve to say to you ..."]
[...]

(Lost account of Enki's advice to build a boat and load it with pairs of living things and Ziusudra's compliance.)

The Deluge

All the evil winds, all stormy winds gathered into one and with them, then, the Flood was sweeping over (the cities of)
the half-bushel baskets
for seven days and seven nights.
After the flood had swept over the country,
after the evil wind had tossed the big boat about on the great waters,
the sun came out spreading light over heaven and earth.

Ziusudra's Offering at End of Flood

All the evil winds, all stormy winds gathered into one
and with them, then, the Flood was sweeping over (the cities of)
the half-bushel baskets
for seven days and seven nights.
After the flood had swept over the country,
after the evil wind had tossed the big boat about on the great waters,
the sun came out spreading light over heaven and earth.

Ziusudra's Offering at End of Flood

Ziusudra then drilled an opening in the big boat.
and the gallant Utu sent his light
into the interior of the big boat.
(140′) Ziusudra, being the king,
stepped up before Utu kissing the ground (before him).
The king was butchering oxen, was being lavish with the sheep
[barley cak]es, crescents together with [...]
[...] he was crumbling for him
[...]
[juniper, the pure plant of the mountains] he filled [on the fire]
and with a [...] clasped to
[the breast he ...]
[...]

(Lost account of Enlil's wrath at finding survivors and his mollification by Enki.)

End of Enki's Speech

"You here have sworn
by the life's breath of heaven
the life's breath of earth
that he verily is allied with you yourself;
you there, An and Enlil,
have sworn by the life's breath of heaven,
the life's breath of earth,
that he is allied with all of you.
He will disembark the small animals
that come up from the earth!"

Ziusudra Rewarded

Ziusudra, being king,
stepped up before An and Enlil
kissing the ground,
And An and Enlil after hono[ring him]
(180′) were granting him life like a god's,
were making lasting breath of life, like a god's, descend into him.
That day they made Ziusudra,
preserver, as king, of the name of the small animals and the seed of mankind,
live toward the east over the mountains
in Mount Dilmun.[18]

was essential for a ruler to know the will of the gods and to act in conformity to it.

[16] The touching of the throat symbolized a wish that it be cut if the person doing it broke his or her oath.

[17] Kiur (KI-ÙR) was the forecourt of Enlil's temple in Nippur. The divine assembly met in a corner of it called Ubshuʾukkinna. The gods would arrive by boat on a canal flowing close by.

[18] Dilmun was the present Bahrain. Here in the tale it seems to have been considered a faraway, half-mythical place.

REFERENCES

Jacobsen 1987a:145-150.

ENKI AND NINMAḪ (1.159)

Jacob Klein

This archaic and still partly incomprehensible myth praises Enki, the god of the subterranean fresh waters, wisdom and magic, for having planned and directed the creation of mankind and for having devised ways in which the physically handicapped could adjust to society. The myth seems to consist of two originally independent stories. The first part tells the story of the creation of man rather briefly (lines 1-43). Man was created from pieces of clay, placed in the womb of the mother-goddesses where he obtained his form and was given birth. He was created for the purpose of relieving the gods from their hard labor, and especially from digging canals for irrigation agriculture. The second part (lines 44-139) tells of a contest between the mother-goddess Ninmah and Enki during a feast celebrating man's creation. At first Ninmah creates a number of crippled and handicapped human beings, challenging Enki to solve their problem. Enki cleverly "decrees their fate," assigning them a function in society whereby they earn their living in an honorable way. When Ninmah gives up, it is Enki's turn to create an abnormal creature. Enki creates a human wreck, whose nature cannot be precisely determined (either an aborted fetus or an old man),[1] and with which Ninmah is unable to cope. The end of the second part is damaged and obscure, but it is clear that Enki prevails over Ninmah in the contest. The myth concludes with the following statement (lines 140-141): "Ninmah did not equal the great lord Enki/ Father Enki, your praise is sweet." In spite of its fragmentary state of preservation, the myth is highly important from the point of view of the history of religion because it is the earliest composition dealing with the theme of man's creation, and as such it is a forerunner to the First Tablet of the Babylonian Story of the Flood (see text 1.130), as well as to the two parallel stories of creation of man in the Bible (Gen 1-2).[2]

Genesis and the Labor of the Gods (lines 1-11)
In those days, in the days
when heaven and earth were [created],
In those nights, in the nights
when heaven and earth were [created],[a]
In those [years], in the years
when the fates [were decreed],[3]
When the Anunna-gods[4] were born,
When the goddesses[5] were taken
in marriage,
When the goddesses were distributed
in heaven and earth,
When the goddesses were inseminated,
became pregnant and gave birth,[b]
The gods who baked their daily-bread,
(and) set therewith their tables —
The senior gods did oversee the work,
while the minor gods were bearing the toil.[6]
The gods were digging the canals,
were piling up their silt in Ḫarali;[7]
The gods were dredging the clay,
they were complaining about their (hard) life.[8] [c]

Rebellion of the Gods Against Enki (lines 12-23)
At that time, the one of immense wisdom,
the creator of all the senior gods,
Enki,[9] in the deep E-engura,[10]
in the flowing water, a place
whose inside no god has ever seen,
Lay on his bed, would not arise
from (his) sleep.[d]
The gods were weeping and were saying:
"He brought about this misery!"
To the sleeping one who lay at rest,
(to him who) would not arise from his sleep,
Nammu,[11] the primeval mother,
the bearer of the senior gods,[e]
Brought the tears of the gods to her son:

a Gen 1:1; 2:4
b Gen 6:1-4
c Gen 2:5
d 1 Kgs 18:27-29; Ps 44:24; Ps 121:4
e Gen 3:20

[1] This creature, which is totally unable to function, is called U$_4$-MU-UL ("the-day-was-far-off" or "my-day-is-far-off"). The name may refer to a prematurely born baby or to a very old man, born long ago. See generally Kilmer 1976.

[2] The following translation of the two most comprehensible episodes from this myth is based on Benito's critical edition (1969). Benito's renderings were considerably modified in the light of Jacobsen's translation of the myth (1987a:151-166) and of further study of the text.

[3] "In those days" etc., i.e., in days of yore etc.

[4] The Anunna-gods (Sum. ^{d}A-NUN-NA-KE$_4$-NE) usually refer to the gods of the universe, and occasionally to the gods of a local pantheon.

[5] In lines 5-7, the text uses for "goddess" the rare and somewhat obscure term *amalu* (= AMA.^{d}INANNA), which was translated into Akk. *amalu(k)tu* and *ištarītu* (see Steinkeller, *JCS* 32 [1980]:30, note 38). Jacobsen translates "goddess-mothers." The term is used here to avoid ambiguity as to the sex of these divine beings, since the regular Sum. word for "god" (DINGIR) refers to both male and female deities.

[6] Reading DÚ-LUM (for normal DU-LUM) "suffering," "toil."

[7] Originally probably a remote country, from where gold was imported to Sumer (cf. Enki and Ninhursag, 51a). Later it was mythologized and regarded as the dwelling place of the gods before they created man (cf. G. Komoróczy, *Acta Orientalia Hungarica* 26 [1972] 113-123; *Iraq* 39 [1977] 67-68).

[8] Engaged in irrigation agriculture, the gods had to clean the rivers and canals of accumulated silt — a rather strenuous task.

[9] The god of the subterranean sweet waters, wisdom and magic, creator of mankind.

[10] É-ENGUR (literally: "The-House-the-Watery-Deep") was the name of Enki's temple in Eridu (cf. Å. Sjöberg, *TCS* III 54-55). Here it is a cosmic location beneath the earth in days of yore.

[11] Elsewhere, Nammu, the primeval mother, is called "The Bearer (birthgiver) of Heaven and Earth." This goddess seems to be the personification of the subterranean depths, the source of the sweet waters, the dwelling of Enki. Accordingly, her name is written with the logogram for Engur "subterranean (sweet) water."

"You are verily slumbering(?),
you are verily sleeping,
[You(?)] of(?) yourself(?)
would [not(?)] arise;
The gods, your 'handiwork,'
are smashing their equipment(?)!
My son, arise from your bed;
and when you have searched out wise
counsel with your ingenuity,
When you have fashioned a worker
comparable(?) to the gods,
may they relax from their toil!"[f]

Enki's Plan as to the Creation of Man (lines 24-37)

Enki, at the word of his mother,
Nammu, arose from his bed,
In Ḫalankug,[12] his room of taking counsel,
he smote(?) his thigh,[13]
The wise and intelligent one,
the custodian of heaven(?) and earth(?),
the-fashioner-of-the-forms of every being,
created two(?) birth-goddesses.[14]
Enki stationed them at his side,
examining them carefully.
And when Enki, the-fashioner-of-the-forms,
pondered by himself their nature,[15]
He said to his mother, Nammu:
"My mother, the creature which you named(?),
will verily exist; impose (on him)
the burden[16] of the gods![g]
When you have mixed the 'heart' of
the clay on top of the Abzu,[17]
The two(?) birth-goddesses shall nip off
pieces of clay.[18] When you yourself
have given (it) form,[19] [h]
Let Ninmah serve as your helper.[20]
And let Ninimma, Shuzianna, Ninmada, Ninbara,
Ninmug, Musardu and Ningunna
Assist you[21] as you activate birthgiving.[22]
My mother, after you decree his fate,
let Ninmah impose on him the burden."[23]

Creation of Man according to Enki's Plan
(lines 38-43)

[Thus(?)] she created mankind
ma[le and female(?) ....].[i]
By the male inseminating [the female(?)],
mankind [will beget(?)] an offspring,[24]
[After(?) nine(?) months(?) of(?)] pregnancy(?)
a man(?) will be [born(?)][25] [j] ...
.... she placed it on alfa-grass,
purified its delivery.[26] [k]

Ninmah Challenges Enki during a Banquet
(lines 52-57)

Enki and Ninmah were drinking beer,
and their heart became elated.
Ninmah said to Enki:
"What(ever) makes the form of man good or
bad — it is within my power;
As my heart prompts me, I can make
(its) 'fate' good or bad!"[27]

f Gen 2:5, 15; 3:17-19
g Gen 1:28-30; 2:15; 3:17-19
h Gen 1:27; 3:19; Pss 30:10; 103:14; Job 10:9; Eccl 3:20
i Gen 1:27; 2:21-23
j Gen 1:28; 2:23-24; 4:1; Jer 30:6
k Ezek 16:4, 9

[12] ḪAL-AN-KUG is equated with *apsûm* "deep" in an OB school-tablet. In the godlist An-Anum, it is an epithet of both Enki and his wife, Damgalnunna (Green 1975:205).

[13] A gesture of deep distress and pondering.

[14] Lit., "he caused the SIG$_7$-EN-SIG$_7$-DU$_{10}$ to emerge." The Sum. compound SIG$_7$-EN-SIG$_7$-DU$_{10}$ appears also in line 32, where the late bilingual version replaces it with ŠÀ-TUR (= Akk. *šassūru)* "womb(s)." Our text refers probably to a pair of birth-goddesses (i.e., divine wombs, matrices), wherein two male and female clay figures were planted, developed and given birth. These correspond to the fourteen (seven and seven) *šassūrātum* of the OB Atra-ḫasis myth, which produced seven males and seven females (Tablet I 277; S iii 9-10; see Lambert and Millard 1969:62) when man was created. Jacobsen (1987a:156, n. 7) reads the Sum. compound IMMA-EN and IMMA-ŠÁR, seeing in these two names, personifications of the female ovaries (see also nn. 20, 22 and 27 below).

[15] Or "its (= the project's) nature."

[16] So Benito and Kramer, who assume that the hapax ZUB-SÌG is a Sum. form of the Akk. *tupšikku* "earth-basket," "mortar-board," "corvée." Jacobsen takes ZUB-SÌG to mean "birth-chair."

[17] The subterranean sweet water ocean (see n. 10 above).

[18] Jacobsen translates: "Imma-en and Imma-shar can make the foetus bigger."

[19] Jacobsen: "And when you have put limbs on it."

[20] Ninmah ("The Lofty Lady") is one of the epithets or manifestations of the Sum. birth-goddess par excellence, Nintu. She acts here as the midwife, assisting Nammu in giving birth/creating man. In the second part of this myth, she competes with Enki and creates a number of crippled human beings.

[21] The minor goddesses listed in lines 34-35 seem not to be connected to birth-giving or midwifery as such. Possibly they represent friends and neighbors of the woman in labor who come to help the midwife in her task (see further Jacobsen 1987a:157, n. 10).

[22] Nammu's role in this myth seems to be that of the chief-midwife, who activated and assisted the "birth-goddesses" in giving birth to Man. Others assume that Nammu actually gave birth to man, translating the Sum. phrase TU-TU-A-ZU "at your giving birth."

[23] See line 30 and n. 16 above.

[24] The restoration of these two lines is highly conjectural. Jacobsen assumes that these lines express the idea that Nammu gave birth to primeval man without the need for a male sperm. He translates accordingly: "'And when, [without any m]ale, you have built it up in it, [may you give birth] to manki[nd]!' [Without] the sperm of a ma[le] she gave [birth] to offspri[ng], to the [em]bryo of mankind." However, in view of the Atra-ḫasis myth, which reports the creation of seven males and seven females (see n. 14 above) and Gen 1:27 ("male and female created He them"), our reconstruction of the story seems to be preferable.

[25] It is assumed here that lines 39-40 are anthropological observations by the mythographer as to the nature of mankind in general (for similar notes cf. Atra-ḫasis I 271-276; S iii 15-21; Lambert and Millard 1969:62). For a radically different interpretation of these lines, see Jacobsen.

[26] First man was created pure, amidst purification rites (cf. Atra-ḫasis I 204-207; Lambert and Millard 1969:56).

[27] As the mother-goddess par exellence, who represents all females in whose wombs the embryo develops and takes its form, Ninmah boasts that she can give birth to any form of human being. The empirical fact that all human beings, including cripples and deformed ones, are formed

Enki answered Ninmah:
"Let me counterbalance the 'fate',
desired by your heart — good or bad!"

Contest Between Ninmah and Enki: The Creation of Cripples and their Social Status (lines 58-78)

Ninmah took in her hand clay
from the top of the Abzu;[28]
She fashioned from it the first man:
one (who) could not bend his stiffened(?)
hands to reach out (for anything).[29]
Enki — upon seeing the first man
(who) could not bend his stiffened(?)
hands to reach out (for anything),
Decreed its fate: he made him stand
in attention at the head of the king.
Second — she fashioned from it one
'deprived of light,' a blind(?) man.[30] [l]
Enki — upon seeing the one 'deprived
of light,' the blind(?) man,
Decreed its fate: he allotted
to it the musical art,
And seated it (as) chief-[musician][31]
in a place of honor,[32] before the king.
Third — [she fashioned from it one la]me
as to [both feet],[33] [m] crippled of feet.
Enki — [upon see]ing the one lame
as to both feet, crippled of feet,
He taught(?) it[34] the work of [the metal-caster]
and silver-smith, his .....
Fourth — she fashioned from it
a man discharging semen.[35] [n]
Enki — upon seeing the man
discharging semen,
Bathed him in water (blessed) with incantation,
and removed Death[36] from his body.
Fifth — she fashioned from it a woman
who could not give birth.
Enki — upon seeing the woman
who could not give birth,[o]
Decreed her fate, he assigned her
to do work in the Women's Quarter.[37]
Sixth — she fashioned from it a man,
in whose body neither male organ
nor female organ was placed.
Enki — upon seeing the man
in whose body neither male organ
nor female organ was placed,[38]
He called him: "Nippurean(?)-the-courtier,"[39]
And decreed him as his fate to stand
in attendance before the king.[p]
Ninmah threw the pinch of clay
in her hand on the ground,
and a great silence fell.
The great lord, Enki, said to Ninmah:
"I have decreed the fate for those
whom you have fashioned,
and given them (their daily) bread.
Now come, let me fashion (one) for you;
and do you decree the fate of that newborn!"

l Lev 21:18; 2 Sam 5:6-8
m 2 Sam 9:13
n Lev 15:2 et passim
o Gen 11:30; 1 Sam 2:5; Isa 54:1
p Gen 40:2; 1 Kgs 22:9; 2 Kgs 20:18; Isa 56:4-5; Jer 38:7; Est 1:10

---

in the female's womb is reflected here.

[28] See n. 17 above.

[29] Reading with Kramer: ŠU ŠÚ-ŠÚ SÁ-SÁ-DÈ NU-GAM. For a radically different rendering of this line, see Jacobsen 1987a:159.

[30] Lit., perhaps: "a seeing man," possibly a euphemism for blindness.

[31] Restoring [NAR]-GAL.

[32] For ZÀ-GU-LA, lit., "the great side," see Sjöberg 1960:63, n. 3.

[33] Restoring [G̃ÌR-MIN Ḫ]UM, lit., "two feet broken" (see Jacobsen 1987a:160; Hallo 1969).

[34] Restoring MI-NI-IN-Z[U](?).

[35] Or "a man leaking urine" (Jacobsen).

[36] Lit., "Fate" (a demon of fatal sickness).

[37] Lit., "The Women's House," normally the queen's household, but according to another version, the reference is to the work of weaving. "The Women's House" could also refer to the royal harem (cf. Esth 2:3 et passim).

[38] The text refers to a eunuch.

[39] So Jacobsen. By a slight emendation of the text one can render: "Enki(?) called his name: 'courtier.'"

REFERENCES

Benito 1969:1-81; Green 1975:170-174; Jacobsen 1987a:151-166; Kramer 1989:188-198; Lambert and Millard 1969:42-70; Pettinato 1971; Sauren 1993.

THE EXALTATION OF INANNA (1.160)

William W. Hallo

This is one of three hymns to the goddess Inanna attributed to Enheduanna in its own text. All three are listed together at the beginning of a literary catalogue, with this composition last (Cohen 1976:131f.). The cycle is a counterpart to The Collection of the Temple Hymns, another cycle attributed to the same author (Sjöberg and Bergmann 1969). If the latter reflects on Sargon, the author's father, founder of the first documented empire in Asia, at peace, the former cycle describes him at war. But it does so in highly metaphoric terms, crediting the victories of the Sargonic dynasty to Inanna, its patron deity. Enheduanna emerges from these and other works (Westenholz 1989) as a genuine creative talent, a poetess as well as a princess, a priestess and a prophetess. She is, in fact, the first non-anonymous and non-legendary author in history. As such she has found her way into contemporary anthologies, especially of women's literature (Barnstone and Barnstone 1980:1-8; Kilmer in Bankier and Lashgari 1983:111-117).

A. Exordium[1]

(i) Inanna and the divine attributes

Lady of all the divine attributes,[2]
resplendent light,
Righteous woman clothed in radiance,
beloved of Heaven and Earth,
Hierodule of An,
(you) of all the great ornaments,
Enamored of the appropriate tiara,
suitable for the high-priesthood,
Whose hand has attained
(all) the "seven" divine attributes,[3]
Oh my lady, you are the guardian
of all the great divine attributes!
You have picked up the divine attributes,
you have hung the divine attributes on your hand,
You have gathered up the divine attributes,
you have clasped the divine attributes to your breast.

(ii) Inanna and An (Heaven)

Like a dragon you have deposited venom on the foreign land.
When you roar at the earth like Thunder,
no vegetation can stand up to you.
A flood descending from its mountain,
Oh foremost one, you are the Inanna of heaven and earth!
Raining the flaming fire down upon the nation,
Endowed with divine attributes by An,
lady mounted on a beast,
Who makes decisions at the holy command of An.
(You) of all the great rites,
who can fathom what is yours?

(iii) Inanna and Enlil

Devastatrix of the lands,
you are lent wings by the storm.
Beloved of Enlil,
you fly about in the nation.
You are at the service of the decrees of An.

a Gen 4:24 et passim

Oh my lady, at the sound of you
you make the foreign lands bow down.
At (your) tempestuous radiance, mankind
In fear and trembling
when it comes before you,
Receives from you its just deserts.
A song of lamentation it begins for you.
It walks toward you along the path
of the house of all the great sighs.

(iv) Inanna and Ishkur[4]

In the van of battle
everything is struck down by you.
Oh my lady, (propelled) on your own wings,
you peck away (at the land).[5]
In the guise of a charging storm you charge
With a roaring storm you roar.
With Thunder you continually thunder.
With all the evil winds you snort.
Your feet are filled with restlessness.
To (the accompaniment of) the harp of sighs
you give vent to a dirge.

(v) Inanna and the Anunna[6]

Oh my lady, the Anunna, the great gods,
Fluttering like bats
Fly off from before you to the clefts,
They who dare not walk in your terrible glance,
Who dare not proceed before your terrible countenance.
Who can temper your raging heart?
Your malevolent heart is beyond tempering.
Lady (who) soothes the reins, lady (who) gladdens the heart,
Whose rage is not tempered,
oh great daughter of Suen!
Lady supreme over the foreign land,
who has (ever) denied (you) homage?

(vi) Inanna and Mt. Ebih[7]

In the mountain where homage is withheld from you
vegetation is accursed.
Its grand entrance you have reduced to ashes.

[1] The rhetorical and other structural divisions imposed on the text are in part modern constructs; they are defended in Hallo and van Dijk 1968, chs. 4-5, and in Hallo 1996, ch. V/3. They are reflected in the current translation as far as possible; for further details see Hallo and van Dijk 1968, ch. 2.

[2] Or: "essences" (ME), from the Sum. verb "to be." They are thought of in physical terms as symbols to be worn or carried. The myth of Inanna and Enki (Text 1.161 below) lists over 125 of them, including many of the "arts of civilization"; it may well be alluded to in this stanza.

[3] "Seven" is here used in the sense of a large, round number, as frequently in BH.

[4] Storm god and embodiment of thunder (cf. above, line 10).

[5] For the winged Inanna in other texts and in art, cf. already lines 17f. (differently Heimpel 1971:233) and Hallo and van Dijk 1968:51.

[6] The deities in general, later conceived as subordinate or chthonic (netherworld) deities in particular.

[7] Presumably this stanza refers to the mountain range marking the northern border of Sumer and Akkad, and later of Babylonia, identified with the Jebel Hamrin, and subject of another of Enheduanna's hymns to Inanna, alluding to Sargonic triumphs on this frontier.

Blood rises in its rivers for you,
its people have nought to drink.
It leads its army captive before you of its own accord.[8]
It disbands its regiments before you of its own accord.[8]
It makes its able-bodied young men parade before you of their own accord.[8]
A tempest has filled the dancing places of its city.
It drives its young adults before you as captives,

(vii) Inanna and Uruk(?)

Because the city has not declared
"The land is yours,"
Because they have not declared
"It is your father's, your begettor's,"[9]
You have spoken your holy command,
have verily turned it back from your path,
Have verily removed your foot from out of its byre.
Its woman no longer speaks of love with her husband.
At night they no longer have intercourse.
She no longer reveals to him her inmost treasures.
Impetuous wild cow, great daughter of Suen,
Lady supreme over An,
who has (ever) denied (you) homage?

(viii) Invocation of Inanna

You of the appropriate divine attributes,
great lady of ladies,
Issued from the holy womb,
supreme over the mother who bore you,
Omniscient sage, lady of all the foreign lands,
Sustenance of the multitudes,
I have verily recited your sacred song!
True goddess, fit for the divine attributes,
it is exalting to acclaim you.
Merciful one, brilliant, righteous woman,
I have verily recited your divine attributes for you!

B. The Argument

(ix) The Banishment from Ur

Verily I had entered my holy cloister[10] at your behest,
I, the high-priestess, I, Enheduanna!
I carried the ritual basket, I intoned the acclaim.
(But now) one has placed me in the leper's ward,[11]
I, even I, can no longer live with you!
They approach the light of day,
the light is obscured about me,
The shadows approach the light of day,
it is covered (as) with a (sand)storm.
My mellifluous mouth is cast into confusion.
My choices features are turned to dust.

(x) The Appeal to Inanna(?)

My fate — it concerns Suen and Lugalanne — [12]
Report it to An! May An release me!
Say but to An "Now!" and An will release me (saying):
"This woman will carry off the fate of Lugalanne.
Mountain (and) flood lie at her feet.
That woman is as exalted (as he) —
she will make the city abandon him."
Surely she will assuage her heartfelt rage for me.
Let me, Enheduanna, recite a prayer to her.
My tears like sweet drink
Let me give free vent to for the holy Inanna,
Let me say "Hail!" to her!

(xi) The Indictment of Lugalanne(?)

I cannot appease Ashimbabbar.[13]
He (Lugalanne?) has altered the lustrations of holy An and all his (rites) whatsoever.
He has verily carried off from An (his temple) Eanna.
He has not stood in awe of King An.
That sanctuary whose attractions are irresistible,
whose beauty is endless,
That sanctuary he has verily brought to destruction.

When he began to enter there,
he became jealous of him.[14]
Oh my divine impetuous wild cow, drive out this man, capture this man!

(xii) The Curse of Uruk[15]

In the "Place of Sustenance" what am I, even I?
(Uruk) is a malevolent rebel against your Nanna —
may An make it surrender![16]
This city — may it be sundered by An!
May it be cursed by Enlil!
May its plaintive child not be placated by his

---

[8] Or: "one by one, one after the other"; cf. B. L. Eichler, *JAOS* 103 (1983) 97 and n. 19.

[9] Translating with D. O. Edzard, *ZA* 66 (1976) 47, n. 190.

[10] I.e., the *gipāru*, the residence of the high-priestess.

[11] Variant: "in a good place" (euphemism?). Note that "grave" uses the same logogram (plus "house").

[12] Enheduanna is the first of a long line of princesses appointed by their royal fathers as high-priestesses of Nanna, the moon-god at Ur, equated with the Akk. Suen. Lugalanne is a rebel against Sargonic rule and a pretender to the rule of Uruk, known also from other sources. The translation follows Wilcke 1976a:88.

[13] Another manifestation of the moon-god.

[14] For TAB-KU$_4$ cf. *CAD S* s.v. *šurrû*. The second half of the line follows Civil 1990b.

[15] For Uruk as the "Place of Sustenance" see Hallo and van Dijk 1968:58 and n. 52. Other cities may share this epithet; see e.g. Shulgi B 41 (Castellino 1972:34f.).

[16] Against the astral reinterpretation of this line by B. Alster, cf. Hallo, *JNES* 37 (1978) 273.

mother!
Oh lady, the (harp of) mourning is placed on the ground.
One had verily beached your ship of mourning
on a hostile shore.
At (the sound of) my sacred song
I am are ready to die.

(xiii) The Indictment of Nanna

As for me, my Nanna takes no heed of me.
In murderous straits,
he has verily given me over to destruction.
Ashimbabbar has not pronounced my judgment.
Had he pronounced it: what is it to me?
Had he not pronounced it: what is it to me?
(Me) who once sat triumphant
he has driven out of the sanctuary.
Like a swallow he made me fly from the window, my life is consumed.
In the bramble of the mountain he made me walk.
The crown appropriate for the high-priesthood
he carried off from me.
He gave me dagger and sword —
"it becomes you," he said to me.

(xiv) Second(?) Appeal to Inanna

Most precious lady, beloved of An,
Your holy heart is lofty,
may it be assuaged on my behalf!
Beloved bride of Ushumgal-anna[17]
Of the heavenly foundations and zenith
you are the "senior" queen.
The Anunna have submitted to you.
From birth on you were the "junior" queen.
Over the great gods, the Anunna,
how supreme you are!
The Anunna with their lips
kiss the ground (in obeisance) to you.
(But) my own sentence is not concluded,
a hostile judgment appears before my eyes as my judgment.
(My) hands are no longer folded on the ritual couch.
The pronouncements of Ningal
I may no longer reveal to man.[18]
(Yet) I am the brilliant high-priestess of Nanna,
Oh my lady beloved of An,
may your heart take pity on me!

(xv) The Exaltation of Inanna[19]

That one has not recited as a "Known! Be it known!" of Nanna,
that one has recited as a "Tis Thine!":

"That you are lofty as Heaven (An) —
be it known!
That you are broad as Earth —
be it known!
That you devastate the rebellious land —
be it known!
That you roar at the land —
be it known!
That you smite the heads —
be it known!
That you devour cadavers like a dog —
be it known!
That your glance is terrible —
be it known!
That you lift your terrible glance —
be it known!
That your glance is flashing —
be it known!
That you are ill-disposed toward the defiant —[20]
be it known!"

That one has not recited (this) of Nanna,
that one has recited it as a "Tis Thine!" —
(That,) oh my lady, has made you great,
you alone are exalted!
Oh my lady beloved of An,
I have verily recounted your fury!

C. Peroration

(xvi) The Composition of the Hymn

One has heaped up the coals (in the censer),
prepared the lustration.
The nuptial chamber awaits you,
let your heart be appeased!
With "It is enough for me, it is too much for me!"
I have given birth, oh exalted lady,
to (this song) for you.
That which I recited to you at (mid)night
May the singer repeat it to you at noon!
(Only) on account of your captive spouse,
on account of your captive child,
Your rage is increased,
your heart unassuaged.

(xvii) The Restoration of Enheduanna

The first lady, the reliance of the throne-room,
Has accepted her offerings.
Inanna's heart has been restored.
The day was favorable for her,
she was clothed sumptuously,
she was garbed in womanly beauty.

[17] Short form of Ama-ushumgal-anna, a manifestation of Dumuzi.

[18] Ningal is the consort of the Moon-god at Ur, and a patroness of dream-interpretation (oneiromancy). In her prophetic function, Enheduanna was apparently an oneiromancer (ENSI = *šāʾiltu*).

[19] In this "magnificat," the Argument reaches its climax as the crucial divine attributes are attributed to Inanna, not Nanna. Her triumph is signalled similarly in another hymn by Enheduanna, and in the historiographic tradition about Sargon's defeat of the great rebellion in his old age. Note that after its opening couplet (lines 123f.), the remainder of the magnificat has a different (i.e., indifferent) sequence of lines in every exemplar.

[20] Cf. *CAD* s.v. *šapṣu*.

Like the light of the rising moon,
how she was sumptuously attired!
When Nanna (Moon) appeared in proper view,
They (all) blessed her (Inanna's) mother Ningal.
(150) The heavenly doorsill called "Hail!"

(xviii) Doxology
For that her (Enheduanna's) speaking to the Hierodule (Inanna)
was exalted —
(To) the devastatrix of the foreign lands,
endowed with divine attributes from An,
(To) my lady wrapped in beauty,
(to) Inanna: Praise!

REFERENCES

Texts: numerous whole or partial duplicates as listed in Hallo and van Dijk 1968:36f. and subsequent reviews. Translations and studies: Barnstone and Barnstone 1980; Hallo and van Dijk 1968; Heimpel 1971; Kilmer 1983; Kramer *ANET* 579-582; Römer 1972; Sauren 1970; Westenholz 1989; Wilcke 1976a.

INANNA AND ENKI (1.161)

Gertrud Farber

The exact date of the origin of this composition is unknown. It has come down to us in only very few sources, all of which stem from the Old Babylonian scribal school of Nippur.[1]

The main topic of the myth is the love goddess Inanna's attempt to increase her city Uruk's and her own power and influence. She therefore wants to bring into her possession the ME, the cultural norms which are the basis of Sumerian civilization and all aspects of life.[2] These cultural norms are stored like concrete objects in Enki's underwater temple in Eridu. During Inanna's visit to Eridu, Enki, the god of wisdom, bestows the ME on her, while he is drunk. She manages to escape with them and securely brings them to her hometown Uruk despite several attempts by Enki to stop her. Unfortunately, the last lines of the text are poorly preserved, and it is still unclear how the conflict between Inanna and Enki is settled.[3]

The importance of "Inanna and Enki" lies in the detailed listing of the ME, which gives us some insight into Sumerian thinking — how they looked on life and how they understood the world.

The composition orginally had some 820 lines. Repetitions and unclear lines are not included in the following translation; (....) marks abridged text.

Introduction: Inanna's praise of her sex appeal and her plan to visit Enki in order to increase her power (Tablet I i and SLTNi 32+)
[.... Inanna] placed the ŠUGURRA, the crown of the steppe, on her head.
As she went outside to the shepherd, to the sheepfold,
[....] was bent down, her vulva was to be wondered at,
[....] was righteously bent down, her vulva was to be admired.[4]
Rejoicing at her wonderful vulva, she started to praise herself.
" (....)
When I will have directed my foot towards god Enki and the Abzu and Eridu,
I will speak coaxingly to Enki, to the Abzu and Eridu. (....)
I, the lady, I, the queen of heaven, I want to go to the Abzu,
to the lord Enki I shall speak a prayer.
Like the sweet oil of the cedar [....]
(....).
On that day, the maid Inanna
directed her step all by herself
towards Enki's Abzu in Eridu.
On that day, the one who has overpowering knowledge, who knows the divine decrees in

[1] For the first identification of the text see Kramer 1944:64-68. For a complete edition see Farber 1973. For collations and new text material see Waetzoldt 1975 and Farber 1995. Other important studies include Alster 1974a and Kramer 1989:57-68, 222-225, with a new translation. The free rendering of the myth by Wolkstein and Kramer 1983:11-27 is not true to the Sum. text and should not be regarded as a scholarly translation.

[2] For a discussion of the ME see Farber 1973:116-213 and Farber 1990:610-613. In some instances in this volume translated "divine attributes," "divine powers," "divine offices."

[3] I still support my original interpretation which is based on grammatical forms and the structure of the dialogue, that Inanna has to give the cultural norms back to Enki. For different and in my opinion grammatically problematic interpretations see Alster 1974a:26, who assumes that although the ME remain in Uruk, both Inanna and her city are severely punished by Enki, and Kramer 1989:68 who thinks that Enki accepts the fact that the ME are no longer in his possesssion and that everybody is rejoicing.

[4] She is probably having sex with her lover, the shepherd-god Dumuzi.

heaven and earth,
who just from his dwelling knows about the plans of the gods,
knew everything (about the plot)
even before the radiant Inanna had approached the temple in Eridu by a mile.

Inanna's visit in Eridu and her acquisition of the cultural norms, the ME (SLTNi 32+ and Tablet I ii - iii)

So Enki, the king of the Abzu,
spoke to his man and gave him instructions:
"Come here, man, listen to my word!
When the young girl Inanna has entered the Abzu and Eridu,
have her eat butter-cake,
let her be served cool water which refreshes the soul,
at the lion gate[5] pour beer for her,
treat her like a friend and a colleague.
At the pure table, at the table of An,
you shall greet the radiant Inanna."
According to these instructions
Isimud, the vizier, follows his king's commands.
He allows the maid Inanna to enter the Abzu and Eridu,
(...)
where she gets butter-cake to eat.
Cool water, refreshing to the soul, is poured for her,
at the lion gate she is served beer.
He treats her like a friend and a colleague.
At the pure table, the table of An,
he greets her.
Enki and Inanna drink beer together in the Abzu,
enjoy the taste of sweet wine.
The bronze AGA-vessels are filled to the rim,
they have a competition, (drinking from the) bronze vessels of Uraš.

[Break of 35 to 40 lines]

Enki apparently gets drunk and presents all the divine norms, or ME, which are stored in his care in the Abzu to his daughter Inanna. The presentation of several items at a time, follows the pattern:

"In the name of my power, in the name of my Abzu,
I will give them all to my daughter, the radiant Inanna, and (this) shall not be [contested]."
The ... (5 to 8 items each time)
the radiant Inanna accepted.

This pattern is repeated fifteen times, of which only six, containing the ME no. 53-94, are preserved. The final listing seems to have more items. The main 94 ME are:

I (1-5) EN-ship, LAGAL-priesthood, godship, the mighty legitimate crown, the throne of kingship,
II (6-10) the noble scepter, staff and rein, the noble dress, shepherdship, kingship,
III (11-15) EGIZI-priestess-ship, NINDINGIR-priestess-ship, IŠIB-priesthood, LUMAḪ-priesthood, GUDU-priesthood,
IV (16-21) truth, ..., ..., descending into the Netherworld, having ascended from the Netherworld, the KURĜARRA-priest,
V (22-27) sword and club, the temple servant SAĜURSAĜ, the black dress, the colorful dress, the ... hair, the ... hair,
VI (28-34) [7 mainly broken ME]
VII (35-40) the standard, the quiver, love making, kissing, prostitution, running (?),
VIII (41-46) speech, slander, cajoling, ..., the cult-prostitute, the pure tavern,
IX (47-52) the holy NIGINĜAR shrine, ..., the hierodule of heaven, the resounding lute, the art of singing, the (wise) state of old age,
X (53-59) heroism, possession of power, dishonesty, righteousness, plundering of cities, singing of lamentations, rejoicing,
XI (60-64) deceit, the rebellious land, kindness, traveling around, the permanent home,
XII (65-72) the craft of the carpenter, the craft of the copper-smith, the art of the scribe, the craft of the smith, the craft of the leather-worker, the craft of the fuller, the craft of the builder, the craft of the mat-weaver,
XIII (73-81) understanding, knowledge, purifying washing rites, the house of the shepherd (?), heaping up of coals, the sheepfold, fear, awe, reverent silence,
XIV (82-88) the bitter toothed ..., kindling of fire, extinguishing of fire, hard work, ..., the assembled family, descendants,
XV (89-94) dispute, triumph, counseling, deliberation, jurisdiction, decision-making.

[Break of approximately 80 lines]

Inanna's departure by boat and Enki's regret (Tablet I iv - vi)

After having received the ME from Enki, Inanna leaves the Abzu while Enki seems to have fallen asleep. While she is (apparently) loading the ME on to her ship, she is listing them again, one by one, following the pattern:

" ... he has given to me."

In this section the ME no. 56-91 are preserved. It seems that she is explaining her behavior to somebody who may have objected that she removed the ME from the Abzu.[6]

[Break of approximately 35 lines]

Enki has woken up and gradually becomes sober again.

[Enki now addresses his vizier Isimud:]

[5] This may refer to the lion dating from the Ur III period which has been excavated in Eridu.

[6] Alster has suggested that this may have been the mysterious frog guarding the entrance to the Abzu who occurs in I vi, 4; 6, see Alster 1974a:24.

["My vizier Isimud, my sweet name of heaven!"]
["My king,] Enki! I am at your service, what is your wish?"
"If she has not yet left for Uruk and Kulab,
if she has not yet left for the place (...) where the sun rises,
I need to get hold of her, because of what I have said."[7]
"The radiant Inanna has already gathered up all the ME, she has boarded the 'boat of heaven,'
and the 'boat of heaven' has left the quay."
When the one who had drunk beer, who had drunk (too much) beer, had thrown up all the beer,
when father Enki, the one who had drunk (too much) beer, had thrown up the beer,
the great lord Enki gave all his attention to [...].
The lord (now) looks thoroughly at his Abzu
and then speaks to his vizier Isimud:
"My vizier Isimud, my sweet name of heaven!"
"My king Enki, I am at your service, what is your wish?"

The sobered Enki now asks Isimud where all his ME have disappeared to. He names them all in groups, following the pattern:

"The ..., where are they?"

Nine of the groups are preserved, listing ME no. 1-52.

[Break of approximately 35 lines]

The 20 poorly preserved lines of column vi can still not be restored properly. They tell about a frog sitting at the entrance door of Enki's temple. Perhaps the frog is being blamed for having let Inanna escape through the door with all her presents.[8]

[Break of 10 to 15 lines]

Enki's futile attempts to retrieve the ME (Tablet II i - iv 17)

The prince speaks to his vizier Isimud,
Enki addresses his "sweet name of heaven":
"My vizier Isimud, my sweet name of heaven!"
"My king Enki, I am at your service, what is your wish?"
"The 'boat of heaven,' how far has it traveled?"
"Right now, it has reached the [...] quay."
"Go! The Enkum shall seize the boat from her!"
The vizier Isimud speaks to the radiant Inanna:
"My lady, your father has sent me to you.
What your father has said is sublime,
what Enki has remarked is sublime.
His important words may not be disregarded."
To this the radiant Inanna answers:
"What did my father say to you? What did he remark to you?
Why may his important speech not be disregarded?"
"My king has said to me,
Enki has instructed me:
'Inanna shall return to Uruk, but you, escort the 'boat of heaven' to Eridu!'"
The radiant Inanna answers the vizier Isimud:
"Why has my father changed his word to me?
Why has he overturned his honest speech to me?
Why has he disgraced his important words to me?
My father has spoken dishonestly to me, he has spoken insincerely to me.
Untruthfully he has made his promises in the name of his power and in the name of his Abzu,
cheatingly he has sent you to me as a messenger!"
Hardly has she finished this speech,
when the Enkum try to seize the "boat of heaven."
The radiant Inanna now says to her vizier Ninshubura:
"Come here, my faithful vizier of the Eanna,
my vizier of good tidings,
my messenger of truthful words!
Water has not touched your hand, water has not touched your foot."[9]
After Inanna has thus saved the ME which had been given to her, and the "boat of heaven,"
the prince speaks to his vizier Isimud a second time,
Enki addresses his "sweet name of heaven."
(...)

In the next 170 lines Enki tries five more times to retrieve the "boat of heaven" loaded with the ME. At the pure [...] the 50 "Giants of Eridu" shall seize the boat, at the hill UL.MA the 50 "LAḪAMA-demons of the Ocean" fail to capture the boat. At the hill "Field" all "Big Fish" are sent out to get the boat. At the [...] the "Guardians of Uruk" are unsuccessful, and at the Iturungal River the "[...] of the Iturungal" fail once more. And so Inanna arrives safely in Uruk, bringing the ME with her.

Inanna's Arrival in Uruk and the Ensuing Celebration (Tablet II iv 18 - 58)

[11 lines mostly destroyed]

Ninshubura does something concerning the "boat of heaven" with her foot and her [hand], then something happens for the seventh time, while Inanna "completes something else to perfection."

Her vizier Ninshubura
[addresses] the radiant Inanna:
"My lady, on the day you [bring] the 'boat of heaven' to the gate ['Joy,' to Uruk-Kulab],
our city will [revel] in abundance,

[7] I think that Enki wants to prevent her from leaving, but Kramer assumed that Enki, being still drunk, was actually assisting her in her departure; see Kramer 1989:64.

[8] For this interpretation see Alster 1974a:24; see also n. 6.

[9] Unfortunately we do not understand the magic procedure used by Ninshubura to save the boat.

(...),
on our [canals] cargo-boats [will ...]."
To that the radiant Inanna answers her:
"On the day I [bring] the 'boat of heaven' to the gate 'Joy,' to Uruk-Kulab,
it shall pass along the [street] magnificently.
[The people] shall stand in the street full of awe.[10]
(...)
The old men [shall receive] prudence,
the old women [shall receive] wise counsel,
to the young men [I will give] the strength [of weapons],
the little children [shall be happy!]
[Break of 6 lines]
[...] the 'boat of heaven,' [there shall be a] festival!
The king shall slaughter oxen, [many sheep he shall bring],
beer he shall pour into the cups.
May he [sound] the drums and timpani,
may he skilfully [play] the sweet TIGI-instruments.
All the lands shall [proclaim] my sublimity,
my people shall praise my glory!"
On the day she brought the "boat of heaven" to the gate "Joy," to Uruk-Kulab,
it passed along the streets magnificently [...].
It reached the house of the maid, and [she determined] its place.
[It passed] the pure well, her main well.
Inanna had the ME which had been bestowed on her and the "boat of heaven" [land] at the gate of the G̃IPAR,
she had them [...] at the entrance of the AGRUN (a divine dwelling).[11]
Shining brightly, the radiant Inanna then [blessed] the place [where] the "boat of heaven" [had docked].

The narrative moves back to Eridu.

The prince now [says] to his vizier Isimud,
Enki [addresses] his "sweet name of heaven":
"My vizier Isimud, my sweet name [of heaven]!"
"My king Enki, I am at your service, [what is your wish]?"
"The 'boat of heaven,' how far has it traveled?"
"It has arrived at the 'White Quay.'"
"Go! admiration shall be [...],
[...] admire the 'boat of heaven.'"
[Break of approximately 5 lines]

The Unloading of the ME in Uruk (Tablet II iv 59 - vi 50)

Isimud has apparently arrived in Uruk at the "White Quay" and is taking part in the festivities. Inanna now starts unloading the ME, and it may be Isimud who lists them individually (line by line)[12] as she takes them from the "boat of heaven," following the pattern:

"The ... you have brought with you."

Following this enumeration of the 94 cultural norms are 16 more items which are only partly preserved. They can either be additional ME or represent a more general description of the goods[13] brought home by Inanna.

"To place [...] on the ground, the charm of all women you have brought with you.
[The ability (?)] to use the ME correctly, you have brought.
[Two lines or items broken.]
The holy percussion instruments TIGI, LILIS, UB, MEZE, and ALA, [and six more items] of An you have brought,
[...] the magnificent [...], as many as there are,
while he was preparing beer,[14] you have brought with you."
[Break of 8 lines]
Full of joy, the woman gave the [...]
the name "the house of the Netherworld has been built."
Like the merchant who had said "fifty shekel,"
then brought them, and there were less,[15]
the place (where this happened) she called "potsherd and rubbish."
The place where the boat had (almost) been turned around
she called "(his) mind has changed."
The place where the boat had docked
she called "the white quay."
The place where she had unloaded [the ME], one by one,
she called "the lapis lazuli quay."

The Settling of the Conflict between Enki and Inanna, perhaps by Enlil (Tablet II vi 51 - 67)

In the meantime Enki has arrived in Uruk. But it seems from the way Enki and Inanna are talking that they are addressing a third person, someone else who has arrived as a *deus ex machina* to settle the conflict. The only arbiter both gods might accept would probably be Enlil.[16]

Enki addresses the radiant Inanna:
"In the name of my power, in the name of my Abzu,
for this woman (here he addresses somebody else, not Inanna) I will place [...][17] in my Abzu."

---

[10] Kramer's interpretation of "high waters sweeping over the street" makes little sense and is grammatically untenable, see Kramer 1989:67.
[11] For *Agrun* as the entrance to a private place see Alster 1972:354 and 1973:102.
[12] For this interpretation see Alster 1974a:25 with n. 7.
[13] See Green 1976:284.
[14] Does this refer to Enki?
[15] The merchant seemingly had been cheating. Is this an allusion to Enki's breach of promise?
[16] For this interpretation, see Farber 1973:94-95; for other interpretations see the discussion in n. 3.
[17] The word missing here might have been crucial for the interpretation of the end of the story.

"Why has this man (Inanna talks about an intruder, not about Enki) now entered here,
[...] taking the ME from me?"
Enlil (?) answers by giving orders including some punishment like the crushing of some women's vulvas. But he also creates a festival.
[7 lines are largely destroyed]
Enlil (?) continues:
"At the gate of the ĜIPAR [your people shall] spend their days,
[at the entrance to the AGRUN], the inhabitants of your city, the inhabitants of Uruk shall live (happily).
And concerning you (addressing Enki), to your city Eridu she has already added [the ME (?)], she has indeed returned them to their original location."

REFERENCES

Alster 1972; 1973; 1974a; Farber 1973; 1990; 1995; Green 1976; Kramer 1944; Kramer and Maier 1989; Waetzoldt 1975; Wolkstein and Kramer 1983.

---

2. HYMNS

TO NANSHE (1.162)

Wolfgang Heimpel

Is it not the city, is it not the city, are its divine powers not proclaimed?
Is it not the city Nina, are its divine powers not proclaimed?
Is it not the city, the pure city, are its divine powers not proclaimed?
Is it not a mountain carried above water, the city, are its divine powers not proclaimed?
Does not the day of the good house appear, has not its destiny been determined?
Does not propriety shine in the city?
Are not the rites[1] of mother Nanshe organized?
Is not its lady, the child born in Eridu,
Nanshe, the lady of precious divine powers, restoring (them)?
The mother — is it not resin? —, the mother — is it not yeast? —,
Is not Nanshe mother of great things?

In the living quarters of the land heavy (things) exist in her presence.
In the stores honey ... like resin.[2]
Vases with everflowing water stood before her.
Boxes with the storables of the land
covered like silt, the thing of the river, the ground before Nanshe.

...

She knows the orphan, she knows the widow.
She knows that person oppresses person. A mother for the orphan,
Nanshe, a caretaker for the widow,
finding a way for houses in debt,
the lady shelters the abducted person,[3]
seeks a place for the weak,
swells him his collecting basket,[4]
(and) makes his collecting vat profitable.
For an honest maid who seized her feet
Nanshe counts a man of good means;
(and) it is the widow that Nanshe endows with an unmarried person
(who is for her) like a roof in a good house.

Does not propriety shine in presence of the lady?
Did not Nanshe — in her presence "hands" are tripled in plenty in Lagash —
call the lord to the holy heart?[5]
The lion of Nanshe, the beloved lord of Lagash, filled the dais in her presence.[6]
She gave the shepherd the mighty scepter.
She perfected Gudea with her precious powers.

---

[1] PA.AN in line 65 is spelled syllabically *bi-lu-da* in line 65 and elsewhere. It is an old loan from Akk. *bēlūtum*. The context of lines 123 and 125 relates it with the expectations of Nanshe of certain priests, and seems to designate the rule of Nanshe and the rules by which her priests act. In line 65, where the context is incompatible with the meaning "rule," and "rite," Jacobsen's translation is used. This meaning is confirmed by the logogram PA.AN "executive + divinity."

[2] Cf. *ELS* 718-720.

[3] My old translation and Jacobsen's "fugitive" would be LÚ-ZÀH. KAR = *ekēmu* = "to take by force, to abduct," generally in war.

[4] ŠU-DU = *kamāsum*. OB Níĝ-gur$_{11}$ *makkūru* 152 (*MSL* 13, 119).

[5] The particular title of the lord of Nanshe here and elsewhere is šennu.

[6] So after Jacobsen. Cf. H. Steible *FAOS* 9/2 (1991) 51:1.

Her shepherd, whom she had called to the holy heart,
Gudea, governor of Lagash,
set (the lyre) Cow Plenty among the drums,
set the silver drum at its side.
While holy songs, harmonious songs, were performed for her,
small copper sickles praise the house.
The chief musician plays her the ibex horn.
The "Has not the house been granted divine powers from Abzu?"[7]
was performed through princely powers of the holy songs of house Sirara.
The dream interpreter[8] brought her the (utensils) of the first fruit (festival);[a]
held the glittering silver cups out to her.
The temple cook [ ];
hot and cold things he brings straight before her.
He brought the ... of the oven before her.
[ ] the great shovel resounds before her.
When meat cuts were brought in large bowls,
when cool water was brought from the Sirara river,
when the festival trappings were brought from (the city) Lagash,[9]
when liquor was brought from the countryside,
her large oven which matches the large hall,
Nanshe's sanctuary of bread distribution,[10] hums.

The lady, the elder woman of Enlil,
Nanshe, the lady who lives in plenty in the land,
..., the child of Enki,
places a person, a good woman for a good house.
After she placed a person, a good woman for a good house,
the daily provisions of the house came straight from the Bursag.[11]
For these rites the barley does not suffice.
The vases were empty, poured no water.
The person who helped with its regular provisions does not receive extra.
What was distributed over and above food and water,
what was left of the regular provisions, what was not used by the house,
what was expended as first item of fish of the tax,[12]
allowing a measure of one acre[13] of canebrake
for each of its (the house's) servants,
what was received in nuts and green plants within the garden,
after it (the above) passed (to the house) no mouth[14] touches it.
Bread of the neighborhood shrines are not carried as bread distribution.
(Before,) a person came for a gift of prime beer: (now) he did not collect[15] cool water.

Its (the house's) established first fruit (festival) is reorganized, (so as) not to cease (again).
There was (now) indeed a fat carrier who passes fat to the house.
There was (now) indeed a cheese carrier who passes cheese to the house,
(and) a courier with fish, a person of daily assignment.
82 Standing in the corners (or) on the sides (instead of helping)
80 when the firewood carrier passed by with what he brought from the steppe
81 to the house of his lady;
83 concealing something,[16] saying something else (will not be effective):
Entering the house of Nanshe from the outside (means) not leaving it from inside.

The caretaker of the house of Nanshe, the child born by Utu,
lord Hendursaga ...

a Num 28:26, etc.

[7] The same as line 232. Both times the title of a composition (incipit) may be involved.

[8] A. L. Oppenheim, *AOS* 32 C 14, quoted *TUT* 256 which records the receipt of barley by Nin-sal-la ensi; that a dream interpreter should be female agrees with the fact that Nanshe herself was the "dream interpreter of the gods" and actually interpreted Gudea's dream (Cyl. A II 1-VI 13). For the translation of ne-saĝ cf. *NABU* 1994 4:72f. No. 83.

[9] In Ur III, Nina and Lagash lie on opposite ends of the district Kinunir-Nina of the province of Lagash. It is conceivable that Gatumdu was joined by the gods along the route to Nina, i.e., Lugal-URUxGÁNA-*tenê*, Dumuzi-Abzu, and Lugal-Dara, and that the New Year was celebrated in Nina for the whole district.

[10] LSU 31: URI$_5^{ki}$ ÈŠ NIDBA-GAL-GAL-LA. NIDBA and *nindabû* designate offerings. According to the etymology, it means "bread distribution." I assume that it was a kind of offering which was prepared in large quantities and redistributed.

[11] The BUR-SAG was a storage-house, or possibly a brewery (Á-SIKIL); see PSD s. vv. [WWH]

[12] In BBVO 10 (1990) 185f., R. Englund pointed to a fish tax which was collected by the enku (ZÀ.HA) for the provincial administration of Umma of which 10% was deducted and sent to Nippur as nisag. It is conceivable that similarly fishes were deducted for the nisag of Nanshe within the district Kinunir-Nina.

[13] The Sumerian IKU was a little smaller than the English acre.

[14] *ELS* 374 s.v. "du$_{11}$-ge," referring to W. H. Ph. Römer, reads KA-GE "mouth" + agentive.

[15] See note 4 above.

[16] For EME-TA ĞÁL-LA cf. the description of Sargon concealing something: "he made it known to his heart, does not let it be on his tongue (EME-NA NU-ĞÁ-ĞÁ), does not talk about it with anyone (*JAOS* 103 [1983]). INIM-KÚR-DI "saying something different" (KÚR = loan translation of Akk. *nakāru*). References and discussion *ELS* 590-593.

The king recognized that which is said (with) good (intention),[17] recognized that which
is said (with) bad (intention);
Hendursaga recognized that which is said (with) good (intention), recognized that
which is said (with) bad (intention).

Those [ ] ... which (could) be obstructed by evil ones he planted her (firmly as) a tree.
Ningublaga, heroic child of noble Sin,
plants it for Nanshe (straight as) a reed in (the face of potential) destructive claims (against) it.

May the lady of right utterance and inalienable divine powers,
may Nanshe be praised in all lands!

On the edge[18] of the year, the day of rites,
the lady poured water in the holy outside.
On the day when the bowls of allotments are inspected
Nanshe inspects the reviewing of servants.
Did not her chief scribe Nisaba
place precious tablets on (her) knees?
She took the gold stylus in hand.
For Nanshe she organized the servants in single file.
The skin-clad enters before her according to his skin;
the linen-clad passes before her according to his linen.
A skin-clad does not enter before her according to his skin,
a linen-clad does not pass before her according to his linen,
a person, registered and ... hired,
about whom eye or ear witnesses,
witnesses of his having disappeared from the house, have spoken,
is terminated in his position at 'the first (stroke) of the drum.'[19]
The king who inquires about the good servants,
Haya, man of tablets,
puts on clay the good servant of his lady who was mentioned,
deletes from clay the maid of his lady who was not mentioned.
Vases not pouring water, 'feet not proceeding straight,'
troughs of dough not cleaned,
fire having gone out in the house of night,
spells interrupted in the house of day —
her prebendary[20] who serves his term (and is responsible for these functions)
is terminated in his position.
When to a prebendary[21] serving his term as person of food allotments against whom a complaint was lodged,
or to a bishop who while living in the house (of Nanshe)
did not let the holy song and her concerns shine,
when to him — he may acknowledge it, he
may not acknowledge it — further allotting is denied,
then the rules of mother Nanshe are made to appear brightly.

No more than this word of words will be established,
nor added to this rule.
No one will superimpose any divine power on this divine power;
No one shall superimpose anything on it.
Superimposing will not enter the house of Nanshe.[22]

...

The ordeal river in the house of Nanshe clears a person.
After the decision has emerged from the holy song, the word of Abzu,
...[23]
(Even) a casually spoken (word), set in excess

[17] Or perhaps: "he kept track of these matters."

[18] ZÀ-MU (*zagmukku*) means "side," or "edge," or "border of the year." It is supposed to designate the New Year. Note, however, that grain rations of the "edge of the year" (ŠE-BA ZÀ-MU-KA) were recorded in Ur III Umma in months I (TPTS 1, 262), V (TENUS 390), VI (SET 175), VII (often, e.g. MVN 13, 191), VIII (SET 169), IX (TENUS 266), X (SET 170), XI (MVN 14, 195), XII (TENUS 372), XIII (Hirose Collection 357). As noted by M. E. Cohen, *The Cultic Calendars of the Near East* (1993) 17, and *KKU* 1:237, offerings for the festival of the 4th month, ITI-NISAĜ "First Fruit month," are designated as SÁ-DU$_{11}$ ZÀ-MU ^{d}ŠÁRA "regular offerings (of) the 'side of the year' (of) Shara" (SNAT 409). The administrative year of Umma in the Ur III period started with the harvest month (ITI ŠE-GUR$_{10}$-KU$_{5}$), yet several texts indeed mark off the year between the 3rd and the 4th month (e.g. YOS 4, 207). Considering the name First Fruit month, the local start of the year seems to have fallen between month III and IV, i.e. in July, so that in this case the "edge of the year" may indeed have been the New Year. The "edge of the year" in Nina is mentioned in the Hendursag hymn (D. O. Edzard and Cl. Wilcke, *Studies Kramer* 144, 28), as here without clue to its timing.

[19] This translation of BALAĜ is not secure. Cf. also line 41.

[20] The prebendary has the title ŠITA-AB-A.

[21] This prebendary has the title SUSBU (Akk. *susbû*).

[22] The transliteration in *JCS* 33 is inaccurate. The line should read as follows:

M [x x x x x]-UN-DIB-BA
T KAR-RA [x] LÚ MU-UN-X-BÉ
U [x x x L]Ú MU-UN-DIB-[x]
W KAR x x L[Ú] MU-U[N-x-x]

[23] D. Charpin, *Clergé* 389: "ENKUM et NINKUM choisissent les rites de purification."

on the lips,
135 will not be added to this word of words.[24]
Refusal and threats did not arise.[25]

A rapacious hand, stretching out a forceful hand,[26]
a hand that keeps up with the mouth,[27] committing violence,
(the case) that (someone) overturned an established line, (the incidence of) an altered demarcation,[28] [b]
140 going ahead[29] (when one should not) to a place of oath,
a first (loaf?) of 2 peck bread which was levied as tax, (of) 2 peck bread that had been distributed,[30]
(the case) that Small Stone lifted the hand for Larger Stone,[c]
that Small Peck lifted the hand for Larger Peck,[31] [c]
that (someone) wants bread who has bread,
145 that (someone) who just ate does not state "I ate,"
that (someone) who just drank does not state "I drank,"
(prompting one to say) "let me set a bowl before you, let me filter beer for you,"
a maid of the deity who was lazy, (and) rebuked (for it) by the house,[32]
an untrustworthy (person) who ... while living in the house,
150 when (a person responsible for any of the above) said "serve (me)! I want to eat,"
said "serve (me)! I want to drink,"
153 Nanshe does not allow the person to eat[33]
152 from bread of fat and white eggs because of the violation.

154 If the violator was allowed to eat he/(Nanshe) will not 'carry the word about it.'
155 With ... eyes, paralyzed mouth, shuffling feet,[34]
he does not fit in, he is no match:
the powerful one [ ] over a person,
the rich one in a reed hut by the street,
one with wife [gave] away his wife for a widow,
160 who laughed one day in his rage,
makes fun another day of his calamity.
Before the lady he cannot raise his ... word.
The lady, caretaker of the provinces,
Innin, mother Nanshe, sees into their hearts.

165 Getting the better[35] of an orphan, ... a widow,
placing a homeless man below a rich man,

b Deut 19:14; 27:17

c Lev 19:35; Deut 25:13-16; Amos 8:5; Mic 6:10; Prov 11:1; 20:10

[24] Cf. Gudea Cyl. A VII 3 according to which Nanshe, having instructed Gudea what do do on behalf of Ningirsu, predicts: TUR DU$_{11}$-GA-ZU MAH DU$_{11}$-GA-ÀM ŠU BA-A-ŠI-IB-TI "he will accept from you your 'small uttered' (word) as a 'large uttered' (word)," which means possibly that Gudea may say anything, even something insignificant, and it will be listened to as if it were something of importance.

[25] Cf. *ELS* 628-629.

[26] See note 4 above.

[27] Hand matched with mouth = skillful, experienced (said of the scribe who can write as fast as one talks) = routinely; or: who is prone to commit violence; quick to jump to action; premeditated. I.e., spoke about it (mouth) and did it (hand).

[28] The context of misdeeds of individuals does not suggest that the two actions in this line are major undertakings, as overturning a foundation (UŠ) would be. It may rather be the line (ÚS) of demarcation (see below) which determined a plot on a field. Nanshe was the "lady of the IN-DUB" (*FAOS* 9/2, 35 note 108). IN-DUB, and IM-DUB, are equated, among other things, with *palāku ša pilki* "to delimit, said of a division of land" or *šapāku ša epri* = "to pile up (said of dirt)." Combining both meanings, DUB may designate piling up and compacting of mud in a line of demarcation between plots. A more elaborate form of this is IM-DÙ-A DUB, the "built up," *pisé*, mud walls surrounding gardens (cf. *MSL* 1, 61:30).

[29] SAĜ-GÍD-I = *šarārum* SAG A I 24 (OB). *šarāru* = GÙ SUM *MSL* 1:77, 74 (K texts): NÍ IN-NA-TE-MA MU-DIĜIR-RA GÙ[GU] LI-BÍ-IN-SUM NAM-ÉRIM NU-UN-KU$_5$ = *iplaḫ-ma ana nīš ili ul išrur mamītam ul itma* — *CAD* s.v. *šarāru* suggests, for one group of references, the meaning "to go ahead." The present context suggests "to go ahead when one should not," in connection with the asseverative oath possibly "to perjure oneself."

[30] Jacobsen reads: SAĜ NINDA-2(BAN)-KA NÍĜ-KU$_5$ AK-A NINDA 2 (BAN) ÍB-TA-BA-A. He suggests that SAĜ designates here "weight adjustment" as in the Ur III wool weighing texts for which he has clarified the term. Assuming that the ban measure of the taxed person was smaller, for example ¾ that of the taxing authority, the weight adjustment would have been 5 quarts. If these 5 quarts were tax exempt, as Jacobsen suggests, the taxing authority would have encouraged tax payers to use small ban measures and harmed itself in the process. My translation implies that the temple taxed bread which it gave out as rations, thereby actually, but not nominally, reducing wages, and that this was seen as an unfair practice. A peck is 8 quarts while the Sumerian ban is 10 quarts.

[31] The occurrence of the dative requires that stone weight and peck were animate beings. The motif of a someone small edging on his larger companion is known from the demonic constables (GALLA) that pursue Dumuzi.

[32] (a) My old translation derived from equation with *lu*ʾʾ*tu*, Jacobsen's from *qâpu*, the new translation from *uṣṣulu* (*AHw* s.v. "gelähmt"), and is based on the assumption that the word does not just describe a person who cannot, but also one who will not, use the hands; lit., "with hanging hands." (b) Lit., "(on whom) word (was) returned from the house." É-TA INIM GI$_4$-A is also known from Gudea Statue B I 13-19: ÉNSI INIM BÍ-ÍB-GI$_4$-A ME [d]NIN-ĜÍR-SU-KA BA-NI-ÍB-LÁ-A SÁ-DU$_{11}$-NA É [d]NIN-ĜÍR-SU-KA-TA INIM HÉ-ÉB-GI$_4$ KA-KA-NI HÉ-KÉŠ "a governor who causes the word to return on them (the previously listed regular provisions for the upkeep of statue B)," i.e., ceases continuation of the endowment, and (thus) "subtracts from the power of Ningirsu — may the word from the house of Ningirsu be returned on his regular provisions."

[33] Lit., "at the place of violation." If the transfer from a spatial to a temporal meaning of KI + genitive + locative is not accepted, we must assume that KI designates the area of jurisdiction of Nanshe.

[34] SAG B 135f. KÌRI-HUM = *hu-um-mu-ṣu* and *ha-am-šu*. Both Akk. words are obscure.

[35] SAĜ-ĜÁ AKA = to act in/on/over a head = "to get the better of someone."

placing a rich man below a poor man,[36] [d]
a mother who screamed violently[37] at her child,
a child who spoke stubbornly[38] to its mother,
170 a younger brother who snarled at his older brother, talked back at the father — the lady, ...
Nanshe, ...
sees into the heart of the land as if it were a split reed.

...

175 Her herald, lord Hendursag, made the contracts for her.
Her angel Old Small Child did not let silence[39] come over it.
The demon, standing ..., watching ...
[ ] her house Sirara where water is sprinkled,

...

181 Did not the one adorned with the staff, trusted in Abzu's interior,
who has no opponent in the high temple[40] (and) house of Nanshe?
184 the king, lord Hendursag, bring forth
183 its command from the house of Nanshe?
185 Like heavy smoke it covers the ground.
Its word spreads over the sky as ... clouds.
The BULUG[41] of spouseship he ... together,
the king, lord Hendursag, he ... together.
He places a good person among good persons,
190 Hands over a bad person to a bad place.
He renders judgement for an orphan,
he also renders judgement for a widow,[e]
(and) he sets right the judgement of a child's mother.
If a mother shared food with her child,
195 shared[42] drink with it,
removed chaff[43] from its mouth:
(By her) whom its (the temple's) person of regular provisions seated by its (the temple's) side,
by its (the child's) mother, the firewood carrier did not pass with what he brought from the steppe, (and) he did not talk to (such a) mother who had given birth in the great city
200 with dry eyes and shrugging shoulders.

If a mother
screamed violently at her child,
a mother ripped its ...
(but) let it drink from her milk filled breast:
205 She, who searches the matter of that mother, searches the matter;
the lady of ...
When the king who loves things straight, Hendursag,
has set the issues straight (and) [x-ed] the eye on its judgement,
(if) he places the blame on the mother of the child,
210 she will not be able to bear the weight of heavy blame, and
such person will have no god to pray to.

If a mother did not share food with her child,
did not share drink with it,
did not remove chaff from its mouth:
215 (By her) whom its (the temple's) person of regular provisions did not seat on its (the temple's) seat,
by its (the child's) mother, the fire wood carrier passed with her share of what he brought from the steppe,
(and) he talked to (such a) mother who had given birth in the great city
with dry eyes and shrugging shoulders.
The king who hates violence, Hendursag,
220 treats such a human being as if she were water in a treacherous place,[44]
rejects her for that child as if she were barley in sterile/soil.
The lady who [determines] the destiny like Enlil,
230 [who] on the dais of Sirara,
has her eyes on her divine powers, the pure.
"Has not the house been granted divine powers from Abzu?"
The gods of Lagash assemble before her in Sirara.
The true stone for weighing silver, the setting

d Lev 19:15

e Exod 22:21; Deut 10:18, etc.

[36] The opposite is expected.

[37] Lit., "talked at her child with raised arm."

[38] KA-DÙ-A = *pûm waštum* (*MSL* 13:244). Cf. for possible alternative interpretations *ELS* 669.

[39] G̃IŠ-LÁ = *qūltu* "silence," or = *tuqumtu* "battle." The choice of the equation in this context is defended in my 1981 commentary. G̃IŠ seems to stand for two words that are distinguished morphemically in Emesal as MU or MU-UŠ. The first is the Emesal word, respectively spelling of the word, "wood," the second occurs as first element of G̃ÉŠTU and G̃IZZAL (Emesal II 183- 184 = *MSL* 4:24). G̃IŠ in G̃IŠ-LÁ = Emesal MU-UŠ (Ur Lamentation 101).

[40] I follow *AHw gegunû* for GI-GUN$_4$-NA. Accordingly it is the shrine on top of a ziqqurat. As Jacobsen notes, it was surrounded by trees. These are the trees that were planted, presumably in containers, on temple towers to give them the look of mountains.

[41] "The needle of matrimony" according to *PSD* 2:274; possibly related to Akk. *mulūgu*, Aram. *m^elôg*; see Levine 1968. [WWH]

[42] I assume that IN-TUK is a frozen form finite verbal form used as noun.

[43] IN-BU$_5$-BU$_5$ Proto Izi I 448 (*MSL* 13:31). BU$_5$ means "to blow," IN-BU$_5$-BU$_5$ "blowing straw," i.e., a product of winnowing, chaff. It consists mainly of bracts of flowers and glumes of the ears of grain. It was inevitable that the breeze that was necessary for winnowing dispersed these parts. I assume that at such occasions, but also at other times, a glume or bract, both of which are often hooked, could get into the mouth of a baby, and that mothers were judged on how they reacted.

[44] For more examples of this idiom cf. *ELS* 587. In the context of the prayer quoted there, the meaning suggested here fits well.

up the true basket,
the peck of true word she presents to all lands.
The shepherd, leader of the land, ... of the provinces,
Ishtaran who lives for straight judgments in the land,
... Ningishzida ...

My lady, your divine powers are great divine powers, are surpassing [(other) divine powers].
Nanshe, your divine powers are not matched by any other divine powers.
King An looks on with joy.
He who sits with Enlil on the dais of destiny determination,
Father Enki, has determined your destiny.
Nanshe, child born in Eridu, to praise you is good.

REFERENCES

Text: Heimpel 1981a. Translations and Studies: Jacobsen 1987a:125-142; Charpin 1986; Gomi and Sigrist 1991:81-95; *ELS*; *KKU*.

THE BLESSING OF NISABA BY ENKI (1.163)

(NIN-MUL-AN-GIM)

William W. Hallo

This hymn in honor of Enki, "the crafty god" (Kramer and Maier 1989), seems to commemorate his blessing of Nisaba, perhaps on the occasion of her (annual ?) visit, in the guise of her statue, to his sanctuary at Eridu. As the personification of both reed and grain, Nisaba was patron-goddess of both scribal art and agriculture, and both characteristics are celebrated in this hymn.

Oh lady, shining like the stars of Heaven,
holding the lapis lazuli tablet,
Nisaba, born in the great sheepfold by the divine Earth,
Wild kid nourished (as) on good milk with pure vegetation,
Mouth-opened by the seven flutes,[1] [a]
Perfected with (all) the fifty great divine attributes.
Oh my lady, the most powerful one in the Ekur —[2]

Dragon, emerging brightly on the festival[3]
Mother-goddess[4] of the nation,
biting off a piece from the clay,[b]
Pacifying the habitat with cool water,
Providing the foreign land with plenty,
Born in wisdom by the great mountain (Enlil),
Righteous woman, chief scribe of Heaven (An),
record-keeper of Enlil,
All-knowing sage of the gods —

In order to make grain and vegetables grow in the furrow,
So that the excellent corn can be marvelled at,
That is, to provide for the seven great throne-daises
By making vegetables shoot forth, making grain shoot forth,
At harvest, the great festival of Enlil,[5]
She in her great princely role has verily cleansed (her) body,
Has verily put the holy priestly garment on (her) torso.

In order to establish oblations where none existed,
And to pour forth great libations of wine
So as to appease X, to appease End[agara],
To appease merciful Kusu and Ezina,[6]
She will appoint a great high-priest,
will appoint a festival,
Will appoint a great high-priest of the nation.
Oh virgin Nisaba, he blesses you in prayer.

He has verily prepared the pure oblation,
Has verily opened the House of Learning of Nisaba,[7]
Has verily placed the lapis lazuli tablet on

a Prov 9:1

b Job 33:6

[1] Variants: counting-reeds; baskets. Perhaps an allusion to the "seven (branches of) learning" alluded to in some royal hymns (e.g. Shulgi C 30; Ishme-Dagan A 73), hence comparable to the "seven pillars of wisdom" (differently Greenfield 1985).

[2] The temple of Enlil at Nippur; became in Akk. a generic term for any temple (see CAD s.v. *ekurru*).

[3] Variant: in the assembly.

[4] Lit., Aruru. For this goddess and her maternal functions, see Wilcke 1976b:235-239; Hallo 1989. For the concept of (her) pinching off clay to create mankind, see *CAD* s.v. *karāšu, kiršu*.

[5] The entire line is a topos, or literary cliche, recurring in other contexts such as line 52 of "The Instructions of Ur-Ninurta" (Alster 1991; cf. below, text 1.177), line 60 of "The Disputation between Summer and Winter" (below, text 1.183), and line 164(a) of the myth of "The Marriage of Sud" (Civil 1983).

[6] Kusu is a purification goddess associated with the censer, Endagara or Indagra (if correctly restored) is her consort (and sometimes identified with Nisaba's consort Haya), and Ezina or Ashnan is the grain goddess. All belong in the circle of Nisaba. (Michalowski 1985:222; 1993:158f.).

[7] Temple of Nisaba at Eridu (and Uruk); later her shrine in the great temple of Marduk in Babylon. See George 1993:91 s.v. É-GESTU-[d]NISSABA.

(her) knee.
Taking counsel with the holy tablet of the heavenly stars,
(As) in Aratta he has placed Ezagin at her disposal,[8]
Eresh he has constructed in abundance.

She is created out of pure little bricks,
She is granted wisdom in the highest degree.
In the Abzu,[9] [c] the great crown(?) of Eridu,
(where) sanctuaries are apportioned,
[In ...], (where) offices(?) are apportioned,
The great princely plowman of the resplendent temple,
the craftsman of Eridu,
The king of lustrations,
the lord of the mask of the great high-priest,
Enki —

The Engur-house[9] when he occupies it,
The Abzu of Eridu when he builds it,
The Halanku[10] when he takes counsel in it,
The house of the box-tree when he fells it,
The sage when his hair is loosened behind him,[11] [d]
The House of Learning when he opens it,

c 1 Kgs 7:23; 2 Chr 4:2

d Judg 5:2; cf. Ezek 44:20

The door of learning when he stands in its street,
The great kettle-drum of cedar when he finishes(?) it,
The ... of date-palm when he perfects (var. holds) it
The drum of ... when he strikes it with the ... — [12]

On Nisaba, the great ..., he invokes seven [blessings(?)]:[13]
Oh Nisaba, (be) a righteous woman, a good woman,
a woman born in the mountain!
Oh Nisaba, in the stall may you be the fat!
In the pen may you be the milk!
In the treasure-house may you be the keeper of the seal!
In the palace may you be the honest steward!
May you heap up grain-piles (as large as) a mound,
grain-piles (as small as) a *māšu*-measure![14]

For the fact that a blessing was invoked on Nisaba by the Prince,
Oh father Enki, your praise is sweet!

Comparable lines already occur in Cylinder A of Gudea (xvii 15f.), and in "Enmerkar and the Lord of Aratta" 321 (text 1.170 below), where Jacobsen weighs a translation by "library" (1987a:301, n. 49).

[8] Lit., "lapis lazuli house" or "blue house," sacred to Nisaba at Eresh but to Ishtar/Inanna at Susa in Iran and at Aratta in Afghanistan(?), source of ancient lapis lazuli; cf. George 1993:158f. s.v. É-ZA-GÍN-(NA).

[9] Lit., "Sea," the temple of Enki at Eridu, sometimes compared to the "molten sea" of Solomon's temple; cf. *ABD* 5:1061f. s.v. "Sea, molten"; George 1993:65 s.v. (É)-ABZU. Also known as "House of the Sweet Waters"; ib. s.v. É-ENGUR.RA.

[10] Another name for Enki's temple at Eridu, or for "his room of taking counsel" there according to line 25 of the myth of "Enki and Ninmah"; see above, text 1.159, with note 12.

[11] This characteristic hairdo was later the mark of certain priests (see *CAD* s.v. *luḫšû*, *sigbarrû*) among others (Jacobsen 1988:127 and n. 13) and in Israel apparently of dedicated warriors.

[12] For these musical instruments in association with Enki, cf. S. N. Kramer, *ActSum* 3 (1981) 5:23.

[13] The restoration is based in part on the seven blessings of the foundations pronounced by Gudea in Cylinder A xx-xxi, although this interpretation of the Gudea passage has been questioned (Suter 1996a; 1996b).

[14] Translation follows *CAD M*/1:401c s.v. *māšu*.

REFERENCES

Text: Hallo 1970a. Translations and studies: Hallo 1970a; Alster 1976:119 and n. 31; Selz, 1989:495.

---

3. PRAYERS AND LETTER-PRAYERS

LETTER-PRAYER OF KING SIN-IDDINAM TO NIN-ISINA (1.164)

William W. Hallo

The genre of letter-prayer combines the format of a letter with the function of a prayer. It is attested first for private petitions in Sumerian, and then developed into a royal mode of communication with the divine, as here. Later examples of the genre occur in Akkadian and perhaps even in Hebrew, notably the "writing" or "letter" of Hezekiah in Isaiah 38. Like that letter, this one is concerned with royal illness; it is addressed to the healing goddess called "lady of Isin," patron deity of the kingdom of Isin, by a king of its chief rival, the kingdom of Larsa.

To Nin-isina, beloved daughter of lofty An (Heaven),
mistress of Egalmah,[1] speak![a]
To the chair-bearer of the Orient,
the counselor of the netherworld,
The beloved (chief) wife of the warrior Pabilsag,
the senior daughter-in-law of Ki'ur,[2]
The senior record-keeper of An and Enlil,
proudest of goddesses,
Who perfects the attributes of Duranki[3] in Nippur,
Who makes their exaltation appear in Egalmah,
the house of her queenship,
Who has founded (in) Larak the Enigingar (and) the (E)ashte,
the Esabad and the Esasumma,[4]
Great healer whose incantation is life,
whose spells restore the sick man,
Mother of the nation, merciful one,
who loves prayer and supplication,
My lady, say furthermore to her —
This is what Sin-iddinam, the king of Larsa, your servant, says:

Since the day of my birth, after you spoke to Utu[5]
(and) he gave me the shepherdship over his nation,
I do not neglect my duties, I myself have been unable to sleep sweetly,
I have sought health (in vain?).
For the gods greatly in my worship
I perform prayers and sacrifices,
I have withheld nothing from them.
(But) Asarluhi spends time (with) the king of Babylon,
the son of Ilurugu (the Ordeal-River) with [...].[6]
Their city against my city daily overruns the land,
Their king seeks out the king of Larsa as an evildoer.
(Though) I, not being the shepherd over their nation,
have not coveted(?) their sacrifices,
A young man stationed himself at my feet at night
in the guise of a dream,
He stood at my head, I myself saw his terrible glance,

a Isa 38:9-20

Carrying a river-oar(?), having cast a spell most evilly.[7]

Since that day, my manhood is not in order,
his hand has seized me.
There is no escaping from my fears by myself,
I am seized by an evil sickness.
My sickness is an unlit darkness, not visible to man.
The physician will not look upon it,
will not s[oothe?] it with a bandage.
The exorcists will not recite the spell,
assuredly my sickness has no diagnosis.
My sickness: its (healing) herb has not sprouted forth
on plain (or) mountain, no one gets it for me.
Healing my sickness is with you (alone),
let me declare your exaltation:
"As my [mother] has abandoned me since my childhood,
I am one who has no [mother],
no one recites my lament to you,
you are my mother!
Except [for you], I do not have another personal goddess,
no one pleads for mercy to you on my behalf.
No one seeks [for mercy?] from you for me,
you are my personal goddess!"

I am verily your constable (and) dog,[8]
I do not cease from being tied to you.
Damu, your beloved son:
I am verily his private soldier (and) weapon holder,
May you plead for mercy for me before him![9]
My sickness has been changed into (worse) sickness,
one does not know how to rectify it.
At midday I cannot be given any sustenance,
by night I cannot sleep.
May you be my very own mot[her?], holy Ninisina,
merciful lady!
With my not sleeping,
let me bring my wailing to you at night:
"Let me behold your favorable glance,
give me sweet life!
[As for me], like a bird fleeing from a falcon,

[1] Lit., "the lofty palace," chief temple of Nin-isina in Isin. This and subsequent temple-names are translated following George 1993, s. v.
[2] Lit., "the levelled place," the temple of Ninlil, whose son Pabilsag was Nin-isina's consort, at Nippur.
[3] "Bond of Heaven and Earth," temple of Inanna at Nippur.
[4] "The established chamber," "the throne house," "the house of the open ear" (or: "the grave"; cf. *CAD* s.v. *qubūru*), and ? respectively.
[5] Sun-god (equated with Akk. Shamash) and patron-deity of Larsa.
[6] Asarluhi is a deity of Kuara near Eridu, a son of Enki, and associated with both the deified Ordeal-River and Marduk, the patron-deity of Babylon.
[7] This difficult line occurs in only one exemplar.
[8] Variant: your little lap dog (lit. chair-dog). Perhaps an allusion to the iconography of Nin-isina (or Gula) enthroned on or beside her sacred dog.
[9] Damu is a healing deity, like his mother. There is an unpublished letter or "address by Nin-isina to Damu on behalf of Sin-iddinam" which seems like the veritable answer to Sin-iddinam's prayer! See Michalowski 1988:266; Keller 1991:310, n. 8.

I am seeking to save my life.
As for me, let me enter your lap in the face of Death,
save me from (its) hand!
I am a young man, I set up lamentation in the face of Death,
my life ebbs away from me."

Like a mother-cow, have mercy on me!
Like a [...], have mercy on me!
Like the mother who bore me,
who verily took me from the womb(?),
have mercy on me!
Hear the ..., (you who are) ill disposed toward the ....
Damu, your beloved son,
the great healer of Enlil,
He knows the plant of life,
he knows the water of life.[10]
[...] the command of the god who created me,
who [can change? it] against you?
Asarluhi, the son of Ilurugu, has verily spoken:
"Let him live!"

[10] The plant of life and water of life are familiar topoi from Sum. and Akk. myths and epics. Cf. e.g. lines 258-263 of "Lugalbanda in the Cave of the Mountain."

REFERENCES

Text: OECT 5:30 and duplicates. Translations and studies: Hallo 1976; Keller 1991; Michalowski 1988.

LETTER-PRAYER OF KING SIN-IDDINAM TO UTU (1.165)

William W. Hallo

Like the preceding letter-prayer, this one is written (as if) by Sin-iddinam, king of Larsa (ca. 1849-1843 BCE) to complain about illness and seek relief. But unlike the former, this one (a) deals with collective illness, (b) addresses Utu, the patron-deity of the dynasty, and (c) survives into Middle Babylonian times in a copy from Emar (Arnaud 1991 No. 101) and into neo-Assyrian times in a copy from Nineveh. The latter substitutes Babylon for Larsa and a royal name, now lost, for Sin-iddinam, and it is a bilingual, i.e., it adds an interlinear translation into Akkadian. But it remains recognizably the old text, and provides at least a chronological bridge to the comparable Biblical genre.

To Utu, my king, lord, senior judge of Heaven and Earth,[1]
Protector of the nation who renders verdicts,
Righteous god who loves to preserve people alive,
who hears prayer,
Long on mercy, who knows clemency,
Loving justice, choosing righteousness - speak!

To the bearded son of Ningal,
(who) wears a lapis lazuli beard,[2]
Opener of the locks of Heaven and Earth,
who makes the dark places bright,[3]
Lord who alone is a resplendent leader,
whose exaltation is unequalled,
Warrior, son born by Ningal,
who guards and gathers together the divine attributes,
Righteous god, prince who determines all fates,
father of the black-headed ones —[4]
say furthermore!
This is what Sin-iddinam, the king of Larsa, your servant, says.

The body of the letter includes a long complaint about the plague which has ravaged Larsa for seven (variant: five) years, protests the king's innocence and cultic fastidiousness, contrasts it with the godlessness of the Shimashkians from Iran who for all that have been spared, and prays for deliverance.

[1] This line, omitting at most "lord," is entered as an *incipit* in an OB catalogue of literary letters; see van Dijk 1989:444:13.

[2] As wife of the moon-god Nanna (Suen/Sin), Ningal was mother of the sun-god Utu (Shamash). The lapis lazuli beard helps show that the reference is to the deity in the form of a statue, with eyes, beard and other portions often inlaid in semi-precious stone such as the prized blue lapis lazuli imported from as far away as Afghanistan.

[3] For the sun-god as opening the locks of heaven by day and illuminating the netherworld by night, see *CAD* s.v. *namzaqu* and esp. Heimpel 1986.

[4] The conventional designation by which the Sumerians (and later the Babylonians) referred to themselves; see *CAD* s.v. *ṣalmāt qaqqadi*.

REFERENCES

Text: OECT 5:25:15-58 and duplicates. Translations and studies: Arnaud 1991:No. 101; Borger 1991; Civil 1996; Hallo 1982; Heimpel 1986.

---

4. LAMENTATIONS

LAMENTATION OVER THE DESTRUCTION OF SUMER AND UR (1.166)

Jacob Klein

Out of the five early Sumerian lamentations hitherto published, two laments commemorate the destruction of Ur, the capital of the Ur III empire. The Third Dynasty of Ur fell in the reign of Ibbi-Sin, its fifth king (ca. 2028-2004 BCE), as a result of a joint attack by the Elamites from the east and the Amorites from the west. The laments were composed not long after the events they record, probably at the initiative of one of the early kings of the Isin Dynasty, which inherited the hegemony over Sumer and began restoring the former capital. The purpose of these laments most probably was to soothe the heart of the city-god, Nanna, so that he allow the restoration of his temple, an undertaking which involved the razing and removal of the ruins of the old temple. The laments also were intended to ensure that the god would prevent the recurrence of the disaster in the future.[1]

The First Ur Lament, parts of which are translated below,[2] seems to have been dedicated to Ninlil, the wife of the city-god Nanna, for she is the dominant figure in the composition: She is pleading for her city in the divine assembly, where its destruction has been decreed; and she laments over it after its destruction. The Second Ur Lament,[3] on the other hand, seems to have been dedicated to the city god, Nanna, for in this poem he is the dominant hero; he pleads for his city to his father, Enlil, in the divine assembly, and when he is informed that his city is doomed, he abandons it, and enables the enemy to take over.

The First Ur Lament is a 436-line long, beautiful poem, divided into eleven cantos.[4] It opens with the enumeration of the major cities and temples of the land which were abandoned by their respective gods and and devastated (Canto 1). Subsequently, the poet addresses the city, uttering a bitter lament over it (Canto 2). Next, the goddess Ningal is introduced, pleading for her city to her husband, Nanna, and to the heads of the pantheon. In her plea she complains that the supreme gods, An and Enlil, doomed her city to destruction and refused to heed her prayer and to take back their decision (Cantos 3-4). At this point, the poet describes the invasion of Sumer by the enemy. On the mythological level, the enemy is described as a merciless "storm" sent by Enlil to destroy the city and annihilate its inhabitants; on the mundane level, we are informed of the attack of the people of Simashki and Elam, who tore down the city and the temple with their axes, slew or exiled its inhabitants, despoiled its treasures and disrupted its economic and cultural life (Cantos 5-6). Ningal flees from her temple like a bird flying away from her ravaged nest, and continues to lament over the city and its people, whom she calls "my beloved children" (Canto 7). Here the poet utters a call to Ningal to return to her abandoned city and temple, and to appeal again to the chief gods to stop the destruction and to put an end to the people's suffering (Canto 8). The lamentation ends with a passionate prayer to Nanna, the city god, that he return to his city and temple, and restore its ruins; that he accept favorably the offerings of the people and purify their hearts; and that he make sure that the destructive "storm" may never come back (Cantos 9-11).[5]

The Gods of Sumer Abandon their Temples (lines 1-6; 13-16; 37-39)

He has abandoned his stable, [a]
  his sheepfold[6] (became) haunted,[7]
The wild ox[8] has abandoned his stable,
  his sheepfold (became) haunted,
The lord of all lands has abandoned it,
  his sheepfold (became) haunted,
Enlil[9] has abandoned the shrine (of) Nippur,
  his sheepfold (became) haunted;
His consort, Ninlil, has abandoned it,
  her sheepfold (became) haunted,
Ninlil has abandoned their house, the Kiur,[10]
  her sheepfold (became) haunted ...

a Judg 6:13; 2 Kgs 21:14; Isa 32:13-14; Jer 12:7; 25:37-38; Pss 78:60-61; 94:14; Lam 2:7

[1] For a summary of the rise and fall of the Ur III empire, see Hallo and Simpson 1971:77-93. For a general survey of Mesopotamian lamentations, see Green 1975:277-371; Krecher 1980-83; Hallo 1995.

[2] See note 5 below.

[3] Michalowski 1989:36-69. See also Kramer, *ANET* 611-619.

[4] The Sum. term for canto or stanza is KI-RU-GÚ, lit., "prostration" (translated freely with Akk. *šēru* "song"). Each canto ends with a one or two-line refrain (Sum. G̃IŠ-GI$_4$-G̃ÁL).

[5] For a critical edition of the lament, see Kramer 1940:16-71. For additional duplicates, not incorporated in this edition, see Gadd and Kramer, UET 6/2 (1966) Nos. 135-139; Kramer and Bernhardt *TMH NF* IV (1967) Nos. 18-25. For translations into German and English, see Falkenstein and von Soden 1953:192-213; Kramer, *ANET*^{2} 1955:455-463; Jacobsen 1987a:447-477.

[6] In lines 1-38, the poet uses a widespread metaphor, likening the temples to stables and sheepfolds, their gods to shepherds, and the people to cattle (see line 38). The gods having abandoned the temples, these are destroyed and turned into ruins haunted by ghosts.

[7] Defective sentence, lacking the predicate, which appears only in line 37 below.

[8] An epithet of Enlil. Jacobsen translates "herder."

[9] The supreme god of the Sumerian pantheon. In the Second Ur Lament he is the one who decrees the destruction of Ur, and the transfer of its hegemony to Isin.

[10] The forecourt of Enlil's temple, where Ninlil's shrine was located.

Nanna has abandoned Ur,
his sheepfold (became) haunted,
Suen[11] has abandoned the Ekishnugal,[12]
his sheepfold (became) haunted;
(15) His consort, Ningal, has abandoned it,
her sheepfold (became) haunted,
Ningal has abandoned her Agrunkug,[13]
her sheepfold (became) haunted ...

Antiphone:
(37) His sheepfold became haunted,[14]
he is grievously groaning over it.
O cow, your lowing does not sound any more
in the stable, the stable does not
cause(?) joy(?) to the Prince![15]

Ningal Pleads for her City to An and Enlil (lines 137-151; 162-172)

"On that day, when that storm[16]
had pounded again and again,
When in the presence of the lady
her city was destroyed,[17]
On that day, when the storm had done(?)
it(?) again and again,
(140) When they[18] ordered the utter
destruction of my city,
When they ordered the utter
destruction of Ur,
When they gave instructions
that its people be killed —
On that day, I verily did not
forsake my city,
I verily did not neglect my Land;
(145) Truly I shed my tears before An,
Truly, I myself uttered supplication
before Enlil:[b]
'May the city not be destroyed!'
I said indeed to them,
'May Ur not be destroyed!'
I said indeed to them,
'May an end not be put to its people!'
I said indeed to them.[c]
(150) But An never changed that word,
Enlil never soothed my heart with that
'It is good; so be it!'...
Verily they gave instructions
that my city be utterly destroyed,
Verily they gave instructions
that Ur be utterly destroyed,
Verily they decreed its destiny
that its people be killed.[d]
(165) Me — in return for that
I gave them my food —
Me they verily also lumped with my city,
My Ur they verily also lumped with me.
An is never to change his word,
Enlil is never to alter
the word he utters!"[e]

Antiphone:
Her city has been destroyed in her face,
her offices vere alienated from her!

The Aftermath of the Destructive Storm (lines 208-228; 240-246)

On that day, the storm[19] was removed from
the city, and that city was in ruins.
O father Nanna, from that city,
all in ruins, it was removed —
the people groan!
(210) On that day, the storm was removed from the
Land, and that city was in ruins![f]
Its people like potsherds[20]
littered its sides.[g]
In its walls breaches were made -
the people groan!
In its high gates where they were wont to
promenade, corpses were piled,
In its boulevards, where feasts were
celebrated, heads lay in heaps(?),
(215) In its streets, where they were wont to
promenade, corpses were piled,
In its places where the country's dances
took place, people were stacked in heaps.[h]
The Land's blood filled all holes
like copper or tin,[21]
Their dead bodies melted away
of themselves, like sheep
fat left in the sun.
Its men who were slain with

b Jer 4:31; Lam 1:2, 16-17; 2:18-19
c Pss 74:19-22; 79:6-11; 83:11-14
d Lam 1:17; 2:1-3, 22
e Num 23:19; 1 Sam 15:29; Isa 40:8; 55:11; Jer 4:27-28; 23:20
f Jer 23:19-20; 25:32; 30:23-24; Amos 1:14; Ps 83:16
g Jer 8:2; 9:21; 16:4; Lam 4:2
h Lam 1:4; 5:14-15

[11] The Semitic name of the moongod Nanna.
[12] "The-House-which-Generates-Light-to-Earth" — Nanna's temple in Ur.
[13] "The-Pure-Storehouse" — Ningal's temple in Ur.
[14] Lit., perhaps "phantoms were placed in his/her sheepfold" or "his/her sheepfold was made into a phantom" (*CAD Z* 58-60, sub *zaqīqu*; Michalowski 1989:98). Others render: "his sheepfold has been delivered to the wind" (Kramer); "in his sheepfold he has had the wind settle" (Jacobsen).
[15] "The Prince" may refer to Nanna, the god of Ur, or to each and every deity mentioned in the preceding lament.
[16] It is assumed that "storm" is here a poetic-theological metaphor for the onslaught of the enemy and the destruction of the city. Further on (lines 173-204), the dispatch of this storm is ascribed to Enlil, and its horrible effects are vividly described. Since, however, the word for "storm" is the same as the word for "day" (Sum. UD), other renderings are possible. Jacobsen translates our line: "In those days, when such (disaster) was being conceived" (see note 31 below).
[17] If the text is not corrupt, than we have here a case of enallage: i.e. Ningal refers to herself exceptionally in the third person, as from a distance.
[18] That is the leaders of the pantheon, An and Enlil, and the assembly of the great gods.
[19] For this metaphoric use of "storm," see notes 16 and 31.
[20] Lit., "(although) not being potsherds."
[21] The poet probably refers to copper and tin ore filling the crevices, or else to melted copper and tin in molds (Jacobsen).

the axe, (their) heads were
not covered with a cloth.
(220) Like gazelles caught in a trap,
(their) mouths bit the dust.
Its men whom the spear had struck down
were not bound with bandages,
As if in the place where their
mother gave birth to them,
they lay in their blood.[i]
Its men who were brought to end
by the battle-mace, were not
bandaged with new(?) cloth
Although they were not beer drinkers,
they drooped neck over shoulder.
(225) He who stood up to the weapon,
was crushed by the weapon
— the people groan!
He who ran away from it,
was overwhelmed(?) by the storm
— the people groan! [j]
In Ur weak and strong
both perished in the famine,[k]
The old men and old women,
who could not leave the house,
were consumed by fire ...
(240) In the storehouses, abounding
in the land, fires were lit,
In its ponds,[22] Gibil,[23] the purifier,
relentlessly did (his) work.[l]
The lofty, untouchable mountain,
the Ekishnugal[24] —
Its faithful house is entirely
devoured by large axes.
The people of Simashki and Elam,
the wreckers, counted its worth
thirty shekels.[25]
(245) They tear down the faithful house
— the people groan!
They make the city a mound of ruins
— the people groan![m]

Ningal's Lament over her Ruined City (lines 254-274; 278-291)

Mother Ningal, like an enemy,
stands outside her city;
(255) The woman bitterly laments
over her ravaged house,
The princess bitterly laments
over her ravaged shrine (of) Ur:[n]
"An has verily cursed my city,
my city has verily been
destroyed before me!
Enlil has verily changed (the destiny)
of my house,[26] it has verily been
smitten by pickaxes!
On my ones coming from the south he
verily hurled fire; alas, my city
has verily been destroyed before me!
(260) Enlil — on my ones coming from
the north he verily hurled flames![o]
Outside the city, the outskirts of the city
were verily destroyed before me;
let me cry 'Alas, my city!'
Inside the city, the inner city was
verily destroyed before me;
let me cry 'Alas, my house!'[p] ...
(265) My city no more multiplied
for me like a fecund ewe,
its faithful shepherd is gone,
Ur no more multiplied for me like a
fecund ewe, its shepherd boy is gone,
My ox no more crouches in its stable,
gone is its oxherd,
My sheep no more crouches in its sheepfold,
gone is its herdsman.
In the river of my city dust has gathered,
it has verily been made into foxholes,[r]
(270) In its midst no flowing water is carried,
its tax-collector is gone.
In the fields of my city there is no grain,
their farmer is gone,
My fields, like fields devastated(?) by the hoe,
have verily grown tangled(?) weed,
My orchards and gardens, full of honey and wine,
have verily grown mountain thorn.
My plain, covered with its luxurious verdure,[27]
have become verily parched[28] like an oven[s] ...
(275) My silver, gems and lapis-lazuli
have verily been scattered about
— let me cry: 'O my possessions!'
My treasures the swamp
has verily swallowed up
— let me cry: 'O my possessions!'
(280) My silver - men who had never known silver
have verily filled their hands with it,
My gems — men who had never known gems
have verily hung them around their necks.[t]
My birds and fowl have verily flown away
— let me cry: 'Alas, my city!'

i Ps 79:3; Lam 4:14
j Ps 79:2-3; Lam 1:15; 4:9
k Deut 28:53-57; Lam 1:11; 2:11-13; 4:4-5, 8-10
l Ps 74:7-8; 79:17; Lam 1:13; 2:3; 4:11
m Ps 74:4-6; 79:1; Lam 2:1-2
n Lam 2:19-22
o Lam 1:13
p Deut32:25; Jer 14:18; Ezek 7:15; Lam 1:20
r Isa 34:13; Jer 9:10; 49:33; Ezek 13:4; Lam 5:18
s Isa 33:9; Jer 23:10; 51:21-23; Joel 1:10-12; Amos 1:2
t Lam 1:10; 4:1

22 Sum. A-NIĜIN.
23 The god of fire.
24 See note 12 above.
25 Lit., "made it thirty shekels" — that is treated it with contempt, or destroyed it easily. See Reiner 1968; 1980.
26 Or "has verily exchanged my house (with another)" (Jacobsen).
27 For GIRI_{17}-ZAL = *tašīltu*, *urqītu*, see Å. Sjöberg, *ZA* 55 (1962):3-4.
28 Or "cracked."

My daughters and sons[29] have verily been
carried off as captives in ships[30]
— let me cry: 'Alas, my city!' ...
[Woe is me! My city] which ceased to exist
— I am no longer its queen,
[Nanna], Ur which ceased to exist
— I am no longer its queen!
Upon the ruins into which my house
verily has been made, upon my city
which has verily been destroyed,
I, the faithful woman - in place of my city
a strange city verily has been built.[u]
Upon the ruins, into which my city
verily has been made, upon my house
which has verily been destroyed,
I, Ningal - in place of my house
a strange house verily has been built!

Curse against the Destructive 'Storm' (lines 388-392; 400-417)

Woe! Storm after storm swept the Land together.
The great storm of heaven, the ever roaring storm,
The malicious storm which swept through the Land[31] —
The city-ravaging storm, the house-ravaging storm,
The stable-ravaging storm,
the sheepfold-burning storm[v] ...
The storm which knows no mother,
the storm which knows no father —
The storm which knows no wife,
the storm which knows no child —
The storm which knows no sister,
the storm which knows no brother —
The storm which knows no neighbor,
the storm which knows no confidant[32] —
The storm which caused the wife to be abandoned,
the storm which caused the child to be abandoned
The storm which caused the Land to perish —
The storm which swept (through the Land)
at Enlil's hateful command —
O Father Nanna, may that storm
swoop down no more upon your city,
May your black-headed people
not see(?) it(?) (again)![33]
May that stormy day, like rain pouring
down from heaven, never recur!
That which smote all living beings of
heaven and earth, the black-headed people,
That storm — may it be entirely destroyed!
Like the great city-gate at night,
may the door be closed tight on it!
May that stormy-day not be placed
in the reckoning,
May its number be taken down
from the peg in Enlil's Temple![34][w]

Antiphone:
Unto distant days, other days,
to the end of the days!

Concluding Penitential Prayer to Nanna (lines 418-424; 430-436)

From days of yore, when the Land was founded,
O Nanna, the humble men,
who lay hold of your feet,
Have brought to you their tears
over the silenced temple, their
chanting (intoned) before you;[35]
May your black-headed people,
who have been cast away,
make obeisance to you,
In your city, which has been made into ruins,
may a wail be set up unto you!
O Nanna, may your restored city
radiate before you,
Like a bright heavenly star,
may it never be destroyed,
may it (always) walk in your sight! ...
May (your) heart relent toward 'the man'
who uttered a prayer for it![36]
And having looked faithfully upon
the 'man of supplication'
who stands here for it,
O Nanna, (you) whose penetrating
gaze searches the bowels,
May the hearts of its people
that committed evil,[37]
be purified before you![x]

u Isa 1:7; Jer 51:51; Hos 7:9; Lam 5:2

v Isa 13:6-10; Jer 23:19-20; 25:32; 30:23-24; Joel 2:1-3; Amos 1:14; Zeph 1:7; Ps 83:16; Lam 1:12

w Jer 20:14-18; Job 3:3-9

x Jer 33:8; Ps 51:12; Lam 5:21

[29] GI_4-IN (Akk. *ardatu*) is rendered (here and in the next line) as "young girls," "daughters"; it may refer to "slave-girls" (Jacobsen).

[30] Collation of the text points to ⌜má⌝-e.

[31] The Sum. word, translated in lines 388-414 as "storm," is UD, usually meaning "day," "weather." Hence, a translation like "stormy-day" would be more accurate (see below lines 409-413). Note further that the expression UD ... BA-E-ZAL-LA-RI, translated in this line as "The storm ... which swept over the land," may also be rendered: "A day ... which dawned." Accordingly, Jacobsen translates this line: "The griveous day that dawned for the country."

[32] The description of the storm in lines 400-404 resembles closely the typological description of various malicious demons in Sum. mythology (see Alster 1972b:104-106).

[33] Translation is based on the deletion of -ZU in IGI-ZU. Kramer translates, maintaining -ZU, as follows: "May you not look (unfavorably) upon your black-headed people!"

[34] Translation follows Jacobsen, who adds the following comment: "The days were thought of as personified and imbued with propensity for good or evil. Removing this (stormy) day from the reckoning, taking it out of the calendar, would mean that it never could be sent out again, would be totally destroyed" (1987a:473, note 36). Other possible translations: "May its (final) account hang on a peg in the house of Enlil" (Falkenstein 1953); or "May its account be hung from a nail outside the temple of Enlil" (Gragg 1973b:35; following Kramer 1940:69).

[35] The "humble man" who represents the people and brings their lament before the god may be the king or the high-priest.

[36] That is: for the city.

[37] Others: "that suffered evil" (Falkenstein and Jacobsen).

May the hearts of your (people) who dwell in the land be good to you!	y Pss 44:8; 74:21; 79:13	O Nanna, in your city again restored, may (your) praise be sung![y]

REFERENCES

Cohen 1981; 1988; Falkenstein and von Soden 1953:192-213; Green 1975; 1978; 1984; Gwaltney 1983; Hallo 1995; Hillers 1992:XXVIII-XXVIX; Jacobsen 1987a:447-477; Kramer 1940; 1991; Kraus 1968:8-13; Krecher 1980-83; McDaniel 1968; Michalowski 1989.

5. INCANTATIONS

A "NON-CANONICAL" INCANTATION (1.167)

William W. Hallo

Incantations were among the earliest literary genres to be fixed in writing. Before they were collected into major canonical series, they circulated in individual formulations, as needed. Sometimes, as here, these were quite short, and to the point, even specifying the source of the problem by name. The name of the client who used the spell was inserted at the appropriate point. The concern here is with the perennial problem of improper burial of a deceased person, which exposed his survivors to the danger of his ghost coming back to haunt them and — worse — to cause them to fall sick.

Moving about by day(?) like a cow in the midst of heaven, a fire(?) rained down from above, Lu-Sukkal, son of Gudea, descended alive into the midst of the watery deep.[1] [a] (5) "Let me not be made to descend!" let him not say before Utu!	*a* 1 Kgs 7:23 etc.	Let him not be one who returns to me! Of So-and-so son of So-and-so whose (personal) god is Enki, (10) and whose personal goddess is Geshtin-anna — [2] Let him not afflict the stomach![3] Conjuration, spell, incantation against colic.[4]

[1] I.e., he drowned; see *CAD* s.v. *apsû*. Alternatively: "into the inner sanctum of the temple"; see *CAD* s.v. *šapsukku* and above, text 1.163, n. 9.

[2] For the concept of the personal or protective goddess, see *CAD* s.v. *amalūtu* and esp. *ištaru*. Geshtin-anna, the sister of Dumuzi, is equated with Belit-seri in Akk.

[3] Alternatively: "distress the heart." There is a whole class of incantations for appeasing the "angered heart" of a deity (Lambert 1974), but here the reference is to distressing the client, and the words used carefully echo those in the "narrative" portion of the incantation (lines 1-4).

[4] So e.g. Cohen 1988:243, 17. Both ŠÀ-GIG in the rubric and ŠÀ-DIB in the text are translated by Akk. *kīs libbi*; see *CAD* s.v. *kīsu* B; the latter also by *muruṣ libbi*, "distress"; see *CAD* s.v. *murṣu*.

REFERENCES

Text: Gurney and Kramer OECT 5 (1976) No. 20. Translations and studies: Scheil 1927; Gurney and Kramer OECT 5 (1976) 31f.; Kutscher 1982.

FROM "EVIL SPIRITS" (1.168)

W. W. Hallo

The formation of systematic ("canonical") series of incantations began as early as Old Babylonian times in the case of the "Evil Spirits" (UDUG-HUL = *utukku lemnūtu*). Again, the concern was with improper burial and its baneful consequences. The present example is a brief incantation out of a reconstruction of second millennium forerunners running to nearly 1000 lines, and these in turn are vastly exceeded in size by the canonical versions of the first millennium.

Oh evil spirit, ghost appearing in the desert,
Oh Namtar, when you touch something evil,[1]
Oh tongue which in its malice binds a man to you,
May you be broken like a pitcher,[2]
may you be split like a measuring vessel!
May you not cross thorugh the door-frame
or over the door-sill!
May you not cross over the threshold(?)!
Oh evil spirit, to your desert!
Oh evil apparition, to your desert![3]
Oh (good ?) spirit dwelling in the house, ...
Oh personal deity,
May the evil spirit and the evil apparition,
like (sherds of) the potter's *burzi*-bowl,
be smashed in the square!
It is an incantation of the evil spirit.

[1] Generically a word for "destiny" or "fate," esp. an evil fate, hence "death," Namtar became a proper name for a demon or virtual "angel of death"; see *CAD* s.v. *namtaru*.

[2] The same image is used of Ur-Nammu, the king of Ur left for dead on the field of battle "like a broken pitcher" and thus perhaps the most famous example of potentially improper burial; see Kramer 1969a:118:59; 1969b:8 and n. 24.

[3] See *CAD* s.v. *alû*.

REFERENCES

Text: PBS I/2:128 ii 8-22. Translations and studies: Falkenstein 1931:87-89; Geller 1985:48-51, 511-522.

6. LOVE POEMS

DUMUZI-INANNA SONGS (1.169)

Yitschak Sefati

The three poems translated below belong to the Sumerian love poetry composed during the Third Dynasty of Ur and early Old Babylonian periods (ca. 2100-1800 BCE). This poetry which is mainly cultic deals with the love affair and marriage of the divine couple, the gods of love and fertility, Dumuzi (the Sumerian name for Tammuz) and Inanna (the Sumerian name for Ishtar). This symbolic marriage commonly known as the "sacred marriage rite" (*hieros gamos*) was believed, according to the Sumerian mythographers and poets, to bring about the fertility of the soil and the fecundity of the womb. It took place, apparently, during the New Year festival. The king, representing Dumuzi, wedded one of the priestesses of high rank, representing Inanna, the alluring fertility goddess. The questions whether the rite took place annually or only occasionally, and who actually represented Inanna during the celebration, remain unanswered.

As in most of Sumerian poetic works, the following poems are ascribed to their appropriate categories by the ancient poets themselves with a special subscript at the end of the composition, resembling the superscript of the biblical psalter. The first two poems are each designated as a "BALBALE (of Inanna)"; the exact meaning of this designation is still unknown, but it seems to indicate that these poems were to be recited, perhaps antiphonally, and heard during certain court or temple festivities. The third poem is designated as TIGI ("kettledrum"), a drum-accompanied hymn; it is subdivided into two sections bearing the labels SA-GÍD-DA and SA-G̃AR-RA, which seem to refer to the tightening or loosening of the skin of the percussion instruments or, if string instruments are involved, to the tuning of the strings (Sumerian SA).

THE WOMEN'S OATH (1.169A) [1]

This poem may be divided into two parts. The first and shorter part (lines 1-12) is in the form of an address (written in the main dialect of Sumerian called Emegir) by Dumuzi to Inanna, the "sister," consisting of epithets of endearment for his beloved. The second part (lines 13-32, written in the Emesal-dialect of Sumerian) consists of Inanna's response, the main point of which is asking her lover to swear that he had no love affairs with other women. The oath is administered by Dumuzi, placing his right hand on her genitals, laying his left hand on her head, bringing his mouth close to her mouth and taking her lips into his mouth. The poem concludes with the same motif with which it began, i.e., the metaphoric description of the beloved. But this time it is Inanna who extols her lover's charms.

Lover (lines 1-12)
My *lubi*,[2] my *lubi*, my *lubi*,
My *labi*, my *labi*, my honey of the mother who bore her,[a]

a Prov 4:3; Cant 6:9

[1] Source: Ni 2489 (*SRT* 31). Edition: Alster 1985:142-146; Jacobsen 1987b:60-63; Sefati 1990. Translation: Jacobsen 1987a:97-98; Kramer 1969c:104-106.

[2] The exact meaning of the words LABI/LUBI is uncertain. In view of the context they seem to be onomatopoeic terms of endearment.

My sappy vine,[b] my honey-sweet, my mellifluous mouth of her mother.

Your eyes — their gaze delights me, come[c] my beloved sister![d]
Your mouth — its utterance delights me,[e] my honey-sweet mellifluous mouth of her mother,
Your lips — their kiss delights me,[f] come my beloved sister!

My sister, your barley — its beer is delicious, my mellifluous mouth of her mother,
Your wort — its liquor(?) is delicious, come my beloved sister!

In the house — your charms [are irresistible], my mellifluous mouth of her mother,
Your charms, my sister, [are irresistible ...] my beloved,
Your house — the storeho[use ...], m[y mellifluous] mouth of her mother,
You, the Princess ... my ...

Girl (lines 13-32)
(You) who gave me life, (you) who gave me life,[3] you will take an oath to me,
Brother of the open country,[4] (you) who gave me life, you will take an oath to me,
You will take an oath to me that you did not lay hands on an alien (woman),
You will take an oath to me that you did not [...] (your) head on an alien (woman).
My one who dons(?) the fine garment for me,[5]
My beloved, the man of [my heart],
[I will make you] take an oath,[6] oh my brother[g] of [beautiful ey]es!
My brother, I will make you take an oath, oh my brother of beautiful eyes!

Your right hand on my nakedness should be placed,[7] [h]
Your left on my head[i] should be laid;
When you have brought your mouth close to my mouth,
When you have seized my lips in your mouth,
By so (doing) you will take an oath to me,
Thus is the "oath(?)[8] of the women," oh my brother of beautiful eyes!

My blossoming one, my blossoming one, sweet is your allure![j]
My blossoming garden of apple trees, sweet is your allure!
My fruitful garden of *celtis*-trees, sweet is your allure!
My(?) "Dumuzi-abzu by his own virtue"(?), sweet is your allure!
My pure figurine, my pure figurine, sweet is your allure!
Alabaster figurine, adorned with the lapis lazuli diadem, sweet is your allure!

(It is a BALBALE-song of Inanna)

b Ps 128:3
c Cant 2:10, 13
d Cant 4:9 et passim
e Cant 4:9, 10, 12; 5:1, 2
f Cant 4:3
g Cant 8:1
h Gen 24:2-9; 47:29
i Cant 2:6; 8:3
j Cant 1:4; 4:10

[3] "Giving life" here is perhaps to be taken as meaning "to bring joy," "to revive the spirit."
[4] It is assumed that the lover (Dumuzi) lives outside the city.
[5] The rendering of the line is uncertain. Perhaps better: "My one who raises the veil(?) of (my) nakedness for me."
[6] Lit., "I will set the oath for you."
[7] Cf. the comparable gesture in connection with oaths in the patriarchal narratives; see Jacobsen 1987a:98, n. 2.
[8] The reading of the Sum. sign is somewhat uncertain.

BRIDEGROOM, SPEND THE NIGHT IN OUR HOUSE TILL DAWN (1.169B)[1]

This poem is a monologue by King Shu-Sin's beloved in which she yearns for him with words of love and expresses her longing for him in requests and wishes. At the conclusion of the song (lines 27-29) there is apparently an invitation to sexual union but in language not adequately clear to us.

Bridegroom[2] of my heart, [my beloved] one,
Your allure is a sweet thing, [is as sweet as] honey;[a]
Dear(?)[3] of my heart, my beloved one,
Your allure is a sweet thing, is as sweet as honey.

You have captivated(?) me, of my own will(?) I will come to you,
Bridegroom, let me run after you to the couch;[b]
You have captivated(?) me, of my own will(?) I will come to you,
Dear(?), let me run after you to the couch.

Bridegroom, I will do to you all the sweet things,
My precious sweet, honey I will bring(?) to you,
In the bedchamber dripping with honey — [c]
Let us enjoy your sweet allure, the sweet things!

a Judg 14:18; Ezek 3:3; Pss 19:11; 119:103; Prov 24:13; Cant 4:11
b Cant 1:4
c Prov 7:17

[1] Source: Ni 2461 (*ISET* 1 90, pl. 32 = *Belleten* 16, pl. 66). Edition: Kramer 1952:360-363; Alster 1985:135-138; Sefati 1985:400-406. Translation: Kramer 1969c:92-93; Jacobsen 1976:171 (lines 1-15); Jacobsen 1987a:88-89; Alster 1993b:22 No. 11 (lines 11-17).
[2] The present rendering "bridegroom" here (as well as in lines 6, 9, 15 and 19) is based on the assumption that the Sum. MU-TI-IN (or perhaps MU-DÌ-IN) is a secondary form derived from the Emesal word MU-UD-NA (NITADAM in Emegir) "beloved, husband." However, MU-TI-IN could alternatively be viewed as a dialectal form of G̃EŠTIN, "grapevine, grapes," in Emesal. Or else, it could be interpreted as "man" (Akk. *zikaru*), see Jacobsen 1987a:88.
[3] The Sum. word GI-RU, which recurs here (in lines 3, 8, 13, 21 and 23) and elsewhere in similar contexts of the Dumuzi-Inanna songs as a parallel to MU-TI-IN (see the previous note), is most probably an epithet of affection for the lover, although its exact meaning and etymology is

Dear(?), I will do to you all the sweet things,
My precious sweet, honey I will bring(?) to you.
Bridegroom, you who have fallen in love with me,
Speak to my mother, (and) I shall offer myself to you,
(Speak) to my father, he will give (me to you) as a gift.

Soothing the reins,[d] the place which soothes the reins, I know,
Bridegroom, spend the night in our house till dawn.

Of your heart, its place which gladdens the heart,[e] I know,
Dear(?), spend the night in our house till dawn.
You, since you have fallen in love with me,
Dear(?), if only you would do to me your sweet things!

The lord my god, the lord my guardian-angel,
My Shu-sin, who cheers Enlil's heart,
If only you would do to me your sweet things(!)![4]
Your "place" (is) sweet as honey — if only you would lay hand on it!

Lay (your) hand upon it for me like a cap(?) on a measuring cup,
Spread(?) (your) hand over it for me like a cap(?) on an old measuring cup.

(It is a BALBALE-song of Inanna)

d Prov 23:16

e Ps 19:9; Prov 15:30; 27:9, 11

quite obscure.

[4] The translation assumes that the "place" (KI sign) preceding "your sweet" (ZÉ-BA-ZU) is most probably a scribal error for "things" (ÈM); cf. line 23. The terms "place" (line 27), and "hand" (lines 27-29), are apparently euphemistic expressions, and this closing passage seems to refer to an invitation to sexual union.

LOVE BY THE LIGHT OF THE MOON (1.169C)

This poem[1] is a dialogue between Inanna and Dumuzi/Ama-ushumgalanna, who woo each other as a young couple prior to their marriage.

The song opens with Inanna's monologue, in which she tells of her chance meeting with Dumuzi and about Dumuzi holding her hand and embracing her (obverse lines 1-8) when spending the previous day in song and dance. Then a dialogue with Dumuzi develops (obverse lines 9-22): Inanna, who is unusually portrayed here as a young and inexperienced maiden, pleads with Dumuzi to let her go home. Apparently she feared the angry reaction of her mother, Ningal, when the latter would realize that she had spent the night away from home in the company of a stranger. Dumuzi, who is revealed here as an enterprising suitor, teaches her "women's deceits"; in other words, he plants deceitful words in her mouth intended to justify her tardiness. Thus they will be able to make love together all night by moonlight. The beginning of the second part (obv. 24 - rev. 3) is highly fragmentary, and we do not know what happened between the couple. One cannot tell whether Inanna responded to Dumuzi's courting or whether, as is more likely, she refused to acquiesce to him like a prostitute, standing in the street. Instead she invited him to her home so that he would properly ask for her hand. When the text becomes intelligible (rev. 4-7), Inanna expresses the wish that Dumuzi turn aside to the gate of her mother Ningal's house where she, too, will joyfully run. Similarly, she expresses a wish (rev. 8-11) that her mother be informed of Dumuzi's arrival so that she would prepare the house for receiving this important guest and sprinkle water on the floor. The song concludes with praise (rev. 14-21), presumably by Inanna's mother, Ningal, for Dumuzi, the future son-in-law. She calls him "the son-in-law of Sin," who makes plants grow abundantly in the plain, and hence he is fit and worthy of Inanna's pure lap. It should be noted that but for the liturgical annotations therein, we would assume it to be a song of purely secular, literary character that was not connected with any cultic ritual but which served as a diverting song for women, to be hummed while they were spinning or weaving or engaged in other chores, in order to while away the time.

Inanna (obverse lines 1-12)
As I, the lady, was passing the day yesterday,
As I, Inanna, was passing the day yesterday,
As I was passing the day, as I was dancing about,
As I was singing songs (from) morning till evening —
He met me, he met me,
The lord, the companion of An met me,
The lord seized me in his hands,
Ushumgalanna[2] embraced me.
"Wild bull(?), set me free, that I may go home!
Companion of Enlil, set me free, that I may go home!
What can I set before my mother as false words?
What can I set before my mother, Ningal, as false words?"
Dumuzi (obverse lines 13-22)
"Let me teach you, let me teach you!
Inanna, let me teach you the women's false words:
'My girlfriend was dancing with me in the

[1] Source: HS 1486 (Bernhardt-Kramer, *TMH NF* III, No. 25). Edition: Kramer 1963:499-500; Sefati:1985, 209-217. Translation: Kramer 1969c:77-78 (obv. 1-22; rev. 4-17); Jacobsen 1976:28-30; 1987a:10-12; Alster 1993b:21-22. No. 10 (rev.6-14)

[2] Ushumgalanna is an abbreviated form of Ama-ushumgalanna, a by-name of Dumuzi.

square,[a]
She ran around with me, playing the tambourine and the recorder,
Her chants, being sweet, she sang for me,
In rejoicing, being sweet, I passed the day there with her' —
This as false words you set before your own mother,
As for us — let me make love with you[b] by the moonlight!
Let me loosen your combs on the pure and luxuriant couch!
May you pass there a sweet day with me in abundance and joy!"

(It is the *sagidda*)

Inanna (obverse lines 24 - reverse 13)
... I, the maid(?), in the alleys(?) ...
With the [wild bu]ll(?), by day, I ...,
(about eleven lines of the obverse and the first three lines of the reverse are broken away)
He is indeed standing at our mother's gate,[c]
I, in joy I am running around;
He is indeed standing at Ningal's gate,
I, in joy I am running around.
Oh, that someone would tell my mother!
May our neighbor sprinkle water on the floor![3]
Oh, that someone would tell my mother, Ningal!
May our neighbor sprinkle water on the floor!
Her dwelling[!] — its fragrance is sweet,
Her words (will) be joyful ones:

Ningal, Inanna's mother (lines 14-21)
"My lord is seemly for the holy lap,
Amaushumgalanna, the son-in-law of Sin,
The lord Dumuzi is seemly for the holy lap,
Amaushumgalanna, the son-in-law of Sin.
My lord, how sweet is your abundance!
How tasty are your herbs and plants in the plain!
Amaushumgalanna, how sweet is your abundance!
How tasty are your herbs and plants in the plain!"
(It is the *sagarra*. It is a *tigi*-song of Inanna)

a Cant 3:2
b Prov 7:18
c Cant 3:4; 8:2

[3] The exact significance of the neighbor sprinkling water is not clear. Alster (1993b:20-21 No. 10) interprets the act of the neighbor as a ritual for purification or apotropaic purposes, to secure happiness for the young couple.

REFERENCES

Alster 1985; 1993b; Civil 1990a; Jacobsen 1975; 1976; 1987a; 1987b; Kramer 1952; 1963; 1969c; Sefati 1985; 1990; Wilcke 1970.

B. ROYAL FOCUS

1. EPIC

ENMERKAR AND THE LORD OF ARATTA (1.170)

Thorkild Jacobsen

The story of Enmerkar and the Lord of Aratta begins in legendary times, before many of the inventions of civilization — such as written communication by letter. Enmerkar ruled in Uruk as "priest-king" (EN), and was the human husband of Inanna, with whom he united yearly in the rite of the sacred marriage. The lord of Aratta ruled in the fabled city of Aratta which lay in the mountains far away to the east. He also was the spouse of Inanna with the responsibilities for the city's prosperity. But Inanna, we are told, loved Enmerkar best.

Enmerkar used this to his advantage in attempting to force the submission of Aratta and the provision of precious stones and other building materials for a temple in Uruk. A drought was brought on the land of Aratta by Inanna. The lord of Aratta, after realizing his dilemma, challenged Enmerkar intellectually. Although the lord of Aratta posed a series of seemingly insurmountable problems, Enmerkar solved them each time. In one particular instance, when his message was too long for his envoy's memory, Enmerkar invented the letter for his envoy to take with him to Aratta. By accident, however, Ishkur (Inanna's brother) happened to bring rain to Aratta which ended the drought. At this the lord of Aratta celebrated and revealed the miraculous origins of his people. Though somewhat fragmentary, the story ends with Enmerkar listing his achievements.

[lines 1-134, omitted here]

Nudimmud's Spell (135-155)

Recite Nudimmud's spell[1]
to him:
"In those days,
there being no snakes,
there being no scorpions,
there being no hyenas,
there being no lions,
there being no dogs or wolves,
there being no(thing) fearful
or hair-raising,
mankind had
no opponents —
in those days
in the countries Subartu,[2]
Hamazi,[3]

a Gen 11:1

bilingual Sumer
being the great country
of princely office,
the region Uri[4]
being a country
in which was
what was appropriate,
the country Mardu[5]
lying in safe pastures,
(in) the (whole) compass
of heaven and earth
the people entrusted (to him)
could address Enlil,
verily, in but a
single tongue.[a]

In those days,
(having) lordly bouts,
princely bouts, and royal bouts —

[1] "Nudimmud's spell" quoted at this point in the tale seems gratuitous. It has no bearing on the situation, is mentioned only, is not repeated later on by the envoy, and plays no role whatever in the plot. Most likely it was a separate, independent myth added by some copyist who thought it might fit.

As it stands, it has been so severely abbreviated that it is difficult to determine either occasion or reason for the act of Enki/Nudimmud which it celebrates: that when mankind had one common language Enki replaced it with the present multiplicity of tongues. Presumably, since Enki is regularly presented as the protector of man — and very particularly so as Nudimmud, man's creator — this act of his will have served to shield mankind. One may conjecture, therefore, that a unilingual mankind somehow had become a threat or a nuisance to Enlil, so that he planned to wipe man out, a catastrophe averted by Enki's clever solution. This would put the story in line with the biblical story of the confusion of languages, where the building of the tower represents a threat to God, and with the myth of Atrahasis, where the noise made by proliferating mankind bothers Enlil to such an extent that he seeks recourse in sending the Deluge.

Here the mass of proliferating unilingual mankind's appeals to Enlil may have become too much for him and Enki, by instituting wars and by dispersing man by his confusion of tongues, will have forestalled a Deluge. See Jacobsen 1992.

[2] In modern terms, approximately northern Iraq.

[3] Not located with any certainty.

[4] The northern part of southern Mesopotamia. The Akk. term for it was Akkad.

[5] The region east of Mesopotamia, also called Amurru.

(did) Enki, (having) lordly bouts,
princely bouts, and royal bouts —
having lordly bouts fought,
having princely bouts fought,
and having royal bouts fought,
did Enki, lord of abundance,
lord of effective command,
did the lord of intelligence,
the country's clever one,
did the leader of the gods,
did the sagacious
omen-revealed[6]
lord of Eridu
estrange the tongues
in their mouths
as many as were put there.
The tongues of men
which were one."

[lines 156-497, omitted here]

The Letter Invented (498)
That day the words
of the lord [...]
seated on [...]
the seed of princes,
[a *mēsu* tree (?)]
grown up singly,
were difficult,
their meaning not to fathom,
and, his words being difficult,
the envoy
was unable to render them.
Since the envoy
— his words being difficult —
was unable to render them,
the lord of Kullab
smoothed clay with the hand
and set down the words on it
in the manner of a tablet.
While up to then
there had been no one
setting down words on clay,
now, on that day,
under that sun,
thus it verily
came to be;
the lord of Kullab
set down wo[rds on clay,]
thus it verily
came to be!

The envoy, like a bird,
was beating the wings,
like a wolf
closing in on a buck
he was hurrying
to the kill.
Five mountain ranges,
six mountain ranges,
seven mountain ranges,
he crossed over,
lifted up the eyes,
he was approaching Aratta;
and joyfully he set foot
in Aratta's courtyard.

His master's preeminence
he proclaimed,
and was decorously speaking
the words he had by heart,
the envoy was translating them
for the Lord of Aratta:
"It being that your father,
[my] master,
has sent me [to you,]
it being that the lord of Uruk,
and lord of Kullab,
has sent me to you ..."

The Lord of Aratta Interrupts
"What is to me
your master's wo[rds?]
What is to me
what he said further?"

"My master — [what] did he say?
what did he say further?
My master,
[des]cendant (?) of Enlil,[7]
grown as high as [...]
abutting [...]
the [... of ...]
who is outstanding
in lordship and kingship,
Enmerkar, son of Utu,
has given me a tablet.
When the Lord of Aratta
has looked at the clay,
and understood from it
the meaning of the words,
and you have told me
what you have to say to me
about it,[8]
let me unto the scion
wearing a lapis lazuli beard,
unto him who was horn
by his sturdy cow(-mother)
in the highland

[6] The accepted candidate for the office of EN was revealed by the taking of omens.
[7] Enlil would be Enmerkar's great-grandfather as father of Suen, the moon god, who in turn was father to Enmerkar's father, Utu.
[8] The messenger addresses the lord of Aratta with his titles and in the third person as a matter of politeness. Thereafter he changes to second person.

of immaculate offices,
unto him who was reared
on Uruk's[9] soil,
unto him who was suckled
with milk
at a good cow's udder,
unto him, who befits
lordship in Kullab,
country of great sacred office,
unto Enmerkar,
son of Utu,
in the Eanna close
announce that message,
in his *gipāru*,
bearing flowers
like the new shoots
of a *mēsu* tree,
let me report
to my master
the lord of Kullab."

After thus he had been telling him,
the Lord of Aratta took
the envoy's piece of clay.
The Lord of Aratta
looked at the clay.
The words were fierce words,
were frowning,
the Lord of Aratta
kept looking
at his piece of clay —

Ishkur Brings Rain

That day
did the crowned lord,
fit for lordship,
Enlil's son,
Ishkur,[10]
the thunderer
of heaven and earth,
the whirling storm,
the great lion,
see fit to come by.
The mountains were shaking,
the mountain ranges
roaring with him
in laughter.
As they met his awe and [g]lory
the mountain ranges
lifted their heads
in delightful verdure,
and on Aratta's parched flanks,
in midst the mountains,
wheat was sprouting of itself,
and vines also were sprouting of themselves.
The wheat, that had sprouted of itself,
they [piled] in piles and heaps
and bro[ught] it in
to the Lord of Aratta,
piled it up before him
in Aratta courtyard.

Rains Attributed to Inanna

The Lord of Aratta
took a look at the wheat,
and in front of all his overseers
was twitting the envoy,
the Lord of Aratta
said to the envoy:
"Most magnificently
Inanna,
queen of all lands,
has not abandoned
her home, Aratta,
has not delivered it up
to Uruk
has not abandoned
her lapis lazuli house,
has not delivered it up
to the Eanna close,
has not abandoned
the mountain
of immaculate offices,
has not delivered it up
to Kullab's brickwork,
has not abandoned
the ornate bed,
has not delivered it up
to the *girin*-flowered bed,
the lord,
her one of the clean hands,
she has not abandoned,
has not delivered him up
to the lord of Uruk,
to the lord of Kullab!
Aratta, right and left,
has Inanna,
queen of all lands,
surrounded for him
as with the waters
of a mighty
burst of a dam.

Miraculous Origins of Aratta's People

Its men are men
chosen from out of men,
are men whom Dumuzi
picked out from men,
they carry out
holy Inanna's commands,
alert champions,
house born slaves of Dumuzi,
they verily are,
Inanna, queen of all lands,

[9] Most likely an ancient scribal mistake for "Aratta's."
[10] The storm god Ishkur usually counted as Inanna's brother and grandson of Enlil, so "son" may here stand for "grandson."

for great love of Dumuzi,	and subjected the country
sprinkled them	to them.[11]
with the water of life,	

[11] A section of the text was apparently lost here in the course of its transmission.

REFERENCES

Jacobsen 1987a:275-319; 1992.

GILGAMESH AND AKKA (1.171)

Dina Katz

The short narrative describes a conflict between two Mesopotamian cities Kish and Uruk. Akka, the ruler of Kish, demanded of the Urukeans to dig wells. Gilgamesh, Akka's dependent lord of Uruk, determined to rebel, ignored the advice of Uruk's assembly of elders and, with the support of his army, freed Uruk from the dominance of Kish and established himself as the independent ruler of Uruk. The copies of this composition, written in Sumerian, date to the Old Babylonian period, and most of them were found in Nippur.[1]

Introduction: Geographical Setting (Lines 1-2)
Akka,[2] the son of Enmebaragesi, sent envoys
From Kish to Gilgamesh, to Uruk.

a 1 Kgs 12:6-15

Gilgamesh Delivers Akka's Message to the Assembly of Elders and Calls on them to Rebel (Lines 3-8)
Gilgamesh, before the elders of his city
Laid the matter, seeking for words:
(5) "To finish the wells, to finish all the wells of the land,
To finish all the shallow wells of the land,
To finish all the deep wells with hoisting ropes,[3]
Let us not submit to the house of Kish
    let us smite it with weapons"

b 1 Kgs 22:26 (The king's son "ben-hamelech") 2 Chr 18:25; 28:7; Jer 36:26

c Isa 2:22

The Elders' Assembly Rejects Gilgamesh's Decision to Rebel (lines 9-14)
The convoked assembly of his city's elders
(10) Answered Gilgamesh:
"To finish the wells, to finish all the wells of the land,
To finish all the shallow wells of the land,
To finish all the deep wells with hoisting ropes,
Let us submit to the house of Kish
    let us not smite it with weapons."

Gilgamesh Does Not Give up and Turns to the Young, Able-bodied, Men (lines 15-23)[4]
(15) Since Gilgamesh, the lord of Kulaba,
Had placed his trust in Inanna,
He did not take to heart the words of his city's elders.[a]
Gilgamesh before the able-bodied men of his city again
Laid the matter, seeking for words:
(20) "To finish the wells, to finish all the wells of the land,
To finish all the shallow wells of the land,
To finish all the deep wells with hoisting ropes,
Let us not submit to the house of Kish
    let us smite it with weapons."

The Young, Able-bodied, Men Decide to Rebel (line 24-29)
The convoked assembly of his city's able-bodied men answered Gilgamesh:
(25) "As they say: to stand up, and to sit down,
To protect the king's son,[b]
And to hold back[5] the donkeys,
Who has breath for that?[6] [c]
Let us not submit to the house of Kish

[1] For the most recent discussion, see Katz 1993.

[2] The reading Akka rather then Agga is supported by some manuscripts which have A-KA or AKA. This name is prevalent in Early Dynastic Fara texts; see Jacobsen 1939:84, n. 99.

[3] This passage, repeated in the speeches of the elders and the able-bodied men, probably contains Akka's demand, since otherwise the reason for this war does not appear in the composition. The verb "finish" is a literal translation, meaning to "drain dry"; however, other translations are possible.

[4] The literary pattern used here, a parallelism between assemblies, one of elders and other of the young, is comparable to the episode narrated in 1 Kgs 12:6-16; see Malamat 1963; Falkenstein 1966. Note that in both cases turning down the advice of the elders and following the advice of the young is justified by divine will.
  Whereas the elders' assembly is widely documented in the Mesopotamian sources, an assembly of young (or able-bodied men) is not attested. Therefore, the assembly of the able-bodied men may have been created here as a fictional literary device to parallel the actual elders' assembly. Through this parallelism Gilgamesh's rebellion seem to have the public's legitimation, in addition to the support he supposedly had from the goddess Inanna. For a detailed discussion, see Katz 1993:23-27.

[5] Or "to spur on."

[6] These three lines constitute a proverb; see below text 1.174 number 1.

let us smite it with weapons.

The Able-bodied Men Nominate Gilgamesh as King (Lines 30-39)
Uruk, the handiwork of the gods,
Eanna, the temple descended from heaven
Whose parts the great gods created,
Its great wall standing on the ground (like) a cloud,
Its lofty abode established by An,
They are entrusted to you, you are king and warrior.[7]
One smashing heads, a prince beloved of An,
His coming would inspire such fear
That its (Kish's) army will dwindle, and scatter in retreat,
And its (Kish's) men be unable to confront him."

The Preparations for the War against Kish (Lines 40-47)
Then Gilgamesh, the lord of Kulaba,
His heart rejoiced at the words of his city's able-bodied men, his spirit brightened.
He said to his servant Enkidu:
"Now let the implements and arms of battle be made ready,
Let the battle mace return to your side,
May they create great fear, terrifying splendor,
That when he comes my great terror overwhelm him,
That his wits become confused[d] and his judgement falter."

The First Confrontation with the Kishite Army (Lines 48-59)
Not five days, not ten days had passed,
When Akka, the son of Enmebaragesi, (and his army) laid siege to Uruk.
Uruk's wits were confused,[d]
And Gilgamesh, the lord of Kulaba,
To its warriors said:
"My warriors, you look alarmed,
(but) let one stout of heart stand up (and say) 'I will go to Akka.'"
Birhurture, his royal bodyguard,
Praised his king (and said):
"I will go to Akka,
That his wits become confused[d] and his judgement falter."
And Birhurture went out through the city gate.

The Second Confrontation with the Kishite Army (Lines 60-83)
As soon as Birhurture went out through the city gate,
They captured him at the entrance of the gate,
And gave Birhurture a thorough beating.

d 1 Sam 21:14; Ps 34:1

e 2 Kgs 9:24

He was brought before Akka,
And to Akka he spoke,
(but) before he had finished speaking the cup-bearer of Uruk mounted the wall
And peered out over the wall.
Akka saw him,
And said to Birhurture:
"Slave, is that man your king?"
"That man is not my king!
Were that man my king.
Were that his dreadful brow,
Were those his bison eyes,
Were that his lapis lazuli beard,
Were those his delicate fingers,
Would not multitudes be cast down, multitudes be raised,
Would not multitudes be smeared with dust,
And would not all the foreign troops be overwhelmed,
Would the mouths of the land not be filled with dust,
Would the prows of the ships not be cut,
And would Akka, the king of Kish, not be taken captive in the midst of his troops?"
They hit him, they strike him,
And give Birhurture a thorough beating.

The Actual War (Lines 84-99)[8]
After the cup-bearer of Uruk, Gilgamesh climbed up the wall,
The terrifying splendor overwhelmed young and old of Kulaba.
It made the able-bodied men of Uruk take up the battle mace,[e]
And throw wide open the city gate's doors.
Enkidu went out through the city gate alone,
Gilgamesh peered out over the wall.
When he looked, Akka saw him (and said to Enkidu):
"Slave, is that man your king?"
"That man is indeed my king (Enkidu answered)."
Just as he (Enkidu) said that,
Indeed multitudes were cast down, multitudes were raised,
multitudes were smeared with dust;
And indeed all foreign troops were overwhelmed,
The mouths of the land were filled with dust,
The prows of the ships were cut,
And Akka, the king of Kish, was taken captive in the midst of his troops.

Gilgamesh Acknowledges his Dependence on Akka in the Past (Lines 100-106)
Gilgamesh, the lord of Kulaba,
Said to Akka:
"Akka my lieutenant, Akka my captain,

[7] The last five lines are understood as a formula for nominating a king. They are partly repeated at the end of the narrative by Akka in his speech acknowledging Gilgamesh as an independent king of Uruk.

[8] For a discussion of the historicity of the composition and the literary traditions concerning the war, see Katz 1993:11-21.

(102a) <Akka my governor, Akka my general,>
Akka my Army commander,
Akka, you have given me breath, Akka you have given me life,
Akka, you have taken the refugee on your lap,[f]
Akka, you have nourished the fleeing bird with grain."

Akka Endorses the Independence of Uruk and Gilgamesh its Ruler (Lines 107-114)
(Akka:) "ʿUruk, the handiwork of the gods,
Its great wall standing on the ground (like) a cloud,
Its lofty abode established by An,
They are entrusted to you. [Repay me m]y favor!"
(Gilgamesh:) "By Utu, I now repay you the former favor."
He set Akka free (to go) to Kish.
Gilgamesh, lord of Kulaba,
Praising you is sweet.

f Num 11:12

REFERENCES

Cooper 1981; Edzard 1959; Falkenstein 1966; Heimpel 1981b; Jacobsen 1970a; 1970b; 1987a:345-355. Katz 1987; 1993; Klein 1976; 1983; Kramer 1949; Lambert 1980; Malamat 1963; Michalowski 1982; Römer 1980; Vanstiphout 1986; 1987a.

---

2. ROYAL HYMNS

THE BIRTH OF SHULGI IN THE TEMPLE OF NIPPUR (1.172)

Jacob Klein

This hymn[1] is part of a rich corpus of Neo-Sumerian "royal hymns" pertaining to Shulgi (ca. 2094-2047 BCE), the second and most important king of the Third Dynasty of Ur.[2] The hymn is dedicated to Enlil, the supreme god of the Sumerian pantheon, and it falls into two main parts: the first part opens with a hymnic praise of Enlil, which is followed by a description of Shulgi's birth and investiture in the Ekur temple; the second part contains blessings and prayers on behalf of Shulgi and the capital city of Ur, both hailed as generous providers of the temple. A three-line epilogue to the hymn reiterates Shulgi's selection by Enlil for a good reign.[3] The hymn was no doubt composed during Shulgi's reign, on the occasion of Shulgi's coronation in Nippur. Subsequently, it may have been put to periodical use in the cult. From the point of view of the history of religion, it is of particular interest that whereas in the first part of the hymn Shulgi is invested with royal insignia, in the second part he fulfills the function of high-priest (EN), offering Enlil and Ninlil their evening meal.[4]

Prologue: Praise to Enlil (lines 1-8)
Enlil, the eminent one, the sovereign (god),
whose utterance is trustworthy,
Nunamnir, the eternal shepherd of the Land,
who hails from the Great Mountain,
The great counselor, the leader of heaven and earth,
who is in control of all the divine offices,
The lord who in accordance with his nobility is laden
with awesome splendor, a perfected heavenly star,
He who takes care of the primeval divine offices,
the choice divine offices, who alone is the lofty god,
The lord, the life-giving light, who guides the multitudes
in a single track, to the whole extent of the earth,
The huge net, spread over heaven and earth,
a rope, stretched over all the lands —
Who ever gave Enlil instructions,
or who ever rivalled him?

[1] The following translation covers only about the first half of the hymn; the rest of it is fragmentary and cannot be fully translated (see Klein 1991:304).

[2] For the Sum. "royal hymns" in general, see Hallo 1963; Römer 1965. For the Shulgi hymns, see Klein 1981a:36-49; 1981b:1-21. For a full edition of the above hymn, see Klein 1991.

[3] Our hymn is designated by the scribe as an ADAB. ADAB-hymns are basically divine prayers. As a rule, they begin with a hymnal address to a deity; the central part of the hymn recounts the divine blessings bestowed upon the king; the hymn usually ends with a three-line prayer to the deity for the king. [The two major parts and the epilogue of our hymn are designated respectively by the following common cultic rubrics: SAGIDDA ("stretched string"), SAGARRA ("loosened string") and URUNE. For these generic subscripts and cultic rubrics, see Wilcke 1975: 252-262].

[4] Apparently Sum. kings, and especially deified kings, could claim the prerogative of high-priesthood, which they exercised on certain cultic festivals or other special occasions. Cf. Ps 110:3-4; 2 Sam 6:14; 1 Kgs 3:4.

The Oracle Predicting Shulgi's Birth (lines 9-14)
He (= Enlil) uttered a great (statement). What is that
which his heart, "the mighty river," has carried?
The hidden(?) plans[5] of his holy word
he brought out from the temple.[a]
That matter is a holy matter, it is a pure matter,
it concerns the offices of the Ekur —
The true cornerstone, (embedded) in the bottom of the deep —
something most precious:
"A 'faithful man' will rebuild the Ekur
(to earn) a lasting name;
The son of (that) 'faithful man' will long hold the scepter,
their throne will not (ever) be overthrown!"[6] [b]

Shulgi's Birth (lines 15-20)
To that end, Ashimbabbar[7] "shone"(?) in the Ekur,
He pleaded(?) with his father, Enlil,
he approached(?) the mother who gave(?) birth(?) to him,[8]
In the "good house" made Nanna,
the noble son, (his) request,
(And) the high-priestess gave birth to a "faithful man,"
from (the semen) which had been placed in her womb.
Enlil, the powerful shepherd,
caused the young man to appear,
A child, most suitable for kingship (and) throne-dais —
it was king Shulgi![9]

Shulgi's Coronation (lines 21-27)
"A lion's seed, who provides the 'highland' generously,
the belo[ved of Nin]lil,
He who was granted authority in the Ekur,
the king of Ur,
(He of) the radiant heart, the shepherd,
the (protective) spirit of the Land" —
gave(?) him(?) (Enlil) as his good name.[10] [c]
Enlil chose Shulgi in (his) pure heart,
he entrusted the people to him.
The lead-rope and the staff he hung on his arm —
he is (henceforth) the shepherd of all the lands.[d]
The immutable scepter of Nanna he placed in his hand,[e]
Upon a royal seat, which may not be overthrown,
he let him raise (his) head heavenward.[f]

Shulgi's Praise of Enlil (lines 28-30)
The day is a blessing, the night is an enchantment,[11]
The Land is a (peaceful) pasture;
Shulgi, the "shepherd of prosperity," he of the lasting name, the "king of the festival,"
The mighty one, the seed engendered by
"a faithful man," praises Enlil.

a Isa 2:3; Mic 4:2

b Gen 15:1-6; 2 Sam 7:4-17; Isa 9:5-6

c Isa 9:5-6

d 2 Sam 5:2; 7:7; Isa 44:28; Ps 78:70-72

e Gen 49:10

f 1 Kgs 2:12; 3:6; 9:5; Pss 2:8-9; 45:7; 110:2-3, 5; 1 Chr 29:23

[5] Sum. LAL-GAR = Akk. *gišḫuru* "plan," "design" etc.

[6] In lines 9-14, the poet refers to a divine plan uttered by the god Enlil and announced in the temple in the form of a Delphian oracle: a "faithful man" will restore the Ekur; as a reward, he will acquire a successor who will secure the continuation of his dynasty. The identity of this successor, namely Shulgi, is revealed in the following passage, which describes his birth in the temple; hence, the "faithful man" must be Ur-Nammu, the founder of the dynasty. The above oracle and the subsequent semi-mythological birth-episode were intended to affirm Shulgi's legitimate right to the throne in view of the political crisis that arose with his father's untimely death in battle, and Shulgi's young age at the time of his coronation.

[7] Epithet of the moon-god Nanna.

[8] I.e., Ninlil, Enlil's wife.

[9] The above birth-episode is beset with philological difficulties, and scholars disagree as to its religious and historical background. According to one opinion, Shulgi was engendered on a high-priestess of the moon-god Nanna in Nippur, in the image of Enlil, during the celebration of the "sacred marriage" rite, in which king Ur-Nammu himself embodied Nanna, the divine bridegroom (Jacobsen, *ZA* 52 [1957], 126-127, note 80; reprint in Jacobsen 1970:387f.). According to another opinion, it is Enlil who engendered Shulgi on his divine spouse, Ninlil, upon the request of Nanna (Kramer, *Iraq* 36 [1974] 93-94). Both of these hypotheses run counter to Ur III royal literature, which consistently mention Lugalbanda and Ninsun as Shulgi's divine parents. According to a third opinion, a major purpose of the "sacred marriage" rite was the engendering of the crown-prince and accordingly Shulgi was engendered in the Ekur, by Ur-Nammu and his first wife, the queen (Hallo 1987:48-52). In our opinion too, Shulgi's birth, in this hymn, takes place only on the human level, ignoring his otherwise professed divine parentage. His birth is requested from Enlil and Ninlil by his city-god, Nanna, and is engendered by Ur-Nammu, his human father, in the temple, on a high-priestess (Klein 1987:101-105).

[10] The long "name" given by Enlil to the new-born crownprince is actually a series of poetic, ad hoc, royal epithets, including the real political title "King of Ur."

[11] The poet seems to stress the bliss and harmony that prevailed on the day of Shulgi's birth and/or coronation.

REFERENCES

Hallo 1963; 1987; Klein 1981a; 1981b; 1987; 1991; Römer 1965; Wilcke 1975:252-262.

THE SACRED MARRIAGE OF IDDIN-DAGAN AND INANNA (1.173)

Thorkild Jacobsen

This hymn was apparently written under Iddin-Dagan, the third king of the dynasty of Isin, for he is mentioned by name in it. It may even be that it was meant for use at the yearly rite of the sacred marriage in which the king took on the identity of the god Ama-ushumgal-anna and as such married Inanna, who was almost certainly incarnated in the reigning queen, as shown by the epithet Nin-egala(k), "queen of the palace," by which she is called in connection with this rite.

The hymn opens with an address to the goddess as morning and evening star followed, in a second canto, by a statement of her powers of office in heaven, on earth, and in the Apsû. From these introductory matters the hymn then moves, with the third canto, into a description of a monthly ritual victory parade in her honor, celebrating her as warrior and goddess of war.

The parade is made up of cult personnel in her service and groups of guards, both of these groups representing warriors and acting out war games in which they cut themselves and each other with knives. In the parade march also young men in neck stocks representing captives, and young and old women who have curled their hair like harlots. They may represent camp followers or women whose providers have fallen in battle and who have had to turn harlots to survive. Beside the parade, or possibly as part of it, march solid citizens of the town, carrying harps and other implements designed to soothe and pacify the goddess.

The end of the sixth canto leads into a new section praising the goddess in her manifestation as the evening star; as such she marks the end of the workday and the quieting down and going to rest of all, men and animals alike. As they sleep, their dream souls appear before her with their requests, and Inanna discerns who is good, who evil.

With the ninth canto the hymn changes its image of the goddess from evening to morning star, and describes the morning offerings to her by people everywhere. Finally, with the tenth canto she is celebrated as the bride in the new year rite of the sacred marriage, in which the king — here Iddin-Dagan-incarnates the bridegroom, Ama-ushumgal-anna — and she, as mentioned, in all likelihood is embodied in the queen. The preparations for the wedding are described, the setting up and readying of the wedding bed, the bride's pre-nuptial bath, the consummation of the marriage, and the magnificent wedding banquet the next morning.

The hymn closes with an envoi with repeated praise of the goddess ending "Great she is, and august, in heroism surpassing." [a]

Proem: Star-rise

The one come forth on high,
the one come forth on high,
I will hail!
The [h]oly one,[1] come forth on high,
I will hail!
The great [queen] of heaven,
Inanna,
I will hail!
The pure torch lit in the sky,
the heavenly light, lighting like day,
the great queen of heaven, Inanna,
I will hail!
The holy one,
queen awe-laden
of the Anunnaki,
noblest one in heaven and earth,
crowned with great horns,[2]
oldest child of the Moon,[3]
Inanna,
I will hail!

Of her grandeur, of her greatness,
of her exceeding nobility,
of her brilliant coming forth
in the evening sky,
of her lighting up in the sky,
a pure torch,
of her stepping up onto the sky
like Moon and Sun,
noted by all lands from south to north,
of the greatness of the holy one of heaven,
to the young lady I will sing!

FIRST PLACE OF COUNTERING[4]

"Her coming forth is (that of) a warrior"

a Ps 45

[1] The Sum. term NU-GIG means lit., "sacred"/"taboo" person. It designates a class of women the function and character of which is not clear. Inanna belonged to this class and typified the women belonging to it. The badge of these women was inlaid with the gems called SHUBA.

[2] The horned crown was an emblem of divinity.

[3] The text treats the moon as divine, as the moon god ^{d}Suen. We translate "Moon" to retain the cosmic implications. Similarly we render ^{d}Utu as "Sun."

[4] The cantos of the composition are — as usual with Sum. antiphonal works — marked off by the nubric "place of countering," and the countering antiphon that follows has at the end the rubric "is its antiphon." In this composition antiphons are specifically indicated only after the first and the eighth cantos. Presumably that means that the first antiphon was to be repeated after each successive canto until, with the eighth canto, the second antiphon replaced it and served to the end.

(is its antiphon)

Powers of Office
She likes wandering in the sky,
being truly Heaven's wild cow,
on earth she is noble, queen of all lands,
in the Deep,[5] in Eridu, she took office,
her father Enki conferred it on her,
laid to her hand lordship and kingship.
With An she has taken her seat
on the great throne dais,
with Enlil she will be making
the decisions for her country.
Monthly, at new moon,
that the offices be carried out properly,
the country's gods gather unto her.
The great Anunnaki, having bowed to her,
are stepping up for prayer, petition, and plaint,
able to voice unto her
the pleas of all lands,
and Milady decides the country's cases,
settling them.
[Inanna] makes the decisions
for the country,
having them carried out.
The dark-headed people[6]
are parading before her.

SECOND PLACE OF COUNTERING

Warrior: Monthly Ritual Triumphal Parade
Algar-instruments,[7] silver inwrought,
they are beating for her,
— before holy Inanna, before her eyes,
they are parading —
The great queen of heaven, Inanna,
I will hail!
Holy tambourines and holy kettledrums
they are beating for her,
— before holy Inanna, before her eyes,
they are parading —
The great queen of heaven, Inanna,
I will hail!
Holy harps and holy kettledrums
they are smiting for her,
— before holy Inanna, before her eyes,
they are parading —
The oldest child of the Moon,
Inanna,
I will hail!

THIRD PLACE OF COUNTERING

The guardsmen[8] have combed
(their hair) for her,
— before holy Inanna, before her eyes
they are parading —
they have made colorful for her
the back hair with colored ribbons,
— before holy Inanna, before her eyes
they are parading —
on their bodies are (sheep)skin (robes)
(the dress) of divinities,[9]
— before holy Inanna, before her eyes,
they are parading —
Fine men, eminent ladies,
the doyenne ot the women sages,
— before holy Inanna, before her eyes
they are parading —
who hold harps and calming instruments,
march beside them.
— Before holy Inanna, before her eyes,
they are parading

They (themselves) are girt
with implements of battle,
— before holy Inanna, before her eyes,
they are parading —
spears, the arms of battle,
are in their hands,
— before holy Inanna, before her eyes,
they are parading

FOURTH PLACE OF COUNTERING

Their right arms are clothed with cloth
in male fashion,[10]
— before holy Inanna, before her eyes
they are parading —
the great queen of heaven, Inanna,
I will hail!
On their left arms they have pulled
the cloth down and off
(63a) — before holy Inanna, before her eyes
they are parading —
(63b) the great queen of heaven, Inanna,
I will hail!
Playfully, with painted buttocks,
they engage in single combat
— before holy Inanna, before her eyes,
they are parading —
the oldest child of the Moon,

[5] The deep (Apsû) refers to the freshwater ocean which the ancients thought underlay the earth, thus forming a triad with the heaven and earth of the preceding lines. It was the domain of Enki, who resided in Eridu, and it surfaced there in Enki's temple and the nearby marshes. A separate myth tells how Inanna received her offices from Enki in Eridu by taking advantage of his generosity when he was in his cups (see text 1.161).

[6] The Sumerians referred to themselves as "the dark-headed people." Why, and in contrast to whom, is not known.

[7] A musical instrument, most likely a small harp with the sides of the sound box covered with drumheads.

[8] The term translated "guardsmen" is the Sum. SAĜ-URSAĜ, which denotes a class of cult personnel in the service of Inanna. Originally apparently a corps of warriors, they developed into actors in ritual performances such as the one here.

[9] The precise meaning of this is not clear. Conceivably by the time the poem was written the old sheepskin mantles, were no longer in common use but were still shown on representations of gods.

[10] This is a reversal of normal usage. Both men and women covered the left shoulder; women also frequently kept both shoulders covered. Leaving the right arm and shoulder bare gave the right arm needed freedom. The significance of the reversal here described is not clear.

Inanna,
I will hail!

FIFTH PLAGE OF COUNTERING

(Captive) lads in neck stocks
bewail to her (their fate)
— before holy Inanna, before her eyes,
they are parading —
maidens and crones, curling the(ir) hair (as harlots)
— before holy Inanna, before her eyes,
they are parading —
daggers and clubs rage before her
— before holy Inanna, before her eyes
they are parading —
the *kurgarû*'s[11] mounted (on chariots),
swing the clubs
— before holy Inanna, before her eyes,
they are parading —
gore is covering the daggers,
blood sprinkles,
— before holy Inanna, before her eyes,
they are parading —
in the courtyard, the (place of) assembly
of the temple administrators,[12]
they are shedding blood,
(as) loudly resounds there
(gay music of) TIGI-harps, tambourines, and lyres.

Inanna as Evening Star

The holy one has seen fit to step up
lone on the clear sky,
and on all lands, teaming
like the nation's dark-headed people,
from heaven's midst Milady
looks kindly down.
August is the queen, the evening star, Inanna.
Fitly (therefore) they praise the maiden Inanna.
August is the queen, the evening star, Inanna,
unto the borders of heaven!

SIXTH PLACE OF COUNTERING

Nightfall
The evening star, the brilliantly rising star,
shedding great light over holy heaven,
the queen, the evening star, has seen fit
to come forth on high,
warrior-like in the sky,
and in all lands the people
are lifting up their faces toward her,
the man is cheering up, the woman is
brightening,
the ox in its yoke is turning the head (homewards),
sheep and goats (?) (shuffling back)
make the dust settle (thick) in their folds.
The numerous (wild) goats and asses of Shakan,[13]
the animals of the desert,
the far-flung four-footed beasts,
the orchard pits, the garden beds,
the green canebrake,
the fish of the deep, the birds of heaven,
Milady is making wend their way
to their lairs.
(All) living beings, the numerous people,
are bending (their) knees to her.

Called by Milady, the old women
are providing plentifully
for great eating and drinking.
(Then) Milady calms down
everything in her country,
the playgrounds of the nation,
the holiday makers;
and the young brave
holds converse with the wife
heart (to heart).[14]

From heaven's midst Milady
looks kindly down,
before holy Inanna, before her eyes,
they walk —
August is the queen, the evening star in the skv,
Inanna.
Fitly (therefore) they praise the maiden Inanna.
August is the queen, the evening star in the sky
unto the borders of heaven!

SEVENTH PLACE OF COUNTERING

Preeminent in the (rose-)tinted sky
the alluring one, befitting broad heaven,
has risen like moonlight at night,
has risen like sunlight at high noon.
Having imposed sweet sleep
on the nation's homes,
— while all lands, the dark-headed ones,
the nation in its entirety,
sleep on roofs, sleep on city walls —
eloquent dream-soul afflati step up to her,
bring her their cases.

Then she discerns the righteous one,
discerns the wicked one.
The wicked one she will hand over

[11] The KURGARÛS, likewise cult personnel, also appear to have been warriors originally. The term may be abbreviated from KURGUGARA "the subjected lands" so that the KURGARÛS symbolized warriors taken captive.

[12] The Sum. term means "the gathering of ENs." Since EN basically denotes "productive manager" and since it forms part of the names for a great many professions of workers on an estate, farmer, head of the plowing teams, cook and baker, washermen, etc., we take "the gathering of ENs" to mean specifically an assembly of administrators in which work plans and other matters relating to the successful functioning of an estate would be discussed and agreed on.

[13] God of goats, gazelles, and wild asses.

[14] A literary stereotype. The quiet talking the day's events over by husband and wife takes place in bed after the day's work is over, for it is almost the only time they have to themselves.

to (serve) a wicked sentence,
the evil one she will do evil to.
On the just one she looks truly,
determines a good fate for him.
From heaven's midst Milady
looks kindly down.
Before holy Inanna, before her eyes,
they walk.
August is the queen
hovering where heaven is founded,
Inanna.
Fitly (therefore) they praise
the maiden Inanna.
August is the queen
going (down) where heaven is founded
unto the borders of heaven!

EIGHTH PLACE OF COUNTERING

Dawn: Inanna as Morning Star

The queen preeminent, the alluring one of heaven,
has seen fit to come out, warrior-like, on high,
lovely is she at An's[15] radiant side,
with An on his august couch
she holds converse heart (to heart).[16]

"May she be found to be
the young brave's and the warrior's only one!"

(is its antiphon)

She is mighty! She is noble! She is elevated to high rank!
Great she is and august, surpassing in heroism!

(is what is sung at its middle)

The queen marveled at by the nation,
the lone star, the morning star,
the queen hovering where heaven is founded,
has seen fit
to come forth warrior-like on high,
and all lands do tremble before her.

Morning Rites

The dark-headed people get up for her.
the young brave traveling the road
sets his course by her,
the ox lifts up its head eagerly
in its yoke.
While at the same time, in the nation's homes
they provide everything aplenty,
hasten to holy Inanna,
and put it out in goodly fashion
for Milady (up in) heaven's midst.

In the clean places, the clear places
of the desert,
on the roofs, on the wall-tops,
[of the dwellers on] wall-tops,
on mankind's smoothed-out spots (for offerings),
they bring her incense
(fragrant) like a cedar forest.
Fine sheep, maned sheep, and grain-fed sheep
they offer up.
For the holy one they clean up a place,
set up handwashing (things) for her.[17]

Ghee, dates, cheese, seven kinds of fruits,
they fill as breakfast,
onto the country's table for her.
Dark beer they pour for her,
light beer [they pour] for her.
With dark beer and [emmer] beer ....
for Milady with (barley) beer and [emmer] beer
SHAGGUBBE-pot[18] and the fermenting vat
bubble, one as the other.
Of paste, liberally enriched with honey and ghee,
and of honey and dates, on cakes,
they make loaves for her,
wine at dawn. Finely ground flour,
honeyed flour,
honey and wine at sunrise they libate for her.
The tutelary gods of the humans step, as their part,
up to her with the food and drink,
and the holy one eats in the pure places,
the clean places.

From heaven's midst Milady
looks kindly down,
before holy Inanna, before her eyes,
they wander.
August where heaven is founded,
is the queen, Inanna.
Fitly (therefore) they praise
the maiden Inanna.
August is the queen
hovering where heaven is founded
unto the borders of heaven!

NINTH PLACE OF COUNTERING

New Year's Sacred Marriage: Inanna as Bride

In the palace,
the house that advises the country
and is a (restraining) yoke[19]
on all foreign lands,

---

[15] I.e., heaven's.

[16] The morning star appearing in the sky is seen as the goddess chatting in bed with the god of heaven before getting up. The line may reflect a momentary lapse into a variant theology which saw Inanna as the wife of An rather than of Dumuzi/Ama-ushumgal-anna. We assume that the term KIMAH, "high place," later used for sepulcher, originally denoted simply a dais on which one would place one's bedding and sleep. We translate it therefore as "couch."

[17] For washing her hands before eating the offerings.

[18] Apparently a vessel used in brewing. Its precise character and use are still to be determined.

[19] Lit., a neck stock.

the house that is the river ordeal[20]
of the dark-headed people,
the nation in its entirety,
a dais has been founded for Ninegalla,
the king, being a god, will sojourn with her on it.

That she may take in charge
the life of all lands,
has on New Year's Day,
the day for rites
for reviewing loyal servants[21]
and performing correctly
the rites of the last day of the month,
a bed been set up for Milady.
Halfa-straw they have been purifying
with cedar perfume,
have been putting it on that bed for Milady.
Over it a bedspread has been pulled straight for her,
a bedspread of heart's delight
to make the bed comfortable.

Milady bathes in water the holy loins,
for the loins of the king
she bathes them in water.
For the loins of Iddin-Dagan
she bathes them in water.
Holy Inanna rubs (herself) with soap,
sprinkles the floor with cedar perfume.

The king goes with (eagerly) lifted head
to the holy loins,
goes with (eagerly) lifted head
to the loins of Inanna.
Ama-ushumgal-anna goes to bed with her:

"O my holy loins! O my holy Inanna!"

After he on the bed, in the holy loins,
has made the queen rejoice,
after he on the bed, in the holy loins
has made holy Inanna rejoice,
she in turn soothes the heart for him
there on the bed:

"Iddin-Dagan, you are verily
my beloved!"

Wedding Banquet
To pure libations, lavers set up,
to gently wafted incense vapors,
to lighted juniper incense,
to food portions standing ready,
to jars standing ready
into his august palace
she enters with him.
His loving consort has the arm
around his shoulders,
holy Inanna has the arm around his shoulders.
shines forth on the arm-lean[22] throne
like the dawn.
With her radiates there, on the long side of the table,
sunlike the king.
Abundance, delicacies, plenty,
they bring straight to her,
a banquet of sweet things
they lay out,
the dark-headed people
bring it straight to her.
The bard has the lute,
that gives tongue from the podium,
the sweet-sounding ALGAR-instruments,
and the lyre, which belongs
where mankind is gay,
prove themselves
in his song of joy of heart.

The king has reached out for food and drink,
Ama-ushumgal-anna has reached out
for food and drink.
The palace is in festive mood,
the king is joyous,
the nation spends the time amid plenty,
Ama-ushumgal-anna is come in joy,
long may he live on this pure throne!
On the royal throne dais she has
(her) head on (his) shoulder.

Envoi
O Milady, you are given praise
to the borders
of heaven and earth!
You being a holy one,
engendered with heaven and earth,
holy passages, pure passages
for a holy one
are put in song!
O (you), chief ornament of the night,
befitting the assembly,
Inanna, oldest child of the Moon,
Queen, evening star, to praise you is sweet!

TENTH PLACE OF COUNTERING

From heaven's midst Milady looks kindly down —
before holy Inanna, betore her eyes,
they walk.
August is the queen, the evening star,
unto the borders of Heaven!
Mighty she is, noble, elevated to high rank,
great she is and august,
in heroism surpassing.

[20] The river ordeal was used as a means to arrive at a divine decision in cases where there was, or could be, no decisive evidence. In metaphoric use, as here, it implies superhuman power to get at the truth and judge rightly.

[21] New Year's Day was a day for reviewing the work of the staff of a temple or estate.

[22] A chair with armrests was comfortable, and so suitable for a throne. Such chairs, used as divine or royal thrones, are often pictured on the monuments.

(is its antiphon)		A song of valor pertaining to Ninsianna.[23]

[23] A name for Inanna as morning and evening Star, it means "heaven's radiant queen."

REFERENCES

Jacobsen 1987a:112-124.

C. INDIVIDUAL FOCUS

1. PROVERBS

SUMERIAN PROVERB COLLECTION 3 (1.174)

*Bendt Alster**

This collection of Sumerian proverbs is known from 40 duplicating cuneiform tablets, most of which come from Nippur, and they (i.e., the tablets, not necessarily the proverbs) date ca. 1900-1800 BCE. As is the case with other major Sumerian proverb collections, this one is known from fragments of multicolumn tablets inscribed with a complete collection, as well as from tablets only containing excerpts. In addition, single entries or very short excerpts are found on small school tablets. These sometimes contain the teacher's handwritten master copy with the pupil's imitated copy, and sometimes lexical or mathematical exercises on the reverse.[1] Yet the proverbs or sayings were unquestionably used for instruction beyond the technical skills of cuneiform writing. The origin of the phrases was not uniform, but many of them were undoubtedly genuine proverbs, that is, anonymous phrases at home in the spoken language and recognized as such by a group of speakers. The daily activities of secular life are in focus rather than those of religion and cult. Unlike the biblical proverbs, there is no clearly expressed concept of "wisdom" embedded in the collections, nor is a clear compositional or ideological principle apparent. Since in origin true proverbs belong to situations arising in a spoken language, they are unsystematic and may well be contradictory, and they are not expressions of coherent philosophical thinking. It was their pregnant linguistic formulation combined with the implicit support of the authority of tradition that made them useful for didactic purposes. In this function, the Sumerian proverbs, like those of other cultures, represent a rather conservative type of social view that basically advises people to remain in the social groups where they belong in society.[2]

1. To stand up and to sit down, to spur the donkeys,
to take care of the king's son,
who has the breath for that?[3]
2. The nurse glances toward the parapet
as if she were a child of the king's.
3. No matter how much water one draws,
the swamps (where it comes from) will still provide water to drink.
4. Unpleasant DULDIN-plants grow toward the good field.
5. Since you are a TIRIGAL-bird, I feed you.
Since you are an TIRIGAL-bird, I give you something to drink,
you are my son, your luck has changed.[4]
6. "Let me go today" is what the herdsman says,
"let me go tomorrow" is what the shepherd boy says,
but "let me go" is "let me go," and the time passes.
7. Possessions are close to the wind.
The ITERDUM-milk, although it is no river mud, cleaves the ground.[5]
8. To serve beer with unwashed hands,
to spit without trampling upon it,
to sneeze without covering it up with dust,
to kiss with the tongue at midday without providing shade,
are abominations[6] to Utu.

9a. The shepherd his penis, the gardener his hair-do.[7]

9b. The unjust heir who does not support a wife, who does not support a son, is not raised to prosperity.[8] [a]

10. Because the shepherd departed, his sheep did

a Prov 11:29

* Some Sum. terms whose exact identity is unknown, such as the DULDIN-plant, the TIRIGAL-bird, and ITERDUM-milk, have not been translated.

1 Cf. Gordon's edition of Collections 1 and 2: Gordon 1959.

2 Cf. Alster 1993a.

3 This saying is quoted in the Sum. Epic tale Gilgamesh and Akka, lines 25-28 (see text 1.171). Cf. below, text 1.175 nn. 1f.

4 It may be assumed that the sound produced by the TIRIGAL-bird reminds of the Sum. words for "I feed you" (ERIBGUE), as well as for "I give you something to drink" (ERIBNAGE). However, the implication of the saying as a whole remains obscure.

5 This apparently hints at cracks that appeared on top of the milk presumably used for cheese production.

6 The Sum. term for "abonimation", NÍG-GIG, also means what is "sacred" to a someone, or "reserved" for someone, especially a god. Cf. Geller 1990. As used in the proverbs, it can be used simply as a synonym for "misconduct, offense, or aberration," but it can also relate to the "sacred and inviolable nature of deity"; cf. Hallo 1985; Klein and Sefati 1988. They translate the fourth abomination by *lehizdawweg* "to copulate"). For other "abominations," see Nos. 118, 161, 168-171, 175 below.

7 A pure guess is that this means that the sexual manners of the gardener were considered more civilized than those of the shepherd.

8 A first millennium BCE translation reads as follows: "A man who does <not> support a wife, a man who does <not> support a son, is

not come back into his custody.
11. Because the clever shepherd got confused, his sheep did not come back into his custody.[b]
12. The herdsman in his weariness cannot recognize his own mother.
13. As long as you have light, grind the flour.
14. The wild bull has detestation for the plough.
15a. To eat modestly does not kill a man, but coveting murders.
15b. To eat a little is to live splendidly. When you walk around, keep your feet on the ground!
16. As long as he is alive, he is his friend. When he is dying, he is his nether-world deputy.[9]
17. Friendship lasts only one day, but the relations of colleagues are eternal.
18. Quarreling belongs to the place of colleagues.[10] Slander finds its way to the place of purification.
19. When travelling a man does not get tired of eating. He picks up food till the end of the day.
20. There are bitter tears in human flesh.
22. A hand will be stretched out toward a hand stretched out. A hand will be opened toward an open hand.
23. He who has money is happy, he who has grain feels comfortable, but he who has live stock cannot sleep.
24. My Enlil, when you rise, my loin cloth is gone.[11]
25. What did Enlil make? Chaff! The lance struck. It went into the flesh.[12]
26. When it is getting dark outside, so that you cannot see a hand in front of you, come in unnoticed!
31. Nanne estimated his old age highly:[13] He built Enlil's temple, but did not complete it. He built a wall around Nippur, but ... He built Eanna, but after it had fallen into neglect he left it. He captured Simurrum, but did not destroy its wall.[14] He never saw mighty kingship. Thus Nanne descended to the underworld with a depressed heart.
33. (He who says) "Let me live today" is bound like a bull to a leash.[15]
34. Ur-Namma [installed] the large mirrors in Enlil's temple.[16]
35. Nanne estimated his old age highly: "It is the 'I' of a man of old age" he said.[17]
37. A slave girl is one who ... the door. A palace-slave-girl is inconsiderate. A palace-slave devours goodwill.[18]
38. A slave girl carried her ransom money with her. She lost(?) thirty *mana* (pounds).
39. You grind with the pestle like a fearful slave girl.
40. The slave girl who neglected to fill the container with barley, grumbled, "it does not fill to the top, it does not fill to the middle."[19]
41. When (the lady) left the house, and (the slave girl) entered from the street, in the absence of her lady the slave girl sat down at a banquet.
42. If there is a dispute at the mill, the slave girl reveals what she has stolen.
44. The pleasure of a daughter-in-law is anger.
55. (As long as you are) alive you should not increase evil by lying, to succumb is your lot.
59. The lord decides in Uruk, but the lady of Eanna decides for him.[20]
60. I am a loyal steward with strong arms.
61. Let the sides be separated, [let] the sides [be united(?)].
62. It is (my) foremanship that makes you charge

b Prov 12:27

a liar who does not support himself," cf. Lambert 1960:255. An Early Dynastic version reads: "He who does not support a wife, he who does not suppoprt a child, his mischief is double bad for him. He grinds flour, he has no rushes (i.e., to sleep on?), he is not reckoned among people"; cf. Alster 1992a:20, 43-48.

[9] The saying quoted here also occurs in a fragmentary historical inscription related to the coronation of a ruler (PBS 5,76). The precise implication and identity of the persons are unknown; cf. Alster 1975:206f.

[10] Var. instead of "colleagues": "big brothers", i.e., the school comrades. So too in the previous proverbs, both of which are also preserved in late bilingual versions; see Lambert 1960:9-15. The Akk. of No. 17 provided the title of *Studies Kutscher* (1993).

[11] The god Enlil is here seen as the wind personified. See no. 23 cf. below, p. 568, n. 8.

[12] Akk. version: "Toward a woman who carried out the ordinances of the gods and multiplied the rules of kingship forever, how did Enlil, the great lord, act? He despised her foundations like chaff." This seems to be an allusion to an unknown woman who acted as king.

[13] Nanne is a name for the eternal loser. Cf. entry No. 35 below.

[14] Var. "but did not subdue it." Perhaps an allusion to the semi-legendary Aanne-pada, king of Ur in the second ED period; see Hallo 1978:73.

[15] Akk. version: "(He who says) 'Let me live one day' (is) a bull upon whom a leash has been thrown."

[16] This allusion to Ur-Namma, the founder of the 3rd Dyn. of Ur, remains obscure.

[17] Cf. entry No. 31 above.

[18] The implication is that those slaves and slave girls who grew up in a palace were less suitable for hard work. Cf. Shuruppak's Instructions 157, quoted below (text 1.176).

[19] This is a so-called wellerism, i.e., a proverb that consists of a quoted cliché plus an implied story.

[20] The lord is the god An, and the lady of Eanna is the goddess Inanna. In other words, "the woman behind the man."

at me.[21]

63. Let the head drop down to the neck with bickering like a swaying reed.
64. The balance set with sinews is a pitfall for the feet.
A man should not take a merchant for his friend.
65. The merchant - how he minimized the silver! [How he minimized] the oil and the barley![22]
67. One cannot drag out the weak, one cannot put the strong to a halt.
68. The smell bitter to us, let it be the smell of leeks, let it not be the smell of beans![23]
69. The insulter will be insulted. The snickerer will be snickered at.
70. A lion caught in the trap of the storehouse is mine in this way:
The owner removes the wood (of the trap).
71. If one cuts a "let-me-stride," its feet will walk to the edge of the desert.[24]
72. A chameleon follows like a snake, like a "let-me-stride."
73. As (if he were) a minor tenant, keeping watch is not what is (most) on his mind.
74. A tenant established a house, ploughing established the field.
75. "I am getting up on my haunches for you," (says) the man (who) is lifting sesame oil.[25]
76. The oath of Ishkur destroys mountains, and yet, it does not overturn a boat.[26]
77. Ishkur splits the mountains, and yet, he does not split the water sack.
79. The run-away slave girl sleeps badly.
82. He moves like a lion toward a louse, but when he has to do a job he moves like a mongoose.
83. By sunrise decisions are made. When the Sun is up, kingship is assigned.
84. Let not the cudgel find your name, let it find your flesh![27]
85. If our smell from plucked leeks is sweet, then it is a stranger that brought them to me.[28]
86. "Give me!" is what the king says. "Do well!" is what the cupbearer says.
87. What characterizes the carpenter is the chisel.
What characterizes the reed weaver is the basket.
What characterizes the smith is the making of "little sides."
What characterizes the singer(?) is UA ALA-LA.
88. He who tosses his head will cross the river.[29]
89. If the foreman does not know how to assign work, his folk will not stop tossing their heads.
91. Enlil's temple is a summation of accounts.
The administration-priest is its foreman.
92. Enlil's temple is totalling(?) wages.
93. Enlil's great punishment is hunger.
94. (If) one does not give the dog something, it will bark at every woman.
95. She grumbles like a dog beaten with a throw stick.
96. That which is made of evil threads grumbles.
97. "Let me speak a word" walks as if it had feet.[30]
Who compares with someone who has a (boasting) mouth?
99. [You], speak to [me], and I will speak to you!
100. In order to do [a job you have] to eat something.
101. You speak with me, and I speak with you.
102. Fools are the lives of the heroes.
103. A fool has a (boasting) mouth.
104. A dog moves, a scorpion moves, but my man does not move.
106. Where there is no grain, it is vengeance turned toward a city.
Where the are no reeds, it is worse than poverty.
107. "I promise!" does not mean "I promised!" "Something is finished" does not mean "It is finished." Things do not change.
108. A vagabond flays (the skin) of the open hand.
109. The two of them are like one man.
110. (If) one finds the place of my refuse heap (one will say): "Do not trespass on it!"
111. Although it never went there, the goat knows the waste land.
112. My mouth cools the hot soup for you.

[21] I.e., presumably, in case one among equals is raised to superiority, it results in animosity among friends.

[22] Variants: Sum. Proverb Collection 1.165: "The merchant - how he carried the silver away! and how he carried the grain away!" Sum. Proverb Collection 17 Sec. B 9: "You merchant, how you minimized the silver, [and] how you minimized the grain!" Aspersions on merchants were frequent in the proverbs; see Hallo 1992:354f. Aspersions on merchants were frequent in the proverbs; see Hallo 1992:534f.

[23] I.e., bitter smell is natural to leeks, but suspicious if it comes from beans. Cf. entry No. 85 below. For the persistent aversion to leeks in the cuneiform tradition, see Hallo 1985:32f.

[24] It may be assumed that "let-me-stride" denotes a type of animal. This also applies to the next entry. For the chameleon, see Sjöberg 1984.

[25] To "lift sesame oil" seems to have been an expression for making a strong effort to the best of one's abilities.

[26] Ishkur is the storm god. Cf. entries Nos. 77 and 136 below.

[27] I.e., let it hit anonymously.

[28] I.e., presumably, if the smell of leeks is sweet, then there is something suspicious about the giver. Cf. entry No. 68 above.

[29] I.e., presumably, the man who shows his impatience will be accepted first on the ferry boat.

[30] Var. "walks on feet".

I pick the bones from the fish for you.[31]
113. My mouth, every month I fill (you, my) mouth.
114. My tongue, like a runaway donkey, does not turn backwards.
115. All day long my food ration is kept away from me, my heart [aches(?)],
but even a dog can satisfy its hunger.
For me (when) it's over, I am happy.
My mother did not allot a second food ration.
117. One should lift in pieces,
and one should put down in a block.
118. (He who says:) "Let me tell you about it" when he knows nothing,
and comes forward as a witness in a case he knows nothing about,
is an abomination to Suen.
119. Flies enter the open mouth.
120. Offerings create life.
121. Punishment is assigned to the quarrelsome one, he is afflicted with diseases.
122. Let him go out.
123. May you hold a kid in your right arm,
and may you hold a bribe in your left arm.[32]
124. The manicurist is himself dressed in dirty rags.
125. He came, he dwelt, he finished,
and did not stand on the ground.[33]
126. He who spoke, but did not [keep his promise(?)], his mouth is a liar.
127. My finger nail that hurts is in my loin.
My foot that hurts is in my sandal.
But who finds my heart that hurts?
128. May Inanna pour oil on my heart that hurts![34]
129. The sail on the mast blocks the river.
130. (When engaged) in a quarrel may an insult reveal itself to you.
(When engaged) in a dispute may a word (of reason) reveal itself to you.
131. If it is too sweet for him, let him eat salt.
If it is not too sweet for him, let him eat "bitter plants."
132. Before the fire has gone out, write your exercise tablet.
134. A man's personal god is a shepherd who finds a grazing ground for him.
Let him lead him like a sheep to the grass he can eat.
135. Until the boasters leave, their(?) mouths bring me "turning eyes."
136. The heavens are destroyed, the earth is shaken. After the heavens were destroyed,
and after the earth was shaken, the people stood by themselves.[35]
137. The rigging is not ship-shape,
and its stern is not seaworthy.
138. He who entered Elam, his mouth is bound.[36]
139. (He who has to live in) Elam, his life is not good.[37]
140. A cake (was) made of GUNIDA-wheat instead of honey.
The nomad (lit., Amorite) ate it, and did not recognize what was in it.
141. He (who) keeps fleeing flees from his own past.
142. The south wind fills my eyes with its sand.
Why does it not strike behind me?
143. Between the basket and the boat are the fields of Simurrum.
144. You keep walking around the storehouse like a pig that has a morsel in its mouth.
145. He who is overwhelmed by Inanna, to forget is what he dreams about.[38]
146. My grain, whether roasted or not roasted,
you have to pour it out.
147. It is characteristic of your harvesting,
it is characteristic of your gleaning that they say, "he is gone, he is gone."
148. "You should serve me," (is what) the purification priests (say).
"Let me turn on your thigh," (is what) the leather workers (say),[39]
To stand in the corners, (is what the) courtesans (do),
"Let me assist you," (is what) the gardener (says),
"I swear by Enki that your garments will not stay long in the house," (is what) the fullers (say).
149. The day became dark, but it did not rain.
It rained, but the sandals were not untied.
The Tigris was confused in its outlet, but no water filled the fields.[40]
150. In Eridu, built in abundance, the monkey sits with longing eyes.
151. Cream and milk are mixed with an axe(?).

[31] Spoken by a husband to his spouse.
[32] The kid was presented as an offering to a temple.
[33] This seems to refer to a restless person, who was unable to settle permanently anywhere.
[34] Inanna is the goddess of love. Cf. entry No. 145 below.
[35] Cf. entry No. 76 above.
[36] I.e., because another language was spoken in Elam. This may refer to a travelling merchant, or possibly to a prisoner of war.
[37] The reference might be to any prisoner of war, or perhaps specifically to King Ibbi-Sin, who was taken captive by the Elamites.
[38] Cf. entry No. 138 above.
[39] Var. "'I bow in (my) hips' (is what) the leather workers (say)."
[40] This is a riddle whose solution seems to be the clouds which produce rain that falls over the rivers, but not on dry land. Cf. Civil 1987:31-32.

152. No matter how unique this one is, its appearances change.
153. The goat spoke in the manner of a (wise) old woman, but acted in the manner of an unclean woman.
154. The clod on the one hand,
the furrow on the other hand,
I am their third.
155. Let me drink diluted beer,
let me sit in the seat of honor!
156. Although it was not dear to him,
he attended the festival.
157. The time passes, what did you gain?
158. The statue is good. The father-in-law rejoices over it: "It is as if it were a human being."
159. A good word is a friend to numerous men.
160. A destructive word is a yoke of four oxen.
161. Putting unwashed hands in the mouth is an abomination.
162. May a clever farmer live with you in the house.
163. What I drink is a river.
The place where I sleep is a place of reed mats.
164. The gekko has a tiara tied to it.[41]
165. "Let me go home" is what he prefers.
166. From my heart which is greater than a garden, the sun does not rise.
167. Bearing up the sky, the earth is hanging in his hands.
168. "Bitter" barley is an abomination to the "ghost-man."[42]
169. Wheat flour is an abomination to his god.
170. If a man sailing downstream demands an inspection,[43]
and if the hand touches the vulva on top of the clothes,
it is an abomination to Utu.
171. To [put(?)] a loaf in the oven while a song is sung is an abomination to Inanna.
174. If the sieve is not shaken, his flour will not drop from it.
175. Coveting and reaching out (in greediness) are abominations to Ninurta.[44]
176. I am confronting Fate:
(Whether I) speak in the way of a just man,
(or I) speak in the way of a wicked man
(it makes no difference).[45]
177. What comes out of one's mouth is not in one's hand.[46]
179. He said "Woe". The boat sank with him.
He said "Hurrah," and the rudder broke.[47]
180. He is walking with his neck "pierced."[48]
181. He makes the turning edge out of the lower edge.[49]
182. He devours (everything) like a field (devoured) by locusts.
183. A released weaver (equals) two slave girls.
A released UNGUR-worker (equals) three slaves.
185. My mouth makes me comparable with men.
186. What is this after you split it?
And this after you split it?
187. When present it is (considered) a loin cloth,
when lost it is (considered fine) clothing.
188. When a leader is being devoured by fire,
those behind him do not say, "Where is the leader?"
189. To cry out louder than(?) the people.
190. When straightforwardness is cut off,
injustice is raised.

[41] There is a pun on the words denoting gekko: MUŠDAGUR, and tiara: MUŠ.

[42] The reference is to funeral offerings. "Bitter" barley was a specific type of barley apparently not used for funeral offerings. The "ghost-man" is the ghost of the deceased. This and the next proverb occur together in the incantation series "Evil Ghosts"; see Hallo 1985:29.

[43] The text has been variously interpreted by a number of scholars. The translation suggested here follows M. Civil 1994:158-163.

[44] Var. Coveting and spying, etc. For similar sentiment in line 55 of the Hymn to Enlil (*Enlil-suraše*), see Jacobsen 1987a:105.

[45] If the logical continuation, "it makes no difference," is justified, the implication is that one cannot avoid Fate.

[46] I.e., the spoken word cannot be recalled.

[47] Cf. Sum. Proverb Collection 7.77: "He said 'Woe.' The boat sank with him. He said 'Hurrah,' and the rudder broke. The young man said 'Oh god,' and the boat reached its destination." Akk. translation: "The young man said 'Woe,' and his boat sank. He said 'Hurrah,' and his rudder broke. The young(?) man said 'Woe,' and his boat reached the bank." There seems to be no inner logic connecting the utterances and their effects. Rather, the point seems to be the joke that an utterance may have totally irrational effects.

[48] The reference may be to a prisoner of war.

[49] The reference is to a cuneiform tablet turned along the incorrect edge by a pupil when passing from the obverse to the reverse.

REFERENCES

Previous edition: Falkowitz 1980; For a complete edition of the Sum. proverbs see Alster 1997. Studies: Alster 1992a; 1993a; Civil 1987; Geller 1990; Gordon 1959; Hallo 1985; Lambert 1960.

PROVERBS QUOTED IN OTHER GENRES (1.175)

Bendt Alster

The proverbs quoted in the Sumerian proverb collections are usually devoid of context indicative of the situations to which they were normally applied. Yet, in some lucky cases, the proverbs listed in the proverb collections coincide with those quoted in literary compositions.[1] On the other hand, a number of proverbs found in literary compositions, in particular in Shuruppak's Instructions (cf. below), were not included in the proverb collections known to us. The presence of proverbs in school dialogues and literary debates suggests that the proverb collections were used as source books which could supply the pupils with a stock of phrases useful for rhetorical debates. Some examples of proverbs quoted in various compositions are listed here.[2]

In the Epic Lugalbanda in Hurrumkurra, the following lines, 158-160, are addressed to the Sun god Utu by the hero Lugalbanda left alone in the unknown mountains. He appeals to the god for help:

An unknown dog is bad, an unknown man is terrible.
But on an unknown road at the verge of the mountains,
Oh Utu, an unknown man is an even worse bad man.[3]

There is an allusion to this proverb in Shuruppak's Instructions, lines 266-268:

An unknown dog is bad, an unknown man is terrible.
On the verge of the mountains, the gods of the mountains eat men!

Sumerian hymns sometimes contain allusions to proverbs. An example is Nanshe Hymn, line 144:

(The man who) after he has acquired something demands more.[4]

This alludes to a proverb quoted elsewhere as follows:

To have and demand more is an abomination to god.[5]

An example of religious instruction is found in the following short didactic poem:[6]

A man without a god does not procure much food, does not procure a little food.
Descending to the river, he does not catch a fish.
Descending to a field, he does not catch a gazelle.
When he boasts, he obtains nothing.
When he runs, he obtains nothing.
However, if his god becomes favorable toward him,
anything that he names will be provided for him.[7]

The function of proverbs to settle a dispute or even a legal issue is illustrated by the disputation between Mother Sheep and Grain, in which the grain takes precedence after the quotation of the following proverb:

He who has silver, he who has precious stones, he who has oxen, he who has sheep, must wait in the city gate for the man who has grain.[8]

[1] This is the case with the following entries of Collection 3 (translated above, previous text): SP 3.1; SP 3.16; SP 3.123; SP 3.134; SP 3.149 (riddle); SP 3.163-169.

[2] Other examples are discussed by Hallo 1990.

[3] Cf. Wilcke 1969:80.

[4] Text 1.162, above (reading NINDA, "bread," instead of NÍG, "something"). See also Heimpel 1981a:90.

[5] UET 6/2 261 and 262.

[6] UET 6/2 251 and 252.

[7] The text translated here is that of UET 6/2 251. There are a number of variants. The briefest form occurs in the poem Man and his God: "a man without a god obtains no food." The whole poem is quoted in a hymn to the deity Hendursage. Cf. Hallo 1990:210, with notes 59 and 60.

[8] Cf. Alster and Vanstiphout 1987:29-30. The implication is that grain is more important than anything else, because he who has grain has something to eat. There are a number of attestations of this proverb: UET 6/2 263 and 266; the love song Ni 4569 with duplicates (Alster, *RA* 79:157); the folktale "Enlil and Namzitarra" 13-18 (Civil 1974 *AfO* 25:65-71); Cohen 1981:64).

REFERENCES

Hallo 1990; Wilcke 1969.

2. INSTRUCTIONS

SHURUPPAK (1.176)

Bendt Alster

In addition to the standard version of this composition, dating around 1900-1800 BCE, an Early Dynastic version dating as early as 2600-2500 BCE, and two partly preserved Akkadian translations, one dating around 1500 BCE, and one dating around 1100 BCE, are known. The excerpts translated here are from the standard version, attested in approximately 80 fragments from Nippur and Ur as well as some other locations. The composition pretends to be addressed by the ante-diluvian ruler Shuruppak to his son Ziusudra, the hero of the flood story who, like Noah, survived the destruction of mankind and became the favorite of the gods. Pertinent to the teaching of Shuruppak are matters relating to secular life, that is, the management of a household, animal husbandry, agricultural work, and social behavior in general, with little emphasis on cult and religion. Many of the sayings quoted preserve the character of genuine proverbs. The imagery referring to daily life with no traces of abstract generalization is noteworthy. The moral perspective is one of modest egoism, in other words, one should not treat others in a way that may instigate them to retaliate to one's own disadvantage. A characteristic type of saying consists of two parts, the first of which contains the advice itself. The second is a motivation clause, similar to those of proverbs in the Hebrew Bible, which makes the consequences of the action described in the first part explicit, frequently in terms of a humorous or exaggerated statement.[1]

The basic edition is by Alster 1974b, with additions by Alster 1987, 1990, 1992a. Cf. Civil 1984 and Wilcke 1978. For a completely revised edition, see Alster 1997.

14. Do not buy a donkey that brays; it will split your people.
15. Do not place a field on a road; ...
16. Do not plow a field where a path begins; ...
17. Do not dig a well in your field; the people will cause you to suffer damage.
18. Do not place your house close to a public square; the heaviest traffic(?) is there.
19. Do not vouch for someone; that man will have a hold on you.[a]
20. And you, let nobody vouch for you; the man will despise you.
21. Do not spy upon a man; the town will make you pay back.
22. Do not loiter about where there is a dispute.
23. Do not appear as a witness in a dispute.
28. Do not steal something; do not kill yourself.
29. Do not break into a house; do not demand the money chest(?).
30. The thief is a dragon, he who has received (what is stolen) is a slave.
31. My son, do not commit robbery, do not cut yourself with an axe.
32. Do not act as the bridegroom's friend in a wedding, do not ... yourself.
33. Do not laugh with a girl who is married; the slander is strong.
34. My son, do not sit (alone) in a chamber with a woman who is married.
35. Do not pick a quarrel; do not humiliate yourself.
36. Do not spit out lies; it causes disrespect.

a Prov 6:1-5; 22:26-27

37. Do not boast; your word stands (forever).
38. Do not give ill advice; you cannot bear a "heavy" eye.
39-41. Do not eat stolen food with a thief; do not sprinkle your hands with blood; after you have apportioned the bones, they will make you restore the ox, they will make you restore the sheep.
42-43. Do not utter nonsense; in the end it will reach out for you like a trap.
44. Do not scatter your sheep into untested grazing grounds.
45. If the "foundation" is not safe, do not hire a man's ox.
46. A safe foundation is a safe road.
47. Do not travel at night; its "heart" is both good and bad.
48. Do not buy an onager; it lasts only one day.[2]
49. Do not have sexual intercourse with your slave girl; she will name you with disrespect.
50. Do not curse with powerful means; they will turn round to your hands.
153. Do not beat a peasant's son; he will "beat" your irrigation canal.
154. Do not buy a prostitute; she is the sharp edge of a sickle.
155. Do not buy a house-born slave; he is an herb that causes stomach-ache.[3]
156. Do not buy a free-born man; he will lean against a wall.
157. Do not buy a palace-slave-girl; the house will be on a bad track.

[1] Cf. Alster 1987:204.

[2] Onagers were too unstable to be tamed, yet they were used for breeding with tame horses.

[3] The point here, as well as in 156-157, is that a slave who grew up as a free man or was used to the good manners of the palace would be

158-164. After you have bought a slave from a foreign country, and after you have taken him home from his unknown place, my son, he will pour water for you, and walk in front of you till sunrise. Since he has no house, he will not go to his house; since he has no town, he will not go to his town; he will not argue with you, he will not be quarrelsome.

unsuitable for hard work. This indicates that the point of view of the sayings is that of ordinary household owners. Cf. Sum. Proverb Collection 3.37, quoted above, text 1.174.

REFERENCES

Alster 1974b; 1987; 1990; 1992a; Civil 1984; Wilcke 1978.

UR-NINURTA (1.177)

Bendt Alster

This composition is best known from a tablet found at Tell Ḥarmal (Baghdad), with two small duplicating fragments from Nippur and two of unknown provenance. The main source is written in a very difficult syllabic orthography, which makes the interpretation of a non-stereotype composition such as this one very difficult. The translation provided here is therefore very tentative. The sections dealing with the just man and the unjust one give the impression that the specific reference is to the king. What is expressed is the royal ideology, according to which a ruler who implements justice in his country and observes the cult of his gods will enjoy a long life, to the benefit of himself as well as his subjects.

Introduction: Ur-Ninurta's kingship (lines 1-17)

1. In days of yore, in days completed long ago,
2. after nights had been become far remote from those distant nights,
3. after years had become remote from remote years,
4. after the flood had swept (the land),
5. the one given wisdom by Enki,
6. the one ... by Nisaba,
7. the one who takes counsel with ... Inanna,
8. — in order to organize the plans of Sumer,
9. in order to abolish wickedness, to implement righteousness,
10. in order to settle the people in their dwelling places,
11. in order to reinforce the foundation of Ur-Ninurta's shepherd[ship],
12. [(Ninurta?),] the king of Eshumesha, born in Nippur,
13. Suen's(?) ...,
14. so that the [(royal throne?)] of [Ur]-Ninurta,
15. could be installed until distant days
16. from Nippur his beloved city,
17. he established it[1] until distant days, forever.

The just man (lines 18-29)

18. So that the days should not [(cease?)] for the sons(?) of the country,[a]
19. The man who knows fear of god,
20. he himself ...
21. [daily(?)] ... he will bring offerings,
22. the god's "name" is dear to him,
23. he keeps(?) (idle?) swearing away from his house.
24. he walks straight from the cult place,
25. what he gives out(?) is satisfactory.
26. Days will be added to his days,[b]
27. the name he has will become even greater,
28. after his death the people will be consolidated.[2]
29. A son will be born to him.[3]

The unjust man (lines 30-37)

30. The man who does not fear the gods,
31. to whom their prayers are not dear,
32. who after he has sworn does not concern himself,
33. his old age will not last long.[b]
34. His inheritance will not be dear to him(?).
35. A son will not be born to him.
36. A man who does not show fear of god, [who has ever] seen him attaining old age? [a]
37. These are the instructions of ...

a Ps 1
b Prov 10:27

[1] I.e., Ur-Ninurta's kingship, cf. line 11.
[2] Variants add: "His old age will last long."
[3] Variants add: "His god will look (with favor) upon him." Further additions not clear.

REFERENCES

Alster 1991; 1992b, No. 83.

3. FABLES

THE HERON AND THE TURTLE (1.178)

Gene B. Gragg

The following composition is contained on a four-column tablet excavated at Nippur in the 1951-1952 season. On this tablet it ends in the middle of the fourth column with a double-ruled line and a colophon giving the number of lines (namely, 115). The composition is similar in style to the literary disputations, but since it contains the story of a quarrel rather than the text of a debate, it may be more properly assigned to the genre of fable. As such it bears comparison with fable-like pericopes identified in the Bible.[a] The conclusion is unfortunately not clear. Two other large tablets had our composition on the obverse, and either a long (at least 90-line) but poorly preserved continuation or related composition, concerning the turtle but with no mention of the heron, on the reverse.[1]

a Judg 9:8-15; 1 Kgs 14:9 = 2 Chr25:18

Prologue 1: The Marshlands of Sumer (lines 1-9)

What does the canebrake say? Its growth is good!
The broad canebrake of Tutub[2] Its growth is good!
The marsh of Kiritab[3] Its growth is good!
The swamp of Akšak[4] Its growth is good!
The dense swamp of Enki[5] Its growth is good!
The small swamp of Eridu[6] Its growth is good!
The *barbar*[7] reeds of Enki Its growth is good!
Ur, the small *zi*-reeds Its growth is good!
Ur, where cows and calves abound Its growth is good!

Prologue 2: The Flora of the Marshlands (lines 10-21)

On that day the water drained from the reeds, and a pen appeared.
The *ardadillu*-plant spreading its seed from the canebreak,
The small *kumul*-plants came out of the earth — they are good little ones.
The small *enbar*-reed grooms her hair, she is a good young maiden.
The *ubzal*-reed goes about the city, he is a good young man.
The *pella*-reed is covered from bottom to top, she is a good daughter-in-law.
The *pella*-reed turns from bottom to top, he is a good young son.
The "artisan"-reed digs the earth, he is a good old man.
The *zi*-reed covers? herself over, she is a good old woman.
The canebreak beautifully raises his head, he is a good Gudea[8]
The poplar tree raises his head by the orchard canal, he is a good king.
The ... with shining branches, he is a good prince.

The Villain Appears (lines 22-31)

On that day, beside the canebrake, one sitting on the bank pleads:
"The heron — I will snatch away her eggs, I will take them away ...
The bird, the gift-giver, will not make a gift.
The heron, the gift-giver, will not make a gift."
This one seized the fish, collected the eggs, he shoved them aside.
The carp in the honey-plant, he shoved them aside.
The marsh-carp in the small *zi*-reeds, he shoved them aside.
The toads in the *liqiliqi*-grass, he shoved them aside.
The *agargara*-fish on the outskirts and its off-spring, he shoved them aside.
The heron, he smashed her eggs, he dashed them in the sea.

The Heron Asks for a Safe Place to Lay Eggs (lines 32-47)

The bird, the gift-giver pleads.
[The heron] enters the temple of King Enki and speaks to him:
"[...] a broad place give me, so that I can lay eggs."
[...] he gave to her.
[...] may he do for her.
[...] it is indeed a ...
[...] in the reed of the bird.
In the [canebrake] she laid eggs.
In the [canebrake of Tutub] she laid eggs.
In the marsh of Kiritab she laid eggs.
In the swamp of Akšak she laid eggs.
In the dense swamp of Enki she laid eggs.

---

[1] Edition and commentary will be found in Gragg 1973a.
[2] Diyala site now known as Ḫafāǧi.
[3] Unidentified site west of Kish.
[4] A small northeastern frontier kingdom.
[5] God of the southern city of Eridu, closely associated with marshes and the underground watery abyss.
[6] Of all the ancient major urban centers, this was the site most closely associated with marshy regions at the head of the Persian Gulf.
[7] No sure identifications can be given for the many types of reeds and other marsh flora mentioned in this text.
[8] Sum. ruler of Lagash, ca. 2175 BCE. His mention here is possibly important for dating the composition.

In the small swamp, the swamp of Eridu she laid eggs.
In the *barbar*-reeds of Enki she laid eggs.
In Ur, among the small *zi*-reeds she laid eggs.
In Ur, where cows and calves abound she laid eggs.

The Turtle Attacks the Heron (lines 48-71)

On that day, the turtle, the quarreler, the man of the cursed way, (said):
"With the heron, with the heron, I will indeed pick a quarrel.
I, the turtle, with the heron, I will indeed pick a quarrel."
He whose eyes are the eyes of a snake, "I will indeed pick a quarrel."
Whose tooth is the tooth of a snake, "I will indeed pick a quarrel."
Whose tongue is the tongue of a snake, "I will indeed pick a quarrel."
Whose bite is the bite of a puppy, "I will indeed pick a quarrel."
(With) dainty hands and dainty feet, "I will indeed pick a quarrel."
The turtle, an oven brick, "I will indeed pick a quarrel."
(Who lives) in the drainage ditch, "I will indeed pick a quarrel."
Who passes his time in the mud like a hoe, "I will indeed pick a quarrel."
An unwashed dirt basket, "I will indeed pick a quarrel."
The turtle, the bird-trapper, the net setter,
Overthrew the heron's reed-construction.
He turned her nest upside down.
He threw her children into the water.
The bird, the dark-eyed one,
The turtle scratched her forehead with his claws.
Its blood covered her chest.
The heron cried, grew pale:
"I, the bird, the ... nest [...]
May my king judge my case, may he decide in my favor!
May Enki judge my case, may he decide in my favor!
(May) the lord of Eridu [...]"

The Turtle (Again) Attacks the Heron (lines 72-105)

For a second time; "The bird, the gift-giver, will not make a gift.
The heron, the gift-giver, will not make a gift."
This one seized the fish, collected the eggs, he shoved them aside.
The carp in the honey-plant, he shoved them aside.
The marsh-carp in the small *zi*-reeds, he shoved them aside.
The toads in the *ligiligi*-grass, he shoved them aside.
The *agargara*-fish on the outskirts and its offspring, he shoved them aside.
... [...] head on high [...].
She cries out to king Enki:
"My king, you have given (your) broad canebrake, there I have laid eggs.
In the broad canebrake of Tutub there I have laid eggs.
In the marsh of Kiritab there I have laid eggs.
In the swamp of Akšak there I have laid eggs.
in the dense swamp of Enki there I have laid eggs.
In the small swamp, the swamp of Eridu, there I have laid eggs.
In the *barbar*-reeds of Enki there I have laid eggs.
In Ur, among the small *zi*-reeds there I have laid eggs.
In Ur, where cows and calves abound there I have laid eggs.

On that day, the turtle, the quarreler, the one of the accursed way,
He whose eyes are the eyes of a snake, the one of the accursed way,
Whose tooth is the tooth of a snake, the one of the accursed way,
Whose tongue is the tongue of a snake, the one of the accursed way,
Whose bite is the bite of a puppy, the one of the accursed way,
(With) dainty hands and dainty feet, the one of the accursed way,
The turtle, an oven brick, the one of the accursed way,
(Who lives) in the drainage ditch, the one of the accursed way,
Who passes his time in the mud like a hoe, the one of the accursed way,
An unwashed dirt basket, the one of the accursed way,
The turtle, the bird-trapper, the net setter,
Overthrew my, the heron's, reed-construction.
He turned my nest upside down.
He threw my children into the water.
I, the bird, the dark-eyed one,
The turtle scratched my forehead with his claws.
My blood covered my chest."

Conclusion: Justice Is Rendered (lines 106-115)

The prince said to (his) vizier, Isimud[9]:
(106a) "My vizier Isimud, my ...
Who stands (in waiting) for King Enki, my perpetual prayer (offerer),
[...] when you have pressed out on the left side,
[...] when you have poured it,

[9] Minor divinity given role of assistant to Enki, pictured on early cylinder seals as two-faced; see *RlA* s.v. Isimu.

[...], you will cover it.
[...] when you have wound,
[...] when you have ...
[...] when you have brought it ...

When you have placed it in the dense swamp of
Enki,
On that day ... may it sit."

REFERENCES

Gragg 1973a:51-72.

4. PIOUS SUFFERER COMPOSITIONS

"MAN AND HIS GOD" (1.179)

Jacob Klein

This Sumerian poem, of about 140 lines, tells a didactic story of a righteous sufferer who remains faithful to his personal god and ultimately is rehabilitated and restored to his former happy status. The poem opens with a brief didactic exhortation, that a man should faithfully praise his god, soothing his heart with lamentations, for "a man without a god would not have anything to eat" (lines 1-10). The rest of the poem is a (fictitious) illustration of this general truth. First the poet introduces the righteous, anonymous, sufferer, describing briefly the various diseases that befell him, whereupon the man utters a bitter lament to his god and pays him homage reverently (lines 11-27). This is followed by the sufferer's lengthy penitential lament, which constitutes the bulk of the composition (lines 28-119). The sufferer begins his lament, describing the ill treatment accorded to him by his fellow men (lines 28-56). Next he expresses the wish that everyone of his friends and family lament ceaselessly on his behalf before his god (lines 64-68). Then he complains about his physical illness and depression (lines 69-81). The sufferer concludes his prayer with a confession of his sins and a heartrending plea for mercy, forgiveness and restoration (lines 82-119). As expected, the drama comes to a happy end: the poet tells us that the god accepted the sufferer's prayer, restored his health, turned his suffering into joy and granted him benevolent guardian angels (lines 120-132). The poem concludes with a thanksgiving praise, uttered by the saved man to his personal god, in which he vows that he will constantly glorify him as long as he lives (lines 133-143).[1]

In many respects, the poem resembles the biblical book of Job. The main difference between the two sources is that the Sumerian composition lacks elements of dialogue. Instead, the complaints and reflections of the hero are expressed in a long personal lamenting monologue, addressed to the deity. And after the hero is restored to health, he utters a short thanksgiving to his merciful and benevolent god. Further, unlike Job, the sufferer has some feelings of guilt, although he is not aware of his sins.[2]

Social Rejection of the Sufferer (lines 28-30; 33-40; 46-47)

I, the young-man,[3] the learned one —
my know[ledge] is of no avail to me;
The truth which I speak
is turned into a lie.
The man of deceipt overwhelms me (like) a
storm, I (am forced to) serve him ...[a]
When I enter the house, heavy is the spirit;

a Ps 35:11-17, 22-26; Job 16:9-11; 19:18-19; 30:1-14

I, the young-man — when I go out to the
street, oppressed is the heart.
I, the valiant[4] — my loyal shepherd
becomes angry with me, (and) looks
upon me with an evil eye.
My herdsman maltreats me, who am
not hostile (toward him),
My companion says not a true word to me,
My friend renders my words,

[1] For an edition of the poem, see Kramer 1955. The selections translated below are based on a revised edition of the text which is in preparation by the author. See for the time being Kramer's slightly revised translation in *ANET* 589-591; for translation of selected portions, see further Jacobsen 1976:153-155.

[2] Hence he can better be described as a "pious sufferer"; see Mattingly 1990. All the manuscripts (cuneiform tablets) from which this poem is reconstructed, can be dated to the later Old Babylonian period (18th-17th centuries BCE). However, many literary elements incorporated in the poem can be traced back to the Old Sumerian preiod (such as e.g., the wisdom proverbs and the penitential lament formulas). Therefore the possibility cannot be excluded that our poem was composed before the Old-Babylonian period, perhaps in the Isin-Larsa period (beginning of the 2nd millennium BCE); see discussion in Hallo 1968:71-82; Jacobsen 1976:152; Klein 1982:297-302.

[3] Sum. GURUŠ, in administrative texts, refers to an adult male, capable of military service or civil work. Here it is the usual poetic, impersonal and typological epithet of the righteous sufferer. In this sense, it is parallel to biblical *gever* (cf. Job 3:3; 4:17; 14:14 et passim; Lam 3:1). Further on, it is occasionally paralleled by the synonymous ŠUL "hero," "valiant." Both Sum. words were translated by Akk. *eṭlu*. A third, parallel, expression used by the poet to refer to the sufferer is LÚ-ULU$_3$ "man."

[4] For the Sum. word ŠUL "valiant," see note 3.

truthfully spoken, a lie.[b]
The man of deceit speaks
insulting words to me;[c]
(But) you, my god,
do not thwart them! ...
Food is all about, (yet) my food is hunger,
On the day shares were allotted to all,
my allotted share was suffering![d]

Complaining of Sickness and Depression (lines 69-80)[e]

"My god, the day shines bright over
The Land, (but) for me the day has darkened,
The bright day has dawned(?) upon(?)
me(?) like a misty(?) day.[5]
Tears, lament, anguish and
depression are lodged within me,
Suffering overwhelms me
like a weeping child.
In the hands of Fate,[6]
(my) features had been changed,
my breath of life had been carried off,
Asag,[7] the evil one, bathes in my body.
In the bitterness and misfortune of my path,
I never see a good dream;
Daily false dreams do not cease (haunting) me!
Anguish embraced me — who am not its spouse,
Wailing spread wide (its) arms (around) me
— who am not its small child,
Lamentation swept over me
like a crushing(?) storm ..."

Confession of Sins and Plea for Mercy (lines 98-119)

"My god, to you, who are my father that
begot me,[8] let me [lift] my eyes,[f]
'Good Cow,'[9] god(?) of mercy
(and acceptance of) supplication,
let me [aquire(?) through(?) you]
lofty strength!
How long will you not care for me,
will you not look after me?
Like an ox I would like to rise toward you,
but you do not let me rise,
You do not let me take the right course.
They say — the wise men
— a word true and right:
'Never has a sinless child
been born to its mother,
A mortal(?) has never been perfect(?),
a sinless man has never existed from old' ...[g]
My god, ... after you will have
let my eyes recognize my sins,
I shall recount at the city(?) gate[10]
those of them that have been forgotten,
and those of them which are visible(?);[11]
I, the young man, shall publicly
declare my sins before you![h]
In the assembly let tears(?) fall,
like a heavy downpour (of rain)!
In your temple, let my merciful mother
continuously weep for me!
I, the valiant, may your holy
[heart have] mercy and take pity on me!
I, the young man — may your heart,
'the terrifying (flood) wave,'
be assuaged toward me!"[12] [i]

Acceptance of the Sufferer's Prayer and his Restoration (lines 120-132)

The man — his god verily heard
his bitter weeping;
After the heart of his god became soothed
toward the young man at his prolonged
lamentation and wailing,
The true words, the artless words,
uttered by him, his god accepted.
His words of supplication,
which the young man expressed,
(And) the pure prayers(?) — pleased
the flesh of his god like fine oil.
(Thereupon) his god withdrew
his hand from the evil matter:
Anguish, which embraced him,
who was not its spouse,
(And) wailing, which spread out wide
its arm (around him) — he annihilated;[13]
Lamentation, which swept over him like
a crushing(?) storm — he dissipated;[14]
Fate, which had been lodged in his body,
he eradicated(?).[15]
He turned the young man's suffering

b Pss 31:12; 38:12-13; 69:9; 88:19; Job 6:15-21, 27; 19:14-17

c Ps 22:7-9

d Job 3:24-26; 7:3-6

e Pss 38:7-11; 88:4-7; Job 7:4-6; 9:25; 14:22; 16:16; 17:1-2, 7; 19:7-11; 30:15-19, 26-31

f Pss 27:10; 22:10-11; 71:5-6

g Gen 6:5-7; Ps 51:7; Job 4:17-18; 7:20-21; 15:17-18;

h Pss 38:3-7, 19; 25:7, 11; 31:11; Job 13:23

i Pss 6:1; 38:2; 39:14; 102:11

[5] Reading tentatively U$_4$-ḪI-DA$^!$-GIM, lit., "like an alloyed/mixed day" (see Hallo 1968:85, n. 106).

[6] Sum. NAM-TAR (Akk. *namtarru*); a netherworld demon of fatal sickness, the harbinger of death.

[7] A demon of sickness, especially causing headaches, and the sickness it causes.

[8] It is hard to assume that the Sumerians considered themselves genetic descendents of their "personal god" (so Jacobsen 1976:157-160). Rather, we take this as a hyperbolic metaphor.

[9] "Good cow" is a frequently attested epithet of mother-goddesses, especially when their mercifulness is stressed; it also refers to divine mothers of Sum. kings (see Sjöberg, *OrSuec* 21 1972:99). Here, exceptionally, it seems to refer to the personal god of the sufferer.

[10] Reading tentatively KÁ-URU(?)-KA. The city-gate served, in the ANE as the place for public assemblies (Sum. UNKEN) and court-trials.

[11] I.e., those sins which were committed unawares, and those which were committed intentionally.

[12] These two lines (lines 118-119), and especially the expression ŠÀ-ZU KI-BÉ ḪA-MA-GI$_4$-GI$_4$ "may your heart be assuaged toward me!" represent a standard concluding formula of personal laments and 'letter-prayers,' attested from the Ur III period on; and it appears already in a hymn, written by Enḫeduanna, the daughter of Sargon of Akkad, in honor of the goddess Inanna (cf. Klein 1982:300-301; text 1.160, above).

[13] Lit., "he scattered them to the wind."

[14] Lit., "he let them to be devoured by the marshes."

[15] See note 6 above.

into joy,
A benevolent UDUG-spirit,[16]
that watches at the (door) opening(?),
set by him (as) a guardian,
He (also) gave him[j] LAMMA-spirits[17]
(of) "good eyes."

j Job 42:10-17; Ps 91:11

[16] Sum. UDUG (Akk. *utukku* or *šēdu*) denotes a demon, which may be either "good" (i.e., protective and benevolent) or "bad" (i.e., evil and harming).

[17] Sum. LAMMA (Akk. *lamassatu*) denotes an anonymous, female protective deity.

REFERENCES

Van Dijk 1953; Hallo 1968; Jacobsen 1976:152-164; Klein 1982; Kramer 1955; *ANET* 589-591; Mattingly 1990; Weinfeld 1988.

5. DISPUTATIONS

THE DISPUTATION BETWEEN EWE AND WHEAT (1.180)

H. L. J. Vanstiphout

This composition is presently the most accessible of the group of poetic disputations, a genre which was very popular in the Old Babylonian scribal schools and, according to the texts themselves, also at the royal court. This piece is remarkable for three reasons: it starts with a very long "cosmogonical" introduction,[1] it is apparently occasioned by a festival (a banquet at harvest time?), and it is a prime example of a consciously poetic stance in composition as well as in performance.[2] The text is available in a provisional edition which utilized the 39 published manuscripts.[3]

When upon the Hill of Heaven and Earth[4]
An had spawned the divine Godlings, —
Since godly Wheat had not been spawned or created with them,
Nor had the yarn of the godly Weaver[5] been fashioned in the Land,
Nor had the loom of the godly Weaver even been pegged out,
For Ewe had not yet appeared, nor were there numerous lambs,
And there was as yet no goat, nor numerous kids,
For Ewe did not drop her twin lambs
And Goat did not drop her triplet kids, —
The very names of Wheat, the holy blade, and of Ewe
Were yet unknown to the Godlings and the greater Divinities.[a]

There was no wheat-of-thirty-days;
There was no wheat-of-forty-days;
There was no wheat-of-fifty-days,
Nor small wheat, nor mountain wheat, nor wheat of the goodly village;
Also there was no cloth to wear;
The godly Weaver not having been born, no royal cap was worn;
Lord herald, the precious lord, had not been born;
Shakan[6] did not go out to the arid lands.

The people of those distant days[7]
Knew not bread to eat,
They knew not cloth to wear;
They went about in the Land with naked limbs
Eating grass with their mouths like sheep,
And drinking water from the ditches.[b]

At that time, at the birthplace of the Gods,
In their home, the Holy Hill, they (the gods) fashioned Ewe and Wheat.

Gathering in the divine dining hall,
Of the bounty of Ewe and Wheat
The Godlings of the Holy Hill
Partook, but were not sated;
Of the sweet milk of their goodly sheepfold
The Godlings of the Holy Hill
Then drank, but were not sated.
And so, for their own well-being in the goodly sheepfold
They gave them to Mankind as sustenance.[c]

a Gen 1:11; Deut 32:2
b Gen 3:18; Exod 10:12
c Exod 16:13

[1] For the status of these introductions see Van Dijk 1953:39; Pettinato 1971; Vanstiphout 1990a:289-295; Bottéro 1991:20-21; Clifford 1994:25-32.

[2] Vanstiphout 1992b.

[3] Alster and Vanstiphout 1987.

[4] The Hill of Heaven and Earth is the primeval birth and dwelling place of the gods. See in general Van Dijk 1964 and Pettinato 1971.

[5] The Weaver is the goddess Uttu. See Vanstiphout 1990b.

[6] The god of the wild animals of the plains.

[7] Where do these people come from?

Then Enki spoke to Enlil:
Father Enlil, Ewe and Wheat
Were well settled on the Holy Hill;
Let us now send Ewe and Wheat down from the Holy Hill."
Enki and Enlil, having agreed on this, their sacred word,
Sent down Ewe and Wheat from the Holy Hill.

Ewe, fenced in by her sheepfold,
They richly endowed in grass and herbs.
For Wheat they made a field
And bestowed on her Plow and Yoke and Team.
Ewe, standing in her sheepfold,
Was a shepherd full of the sheepfold's splendor;
Wheat, standing in her furrow,
Was a shapely girl radiating beauty [d]
Lifting her noble head high above the field
She was suffused with bounty from the skies.

Thus both Ewe and Wheat were radiant in appearance
And among the gathered people they caused abundance,
And in the Land[8] they brought well-being.
The ordinances of the Gods they fulfill with care;
The store-rooms of the Land they fill with abundance,
So that the barns of the Land are bulging with them.
Even in the home of the needy, who are crouching in the dust,
When they enter there, they bring about wealth.
Both of them, wherever they direct their steps,
Add to the riches of the household;
Wherever they stand, they bring satisfaction;
Wherever they sit, they are embellishment.[9]
And so they gladden the heart of An and the heart of Enlil.

They drank sweet wine,
They drank tasty beer;
And when they had drunk sweet wine
And sated themselves on tasty beer
They started a quarrel in the midst of the watered fields;
They held a wrangle in the Dining Hall.[10] [e]

Wheat calls out to Ewe:

"Sister, I am your better; I take precedence!
I am the most splendid of the jewels of the Land!

I give strength to the Chief Warrior
So that he fills the palace with awe,
And people spread his fame to the confines of the Land!
I am a gift of the Gods;
I am the strength of princes!

When I grant my power to the warrior
And he enters the lists,
He knows not fear nor faltering,
For I make him march out as to a playing field.
Yet I also foster neighborliness and friendship,
As I sort out neighbors' quarrels. [f]
And when I come out to the captive youth,
And give him my blessing,
He forgets his despondent heart
As if I broke his fetters and shackles.

I, I am wheat, the Holy Blade; I am Enlil's daughter (everywhere),
In the shacks, in the shepherds' huts, scattered over the plain,

What can you put against this? What can you reply? Answer me that!"

Thereupon Ewe replied to Wheat:

"Sister, what are you saying?
An, king of the Gods,
Made me descend from the holy and most precious place!

All the yarns of the divine Weaver, the splendor of royalty, are mine! Shakan, lord of the Mountain,
Adorns the king's emblem with incrustations,
And puts his implements in order.
Against the mighty peaks of the rebel land he twists a rope,[11]
He readies the big sling, the quiver and the long-bow.
Also the watch over the elite troops is mine,
As is the sustenance of the workers in the field,
And the water-skin of refreshing drink and the sandals — all that is mine!

Sweet oil, the fragrance of the Gods,
Mixed oil, pressed oil, herbal oil, cedar oil of the offerings — these are mine!
In his gown, which is my cloth of shining wool,
The king rejoices on the throne
My sides gleam on the flesh of the Great gods! [g]
Together with the bathed purification and incantation priests
When they have dressed for purifying me,
I walk to my holy meal! [h]

d Cant 7:3
e Hab 2:15
f Ps 78:25; Hos 9:4; Prov 12:9
g Lev 16:4; 16:32; Num 4:6-8
h Jer 11:19; Isa 5:37; Ps 44:23

[8] The Land (Sumerian KALAM) always refers to Babylonia (or Sumer and Akkad).
[9] The pair "to sit/to stand" is a frequent expression denoting the totality of all possible situations and actions.
[10] Apparently the banquet is held at the same time in heaven (the gods partake) and *sur l'herbe*, in the midst of the fields. Was the actual festival also held in the fields?
[11] Very probably an allusion to Mount Ebikh, the first line of mountains to the east of the Mesopotamian plain, which is said to contain the rebellious mountaineers. It is also a mythological being in its own right. See Vanstiphout 1991b.

But your harrow, plowshare, rein —
These are but tools of the all-devouring bog!

What can you put against this? What can you reply? Answer me that!"

Again Wheat addressed Ewe:

"When the beer bread has been well cooked in the oven,
Yea, when the mash has been prepared in the oven,
Ninkasi[12] herself mixes them for me.
Your big billy-goats and rams
Are then finished for my banquet.
On their thick legs they stand apart from my produce,
And even your shepherd from the desert lifts his eyes towards my things!

As to me, when I stand in the furrow in the midst of the field
My farmer chases away your shepherd's lad with his cudgel.
When they are looking for you in fields and desolate places,
Fear does not leave you.
Snakes, scorpions, robbers that dwell in the plain —
They all threaten your life in the high desert!

Every day your number is totalled
And your tally-stick put up,
So that your shepherd can tell how many ewes are left, and how many lambs;
How many goats and how many kids!

When the breeze passes through the towns,
And the strong winds are buffeting,
They have to construct a shed for you.
But when the breeze passes through the towns,
And the strong winds are buffeting,
Then I, as an equal, stand up to Ishkur![13]

I, I am Wheat, born for the warrior; I do not give up!
The churn, the vat on legs, those adornments of herding, these are your attributes!

What can you put against this? What can you reply? Answer me that!"

Again Ewe replied to Wheat:

"You, like heavenly holy Inana,
You love horses![14]
The criminal and his mate, the foreign slave,
And the forced laborer, those of the poor wives and indigent children,
When, bound with the elbow-rope,
They come to the threshing floor,
Or are taken away from the threshing-floor,
When their flail hits your face, strikes your mouth,
Then your ears ... like a pestle ...
And you are carried away by the south or the north wind.
The millstone ...
It makes your body into flour as if it were pumice,
In order to fill the kneading trough.
Then the baker's girl flattens you out broadly,
And you are put in the oven
And taken out of the oven again.
"When you are finally put on the table,
I come before you, and you are behind!

Wheat, watch yourself!
You, just as I, are meant to be eaten.
Therefore, looking at what you really are,
Why should I come second?
The miller, is he not evil to you?

What can you put against this? What can you reply?"

Then wheat was hurt in her pride; she bowed her head for another attack.
Wheat replied to Ewe:

"You, Ishkur is your master, Shakan your herdsman, and your bed is the arid wasteland!
Like fires beaten out in houses and fields,
Like sparrows chased from the door of a house,
You are turned into the lame and the weak of the Land!
I can indeed bow my neck to the ground;
But you are put into various containers;
When your innards are taken away by the buyers in the market,
And your neck is wrapped with your very own loin-cloth,
One man says to the other: 'Fill the measure with grain for my sheep!'"

Thereupon Enki spoke to Enlil:
"Father Enlil, Ewe and Wheat, both of them,
Should walk together!
Of their combined metal [the alloy] should never cease;
Yet of these two Wheat should be the greater!
May the other one kneel before Wheat;
May ... kiss her feet!
And from sunrise to sunset
The name of Wheat be praised!"

[12] The goddess of beer.
[13] God of wind and storm.
[14] See *Gilgamesh Epic* VI ii 53-56.

[May you put Ewe's neck to the yoke] of Ashnan!
For whosoever has gold, or silver, or cattle, or
    sheep,
(190) Shall ever wait at the door of him who has
    grain, and so pass his days!"[15]
	Dispute of Ewe and Wheat
	Because Ewe is left behind and Wheat comes out
	    (winning),
	Praise be to father Enki!

[15] These lines are known as an independent proverb. See Alster 1975:155 and above text 1.175 and n. 8.

REFERENCES

Alster and Vanstiphout 1987; Bottéro 1991:7-22; Clifford 1994; Pettinato 1971; van Dijk 1953; 1964; Vanstiphout 1990a; 1990b; 1991b; 1992a; 1992b.

THE DISPUTATION BETWEEN THE HOE AND THE PLOW (1.181)

H. L. J. Vanstiphout

This piece is undoubtedly the finest example of the genre. It has long been recognized as one of the first poetic, if heavily rhetorical, statements of the case of the common man against the rich and mighty.[1] But its most striking qualities are the sheer excellence of the argumentation (plow is deftly hoist with its own petard),[2] the heavy satire on the pretences of the mighty, the earthy but clever humor,[3] and most of all the irreverent but highly effective "reworking" of the format: the traditional cosmogonic introduction is turned into a story the workmen tell at night, when resting and drinking! It is to be regretted that we still have no adequate edition.[4] The present translation is based upon all published texts[5] and some quotes from secondary literature.

(1) Hey! Hoe, Hoe, Hoe, tied up with string;
Hoe, made from poplar, with a tooth of ash;
Hoe, made from tamarisk, with a tooth of sea-
    thorn;
Hoe, double-toothed, four-toothed;
(5) Hoe, child of the poor, *bereft even of a loin-
    cloth*;
Hoe picked a quarrel with Plow.
Hoe and Plow — this is their dispute.
Hoe cried out to Plow
"O Plow, you draw furrows — what is your fur-
    rowing to me?
(10) You make clods — what is your clod making
    to me? *a*
You cannot dam up water when it escapes.
You cannot heap up earth in the basket.
You cannot press clay or make bricks.
You cannot lay foundations or build a house.
(15) You cannot strengthen an old wall's base.
You cannot put a roof on a man's house.
O Plow, you cannot straighten a street! *b*
O Plow, you draw furrows — what is your fur-
    rowing to me?
You make clods — what is your clod making to
    me?"
	a Ezek 17:14;
	29:14-15;
	Dan 7:24
	
	b Isa 32:19
	
	c Ps 96:11;
	Prov 8:16;
	1 Chr 16:31
		(20) The Plow cries out to the Hoe
		
		"I, I am Plow, I was fashioned by the great
		    powers, assembled by noblest hands!
		I am the mighty registrar of the god Enlil!
		I am the faithful farmer of Mankind!
		At the celebration of my harvest-festival in the
		    fields,
		(25) Even the King slaughters cattle for me, adding
		    sheep!
		He pours out libations for me, and offers the
		    collected liquids!
		Drums and tympans sound!
		(30) The king himself takes hold of my handle-bars;
		My oxen he harnesses to the yoke;
		Great noblemen walk at my side;
		The nations gaze at me in admiration,
		The Land watches me in joy![6] *c*
		
		(35) The furrow I draw is set upon the plain as an
		    adornment;
		Before my sheaves, erected in the fields,
		Even the teeming herds of Shakan kneel down!
		Before my ripened grain, ready for harvesting
		...
		(40) ...[7]

---

[1] See Kramer 1981:342-347 and Vanstiphout 1992a:344-347.

[2] See Vanstiphout 1984 *passim*.

[3] See Vanstiphout 1991a *passim*.

[4] M. Civil's 1960 dissertation remains unpublished. Provisionally the fullest rendering is Kramer 1975.

[5] See Vanstiphout 1984:239. All known material can be found in Attinger 1993:38-39.

[6] This passage apparently alludes to a ceremony, probably at the beginning of the plowing season, and alluded to in a calendrical text. The point is that Hoe will turn the *cameo* into its opposite image in lines 91ff.

[7] These two lines I cannot understand on the basis of the published material.

The shepherd's churn is filled to the brim;
With my *sheaves* scattered over the fields
The sheep of Dumuzi are sated.

My stacks adorning the plains
Are like so many yellow hillocks inspiring awe.[d]
Stacks and mounds I pile up for Enlil;
Dark emmer I amass for him.
I fill the storehouses of Mankind;
Even the orphans, the widows and the destitute
Take their reed baskets
And glean my scattered *grains*.[e]
My straw, piled up in the fields
People even come to *collect* that,
While the beasts of Shakan go about.

O Hoe, miserable hole-digger, with your pathetic long tooth,
O Hoe, always burrowing in the mud,
O Hoe, whose head is always in the dust,
O Hoe-and-brickmold, you spend your days in mud, nobody ever cleans you!

Dig holes! Dig crevices! O navel-man, dig!
O Hoe, you of the poor man's hand, you are not fit for the hand of the noble!
The slave's hand is adorned with your head!
And you dare to insult me?
You dare to compare yourself to me?
When I go out to the plains, *every eye is full of admiration*,
...
..."[8]

Then the Hoe cried out to the Plow

"O Plow, my smallness — what is that to me? My humble state — what is that to me?[f]
My dwelling at the river bank - what is that to me?
At Enlil's place, I precede you!
In Enlil's temple, I stand in front of you!

I make ditches, I make canals;
I fill the meadows with water;
And when the water floods the canebrake,
My small baskets carry it away.
When a canal is cut, or a ditch,
And the water rushes out as a rising flood,
Making everything into a swamp,
I, the Hoe, dam it in,
So that neither southern nor northern storm can *blow it away*.

The fowler samples eggs;
The fisherman catches fish;
And they all empty bird-traps

d Deut 24:19; Cant 7:3

e Exod 22:21; Ruth 2:7; 2:15

f Isa 10:33; Prov 16:11; 29:23

Thus is wealth spread everywhere by my doing.

Moreover, after the water is drained from the meadows
And the work in the moist earth is to be taken in hand,
O Hoe, I come out to the field before you!
The opening up of the field — I start that before you!
The sides and the bottom of the dyke I clean for you!
The weeds in the field I heap up for you!
Stumps and roots I heap up for you!
Only then you work the field, you have your go!
Your oxen are six, your people four — you yourself are merely the eleventh!
The side-boards *take away* the field.
And you want to compare yourself with me?

When you finally come down to the field after me,
Your single furrow already gladdens your eye!
When you finally put your head to the task,
Your *tongue gets caught* by brambles and thorns.
Your tooth *breaks*, and your tooth is renewed;
You will not keep it for long.
Your plowman calls you "This Plow is broken again!"[9]
And, again, carpenters have to be hired, people ...
The whole chapter of workers is milling around you.
The harness-makers scrape another green hide for you,
Twisting it with pegs for you.
Without stopping they turn the tourniquet for you,
And finally a foul hide is put upon your head.[10]

Your *work* is slight, though your ways are great!
My turn of duty is twelve months;
Your effective term is four months;
The time you are idle is eight months;
So you are absent twice as long as you are present!

And then, on the boat you make a hut;
When you are put aboard, your 'hands' sever the boards
So that your face has to be pulled out of the water like a wine-jar.
And only after I have made a pile of logs
Can my smoke and fire dry you out!
Your seeding-funnel — what is then its importance?
Your 'important ones' are thrown upon a pile

[8] See previous note.
[9] For the passage 95-99 see Civil 1994:74-75.
[10] For 103-105 see now Civil 1994:73.

As implements to be destroyed.
But I, I am the Hoe, and live in your city!
No one is more honored than I am.
I am but a servant following his master;
I am but the one who builds the house for his king;
I am but the one who broadens the stalls, who expands the sheepfolds!

I press clay, I make bricks;
I lay foundations, I build houses;
I strengthen the base of an old wall;
I repair the roof of the honest man;
I, I am Hoe, I lay out the streets!

When I have thus gone through the city and built its solid walls,
And have made appear the temples of the great gods therein,
Embellished them with red, yellow and streaked wash,
I go to construct the royal dwelling in the city,
Where overseers and captains dwell.

When the weakened clay has been built up, the fragile clay buttressed,
They can rest because of me in a cool, well-built dwelling.
And when the fire-side makes the hoe gleam, and they lie on their side,
You are not to go to their feast!
They eat and drink;
Their wages are paid out to them
Thus I enable the laborer to support his wife and children.[g]

For the boat-man I make an oven, I heat pitch for him;
And when I have fashioned Magur and Magilum boats,
I have enabled the boatman to support his wife and children.

For the householder I plant the garden;
And when the garden has been encircled, the fences been put up,
the agreements reached,
People again take up the hoe.
When wells have been dug, and poles set up,
The bucket-bar hung, I straighten the beds
And fill their ditches with water.
When the apple-tree has blossomed and the fruits appear,
These fruits are put up as an ornament in the temples of the gods.
Thus I enable the gardener to support wife and children!

When I work at the river with the plow, strengthening the banks,
Building a hut on its banks,
Those who have passed the day in the fields
And the shift which has done the same at night,
They enter their huts.
They revive themselves as in a well-built city;
The water-skins I made they use to pour water
And so they put life into their hearts again.

g Prov 12:11

And you, Plow, think to insult me (by saying) 'Go, dig a hole!?'
On the plains, where no moisture is found,
When I have dug up the sweet water,
The thirsty ones come back to life at the side of my wells!

And what then says the one to the other?
What do they tell one another?[11]
'The shepherd's hoe is surely set up as an ornament on the plains!
For when An had ordered his punishment,
And the bitterness had been ordained over Sumer,
And the waters of the well-built house had collected in the swamp,
And Enlil had frowned upon the Land,
Even the shepherd's crook of Enlil had been made felt,
When great Enlil had acted thus,
Enlil did not restrain his hand.
Then the Hoe, with its single tooth, struck the dry earth!

As for us, the winter's cold, as the locust swarm, you lift!
The heavy hand of summer as of winter you take away.
O Hoe, you binder, you bind the sheaf!
O bird-trap, you binder, you bind the reed-basket!
The lone workman, even the destitute, is provided for;
The grains ... are spread.'"
Then the Storm[12] spoke a word

"The millstone lies still, while the pestle pounds!
From side-plate and foot-plate good results may be had!
Why should the sieve quarrel with the strainer?
Why make another angry?
Ashnan, can a single one reap your neck?
Ripe grain, why should you compare?"

Then Enlil spoke to the Hoe

"O Hoe, do not be so angry!
Do not cry out so loud!
Of the Hoe, is not Nisaba its overseer, its captain?
Hoe, whether five or ten shekel make your price,
Or whether one-third or one half mina,
Like a maid-servant, always ready, you will

[11] Civil 1994:140 interprets this passage as referring to "a catastrophic flood, menacing the harvest." This is almost certainly right as it stands; but the point is that the workmen interpret it as a cosmic or primeval flood *at the same time*.
[12] Probably here an epithet for Enlil.

fulfill your task!"
Dispute of the Hoe and the Plow.

Because the Hoe was greater than the Plow,
Praise be to Nisaba.

REFERENCES

Attinger 1993; Civil 1994; Kramer 1975; 1981; Vanstiphout 1984; 1991a; 1992a.

THE DISPUTATION BETWEEN BIRD AND FISH (1.182)

H. L. J. Vanstiphout

This composition is remarkable not only because it stresses the importance of pleasant and beautiful things in life over dour seriousness,[1] but also because of its peculiar format. It intentionally mixes the generic features of the disputation with those of a fable.[2] Since fish is unable to win by force of argument, it attempts to do so by force *tout court*. Fish's violent attack introduces an element of narrativity which breaks through the argumentative structure. The burden seems to be that stern moral righteousness can never excuse violence anyway. Apart from a couple of more or less complete translations[3] there is no edition, though barring a few possibly crucial lines at the end the text can be reconstructed almost completely. The present translation is based upon an edition prepared for the *PSD* project, and uses unpublished material.[4]

[In long gone, far off days], after the kind fate had been decreed,
[After An and Enlil] had set up the rules of heaven and earth,[a]
[Nudimmud,[5] noble prince], the lord of broad insight, —
[Lord Enki,] decreeing [the fates], their third one he surely is! —
[The waters ...] he collected, founded dwelling-places;
[Life-giving (waters)?] which beget fecund seed he held in hand;
[Tigris and] Euphrates he laid out side by side, and brought in them (the water of) the mountains;
[The smaller] streams he scoured, and put in ditches too.

[Father] Enki also made wide pens and stalls, and provided shepherd and herdsman;
He founded cities and villages, and so made mankind thrive;
A king he gave them for shepherd, and raised him to sovereignty over them; [b]
The king rose as daylight over the countries.

[Father] Enki tied up the marshes, growing there reeds young and old;[5a]
[In ...] ponds and large lakes he made birds and fishes teem; [c]

a Ps 139:24
b 2 Sam 7:7
c Ps 89

[In the lagoons?] he gave all kinds of living creatures as their sustenance,
[...] and so placed the abundance of the gods in their charge.

Nudimmud, noble prince, the lord of broad insight,
When he had fashioned Bird and Fish,
He filled canebrake and marsh with Fish and Bird,
Selected their stations
And made them acquainted[6] with their rules.
Upon that time Fish laid its eggs in the swamp;
Bird built its nest in an opening of the thicket.
But Bird frightened Fish (dwelling) among its property.

[Fish to Bird] cried out;
[...] started a wrangle.
[Fish ...] stood up in pride,[7]
[...] shouted at him, turning up his nose:

"[...] who knows no peace;
[...] constantly wailing;
[...] face? [...] heart dripping with evil!

Standing on the plain you keep picking — they chase you away!
In the furrows the farmer's sons lay a snare for your neck;
The gardener in garden and orchard sets up a net against you!

---

[1] See Vanstiphout 1992a:347-348.
[2] There should be no longer a misunderstanding about the difference between a fable, which is essentially a *narrative* form, and a disputation, which is essentially a *rhetorical* form. Therefore the chapter heading "Fables or Contest Literature" in Lambert (1960) is misleading, doubly so since in that chapter we find only disputations, while the real fables appear in the two subsequent chapters ("Popular Sayings" and "Proverbs").
[3] Kramer 1964 and Krispijn 1993:138-144.
[4] For the material see Attinger 1993:49-50 and Vanstiphout 1991c.
[5] An epithet of the god Enki.
[5a] See the "Epic of Creation," text 1.111, p. 390 above.
[6] Lit., perhaps "made them face the rules."
[7] Perhaps better "in an overbearing manner."

(35) He cannot rest his arm from the sling, cannot sit down in peace!

For in the vegetable rows you cause damage; you are unpleasing;
On the fields along the banks there are your unpleasing[8] footprints.
Bird, you know no shame; you fill the courtyard with your droppings
The sweeper-boy, who cleans the courtyard, chases you with ropes!

(40) By your call the household is disturbed; they flee from your din; [d]
And enter the house of the shrine!
Mooing like cattle, bleating like sheep
They pour out cool water in narrow jugs for you
And then drag you away to the daily sacrifice!
(45) The fowler carries you away with fettered wings,
(The fisherman brings you to the palace;)
Having bound your wings and beak.

Chatterer, whose mooing has no ...; what are you flapping about?
With your ugly screech you disturb[9] the night; no one sleeps sweetly.
(...)[10]
(52) Bird, get out of the swamp! Take this racket of yours off my back!
Go, creep into your hole on top of the rubbish heap — this befits you!"
Thus did Fish insult Bird on that day.

(55) But Bird, with dappled coat and glittering face, and convinced of its own beauty,[e]
Took not to heart the insults Fish had hurled at it.
As if it had been but a nursemaid singing a lullaby,
It did not give in to that speech, but still angry words rose from it.[11]

And then did Bird answer Fish:

(60) "How has your heart become so arrogant, while you yourself are so lowly?
Your mouth is a hillock; your mouth goes all the way round, but you cannot see behind you.
Your hips are cut off, as are your arms, hands and feet — try to put your neck to your feet!
Your smell is awful; you make people throw up, they wrinkle their nose at you!
No trough would hold the kind of prepared food you eat;
(65) And he who has carried you dares not let his hand touch his skin!

d Ezek 3:12; Job 39:24

e Isa 33:17; Ezek 28:12; 28:17; Ps 45:12

In the great swamp and the broad marshes, I am your persecuting demon;
The sweet plants there you cannot eat, they are near to my mouth!
You cannot travel with safety in the river, my storm-cloud covers you.
Underneath my eyes you wriggle through all the reeds!

(70) Your young, every one of them, constitute my daily allotment; you give them to me for my food.
Your big ones are just as certain my *provision* at my banqueting hall.

While I, I am beautiful Bird, the wise one!
Beautiful artistry was put into (the finishing of) my adornment
But no skill has been applied even to begin your rough shaping!
(75) Strutting about in the Royal Palace befits me;
My warbling is as a decoration in the courtyard;
The sound I produce, the sweet chanting of my voice,
Is made into a delicious ornament for Shulgi's[12] person!
Produce and fruits of all orchard and gardens are my plentiful daily ration;
(80) Finest groats, peeled barley, emmer wheat and dates are sweet things to my mouth.
How do you not recognize my greatness ? Bow your neck to the ground!"

Thus Bird insulted Fish on that day.

Fish became angry and, trusting in its heroic strength and worthiness,
Swept over the bottom like a heavy rain cloud. It took up the quarrel.
(85) It took not to heart the insults Bird had hurled at it.
"Upon your own neck be it!" it spoke unrestrainedly,

And again did Fish reply to Bird:

"Long beak, long legs, dwarfed feet, cleft bill, slit mouth!
You are clattering from ignorance; you have not reflected!
(90) Glutton, freak(?), filling the courtyard with droppings —
The little sweeper-boy sets nets in the house and chases you with ropes! —

[8] A sly hint in reverse? We know that Fish will be the loser because it is much too proud and self-opinionated; is this an allusion to the chicken-track aspect of cuneiform signs?

[9] Lit., "you frighten." But since there is no personal direct object the literal translation ["you frighten the night"] would be nonsense.

[10] Study by autopsy of the tablets has revealed that the line numbering of the translations and consequently also that of quotes in secondary literature is out by two numbers from line 48 onwards. Still, since there is no edition it is better provisionally to keep to the traditional numbering.

[11] I.e. from Bird.

[12] Shulgi is the greatest king of the Third Dynasty of Ur.

The baker, the brewer, the porter, all those who live in the house are annoyed with you![13]

Bird, you did not examine(?) the case of my greatness, you did not take due account of its nature;
My weakness and my strength you did not consider; yet you spoke inflammatory words!
Once you have really looked into my achievements, you will humble yourself exceedingly!
Now your speech contains grave errors; you have not thought about it!

I, I am Fish; I deliver altogether the abundance of the pure shrine,
Even to the great offerings to lustrous Ekur — I stand proudly with my head raised high!
Just like Ashnan I am here to satisfy the hunger of the Land — I am her aide!
And therefore people pay attention to me, they keep their eyes upon me!
As at the harvest festival, they always rejoice over me, and take care of me!

Bird, whatever great deeds you may have done, I will teach you their pretense!
The harshness and evil speech you held, I shall hand back to you!"

Thereupon Fish conceived an evil plot against Bird.[f]
Silently, furtively, it slithered alongside
And when Bird arose from its nest to fetch food for its young
Fish searched for the most discreet of the silent places.

Its well-built nest, made from brushwood it made into a derelict house;
Its well-built house it destroyed, tore down the storeroom;
The eggs it had laid it smashed, and threw them into the sea.
Thus did Fish strike at Bird — and then fled into the waters.

Then came Bird, lion-faced, and with an eagle's talons,
Winging towards its nest. It stops in mid-flight;
Like a hurricane whirling in the midst of heaven, it circles in the sky;
Bird, looking about for its nest spreads open wings and legs.

Its well-built nest, made from brushwood, it now tramples over it as if it were the broad plain.
Its mouth cries out in the midst of heaven as does the priestess!

[f] Exod 15:7; Zech 10:11

Bird now seeks around for Fish, searching the marshes;
Bird peers into the river, watches it closely.

As if snatching into the water, it stretched out its legs,
Clasped its *claws*[?] together and did not open them again.
Thus Bird took vengeance.

Again did Bird reply to Fish:

"Utter fool, dumb one, muddle-headed one, Fish, you are out of your mind!
Those who circle the quay — their mouths never eat enough; you spend your day with fodder!
Swine, rascal, gorging yourself upon your own dung, *freak*[?]!
You are like a watchman living on top(?)[14] of a house, dripping(?) by itself!
Fish, you kindled something like fire against me, you planted henbane;
Your stupidity caused devastation; you have sprinkled your hands with blood!
Your arrogant heart, by its own deeds, will destroy itself!

But I, I am Bird, flying in heaven and walking upon earth;
Wherever I travel, I am there for the joy of everyone[15] under the sky;
[...] o Fish, the greatest princes gave them.
[...] New Year(?) [...] my [...] it is the first born young; [...] to [...] of Enlil.
[...] walks with uplifted head;
[...] ... until distant days.
[...] ... he speaks to the multitudes.
[How] can you not recognize my pre-eminence?
Bow your neck to the ground!"

Thus again Bird had hurled insults at Fish.

Then did Fish shout at Bird, looking at it in anger:

"Let not words ...! Our judge should take it up[?]!
To our judge and umpire, to Enki, let us take our case!"

And so the two of them, jostling and continuing the evil quarrel,
In order to establish, the one over the other, his pre-eminence,
In ... Eridu (they?) registered the litigation, and, having performed the argumentation,
[...] confused(?), as if by their (own) noise,
[...] crept (before him) like ...;

[13] Or perhaps "are fleeing from you"?
[14] "Top" or "roof" is normally ÙR, while the text has ÚR "base." I do not understand the second hemistich, and the translation is merely an (unlikely) approximation.
[15] Lit., "everyone named."

[From Shulgi], son of Enlil,
(149) [...] peace, they request a verdict.

(150) ["You (Enki),[16] whose] speech is true — Please, your ear to my words!
I had placed [my nest in the marshes]; eggs had been laid.
[Food(?) of the marshes(?)] was given for free, was put there for their sustenance.
[After Fish] had set up [the quarrel(?)]
[...] it has destroyed my house;
(155) [My well-built nest] made from brushwood he made into a derelict house;
[My well-built house he destroy]ed, my storeroom he tore down;
[The eggs I laid he] smashed and threw them into the sea.
[O judge ...[17]] examine my speech, return my verdict!"

[Before(?) the judge who was(?)] looking closely into [the matter, he] prostrated himself to the ground.
(160) Now [their judge] announces(?) the word;
[He whose word is] great, spoke from the heart
["...] I am accepting their appeal!"[18]
[The contestants,] quarrelling, come along.
Like one passing (?) a [...], (one) came out supreme.
(165) Like goring [oxen(?)] they jostled each other.
"[Whatever word you speak], let it be favorable to me!
You know the rules and ordinances of the broad earth!
When you search for the right decision, you are immensely wise in knowing the (right) word for that!"

He answered Bird and Fish

(170) "To stand in the Ekur is fitting for Bird, its voice is sweet [indeed].
At Enlil's holy table, Bird should take precedence over you [...]!
In the temple of all the great gods (Bird's) voice is pleasing;
The Anunna-gods rejoice in its voice.
It is suitable for the banquets in the great dining hall of the gods;
(175) It [provides] good cheer in Shulgi's palace.
It should stand with raised head, in the [house] of Shulgi, son of Enlil!"
King Shulgi[19] [...]

[...]
Fish [...]
(180) Thereupon[20] [...] ...[21]
(190) In the dispute held by Bird and Fish,
Because Bird was victorious over Fish,
Father Enki be praised!

[16] Or perhaps (Shulgi)?
[17] Or perhaps (Shulgi)?
[18] Lit., "[...] their appeal is surely sweet to my mouth!"
[19] Direct speech or narrative?
[20] Clearly a new and final narrative episode.
[21] There are a number of missing lines. The tablet which contained the immediately preceding lines could easily have had ten lines before the end.

REFERENCES

Attinger 1993:49-50; Kramer 1964; Krispijn 1993:131-148; Lambert 1960; Vanstiphout 1991c; 1992a.

THE DISPUTATION BETWEEN SUMMER AND WINTER (1.183)

H. L. J. Vanstiphout

As far as we know, this altercation between the two most natural opposites imaginable, was the longest of all Sumerian disputations.[1] But it is in a much worse state of preservation than the previous three pieces.[2] Here also there is a mixture of generic features: the text starts with a long list of "destinies" or proprieties allotted to the contestants by the gods. It is obvious from the start that basically the two contestants are equal in value, and that the quarrel can only start because of unwarranted jealousy (indeed, it starts on a point of procedure, or literally precedence). The dispute as such remains unresolved, since the verdict insists that they are complementary and should remain so. Yet the matter is resolved on a point of simple justice: Winter (Enten) ought not to be jealous of Summer (Emesh), but Summer should not be allowed to profit from Winter's efforts. So the main feature of this piece is that it is about undue rivalry resolved.[3]

[1] 318 lines have been calculated.
[2] For the published material see Vanstiphout 1987b.
[3] See Vanstiphout 1992a.

(1) The Lord lifted his head in pride, bountiful days arrived.

Heaven and earth he regulated, and the population spread wide;

Enlil, like a mighty bull, placed his feet on the earth.

To make bountiful times of abundance,[a]

(5) To make manifest ... nights of splendor,

To make legumes grow, to make wheat spread out,

To make 'the' carp-flood[4] appear regularly at the quays,

To make the people lengthen their days in abundance,

To make Emesh bind the dykes of heaven,

(10) To make Enten show regularly the abundant waters at the quays,

— This was what Enlil, king of the Mountainland, wanted to achieve.[5]

With the great Hursag-hill he copulated, yes, gave that mountain her share;

He thus made her pregnant with Emesh and Enten, welfare and life of the Nation;

Enlil, when he copulated, roared like a bull;

(15) Hursag spent the day at that place, and at night she opened her loins.[6]

Emesh and Enten she bore as (smoothly as with) princely oil;[b]

As great bulls (s)he made them eat pure plants in the enclosures of the hills;

(S)he reared them in the mountain meadows.

Then Enlil cast the lots for Emesh and Enten[7]

(20) To Emesh the founding of settlements;

The bringing in of abundant harvests to great mountain Enlil;[c]

To send out laborers to the great fields; to make settle the ox on the acre.

To Enten abundance, the early flooding, the bounty and life of the Nation;[c]

The placing of wheat on the fruitful acres; to gather in everything.

(25) This Enlil decided for Emesh and Enten as their destiny.

Enten, from the brink of the hill country

Took in hand the early flooding, bounty and life of the Nation.

He set his foot upon Tigris and Euphrates like a big bull,

And let them free upon the fruitful fields of Enlil.

(30) The sea he fashioned (into) ....

(margin references:)
a Prov 3:10

b Ps 74:17

c Prov 10:5

d Deut 28:4-5; Ezek 16:13

Enten (also) brought forth ....

The bull (he) surrounded with reeds both young and old (...).

Ninurta, Enlil 's heroic son,

Took away the water from the great fields

(35-45 broken)

(46) The ox shakes its head in the yoke.

(47-49 broken)

(50) ... the goat (bore) kids.

Cows and calves he made teem; he gathered ghee and milk;

In the high steppe deer and buck rejoice.

The birds of heaven build their nests all over.

The fish of the swamps lay their eggs in the reed thickets.

(55) In the orchards honey and wine are dripping onto the ground;[d]

The orchards are in full fruit.

The gardens grow legumes and sprout vegetables.

The grain becomes heavy in the furrow

Ashnan appears as a fair young maid[8];

(60) And thus did the Harvest, the great feast of Enlil, raise its head towards heaven.

Emesh made a barn; he widened sheepfold and stall;

He added to the abundance in the great fields;

And all the produce he put aside ....

The abundant harvest he brought into the estate, he gathered the heaps of grain.

(65) He founded cities and villages; he built the temple of the Nation.

He caused the House of the gods to appear like a hill on a pure place.

The House-of-Life, holy abode of kingship, fit for the lofty dais,

He founded in abundance for great mountain Enlil.

Emesh, heroic son of Enlil,

(70) Then decided to bring offerings to the House-of-Life, Enlil's abode.

Wild animals, cattle and sheep of the hill country,

Wild rams, deer and buck, all fully grown,

Mountain sheep, noble sheep, fat-tailed sheep he brought.

Pigs grown fat in the midst of the reed thicket, porcupine and tortoise,

(75) Birds on their nest, brooding their eggs.

All harvest produce, flour and malt for mixing, ghee and milk from sheepfold and stall;

Rye, egg-beans, small beans, large beans in

---

[4] The traditional name of the all-important flooding at the beginning of the agricultural cycle.

[5] In a way this is somewhat strange. Usually it is the god Enki who explains the purpose behind his creative acts.

[6] For this motif (and the lines 12-15) see Cooper 1989.

[7] The following passage is reminiscent of Enki's actions in the programmatic piece "Enki Orders the World," for which see most recently Bottéro and Kramer 1989:165-188.

[8] See the Disputation between Ewe and Wheat (text 1.180 above) lines 49-52.

basketfuls;
Onions which took sweetness when in their furrows, garlic and shallots,
Beet, cress, ...

(80-89 broken)

(90) Enten, proud son of Enlil,

(91 broken)

(92) For the sheep which is being disputed — it is fattened but at its side there is a scorpion[9]

(93-98 broken)

The fattened Bibra-bird, the Esig-bird, the Shurra-bird and the Ushtur-bird,[10]
(100) The carp ... which Enlil made grow up;
The pomegranates which he gathered ...;
Large beets, a large GUG-loaf cut, garlic cut with the cleaver;
Enten himself carried the offerings he brought.

Emesh, heroic son of Enlil
(105) Then decided to bring offerings to the House-of-Life, Enlil's abode
Bucks and lambs of the mountain-sheep.

Emesh and Enten drove together the gift of young cattle;
The two of them, like butting bulls they reared themselves for battle.
Enten, because of his tired arms and shoulders
(110) From all the grain grown heavy in the furrow which he had been watering,
Turned from them as (from) a stranger; he did not want to draw near.
Anger overcame Enten, and he started a quarrel with Emesh.[e]

"Emesh, my brother, do not praise yourself![11]
Whatever you carry to the Palace as a gift
(115) Has not been made through your effort - Do not brag!
As if you yourself had done the hard work;
As if you yourself had done the farming work;
As if your own water-inspection at the early flood had brought life to the Nation;
As if you yourself had caused grain to appear on the fields with the dew from the skies —
(120) You are about to enter the Palace in this way with my efforts!
As if you yourself had brought ... the wild animals, the cattle and sheep from the hill country";

(122-139 broken; 140-152 very fragmentary)

Thus had Enten then insulted Emesh.

Emesh, the hero whom one does not ..., he searched for rude insults;
(155) On harvest day he trusted in his heart, he left;
Like a mighty bull, he ate hay, and raised his head.

Emesh thereupon replied to Enten:

"Enten, do stay at the side of the oven ...; when ... their words;
You should not place these heavy insults (against one?) who does not lead a sitting life;

(160) For carrying out the task, with its difficulties, of furrowing the Nation
You do not raise the cry in the GUNE, you do not inspect the estate.
The young scribe is absent, which is an abomination; no grass is pulled out for the bed.
The singer does not embellish the banquet; at its side ....

Enten, do not speak insults; to the steppe ....
(165) I shall reveal my force to the estate, so that even you may perceive it!
In my working tour of seven months in a year
... does not whisper softly to ....

(168-171 broken)

(173) Enten, do not ... noise ....
When you have taken away the water from the fields, when the tubs are placed,
(175) When you have made ready the fishing places, and heaped up the fish,
I am Enlil's great comptroller;
And I harrow the field into a fruitful field!
When the oxen have stopped working the field
When I have put force to the damp earth; when I have fulfilled the necessary assignment,
(180) I do not work for you in the fields and plantations early in the season.[12]
The early grain will bend its neck in the hollow of the furrow; but no one makes a fence.
Your plowboy, wherever he walks the ox, will not make the ox angry with me."

(183-188 fragmentary)

Enten thereupon replied to Emesh:

(190) "Emesh, the mule grazing on the harvest-field makes an ear-splitting noise!

(191 broken)

The harvest ox which chafes its neck at the yoke-block shakes its head!
The ale-seller going down to the harvest field is holding the jug!
The flour-roaster ...
(195) The laborer though constantly boasting does

e Amos 3:15

[9] Note that in the Disputation between Ewe and Wheat the same notion occurs; see above, text 1.180, line 127.
[10] We do not know exactly which birds these are.
[11] Note that Emesh has not been bragging so far.
[12] See Civil 1994:79 and 83 for this line and the next.

not know the extent of the field![f]
Emesh, my brother, after you have boasted with my exertions,
At the end of the year the grain is brought in to the estate, and the granaries are filled up.
After you have brought the excess, and your Bardul and your Niglam[13] garments are woven,
An axe ... to your strength[?] ....
Emesh, opening up the field, do not forget the wet earth!

(201-207 broken)

Reed-cutter about to prune with the Barhuda,[14] split the grown reed!

(209 broken)

Potter, dig up clay, light the fire, carry faggots, and ... the pot!
Weaver, weave your Bardul garment with the strength[?] of your Aktum cloth!
Brewer, bake beer bread at the harvest place as is your assignment!
... let Emesh leave!
... he threw ....
Men wear boots and sandals ....

Emesh, my brother, as long as you go with[?] my own tour of duty,
Small and great order you about; your string is never cut.
Though you have gathered all things in the Nation, and filled the granaries,
It is with my effort of your capital[?], I am completely the rightful owner!

When the clouds brought abundance down from the skies,
And the water for the first greening had descended from the hillsides;
When the new grain, being added to the old grain, is put in the granary;
The good farmer, having seen to his fields, shouts for joy,
Harnesses his carrier donkeys, and sets out proudly for the city.

My brother, when you have put away the holy plow in the barn,
The granary, all that you have gathered, you make roar like fire[?];
You sit down to plentiful food and drink;
You obtain the choicest goods from the Nation.
The king named by Nanna, son of Enlil,
Ibbi-Sîn,[15] when you have clothed him with the Shutur and the Hursag[16] garments,
Adorned him with the Bardul and the Niglam garments,
When you have made a perfect feast for the gods,
The Anuna clothe their holy bodies with a garment.
And in his House-of-Life, the holy abode of kingship founded by An,
When you have prepared at that place of heart's content a succulent banquet;
With tambourine, drum, trumpet and lute playing for him as by themselves,
And Tigi and Zamzam[17], they who gladden your heart, while away the day,
It is I who have made the plentiful wine, who deliver lots of drink;
I who perfect the garments with fine oil;
I who bring out the [...], the Shutur and the Aktum cloths!
In order to safeguard[?] them for Emesh, the first in Sumer, at the heavy ....
That resting place in the bosom of the Blackheads, where they were put away,
Moths have destroyed the blankets, eaten the Aktum carpet for you!

(244-253 fragmentary; 254-256 broken)

The gardener does not know how to grow purslain, your basket for cut (vegetables) ...;
You, how can you compare with me, while seeking a roof for resting?"

Thus had Enten then insulted Emesh.

Emesh, heroic son of Enlil
Was convinced of his own power, and trusted in his heart.
To the insults Enten had spoken to him
It was as if he acted friendly.

Emesh thereupon replied to Enten:

"Enten, do not yourself praise your overriding force after you have explained your importance!
In the city I shall speak about your abode, which I shall always protect[?];

You may seem a chief, but you are a helpless one.
Your faggot is for brazier, hearth and oven,
So shepherd's boy and shepherd with your heavy sheep
The helpless ones, from brazier to oven, from oven to brazier
They run about like sheep in your ....
In sunshine you lay your plans ...;
But now in the city teeth are chattering because of you.[g]
When the day is only half, nobody walks the streets.

f Isa 10:15; 60:21
g Amos 3:15

[13] We do not know precisely what kinds of garment these are.
[14] An agricultural implement; mattock?
[15] Last king of the Ur III Dynasty.
[16] Unknown garments.
[17] Musical instruments.

The servant, glad of his oven, (remains) in the house till the sun sets.
The maid, not employed in the flooded fields, passes the day with (making?) garments;
In the field, which Enten does not work,[18]
Where no furrows have been cut,
Its grain, not being put in its wholesome place, is taken away by the fat crow;
The produce of the vegetable cutter — of these vegetables the market-price is bad;
Bearing only old reeds, the reed-bearers get cuts in their bare feet.
Do not speak about overriding power — I will make known its shape and essence!"

Emesh thus replied to Enten.

Then ... Sumer in abundance,
Both of them stretch their legs, stand up as for a fight.
(285a) Enten ... a word ... raises his head:

"Father Enki, you gave me the control of the watership, you brought me the water of abundance!

(287-290 fragmentary)

The grain grew heavy in the furrows.

(292-295 broken)

(296) Enten admires the heart of your ... in words."

Emesh collects everything in his head, and calms down.
Emesh speaks respectfully to Enlil:
"Enlil, your judgment is overpowering, your word is the highest.
Your verdict cannot be altered - who could change it?
Brother has started a quarrel with brother, but now they are calm again.
As long as you enter the palace the people will speak their awe.
When you live there, I shall not mock anything, but praise everything."

Enlil replies to Emesh and Enten:

"Of the life-giving waters from the midst of the mountains, Enten is the director.
The farmer of the gods, who gathers everything.
Emesh, my son, how can you compare with Enten, your brother?"

Enlil — the gist of his mighty word is perfect;
The verdict he pronounced cannot be altered — who could change it?

Emesh bowed before Enten, said prayers to him.
In his house he prepared beer and wine for him.
At its side they pass the day with a succulent banquet.
Emesh gives gold and silver to Enten;[h]
In brotherly love and friendship they will alternate
And they shall comfort their minds by speaking sweet words, and so gratify each other.[i]

In the disputation between Emesh and Enten
Enten, the farmer of the gods, was greater than Emesh;
Therefore great mountain Enlil be praised.

h Job 42:11
i Zech 14:8

[18] Obviously, which are not worked in winter; see Civil 1994:79.

REFERENCES

Bottéro and Kramer 1989; Civil 1994; Cooper 1989:87-89; van Dijk 1957b; Vanstiphout 1987b:15-16; 1992a.

6. SCHOOL DIALOGUES

This section has been included for a very special reason. The Scriptural parallels here might be few in number, and inherently vacuous, if not nugatory. And that is precisely the point: the rich 'school literature' in Sumerian from Old Babylonian Mesopotamia shows a striking and very meaningful contrast between the two cultures. In the Mesopotamian case the perception, ordering and evaluation of conscious culture is governed by an organized system of education in the scribal school, or Eduba, as is shown by its structure, its curriculum, and its products. What is more, in a significant number of compositions they have laid down — though mostly in a jocular vein — their *attitudes* towards this system, including that of intellectual freedom, with its consequent cynicism, within the closed group of *literati*. This unexpectedly 'modern' idea is absent from the neighboring cultures, and only represented in a much watered down version in Mesopotamia itself after the Kassite period. The only meaningful point(s) of comparison would be some periods in Egyptian cultural history. And this is all the more reason for including, by way of stark contrast, some samples in this collection.[1] The three pieces have been chosen because each of them

[1] On the schools in general, their curriculum and their methods, see Van Dijk 1953:21-27; Gadd 1956; Sjöberg 1975; Römer 1977; Vanstiphout 1979 with earlier literature; Civil 1985; Waetzoldt 1986, 1988 and 1989.

highlights a different aspect, not only of the school, but of the internal and external implications of being a "scholar"; furthermore, they present a marked gradation in subject matter and seriousness for the pupils involved.

THE DIALOGUE BETWEEN TWO SCRIBES (1.184)

H. L. J. Vanstiphout

This provisionally fragmentary[1] composition focuses on the competition between two scribes, one being more advanced than the other, and using his seniority to bully and insult the younger one — after which the teacher, apparently a stickler for school tradition, takes the side of the senior student (the "Big Brother"). But in the meantime we learn a number of practical and methodological details about schooling, its aims and its eventual rewards. The two opponents in this quarrel are identified by name. And the piece cleverly takes over some of the structural features of a poetical disputation.[2]

(GIRINE-ISAG)
"Well fellow student, what shall we write today on the back of our tablet[3]?"

(ENKI-MANSUM)
"Today we will not even write a single word from our lesson!"

(GIRINE-ISAG)
"But then surely the teacher will know and be angry with us because of you!
What will we say to him?"

(ENKI-MANSUM)
"Come now, I shall write what I want! I will set the task!"

(GIRINE-ISAG)
"If you set the task, I am not your 'big brother'!
Why do you encroach on my status of 'big brother'?
I have become excellent in the scribal art; I have fulfilled the function of 'big brother' to perfection!
You are slow of understanding and hard of hearing; you are but a novice in the school!
You are deaf to the scribal art, and silent in Sumerian!
Your hand is crippled; it is unfit for the writing reed
And unfit for the clay; (your) hand cannot keep up with the mouth.
And you would be a scribe like me?"

(ENKI-MANSUM)
"[Why should I] not be a scribe like you?"

(15-18 lost or fragmentary)

(GIRINE-ISAG)
"You wrote a tablet, but you cannot grasp its meaning.
You wrote a letter, but that is the limit for you!
Go to divide a plot, and you are not able to divide the plot;
Go to apportion a field, and you cannot even hold the tape and rod properly.
The field pegs you are unable to place; you cannot figure out its shape,
So that when wronged men have a quarrel you are not able to bring peace,
But you allow brother to attack brother.[a]
Among the scribes, you (alone) are unfit for the clay.
What are you fit for? Can anybody [tell] us?"

(ENKI-MANSUM)
"Why should I be good for nothing?
When I go to divide a plot, I can divide it;
When I go to apportion a field, I can apportion the pieces,
So that when wronged men have a quarrel, I soothe their hearts and [...].
Brother will be at peace with brother, the(ir) hearts [...]."

(33-58 lost or fragmentary)

(GIRINE-ISAG) (?)
"As to subtracting and adding the daily quota of the weaving girls,
And the finished order of the apprentice smith[4] of his master — I know its procedure.
My father speaks Sumerian; I am the son of a scribe;
But you are the son of a vile one, a barbarian.
You cannot shape a tablet, nor knead an exercise tablet.
You cannot even write your own name; the clay is

a [Talmud: *sin^{c}at chinnam*!]

[1] For the published material, see Römer 1988:235. He gives a partial edition of the text based on the published manuscripts, and cites earlier studies.

[2] More or less balanced speaking time; arguments which are answered point for point in places; intervention of a "judge" — although his decision seems to be left in abeyance.

[3] Also possible "after our tablet." But since the back of exercise tablets is regularly used for other texts than the front this translation seems to make better sense.

[4] The meaning is probably that he is able to calculate the relation in weight or value between the raw material the apprentice smith has received and the finished product.

not suited to your hand.
Stop hacking away! Is it a hoe you are wielding?[5]
Clever fool, cover your ears, cover them!
Do you pretend to speak Sumerian as I do?"

(ENKI-MANSUM) (?)
"Why do you keep repeating to me 'cover your ears, cover them?'"

(68-133 lost or fragmentary)

"Why do you act like this?[6]
Why do you push one another, and hurl insults at one another?
You raise a clamor in the school!
I have been teaching Sumerian as required,"

(138-139 fragmentary)

"Even in those long gone days, when you were still beaten and ...,
No shouting reached me (like this)!
Why, to him who is your 'big brother,'
Who knows more about the scribal art than you,
Why have you spoken to him so arrogantly,
And cursed and insulted him?"

The teacher, who knew about everything
Frowned sternly (saying) "Do as you wish!"

(GIRINE-ISAG?)
"If I could really do as I wished,
Then a fellow acting like you, attacking his 'big brother,'
After I had given him 60 strokes with the cane,
Put his feet in fetters,
Confined him to the house so that he cannot go out for two months,
Your (his!) crime would certainly not yet have been expiated!"[7]

As from this day, their eyes keep staring (in hatred).
The one acts meanly towards the other.
Brother fights with brother, takes him on.
Since between the quarreling Enki-Mansum and Girine-Isag, both of them,
The teacher will give the verdict,
Praise be to Nisaba!

[5] This seems a clever allusion to the Dispute between the Hoe and the Plow (text 1.181 above), where one of the underlying ideas may have been that the work of the Hoe in the soft earth is to be compared (also in importance) to that of the stylus on clay!
[6] Perhaps the teacher himself or one of his senior staff is speaking now. But it is also possible, and perhaps more plausible in view of lines 146-147, that this is the Big Brother upbraiding the pupil in front of the teacher.
[7] The different manuscripts show some hesitation between the 2nd and the 3rd person in these lines.

THE DIALOGUE BETWEEN A SUPERVISOR AND A SCRIBE (1.185)

H. L. J. Vanstiphout

This piece is not unlike the preceding one in that it consists of an altercation between a senior and a junior member of the Eduba. Still, the relationship is subtly different: the senior one is not just a more mature student, but a regular supervisor (an UGULA). He submits the pupil, who is obviously aspiring to higher things at this moment, to a kind of examination which deals not only with the capabilities ensuing from the pupil's schooling, but also with his moral stance within the Eduba system. If one were to posit a background or location in reality, the examination could represent a test of Sumerian style and rhetoric. The final part consists of a eulogy of the pupil, who has apparently done well. There is no edition as yet; this translation is based upon the published material, with the proviso that unpublished material shows the existence of another and appreciably longer version.[1]

(*Supervisor*)
"(Old) schoolboy, come here, come to me quickly!
What my teacher taught me, I will teach you.

Like you, I was once a youth, who had a big brother.
[The teacher] selected me from the other men, and assigned me a task.
Like the trembling reed I trembled, [a] but I applied myself to the work.
The [word] of my master I did not forget; I did not ...
My big brother was delighted with my (work at the) assignation.
My humility made him so happy that he spoke ...
Whatever I was ordered to do, I did; and everything was always in its place.
From his counsels only a fool would deviate.
He guided my hand properly on the clay, and kept

[a] 1 Kgs 14:15

[1] The published texts are A: HS 1546+1582 = *TMH NF* III 38 + IV 77; B: Ni 4243 + Ni 4092 = *SLTNi* 114 + *ISET*, 84; C: Ni 2507 = *SRT* 28; D: HS 1441 = *TMH NF* III 37; E: CBS 13106 = *HAV* 19; F: CBS 14070 = *SEM* 59; G: Ni 2506 = *SRT* 27; H: Ni 4133 = *ISET* 1, 135; I: Ni 9679 = *ISET* 2, 84; a: 3N-T 917, 388 = *SLFN* 47; b: 3N-T 917, 399 = *SLFN* 47; c: 3N-T 906, 231 = *SLFN* 47; d: 3N-T 927, 517 = *SLFN* 47.

me on the straight line.
He opened my mouth to all the words; he showed me the (wisest) counsels.
He filled my eyes with the rules of him who correctly fulfills the assignment.
Zeal is the lot of the assignee; time-wasting is a shame.
(15) He who tarries (on his way) to the place of work neglects his duty.
One should not not exalt one's knowledge, but should control one's speech.
When one exalts one's knowledge in splendor, people raise their eyes in astonishment. [b]
Do not idle away the day! Do not rest in the evening! Go to work this moment!
[Neither graduate nor] freshman may give himself over to levity!
(20) ... your words must be serious.
Again, do not put your trust in your own unopened eyes
Thus you would greatly scorn obedience, which is the honor of humanity.
[A modest man] has a peaceful heart; his sins are absolved.
A poor man's gift is honorable to all minds.
(25) Even he who has nothing still kneels and holds the sacrificial kid to his breast
Bowing to the powers that be, and containing myself — that is what gratifies me!

These things my teacher taught me, I recited them to you; do not scorn them!
Pay attention; take these thing to heart; this will be to your profit."

The learned scribe respectfully answered his master:

(*Scribe*)
(30) "Now you have recited, incantation-like, I shall give you the response thereto.[2]
And to your bullish "sweet chant" its rebuttal.
You shall not turn me into a know-nothing; I shall answer but once.

Once a puppy, my eyes are wide open now, I act with humanity.
So why is it that you keep setting up rules for me, as if I were a shirker?
(35) Those who hear your words will revile me!

Whatever you showed me from the scribal art has been given back to you!
You appointed me over your household; you cannot accuse me of a single instance of neglect.[3]
I always assigned the tasks of the slave girls, the slaves and other personnel of your household.
I soothed their hearts with rations of food, clothing and oil.
(40) I assigned the order of their tasks. It is said "Do not pursue the servant in the house of the master!"
But every morning I did — I followed them like sheep.
You ordered the preparations for the offerings; and on the same day I performed them for you.
I prepared the sheep and the banquets expertly, so that your god was overjoyed.
The day when the ship of your god arrived it was greeted with great respect.
(45) You ordered me to the edge of the field; the work force was already toiling there.
In the contest of labor there was no rest, night or day.
The journeymen, sons of the plowmen, were strongest.
I brought back quality to your field; but the people admire [you!]
However great the assigment for the oxen, I always brought in more; their burden [...]

(50) Since my youth you have watched me, and inspected my ways.
I am polished like fine metal; a better product [there is not?]
I do not use big words, as is your mistake; I wait upon you.
Belittling oneself is what causes people to be ignored; therefore I want to make (my true worth?) apparent for you: learn this!"[4]

(*Supervisor*)
"Earlier, you were but a child. Now, hold up your head!
(55) Your hands were turned to the grown-ups; now fulfill (your own) task!
Accept this prayer of blessing; [a good?] fate [I will proclaim?]
Your counsels have penetrated my body as if I had taken milk and oil.
[Your] unceasing service [...]
May the good results thereof be regular; the bad results [...]
(60) May the teachers, these wise men, encourage you (further).
In this house, that foremost place, may [...]
Your name may be elected with honor; its power and excellence [...]
The cattlemen may [fight for?] for your pleasurable songs;
I myself want to fight for your pleasurable song; I want to [...]
(65) The teacher with joyous heart will bless you.

b Prov 15:12

[2] See Vanstiphout 1996:1-2 for this and the next two lines.
[3] See Vanstiphout 1996:2.
[4] See Vanstiphout 1996:2.

You are a young man who listened to my words; my heart is glad.
The worthiness of Nisaba which the teacher has placed in your hands
(Makes you) into the good hand of Nisaba; [lift up?] your head to heaven!
Let this become (your) fate with a joyous heart; let downheartedness [lift?].
The Eduba, the place of all wisdom there is [...][5]

[5] There follow half a dozen fragmentary lines.

THE DIALOGUE BETWEEN AN EXAMINER AND A STUDENT (1.186)

H. L. J. Vanstiphout

In this composition we again have a dialogue, but now it takes the form of a *viva voce* examination. One might say that it looks like a final examination, wherein the student may be said to try for graduation. Apparently it takes place before an external examiner: the student keeps referring to his teacher. In a second part, not translated here, the piece takes on the format of a flyting — which in various guises can also be found in other, related compositions. There is a very good edition of the first part of the text.[1]

(Examiner and Student)
"Young man, [are you a student?" — "Yes, I am a student."]

(Examiner)
"If you are a student
Do you know Sumerian?"

(Student)
"Yes, I can speak Sumerian."

(Examiner)
"You are so young; how is it you can speak so well?"

(Student)
"I have listened constantly to the words of my teacher;
So I can answer you."

(Examiner)
"All right, you may be able to answer me, but what do you write?"

(Student)
"If you would just examine what I write!
[The time] I still have to spend in school is less than three months.
The [texts] in Sumerian and Akkadian, from A-A ME-ME[2]
[To ...] I can read and write.
All lines from ^{d}INANA-TEŠ$_2$ [3]
Till the 'beings of the plain' at the end/beginning of LU$_2$-*šu* I wrote.[4]
I can show you my signs,
Their writing and their interpretation; and this is how I pronounce them."

(Examiner)
"Right, follow me!
I will not give you things that are too complicated."

(Student)
"Even if I am assigned LU$_2$=*šu* on an exercise tablet
I can give the 600 LU$_2$ entries in their correct sequence.[5]
The schedule of my schooling was like this:
My holidays were three every month;
Various feasts averaged three per month;
With all that, there were 24 days per month
That I spent in school. But this time never seemed long.
In a single day the teacher would give me the same *pensum* four times.
In the final reckoning, what I know of the scribal art will not be taken away!
So now I am master of the meaning of tablets, of mathematics, of budgeting,
Of the whole scribal art, of the disposition of lines, of evading omissions, of ....
My teacher approved (my) beautiful speech.
The companionship (in the school) was a joyful thing.
I know my scribal art prefectly;
Nothing flusters me.
My teacher had to show me a sign only once,
And I could add several from memory.

[1] Civil 1985.
[2] A beginner's sign list.
[3] A lexical list.
[4] A lexical list. See Civil 1985:74 for this line.
[5] There are no 600 entries in the lexical series LÚ-*šu*(*šá*)!

Having been in school for the required period,
I am now an expert in Sumerian, in the scribal art, in interpretation, and in budgeting.
I can even speak Sumerian."

(Examiner)
"That may be so, but the sense of the Sumerian is hidden from you!"

(Student)
(40) "I desire to start writing tablets (professionally);
Tablets of one measure of grain till those of 600 measures;
Tablets of one shekel till those of twenty minas;
Also any marriage contracts they may bring;
And partnership contracts — I can specify verified weights up to a talent,
(45) And also deeds for the sale of houses, gardens, slaves,
Financial guarantees, field hire contracts, ...
Palm growing contracts, ...
Adoption contracts — all those I can draw up."

(49-55 fragmentary)

(Examiner? Student?)
"We are of the same birth, we are ....[6]
He and I have [compared] our hand tablets
Both have drawn up budgets ...
And regarding the budget ...
(60) The budget ...
He who cannot understand the accounts like scribes ....
About the tablets' meaning, the scribal art, the signs with difficult readings,
Let them have a fight.
If he wins, he shall take whatever is mine;
(65) But if I win, what shall I get?"

(66-69 fragmentary)

(70) "We will shout insults at one another!
One will exchange insults with the other!"

[6] It is certainly possible that the real or imaginary situation is that the pupil of our text is applying for a job at an administrative center, and that in the lines lost just before the examiner has told him that there is another candidate — whence the sudden change of tack in the composition which ends in a string of insults.

REFERENCES

Civil 1985; Gadd 1956; Römer 1977; 1988; Sjöberg 1975; Van Dijk 1953; Vanstiphout 1979; 1996; Waetzoldt 1986; 1988; 1989.

SUMERIAN BIBLIOGRAPHY

ALSTER, B.
1972a "A Sumerian Incantation against Gall." *Or* 41:349-358.
1972b *Dumuzi's Dream*. Copenhagen: Akademisk Forlag.
1973 "An Aspect of 'Enmerkar and the Lord of Aratta.'" *RA* 67:101-110.
1974a "On the Interpretation of the Sumerian Myth 'Inanna and Enki.'" *ZA* 64:20-34.
1974b *The Instructions of Suruppak*. Mesopotamia. Copenhagen Studies in Assyriology 2. Copenhagen: Akademisk Forlag.
1975 "Paradoxical Proverbs and Satire in Sumerian Literature." *JCS* 27:201-230.
1976 "On the Earliest Sumerian Literary Tradition." *JCS* 28:109-126.
1985 "Sumerian Love Songs." *RA* 79:127-159.
1987 "Additional Fragments of the Instructions of Shuruppak." *AO* 5:199-206.
1990 "Additional Lines Identified in the Early Dynastic Version." *ZA* 80:15-19.
1991 "The Instructions of Ur-Ninurta and Related Compositions." *Or* 60:141-157.
1992a "Early Dynastic Proverbs and Other Contributions to the Study of Literary Texts from Abū Ṣalābīkh." *AfO* 38:1-51.
1992b "Corrections to The Instructions of Urninurta and Related Compositions." *NABU* 3:63, No. 83.
1993a "Proverbs From Ancient Mesopotamia: Their History and Social Implications." In *Proverbium. Yearbook of International Proverb Scholarship*. University of Vermont, 10:1-19.
1993b "Marriage and Love in the Sumerian Love Songs." Pp. 15-27 in *Studies Hallo*.
1997 *Proverbs of Ancient Sumer: The World's Earliest Proverb Collections*. Bethesda, MD: CDL Press.

ALSTER, B., and H. L. J. VANSTIPHOUT.
1987 "Lahar and Ashnan. Presentation and Analysis of a Sumerian Disputation." *ActSum* 9:1-43.

ARNAUD, D.
1991 *Textes syriens de l'âge du bronze récent*. AOSup 1.

ATTINGER, P.
1993 *Eléments de linguistique sumérienne*. OBO Sonderband. Göttingen: Vandenhoeck & Ruprecht.

BARNSTONE, A., and W. BARNSTONE, editors.
1980 *A Book of Women Poets from Antiquity to Now*. New York: Schocken.

BENITO, C. A.
1969 *"Enki and Ninmah" and "Enki and the World Order"*. Ph.D. Dissertation. University of Pennslyvania. Philadelphia.

BORGER, R.
1991 "Ein Brief Sîn-idinnams von Larsa an den Sonnengott ...." *Nachrichten der Akademie der Wissenschaften in Göttingen I. Phil.-hist. Kl.* 1991/2:39-81 + 2 pls.

BOTTÉRO, J.
1991 "La 'tenson' et la réflexion sur les choses en Mésopotamie." Pp. 7-22 in *Dispute Poems and Dialogues in the Ancient and Mediaeval Near East*. Ed. by G. Reinink and H. Vanstiphout. OLA 42. Leuven: Peeters.

BOTTÉRO, J. and S. N. KRAMER.
1989 *Lorsque les dieux faisaient l'homme: Mythologie mésopotamienne*. Bibliothèque des histoires. Paris: Gallimard/NRF.

CASTELLINO, G. R.
1972 *Two Šulgi Hymns (BC)*. Studi Semitici 42.

CHARPIN, D.
1986 *Le Clergé d'Ur au siècle d'Hammurapi*. Geneva and Paris: Droz.

CIVIL, M.
1969 "Review of *CT* 44." *JNES* 28:70-72.
1976 "The Song of the Plowing Oxen." Pp. 83-95 in *Studies Kramer*.
1983 "Enlil and Ninlil: the Marriage of Sud." *JAOS* 103:43-66; republ. in *Studies Kramer*[2] (1984) 43-66.
1984 "Notes on the 'Instructions of Šuruppak.'" *JNES* 43:281-298.
1985 "Sur les 'livres d'écolier' à l'époque paléo-babylonienne." Pp. 67-78 in *Miscellanea Babylonica*. Ed. by J.-M. Durand. Paris: Éditions Recherche sur les Civilisations.
1987 "Sumerian Riddles: a Corpus." *AO* 5:17-37.
1990a "From Vienna to Manchester." *NABU* 14-15.
1990b "Ninmešarra 90 and Qinu 'Jealousy, Anger.'" *NABU* 1990:44f.
1994 *The Farmer's Instructions. A Sumerian Agricultural Manual*. AOSup 5. Sabadell: Editorial Ausa.
1996 "Sin-iddinam in Emar and SU.A = Šimaški." *NABU* 1996:3-8.

CLIFFORD, R. J.
1994 *Creation Accounts in the Ancient Near East and in the Bible*. CBQMS 26. Washington DC: Catholic Biblical Association of America.

COHEN, M. E.
1976 "Literary Texts from the Andrews University Archaeological Museum." *RA* 70:129-144.
1981 *Sumerian Hymnology, the Eršemma*. Cincinnati: Hebrew Union College.
1988 *The Canonical Lamentations of Ancient Mesopotamia*. 2 vols. Potomac, MD: CDL.

COOPER, J. C.
1981 "Gilgamesh and Akka: A Review Article." *JCS* 33:224-239.
1989 "Enki's Member: Eros and Irrigation in Sumerian Literature." Pp. 87-89 in *Studies Sjöberg*.

VAN DIJK, J.
1953 *La sagesse suméro-accadienne*. Leiden: Brill.
1957 "La découverte de la culture littéraire sumérienne ...." *Orientalia et Biblica Lovaniensia* 1:5-28.
1964 "Le motif cosmique dans la pensée sumérienne." *ActOr* 28:1-59.
1980 *Texte aus dem Rēš-Heiligtum in Uruk-Warka*. *BaM* Beiheft 2. Berlin: Gebr. Mann.
1989 "Ein spätbabylonischer Katalog einer Sammlung sumerische Briefe." *Or* 58:411-452.

EDZARD, D. O.
1959 "Enmebaragesi von Kish." *ZA* 53:9-26.
EICHLER, B. L.
1983 "Of slings and shields, throw-sticks and javelins." *JAOS* 103:95-102; republ. in *Studies Kramer*[2] (1984) 95-102.
FALKENSTEIN, A.
1931 *Die Haupttypen der sumerischen Beschwörung literarisch untersucht*. LSS n.F. 1.
1963 "Sumerische religiöse Texte." *ZA* 55:11-67.
1966 "Zu Gilgamesh und Agga." *AfO* 21:47-50.
FALKENSTEIN, A., and W. VON SODEN.
1953 *Sumerische und Akkadische Hymnen und Gebete*. Zürich and Stuttgart: Artemis.
FALKOWITZ, R. S.
1980 *The Sumerian Rhetoric Collections*. Ph.D. Dissertation. University of Pennsylvania, Philadelphia.
FARBER, G.
1973 (published under double name Farber-Flügge) *Der Mythos "Inanna und Enki" unter besonderer Berücksichtigung der Liste der me*. Studia Pohl 10. Rome: Biblical Institute Press.
1990 "me (ĝarza, *parṣu*)." *RlA* 7:610-613.
1995 "'Inanna and Enki' in Geneva: a Sumerian Myth Revisited." *JNES* 54:287-292.
forthcoming "'Das Lied von der Hacke,' ein literarischer Spaß?" In "Berliner Beiträge zum Vorderen Orient": paper read at the Rencontre Assyriologique Internationale, 1994, Berlin.
FOSTER, B. R.
1983 "Self-Reference of an Akkadian Poet." *JAOS* 103:123-130; republ. in *Studies Kramer*[2] (1984) 123-130.
1993 *BM*.
1995 *FDD*.
GADD, C. J.
1956 *Teachers and Students in the Oldest Schools*. London: School of Oriental and African Studies.
GELLER, M. J.
1985 *Forerunners to Udug-hul: Sumerian Exorcistic Incantations*. FAS 12.
1990 "Taboo in Mesopotamia." *JCS* 42:105-117.
DE GENOUILLAC, H.
1930 *Textes réligieux sumériens du Louvre 2*. TCL 16. Paris: Geuthner.
GEORGE, A. R.
1993 *House Most High: the Temples of Ancient Mesopotamia*. Winona Lake, IN: Eisenbrauns.
GOMI T., and M. SIGRIST.
1991 *The Comprehensive Catalogue of Published Ur III Tablets*.
GORDON, E. I.
1959 *Sumerian Proverbs. Glimpses of Everyday Life in Ancient Mesopotamia*. With a Chapter by Th. Jacobsen. University Monographs. Philadelphia: University of Pennsylvania.
GRAGG, G.
1973a "The Fable of the Heron and the Turtle." *AfO* 24:51-72.
1973b *Sumerian Dimensional Infixes*. AOATS 5. Neukirchen-Vluyn: Neukirchener Verlag.
GREEN, M. W.
1975 *Eridu in Sumerian Literature*. Ph.D. Dissertation University of Chicago, 1975.
1976 "Review of Farber 1973." *JAOS* 96:283-286.
1978 "The Eridu Lament." *JCS* 30:127-167.
1984 "The Uruk Lament." *JAOS* 104:253-279.
GREENFIELD, J. R.
1985 "The Seven Pillars of Wisdom (Prov 9:1) — a Mistranslation." *JQR* 76:13-20.
GURNEY, O. R., and S. N. KRAMER.
1982 *Sumerian Literary Texts in the Ashmolean Museum*. OECT 5.
GWALTNEY, W. C., JR.
1983 "The Biblical Book of Lamentations in the Context of Near Eastern Lament Literature." Pp. 191-211 in *SIC* 2.
HALLO, W. W.
1963 "Royal Hymns and Mesopotamian Unity." *JCS* 17:112-118.
1968 "Individual Prayer in Sumerian: the Continuity of a Tradition." *JAOS* 88:71-89; repr. in *Studies Speiser*.
1969 "The Lame and the Halt." *EI* 9:66-70 (Albright Volume).
1970a "Antediluvian Cities." *JCS* 23:57-67.
1970b "The Cultic Setting of Sumerian Poetry." *RAI* 17:116-134.
1971 "Gutium." *RlA* 3/9:708-720.
1973 "Choice in Sumerian." *JANES* 5:165-172.
1976 "The Royal Correspondence of Larsa: I. A Sumerian Prototype for the Prayer of Hezekiah?" Pp. 209-224 in *Studies Kramer*.
1978 "Simurrum and the Hurrian Frontier." *RHA* 36:71-83.
1982 "The Royal Correspondence of Larsa: I. The Appeal to Utu." Pp. 95-109 in *Studies Kraus*.
1985 "Biblical Abominations and Sumerian Taboos." *JQR* 76:21-40.
1987 "The Birth of Kings." Pp. 45-52 in *Studies Pope*.
1989 "Nippur Originals." Pp. 237-247 in *Studies Sjöberg*.
1990 "Proverbs Quoted in Epic." Pp. 203-217 in *Studies Moran*.
1991 *BP*.
1992 "Trade and Traders in the Ancient Near East: Some New Perspectives." *RAI* 38:351-356.
1995 "Lamentations and Prayers in Sumer and Akkad." in *CANE* 3:1876-1881.
1996 *Origins*. Leiden: Brill.

HALLO W. W., AND J. J. A. VAN DIJK.
1968 *The Exaltation of Inanna*. YNER 3. New Haven/London: Yale University Press. repr. 1982. New York: AMS Press.
HALLO, W. W., AND W. K. SIMPSON.
1971 *The Ancient Near East: A History*. New York: Harcourt and Brace.
HEIMPEL, W.
1971 "Review of Hallo and van Dijk 1968." *JNES* 30:232-236.
1981a "The Nanshe Hymn." *JCS* 33:65-139.
1981b "A Note on Gilgamesh and Agga." *JCS* 33:242-243.
1986 "The Sun at Night and the Doors of Heaven in Babylonian Texts." *JCS* 38:127-151.
HUNGER, H.
1968 *Babylonische und assyrische Kolophone*. AOAT 2.
JACOBSEN, T.
1939 *The Sumerian King List*. AS 11. Chicago: University of Chicago Press.
1946 "Sumerian Mythology, a Review Artcle." *JNES* 5:128-152.
1970a "Primitive Democracy in Ancient Mesopotamia." Republished in W. L. Moran, ed., Jacobsen, Th. *Toward the Image of Tammuz and other Essays on Mesopotamian History and Culture*. Cambridge, Mass.: 157-170 (first published in 1943).
1970b "Early political Development in Mesopotamia." Reprint, *Ibid.*, 132-157 (first published in 1957).
1975 "Religious Drama in Ancient Mesopotamia." Pp. 65-97 in *Unity and Diversity*.
1976 *The Treasures of Darkness. A History of Mesopotamian Religion*. New Haven and London: Yale University Press.
1984 "The Harab Myth." *SANE* 2:99-120.
1987a *The Harps that Once .... Sumerian Poetry in Translation*. New Haven and London: Yale University Press.
1987b "Two bal-bal-e Dialogues." Pp. 57-63 in *Studies Pope*.
1988 "God or Worshipper." Pp. 125-130 in *Studies Kantor*.
1992 "The Spell of Nudimmud." Pp. 403-416 in *Studies Talmon*.
KATZ, D.
1987 "Gilgamesh and Akka: Was Uruk Ruled by Two Assemblies?" *RA* 81:105-114.
1993 *Gilgamesh and Akka*. Groningen: STYX.
KELLER, S.
1991 "Written Communications Between the Human and Divine Spheres in Mesopotamia and Israel." Pp. 299-309 in *SIC* 4.
KILMER, A. D.
1976 "Speculations on Umul, the First Baby." Pp. 265-270 in *Studies Kramer*.
1983 *Women Poets of the World*. Ed. by J. Bankier and D. Lashgari. New York: Macmillan.
KLEIN, J.
1976 "Shulgi and Gilgamesh: Two Brother Peers (Shulgi hymn O)." Pp. 271-292 in *Studies Kramer*.
1981a *Three Šulgi Hymns: Sumerian Royal Hymns Glorifying King Šulgi of Ur*. Ramat-Gan: Bar-Ilan University Press.
1981b *The Royal Hymns of Shulgi King of Ur: Man's Quest for Immortal Fame*. Transactions of the American Philosophical Society 71/7. Philadelphia.
1982 Personal God and Individual Prayer in Sumerian Religion." *AfO* 19:295-306.
1983 "The Capture of Akka by Gilgamesh (GA 81 and 99)." *JAOS* 103:201-203.
1987 "The Birth of a Crownprince in the Temple: A Neo-Sumerian Literary Topos." Pp. 97-106 in *La femme dans le Proche-Orient Antique*. *RAI* 33. Ed. by J.-M. Durand. Paris: Editions Recherche sur les Civilisations.
1991 "The Coronation and Consecration of Šulgi in the Ekur (Šulgi G)." Pp. 292-313 in *Studies Tadmor*.
KLEIN, J., and Y. SEFATI.
1988 "The Concept of 'Abomination' in Mesopotamian Literature and the Bible." *Beer-Sheva* 3:131-148 (in Hebrew with English Summary pp. 12*-13*).
KRAMER, S. N.
1940 *Lamentation Over the Destruction of Ur*. AS 12. Chicago: University of Chicago Press.
1944 *Sumerian Mythology*. Philadelphia: The American Philosophical Society.
1949 "Gilgamesh and Akka." *AJA* 53:1-18.
1952 "Five New Sumerian Literary Texts." *Belleten* 16:345-365.
1955 "Man and his God: a Sumerian Variation on the 'Job' Motif." Pp. 170-182 + pls. i-iv in *Studies Rowley*.
1963 "Cuneiform Studies and the History of Literature: The Sumerian Sacred Marriage Texts." *PAPS* 107:485-527.
1964 "Sumerische Litteraire Teksten uit Ur." *Phoenix* 10/1:99-108.
1969a "The Death of Ur-Nammu and his Descent to the Netherworld." *JCS* 21:104-122.
1969b "Sumerian Similes." *JAOS* 89:1-10.
1969c *The Sacred Marriage Rite: Aspect of Faith, Myth, and Ritual in Ancient Sumer*. Bloomington: Indiana University Press.
1969d "Hymnal Prayer of Enheduanna: the Adoration of Inanna in Ur." *ANET*, 579-582.
1975 *Sumerian Culture and Society*. Menlo Park (14-16)
1981 *History Begins at Sumer*. 3rd Revised Edition. Philadelphia: University of Pennslyvania Press.
KRAMER, S. N., and J. MAIER.
1989 *Myths of Enki, the Crafty God*. New York and Oxford: Oxford University Press.
KRAUS, H.-J.
1968 *Klagelieder (Threni)*³. BKAT. Neukirchen-Vluyn: Neukirchener Verlag.
KRECHER, J.
1980-83 "Klagelied." *RlA* 6:1-8.
KRISPIJN, Th. J. H.
1993 "Dierenfabels in het oude Mesopotamië." Pp. 131-148 in *Mijn naam is haas. Dierenverhalen in verschillende culturen*. Ed. by E. L. Idema, et al. Baarn: Ambo.
KUTSCHER, R.
1982 "Review of OECT 5." *BiOr* 39:583-590.

LAMBERT, W. G.
1960 *BWL.*
1974 "Dingir.ša.dib.ba Incantations." *JNES* 33:267-322.
1980 "Akka's Threat." *Or* 49:339-340.
LAMBERT, W. G., and A. R. MILLARD.
1969 *Atra-Ḫasīs: The Babylonian Story of the Flood.* Oxford: Clarendon Press.
LEICHTY, Erle
1964 "The Colophon." Pp. 147-154 in *Studies Oppenheim.*
LEVINE, B. A.
1968 "Mulūgu/Melûg: the Origins of a Talmudic Legal Institution." *JAOS* 88:271-285.
LIPIŃSKI, E.
1988 "Ea, Kothar et El." *UF* 20:137-143.
LIVINGSTONE, A.
1980 "A Fragment of a Work Song." *ZA* 70:55-57.
1989 *Court Poetry and Literary Miscellanea.* SAA 3.
LONGMAN, T. III
1991 *Fictional Akkadian Autobiography.* Winona Lake, IN: Eisenbrauns.
MALAMAT, A.
1963 "Kingship and Council in Israel and Sumer: a Parallel." *JNES* 22:247-252.
MATTINGLY, G. L.
1990 "The Pious Sufferer: Mesopotamia's Traditional Theodicy and Job's Counselors." Pp. 305-348 in *SIC* 3.
MCDANIEL, T. F.
1968 "The Alleged Sumerian Influence upon Lamentations." *VT* 18:198-209.
MICHALOWSKI, P.
1982 "Review of Römer 1980." *BSOAS* 45:557-578.
1985 "On Some Early Sumerian Magical Texts." *Or* 54:216-225.
1988 "Sin-iddinam and Iškur." Pp. 265-527 in *Studies Sachs.*
1989 *The Lamentation Over the Destruction of Sumer and Ur.* Mesopotamian Civilizations 2. Winona Lake, IN: Eisenbrauns.
1993 "The Torch and the Censer." Pp. 152-162 in *Studies Hallo.*
PETTINATO, G.
1971 *Das altorientalische Menschenbild und die sumerischen und akkadischen Schöpfungsmythen.* Heidelberg: Winter.
REINER, E.
1968 "Thirty Pieces of Silver." *JAOS* 88:186-190; repr. in *Studies Speiser.*
1980 "Thirty Pieces of Silver." *University of Chicago Record* 14:172-184.
1985 *Your Thwarts in Pieces Your Mooring Rope Cut: Poetry from Babylonia and Assyria.* Michigan Studies in the Humanities 5. Ann Arbor: University of Michigan.
RÖMER, W. H. Ph.
1965 *Sumerische 'Königshymnen' der Isin-Zeit.* Leiden: E. J. Brill.
1972 "Review of Hallo and van Dijk 1968." *UF* 4:173-206.
1977 *Iets over School en Schoolonderricht in het Oude Mesopotamië.* Assen.
1980 *Das Sumeriche Kurzepos "Gilgamesh und Akka".* AOAT 290/1. Neukirchen-Vluyn.
1988 "Aus einem Schulstreitsgespräch in sumerischer Sprache." *UF* 20:233-245.
SAUREN, H.
1970 "Review of Hallo and van Dijk 1968." *BiOr* 27:38-41.
1993 "Nammu and Enki." Pp. 198-208 in *Studies Hallo.*
SCHEIL, V.
1927 "Formule magique avec allusion historique." *RA* 24:42.
SEFATI, Y.
1985 *Love Songs in Sumerian Literature: Critical Edition of the Dumuzi-Inanna Songs.* Ph.D. Dissertation. Bar-Ilan University. (in Hebrew).
1990 "An Oath of Chastity in a Sumerian Love Song (SRT 31)?" Pp. 45-63 in *Bar-Ilan Studies in Assyriology Dedicated to Pinḥas Artzi.* Ed. by J. Klein and A. Skaist. Ramat-Gan: Bar-Ilan University Press.
SELZ, G. J.
1989 "Nissaba(k), 'die Herrin der Getreidezuteilungen'." Pp. 491-497 in *Studies Sjöberg.*
SJÖBERG, Å.
1960 *Der Mondgott Nanna-Suen in der sumerischen Überlieferung, I. Teil: Texte.* Stockholm: Almqvist & Wiksell.
1975 "The Old Babylonian Edubba." Pp. 159-179 in *Studies Jacobsen.*
1984 "Eve and the Chameleon." Pp. 217-225 in *Studies Ahlström.*
SJÖBERG, Å. W. AND E. BERGMANN, S. J.
1969 *The Collection of the Sumerian Temple Hymns.* TCS 3. Locust Valley, NY: J. J. Augustin.
SUTER, Claudia E.
1996a "Blessings of Ziggurat?" American Oriental Society meeting 206 (unpubl.)
1996b "Gudea's Segnung des Eninnu." *RAI* 43 (unpubl.).
VANSTIPHOUT, H.
1979 "How Did They Learn Sumerian?" *JCS* 31:118-126.
1984 "On the Sumerian Disputation between the Hoe and the Plough." *AO* 2:239-251.
1986 "Towards a Reading of 'Gilgamesh and Agga,' Part II: Construction." *OLP* 17:33-50.
1987a "Towards a Reading of 'Gilgamesh and Agga.'" *AO* 5:129-141.
1987b "Joins proposed in Sumerian Literary Compositions." *NABU* 1987/3 87:46-47.
1990a "The Mesopotamian Debate Poems. A General Presentation (Part I)." *ASJ* 12:271-318.

1990b "A *double entendre* Concerning Uttu." *NABU* 1990/2 57:40-44.

1991a "Lore, Learning and Levity in the Sumerian Disputations: a Matter of Form, or Substance?" Pp. 23-46 in *Dispute Poems and Dialogues in the Ancient and Mediaeval Near East*. Ed. by G. Reinink and H. Vanstiphout. OLA 42. Leuven: Peeters.

1991b "A Further Note on Ebih." *NABU* 1991/4 103:71-72.

1991c "A Note on the Format of 'Bird and Fish'." *NABU* 1991/4 104:72-73.

1992a "The Mesopotamian Debate Poems. A General Presentation. Part II. The Subject." *ASJ* 14:339-367.

1992b "The Banquet Scene in the Sumerian Debate Poems." *Res Orientales* 4:37-63.

1996 "Remarks on 'Supervisor and Scribe' (or Dialogue 4, or Eduba C)." *NABU* 1996/1 1:1-2.

WAETZOLDT, H.

1975 "Review of Farber 1973." *BiOr* 32:382-384.

1986 "Keilschrift und Schulen in Mesopotamien und Ebla." Pp. 36-49 in *Erziehungs- und Unterrichtsmethoden im historischen Wandel*. Ed. by L. Kriss-Rettenbeck and M. Liedtke. Bad Heilbrunn: Klinkhardt.

1988 "Die Entwicklung der Naturwissenschaften und des Naturwissenschaftlichen Unterrichts in Mesopotamien." Pp. 31-49 in *Naturwissenschaftlicher Unterricht und Wissenskumulation*. Ed. by J. G. Prinz von Hohenzollern and M. Liedtke. Bad Heilbrunn: Klinkhardt.

1989 "Der Schreiber als Lehrer in Mesopotamien." Pp. 33-50 in *Schreiber, Magister, Lehrer*. Ed. by J. G. Prinz von Hohenzollern and M. Liedtke. Bad Heilbrunn: Klinkhardt.

WEINFELD, M.

1988 "Job and its Mesopotamian Parallels." Pp. 217-226 in *Studies Fensham*.

WESTENHOLZ, J. G.

1989 "Enḫeduanna, en-priestess, hen of Nanna, spouse of Nanna." Pp. 539-556 in *Studies Sjöberg*.

WILCKE, C.

1969 *Das Lugalbandaepos*. Wiesbaden: Otto Harrassowitz.

1970 "Die akkadischen Glossen in TMF NF 3 no. 25 und eine neue Interpretation des Textes." *AfO* 23:84-87.

1972 "Hacke - B. Philologisch." *RlA* 4:33-38.

1975 "Formale Gesichtspunkte in der sumerischen Literatur." Pp. 205-316 in *Studies Jacobsen*.

1976a "Nin-me-šar-ra — Probleme der Interpretation." *WZKM* 68:79-92 + 1 pl.

1976b "Formale Gesichtspunkte in der sumerischen Literatur." Pp. 205-316 in *Studies Jacobsen*.

1978 "Philologische Bemerkungen zum Rat des Šuruppag." *ZA* 68:196-232.

WOLKSTEIN, D., and S. N. KRAMER.

1983 *Inanna, Queen of Heaven and Earth*. New York: Harper and Row.